The Cambridge Handbook of Personal Relationships

The *Cambridge Handbook of Personal Relationships* serves as a benchmark of the current state of scholarship in this dynamic field, synthesizing the extant theoretical and empirical literature, tracing its historical roots, and making recommendations for future directions. The volume addresses a broad range of established and emerging topics, including theoretical and methodological issues that influence the study of personal relationships; research and theory on relationship development; the nature and functions of personal relationships across the life span; individual differences and their influences on relationships; relationship processes such as cognition, emotion, and communication; relational qualities such as satisfaction and commitment; environmental influences on personal relationships; and maintenance and repair of relationships. The authors are experts from a variety of disciplines, including several subfields of psychology, communication, family studies, and sociology, who have made major contributions to the understanding of relationships.

Anita L. Vangelisti is a professor in the Department of Communication Studies at the University of Texas at Austin. Her work focuses on the associations between communication and emotion in the context of close, personal relationships. She has published numerous articles and chapters and has edited several books. Vangelisti has served on the editorial boards of more than a dozen scholarly journals and has received recognition for her research from the National Communication Association and the International Society for the Study of Personal Relationships.

Daniel Perlman is an academic psychologist with broad, applied interests that cut across social, developmental, and clinical psychology as focused on the study of close relationships. He is a professor of Family Studies and also teaches in the Department of Psychology at the University of British Columbia. He was president of the International Society for the Study of Personal Relationships and the Canadian Psychological Association. He has authored more than 50 articles, edited or authored 15 books, and been the editor or associate editor for four journals.

The Cambridge Handbook
of Personal Relationships

Edited by

Anita L. Vangelisti
and
Daniel Perlman

CAMBRIDGE UNIVERSITY PRESS
Cambridge, New York, Melbourne, Madrid, Cape Town, Singapore, São Paulo

Cambridge University Press
40 West 20th Street, New York, NY 10011-4211, USA

www.cambridge.org
Information on this title: www.cambridge.org/9780521826174

© Cambridge University Press 2006

First published 2006

Printed in the United States of America

A catalog record for this publication is available from the British Library.

Library of Congress Cataloging in Publication Data

The Cambridge handbook of personal relationships / edited by Anita L. Vangelisti,
Daniel Perlman.
   p. cm.
Includes bibliographical references and index.
ISBN-13: 978-0-521-82617-4 (hardcover)
ISBN-10: 0-521-82617-9 (hardcover)
ISBN-13: 978-0-521-53359-1 (pbk.)
ISBN-10: 0-521-53359-7 (pbk.)
1. Interpersonal relations – Handbooks, manuals, etc. 2. Interpersonal
communication – Handbooks, manuals, etc. 3. Social psychology –
Handbooks, manuals, etc. I. Vangelisti, Anita L. II. Perlman, Daniel.

ISBN-13   978-0-521-82617-4 hardback
ISBN-10   0-521-82617-9 hardback

ISBN-13   978-0-521-53359-1 paperback
ISBN-10   0-521-53359-7 paperback

Contents

Preface

For volumes that review the present state of knowledge in dynamic, rapidly evolving fields, the label *handbook* seems only marginally appropriate. When one thinks of a handbook, one visualizes a person holding a plumbing manual in one hand and a wrench in the other and, after the leaky pipe has been fixed, putting the manual away for use another day, confident that the principles of plumbing will not change substantially from one year to the next or even very much from one decade to the next. Relationship science, in contrast, is a large and still loosely organized field that continues to expand rapidly in all directions, its momentum fueled partly by the internal combustion provided by the theorists and researchers who form the core of the field and partly by scholars in other fields who recognize the relevance of relationship theory and research to their own problems. Relationship science is, in short, a nova in the heavens of the social, behavioral, and biological sciences.

Not so long ago, the future of a field devoted to understanding interpersonal rela-

tionships was in doubt. As a consequence, and to be on the safe side, many of us adopted the convention of referring to the relationship field as "emerging," a practice noted with exasperation in the late 1980s by Steve Duck, the editor of the first relationship handbook, the *Handbook of Personal Relationships* (1988). In his introductory remarks, Duck took a deep breath and dared to declare that the field *had* emerged, putting its birth about 10 years earlier, in the late 1970s. A second edition of that first handbook appeared 10 years later (Duck, 1997) and only 3 years after that a relationship "sourcebook" edited by Clyde and Susan Hendrick (2000) was published. In between and since, several edited topical "mini-handbooks" have been published, each devoted to a subject of special interest to relationship researchers, as Dan Perlman and Duck note in their historical review chapter in this book.

The continuing high volume of activity in the relationship field places a heavy burden on relationship scholars. There is too much to learn, and far too little time in which to learn it, for most of us to feel that we have anything but a tenuous grasp of the breadth and depth of the field or more than a dim appreciation of its current trajectory. There are too many books, too many journal articles, and too many conferences, preconferences, and workshops for anyone to take in. Hence the need for volumes that periodically, comprehensively, and concisely describe current activities in the field – handbooks, in other words, or perhaps more accurately, status reports – to help us fend off the feelings of defeat that precede retreat into more settled areas of inquiry.

A Book of Bets

In addition to surveying present activities in areas of interest to relationship scholars, many handbook contributors briefly describe the history of the area and some also attempt to predict its future. Historical remarks are useful to newcomers to the field who, entering the relationship movie midstream, often wonder how the relationship field got to where it is (and why it took so long to get here). Forecasts of profitable future activities are especially useful to new recruits, many of whom are in the process of deciding where they might most profitably invest their scholarly efforts. A "bookmaker's book of bets" is, in fact, a secondary definition of the word handbook (*Webster's Collegiate Dictionary*, 10th ed., p. 526). Indeed, and apart from the explicit predictions of future activity that some handbook contributors make, their descriptions of current activities in a specific problem area can be viewed as surveys of the bets individual researchers are currently making – where, in other words, one's colleagues are gambling their professional and personal resources in the expectation that their investments will pay off by advancing relationship knowledge. It perhaps does not need saying that in performing the triage necessary for a concise report, some surveyors are better than others in identifying which current activities are likely to be rewarding and which can

be omitted from their report because they promise to be a waste of time or, of course, that some researchers invest their resources more wisely than others. Histories of disciplines, in fact, are simply accounts of scholars' bets that paid off. Lost wagers are rarely mentioned.

It is to the prediction of profitable future activities that I address the remainder of these prefatory remarks because, like it or not, all scholars must be gamblers. To decide where to invest their time, energy, and other resources, they must make predictions about the kinds of theoretical, research, and service activities that are the surest bets to advance the field. This kind of gambling is a high-stakes activity, both for the individual and for the field, which perhaps is why so many scholarly conferences devote at least one session to "future directions" or some variant on that theme and so many journals periodically publish "forecast" articles and issues.

The Wild Cards

Making accurate predictions about a field's future, especially predictions about the specific research paths that will yield a significant payoff, is extraordinarily difficult. It is hazardous, in fact. My thesis here is that the wild cards that so often trump the most carefully considered forecasts are dealt by powerful, pervasive, and slow-moving macroforces. Because these forces intensify so gradually (think of a hand in a bucket of water in which the temperature is slowly and imperceptibly increased to the boiling point), they are hard to identify even as they are exerting their massive and inexorable influence on scholars' activities. I illustrate the point by describing some of the macroforces that, I now see in retrospect, were beginning to gather strength when I became involved in relationship research more than half a century ago.

The seeds of at least three macroforces that would influence all of the social and behavioral sciences were beginning to germinate when, as an undergraduate English major vaguely intending to go on to law school, I impulsively enrolled in a new seminar offered by the psychology department titled Perception and Cognition. I signed up for the seminar expecting it (don't ask me why) to be a course in extrasensory perception and precognition. Although I spent much of the semester wondering when we were going to get to the interesting part, I wisely refrained from asking the professor, Paul Secord, for clarification and, persevering to the very end, I did well enough that Secord asked me if I would like a job as his research assistant. I had no idea what a research assistant did, but with another boring secretarial job looming on the summer horizon, I was pleased to give it a whirl.

Secord could offer me a job as a research assistant because during the semester in which I was impatiently tapping my foot waiting to learn the secrets of clairvoyance, mind reading, and spoon bending, he had received word that he was to receive a research grant from the National Institute of Health–Public Health Service. I learned years later that both the topic of Secord's seminar and his grant proposal had been influenced by his recent participation in the seminal symposium sponsored by the Office of Naval Research held at Harvard in March of 1957, resulting in the classic volume edited by Tagiuri and Petrullo, *Person Perception and Interpersonal Behavior* (1958). Secord's grant was among the first federal research grants ever made to the social and behavioral sciences. The gradual infusion of increasing amounts of federal research funds into the social and behavioral sciences that followed was to have enormous impact on what researchers in these disciplines did and how they did it.

Person perception and interpersonal attraction are intimate companions that together formed an important part of the nucleus of relationship science. My first task as a research assistant thus thrust me into relationship research. My job was to hand out slips of paper to a group of students, all strangers to one another, sitting around in a circle about to begin a discussion (of

pedagogical reform, no less). Each individual's slip listed certain other persons in the group who, supposedly as revealed by a personality test taken earlier, probably would like the individual. After their (embarrassingly desultory) discussion, I handed out questionnaires that asked each person whom he or she liked now that they had become acquainted with the other group members. I learned later that the experiment had been stimulated by the proposition, advanced independently by Renato Tagiuri and Theodore Newcomb, that a fundamental characteristic of the dyad is "congruency," a prominent instance of which was believed to be the tendency for people to like those who like them. Backman and Secord's (1959) results revealed that perception of another's liking caused liking the other in return at first but the effect evaporated upon further interaction (and the additional information it provided).

The seeds of the second macroforce, one that was to transform research activities in all of the sciences, were reflected in another of my initial tasks. Sitting by a window, I was to take two cards from a box of rectangular cards on which someone had punched a lot of holes, sandwich them together, and then hold the pair up to the light and count the number of holes through which the sun shone. This took a very long time. A very, very long time. With his usual perspicacity, Secord had recognized the possibilities that lie in the university's purchase of a card-punching machine. Unfortunately, no machine was available to make the comparisons he needed, nor was there available a machine that could compute the needed statistics on the "similarity-of-holes" data (what it actually represented, I never knew). I was to accomplish the latter by depressing the appropriate numbered keys on the top of a Friden calculating machine, which was about as large as a breadbox but considerably heavier, and then pulling the crank on its side almost 180 degrees to enter the numbers into the gizzards of the machine. Several days of frenzied crank-pulling to obtain what seemed an endless series of correlation coefficients later sent me to the orthopedic surgeon with what was diagnosed as "tennis elbow."

Along with what has been called the golden age of federal research funding and the advent of the computer age, the seeds of the third potent macroforce were reflected in my own gender, which turned out to be a harbinger of the great migration of women into the sciences. Redress of the lopsided sex ratio of researchers in the social and behavioral sciences almost surely influenced the development of relationship research, for researchers usually enjoy working on problems they personally care about; women, it has been documented, are more interested in personal relationships than men are. The entry of the other half of the human population into competition for graduate training and for jobs had another effect: It almost surely increased the quality of researchers in the disciplines that were to contribute to relationship science. Competition for admission to graduate schools became increasingly intense, and today most applicants' vitas are brimming with research publications, computer and statistical expertise; perfect grade point averages; outstanding GRE scores; extensive undergraduate coursework in psychology, sociology, and allied fields; and incredible (sometimes literally) letters of recommendation. Many of my age cohort (including yours truly) suspect they would not be let in the door today.

Reflecting on the changes that have occurred over the past 50 years in the study of interpersonal relationships, it thus seems to me that the major transforming agents have been only secondarily individual theorists and researchers. Rather, the prime movers in any field that influence who the theorists and researchers are (their personal characteristics and, indeed, their very number), what these theorists and researchers do, and how they do it – and, therefore, the number, nature, and quality of the advances made in a field – are powerful, pervasive, slow-moving macroforces. These are almost impossible to identify in prospect and difficult to identify even when they are quietly exerting their vast power. Indeed, their influence is rarely acknowledged even in retrospect. Their monumental impact illustrates that relationship science, like a relationship itself, is an open system sensitive to perturbations not only in the systems that relationship science encompasses (e.g., the scholars working in each of the problem areas that comprise relationship science) but also in the larger, societal systems in which relationship science is nested. It is the forces generated within these larger systems that so often crush the individual researcher's bets on the future.

Variegated Effects of Macroforces

Each of the individual macroforces I have named as influencing the relationship field over the past half century (and I make no claim the list is exhaustive) represents a broad category of the types of changes that may forever alter the course of a research discipline – namely, changes in researchers' monetary, time, or other resources to do what they do; changes in technology that affect how they do it; and changes in the number and characteristics of the researchers themselves. Each macroforce has had variegated effects; most have facilitated the field's advance, but some have impeded it and are continuing to do so. For example, the effects of federal research funding for social and behavioral research have not been wholly beneficial. One of its most unfortunate effects is that as universities have become increasingly dependent on federal monies, many have come to see their researchers more as revenue-generating agents than as knowledge-generating scholars. Their employers' view not only influences researchers' choice of problem (increasingly determined by the vagaries of politics and the federal "social problem du jour" as opposed to research addressed to fundamental problems in the field) but also researchers' approach to the problem (e.g., a quick return to be itemized in the next "progress report" to ensure continued support).

Changes in technology are, of course, particularly potent forces. The increasing power and sophistication of the computer not only has dramatically facilitated complex statistical analyses of data, it has also made possible the development of new methods to investigate both new and old hypotheses. For example, a decade or so after Backman and Secord's (1959) experiment, the failure to find evidence of liking reciprocity in a data set led a graduate student named David Kenny to develop what he called the social relations modeling (SRM) method (Kenny, 1994, p. 101); the liking reciprocity hypothesis was the first he investigated with the new method (Kenny & La Voie, 1982, 1984). The availability of the computer surely played a silent role, for one does not like to think about analyzing SRM data on a Friden calculator.

One especially does not like to think about performing the multiple regression analyses now endemic in relationship research on a Friden calculator, although it must be said that the old iron breadbox had its virtues. Because calculating a correlation coefficient was laborious, one did not undertake the task unless one had ascertained, first, that the data met the necessary assumptions and, second, that one really, truly needed those coefficients, which meant that one knew exactly what one was going to make of them. Moreover, by the time one had finished calculating all the necessary statistics on a data set, one had gained great familiarity with it, including its warts and anomalies, which often tempered interpretation of those statistics and sometimes even precluded their report. Today, extraordinary amounts of data are automatically fed into a statistical software program (often selected by what is now commonly called a technical advisor) that effortlessly but mindlessly churns out cornucopias of statistics, some of which have little or no real meaning but are interpreted as though they did.

The effects of one macroforce often interact with the effects of another. For example, the researcher's need for federal research funding often interacts with the computerization of statistical analysis to produce a sit-uation social psychologist William McGuire (1973) described some time ago:

> The affluent senior researcher often [carries] out his work through graduate assistants and research associates, who, in turn, often have the actual observations done by parapsychological technicians or hourly help, and the data they collect go to card-punchers who feed them into computers, whose output goes back to the research associate, who might call the more meaningful outcomes to the attention of the senior researcher, who is too busy meeting the payrolls to control the form of the printout or look diligently through it when it arrives. (p. 555)

Or, it should be added, too busy to certify that the data shoveled into the computer's furnace meet each statistic's assumptions. The need to meet a statistic's assumptions was brought home to me early in a searing experience. After doing exactly what students are warned never to do – collecting data without first determining how they would be analyzed – Marshall Dermer and I belatedly discovered there were no time-series statistics available at that time to analyze our activation-level diary data (Dermer & Berscheid, 1972). Happily, Marshall found a team of biological rhythm statisticians working in the rabbit warren of rooms under the football stadium; taking pity on us, they agreed to make us some statistics (and thus act as our technical advisors). Unhappily, when we got around to looking these statisticans' gift horse in the mouth, we discovered that one of the mathematical assumptions underlying their statistics required our human subjects to be dead at least once a day. Even more unhappily, we made this discovery after we had interpreted our results to our satisfaction and were on the brink of publishing our report – yet another illustration that a researcher's facile and creative mind usually can see a rational pattern in any random display.

The fact that violation of a statistic's assumptions is hard to discern in the obtained statistic represents a special danger for relationship researchers who often find themselves in the uncomfortable position of trying to make causal inferences from regression analyses performed on nonexperimental data. Many of the variables of interest in relationship research are causally bidirectional and highly correlated with each other (e.g., trust, love, commitment; see Attridge, Berscheid, & Simpson, 1995). This highly glutinous mass often makes it difficult for relationship researchers to meet the assumptions that causal inference from such data requires (see Berscheid & Regan, 2005, pp. 79–81; McKim & Turner, 1997). Thus, my first prediction for relationship science is that making causal inferences from nonexperimental data will continue to be a problematic activity, barring the emergence of an statistical alchemist and the services of a statistical auditing firm to weed out spurious results in previously published reports.

Some Other Predictions

My other predictions about the future of the relationship field and profitable avenues of research follow from consideration of the three broad categories of macroforces I have named. First, and with respect to resources, one can predict that threats to federal funding for the social and behavioral sciences will increase in frequency and severity as the nation's financial solvency deteriorates and its financial obligations increase. Indeed, funding from the National Institutes of Health for much basic social scientific research, including research vital to an understanding of relationships, is in jeopardy as this *Handbook* goes to press (see Carpenter, 2005; Fiske, 2005).

Second, and with respect to technological changes, my predictions are more positive. Advances in neuroscience as a result of the development of functional magnetic resonance imaging (fMRI) and the increasing availability of the necessary magnets represent enormous opportunities for relationship researchers (see Berscheid, 2004). These are only now beginning to be mined (e.g., Fisher et al., 2003). Aron (in press) detailed several contributions that fMRI can make to relationship science and asserted that, in turn, relationship science may have

an even greater potential to contribute to neuroscience. His arguments may even be understated because it has become increasingly clear that the operations of the brain cannot be understood without significant advances in affective neuroscience; advances in affective neuroscience, in turn, require the development of a robust social neuroscience, which requires advances in relationship science because it is within our relationships with others that we humans most frequently and intensely experience emotion and process stimuli heavily saturated with affect.

The methods of neuroscience are only one way to understand the unconscious mind; the methods of cognitive social psychology are another. Unfortunately, the latter have yet to exert much influence on the relationship field. For example, social cognitive psychologist James Uleman (2005) observes that contemporary theory of mind "is remarkably absent from most research on person perception" (p. 11), which remains as important to the understanding of relationships as it was 50 years ago. Even well-established research findings on the nature of the human mind have yet to be recognized by many relationship scholars. Psychologist and computer scientist Roger Schank ("God . . .," 2005) opined, for example:

> I do not believe that people are capable of rational thought when it comes to making decisions in their own lives. People believe they are behaving rationally and have thought things out, of course, but when major decisions are made – who to marry, where to live, . . . people's minds simply cannot cope with the complexity. When they try to rationally analyze potential options, their unconscious, emotional thoughts take over and make the choice for them. (p. F3)

If Schank and the conclusions of many cognitive social psychologists are correct (see Hassin, Uleman, & Bargh, 2005, who described the *new unconscious*), we relationship scholars are trying to identify and understand the determinants of a person's "major decisions," such as mate selection or whether to maintain or dissolve a relationship, primarily through self-report even though the answers to many of our questions are not available to our respondents to report (although they always do report something).

New understandings of the human mind have additional implications for us researchers; that is, we ourselves are not immune from the limitations of our conscious minds when thinking about the highly complex system in which people's relationship decisions and other behaviors are embedded. More than 30 years ago, McGuire called for new conceptual models "that involve parallel processing, nets of causally interrelated factors, feedback loops, bidirectional causation, etc." (1973, p. 452) to deal with complex cognitive and social systems in which multiple causes interact with each other to produce an effect and in which effects act to change their original causal conditions. McGuire also warned, however, that "We shall all shy away from the mental strain of keeping in mind so many variables, so completely interrelated" (p. 452). He was right; we relationship scholars do shy away from the exercise. But he was wrong to blame "mental strain" for our avoidance; our conscious minds can strain until our noses bleed, but most of us still can't do it. Perhaps the epistemology of relationship research could use some attention.

Finally, with respect to macroforces that result in changes in the characteristics of research personnel, one can confidently predict that relationship researchers will become more racially and culturally diverse for a variety of reasons and that fewer will be men (if recently reported sex ratios of college undergraduates is any indication), all of which will influence the kinds of relationship problems that receive attention. One might also predict that as present researchers grow older, their interest in phenomena associated with young relationships (e.g., romantic love) will wane and the joys and problems of older relationships will gain more representation in relationship theory and research.

Only time will tell what the future holds for relationship research. We can all bet on that – and pray that the forces be with us.

ELLEN BERSCHEID
University of Minnesota

References

Aron, A. (in press). Relationship neuroscience: Advancing the social psychology of close relationships using functional neuroimaging. In P. A. M. Van Lange (Ed.), *Bridging social psychology: Benefits of transdisciplinary approaches*. Mahwah, NJ: Erlbaum.

Attridge, M., Berscheid, E., & Simpson, J. A. (1995). Predicting relationship stability from both partners versus one. *Journal of Personality and Social Psychology, 69*, 254–268.

Backman, C. W., & Secord, P. F. (1959). The effect of perceived liking on interpersonal attraction. *Human Relations, 12*, 379–384.

Berscheid, E. (2004). Lighting up the brain to illuminate the mind [Review of *Foundations in social neuroscience*]. *Contemporary Psychology: APA Review of Books, 49*, 713–716.

Berscheid, E., & Regan, P. (2005). *The psychology of interpersonal relationships*. New York: Prentice-Hall.

Carpenter, S. (2005, February). Hitting the bricks. *Aps Observer, 18*(2), pp. 12–19.

Dermer, M., & Berscheid, E. (1972). Self-report of arousal as an indicant of activation level. *Behavioral Science, 17*, 420–429.

Duck, S. (Ed.). (1988). *Handbook of personal relationships: Theory, research and interventions*. Oxford, England: Wiley.

Duck, S. (Ed.) (1997). *Handbook of personal relationships* (2nd ed.). Chichester, England: Wiley.

Fisher, H., Aron, A., Mashek, D., Strong, G., Li, H., & Brown, L. L. (2003, November). *Early state intense romantic love activates cortical-basal-ganglia reward/motivation, emotion and attention systems: An fMRI study of a dynamic network that varies with relationship length, passion intensity and gender*. Paper presented at Society for Neuroscience, New Orleans.

Fiske, S. (2005, March). Advice to social psychology grant writers. *APS Observer, 18*, p. 14.

Fiske, S. God (or not), physics and, of course, love: Scientists take a leap (January 4, 2005). *New York Times*, p. F3.

Hassin, R. R., Uleman, J. S., & Bargh, J. A. (2005). *The new unconscious*. New York: Oxford University Press.

Hendrick, C., & Hendrick, S. S. (Eds.). (2000). *Close relationships: A sourcebook*. Thousand Oaks, CA: Sage.

Kenny, D. A. (1994). *Interpersonal perception: A social relations analysis*. New York: Guilford Press.

Kenny, D. A., & La Voie, L. (1982). Reciprocity of interpersonal attraction: A confirmed hypothesis. *Social Psychology Quarterly*, 45, 54–58.

Kenny, D. A., & La Voie, L. (1984). The social relations model. In L. Berkowitz (Ed.), *Advances in experimental social psychology* (Vol. 18, pp. 142–182). Orlando, FL: Academic Press.

McGuire, W. J. (1973). The yin and yang of progress in social psychology: Seven koan. *Journal of Personality and Social Psychology*, 26, 446–456.

McKim, V. R., & Turner, S. P. (Eds.). (1997). *Causality in crisis? Statistical methods and the search for causal knowledge in the social sciences.* Notre Dame, IN: Notre Dame Press.

Tagiuri, R., & Petrullo, L. (Eds.). (1958). *Person perception and interpersonal behavior.* Stanford, CA: Stanford University Press.

Uleman, J. S. (2005). Introduction: Becoming aware of the new unconscious. In R. R. Hassin, J. S. Uleman, & J. A. Bargh (Eds.), *The new unconscious* (pp. 3–15) New York: Oxford University Press.

Contributors

GRAHAM ALLAN
School of Social Relations
Keele University
Staffs ST5 5BG
G.Allan@keele.ac.uk

DONNA M. ALLEN
Department of Business
Northwest Nazarene University
623 Holly Street
Nampa, ID 83686-5897
dmallen@mnu.edu

IRWIN ALTMAN
Department of Psychology
University of Utah
390 S. 1530 E.
Salt Lake City, UT 84112-0251
irwin.altman@m.cc.utah.edu

ARTHUR ARON
Department of Psychology
SUNY at Stony Brook
Stony Brook, NY 11794-2500
Arthur.Aron@sunysb.edu

DONALD H. BAUCOM
259 Davie Hall, CB #3270
Psychology Department
UNC-CH
Chapel Hill, NC 27599-3270
don_baucom@unc.edu

STEVEN R. H. BEACH
Institute for Behavioral Research
157 Psychology
University of Georgia
Athens, GA 30602-3013
sbeach@egon.psy.uga.edu

ELLEN BERSCHEID
Department of Psychology
University of Minnesota
75 East River Road
Minneapolis, MN 55455
Bersc001@umn.edu

ROSEMARY BLIESZNER
Department of Human Development
  (0416)
Virginia Polytechnic Institute and State
  University
Blacksburg, VA 24061
rmb@vt.edu

JEFFREY BOASE
Department of Sociology
University of Toronto
725 Spadina Ave.
Toronto, ON, M5S 2J4
Canada
jeff.boase@utoronto.ca

TYFANY M. J. BOETTCHER
Human Development and Family Sciences
The University of Texas at Austin
1 University Station A2700
Austin, TX 78712-0141
tyfany21@aol.com

BARBARA B. BROWN
University of Utah
Department of Family and Consumer Studies
225 South 1400 East, Room 228 AEB
Salt Lake City, UT 84112-0080
barbara.brown@fcs.utah.edu

ABRAHAM P. BUUNK
Department of Psychology
University of Groningen
Grote Kruisstraat 2/1
9712 TS Groningen
The Netherlands
a.p.buunk@ppsw.rug.nl

LORNE CAMPBELL
Department of Psychology
University of Western Ontario
London, Ontario, Canada N6A 5C2
lcampb23@uwo.ca

DANIEL J. CANARY
Hugh Downs School of Human Communication
Arizona State University
Tempe, AZ 85287-1205
dan.canary@asu.edu

RODNEY CATE
Department of Family Studies and Human
   Development
University of Arizona
Tucson, AZ 85721-0033
rcate@ag.arizona.edu

JOHN P. CAUGHLIN
Department of Speech Communication
University of Illinois
702 S. Wright Street, 127 Lincoln
Urbana, IL 61801
caughlin@uiuc.edu

MAHNAZ CHARANIA
Department of Psychology
Box 19528
University of Texas at Arlington
Arlington, TX 76019-0528
mahnazr10@hotmail.com

JENNIE Y. CHEN
Department of Psychology
Texas A&M University
4235 TAMU
College Station, TX 77843-4235
pookiesoup@tamu.edu

F. SCOTT CHRISTOPHER
Department of Family Resources
Arizona State University
Tempe, AZ 85287-2502
scott.christopher@asu.edu

JENNIFER A. CLARKE
Department of Behavioral Sciences and
   Leadership
HQ USAF/DFBL
2354 Fairchild Drive, Suite 6J133
USAFA, CO 80840-6228
clarkej@email.unc.edu

MARILYN COLEMAN
Department of Human Development and
   Family Studies
411 Gentry
University of Missouri
Columbia, MO 65211
ColemanMa@missouri.edu

W. ANDREW COLLINS
Institute of Child Development
University of Minnesota
51 E. River Road
Minneapolis, MN 55455-0345
wcollins@umn.edu

MICHAEL K. COOLSEN
Department of Management and
   Marketing
The John L. Grove College of Business
Shippensburg University
1871 Old Main Drive
Shippensburg, PA 17257-2299
mkcool@wharf.ship.edu

NATHAN R. COTTLE
Development of Family Studies and Early
   Childhood Education
Matthews Hall 119A
University of North Texas
PO Box 310829
Denton, TX 76203-0829
NCottle@coe.unt.edu

CAROLYN E. CUTRONA
ISBR
2625 N. Loop Drive Suite 500
Ames, IA 50010
ccutrona@iastate.edu

MARIANNE DAINTON
Associate Professor of Communication
La Salle University
Philadelphia, PA 19141
dainton@lasalle.edu

VALERIAN J. DERLEGA
Department of Psychology
Old Dominion University
Norfolk, VA 23529-0267
vderlega@odu.edu

LISA M. DIAMOND
Department of Psychology
University of Utah
380 South 1530 East, Room 502
Salt Lake City, UT 84112-0251
diamond@psych.utah.edu

PIETERNEL DIJKSTRA
Slochtermeenteweg 44
9621 CP Slochteren,
The Netherlands
dijkstrap@planet.nl

STEVE DUCK
Department of Communication Studies
151 BCSB
University of Iowa
Iowa City, IA 52242-1498
steve-duck@uiowa.edu

PEARL A. DYKSTRA
NIDI, P.B. 11650
2502 AR The Hague
The Netherlands
dystra@nidi.nl

NORMAN B. EPSTEIN
Department of Family Studies
University of Maryland
College Park, MD 20742
ne4@umail.umd.edu

BEVERLEY FEHR
Psychology Department
University of Winnipeg
515 Portage Avenue
Winnipeg, Manitoba R3B 2E9
bfehr@uwinnipeg.ca

FRANK D. FINCHAM
FSU Family Institute
Department of Child and Family Science
Florida State University
211 Sandels Building
Tallahassee, FL 32306-1491
ffincham@fsu.edu

HELEN E. FISHER
Department of Anthropology
Rutgers University
Office: 4 East 70th Street
New York City, NY 10021
HelenFisher@HelenFisher.com

JULIE FITNESS
Psychology Department
Macquarie University
Sydney 2109, Australia
Jfitness@psy.mq.edu.au

GARTH J. O. FLETCHER
Department of Psychology
University of Canterbury
Christchurch, New Zealand
g.fletcher@psyc.canterbury.ac.nz

MYRON D. FRIESEN
Department of Psychology
University of Canterbury
Private Bag 4800
Christchurch 8020, New Zealand
mdf26@student.canterbury.ac.nz

LAWRENCE GANONG
Sinclair School of Nursing and Department
of Human Development and Family
Studies
409 Gentry
University of Missouri
Columbia, MO 65211
Ganongl@missouri.edu

KELLI A. GARDNER
Psychology Department
Iowa State University
Ames, IA 50011-3180
kbendick@iastate.edu

JENNY DE JONG GIERVELD
The Netherlands Interdisciplinary Demographic
Institute
Lange Houtstraat 19
P.O. Box 11650
NL-2502 AR The Hague
The Netherlands
gierveld@nidi.nl

ROBIN GOODWIN
Department of Human Sciences
Brunel University
Uxbridge, Middlesex
London UB8 3PH
United Kingdom
Robin.Goodwin@brunel.ac.uk

CHRISTINE R. GRAY
Human Development and Family
Sciences
The University of Texas at Austin
1 University Station A2700
Austin, TX 78712-0141
crgray@mail.utexas.edu

KATHRYN GREENE
Department of Communication
Rutgers University
New Brunswick, NJ 08091-1071
kgreene@scils.rutgers.edu

DAVID W. HARRIS
Department of Psychology
Michigan State University
East Lansing, MI 48824
harri523@msu.edu

WILLARD W. HARTUP
Institute of Child Development
University of Minnesota
51 E. River Road
Minneapolis, MN 55455
hartup@umn.edu

JOHN H. HARVEY
Ell Seashore Hall
University of Iowa
Iowa City, IA 52242
john-harvey@uiowa.edu

KATHI L. HEFFNER
Department of Psychology
Ohio University
209 Porter Hall
Athens, OH 45701
heffner@ohio.edu

TED L. HUSTON
Department of Human Ecology
Gearing 117
University of Texas at Austin
Austin, TX 78712
huston@mail.utexas.edu

WILLIAM J. ICKES
Department of Psychology
University of Texas at Arlington
Arlington, TX 76019-0528
ickes@uta.edu

EMILY A. IMPETT
Center for Research on Gender and Sexuality
San Francisco State University
2017 Mission Street #300
San Francisco, CA 94110
eimpett@sfsu.edu

MICHAEL P. JOHNSON
Associate Professor of Sociology, Women's
    Studies, and African and African American
    Studies, Department of Sociology
The Pennsylvania State University
University Park, PA 16802-6207
mpj@psu.edu

DEBORAH J. JONES
CB #3270, Davie Hall
Psychology Dept. UNC-CH
Chapel Hill, NC 27599-3270
djjones@email.unc.edu

DEBORAH A. KASHY
Department of Psychology
Michigan State University
East Lansing, MI 48824
kashyd@pilot.msu.edu

JANICE K. KIECOLT-GLASER
Department of Psychiatry
Ohio State University College of Medicine
1670 Upham Drive
Columbus, OH 43210-1228
kiecolt-glaser.1@osu.edu

JEFFREY L. KIRCHNER
308 Davie Hall
Psychology Department
University of North Carolina at Chapel Hill
Chapel Hill, NC 27599-3270
jkirch@email.unc.edu

BRIGHID M. KLEINMAN
University of Miami
Department of Psychology
P.O. Box 248185
Coral Gables, FL 33124-0751
b.kleinman@umiami.edu

GALENA H. KLINE
University of Denver
Department of Psychology
Frontier Hall, 2155 S. Race St.
Denver, CO 80208
gakline@du.edu

MARK L. KNAPP
Department of Communication Studies
University of Texas at Austin
1 University Station A1105
Austin, TX 78712-0115
mlknapp@mail.utexas.edu

ASCAN KOERNER
Department of Communication Studies
244 Ford Hall
University of Minnesota
Minneapolis, MN 55455
koerno11@umn.edu

JEAN-PHILIPPE LAURENCEAU
University of Delaware
Department of Psychology
108 Wolf Hall
Newark, DE 19716-2577
jlaurenceau@psych.udel.edu

KIM LEON
Human Development & Family Studies
College of Human Environmental Sciences
University of Missouri-Columbia
407 Gentry Hall
Columbia, MO 65211-7040
leonk@missouri.edu

TIMOTHY J. LOVING
University of Texas at Austin
Department of Human Ecology
1 University Station A2700
Austin, TX 78712-0141
tjloving@mail.utexas.edu

STEPHANIE D. MADSEN
Psychology Department
McDaniel College
Westminster, MD 21157-4390
smadsen@mcdaniel.edu

HOWARD J. MARKMAN
University of Denver
Department of Psychology
Frontier Hall, 2155 S. Race St.
Denver, CO 80208
hmarkman@du.edu

ALICIA MATHEWS
Old Dominion University
Department of Psychology
Norfolk, VA 23529-0267
amath003@odu.edu

MARIO MIKULINCER
Department of Psychology
Bar-Ilan University
Ramat Gan 52900
Israel
mikulm@mail.biu.ac.il

PATRICIA NOLLER
Department of Psychology
University of Queensland
Brisbane, QLD 4072
Australia
pn@psy.uq.edu.au

NICKOLA C. OVERALL
Department of Psychology
University of Auckland
Private Bag 92019
Auckland, New Zealand
n.overall@auckland.ac.nz

LETITIA ANNE PEPLAU
Department of Psychology
Box 951563
University of California, Los Angeles
Los Angeles, CA 90095-1563
lapeplau@ucla.edu

DANIEL PERLMAN
School of Social Work and Family
    Studies
University of British Columbia
Vancouver, BC
Canada V6T 1Z2
d.perlman@ubc.ca

SALLY PLANALP
Department of Communication
The University of Utah
255 S. Central Campus Drive,
    Room 2400
Salt Lake City, UT 84112
Sally.Planalp@utah.edu

URMILA PILLAY
54 Ratcliffe Close
Uxbridge UB8 2DD
U.K.
urmilapillay@msn.com

NICOLE D. PLEASANT
University of Denver
Department of Psychology
Frontier Hall
Denver, CO 80208
npleasan@du.edu

CARYL E. RUSBULT
Department of Social Psychology
Vrije Universiteit
Van der Boechorststraat 1
Amsterdam 1081 BT
The Netherlands
ce.rusbult@psy.vu.nl

BARBARA R. SARASON
Department of Psychology
Box 351525
University of Washington
Seattle, WA 98195
bsarason@u.washington.edu

IRWIN G. SARASON
Department of Psychology
Box 351525
University of Washington
Seattle, WA 98195
isarason@u.washington.edu

PHILLIP R. SHAVER
Department of Psychology
University of California
One Shields Avenue
Davis, CA 95616-8686
prshaver@ucdavis.edu

ALAN L. SILLARS
Department of Communication Studies
University of Montana
Missoula, MT 59812
sillars@selway.umt.edu

JEFFRY A. SIMPSON
Department of Psychology
University of Minnesota
Minneapolis, MN 55455-0344
simps108@umn.edu

SUSAN SPRECHER
Department of Sociology-Anthropology
Illinois State University
Normal, IL 61790-4660
sprecher@ilstu.edu

SUSAN STANTON
238 Davie Hall
Psychology Dept. UNC-CH
Chapel Hill, NC 27599-3270
sstanton@email.unc.edu

GREG STRONG
Department of Psychology
SUNY at Stony Brook
Stony Brook, NY 11794-2500
gregjstrong@hotmail.com

CATHERINE A. SURRA
University of Texas at Austin
Department of Human Ecology
Gearing 115
Austin, TX 78712
surra@mail.utexas.edu

ANITA L. VANGELISTI
Department of Communication Studies
College of Communication
1 University Station A1105
Austin, TX 78712
a.vangelisti@mail.utexas.edu

C. ARTHUR VANLEAR
Department of Communication
    Sciences
University of Connecticut
Box U-85
Storrs, CT 06269-1085
vanlear@uconn.edu

THEO VAN TILBURG
Faculty of Social Sciences
Vrije Universiteit
De Boelelaan 1105
Amsterdam NL-1081HV
The Netherlands
TG.van.Tilburg@fsw.vu.nl

BARRY WELLMAN
Centre for Urban & Community Studies
University of Toronto
455 Spadina Avenue
Toronto, ON, Canada M5S 2G8
wellman@chass.utoronto.ca

AMY WENZEL
Psychopathology Research Unit
Department of Psychiatry
University of Pennsylvania
3535 Market St., Room 2032
Philadelphia, PA 19104
awenzel@mail.med.upenn.edu

CAROL M. WERNER
Department of Psychology
University of Utah
380 South 1530 East, Room 502
Salt Lake City, UT 84112-0251
carol.werner@psych.utah.edu

ADAM R. WEST
The University of Texas at Austin
Division of Human Development and Family
    Sciences
SEA 2.412/A2700
One University Station
Austin, TX 78712
adamwest@mail.utexas.edu

SARAH W. WHITTON
Judge Baker Children's Center
53 Parker Hill Avenue
Boston, MA 02120
swhitton@jbcc.harvard.edu

HEIKE A. WINTERHELD
Department of Psychology
N307 Elliott Hall
University of Minnesota
Minneapolis, MN 55455
winte216@umn.edu

Part I

INTRODUCTION

CHAPTER 1

Personal Relationships: An Introduction

Daniel Perlman
Anita L. Vangelisti

In a classic series of studies, Reed Larson and his colleagues (Larson, Csikszentmihalyi, & Graef, 1982) had 179 teenagers and adults carry electronic pagers with them wherever they went for 1 week. Once every 2 hours of their waking day, Larson beeped these individuals, asking them to indicate what they were doing and who, if anyone, was with them. More than 70% of the times they were paged, these individuals were in the presence of other people. Worked out over the course of a lifetime, from age 18 to 65, this means people are likely to spend 203,585 hours in the presence of others. As far back as Aristotle, humans have been recognized as social animals. Obviously, personal relationships are a salient and important aspect of our lives.

What precisely do we mean when we refer to personal relationships? Two classic definitions that specify the domain of this volume are as follows:

> *Two people are in a relationship with one another if they impact on each other, if they are interdependent in the sense that a change in one person causes a change in the other and vice versa. (Kelley et al., 1983)*

> *A relationship involves a series of interactions between two individuals known to each other. Relationships involve behavioural, cognitive, and affective (or emotional) aspects. Formal relationships are distinct from personal relationships. Relationships in which most of the behaviour of the participants is determined by their position in society, where they do not rely on knowledge of each other, are role or formal relationships. (Hinde, 1979)*

Personal relationships, in short, have a holistic quality. They are more than isolated interactive moments. They are more than highly scripted role-relations. Personal relationships include a range of relationships, including, but not exclusive to our most intimate relationships.

There are several reasons why personal relationships are important and why they are studied. When people are asked about what makes their lives meaningful, what contributes to their happiness, and what they value, they frequently identify close relationships. People have a pervasive, nearly universal need to belong (Baumeister & Leary, 1995). Research suggests that we are eager to form new bonds but dislike breaking them. Similarly, we devote considerable cognitive processing to interpersonal interactions and relationships (Fletcher, Overall, & Friesen, this volume). Finally, relationships are a key to our well-being. A plethora of evidence shows that close relationships are indeed vital to various indicators of well-being, including happiness, mental health, physical health, and even longevity (Berkman, 1995; Myers, 1999). As the slogan for a California public service program proclaims, "friends are good medicine." Undoubtedly, there are exceptions to these generalizations, and it is difficult to know for sure whether relationships are the cause of these outcomes. Nonetheless, the association of sociability with well-being cuts across time, cultures, measures of sociability, and indicators of well-being, and the association is a statistically strong one (Sarason & Sarason, ch. 23, this volume). In the health domain, cigarette smoking is one of the most widely studied and clearest hazards to health and longevity. Research demonstrates that sociability has as strong, probably even a stronger, association with well-being than does smoking. Stop smoking and have successful friendships: You'll live a long, happy life. Indeed one can argue that without relationships and social groups, humans would not be able to reproduce and survive (Reis, Collins, & Bersheid, 2000). The advances humans have made depend heavily on collective action.

Of course, relationships are not always positive experiences. There is a dark side to close relationships (Cupach & Spitzberg, 1994; Spitzberg & Cupach, 1998). Personal relationships can serve as a context for a variety of negative emotions, including jealousy (Guerrero & Anderson, 1998) and hurt (Leary, Springer, Negel, Ansell, & Evans, 1998). Furthermore, people can experience psychological (Straus & Field, 2003) or physical abuse (Johnson, this volume) at the hands of a loved one. Yet even when problematic, relationships are significant to us.

General Description

Because relationships are so central to people's lives, they have garnered the attention of researchers and theorists from a number of disciplines. Indeed, scholars have devoted a great deal of time and effort to understanding the antecedents, processes, and outcomes of close, interpersonal relationships.

The purpose of the *Handbook of Personal Relationships* is to present a synthesis of cutting-edge research and theory. This book integrates the varying perspectives and issues addressed by those who study how people relate to one another. To capture the breadth and depth of the literature in this area, the work of scholars from a variety of disciplines – including several subfields of psychology (e.g., social, developmental, personality, clinical), communication, family studies, and sociology – is highlighted.

The first section of the book comprises the current introduction. Following this editorial introduction, the second section offers a foundation for studying personal relationships. The history of the field is examined, as are the theories most frequently employed by researchers to explain processes associated with the development, maintenance, and decline of personal relationships. In this section of the book, there is an emphasis on introducing and comparing dominant theories (e.g., social exchange, attachment, evolutionary); the role of various theories in generating research is noted throughout the volume. Both qualitative and quantitative methods are discussed in terms of their unique applications and contributions to the relevant literature. In addition, the second section illuminates the ways relationships have been divided into types. The concerns raised in this section provide a foundation for examining personal relationships because they set the baseline for the ways that researchers observe, explain, and evaluate relationships.

The third section focuses on research and theory explicating the development of personal relationships, from when people meet until when relationships end. Chapters focus on issues such as courtship, marriage, and divorce. Although the developmental course of relationships may be viewed as somewhat linear, much of the research covered in this section points to the complex, multifaceted nature of relationship development.

The fourth section focuses on relationships across the life span. The nature and functions of relationships vary depending, in part, on the age of relational partners. Children have different ways of relating and they develop relationships for different reasons than do adolescents or adults. People dealing with the tasks of middle age maintain different sorts of relationships than do the elderly. Chapters in this section describe some of the special concerns reflected in personal relationships in various life stages.

In the fifth section, individual differences that influence personal relationships are examined. People approach and enter relationships with some relatively stable characteristics. Whether those characteristics involve personality traits, attachment styles, biological sex, sexual orientations, or mental health, they affect the developmental course of people's relationships. The material covered in this section describes the effects of individual differences on personal relationships.

The sixth and seventh sections present relationship processes. In the sixth section, communication, cognition, emotion, and psychophysiology are discussed. These are fundamental processes that influence, and are influenced by, relationships as well as other arenas of life. The seventh section deals with processes that involve interpersonal interaction. These include disclosure, social support, conflict, and sexual behavior.

Over the past dozen years, researchers have focused attention on the problematic aspects of personal relationships. People involved in close relationships experience stress because of circumstances that occur outside their relationship as well as events inside the relationship that the partners themselves instigate. Relational partners sometimes feel jealous or lonely. They often lie to each other. They may engage in extradyadic liaisons and may even physically or psychologically abuse each other. Some relational threats are common and their successful navigation actually may add to partners' confidence in their union. Other threats not only damage the relationship, they may jeopardize the physical and psychological well-being of one or both partners. The eighth section of the *Handbook* covers several of the more widely studied threats to personal relationships.

The ninth section examines the major qualities that suggest how well relationships are doing. The study of relational satisfaction began in the 1920s and more recently has been augmented by investigations of love, commitment, and intimacy. This section addresses the antecedents and dynamics associated with these phenomena as well as the challenges that researchers face as they attempt to conceptualize and operationalize the qualities of personal relationships.

Of course, relationships do not happen in a vacuum. They are influenced by physical, social, and cultural contexts. The tenth section deals with some of the factors outside individuals and relationships that affect the bonds between partners. This section includes classic (e.g., social networks) as well as leading-edge topics (e.g., computer-mediated relationships).

Although the focus of much of the research deals with the initiation and establishment of relationships, relationships actually persist for a long time, sometimes with problems. The final section of the volume covers how people sustain their relationships over time and how therapists can intervene to repair problematic relationships.

To ensure consistency across the volume in terms of scope and coverage, authors were guided in the following ways. First and foremost, they were asked to provide an integrative synthesis of existing theory and research, featuring classic and cutting-edge references where appropriate. Authors were encouraged to provide an historical or conceptual framework for organizing the literature and to make note of any important conceptual shifts. Second, they were instructed to comment on basic paradigms and research issues and to evaluate critically the area's methods. Third, authors were asked to provide judicious coverage of, and endeavor to resolve, any conflicts in the literature. Fourth, although this volume is primarily retrospective, authors were asked to signal directions for future research.

Authors

The individuals who contributed to the *Handbook* were selected as authors because they are recognized for the outstanding theoretical and empirical contributions they have made to the study of personal relationships. The contributors, in short, are distinguished, internationally known scholars. They herald from a variety of disciplines and approach personal relationships from a number of perspectives. They focus on topics ranging from the beginning to the ending of relationships, from micro to macro forces, and from the problematic to the sublime. Readers will find that the authors are adroit at expressing themselves in a scholarly yet readable fashion

Audience

Because the contributors offer sophisticated, new perspectives on extant literature as well as important theoretical and methodological recommendations for future research, the *Handbook* is an important volume for individual researchers and theorists to have on their shelves. Graduate students in social psychology, communication, family studies, sociology, and clinical psychology also will need to know the material published in this book. They may use the volume as a text in one of their courses or as an advanced introduction to the study of close relationships. Additionally, practitioners will be served by the volume. They will find that the theory and research presented provides a foundation for understanding relationships seminal to their therapeutic work with individuals confronting relationship issues, couples, and families.

Readers who are familiar with the literature on personal relationship will note that the current volume is one of three published in the last decade that summarizes research on personal relationships. In part, this is because of the speed with which the field has advanced. One of the other two books, also titled the *Handbook of Personal Relationships*, was edited by Steve Duck (1997) and published by Wiley. The other, *Close Relationships: A Sourcebook*, was edited by Clyde Hendrick and Susan S. Hendrick (2000) and was published by Sage. Both of these volumes serve as benchmarks for the field. The Duck *Handbook* conceives of the field of personal relationships as relatively new, and, as a consequence, its chapters provide researchers with compelling directions for future study. The Hendrick and Hendrick *Sourcebook* offers what they term a "panoramic view of close relationships research" (p. xxii); it provides an important overview of the literature. The current *Handbook* was conceived as a complement and an update to both of the prior volumes. It characterizes the field as relatively mature and highlights the established body of theory and research that has been generated over the past 3 decades. It offers readers a relatively detailed, sophisticated synthesis of existing literature. It is our hope that the insights and commentaries offered by the authors in *Handbook of Personal Relationships* will do as much to generate research and to advance the field as did the prior two volumes.

We believe social-science knowledge is best when it can be given away. If this volume is to succeed, it must engage you and leave you, the reader, wiser. Whether it is for your personal life, a course, your professional practice, or for conducting the next generation of research, the chapters should leave you better informed about, and with better tools for understanding, close relationships. We hope that you will develop an intimate relation with the contributors' ideas and join with us in helping to disseminate, apply, or empirically advance their wisdom.

Acknowledgments

We are indebted to many people for the important contributions they have made to this volume. This project came to fruition because of the work of a group of outstanding authors. The time, expertise, and careful thought that the authors willingly dedicated to writing chapters made this *Handbook* possible. We also are grateful to our editor, Philip Laughlin, who had the vision for this project. His willingness to respond to what must have seemed like an infinite number of questions, his patience, and his sense of humor made our work a pleasure.

To our universities we owe a debt of gratitude for their good libraries, for their computer systems, and for providing an environment that facilitates productivity. The project was started when Dan spent a very pleasant semester as a sabbatical visitor with the University of Texas Human Development and Family Sciences program. We also want to thank low-cost long-distance calling services for allowing us to work together on the phone for long periods without concern about telephone bills.

Being editors of a book about relationships, we are especially sensitive to how relationships enhance our lives and how there are trade-offs between work and family. We would like to thank our partners, John Daly and Lorrie Brubacher, for their support and understanding during the 3-year journey that the book has required. We also thank Abigail for reminding us, as young children will do, that relationships should come first.

References

Baumeister, R. F., & Leary, M. R. (1995). The need to belong: Desire for interpersonal attachments as a fundamental human motivation. *Psychological Bulletin, 117,* 497–529.

Berkman, L. F. (1995). The role of social relations in health promotion. *Psychosomatic Medicine, 57,* 245–254.

Cupach, W. R., & Spitzberg, B. H. (1994). (Eds.). *The dark side of interpersonal communication.* Hillsdale, NJ: Erlbaum.

Duck, S. W. (Ed.). (1997). *Handbook of personal relationships.* Chichester, England: Wiley.

Guerrero, L. K., & Andersen, P. A. (1998). Jealousy experience and expression in romantic relationships. In P. A. Andersen & L. K. Guerrero (Eds.), *Handbook of communication and emotion* (pp. 155–188). San Diego, CA: Academic Press.

Hendrick, C., & Hendrick, S. S. (Eds.). (2000). *Close relationships: A sourcebook.* Thousand Oaks, CA: Sage.

Hinde, R. A. (1979). *Towards understanding relationships.* London: Academic Press.

Kelley, H. H., Berscheid, E., Christensen, A., Harvey, J. H., Huston, T. L., Levinger, G., et al. (1983). *Close relationships.* New York: Freeman.

Larson, R., Csikszentmihalyi, M., & Graef, R. (1982). Time alone in daily experience: Loneliness or renewal? In L. A. Peplau & D. Perlman (Eds.), *Loneliness: A sourcebook of current theory, research, and therapy* (pp. 40–53). New York: Wiley Interscience.

Leary, M. R., Springer, C., Negel, L., Ansell, E., & Evans, K. (1998). The causes, phenomenology, and consequences of hurt feelings. *Journal of Personality and Social Psychology, 74,* 1225–1237.

Myers, D. G. (1999). Close relationships and the quality of life. In D. Kahneman, E. Diener, & N. Schwartz (Eds.), *Well-being: The foundations of hedonic psychology* (pp. 374–380). New York: Russell Sage Foundation.

Reis, H. T., Collins, W. A., & Bersheid, E. (2000). The relationship context of human behavior and development. *Psychological Bulletin, 126,* 844–872.

Spitzberg, B. H., & Cupach, W. R. (Eds.). (1998). *The dark side of close relationships.* Hillsdale, NJ: Erlbaum.

Straus, M. A., & Field, C. J. (2003). Psychological aggression by American parents: National data on prevalence, chronicity, and severity. *Journal of Marriage and Family, 65,* 795–808.

Part II

FOUNDATIONS FOR STUDYING RELATIONSHIPS

CHAPTER 2

The Seven Seas of the Study of Personal Relationships: From "The Thousand Islands" to Interconnected Waterways

Daniel Perlman
Steve Duck

In 1985, we wrote a projective overview of the field of personal relationships, describing it as a thousand islands of separate research traditions and practices that were in the process of coming together (Duck & Perlman, 1985). We now look out on a research world 20 years later, and we notice the connections – the oceans – rather than the separations. This chapter attempts historical overview of these developments and of previous tides and currents that led the research scholarship to today's position.

Whereas any historians – of an academic field or anything else – are necessarily selective and so offer only one perspective on history, the fact that we start from two or three or four disciplines (D. P. from social psychology and family studies; S. D. from communication studies and social psychology) ought to broaden our vision. Quite frankly, it has led to some friendly disputes between us about the placement of emphasis or precedence for ideas. We are aware, both in the abstract and through concrete experience, then, that there are differences in the points of view of researchers looking at the last 20 years, let alone the last

century of research on personal relationships. Readers, too, especially those who have labored in the field during the last 20 years, may have their own favorite ways of looking at the progress that has been made, as well as regrets about the roads less traveled. These observations therefore place us in an interesting dualistic relationship to the study of personal relationships and those who conduct it. First, our personal perspectives are individual and yet share some common space; second, our interpersonal attempts to create consensus about the venture reflect what happens when two people enter a friendship or romance. The trick is to end up with both sides agreeing more than they disagree.

In this chapter, we discuss 20th century trends in the study of personal relationships. We do this using the period in the late 1960s and early 1970s as a reference point. At that time, most work that is identifiably "relational" was done by social psychologists, sociologists, and family scientists, with the clearest lead being taken by social psychologists of attraction (Levinger, Newcomb) and scholars concerned with trait complementarily (e.g., sociologist Robert Winch). Social psychologists were focused on experimental investigations of interpersonal attraction (e.g., the question of liking), whereas the other two disciplines tended to be most interested in demographic and normative–performative aspects of relationships (Tharp, 1963, and Barry, 1970, provide reviews of the psychological literature done in this era and Broderick, 1970, instituted the important tradition of the *Journal of Marriage and the Family*'s decade review series). By the turn of the millennium, a variety of scholars was exploring the ways in which real-life relationships were developed, maintained, dissolved, carried on in the networks of other relationship in which they occurred naturally, and had a bearing on such other life issues as health (see Loving, Heffner, & Kiecolt-Glaser, this volume), coping with stress (Cutrona & Gardner, this volume), drug and tobacco usage (e.g., Farrell & White, 1998), and successful parenting (Kuczynski, 2003).

Against this broad canvas, we begin with a short early history of the field before the 1960s, discuss the 1960s and 1970s, and then cover trends since that time. Our analysis focuses on key contributors to the field, the methods of research being used, the dominant theoretical perspectives, and the substantive concerns being addressed. As the reader will see, however, the decision to select what are the key issues can be differently decided in different disciplines: Whereas a psychologist emphasizes inner activity, a communication researcher emphasizes interaction, a sociologist emphasizes embeddedness within a larger system, and a developmentalist the progressions made during the life span. We mention this point several times in review, because an interdisciplinary field has to be just that – one with its own developing sense of selfhood, and one that attempts not to privilege one type of research focus over others.

Our goal in this chapter is to provide a general historical picture. Many of the other authors in this volume highlight key developments and contributors of significance to more narrowly defined areas of work.

As part of the analysis, we report citation data and empirical analyses of the publication literature. To some extent, this grounds the analysis in objective evidence, yet any commentary on trends is necessarily highly selective and subjective. For example, citation indices are a measure of a person's visibility but require the assumption that every author reads and duly cites relevant work from all suitable places. Where authors do not read or research outside their own disciplinary boundaries, then these indices reflect the tendency to credit one's own. Because it is our major case that interdisciplinarity and multidisciplinarity (Acitelli, 1995) have evolved in the last 20 to 25 years, some of the sliding of previously prominent authors in the index lists can be attributed to the "dilution" effect produced by a newer and more diverse group of citing authors who cite, as classic work, different sorts of sources. Tracking the dilution effect is difficult, but the field has now moved to the point where collaboration among and the contribution of various disciplines is being recognized and folded into the development of the field.

With scholars from several disciplines contributing to the study of relationships and sharing elements of a common history of ideas, they often run in parallel without much crossover. To some extent, these scholars communicated and influenced one another, but the pressures to gain tenure in an existing discipline, using its familiar outlets and sources, tended to isolate people within their own intellectual traditions and emphases in practice, but without formally ruling out possible connectedness. Perhaps such pressures still exist to some extent. Yet as we noted in 1985 (Duck & Perlman, 1985), one of the great excitements in the early 1980s was the dawning recognition of the possibility that connectedness could be soundly established between different traditions.

This chapter focuses on what is currently called the area of close or personal relationships, the central concern for members of the International Association for Relationship Research (IARR) formed from the amalgamation of the previous International

Society for the Study of Personal Relationships (ISSPR) and the International Network on Personal Relationships (INPR). Our approach is linked most tightly with the disciplines of psychology and communication, especially in North America. This complements the current state of relationships field; Hoobler (1999) recently found that 85% of senior authors of articles in the field's two leading journals (*Journal of Social and Personal Relationships* and *Personal Relationships*) between 1989 and 1998 were either psychologists (62%) or communication scholars (23%). Increasingly, psychologists cite communication (Acitelli, 1995) and each discipline adapts some of its own traditions by acknowledging the values and research techniques of other disciplines, such as health communication and biology. If this chapter had been written by scholars from a different background (e.g., a family scientist, a social gerontologist or a sociologist), the analysis would undoubtedly refer to a somewhat different body of literature and reach somewhat different conclusions. Adams (1988), Bahr (1991), and Nye (1988), for example, provided analyses that complement this one, but they focus on family relationships (rather than close relationships more generally) and work from a family sociology or family studies perspective. Similarly, Cooper and Sheldon (2002) presented a content-analytically based overview of research since the 1930s on romantic relationships done by personality psychologists. These other disciplines and specialties within psychology mark out the progress of the field in different ways (Duck, Acitelli, & Nicholson, 2000), but one general truth is that each discipline has its heroes in the development of the field.

The History of Research on Close Relationships Before the 1960s

Philosophical Beginnings

More than 2,300 years ago, Aristotle wrote:

> One person is a friend to another if he is friendly to the other and the other is friendly

> to him in return.... People are also friends if the same things are good and bad for them, or if they are friends to the same people and enemies to the same people.... We are also friendly to those who have benefited us.... Also to those who are friends of our friends and those who are friendly to the people to whom we ourselves are friendly. (Aristotle, 330 B.C. trans. 1991, pp. 72–73)

Aristotle's writings, along with other materials from the same general period, testify that concern with relationships dates back a long time. In his *Nicomachean Ethics* and his treatise on *Rhetoric*, Aristotle addressed a number of topics, including the definition and types of friendship, the functions of friendship, the role of friendship in maintaining a stable society, who we select as friends, the role of individual differences in our friendships, the breakdown of relationships, and so on. Other Greek philosophers dealt with shyness, jealousy, love, bereavement, and the like. Although consideration of relationships is not new, it remains true that empirical testing and development of an understanding of factors that are important in relationships has grown enormously in the last two decades.

The philosophical approach that Aristotle used dominated the analysis of close relationships until the late 1880s (see Reisman, 1979, ch. 2, and Blieszner & Adams, 1992, ch. 2, for brief histories of the analysis of friendship; see Pakaluk, 1991, for selected writings). In the late 1880s and early 1900s, founding figures in the modern social sciences began developing their viewpoints. Their ideas had implications for our understanding of relationships. For example, Freud wrote on the role of parent–child relationships in personality development (see Hall & Lindzey, 1957, ch. 2). His analysis has led some to believe that we transfer onto adult relationships feelings and expectations based on childhood experiences and may seek a marital partner similar to our opposite-sex parent. James (1981) contended that the self-concept is defined in our relationships with others. Durkheim (1897/1963) was concerned with social organization. In what was one of his most influential publications, he argued that being socially marginal was the key antecedent of suicide. Thus, Durkheim's work focused attention on the detrimental consequences of social isolation, or what he called *anomie*. Simmel (1950), writing circa 1900, examined the unique properties of dyads, partnerships that involve just two people, noting significantly that they require consensus to work, but they can be ended by individual action. Darwin (1859) wrote his *Origins of the Species* that would come to be a key underpinning for modern evolutionary positions such as those developed by Buss (1998). All these scholars, from different disciplines, had something to say about personal relationships, and one of the major developments of modern research in personal relationships has been the validation and recognition of the insights of these various disciplines to the whole picture of "relationships."

The Rise of Empiricism

At about this same time, a major revolution occurred in social analysis – namely, the use of empirical investigations gained a toehold. For example, in his analysis of how a lack of social integration leads to suicide, Durkheim (1897/1963) supported his argument with statistics that introduced one of the first social scientific (as opposed to simple impressionistic) data to the question of personal relationships. In a 1898 article, Will S. Monroe asked 2,336 children in western Massachusetts to identify the traits and habits they considered to be important in selecting friends. (They mentioned such attributes as kindness, cheerfulness, and honesty.) This simple procedure marked a significant shift in the study of relationships – a change from analyses that were primarily philosophical analysis of terminology or introspections, to those that were grounded in data and empirical evidence.

In 1912, Harris reviewed a number of statistical facts on human mating to conclude that on "average, similar individuals tend to marry" (p. 492). Harris called this assortative mating. In 1929, Katherine Davis

published her volume *Factors in the Sex Life of 2200 Women*. As implied in her title, her study examined sexual behavior but, importantly, also included an early measure of marital satisfaction.

In the mid-1920s, Ernest Burgess (1926) conducted a painstaking survey of the available literature on the family. From his perspective, there was not yet "a single work that even pretended to study the modern family as behavior or as a social phenomenon" (p. 3). In this essay, he went on to define the family and outline the conceptual elements that he believed were needed in its analysis. Some consider Burgess's article to have launched the modern field of family relations (Broderick, 1988).

A number of developments occurred during the 1930s (see Broderick, 1988, for those in family studies). At the substantive level, there were noteworthy investigations such as Moreno's (1934) sociometric studies of popularity and cliques among school children. Jessie Bernard (1933) developed a measure of marital adjustment; E. Lowell Kelly, Louis Terman, Ernest Burgess, and others began their longitudinal studies of marital success (see Karney & Bradbury, 1995). Personality psychologists were studying assortative mating as well as the links between personality traits and marital satisfaction (Cooper & Sheldon, 2002). Waller (1937) published his classic article, "The Rating and Dating Complex," an analysis of what college students desire in a mate. A year later, in his early family text, Waller (1938) discussed his principle of least interest (i.e., that the partner with the least interest in the relationship has the greatest power).

At the organizational level, there were also important steps forward. Scholars interested in studying marriage and the family founded the National Council on Family Relations (NCFR). One of NCFR's first activities was establishing in 1939 their flagship publication, *Marriage and Family Living* (or the *Journal of Marriage and the Family* as it is now called). Although only a small journal at first, its arrival testified that there was a growing flow of studies to be reported. The Groves Conferences on Marriage and

Family Life began in 1934, and what is now the American Association for Marriage and Family Therapy started in 1945 (see Baucom, Epstein, & Stanton, this volume).

The Second World War undoubtedly slowed the study of relationships. One of the serendipitous findings of the massive work on the American soldier was the importance of peer relationships to the combat effectiveness of U.S. troops (Stouffer, Suchman, Devinney, Star, & Williams, 1949). As the war ended, social psychologists (e.g., Asch, 1946) were doing classic studies of how we form first impressions of new acquaintances. In 1950, Festinger, Schachter, and Back published their well-known study of married student housing at the Massachusetts Institute of Technology. Echoing Bossard's (1932) earlier findings on the role of propinquity in mate selection, they found that the closer residents lived to one another in functional terms, the more they tended to like one another.

In the 1940s and 1950s, sociologists conducted studies on human interaction in specific contexts and speculated on the place of relationships in U.S. society (see Lopata, 1981). An example of each of these genres, respectively, is William Foote Whyte's (1955) *Street Corner Society* and Riesman, Glazer, and Denney's (1953) *The Lonely Crowd*.

In the post-WWII period, research to related close relationships enjoyed a new prominence both publicly and within the discipline of psychology. The leading U.S. news magazine in that era, *Time*, featured Alfred Kinsey and his pioneering research on sexual practices as a cover story (August 24, 1953). Three presidents of the American Psychological Association (APA) gave their presidential addresses on topics related to relationships. Robert Sears (1951) argued that to best understand personality and social behavior, we need to examine not only individual but also dyadic influences. Harry Harlow (1958) indicated the importance of mother love to the development of monkeys. Arguably, Theodore Mead Newcomb is the APA president whose work is most directly related to what we now consider

the study of personal relationships. In his presidential address, Newcomb (1956) spoke on the question of interpersonal attraction, or who likes whom. He reported the preliminary findings from a study in which he had provided housing to a small group of Michigan students in return for their allowing him to study the friendships that developed in the group. Five years later, Newcomb (1961) published a monograph in which he gave a full report of his findings, and he also offered a balance-type theoretical perspective that he discussed in terms of systems of orientation (AB-X) for understanding what he had found. For example, he concluded that Person A will like Person B when, in Person A's mind, both A and B like the same things X.

The Study of Interpersonal Attraction in the 1960s and 1970s

Around the time of Newcomb's Michigan study, an important shift was occurring within the field of social psychology. Up until the 1950s, most social psychological studies were nonexperimental (70% circa 1949, Higbee & Wells, 1972). But by the end of the 1960s, more than 8 of 10 articles in social psychology's premier publication outlet, the *Journal of Personality and Social Psychology*, involved an experimental manipulation. The social psychological study of relating appears to have followed this trend. Focusing on the readily manipulable, researchers studied initial attraction or liking rather than long-term relationships as ongoing processes. In the earliest days of this work, *attraction* was not always differentiated from *relating*, leading to some misunderstandings about the varying goals of different work and, more important, to some arguments about the relevance of work on attraction to the understanding of longer term relationships that were almost entirely the result of failing to make this distinction (Levinger, 1972). The study of interpersonal attraction also grew within social psychology. By end of the 1960s, it was a recognized subarea of the field. This new stature was marked by the publication of two texts (Berscheid & Hatfield Walster, 1978 [first edition 1969]; Rubin, 1973) and two syntheses in the *Annual Review of Psychology* (Byrne & Griffitt, 1973; Huston & Levinger, 1978).

A Who's Who Analysis of the 1970s

METHODS FOR IDENTIFYING AND RANKING EMINENT CONTRIBUTORS

To do a more empirically based examination of trends in the study of personal relationships during the late 1960s and the early 1970s, we did a citation analysis of the aforementioned publications. We selected them because the texts presumably provided a synthesis of the important knowledge in the field suitable for informing students and the *Annual Review* chapters represented seminal summaries of the scientific literature at that time. To get an initial pool of contributors whose work was prominent in the 1970s, we used each publication's author index to identify approximately the 40 most cited scholars in each data source. We counted the number of text pages (excluding prefaces and bibliography pages) on which scholars were mentioned. Because these publications differed in whom they cited most, across the four publications, this provided a pool of 103 names. We then counted and summed the number of pages in all four sources on which every so identified scholar was cited.[1] Because the mean and standard deviation of the number of pages on which the pool of scholars was cited in the four data sources differed, in deciding on an index, we calculated the sum of each scholar's standardized score across all four sources. Because these standardized scores correlated 0.97 with the simple number of pages on which scholars were cited across the four texts, we decided to use the total number of pages as our eminence index. To avoid any tendency the seven authors of the data sources (Berscheid, Byrne, etc.) might have to unduly cite themselves, we replaced their self-citations with the number of citations of them one would expect based on a regression analysis using the other three sources as the predictor variables. All citation counts were done twice, once by the senior author and once by an undergraduate student, with any inconsistencies resolved by senior author. In earlier publications, albeit involving a larger number of data sources, Perlman established reasonable reliability and validity for such citation counts as an eminence measure (Perlman, 1979, 1980; Perlman & Lipsey, 1978).

THEORETICAL EMPHASES

Table 2.1 shows the 40 most eminent personal relationship scholars in the mid-1970s. Most of the individuals listed in this table were psychologists, although the set of prominent scholars also includes a few sociologists (Blau, Burgess, Homans, Kerckhoff, Back, Goffman, Wallin, and Waller). By considering the work for which they were cited, the names in this table can be used as clues to the theoretical perspectives and the topics of interest in the 1960s and 1970s.

According to this technique, the most eminent scholar was Donn Byrne, noted for his studies showing that liking is a function of the reinforcement value of attitude similarity. Byrne, along with his coauthors such as Lamberth, Clore, and Griffitt, interpreted attitude similarity and its role in attraction via a linear function. Along somewhat similar theoretical lines, Lott and Lott contended that "liking for a person will occur under those conditions in which an individual experiences *reward in the presence of that person*, regardless of the relationship between the other person and the reward event" (Lott & Lott, 1974, p. 172). In his gain–loss studies, Aronson asked how the sequencing of rewards influenced initial attraction (Aronson & Linder, 1965). In this period, then, there is evidence of a reinforcement or reward framework shaping a good deal of the thinking on initial attraction.

The emphasis on reinforcement can undoubtedly be seen as an extension of the reinforcement theoretical perspectives of Hull, Skinner, and others who were regnant at that time in experimental psychology. For example, the Lotts were seeing if the principles of classical conditioning à la Hull (1952) could be applied to attraction.

Table 2.1. *Eminence Among Personal Relationship Scholars in the 1970s*

Citations	Scholar
39	Byrne, D.*
37	Hatfield Walster, E.*
35	Schachter, S.
28	Aronson, E.
26	Berscheid, E.*
25	Davis, K.
25	Newcomb, T.
23	Jones, E.
21	Heider, F.
21	Rubin, Z.*
20	Kelley, H.
18	Festinger, L.
18	Levinger, G.*
18	Walster, G. W.
17	Murstein, B.
15	Allport, G.
15	Deutsch, M.
15	Lamberth, J.
15	Lott, A. J.
15	Zajonc, R.
14	Clore, G. L.
14	Maslow, A.
13	Blau, P.
13	Burgess, E.
13	Homans, G.
13	Kerckhoff, A.
13	Lerner, M.
13	Lott, B. E.
12	Back, K.
12	Goffman, E.
12	Griffitt, W.
12	Wallin, P.
11	Waller, W.
10	Altman, I.
10	Darley, J.
10	Freud, S.
10	Lorenz, K.
10	Mehrabian, A.
10	Reik, T.
10	Zimbardo, P.

* Self-citations replaced with regression-predicted citation score.

Similarly, Byrne linked his model with classical conditioning.

Two other theoretical perspectives, broadly defined, were also prominent in this period. Several eminent researchers offered some form of a cognitive model. Heider and Newcomb had similar balance theories, giving a cognitive consistency type (as opposed to Byrne's reinforcement) explanation of why attitude similarity produces liking. Festinger was noted for his dissonance formulation that the inconsistencies in our cognitions motivate a change in either those cognitions or our behavior. Heider, Jones, Davis, and Kelley all contributed to attribution theory, or how we explain the causes of behavior. Social exchange models rounded out the theoretical perspectives (e.g., equity views expressed especially by Hatfield as well as by Berscheid, G. W. Walster, Homans, and Blau, plus Kelley and Levinger's interdependence formulations). Both these exchange theories are concerned with the outcomes and costs of relationships, but they differ in that equity theorists are more concerned with the fairness in the rate of return partners receive whereas interdependence theorists believe people compare different relationships to find those from which they can get the best outcomes.

SUBSTANTIVE FOCI

In terms of topics, it is significant that two of the four seminal publications on which the citation counts were based used the term *interpersonal attraction* as their title (Berscheid & Hatfield Walster, 1978; Byrne & Griffitt, 1973). This was the central focus of research in this era. Berscheid and Hatfield Walster (1978, p. 20) defined interpersonal attraction as "an individual's tendency or predisposition to evaluate another person or symbol of that person in a positive (or negative) way." A few other prominent topics included love (Rubin, Hatfield, Maslow, Reik), affiliation in humans (Schachter, Zimbardo) and animals (Lorenz), physical attractiveness (Berscheid & Hatfield), ingratiation (Jones), relationship development (Davis, Levinger, Murstein, Kerckhoff), the mere exposure effect (Zajonc), and self-disclosure (Altman).

Similar trends were occurring in communication studies also in which the focus on initial attraction was early on criticized for assuming that personality characteristics and attitudes measured on a researcher's tests would necessarily be communicated and available through the communication that occurs in everyday life (Bochner, 1984; Duck, 1986; Sunnafrank, 1983). Although communication studies research on interpersonal communication was influenced by the events in social psychology, the first signs of resistance to the confusion of attraction and relationship were registered by Bochner (1984), along with the beginning of attention to the interaction processes by which personality traits exerted their effects in conversation (Burleson, 1990). Furthermore, theorists lead by Berger and colleagues (Berger & Bradac, 1982; Berger & Calabrese, 1975) were busy developing an understanding of the ways in which people gathered and marshaled knowledge during the process of attraction. Their work resulted in the publication of their influential uncertainty reduction theory (Berger & Bradac, 1982).

The Predominant Paradigm of the 1960s and 1970s

A REPRESENTATIVE STUDY: BYRNE (1961)

As a representative study from this era, let us discuss one of Byrne's (1961) early investigations. In the introduction of his report, Byrne acknowledged that "a number of studies have found greater similarity among friends than among nonfriends" (p. 713). But this was not sufficient. Byrne embarked on his investigation "to test the proposition that the effect of attitude similarity is a causative one." The subjects were 64 introductory psychology students at the University of Texas (36 men and 28 women). Subjects were first asked to complete a questionnaire assessing their attitudes toward 26 issues. Byrne (1961, p. 714) described the main part of his study as follows:

> Two weeks later they were falsely informed that the attitude scale had been given as part of a study in interpersonal prediction. They were told that the individuals in another class had been given the same scale that they took, students in the two classes were matched on the basis of sex, and they were given each other's tests (names

removed) in order to determine how much they could learn about one another from this information alone.

> Actually the questionnaire they received at this time was a fake one made up by the experimenter. The subjects were randomly divided into ... groups: one group received attitude scales filled out exactly the same as theirs, one received scales exactly the opposite as theirs had been. ... As a measure of interpersonal attraction, subjects were asked to indicate how well they felt they would like this person and whether they believed they would enjoy working with him (or her) as a partner in an experiment. ...

> [The] hypothesis was overwhelmingly confirmed for each of the two attraction scales. The group with attitude scales filled out the same as their own (SA) indicated significantly more positive feelings toward the "stranger" than did the group which received scales indicating dissimilar attitudes (DA). [For Personal Feelings, the means were 6.53 vs. 1.76 and for Desirability as a work partner, they were 6.47 vs. 2.65.] Each difference was significant at less than the 0.001 level.

PROTOTYPICAL FEATURES

Byrne went on to do numerous studies of attraction using various methods and populations (see Byrne, 1971, 1997). As we looked at the 1961 study, however, we believe many of its features are prototypical of the era. We see the following noteworthy aspects of Byrne's study:

- Byrne was a North American scholar, publishing his work primarily for an audience of social psychologists.
- His article was three pages long, reported just one study (with a total of four conditions rather than just the two we have described) and contained 11 references.
- His scientific goal was causal inference.
- Byrne performed an experiment in which he manipulated his independent variable, attitude similarity, and randomly assigned subjects to experimental conditions.
- The experiment involved a fallacious cover story.

- His subjects were introductory psychology students who were presumably middle-class Caucasians.
- The study involved strangers who never actually interacted.
- Interpersonal attraction was the dependent variable.
- Byrne was concerned with one person's – the subject's – attraction.
- Byrne used between group *t* tests to perform his statistical analyses.
- Byrne was only concerned with the outcome of how well subjects liked the stranger, not with the processes involved in their becoming friendly.
- Byrne was not concerned with such variables as the subjects' other relationships or the subjects' stage in the life cycle. He did not consider stages of relationships. He neither examined sex differences nor discussed practical implications of his findings, although his later work (e.g., Byrne, 1971) did both.
- Because Byrne employed an experimental design with random assignment of subjects to conditions, he was able to have greater confidence in his causal inferences, but because the study was conducted in a laboratory, he was less confident in the external generality of his results.

EMPIRICAL EVIDENCE FOR THE PROTOTYPICAL FEATURES

Although not all these features have been examined, some of them have been empirically documented, at least for social psychology in general. Sears (1986) summarized key findings from these archival investigations of publication practices saying, "By the 1960s, this conjunction of college student subject, laboratory site, and experimental method, usually mixed with some deception, had become the dominant methodology in social psychology, as documented in several systematic content analyses of journal articles" (p. 516). For instance, Higbee and Wells (1972) found that 75% of studies in the *Journal of Personality and Social Psychology*

(c. 1969) used college students as subjects, 40% used *t* tests, and 79% performed analyses of variance. Within the relationships literature per se, Huston and Levinger (1978) ascertained that by the mid-1970s, "More than two thirds of the studies focus on impressions after a person is given information or after a brief encounter" (p. 117).

Trends Between the Late 1970s and the 1990s

Duck and Perlman's Analysis

By the time Huston and Levinger's 1978 *Annual Review* chapter was published (on interpersonal attraction and relationships), the winds of change seemed to be blowing across the field. In comparing Huston and Levinger's review with Byrne and Griffitt's earlier chapter, Huston and Levinger covered more ground and attended more to the development and decline of relationships including for the first time in such a review the term "relationships." In the mid-1980s, we (Duck & Perlman, 1985) commented on the changes that we saw occurring in the field. First, we noted what might be called the organizational growth of personal relationships as a specialized area of work. In 1981, Duck and Gilmour (1981a, 1981b, 1981c) had published the first three of a five volume series that was the first to be entitled "Personal Relationships." These three were devoted to individuals in relationships, developing relationships, and relationships in disorder, with two later volumes devoted to relationship dissolution and relationship repair, respectively (Duck, 1982, 1984; Duck & Gilmour, 1981a, 1981b, 1981c). At nearly the same time, Gilmour and Duck initiated the first two International Conferences on Personal Relationships at Madison Wisconsin, 1982 and 1984, with barely 110 participants at each (see Figure 2.1). The first journal for the field, *Journal of Social and Personal Relationships*, was published in March 1984. In 1986 and 1987, the ISSPR and INPR were founded with a commitment to the study of personal relationships being an international, multidisciplinary activity. Through the organization of, effectively, annual conferences sustaining roughly 300 delegates each year and a strong emphasis on the development of young scholars with an early appreciation for multidisciplinary reading and research, these developments increasingly served as a basis for consolidation and development of the field. By 2002, when ISSPR and INPR merged into IARR, the merger conference in Halifax, Nova Scotia, was host to some 320 participants from more than a dozen countries and to such disciplines as family studies, communication studies, sociology, leisure studies, biology, and several branches of psychology from social to developmental to cognitive.

We (Duck & Perlman, 1985, p. 3) also noted that "Methodological innovations have featured prominently since 1978." At the time we wrote that statement, we focused on such innovations as daily diary and experience sampling (or pager) techniques (see Duck, Rutt, Hurst, & Strejc, 1991; Larson, Csikszentmihalyi, & Graef, 1982; Reis & Wheeler, 1991). We saw in these techniques a trend to move out of the laboratory in an increased effort to understand people's everyday lives. From today's vantage point, we would also certainly identify the rise in some quarters of qualitative methods, note concern with the individual versus the dyad as the level of analysis (Bulcroft & White, 1997) and the insider versus outsider issue (Duck & Sants, 1983; Olson, 1977; Surra & Ridley, 1991), mention concern with conducting longitudinal studies (Shebilske & Huston, 1996), pass along a popular book on relationship measures (Rutter & Schwartz, 1998), and note a variety of statistical advances, including

  meta-analysis for combining the results across multiple studies,
  structural equation modeling (e.g., LISREL);
  Kenny's social relations model for determining how much the person, his or her partner, and the interaction between them contribute to their interactions (Kenny & La Voie, 1984); and

procedures for dealing with the problem of the nonindependence of data collected from relationship partners (Gonzalez & Griffin, 1997), and, as we entered the 21st century, hierarchical linear modeling (Kashy, Campbell, & Harris, this volume).

Additionally, in such disciplines as communication studies, sociology, and family studies, there has been a notable growth in interview techniques, often involving the long-term systematic gathering of data in the subjects' own homes. For example, Veroff's Early Years of Marriage (EYM) project has been investigating 373 couples since 1986. It involved in-home interviews, telephone interviews, and the innovative joint narrative technique of having couples jointly tell the story of their relationship. Via these methods, the EYM project has developed a number of important insights into the dynamics of marriage and some early indicators of the marriage's likely success or failure. Members of the extended EYM team have also uncovered important stylistic differences in the husbands' and wives' typical responses to talk about their relationship and also some important elements of the dynamics of conflict management (Acitelli, Douvan, & Veroff, 1993; Crohan, 1992; Ruvolo & Ruvolo, 2000). Baxter's work on a dialectical model of relationships (e.g., Baxter & Montgomery, 1996) has also been influential in broadening the understanding of the ways in which partners in a dyad contend with the different forces that are at play in relational conduct, such as the urge for personal autonomy as it must be balanced with needs for interdependence in any relationship. Such work has typically been carried out in real-life networks, families, or long-distance relationships; with an emphasis on qualitative data from which themes are derived by repeated review rather than by the investigator's intuitions.

In our 1985 analysis, we also observed several other trends:

  a shift away from studies of initial acquaintance to studies of longer term relationships;

Figure 2.1. Keynote speakers at the 1982 International Conference on Personal Relationships held in Madison, Wisconsin. Front row: Harold Kelley, Elaine Hatfield, Steve Duck, Ted Huston, John Harvey; second row: Ellen Berscheid, Jerry Ginsberg, Robert Hinde, Daniel Perlman; back row: Wolfgang Stroebe and Michael Argyle. Photo courtesy of Robin Gilmour.

a shift away from the simple question of attraction to a broader set of topics such as shyness, jealousy, loneliness, peer relationships, and social support, but also to a focus on process rather than snapshots;

a greater concern with mediating variables and relationship processes in the longer term;

more vigorous efforts to differentiate and taxonomize relationships (see VanLear, Koerner, & Allen, this volume);

new interest in role and sex differences in relationships (see Impett & Peplau, this volume),

greater recognition that dyadic relationships are part of larger networks of relationships (see Allan, this volume); and

greater concern with health (see Loving, Heffner, & Kiecolt-Glaser, this volume) and applied issues.

Although we then saw social cognition as a substantial concern, there were other trends emerging elsewhere at the same time.

In social psychology, the focus of its work on cognition over the next decade led Berscheid to devote the "lion's share" of her 1994 *Annual Review* chapter to relationship cognition (cf. Berscheid & Reis, 1998, pp. 216–222). We also stated that "there appears to be a greater use of diverse subject populations; more intensive use of multivariate statistical approaches…less use of deception; less direct manipulation of variables; and more concern for external validity" (Duck & Perlman, 1985, p. 6).

Empirical Evidence and a Second View

Complementing the impressionistic analysis we did in the mid-1980s of trends in the personal relationship area, Reis and Stiller (1992) did a quantitative analysis of trends in *Journal of Personality and Social Psychology* (*JPSP*) articles for the 20-year period 1968 to 1988. As shown in Table 2.2, they found evidence of a growing complexity in the work published. For instance, they reported the number of pages per article increased from 4.35 to 10.30, the number of references went

Table 2.2. *Journal of Personality and Social Psychology Publication Trends*

Variable	1968	1988
Pages	4.35	10.30
Tables	2.80	3.90
References	14.70	42.50
Studies reported	1.30	1.80
Subjects	141	200
Grant support	71%	59%

Note: From "Publication trends in JPSP: A three-decade review," by H. T. Reis and J. Stiller, 1992, *Personality and Social Psychology Bulletin,* 18, p. 467. Copyright by the Society for Personality and Social Psychology. Adapted with the permission of the authors.

from 14.65 to 42.52, and the number of studies reported in each article climbed from 1.27 to 1.78. Consistent with the views we espoused about a shift away from experimental designs, Reis and Stiller found that the use of analysis of variance declined in *JPSP*, but the use of multivariate techniques (e.g., correlation, regression, factor analysis, path analysis) increased. In the same vein, Cooper and Sheldon (2002) found that in personality research on romantic relationships, there was a steady increase in the use of more complex statistical designs from the 1960s until the end of their investigation. Simple studies do, however, still persist: Hoobler (1999) reported that in the 1990s, 38% of relationship articles were exploratory or descriptive in nature and cross-sectional personality studies relying exclusively on self-report from a single individual are as prevalent as ever (Cooper & Sheldon, 2002). Reis and Stiller found that the number of subjects per study increased (from 140.6 to 199.9), but they did not systematically analyze the type of individuals recruited for studies. Sears (1986) reported a complementary piece examining the Interpersonal Relations and Group Processes section of the *Journal of Personality and Social Psychology* for the period 1980 to 1985. He showed that the percent of articles based on U.S. undergraduate students and the use of the lab as a research site was declining (from 78% to 58%, and from 69% to 66%, respectively), whereas the use of adults and natural habitats was increasing (19% to 32%

and 31% to 34%). A decade later, de Jong Gierveld (1995) showed that only 51% of the empirical articles published in the *Journal of Social and Personal Relationships* (1984–1994) were based on university student samples (cf. Hoobler, 1999), although she did not break those studies down by methods or populations employed.

At roughly the same time as we (Duck & Perlman, 1985) reflected on trends in the field, so, too, did Ellen Berscheid (1985). This is how she summed up what she saw:

> *Investigators are turning from a focus upon attraction phenomena as they occur in initial encounters between strangers to the study of attraction in the context of ongoing relationships; from a view of attraction as a monolithic global construct to a recognition that it is fruitful to differentiate varieties of attraction; from an exclusive study of mild forms of attractions (e.g., liking) to studies that include more intense forms (e.g., love); from investigations of a single stimulus at a single point in time and its influence upon attraction to an interest in how a variety of casual conditions may contribute to an attraction phenomena and how they all may evolve and change over time; from an exclusive focus upon how the characteristics of the individual (or of the other, or of their combination) influence attraction to a consideration of how these characteristics may interact with environmental variables, both physical and social, to affect attraction and how attraction itself may subsequently influence all of these variables. (Berscheid, 1985, pp. 417–418)*

Thirteen years later, in 1998, she would add, "Today, all of these transitions have been made" (Berscheid & Reis, 1998, p. 193).

The Study of Personal Relationships in the Late 1990s

Who's Who in the 1990s

To determine the most frequently cited contributors of the 1990s, we did another citation analysis, employing the same general procedures as were used for the publications analyzed in the 1970s. For the era of the 1990s, we used seven data sources: three summaries of the field for professionals and advanced students (Berscheid and Reis's 1998 *Handbook of Social Psychology* chapter, Duck's 1997 *Handbook of Personal Relationships*, and C. Hendrick and S. Hendrick's *Close Relationships: A Sourcebook*, 2000), and four textbooks (Brehm, 1992; Cramer, 1998; Hinde, 1997; Weber & Harvey, 1994). For each of the main editors or authors (e.g., Berscheid, Brehm), we again replaced their self-citations with a regression-predicted citation score. Three of the sources had chapter authors (Duck, 1997; Hendrick & Hendrick, 2000; Weber & Harvey, 1994). In the book(s) for which scholars wrote a chapter(s), we assigned them a citation score in that volume equal to the number of times they were cited in that volume by others plus 0.33 times their self-citations. (We arrived at this adjustment in light of finding for the text authors that, on average, their actual self-citations were almost exactly 3 times their regression-predicted citations.) This made some use of the available independent citation of these scholars but guarded against inflation due to self-citation. In this case, selecting the 40 most frequently cited scholars in these seven works produced an initial pool of just over 160 names. Again, a preliminary sum of normalized citation scores correlated very highly ($r = 0.99$) with the simple number of pages on which each scholar was cited across the seven data sources. We again decided to use the total number of pages as our eminence index. As an indicator of the "split half" reliability of this index, we correlated the sum of the scores in four works (Berscheid & Reis, Brehm, Cramer, and Duck) with the remaining three works; the resulting correlation was 0.72.

Table 2.3 shows the 60 most eminent personal relationship scholars in the mid- to late-1990s. Ten members of this group are individuals who were also identified as eminent in the 1970s: Altman, Berscheid, Byrne, Davis, Hatfield, Kelley, Levinger, Murstein, Rubin, and G. Walster. The eminent individuals of the 1990s are primarily psychologists, with a few scholars with training or appointments in communications (Baxter, Canary, Cupach, Dindia, Duck, Montgomery, Wood), sociology (Johnson, Schwartz, Spanier, Sprecher, G. Walster), and family studies (Cate, Huston, Milardo, Surra). A subset of the psychologists has clinical training (Bradbury, Christensen, Fincham, Gottman, Jacobson, Markman, O'Leary). The large majority of scholars are employed within the United States with exceptions being Bowlby (United Kingdom, deceased), Buunk (the Netherlands), Fletcher (New Zealand), Holmes (Canada), and Noller (Australia). The scholars in Table 2.3 again give clues as to the theoretical perspectives and the topics of recent and current interest.

THEORETICAL EMPHASES

Ellen Berscheid and Harold Kelley are now the two most frequently cited scholars. One of the striking features of the table is that five other scholars in the top 30 were coauthors with Kelley and Berscheid of the seminal 1983 volume, *Close Relationships* (Peplau, Huston, Levinger, Harvey, and Christensen). Three or four other scholars in the table (Rusbult, Holmes, Thibaut, and, to a lesser extent, Buunk) have been associated with interdependence theory. The interdependence viewpoint advanced in Kelley et al.'s (1983) volume has clearly become an important perspective for understanding relationships. Other theoretical perspectives espoused by currently eminent scholars include equity theory (Hatfield, Sprecher, G. Walster), attachment theory (Shaver, Hazan, Noller, Simpson, Bowlby, and Weiss), attribution theory (Kelley, Fincham, Bradbury, and Harvey), and dialectical theory (Baxter, Montgomery, and, extending beyond those in Table 2.3, Rawlins, 1992). Buss is within the set of the top 20 most eminent scholars, as is Simpson. An evolutionary perspective is one that was growing in significance at the end of the 20th century. Byrne is now the 33rd scholar in terms of eminence; contributors such as Aronson, Clore, Griffitt, and the Lotts are no longer

Table 2.3. *Eminence Among Personal Relationships Scholars in the 1990s*

Citations	Scholar
133	Berscheid, E.
128	Kelley, H.
125	Gottman, J.
102	Duck, S.[a,c]
102	Shaver, P.
101	Hatfield, E.
87	Baxter, L.
87	Peplau, L. A.
84	Rusbult, C.
81	Huston, T.
70	Levinger, G.
64	Rubin, Z.
62	Hendrick, S. S.
58	Simpson, J.
58	Sprecher, S.[c,d]
57	Altman, I.
57	Buss, D.
57	Fincham, F.
55	Kurdek, L. A.
55	Noller, P.
54	Aron, A.[b,c]
54	Bradbury, T.
54	Harvey, J.[a,d]
54	Reis, H.
54	Thibaut, J.
49	Buunk, B.
48	Bowlby, J.
48	Davis, K. E.
47	Christensen, A.
47	Kenny, D.
46	Hazan, C.
46	Surra, C.
45	Byrne, D.
45	Hendrick, C.
45	Murstein, B.
44	Holmes, J.
42	Cate, R.
42	Markman, H. J.
41	Schwartz, P.
39	Clark, M. S.
39	Jacobson, N. S.
38	Milardo, R. M.[b,d]
38	Weiss, R. S.
37	Montgomery, B. M.[b,c]
37	Hill, C. T.
37	Snyder, M.
36	Spanier, G. B.
35	Canary, D. J.
35	Fletcher, G. J. O.
34	Berg, J. H.
34	Cupach, W. R.

Citations	Scholar
34	O'Leary, K. D.
34	Tesser, A.
34	Walster, G. W.
34	Aron, E. N.[b,c]
34	Johnson, M. P.
34	Ickes, W. J.[b,c]
33	Wood, J. T.
33	Dion, K. K.
33	White, G. L.
33	Veroff, J.
33	Dindia, K.[b,d]

[a] Self-citations replaced with regression-predicted citation score. [b] Includes at least one adjusted chapter author score adjusted where the scholar's score for Duck's *Handbook* was the sum of times other authors in that volume cited the scholar plus 0.33 times the scholar's self-citations. [c] Includes at least one adjusted chapter author score adjusted where the scholar's score for Weber and Harvey's text was the sum of times other authors in that volume cited the scholar plus 0.33 times the scholar's self-citations. [d] Includes at least one adjusted chapter author score adjusted where the scholar's score for C. Hendrick and S. Hendrick's *Sourcebook* was the sum of times other authors in that volume cited the scholar plus 0.33 times the scholar's self-citations.

on the list, although Jacobson, Christensen, and O'Leary are associated with behaviorally oriented marital therapy approaches. The reward or reinforcement tradition appears to have dropped in prominence and, even within the couples therapy area, purely behavioral models have been replaced by more integrative approaches (see Baucom et al., this volume).

SUBSTANTIVE FOCI

Looking at Table 2.3, supplemented by our judgments, the range of topics seems broader than in the 1970s. A few prominent topics of the 1970s continue to be of interest: love (Hatfield, Rubin, S. Hendrick and C. Hendrick, Shaver, Kelley, Aron), physical attractiveness (Berscheid, Hatfield, Reis, Sprecher), relationship development (Bradbury, Levinger, Huston, Surra, Murstein), and self-disclosure (Altman). Other topics include marital interaction and satisfaction (Gottman, Noller, Fincham, Bradbury); communication (Baxter, Duck, Gottman, Noller), commitment (Rusbult,

Kelley, Surra), trust (Holmes), conflict and dissatisfaction (Canary, Johnson, Milardo, Rusbult, Kelley), breakdown, dissolution, and loss of relationships (Duck, Rusbult, Levinger, Baxter, Harvey, Peplau, Rubin), the dark side of relationships (Cupach), communal versus exchange relationships (Clark), sex differences and sexual orientation in relationships (Peplau, Kurdek, Wood, Canary, Dindia), sexuality (Sprecher, C. Hendrick and S. Hendrick, Simpson), dating and mate selection (Buss, Surra), jealousy (Buss, Buunk, Cupach), loneliness (Peplau, Shaver, Cupach, Weiss), positive illusions in relationships (Holmes), and data-analytic procedures (Kenny).

Further work has applied relationship theories to the practical management of relationship issues in ill-health (Lyons, Sullivan, Ritvo, & Coyne, 1995), long distance relationships (Rohlfing, 1995; Sahlstein, 1998; Stafford, 2004), Comforting (Barbee, 1990; Burleson, 1990), face threat (Metts, 2000), hurtful messages (Vangelisti, 1994), shyness (Bradshaw, 1998), and even the role of history (Duck, 2002).

Where Next for the Study of Personal Relationship?

In the late 1970s and the early 1980s, we had a clear sense of the field changing course. In an important way, we believe a paradigm shift away from the type of research we illustrated with Byrne's study has occurred. At present, we see the area as being more diversified methodologically. Because of that, we do not anticipate sweeping changes in the foreseeable future. Instead, we suspect a gradual evolution is more likely to occur over the next few years. We expect the internal evolution of ideas, methodological innovations, pressures from universities and granting agencies, and the changing nature of relationships in society will be among the factors that influence the directions of future relationship research. What we see at present are some emerging lines of work and some prescriptions for where the field should go.

In the late 1990s, two emerging lines of work that attracted our attention were on maintenance (Canary, Rusbult, Harvey, Dindia, Baxter) and on the dark side of relationships (Felmlee & Sprecher, 2000, also noted this later trend). Close relationships continue for 10, 20, or even 60 years, although for most of the 20th century, researchers seemed to focus more on their initiation or ending rather than their persistence. We are glad that new work is illuminating how people keep relationships going (Canary & Dainton, this volume). In a broad sense, the dark aspects of relationships are the opposite side of their positive elements. The dark side is clearly important in its own right, but work on toxicity (e.g., Cupach & Spitzberg, 1994; Kowalski, 1997; Spitzberg & Cupach, 1998) may help us illuminate how to have more successful relationships.

Most of the contributors to this volume identify recent developments and trends in their own areas. From our perspective, we see a general difference in the approach of this volume compared with its earliest predecessor (Duck, 1988): The initial handbook was more prospective, whereas the current volume is more of a retrospective of what has been accomplished. Indeed, the field has now matured to the point where handbooks on specialized subtopics are appearing (Harvey, Wenzel, & Sprecher, 2004; Mashek & Aron, 2004). In terms of specific topics, chapters such as those on physiology (Loving, Heffner, & Kiecolt-Glaser; cf. Aron, Fisher, & Strong), online relationships (Boase & Wellman) and relationships, culture and social change (Goodwin & Pillay; cf. Allan and de Jong Gierveld, van Tilburg, & Dykstra) represent new thrusts. Beyond this volume, noteworthy evolving interests at the beginning of the 21st century included foregiveness, featured in Fincham's (2000) invited *Personal Relationships* article, and compassionate love. The Fetzer Institute (http://www.fetzer.org) funded 26 research projects on the later topic and cosponsored with the International Association of Relationship Research and Illinois State University the 2003 Conference on Compassionate Love coordinated by Susan Sprecher (for the program see "Detailed Conference Program," n.d.).

Several authors have recently given their prescription for where the field should be going (see Sarason, Pierce, & Sarason, 1995, including Rook's 1995 summary). For instance, Hinde (1997, ch. 29) argued that the field needs an integration of its activities and analyses. Berscheid (1995) called for a grand, unifying theory of relationships that "would address the principal relationship types, delineating the similarities and differences among them with respect to the causal conditions associated with various relationship phenomena" (p. 529). Felmlee and Sprecher (2000) advocated developing better connections between the increasingly specialized conceptualization used to address narrow topics and the broader, more general theories available in, for example, sociology. Duck, West, and Acitelli (1997) suggested that we should study relationships in their full complexity as lived experiences and therefore should not "overlook the importance of 'context' in modifying and influencing the ways in which relating is carried out" (p. 2). In an article on the state of the field from a sociological perspective, Felmlee and Sprecher (2000) argued for further study of the social environmental context of relationships, especially the social networks in which they are embedded. Aron and Aron (1995) believe relationship researchers should attend to "deep, passionate relational experiences"; take theoretical perspectives that integrate cognitive and emotional elements; and see not only how basic disciplines can contribute to the understanding of relational phenomena but also how the study of relationships can contribute to basic disciplines. Other suggestions (see Rook, 1995) include the following:

more descriptive efforts,

greater attention to the sociocultural or historical context in which relationships occur (cf. Felmlee & Sprecher, 2000),

more attention to the socially constructed nature of relationships and the way we tell our stories about them, and

continued efforts to apply our existing knowledge of relationships.

Limitations?

These days many empirical reports abruptly break off at this point with touching modesty to deal with the limitations of the study – just before the conclusion proceeds to ignore them! We don't believe that the failures of the field should be ignored, and indeed they represent part of our guidance for future work, but we do see some areas of the field that have been notable failures. Despite early calls for a descriptive base of relationships (Hinde, 1979), it is evident that the geography of relational activity has never been established. Apart from some notable diary and experience sampling studies (e.g., Reis, Lin, Bennett, & Nezlak, 1993), we really cannot say how people spend their relational time, nor whether researchers are right to emphasize the topics that have excited some. As one brave example, we observe that although hundreds of research articles have been published on self-disclosure, studies of its occurrence in real life (Dindia, Fitzpatrick, & Kenny, 1989) report its occurrence as dramatically small (2%). Of course, the 2% of occasions when it occurs could exert powerful leverage on the relationships that justifies the large investment of research, but that has not been demonstrated, nor has it been demonstrated in the multivariate context of everyday life influences. In 1985, we were able to applaud the work of Davis and Todd (1985) or Argyle and Henderson (1984) in drawing up maps of differences among types of relationship, now extended by VanLear, Koerner, and Allen (this volume). Nonetheless, these promising developments have been left largely untranslated into maps of real world, everyday relational behaviour. The truth is that we do not know how relaters actually spend their time, although – a different issue – we do know a great deal about the features of prototypes of relationships that participants claim to give weight (e.g., Fehr, 1988).

In addition to limitations on our descriptive base of real behaviors, there are astonishing and disconcerting divergences in basic descriptive units. For example, participants are most often left to self-select their relational involvement category, and researchers often mix participants from various groups, leading to unknown bandwidths of eccentricity being included in the same study of "dating" or "close relationships" (see Surra, Gray, Cottle, & Boettcher, 2004). Equally, there are many definitions of such concepts as self-disclosure (e.g., Altman & Taylor, 1973; Dindia, 2000; Spencer, 1994), commitment (e.g., Kelley et al., 1983; Reis & Shaver, 1988; Rusbult & Buunk, 1983), and privacy (Altman & Taylor, 1973, Kelvin, 1977, see Petronio, 2002 for a review). When we commend such inventiveness, we should also remember how hard this makes it to compare results of different studies in a way that renders us more likely to accumulate knowledge rather than add argumentative confusion. Before cooking the relational hares, we should adopt Mrs. Beeton's 19th century advice to cooks and "first catch your hare" or at least decide on an agreed description of what one looks like. An establishment of agreement about the units of analysis in this field, as in any other, cannot be a bad thing.

Once there is some consensus about the denotation of key terms across originating disciplines, then we can move to the sort of truly interdisciplinary work for which Acitelli (1995) pleaded, and away from the "disciplines at parallel play" that she observed at the time. Such a move allows not only greater intellectual interplay between disciplines but permits a clearer view of the methodological and practical inputs that can be expected from each as a contribution to the whole picnic. It is less valuable to expect everyone to bring the same dish to picnics and more useful when some are designated to provide dessert and others to provide beverages. The success of the picnic depends on division of provender and on the various contributions of each to the whole.

A further limitation to the field is the ambiguity that exists in the matter of application, or, to phrase it differently, the question of relevance. What is the ultimate purpose of research on relationships? The clarification of "best methods"? The offering to society of some benefits in terms of social education or increased pursuit of happiness? The sophistication of research? Are we fishing in inland coves, navigating between islands, or doing commerce across the broad oceanic expanse?

Conclusions

Wherever the field of personal relationships is headed in the future, the last 25 years have been a period of exciting growth. As Berscheid and Reis (1998, p. 253) stated:

> The sheer volume of recent research on interpersonal relationships within social psychology and allied disciplines reflects the fact that relationship science in the latter half of the 1990s resembles a boomtown during the gold rush days of the American West. Relationship science is young, sprawling, dynamic, [and] enthusiastic.

We are encouraged by this activity. Relationship scholars are collecting impressive evidence that relationships are crucial to our well-being and are among the things we consider most important in life. Baumeister and Leary (1995) have contended that even in a world where the nature of relationships may be changing, belongingness is a key, universal human motive. We think it is crucial for us personally and as a species that we understand and foster our relationships.

Are we making progress in our analysis? We believe we are. More than 40 years ago, Crutchfield and Krech (1962, p. 10) wrote:

> We seem to detect a tendency for thinking on the problem to go full circle. But this usually turns out to be not really a circle, not simply a regression to an earlier stage. Instead, there is a kind of spiral, a recurrence of older conceptions but at a more advanced level of complexity and sophistication.

They were reflecting on the history of psychology more generally, but we, like

Broderick (1988), think their remarks apply to the study of personal relationships as well.

The research on interpersonal attraction done by social psychologists in the late 1960s had a special emphasis on experimental studies with college sophomores. Nonetheless, a trend toward a broader array of methods seems to actually be returning us to techniques and populations that were used earlier in the 20th century.

Going even further back in history, we see two noteworthy ways the study of relationships has remained constant. First, many of the issues and questions that intrigued the earliest social analysts are still of concern today. For instance, Aristotle was concerned with the functions that relationships serve in our lives, the types of relationships that exist, age and individual differences in friendships, the antecedents of friendship choice, the speed with which relationships develop, how the larger patterning of relationships (e.g., social networks) influences an individual's friendships, and the deterioration of relationships. All these concerns can be found in the recent study of relationships. Some of the particulars of Aristotle's analysis (e.g., his typology of friendships) were even tested in the 20th century (Murstein & Spitz, 1973–1974). Similarly, Art Aron (personal communication, October 18, 2004) considers Plato's "*Symposium* to be one of the seminal sources of the ideas for the self-expansion model."

A second way the study of friendship has remained constant has been that some of the same basic ideas about friendships seem to keep reappearing, albeit expressed in slightly different words. For example, recall Aristotle's view that similarity fosters friendship ("Those, then, are friends to whom the same things are good and evil"). More than 2,000 years later, Newcomb (1956) echoed this same notion in his APA presidential address: "Interpersonal attraction always and necessarily varies with perceived similarity regarding important and relevant objects" (p. 579). Similarly, in his *Symposium* Plato discussed the important role beauty has in fostering love. This same emphasis can be found today in the eros dimension of Hendricks's love scales (Hendrick & Hendrick, 1986).

Yet the other component of Crutchfield and Krech's view is the belief that changes have occurred in social analysis. Our concepts continually advance. Not only do they become more complex and sophisticated, they also become better understood, more useful, and more precise as time passes. In terms of statistical jargon, the social sciences have gone beyond the search for simple, main outcomes to the search for mediating variables and interaction effects. In other words, social scientists have replaced the hunt for a few universal principles that should hold under all conditions with efforts to determine how various forces in our lives combine to impinge on us. As a result of this shift in emphasis, social scientists now more fully appreciate that a given force may operate only under some circumstances and that its impact may be enhanced (diminished) by third factors and the like. As the statistical methods of the social sciences have become more complex, it has also been important to have theories which could help us predict and understand the more complex patterns of evidence that were being uncovered. As we go forward into the new millennium, we hope Crutchfield and Krech's image of our understanding of relationships as a spiral spinning a wider and higher level of knowledge will become a reality. Looking backward to predict the future, we think there is a good probability that such an upward, expanding spiral will occur.

Author Note

This chapter evolved from the first author's International Society for the Study of Personal Relationships presidential address given at the Second Joint Conference of ISSPR and INPR in Brisbane, Australia, June 30, 2000, and an invited address he gave at the VII Mexican Congress of Social Psychology and the III Latin American Reunion of Cross Cultural Psychology, Toluca, México, October 21–23, 1998

(Perlman, 1999). We wish to express our thanks to Kelly Campbell, Ming Sze Lai, and Nima Tabloei for their assistance in doing citation counts and for several colleagues including Donn Byrne, Susan Hendrick, David Kenny, George Levinger, Robert Milardo, and Susan Sprecher – among others – who provided constructive comments on earlier versions of the paper.

Footnote

1. Because Byrne and Griffitt's review was quite brief, the initial pool of frequently cited scholars from this source was smaller ($N = 28$) than those from the others. Rubin used a footnote system rather than a standard reference list. For his volume, citations on both text and footnote pages were counted because the footnotes sometimes expanded on the text or were the only place where an author was mentioned by name. In calculating Elaine Hatfield's citation impact, references to her present and her former names (E. Walster) were counted. For Buunk, references to B. Buunk and A. P. Buunk were combined because Buunk has used both sets of initials.

References

Acitelli, L. K. (1995). Disciplines at parallel play. *Journal of Social and Personal Relationships, 12,* 589–596.

Acitelli, L. K., Douvan, E., & Veroff, J. (1993). Perceptions of conflict in the first year of marriage: How important are similarity and understanding? *Journal of Social and Personal Relationships, 10,* 5–19.

Adams, B. N. (1988). Fifty years of family research: What does it mean? *Journal of Marriage and the Family, 50,* 5–17.

Altman, I., & Taylor, D. (1973). *Social penetration: The development of interpersonal relationships.* New York: Holt, Rinehart & Winston.

Argyle, M., & Henderson, M. (1984). The rules of friendship. *Journal of Social and Personal Relationships, 1,* 211–237.

Aristotle (1991). Rhetoric (II.4). In M. Pakaluk (Ed.), *Other selves: Philosophers on friendship* (pp. 72–76). Indianapolis, IN: Hackett.

Aron, A., & Aron, E. (1995). Three suggestions for increased emphasis in the study of personal relationships. *Journal of Social and Personal Relationships, 12,* 559–562.

Aronson, E., & Linder, D. (1965). Gain and loss of esteem as determinants of interpersonal attractiveness. *Journal of Experimental Social Psychology, 1,* 156–171

Asch, S. E. (1946). Forming impressions of personality. *Journal of Abnormal and Social Psychology, 41,* 258–290.

Bahr, S. J. (Ed.). (1991). *Family research: A sixty-year review, 1930–1990.* Lexington, MA: Lexington Books.

Barbee, A. P. (1990). Interactive coping: The cheering up process in close relationships. In S. W. Duck (with R. S. Cohen) (Eds.), *Personal relationships and social support* (pp. 46–65). London: Sage.

Barry, W. A. (1970). Marriage research and conflict: An integrative review. *Psychological Bulletin, 73,* 41–54.

Baumeister, R. F., & Leary, M. R. (1995). The need to belong: Desire for interpersonal attachments as a fundamental human motivation. *Psychological Bulletin, 117,* 497–529.

Baxter, L. A., & Montgomery, B. M. (1996). *Relating: Dialogues and dialectics.* New York: Guilford Press.

Berger, C. R., & Bradac, J. J. (1982). *Language and social knowledge: Uncertainty in interpersonal relationships.* London: Edward Arnold.

Berger, C. R., & Calabrese, R. J. (1975). Some explorations in initial interaction and beyond: Toward a developmental theory of interpersonal communication. *Human Communication Research, 1,* 99–112.

Bernard, J. (1933). An instrument for the measurement of success in marriage. *American Sociological Society Publication, 27,* 94–106.

Berscheid, E. (1985). Interpersonal attraction. In G. Lindzey & E. Aronson (Eds.), *The handbook of social psychology: Vol. II. Special fields and applications* (3rd ed., pp. 413–484) New York: Random House.

Berscheid, E. (1994). Interpersonal relationships. *Annual Review of Psychology, 45,* 79–129.

Berscheid, E. (1995). Help wanted: A grand theorist of interpersonal relationships, sociologist or anthropologist preferred. *Journal of Social and Personal Relationships, 12,* 529–533.

Berscheid, E., & Hatfield Walster, E. (1978). *Interpersonal attraction* (2nd ed.). Reading, MA: Addison-Wesley.

Berscheid, E., & Reis, H. (1998). Attraction and close relationships. In D. T. Gilbert, S. T. Fiske, & G. Lindzey (Eds.), *The handbook of social psychology* (4th ed., pp. 193–281). New York: McGraw-Hill.

Blieszner, R., & Adams, R. G. (1992). *Adult friendship*. Newbury Park, CA: Sage.

Bochner, A. P. (1984). The functions of communication in interpersonal bonding. In C. Arnold & J. Bowers (Eds.), *The handbook of rhetoric and communication* (pp. 544–621). Boston: Allyn and Bacon.

Bossard, J. H. S. (1932). Residential propinquity as a factor in mate selection. *American Journal of Sociology, 38*, 219–224.

Bradshaw, S. D. (1998). I'll go if you will: Do shy persons utilize social surrogates? *Journal of Social and Personal Relationships, 15*, 651–669.

Brehm, S. S. (1992). *Intimate relationships* (2nd ed.). New York: McGraw-Hill.

Broderick, C. B. (1970). Editorial. *Journal of Marriage and the Family, 32*, 495.

Broderick, C. B. (1988). To arrive where we started: The field of family studies in the 1930s. *Journal of Marriage and the Family, 50*, 569–584.

Bulcroft, R. A., & White, J. M. (1997). Family research methods and levels of analysis. *Family Science Review, 10*, 136–153.

Burgess, E. W. (1926). Topical summaries of current literature: The family. *American Journal of Sociology, 32*, 104–115.

Burleson, B. R. (1990). Comforting as social support: Relational consequences of supportive behaviors. In S. W. Duck (with R. S. Cohen) (Eds.), *Personal relationships and social support* (pp. 66–82). London: Sage.

Buss, D. M. (1998). Sexual strategies theories: Historical origins and current status. *Journal of Sex Research, 35*, 19–31.

Byrne, D. (1961). Interpersonal attraction and attitude similarity. *Journal of Abnormal and Social Psychology, 62*, 713–715.

Byrne, D. (1971). *The attraction paradigm*. New York: Academic Press.

Byrne, D. (1997). An overview (and underview) of research and theory within the attraction paradigm. *Journal of Social and Personal Relationships, 14*, 417–431.

Byrne, D., & Griffitt, W. (1973). Interpersonal attraction. *Annual Review of Psychology, 24*, 317–336.

Cooper, M. L., & Sheldon, M. S. (2002). Seventy years of research on personality and close relationships: Substantive and methodological trends over time. *Journal of Personality, 70*, 783–812.

Cramer, D. (1998). *Close relationships: The study of love and friendship*. London: Arnold.

Crohan, S. E. (1992). Marital happiness and spousal consensus on beliefs about marital conflict: A longitudinal investigation. *Journal of Social and Personal Relationships, 9*, 89–102.

Crutchfield, R. S., & Krech, D. (1962). Some guides to the understanding of the history of psychology. In L. Postman (Ed.), *Psychology in the making* (pp. 3–27). New York: Knopf.

Cupach, W. R., & Spitzberg, B. H. (Eds.). (1994). *The dark side of interpersonal communication*. Hillsdale, NJ: Erlbaum.

Darwin, C. (1859). *On the origins of the species by means of natural selection, or preservation of favoured races in the struggle for life*. London: Murray.

Davis, K. (1929). *Factors in the sex life of 2200 women*. New York: Harper & Row.

Davis, K. E., & Todd, M. J. (1985). Assessing friendship: Prototypes, paradigm cases and relationship description. In S. W. Duck & D. Perlman (Eds.), *Understanding personal relationships* (pp. 17–38). London: Sage.

De Jong Gierveld, J. (1995). Research into relationship research designs: Personal relationships under the microscope. *Journal of Social and Personal Relationships, 12*, 583–588.

Detailed conference program [2004 International Association for Relationship Research Conference]. (n.d). Retrieved September 19, 2004, from http://iarrc.commarts.wisc.edu/Program/PDFs/Section%203%20Detailed%20Program.pdf

Dindia, K. (2000). Self-disclosure, identity, and relationship development: A dialectical perspective. In K. Dindia & S. W. Duck (Eds.), *Communication and personal relationships* (pp. 147–162). Chichester, England: Wiley.

Dindia, K., Fitzpatrick, M. A., & Kenny, D. A. (1989, May). *Self-disclosure in spouse and stranger dyads: A social relations analysis*. Paper presented at the meeting of the International Communication Association, San Francisco.

Duck, S. (Ed.). (1988). *Handbook of personal relationships: Theory, research and interventions.* Oxford, England: Wiley.

Duck, S. (Ed.). (1997). *Handbook of personal relationships* (2nd ed.). Chichester, England: Wiley.

Duck, S., & Perlman, D. (1985). The thousand islands of personal relationships: A prescriptive analysis for future explorations. In S. Duck & D. Perlman (Eds.), *Understanding personal relationships* (pp. 1–15). London: Sage.

Duck, S., West, L., & Acitelli, L. K. (1997). Sewing the field: The tapestry of relationships in life and research. In S. Duck (Ed.), *Handbook of personal relationships* (2nd ed., pp. 1–23). Chichester, England: Wiley.

Duck, S. W. (Ed.). (1982). *Personal relationships 4: Dissolving personal relationships.* London: Academic Press.

Duck, S. W. (Ed.). (1984). *Personal relationships 5: Repairing personal relationships.* London: Academic Press.

Duck, S. W. (1986). *Human relationships.* London: Sage.

Duck, S. W. (2002). Hypertext in the key of G: Three types of "history" as influences on conversational structure and flow. *Communication Theory, 12,* 41–62.

Duck, S. W., Acitelli, L. K., & Nicholson, J. H. (2000). Families as an experiential quilt. In *Families as relationships* (pp. 175–189). R. M. Milardo & S. W. Duck (Eds.), Chichester, England: Wiley.

Duck, S. W., & Gilmour. R. (Ed.). (1981a). *Personal relationships 1: Studying personal relationships.* London: Academic Press.

Duck, S. W., & Gilmour. R. (Ed.). (1981b). *Personal relationships 2: Developing personal relationships.* London: Academic Press.

Duck, S. W., & Gilmour. R. (Ed.). (1981c). *Personal relationships 3: Personal relationships in disorder.* London: Academic Press.

Duck, S. W., Rutt, D. J., Hurst, M., & Strejc, H. (1991). Some evident truths about conversations in everyday relationships: All communication is not created equal. *Human Communication Research, 18,* 228–267.

Duck, S. W., & Sants, H. K. A. (1983). On the origin of the specious: Are personal relationships really interpersonal states? *Journal of Social and Clinical Psychology, 1,* 27–41.

Durkheim, E. (1963). *Suicide.* New York: Free Press. (Original work published 1897).

Farrell, A. D., & White, K. S. (1998). Peer influences and drug use among urban adolescents: Family structure and parent–adolescent relationship as protective factors. *Journal of Consulting and Clinical Psychology, 66,* 248–258.

Fehr, B. (1988). Prototype analysis of the concepts of love and commitment. *Journal of Personality and Social Psychology, 55,* 557–579.

Felmlee, D., & Sprecher, S. (2000). Close relationships and social psychology: Intersections and future paths. *Social Psychology Quarterly, 63,* 365–376.

Festinger, L., Schachter, S., & Back, K. (1950). *Social pressures in informal groups: A study of human factors in housing.* New York: Harper & Row, 1950.

Fincham, F. D. (2000). The kiss of the porcupines: From attributing responsibility to forgiving. *Personal Relationships, 7,* 1–23.

Gonzalez, R., & Griffin, D. (1997). On the statistics of interdependence: Treating dyadic data with respect. In S. Duck (Ed.), *Handbook of personal relationships* (2nd ed., pp. 271–302). Chichester, England: Wiley.

Hall, C. S., & Lindzey, G. (1957). *Theories of personality.* New York: John Wiley.

Harlow, H. F. (1958). The nature of love. *American Psychologist, 13,* 673–685. Retrieved June 14, 2005, from http://psychclassics.yorku.ca/Harlow/love.htm

Harris, J. A. (1912). Assortive mating in man. *Popular Science Monthly, 80,* 476–492.

Harvey, J., Wenzel, A., & Sprecher, S. (Eds.). (2004). *Handbook of sexuality in close relationships.* Mahwah, NJ: Erlbaum.

Hendrick, C., & Hendrick, S. S. (1986). A theory and method of love. *Journal of Personality and Social Psychology, 50,* 392–402.

Hendrick, C., & Hendrick, S. S. (Eds.). (2000). *Close relationships: A sourcebook.* Thousand Oaks, CA: Sage.

Higbee, K. L., & Wells, M. G. (1972). Some research trends in social psychology during the 1960s. *American Psychologist, 27,* 963–966.

Hinde, R. A. (1979). *Towards understanding relationships.* London: Academic Press.

Hinde, R. A. (1997). *Relationships: A dialectical perspective.* East Sussex, England: Psychology Press.

Hoobler, G. D. (1999, June). *Ten years of personal relationships research: Where have we been and where are we going?* Paper presented at the annual meeting of the International Network on Personal Relationships and International Society for the Study of Personal Relationships, Louisville, KY.

Hull, C. L. (1952). *A behavior system*. New Haven, CT: Yale University Press.

Huston, T. L., & Levinger, G. (1978). Interpersonal attraction and relationships. *Annual Review of Psychology, 29*, 115–156.

James, W. (1981). *Principles of psychology*: Volumes 1 and 2. Cambridge, MA: Harvard University Press. (Original work published 1890.)

Karney, B. R., & Bradbury, T. N. (1995). The longitudinal course of marital quality and stability: A review of theory, method, and research. *Psychological Bulletin, 118*, 3–34.

Kelley, H. H., Berscheid, E., Christensen, A., Harvey, J. H., Huston, T. L., Levinger, G., et al. (1983). *Close relationships*. New York: Freeman.

Kelvin, P. (1977). Predictability, power, and vulnerablity in interpersonal attraction. In S. W. Duck (Ed.), *Theory and practice in interpersonal attraction* (pp. 355–378). London: Academic Press.

Kenny, D. A., & La Voie, L. (1984). The social relations model. *Advances in Experimental Social Psychology, 18*, 142–182.

Kowalski, R. M. (Ed.). (1997). *Aversive interpersonal behaviors*. New York: Plenum.

Kuczynski, L. (Ed.). (2003). *Handbook of dynamics in parent–child relations*. Thousand Oaks CA: Sage.

Larson, R., Csikszentmihalyi, M., & Graef, R. (1982). Time alone in daily experience: Loneliness or renewal? In L. A. Peplau & D. Perlman (Eds.), *Loneliness: A sourcebook of current theory, research, and therapy* (pp. 40–53). New York: Wiley-Interscience.

Levinger, G. (1972). Little sand box and big quarry: Comment on Byrne's paradigmatic spade for research on interpersonal attraction. *Representative Research in Social Psychology, 3*, 3–19.

Lopata, H. Z. (1981). Friendship: Historical and theoretical introduction. In H. Z. Lopata & D. Maines (Ed.), *Research in the interweave of social roles: Friendship* (Vol. 2, pp. 1–19). Greenwich, CT: JAI Press.

Lott, A. J., & Lott, B. E. (1974). The role of reward in the formation of positive interpersonal attitudes. In T. L. Huston (Ed.), *Foundations of interpersonal attraction* (pp. 171–192). New York: Academic Press.

Lyons, R., Sullivan, M., Ritvo, P., & Coyne, J. (1995). *Relationships in chronic illness and disability*. Thousand Oaks, CA.: Sage.

Mashek, D. J., & Aron, A. (Eds.). (2004). *Handbook of closeness and intimacy*. Hillsdale, NJ: Erlbaum.

Metts, S. (2000). Face and facework: Implications for the study of personal relationships. In K. Dindia & S. W. Duck (Eds.), *Communication and personal relationships* (pp. 72–94). Chichester, England: Wiley.

Monroe, W. S. (1898). Discussion and reports. Social consciousness in children. *Psychological Review, 5*, 68–70.

Moreno, J. L. (1934). *Who shall survive? A new approach to the problem of human interrelationships*. Washington, DC: Nervous and Mental Disease Publishing.

Murstein, B. I., & Spitz, L. T. (1973–1974). Aristotle and friendship: A factor-analytic study. *Interpersonal Development, 4*, 21–34.

Newcomb, T. M. (1956). The prediction of interpersonal attraction. *American Psychologist, 11*, 575–586.

Newcomb, T. M. (1961). *The acquaintance process*. New York: Holt, Rinehart & Winston.

Nye, F. I. (1988). Fifty years of family research: 1937–1978. *Journal of Marriage and the Family, 50*, 305–316.

Olson, D. H. (1977). Insiders' and outsiders' views of relationships: Research studies. In G. Levinger & H. Rausch (Eds.), *Close relationships: Perspectives on the meaning of intimacy* (pp. 115–135). Amherst: University of Massachusetts Press.

Pakaluk, M. (Ed.). (1991). *Other selves: Philosophers on friendship*. Indianapolis, IN: Hackett.

Perlman, D. (1979). Rear end analysis: The uses of social psychology textbook citation data. *Teaching of Psychology, 6*, 101–104.

Perlman, D. (1980). Who's who in psychology: Endler et al.'s SSCI scores vs. a textbook definition. *American Psychologist, 35*, 104–106.

Perlman, D. (1999). Tendencias actuales en el estudio de las relaciones cercanas. Un vistazo hacia el pasado para predecir el futuro [Current trends in the study of close relationships: Glancing backward to forecast the future]. *Revista de Psicologia Social y Personalidad, 15*, 157–178.

Perlman, D., & Lipsey, M. (1978). Who's who in social psychology: A textbook definition.

Personality and Social Psychology Bulletin, 4, 212–216.

Petronio, S. (2002). *Boundaries of privacy.* Albany: SUNY Press.

Rawlins, W. K. (1992). *Friendship matters: Communication, dialectics, and the life course.* New York: de Gruyter.

Reis, H. T., Lin, Y., Bennett, M. E., & Nezlek, J. B. (1993). Change and consistency in social participation during early adulthood. *Developmental Psychology, 29,* 633–645.

Reis, H. T., & Shaver, P. R. (1988). Intimacy as an interpersonal process. In S. W. Duck (Ed.), *Handbook of personal relationships: Theory, research and interventions* (pp. 367–390). Chichester, England and New York: Wiley.

Reis, H. T., & Stiller, J. (1992). Publication trends in *JPSP:* A three-decade review. *Personality and Social Psychology Bulletin, 18,* 465–472.

Reis, H. T., & Wheeler, L. (1991). Studying social interaction with the Rochester Interaction Record. *Advances in Experimental Social Psychology, 24,* 269–318.

Reisman, J. M. (1979). *Anatomy of friendship.* New York: Irvington.

Riesman, D., Glazer, N., & Denney, R. (1953). *The lonely crowd: A study of the changing American character* (abridged ed.). Garden City, NY: Doubleday.

Rohlfing, M. (1995). "Doesn't anybody stay in one place any more?" An exploration of the understudied phenomenon of long-distance relationships. In J. T. Wood & S. W. Duck (Eds.), *Under-studied relationships: Off the beaten track. Volume 6: Understanding relationship processes* (pp. 173–196). Newbury Park, CA, Sage.

Rook, K. S. (1995). Relationship research at the crossroads: Commentary on special section. *Journal of Social and Personal Relationships, 12,* 601–606.

Rubin, Z. (1973). *Liking and loving: An invitation to social psychology.* New York: Holt, Rinehart, & Winston.

Rusbult, C. E., & Buunk, A. P. (1993). Commitment processes in close relationships: An interdependence analysis. *Journal of Social and Personal Relationships, 10,* 175–203.

Rutter, V., & Schwartz, P. (1998). *The love test: Romance and relationship self-quizzes developed by psychologists and sociologists.* New York: Berkley.

Ruvolo, A. P., & Ruvolo, C. M. (2000). Creating Mr. Right and Ms. Right: Interpersonal ideals and personal change in newlyweds. *Personal Relationships, 7,* 341–362.

Sarason, I. G., Pierce, G. R., & Sarason, B. R. (Eds.). (1995). On the study of relationships [Special section]. *Journal of Social and Personal Relationships, 12,* 521–619.

Sahlstein, E. (1998, April). *Long-distance relationships: What are they?* Paper presented at the annual convention of the Central States Communication Association, Chicago.

Sears, D. O. (1986). College sophomores in the laboratory: Influences of a narrow data base on social psychology's view of human nature. *Journal of Personality and Social Psychology, 51,* 515–530.

Sears, R. R. (1951). A theoretical framework for personality and social behavior. *American Psychologist, 6,* 476–482.

Shebilske, L., & Huston, T. (Organizers). (1996, August). *Designing and carrying out a longitudinal study of relationships: Lessons from the Pair Project.* Workshop presented at the meeting of the International Society for the Study of Personal Relationships, Banff, Canada.

Simmel, G. (1950). *The sociology of Georg Simmel* (K. H. Wolff, Trans and Ed.). Glencoe, IL: Free Press.

Spencer, E. E. (1994). Transforming relationships through ordinary talk. In S. W. Duck (Ed.), *Understanding relationship processes 4: Dynamics of relationships* (pp. 58–85). Newbury Park, CA: Sage.

Spitzberg, B. H., & Cupach, W. R. (Eds.). (1998). *The dark side of close relationships.* Hillsdale, NJ: Erlbaum.

Stafford, L. (2004). *Maintaining long-distance and cross-residential relationships.* Mahwah, NJ: Erlbaum.

Stouffer, S. A., Suchman, E. A., Devinney, L. C., Star, S. A., & Williams, R. M., Jr. (1949). *The American soldier: Adjustment during army life.* (Studies in social psychology in World War II, Vols. 1–2.). Princeton, NJ: Princeton University Press.

Sunnafrank, M. (1983). Attitude similarity and interpersonal attraction in communication processes: In pursuit of an ephemeral influence. *Communication Monographs, 50,* 273–284.

Surra, C. A., Gray, C. R., Cottle, N., & Boettcher, T. M. J. (2004). Research on mate selection and premarital relationships: What do we really know? In A. L. Vangelisti (Ed.), *Handbook of family communication* (pp. 53–82). Mahwah, NJ: Erlbaum.

Surra, C. A., & Ridley, C. (1991). Multiple perspectives on interaction: Participants, peers, and observers. In B. M. Montgomery & S. W. Duck (Eds.), *Studying interpersonal interaction* (pp. 35–55). New York: Guilford Press.

Tharp, R. G. (1963). Psychological patterning in marriage. *Psychological Bulletin, 60*, 97–117.

Vangelisti, A. L. (1994). Messages that hurt. In W. R. Cupach & B. H. Spitzberg (Eds.), *The dark side of communication* (pp. 53–82). New York: Guilford Press.

Waller, W. (1937). The rating and dating complex. *American Sociological Review, 2*, 727–734.

Waller, W. (1938). *The family: A dynamic approach.* New York: Dryden Press.

Weber, A. L., & Harvey, J. H. (Eds.). (1994). *Perspectives on close relationships.* Boston: Allyn and Bacon.

Whyte, W. F. (1955). *Street corner society: The social structure of an Italian slum* (2nd ed.). Chicago: University of Chicago Press.

CHAPTER 3

Theoretical Perspectives in the Study of Close Relationships

John H. Harvey
Amy Wenzel

The purpose of this chapter is to provide a selective review and evaluation of major theoretical perspectives, or systematic networks of ideas and findings, in the study of close relationships. We stress at the outset that given the extensiveness of theoretical work on close relationships, our reviews of major theories are brief and do not do justice to the nuances of these approaches. In addition, we acknowledge that some theories are broad and cover all of the passages of relationships. In contrast, others are narrower and restricted to certain passages such as the beginning, middle, or ending periods. We emphasize perspectives that are broader, with the presumption that their concepts are applicable across relationship passages and types of events. Moreover, we should note that other chapters in this handbook (e.g., Planalp, Fitness, & Fehr) also address theories as applied to relationships in a less general fashion than is true in the present chapter. In the sections that follow, we discuss four major systems of theoretical analyses of close relationships: the evolutionary psychology approach, the social exchange approach, the cognitive–behavioral approach, and the

attachment approach. Strengths and weaknesses associated with each approach are highlighted, and a final section attempts to integrate aspects of these theories into a unifying framework.

Evolutionary Psychology Approaches

Evolutionary theorists argued that people need close relationships to survive and that many aspects of dating and mating phenomena, including sexual attraction and mate selection strategies, may be understood by reference to evolved tendencies geared to facilitate survival of the species (Buss, 1994). In general, the major goal of evolutionary theory involves explaining the survival of the species via processes of natural selection. Evolutionary theorists and researchers in the area of close relationships have attempted to explain why men and women have different, and to some extent conflicting, dating and mating strategies. Without question, the evolutionary approach has become the most controversial theoretical perspective in the field of close relationships. For example,

Thornhill and Thornhill (2000) ignited a dialogue by arguing that rape has a genetic basis, the idea in brief being that rapists are spreading their seeds and hence perpetuating their species. As we will see, this "spreading seed to perpetuate the species" idea is central to evolutionary psychology's approach to dating and mating phenomena.

Evolutionary positions on close relationships sprang from sociobiology. The first work that presented the sociobiology position was the biologist Edward Wilson's *Sociobiology: The New Synthesis* in 1975. Another work in this genre is the biologist Donald Symons's (1979) *The Evolution of Human Sexuality*. In simple terms, evolutionary theorists propose that men and women are wired differently genetically. Throughout the immensely long hunting-and-gathering phase of human evolutionary history, as the argument goes, the sexual desires and dispositions that were adaptive for one sex were a ticket to reproductive oblivion for the other. The most controversial implication of this evolutionary reasoning is that the "double standard" (i.e., men can have outside sexual relations, but women cannot) is almost built into people's genes. It is further implied that men and women possess brain anatomy and functioning that contribute to their sexual differences. Evolutionary psychology does not focus on so-called proximate causes of behavior, or causes that are the factors that many of us in the close relationship field embrace, including particular patterns of thought, feeling, other behavior, and one's environmental context. Instead, evolutionary psychology is concerned with causality over the long term, or how the organism and psyche have evolved over thousands of years. Evolution is believed to be always changing the organism and behavior in gradual, subtle ways.

Buss (1988, 1989, 1994) made the major extrapolations of evolutionary psychology logic to situations involving male–female close relationships. For example, in this work, he has used the evolutionary position to predict that in general, men will prefer relationships with women who are youthful and reproductively vital (so that they can bear offspring). Men also should prefer women who can give them confidence in their paternity, who are physically attractive, and who show intelligence, social skills, and resourcefulness (i.e., cues regarding the woman's parental abilities). On the other hand, women in general should prefer relationships with men who show the ability and resources to support offspring. Such men may have a great deal of status and money and buy the woman gifts, as well as show qualities the woman believes would make for a good father. Or, if younger, they may show a lot of ambition and industriousness, suggesting that they have good potential to attain resources. Strangely, it is not argued that women will also prefer physically attractive and youthful mates. Presumably, resources are their main agenda. Buss and colleagues have provided much data that are claimed to support these hypotheses (see Buss, 1994, for a review). Most of these data concern women and men's differential preferences for dating and mating qualities and sexual inclinations. They are, therefore, quite far removed from any type of direct investigation of slow unfolding of biologically driven evolutionary processes. For example, Shackelford and Buss (1997) asked spouses to rate the likelihood that they will have an affair or engage in a certain number of extramarital behaviors. Men were found to rate the likelihood higher in most situations than were women. Not only are such measures indirect tests of evolution, they also are hypothetical in nature, with an unclear link to the frequency of actual affairs in this case.

Critics have suggested that evolutionary psychology makes apologies or excuses for male philandering and contributes to gender stereotyping (Bem, 1993). We do not doubt the involvement of evolution in dating and mating behavior. But the theory is so gross that it does not attempt to explain the countless variations on male and female mating preferences, or the many strategies they develop to woo the opposite sex. It is, in effect, too simplistic to understand the often convoluted patterns of mating behavior. Finally, the theory does not recognize further evolved patterns of similarity between the sexes. These patterns may have evolved because they get the job done – are adaptive – and cut across issues such as attractiveness, health, intelligence, child-rearing inclinations, and so on (Bem, 1993).

Many of these criticisms of evolutionary psychology have been posited by researchers who adopt the social constructivist perspective. In general, feminists such as Bem (1993) argue that people develop their romantic and sexual relationships through their thoughts, feelings, and interactions. This idea is the essence of social constructionism, which emphasizes social processes as more than innate, biological processes in human development and behavior. Tiefer (1995) took a similar position in arguing that people *learn* how to be sexual creatures and how to be satisfied in sexual matters. She contended that many people accept that sex can be explained purely from a biological perspective because this perspective accesses and maintains prevailing scientific-medical authority. It may not necessarily be correct, however. Sexual mores change over time. To illustrate, witness the increasing acceptance of homosexuality and the greater acceptance over the last four decades of women having many sexual partners before being married (Ehrenreich, Hess, & Jacobs, 1986; McCormick, 1994; Reiss, 1990). Thus, what is "normal" and "natural" often changes because of changes in human attitudes, values, beliefs, and behavior. Tiefer implied some obvious logic that too often is neglected in the posture-taking among opposing camps on human mating: Just as they differ in certain areas, men and women share a lot of characteristics in their motives and social psychological dynamics regarding dating and mating.

Although evolutionary theory is strangely mute regarding why some people initially develop homosexual preferences, it argues that male homosexuals often show behavioral patterns that support the theory. In a study involving a convenience sample of homosexual and heterosexual men and women, Bailey, Gaulin, Agyei, and Gladue (1994) found evidence consistent with evolutionary theory in that homosexual respondents obtained similar scores on measures such as interest in uncommitted sex as did same-sex heterosexual respondents. They argued that this similarity suggests similar biological determinants of certain aspects of mating psychology. However, Bailey et al.'s study does not speak directly to the question of how homosexual mating and dating tendencies, as compared with heterosexual mating and dating tendencies, facilitate major principles of evolutionary theory such as survival of the species. Nor at this time is the theory clear regarding how the brain development of homosexual and heterosexual persons may have evolved such that brain development differs for heterosexual and homosexual persons of the same sex but is similar in heterosexual and opposite-sex homosexual persons (Bailey et al., 1994; LeVay, 1993).

There is evidence from the American Couples Study by Blumstein and Schwartz (1983) that homosexual men have by far the greatest number of sexual partners. Symons (1979) suggested that the number of partners gay men had in the San Francisco Bay Area in the late 1970s averaged in the hundreds; 28% had had more than 1,000 sex partners in their lives. Symons also indicated that whereas heterosexual and lesbian women did not begin to report such large numbers, their numbers of sexual partners, too, were growing in the late 1970s. With the advent of AIDS, it is likely this analysis about people's quest to "score" a lot is much less tenable at the present time. Evolutionists such as Symons suggest that this possible propensity for gay men to engage in considerable extra-dyadic sexual activity is a mark of males' true inclinations regarding infidelity, following from the evolutionary theory of dating behavior. Such logic does not explain why the homosexual behavior occurs in the first place, given that it has no potential to preserve genetic material of the involved persons.

One conclusion on the value of evolutionary perspectives as applied to close relationships is that they have provided a fertile ground for theory and research during the last two decades. For example, the theory has stimulated much research on mate preferences; gender differences in variables such as sexual desire, jealousy, conflict, and abuse in close relationships. Increasingly, evolutionary thinking has embraced more interactive positions, such as the recent contention that evolution and contemporary social psychological mechanisms (e.g., a person's thoughts and feelings in making dating selections) are both necessary to understand close relationships (e.g., Buss, Haselton, Shackelford, Bleske, & Wakefield, 1999). It is not clear whether this "evolutionary psychology interacting with contemporary social–cognitive–behavioral processes" will be as influential in its impact on relationships theory and research, as has been true for the more extreme version of evolutionary psychology applied to the study of relationships. Nonetheless, the "evolved" version of this theory does strike a more reasoned chord about dating and mating activities and hence is likely to remain the preferred version of the theory among relationships scholars. In addition, more conclusive work to verify evolutionary perspectives awaits advances in studying how DNA changes over time are correlated with molar social events such as those involved in close relationships. Even with the advances in biotechnology that characterize the 21st century, this linkage with how people carry out their close relationships may not occur for decades into the future.

Social Exchange and Equity Approaches

Social exchange and equity represent rule-based perspectives that traditionally were important in the field of close relationships (Berscheid & Walster, 1978). The essence of this position is that people operate so as to gain rewards and avoid punishments or costs. Canary and Stafford (2001) defined an equitable relationship as one in which the ratios of outcomes divided by inputs are equal for both parties. To the extent that one person's outcome–input ratio is larger than the partner's, that person is overbenefited. To the extent that one person's outcome–input ratio is less than the parter's, that person is underbenefited. The most satisfying associations to the individual making the assessment are equitable ones, followed by overbenefited ones, and followed finally by underbenefited ones (Hatfield, Utne, & Traupmann, 1979).

Kelley and colleagues' articulation of interdependence theory (Kelley & Thibaut, 1978; Kelley et al., 1983) represents another view of social exchange. According to this view, relational outcomes are dependent on the rewards and costs that relational partners experience. The theory suggests that outcomes are evaluated relative to expectations and that individuals hold out for what they feel they deserve. Outcomes are compared with a personal standard or expectation of what constitutes acceptable outcomes, known as the comparison level. The satisfaction level is a function of the comparison level and current relationship outcomes. When outcomes surpass the comparison level, the person is satisfied with the relationship. The person is unsatisfied when outcomes fall short of this perceived standard. Kelley and colleagues have developed rather complex ideas about how the transformation of matrices of outcomes helps explain relationships in which the welfare of the couple as a unit may take precedence over the individual's own outcomes.

As discussed by Canary and Stafford (2001), people who perceive themselves in inequitable relationships often engage in a variety of strategies to restore equity. For example, when married women perceive that they are taking on an inequitable load of household and child-caretaking responsibilities, they may seek to restore equity by decreasing their inputs, or cutting back on what they do for the family. They may also increase their outcomes by making time for themselves. They can persuade their partner to take on more responsibilities, and they can engage in various cognitive strategies such as distorting reality or comparing themselves with women who have even more inequitable situations. Equity theory remains a central approach to understanding social exchange in close relationships. Equity rules do not appear to always dominate the exchange process, however (e.g., Mills & Clark, 1982). As we discuss next, communal love theory provides an important complement to equity theory in helping us understand relationships, such as those of many parents and children that do not appear to follow equity rules.

According to Clark and Mills, a close, romantic relationship is a relationship in which each member has a concern for the welfare of the other (Clark & Mills, 2001; Mills & Clark, 1982, 1994). In such a communal relationship, benefits are given to the other based on the need of other, presumably without concern about the quid pro quo quality of the exchange. Members of a communal relationship are motivated to provide benefits to the other without expecting a specific benefit in return, as would be the case in an exchange relationship. A benefit is defined as something one person intentionally gives to another, or does for another and that is of use to the other. The communal love position represents a necessary complement to equity theory, because relationships between parents and children and sometimes between romantic partners often show more of a communal quality than a social exchange or equity quality.

Another unique exchange theory was developed by Foa and Foa (1974), who emphasized the "societal structures of the mind." According to the Foas, as part of the socialization process, people learn what is acceptable to give to (or take away from) one another in various types of relationships. Their approach is unique in that it focuses on the content of exchanges rather than the process of exchange. In their view, people give one another status, love, services, goods, money, and information. These resources are seen as ordered on the dimensions of particularism and concreteness. Love, for example, is the most particular resource; it mat-

ters a great deal from whom we receive love. Money, on the other hand, is the least particularistic and most concrete resource. The resources of status and services are less particularistic than is love. With regard to our understanding of love, the Foas suggest that people learn that concrete resources such as money should not be given to get love in return. To get love from other, one must give love, or possibly status – which the Foas have shown to be close to love in people's mental maps of relations among interpersonal resources. An intriguing proposition of the Foas' analysis is that when one gives love to another, one receives in return love from the very act of giving, supporting the biblical saying "It is more blessed to give than receive."

Relationship commitment also has been linked to the social exchange logic. Commitment is typically conceived as a general desire for a combined relational future. However, the concept appears to be a multifaceted one that overlaps with other related variables such as satisfaction and love (Fehr, 1988). Typically theorized from a social exchange or interdependence perspective, three bases of commitment have been identified: (a) "want to" commitment, or a person's desire and choice to stay in a relationship because of positive feelings toward the partner and the rewards inherent in those feelings; (b) "ought to" commitment, or a felt obligation to stay in a relationship because of promises made or others' expectations and the anticipated costs incurred through guilt or disapproval should that obligation not be met; and (c) "have to" commitment, or a resolution to stay in a relationship because there are no better alternatives as sources of profit (D. J. Johnson & Rusbult, 1989).

The concepts of commitment and interdependence are integrated in Rusbult and colleagues' writing. These scholars (e.g., Rusbult, Olsen, Davis, & Hannon, 2001) have used interdependence theory (cf. Kelley & Thibaut, 1978) to posit that dependence is a fundamental property of relationships. Dependence level describes the degree to which an individual needs his or her relationship or the extent to which the individual's well-being is influenced by involvement in the relationship. Rusbult and colleagues argue that people become dependent to the degree that (a) satisfaction is high, or the relationship fulfills an individual's important needs; (b) the quality of alternatives is poor, or the individual's most important needs could not be fulfilled independent of the relationship; or (c) investment size is high, or many important resources have become attached to the relationship, including resources that would be lost or decline in value if the relationship were to end.

Le and Agnew (2003) provided a useful meta-analysis of commitment and its theorized determinants. In this study, commitment was found to be a significant predictor of relationship breakup. Le and Agnew focused attention on Rusbult and colleagues' investment model of commitment. In this model, satisfaction level, quality of alternatives, and investment size are posited to be both individually and collectively the antecedents of commitment. The investment model accounted for a substantial portion of the variance in commitment, but other factors unaccounted for by the model appear to be important as well. For example, dispositional factors such as attachment style (Morgan & Shaver, 1999) are associated with commitment, but not a part of this model.

The social exchange theoretical system has wielded major influence on the field for decades. It is less influential now, and ideas such as the communal love idea have come along to complement the basic idea of exchange or equity. It remains a fundamental system of logic in the analysis of close relationships. It has been argued that even communal relationships involve implicit considerations of equity or reciprocity (Harvey & Weber, 2002). The interdependence model as applied to social exchange represents a sophisticated approach to understanding how individuals address both their own and the couple's needs and expectations in close relationships.

Cognitive–Behavioral Approaches

Several classic treatments of cognition in liking behavior provide a foundation for this vast arena of contemporary work in the close relationships field. Newcomb's (1961) and Heider's (1958) balance theories and Festinger's (1957) dissonance theory are illustrative of these early cognitive approaches. Both balance theories and dissonance theory rely on the assumption that people desire to have consistent cognitions about their attitudes and behavior. People are constantly thinking about and acting toward individuals whom they like or dislike. According to these theories, people will change attitudes about the extent to which they like another person, or how they act toward the person, so as to accommodate a balanced cognitive system. Consistency theories were highly influential in the first two decades of work on liking but have not been pursued to any significant degree in the last two decades.

According to extant cognitive–behavioral approaches to close relationships, the manner in which individuals perceive and interpret events in their relationship has a profound influence on their subjective emotional experience and their subsequent behavior (cf. Beck, 1988; Gottman, 1994, 1995). Because of the extensive history that couples develop, seemingly minute relationship events often hold a great deal of meaning to one or both partners, which can prompt behavior that is much more extreme than would seem warranted to an outside observer. Moreover, the beliefs and expectations that individuals have for their relationships often bias the manner in which they explain events in their relationship and evaluate their relationship's quality (for a review, see Epstein & Baucom, 1993). Not surprisingly, cognitive–behavioral therapy is often a logical intervention choice for distressed couples (e.g., Baucom & Epstein, 1990) because it targets the modification of such maladaptive cognitions and trains couples in specific communication and problem-solving skills to negotiate relationship conflict.

A large portion of the empirical work designed to validate aspects of cognitive–behavioral theories of close relationships focuses on the attributions that individuals make for events that occur in their relationship. As described in Bradbury and Fincham's (1990) seminal review paper, individuals in healthy relationships attribute positive relationship events to internal (vs. external), global (vs. specific), and stable (vs. unstable) characteristics of their partner, whereas individuals in distressed relationships downplay their partner's positive behavior, attributing it to external, specific, and unstable factors. Conversely, individuals in healthy relationships attribute negative relationship events to external, specific, and unstable factors, whereas individuals in distressed relationships attribute negative relationship events to internal, global, and stable characteristics of their partner. Together, these attributions form a category called *causal attributions*, which "focus on who or what caused an event or condition" (M. D. Johnson, Karney, Rogge, & Bradbury, 2001, p. 175). Bradbury and Fincham (1990) also noted the importance of responsibility attributions, which are "judgments that presuppose a causal attribution and concern an individual's accountability or answerability for some event" (p. 17). An impressive program of research by Bradbury, Fincham, and their colleagues has demonstrated that both types of maladaptive attributions predict marital satisfaction longitudinally even when initial levels of satisfaction are controlled (e.g., Fincham & Bradbury, 1993) and that they are associated with the use of ineffective problem solving strategies (e.g., Bradbury & Fincham, 1992).

Despite the magnitude of this systematic line of research, there is still little direct empirical evidence to support the notion that cognition indeed *causes* maladaptive relationship behavior (cf. M. D. Johnson et al., 2001). To take the first step in addressing this issue, Johnson et al. examined data from their laboratory to determine whether the influence of attributions on relationship satisfaction is best characterized by a mediating model (i.e., attributions => behaviors => change in relationship satisfaction) or a moderating model (i.e., attributions and behaviors interact to explain changes in relationship satisfaction). Their data provided no evidence to support a mediating model and partial support for a moderating model, such that attributions were related to a change in relationship satisfaction in the context of negative, but not positive, behavior. It now has long been established that maladaptive attributions are associated with a host of negative relationship outcomes; this analysis makes it clear that researchers who study attributions made for relationship events are now moving toward the construction of causal models to isolate the influence of attributions in explaining relationship satisfaction over time.

In contrast to the extensive line of research examining attributions and relationship quality, work done to observe the influence of other cognitive variables on relationship behavior has been less programmatic (cf. Fincham, 1994). Recently, Fincham and Beach (1999) noted a growing disconnect between social cognition research and clinical research that examines distorted cognition in the context of relationship distress. They observed that social cognition researchers have moved toward the study of cognitive structure (i.e., the manner in which people form mental representations of information) and information processing, whereas clinical researchers have focused primarily on cognitive content (i.e., what people are actually thinking). To demonstrate that phenomena of interest to social cognition researchers indeed have bearing on the effects typically observed in the clinical literature, they presented data showing that priming affects relationship behavior and that the accessibility of marital quality moderated relations between self-reported marital quality and particular relationship behaviors. That is, they showed that many of social cognitive variables that have been discounted by clinical researchers alter associations between many relationship variables that are now considered to be well established. We agree with Fincham and Beach that the future of cognitive–behavioral conceptualizations of relationship quality must be expanded beyond the examination of cognitive content to account for the manner in which couples represent, access, remember, and act on relationship-relevant information.

Cognitive–behavioral models of relationship functioning provide a great deal of explanatory power to account for subjective relationship experiences and the escalation of relationship conflict. Certainly, cognitive–behavioral couples therapy is among the most effective intervention approaches for couple distress (e.g., Baucom, Epstein, & Stanton, this volume; Baucom & Lester, 1986; Baucom, Sayers, & Sher, 1990), particularly in its efficacy to restructure maladaptive attributions and expectancies. Nonetheless, future researchers can expand the parameters of these models and link them with other relationship theories that include a cognitive component in a number of ways. For example, according to attachment theorists, individuals have attachment working models that subsequently influence the manner in which they perceive events in their adult close relationships (cf. Baldwin, Keelan, Fehr, Enns, & Koh-Rangarajoo, 1996). This supposition clearly suggests that there are distinct knowledge structures and information-processing styles associated with different attachment styles, although only recently has research been conducted to link such cognitive variables with attachment styles (e.g., Collins, 1996), and few studies have examined the extent to which maladaptive attributions in particular influence relationship functioning in the context of the different attachment styles. There is some evidence that attributions mediate the effects of attachment style on relationship adjustment (Gallo & Smith, 2001), suggesting that consideration of relationship variables across a number of theoretical approaches might be useful in capturing additional variance in relationship quality.

Another limitation of the extant empirical research designed to validate aspects of the cognitive–behavioral approach to understanding relationships is the much heavier focus on cognitive variables than on behav-ioral variables. Most of the research in this area is designed to elucidate the specific attributions, beliefs (e.g., Bradbury & Fincham, 1993), and schemata (e.g., Baldwin, 1992) that are associated with broad domains of problematic behavior, such as deficits in problem-solving ability. We argue that it is just as important to examine individual differences in one's knowledge of and ability to implement adaptive relationship behaviors, ranging from skills to manage conflict to skills necessary to maintain and enhance the relationship. Baucom, Epstein, Rankin, and Burnett (1996) presented a taxonomy of cognitions associated with marital relationships; we believe it is equally important to compile a unified taxonomy of behaviors that characterize marital interactions. Moreover, as discussed earlier, it is important to demonstrate empirically that maladaptive cognitions affect behavior in a unidirectional manner; at this point, we cannot rule out the possibility that engaging in particular adaptive or maladaptive relationship behaviors activate or intensify adaptive or maladaptive cognitions. If a bidirectional relationship were elucidated, it would follow that behavioral skills interventions would have a substantial impact on the types of cognitions that are activated in relationship interactions, although to date comparisons of behavioral marital therapy with cognitive–behavioral marital therapy suggest that only the cognitive–behavioral approach reduces maladaptive cognitions (e.g., Baucom & Lester, 1986; Baucom et al., 1990). Alternatively, it could be that the degree of activation of maladaptive cognitions and the inability to use effective relationship management skills *both* covary with a third variable that underlies the propensity to experience relationship distress, such that maladaptive cognitions and maladaptive behaviors are epiphenomena of a more fundamental type of relational dysfunction.

Attachment Approaches

Personality approaches to the study of close relationships rest on the assumption that individual differences in various traitlike constructs account for variance in relationship quality. One construct that has received an enormous amount of attention over the past 2 decades is adult attachment (see Shaver and Mikulincer's chapter in this volume). Hazan and Shaver (1987) developed the provocative idea that people's adult style of close relationship or love is premised on their early attachment experiences with their parents; these researchers later proposed that adult attachment could serve as an organizational scheme to encompass much of the field of close relationships (Hazan & Shaver, 1994). Specifically, Hazan and Shaver (1987) proposed that the formation of adult romantic relationships is a biosocial attachment process analogous to the development of child–caregiver bonds during infancy (Bowlby, 1969, 1973). Just as infants can be described as having a secure, anxious–ambivalent, or avoidant attachment to a primary caregiver, adults can be similarly depicted in their typical approaches to close relationships.

In their early work, Hazan and Shaver (1987) asked people to select the one attachment style that best described their feelings and experiences. About 55% selected the *secure* style of attachment (i.e., "I find it relatively easy to get close to others and am comfortable depending on them and having them depend on me."). Approximately 25% chose the *avoidant* style (i.e., "I am somewhat uncomfortable being close to others; I find it difficult to trust them completely, difficult to allow myself to depend on them. I am nervous when anyone gets too close . . . "). Finally, another approximate 20% selected the *anxious–ambivalent* style (i.e., "I find that others are reluctant to get as close as I would like. I often worry that my partner doesn't really love me or won't want to stay with me."). Although approximately 70% of individuals report stable attachment styles over time periods ranging from 8 months to 2 years (Simms, 2002), at least some degree of attachment change occurs through a variety of contextual (e.g., partners' attachment representations), social–cognitive (e.g., perception of marital satisfaction), and individual difference factors (e.g., personality disturbance;

Davila, Karney, & Bradbury, 1999). Davila, Burge, and Hammen (1997) even speculated that change in attachment style may reflect an individual difference tendency; they found that some women (particularly those similar to women with consistently insecure attachments) were more prone to attachment fluctuations, possibly reflecting earlier adverse experiences.

Compared with the original ideas and method for studying attachment and close relationships, Bartholomew and Horowitz (1991) developed finer distinctions of attachment types and a questionnaire approach to assessing attachment type, both based on orthogonal dimensions of a working model of the self and a working model of others. Their proposed attachment styles were as follows: (a) secure (i.e., positive feelings about self and others); (b) dismissing (i.e., positive feelings about self, negative feelings about others); (c) preoccupied (i.e., negative feelings about self, positive feelings about others); and (d) fearful (i.e., negative feelings about self and others). According to Brennan, Shaver, and Tobey (1991), the Bartholomew and Horowitz (1991) attachment scheme corresponds roughly to the Hazan and Shaver (1987) attachment scheme, such that individuals who are classified as secure according to one scheme are also regarded as secure by the other. Although classification of individuals according to these typologies has yielded fruitful data in this line of research, it is currently accepted that adult attachment is measured most effectively along two continuous dimensions: anxiety over relationships and discomfort with closeness (Brennan, Clark, & Shaver, 1998; Fraley & Waller, 1998).

Since the original work by Hazan and Shaver, whole research programs have been developed to examine the correlates and sequelae of these attachment styles. For example, it has been found that attachment styles predict both one's own relationship satisfaction as well as one's partner's relationship satisfaction (Collins & Read, 1990). Secure individuals experience greater satisfaction in close relationships and tend to report more positive love experiences than do either avoidant or anxious–ambivalent individuals (e.g., Fraley & Shaver, 1999). Moreover, securely attached individuals generally are rated as having high self-esteem and as being well adjusted (e.g., Feeney & Noller, 1990). In contrast, avoidant individuals tend to hold permissive views toward casual sex (Feeney, Noller, & Patty, 1993) and keep individuals with whom they are in close relationships at a distance (Keelan, Dion, & Dion, 1998). Anxious–ambivalent individuals report little confidence in their ability to achieve sexual competence and fears that their partners will become distant (Feeney & Noller, 2004). Thus, many programs of research converge to suggest that securely attached individuals subjectively experience higher quality relationships and objectively exhibit more adaptive relationship behaviors than individuals classified as avoidant or anxious/ambivalent. Moreover, research has demonstrated that attachment style predicts the manner in which individuals adapt to nonrelational stressors. For example, Mikulincer, Florian, and Weller (1993) found that in Israel at the time of the Gulf War, securely attached individuals coped with war-related stress by reaching out to their social support system, whereas anxious–ambivalent individuals used emotion-focused skills to regulate their subjective experience of being overwhelmed, and avoidant individuals used techniques including somatization, hostility, and emotional distancing.

Perhaps the most daunting continuing challenge for attachment–close relationship work is to agree on a standard approach to the measurement of adult attachment. In fact, Baldwin and Fehr (1995) wondered whether there is variability in the underlying construct itself, because approximately 30% of their respondents, particularly anxious–ambivalent respondents, changed their attachment style classification over a period of time from 1 week to several months. Although many researchers have concluded that there is weak convergence among adult attachment measures (e.g., Crowell & Treboux, 1995), Bartholomew and Shaver (1998) concluded that there is

a "set core of relational tendencies underlying responses to the various attachment measures" (p. 41), particularly when the differences in methods (e.g., interview vs. self-report) and subtleties associated with different conceptual schemes of adult attachment (e.g., clinical psychology perspective vs. personality or social psychology perspective) are taken into account. They created a continuum of adult attachment measures ranging from ones based on retrospective reports of relationships with one's parents to reports of relationships with one's romantic partner. Not surprisingly, they speculated that internal working models of relationships with parents are different from internal working models of partner relationships, making measures assessing these aspects of attachment far apart on the continuum and likely achieving only moderate levels of convergence. They recommended that attachment researchers should measure this construct using multiple measures to tap the underlying attachment mechanism and that attachment measures should be selected based on the domain of interest to the research question (e.g., parental relationships, romantic relationships). A related challenge is that people apparently remember past adult attachment patterns as similar to their current attachment pattern (Scharfe & Bartholomew, 1998). This finding may reflect the general tendency of people to reconstruct past experiences to be consistent with present experiences (Ross, 1989).

Attachment theory shows great promise to live up to its goal of becoming the prominent approach to conceptualizing close relationships from a psychosocial perspective. Many researchers have demonstrated that adult attachment has impressive construct validity by verifying that the attachment styles match up to certain personality, cognitive, and behavioral variables in the expected manner (e.g., Bartholomew, Kuong, & Hart, 2001). Moreover, it has roots in a tradition from developmental psychology (e.g., Bowlby, 1969, 1973) that has had a profound influence in the manner in which infant behavior is predicted and explained. Nevertheless, it is important for attachment researchers to move beyond the use of convenience samples, such as college students, to ensure that findings generalize to couples representing different ethnicities, nationalities, age groups, and sexual orientations (cf. Kurdek, 1998). Moreover, investigation into the mechanism by which attachment styles influence relational quality has the potential to provide a unifying framework for the field of close relationships. In but one example, Kurdek (2002) found that attachment dimensions (e.g., anxiety, closeness) affected relational quality only indirectly through the activation of relationship-relevant schemas. Such research has the potential to contribute to a model that incorporates findings from a number of traditions in the close relationships field.

Comparison and Conclusions

The study of close, romantic relationships is grounded richly in theories that speak to biological, intrapersonal, dyadic, familial, and societal levels of analysis. Together, these theories provide compelling explanations for our attraction to certain people rather than others, reasons our relationships are satisfying or unsatisfying, and changes in accepted relationship and sexual behaviors over time. Each theory by itself makes a unique contribution to understanding the development, maintenance, and dissolution of close relationships; however, each theory also is inherently limited in accounting for the subtle interactions between individual and couple characteristics that form the trajectory of a relationship. We argue that the field is ripe for a model to unify these approaches to the understanding of close relationships in a societal context, and we attempted to highlight several ways in which the underlying processes associated with close relationships are elucidated only by measuring relationship variables associated with more than one theoretical approach.

Evolutionary theory provides a general, compelling explanation for the manner in which our behavioral tendencies in close relationships developed across generations and points to evolved biological mechanisms for gender differences in dating and mating preferences. It does not account, however, for individual differences in the manner in which people cope with relationship events, both positive and negative. Attachment theory, an approach that itself has evolutionary undertones, is but one perspective in explaining these individual differences. Early experiences with the primary caregiver are the chief contributor to the development of an internal working model about the trustworthiness and dependability of others and the worthiness of oneself to be included in a close relationship. By definition, each individual's working model will be unique because no two people have identical experiences with their caregivers. It can be argued that attachment theory can explain, at least in part, the types of partners that individuals seek out (cf. Bartholomew et al., 2001) and the sexual behavior in which they engage (cf. Feeney & Noller, 2004). That is, attachment dimensions could moderate the dating and mating behaviors predicted by evolutionary theory.

As discussed previously, it is increasingly being acknowledged that different attachment styles are associated with distinct patterns of cognition and relational schemas. Thus, the cognitive–behavioral approach to understanding close relationships is not mutually exclusive from the adult attachment approach. Cognitive–behavioral researchers have been meticulous in conducting a systematic program of research to demonstrate that cognition predicts relationship quality above and beyond a number of individual difference variables, such as neuroticism (e.g., Karney, Bradbury, Fincham, & Sullivan, 1994). Attachment theory provides a context to explain the types of cognitions to which certain individuals are prone, both independently of a particular relationship as well as within a particular relationship. Moreover, attachment theory has the potential to serve as the basis of a taxonomy of relational schemas and the ease with which they are activated during specific relational events. Specific relational behaviors also can be predicted by attachment theory, and there is preliminary evidence that activation of certain cognitions mediates the relation between attachment style and behavior (e.g., Kurdek, 2002). In all, we argue that the examination of cognitive and behavioral variables from an attachment perspective has the potential to broaden the cognitive–behavioral approach to understanding close relationships by accounting for the attachment histories of each individual and their relationship cognitions that are particularly salient.

These theoretical approaches are not inconsistent with the social exchange and equity perspectives. As mentioned previously, the equity analyses appear to be less influential now in the close relationships field, in part because they cannot readily account for the maintenance of relationships in which the ratio of rewards and costs is out of balance. The communal love theory helped to overcome this limitation because it proposes that individuals will provide benefits to their partners in the name of love, rather than expecting a benefit in return. Although the communal love theory certainly captures romantic relationships in their ideal, many individuals in distressed relationships lack the trust and compassion to continue functioning on this level. It is possible that certain cognitions, such as attributions of blame and responsibility for relationship transgressions, reduce the propensity for the couple to engage in communal behavior. Indeed, when a relationship becomes distressed, it is possible that each individual focuses his or her attention on the quid pro quo of social exchange and is quick to identify instances of relationship inequity. Interdependence theory appears to offer promise in helping us understand how individuals balance own versus couple's needs and expectations. From an attachment perspective, it is likely that there are individual differences in the ability to engage in a communal relationship. It is not difficult to imagine the manner in which an avoidant or anxious–ambivalent attachment style would interfere with giving or receiving selfless benefits from one's partner.

It is important to acknowledge that all of these relational processes take place in a societal context. Expectations regarding acceptable relationship and sexual behavior change over time. These trends have the potential to influence dating and mating choices, the activation of certain relationship cognitions, and the choice of benefits one gives to his or her partner. As advances are made in psychotherapeutic interventions, it is becoming increasingly possible to get help in altering maladaptive relationship attributions, standards, and beliefs (e.g., Baucom & Epstein, 1990) and even mold a more secure attachment style (e.g., Slade, 1999). Thus, theory about the mechanism of relational maintenance must be interpreted in light of societal mores and will be ever changing in a dynamic interplay between these intrapersonal, interpersonal, and societal factors.

References

Bailey, J. M., Gaulin, S., Agyei, Y., & Gladue, B. A. (1994). Effects of gender and sexual orientation on evolutionarily relevant aspects of human mating psychology. *Journal of Personality and Social Psychology, 66*, 1081–1093.

Baldwin, M. W. (1992). Relational schemas and the processing of social information. *Psychological Bulletin, 112*, 461–484.

Baldwin, M. W., & Fehr, B. (1995). On the instability of attachment style ratings. *Personal Relationships, 2*, 247–261.

Baldwin, M. W., Keelan, J. P. R., Fehr, B., Enns, V., & Koh-Rangarajoo, E. (1996). Social cognitive conceptualization of attachment working models: Availability and accessibility effects. *Journal of Personality and Social Psychology, 71*, 94–106.

Bartholomew, K., & Horowitz, L. M. (1991). Attachment styles among young adults: A test of a four-category model. *Journal of Personality and Social Psychology, 61*, 226–244.

Bartholomew, K., Kuong, M. J., & Hart, S. D. (2001). Attachment. In W. J. Livesley (Ed.), *Handbook of personality disorders* (pp. 196–230). New York: Guilford Press.

Bartholomew, K., & Shaver, P. R. (1998). Methods of assessing adult attachment: Do they converge? In J. A. Simpson & W. S. Rhodes

(Eds.), *Attachment theory and close relationships* (pp. 25–45). New York: Guilford Press.

Baucom, D. H., & Epstein, N. (1990). *Cognitive-behavioral marital therapy*. New York: Brunner/Mazel.

Baucom, D. H., Epstein, N., Rankin, L., & Burnett, C. K. (1996). Understanding and treating marital distress from a cognitive–behavioral orientation. In K. S. Dobson & K. D. Craig (Eds.), *Advances in cognitive–behavioral therapy* (pp. 210–236). Thousand Oaks, CA: Sage.

Baucom, D. H., & Lester, G. W. (1986). The usefulness of cognitive restructuring as an adjunct to behavioral marital therapy. *Behavior Therapy, 17*, 385–403.

Baucom, D. H., Sayers, S. L., & Sher, T. G. (1990). Supplementing behavioral marital therapy with cognitive restructuring and emotional expressiveness training: An outcome investigation. *Journal of Consulting and Clinical Psychology, 58*, 636–645.

Beck, A. (1988). *Love is never enough*. New York: Harper & Row.

Bem, S. L. (1993). *The lens of gender: Transforming the debate on sexual inequality*. New Haven: Yale University Press.

Berscheid, E., & Walster, E. (1978). *Interpersonal attraction* (2nd ed.), Needham, MA: Addison-Wesley.

Blumstein, P., & Schwartz, P. (1983). *American couples*. New York: Simon & Schuster.

Bowlby, J. (1969). *Attachment and loss: Vol. 1. Attachment*. New York: Basic Books.

Bowlby, J. (1973). *Attachment and loss: Vol. 2. Separation: Anxiety and anger*. New York: Basic Books.

Bradbury, T. N., & Fincham, F. D. (1990). Attributions and marriage: Review and critique. *Psychological Bulletin, 107*, 3–33.

Bradbury, T. N., & Fincham, F. D. (1992). Attributions and behavior in marital interaction. *Journal of Personality and Social Psychology, 63*, 613–628.

Bradbury, T. N., & Fincham, F. D. (1993). Assessing dysfunctional cognition in marriage: A reconsideration of the Relationship Belief Inventory. *Psychological Assessment, 5*, 92–101.

Brennan, K. A., Clark, C. L., & Shaver, P. R. (1998). Self-report measurement of adult attachment: An integrated overview. In J. A. Simpson & W. S. Rhodes (Eds.), *Attachment theory and close relationships* (pp. 46–76). New York: Guilford Press.

Brennan, K. A., Shaver, P. R., & Tobey, A. E. (1991). Attachment styles, gender, and parental problem drinking. *Journal of Social and Personal Relationships, 8*, 451–466.

Buss, D. M. (1988). The evolution of human intrasexual competition: Tactics of mate selection. *Journal of Personality and Social Psychology, 54*, 661–728.

Buss, D. M. (1989). Sex differences in human mate preferences: Evolutionary hypotheses tested in 37 cultures. *Behavioral and Brain Sciences, 12*, 1–14.

Buss, D. M. (1994). *The evolution of desire*. New York: Basic Books.

Buss, D. M., Haselton, M. G., Shackelford, T. K., Bleske, A. L., & Wakefield, J. C. (1999). Interactionism, flexibility, and inferences about the past. *American Psychologist, 54*, 443–445.

Canary, D. J., & Stafford, L. (2001). Equity in the preservation of personal relationships. In J. H. Harvey & A. Wenzel (Eds.), *Close romantic relationships: Maintenance and enhancement* (pp. 133–151). Mahwah, NJ: Erlbaum.

Clark, M. S., & Mills, J. (2001). Behaving in such a way as to maintain and enhance relationship satisfaction. In J. H. Harvey & A. Wenzel (Eds.), *Close romantic relationships: Maintenance and enhancement* (pp. 13–26). Mahwah, NJ: Erlbaum.

Collins, N. L. (1996). Working models of attachment: Implications for explanation, emotion, and behavior. *Journal of Personality and Social Psychology, 71*, 810–832.

Collins, N. L., & Read, S. J. (1990). Adult attachment, working models, and relationship quality in dating couples. *Journal of Personality and Social Psychology, 58*, 644–653.

Crowell, J., & Treboux, D. (1995). A review of adult attachment measures: Implications for theory and research. *Social Development, 4*, 294–327.

Davila, J., Burge, D., & Hammen, C. (1997). Why does attachment style change? *Journal of Personality and Social Psychology, 73*, 826–838.

Davila, J., Karney, B. R., & Bradbury, T. N. (1999). Attachment change processes in the early years of marriage. *Journal of Personality and Social Psychology, 76*, 783–802.

Ehrenreich, B., Hess, E., & Jacobs, G. (1986). *Remaking love: The Feminization of sex*. New York: Anchor/Doubleday.

Epstein, N., & Baucom, D. H. (1993). Cognitive factors in marital disturbance. In K. S. Dobson

& P. C. Kendall (Eds.), *Psychopathology and cognition* (pp. 351–385). San Diego, CA: Academic Press.

Feeney, J. A., & Noller, P. (1990). Attachment style as a predictor of adult romantic relationships. *Journal of Personality and Social Psychology, 58*, 281–291.

Feeney, J. A., & Noller, P. (2004). Attachment and sexuality in close relationships. In J. H. Harvey, A. Wenzel, & S. Sprecher (Eds.), *Handbook of sexuality in close relationships* (pp. 183–201). Mahwah, NJ: Erlbaum.

Feeney, J. A., Noller, P., & Patty, J. (1993). Adolescents' interaction with the opposite sex: Influence of attachment and gender. *Journal of Adolescence, 16*, 169–186.

Fehr, B. (1988). Prototype analysis of the concepts of love and commitment. *Journal of Personality and Social Psychology, 55*, 557–579.

Festinger, L. (1957). *A theory of cognitive dissonance*. Stanford, CA: Stanford University Press.

Fincham, F. D. (1994). Cognition in marriage: Current status and future challenges. *Applied and Preventative Psychology, 3*, 185–198.

Fincham, F. D., & Beach, S. R. H. (1999). Marriage in the new millennium: Is there a place for social cognition in marital research? *Journal of Social and Personal Relationships, 16*, 685–704.

Fincham, F. D., & Bradbury, T. N. (1993). Marital satisfaction, depression, and attributions. *Journal of Personality and Social Psychology, 64*, 442–452.

Foa, U. G., & Foa, E. B. (1974). *Social structures of the mind*. Springfield, IL: Charles C Thomas.

Fraley, R. C., & Shaver, P. (1999). Loss and bereavement: Attachment theory and recent controversies concerning grief work and the nature of detachment. In J. Cassidy & P. Shaver (Eds.), *Handbook of attachment* (pp. 735–759). New York: Guilford Press.

Fraley, W. C., & Waller, N. G. (1998). Adult attachment patterns: A test of the typological model. In J. A. Simpson & W. S. Rhodes (Eds.), *Attachment theory and close relationships* (pp. 77–144). New York: Guilford Press.

Gallo, L. C., & Smith, T. W. (2001). Attachment style in marriage: Adjustment and responses to interaction. *Journal of Social and Personal Relationships, 18*, 263–289.

Gottman, J. (1994). *What predicts divorce? The relationship between marital processes and marital outcomes*. Hillsdale, NJ: Erlbaum.

Gottman, J. (1995). *Why marriages succeed or fail*. New York: Fireside Books.

Harvey, J. H., & Weber, A. L. (2002). *Odyssey of the heart* (2nd ed.). Mahwah, NJ: Erlbaum.

Hatfield, E., Utne, M. K., & Traupmann, J. (1979). Equity theory and intimate relationships. In R. L. Burgess & T. L. Huston (Eds.), *Social exchange in developing relationships* (pp. 99–133). New York: Academic Press.

Hazan, C., & Shaver, P. (1987). Romantic love conceptualized as an attachment process. *Journal of Personality and Social Psychology, 52*, 511–524.

Hazan, C., & Shaver, P. R. (1994). Attachment theory as an organizing framework for research on close relationships. *Psychological Inquiry, 5*, 1–22.

Heider, F. (1958). *The psychology of interpersonal relations*. New York: Wiley.

Johnson, D. J., & Rusbult, C. E. (1989). Resisting temptation: Devaluation of alternative partners as a means of maintaining commitment in close relationships. *Journal of Personality and Social Psychology, 57*, 967–980.

Johnson, M. D., Karney, B. R., Rogge, R., & Bradbury, T. N. (2001). The role of marital behavior in the longitudinal association between attributions and marital quality. In V. Manusov, & J. H. Harvey (Eds), *Attributions, communication behavior, and close relationships* (pp. 173–192). New York: Cambridge University Press.

Karney, B. R., Bradbury, T. N., Fincham, F. D., & Sullivan, K. T. (1994). The role of negative affectivity in the association between attributions and marital satisfaction. *Journal of Personality and Social Psychology, 66*, 413–424.

Keelan, J. P. R., Dion, K. K., & Dion, K. L. (1998). Attachment style and relationship satisfaction: Test of a self-disclosure explanation. *Canadian Journal of Behavioural Science, 30*, 24–35.

Kelley, H. H., Berscheid, E., Christensen, A., Harvey, J. H., Huston, T., Levinger, G., McClintock, E., Peplau, L. A., & Peterson, D. (1983). *Close relationships*. San Francisco: Freeman.

Kelley, H. H., & Thibaut, J. W. (1978). *Interpersonal relations: A theory of interdependence*. New York: Wiley.

Kurdek, L. A. (1998). Relationship outcomes and their predictors: Longitudinal evidence from heterosexual married, gay cohabiting, and lesbian cohabiting couples. *Journal of Marriage and the Family, 60*, 553–568.

Kurdek, L. A. (2002). On being insecure about the assessment of attachment styles. *Journal of Social and Personal Relationships, 19*, 811–834.

Le, B., & Agnew, C. R. (2003). Commitment and its theorized determinants: A meta-analysis of the investment model. *Personal Relationships, 10*, 37–57.

LeVay, S. (1993). *The sexual brain.* Cambridge, MA: MIT Press.

McCormick, N. (1994). *Sexual salvation: Affirming women's sexual rights and pleasures.* Westport, CT: Praeger.

Mikulincer, M., Florian, V., & Weller, A. (1993). Attachment styles, coping strategies, and post-traumatic psychological distress: The impact of the Gulf War in Israel. *Journal of Personality and Social Psychology, 64*, 817–826.

Mills, J., & Clark, M. S. (1982). Exchange and communal relationships. In L. Wheeler (Ed.), *Review of personality and social psychology* (pp. 121–144). Beverly Hills, CA: Sage.

Mills, J., & Clark, M. S. (1994). Communal and exchange relationships: New research and old controversies. In R. Gilmour & R. Erber (Eds.), *Theoretical approaches to personal relationships* (pp. 29–42). Hillside, NJ: Erlbaum.

Morgan, H. J., & Shaver, P. R. (1999). Attachment processes and commitment to romantic relationships. In W. H. Jones & J. M. Adams (Eds.), *Handbook of interpersonal commitment and relationship stability* (pp. 109–124). New York: Plenum.

Newcomb, T. M. (1961), *The acquaintance process.* New York: Holt, Rinehart & Winston.

Reiss, I. L. (1990). *An end to shame: Shaping our next sexual revolution.* Amherst, NY: Prometheus.

Ross, M. (1989). Relation of implicit theories to the construction of personal histories. *Psychological Review, 96*, 341–357.

Rusbult, C. E., Olsen, N., Davis, J. L., & Hannon, P. A. (2001). Commitment and relationship maintenance mechanisms. In J. H. Harvey & A. Wenzel (Eds.), *Close romantic relationships: Maintenance and enhancement* (pp. 87–113). Mahwah, NJ: Erlbaum.

Scharfe, E., & Bartholomew, K. (1998). Do you remember?: Recollections of adult attachment patterns. *Personal Relationships, 5*, 219–234.

Shackelford, T. K., & Buss, D. M. (1997). Cues to infidelity. *Personality and Social Psychology Bulletin, 23*, 1034–1045.

Simms, L. J. (2002). The application of attachment theory to individual Behavior and functioning in close relationships: Theory, research, and practical applications. In J. H. Harvey & A. Wenzel (Eds.), *A clinician's guide to maintaining and enhancing close relationships* (pp. 63–79). Mahwah, NJ: Erlbaum.

Slade, A. (1999). Attachment theory and research: Implications for the theory and practice of individual psychotherapy with adults. In J. Cassidy & P. R. Shaver (Eds.), *Handbook of attachment: Theory, research, and clinical applications* (pp. 575–594). New York: Guilford Press.

Symons, D. (1979). *The evolution of human sexuality.* New York: Oxford University Press.

Thornhill, R., & Thornhill, N. (2000). *Biological bases of sexual coercion.* Cambridge, MA: MIT Press.

Tiefer, L. (1995). *Sex is not a natural act.* Boulder, CO: Westview.

Wilson, E. O. (1975). *Sociobiology: The new synthesis.* Cambridge, MA: Belknap Press of Harvard University Press.

CHAPTER 4

Research Methods for the Study of Personal Relationships

Mahnaz Charania
William J. Ickes

Suppose that we are interested in enhancing our knowledge of the dynamics of a *dysfunctional* family. How do we decide which questions to ask? Should the focus be on the relationship of the married couple, the relationship between the parents and their child, or both? Should the researcher invite these individuals into a laboratory, ask them to independently complete mail-in survey questionnaires, or observe them in their home? There are no clear-cut answers to such questions. Rather, a variety of factors must be taken into account when deciding which questions to address and how to best address them.

Ultimately, the value of the approach one uses to collect data lies in its applicability to the particular research question being addressed (see Canary, Cupach, & Messman, 1995). The methodology that is selected will affect not only the quality of the data that are collected but also one's ability to interpret the data effectively. As Caspi and Bem (1990) noted, "Stability and predictive utility are not, of course, the only reasons for favoring particular kinds of data. Different

kinds of data are also differentially suited for answering different questions" (p. 555).

The field of relationship research has become increasingly multidisciplinary, with contributions and advances in research methodology from scholars in psychology, sociology, marital and family therapy, and communication (see Berscheid, 1994). A sociologist, for example, might approach the dynamics of a dysfunctional family by examining the macrolevel forces that impact the relationship among the family members, whereas a clinical psychologist might examine the meso- or even micro-level processes that characterize the family members' interaction pattern.

Researchers have traditionally benefited from adopting a social science approach when choosing methods to study personal relationships. Compared with case history, anecdotal, or impressionistic approaches, the social science approach seeks to obtain more objective and generalizable results through the use of structured research instruments that enable the researcher to translate participant responses effectively into numerically interpretable data. The methods we review support this quantitative approach to relationship research, in contrast to more qualitative approaches (see Allen & Walker, 2000, for a review of the qualitative approaches).

The purpose of the present chapter is to provide an overview of the various methods by which personal relationships may be (and have been) studied, as well as to consider methods for studying some special types of relationships that researchers have begun to explore during the past decade. We also highlight an integrated approach that enables researchers to simultaneously capitalize on the strength of various methods while minimizing the limitations they present.

The Trade-Off Problem

Not surprisingly, certain valuable information may be omitted because of the method of investigation in any attempt to capture what the researcher may deem to be the most relevant or important data. Because every research method has at least some limitations, a thorough understanding of different research methods combined with a clear set of hypotheses should enable researchers to maximize the validity and informativeness of their studies. We begin our review by discussing some of the typical trade-offs that researchers and practitioners must consider before selecting the method(s) by which they will address their respective research questions.

Correlational Versus Experimental Research

The first major trade-off that researchers confront typically occurs when they decide to conduct a correlational versus an experimental study. Correlational research is used to establish a relationship between two or more naturally occurring variables, whereas experimental research allows us to directly test hypotheses about the causes of behavior. Relationship researchers have primarily relied on these two methods when studying

interpersonal processes, although they have also benefited from other types of methods, such as the use of descriptive statistics (e.g., of the type obtained through public opinion polls), or the use of quasi-experimental designs in situations in which conducting a true experiment is not ethical or feasible (see Leary, 2004).

Correlational research has been used extensively to study the dynamics of personal relationships by examining the empirical relations among variables such as satisfaction in romantic relationships and the perception of love (Aron & Westbay, 1996), feelings of closeness, and the level of self-disclosure among friends (Hacker, 1981). It has also been used to explore how various personality dimensions are related to various relationship dimensions (Ickes, Hutchison, & Mashek, 2004). In most cases, the researcher assesses the direction, magnitude, and reliability of the relationship between two or more variables by first measuring them through self-report methods. However, the nature of the causal relations among these variables (if any) cannot be established in any definitive way.

In contrast, experimental methods in relationship research are used to determine whether changes in the level of certain independent variables (e.g., level of self-disclosure) *cause* corresponding changes to be observed in the level of one or more dependent variables (e.g., level of perceived closeness). In any application of the experimental method, the independent variables are the ones that are systematically manipulated by the experimenter, whereas the dependent variables are the ones that are subsequently measured by the experimenter. For a study to qualify as a true experiment, two criteria must be met. First, the experimenter must manipulate, or systematically vary, the level of the independent variable (the specific treatment that subjects receive) across the set of experimental conditions. Second, the experimenter must randomly assign the subjects (as individuals, dyads, groups, etc.) to each of the experimental conditions. Only through a rigorous (i.e., nonconfounded) application of the experimental method can the investigator determine whether a causal relationship exists between two variables.

For example, Mashek (2002) conducted an experiment with undergraduate dating couples to test the hypothesis that a romantic partner's threat to one's personal control leads one to desire less closeness from the partner. The couples were randomly assigned to either the experimental condition, in which one member of the dyad threatened his or her romantic partner's control, or to the control condition, in which a stranger threatened the target person's control. Mashek found that when a romantic partner threatened control, the target person desired significantly less closeness with his or her partner than when the threat was received from a stranger.

In many cases, it may not be financially or ethically feasible to conduct a true experiment. In such cases, researchers have frequently relied on "causal modeling" techniques, which permit the researcher to apply statistical controls to make stronger causal inferences from correlational data.

Convenience Versus Nonstudent Samples

A second major trade-off that relationship researchers confront concerns their decision to use convenience samples (typically college students) or the more difficult-to-obtain nonstudent samples. Sounding a strong cautionary note, Sears (1986) argued that social psychologists may have saturated the research enterprise with unrepresentative findings having only limited generality through their many studies of college students who are tested in laboratory situations. He believes that college students are distinctive because of two powerful demographic variables, age and education. Both of these variables may influence attitudes and attitude-related decisions, which are presumed to be unstable at such an age. This assessment, if true, would be alarming when one considers that nearly 45% of the articles published on close relationships since the 1930s have focused college-student samples (Cooper & Sheldon, 2002).

So why do researchers continue to use these convenience samples? The consensus within the field of psychology seems to be that reliance on college student samples does not have major negative consequence (Sears, 1986). Furthermore, given the incentives for frequent publications and the relative ease of implementing laboratory studies with college student populations, many researchers have strong motives to continue using them as their primary participants.

Despite these strong motives, we think that researchers should more carefully evaluate the trade-off between control versus representativeness. The recommendations provided by Sears (1986) include not only moving beyond the student population, but moving beyond the laboratory as well. It is probably not feasible to replicate all past findings in different research settings and with different subject populations. However, researchers should be encouraged (and even admonished) to review critically those findings that are potentially misleading because of the nature of the population sampled and to attempt to replicate these findings in ways that test the limits of their generality to different settings and different subject populations.

Individual Versus Dyad-Level Analyses

A third, and in many ways the most important, trade-off in the study of personal relationships concerns the researcher's decision about whether to assess the phenomena of interest at the level of the individual or the level of the dyad (Ickes, 2002). The marital dyad, for instance, is a dynamic interpersonal system in which the husbands' and wives' thoughts, feelings, and behavior are interdependent rather than independent. For this reason, it is just as important to consider the intersubjective aspects of personal relationships as to consider the subjective realities of the individual partners (cf. Ickes, 2002; Simpson, Oriña, & Ickes, 2003).

With only rare exceptions (e.g., Rutter, 1984), theorists and researchers acknowledge the strong mutual influences that dyad and group members can have on each other's cognitions, emotions, and behaviors (e.g., Ickes, 2002; Kenny, 1996; Rusbult & Arriaga, 1997; Simpson et al., 2003). For example, Ickes, Tooke, Stinson, Baker, and Bissonnette (1988) showed that the inter-partner correlations computed for differ-ent aspects of the thought and feeling con-tent reported by dyad members can be used to identify the "intersubjective themes" that characterize their current interaction episode. Given the increasing evidence for genuinely intersubjective phenomena such as this (see Ickes, 2002), several writers have stressed the importance of developing research paradigms that will allow the inter-dependent nature of the relationship to be uncovered (Campbell & Kashy, 2002; Gon-zalez & Griffin, 2000; Ickes, 2002; Ickes & Gonzalez, 1994, 1996; Kenny, 1988).

We closely examine one such paradigm, developed by William Ickes and his col-leagues (Ickes, Bissonnette, Garcia, & Stin-son, 1990; Ickes, Robertson, Tooke, & Teng, 1986) in a later section ("The Integrated Approach") of this chapter. This change of focus requires us, however, to consider the various kinds of data that relationship researchers typically collect and the more specific methods by which these specific forms of data collection typically occur. Accordingly, we now turn our attention to the trade-offs that researchers must con-front when deciding whether to use self-report methods, peer-report methods, obser-vational methods, physiological methods, archival methods, integrated methods, or a combination of these in their relation-ship research.

Self-Report Methods

A review by Cooper and Sheldon (2002) of 477 abstracts published since 1932 on the topic of personality and close (roman-tic) relationships revealed that 77% of these studies relied solely on self-report methods. The primary reason for this not-so-surprising finding is that self-report methods pro-vide the easiest and most efficient way to assess individuals' attitudes, beliefs, and self-

perceived behaviors. All the researcher has to do is ask the participants to respond to a relevant set of questions, whether this is done in face-to-face interviews, over the telephone, through paper-and-pencil ques-tionnaires, or through "electronic question-naires" that participants complete on the Internet.

There are at least three major advan-tages to using self-report methods to study relationships (see Harvey, Christensen, & McClintock, 1983; Harvey, Hendrick, & Tucker, 1988; Ickes, 1994):

1. *Self-reports are relatively easy, efficient, and inexpensive to obtain.*
2. *Self-reports represent the only way resear-chers currently have to access purely subjec-tive events.*
3. *Self-reports enable researchers to obtain the participants' reports of certain overt behav-iors that are typically private and may remain inaccessible otherwise.*

It is important to note, however, that seri-ous biases can be associated with obtain-ing retrospective reports from participants of events that may lie far in the past. For example, McFarland and Ross (1987) con-ducted a study in which members of dat-ing couples rated self and partner on a num-ber of dimensions such as kindness, honesty, and intelligence. Two months later, the par-ticipants were asked to provide ratings of self and partner on the same seven dimen-sions and to attempt to recall their previ-ous ratings as well. The authors found a significant consistency effect in recall, such that participants who became more nega-tive about themselves recalled their past rat-ings as being more negative, whereas par-ticipants who became more positive about themselves recalled their previous ratings as having been more positive than they actu-ally were. Similar findings were obtained for both self and partner ratings. Thus, aspects of one's relationship are often reported as being more consistent over time than they truly are, and this seems to occur because par-ticipants attempt to impose consistency on their ratings across time, because they often cannot remember what they reported initially, or both.

Although such instances of memory affecting recall can adversely affect the integrity of the data collected, we review here several techniques that can be used to minimize such effects, such as obtaining participant responses at more "behavior proximal" times (e.g., through diary accounts or interaction record studies). Because self-report data offer a crucial window into a person's private experience, most studies of personal relationships will probably involve the collection of self-report data, either as the primary data or as secondary data, that will complement the other sources of data we review. The following subsections address many of the specific methods by which self-report data have been collected.

Questionnaires and Surveys

A popular adage notwithstanding, the consensus of most relationship researchers is that, generally speaking, *opposites don't attract*. For example, in their recent survey study described on CNN.com ("Scientists," 2003), researchers Buston and Emlen concluded that "both sexes are most likely to attract individuals who look like them, have the same wealth, social status and share the same outlook towards family and fidelity." These conclusions were based on the data obtained by administering a self-report questionnaire to 978 college students between the ages of 18 and 20. Compatibility researchers have repeatedly benefited from the survey methodology in determining which types of couples are better suited for each other, by assessing attributes such as gender roles (Ickes, 1993), attachment styles (Hazen & Shaver, 1987), and communication styles (Swann, Rentfrow, & Gosling, 2003).

For decades, relationship researchers have exploited other ways of collecting questionnaire data outside of the traditional laboratory setting. As a consequence, some useful guidelines are now available for collecting self-report data through media such as magazines (Athanasiou, Shaver, & Tavris, 1970; Tavris & Sadd, 1977), newspapers

(see Shaver & Rubenstein, 1983) and, more recently, the Internet (Buchanan, 1998).

Collecting data through the Internet is increasing in popularity as a result of the flexibility and efficiency that this method offers to both the researcher and the participants. According to Stewart (2002), much of the escalated interest is due to the ease with which "data mapping" takes place (i.e., the data are automatically transferred to a data file, thereby eliminating the time and effort that researchers must typically devote to entering, correcting, and "cleaning" their raw data). Not surprisingly, this method holds particular appeal for technologically savvy researchers. As Buchanan (2000) warned, however, obtaining a representative sample via the Internet is frequently problematic. Buchanan therefore suggested that researchers who wish to use the Internet should recruit a very large sample, gather relevant demographic information, and then use that information to select a subsample having a composition similar to that of the population of interest.

As Internet-based dating and compatibility-matching services proliferate, questions will inevitably arise about their effectiveness. The results of at least one early study (Rehmatullah & Ickes, 2004) suggest that compatibility matching has the potential to be quite effective when marital satisfaction is used as the outcome measure.

Face-to-Face and Telephone Interviews

An alternative to asking participants to fill out questionnaires is to interview them in person or on the telephone. Chen (1996) suggested that researchers evaluate the potential benefits of using telephone surveys by asking themselves the following questions:

1. *Do many of the questions to be asked depend the respondents' answers to previous questions?*
2. *Must the survey be conducted at a specific time?*
3. *Are some of the survey questions quite complex?*

Responding "yes" to some or all of these questions should increase the researcher's confidence in choosing the telephone interview as a viable medium through which the desired data can be collected. Moreover, contacting prospective participants through the telephone can be useful in determining their eligibility and willingness to participate in the research. For example, in a study examining social support and social undermining from the spouse as potential moderators of the relationship between perceived stress and depressive symptoms, Cranford (2004) used telephone interviews to systematically select participants who were then asked to complete mail-in surveys.

Although this method is cost-effective, both financially and in regard to time (Aneshensel, Frerichs, Clark, & Yokopenic, 1982; Chen, 1996), it may not be the ideal choice if the prospective respondents must be interviewed at a special location, if they must be shown something, or if the questionnaire is lengthy (Chen, 1996). In cases such as these, the face-to-face interview procedure may prove to be the preferred research method. Antill (1983), for example, conducted in-home interviews with 108 married couples after recruiting them as potential participants from theaters and shopping centers in and around Sydney, Australia. The results of these in-person interviews allowed Antill to conclude that the marital satisfaction of both the husbands and wives was predicted by the degree to which they viewed their partners as having traditionally feminine traits.

Some disadvantages of the face-to-face interview technique may help to explain why this methodology is seldom used in the study of personal relationships. Stewart (2002) argued that issues such as staffing costs, possible researcher effects, marketing anxiety, and issues of liability often offset the method's apparent advantages, such as item variety and the development of rapport between the interviewer and the interviewee.

Mangione, Hingson, and Barrett (1982) reported a study in which they compared in-person interviewing with two alternative methods. The first alternative consisted of dropping off and then picking up a self-administered questionnaire, whereas the second alternative consisted of a telephone interview with an in-person follow-up. Mangione et al. (1982) concluded that when researchers are collecting sensitive data, a combined telephone and in-person follow-up can be an effective research method, particularly when there is a lack of phone ownership among the participants or when the data are collected in geographic regions where the telephone is not a practical mode of communication.

Diary Accounts

In a recent study, Ducharme, Doyle, and Markiewicz (2002) used a diary technique to investigate the attachment security, affect, and behavior of 15- and 16-year-olds with respect to their parents and peers. The adolescent participants were asked to maintain a 1-week diary in which they were to record all positive and negative interactions with their parents and peers. The results indicated that adolescents who were securely attached to at least one parent reported significantly more positive and fewer negative interactions with their parents than teens who were insecurely attached to both parents. Furthermore, the teens' attachment security with their father directly affected their peer relations.

Because the diary method is an excellent way to track individuals over time, there should be no surprise that it has been used in conjunction with longitudinal studies. For example, Kirchler (1988) asked couples to complete a 4-week diary to study their marital happiness and interaction. By having them record the frequency and valence of the couples' interaction six times a day, Kirchler was able to determine that marital happiness was inversely related to the frequency of conflict but was positively correlated with the frequency, positivity, and effectiveness of spousal interaction and with the accuracy of perception of the partner's motivational state.

Interaction Record Studies

Similar to diary studies, interaction record studies permit the investigator to obtain descriptive data from the participants about their daily social interaction experiences. These "interaction records" typically require the participants to record both objective facts about their daily social interactions and the subjective experiences that accompany these interactions. As Wiederman (2004) suggested, a good way to improve on asking participants to remember past experiences, or to compare the past to the present, is to have them report the experiences shortly after they occur and thereby minimize the chance of omission or distortion of data. Two well-known examples, both employing event-contingent recording procedures, are the Rochester Interaction Record (RIR; Wheeler & Nezlek, 1977) and the Iowa Communication Record (ICR; Duck, Rutt, Hurst, & Strejc, 1991).

The RIR requires participants to report the time and place of their interaction, the number of partners present, the length of interaction, and the participants' evaluation of the interaction (assessed on multiple dimensions). The ICR, which was introduced 11 years later, further requires the participants to estimate the impact of their interactions on the future of their relationships (Duck, 1991).

Interest in this research method was stimulated by a series of studies conducted by Ladd Wheeler, John Nezlek, Harry Reis, and their colleagues at the University of Rochester (Reis & Wheeler 1991). In these studies, college-age subjects used the RIR to make a record of each of their social interactions that lasted 10 minutes or longer. The subjects were asked to keep these records for an extended period of time (typically, 10 to 14 days) to sample adequately their general pattern of social activity.

To date, the RIR (or one of its variants) has been used to study a wide range of topics, including loneliness (Wheeler, Reis, & Nezlek 1983), clinical depression (Nezlek, Hampton, & Shean, 2000), the impact of physical attractiveness on one's social life (Reis, Nezlek, & Wheeler, 1980), the tendency to withdraw from other relationships during the later stages of courtship (Milardo, Johnson, & Huston, 1983), and the psychological well-being of older adults (Nezlek, Richardson, Green, & Schatten-Jones, 2002).

Interaction record studies using the RIR and the ICR are *event-contingent*, requiring respondents to report their experience each time an appropriate event (e.g., an interaction at least 10 minutes long) has occurred. In contrast, other interaction record studies have been *interval-contingent*, requiring respondents to report at regular, predetermined intervals, or *signal-contingent*, requiring respondents to report whenever signaled by the researcher (Wheeler & Reis, 1991). For example, Dirk Revenstorf and his colleagues used an interval-contingent interaction record study when they asked couples involved in marital therapy to make daily ratings of six aspects of their relationship (Revenstorf, Hahlweg, Schindler, & Kunert, 1984). These data were subsequently analyzed using time-series statistics to assess the changes that occurred in the couples' relationships over time.

Signal-contingent studies require subjects to complete an interaction record whenever the experimenter signals them by means of a telephone call or the beeping of an electronic pager. In an elegant study using telephone calls both to signal the subjects and to record their responses, Ted Huston and his colleagues phoned married couples nine times during a 2- or 3-week period. During these calls, each spouse was asked to report on activities in the past 24 hours that included household tasks, leisure activities, positive and negative interaction events, conflict, and conversations (Huston, Robins, Atkinson & McHale, 1987). In a study that sampled the day-to-day experiences of 170 high school students, Maria Mei-Ha Wong and Mihaly Csikszentmihalyi (1991) used preprogrammed electronic pagers to signal their teenage subjects to complete a behavioral self-report measure at randomly determined intervals. One of their strongest findings was that the girls spent more time with friends and less time alone than the boys.

Written Correspondence

An analysis of letters (e.g., epistles) and other forms of written correspondence (e.g., electronic mail) represents another way in which self-report data can be used to study relationships. For example, Banks, Louie, and Einerson (2000) analyzed a collection of holiday letters and discussed the ways in which these letters can help to create a positive identity for the writer and his or her intimates. Because written correspondence is also a mode of relating to others, epistolary studies may have much to teach us about the dynamics of personal relationships as they are expressed in this as well as in other modes (Mamali, 1992).

Similarly, because e-mail is a mode of relating as well as a written record of the e-mail interaction, it offers a rich source of insights into relationship processes. Boneva and her colleagues, for instance, compared the e-mails of men and women and learned that women are more likely than men to maintain kin relationships via e-mail (Boneva, Kraut, & Frohlich, 2001). Other researchers have studied the written correspondence between individuals who subscribe to various computer-mediated social support networks. For example, in a study by Dunham and his colleagues (1998), single mothers with young infants were given access to an online network concerning parental issues. After reviewing the mothers' private e-mails and message postings, the researchers concluded that these women relied on the network for emotional support and were able to develop close personal relationships with other network subscribers.

Peer Report Methods

Whereas self-report research tends to focus on the different subjective reactions of the individual members of a relationship, peer report research tends to focus on the shared, intersubjective reactions of a set of peers who all view the relationship from the outside, as observers and knowledgeable informants. For example, the use of peer nominations is becoming increasingly popular in studies of children's social behavior. Children are typically provided with a list of statements and asked to nominate a specific number of peers that the statements most accurately characterize.

In one of these studies, Bellmore and Cillessen (2003) examined fourth graders' meta-perceptions and meta-accuracy judgments about acceptance and rejection in their peer group. The children were asked to nominate same-sex or other-sex peers in response to questions such as, "Who likes you the most?" and "Who likes you the least?" The authors then obtained meta-accuracy scores by comparing children's perceived acceptance and rejection with their peer's actual acceptance and rejection nominations. Using this procedure, Bellmore and Cillessen (2003) gained more accurate information about the children's social relationships than if they had simply asked each child to respond independently.

Although peer reports are seldom used by researchers who study personal relationships, many have found this methodology to be useful in combination with other methods, such as self-reports. Burton and Krantz (1990), for example, attempted to predict the level of self-control, perception of self-control, and emotional distress reported by third, fourth, and fifth graders with information obtained previously through both self-reports and teacher ratings. Clearly, if researchers are willing to invest the time and effort required, they can learn much by asking knowledgeable observers of a given relationship to complete questionnaires, answer interview questions, provide written accounts, keep interaction records, or allow their own correspondence about the relationship to be examined.

Observational Methods

In the social sciences, there are two types of data: (a) those that are reported to the researcher and (b) those that are observed directly by the researcher (Metts, Sprecher, & Cupach, 1991). Observational studies involve summary judgments or behavioral records made by trained raters or by automatic recording devices (Ickes, 1994). To the extent that observational data can be collect in an unobtrusive and nonreactive way, the observational method becomes especially attractive to researchers who are interested in studying people's behavior as it naturally occurs within a variety of settings.

Although many observational studies are conducted in laboratory settings (e.g., Gottman, Markman, & Notarius, 1977; Ickes, 1984), many others are conducted in real-world settings as diverse as a hospital delivery room (Leventhal & Sharp, 1965), a police station (Holdaway, 1980), a subway train (Fried & DeFazio, 1974), and the United Nations building (Alger, 1966).

Whatever setting is chosen, it is important that the observation itself be as unobtrusive as possible. Recording the subjects' interaction by means of a hidden video camera for later analysis (Ickes, 1983; Ickes et al., 1990) provides one means of ensuring that the subjects' behavior will not be biased by the presence of trained raters on the scene. Having college roommates start an audiotape recorder in their dormitory room whenever they begin a conversation is also a relatively unobtrusive way to study their naturally occurring interactions (Ginsberg & Gottman, 1986). However, putting directional microphones in subjects' faces and requiring them to interact in front of a camera crew or in the presence of trained raters will virtually guarantee that their behavior will be altered or interfered with by the recording process itself.

Another question to consider is whether the behavior of interest warrants observational time periods that are very short (e.g., microbehaviors such as eye blinks), somewhere in the middle range (e.g., mutual gazes, frequency and duration of phone calls following dates), or relatively long (e.g., periods of marital separation). Although the timescale of the behaviors themselves typically dictates the answer to this question,

researchers must also rely on both their own intuitions and the reported experiences of previous researchers in making the relevant judgment calls.

Physiological Methods

The rising interest among researchers in studying how the quality of personal relationships is related to health status and health outcomes has led to the increased use of physiological measures in relationship research (Feeney, 2000; Loving, Heffner, & Kiecolt-Glaser, this volume). Although this method can be costly in terms of time, knowledge, and equipment (Ickes, 1994), it permits unique insights into the physiological processes that underlie human behavior, and it encourages work at the interfaces of biology, psychology, physiology, and medicine.

Physiological measures have been used to study marital abuse and marital conflict behaviors (Gottman, Jacobson, Rushe, & Shortt, 1995; Levenson & Ruef, 1992; Ruef, 2001), the health consequences of interpersonal interactions (McGuire & Kiecolt-Glaser, 2000), and the factors that predict husbands' and wives' retirement satisfaction (Kupperbusch, Levenson, & Ebling, 2003).

For example, Gottman and Levenson (1985, 1986; Levenson & Gottman, 1983, 1985) explored the link between marital conflict and marital distress by adding a physiological component to the observational method. In their studies, couples initially discussed either a high-or low-conflict situation while continuous measures of their heart rate, circulation, and general somatic activity were collected. Several days later, the partners returned to the lab to watch the recorded videotapes of their previous conflict interaction while the same physiological measures were taken once again. One widely cited finding from Levenson and Gottman's (1983) research was that physiological linkage (how closely the spouses' physiological responses covaried during the conflict interaction) accounted for 59% of the variance in their marital satisfaction scores (cf. Weiss & Heyman, 1990).

Archival Methods

A less frequently used, yet highly efficient, method of collecting data involves the secondary analysis of data that were collected for different purposes by previous researchers or institutions. Although the current researcher typically has no control over how such data were collected or what types of data are available, he or she may have access to a large volume of data that can be profitably mined to address research questions that were not considered in the original investigations. For example, researchers frequently request access to raw data from institutions such as the University of Chicago's National Opinion Research Center (NORC) and the University of Michigan's Survey Research Center (Rosenthal & Rosnow, 1991).

A good example is the archival study by Frank Trovato of the relationship between divorce and suicide in Canada (Trovato, 1986, 1987; Trovato & Lauris 1989). Hendrick and Hendrick (1992) have described this study as follows:

> Trovato used census-type demographic data from all the Canadian provinces to assess the impact of divorce on suicide, taking into consideration the effects of other variables such as educational level, religious preferences, marriage rates, and geographical mobility between provinces. He determined that divorce has a substantial effect on suicide rate (1986), and he did this without administering a single questionnaire or making even one behavioral observation. (pp. 14–15)

Trovato's findings were similar to those of Steven Stack, who used the same kinds of archival data to test the relationship between divorce and suicide in the United States (Stack, 1980, 1981) and in Norway (Stack, 1989). As this set of studies illustrates, data concerning major life events can be obtained from national agencies that compile statistics from official records such as divorce decrees and birth, marriage, and death certificates. Researchers such as Stack and Trovato can then use these archival data to test important hypotheses about personal relationships without having any direct contact with the subjects of their research. Of all of the methods available for conducting relationship research, the archival methods are the least obtrusive. For this reason, they are the least likely to be biased by the subjects' reactions to the researcher.

Archival studies are not universally valued, however. In fact, Larson and Holman (1994) have recommended that researchers avoid the use of such secondary data, especially if the original survey was not designed to address the specific issues that the current researcher is investigating. A stronger emphasis Holman et al. (2001) argued should be placed on designing studies with a particular purpose and predetermined elements of investigation.

Experimental Methods

Ickes, Patterson, Rajecki, and Tanford (1982) conducted a study in which one member of each pair of male strangers (the perceiver) was randomly assigned to receive one of one of three kinds of preinteraction information about the other member (the target). Specifically, some perceivers were led to expect that their target partners would act very friendly; others were led to expect that their partners would act very unfriendly, and a third (control) group was given no expectancy information. Of course, the information the perceivers received was in no case based on what their interactional partners were actually like; it was instead manipulated independently by the experimenters.

The results of the study converged to suggest that, relative to the no-expectancy perceivers, the friendly-expectancy perceivers adopted a reciprocal interaction strategy (one designed to reciprocate the friendly behaviors they expected their partner to display), whereas the unfriendly-expectancy perceivers adopted a compensatory inter-action strategy (one designed to com-pensate for the unfriendly behaviors they expected their partner to display). Because the experimenters determined what kind of expectancy information the perceivers received, and the subjects (perceivers and targets) were randomly assigned to the three expectancy conditions, the differences in the perceivers' behavior in the three con-ditions could be attributed to the differ-ent expectancies that were created rather than to differences in the types of subjects assigned to the three conditions. In other words, the only plausible cause of the dif-ference in the perceivers' behavior in the three conditions was the difference in the expectancies which the experimenters had established.

As this example suggests, researchers who use the experimental method in relation-ship research often seek to identify those independent variables whose manipulation establishes the varying conditions in which different types of relational phenomena (for example, reciprocity vs. compensation) will be observed. Occasionally, however, exper-imenters may pursue the opposite goal of manipulating the presence or absence of certain relational phenomena to assess their effects on subjects' perceptions of the relationship (e.g., Clark, 1985; Clark & Mills 1979).

The Integrated Approach

The unstructured dyadic interaction para-digm (Ickes, 1983; Ickes & Tooke 1988; Ickes et al., 1990) provides a useful example of an integrated approach that successfully com-bines the benefits of an observational study with the structure of a laboratory setting. In this procedure, the members of each dyad – who can be strangers, acquaintances, or inti-mates, depending on the purposes of the study – are led into a waiting room and left there together in the experimenter's absence. During the time in which the sub-jects are ostensibly waiting for the experi-ment to begin, their verbal and nonverbal behaviors are unobtrusively audio and video-taped. When the experimenter returns at the end of the observation period, the subjects are partially debriefed and asked for their signed consent to release the videotape of their interaction for use as data. They are also asked to participate in a second part of the study that concerns the specific thoughts and feelings they had during the interaction.

If their signed consent is given, the sub-jects are then seated in separate but identical cubicles where they are each instructed to view a videotaped copy of the interaction. By stopping the videotape with a remote start–pause control at those points where they remember having had a specific thought or feeling, each subject makes a written, time-logged listing on a standardized form of these *actual thought–feeling entries*. The subjects are then instructed to view the videotape a second time, during which the tape is stopped for them at each of those points at which their interaction partner reported a thought or feeling. The subject's task during this pass through the tape is to infer the con-tent of their partner's thoughts and feelings and provide a written, time-logged listing on a second, standardized form of these *inferred thought feeling entries*. When both subjects have completed this task, they are asked to complete a posttest questionnaire assessing their perceptions of themselves and their partner during the interaction. They are then debriefed more completely, thanked, and released.

The unstructured dyadic interaction paradigm combines a number of the meth-ods already described in this chapter. First, the observational method is used when the participants' interaction behavior is unob-trusively recorded on audio and videotape for later analysis. Second, the subjects are cued by the events recorded on the video-tape to make an event-contingent self-report interaction record of their own thoughts and feelings during the interaction. Third, they are then cued by the same videotape to make an event-contingent peer-report interaction record of the inferred thoughts and feel-ings of their interaction partners. Fourth, the subjects complete a posttest questionnaire in which they provide additional self-report and peer-report data. Fifth, in some cases the experimental method can be incorporated into this procedure, as illustrated by the previously described study in which one male dyad member was randomly designated to receive false feedback about the friendliness or unfriendliness of the other male dyad member before their interaction took place (Ickes, Patterson, et al. 1982, Experiment 1). Sixth, the paradigm can even be used to answer important cross-cultural questions, as in a recent study that compellingly documented what the researchers have described as the Hispanic social advantage (Holloway, Waldrip, & Ickes, 2005).

Even more important, an integrated method such as the unstructured dyadic interaction paradigm can be used to address fundamental questions about relationship partners' behavioral and cognitive interdependence. As examples of the latter, the paradigm has been used to explore intersubjective phenomena that include dyadic intersubjectivity (Ickes et al., 1988) and empathic accuracy (Ickes, 1997). According to the operational criteria proposed by Ickes and Gonzalez (1994, 1996), these phenomena are intersubjective because they involve both (a) the assessment of the cognitive responses of both dyad members and (b) the assessment of the degree of convergence, matching, or similarity in these cognitive responses.

Longitudinal Analysis

Studies using longitudinal data are increasingly being conducted in an attempt to predict the long-term quality of close relationships. Over the last 50 years, a great deal of attention has been focused on predicting marital quality and satisfaction by studying a reasonably large sample of couples over an extended period of time (see Holman et al., 2001). A recent and comprehensive study involves 376 couples who responded to the PREP-M (PREParation for Marriage) questionnaire (Holman, Busby, & Larson, 1989) between 1989 and 1993. These couples, who

were either seriously dating or engaged to be married at the time of their initial assessment, completed a follow-up questionnaire in early 1997. Holman et al. (2001) provided an extensive overview of the results of this study in their book, which includes an investigation of how premarital factors help us understand the differences between partners who broke up premaritally, those who married and later divorced, those who married but were currently dissatisfied, and those who married and remained highly satisfied.

Longitudinal designs have been a mainstay of developmental researchers who are interested in studying children's ability to form close relationships (Dodge & Feldman, 1990; Kagan, Snidman, & Arcus, 1998). In many cases, these studies reflect a more specific interest in the links between the child's early attachment to its primary caregiver and its later relationships with peers and romantic partners (Kochanska, 2002). The success of longitudinal studies lies in the researcher's ability to predict more accurately the temporal relationship between the variables of interest, a process that would at best be incomplete, and at worst impossible, without information provided by the participants on multiple occasions.

The primary advantages of longitudinal studies are (a) their assessments of *current* behaviors, beliefs, feelings, and attitudes at different points in time, and (b) their prospective (as opposed to retrospective) focus. Unlike retrospective designs, which require the participants to report events that occurred in the (sometimes distant) past, longitudinal designs allow the participants to reveal their attitudes, feelings, or behaviors at the specific times that each of the multiple assessments take place. The major drawback of such studies, however, is the difficulty of obtaining a sample of respondents who will agree to participate long-term and on multiple occasions, thereby creating a discrepancy between the original sample size and the sample left in the final follow-up.

Although respondent mortality is the most serious disadvantage of the longitudinal approach (Shaughnessy & Zechmeister, 1997), it is one that can be minimized by obtaining a very large initial sample of respondents and then assertively recruiting their continued participation throughout the subsequent waves of data collection. Call (1990) recommended that researchers obtain the names and addresses of friends or relatives of the participants during the initial data collection phase whom the researchers may later contact in the event the participant moves. This process will enable researchers to minimize the impact of losing participants over time. In addition, researchers must acknowledge that the length of the time frames they study can influence the results they obtain. For example, studying changes in marital satisfaction over the first few years of marriage could yield changes that are both quantitatively and qualitatively different from those that occur in marriages during the later years or over longer periods of time. Collins and Sayers (2000) proposed a measurement model to address more effectively this issue of "growth" in longitudinal research.

Meta-Analysis

The study of close relationships dates at least as far back as 1932, when Schiller published a paper on assortative mating on the basis of temperament and emotional traits (Cooper & Sheldon, 2002). Given the worldwide explosion of relationship research by investigators who span a wide range of academic disciplines, one can only imagine the amount of information that has accumulated since then. Meta-analysis provides an exceptionally valuable tool by which researchers can integrate and summarize the results of both correlational and experimental studies.

The results of a meta-analysis, which integrates the findings from a set of studies that have investigated the same (or conceptually similar) independent or dependent variable(s) (or both), are summarized using measures of effect size. These measures enable meta-analytic researchers to compare and contrast subsets of conceptually related findings that have first been

converted to a common metric (i.e., the metric of effect size). Using the effect-size estimates as their dependent variables, meta-analysts can apply standard statistical analyses to explore how the average size of a given effect across a set of studies is moderated by relevant "boundary variables," such as sociodemographic and personality characteristics, situational and context variables, and methodological differences (Shaugnessy & Zechmeister, 1997).

Two ambitious meta-analyses conducted by Amato and Keith (1991a, 1991b) assessed the effect of parental divorce on the well-being of adults, as well as children, who grew up in divorced families. In the first of these meta-analyses, effect size was calculated for 15 outcome variables across 37 studies involving over 81,000 individuals. The results indicated that adults who had experienced parental divorce as children exhibited lower levels of well-being than did adults whose parents were continuously married. The second meta-analysis integrated the results of 92 studies that compared children living in divorced, single-parent families with children living in intact families on various measures of well-being. The results indicated that children of divorced parents had poorer social adjustment (in particular, they were less popular and cooperative) than were children who did not experience parental divorce.

More recently, following their review of 10 relevant studies, Graham and Ickes (1997) speculated that gender differences in empathic accuracy might be due to differential motivation rather than differential ability. This speculation was tested more rigorously in a meta-analysis by Ickes, Gesn, and Graham (2000), who examined effect sizes for the gender differences obtained in a larger set of 15 empathic accuracy studies. Consistent with Graham and Ickes's (1997) earlier speculation, Ickes and his colleagues concluded that reliable gender differences in empathic accuracy are found only in situations in which empathy-relevant gender-role expectations are made salient – expectations that appear to enhance the motivation of female, but not male, perceivers.

As these examples illustrate, meta-analysis permits the investigator to identify both the "main effects" that hold across multiple studies and the "interaction effects" that hold for some categories of studies but not others. The researcher's ability to detect these effects owes much to the statistical sensitivity that results from summarizing the data from each study in the form of a single effect-size estimate (Rosenthal & Rosnow, 1991). An important caveat should be noted, however: The integrity of a meta-analysis depends on the reviewer's judgment of which studies to include and how to define the scope and parameters of the current investigation (see Schneider, 1991).

Special Cases

Increasingly, relationship researchers have taken an interest in extending their work to "understudied" populations. At the same time, they have become more mindful of the importance of testing the generality of their findings across different ages, genders, and cultural groups. Here, we comment briefly on three emerging areas of research and the important methodological implications that apply to them.

Studying Selected Groups: Children and the Elderly

Human relationships in the middle of the life span, ranging from adolescence to adulthood, are overstudied in comparison to relationships at the beginning and end of the life span (see Cooper & Sheldon, 2002). Many factors are responsible for this outcome. They include some unique ethical issues in addition to the more practical problems associated with identifying and recruiting representative samples, obtaining informed consent, and providing transportation for very young or very old participants who often rely on others for transportation. Fortunately, however, researchers have developed many effective strategies for dealing with such issues, while emphasizing the importance of increasing the research that is conducted with these understudied populations.

According to Graue and Walsh (1998), "Studying children is a difficult and more problematic endeavor from studying adults, and studying young children is even more so" (p. 95). Generally, the researcher must obtain permission from the parents before interviewing the child, and once this permission is granted, the researcher faces the difficulty of establishing a trusting relationship with the child to obtain the information of interest. Several methods have been used successfully to obtain data from children. These include conducting observational studies by bringing children into the laboratory (Ainsworth, 1973), conducting structured and unstructured interviews with the child (Murphy & Eisenberg, 2002), and (most commonly) using information obtained from teachers, peers, or parents about the child participant.

When studying the elderly, researchers have frequently relied on medical records to sample rare populations, such as those suffering from serious illness, living alone, or recently institutionalized (see Palmore, 1989). Obtaining permission continues to be an issue, especially when family members act as "gatekeepers" (Lawton & Herzog, 1989) who want to protect their parents or spouses from the interviewer.

Study Issues on the Dark Side of Relationships

Although some scholars focus their work on the more obvious issues that define the dark side of human relationships, such as conflict, obsessions, abuse, rape, and divorce (see Harvey & Weber, 2002), other researchers have focused on the more subtle, negative influences on relationships, such as inappropriate and forbidden relationships (Goodwin & Cramer, 2002) or the discrepancies between partners' levels of perceived and desired closeness (Ickes et al., 2004). Theorists and researchers who wish to study such phenomena are often faced with formidable challenges as they address issues of social desirability, self-selection, and distorted memories among populations that are highly motivated to conceal the true nature of such socially disapproved relationships.

In most cases, the observational method cannot be ethically applied to the study of abusive relationships. For that reason, we recommend employing face-to-face interview techniques as an alternative to the self-report, as previously suggested by Bentovim, Bentovim, Vizard, and Wiseman (1995). Specifically, Bentovim et al. (1995) discussed different approaches that might be used to investigate potential sexual abuse, especially when interviewing children. These approaches include using different forms of questioning, examining the respondent's artwork, analyzing the respondent's behavior during free and structured play, and using anatomically correct dolls to stimulate projective responses.

Extensive research using diverse methods has also been conducted on issues such as spousal abuse. Coan and his colleagues (Coan, Gottman, Babcock, & Jacobson, 1997), for instance, used an experimental study to compare nonviolent, distressed couples with couples who were experiencing domestic violence. The purpose of the study was to assess the extent to which domestically violent men reject influences from their wives. Their experimental design allowed Coan and his colleagues to better understand the motivations of Type 1 batterers, who were suspected to reject their wives' influence as a means of maintaining power and control. A second study, also focused on studying violent interspousal relationships, benefited from the use archival data that were previously obtained in a national survey (Whitchurch, 2000). In this study, specific violent behaviors and critical incidents, such as escalation and physical violence, were examined to identify differences among four couple types and to explain the discrepancies that had been identified in the relevant research literature.

The Cross-Cultural Perspective

The search for the universals of social behavior remains a long-standing goal of rela-

tionship researchers across many disciplines and is a particular concern of evolutionary psychology (Buss, 1994; Daly, Wilson, & Weghorst, 1982; Tooby & Cosmides, 1992). An important contrasting goal, however, is to further our understanding of the *variability* between different societies or cultural groups. Accordingly, the cross-cultural perspective has recently emerged as an important conceptual framework for relationship research (see Goodwin & Pillay, this volume).

It is conventional to divide cross-cultural studies of personal relationships into two broad categories: those seeking to identify differences among cultures or subcultures *within* a given society and those seeking to identify differences *between* the cultures found in different societies or nations. While acknowledging this distinction, we proceed with the assumption that these two types of studies are not mutually exclusive. Indeed, both present similar methodological problems to the cross-cultural researcher.

One issue that repeatedly arises as a source of concern is the applicability of a particular questionnaire or research instrument from one culture to another. Because self-report is the primary method by which relationship data are collected (Cooper & Sheldon, 2002), it is extremely important to ensure that the instruments used across cultures are presented as comparable yet culture-specific, making valid cross-cultural comparisons possible (Banville, Desrosiers, & Genet-Volet, 2000). The trick of balancing the conceptual equivalency of the measures with their cultural specificity is a delicate one, leading Suchman (1964) to caution that "A good design for the collection of comparative data should permit one to assume as much as possible that the differences observed . . . cannot be attributed to the differences in the method being used" (p. 135).

In an attempt to minimize the risk of arriving at inaccurate conclusions in cross-cultural research, Vallerand (1989) developed a rigorous methodology that consists of seven steps leading to the translation and validation of an appropriate research instrument. Although a detailed discussion of his methodology is beyond the scope of this chapter, we recommend it as a source of useful guidelines for any investigators who wish to do cross-cultural research.

Summary

The benefit of obtaining multiple perspectives, through multiple methods is invaluable when conducting research on personal relationship. Some writers (e.g., Aronson, Wilson, & Brewer, 1998) have called for more *programmatic research*, in which different research procedures are applied in different settings to explore the same relationship(s). Other writers (e.g., Dillman & Tarnai, 1988) have recommended the use of *mixed-mode surveys* that combine multiple data-collection methods with the same population.

We have also reviewed another eclectic approach as a solution to the trade-off problem. This approach, the unstructured dyadic interaction paradigm described earlier in this chapter, combines different methods in such a way that they build on each other's strengths and compensate for each other's weaknesses. When this strategy is successfully applied, the integration of various methods within a single research project may enable researchers to demonstrate a convergence or triangulation of results across the various methods. It may also broaden the researchers' view of the relational phenomena they are studying in ways that can help them to account for any discrepancies in the patterns of results obtained by one method versus another. Obtaining these important advantages also requires a trade-off, however, in that eclectic approaches often require a greater investment of time, effort, and other resources than single-method approaches require.

Accordingly, each researcher must determine which combination of methods is most appropriate for the research question being addressed. As the field of relationship research becomes increasingly mature and multidisciplinary, we expect that eclectic approaches in methodology will be used more often, and that they will help researchers to identify and explore exciting new directions for studying the dynamics of personal relationships.

References

Ainsworth, M. D. S. (1973). The development of infant–mother attachment. In B. M. Cadwell & H. N. Ricciuti (Eds.), *Review of child development research: Vol. 3. Child development and social policy* (pp. 1–99). Chicago: University of Chicago Press.

Alger, C. E. (1966). Interaction in a committee of the United Nations General Assembly. *Midwest Journal of Political Science, 10*, 411–447.

Allen, K. R., & Walker, A. J. (2000). Qualitative research. In C. Hendrick & S. S. Hendrick (Eds.), *Close relationships: A sourcebook* (pp. 19–30). Thousand Oaks, CA: Sage.

Amato, P. R., & Keith, B. (1991a). Parental divorce and adult well-being: A meta-analysis. *Journal of Marriage and the Family, 53*, 43–58.

Amato, P. R., & Keith, B. (1991b). Parental divorce and the well-being of children: A meta-analysis. *Psychological Bulletin, 110*, 26–46.

Aneshensel, C. S., Frerichs, R. R., Clark, V. A., & Yokopenic, P. A. (1982). Measuring depression in the community: A comparison of telephone and personal interviews. *Public Opinion Quarterly, 46*, 110–121.

Antill, J. K. (1983). Sex role complementarity versus similarity in married couples. *Journal of Personality and Social Psychology, 45*, 145–155.

Aron, A., & Westbay, L. (1996). Dimensions of the prototype of love. *Journal of Personality and Social Psychology, 70*, 535–551.

Aronson, E., Wilson, T. D., & Brewer, M. B. (1998). Experimentation in social psychology. In S. T. Fiske & G. Lindzey (Eds.), *The handbook of social psychology* (4th ed., Vol. 1, pp. 99–142). New York: McGraw-Hill.

Athanasiou, R., Shaver, P., & Tavris, C. (1970). Sex. *Psychology Today, 4*, 37–52.

Banks, S. P., Louie, E., & Einerson, M. (2000). Constructing personal identities in holiday letters. *Journal of Social and Personal Relationships, 17*, 299–327.

Banville, D., Desrosiers, P., & Genet-Volet, Y. (2000). Translating questionnaires and inventories using a cross-cultural translation technique. *Journal of Teaching in Physical Education, 19*, 374–387.

Bellmore, A. D., & Cillessen, A. N. (2003). Children's meta-perceptions and meta-accuracy of acceptance and rejection by same-sex and other-sex peers. *Personal Relationships, 10*, 217–233.

Bentovim, A., Bentovim, M., Vizard, E., & Wiseman, M. (1995). Facilitating interviews with children who may have been sexually abused. *Child Abuse Review, 4*, 246–262.

Berscheid, E. (1994). Interpersonal relationships. *Annual Review of Psychology, 45*, 79–129.

Boneva, B., Kraut, R., & Frohlich, D. (2001). Using e-mail for personal relationships: The difference gender makes. *American Behavioral Scientist, 45*, 530–549.

Buchanan, T. (1998, November). *Internet research: Self-monitoring and judgments of attractiveness.* Paper presented at the 1998 Society for Computers in Psychology Conference, Dallas, TX.

Buchanan, T. (2000). Potential of the Internet for personality research. In M. H. Burnham (Ed.), *Psychological experiments on the Internet* (pp. 121–140). San Diego, CA: Academic Press.

Burton, C. B., & Krantz, M. (1990). Predicting adjustment in middle childhood from early peer status. *Early Child Development and Care, 60*, 89–100.

Buss, D. M. (1994). *The evolution of desire: Strategies of human mating.* New York: Basic Books.

Call, V. R. A. (1990). *Respondent cooperation and requests for contacts in longitudinal research: A national survey of families and households* (NSF Working Paper No. 35). Madison: University of Wisconsin, Center for Demography and Ecology.

Campbell, L., & Kashy, D. A. (2002). Estimating actor, partner, and interaction effects for dyadic data using PROC MIXED and HLM: A user-friendly guide. *Personal Relationships, 9*, 327–342.

Canary, D. J., Cupach, W. R., & Messman, S. J. (1995). *Relationship conflict: Conflict in parent–child, friendship, and romantic relationships.* Thousand Oaks, CA: Sage.

Caspi, A., & Bem, D. J. (1990). Personality continuity and change across the life course. In L. A. Pervin (Ed.), *Handbook of personality: Theory and research* (pp. 549–575). New York: Guilford Press.

Chen, P. Y. (1996). Conducting telephone surveys. In F. T. Leong & J. T. Austin (Eds.), *The psychology research handbook: A guide for graduate students and research assistants* (pp. 139–154). Thousand Oaks, CA: Sage.

Clark, M. S. (1985). Implications of relationship type for understanding compatibility In W. Ickes (Ed.), *Compatible and incompatible relationships* (pp. 119–40). New York: Springer-Verlag.

Clark, M. S., & Mills, J. (1979). Interpersonal attraction in exchange and communal relationships. *Journal of Personality and Social Psychology, 37*, 12–24.

Coan, J., Gottman, J. M., Babcock, J., & Jacobson, N. (1997). Battering and the male rejection of influence from women. *Aggressive Behavior, 23*, 375–388.

Collins, L. M., & Sayer, A. G. (2000). Modeling growth and change processes: Design, measurement, and analysis for research in social psychology. In H. T. Reis & C. M. Judd (Eds.), *Handbook of research methods in social and personality psychology* (pp. 478–495). New York: Cambridge University Press.

Cooper, M. L., & Sheldon, M. S. (2002). Seventy years of research on personality and close relationships: Substantive and methodological trends over time. *Journal of Personality, 70*, 783–812.

Cranford, J. A. (2004). Stress-buffering or stress-exacerbation? Social support and social undermining as moderators of the relationship between perceived stress and depressive symptoms among married people. *Personal Relationships, 11*, 23–40.

Daly, M., Wilson, M., & Weghorst, S. J. (1982). Male sexual jealousy. *Ethology and Sociobiology, 3*, 11–27.

Dillman, D. A., & Tarnai, J. (1988). Administrative issues in mixed mode surveys. In R. M. Groves, P. P. Biemer, L. E. Lyberg, J. T. Massey, Nicholls W. L., II, & J. Waksberg (Eds.), *Telephone survey methodology* (pp. 509–528). New York: Wiley.

Dodge, K. A., & Feldman, E. (1990). Issues in social cognition and sociometric status. In S. R. Asher & J. D. Coie (Eds.), *Peer rejection in childhood* (pp. 119–155). New York: Cambridge University Press.

Ducharme, J., Doyle, A., & Markiewicz, D. (2002). Attachment security with mother and father: Associations with adolescents' reports of interpersonal behavior with parents and peers. *Journal of Social and Personal Relationships, 19,* 203–231.

Duck, S. (1991). Diaries and logs. In B. M. Montogomery & S. Duck (Eds.), *Studying interpersonal interaction* (pp. 141–161). New York: Guilford Press.

Duck, S., Rutt, D. J., Hurst, M. H., & Strejc, H. (1991). Some evident truths about conversations in everyday relationships: All communications are not created equal. *Human Communication Research, 18,* 228–267.

Dunham, P. J., Hurshman, A., Litwin, E., Gusella, J., Ellsworth, C., & Dodd, P. (1998). Computer-mediated social support: Single young mothers as a model system. *American Journal of Community Psychology, 26,* 281–306.

Feeney, J. A. (2000). Implications of attachment style for patterns of health and illness. *Child: Care, Health and Development, 26,* 277–288.

Fried, M. L., & DeFazio, V. J. (1974). Territoriality and boundary conflicts in the subway. *Psychiatry, 37,* 47–59.

Ginsberg, D., & Gottman, J. M. (1986). Conversations of college roommates: Similarities and differences in male and female friendship. In J. M. Gottman & J. G. Parker (Eds.), *Conversations of friends* (pp. 241–91). New York: Cambridge University Press.

Gonzalez, R., & Griffin, D. (2000). On the statistics of interdependence: Treating dyadic data with respect. In W. Ickes & S. Duck (Eds.), *The social psychology of personal relationships* (pp. 181–213). Chichester, England: Wiley.

Goodwin, R., & Cramer, D. (Eds.). (2002.). *Inappropriate relationships: The unconventional, the disapproved, and the forbidden.* Mahwah, NJ: Erlbaum.

Gottman, J. M., Jacobson, N. S., Rushe, R. H., & Shortt, J. W. (1995). The relationship between heart rate reactivity, emotionally aggressive behavior, and general violence in batterers. *Journal of Family Psychology, 9,* 227–248.

Gottman, J. M., & Levenson, R. W. (1985). A valid procedure for obtaining self-report of affect in marital interaction. *Journal of Consulting and Clinical Psychology, 53,* 151–160.

Gottman, J. M., & Levenson, R. W. (1986). Assessing the role of emotion in marriage. *Behavioral Assessment, 8,* 31–48.

Gottman, J. M., Markman, H., & Notarius, C. (1977). The topography of marital conflict: A sequential analysis of verbal and nonverbal behavior. *Journal of Marriage and the Family, 39,* 461–77.

Graham, T., & Ickes, W. (1997). When women's intuition isn't greater than men's. In W. Ickes (Ed.), *Empathic accuracy* (pp. 117–143). New York: Guilford Press.

Graue, M. E., & Walsh, D. J. (1998). *Studying children in context: Theories, methods, and ethics.* Thousand Oaks, CA: Sage.

Hacker, H. M. (1981). Blabbermouths and clams: Sex differences in self-disclosure in same-sex and cross-sex friendship dyads. *Psychology of Women Quarterly, 5,* 385–401.

Harvey, J. H., Christensen, A., & McClintock, E. (1983). Research methods. In H. H. Kelley, E. Berscheid, A. Christensen, J. H. Harvey, T. L. Huston, G. Levinger, et al. (Eds.), *Close relationships* (pp. 449–485). New York: Freeman.

Harvey, J. H., Hendrick, S. S., & Tucker, K. (1988). Self-report methods in studying personal relationships. In S. Duck, D. F. Hay, S. E. Hobfall, W. Ickes, & B. M. Montgomery (Eds.), *Handbook of personal relationships: Theory, research, and interventions* (pp. 99–113). Chichester: Wiley.

Harvey, J. H., & Weber, A. L. (2002). *Odyssey of the heart: Close relationships in the 21st century* (2nd ed.). Mahwah, NJ: Erlbaum.

Hazan, C., & Shaver, P. (1987). Romantic love conceptualized as an attachment process. *Journal of Personality and Social Psychology, 52,* 511–524.

Hendrick, S., & Hendrick, C. (1992). *Liking, loving and relating* (2nd ed.). Pacific Grove, CA: Brooks/Cole.

Holdaway, S. (1980). The police station. *Urban Life, 9,* 79–100.

Holloway, R. A., Waldrip, A. M., & Ickes, W. (2005). *Evidence for the Hispanic social advantage in same- and mixed-sex interactions: A self schema* approach. Manuscript in preparation.

Holman, T. B., Birch, P. J., Carroll, J. S., Doxey, C., Larson, J. H., & Linford, S. T. (2001). *Premarital prediction of marital quality or breakup: Research, theory, and practice.* New York, NY: Kluwer Academic.

Holman, T. B., Busby, D. M., & Larson, J. H. (1989). *PREParation for marriage* [questionnaire]. Provo, UT: Brigham Young University.

Huston, T. L., Robins, E., Atkinson, J., & McHale, S. M. (1987). Surveying the landscape of marital behavior: A behavioral self-report approach to studying marriage. *Applied Social Psychology Annual, 7,* 45–72.

Ickes, W. (1983). A basic paradigm for the study of unstructured dyadic interaction. In H. T. Reis (Ed.), *New directions for methodology of social and behavioral science: Naturalistic approaches to studying social interaction* (pp. 5–21). San Francisco: Jossey-Bass.

Ickes, W. (1984). Compositions in black and white: Determinants of interaction in interracial dyads. *Journal of Personality and Social Psychology, 47,* 330–341.

Ickes, W. (1993). Traditional gender roles: Do they make, and then break, our relationships? *Journal of Social Issues, 49*(3), 71–85.

Ickes, W. (1994). Methods of studying close relationships. In A. L. Weber & J. H. Harvey (Eds.), *Perspectives on close relationships* (pp. 18–44). Boston: Allyn & Bacon.

Ickes, W. (Ed.). (1997). *Empathic accuracy.* New York: Guilford Press.

Ickes, W. (2002). Subjective and intersubjective paradigms for the study of social cognition. *New Review of Social Psychology, 1,* 112–121.

Ickes, W., Bissonnette, V., Garcia, S., & Stinson, L. (1990). Implementing and using the dyadic interaction paradigm. In C. Hendrick & M. S. Clark (Eds.), *Research methods in personality and social psychology* (pp. 16–44). Thousand Oaks, CA: Sage.

Ickes, W., Gesn, P. R., & Graham, T. (2000). Gender differences in empathic accuracy: Differential ability or differential motivation? *Personal Relationships, 7,* 95–109.

Ickes, W., & Gonzalez, R. (1994). "Social" cognition and social cognition: From the subjective to the intersubjective. *Small Group Research, 25,* 294–315.

Ickes, W., & Gonzalez, R. (1996). "Social" cognition and social cognition: From the subjective to the intersubjective. In J. L. Nye & A. M. Brower (Eds.), *What's social about social cognition? Research on socially shared cognition in small groups* (pp. 285–308). Thousand Oaks, CA: Sage.

Ickes, W., Hutchison, J., & Mashek, D. (2004). Closeness as intersubjectivity: Social absorption and social individuation. In D. J. Mashek & A. Aron (Eds.), *Handbook of closeness and intimacy* (pp. 357–373). Mahwah, NJ: Erlbaum.

Ickes, W., Patterson, M. L., Rajecki, D. W., & Tanford, S. (1982). Behavioral and cognitive consequences of reciprocal versus compensatory responses to pre-interaction expectancies. *Social Cognition, 1,* 160–190.

Ickes, W., Robertson, E., Tooke, W., & Teng, G. (1986). Naturalistic social cognition: Methodology, assessment, and validation. *Journal of Personality and Social Psychology, 51,* 66–82.

Ickes, W., & Tooke, W. (1988). The observational method: Studying the interaction of minds and bodies. In S. W. Duck, E. D. Hay, S. E. Hobfoll, W. Ickes, & B. M. Montgomery (Eds.), *Handbook of personal relationships: Theory, research and interventions* (pp. 79–97). Chichester, England: Wiley.

Ickes, W., Tooke, W., Stinson, L., & Baker, V. L., & Bissonnette, V. (1988). Naturalistic social cognition: Intersubjectivity in same-sex dyads. *Journal of Nonverbal Behavior, 12,* 58–84.

Kagan, J., Snidman, N., & Arcus, D. (1998). Childhood derivatives of high and low reactivity in infancy. *Child Development, 69,* 1483–1493.

Kenny, D. A. (1988). The analysis of data from two person relationships. In S. W. Duck, D. E. Hay, S. E. Hobfoll, W. Ickes, & B. M. Montgomery (Eds.), *Handbook of personal relationships: Theory, research, and interventions* (pp. 57–77). Chichester, England: Wiley.

Kenny, D. A. (1996). Models of non-independence in dyadic research. *Journal of Social and Personal Relationships, 13,* 279–294.

Kirchler, E. (1988). Marital happiness and interaction in everyday surroundings: A time-sample diary approach for couples. *Journal of Social and Personal Relationships, 5,* 375–382.

Kochanska, G. (2002). Mutually responsive orientation between mothers and their young children: A context for the early development of conscience. *Current Directions in Psychological Science, 11,* 191–195.

Kupperbusch, C., Levenson, R. W., & Ebling, R. (2003). Predicting husbands' and wives' retirement satisfaction from the emotional qualities of marital interaction. *Journal of Social and Personal Relationships, 20,* 335–354.

Larson, J. H., & Holman, T. B. (1994). Premarital predictors of marital quality and stability. *Family Relations: Interdisciplinary Journal of Applied Family Studies, 43,* 228–237.

Lawton, M. P., & Herzog, A. R. (1989). *Special research methods for gerontology.* New York: Baywood.

Leary, M. R. (2004). *Introduction to behavioral research methods* (4th ed.). Boston: Pearson Education.

Levenson, R. W., & Gottman, J. M. (1983). Marital interaction: Physiological linkage and affective exchange. *Journal of Personality and Social Psychology, 45,* 587–597.

Levenson, R. W., & Gottman, J. M. (1985). Physiological and affective predictors of change in relationship satisfaction. *Journal of Personality and Social Psychology, 49,* 85–94.

Levenson, R. W., & Ruef, A. M. (1992). Empathy: A physiological substrate. *Journal of Personality and Social Psychology, 63,* 234–246.

Leventhal, H., & Sharp, E. (1965). Facial expressions as indicators of distress. In S. S. Tompkins & C. E. Izard (Eds.), *Affect, cognition, and personality* (pp. 296–318). New York: Springer.

Mamali, C. (1992, March). *Correspondence and the reconstruction of social dynamics: The correspondentogram of a nuclear family.* Paper presented at the Workshop on Theoretical Analysis, Department of Sociology, University of Iowa, Iowa City, Iowa.

Mangione, T. W., Hingson, R., & Barrett, J. (1982). Collecting sensitive data: A comparison of three survey strategies. *Sociological Methods and Research, 10,* 337–346.

Mashek, D. J. (2002). Feeling too close in romantic relationships: A consequence of threat to control? *Dissertation Abstracts International, 64 (1-B).* (UMI No. 3078570)

McFarland, C., & Ross, M. (1987). The relation between current impressions and memories of self and dating partners. *Personality and Social Psychology Bulletin, 13,* 228–238.

McGuire, L., & Kiecolt-Glaser, J. K. (2000). Interpersonal pathways to health. *Psychiatry: Interpersonal and Biological Processes, 63,* 136–139.

Metts, S., Sprecher, S., & Cupach, W. R. (1991). Retrospective self-reports. In B. M. Montgomery & S. Duck (Eds.), *Studying interpersonal interaction* (pp. 162–178). New York: Guilford Press.

Milardo, R. M., Johnson, M. P., & Huston, T. L. (1983). Developing close relationships: Changing patterns of interaction between pair members and social networks. *Journal of Personality and Social Psychology, 44,* 964–976.

Murphy, B. C., & Eisenberg, N. (2002). An integrative examination of peer conflict: Children's reported goals, emotions, and behaviors. *Social Development, 11,* 534–557.

Nezlek, J. B., Hampton, C. P., & Shean, G. D. (2000). Clinical depression and day-to-day social interaction in a community sample. *Journal of Abnormal Psychology, 109,* 11–19.

Nezlek, J. B., Richardson, D. S., Green, L. R., & Schatten-Jones, E. C. (2002). Psychological well-being and day-to-day social interaction among older adults. *Personal Relationships, 9,* 57–71.

Palmore, E. B. (1989). Medical records and sampling frames and data sources. In M. P. Lawton & A. R. Herzog (Eds.), *Special research methods for gerontology* (pp. 127–135). New York: Baywood.

Rehmatullah, M., & Ickes, W. (2004). *Compatibility matching and marital satisfaction: Some encouraging findings.* Manuscript in preparation, University of Texas at Arlington.

Reis, H. T., Nezlek, J., & Wheeler, L. (1980). Physical attractiveness in social interaction. *Journal of Personality and Social Psychology, 38,* 604–617.

Reis, H. T., & Wheeler, L. (1991). Studying social interaction with the Rochester Interaction Record. *Advances in experimental social psychology, 24,* 269–318.

Revenstorf, D., Hahlweg, K., Schindler, L., & Kunert, H. (1984). The use of time series analysis in marriage counseling. In K. Hahlweg & N. S. Jacobson (Eds.), *Marital interaction: Analysis and modification* (pp. 199–231). New York: Guildford Press.

Rosenthal, R., & Rosnow, R. L. (1991). *Essential of behavioral research: Methods and data analysis* (2nd ed.). New York: McGraw-Hill.

Ruef, A. M. (2001). Empathy in long-term marriage: Behavioral and physiological correlates. *Dissertation Abstracts International, 62 (1-B).* (UMI No. 3002245)

Rusbult, C. E., & Arriaga, X. B. (1997). Interdependence theory. In S. Duck (Ed.), *Handbook of personal relationships: Theory, research, and interventions* (2nd ed., pp. 221–250). New York: Wiley.

Rutter, D. (1984). *Looking and gazing: The role of visual communication in social interaction.* Chichester, England: Wiley.

Schneider, B. H. (1991). Reviewing previous research by meta-analysis. In B. M. Montgomery & S. Duck (Eds.), *Studying interpersonal interaction* (pp. 303–320). New York: Guilford Press.

Scientists: Opposites don't attract. (2003, July 1). *CNN.com.* Retrieved June 2004 from http://www.cnn.com/2003/TECH/science/07/01/potentials.attract/index.html

Sears, D. O. (1986). College sophomores in the laboratory: Influences of a narrow data base on social psychology's view of human nature. *Journal of Personality and Social Psychology, 51,* 515–530.

Shaughnessy, J. J., & Zechmeister, E. B. (1997). *Research methods in psychology* (4th ed.). Boston: McGraw Hill.

Shaver, P., & Rubenstein, C. (1983). Research potential of newspaper and magazine surveys. In H. T. Reis (Ed.), *Naturalistic approaches to studying social interaction: New directions for methodology of social and behavioral science, no. 15* (pp. 75–91). San Francisco: Jossey-Bass.

Simpson, J. A., Orina, M. M., & Ickes, W. (2003). When accuracy hurts, and when it helps: A test of the empathic accuracy model in marital interactions. *Journal of Personality and Social Psychology, 85,* 881–893.

Stack, S. (1980). The effects of marital dissolution on suicide. *Journal of Marriage and the Family, 42,* 83–91.

Stack, S. (1981). Divorce and suicide: A time series analysis, 1933–1970. *Journal of Family Issues, 2,* 77–90.

Stack, S. (1989). The impact of divorce on suicide in Norway, 1951–1980. *Journal of Marriage and the Family, 51,* 229–238.

Stewart, T. D. (2002). *Principles of research in communication.* Boston: Allyn & Bacon.

Suchman, E. A. (1964). The comparative method in social research. *Rural Sociology, 29,* 123–137.

Swann, W. B., Rentfrow, P. J., & Gosling, S. D. (2003). The precarious couple effect: Verbally inhibited men + critical, disinhibited women = bad chemistry. *Journal of Personality and Social Psychology, 85,* 1095–1106

Tavris, C., & Sadd, S. (1977). *The redbook report on female sexuality.* New York: Delacorte Press.

Tooby, J., & Cosmides, L. (1992). Psychological foundations of culture. In J. Barkow, L. Cosmides, & J. Tooby (Eds.), *The adapted mind:*

Evolutionary psychology and the generation of culture (pp. 19–136). New York: Oxford University Press.

Trovato, F. (1986). The relation between marital dissolution and suicide: The Canadian case. *Journal of Marriage and the Family, 48,* 341–348.

Trovato, F. (1987). A longitudinal analysis of divorce and suicide in Canada. *Journal of Marriage and the Family, 49,* 193–203.

Trovato, F., & Lauris, G. (1989). Marital status and mortality in Canada: 1951–1981. *Journal of Marriage and the Family, 51,* 907–922.

Vallerand, R. J. (1989). Vers une methodologie de validation trans-culturelle de questionnaires psychologiques: Implications pour la recherché en langue francaise. *Canadian Psychology, 30,* 662–680.

Wiederman, M. W. (2004). Methodological issues in studying sexuality in close relationships. In J. Harvey, A. Wenzel, & S. Sprecher (Eds.), *Handbook of sexuality in close relationships* (pp. 31–56). Mahwah, NJ: Erlbaum.

Weiss, R. L., & Heyman, R. E. (1990). Observation of marital interaction. In F. D. Fincham & T. N. Bradbury (Eds.), *The psychology of marriage: Basic issues and applications* (pp. 87–117). New York: Guildford Press.

Wheeler, L., & Nezlek, J. (1977). Sex differences in social participation. *Journal of Personality and Social Psychology, 35,* 742–754.

Wheeler, L., Reis, H., & Nezlek, J. B. (1983). Loneliness, social interaction, and sex roles. *Journal of Personality and Social Psychology, 45,* 943–953.

Wheeler, L., & Reis, H. T. (1991). Self-recording of everyday life events: Origins, types, and uses. *Journal of Personality, 59,* 339–354.

Whitchurch, G. G. (2000). Violent critical incidents in four types of violent interspousal relationships. *Marriage and Family Review, 30,* 25–47.

Wong, M. M., & Csikszentmihalyi, M. (1991). Affiliation motivation and daily experience: Some issues on gender differences. *Journal of Personality and Social Psychology, 60,* 154–164.

CHAPTER 5

Advances in Data Analytic Approaches for Relationships Research: The Broad Utility of Hierarchical Linear Modeling

Deborah A. Kashy
Lorne Campbell
David W. Harris

CLEOPATRA
O my lord, my lord,
Forgive my fearful sails! I little thought
You would have followed.

ANTONY
Egypt, thou knew'st too well
My heart was to thy rudder tied by th'
strings,
And thou shouldst tow me after. O'er my
spirit
Thy full supremacy thou knew'st, and that
Thy beck might from the bidding of the gods
Command me.
(Antony and Cleopatra, Act III, Scene 11)

This exchange between Antony and Cleopatra as envisioned by Shakespeare eloquently portrays the power and influence intimates can have over one another in romantic relationships. Although love and relationships have been focal points for poets and philosophers for thousands of years, these topics have been largely ignored by scientists until recent times. It was only 2 decades ago that a strong theoretical approach to the study of love and close relationships was called for by Harold Kelley and his colleagues (1983). Following his beloved Cleopatra to Egypt,

Antony's perilous journey symbolizes what Kelley et al. firmly stated was the defining feature of a close relationship: interdependence, or the existence of connections between one partner's activities or qualities and the other partner's outcomes.

Relationship research has since made great gains as a field of scientific study, establishing over the past 2 decades what has recently been labeled the *New Science of Intimate Relationships* (Fletcher, 2002). One consequence of this fact is that two journals dedicated solely to the study of close relationships are thriving (the *Journal of Social and Personal Relationships*, begun in 1984, and *Personal Relationships*, begun in 1994). As relationships research has grown, a number of research methodologists (e.g., R. Gonzalez, J. M. Gottman, and D. A. Kenny) have turned their attention to developing data analytic models and methods that are specifically designed for the challenges inherent in the study of close relationships (see, for example, Gonzalez & Griffin, 2002; Gottman, Murray, Swanson, Tyson, & Swanson, 2002; Kenny, 1996). These analytic strategies help bridge the gap between the theoretical notion of interdependence in relationships and the empirical study of this phenomenon.

Consider first the question of why specific analytic strategies are even necessary in the field of relationship science. Interdependence between individuals implies that the thoughts, feelings, or behaviors of related individuals will be especially similar to one another (i.e., more similar than the thoughts, feelings, or behaviors of two unrelated individuals would be).[1] That is, the scores from individuals who are involved in a relationship will not be independent. Yet many traditional statistical techniques, such as analysis of variance and multiple regression, assume that each observation is completely independent of every other observation in a data set.

There are two major issues involved in the analysis of nonindependent data. The first issue is that of bias in hypothesis testing. Speaking somewhat generally, if a statistical technique that assumes independence (e.g., analysis of variance or regression) is used with nonindependent data, the alpha level associated with the inferential statistics generated will not accurately reflect the true probability of making a Type I error. As Kenny and his colleagues (Kenny, 1995; Kenny, Kashy, & Bolger, 1998) have shown, in some instances the statistical tests will be overly liberal (too many false positives), and in other instances the tests will be overly conservative (too many false negatives).

The second issue concerns the types of questions that can be addressed. In particular, one of the most important advantages of gathering nonindependent data (data from both or all partners involved in a relationship) is that researchers can examine not only how a person's characteristics affect his or her own behavior, but also how that person's characteristics affect his or her partner's behavior. Much of the methodological work that has been done in recent years has been focused on developing data analytic techniques that model interpersonal influence in relationships (e.g., Gonzalez & Griffin, 1997; Kenny, 1996).

As we considered what we wanted to include in this chapter concerning "advances in data analytic methods for relationships research," we decided that we first wanted to know how the field has responded to the many published papers detailing new analytic methods for relationships research. In pursuit of this goal, we surveyed relationships research from five prominent journals that publish relationships research: *Personal Relationships, Journal of Social and Personal Relationships, Journal of Personality and Social Psychology – Interpersonal Relations and Group Processes, Personality and Social Psychology Bulletin*, and *Journal of Marriage and Family*. To determine the extent to which researchers have been applying these new analytic methods and to ascertain how the application of these analytic methods has shifted over time, we examined all research publications within the close relationships domain from these journals for the years 1994 ($n = 157$) and 2002 ($n = 181$). We were specifically interested in two aspects of the research: the unit from which the data were collected and the data analytic strategy applied.

For the purposes of our survey, we classified each study according to the type of data that were gathered. Specifically, we determined whether each study collected data from one individual in a given relationship, both members of a dyadic relationship, or from multiple family members or members of other relationship groups (e.g., friendship groups in which group size is greater than two). This is admittedly a rather simple coding scheme. That is, our individual data code includes studies in which an individual provided data at one time point about one relationship as well as studies in which an individual provided data at many time points about one or many relationships. The key element of the individual code is only that one individual's perspective on the relationship(s) in question was obtained. Thus, for the studies with individual data, there is typically no violation of independence of data from person to person, and a variety of standard analytic methods are available for such data.

Table 5.1. *Frequency (and Percentage) of Studies Reporting Individual (Indiv), Dyadic, and Group and Family Data Reported in Relationships Publications From Five Journals in 1994 and 2002*

Journal	1994			2002		
	Indiv	Dyad	Group	Indiv	Dyad	Group
Pers Rel	22 (75.9)	5 (17.2)	2 (6.9)	28 (73.7)	10 (26.3)	0 (0.0)
J Soc Pers Rel	22 (62.9)	13 (37.1)	0 (0.0)	19 (65.5)	10 (34.5)	0 (0.0)
J Marr Fam	59 (81.9)	10 (13.9)	3 (4.2)	53 (77.9)	11 (16.2)	4 (5.9)
J Pers Soc Psych	8 (47.1)	7 (41.2)	2 (11.8)	19 (79.2)	5 (20.8)	0 (0.0)
Pers Soc Psych Bull	3 (75.0)	1 (25.0)	0 (0.0)	14 (63.6)	8 (36.4)	0 (0.0)
Totals	114 (72.6)	36 (22.9)	7 (4.5)	133 (73.5)	44 (24.3)	4 (2.2)

Note: Of the 11 reported group studies, 9 involved families and two were nonfamily group studies. *J Marr Fam* = *Journal of Marriage and family; J Pers Soc Psych = Journal of Personality and Social Psychology; J Soc Pers Rel = Journal of Social and Personal Relationships; J Soc Psych Bull = Journal of Social Psychology Bulletin; Pers Rel = Personal Relationships.*

The reader can perhaps anticipate that our real interest was in the more complex and challenging data structures that arise when all members of dyads and groups provide data. These are the instances in which the standard assumption of independence of data is violated, and, more important, these are the instances unique to the study of interpersonal relationships. These are also the data structures that have been extensively addressed by research methodologists such as Kenny (e.g., 1994, 1995, 1996; Kenny & Cook, 1999; Kenny, Kashy, & Bolger, 1998) and Griffin and Gonzalez (e.g., 1995; Gonzalez & Griffin, 1997, 1999, 2002). Table 5.1 contains the results of our survey.

Two findings are readily apparent in Table 5.1. First (and in our view somewhat surprisingly), the pattern of data type is highly stable across the two time points sampled. Second, individual-level data are clearly the dominant data type reported such that individual-level data account for about 70% of data published in relationships journals during the 2 years sampled. Less than one quarter of the relationships-oriented research published in the journals sampled involved dyadic data in both 1994 and 2002 – despite the fact that a quintessential feature of relationships is that partners' thoughts, feelings, and behaviors are causally connected (Kelley et al., 1983). Less than 5% of data are generated by families or other small groups.

Although the proportion of dyadic and family data collected does not appear to have changed much over time, it may be that the data analytic approaches taken with these data structures have changed over time. That is, researchers who collect dyadic, family, or group data today may be using more sophisticated and appropriate data analytic techniques with dyadic, family, and group data than researchers did a decade ago. Thus, the next question we investigated in our survey was the type of data analytic approach used in each study that collected either dyadic, family, or group data.

Table 5.2 presents the frequencies of the various data analytic approaches applied to dyadic and group data during the 2 years surveyed. The table is organized in order of increasing appropriateness and complexity. The first strategy in the table involves treating dyadic, family, or group data as if they were simply data from individuals, ignoring nonindependence and therefore violating the independence assumption. We were pleased to see that only three published studies used this approach, and they were all published in 1994. In the second strategy, researchers computed a mean for each dyad or group and then treat dyad or group as the unit of analysis. Although this approach does not violate statistical assumptions, it is often wasteful because useful and interesting information may be lost when the data are averaged. In addition, statistical

Table 5.2. *Frequencies of Various Analytic Approaches Applied to Dyadic and Group Data in 1994 and 2002*

Analysis Strategy	1994	2002
Nonindependence ignored – independence assumption violated	3	0
Means for each dyad or group computed and analyzed with dyad or group as unit of analysis	6	3
Separate analyses conducted for different dyad or group member types (e.g., men and women)	9	8
Separate analyses conducted for dyad or group member types and partner variables included as predictors as well	7	4
Standard analyses treating dyad or group as the unit of analysis	13	15
Social relations model	2	0
Structural equation modeling with dyad or group as the unit of analysis	2	4
Actor–partner interdependence model	0	6
Hierarchical linear modeling	1	8

relationships that emerge for mean values may differ from those at the individual level. For example, it may be that couples who are higher in income on average are happier in their relationships on average, but that within a couple, the higher earning person may be less happy than the lower earning person. Like ignoring nonindependence, analysis of group means is a relatively rare data analytic approach.

The third analysis strategy is neither rare nor is it showing any real decline over time. In this approach, separate analyses are conducted for each "type" or "class" of dyad member. The prototypical example of this would be a study of married couples in which researchers conduct separate analyses for husbands and wives. For example, researchers examining issues of trust and satisfaction might compute a regression for the wives in which how much the women trust their husbands is used to predict their satisfaction. A similar regression would be computed for husbands. Because the data from dyad members are not pooled, there is no violation of independence; however, there are problems with this approach. One of the most important is that researchers tend to interpret differences between results from the two analyses as indicative of significant differences between the types of dyad members (e.g., husbands and wives). Thus, one might find that for men the relationship between trust and satisfaction is

characterized by $b = 0.50, p < 0.05$ but that for women this relationship is characterized by $b = 0.30, ns$. Too often researchers interpret such results as indicating that men and women differ in the degree to which trust is an important predictor of satisfaction. Just because one coefficient is significantly different from zero and the other is not does not imply that the two differ from each other. Researchers often fail to conduct any direct tests to address this problem and often make fundamental errors in interpreting their results (e.g., Onishi & Gjerde, 2002). In general, the separate analysis strategy places a great deal of emphasis on gender differences without ever testing whether such differences exist. Another problem with this data analytic approach is that it promotes a view that a person's relationship outcomes are solely determined by characteristics of the person and does not take partner effects into account.

As can be seen in the next row of Table 5.2, some researchers do make the improvement over the previously mentioned strategy by including partner variables as predictors. So extending our example of trust, this approach involves computing a regression for the wives in which their satisfaction is a function of both how much they trust their husbands and how much their husbands trust them. A similar regression is computed for the men. This is a step up from the previous category in that there is some accommodation for mutual influence. Nonetheless, because separate analyses are still being conducted for each "type" of dyad member (i.e., one analysis for wives but including some husband variables as predictors of wives' outcomes, and a parallel analysis for husbands), this analysis promotes the interpretation of differences between dyad member types even if such differences do not exist.

The next category in Table 5.2 is a broad aggregation of research that uses standard data analytic techniques treating dyad or group as the unit of analysis so that the assumption of independence is not violated. Notably this is the most frequent analysis strategy in the table, and it appears to be stable over time. Examples of such analyses include related groups t tests for gender differences in married couples or dating couples and mixed model analysis of variance where the within-groups factor is sex. Simple correlational research in which partners' scores are correlated with each other also falls into this group.

In the bottom part of the table, we come to the four most complex and sophisticated data analytic tools applied in relationships research, and we were pleased to see that three of the four appear to be growing in frequency of use. The social relations model (SRM; Kenny, 1994) is a model of dyadic and group behavior that suggests that dyadic behavior can be partitioned into group-, dyad-, and individual-level effects.

As an example, consider a study of self-disclosure among friends. The SRM suggests that how much one friend, Cheryl, discloses to another, say Juli, is a function of four effects. First there is the *group mean*, which is the average level of self-disclosure that occurs in a particular friendship group – some groups are higher in disclosure on average than others. Next is the *actor effect*, which is a person's general tendency to disclose to all partners. How much Cheryl discloses to Juli in part reflects Cheryl's tendency to self-disclose a great deal to all of her friends. Cheryl's disclosure to Juli is also a function of Juli's *partner effect*. The partner effect is a person's tendency to elicit a behavior

from all partners; in the example, everyone in the friendship group may self-disclose to Juli. Finally, there is a unique component to Cheryl's disclosure with Juli, which is known as the *relationship effect*. Cheryl's relationship effect with Juli is Cheryl's tendency to self-disclose a unique amount to Juli after controlling for Cheryl's general tendency to disclose to all partners and after controlling for Juli's tendency to elicit disclosure from all partners.

One challenge in applying the SRM is that each person must be paired with multiple partners. Typically this occurs in small groups in which each individual interacts with or rates every other person in a group, and so it cannot be applied to the standard couple's research design in which each person is a member of only one dyad. Within the relationships domain, the SRM has been used to study several aspects of friendship (e.g., Kenny & Kashy, 1994; Simpkins & Parke, 2002) as well as communication within married couples (e.g., Fitzpatrick & Dindia, 1986; Sabatelli, Buck, & Kenny, 1986). One area that has found the SRM to be particularly useful is the study of families (e.g., Cook, 2000, 2001; Delsing, Oud, De-Bruyn, & van-Aken, 2003)

Structural equation modeling (SEM), treating the dyad or group as the unit of analysis, is a data analytic approach that is growing somewhat over time. SEM techniques offer researchers ways to estimate and test theoretical models based on correlational data. The SEM approach offers several advantages that are generally not available with more traditional data analytic techniques (for a review, see MacCallum & Austin, 2000). For instance, researchers can generate latent factors using multiple measures of the same psychological construct and thus generate error-free estimates of the relationships between these constructs. In particular, researchers increasingly seem to be using latent growth curve analysis (e.g., Duncan, Duncan, Strycker, & Alpert, 1999). Additionally, researchers can move beyond testing the statistical significance of single relationships between two or more variables and can test the relative fit of models that contain a variety of direct and indirect relationships between the study variables. For example, in a study of satisfaction in marriage, a researcher can compare the relative fit of models that specify no gender differences with ones that do to determine whether marital satisfaction is related in a similar fashion to certain variables for men and women (e.g., Murray, Holmes, & Griffin, 1996a).

Perhaps most intriguing are the results for hierarchical linear modeling (HLM; also called multilevel modeling) and analyses in which actor and partner effects are estimated in analyses treating dyad as the unit of analysis. These data analytic methods were virtually unknown to the relationships community in 1994 but are being applied more and more today. The actor–partner interdependence model (APIM) is really more of a conceptual model than a data analytic method because its parameters can be estimated using structural equation modeling, hierarchical linear modeling or by pooling regression analyses (see Campbell & Kashy, 2002; Kashy & Kenny, 2000). This model treats dyad as the unit of analysis and simply proposes that a person's outcomes are a function of his or her own predictor variables as well as his or her partner's predictor variables. For example, if the effects of commitment on marital satisfaction are of interest, the actor effect from the APIM estimates the degree to which a person's own commitment predicts that person's satisfaction. The partner effect estimates the degree to which the partner's commitment predicts the person's satisfaction. Clearly this is an appealing model for relationships researchers.

Finally, of all these more complex data analytic approaches, HLM is arguably the most flexible in terms of its ability to accommodate a wide variety of data structures that commonly occur in relationships research. It is a technique that allows researchers to examine simultaneously the effects of individual-, dyad-, and even group-level variables, and it can also be used to examine longitudinal data both for individuals and for dyads.

Because of the potential of HLM to assist researchers in analyzing complex data

structures, we decided to focus the remainder of this chapter on some of the possible uses that HLM has in relationships research. We provide a brief overview of HLM and cite examples of some excellent research that is beginning to take advantage of this powerful new analytic tool. Although the possible uses we discuss are not exhaustive, they focus on some of the more common data structures that we observed from our analysis of recently published relationships research.

A Basic Introduction to HLM

As the name implies, a hierarchical data structure contains multiple levels within the data. The most elementary multilevel data structures contain two levels, and there are two classic cases that generate multilevel data. In the first case, individuals are nested within groups, such as students within a classroom – here students are the lower-level unit and classrooms the upper-level unit. Dyadic data have this form because the two partners are nested within couple. In the second case, repeated measures are obtained from each individual – here observation is the lower-level unit and person is the upper-level unit. A common example of this is diary research in which each individual provides multiple data points over time or events. In HLM analyses, the outcome (dependent) variable is measured at the lower level (e.g., for each student, partner, or diary). Although within an upper-level unit, observations at the lower level are not assumed to be independent of one another (i.e., within the same classroom, two students' scores on an English achievement test are not assumed to be independent; a husband's satisfaction and his wife's satisfaction are not assumed to be independent; a man's reports of his extroversion-related behaviors on Monday are not independent of his reports on Tuesday), independence is assumed to exist between upper-level units (i.e., there is independence from classroom to classroom, couple to couple, and person to person in our three examples).

In introducing HLM, we begin with a discussion of how it is applied with data that have been collected from independent individuals over time (i.e., repeated measurements), as would be the case in a typical diary study (e.g., DePaulo & Kashy, 1998; Fournier, Moskowitz, & Zuroff, 2002). We then turn to HLM models for dyadic data, and we conclude by integrating both types of data structures into a three-level HLM design. We provide just a basic overview of these topics and urge readers who are not familiar with HLM to consult Kenny, Bolger, and Kashy (2001) for a more extensive introduction and Kreft and deLeeuw (1998), or Raudenbush and Bryk (2002) for a thorough discussion of the topic.

HLM With Data From Independent Individuals Over Time

Consider first a hypothetical study examining factors that affect daily mood. In the study, in addition to having participants report on their daily mood, individuals complete a measure of the level of conflict in their interactions with close friends and dating partners; these measures are completed at the end of each day for a period of 14 consecutive days. One central question addressed in the research could be the degree to which perception of conflict with close partners affects mood. In the standard notation of HLM, daily mood (the outcome variable in this example) is denoted as Y, and conflict is denoted as X. Both X and Y are lower-level variables, and every participant has 14 observations for each. Say that an additional question for the research is whether the conflict–mood relationship varies as a function of a person's sensitivity to rejection. That is, individuals who are more sensitive to rejection may be more reactive in terms of their mood when there is conflict. Rejection sensitivity is an upper-level predictor variable (i.e., it is a person-level variable), denoted as Z, and is assessed once for each participant. To reiterate, the upper-level unit in this hypothetical study is individual, and the lower-level unit is day. The upper-level predictor (Z) is rejection sensitivity, the lower-level

predictor (X) is level of conflict each day, and the outcome (Y) is daily mood. In describing HLM, we first present an overview of the fixed and random effects that are estimated by this data analytic approach. Then we introduce the more formal HLM equations.

FIXED AND RANDOM EFFECTS

A number of questions can be addressed with this data set using HLM. First, a researcher can estimate the general effects of X and Z, as well as their interaction (XZ), on Y across the sample. These average effects of the predictors on the outcome (averaging over days and persons) are known as fixed effects. For our example, one fixed effect measures whether individuals who are higher in rejection sensitivity have more negative moods in general (Z predicting Y). Another fixed effect measures whether days during which there are higher levels of conflict are associated with more negative moods (X predicting Y). The effect of the interaction assesses the degree to which relationship between perceived daily conflict and mood differs depending on a person's level of rejection sensitivity (XZ predicting Y).

In addition to estimating fixed or average effects, HLM allows researchers to estimate the degree of variability in these effects, known as random effects. For example, there may be individual differences in average mood after controlling for rejection sensitivity (i.e., variance in average Y across the upper-level units after controlling for variance in Z). It may also be the case that there is variation from person to person in the relationship between perceived conflict and daily mood after controlling for rejection sensitivity (i.e., variance in the X–Y relationship across upper-level units after controlling for Z). Note that in this discussion, we have assumed that conflict (X) and rejection sensitivity (Z) have each been centered around their respective grand means. Centering is an important issue in HLM because how the predictor variables are centered can have a major effect on the way coefficients should be interpreted. Hofmann and Gavin (1998) and Kreft, DeLeeuw, and Aiken (1995) provided very thorough discussions of this important topic.

THE HLM EQUATIONS

In the simplest sense, estimation in HLM can be seen as comprising two steps. In the first step, the lower-level outcome variable is regressed on the lower-level predictor variable(s) separately for each upper-level unit. In our example, daily mood would be regressed on daily perceived conflict for each upper-level unit (i.e., individual), generating a slope and an intercept for each person. A prototypical lower-level equation with one predictor variable is as follows:

$$Y_{ij} = b_{oi} + b_{1i}X_{ij} + e_{ij}. \qquad (5.1)$$

In this equation, Y_{ij} is person i's mood on day j, and X_{ij} is person i's conflict on day j. This equation shows that a separate intercept and slope are estimated for each person (i.e., b_{oi} and b_{1i}). Because daily conflict (X) is centered around the grand mean, b_{oi} estimates person i's average mood (Y), and b_{1i} estimates the relationship between daily conflict and mood for person i.

In the second step, the regression coefficients from the first step analyses are aggregated across the upper-level units (the individuals). It is during this stage of the analysis that the effects of upper-level predictor variables (i.e., Z variables) are assessed and significance tests are conducted. Because our example generated two coefficients for each upper-level unit, b_{oi} and b_{1i}, there are in some sense two analyses in the second step. In one analysis, the intercepts generated in the first step would be regressed on rejection sensitivity:

$$b_{oi} = a_o + a_1 Z_i + d_i. \qquad (5.2)$$

In this equation, a_o represents the average intercept across the upper-level units. Because X and Z are grand mean centered, a_o equals the grand mean for daily mood. Note that a_o is a fixed effect parameter. The regression coefficient, a_1 estimates the relationship between rejection sensitivity (Z) and daily mood (Y) across the sample. The estimate and test of a_1 answers one of the fixed effect questions posed earlier: Do individuals who are higher in rejection sensitivity have more negative moods? The term d_i represents the unexplained component in the average daily mood from person to person. The variance in d_i (with some additional computational work) forms the basis of the random effect that estimates the degree to which average mood varies from person to person after controlling for rejection sensitivity.

In the second analysis, the slopes generated in the first step (Equation 5.1) are regressed on rejection sensitivity:

$$b_{1i} = c_o + c_1 Z_i + f_i. \qquad (5.3)$$

In this equation, c_o represents the average of the first-step slopes across persons. Because Z is grand mean centered, this equals the average relationship between X and Y. In the hypothetical example c_o estimates the answer to the fixed effect question: On days in which there are higher levels of conflict, do people generally have more negative moods? The last fixed effect question is the interaction between X and Z and is estimated by c_1. In the example c_o estimates the degree to which the relationship between daily conflict and mood varies as a function of rejection sensitivity. For example, the relationship between perceived daily conflict and mood may be particularly strong for people who are highly rejection sensitive. The term f_i represents the component in the slopes that is not explained by Z. The variance of f_i (again with some additional computational work) forms the basis of the random effect that estimates the degree to which the conflict–mood relationship varies from person to person after controlling for rejection sensitivity. Thus, four fixed effects and two random effects are estimated in this HLM analysis.

An important aspect of HLM is how the lower-level estimates are combined across upper-level units. It may be the case that some lower-level regression estimates are of higher quality than others. This can occur if there are unequal numbers of observations within each upper-level unit. It can also occur if there is differential variation in the lower-level predictor variables (X) for each upper-level unit. Thus, the second step analyses need to weight the first-step results by indices of the first-step results' quality. That is, lower-level regression coefficients from upper-level units with a great deal of data and large variance in X should be treated as more accurate than coefficients from upper-level units with small amounts of data or small variance in X.

Most data analytic programs use as their default restricted maximum likelihood (REML) estimation for multilevel analyses. This estimation procedure actually does the analysis in a single step rather than in the two steps we have described. In REML the weights are a function of the standard errors of the lower-level regression coefficients and the variance of the term being estimated. For example, the weight given to a particular b_{oi} is a function of its standard error and the variance of d_i. Several specialized stand-alone computer programs have been written that use these methods to derive estimates for multilevel data: HLM (Raudenbush, Bryk, Cheong, & Congdon, 2001), and *MLwiN* (Goldstein et al., 1998). Within major statistical packages, SAS's PROC MIXED and SPSS Mixed Model can be used to estimate multilevel models.

AN EXAMPLE: LYING IN CLOSE RELATIONSHIPS

In research by DePaulo and Kashy (1998), two diary studies were conducted, one examining lying behavior in undergraduates and the other examining lying in a community sample. Participants were asked to complete a brief questionnaire every time they interacted with another person for 10 minutes or longer. They were also asked to complete a deception questionnaire every time they "intentionally tried to mislead someone." This deception questionnaire asked a series of questions concerning the content of the lie and the reason for the lie, as well as the liar's level of distress when lying. At the end of the study, participants identified how close they felt to each of the partners with whom they had interacted,

how long they had known each partner, and they identified whether each partner was a best friend, friend, acquaintance, stranger, parent, spouse, child, brother, sister, or other relative.

To simplify our discussion, we consider only one outcome variable from this research: rate of lying to a partner. This variable is the number of lies told to the partner divided by the number of social interactions with the partner. Clearly we have multilevel data – each person interacted with a number of partners and so partner is the lower-level unit and subject is the upper-level unit. In one HLM analysis, the rate of lying to the partner (Y) was predicted to be a function of the closeness to the partner (X). Participant gender (effect coded so that men were coded as -1 and women were 1) was included as an upper-level predictor variable (Z). Results indicated that for both the college and community samples, rates of lying were lower when participants were interacting with partners to whom they felt closer. Notably, participant gender did not moderate this finding in either sample. Results also indicated that relative to other interaction partners, participants were especially likely to lie to their mothers and dating partners, but participants who were married told few lies to their spouses.

HLM With Dyadic Data

As mentioned, data collected from both members of a dyad has a multilevel structure because the two individuals are nested within a dyad. Therefore, with dyadic data, individuals are the lower-level units and the dyad is the upper-level unit. As before, the outcome variable (Y) is measured once for each lower-level unit, and so each person within the dyad provides a score on Y. Predictor variables that vary across the two partners within a dyad represent lower-level predictor variables (Xs), whereas predictor variables that vary between dyads (so that both members of any given dyad have the same score but members of two different dyads may differ) represent upper-level variables (Zs).

As an example, consider a study in which researchers want to examine the effects of relational self-construal (RSC; the degree to which individuals incorporate important others into the self-concept; Cross, Bacon, & Morris, 2000) on intimacy in same-sex friend dyads. Specifically, do people report more intimacy in same-sex friendships when they also incorporate others into their self-concept (high RSC)? Say that the researchers are also interested in testing whether the relationship between RSC and intimacy differs depending on the gender of the two friends. In this example, intimacy is the outcome (Y) and is measured for both partners in every dyad. The lower-level predictor variable (X) is RSC, and it, too, is measured for both partners. Gender of the dyad is an upper-level predictor variable (Z) because the dyads are either pairs of male best friends or pairs of female best friends. Note that gender should be effect coded (1, −1) and that RSC scores should be centered around the grand mean so that interactions among the predictors can be estimated.

Turning now to the specific HLM models, we can apply Equations 5.1, 5.2, and 5.3 to the dyadic case with some minor changes. Consider Equation 5.1 first. If we apply this equation to the present example, Y_{ij} is the intimacy score for person j in dyad i, and X_{ij} is the RSC score for person j in dyad i. Because RSC (X) is centered around the grand mean, b_{0i} estimates the average intimacy for dyad i, and b_{1i} estimates the relationship between RSC and intimacy mood for dyad i.

Equation 5.2 involves predicting the dyad average on intimacy, b_{0i}, using the gender of the friends, Z, as the predictor (coded −1 for pairs of male friends and 1 for pairs of female friends). This results in two fixed effects: an intercept, a_0, which is the grand mean for intimacy, and a slope, a_1, the effect of gender on intimacy. The random component of the model, d_i, specifies that the average level of intimacy may vary from dyad to dyad.

With Equation 5.3 comes an important change from our earlier example. A restriction must be placed on the random effects component of this model (predicting the

dyad slopes) when there are only two observations within each upper-level unit, as is the case with dyadic data. With only two replications within each upper-level unit, there is not enough information in the data to estimate a variance in the slopes. Thus, we must assume that the relationship between RSC and intimacy is the same from dyad to dyad. More exactly, the random component, f_i, must be omitted from Equation 5.3 in the dyadic case.[2] Nevertheless, both fixed effect components of Equation 5.3 can be estimated for the dyadic case. Thus, c_0 estimates the average effect of RSC on intimacy across the dyads, and c_1 estimates the interaction effect between gender and RSC on intimacy.

Although the method of using multilevel models is particularly useful when members of the dyads are indistinguishable (e.g., same-sex friends), it is not as useful when dyad members are distinguishable (e.g., married couples). There are several strategies for handling dyadic data within multilevel modeling when members are distinguishable. We discuss two strategies, the first of which is the simplest.

The first strategy follows directly from our initial discussion, except that a second lower-level predictor variable is added to code for the distinguishing variable. If our example had involved mother–daughter dyads rather than same-sex friends, we could have included family role as an effect coded lower-level predictor variable (an X variable) in the model. We can then test whether the effects of our key lower-level predictor variables differ across the distinguishing variable (family role) by including interaction terms among these lower-level variables (e.g., does the strength of the link between RSC and intimacy differ for mothers and daughters). Most HLM programs also allow for heterogeneous compound symmetry, which results in estimation of separate random effects across a distinguishing variable. Thus, we need not assume that the variance in average intimacy for mothers is the same as that for daughters.

Another strategy for handing distinguishable dyad members was originally suggested by Raudenbush, Brennan, and Barnett (1995). This model is sometimes referred to as the *two-intercept model* (e.g., Kenny, Kashy, & Cook, 2005). The following equation is estimated for member j of dyad i:

$$Y_{ij} = a_i X_{1i} + b_i X_{2i},$$

where Y_{ij} would be the individual's intimacy score, X_1 is a dummy variable that is coded 1 for partner 1 and 0 for partner 2 whereas X_2 is a dummy variable coded 0 for partner 1 and 1 for partner 2. Within the model, the effects of X_1 and X_2 are random variables (both a and b have an i subscript). Note also that there is no intercept in the model and no error term and so this is an unusual model. For this model, there is a variance–covariance matrix of a_i and b_i with three elements: the variance of a_i or s_a^2, the variance of b_i or s_b^2, and the covariance between the two or s_{ab}. We can test whether the two variances are equal and whether the covariance is statistically different from zero.

The two-intercept model, as we have described it, only estimates the effects of the distinguishing variable on the outcome. When there are additional X or Z variables of interest, they can be added to the model. Adding lower-level predictor variables to the analysis requires that the additional X variables be multiplied by each of the two X dummies. In that way, we can test whether the effect of the X variable is the same for the two types of members.

THE ACTOR–PARTNER INTERDEPENDENCE
MODEL – AN APPLICATION OF HLM TO DYADIC DATA

One application of multilevel modeling with dyads is the APIM described by Kenny and his colleagues (Kashy & Kenny, 2000; Kenny, 1988, 1990, 1996; Kenny & Cook, 1999). The APIM suggests that a person's independent variable score affects both his or her own outcome score (known as the actor effect) and his or her partner's outcome score (known as the partner effect). The partner effect from the APIM directly models the mutual influence that may occur between individuals involved in a dyadic relationship.

In the example discussed previously for same-sex friends, in addition to the possibility that a person's own relational self-construal affects his or her intimacy in a relationship, it is also possible that the person's friend's relational self-construal affects his or her intimacy. This is simply an extension of the multilevel model for dyadic data. In this new model, a person's intimacy (Y) is predicted by two X variables: One X is his or her own RSC score, and the other X is his or her partner's RSC score. Because in this example gender is a Z variable, interactions between gender and the actor effect would suggest that the relationship between a person's RSC and that person's intimacy differs for male–male friend dyads and female–female friend dyads. Interactions between gender and the partner effect would suggest that the relationship between a person's intimacy and his or her partner's RSC differs for the two dyad types. If, on the other hand, gender were a within-dyads variable (e.g., if the couples were heterosexual dating couples) gender could be entered as an X variable that interacts with both the actor and partner effects to determine whether the relationship between X and Y differs for men and women within dyads. Campbell and Kashy (2002) provided a detailed discussion of how to estimate the APIM using HLM. Encouragingly, some relationships research is beginning to estimate these more complex models (e.g., Campbell, Simpson, Kashy, & Fletcher, 2001; Murray, Holmes, & Griffin, 1996a; 1996b; Robins, Caspi, & Moffitt, 2000).

AN EXAMPLE: EMPATHIC ACCURACY
IN MARITAL INTERACTIONS

In this research, Simpson, Orina, and Ickes (2003) hypothesized that people would feel closer to their partners when they more accurately inferred their partner's mundane thoughts and feelings but feel less close when they accurately inferred their partner's relationship threatening thoughts and feelings. Ninety-five married couples were asked to discuss a problem area in their relationship while being videotaped and were then asked to view the interaction privately and list the thoughts and feelings they recalled having during the interaction. They were also asked to list how threatening–destabilizing they perceived each thought and feeling was to the relationship. Participants were then asked to view the interaction a second time and to infer their partner's thoughts and feelings at the times their partners reported having a specific thought or feeling. An empathic accuracy (EA) score, reflecting how accurately people's inferences reflected their partner's thoughts and feelings, was computed from ratings made by independent raters.

The researchers employed HLM to assess the degree to which people's own empathic accuracy as well as their partner's empathic accuracy predicted how close they felt to the partner. An important predictor variable these researchers examined was the degree to which people's thoughts and feelings during the discussion were threatening. A negative actor effect for this variable predicting closeness to the partner would indicate that individuals whose thoughts and feelings were more threatening felt less close to their partner. A negative partner effect would indicate that individuals whose partner's thoughts and feelings were more threatening felt less close to their partner. An effect-coded dummy variable representing gender was included in all analyses, as was the interaction between gender and the actor and partner effects in the model. No interactions with gender emerged, and the results were presented pooled across gender. Consistent with the hypothesis, a key result from this study indicated that when people accurately inferred their partner's more threatening thoughts and feelings, they felt less close to their partners; however, people felt closer to their partners when they more accurately inferred less threatening thoughts and feelings.

Growth Curve Modeling

The growth curve model is a special case of HLM in which time is the lower-level predictor variable. In many ways, our discussion of HLM with individual diary data is directly applicable to the growth curve model. Because this model has been particularly

useful in relationships research, however, we review it briefly here. A more extensive discussion of issues involved in growth curve modeling can be found in Karney and Bradbury (1995).

In a growth curve model, the nature of how people change is specified in the lower-level model via the form in which the predictor variable, time, occurs. Time can be included as a linear predictor (as is most commonly the case), or it can be included in other functional forms such as a polynomial (i.e., including time-squared as a predictor along with a linear time component). The complexity of the functional form for time is to some degree limited by the number of time points collected for each individual so that with relatively small numbers of observations for each person, the researcher may be limited to a linear model of time. An example of the lower-level model with time as a linear predictor would be the following:

$$Y_{ij} = b_{0i} + b_{1i}(Time)_{ij} + e_{ij}. \qquad (5.4)$$

In this equation, Y_{ij} is person i's outcome score at time j. As before, this equation shows that an intercept and a slope are estimated for each person. The intercept, b_{0i}, estimates the person's outcome when time $= 0$, and the meaning of this depends completely on how time is scaled. As Karney and Bradbury (1995) suggested, it may be useful to define the lower-level predictor variable, X, as the amount of time elapsed since initial measurement so that the intercept becomes the outcome score at the initial time of measurement. Other definitions are also possible, however, and the researcher needs to choose the one that best suits his or her research goals. The slope, b_{1i}, estimates the rate of linear change on Y for person i.

As was the case in our previous discussions of HLM, the lower-level intercepts and slopes can be predicted by upper-level predictor variables (Zs). Of key interest is the analysis predicting slopes, which address the question of whether different contexts or personality types (whatever the Z variable happens to be) show different rates of change over time.

AN EXAMPLE: FLUCTUATIONS IN SATISFACTION
IN NEWLY DATING COUPLES

In Arriaga's (2001) research two studies of undergraduates were conducted to examine the association between relationship satisfaction and later breakup status. Individuals (but not their partners) reported on their relationship satisfaction once each week for a period of 10 weeks. Approximately 4 months later, they were contacted and asked to report whether the relationship had ended.

A linear model of change in satisfaction over time was applied to the data, resulting in a set of intercepts (the persons' initial level of satisfaction), slopes (linear change in satisfaction over time), and indices of variability of scores around their regression line (i.e., the error in prediction for each person). These values were then used to predict breakup status. Consistent with expectations, individuals with greater levels of variability or fluctuation in satisfaction were more likely to break up.

HLM With Dyads and Repeated Measurements

Thus far we have limited our discussion to two-level multilevel models. An additional layer of complexity is added when repeated measures are assessed from both members of a dyadic relationship. In such a case, the repeated measurements are nested within individual and individuals are nested within dyads, resulting in a three-level model.

A recent example of this data structure is provided by research of Murray, Bellavia, Rose, and Griffin (2003). They recruited 152 married and 2 cohabitating couples to participate in a daily diary study for a period of 21 consecutive days. Guided by their dependency-regulation model, Murray et al. (2003) tested the notion that people who chronically felt less valued by their partners would read too much into negative relationship events and subsequently feel less valued, more hurt and rejected, and more anxious about their partner's acceptance than people who chronically felt more valued by their partners.

In one model, perceptions of felt-rejection by a partner each day served as a lower-level outcome variable, level of conflict on the prior day served as a lower-level predictor variable, and chronic perceived regard served as an upper-level predictor variable. The interaction between chronic perceived regard and daily perceptions of conflict estimated the degree to which people who chronically felt less valued felt more rejected on days following relatively high levels of conflict. In essence, the model estimated in this research combines the "two intercept model" for dyadic data with a standard HLM for individual data. Thus, in the model, estimates were calculated simultaneously for men and women and compared to test for gender differences, but no gender differences were evident. The predicted interaction between chronic perceived regard and perceptions of conflict emerged such that on days following high levels of conflict, people who chronically felt less valued felt more rejected.

Another example of a three-level model is Campbell, Simpson, Boldry, and Kashy (2004). They recruited 103 dating couples to participate in a diary study for a period of 14 days. Both partners completed diaries each day during the study. Guided by attachment theory, one of the hypotheses tested by Campbell et al. (2004) was that more anxiously attached individuals would feel less confident about the future of their relationship on days when they perceived more conflict with their partners. In this model, daily perceptions of the future of the relationship was a lower-level outcome variable, daily perceptions of relationship conflict was a lower-level predictor variable, and attachment anxiety was an upper-level predictor variable. An additional upper-level predictor variable was the partner's score on the anxious attachment dimension, and so this research combines the APIM approach with a standard HLM for individuals. As predicted, a cross-level interaction emerged, showing that more anxiously attached individuals reported less confidence about the future of their relationships, more so on days when they perceived more relationship-based conflict.

Finally, consider recent research conducted by Karney and Frye (2002; Study 1), in which both members of newly married couples were asked to rate their satisfaction with their relationship every 6 months for 4 years and were then asked to recall the trajectory of their satisfaction over that time period. From each participant, 8 data points were collected prospectively, and an additional 8 data points were collected retrospectively. Both sets of repeated measures of satisfaction represent lower-level variables that were nested within the upper-level units (individuals). With these data, Karney and Frye could assess actual trajectories of marital satisfaction over time compared with the trajectories people recalled at the end of the 4-year period. This analysis was accomplished by combining the "two-intercept model" with a growth curve model that included a nonlinear component for time (i.e., time-squared). Karney and Frye used "prospective" and "retrospective" as the two groupings of data in their two-intercept model, and they computed separate analyses for husbands and wives. As they described in a footnote, this allowed them to compare directly the prospective and retrospective results. Interestingly, whereas people reported a steady decline in marital satisfaction over time, their retrospective reports showed that they believed their marriages were improving across the last few measurement sessions.

Conclusions

When we first considered what we wanted to discuss in this chapter, we intended to spend about half the chapter discussing data analytic techniques appropriate for family data. Our survey of the relationships literature suggested, though, that such a discussion might have little utility for relationships researchers. For instance, less than 5% of the published relationships research in 1994 and 2002 (in the five journals we sampled) contained data that were collected from multiple group or family members. We were also somewhat surprised that less than 25% of the research in our survey collected data from

both members of the dyadic relationship under investigation. It appears from our survey of the literature that researchers are well aware of the biasing effects of nonindependence and are perhaps attempting to circumvent this problem by focusing on individuals' perceptions of their relationships, a data structure that does not violate the independence assumption of traditional data analytic strategies. It is important to stress that whereas individual level-hypotheses can be tested with more complex data structures, it is not possible to model directly the interdependence that exists in relationships with data collected from one member of the dyad.

A number of researchers, however, recognize the benefits of collecting data from both members of a dyadic relationship and make a concerted effort to do so. There are challenges inherent in analyzing these more complex data structures, and many statistical methods have been introduced to assist researchers. Nonetheless, our survey suggests that these statistical methods do not currently enjoy widespread use. For instance, relationships researchers often adopt the practice of analyzing the data for men and women separately when they have data from heterosexual dating or married couples. We were heartened by the fact that when dyadic data have been collected, there appears to be a shift toward adopting more complex and appropriate statistical data analytic strategies. For that reason, we chose to focus on what we think is the most powerful new data analytic tool available in the study of close relationships: hierarchical linear modeling.

A goal of this chapter was to demonstrate that HLM is a flexible data analytic strategy that can handle a variety of nested data structures relevant to relationships researchers. Given that most theoretical approaches to the study of interpersonal relationships stress the importance of interdependence (e.g., Kelley et al., 1983) and the influence of variables at the individual and relationship level on a variety of outcomes, HLM is well suited to assist relationships researchers studying such processes. Another goal of this chapter was to show the ease with which HLM can be implemented. Conceptually, the effects estimated by HLM are fairly straightforward; practically, a number of software programs that can estimate hierarchical linear models are currently available to researchers. For these reasons, we anticipate that HLM will become a standard data analytic tool for relationships researchers.

Our discussion of HLM is admittedly topical, partly because we wanted to illustrate how HLM can be, and has been, applied with complex data sets and partly because many of the technical issues associated with HLM deserve a great deal more attention than we could spare in this chapter. We hope this chapter inspires relationships researchers to begin, or continue, to collect complex data sets and to employ data analytic strategies such as HLM to model the interdependence that exists in relationships, but we strongly encourage researchers to first educate themselves more thoroughly on the many important issues associated with this method.

Footnotes

1. In some instances, interdependence can actually be negative, implying that scores from related individuals will be especially dissimilar to one another (i.e., more dissimilar than scores of two unrelated individuals).
2. Newsom and Nishishiba (2002) discussed problems in estimating HLM models with dyadic data. The problems they described arise when the random slope component is not omitted from the model as we have suggested.

References

Arriaga, X. B. (2001). The ups and downs of dating: Fluctuations in satisfaction in newly formed romantic relationships. *Journal of Personality and Social Psychology, 80*, 754–765.

Campbell, L., & Kashy, D. A. (2002). Estimating actor, partner, and interaction effects for dyadic data using PROC MIXED and HLM: A guided tour. *Personal Relationships, 9*, 327–342.

Campbell, L., Simpson, J. A., Boldry, J. G., & Kashy, D. A. (2004) *Perceptions of conflict and support in romantic relationships: The role of attachment anxiety.* Unpublished manuscript, University of Western Ontario, London, Ontario, Canada.

Campbell, L., Simpson, J. A., Kashy, D. A., & Fletcher, G. J. O. (2001). Ideal standards, the self, and flexibility of ideals in close relationships. *Personality and Social Psychology Bulletin, 27*, 447–462.

Cook, W. L. (2000). Understanding attachment security in family context. *Journal of Personality and Social Psychology, 78*, 285–294.

Cook, W. L. (2001). Interpersonal influence in family systems: A social relations analysis. *Child Development, 72*, 1179–1197.

Cross, S. E., Bacon, P., & Morris, M. (2000). The relational–interdependent self-construal and relationships. *Journal of Personality and Social Psychology, 78*, 791–808.

Delsing, M. J. M. H., Oud, J. H. L., De-Bruyn, E. E., & van-Aken, M. A. G. (2003). Current and recollected perceptions of family relationships: The social relations model approach applied to members of three generations. *Journal of Family Psychology, 17*, 445–459.

DePaulo, B. M., & Kashy, D. A. (1998). Everyday lies in casual relationships. *Journal of Personality and Social Psychology, 74*, 63–79.

Duncan, T. E., Duncan, S. C., Strycker, L. A., Li, F., & Alpert, A. (1999). *An introduction to latent variable growth curve modeling: Concepts, issues, and applications.* Mahwah, NJ: Erlbaum.

Fitzpatrick, M. A., & Dindia, K. (1986). Couples and other strangers: Talk time in spouse–stranger interaction. *Communication Research, 13*, 625–652.

Fletcher, G. J. O. (2002). *The new science of intimate relationships.* Oxford: Blackwell.

Fournier, M. A., Moskowitz, D. S., & Zuroff, D. C. (2002). Social rank strategies in hierarchical relationships. *Journal of Personality and Social Psychology, 83*, 425–433.

Goldstein, H., Rasbash, J., Plewis, I., Draper, D., Browne, W., Yang, M., Woodhouse, G., & Healy, M. (1998). *A user's guide to MLwiN.* Institute of Education, University of London.

Gonzalez, R., & Griffin, D. (1997). On the statistics of interdependence: Treating dyadic data with respect. In S. Duck (Ed.), *Handbook of personal relationships: Theory, research and interventions* (2nd ed., pp. 271–302). New York: Wiley.

Gonzalez, R., & Griffin, D., (1999). The correlational analysis of dyad-level data in the distinguishable case. *Personal Relationships*, 6, 449–469.

Gonzalez, R., & Griffin, D. (2002). Modeling the personality of dyads and groups. *Journal of Personality*, 70, 901–924.

Gottman, J. M., Murray, J. D., Swanson, C. C., Tyson, R., & Swanson, K. R. (2002). *The mathematics of marriage: Dynamic nonlinear models*. Cambridge, MA: MIT Press.

Griffin, D., & Gonzalez, R. (1995). Correlational analysis of dyad-level data in the exchangeable case. *Psychological Bulletin*, 118, 430–439.

Hofmann, D. A., & Gavin, M. B. (1998) Centering decisions in hierarchical linear models: Implications for research in organizations. *Journal of Management*, 24, 623–641.

Karney, B. R., & Bradbury, T. N. (1995). Assessing longitudinal change in marriage: An introduction to the analysis of growth curves. *Journal of Marriage and the Family*, 57, 1091–1108.

Karney, B. R., & Frye, N. E. (2002). "But we've been getting better lately": Comparing prospective and retrospective views of relationship development. *Journal of Personality and Social Psychology*, 82, 222–238.

Kashy, D. A., & Kenny, D. A. (2000). The analysis of data from dyads and groups. In H. T. Reis & C. M. Judd (Eds.), *Handbook of research methods in social psychology* (pp. 451–477). New York: Cambridge University Press.

Kelley, H. H., Berscheid, E., Christensen, A., Harvey, J. H., Huston, T. L., & Levinger, G., et al. (1983). Analyzing close relationships. In H. H. Kelley, E. Berscheid, A. Christensen, J. H. Harvey, T. L. Huston, G. Levinger, et al. (Eds.), *Close relationships* (pp. 20–67). New York: Freeman.

Kenny, D. A. (1988). The analysis of data from two person relationships. In S. Duck (Ed.), *Handbook of interpersonal relationships* (pp. 57–77). London: Wiley.

Kenny, D. A. (1990). Design issues in dyadic research. In C. Hendrick & M. S. Clark (Eds.), *Review of personality and social psychology: Research methods in personality and social psychology* (pp. 164–184). Newbury Park, CA: Sage.

Kenny, D. A. (1994). *Interpersonal perception: A social relations analysis*. New York: Guilford Press.

Kenny, D. A. (1995). The effect of nonindependence on significance testing in dyadic research. *Personal Relationships*, 2, 67–75.

Kenny, D. A. (1996). Models of interdependence in dyadic research. *Journal of Social and Personal Relationships*, 13, 279–294.

Kenny, D. A., Bolger, N., & Kashy, D. A. (2001). Traditional methods of estimating multilevel models. In D. S. Moskowitz & S. L. Hershberger (Eds.), *Modeling intraindividual variability with repeated measures data: Methods and applications*. Mahwah, NJ: Erlbaum.

Kenny, D. A., & Cook, W. (1999). Partner effects in relationship research: Conceptual issues, analytic difficulties, and illustrations. *Personal Relationships*, 6, 433–448.

Kenny, D. A., & Kashy, D. A. (1994). Enhanced co-orientation in the perception of friends: A social relations analysis. *Journal of Personality and Social Psychology*, 67, 1024–1033.

Kenny, D. A., Kashy, D. A., & Bolger, N. (1998). Data analysis in social psychology. In D. T. Gilbert, S. T. Fiske, & G. Lindzey (Eds.), *The handbook of social psychology* (4th ed., Vol. 1, pp. 223–265). New York: McGraw-Hill.

Kenny, D. A., Kashy, D. A., & Cook, W. (2005). *The analysis of dyadic data*. New York: Guilford Press.

Kreft, I. G. G., & DeLeeuw, J. (1998). *Introducing multilevel modeling*. London: Sage.

Kreft, I. G. G., DeLeeuw, J., & Aiken, L. S. (1995). The effect of different forms of centering in hierarchical linear models. *Multivariate Behavioral Research*, 30, 1–22.

MacCallum, R. C., & Austin, J. T. (2000). Applications of structural equation modeling in psychological research. *Annual Review of Psychology*, 51, 201–226.

Murray, S. L., Bellavia, G. M., Rose, P., & Griffin, D. W. (2003). Once hurt, twice hurtful: How perceived regard regulates daily marital interactions. *Journal of Personality and Social Psychology*, 84, 126–147.

Murray, S. L., Holmes, J. G., & Griffin, D. W. (1996a). The benefits of positive illusions: Idealization and the construction of satisfaction in close relationships. *Journal of Personality and Social Psychology*, 70, 79–98.

Murray, S. L., Holmes, J. G., & Griffin, D. W. (1996b). The self-fulfilling nature of positive illusions in romantic relationships: Love is not blind, but prescient. *Journal of Personality and Social Psychology*, 71, 1155–1180.

Newsom, J. T., & Nishishiba, M. (2002). *Non-convergence and sample bias in hierarchical linear modeling of dyadic data*. Retrieved from http://www.upa.pdx.edu/IOA/newsom/mlrdyad4.doc, June 22, 2004. Unpublished manuscript.

Onishi, M., & Gjerde, P. F. (2002). Attachment strategies in Japanese urban middle-class couples: A cultural theme analysis of asymmetry in marital relationships. *Personal Relationships, 9*, 435–455.

Raudenbush, S. W., Brennan, R. T., & Barnett, R. C. (1995). A multivariate hierarchical modeling for studying psychological change within married couples. *Journal of Family Psychology, 9*, 161–174.

Raudenbush, S. W., & Bryk, A. S. (2002). *Hierarchical linear models: Applications and data analysis methods* (2nd ed.). Thousand Oaks, CA: Sage.

Raudenbush, S. W., Bryk, A. S., Cheong, Y. F., & Congdon, R. (2001). *HLM 5: Hierarchical linear and nonlinear modeling* (2nd ed.). Lincolnwood, IL: Scientific Software International.

Robins, R. W., Caspi, A., & Moffitt, T. E. (2000). Two personalities, one relationship: Both partners' personality traits shape the quality of their relationship. *Journal of Personality and Social Psychology, 79*, 251–259.

Sabatelli, R. M., Buck, R., & Kenny, D. A. (1986). A social relations analysis of nonverbal communication accuracy in married couples. *Journal of Personality, 53*, 513–527.

Simpkins, S., D., & Parke, R. D. (2002). Do friends and nonfriends behave differently? A social relations analysis of children's behavior. *Merrill Palmer Quarterly, 48*, 263–283.

Simpson, J. A., Orina, M. M., & Ickes, W. (2003). When accuracy hurts, and when it helps: A test of the empathic accuracy model in marital interactions. *Journal of Personality and Social Psychology, 85*, 881–893.

CHAPTER 6
Relationship Typologies

C. Arthur VanLear
Ascan Koerner
Donna M. Allen

If we are to build a coherent science of human relationships, we must have a structure within which to organize our observations and knowledge claims. Robert Hinde (1996) pointed out that the advance of biology as a science and evolution as a theory was facilitated by the development of the biological taxonomy. One of the major lessons of that history is the intimate linkage between the development of a typology and our theoretical understanding of the phenomenon. Biological organisms could have been organized by size, color, diet, or habitat. Whereas some of these are useful, they are isolated and do not facilitate an integration of knowledge that is made possible by a typology that is based on the theory of evolution and that links the typology to a significant body of knowledge. At present, the field of personal relationships is a multiparadigmatic science, and so we have a multitude of potential typologies from which to choose. A typology may prove to be a necessary foundation on which to build a science of human relationships. The selection of typologies, however, may depend on the theoretical orientation of the researcher. This chapter reviews the major issues and approaches to typing personal relationships at both general and specific levels.

Types Versus Dimensions

Some scholars have argued that using multidimensional scales to describe relationships is superior to a typological approach (Griffin & Bartholomew, 1994). The argument is that locating a relationship on a series of dimensional scales provides a more precise description than a nominal categorization, which is often a simplification of several scalar measures and therefore throws away information. This argument ignores the basic point of typologies.

Many typologies are a form of data reduction. Just as factor analysis reduces a number of scalar items to a smaller number of more general dimensions, many typologies reduce scores on a set of dimensions to a nominal categorization. A good typology can improve our understanding of the phenomenon as well as provide useful and interpretable information about specific cases.

Most of us find it difficult to form a clear conception of a relationship by trying to identify it as a point in multidimensional "hyperspace." When most people think about relationships, they identify them as types or kinds of relationships, not as points along a set of continuous dimensions (Haslam, 1994). Typologies are useful for building theory; for teaching about relationships; and for clinical therapy, counseling, or relational enrichment training.

Typologies are not only convenient simplifications. They are more appropriate when cases are not evenly distributed in the multidimensional space but form clusters so that certain values on one dimension are associated with specific values on other dimensions (Haslam, 1999). If cases are evenly distributed across all levels of all dimensions, however, then the variation within categories of a typology may be as important as the variation between or among categories, and a dimensional approach is appropriate.

Methods for Typing Relationships

The hallmark of science is that theory is supported by empirical evidence and so a typology of human relationships should be supported empirically. A detailed discussion of methods of typing is beyond the scope of this chapter, but a brief review is in order. Whereas some types are identified by the participants' reactions to experimental conditions – Ainsworth's strange situation (Ainsworth, Blehar, Waters, & Wall, 1978) or Reiss's (1981) card-sort problem-solving procedure – or patterns of behavioral interaction (e.g., Gottman, 1993), most typologies rely on analyses of participants' self-reports. There are two general types of methods – those that help to generate types inductively and those that are used to confirm hypothesized types.

Inductive Methods

One method used to generate categories from scratch is a Q-sort method (Stephen-son, 1953). "Judges" are given examples and asked to sort them into groups of similar types. Of course, different judges may use different criteria for sorting.

The most popular inductive method is to measure participants on self-reports designed to tap several dimensions (often generated by exploratory factor analysis of the items) and apply cluster analysis to the resulting factors to come up with the categories of the typology. Haslam (1999) pointed out several limitations to this method. First, because there are many clustering algorithms, different methods can yield different results. All too often the default or most popular method is used without careful consideration of the appropriate choices. Second, cluster analyses have been criticized for their inability to uncover actual categories in the data (Meehl, 1995). Third, cluster analyses will always generate categories even when the data are best represented as continuous dimensions. Of course, any typology generated by any inductive technique should be supported by confirmatory analyses on additional data.

Confirmatory Methods

One can usually regenerate a previous typology by using the estimates from the prior analysis as a starting point to cluster new data. This is not strong confirmation of a typology because initializing to the previous results biases the results in favor of the prior categories. This approach may, however, be acceptable to type cases from a previously well-validated typology. A strong confirmatory approach should demonstrate that the proposed categories represent true discontinuities in the underlying dimensions. Although intuitively appealing, a simple test of bimodality is not a reliable indicator of the discreteness of a categorical distinction (Haslam, 1999). Haslam proposed two types of methods, taxometric procedures and an admixture–commingling analysis as confirmatory approaches to support the discreteness of proposed typological distinctions. He used these methods to demonstrate that the Fiske (1991) typology is not based on continuous dimensions. Using a similar approach, Fossati et al. (2003) used multivariate normal mixture analysis for testing a single population versus a two-cluster solution on the Attachment Style Questionnaire (ASQ). They failed to find that a categorization of secure versus insecure attachment provided a better representation of their data than the continuous dimensions of the ASQ. A disadvantage of taxometric and admixture techniques is that they are somewhat complex and not well known.

Koerner and Fitzpatrick (2002b) argued that if the dimensions of a proposed typology consistently show interaction effects in predicting important dependent variables, then a typological approach in which the dimensions are ordinalized is validated. They argued that the conformity and conversation orientation dimensions of family communication consistently show such interaction effects on important dependent variables, thus supporting the typological approach to McLeod and Chaffee's (1972) family communication patterns.

Distinctions Among Relationship Typologies

The classification of relationships is fundamental in building a science of relationships (Hinde, 1996). Some typologies are primarily deductively derived from theory, whereas others are primarily inductively derived through empirical study. Typologies also differ in their use of common language labels (e.g., family, marriage) or the extent to which they apply to the way relational participants understand their own relationships. Some typologies treat relationships as static categories, and others view them as passing through different types over time.

The most fundamental differences between typologies are the bases of classification. One reason there are so many typologies of marriage is that scholars focus on different variables. A number of scholars have attempted to identify the fundamental dimensions and topoi of relationships (Burgoon & Hale, 1984, 1987; Foa & Foa,

1974; Haslam, 1995; Schutz, 1958). The dimensions that are central to one author may not be to another, the key variables of one theory may be ignored by another, and even the pivotal concepts of one discipline may be less important to another discipline (Weiss, 1998). We believe that typologies based on multiple dimensions that are central to multiple disciplines will have the greatest degree of general applicability.

Weiss (1998) argued that a typology of relationships ought to be based on the "determinants of relationships," which from his attachment perspective lies in *understandings* and *emotions*. Operating from a social cognition perspective, Fitzpatrick (1988) and Haslam (1994) argued that the basis of relationship types are the differences in cognitive "scripts" that people learn, develop, and attempt to apply in enacting their relationships. By mentally representing relationships as types, people use those schemata as guides for acting and responding to others (Fitzpatrick, 1988; Haslam, 1994; Koerner & Fitzpatrick, 2002a). Typologies may also be based on the structural (e.g., sexual composition) or functional (e.g., instrumental, romantic) characteristics of relationships. Other scholars operating from a relational pragmatics perspective hold that relationships are open systems that are always in the process of becoming (Bateson, 1972; Fisher & Adams, 1994; Lederer & Jackson, 1968; Watzlawick, Beavin, & Jackson, 1967). If a relationship type can be identified, it is always emergent, based on the redundancies in the patterns of interaction over time.

Typologies differ in the extent to which they are based on the matched characteristics of the individuals in or the nonsummative properties of the relationship. At one extreme, we have relationships typed based on matching individual characteristics that predate the relationship (e.g., attachment styles, interpersonal needs). The assumption underlying such an approach is that the characteristics of the individuals in the system determine the nature of the system. At the other extreme, we have relationships typed at the relational level (e.g., symmetry, complementarity, stability) that are not divisible into individual characteristics apart from the relationship and only emerge over time. The first approach has come under fire for being too deterministic (Fisher & Adams, 1994). The nonsummative approach has been criticized for not allowing for individual differences in shaping the nature of the system (Hewes, 1979). A third approach identifies individuals' orientations to a particular relationship, types both the partners, and matches them for similarity or differences to arrive at couple types (e.g., Fitzpatrick, 1988). To the extent that a pre-existing schema influences each person's orientation, it is captured in the typology, and to the extent that a person's orientation emerges from his or her experience in that relationship, that, too, is captured.

Beginning with Leary's (1955) affect–control circumplex, a long line of circumplex models has been used to type relationships, including Foa and Foa (1974), Kiesler (1983), Olson (1981, 1993), and others. Haslam (1995) has shown that Fiske's (1991) typology, although not formulated as such, can also be fit to a circumplex pattern.

Typologies are often hierarchically organized, but the basis of that organization may differ. Koerner and Fitzpatrick (2002a) suggested a hierarchical organization of schema beginning with general social schema, relationship type schemas (e.g., family, friends, colleagues), and relationship-specific schemas. A systems approach would consider individuals nested within dyadic relationships (e.g., marriages, siblings, mother–child), nested within larger social organizations (e.g., families, social networks), and so on. Some typologies consider certain distinctions as more fundamental than others, such that the most fundamental forms the first division and then that is further subdivided on the basis of other distinctions. Other typologies treat each category as having equal status.

Our review of relationship typologies has raised the following questions. First, does the typology represent fundamental psychological processes underlying human relationships? These may be motivations and emotions or the cognitive structures and understandings of participants within relationships (or a combination of these). Second, does the typology represent social–cultural structures organizing relationships? The typology may represent cross-cultural variations in relationship forms or cross-cultural universals (i.e., archetypes or deep structures). Third, does the typology discriminate between variations in the behaviors and interaction patterns across relationships?

General Typologies

General typologies are those classification schemes that attempt to identify the fundamental features of the whole length and breadth of human relationships. Of course, any dimension can be dissected to form a typology, and any set of dimensions can be combined to increase the complexity. Our review is limited to those typologies that have had or promise to have a major impact on our understanding of human relationships. In our view, a general typology of human relationships should make distinctions that are fundamental or basic to human relationships. Distinctions are fundamental or basic if they apply across disciplinary boundaries. They should serve to organize relationships at a societal level, at an individual psychological level (e.g., cognitively and emotionally), and in terms of patterns of behavioral interaction. Fundamental distinctions are likely to provide a bridge between the sociological and psychological realities of human relationships as well as the biological imperatives responsible for their ancient evolution into a primal characteristic of our species. They should apply cross-culturally – they may either be found in all cultures or they may explain cross-cultural variation.

We begin by identifying some of the simple divisions that have traditionally been made between human relationships. The title of this book, the titles of our journals, and the organization of our scholarly societies imply either implicitly or explicitly a division of relationships into

	Personal Relations	Social Relations
Voluntary	Marriage Best Friends Cohabiting Couple Adoptive/Foster Family	Acquaintances Casual Friends Relational Marketing
Exogenously Established	Parent–Child Siblings Grandparent–Child	Distant Relatives Work Relationships Monopoly Provider–Client

Figure 6.1. Types of relationships based on volition and intimacy.

personal and *social*. The most obvious dimensions on which this distinction is based are intimacy, closeness, or interdependence, with personal relationships being closer, more intimate, and interdependent and social relationships being more superficial and impersonal. Argyle and Henderson (1985) found that intimacy discriminated between differences in relationships based on relational rules in four countries. Marwell and Hage (1970) found intimacy accounted for 50% of the variance across 100 role relationships. Many typologies identify a "disengaged," "detached," "independent," or "separate" relationship type and "interdependent," "companionate," "attached," or "enmeshed" relationships. Intimacy and interdependence are highly correlated and may belong to a single more abstract second-order factor such as "solidarity" or "closeness."

Another common distinction is between voluntary (i.e., open field) relationships and those that exist because of exogenous factors (e.g., born into them, employment). Some think that there is a qualitative difference between relationships that people choose for themselves and those that are chosen for them or controlled by exogenous factors (e.g., by law, biology, or external necessity). Figure 6.1 shows how these two distinctions can serve to identify certain types of relationships in their prototypical form.

Similarly, Toennies (1957) made a distinction between *Gemeinschaft* (community) and *Gesellschaft* (society) relationships.

Gemeinschaft relationships are based on kinship, loyalty, friendship, and tradition. *Gesellschaft* relationships are based on legal contract, public opinion, rationality, and exchange. Using this distinction, Marwell and Hage (1970) proposed an inductively derived empirically based typology of "role-relationships," based on three dimensions: (a) intimacy, (b) visibility, and (c) regulation (by society). They then posited four levels of both Gemeinschaft and Gesellschaft relationships (i.e., *Uncontrolled, Regulated, Visible,* and *Mixed*). This typology, however, has not produced a large body of systematic empirical study and does not necessarily apply across most cultures; further, it is unclear whether it has any "psychological reality" for everyday social actors in organizing their own behavior.

Bateson (1972) and others (Lederer & Jackson, 1968; Watzlawick et al., 1967) have observed two types of mutually causal interaction sequences, which have often been suggested as the basis of a typology of relationships. *Reciprocity*, in which behaviors of similar function are redundantly exchanged, leads to enactment of a *symmetrical* relationship (e.g., reciprocation of affection leading to mutual attraction). Redundant *compensation*, in which behaviors of maximally different functions are exchanged, leads to enactment of a *complementary* relationship (e.g., leadership–subordination, teacher–student). A *parallel* relationship is characterized by flexible interaction such that (a) the participants engage in both reciprocity and compensation (Fisher & Adams, 1994), or (b) when compensatory patterns are enacted, participants do not always perform the same behavioral function (VanLear, 1985). Hinde (1996) suggested that relationships are more than the patterns of behavioral exchange. They include memories, perceptions, emotions, and judgments about each other. These patterns of interaction have been, and will continue to be, useful in discriminating among different kinds of relationships (e.g., Williamson & Fitzpatrick, 1985), but a relational typology should probably also include the psychological bases of relationships.

Alan Fiske (1991) proposed what has become one of the most widely researched and often used general typologies of human relationships. Fiske (1991, 1992) made the claim that people in all cultures use just four basic "models" to organize their thinking and behavior regarding most aspects of their associations with other people. The four models are *communal sharing* (CS), *authority ranking* (AR), *equality matching* (EM), and *market pricing* (MP). In a CS *relationship*, people have a feeling of equivalence and are oriented to their commonality and the common good, not their differences or individuality. Participants in a CS relationship constitute the "in-group" and are seen as belonging together and acting as one social actor. AR *relationships* are organized in a linear status hierarchy like a "chain of command" in which privileges and responsibilities are based on relative rank. In *EM relationships*, reciprocal exchange is used to ensure equity and balance. Participants in EM relationships perceive themselves as individuals who are relating with one another as equals. Finally, *MP relationships* are concerned with socially meaningful ratios such as costs to rewards according to a distributive justice of entitlements in proportion to one's investments. Participants in MP relationships perceive themselves as individuals with potentially dissimilar valuations.

Fiske and his colleagues have explored the cross-cultural application of these four models and their role in social cognition. When people make errors in remembering people or interactions, the four relational models better predict the erroneous substitution of other people than do personal characteristics in samples across five cultures (Fiske, 1993, 1995; Fiske, Haslam, & Fiske, 1991). When people intentionally substitute a new person to do something with over an original choice, the four models best predict the person substituted (Fiske & Haslam, 1997). When people are asked to categorize their own relationships, or rate their similarity, the clusters that are obtained correspond to the four relational models (Haslam & Fiske, 1992). Fiske and Haslam (Fiske & Haslam, 1996; Haslam, 1994) provided evidence that the four models more closely resemble how people think about their relationships than the affiliation–control circumplex (Kiesler, 1983), Parsons's pattern variables (Parsons & Shils, 1951), Foa and Foa's (1974) resource exchange, or Clark and Mills's (1979) communal versus exchange distinction. Other species display evidence of CS and AR relationships, but MP and possibly EM are patterns unique to human relationships (Haslam, 1997) because people can calculate value.

According to Fiske (2000), people can use different models simultaneously in dealing with different aspects of the same relationship or even the same interaction. Whereas this flexibility provides added complexity to the fabric of human relationships, it makes specifying the parameters of the theory difficult and indicates that the four models may not be as mutually exclusive as they first appear.

Robert Weiss (1998) argued that Fiske's typology is not based on the essential determinants of relationship because its main distinction is based on the distribution and allocation of resources between relationship participants – the system does not explain why people maintain communal sharing, authority ranking, market pricing, or equity matching in their relationships.[1]

This brings us to the theoretical taxonomy of relationships proposed by Weiss (1974, 1998). Weiss's system is based on his view of the "essential determinants" of relationships – emotion (e.g., security) and cognition (e.g., expectations, understandings). In contrast to Bateson (1972) and Hinde (1996), Weiss (1998) viewed the "relationship" as an aspect of the individual's orientation toward the other.

The fundamental distinction that Weiss's (1998) typology makes is between *attachments* and *affiliations*. Drawing from attachment theory (Ainsworth, 1969; Bowlby, 1969), Weiss (1998) argued that one of the principle bases for human relationships is security. Because human beings are born developmentally immature, there must be an instinctual biological attachment between a child and its caregiver (Buck, 1989). The attachment goes both ways: The child is dependent on the caregiver for security, and the caregiver is instinctually motivated to protect the child. If a secure attachment relationship is established, the child has a secure psychological base from which to explore the world, and this eventually fosters a healthy independence in later life. If a secure attachment relationship is not established, then this can have severe consequences for cognitive and emotional development as well as the ability to establish healthy relationships later in life (Ainsworth, 1969). Later in life, adults develop emotional attachments to specific others based on similar neurochemical brain systems (Buck, 1989). Further, the attachment styles that children display in relation to their parents (e.g., secure, anxious, or avoidant) seem to be reflected, with modification, in adult relationships later in life (Hazan & Shaver, 1987).

It is not the attachment styles of either children or adults that form the basis for Weiss's (1998) distinctions between the types of attachment relationships, however. In addition to the *child's attachment to the parents*, adult attachment relationships take three forms according to Weiss: (a) *pair-bond relationships*, (b) *parental relationships*, and (c) *guidance-obtaining relationships*, which link feelings of security and accessibility with the presence of a specific other. *Pair-bonds* are persistent and marked by the same separation anxiety displayed by children in the absence of the parent. The "cognitive

modules" of the pair-bond are, however, quite different from children's relationships: The roles of provider and beneficiary are fulfilled by both parties. Weiss referred to *the parental relationship* from the perspective of the parents' bonds of attachment to their children noting the distress that comes with separation or loss of custody and the parents' feelings of protection toward their child. *Adult guidance-obtaining relationships* are relationships in which the adult attaches to another who is seen as stronger or wiser (e.g., a client–therapist relationship).

Affiliations, on the other hand, are not based on feelings of security or separation anxiety attached to a specific other but alliances based on "common interests" and "mutual advantage." Whereas the mutual benefits of some affiliations (e.g., friendship) may be based on sheer pleasure of companionship with a specific other, separation will, by definition, not evoke feelings of insecurity for an affiliation. Likewise, whereas some affiliations are entered into for the purposes of mutual security, the need is not inherently tied to the specific individual but comes from "augmentation of resources." Weiss (1998) included *friendships*, *work relationships*, and *kinship ties* as categories of affiliations based on the nature of the "common interests" and the cognitive models they require. Of course, an attachment bond could potentially be found in any of these relationships (e.g., best friends who feel inseparable or siblings who become dependent on each other as either a pair-bond or a guidance-obtaining relationship).

One of the virtues of this typology is that it is based on what many believe to be a fundamental distinction with roots in biological evolution. Both attachments and affiliations can also be observed as the basis of relationships between other mammals. Mammals are born immature and therefore possess the capacity for instinctual bonds of attachment (Buck, 1989). Reptiles apparently do not (Buck, 1989). Anyone who has dogs knows that adult mammals can transfer their attachment to another. Likewise, herd animals appear to form associations where they may work together to hunt or protect the herd but do not suffer great anxiety or grief when a member of the herd is lost.

Weiss's (1998) typology has its limitations. Many scholars believe that a relationship is something that exists *between* people, not in the needs, motivations, or understandings of one of the participants (Fisher & Adams, 1994). A useful distinction is whether both parties have an attachment motivation (parent–child and pair-bonds) or only one of the parties (the beneficiary) holds a true attachment (e.g., guidance-obtaining relationship).

Weiss's taxonomy has not yet generated much research. Our view is that the distinction between *attachments* and *affiliations* is fundamental and useful, but other subdivisions (maybe Fiske's four models) may prove more useful for organizing research.

Specific Relationship Types and Typologies of Specific Relationships

The headings of the sections to follow were selected because they are the most common groupings in the literature, and they are the types for which specific typologies are most frequently proposed. They are also types of relationships recognized and understood by laypersons outside the scholarly community. For this book, we have chosen to focus on types of "personal relationships" instead of "social relationships."

Family Typologies

Often family typologies are based on determinations made by the researchers reflecting structural properties of families, such as parents' marital or work status (e.g., Crouter & Manke, 1997). Other externally determined typologies compare normative or well-functioning families to nonnormative or dysfunctional families. Typologies of alcoholic versus nonalcoholic dysfunctional and functional families (Harrington & Metzler, 1997) or of families headed by heterosexual versus homosexual parents (Allen & Burrell, 1996) are examples. Although types in these typologies are often labeled based

on specific characteristics or outcomes, the behavioral patterns associated with that characteristic or outcome often become part of the definition of the type. For example, in the Vuchinich and Angelelli (1995) family typology, low problem-solving families are not only poor at solving problems, they are also characterized by strong father–mother alliances.

Not all family typologies, however, are based mainly on structural properties. Frequently, typologies base their categorizations on communication behaviors and patterns of family members. Typically, observed behaviors or outcomes associated with the behaviors are judged against some externally established standard that makes some types of families more desirable. Examples include Kantor and Lehr's (1976) typology of closed, open, and random families, where open families are seen as most functional, or Reiss's (1981) typology of consensus–sensitive, interpersonal distance-sensitive, and environment-sensitive families, in which environment-sensitive families are best for the mental health of children. Other examples of such typologies include Baumrind's (1967, 1971) typology of *authoritative, authoritarian*, and *permissive* families based on parenting style and its extensions by Maccoby and Martin (1983), who further divided the permissive type into *neglectful* and *indulgent*, and Slicker (1998), who proposed a five-category typology with the addition of midrange parenting styles.

Olson's (1981, 1993) typology based on his circumplex model of marital and family communication is also in this class. Here, 16 family types are identified based on the two orthogonal dimensions of cohesion (enmeshed, connected, separated, disengaged) and flexibility (chaotic, flexible, structured, rigid). Families moderate on both dimensions (connected or separated and flexible or structured, respectively) are labeled *balanced* and are seen as most functional, families extreme on both dimensions (enmeshed or disengaged and chaotic or rigid) are labeled *unbalanced* and least functional, and families extreme on one dimension but moderate on the other are of intermediate functioning. Communication is viewed as a third, facilitating dimension that allows families to move along the cohesion and flexibility dimensions and is, therefore, particularly relevant for family therapy designed to enhance family functioning. Olson used the same dimensions to type marriages (Lavee & Olson, 1993; Olson & Fowers, 1993).

There are also family typologies that are based on perceptions or judgments family members make about their own families rather than on perceptions and judgments made by external observers. Some focus on psychosocial outcomes, such as typologies of satisfied versus dissatisfied families. Others focus on the behavior that families perceive themselves (Moos & Moos, 1976). One example is the typology based on family communication patterns first described by McLeod and Chaffee (1972) and further developed by Fitzpatrick and her associates (Fitzpatrick & Ritchie, 1994; Koerner & Fitzpatrick 2002b, 2004; Ritchie & Fitzpatrick, 1990). These researchers have argued that family communication patterns are created by different strategies that families use to establish shared social realities and that are part of more complex family communication schemata. Communication behaviors and family communication schemata, in turn, have been linked to various outcomes of family communication, including conflict style and resolution (Koerner & Fitzpatrick, 1997, 2002c), resiliency (Fitzpatrick & Koerner, in press), and other-orientation (Koerner & Cvancara, 2002).

According to the typology, families that focus on concepts when creating social reality are conversation-oriented in their family communication, and families that focus on relationships when creating social reality are conformity-oriented in the family communication. Thus, the typology is based on two dimensions (conversation orientation and conformity orientation) that evoke the two dimensions of affiliation and power that are central to most if not all interpersonal relationships (Haslam, 1994). Families making frequent use of both strategies have a *consensual* family communication schema.

Their interactions are characterized by a tension between conforming to one another on one hand, and open communication and exploring new ideas on the other. Families oriented more toward conversation than toward conformity have a *pluralistic* family communication schema. Their interactions are characterized by open, unconstrained discussions that are open to and involve all family members. Families oriented more toward conformity than conversation have a *protective* family communication schema. Their communication is characterized by an emphasis on obedience to parental authority and by little concern for conceptual matters or for open communication within the family. Finally, families not oriented toward either strategy have a *laissez-faire* family communication schema. Their communication is characterized by fewer, and often uninvolving interactions about only a limited number of topics.

Although distinct, family communication in these four types is generally functional with each type having particular strengths and weaknesses. For example, whereas conflict in consensual families is usually less frequent and less stressful for family members than conflict in pluralistic families, children of consensual families have more problems with conflict in subsequent romantic relationships than children of pluralistic families (Koerner & Fitzpatrick, 2002c). In other words, in this typology, functionality is relative, meaning that families achieve acceptable outcomes in different ways, based on how they perceive their social environments.

Marital Typologies

Like family typologies, some marriage typologies focus on structure and are more meaningful to the researcher than to the participants. Most marital typologies, however, focus not as much in structural differences as on differences in behaviors. For example, Rosenfeld, Bowen, and Richman's (1995) typology of dual-career families classified marriages as collapsing, work-directed, and traditional role marriages based on spouses' participation in family- and work-related activities. Similarly, Gottman's (1993, 1994) marital typology is based on conflict behaviors and identifies three functional (i.e., validating, volatile, and avoidant) and two dysfunctional types (i.e., hostile and hostile-detached). The main payoff of these typologies is that they have increased, in some cases substantially, our understanding of important relational processes and the relational and social consequences of certain types of behaviors and patterns.

Of the typologies that are based not only on behavioral differences but also on how relationships are represented cognitively by participants, one of the first and probably still the most influential is Fitzpatrick's (1988) marital typology (Fincham, 2004). Based on spouses' reports of their ideology, interdependence, and conflict avoidance, marriages are categorized into one of the three types: *traditionals* (conventional ideology, high interdependence, low conflict avoidance), *independents* (unconventional ideology, high interdependence and sharing, low conflict avoidance), or *separates* (conventional ideology, low interdependence, high conflict avoidance). In about two thirds of marriages, both spouses have the same marital type; the remaining marriages fall into a mixed type (most frequently a traditional wife and a separate husband). Noller and Hiscock (1989) replicated Fitzpatrick's typology on Australian couples, relabeling traditionals as "connecteds."

The strength of this typology is that it is based on both theory (the dimensions were identified based on prevailing marital theories) and empirical validation (the three types represent naturally occurring clusters in the conceptual space of eight possible types defined by the three dimensions). In addition, it also recognizes that different marriages achieve similarly satisfactory or functional outcomes in different ways that produce a different set of advantages and challenges for each type. For example, independent and separate spouses cultivate close relationships outside of marriage that are sources of emotional support from them, whereas traditional spouses focus almost exclusively on the marital relationship as a source of emotional support and often neglect external friendships. Thus, spouses in all marriage types are generally able to receive emotional support in times of need, although death of a spouse or divorce are more challenging in traditional marriages, whereas the stresses of moving to a different location and a new social network are more challenging in independent and separate marriages. Probably the greatest weakness of the typology is that about a third of all couples fall into the mixed category (i.e., spouses disagree about their marriage type). Although there are six types of mixed couples that should be expected to vary greatly in their communication, they are usually treated as similar, which is not only an oversimplification, but also a lost opportunity to study the consequences of divergent perceptions of relationship among married couples.

Fitzpatrick's marital typology is closely related to McLeod and Chaffee's (1972) family typology. Fitzpatrick and Ritchie (1994) have shown that families headed by traditional couples are usually consensual, those headed by independents are pluralistic, families headed by separates are protective, and those headed by mixed couples are laissez-faire. These associations are expected given the parents' influence on family communication, and they do make a strong case for the validity of the respective typologies.

Divorce Typologies

Because the communication of divorcing couples is focused on renegotiating the relationship and accomplishing tasks such as child care and household dissolutions, a logical focus for typologies of divorcing couples is on the conflict communication of couples. An early example is Kressel, Jaffee, Tuchman, Watson, and Deutsch's (1980) typology, which used the dimensions of ambivalence about the divorce, frequency and openness of communication, and level of conflict to distinguish between enmeshed (high ambivalence, high communication, high conflict), autistic (high ambivalence, low communication, low conflict), direct-conflict (moderate ambivalence, high communication, high conflict), and disengaged couples (low ambivalence, low communication, low conflict). Couples that were in direct conflict or disengaged had more amiable separations than enmeshed and autistic couples. Similarly based on different conflict styles are typologies by Parkinson (1987), who distinguished between semidetached couples, avoidant couples, couples battling for power, push–pull couples, confronting couples, enmeshed couples, and violent couples, and by Weingarten and Leas (1987), whose five couple types are determined by the intensity of conflict and range from couples with specific problems to solve to couples at war. To predict the success of mediation was the purpose of Cohen, Luxenburg, Dattner, and Matz's (1999) typology, who identified seven couple types based on commitment to divorce, prior litigation, relationship quality, ability to communicate, and commitment to children. Their couple types include semiseparated couples, emotionally withdrawn and noncommunicative couples, couples in a power struggle, leaver–left couples, battling couples, enmeshed couples, and violent couples.

Unlike these typologies describing couples during separation and divorce, Ahrons's (1994) typology describes postdivorce relationships. Based mainly on their communication behaviors, Ahrons identified couples who maintain positive relationships as *cooperative colleagues* or *perfect pals*, whereas couples that interact with one another but do so in poor relationships are *angry associates* or *fiery foes*. Couples who do not maintain a relationship after divorce are called *dissolved duos*.

Parent–Child Typologies

Because family typologies are frequently based on parent–child relationships, there is much overlap between family typologies and parent–child typologies that need not be repeated here. Some classification schemes, however, have been more specifically defined for parent–child dyads without concern for the family context, most notably attachment styles. Based on attachment theory (Bowlby, 1969), Ainsworth, Blehar, Waters, and Wall (1978) classified children as *secure, anxious–ambivalent*, or *avoidant*. Similarly, Furman, Simon, Shaffer, and Bouchey (2002) identified categories of *secure, dismissing*, and *preoccupied* based on both attachment styles and working models. Also based on internal working models of self and other, Bartholomew (1990) developed a system of four attachment styles: secure, dismissive, preoccupied, and fearful avoidant. Expanding attachment theory to include labels for parents as well as children, Zeanah et al. (1993) used a three-category model for both parents and children with infants classified as *secure, avoidant*, or *resistant* and parents classified as *autonomous, dismissing*, or *preoccupied*.

Later research expanded attachment types to include secondary caregivers as well (Bretherton, 1985). Dufour and Bouchard's (2003) typology of fathers classifies them as either *proactive* (modern) or *reactive* (traditional). Proactive fathers were further defined as accommodating, guiding, or pragmatic; reactive fathers were further classified as *family men* or *worried*.

In regard to the correlation between attachment style and family types, we would expect that based on the warmth of the parent–child interaction and the concern that parents show for their children, it is most likely that children of consensual and pluralistic families are securely attached, children of protective families are preoccupied, and children of laissez-faire families are avoidant. The way in which parents handle authority and responsiveness and the attachment style of the child seem to be the two major issues in parent–child typologies.

Sibling Typologies

Sibling relationships often last a lifetime and go through significant changes over time (Mares, 1995), suggesting different typologies for different life stages. Examples include Stewart, Verbrugge, and Beilfuss's (1998) typology of adult siblings and Gold's (1989) typology of siblings in old age.

Stewart's typology classified siblings as *caretakers*, *buddies*, or *casual*, but added another category (*loyal–unresolved*) for the older siblings. As with family typologies, there are sibling typologies based on structural properties and others based on interpersonal processes such as affect, conflict, control, support, and involvement. Typologies based on structure include Gibbs, Teti, and Bond's (1987) widely spaced and closely spaced dyads, Dunn and Kendrick's (1981) same-sex and different-sex dyads, and those based on birth order (Stocker & McHale, 1992). Typologies based on psychological and behavioral variables include Stewart et al.'s (2001) classification of adult sibling relationships as *supportive, longing, competitive, apathetic*, and *hostile*, and Gold's (1989) typology of older siblings as *intimate, congenial, loyal, apathetic*, and *hostile*.

Given the similarities in underlying dimensions, it is reasonable to presume associations between sibling and general family types. For example, Stormshak, Bellanti, and Bierman's (1996) typology of siblings as *conflictual, supportive*, or *involved* is based on combinations of conflict and warmth, which relate to Fitzpatrick and Ritchie's (1994) conformity orientation and conversation orientation. Thus, we would expect siblings from consensual families to be involved during conflict, siblings from pluralistic families to be supportive, and siblings from protective families to be conflictual.

Romantic and Premarital Relationships

There is a great deal of variance in romantic and premarital relationships. Neither romance nor marriage necessarily implies equality so that we may find romantic authority-ranking relationships or communal-sharing relationships. We can distinguish between flirtations, casual dating, serious or exclusive dating ("going steady"), and committed relationships (e.g., cohabitation or engagement). Even among cohabiting couples we can distinguish between those who are *premarriage* (i.e., who are engaged, intend to be married, or are using cohabitation as a "trial" for marriage), those who view cohabitation as an alternative to marriage (i.e., *common law marriages*), and those who cohabit without any agreed-on long-term plans (i.e., who are living together for the sake of convenience). We can also distinguish between heterosexual and homosexual relationships.

In some ways romantic relationships can be conceptualized as occupying a middle ground between friendship and marriage. A romantic relationship, at least in its own paradigm case, may potentially contain all of the elements of a friendship, plus a mutually acknowledged sexual attraction. A marriage, at least in its paradigm case, *may* contain all the elements of a romantic relationship, plus a legally recognized commitment. If this is true, then we might expect to find parallels between types of friendships and types of romantic relationships (Shulman & Knafo, 1997) on one hand, and among types of romantic relationships and types of marriages on the other.

Shulman and Knafo (1997) considered studies in which adolescent romantic relationships were typed using the same methods as they used to type and evaluate adolescent friendships. The same two principle types emerged: *interdependent romances* and *disengaged romances* (also similar to some marital types). Whereas the two friendship types did not yield differences in the intimacy dimensions, interdependent romantic relationships did have greater emotional closeness than disengaged romances.

The opposite sex composition of heterosexual romantic or premarital relationships invites distinctions based on gender-role and gender-trait orientations. Gaines (1995), for example, used such variables to create a three category typology: *respect-giving reversed* (men viewed themselves as respectful of women), *affectionate* (women and men view themselves as affectionate and reject gender roles, men low in respect giving), and *traditional* (both sexes accept gender roles, women expressive, and men instrumental). Similar distinctions are made in some marriage typologies.

Fowers and Olson (1992) used a premarital couples inventory to create a four-category typology. *Visualized* couples have high levels of satisfaction, affection and sex, and openness in communicating about feelings and problems. They spend time together and prefer egalitarian roles, but may have unrealistic expectations. *Harmonious couples* have moderate levels of relational quality but are satisfied with each other's personality, amount of time together, amount of sex, and the other's friends and family. They are also somewhat unrealistic about marriage and have not decided how many children to have. *Traditional couples* are moderately dissatisfied with their interaction (uncomfortable with discussing feelings or conflict) but are strong in decision making and planning, have consensus about children, and tend to be realistic about marriage. Olson and colleagues found a similar marital typology (Lavee & Olson, 1993; Olson & Fowers, 1993).

Friendship Typologies

Friendship is usually distinguished from *friendly relations* (Kurth, 1970) or *acquaintances*. There seems to be a consensus that a "true friendship" involves some degree of intimacy and is voluntary, and this appears to be true across cultures (Argyle & Henderson, 1985; Davis & Todd, 1985). Likewise, friendship is usually distinguished from "romantic relationships" even though a romantic relationship may possess all of the characteristics of a true friendship (Shulman & Knafo, 1997) plus a mutually acknowledged sexual attraction. This is evidenced in statements such as "my wife/husband is my best friend." Davis and Todd specified the "prototypical" characteristics of friendship. Friends (a) are equals, (b) enjoy each other, (c) have mutual trust, (d) provide mutual support, (e) have mutual acceptance, (f) have mutual respect, (g) are themselves, (h) posses mutual understanding, and (i) display mutual intimacy or sharing. This model emphasizes the "mutuality" of friendship.

Based on this discussion, one might expect prototypical friendships to be communal sharing relationships, and casual friendships might be equity-matching or even market-pricing relationships. Whereas some very close relationships may obtain the status of "attachments," most friendships

are associations. Likewise, although friends often reciprocate intimacy and affection, control patterns are characteristic of a *parallel relationship* (VanLear, 1985).

Therefore, one way to approach a typology of friendship would be to examine various ways in which a "friendship" can deviate from the "paradigm" case. *Reciprocal friendships*, in Reisman's (1981) typology of adult friendships, are very similar to the paradigm case of friendship. These are intimate, peer relationships between equals, characterized by loyalty and commitment. *Associative friendships* are relationships that, although often referred to as "friendship" are more like "friendly relations." They are pleasurable but lack loyalty or commitment and do not endure far beyond the external circumstances or instrumental goals that brought the parties together. A *receptive friendship* is not a true peer relationship but is characterized by a status difference that is recognized by both parties (Reisman, 1981), similar to an authority-ranking relationship.

The literature on adult friendships tends to display a positivity bias. Close relationships like friendships provide ample opportunity for conflict (Altman & Taylor, 1973), however. Further, people often choose to stay in difficult relationships because of fear of loneliness, perceived lack of better alternatives, or simply because some people have a tolerance for conflict. Therefore, the kind of *volatile* relationships observed between some marital couples might be added to a typology of adult friends. There is also considerable variability in the extent of interdependence within friendships (Shulman & Knafo, 1997). We might expect some friendships to be highly *interdependent* and others to be more *disengaged* (Shulman & Knafo, 1997).

People must learn to be friends. There is a growing body of intriguing literature on childhood friendships and how they develop with age. Kerns (2000) identified distinctions between types of preschool friendships. The three-cluster solution included (a) a *harmonious/interactive* group, which was affectively positive group with a high level of interactive play; (b) a *disjointed* group, which displayed low harmony, high control, and low levels of coordinating in their play; and (c) a *harmonious and independent* group, which was positive in the orientations but engaged in less interactive play. The five-cluster solution added *conflictual/interactive* and *highly conflictual* types. There was some evidence that these clusters also discriminated among various attachment combinations and future stability. Most intriguing is the proposition that children learn to enact "true" friendship. The most frequent category for preschoolers in both three- and five-cluster solutions is the *harmonious/interactive*, which is the closest in description to the paradigm case of friendship for adult dyads.

Shulman (1995; Shulman & Knafo, 1997) argued that as children grow up, they develop their methods of coping with the dialectic of closeness and individuality through their friendships. Shulman and colleagues examined the close friendships of early and middle adolescents to identify two major friendship types. *Interdependent friends* cooperate by freely accepting one another's solutions and respecting the needs of both individuals and report enjoying working with the other in a cooperative interaction. *Disengaged friends*, on the other hand, tend to work independently, are competitive, and only cooperate if they need to.

It is noteworthy that most early-adolescent friends fit the criteria for *disengaged* (69%), whereas most of the friendships in middle adolescence were *interdependent* (61%). Shulman and Knafo (1997) saw the increase in interdependent friendships in middle adolescence as an indication of a maturing in the ability to handle the individuality closeness dialectic. It also appears that as adolescents mature, they are more likely to enact friendships closer to the ideal of the "paradigm case."

Conclusions

Basic Distinctions

The distinction between social and personal relationships based either on intimacy or interdependence will probably continue to have utility for typing human relationships. This distinction may be important for social cognitive theorists because the scripts and schemas for social and personal relationships are likely to differ. We believe, however, that the distinction between attachments and affiliations also has a strong theoretical and ontological basis. Although all attachments probably qualify as personal relationships and all social relationships are clearly affiliations, there may be cases in which relationships normally thought of as "personal" (on the basis of intimacy or interdependence) would not meet the criteria for an attachment.

In addition to a solidarity or closeness (or attachment) dimension,[2] analyses of relationships consistently identify a control–power dimension (Burgoon & Hale, 1984; Foa & Foa, 1974; Haslam, 1995; Leary, 1955; Schutz, 1958). This could be displayed as dominance versus deference on the individual level, but at the relational level, it is displayed as symmetry (equity) versus asymmetry (inequity–complementarity) of control. Authority-ranking and probably market-pricing relationships, conformity-protection-oriented families, authoritarian parenting, caretaker siblings, traditional marriages, and receptive friendships usually display asymmetry of control, whereas equity-matching relationships, consensual pluralistic families, reciprocal, or paradigm case friendships display equity of power and control. We suspect that communal sharing relationships display a parallel pattern of exchange. Figure 6.2 locates the general typology categories on the basis of these distinctions. Although we do not suggest that Figure 6.2 offers a perfect fit to all of these typologies, it does provide a good picture of the major overlapping distinctions.

Closeness and equity of control dimensions capture distinctions among most of the relationship types reviewed. The addition of a conflict dimension is likely to capture most of the remaining types. Some families, marriages, siblings, or friends readily engage in conflict, and some avoid it; many of the

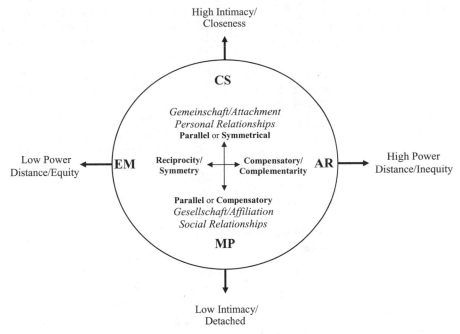

Figure 6.2. Conceptual space defined by dimensions of intimacy/ and closeness and power distance of general typologies of Toennies, Bateson, Fiske, and Weiss. *Note:* AR = authority ranking; CS = communal sharing; EM = equality matching; MP = market pricing.

typologies reviewed have categories that discriminate among degree of conflict or the expression of negative affect.

Variations in cognitive schema used to guide behavior in and make sense out of social relationships appear to distinguish between relationship types. People learn these schemas from observing and participating in relationships within their culture and then reproduce the cultural patterns. Koerner and Fitzpatrick (2002a) suggested that such scripts and schema are hierarchically organized from general social schemata, to relationship-specific schemata, with relationship type schemas occupying the middle of the hierarchy. Fiske's (1991) four models represent knowledge structures that can operate at any level of this hierarchy, from general social schema that motivate reciprocity or compensation, to relationship types that identify cultural–societal prototypes, to redundant patterns within a specific relationship that provide the gestalt for the character of that relationship or for specific aspects of that relationship.

Weiss's (1998) basic distinction between attachment and affiliation is probably at the top of the hierarchy. His subdivisions are various cognitive models that occupy the middle level.

We now have many typologies to classify relationships from general to very specific. At this point it is probably more productive to study the relationships between them and to research their respective merits, than to continue to proliferate typologies.

Uses of Typologies

Typologies can be used as either independent variables, dependent variables, and, by implication, intervening variables, as well as moderating or contingency variables. If one takes the position that relationships are always emergent, then the question becomes which exogenous variables and which processes lead to the emergence of a relationship as a particular type? Children may learn certain schema for marriage from watching their parents and reproduce those forms in their own marriage (VanLear, 1992). Thus, parents' behavior may be the independent variable and children's marital type the dependent variable.

Typologies can also be viewed as independent variables. For example, the type of marriage may predict marital behaviors and interaction patterns (Williamson & Fitzpatrick, 1985), marital satisfaction (Fitzpatrick & Best, 1979), or marital stability (Gottman, 1994). The type of parent–child relationship may predict aspects of the child's future relationships later in life (Hazan & Shaver, 1987), or the type of marriage a child's parents have may affect how the child enacts his or her own marriage (VanLear, 1992).

Finally, relationship typologies can be used as moderator variables. For example, VanLear and Zietlow (1990) proposed a contingency model of marital interaction and provided evidence that the behaviors and interaction patterns that are satisfying in one type of marriage are dissatisfying when enacted in a different type of marriage.

Typologies act as tools for organizing our knowledge and understanding about human relationships. They act as theoretically important variables in their own right. Finally, they provide parameters and limits for generalizations about human relationships.

Footnotes

1. Not all of us agree with Weiss's critique. Fiske considers the four types intrinsically rewarding.
2. The use of the term *dimension* to refer to these distinctions does not imply a continuous dimension.

References

Ahrons, C. (1994). *The good divorce*. New York: HarperCollins.

Ainsworth, M. D. S. (1969). Object relations, dependency, and attachment: A theoretical review of the infant–mother relationship. *Child Development, 40*, 969–1025.

Ainsworth, M. D. S., Blehar, M. C., Waters, E., & Wall, S. (1978). *Patterns of attachment: A psychological study of the strange situation*. Hillsdale, NJ: Erlbaum.

Allen, M., & Burrell, N. (1996). Comparing the impact of homosexual and heterosexual parents on children: Meta-analysis of existing research. *Journal of Homosexuality, 32*, 19–35.

Altman, I., & Taylor, D. A. (1973). *Social penetration: The development of interpersonal relationships*. New York: Holt, Rinehart & Winston.

Argyle, M., & Henderson, M. (1985). The rules of relationships. In S. Duck & D. Perlman (Eds.), *Understanding personal relationships: An interdisciplinary approach* (pp. 63–84). Beverly Hills, CA: Sage.

Bartholomew, K. (1990). Avoidance of intimacy: An attachment perspective. *Journal of Social and Personal Relationships, 7*, 147–178.

Bateson, G. (1972). *Steps to an ecology of mind*. New York: Ballantine.

Baumrind, D. (1967). Child care practices anteceding three patterns of preschool behavior. *Genetic Psychology Monographs, 75*, 43–88.

Baumrind, D. (1971). Current patterns of parental authority. *Developmental Psychology Monographs, 4* (Part 2), 99–102.

Bowlby, J. (1969). *Attachment and loss: Vol. 1. Attachment*. New York: Basic Books.

Bretherton, I. (1985). Attachment theory: Retrospect and prospect. *Monographs of the Society for Research in Child Development, 50*, 3–35.

Buck, R. (1989). Emotional communication in personal relationships: A developmental–interactionist view. In C. Hendrick (Ed.), *Close relationships* (pp. 44–76). Beverly Hills, CA: Sage.

Burgoon, J. K., & Hale, J. L. (1984). The fundamental topoi of relational communication. *Communication Monographs, 51*, 173–214.

Clark, M. S., & Mills, J. (1979). Interpersonal attraction in exchange and communal relationships. *Journal of Personality and Social Psychology, 37*, 12–23.

Cohen, O., Luxenburg, A., Dattner, N., & Matz, D. E. (1999). Suitability of divorcing couples for mediation: A suggested typology. *American Journal of Family Therapy, 27*, 329–344.

Crouter, A. C., & Manke, B. (1997). Development of a typology of dual-earner families: A window into differences between and within families in relationships, roles, and activities. *Journal of Family Psychology, 11,* 62–75.

Davis, K. E., & Todd, M. J. (1985). Assessing friendship: Prototypes, paradigm cases and relationship description. In S. Duck & D. Perlman (Eds.), *Understanding personal relationships: An interdisciplinary approach* (pp. 17–38). Beverly Hills, CA: Sage.

Dufour, S., & Bouchard, C. (2003). Promoting children's mental health in disadvantaged areas: Profiles of fathers [electronic version]. *Fathering, 1,* 263 (20).

Dunn, J., & Kendrick, C. (1981). Social behavior of young siblings in the family context: Differences between same-sex and different-sex dyads. *Child Development, 52,* 1265–1273.

Fincham, F. D. (2004). Communication in marriage. In A. L. Vangelisti (Ed.), *Handbook of family communication* (pp. 83–103). Mahwah, NJ: Erlbaum.

Fisher, B. A., & Adams, K. (1994). *Interpersonal communication: A pragmatic perspective.* New York: McGraw-Hill.

Fiske, A. P. (1991). *Structures of social life: The four elementary forms of human relations.* New York: Free Press.

Fiske, A. P. (1992). The four elementary forms of sociality: Framework for a unified theory of social relations. *Psychological Review, 99,* 689–723.

Fiske, A. P. (1993). Social errors in four cultures: Evidence about universal forms of social relations. *Journal of Cross-Cultural Psychology, 24,* 463–494.

Fiske, A. P. (1995). Social schemata for remembering people: Relationships and person attributes that affect clustering in free recall of acquaintances. *Journal of Quantitative Anthropology, 5,* 305–324.

Fiske, A. P. (2000). Relational models theory overview: Human sociality. Retrieved November 7, 2003, from http://www.sscnet.ucla.edu/anthro/faculty/fiske/relmodov.htm

Fiske, A. P., & Haslam, N. (1996). Social cognition is thinking about relationships. *Current Directions in Psychological Science, 5,* 131–148.

Fiske, A. P., & Haslam, N. (1997). The structure of social substitutions: A test of relational models theory. *European Journal of Social Psychology, 27,* 725–729.

Fiske, A. P., Haslam, N., & Fiske, S. (1991). Confusing one person with another: What errors reveal about the elementary forms of social relations. *Journal of Personality and Social Psychology, 60,* 656–674.

Fitzpatrick, M. A. (1988). *Between husbands and wives: Communication in marriage.* Beverly Hills, CA: Sage.

Fitzpatrick, M. A., & Best, P. (1979). Dyadic adjustment in traditional, independent, and separate relationships. *Communication Monographs, 46,* 167–178.

Fitzpatrick, M. A., & Koerner, A. F. (2005). Family communication schemata: Effects in children's resiliency. In S. Dunwoody, L. B. Becker, D. McLeod, & G. Kosicki (Eds.), *The evolution of key mass communication concepts: Honoring Jack M. McLeod* (pp. 115–139). Cresskill, NJ: Hampton Press.

Fitzpatrick, M. A., & Richie, L. D. (1994). Communication schemata within the family: Multiple perspectives on family interaction. *Human Communication Research, 20,* 275–301.

Foa, U. G., & Foa, E. B. (1974). *Societal structures of the mind.* Springfield, IL: Charles C Thomas.

Fossati, A., Feeney, J. A., Donati, D., Donini, M., Novella, L., Bagnato, M., et al. (2003). On the dimensionality of the attachment style questionnaire in Italian clinical and nonclinical participants. *Journal of Social and Personal Relationships, 20,* 55–79.

Fowers, B. J., & Olson, D. H. (1992). Four types of premarital couples: An empirical typology based on PREPARE. *Journal of Family Psychology, 6,* 10–21.

Furman, W., Simon, V. A., Shaffer, L., & Bouchey, H. A. (2002). Adolescents' working models and styles for relationships with parents, friends, and romantic partners. *Child Development, 73,* 241–255.

Gaines, S. O. (1995). Classifying dating couples: Gender as reflected in traits, roles, and resulting behavior. *Basic and Applied Social Psychology, 16,* 75–94.

Gibbs, E. D., Teti, D. M., & Bond, L. A. (1987). Infant–sibling communication: Relationships to birth-spacing and cognitive and linguistic development. *Infant Behavior and Development, 10,* 307–323.

Gold, D. T. (1989). Sibling relationships in old age: A typology. *International Journal of Aging and Human Development, 28,* 34–54.

Gottman, J. M. (1993). The roles of conflict engagement, escalation, and avoidance in marital interaction: A longitudinal view of five types of couples. *Journal of Consulting and Clinical Psychology, 61*, 6–15.

Gottman, J. M. (1994). *What predicts divorce: The relationship between marital process and marital outcomes.* Hillsdale, NJ: Erlbaum.

Griffin, D. W., & Bartholomew, K. (1994). The metaphysics of measurement; the case of adult attachment. In K. Bartholomew & D. Perlman (Eds.), *Attachment processes in adulthood. Advances in personal relationships* (Vol. 5, pp. 17–52). Philadelphia: Kingsley.

Harrington, C., & Metzler, A. (1997). Are ACOAs different from adult children of dysfunctional families without alcoholism: A look at committed intimate relationships. *Journal of Counseling Psychology, 44*, 102–107.

Haslam, N. (1994). Mental representation of social relationships: Dimensions, laws, or categories? *Journal of Personality and Social Psychology, 67*, 575–584.

Haslam, N. (1995). Factor structure of social relationships: An examination of relational models and resource exchange theories. *Journal of Social and Personal Relationships, 12*, 217–227.

Haslam, N. (1997). Four grammars for primate social relations. In J. Simpson & D. Kenrick (Eds.), *Evolutionary social psychology* (pp. 297–316). Hillsdale, NJ: Erlbaum.

Haslam, N. (1999). Taxometric and related methods in relationships research. *Personal Relationships, 6*, 519–534.

Haslam, N., & Fiske, A. P. (1992). Implicit relationship prototypes: Investigating five theories of the cognitive organization of social relationships. *Journal of Experimental Social Psychology, 28*, 441–474.

Hazan, C., & Shaver, P. R. (1987). Romantic love conceptualized as an attachment process. *Journal of Personality and Social Psychology, 52*, 511–524.

Hewes, D. E. (1979). The sequential analysis of social interaction. *Quarterly Journal of Speech, 65*, 56–73.

Hinde, R. A. (1996). Describing relationships. In A. E. Aughagen & M. von Salisch (Eds.), *The diversity of human relationships* (pp. 7–35). Cambridge, England: Cambridge University Press.

Kantor, D., & Lehr, W. (1976). *Inside the family.* San Francisco: Jossey-Bass.

Kerns, K. A. (2000). Types of preschool friendships. *Personal Relationships, 7*, 311–324.

Kiesler, D. J. (1983). The 1982 interpersonal circle: A taxonomy for complementarity in human transactions. *Psychological Review, 90*, 185–214.

Koerner, A. F., & Cvancara, K. E. (2002). The influence of conformity orientation on communication patterns in family conversations. *Journal of Family Communication, 2*, 132–152.

Koerner, A. F., & Fitzpatrick, M. A. (1997). Family type and conflict: The impact of conversation orientation and conformity orientation on conflict in the family. *Communication Studies, 48*, 59–75.

Koerner, A. F., & Fitzpatrick, M. A. (2002a). Toward a theory of family communication. *Communication Theory, 12*, 70–91.

Koerner, A. F., & Fitzpatrick, M. A. (2002b). Understanding family communication patterns and family functioning: The roles of conversation orientation and conformity orientation. *Communication Yearbook, 26*, 37–69.

Koerner, A. F., & Fitzpatrick, M. A. (2002c). You never leave your family in a fight: The impact of families of origins on conflict-behavior in romantic relationships. *Communication Studies, 53*, 234–251.

Koerner, A. F., & Fitzpatrick, M. A. (2004). Communication in intact families. In A. L. Vangelisti (Ed.), *Handbook of family communication* (pp. 177–195). Mahwah, NJ: Erlbaum.

Kressel, K., Jaffee, N., Tuchman, B., Watson, C., & Deutsch, M. (1980). A typology of divorcing couples: Implications for mediation and the divorce process. *Family Process, 19*, 101–116.

Kurth, S. (1970). Friendships and friendly relations. In G. J. McCall (Ed.), *Social relationships.* Chicago: Aldine.

Lavee, Y. & Olson, D. H. (1993). Seven types of marriage: Empirical typology based on ENRICH. *Journal of Marital and Family Therapy, 19*, 325–340.

Leary, T. (1955). The theory and measurement methodology of interpersonal communication. *Psychiatry, 18*, 147–161.

Lederer, W. J., & Jackson, D. D. (1968). *The mirages of marriage.* New York: Norton.

Maccoby, E. E., & Martin, J. A. (1983). Socialization in the context of the family: Parent–child interaction. In E. Hetherington (Vol. Ed.), P. H. Mussen (Series Ed.), *Handbook of child psychology* (Vol. 4, pp. 1–101). New York: Wiley.

Mares, M. L. (1995). The aging family. In M. A. Fitzpatrick & A. L. Vangelisti (Eds.), *Explaining family interaction* (pp. 344–374). Thousand Oaks, CA: Sage.

Marwell, G., & Hage, J. (1970). The organization of role-relationships: A systematic description. *American Sociological Review, 35*, 884–900.

McLeod, J. M. & Chaffee, S. H. (1972). The construction of social reality. In J. Tedeschi (Ed.), *The social influence process* (pp. 50–59). Chicago: Aldine-Atherton.

Meehl, P. E. (1995). Bootstraps taxometrics: Solving the classification problem in psychopathology. *American Psychologist, 50*, 266–275.

Moos, R. H., & Moos, B. S. (1976). A typology of family environments. *Family Process, 15*, 357–371.

Noller, P., & Hiscock, H. (1989). Fitzpatrick's typology: An Australian replication. *Journal of Social and Personal Relationships, 6*, 87–91.

Olson, D. H. (1981). Family typologies: Bridging family research and family therapy. In E. E. Filsinger & R. A. Lewis (Eds.), *Assessing marriage: New behavioral approaches* (pp. 74–89), Beverly Hills, CA: Sage.

Olson, D. H. (1993). Circumplex model of marital and family systems. In F. Wals (Ed.), *Normal family processes* (2nd ed.). New York: Guilford Press.

Olson, D. H. & Fowers, B. J. (1993). Five types of marriage: An empirical typology based on ENRICH. *Family Journal, 3*, 196–207.

Parkinson, L. (1987). *Separation, divorce, and families*. London: Macmillan Education.

Parsons, T., & Shils, E. A. (Eds.). (1951). *Toward a general theory of action*. Cambridge, MA: Harvard University Press.

Reisman, J. M. (1981). Adult friendships. In S. Duck & R. Gilmour (Eds.), *Personal relationships 2: Developing personal relationships* (pp. 205–230) London: Academic Press.

Reiss, D. (1981). *The family's construction of reality*. Cambridge, MA: Harvard University Press.

Ritchie, L. D., & Fitzpatrick, M. A. (1990). Family communication patterns: Measuring interpersonal perceptions of interpersonal relationships. *Communication Research, 17*, 523–544.

Rosenfeld, L. B., Bowen, G. L., & Richman, J. M. (1995). Communication in three types of dual-career marriages. In M. A. Fitzpatrick & A. L. Vangelisti (Eds.), *Explaining family interaction* (pp. 257–289). Thousand Oaks, CA: Sage.

Schutz, W. C. (1958). *The interpersonal underworld*. Palo Alto, CA: Science and Behavior Books.

Shulman, S. (1995). Typology of close friendships, relationship models and friendship reasoning in early adolescence. In S. Shulman (Ed.), *Close relationships and socioemotional development* (pp. 109–127). Norwood, NJ: Ablex.

Shulman, S., & Knafo, D. (1997). Balancing closeness and individuality in adolescent close relationships. *International Journal of Behavioral Development, 21*, 687–702.

Slicker, E. K. (1998). Relationship of parenting style to behavioral adjustment in graduating high school seniors [electronic version]. *Journal of Youth and Adolescence, 27*, 345.

Stephenson, W. (1953). *The study of behavior*. Chicago: University of Chicago Press.

Stewart, R. B., Kozak, A. L., Tingley, L. M., Goddard, J. M., Blake, E. M., & Cassel, W. A. (2001). Adult sibling relationships: Validation of a typology. *Personal Relationships, 8*, 299–324.

Stewart, R. B., Verbrugge, K. M., & Beilfuss, M. C. (1998). Sibling relationships in early adulthood: A typology. *Personal Relationships, 5*, 59–74.

Stocker, C. M., & McHale, S. M. (1992). The nature and family correlates of preadolescents' perceptions of their sibling relationships. *Journal of Social and Personal Relationships, 9*, 179–195.

Stormshak, E. A., Bellanti, C. J., & Bierman, K. L. (1996). The quality of sibling relationships and the development of social competence and behavioral control in aggressive children. *Developmental Psychology, 32*, 79–89.

Toennies, F. (1957). *Community and society* (C. P. Loomis, Trans.). New York: Harper and Row.

VanLear, C. A. (1985). *The formation of social relationships: A longitudinal comparison of linear and nonlinear models*. Unpublished doctoral dissertation, University of Utah, Salt Lake City.

VanLear, C. A. (1992). Marital communication across the generations: Learning and rebellion, continuity and change. *Journal of Social and Personal Relationships, 9*, 103–124.

VanLear, C. A., & Zietlow, P. H. (1990). Toward a contingency approach to marital interaction: An empirical integration of three approaches. *Communication Monographs, 57*, 202–218.

Vuchinich, S., & Angelelli, J. (1995). Family interaction during problem solving. In M. A. Fitzpatrick & A. L. Vangelisti (Eds.), *Explaining family interaction* (pp. 177–205). Thousand Oaks, CA: Sage.

Watzlawick, P., Beavin, J., & Jackson, D. D. (1967). *Pragmatics of human communication.* New York: Norton.

Weingarten, H., & Leas, S. (1987). Levels of marital conflict model: A guide to assessment and intervention. *American Journal of Orthopsychiatry, 58,* 407–417.

Weiss, R. S. (1974). The provisions of social relationships. In R. Zick (Ed.), *Doing unto others: Joining, molding, conforming, helping, loving* (pp. 17–26). Englewood Cliffs, NJ: Prentice Hall.

Weiss, R. S. (1998). A taxonomy of relationships. *Journal of Social and Personal Relationships, 15,* 671–683.

Williamson, R. N., & Fitzpatrick, M. A. (1985). Two approaches to marital interaction: Relational control patterns in marital types. *Communication Monographs, 52,* 236–252.

Zeanah, C. H., Benoit, D., Barton, M., Regan, C., Hirshberg, L. M., & Lipsitt, L. P. (1993). Representations of attachment in mothers and their one-year-old infants [electronic version]. *Journal of the American Academy of Child and Adolescent Psychiatry, 32.*

Part III

DEVELOPMENT OF RELATIONSHIPS

CHAPTER 7

From Courtship to Universal Properties: Research on Dating and Mate Selection, 1950 to 2003

Catherine A. Surra
Christine R. Gray
Tyfany M. J. Boettcher
Nathan R. Cottle
Adam R. West

For several decades, dating and mate selection have been cornerstones of research on the sociology of the family, social psychology, interpersonal communication, and the hybrid of all of these fields, family studies. Traditionally, researchers have focused on the formation of marital unions, although the focus has broadened to include nonmarital romantic relationships more generally, as the institution of mate selection has become less orderly and predictable in its movement toward marriage. The goal of contemporary scholarship is to understand the forces that draw heterosexual and homosexual partners to one another in the first place and, ultimately, to understand the mechanisms by which partners form long-term stable and satisfying romantic unions of any type. In this chapter, we formally investigate changes in research over the last fifty years, with special attention to a recent decade. Then we review key areas of research to elucidate the implications of the trends identified.

We investigated trends in the study of dating and mate selection in two ways. First,

we obtained a historical view by researching major outlets for reviews in the fields of study just described. Our assumption here was that major reviews are repositories of, and therefore reflect, the dominant theoretical and empirical trends that take hold within disciplines. The outlets we examined included the *Annual Review of Psychology* from 1950 to 2003 and the *Annual Review of Sociology* from when it was first published in 1975 to 2003. We also researched the decade reviews of the *Journal of Marriage and Family* from when they were first published in 1970 to the most recent issue, 2000. We looked for information pertaining to heterosexual or homosexual relationships, close or interpersonal relationships, dating, attraction, homosexuality or gay relationships, and mate selection by examining titles of articles, abstracts when available, and the index of each volume. Second, we researched eight major journals that publish papers on dating and mate selection for a recent decade, 1991 to 2000, to investigate contemporary trends in topics researched.

A Brief History of the Study of Dating and Mate Selection, 1950 to 2003

Our investigation of the major published reviews of research on dating and mate selection uncovered eight papers that dealt exclusively with mate choice, premarital relationships, or personal relationships with a strong focus on romantic relationships. These articles are the source of the conclusions reached in this section. In addition to these, we uncovered 20 articles, not included here, in which nonmarital romantic relationships were addressed as part of a larger review on broader topics, such as personality, group dynamics, adolescence, or social networks.

A Major Change in Research on Dating and Mate Selection

Our review revealed a major shift in emphasis: The topic of relationship development with an emphasis on progress toward marriage, a leading focus of research for several decades, has rather suddenly vanished from reviews published in major outlets. This theme concerns research on how and why relationships progress toward deeper involvement or marriage. It also concerns the opposing question: Why do relationships deteriorate in involvement, and, in some cases, break up? Five of the six major reviews published from 1970 to 1990 were entirely or mostly devoted to the topic. In their review of research conducted during the 1960s, Moss, Apolonio, and Jensen (1971) focused on studies of the courtship continuum, or how relationships progress toward marriage. Burchinal (1964) first discussed the idea of a courtship continuum, explaining that research of his era made a sharp distinction between dating and courtship based on their unique roles and functions. Up to and including 1990, all reviews since this early treatment incorporated relationship development, although the emphasis shifted for some from courtship that results in marriage to a more general understanding of how relationships are formed and

change (Blumstein & Kollock, 1988; Huston & Levinger, 1978; Murstein, 1980; Surra, 1990). Although some scholars may assume that the push for cross-cultural studies is new, sections on cultural variation were included in two of the earliest reviews (Moss et al., 1971; Murstein, 1980), but not later ones.

In reviews published so far during the decade of 2000, the theme of courtship development has faded away. More recent reviews instead have been devoted entirely to cohabitation (Smock, 2000) or to summaries of theories that apply across different types of relationships, including, but not limited to, nonmarital romantic relationships (e.g., Rusbult & Van Lange, 2003). The strongest evidence that these themes are no longer a major force in research on nonmarital relationships comes from tracking the decade reviews in *Journal of Marriage and Family*. Every 10 years since 1970, this journal has published an issue or issues devoted to major research topics of the decade. The decade review issues included an article on mate selection and premarital relationships in 1970, 1980, and 1990 (Moss et al., 1971; Murstein, 1980; Surra, 1990). In addition, the decade reviews of 1970 and 1980 each had a separate review of research on premarital sex (Cannon & Long, 1971; Clayton & Bokemeier, 1980). Thus, premarital topics of some sort were a vibrant research focus for three decades; 5 of the 33 reviews published during that time were devoted exclusively to premarital topics. The decade review issue of 2000, however, had no article on dating topics, and the only discussion of dating or premarital topics is found within more general reviews on sexuality (Christopher & Sprecher, 2000) and violence (Johnson & Ferraro, 2000).

It may appear that research devoted to the courtship continuum and relationship development in nonmarital romantic relationships is declining. As we show later, however, the decline has more to do with a shift in emphasis than it does the number of studies conducted that are relevant to dating and mate selection.

The Study of Universal Processes: Predominant Topics Across Disciplines

Our investigation of major reviews also showed a good deal of commonality and consistency in topics relevant to dating and mate section. Research on the topics of similarity, homogamy, and assortative mating has been conducted for more than 50 years, and it continues to be a subject of interest. The hypothesis that similarity breeds attraction, progress toward deeper involvement, and the decision to wed is pervasive in all of the disciplines that we investigated and has received considerable support. Researchers have also examined the conditions responsible for this association, most notably the structure of the social environment (e.g., the availability of individuals similar to oneself within the population), residential propinquity, and the factors that moderate or modify the association (e.g., the length of the relationship, the sex of the target). The counterpoint to homogamy, the hypothesis that opposites or complementary partners attract, received a great deal of attention early on but has declined in significance in recent decades. Nevertheless, studies in support of the complementarity hypothesis still appear in the literature (see, for example, Dryer & Horowitz, 1997; Pilkington, Tesser, & Stephens, 1991).

Love, commitment, and intimacy have been topics of interest to researchers from different disciplines for several decades. Even the earliest reviews of research conducted during the 1960s (Moss et al., 1971) identified love and empathy as two of the major forces in the development of relationships to marriage. In their review of research around the 1960s and 1970s, Huston and Levinger (1978) discussed the role of love in building commitment to marriage and the correlates of commitment. Similarly, Clark and Reis (1988) reviewed research on the definition and implications of intimacy for the well-being of individuals and relationships. Nearly all major reviews of premarital relationships and personal relationships have identified love, commitment, intimacy, or all of these as major constructs.

Topics related to social exchange theory, or derivative from it, also are consistently studied in research on dating and mate selection, although the emphasis has shifted from norms that govern tit-for-tat exchanges to those that motivate a more cooperative stance. From the earliest to the most recent reviews in psychology and sociology, questions about how justice norms apply in dating and romantic relationships have carried weight in the literature (Blumstein & Kollock, 1988; Clark & Reis, 1988; Murstein, 1980; Surra, 1990). Equity, fairness, and the magnitude and equality of rewards and costs have been examined as they pertain to both the functioning and outcomes of nonmarital romantic relationships. More recently, research has focused on how partners respond to one another's needs, particularly when the needs of coupled partners do not correspond, the welfare of the relationship is at stake, or each partner has a concern for the welfare of the other. Research on these topics has been the subject of reviews on interdependence theory and communal versus exchange relations (Clark & Reis, 1988; Rusbult & Van Lange, 2003).

Our review of reviews published in the last 50 years showed sustained interest in topics specific to dating, such as assortative mating, as well as topics that explain a variety of relationships, such as love, intimacy, and social exchange. Recently, major theorists in psychology and sociology have exhorted researchers to shift their emphasis even further, away from the study of specific types of relationships and toward dimensions of relationships that apply to close relationships generally (e.g., Berscheid, 1995; Blumstein & Kollock, 1988; Hinde, 1987, 1996). Such a shift is seen as a means of bringing greater understanding of all types of close, personal relationships, rather than a piecemeal emphasis on a particular type of relationship. Similarly, Ross (1995) argued that the study of marital status may be outdated, and relationships might be more profitably studied as a continuum of social attachment that includes marriage itself, living together with a partner, not living together and having a partner, and not having a partner. A more universal approach also has the advantage of drawing together research from different disciplines so that psychology would benefit from a stronger sociocultural perspective (Berscheid, 1995; Blumstein & Kollock, 1988), and sociology would benefit from a greater understanding of relationships not defined by formal roles, such as cohabitation instead of marriage (Blumstein & Kollock, 1988).

The apparent decline in research on the courtship continuum, combined with the call for an emphasis on more universal approaches, led us to wonder about how research on dating and mate selection is changing. We especially wanted to know whether the amount of research has been declining overall. In addition, we asked: Is the emphasis of studies truly shifting from those specific to mate selection to more universal topics and, if the emphasis is shifting, is it doing so across disciplines?

Changes in Research on Dating and Mate Selection, 1991–2000

To understand better the changes in research on dating and mate selection, we systematically examined articles published over the last 10 years. We report on topics studied in eight major journals and how the amount and nature of attention to research on dating and mate selection has changed over the years.

Method

To identify studies done on dating and mate selection from 1991 to 2000, we read the title and abstract of papers published in eight major journals: *American Sociological Review, American Journal of Sociology, Communication Monographs, Human Communication Research, Journal of Marriage and Family*, the sections on Interpersonal Relationships and Group Processes and on Personality Processes and Individual Differences in the *Journal of Personality and Social Psychology, Journal of Social and Personal Relationships*, and *Personal Relationships*. Because

Personal Relationships was first published in 1994, we examined articles published since that time. Of course, these journals do not include all journals that publish articles on dating and mate selection, nor do they necessarily include the journals that publish the most articles. However, as the major journals in sociology, psychology, communication, and interdisciplinary fields that publish articles on dating and mate selection, they should represent well the changes we wished to examine. Despite the publication of a number of important books related to dating and mate selection during the decade (e.g., Buss, 1994; Cate & Lloyd, 1992; Holman, 2001; Lloyd & Emery, 2000), we included only journal articles in our sample to limit the scope of our research.

From the outset, an important task was to determine the boundaries of the domain of research on dating and mate selection. We wanted to be sure to include two groups of studies: those that investigated romantic relationships specifically and those that examined more general properties that operate in dating relationships as well as other types of relationships. We wanted to include, for example, a paper on intimacy in personal relationships, even if it did not specifically focus on intimacy in romantic relationships. To define clearly the boundaries of what to include, we devised two definitions to guide our investigations, one for mate selection and one for dating properties. Articles were included if they fit either definition.

We defined the study of mate selection as research into the processes by which individuals choose their heterosexual or homosexual romantic partners or of the factors that predict whether romantic relationships progress, maintain, or dissolve over time. Study of mate selection includes traditional topics, such as courtship, as well as cohabitation, union formation, and other statuses and forms relevant to nonmarital romantic relationships. To tap into more general relational phenomena, we defined the study of dating relationships as investigation of the properties that pertain to the nature of romantic heterosexual or homosexual relationships and the factors that affect relational properties, including their cognitive, affective, or behavioral characteristics. This definition includes the study of relational phenomena, such as conflict, communication, or interpersonal attitudes (e.g., trust). The definition made it possible for us to include articles on universal properties of relationships that apply to dating. Both definitions include individual, social, and structural influences. Whenever questions arose as to whether a particular article should be included, we referred to these definitions. We included articles on dating or mate selection at all stages of the life span (e.g., adolescent dating), although we did not systematically code this information.

Although our definitions were well circumscribed, they did present certain limitations. If the abstract, for example, described a study about self-disclosure in friendship, we excluded it. If, on the other had, it was described more generally as a study of self-disclosure, it was included because it would apply to dating. In the latter case, however, we might have discovered later in our coding that self-disclosure was indeed studied using a sample of friends. Thus, we were guided primarily by authors' own descriptions of the emphasis the study as presented in the abstract. This procedure probably means that we included in our sample some studies on topics that were applicable to dating, but were, in fact, investigated in nondating relationships. Studies of marriage were included only if authors made reference in the abstract to mate selection or dating; for example, a study of marriage was included because it concluded that spouses must select on the basis of homogamy during mate selection, rather than increase their similarity to one another after marriage (Tambs & Moum, 1992). Studies of individual attitudes were excluded if they pertained to attitudes that lie outside of a specific relationship (e.g., changes over time in attitudes toward premarital sex).

This procedure yielded a sample of 531 articles, 47 of which were nonempirical essays or reviews. We then met in groups of three or four to code the topic of each article into 1 of 36 categories (see Table 7.1). If the

Table 7.1. *Distribution of Articles by Topic, 1991 to 2000*

Topic	%	n
Attachment	10.0	53
Violence	7.2	38
Marriage markets and union formation	7.2	38
Cohabitation	6.0	32
Communication	5.8	31
Relationship development and outcomes	5.6	30
Love	5.5	29
Cognitions and perceptions	5.5	29
Homogamy and matching	3.8	20
Self and identities	3.4	18
Gay relationships	3.2	17
Jealousy and extradyadic relationships	2.4	13
Conflict	2.3	12
Family of origin	2.3	12
Sex	2.3	12
Social networks and other contexts	2.3	12
Attraction and liking	2.1	11
Evolutionary and biological processes	2.1	11
Other	2.1	11
Individual characteristics	1.9	10
Intimacy	1.7	9
Maintenance	1.7	9
Grand theories	1.7	9
Breakups	1.5	8
Commitment	1.5	8
Gender and sex differences	1.3	7
Power	1.1	6
Trust	1.1	6
Depression	0.9	5
Emotion	0.9	5
Narratives and archival data	0.9	5
Partner preferences	0.8	4
Activity participation	0.6	3
Accommodation	0.6	3
Illusions	0.6	3
Forgiveness	0.4	2
Total	100.0	531

Table 7.2. *Distribution of Articles by Journal, 1991 to 2000*

Journal	% on dating and mate selection[a]	n[a]	% on dating and mate selection out of total published in journal[b]	n[b]
Sociology				
American Journal of Sociology	2.1	11	2.9	378
American Sociological Review	3.4	18	3.2	554
Psychology				
Journal of Personality and Social Psychology[c]	20.7	110	8.3	1330
Communication				
Communication Monographs	2.3	12	5.3	227
Human Communication Research	3.2	17	7.6	224
Interdisciplinary				
Journal of Marriage and Family	22.6	120	14.8	809
Journal of Social and Personal Relationships	27.9	148	36.5	406
Personal Relationships	17.9	95	56.2	169
Total	100.0	531		

[a] Based on total number of articles published on dating and mate selection in journals reviewed ($N = 531$).
[b] Based on total number of articles published in the journal, excluding book reviews and commentaries.
[c] Sections on Interpersonal Relationships and Group Processes and on Personality Processes and Individual Differences.

article was a multivariate study, we coded it according to the phenomenon the authors were trying to explain.

Results

The distribution of articles showed that the five most prevalent topics were attachment in adult relationships, violence, marriage markets and union formation, cohabitation, and communication (see Table 7.1). Most of the articles had to do with heterosexual relationships, and 3.2% addressed gay relationships in some manner.

Of all articles published on dating and mate selection included in our sample, most are found in one of the three interdisciplinary journals (*Journal of Social and Personal Relationships*, *Journal of Marriage and Family*, and *Personal Relationships*, even though the latter began publishing in 1994), or in the *Journal of Personality and Social Psychology* (see Table 7.2). The major journals in sociology and communication were the least likely to publish articles on dating and mate selection, publishing 2% to 3% of

the articles in our sample and 3% to 8% of all articles published in the journal. These findings are not surprising, given that these journals typically publish papers in their respective root disciplines. Out of all articles published in the journal, the highest percentage of articles on dating and mate selection (56%) is found in *Personal Relationships*. What is surprising perhaps is that one of the major outlets for published work in the root discipline of social psychology, the *Journal of Personality and Social Psychology*, was among the most active in terms of publishing papers on dating and mate selection (21% of our sample), but, in the two sections of the journal that we studied, only about 8% of the articles published addressed dating and mate selection.

The number of articles on dating and mate selection published over the years was stable. We found no significant trends over time. On average, about 53 articles were published each year. The years 1995 and 1998 were particularly productive, as 63 articles were published in 1995 and 70 in 1998.

Table 7.3. *Major Topics of Research on Dating and Mate Selection*

Major topic	Subtopic
Mate choice	Relationship development and outcomes
	Maintenance
	Marriage markets and union formation
	Homogamy and matching
	Cohabitation
	Partner preferences
	Breakups
Relationship processes	Love
	Accommodations
	Trust
	Commitment
	Illusions
	Power
	Violence
	Emotion
	Cognitions and perceptions
	Narratives and archival data
	Attraction and liking
	Intimacy
	Communication
	Conflict
	Jealousy and extradyadic relationships
	Forgiveness
	Activity participation
Causal conditions	Attachment
	Family of origin
	Gender and sex differences
	Depression
	Self and identities
	Individual characteristics
	Evolutionary and biological processes
	Social networks and other contexts

Note: Gay relationships, grand theories, sex, and other were excluded from the major topics.

To examine the extent to which emphasis has shifted from mate choice to universal relationship processes, we examined how the distribution of topics has changed over the years. We first collapsed topics into three major themes: mate choice, relationship processes, and causal conditions (see Table 7.3). Mate choice includes topics that focus on nonmarital romantic relationships, such as the courtship continuum,

changes in relationship status, cohabitation, and homogamy. Relationship processes are topics that reflect more universal process because they apply to a variety of close relationships, such as attraction, communication, power, and emotion. Causal conditions include topics that lie outside of the dyad, such as individual differences, family of origin effects, and contextual influences. We dropped articles on three topics because their breadth of coverage made it impossible to categorize them into one of the three themes: gay relationships, grand theory, and sex. We excluded articles that fit the miscellaneous "other" category because they were too narrow.

This analysis revealed a significant trend over time toward a steadily decreasing emphasis on mate choice and a fairly steady increase in research on relationship processes (see Table 7.4). The percentage of articles published on mate choice, out of the total published each year, declined from 1991 to 2000, from a high of 44% to a low of 16%. This change was accompanied by a fairly steady increase in the percentage of articles published on relationship processes over the same period, from lows of about 37% early in the decade to a high of more than 50% of the articles published in the last 2 years we investigated. The percentage of articles devoted to causal conditions also increased, particularly when the last 8 years are compared with the earliest 2 years.

The association between topics investigated and journal of publication was also significant (see Table 7.5). Sociology journals published the highest percentage of articles on mate choice (70%), compared with the remaining two topics, with interdisciplinary journals publishing about 33% of their articles on mate choice, nearly 40% less than those published in sociology. Sociologists tend to preserve distinctions among relationships of different social statuses, which may account, in part, for these findings. Communication journals, in contrast, published the vast majority of their papers (80%) on universal relationship processes, with psychology and interdisciplinary journals doing so about 43% of the time. Perhaps because

Table 7.4. *Percentage of Articles by Topic and Year of Publication*

Topic	Year of Publication				
	1991–1992	1993–1994	1995–1996	1997–1998	1999–2000
Mate choice	44.3	34.9	27.5	26.1	16.3
Relationship processes	38.6	37.3	48.0	43.2	52.0
Causal conditions	17.0	27.7	24.5	30.6	31.6
Total	99.9	99.9	100.0	99.9	99.9

Note: χ^2 (8, $N = 482$) = 21.90, $p < 0.01$.

of their emphasis on individual differences and characteristics, psychology journals also published a higher percentage of papers on causal conditions (about 40%) than did any of the remaining journals.

Summary of Changes in Research on Dating and Mate Selection

Our coding of studies on dating and mate selection published in eight journals revealed consistent trends. The amount of attention to research has remained steady from 1991 to 2000. Both our study of major reviews and our coding of journals, however, showed a dramatic shift in focus away from the study of mate choice to the study of universal relationship processes, even when mate choice is broadly defined to include cohabitation, dating statuses, and courtship processes. Our investigation of major review outlets also showed that the study of universal processes has been a focus for several decades but that it now dominates the empirical literature. The once dominant topic of mate selection, particularly

the focus on courtship leading to marriage, declined in importance, with the possible exception of the focus on cohabitation in sociology.

Implications of Changes in Research for Specific Topics

To elucidate the impact of these changes, we review research on four topics relevant to mate selection (marriage markets and union formation, cohabitation, evolutionary approaches, and social exchange and related theories) and one causal condition (romantic attachment). The goal is to review literature to highlight how the trends uncovered in the chapter affect the research enterprise and findings. As a result, the reviews are selective and illustrative, rather than exhaustive (for a more thorough review, see Surra, Gray, Cottle, & Boettcher, 2004).

Marriage Markets and Union Formation

The topic of marriage markets and union formation contributed to the overall decline in

Table 7.5. *Percentage of Articles by Topic and Discipline*

	Journal			
	Sociology	Psychology	Communication	Interdisciplinary
Mate choice	70.4	15.2	0.0	32.6
Relationship processes	22.2	43.8	80.0	43.4
Causal conditions	7.4	41.0	20.0	24.0
Total	100.0	100.0	100.0	100.0

Note: χ^2 (6, $N = 482$) = 54.60, $p < 0.001$.

research on mate selection. Although this topic had the most articles of any other topic within the theme of mate choice, the number decreased over time, from 12 in 1991 to 1992, to 4 in 1999 to 2000.

Part of the decrease in research on this topic may be attributable to demographic changes in marriage behavior that may lead to the conclusion that marriage is much less of an option in mate choice now than previously (see Surra, Boettcher, Gray, West, & Cottle, 2004). Although the rate of marriage has declined slightly for some racial and educational groups (Goldstein & Kenney, 2001; Teachman, Tedrow, & Crowder, 2000), the increase in the age at marriage sometimes leads to the misconception that the marriage rate has dropped dramatically. The median age of first marriage has increased from 1970 to 2000 for men and women, 3.6 years for men from 23.2 to 26.8 years, and 4.3 years for women from 20.8 to 25.1 years (U.S. Bureau of the Census, 2001). Nevertheless, by age 65, 95% of men and women are married (Fields & Casper, 2001). Forecasts of eventual marriage for women born in the 1950s and 1960s are that almost 90% will eventually wed, a figure that is comparable to figures from the early years of the 20th century (Goldstein & Kenney, 2001). In addition, individuals increasingly have formed cohabiting relationships, which, for some, replace marriage entirely (Bernhardt & Goldscheider, 2001; Sassler & Schoen, 1999). Accompanying the increases in cohabitation is the formation of families through nonmarital childbirth, which have increased such that one in three births are to unmarried women (South & Lloyd, 1992; U.S. Bureau of the Census, 2003). These trends may have diverted attention from choice of a spouse to the study of universal processes and other relationship statuses, such as cohabitation.

During the decade we investigated, however, research on marriage markets and the factors that affect marital timing remained an important topic within sociology. Marriage markets are local, community areas in which individuals are likely to make the transition to first marriage (Lichter, LeClere, & McLaughlin, 1991). Because these marriage markets are relatively small geographic areas, they operate on the principles of propinquity, defined as proximity in location and time, and mate availability (Fossett & Kiecolt, 1991). When a large number of attractive potential mates is available in a given market, more individuals are likely to marry. Conversely, a shortage of attractive mates of either sex will produce a marriage squeeze for the opposite sex. Women, especially African American women, are much more likely to experience this squeeze due to a scarcity of eligible men (South & Lloyd, 1992).

The effects of the marriage squeeze have been measured using the sex ratio, calculated as the number of men divided by the number of women in a marriage market. This measure can be refined using factors such as race, age, employment, marital status, or institutionalization to limit the count of men and women to include only those who are potential mates (Fossett & Kiecolt, 1991). Using the sex ratio, researchers have predicted a number of outcomes, including marriage rates, nonmarital fertility, and sexual behavior (Fossett & Kiecolt, 1991). In support of the principle of endogamy, or the tendency of individuals to marry within their social group, research has shown that marriage rates are affected when imbalances in the sex ratio exist within racial groups (Fossett & Kiecolt, 1993; South & Lloyd, 1992). For example, although African American women desire and expect to marry (Bulcroft & Bulcroft, 1993), they have been found to have a smaller pool of available mates from which to choose (South & Lloyd, 1992). Research also has shown that the shortage of favorable mates results partly from a greater number of interracial relationships involving African American men than African American women, especially men of higher socioeconomic status (Crowder & Tolnay, 2000).

The economic opportunities of both men and women, such as employment, income, and socioeconomic status, have been shown to have effects on marriage rates and marital timing for first marriages (Fossett & Kiecolt, 1991; Lichter et al., 1991; Sassler & Schoen, 1999; South & Lloyd, 1992). Although some researchers have found that marriage rates have decreased over time (Schoen & Weinick, 1993b), marriage rates for women who obtain a college education have increased, even though the timing of their marriages may be later than the timing for those who do not attend college (Goldstein & Kenney, 2001; Qian & Preston, 1993).

The study of universal properties has not yet permeated research on marriage markets or timing. Only 2 of the 38 articles addressed the effects of universal properties on union formation (e.g., Mastekaasa, 1992). As investigators broaden their definitions of mate choice to include statuses other than marriage, we expect studies of universal properties, such as love, commitment, and trust, and their impact on union formation and marriage to become much more prevalent. When combined with studies of market factors, the study of universal properties will provide a more complete picture of how macro and micro factors combine to affect the varieties of mate choice.

Cohabitation

It used to be that choosing a mate meant choosing a marriage partner. Patterns of contemporary mate selection are broader than just marriage, however. No pattern has changed contemporary mate selection more than cohabitation. The number of cohabiting couples has increased dramatically, from around 500,000 in 1960, to 4.2 million in 1998 (U.S. Bureau of the Census, 1999). Nearly half of all first marriages are preceded by some cohabitation experience (Bumpass, 1990). The magnitude of the phenomenon has challenged researchers to figure out where cohabitation fits into the courtship continuum and into dating and mate selection more generally.

Investigators frequently have met the challenge by comparing cohabitation to other statuses or states, notably, cohabitation as marriagelike, as a transitional stage on the path to marriage, and as singlehood and, therefore, more like dating (Manning, 1993; also see Casper & Sayer, 2000). Cohabitation as an alternative form of marriage is supported by research demonstrating that individuals cohabit at nearly the same age as earlier generations married (Bumpass, Sweet, & Cherlin, 1991). Findings also show, however, that cohabitors differ from those married with respect to greater heterogamy on religion and age and greater homogamy on education (Schoen & Weinick, 1993a). If cohabitation is a transition or stage on the path to marriage, pregnant cohabiting women would be expected to be more likely to marry their partners than pregnant single women (Manning, 1993). This hypothesis was supported for white women in their 20s. The premise that cohabitation is similar to singlehood was supported by studies showing that cohabitors are similar to single persons in plans for fertility, employment, likelihood of being a student, home ownership (Rindfuss & Vanden-Heuval, 1990), and employment (Landale & Fennelly, 1992).

As the research suggests, cohabitation takes on a variety of forms and individuals who cohabit do so for a variety of reasons. Two variables are particularly powerful in differentiating types of cohabitors: plans to marry the cohabiting partner and individuals' union history. Casper and Sayer (2000) examined patterns of cohabitation and found that individuals who regard cohabitation as an alternative form of marriage were the most likely to remain cohabiting over a roughly 5- to 7-year period. Those who identified their cohabitation as a stage toward marriage were the most likely to shift to a legally recognized marriage. Cohabitors classified as a trial for evaluating a relationship with no plans to marry and those classified as a serious dating relationship were the most apt to end their cohabiting relationships. Although cohabitors, in general, have lower relationship quality than marrieds on several indicators, cohabitors with plans to marry have relationship quality similar to marrieds (Brown & Booth, 1996). Studies have shown that some ill effects of cohabitation, such as greater perceived relationship instability (DeMaris & MacDonald, 1993) and likelihood of marital separation (DeMaris & Rao, 1992; Teachman, 2003), were tempered or fully negated when one accounted for serial cohabitation, in which respondents' cohabitation experience included others in addition to the existing partner.

Future research should take into account such variables as marriage plans, commitment, and union history to understand cohabitation. The study of universal properties will also be useful for differentiating types of cohabiting relationships from one another and for comparing cohabitation to other statuses.

Evolutionary and Biological Processes

Evolutionary approaches to dating and mate selection have captured increasing attention during the decade of research that we reviewed, although the percentage of articles devoted to this topic is still relatively small (2%, see Table 7.1). Some articles that employ an evolutionary perspective were sometimes coded as another topic (e.g., jealousy and extradyadic relationships), depending on their emphasis.

Evolutionary approaches posit that mate choices are directed by innate mechanisms based on Darwin's theory of natural selection (Kenrick, Groth, Trost, & Sadalla, 1993; Simpson & Gangestad, 2001). As a result, evolutionary approaches have focused on gender differences in mate preferences and have tried to explain them in terms of the respective reproductive concerns of men and women. Individuals are thought to select mates on the basis of their potential to provide reproductive success and to rear healthy offspring. Men are thought to be more concerned about their ability to reproduce to ensure that their genetic heritage is passed on, whereas women, because of their greater physical investment in childbearing (e.g., gestation) and child rearing (e.g., nursing), are thought to be more concerned about the long-term survival of their offspring. Thus, men have been shown to have stronger

preferences than women for partners who are youthful, attractive, and thinner (Ben Hamida, Mineka, & Bailey, 1998). Additionally, men have been found to exhibit more jealousy (Bailey, Gaulin, Agyei, & Gladue, 1994) and to be more permissive in their sexual behavior and willingness to participate in short-term sexual relationships (Schmitt & Buss, 1996; Simpson & Gangestad, 1991). Women have been found to prefer partners who are healthy, strong, and possess wealth (Ben Hamida et al., 1998; Buss, Shackelford, Kirkpatrick, & Larsen, 2001). Women are thought to be more selective in choosing a mate (Booth, Carver, & Granger, 2000; Kenrick et al., 1993), and have been found to be less permissive in their sexual behavior (Schmitt & Buss, 1996; Simpson & Gangestad, 1991). These hypothesized, innate preferences and sexual behaviors, however, have been found to change over time as a result of economic, demographic, and social trends (Buss et al., 2001).

Consistent with the movement toward the study of universal properties, research employing an evolutionary approach typically addresses a variety of romantic relationships, ranging from initial encounters to marital relationships. Evolutionary researchers often assume that mate preferences are universal and operate similarly in all types of romantic relationships. In a comparison of mate preferences of heterosexual and homosexual men and women, for example, many mate preferences were more closely tied to an individual's sex than they were to their sexual orientation, suggesting that evolutionary approaches may also apply to homosexual relationships (Bailey et al., 1994). Little mention, however, is made about how preferences may influence nonromantic relationships, including cross- and same-sex friendships. Additionally, more research is needed to test the universality of mate preferences and to explore possible differences in mate preferences according to the status or depth of the relationship. Some research, for example, has found that men show increasing levels of discrimination in their mate preferences when they consider partners for more long-term, committed relationships (Kenrick et al., 1993; Kenrick, Sundie, Nicastle, & Stone, 2001).

Social Exchange, the Investment Model, and Interdependence

A key focus of research on mate selection is to understand why partners in nonmarital romantic relationships become more or less involved, satisfied, or committed over time. Related to this issue are the predictors of why couples break up versus stay together. As shown in Table 7.1, research on this topic, which we coded as relationship development and outcomes, was among the most investigated topics of the decade, constituting 5.6% of the articles published. Research on this topic falls squarely into the larger purview of mate choice (see Table 7.3), because the goal of this work is to explain factors that contribute to deeper or weaker involvement between nonmarital romantic partners.

Theories used to examine these questions have been primarily derived from social exchange theory, Rusbult's investment model (1980, 1983; Rusbult, Martz, & Agnew, 1998), and interdependence theory. According to these theories, nonmarital romantic relationships should be more satisfying, committed, and stable to the extent that the rewards partners derive from interaction are high; costs are low; alternatives to the relationship are perceived as providing fewer rewards and greater costs, compared with those derived from the relationship itself; partners' investment of resources (e.g., time and effort) in the relationship is great; and the contribution of partners' resources is perceived as equitable or fair. Although these properties have broad applicability to a variety of voluntary relationships, most of the research examines heterosexual, nonmarital romantic unions. Just like other research, however, studies of these properties seem to be moving toward voluntary relationships generally.

Research on what makes for satisfying and committed relationships has shown that rewards partners derived from interaction are arguably the strongest predictor.

Rewards predicted satisfaction regardless of whether they were measured in terms of specific rewards that partners glean from interactions (e.g., the other's intelligence), rewards obtained from the exchange of specific resources, measures of attractions to the relationship, or more general assessments of how rewarding the relationship is (Rusbult, 1983; Sprecher, 2001). In addition, the reward value of resources exchanged in interaction predicted increases in satisfaction over a 6-month (Sprecher, 2001) and a 9-month period (Rusbult, 1983). Some findings show that rewards predict commitment better for men than women (Rusbult, 1983; Sprecher, 2001).

The perceived quality of alternatives to and investments in the relationship are strong predictors of both satisfaction and commitment. In cross-sectional analyses, alternatives and investments predicted commitment for both men and women (Rusbult et al., 1998; Sprecher, 2001), and higher levels of investments predicted increases in commitment over time for women (Sprecher, 2001). Although alternatives were uniquely related to satisfaction at one point in time, neither alternatives nor investments predicted changes in satisfaction over time (Sprecher, 2001). Of all of the variables in the investment model, initial high levels of investment predicted increases in commitment over time for women only. For men, the best predictor of satisfaction was less underbenefiting inequity, or individuals' perception that the partner is getting a better deal in the exchange of resources. Greater initial equity predicted increases in satisfaction and commitment over consecutive 1-year waves (Sprecher, 2001). Composite measures of dependence, consisting of satisfaction, alternatives, and investments, predicted commitment in cross-sectional analyses, but prediction of changes in commitment was weak (Weiselquist, Rusbult, Agnew, & Foster, 1999).

With respect to relationship dissolution, studies have shown that commitment itself predicts whether relationships break up after 2 to 5 months as well as or better than the individual predictors of satisfaction, alternatives, and investments and that commitment mediates the association between the investment model variables and break up (Rusbult, 1983; Rusbult et al., 1998). Likewise, Sprecher (2001) showed that the best predictor of breakups over 5 years was women's commitment.

Consistent with our finding that research on dating and mate selection is moving toward the study of universal properties, recent studies, in particular, have emphasized how the properties just described operate in relationships other than heterosexual nonmarital unions. An illustration of this approach is found in a series of studies by Kurdek (1991, 1992, 1998) in which he examined how properties derived from the investment model and interdependence theory explain outcomes in gay relationships. He showed that among gay and lesbian couples rewards predicted satisfaction in cross-sectional analyses (Kurdek, 1991), but changes in rewards did not predict changes in satisfaction over time (Kurdek, 1992). For gay partners, changes in relationship satisfaction were predicted by changes in the quality of alternatives and in investments over a 4-year period (Kurdek, 1992). The findings for costs suggest that they may predict satisfaction somewhat better in the relationships of gay and lesbian partners than in heterosexual relationships. Over a 4-year period, the best predictor of breakups was lower initial investments (Kurdek, 1998).

Other evidence that variables derived from social exchange theory and related models are increasingly viewed as universal properties is found in the samples used to investigate these variables. The samples used to investigate universal properties frequently are unspecified with respect to dating status, the assumption apparently being that status is irrelevant to the property under investigation (Surra, Boetcher, et al., 2005; Surra, Gray, et al. 2004). Our review of the empirical articles on the universal property of love, for example, showed that in the overwhelming majority of studies, the researchers either did not report relationship status at all or described it partially, for example, as heterosexual romantic rela-

tionships, with no distinction between dating or married. A similar trend is true for research on social exchange and the investment model, where, in early work, (e.g., Rusbult, 1983), samples were almost always composed entirely of partners in dating relationships, but in recent investigations dating and married couples are treated as the same and combined into one sample (e.g., Rusbult et al., 1998; Weiselquist et al., 1999). The use of unspecified and mixed samples is consistent with the idea that variables derived from interdependence theory and social exchange theory have the potential to explain a variety of types of voluntary relationships.

Attachment As a Causal Condition

From 1991 to 2000, research on dating and mate selection witnessed an increase in attention paid to causal conditions (see Table 7.4). Of the topics classified as causal conditions, adult romantic attachment style received, by far, the most attention, constituting 10% of the entire sample of articles.

Researchers have tested three rival hypotheses pertaining to attachment and mate choice. They are that individuals will be most attracted to and select romantic partners who (a) provide an opportunity to form a secure attachment bond (attachment-security hypothesis), (b) endorse models of self and others similar to their own (similarity hypothesis), or (c) endorse models of self and others that complement their own (complementarity hypothesis). The data provide mixed support for the hypotheses.

The attachment-security hypothesis is supported by data showing that established couples, either seriously dating or married, report a higher proportion of secure individuals than studies that do not use relationship involvement as a criterion for inclusion in the study (Kirkpatrick & Davis, 1994; Kobak & Hazan, 1991). These data suggest that providing security may be linked to sustaining a committed romantic relationship. Individuals, regardless of their own attachment style, rated hypothetical secure partners as the most ideal partner, followed by preoccupied partners and then avoidant partners (Latty-Mann & Davis, 1996). Experimental studies have shown that individuals who imagined a secure partner, compared with an insecure partner, reported more positive and less negative feelings about the hypothetical relationship, a greater likelihood that the relationship would result in marriage, more liking for the partner and enjoyment of the relationship (Pietromonaco & Carnelley, 1994), and fewer negative and more positive emotions (Chappell & Davis, 1998).

In contrast to data showing preference for secure partners, other data support the idea that individuals prefer a similar or a complementary partner with respect to attachment style. Both secure individuals and anxious individuals were more likely to be dating partners and more satisfied with partners who had attachment styles similar to their own (Frazier, Byer, Fischer, Wright, & DeBord, 1996). Findings from experimental studies of hypothetical partners also indicate that anxious and avoidant subjects were more likely to choose partners with similar styles (Frazier et al., 1996). In support of the complementarity hypothesis are data showing that over a 4-year period couples with avoidant men and anxious–ambivalent women were as stable as, although less satisfied than, couples with partners who were both secure (Kirkpatrick & Davis, 1994). Contrary to the similarity hypothesis, two pairings did not exist in this sample of established couples, anxious pairs and avoidant pairs.

In addition to mate choice, researchers have investigated how attachment style affects universal properties. For example, of the 53 attachment articles we coded, 15 explored communication and conflict. In their study on attachment style and patterns of self-disclosure, for instance, Mikulincer and Nachshon (1991) found that securely attached individuals, compared with ambivalent and avoidant individuals, reported more disclosure flexibility and topical reciprocity with romantic partners, friends, and family members. Such findings suggest that the effects of attachment style are congruent across different types

of relationships. Other research has indicated, however, that anxiously attached married men have less positive perceptions of their partners than do men who are dating (Young & Acitelli, 1998). Thus, researchers still need to pay careful attention to relationship status in studies of the effects of romantic attachment on universal properties of relationships.

Conclusions

Research on dating and mate selection has shifted its emphasis away from traditional mate choice and the courtship continuum and toward properties that apply universally across close relationships. The shift may be a response, in part, to a three-pronged challenge posed by theorists from different disciplines to (Berscheid, 1995; Blumstein & Kollock, 1988; Hinde, 1987, 1996) (a) forego an approach to the study of relationships that is narrowly aimed at understanding a particular type of relationship, (b) replace this approach with one aimed at identifying the universal qualities that explain behavior in a variety of close relationships, and (c) identify the varied ways that universal properties operate in different relationships. Clearly, research on dating and mate selection is responding to the first two prongs of the challenge, but results from other studies we have conducted indicate that research often ignores the third (Surra, Boettcher, et al., 2005; Surra, Gray et al., 2004). We have found, for example, that in a large percentage of studies relevant to dating and mate selection, researchers ignore relationship type and status in several features of research design, including sampling, procedure, and analysis. It is fairly common practice to collapse different relationship statuses (e.g., daters, married, cohabitors, friends) into one sample, to gather data by asking questions that ignore or combine different relationship statuses or types, or to fail to report the relationship status or type of study participants. Such practices may be due in part to the sheer practical difficulties associated with recruiting large samples of individuals in nonmarital or other relationships and maintaining distinctions among different statuses in research designs and analyses. The practical and monetary expense of doing research on contemporary mate selection alone may explain the increasing preference for study of universal properties in mate choice.

Research undoubtedly is responding to the context in which it occurs. It used to be that individuals took one route to marriage, and that was from casual to more serious involvement to formal engagement. Not only have the pathways toward marriage multiplied, but also their fluid end points, which now must include same- and opposite-sex marriages; short-term, long-term, and serial cohabitations; and civil unions. The study of universal properties is an increasingly attractive scholarly tool for dealing with the variety. The danger of such an approach is that if it is not carefully executed we will know nothing about particular types or pathways of relationships, and most certainly, nothing about dating and mate selection in the postmodern age.

Author Notes

The authors would like to thank Susan Robison, Amber Peters, Alyssa Wheeler, Leah Smith, and the many undergraduate research assistants who helped us with this project.

References

Bailey, J. M., Gaulin, S., Agyei, Y., & Gladue, B. A. (1994). Effects of gender and sexual orientation on evolutionary relevent aspects of human mating psychology. *Journal of Personality and Social Psychology*, 66, 1081–1093.

Ben Hamida, S., Mineka, S., & Bailey, J. M. (1998). Sex differences in perceived controllability of mate value: An evolutionary perspective. *Journal of Personality and Social Psychology*, 75, 953–966.

Bernhardt, E. M., & Goldscheider, F. K. (2001). Men, resources, and family living: The determinants of union and parental status in the United States and Sweden. *Journal of Marriage and Family*, 63, 793–803.

Berscheid, E. (1995). Help wanted: A grand theorist of interpersonal relationships, sociologist or anthropologist preferred. *Journal of Social and Personal Relationships*, 12, 529–533.

Blumstein, P., & Kollock, P. (1988). Personal relationships. *Annual Review of Sociology*, 14, 467–490.

Booth, A., Carver, K., & Granger, D. (2000). Biosocial perspectives on the family. *Journal of Marriage and the Family*, 62, 1018–1034.

Brown, S. L., & Booth, A. (1996). Cohabitation versus marriage: A comparison of relationship quality. *Journal of Marriage and the Family*, 58, 668–678.

Bulcroft, R. A., & Bulcroft, K. A. (1993). Race differences in attitudinal and motivational factors in the decision to marry. *Journal of Marriage and the Family*, 55, 338–355.

Bumpass, L. L. (1990). What's happening to the family? Interactions between demographic and institutional change. *Demography*, 27, 483–498.

Bumpass, L. L., Sweet, J. A., & Cherlin, A. (1991). The role of cohabitation in declining rates of marriage. *Journal of Marriage and the Family*, 53, 913–927.

Burchinal, L. G. (1964). The premarital dyad and love involvement. In H. T. Christensen (Ed.), *Handbook of marriage and the family* (pp. 623–674). Chicago: Rand-McNally.

Buss, D. M. (1994). *The evolution of desire: Strategies of human mating*. New York: Basic Books.

Buss, D. M., Shackelford, T. K., Kirkpatrick, L. A., & Larsen, R. J. (2001). A half century of mate preferences: The cultural evolution of values. *Journal of Marriage and the Family*, 63, 491–503.

Cannon, K. L., & Long, R. (1971). Premarital sexual behavior in the sixties. *Journal of Marriage and the Family*, 33, 36–49.

Casper, L. M., & Sayer, C. (2000). *Cohabitation transitions: Different attitudes and purposes, different paths*. Paper presented at the Annual Meeting of the Population Association of America, Los Angeles, CA.

Cate, R. M., & Lloyd, S. A. (1992). *Courtship*. Newbury Park, CA: Sage.

Chappell, K. D., & Davis, K. E. (1998). Attachment, partner choice, and perception of romantic partners: An experimental test of the attachment-security hypothesis. *Personal Relationships, 5,* 327–342.

Christopher, F. S., & Sprecher, S. (2000). Sexuality in marriage, dating, and other relationships. *Journal of Marriage and the Family, 62,* 999–1017.

Clark, M. S., & Reis, H. T. (1988). Interpersonal processes in close relationships. *Annual Review of Psychology, 39,* 609–672.

Clayton, R. R., & Bokemeier, J. L. (1980). Premarital sex in the seventies. *Journal of Marriage and the Family, 42,* 759–775.

Crowder, K. D., & Tolnay, S. E. (2000). A new marriage squeeze for black women: The role of interracial marriage by black men. *Journal of Marriage and the Family, 62,* 792–807.

DeMaris, A., & MacDonald, W. (1993). Premarital cohabitation and marital instability: A test of the unconventionality hypothesis. *Journal of Marriage and the Family, 55,* 399–407.

DeMaris, A., & Rao, K. V. (1992). Premarital cohabitation and subsequent marital stability in the United States: A reassessment. *Journal of Marriage and the Family, 54,* 178–190.

Dryer, D.C., & Horowitz, L. M. (1997). When do opposites attract? Interpersonal complementarity versus similarity. *Journal of Personality and Social Psychology, 72,* 592–603.

Fields, J., & Casper, L. M. (2001). *America's families and living arrangements: March 2000* (Current Population Reports, P 20–537). Washington, DC: U.S. Census Bureau.

Fossett, M. A., & Kiecolt, K. J. (1991). A methodological review of the sex ratio: Alternatives for comparative research. *Journal of Marriage and the Family, 53,* 941–957.

Fossett, M. A., & Kiecolt, K. J. (1993). Mate availability and family structure among African Americans in the U.S. metropolitan areas. *Journal of Marriage and the Family, 55,* 288–302.

Frazier, P. A., Byer, A. L., Fischer, A. R., Wright, D. M., & DeBord, K. A. (1996). Adult attachment style and partner choice: Correlational and experimental findings. *Personal Relationships, 3,* 117–136.

Goldstein, J. R., & Kenney, C. T. (2001). Marriage delayed or marriage forgone? New cohort forecasts of first marriage for U.S. women. *American Sociological Review, 66,* 506–519.

Hinde, R. (1987). *Individuals, relationships, and culture: Links between ethology and the social sciences.* Cambridge, England: Cambridge University Press.

Hinde, R. A. (1996). Describing relationships. In A. E. Augagen & M. von Salisch (Eds.), *The diversity of human relationships* (pp. 7–35). Cambridge, England: Cambridge University Press.

Holman, T. B. (2001). *Premarital prediction of marital quality or breakup: Research, theory, and practice.* New York: Kluwer Academic/Plenum.

Huston, T. L., & Levinger, G. (1978). Interpersonal attraction and relationships. *Annual Review of Psychology, 29,* 115–156.

Johnson, M. P., & Ferraro, K. J. (2000). Research on domestic violence in the 1990s: Making distinctions. *Journal of Marriage and the Family, 62,* 948–963.

Kenrick, D. T., Groth, G. E., Trost, M. R., & Sadalla, E. K. (1993). Integrating evolutionary and social exchange perspectives on relationships: Effects of gender, self-appraisal, and involvement level on mate selection criteria. *Journal of Personality and Social Psychology, 64,* 951–969.

Kenrick, D. T., Sundie, J. M., Nicastle, L. D., & Stone, G. O. (2001). Can one ever be too wealthy or too chaste? Searching for nonlinearities in mate judgments. *Journal of Personality and Social Psychology, 80,* 462–471.

Kirkpatrick, L. A., & Davis, K. E. (1994). Attachment style, gender, and relationship stability: A longitudinal analysis. *Journal of Personality and Social Psychology, 66,* 502–512.

Kobak, R., & Hazan, C. (1991). Attachment in marriage: Effects of security and accuracy in working models. *Journal of Personality and Social Psychology, 60,* 861–869.

Kurdek, L. A. (1991). Correlates of relationship satisfaction in cohabiting gay and lesbian couples: Integration of contextual, investment, and problem-solving models. *Journal of Personality and Social Psychology, 61,* 910–922.

Kurdek, L. A. (1992). Relationship stability and relationship satisfaction in cohabiting gay and lesbian couples: A prospective test of the contextual and interdependence models. *Journal of Social and Personal Relationships, 9,* 125–142.

Kurdek, L. A. (1998). Relationship outcomes and their predictors: Longitudinal evidence from heterosexual married, gay cohabiting, and lesbian cohabiting couples. *Journal of Marriage and the Family, 60,* 553–568.

Landale, N. S., & Fennelly, K. (1992). Informal unions among mainland Puerto Ricans: Cohabitation or an alternative to marriage? *Journal of Marriage and the Family, 54,* 269–280.

Latty-Mann, H., & Davis, K. E. (1996). Attachment theory and partner choice: Preference and actuality. *Journal of Social and Personal Relationships*, 13, 5–23.

Lichter, D. T., LeClere, F. B., & McLaughlin, D. K. (1991). Local marriage markets and the marital behavior of black and white women. *American Journal of Sociology*, 96, 843–867.

Lloyd, S. A., & Emery, B. C. (2000). *The dark side of courtship: Physical and sexual aggression.* Thousand Oaks, CA: Sage.

Manning, W. D. (1993). Marriage and cohabitation following premarital conception. *Journal of Marriage and the Family*, 55, 839–850.

Mastekaasa, A. (1992). Marriage and psychological well-being: Some evidence on selection into marriage. *Journal of Marriage and the Family*, 54, 901–911.

Mikulincer, M., & Nachshon, O. (1991). Attachment styles and patterns of self-disclosure. *Journal of Personality and Social Psychology*, 61, 321–331.

Moss, J. J., Apolonio, F., & Jensen, M. (1971). The premarital dyad during the sixties. *Journal of Marriage and the Family*, 33, 50–69.

Murstein, B. I. (1980). Mate selection in the 1970s. *Journal of Marriage and the Family*, 42, 777–792.

Pietromonaco, P. R., & Carnelley, K. B. (1994). Gender and working models of attachment: Consequences for perceptions of self and romantic relationships. *Personal Relationships*, 1, 63–82.

Pilkington, C. J., Tesser, A., & Stephens, D. (1991). Complementarity in romantic relationships: A self-evaluation maintenance perspective. *Journal of Social and Personal Relationships*, 8, 481–504.

Qian, Z., & Preston, S. H. (1993). Changes in American marriage 1972 to 1987: Availability and forces of attraction by age and education. *American Sociological Review*, 58, 482–495.

Rindfuss, R. R., & VandenHeuvel, A. (1990). Cohabitation: A precursor to marriage or and alternative to being single? *Population and Development Review*, 16, 703–726.

Ross, C. E. (1995). Reconceptualizing marital status as a continuum of social attachment. *Journal of Marriage and the Family*, 57, 129–140.

Rusbult, C. E. (1980). Commitment and satisfaction in romantic associations: A test of the investment model. *Journal of Experimental Social Psychology*, 16, 172–186.

Rusbult, C. E. (1983). A longitudinal test of the investment model: The development (and deterioration) of satisfaction and commitment in heterosexual involvements. *Journal of Personality and Social Psychology*, 45, 101–117.

Rusbult, C. E., Martz, J. M., & Agnew, C. R. (1998). The investment model scale: Measuring commitment level, satisfaction level, quality of alternatives, and investment size. *Personal Relationships*, 5, 357–391.

Rusbult, C. E., & Van Lange, P. A. M. (2003). Interdependence, interaction, and relationships. *Annual Review of Psychology*, 54, 351–375.

Sassler, S., & Schoen, R. (1999). The effect of attitudes on economic activity on marriage. *Journal of Marriage and the Family*, 61, 147–159.

Schmitt, D. P., & Buss, D. M. (1996). Strategic self-promotion and competitor derogation: Sex and context effects on the perceived effectiveness of mate attraction tactics. *Journal of Personality and Social Psychology*, 70, 1185–1204.

Schoen, R., & Weinick, R. M. (1993a). Partner choice in marriages and cohabitation. *Journal of Marriage and the Family*, 55, 408–414.

Schoen, R., & Weinick, R. M. (1993b). The slowing metabolism of marriage: Figures from 1988 U.S. marital status life tables. *Demography*, 30, 737–745.

Simpson, J. A., & Gangestad, S. W. (1991). Individual differences in sociosexuality: Evidence for convergent and discriminant validity. *Journal of Personality and Social Psychology*, 60, 870–883.

Simpson, J. A., & Gangestad, S. W. (2001). Evolution and relationships: A call for integration. *Personal Relationships*, 8, 341–355.

Smock, P. J. (2000). Cohabitation in the United States: An appraisal of research themes, findings, and implications. *Annual Review of Sociology*, 26, 1–20.

South, S. J., & Lloyd, K. M. (1992). Marriage opportunities and family formation: Further implications of imbalanced sex ratios. *Journal of Marriage and the Family*, 54, 440–451.

Sprecher, S. (2001). Equity and social exchange in dating couples: Associations with satisfaction, commitment, and stability. *Journal of Marriage and the Family*, 63, 599–613.

Surra, C. A. (1990). Research and theory on mate selection and premarital relationships in the

1980s. *Journal of Marriage and the Family, 52,* 844–865.

Surra, C. A., Boettcher, T. M., Gray, C. R., West, A., & Cottle, N. (2005). *On the treatment of relationship status in research on dating and mate selection.* Manuscript submitted for publication.

Surra, C. A., Gray, C. R., Cottle, N., & Boettcher, T. M. J. (2004). Research on mate selection and premarital relationships: What do we really know? In A. Vangelisti (Ed.), *Handbook of family communication* (pp. 53–82). Mahwah, NJ: Erlbaum.

Tambs, K., & Moum, T. (1992). No large convergence during marriage for health, lifestyle, and personality in a large sample of Norwegian spouses. *Journal of Marriage and the Family, 54,* 957–970.

Teachman, J. (2003). Premarital sex, premarital cohabitation, and the risk of subsequent marital dissolution among women. *Journal of Marriage and Family, 65,* 444–455.

Teachman, J. E., Tedrow, L. M., & Crowder, K. D. (2000). The changing demography of America's families. *Journal of Marriage and the Family, 62,* 1234–1246.

U.S. Bureau of the Census. (1999). *Statistical Abstract of the United States.* Washington, DC: U.S. Government Printing Office.

U.S. Bureau of the Census. (2001). *America's families and living arrangements* (Current Population Reports, Series P20, No. 537). Washington, DC: U.S. Government Printing Office.

U.S. Bureau of the Census. (2003). *Fertility of American women* (Current Population Reports, Series P20, No. 548). Washington, DC: U.S. Government Printing Office.

Weiselquist, J., Rusbult, C. E., Agnew, C. R., & Foster, C. A. (1999). Commitment, prorelationship behaviors, and trust in close relationships. *Journal of Personality and Social Psychology, 77,* 942–966.

Young, A. M., & Acitelli, L. K. (1998). The role of attachment style and relationship status of the perceiver in the perceptions of romantic partner. *Journal of Social and Personal Relationships, 15,* 161–173.

CHAPTER 8

The Affective Structure of Marriage

John P. Caughlin
Ted L. Huston

Scholarly research on marital well-being has a long and rich history (e.g., Burgess & Wallin, 1953; Terman, Buttenwieser, Ferguson, Johnson, & Wilson, 1938; Waller, 1938). From its inception, writings on the topic have been diverse, with early scholars focusing on a range of factors affecting marital success, including couples' courtship experiences (Burgess & Wallin, 1953), spouses' personality traits (e.g., Terman et al., 1938), and cognitive processes such as selective attention to partners' good qualities (e.g., Waller, 1938). As the divorce rate increased and plateaued at a historically high level (Teachman, Tedrow, & Crowder, 2000), scholarly and popular interest in marital satisfaction, distress, and divorce intensified (Bradbury, Fincham, & Beach, 2000). The resulting literature on marriage is colossal and multifarious with literally hundreds of variables examined (Karney & Bradbury, 1995).

Obviously, no single chapter can give a thorough review of research on marriage, and that is not our goal here. For instance, space does not allow us to discuss the extensive work connecting demographic characteristics such as young age at marriage,

premarital births, and low socioeconomic status to marital instability (for a review, see Faust & McKibben, 1999). Instead, our discussion focuses primarily on the dynamics within marriage and contextual factors that influence such dynamics. As such, this chapter draws on what Fincham and Bradbury (1990) referred to as the "behavioral" and "mediational" traditions of research; that is, our focus is both on observable behaviors and subjective factors (e.g., affect) in marriage.

In particular, our aims are to provide a conceptual overview of the literature and to suggest directions that may lead to a better understanding of how and why marriages change. This focus on change in marriage reflects the fact that it has become the central focus of research on marriage over the past quarter of a century (see Rogge & Bradbury, 2002, p. 228). In the first main section of the chapter, we describe the emotional climate of marriage, arguing that it is crucial to make a distinction between positive and negative affect in marriage. Next, we discuss the importance of taking a developmental perspective for understanding marriage, and then we review and critique various theoretical models of how marriages change. We also discuss several factors that influence why marriages change in particular ways. Finally, we draw a number of conclusions and make recommendations based on current findings, including the emerging evidence that there are multiple distinct trajectories that lead to marital distress and divorce.

Emotional Climate of Marriage

Examining change in marriages requires specifying *what* changes (Rogge & Bradbury, 2002). One construct that is useful in summarizing much of what changes is the "emotional climate," a phrase we use to capture the mix of positive and negative affect that characterizes particular marriages and differentiates them from one another. Emotional climate is a broad umbrella term that covers spouses' affective experiences (e.g., love, hostility) and the overt expression of affect in a couples' day-to-day life together (e.g., interest, warmth, support, antagonism, anger).

The overall emotional tenor of a marriage is, of course, unlikely to be evident in any single encounter, and the affect couples experience and express fluctuates some on a day-to-day basis, making it difficult to assess it accurately without "sampling" the marriage across time and place. Spouses who might ordinarily be poor listeners are sometimes uncharacteristically attentive; a particular kind of situation might bring out a couple's propensity toward antagonism but afford little opportunity for them to show affection.

As noted in Figure 8.1, the emotional climate of a marriage can be summarized in the context of two core constructs, *affection* and *antagonism*. Although a couple can be located anywhere in the two-dimensional space created by the affection and antagonism dimensions, the four corners represent archetypical emotional climates: warm (i.e., high affection and low antagonism), tempestuous or stormy (i.e., high affection and high antagonism), hostile (i.e., low affection and high antag-

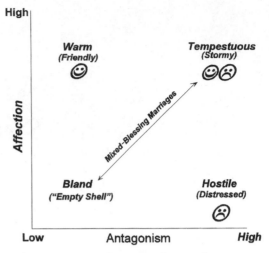

Figure 8.1. A two-dimensional space for describing the emotional climate of marriages.

onism), and bland (i.e., low affection and low antagonism).[1] Figure 8.1 also depicts a diagonal corridor that ranges from bland, or "empty shell," to tempestuous marriages. This corridor represents marriages that are mixed blessings in terms of emotional climate; that is, they have a fairly equal ratio of positive and negative elements.

Our focus on two separate dimensions of emotional climate represents a departure from most research on marital change. The majority of longitudinal research on marriages has assessed changes in one construct, marital satisfaction (Noller & Feeney, 2002; Rogge & Bradbury, 2002), and much of this research has assumed that conflict and antagonism are *the* key predictors of marital satisfaction (e.g., Christensen & Walczynski, 1997; Notarius, Lashley, & Sullivan, 1997). There is growing recognition, however, that enduringly happy relationships involve more than just the absence of antagonism and strife – affectionate and supportive behaviors are also important (Bradbury, Cohan, & Karney, 1998; Gottman & Levenson, 2000; Huston & Houts, 1998; Huston & Vangelisti, 1991; Reis & Gable, 2003; Vangelisti, 2002).

Indeed, the distinction between positive and negative affect is crucial. Treating affection and antagonism as if they could be described along one continuum would imply that dyads who are high in affection are low in antagonism, and vice versa, but affection coexists in varying degrees with antagonism (Gottman, 1994; Huston & Houts, 1998; Huston & Melz, 2004). Indeed, the correlations between affectionate and antagonistic marital behaviors are often quite low, and factor analyses have supported the empirical distinction between positive and negative aspects of marriage (Huston & Vangelisti, 1991; Smith, Vivian, & O'Leary, 1990). Similarly, Gable, Reis, and Elliot (2003) have argued that positive and negative emotions comprise two distinct systems, and Fincham and Beach (this volume; Fincham, Beach, & Kemp-Fincham, 1997) have argued that global measures of marital quality are actually composed of empirically separable positive and negative elements. Moreover, the effects of affectionate and antagonistic dimensions on marital satisfaction are not additive: Aversive behaviors and affectionate behaviors often interact so that the unsatisfying impact of antagonistic interactions is heightened when it occurs in a context of low affection and alleviated when it appears in an otherwise affectionate relationship (Caughlin & Huston, 2002; Gottman, 1994; Huston & Chorost, 1994).

As suggested by the evidence that the impact of antagonism on satisfaction is buffered by high affection, spouses do not merely experience the emotional climate of marriage, they also interpret and evaluate it. Antagonistic behaviors are taken to mean something different to spouses when they are embedded in an affectionate relationship than when they take place in a marriage largely devoid of affection (Caughlin & Vangelisti, in press). Thus, although our focus in this chapter is on the connections between the emotional climate and marital satisfaction and stability, it is worth keeping in mind that these connections are mediated or moderated (or both) by various cognitive processes (see Fletcher, Overall, & Friesen, this volume, for a review).

Indeed, the overall emotional climate of a marriage (e.g., affectional expression, antagonism) is associated with spouses' perceptions of their partner's responsiveness and contrariness (Huston & Houts, 1998), and perceived partner responsiveness, in turn, is linked to relational outcomes (Reis, Clark, & Holmes, 2004). Not surprisingly, the association between affectionate marital behavior and marital satisfaction is at least partly mediated by perceptions of partners' responsiveness (Miller, Caughlin, & Huston, 2003). Given the connection between warm and responsive behaviors and secure attachment styles (Reis et al., 2004), it is likely that the emotional climate would influence (and be influenced by) spouses' working models of attachment, as well as by their working model of their spouses' dispositions toward them (Feeney, Noller, & Roberts, 2000).

Importance of a Developmental Perspective

Assessing affection and antagonism at any given point in time provides a snapshot view of the emotional tenor of marriage, but such snapshots also can be mapped over time to provide a more developmental perspective. Given the widespread interest in changes in marital satisfaction, it might seem like developmental issues would be central to the marital literature. However, limitations in much of the marital research may obscure our understanding of how marriages change over time. To explain why this is so, it is useful to consider five couples shown in Figure 8.2. Each couple is represented by a particular type of shape (e.g., heart, octagon).

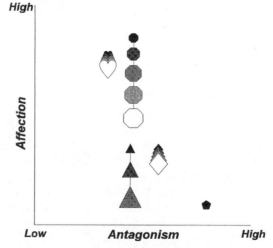

Figure 8.2. The early marital trajectories of emotional climate for five couples.

The placement of each shape represents the couples' levels of affection and antagonism at a particular point in time. Most of the shapes appear in a sequence representing the time dimension. The five smallest (and darkest) shapes represent the newlywed period for the five couples. Each lighter (and larger) shape signifies a later assessment at annual intervals. The series of octagons, for example, shows a couple who began marriage with a high level of affection that declined sharply over the first few years of marriage. The single pentagon stands alone in the figure (rather than in a sequence like the others), indicating that the couple divorced before the emotional climate of their marriage could be assessed a second time.

Although the five couples depicted in Figure 8.2 are hypothetical, the trajectories are based loosely on different outcomes observed in the Process of Adaptation in Intimate Relationships (PAIR) Project, a 13-year longitudinal study of marriages (Huston, Caughlin, Houts, Smith, & George, 2001).[2] The placements of the couples in the figure approximate the mix of affectionate and antagonistic elements of couples who experienced different relational outcomes: The hearts are similar to the Married–Happy couples (who were still married and reported being satisfied after 13 years), the diamonds are comparable to the Married–Not Happy couples (who were still married after 13 years but did not report being satisfied), the pentagon is like the group of couples who quickly divorced (before their second anniversary), the triangles are akin to the Divorced–Early couples (who divorced between 2 and 7 years), and the octagons correspond to the Divorced–Later couples (who stayed married at least 7 years but divorced before 13 years).

The main differences among these outcome groups are illustrated by the representative shapes. Those who quickly divorced, like the pentagon, were distinguished as newlyweds by high levels of antagonism and low levels of affection; that is, their emotional climate was quite hostile compared with other couples. The Married–Happy and Divorced–Later couples, like the darkest (smallest) heart and darkest (smallest) octagon, began marriage with a great deal of affection and moderate levels of antagonism. That is, these groups were similar to each other as newlyweds, although the Divorced–Later couples were even higher than the Married–Happy couples in terms of affectionate interaction. Over the first few years of marriage, however, the Divorced–Later group dropped precipitously in levels of affection, whereas the Married–Happy groups remained nearly stable in terms of affection and antagonism. The Divorced–Early group and the Married–Not Happy group (like the darkest triangle and darkest diamond) had very similar emotional climates as newlyweds. These couples' marriages started off with more of a "mixed-blessing" marriage than did the other groups; they generally were less affectionate than the Married–Happy and Divorced–Later couples, but more affectionate than the couples who quickly divorced. The Married–Not Happy and Divorced–Early couples also were less antagonistic than those who quickly divorced. The Married–Not Happy group was slightly, but significantly, more antagonistic than the Married–Happy couples were as newlyweds. In short, the Married–Not Happy and Divorced–Early groups began marriage with comparable climates. They were distinguished over the first few years of marriage, however, by a steep drop in affection for the Divorced–Early couples, whereas the Married–Not Happy group retained a fairly stable emotional climate.

Some of the details from the PAIR Project findings are discussed in more detail later in this chapter, but the overview of the results just summarized (and roughly illustrated in Figure 8.2) is sufficient to underline the importance of a developmental perspective. First, consideration of developmental issues highlights the need to assess the emotional climate periodically. Most longitudinal studies of marriage do not do so; for instance, studies assessing marital interaction usually look in on marriage at a single time point to predict subsequent changes in satisfaction (Noller & Feeney, 2002). Studies of this general design have produced unquestionably important results, but they provide an incomplete, sometimes misleading, basis for understanding how and why marriages change. Consider, for example, a hypothetical study of the couples summarized in Figure 8.2. For the sake of argument, assume that each shape in the figure represents enough couples that group differences would be statistically and substantively significant. Imagine that this hypothetical study assessed the emotional climate only when the couples were newlyweds and then followed up with the couples after the pentagons, diamonds, and octagons divorced. Such a study, which would have data only on the darkest shapes depicted in Figure 8.2, probably would suggest that high antagonism predicts divorce, and this would be an accurate conclusion because high antagonism was characteristic of the pentagon couples. This conclusion would also be somewhat misleading, however, because neither of the other two divorced groups – the octagons and the triangles – were particularly antagonistic as newlyweds.

Moreover, this hypothetical study probably would fail to reveal much of a connection between newlywed affection and divorce, as the couples highest and lowest in affection both ended up divorcing. Only a study that samples the emotional climate over time can reveal the importance of declining affection as a precursor of divorce. Such changes in the emotional tenor of marriages are important because individuals' judgments of marriage are not based only on a single point in time. Spouses' perceptions of how their marriage has changed give them information about the likely future of the marriage, and this projection, coupled with the sense of what the marriage once was like, can shape their evaluations of the current state of the relationship (Huston & Burgess, 1979; Karney & Frye, 2002). Compare, for instance, the clear (largest) octagon to the clear (largest) diamond in Figure 8.2. With a snapshot assessment at that time, both would be characterized as having somewhat of a mixed-blessing marriage, with the octagon's marriage being slightly warmer than that of the diamond couple. A single assessment might suggest that these couples would likely have similar outcomes or that the octagons were headed for a more successful relationship, but a more complete developmental view suggests that the octagon actually represents a couple headed toward divorce (Huston et al., 2001), possibly because the perceived (and actual) loss of affection influences the way the octagon couples might view their current marriage.

Notice also that if one examines the emotional climate only one time, the particular time selected can greatly influence the findings. If a different hypothetical investigation examined the third point for each shape instead of the first, for instance, the results would be very different. The pentagon couples would not be assessed at all because they would have divorced before the sampling period; consequently, the study would reveal little association between antagonism and divorce. However, by the third time period, the octagons and triangles would have begun their steep drops in affection, meaning that the study might conclude that the absence of affection was associated with divorce. In other words, the results would be essentially contradictory to those obtained with a single assessment of the same couples a few years earlier.

This problem with the timing of a single assessment is compounded in studies in which the assessments of affection and antagonism are made at various developmental stages for couples within a sample (Huston et al., 2001). In such cases, the conclusions about the significance of affection and antagonism in accounting for distress or divorce may reflect the composition of the sample in terms how long the typical couple has been married when the study began. When many of the couples studied have been married for a number of years, for example, a large portion of the couples who are headed for divorce may have already experienced changes in the emotional climate and declines in satisfaction. In such cases, it is impossible to determine whether some aspect of the emotional climate of the marriage caused the distress or divorce or whether an unaffectionate and antagonistic climate is a symptom of rising dissatisfaction (Bradbury et al., 1998; Huston et al., 2001; Noller & Feeney, 2002).

Finally, little of the research on predictors of marital stability has considered life-stage issues. This is somewhat surprising given the copious research on the transition to parenthood on marriage (for review, see Huston & Holmes, 2004) and the work documenting overall declines in satisfaction over the course of marriage (Johnson, Amoloza, & Booth, 1992; Vaillant & Vaillant, 1993; VanLaningham, Johnson, & Amato, 2001). The few studies that have investigated emotional climate at various life stages suggest that the connections between emotional climate and marital outcomes probably depend on how long couples have been married. Zietlow and Sillars (1988), for example, compared long-term marriages to those of shorter duration and found that couples who had been married at least 30 years engaged in more frequent reciprocal confrontation (e.g., personal criticisms, hostile questions) when discussing salient conflict issues. That is, couples who had been married for a long period exhibited high levels of negative reciprocity, which often is implicated as one of the best predictors of dissatisfaction and divorce (e.g., Gottman, 1998). Given that most couples already married 30 years will stay married (U.S. Census Bureau, 2002), Zietlow and Sillars's work suggests that negative reciprocity probably does not predict divorce among long-term couples. Along similar lines, Pasupathi, Carstensen, Levenson, and Gottman's (1999) research comparing older couples with younger couples suggests that responsive listening is connected to marital satisfaction among younger couples but not among long-term couples.

Although the existing research from across the life course highlights the potential importance of developmental issues, there are some challenges in interpreting such work. Because few investigations have lasted for much more than a decade (cf. Kelly & Conley, 1987), it is difficult to separate cohort effects from developmental changes (Zietlow & Sillars, 1988). Also, different associations between measures of emotional climate and marital satisfaction among marriages of different length could reflect the fact that groups of long-term couples, by definition, do not include couples who divorced in the early or middle years of marriage. Caughlin (2002), for example, suggested that there are probably different styles of enacting particular patterns of interaction and that only some of these styles are related to divorce. Gottman, Coan, Carrere, and Swanson (1998) found that some forms of negativity (e.g., expressions of belligerence, contempt, and defensiveness) forecast divorce, but other forms of negativity were not significantly associated with marital stability. It is possible that couples who exhibit the more pernicious forms of negative reciprocity would have divorced before they could participate in a study of long-term couples such as that by Zietlow and Sillars. Thus, the lack of connection between negative reciprocity and dissatisfaction among older couples might be due to these couples, engaging primarily in a fairly harmless form of the pattern.

Clearly, more research is needed to understand whether (and why) the connection between emotional climate and marital outcomes depends on the life stage of the marriage. Nevertheless, this possibility further highlights the importance of considering developmental issues in marriage, even when the available data are not perfect (e.g., when developmental and cohort effects cannot be separated). Of course, considering developmental issues requires an understanding of what changes over the course of marriage and when. Our review thus far implies that it is important to examine the emotional climate of marriage over time, but the literature suggests at least four ways that the climate may change.[3]

Models of Marital Change

Emergent Distress Model

The most prevalent account of why marriages change is rooted in social learning, or behavioral models, which focus on how positive and negative behavior shapes how spouses come to feel about one another (Bradbury et al., 1998; Fincham & Beach, 1999; Karney & Bradbury, 1995). Although scholars sometimes discuss the role of positive behaviors, numerous studies in this tradition have found that the levels of negative behaviors are correlated with satisfaction more strongly than are the levels of positive behaviors (Gottman, 1994; Huston & Vangelisti, 1991; Kurdek, 1995; Wills, Weiss, & Patterson, 1974). Consequently, research taking a behavioral perspective has tended to focus on negative behaviors, usually as they occur within the context of relational conflict (Bradbury et al., 1998).

This view of marital relationships implies a model of change that has been summarized most explicitly as the erosion model (Clements, Cordova, Markman, & Laurenceau, 1997; Clements, Stanley, & Markman, 2004; Markman, 1979). This model presumes that marriages begin with "high degrees of positive factors, such as attraction, love, commitment, trust, friendship, and intimacy" (Clements et al., 1997, p. 342). This affection, however, is not seen as predictive of ultimate relational outcomes; as Notarius and his colleagues (1997) argued, "it is not how loving the partners are to each other in good times that make or breaks a marriage; it is how the partners deal with conflict" (p. 219). The emergent distress model suggests that antagonistic behaviors – particularly during conflict – erode the positive aspects of marriage over time (Clements et al., 2004).

Probably the best known variant of an emergent distress model is Gottman's (1993, 1994) cascade model of divorce. In this model, Gottman (1994) suggested that divorce typically results from a sequential process, beginning with a decline in marital satisfaction, "which leads to consideration of separation or divorce, which leads to separation, which leads to divorce" (p. 88). Gottman proposed that this process is impelled by marital interaction that is more negative than positive. Although the cascade model implies a role for affectionate behaviors, Gottman identified four antagonistic

and uncooperative behaviors (criticizing, showing contempt, expressing defensiveness, and stonewalling) as "integral in powering the cascade" (p. 110).

Implicit in much of the research taking an emergent distress perspective is the assumption that the negative behaviors that erode affection result from poor conflict management skills (Clements et al., 2004; Kline, Pleasant, Whitton, & Markman, this volume). The assumption that a lack of skills is at the root of negative behaviors is so pervasive that authors frequently use the phrases *communication skills* and *conflict behaviors* synonymously (e.g., Cohan & Kleinbaum, 2002; McNulty & Karney, 2004). Consequently, marital interventions based on the emergent distress model focus largely on building skills to manage conflicts (for a review of divorce prevention programs, see Monarch, Hartman, Whitton, & Markman, 2002).

ANALYSIS AND CRITIQUE

In many ways, research based on the emergent distress model has been successful. Scholars have identified antagonistic behaviors in couples that foretell diminished satisfaction and divorce at rates statistically greater than chance (e.g., Clements et al., 2004; Gottman, 1994). Also, divorce prevention programs based on the emergent distress model, such as the Prevention and Relationship Enhancement Program, provide benefits such as reducing antagonistic conflict behaviors and diminishing the divorce rate (Hahlweg, Markman, Thurmaier, Engl, & Eckert, 1998; Kline et al., this volume; Markman, Renick, Floyd, Stanley, & Clements, 1993).

There is also evidence that the emergent distress model is far from complete, however. Although the antagonistic behaviors highlighted by the emergent distress model are associated with declining satisfaction, they account for only a relatively small percentage of variation in marital satisfaction (Bradbury, Rogge, & Lawrence, 2001). This is partly because few studies have simultaneously taken into account both of the two broad affective dimensions of the emotional climate of marriage. Unless high levels of antagonism are accompanied by low levels of affection, marital satisfaction does not decline much, if at all (Huston & Chorost, 1994).

Moreover, studies that have used antagonistic behaviors to classify couples as divorced or still married often have implied that this would allow the scholars to predict divorce in other couples at very high rates, often exceeding 90% (e.g., Gottman, 1994; Gottman et al., 1998). However, correct classification rates (whatever data they may be based on) in a particular sample do not indicate prediction rates for couples outside that sample (Clements et al., 2004); indeed, Heyman and Smith Slep (2001) found that variables that were able to predict divorce in one group 69% of the time were only accurate 29% of the time in a second cross-validated sample. Furthermore, the overall prediction of marital stability combines the success of predicting who will remain married with the success of predicting who will divorce. When they examined each of these components separately, Heyman and Smith Slep were considerably more successful at identifying those who remained married than those who divorced. Thus, although the antagonistic behaviors are related to divorce more than would be expected by chance, their predictive utility is more limited than is often portrayed in the literature.

Additionally, some of the tenets of the emergent distress model are untenable. The assumption that all marriages begin with high levels of positive affect, for example, is inconsistent with studies of premarital and newlywed couples, which show that a meaningful minority of couples come to marriage without being particularly satisfied (Clements et al., 2004) and without high levels of love and affectionate interaction (Huston, 1994, Huston et al., 2001; Surra & Hughes, 1997).

Also, although the utility of skills-based interventions suggests that a lack of skills is at least a partial explanation for any emerging distress, antagonistic behaviors in marriage frequently result from factors other than a lack of skills (Canary, 2003; Sillars & Weisberg, 1987). Sometimes antagonistic behaviors reflect existing dissatisfaction. The few studies that have included assessments of marital interaction at multiple points in a marriage suggest that dissatisfaction foreshadows increasing levels of antagonistic elements like criticisms and the demand–withdraw pattern of communication (Huston & Vangelisti, 1991; Noller & Feeney, 1998). Additionally, dissatisfied spouses evince communication skills with strangers that they do not with their partner (Birchler, Weiss, & Vincent, 1975; Noller, 1984), and Burleson and Denton's (1997) research demonstrated that the link between antagonistic behaviors and marital dissatisfaction is not mirrored by a similar one between communication skills and satisfaction. Such findings led Burleson and Denton to conclude that antagonism in marriage "may result more from ill will than poor skill" (p. 897).

Disillusionment Model

Like the emergent distress model, the disillusionment model presumes that couples are highly affectionate as newlyweds. Indeed, this assumption is so widespread in Western culture that the authors of a prominent textbook on intimate relationships suggest that "the prototypical North American marriage occurs when people. . . who are flushed with romantic passion pledge to spend the rest of their lives together" (Brehm, Miller, Perlman, & Campbell, 2002, p. 241). Individuals in such blissful relationships are motivated to sustain the romance by idealizing their partner (Miller et al., 2003; Murray & Holmes, 1993; Waller, 1938) and by "minimizing or ignoring information that should give them pause" (Brehm et al., p. 242). Moreover, individuals during courtship and the early part of marriage may engage in impression management behaviors (Huston, 1994; Waller, 1938). Partners may, for example, conceal potential difficulties or uncertainties by dodging certain issues or by engaging in exaggerated displays of affection (Huston, 1994; Miller et al., 2003).

According to the disillusionment model, idealized views of one's partner become more difficult to sustain as spouses' wedding day recedes into the past. Increased interdependence makes it more difficult to conceal problems or maintain exaggerated affection (Huston et al., 2001). Spouses also may become disillusioned if they find that marriage alone does not solve the problems that could be dismissed as "prewedding jitters" during courtship. Additionally, partners' self-verification motives (i.e., the desire to let their spouse see their "authentic" self) may increase after marriage, even if self-verification means that the spouse discovers unflattering qualities (Swann, De La Ronde, & Hixon, 1994). Such factors are viewed as priming couples for declines in affection.

Disenchantment can occur because the loss of affection itself is disillusioning (Kayser, 1993). People marry for love and the hope that they and their mate will retain their ardor over time. When love (Huston et al., 2001; Sprecher & Regan, 1998) and satisfaction (Johnson et al., 1992; Vaillant & Vaillant, 1993; VanLaningham et al., 2001) decline over time, as they usually do, the spouses are disappointed. Some suggest, thus, that when newlywed partners entertain unrealistic fantasies about marriage, they are set up for disappointment. Alternatively, Huston et al. (2001) suggested that some couples who end up divorcing may not so much idealize their partner as fail to see their partner's serious shortcomings. With time such people may find it increasingly difficult to set aside their doubts about their partner, losing hope, for instance, that their inexpressive partner will warm up or that their difficult partner will settle down.

Other scholarship suggests that there is great variation in the extent to which spouses experience disillusionment or disaffection. Neff and Karney (2002) argued, for example, that some marital partners may be able to sustain general illusions that enhance affect, even if they uncover some specific undesirable qualities about each other. Similarly, Murray and her colleagues' (Murray, Bellavia, Rose, & Griffin, 2003; Murray, Rose, Bellavia, Holmes, &

Kusche, 2002) research suggests that individuals' self-esteem and beliefs about whether their partner regards them positively influence how they react to problems or stressors in their relationship: People with high self-esteem who believe their partner regards them highly are less likely than others to see specific problems as a sign of overall relational rejection and are less likely to respond in negative ways to specific stressors. That is, self-esteem and perceptions of the partner's positive regard may protect individuals from general disillusionment, even when specific problems are noticed.

ANALYSIS AND CRITIQUE

Despite the fact that the popular Western view of marriage is consistent with the disillusionment model, the possibility of disillusionment being the root of marital distress and divorce is understudied in the scholarly literature. Considering the importance placed on love by American couples (Brehm et al., 2002), there are shockingly few studies that have assessed constructs such as affectionate behavior and love over time in marriage (Huston, 2000; Noller & Feeney, 2002; also see Aron, Fisher, & Strong, this volume). This makes it difficult to assess the disillusionment model thoroughly.

Nevertheless, the extant research supports two general conclusions about the disillusionment model. First, as noted earlier, studies of premarital and newlywed couples indicate that there is considerable variation early in relationships in terms of affection and satisfaction (Clements et al., 2004; Huston et al., 2001). That is, the disillusionment model assumption that couples typically begin their marriage in a state of bliss is not supported by the existing research.

Second, even though the "blissful beginning" portion of the disillusionment model appears to be, at best, an overstatement, disillusionment does appear to occur in some couples, and the extent of disillusionment is associated with increasing dissatisfaction and with divorce. Much of the research pertaining to this model is based on accounts from formerly married individuals, who frequently identify the loss of affectionate elements as the most salient precursors of divorce (Kayser, 1993; Kitson, 1992). Also, declines in marital satisfaction in the early years of marriage are associated with overly romantic accounts of courtship, like the experience of love at first sight and avid pursuit (Holmberg, Orbuch, & Veroff, 2004). Such studies suggest that the loss of idealization and affection are precursors of declining satisfaction and divorce.

One study that examined love and affectionate behaviors over time was the aforementioned study by Huston and his colleagues (2001). As summarized earlier (and depicted loosely by the pentagon in Figure 8.2), one group of couples began marriage with high antagonism and low affection, then divorced. Clearly, these couples did not idealize their partners as newlyweds, and a hostile marital climate (not disillusionment) foreshadowed divorce for them. However, among the couples who remained married for at least 2 years, a decline in affection over the first 2 years of marriage was the most salient predictor of their eventual divorce (see the octagons and triangles in Figure 8.2 for an illustration). The timing of divorce was predicted by where they began, with couples who divorced early (i.e., between 2 and 7 years) starting marriage with lower levels of affection than couples who divorced later. Because the couples who divorced early were not highly affectionate as newlyweds, their marriages are not described precisely by the disillusionment model, but the declines in affection were reminiscent of disillusionment. The couples who divorced after at least 7 years, on the other hand, evinced both the elevated initial levels of affection and the steep drops in affection described by the disillusionment model. Perhaps the couples who divorced later simply had farther to fall before they became disillusioned, or maybe such couples hung on longer because of the possibility that they could recapture their former, extremely affectionate relationship. Regardless, Huston et al.'s (2001) study strongly suggests that disillusionment foreshadows divorce (except in the couples who divorced

almost immediately afer the wedding). This disillusionment did not appear to result from antagonism, as the emergent distress model would predict: There was no evidence that increases in antagonism were associated with the declines in affection that presaged divorce.

Combined with the studies taking the emergent distress perspective, the evidence for the disillusionment model implies that there are qualitatively distinct pathways to divorce (rather than a single process like the cascade model). Gottman and Levenson (2000, 2002), for example, found that the predictors of divorce within the first 7 years of a 14-year study were different from the predictors of divorce after at least 7 years: Whereas antagonistic behaviors prefigured earlier divorces, the absence of positive expressions, or a neutral affective style, foreshadowed the later divorces. Given that Gottman and Levenson's research included couples who had been married for a number of years before the first phase of the study, the absence of affection could easily represent a later stage in the disillusionment process – after the drop in affection.

Enduring Dynamics Model

The third general model of marital change has been referred to as the perpetual problems model (Huston & Houts, 1998), the maintenance hypothesis (Karney & Bradbury, 1997), and the enduring dynamics model (Caughlin, Huston, & Houts, 2000). Unlike the previous two models, the enduring dynamics perspective suggests that the view of courtship as a period of extreme impression management and idealization is a cultural myth (Surra, Batchelder, & Hughes, 1995). Rather than coming to marriage with uniform bliss, newlyweds have developed views about each other based on their courtship and the stable dispositions that each partner brings to their union (Burgess & Wallin, 1953; Huston & Houts, 1998). That is, rather than having idealized perspectives of each other, newlyweds come to marriage well aware of each other's character flaws and strengths. This model assumes that patterns of behavior emerge in courtship and continue into marriage; thus, the ultimate fate of the relationship is largely determined before the marriage.

ANALYSIS AND CRITIQUE

As noted earlier, there is compelling evidence that engaged and newlywed couples vary meaningfully in terms of affection and antagonism (Clements et al., 2004; Huston, 1994; Huston et al., 2001; Surra & Hughes, 1997). More important, the variation among newly formed couples presages the quality of the relationships years later. The extent of conflict before marriage is positively related to the amount of conflict later in marriage (Huston & Houts, 1998). Also, high satisfaction after more than a decade of marriage is foreshadowed by high levels of love and affectionate communication during the newlywed period (Huston et al., 2001) and by high satisfaction during courtship (Clements et al., 2004). In contrast, antagonism (e.g., feelings of ambivalence and expressions of negativity) among newlyweds is higher among couples who are unhappy after 13 years of marriage than among couples who are happy after the same period (Huston et al., 2001). In short, enduring dynamics appear to account fairly well for variations in satisfaction among couples who stay married.

The notion of enduring dynamics is less useful in predicting divorce, however. If the roots of divorce were apparent early in a relationship, couples who end up divorcing would be lower in affection or higher in antagonism as newlyweds than are couples who stay married. Although Huston et al. (2001) reported that couples who divorced very early in marriage (less than 2 years after the wedding) were particularly high in antagonism and low in affection, this pattern was not evident for the majority of couples who divorced. Indeed, couples who divorced after at least 7 years of marriage were particularly high in affection as newlyweds, even compared with couples who stayed happily married for at least 13 years (Huston et al., 2001). Some explanation besides enduring dynamics (e.g., disil-lusionment) seems necessary to explain such findings.

Accommodation Models

There are at least two broad notions of accommodation in the marriage literature. The first is based on a life cycle notion and suggests that after marriage, some personality difficulties or compatibility issues surface in nearly all marriages. Unlike the disillusionment model, however, an accommodation perspective suggests that these problems are overcome as spouses adapt to each other (Huston, 1994; Waller, 1938). For example, people married to moody spouses may learn to take what their partner says with a grain of salt. Thus, the early part of marriage is portrayed as a time of heightened conflict and negativity, but such antagonism would decline as spouses adjust to each other.

The second notion of accommodation is tied to particular stressful events or behaviors that may arise at varying points in a marriage. We refer to this perspective as the life events form of accommodation. The life events perspective refers both to stressors that originate outside the marital dyad (e.g., economic hardship) and to circumstances that originate inside the dyad (e.g., dissatisfaction caused by one spouse's hurtful behavior).

The particular events or circumstances may vary widely, but this general perspective assumes that there are key periods when relationships are tested and that the way couples adapt or accommodate to those important periods foretells the future course of relationships. Perhaps the most formal model in this genre is Karney and Bradbury's (1995) vulnerability–stress–adaptation model. According to this model, people come to marriage with varying levels of enduring vulnerabilities (e.g., poor conflict-management skills, dysfunctional personality traits). During many periods of marriage, such vulnerabilities may have little impact on marriage (Fincham & Beach, 1999); however, when stressful events occur, couples adapt to those events. According to Karney and Bradbury's (1995) model, the nature and success of spouses' adaptations will be largely determined by the stressful event and by the enduring vulnerabilities that the spouses brought to the union. Barring an exceptionally disruptive stressful event, couples with few enduring vulnerabilities may experience temporary perturbations in their relationship, but usually would adapt so that any declines in relational quality (e.g., declines in affection or rises in antagonism) would be minimal or temporary. In contrast, for couples with extensive vulnerabilities, stressful events would likely serve as a catalyst for relational deterioration and eventual divorce.

ANALYSIS AND CRITIQUE

Overall, the existing evidence contradicts the broad life cycle notion of accommodation; that is, the transition to marriage does not appear to be a time of heightened antagonism or diminished affection that improves as couples adjust. Negativity, on average, does decline in the early years of marriage, but not nearly to the degree that affection declines (Huston et al., 2001). Also, the life cycle accommodation notion would imply that spouses would adapt to any personality issues shortly after marriage, but enduring qualities such as high trait anxiety (or neuroticism) predict antagonistic behaviors early in marriage, and these associations remain remarkably steady for more than a decade (Caughlin et al., 2000). In short, there is little evidence supporting the view that spouses typically accommodate to each other after the transition to marriage.

There is, however, support for a life events perspective of accommodation. Conger and his colleagues (Conger et al., 1990; Conger, Rueter, & Elder, 1999; Cutrona et al., 2003) have conducted a series of investigations showing that the connection between economic hardship and marital distress is mediated by factors such as supportive behaviors between spouses and constructive discussions of conflicts. Although Conger et al. (1999) refered to such mediators as protective factors, they also can be conceptualized as accommodative factors

(i.e., processes by which successful couples are able to adapt to economic difficulties so that marital dissatisfaction is temporary or minimized).

As noted earlier, life events also can involve circumstances that spouses bring on themselves, such as betrayals or other relational transgressions (Arriaga & Rusbult, 1998; Rusbult, Bissonette, Arriaga, & Cox, 1998). Some sort of relational transgression (ranging from mundane to serious) probably happens periodically in most relationships (Arriaga & Rusbult, 1998). Spouses who are willing and able to engage in constructive accommodations to their partner's transgressions can promote relational satisfaction by helping to ensure that transgressions become temporary difficulties rather than catalysts that begin reciprocal destructive behaviors (Arriaga & Rusbult, 1998; Rusbult et al., 1998). According to this perspective, accommodation is not exclusively behavioral because the willingness to act in a prosocial manner (e.g., by forgiving the partner) is based on how spouses interpret transgressions and how those interpretations influence their behavioral preferences (Finkel, Rusbult, Kumashiro, & Hannon, 2002). Factors such as high relational commitment and the tendency to take the partner's perspective shape individuals' reactions to transgressions, making the attributions and emotions about them more positive and the behavioral responses to them more constructive (Arriaga & Rusbult, 1998; Rusbult et al., 1998).

Comparison of the Models

The main characteristics of and distinctions among the models are adumbrated in Table 8.1. Overall, our discussion of the various models suggests that there is partial – but only partial – support for various models. Given that the models imply distinct portraits of change in marriage, how can this be? First, it is important to recognize that the life events form of the accommodation perspective does not refer to the same period in marriage as do the other models. The events that give rise to important accommodation

Table 8.1. *Summary of the Models of Marital Change*

	Model of Change				
Defining features	Emergent distress	Disillusionment	Enduring dynamics	Accommodation Life cycle	Accommodation Life events
Characterization of newlywed period	Highly affectionate	Highly affectionate	Varied according to couples' strengths and flaws	Highly antagonistic	Model makes no claims about early marriage
Critical period for changes	Early years of marriage	Early years of marriage	Courtship (when marital dynamics are established)	Early years of marriage	Periods during and after disruptive events
Crucial changes	Increases in antagonism	Loss of affection	None (strengths and flaws maintained)	Declining antagonism	Disruptive events and how couples adapt to them
Outcomes that model appears to explain best	Very quick or imminent divorce	Divorce after at least several years	Satisfaction among stable marriages	None	Outcomes that are not foreshadowed early in marriage

opportunities can come at various stages in marriage, and they would be unlikely to all occur at the same time in any given sample. At any given time, some couples within a given sample may be experiencing a particular event, but others would not be. If a study examines this same group at different times, other couples may be experiencing important events. Over a large enough sample, the effect of such events would not have an obvious influence on sample averages because there would always be a certain portion of the couples experiencing some potentially troubling event. Thus, studies such as the PAIR Project (which assess couples at regular intervals) are unlikely to uncover broad samplewide evidence of accommodation at any particular time. If the goal of a study is to examine accommodation to life events rather than sampling couples at regular intervals, it probably makes more sense to time the study to coincide with particu-

lar events. In short, the life events version of accommodation is not directly comparable to the other models of change. This discrepancy in time frame among the models emphasizes the importance of carefully considering the timing of phases in longitudinal research on marriage (see Robins, 1990).

Second, different models may best describe changes in different couples. In the PAIR Project, for example, enduring dynamics seem to best explain the differences among couples who continued to be married after 13 years: Happy couples, compared with those who were not happy later, tended to be more affectionate and less antagonistic as newlyweds (Huston et al., 2001), and these differences are tied to enduring qualities that spouses bring to marriage (Caughlin et al., 2000; Miller et al., 2003). Disillusionment appears to be a better description of change in couples who divorced after at least 7 years: They were highly affectionate as newlyweds and experienced steep declines in affection early in marriage (Huston et al., 2001). Disillusionment also seems to partially describe couples who divorced between 2 and 7 years because they did evince sharp declines in affection over time; however, they did not begin their marriage with the highly affectionate quality predicted by the disillusionment model (Huston et al., 2001). Thus, declining affection appears to forecast divorce after at least 2 years of marriage, and the timing of divorce appears to depend on the emotional climate of the marriage early on, with dyads who are very high in initial affection taking longer to divorce (Huston et al., 2001). Also, the few couples who were married less than 2 years in the PAIR Project were exceedingly high in antagonism as newlyweds, which is reminiscent of the final stages of the emergent distress model (Huston et al., 2001). Coupled with other research showing that antagonism predicts divorce in some couples (e.g., Gottman, 1994), emergent distress may indicate the end stage of marriage for some couples. Finally, although the early marital dynamics were related significantly to outcomes such as divorce and dissatisfaction, there were couples in the various groups who did not evince the typical pattern for their group. Perhaps these couples' outcomes are best explained by accommodations made in response to life events; for instance, the few couples who divorced later who were not exceedingly high in newlywed levels of satisfaction may have divorced because of unsuccessful coping with life events.

In short, various models of marital change are useful because no single pathway describes changes in all, or even most, marriages. Even among couples sharing a similar outcome (e.g., divorce), there is considerable variation in the course toward that outcome. This implies that attempts to develop a single explanation or description of divorce are likely to be, at best, incomplete. Concluding that multiple models are useful is merely recognizing that there are multiple developmental processes in marriage.

Predicting Changes in the Emotional Climate of Marriages

The predominant perspective of change in marriage has examined various predictors of marital satisfaction and divorce. Such studies, which typically assess the predictor variables at only one point in time (Noller & Feeney, 2002), are extremely useful but also obscure some developmental aspects of marital dissatisfaction and divorce. Studies that examine predictors of satisfaction at only one time, for instance, cannot demonstrate the importance of disillusionment, which is a notable addition to our understanding of why some couples divorce (Huston et al., 2001). Existing research cataloging predictors of dissatisfaction and divorce must be augmented with more investigations of why the emotional climates of various marriages begin the way they do and why they change in various ways over time. The research that already has been conducted suggests the factors that shape changes in emotional climate include a couple's courtship history, spouses' enduring characteristics, and the life events that couples encounter.

Courtship

Couples come to marriage with a joint history, and that history can presage the course of their union. In the PAIR Project, for instance, couples who divorced very early in marriage (i.e., before their second anniversary) experienced courtships that can be described as rocky and turbulent (Huston & Melz, 2004). The length of their courtships (i.e., the time from when they first started dating to when they verbally committed to marriage) tended to be longer than the average couple's, and they tended to have more downturns (i.e., instances when their commitment declined) than did other couples (Huston, 1994). Qualitative descriptions of their relationships before marriage suggested that they had courtships similar to what Surra and Hughes (1997) called "event-driven" courtships; that is, they were filled with drama, including distress over potential rivals, anger caused by various transgressions, and ambivalence about whether the partner would really make a suitable spouse (Huston & Melz, 2004).

Although the courtships of the PAIR Project couples married only briefly were particularly long, there was not a simple association between the duration of courtship and divorce. Instead, the couples who eventually divorced after being married at least 7 years had significantly shorter courtships than did the other couples in the PAIR Project (Huston & Melz, 2004). These passionate courtships were distinguished by having sex early in the relationship, by falling quickly in love, and by deciding to get married after only a few months of dating. Given this history, partners in such couples may have entered marriage with idealized views of each other, which would have primed them for the disillusionment observed in this group of couples (Huston et al., 2001).

Finally, couples who were still married and happy after 13 years of marriage had courtships that were similar to what Surra and Hughes (1997) called relationship-driven courtships. These courtships tended to be undramatic, and in some ways even mundane; for example, simply spending more time together was a common reason for heightened relational commitment, and these couples were unlikely to experience dramatic events such as temporary breakups (Huston & Melz, 2004). In short, the enduring steadiness that these couples exhibited in their emotional climate over the first years of marriage was forecast by very steady courtships in which feelings of commitment generally increased steadfastly until the partners decided to marry.

Enduring Characteristics of Spouses

Individuals' relatively stable and enduring characteristics (e.g., personality traits and attachment styles) influence their relationships (Simpson, Winterheld, & Chen, this volume). There is ample evidence, for example, that trait anxiety or neuroticism, which involves being prone to negative moods and being emotionally labile, is associated with dissatisfaction (Bouchard, Lussier, & Sabourin, 1999; Caughlin et al., 2000; Karney & Bradbury, 1997) and divorce (Kelly & Conley, 1987; Kurdek, 1993; Tucker, Kressin, Spiro, & Ruscio, 1998). A complete review of the literature on personality in marriage is beyond the scope of this chapter; however, two points are important here.

First, although there are now well-documented associations between certain personal qualities and marital dissatisfaction and/or divorce, very few investigations have studied the processes underlying such associations. The research that does exist suggests that the association between personality traits and the emotional climate of marriage is varied and complex. One way that individual differences influence marital outcomes is through behaviors. Trait anxiety (aka neuroticism), for example, is associated with antagonistic behaviors that are, in turn, related to marital dissatisfaction (Buss, 1991; Caughlin et al., 2000). Trait anxiety in one partner also elicits negative behaviors and emotions from the other spouse (Buss, 1991; Caughlin et al., 2000). Additionally, one person's disposition can influence the entire interpersonal tenor of a relationship; for instance, trait anxiety is associated with dyadic patterns of behavior, such as the demand–withdraw conflict pattern (Caughlin & Vangelisti, 2000).

Not only do personal characteristics influence behaviors in marriage, they influence the evaluations of those behaviors. People with an expressive (aka psychologically feminine) personality, for example, are likely to see the best in their partner (Miller et al., 2003). Also, Côté and Moskowitz (1998) found that when behavior was discrepant from individuals' dispositional tendencies, they experienced more negative affect than did people for whom the behavior was concordant. Thus, not only are spouses high in trait anxiety likely to engage in more antagonistic behaviors than are other spouses, but they may experience less positive affect than do other spouses when they or their partner engage in affectionate behaviors.

Moreover, the varied processes connecting personality to the emotional climate in marriage (and to various marital outcomes) are further complicated by the fact that the impact of one's personal qualities probably depends on the particular relational situation. Johnson and Booth (1998) compared individuals who remained married over a 12-year period to people who divorced and remarried during the same period. Although the remarried individuals showed more stability in dispositions than would be expected by chance, the connections between a problematic disposition and marital quality varied widely across remarried individuals' two marriages. Johnson and Booth concluded that either the effects of a problematic personality are "influenced by the spouse's characteristics" or different marital relationships make "certain personality traits more or less salient in their influence on marital problems" (p. 900). In sum, the connections between personality and the emotional climate and outcomes of a marriage are undoubtedly complex, and considerably more research is needed to understand this complexity.

The second point regarding individuals' enduring characteristics and marital development is that individual differences may be related to some aspects of development but not to others. Both Karney and Bradbury (1997) and Caughlin et al. (2000) reported that trait anxiety or neuroticism was related to initial levels of dissatisfaction but was not an important predictor of changes in satisfaction. In the PAIR Project, newlywed measures of trait anxiety were related to dissatisfaction both when the couples were newlyweds and 13 years later (Caughlin et al., 2000). Such findings suggest that neuroticism might be most related to enduring dynamics in marriage (rather than to accommodation, disillusionment, or emergent distress).[4] Also, the characteristics that are associated with divorces early in marriage are not necessarily the ones that predict divorces later. Being high in conscientiousness (i.e., the tendency to adhere to moral standards and norms and to be responsible and persistent) appears to diminish the chances that one will divorce early in marriage but does not appear to prevent eventual divorce (Bartolic, Jarvis, & Huston, 2003; Tucker et al., 1998).

Life Events

Various life events can influence the developmental course of marriage. The term life events is usually conceptualized as referring to external stressors (Bradbury et al., 1998; Fincham & Beach, 1999), but some important life events are instigated by couples. For example, premarital childbirth is a predictor of subsequent dissatisfaction and instability (e.g., Billy, Lentil, & McLaughlin, 1986; Kurdek, 1991). Most research on life events has catalogued whether certain events are related to satisfaction and divorce without examining whether such events are associated with early marital climate or changes in that emotional climate.

Presumably, events that predict divorce do so, in part, because they provoke increased antagonism. Consistent with this possibility, Orbuch, Veroff, Hassan, and Hayricks (2002) reported that premarital childbirth is associated with destructive conflict in marriage. Also, economic hardships can lead to heightened hostility in marriage (Conger et al., 1990, 1999). However, the research by Conger and his colleagues suggests that couples who accommodate such events successfully (e.g., by engaging in constructive conflict resolution) are likely to experience such events as temporary perturbations, whereas other couples may begin to experience emergent distress. That is, even negative life events that are associated with divorce are probably not related to marital dissolution in a simple deterministic manner. Instead, life events are likely to serve as catalysts for change, and different couples will adapt to such changes in various ways (Karney & Bradbury, 1995).

Conclusions and Future Directions

Considering the Impact of Ethnicity

Although there has been much progress understanding how and why marriages change, there are some important issues that need to be addressed in future research. Despite the surge in longitudinal research on marriage, little is known about how developmental processes differ across various ethnic groups (Karney, Kreitz, & Sweeney, 2004; Veroff, Devine, & Hachette, 1995). There are some exceedingly difficult challenges involved with addressing this issue, but the existing research suggests that entry into marriage, marital lifestyles, and the factors that affect developmental processes are affected by the ethnic and social context of couples. There are differences across ethnic groups in the overall divorce rate, and ethnic differences in age at marriage, premarital childbirth, and education, all of which have been found to be associated with divorce (Sweeney & Phillips, 2004). More important, various predictors of the developmental course of marriage appear to operate differently in different ethnic and subcultural groups. The connection between discord and having a shorter marriage, for example, may be stronger for Black couples than for White couples (Adelmann, Chadwick, & Baerger, 1996). Also, high negativity from wives, which is known to presage declining satisfaction in White couples, does not appear to do so in Black couples (Veroff et al., 1995). This suggests that the meaning of (and therefore the outcomes of) a particular emotional climate is shaped by one's ethnic background (Orbuch & Veroff, 2002). In short, notwithstanding the considerable challenges involved in gathering data about marital development in ethnically diverse samples, there is little doubt that future research would benefit from greater attention to ethnicity in marriage (Karney et al., 2004).

Methodological Issues That Are Highlighted by the Heightened Focus on Positive Elements of Marriage

As implied by our distinction between affection and antagonism, a salient trend in the literature is to pay greater attention to the positive elements in marriage (Bradbury et al., 1998; Huston et al., 2001; Reis & Gable, 2003; Vangelisti, 2002). Considering that the Western ideal in marriage revolves more around positive elements (e.g., love) than around the absence of negative elements, this is an overdue development.

This trend also highlights the importance of some conceptual and methodological cautions that have been made about research on marital interaction more broadly. As Noller and Feeney (2004) noted, there is a bias favoring observational methods for gathering data about marital interaction, even when such measures are not necessarily the most valid indicator conceptually. This problem is likely to be particularly acute when assessing positive aspects of marriage. Obviously, laboratory studies would not adequately capture the level of affection that takes place in couples' day-to-day life together. Although we would observe many instances of verbal support, smiling, and the like in the laboratory, we would miss other, perhaps more telling, forms of affection, such as how often spouses hug, kiss, and express their affection in overtly sexual ways.

Some positive behaviors can be usefully observed in laboratories. For instance, Pasch and Bradbury (1998) developed a clever technique for eliciting social support interactions: One spouse (the helpee) was instructed to think about something that he or she would like to change about him or herself, and the other (the helper) was told to respond however he or she wanted (also see Cobb, Davila, & Bradbury, 2001). This procedure is clearly valuable in some instances; indeed, Pasch and Bradbury found that the measure of social support explained variation in satisfaction that was not explained by observations of conflict behaviors. Moreover, because some supportive behaviors in marriage are unlikely to be recognized as such by the spouses (Gottlieb, 1985; Story & Bradbury, 2004), outside observations can be important.

Still, there are a number of conceptual reasons to believe that laboratory measures of support are likely to be less than optimal assessments of much of what is most important about social support. First, any measure based on frequencies of supportive comments loses out on potentially important distinctions in the quality of the messages: A long history of research shows that some social support messages tend to be more effective than others (for reviews, see Burleson & Goldsmith, 1998; Goldsmith, 2004). Second, most observational methods used to assess social support (particularly those that occur outside the context of naturally occurring support) will have threats to their external validity. There is an ongoing debate on a similar issue regarding observations of marital conflict (e.g., Noller & Feeney, 2004), but this potential problem is even more serious with social support. Unlike conflict, which often revolves around ongoing and long-term issues (Roloff & Johnson, 2002), supportive communication is often tied to particular events, and the nature of the event impacts the utility of various support strategies. What is considered effective support in a standardized laboratory situation is unlikely to be the most effective strategy in response to more serious crises, which may be the ones with the greatest potential to affect relationships (Bolger, Foster, Vinokur, & Ng, 1996). Third, the provision of support can be threatening to one's identity and self-esteem because it can imply that the person receiving support is unable to deal with the problem alone (Bolger, Zuckerman, & Kessler, 2000; Goldsmith, 2004). Consistent with this possibility, Bolger et al.'s (2000) diary investigation indicated that individuals studying for the bar examination experienced increased distress when they reported receiving support from their partner, but they experienced diminished stress when their partner reported support that was not perceived by the exam candidate. Bolger et al. (2000) concluded that the most effective type of support was *invisible support*, which is helpful without incurring the costs associated with more obvious support. Invisible support may include actions that take place outside the recipients' awareness (e.g., the support provider takes care of a problem that the partner would have otherwise had to handle) or may involve supportive actions that are "accomplished in such a skillful way that, although the information about the transaction is available to the recipient, the transaction is not coded as enacted support" (p. 959). Clearly, such indirect and covert support would be diffi-

cult to assess in a laboratory setting. Moreover, Bolger et al.'s (2000) research suggests that the most obvious (and observable) social support may be counterproductive, which further undermines the assumption that the frequency of social support acts is a useful way to summarize supportive interaction.

There are additional reasons to question whether observational methods are always the best choice for assessing support (e.g., see Goldsmith, 2004), but our purpose is not to suggest that such methods are inappropriate. Instead, it is important to question the assumption that observational procedures are inherently superior or that they represent an advance in and of themselves (e.g., Story & Bradbury, 2004). In fact, some of the ingredients of the emotional life of a marriage – the good (e.g., sexual ardor) and the bad (e.g., violence) – are unlikely to show themselves in laboratory research. The behavioral tradition, more generally, assumes that encounters can be set up in a laboratory that distill the interpersonal essence of a marriage. This seems unlikely. We know from courtship data that single events often transform relationships, moving couples toward marriage, or leading them to break up (Surra & Hughes, 1997). Retrospective interviews gathered from divorced individuals (e.g., Weiss, 1975) suggest that the path to divorce can sometimes be tortured, with periods of emotional upheaval punctuating relatively quiescent periods. Other marriages end, though, with little more than a few angry flare-ups. Single events – such as an affair – can transform the emotional climate of a marriage, but they do not always have such an impact. All of these observations suggest the importance of knowing and tracking the long-term history of the marriage, so that we can understand why particular events might prove to be a turning point in some marriages and not others.

Future research, particularly that with the relatively new focus on positive elements in marriage, should begin with the recognition that different methods (and sometimes multiple methods) are appropriate in different circumstances and that the investigators' research questions (not methodological biases rooted in the behavioral tradition) should drive measures and methods (see Noller & Feeney, 2004).

The Multiple Pathways to Dissatisfaction and/or Dissolution

Finally, one of the most exciting nascent trends in the marital literature involves the recognition that there is not a single unitary process leading to marital distress and divorce (Clements et al., 2004; Gottman & Levenson, 2000; Huston et al., 2001). Some couples begin marriage with lower marital satisfaction than most other couples but remain married indefinitely, whereas other couples begin marriage very satisfied but end up divorcing. Moreover, the predictors of dissatisfaction and divorce are not always the same; for instance, stable characteristics such as trait anxiety appear to be more strongly related to satisfaction than they are to divorce (Caughlin et al., 2000). Even the processes leading to divorce are not uniform, with some couples who eventually divorce beginning marriage with high levels of hostility and divorcing quickly, others beginning marriage with moderate amounts of both positive and negative elements before becoming quite low in affection, and still others beginning marriage with exceedingly high levels of affection that are not sustained over the early years of marriage. Also, the predictors of divorce are different for divorces that occur earlier in marriage compared with those that happen later in marriage. For instance, heightened negativity may presage divorces that happen early in marriage whereas low levels or declining levels of affection forecast later divorces (Gottman & Levenson, 2000; Huston et al., 2001).

Such findings are important theoretically because they provide a more thorough account of divorce. They also have potentially significant practical implications. If very different aspects of the emotional climate lead to divorce in different couples, this would suggest the need for very different intervention and prevention programs, depending on couples' particular weaknesses. Couples who begin marriage with very high levels of antagonism might benefit from traditional conflict skills training programs (see Kline et al., this volume). If a couple appears to be most susceptible to declining affection, however, skills training may be ineffective, whereas a program designed to maintain affection might be more useful. Obviously, the details of such programs would need to be developed and tested systematically, but one promising theoretical framework for developing such work is Aron's self-expansion model (Aron, Fisher, & Strong, this volume; Aron, Norman, Aron, McKenna, & Heyman, 2000). Although spouses who enter marriage with unsustainable idealized views of their partner probably cannot help but experience some loss in affection, perhaps engaging in novel and exciting activities with one's partner can minimize the loss – or help replace idealized views of one's partner with other positive judgments that are based more firmly in the partner's actual character. Regardless of the details of any particular program, the possibility that different couples might require different types of interventions emphasizes the crucial need for future research to recognize that there is not one single process leading to distress and divorce.

Footnotes

1. To simplify our discussion, high and low values in Figure 8.1 should be thought of in comparison to other couples (i.e., as if the values were all standardized). That is, a hostile couple is defined by being much higher than most couples in antagonism and much lower than most couples in affection. The position of a particular couple in this two-dimensional space depends, in principle, on both the intensity and the frequency of affection (positive affect) and antagonism (negative affect).

2. The sample was originally identified by license records of marriages in a four county area of central Pennsylvania. The 168 couples were similar to other couples in the region in terms of ethnicity (98.8% were White), age on the

wedding day (23.5 years for husbands, 21 years for wives) and parents' occupations. Data were gathered from the couples on three occasions, spaced about a year apart, beginning when they were newlyweds (i.e., married about 2 months).

3. If one counts the two forms of accommodation separately, there are five distinct models, as summarized in Table 8.1.

4. Of course, given that several other studies have shown a connection between neuroticism and divorce, the enduring dynamics perspective cannot completely describe the impact of neuroticism on marriage.

References

Adelmann, P. K., Chadwick, K., & Baerger, D. R. (1996). Marital quality of Black and White adults over the life course. *Journal of Social and Personal Relationships, 13*, 361–384.

Aron, A., Norman, C. C., Aron, E. N., McKenna, C., & Heyman, R. E. (2000). Couples' shared participation in novel and arousing activities and experienced relationship quality. *Journal of Personality and Social Psychology, 78*, 273–284.

Arriaga, X. B., & Rusbult, C. E. (1998). Standing in my partner's shoes: Partner perspective taking and reactions to accommodative dilemmas. *Personality and Social Psychology Bulletin, 24*, 927–948.

Bartolic, S., Jarvis, M. O., & Huston, T. L. (2003, November.) *How does personality shape connubial bonds?* Paper presented at the meeting of the National Council on Family Relations, Vancouver, British Columbia.

Billy, J. O. G., Lentil, N. S., & McLaughlin, S. D. (1986). The effect of marital status at first birth on marital dissolution among adolescent mothers. *Demography, 23*, 329–349.

Birchler, G. R., Weiss, R. L., & Vincent, J. P. (1975). Multimethod analysis of social reinforcement exchange between maritally distressed and nondistressed spouse and stranger dyads. *Journal of Personality and Social Psychology, 31*, 349–360.

Bolger, N., Foster, M., Vinokur, A. D., & Ng, R. (1996). Close relationships and adjustment to a life crisis: The case of breast cancer. *Journal of Personality and Social Psychology, 70*, 283–294.

Bolger, N., Zuckerman, A., & Kessler, R. C. (2000). Invisible support and adjustment to stress. *Journal of Personality and Social Psychology, 79*, 953–961.

Bouchard, G., Lussier, Y., & Sabourin, S. (1999). Personality and marital adjustment: Utility of the five-factor model of personality. *Journal of Marriage and the Family, 61*, 651–660.

Bradbury, T. N., Cohan, C. L., & Karney, B. R. (1998). Optimizing longitudinal research for understanding and preventing marital dysfuction. In T. N. Bradbury (Ed.), *The developmental course of marital dysfunction* (pp. 279–311). New York: Cambridge University Press.

Bradbury, T. N., Fincham, F. D., & Beach, S. R. H. (2000). Research on the nature and determinants of marital satisfaction: A decade in review. *Journal of Marriage and the Family, 62*, 964–980.

Bradbury, T., Rogge, R., & Lawrence, E. (2001). Reconsidering the role of conflict in marriage. In A. Booth, A. C. Crouter, & M. Clements (Eds.), *Couples in conflict* (pp. 59–81). Mahwah, NJ: Erlbaum.

Brehm, S. S., Miller, R. S., Perlman, D., & Campbell, S. M. (2002). *Intimate relationships* (3rd ed.). Boston: McGraw-Hill.

Burgess, E., & Wallin, P. (1953). *Engagement and marriage*. Philadelphia: Lippincott.

Burleson, B. R., & Denton, W. H. (1997). The relationship between communication skills and marital satisfaction: Some moderating effects. *Journal of Marriage and the Family, 59*, 884–902.

Burleson, B. R., & Goldsmith, D. J. (1998). How the comforting process works: Alleviating emotional distress through conversationally induced reappraisals. In P. A. Anderson & L. K. Guerrero (Eds.), *Handbook of communication and emotion* (pp. 245–280). San Diego, CA: Academic Press.

Buss, D. M. (1991). Conflict in married couples: Personality predictors of anger and upset. *Journal of Personality, 59*, 663–688.

Canary, D. J. (2003). Managing interpersonal conflict: A model of events related to strategic choices. In J. O. Greene & B. R. Burleson (Eds.), *Handbook of communication and social interaction skills* (pp. 515–549). Mahwah, NJ: Erlbaum.

Caughlin, J. P. (2002). The demand/withdraw pattern of communication as a predictor of marital satisfaction over time: Unresolved issues and future directions. *Human Communication Research*, 28, 49–85.

Caughlin, J. P., & Huston, T. L. (2002). A contextual analysis of the association between demand/withdraw and marital satisfaction. *Personal Relationships*, 9, 95–119.

Caughlin, J. P., Huston, T. L., & Houts, R. M. (2000). How does personality matter in marriage?: An examination of trait anxiety, interpersonal negativity, and marital satisfaction. *Journal of Personality and Social Psychology*, 78, 326–336.

Caughlin, J. P., & Vangelisti, A. L. (2000). An individual difference explanation of why married couples engage in the demand/withdraw pattern of communication. *Journal of Social and Personal Relationships*, 17, 523–551.

Caughlin, J. P., & Vangelisti, A. L. (in press). Conflict in dating and married relationships. In J. Oetzel & S. Ting-Toomey (Eds.), *The Sage handbook of conflict communication*. Thousand Oaks, CA: Sage.

Christensen, A., & Walczynski, P. T. (1997). Conflict and satisfaction in couples. In R. J. Sternberg & M. Hojjat (Eds.), *Satisfaction in close relationships* (pp. 249–274). New York: Guilford Press.

Clements, M. L., Cordova, A. D., Markman, H. J., & Laurenceau, J. (1997). The erosion of marital satisfaction over time and how to prevent it. In R. J. Sternberg & M. Hojjat (Eds.), *Satisfaction in close relationships* (pp. 335–355). New York: Guilford Press.

Clements, M. L., Stanley, S. M., & Markman, H. J. (2004). Before they said "I do": Discriminating among marital outcomes over 13 years. *Journal of Marriage and Family*, 66, 613–626.

Cobb, R. J., Davila, J., & Bradbury, T. N. (2001). Attachment security and marital satisfaction: The role of positive perceptions and social support. *Personality and Social Psychology Bulletin*, 27, 1131–1143.

Cohan, C. L., & Kleinbaum, S. (2002). Toward a greater understanding of the cohabitation effect: Premarital cohabitation and marital communication. *Journal of Marriage and Family*, 64, 180–192.

Conger, R. D., Elder, G. H., Jr., Lorenz, F. O., Conger, K. J., Simons, R. L., Whitbeck, L. B., et al. (1990). Linking economic hardship to marital quality and instability. *Journal of Marriage and the Family*, 52, 643–656.

Conger, R. D., Rueter, M. A., & Elder, G. H., Jr. (1999). Couple resilience to economic pressure. *Journal of Personality and Social Psychology*, 76, 54–71.

Côté, S., & Moskowitz, D. S. (1998). On the dynamic covariation between interpersonal behavior and affect: Prediction from neuroticism, extraversion, and agreeableness. *Journal of Personality and Social Psychology*, 75, 1032–1046.

Cutrona, C. E., Russell, D. W., Abraham, W. T., Gardner, K. A., Melby, J. N., Bryant, C., & Conger, R. D. (2003). Neighborhood context and financial strain as predictors of marital interaction and marital quality in African American couples. *Personal Relationships*, 10, 389–409.

Faust, K. A., & McKibben, J. N. (1999). Marital dissolution: Divorce, separation, annulment, and widowhood. In M. Sussman, S. K. Steinmetz, & G. W. Peterson (Eds.), *Handbook of marriage and the family* (2nd ed., pp. 475–499). New York: Plenum Press.

Feeney, J. A., Noller, P., & Roberts, N. (2000). Attachment and close relationships. In C. Hendrick & S. S. Hendrick (Eds.), *Close relationships: A sourcebook* (pp. 185–201). Thousand Oaks, CA: Sage.

Fincham, F. D., & Beach, S. R. H. (1999). Conflict in marriage: Implications for working with couples. *Annual Review of Psychology*, 50, 47–77.

Fincham, F. D., Beach, S. R. H., & Kemp-Fincham, S. I. (1997). Marital quality: A new theoretical perspective. In R. J. Sternberg & M. Hojjat (Eds.), *Satisfaction in close relationships* (pp. 275–304). New York: Guilford Press.

Fincham, F. D., & Bradbury, T. N. (Eds.). (1990). *The psychology of marriage: Basic issues and applications*. New York: Guilford Press.

Finkel, E. J., Rusbult, C. E., Kumashiro, M., & Hannon, P. (2002). Dealing with betrayal in close relationships: Does commitment promote forgiveness? *Journal of Personality and Social Psychology*, 82, 956–974.

Gable, S. L., Reis, H. T., & Elliot, A. J. (2003). Evidence for bivariate systems: An empirical test of appetition and aversion across domains. *Journal of Research in Personality*, 37, 349–372.

Goldsmith, D. J. (2004). *Communicating social support*. New York: Cambridge University Press.

Gottlieb, B. H. (1985). Social support and the study of personal relationships. *Journal of Social and Personal Relationships, 2*, 351–375.

Gottman, J. M. (1993). A theory of marital dissolution and stability. *Journal of Family Psychology, 7*, 57–75.

Gottman, J. M. (1994). *What predicts divorce?* Hillsdale, NJ: Erlbaum.

Gottman, J. M. (1998). Psychology and the study of marital processes. *Annual Review of Psychology, 49*, 169–197.

Gottman, J. M., Coan, J., Carrere, S., & Swanson, C. (1998). Predicting happiness and stability from newlywed interactions. *Journal of Marriage and the Family, 60*, 5–22.

Gottman, J. M., & Levenson, R. W. (2000). The timing of divorce: Predicting when a couple will divorce over a 14-year period. *Journal of Marriage and the Family, 62*, 737–745.

Gottman, J. M., & Levenson, R. W. (2002). A two-factor model for predicting when a couple will divorce: Exploratory analyses using 14-year longitudinal data. *Family Process, 41*, 83–96.

Hahlweg, K., Markman, H. J., Thurnmaier, F., Engl, J., & Eckert, V. (1998). Prevention of marital distress: Results of a German prospective longitudinal study. *Journal of Family Psychology, 12*, 543–556.

Heyman, R. E., & Smith Slep, A. M. (2001). The hazards of predicting divorce without cross-validation. *Journal of Marriage and Family, 63*, 473–479.

Holmberg, D., Orbuch, T. L., & Veroff, J. (2004). *Thrice told tales: Married couples tell their stories.* Mahwah, NJ: Erlbaum.

Huston, T. L. (1994). Courtship antecedents of marital satisfaction and love. In R. Erber & S. Duck (Eds.), *Theoretical frameworks for personal relationships* (pp. 43–65). Hillsdale, NJ: Erlbaum.

Huston, T. L. (2000). The social ecology of marriage. *Journal of Marriage and the Family, 62*, 209–320.

Huston, T. L., & Burgess, R. L. (1979). Social exchange in developing relationships: An overview. In R. L. Burgess & T. L. Huston (Eds.), *Social exchange in developing relationships* (pp. 3–28). New York: Academic Press.

Huston, T. L., Caughlin, J. P., Houts, R. M., Smith, S. E., & George, L. J. (2001). The connubial crucible: Newlywed years as predictors of marital delight, distress, and divorce. *Journal of Personality and Social Psychology, 80*, 237–252.

Huston, T. L., & Chorost, A. (1994). Behavioral buffers on the effect of negativity on marital satisfaction: A longitudinal study. *Personal Relationships, 1*, 223–239.

Huston, T. L., & Holmes, E. K. (2004). Becoming parents. In A. L. Vangelisti (Ed.), *Handbook of family communication* (pp. 105–133). Mahwah, NJ: Erlbaum.

Huston, T. L., & Houts, R. M. (1998). The psychological infrastructure of courtship and marriage: The role of personality and compatibility in romantic relationships. In T. N. Bradbury (Ed.), *The developmental course of marital dysfunction* (pp. 114–151). Cambridge, England: Cambridge University Press.

Huston, T. L., & Melz, H. (2004). The case for (promoting) marriage: The devil is in the details. *Journal of Marriage and Family, 66*, 943–958.

Huston, T. L., & Vangelisti, A. L. (1991). Socioemotional behavior and satisfaction in marital relationships: A longitudinal study. *Journal of Personality and Social Psychology, 61*, 721–733.

Johnson, D. R., Amoloza, T. O., & Booth, A. (1992). Stability and developmental change in marital quality: A three-wave panel analysis. *Journal of Marriage and the Family, 54*, 582–594.

Johnson, D. R., & Booth, A. (1998). Marital quality: A product of the dyadic environment or individual factors? *Social Forces, 76*, 883–904.

Karney, B. R., & Bradbury, T. N. (1995). The longitudinal course of marital quality and stability: A review of theory, method, and research. *Psychological Bulletin, 118*, 3–34.

Karney, B. R., & Bradbury, T. N. (1997). Neuroticism, marital interaction, and the trajectory of marital satisfaction. *Journal of Personality and Social Psychology, 72*, 1075–1092.

Karney, B. R., and Frye, N. E. (2002). "But we've been getting better lately": Comparing prospective and retrospective views of relationship development. *Journal of Personality and Social Psychology, 82*, 222–238.

Karney, B. R., Kreitz, M. A., & Sweeney, K. E. (2004). Obstacles to ethnic diversity in marital research: On the failure of good intentions. *Journal of Social and Personal Relationships, 21*, 509–526.

Kayser, K. (1993). *When love dies: The process of marital disaffection.* New York: Guilford Press.

Kelly, E. L., & Conley, J. J. (1987). Personality and compatibility: A prospective analysis of marital stability and marital satisfaction. *Journal of Personality and Social Psychology, 52*, 27–40.

Kitson, G. C. (1992). *Portrait of divorce: Adjustment to marital breakdown.* New York: Guilford Press.

Kurdek, L. A. (1991). Marital stability and changes in marital quality in newlywed couples: A test of the contextual model. *Journal of Social and Personal Relationships, 8*, 27–48.

Kurdek, L. A. (1993). Predicting marital dissolution: A 5-year prospective longitudinal study of newlywed couples. *Journal of Personality and Social Psychology, 64*, 221–242.

Kurdek, L. A. (1995). Predicting change in marital satisfaction from husbands' and wives' conflict resolution styles. *Journal of Marriage and the Family, 57*, 153–164.

Markman, H. J. (1979). Application of a behavioral model of marriage in predicting relationship satisfaction of couples planning marriage. *Journal of Consulting and Clinical Psychology, 47*, 743–749.

Markman, H. J., Renick, M. J., Floyd, F. J., Stanley, S. M., & Clements, M. (1993). Preventing marital distress through communication and conflict management training: A 4- and 5-year follow-up. *Journal of Consulting and Clinical Psychology, 61*, 70–77.

McNulty, J. K., & Karney, B. R. (2004). Positive expectations in the early years of marriage: Should couples expect the best or brace for the worst? *Journal of Personality and Social Psychology, 86*, 729–743.

Miller, P. J., Caughlin, J. P., & Huston, T. L. (2003). Trait expressiveness and marital satisfaction: The role of idealization processes. *Journal of Marriage and Family, 65*, 978–995.

Monarch, N. D., Hartman, S. G., Whitton, S. W., & Markman, H. J. (2002). The role of clinicians in the prevention of marital distress and divorce. In J. H. Harvey & A. Wenzel (Eds.), *A clinician's guide to maintaining and enhancing close relationships* (pp. 233–258). Mahwah, NJ: Erlbaum.

Murray, S. L., Bellavia, G. M., Rose, P., & Griffin, D. W. (2003). Once hurt, twice hurtful: How perceived regard regulates daily marital interactions. *Journal of Personality and Social Psychology, 84*, 126–147.

Murray, S. L., & Holmes, J. G. (1993). Seeing virtues in faults: Negativity and the transformation of interpersonal narratives in close relationships. *Journal of Personality and Social Psychology, 65*, 707–722.

Murray, S. L., Rose, P., Bellavia, G. M., Holmes, J. G., & Kusche, A. G. (2002). When rejection stings: How self-esteem constrains relationship-enhancement processes. *Journal of Personality and Social Psychology, 83*, 556–573.

Neff, L. A., & Karney, B. R. (2002). Self-enhancement in close relationships: A model of global enhancement and specific verification. In P. Noller & J. A. Feeney (Eds.), *Understanding marriage: Developments in the study of couple interaction* (pp. 32–58). New York: Cambridge University Press.

Noller, P. (1984). *Nonverbal communication and marital interaction.* New York: Pergamon Press.

Noller, P., & Feeney, J. A. (1998). Communication in early marriage: Responses to conflict, nonverbal accuracy, and conversational patterns. In T. N. Bradbury (Ed.), *The developmental course of marital dysfunction* (pp. 11–43). New York: Cambridge University Press.

Noller, P., & Feeney, J. A. (2002). Communication, relationship concerns, and satisfaction early in marriage. In A. L. Vangelisti, H. T. Reis, & M. A. Fitzpatrick (Eds.), *Stability and change in relationships* (pp. 129–155). New York: Cambridge University Press.

Noller, P., & Feeney, J. A. (2004). Studying family communication: Multiple methods and multiple sources. In A. L. Vangelisti (Ed.), *Handbook of family communication* (pp. 31–50). Mahwah, NJ: Erlbaum.

Notarius, C. I., Lashley, S. L., & Sullivan, D. J. (1997). Angry at your partner? Think again. In R. J. Sternberg & M. Hojjat (Eds.), *Satisfaction in close relationships* (pp. 219–248). New York: Guilford Press.

Orbuch, T. L., & Veroff, J. (2002). A programmatic review: Building a two-way bridge between social psychology and the study of the early years of marriage. *Journal of Social and Personal Relationships, 19*, 549–568.

Orbuch, T. L., Veroff, J., Hassan, H., & Hayricks, J. (2002). Who will divorce: A 14-year longitudinal study of Black couples and White couples. *Journal of Social and Personal Relationships, 19*, 179–202.

Pasch, L. A., & Bradbury, T. N. (1998). Social support, conflict and the development of marital dysfunction. *Journal of Consulting and Clinical Psychology, 66*, 219–230.

Pasupathi, M., Carstensen, L. L., Levenson, R. W., & Gottman, J. M. (1999). Responsive listening in long-married couples: A psycholinguistic perspective. *Journal of Nonverbal Behavior, 23*, 173–193.

Reis, H. T., Clark, M. S., & Holmes, J. G. (2004). Perceived partner responsiveness as an organizing construct in the study of intimacy and closeness. In D. J. Mashek & A. Aron (Eds.), *Handbook of closeness and intimacy* (pp. 201–225). Mahwah, NJ: Erlbaum.

Reis, H. T., & Gable, S. L. (2003). Toward a positive psychology of relationships. In C. L. Keyes & J. Haidt (Eds.), *Flourishing: Positive psychology and the life well-lived* (pp. 129–159). Washington, DC: American Psychological Association.

Robins, E. (1990). The study of interdependence in marriage. In F. D. Fincham & T. N. Bradbury (Eds.), *The psychology of marriage: Basic issues and applications* (pp. 59–86). New York: Guilford Press.

Rogge, R. D., & Bradbury, T. N. (2002). Developing a multifaceted view of change in relationships. In A. L. Vangelisti, H. T. Reis, & M. A. Fitzpatrick (Eds.), *Stability and change in relationships* (pp. 228–253). New York: Cambridge University Press.

Roloff, M. E., & Johnson, K. L. (2002). Serial arguing over the relational life course: Antecedents and consequences. In A. L. Vangelisti, H. T. Reis, & M. A. Fitzpatrick (Eds.), *Stability and change in relationships* (pp. 107–128). New York: Cambridge University Press.

Rusbult, C. E., Bissonette, V. L., Arriaga, X. B., & Cox, C. L. (1998). Accommodation processes during the early years of marriage. In T. N. Bradbury (Ed.), *The developmental course of marital dysfunction* (pp. 74–113). New York: Cambridge University Press.

Sillars, A. L., & Weisberg, J. (1987). Conflict as a social skill. In M. E. Roloff & G. R. Miller (Eds.), *Interpersonal processes: New directions in communication research* (pp. 140–171). Newbury Park, CA: Sage.

Smith, D. A., Vivian, D., & O'Leary, K. D. (1990). Longitudinal prediction of marital discord from premarital expressions of affect. *Journal of Consulting and Clinical Psychology, 58*, 790–798.

Sprecher, S., & Regan, P. C. (1998). Passionate and companionate love in courting and young married couples. *Sociological Inquiry, 68*, 163–185.

Story, L. B., & Bradbury, T. N. (2004). Understanding marriage and stress: Essential questions and challenges. *Clinical Psychology Review, 23*, 1139–1162.

Surra, C. A., Batchelder, M. L., & Hughes, D. K. (1995). Accounts and the demystification of courtship. In M. A. Fitzpatrick & A. L. Vangelisti (Eds.), *Explaining family interactions* (pp. 112–141). Thousand Oaks, CA: Sage.

Surra, C. A., & Hughes, D. (1997). Commitment processes in accounts of the development of premarital relationships. *Journal of Marriage and the Family, 59*, 5–21.

Swann, W. B., De La Ronde, C., & Hixon, J. G. (1994). Authenticity and positivity strivings in marriage and courtship. *Journal of Personality and Social Psychology, 66*, 857–870.

Sweeney, M. M., & Phillips, J. A. (2004). Understanding racial differences in marital disruption: Recent trends and explanations. *Journal of Marriage and Family, 66*, 639–650.

Teachman, J. D., Tedrow, L. M., & Crowder, K. D. (2000). The changing demography of America's families. *Journal of Marriage and the Family, 62*, 1234–1246.

Terman, L. M., Buttenwieser, P., Ferguson, L. W., Johnson, W. B., & Wilson, D. P. (1938). *Psychological factors in marital happiness*. New York: McGraw-Hill.

Tucker, J. S., Kressin, N. R., Spiro, A., III., & Ruscio, J. (1998). Intrapersonal characteristics and the timing of divorce: A prospective investigation. *Journal of Social and Personal Relationships, 15*, 211–225.

U.S. Census Bureau. (2002). *Number, timing, and duration of marriages and divorces: Fall 1996* (Current Population Reports No. P70-80) [Electronic version]. Washington, DC: U.S. Government Printing Office.

Vaillant, C. O., & Vaillant, G. E. (1993). Is the U-curve of marital satisfaction an illusion? A 40-year study of marriage. *Journal of Marriage and the Family, 55*, 230–239.

Vangelisti, A. L. (2002). Interpersonal processes in romantic relationships. In M. L. Knapp & J. A. Daly (Eds.), *Handbook of interpersonal communication* (3rd ed., pp. 643–679). Thousand Oaks, CA: Sage.

VanLaningham, J., Johnson, D. R., & Amato, P. (2001). Marital happiness, marital duration, and the U-shaped curve: Evidence from a five-wave panel study. *Social Forces, 79*, 1313–1341.

Veroff, J., Devine, E., & Hachette, S. J. (1995). *Marital instability: A social and behavioral study of the early years.* Greenwich, CT: Greenwood.

Weiss, R. S. (1975). *Marital separation.* New York: Basic Books.

Waller, W. (1938). *The family: A dynamic interpretation.* New York: Cordon.

Wills, T. A., Weiss, R. L., & Patterson, G. R. (1974). A behavioral analysis of the determinants of marital satisfaction. *Journal of Consulting and Clinical Psychology, 42,* 802–811.

Zietlow, P. H., & Sillars, A. L. (1988). Life-stage differences in communication during marital conflicts. *Journal of Social and Personal Relationships, 5,* 223–245.

CHAPTER 9

Divorce and Postdivorce Relationships

Marilyn Coleman
Lawrence Ganong
Kim Leon

Public and social scientific attitudes about divorce fall along a continuum. At one end are those that see divorce as the shattering of a family and the cause of most social ills, and at the other end of the continuum are those that see divorce as a stressful but normative life transition (Amato, 2004; Popenoe, 1996). Regardless of where an individual might locate his or her attitudes toward divorce on this continuum, divorce is a common occurrence in Western cultures.

Demographers have estimated that about half of all marriages in the United States end in divorce (Kreider & Fields, 2002). This may be an underestimate of the proportion of marriages that dissolve because many marriages, especially among non-Hispanic Black and Hispanic women, end in permanent separation, rather than divorce (Bramlett & Mosher, 2001). Divorce rates in the United States are higher than in Europe (i.e., 3.9 per 1,000 population in 2003 compared with an average of 1.9 per 1,000 in European countries), but so are marriage rates. In general, divorce rates in Europe, North America, Australia, and New Zealand have followed similar trends over the past

few decades (Allan, Hawker, & Crow, 2004; Goode, 1993).

In this chapter, we examine research and theory on postdivorce relationships. Given the enormous volume of writing on divorce over the last 3 decades, this review is necessarily selective – we do not include research on the effects of divorce on children's well-being, and we examine adults' adjustment only in conjunction with how their reactions to divorce affect subsequent relationships. Space restrictions have led us to ignore, for the most part, the causes of marital dissolution (see Caughlin & Huston, this volume), although postdivorce relationships are clearly tied to predivorce family and couple dynamics. Another self-imposed limitation is that we write as if people experience a single divorce only – this is done for ease of presentation and because most researchers have done the same. The reality for many people is multiple divorces, but this adds so much complexity to the issue of postdivorce relationships that we would need a whole volume to describe it. Finally, we note that the review contains both old and new work – we like typological approaches to research because we think considering patterns and profiles are more informative ways to think about family processes and relationships than the more standard variable approach to describing studies. Consequently, we include a fair number of mature (and some new) typologies in this review.

The Process of Divorce

Although divorce is eventful, it is not a discrete event. Divorce is a process that often begins long before and continues long after the legal decree ending a marriage is filed, especially if the divorcing couple has children. Rather than occurring in an orderly, sequential manner, the process of divorcing is typically experienced as a disorganized and seemingly random unfolding of events, at least until motives are assigned by the divorcing individuals (Hopper, 1993).

Hopper (2001) documented two dominant vocabularies of motive for divorce, but these motives emerged *after* the decision to divorce had been made. Because marriage is seen as both a personal accomplishment and an institution that is supposed to last forever, divorcing individuals feel the need to offer accounts that explain their point of view in such a way as to reduce their responsibility for the marriage ending and to provide culturally acceptable reasons for the divorce. Those who initiated the divorce emphasized individualism over commitment, stressing the need for personal development and fulfillment, areas that they perceived were stifled by marriage. The noninitiators articulated a moralistic vocabulary about commitment and the need to stick with the marriage at all costs. However, both initiators' and nonitiators' accounts for divorce appeared to be unrelated to their feelings regarding the marriage – both groups reported feeling indecisive and ambivalent about the marriage. There also was no pattern in the accounts that distinguished which spouse was ultimately the initiator and which the noninitiator of the

legal divorce. In other words, the one who was most upset by the divorce was not necessarily the noninitiator, and these stances emerged *after* the decision to divorce had been made.

The divorce process is complex regardless of who initiated the separation and regardless of how individuals account for and explain the dissolution to others. Divorce is multifaceted, involving every aspect of a person's life. Bohannan's (1970) model of divorce, the six stations of divorce (i.e., emotional, legal, co-parental, economic, social, and psychic), was an early attempt to capture the complex and comprehensive nature of divorce.

Emotional Divorce

Divorced people can often identify when their marriages began to deteriorate, sometimes years before the decision to divorce. Bohannan argued that the dissolution process begins with emotional divorce, a progression that Kayser (1993) termed *marital disaffection*. Marital disaffection is a weakening over time of the emotional attachment to the partner. Positive feelings become more neutral; the person becomes estranged from and indifferent to the spouse. When couples cannot effectively manage conflicts they may become emotionally disengaged, and affective disengagement is associated with lower marital satisfaction (Smith, Vivian, & O'Leary, 1990). Longitudinal research on marital satisfaction and stability has identified a common pattern in which negative ways of handling conflict (e.g., criticism, defensiveness, contempt) lead to affective disengagement, which is highly predictive of divorce (Gottman, 1994).

Although emotional divorce and marital disaffection do not necessarily lead to legal divorce, a marriage in which there is increasing emotional disengagement between partners becomes less stable and morphs into what Sternberg (1986) called *empty love*. That is, the relationship is maintained because of commitment to the institution of marriage, but the couple no longer experiences passion or intimacy. Cuber and Harroff (1965) described a similar process of movement from a vital to a devitalized marriage, in which the initial excitement, romance, physical attraction, and sharing wanes, leaving only commitment to the institution of marriage. Cuber and Harroff referred to such marriages as *habit cages* – the couple essentially lives like roommates rather than romantic partners and has little in common except perhaps children and their shared memories. Although the gradual shift from vital to devitalized couples has been attributed to change in the partners over time, this is unlikely to be the sole problem. In satisfying marriages, partners may grow in new directions, but they also become more interdependent. The shift from a vital to a devitalized relationship may involve a process of affective disengagement.

A common response to emotional divorce is grief. The absence of a loved one or the loss of the ideal of the perfect marriage and family is a kind of death. Unlike death, however, divorce usually initially involves rejection of one partner by another. Additionally, there is seldom the same level of community support for divorcing individuals that is experienced by a bereaved spouse. There is no mourning ritual such as a funeral or memorial service to bring closure to the process. Friends, not wanting to choose sides, may abandon both divorcing partners, making divorce a very lonely process often accompanied by hurt and anger.

Legal Divorce

In Western culture the courts are responsible to dissolve a marriage because marriage is a legal relationship. In other cultures, this may be handled by a religious group or by contract. In the United States, legal divorce has changed from a fault to a no-fault system, meaning that spouses do not have to provide grounds for divorce.

In recent years, a movement has grown that is akin to returning to fault divorce. Covenant marriage laws that have been enacted in a few states offer couples an option of choosing a marriage with more stringent legal requirements than the standard marriage. Requirements for covenant marriage include premarital and marital counseling and a 2-year separation period preceding divorce, except in cases where marital fault can be established (Nock, Wright, & Sanchez, 1999). It is too early to tell if covenant marriages will lower the divorce rate or even if they will be widely accepted. Currently, covenant marriage laws have only been passed in Arizona, Arkansas, and Louisiana, and few people have chosen this option – fewer than 5% in Louisiana (Hawkins, Nock, Wilson, Sanchez, & Wright, 2002). Feminist scholars have raised concerns about the possibility of covenant marriages trapping women in abusive relationships (women would have to substantiate allegations of abuse in court) or that the legal costs of having to show cause would create financial burdens for women (Carriere, 1998; Stewart, 1999).

Even though marital dissolution is a rather simple legal procedure, this aspect of divorce frequently bewilders divorcing persons. Expecting justice for perceived wrongs by the other, divorcing people sometimes feel betrayed that legal decisions that seem unfair are nonetheless legal (Mandell, 2002). Aspects of the legal divorce that are relatively new include court-ordered parenting plans that spell out arrangements regarding the child and mandated mediation for couples who cannot agree on custody and child support (Mason, Fine, & Carnochan, 2004).

Co-Parental Divorce

The most emotionally painful and lingering aspect of divorce is often co-parental divorce. In the United States, joint legal custody has been mandated in many states unless there is cause to not do so. This means that both parents have input into decisions regarding the child's education, religious training, and health care. Joint physical custody, which allows both parents to spend considerable time with the child, is rapidly becoming the preference of courts. Sharing legal or physical custody (or both) requires parents to work together in some fashion. For some, co-parenting is not difficult, but for many, perhaps most, co-parenting is challenging or impossible.

It is important for children's well-being for divorced parents to figure out ways to co-parent without acrimony. Children who have the worst outcomes after parental separation are those whose parents were in high conflict during the marriage and continue fighting after divorce (Amato & Booth, 1996). Children are especially harmed if they perceive that parents' fighting is about them. The best predictor of child outcomes after divorce is parental conflict (Cummings & Davies, 1994). Children whose parents can be *cooperative colleagues* (Ahrons, 1994) and establish a reasonably businesslike working arrangement as co-parents do about as well as those whose nondivorced parents engage in low levels of conflict. It appears to be parental conflict more so than divorce that affects children negatively (Hetherington & Kelly, 2002).

Economic Divorce

The economic divorce often leaves both partners feeling cheated, but dividing up resources is essential because the husband and wife are legally recognized as an economic unit in the United States. The extent to which the couple is considered a single economic unit varies from state to state, however. In some states the couple is considered legally to be one person. In those states, all assets are considered marital assets no matter who brought the resources to the marriage. Couples often do a lot of fighting over money, both before and after divorce. It is likely that many of these heated arguments are not really about money, however, but rather represent underlying issues of power and control.

Once assets have been divided, husbands and wives are usually economically free of each other unless they have minor-aged children together. Despite alterations in legal custody arrangements, mothers still tend to be awarded physical custody of children (Grall, 2000). Consequently, fathers are often legally required to pay child support to their former wives.

Parents paying child support often complain that they pay too much, and parents receiving child support complain that they do not receive enough money to provide for the children. There is truth in both arguments, although parents seldom have accurate ideas regarding the costs of raising a child, and it is rare that both divorced parents do not suffer financially (McManus & DiPrete, 2001). Despite stiffer child support laws, only 45% of parents received the full amount of child support in 2001, 8% more than in 1993 (U.S. Census Bureau Press Release, 2003).

Community Divorce

The community divorce is when partners detach from their old couple friends but have yet to begin the search for a new social support system. Often a time of both anger and despair, people commonly find that when they are not part of a couple, they are no longer invited to social events. Their friends may make them feel uncomfortable and unsupported. Seeking new partners, especially for men, is a frequent means of overcoming the discomfort of dealing with the loss of the social life. In the community divorce, individuals become cognizant of the lack of support they receive from social institutions such as religious groups, school, the legal system, and the health care system.

Psychic Divorce

Psychic divorce is the separation of self from the personality and influence of the former spouse (Hagestad & Smyer, 1982). Weddings are accompanied by rituals and ceremonies attended by friends and family – showers, bachelor parties, rehearsal dinners, the marriage ceremony itself. Divorce has no such ceremonies. It is a difficult time, especially for the noninitiators of the divorce for whom the transition is unexpected and often unwanted and for those who have been married a long time. Divorce at middle age or older is an off-time process in the life course and is likely to be viewed more often as a crisis than is divorce that occurs when individuals are younger. Divorce often occurs early; a third of first marriages end within 10 years and 20% within 5 years (National Center for Health Statistics, 1993).

Three kinds of bonds have to be dissolved when partners end a marriage (Hagestad & Smyer, 1982). First, partners must let go of their emotional attachment to the other person. This bond is the emotional energy that is invested in the relationship. The emotional cathexis is built during the dating period, and dissolving those bonds is a bit like reversing the courtship process.

The second type of bond that must be dissolved is role attachment. The social marker establishing this bond is engagement, represented by the giving of the engagement ring. Married persons, especially those who have long been married, may be attached to the role of spouse, independent of their feelings toward their spouse. They may want to keep "husband" or "wife" in their role portfolio – it is a key part of their identity. DeGarmo and Kitson (1996) found the divorce adjustment was easier for women who were less heavily invested in their role as wife. Not long ago, women's identities were almost completely obliterated by marriage. Women took the husband's name and became Mrs. John Doe, signing letters and introducing themselves this way. Divorce, therefore, meant a loss of identity as well as social status. Even today, divorced and single adults are not accorded the same social status as are married adults.

The final bond that must be dissolved is that of routines. Marriage typically includes established habits and routines. For example, a division of labor is common. As a result, divorce is often accompanied by feelings of incompetence for those who have never done their own laundry or cooking or for those who know nothing about procuring insurance or cleaning out the gutters. Individuals experience a sense of loss when they cannot rely on established routines.

Spiritual Divorce

Kaslow (2000) added religious or spiritual dimensions to the divorce process. For many

people, marriage is a sacred institution, and marital dissolution is a wrenching experience because it represents a religious transgression that involves cutting ties with formal and informal social support networks, a crisis in beliefs, and feelings of guilt and blame. Little research has been done on this aspect of divorce.

Adjustment of Divorced Persons and Postdivorce Relationships

It has been well established that divorced individuals differ from married people on a number of variables. Some of these factors (e.g., lower income, more social isolation, greater number of negative life events) contribute to divorce, but they also can be the result of divorce (Lorenz et al., 1997; Marks, 1996). For example, alcohol abuse often goes up among men and depression increases among women following divorce (Wu & Hart, 2002). Some patterns of less stable behavior that occur after divorce (e.g., engaging in casual sex) appear to be temporary, however, and the lives of others, primarily women, improve. Amato (2000) concluded from his review of research that differences in well-being between divorced and married adults were due to difficulties with solo parenting, a conflictual relationship with the former spouse, economic hardship, and declines in support.

Gender Issues

Although one might think that divorce would be more difficult for women than men, this does not appear to be the case for women as a group. Acock and Demo (1994) reported that mothers perceived their social life, career opportunities, and personal happiness to improve after divorce. Others have reported that women feel more in control after divorce (e.g., even if their income is less, they have control over how it is spent) and that their self-esteem improves (Riessmann, 1990). Divorce may be more difficult for specific groups of women, however, – middle-aged or older women, especially those with little work experience, and the spouse who was left, rather than the leaver, seem to suffer the most (Sweeney, 2002).

Women are considerably more likely to initiate divorce than men (England, 2000; Hetherington & Kelly, 2002). In fact, Hetherington reported that women initiated 68% of the divorces in her samples of middle-class White mothers. This does not necessarily mean that the divorce process is easy for women. Perhaps women are more likely to initiate divorce because they monitor relationships more closely, are more aware when there are problems with the relationship (Gottman, 1994), and feel that they have more to lose by staying in a relationship that they view as unsatisfactory. For example, about half of the women in Hetherington's studies indicated that lack of marital communication and affection stimulated their decision to divorce.

Divorce does take a toll on women, but no more so than do unhappy marriages. Kiecolt-Glaser and Newton (2001) found that women's immune systems are more disrupted than men's during marital conflict, that unhappily married and recently divorced women frequented doctors or hospitals 3 times more often than happily married women, and that they reported more health problems (e.g., headaches, fatigue, colds, and flu) than happily married women.

Adjustment difficulties often have serious implications for postdivorce relationships, both for the maintenance of ties with children and co-parents and for the creation of new romantic relationships (and relationships that may accompany a new partner, such as new in-laws and stepchildren). Some adjustment problems, such as depression and substance abuse, hinder the maintenance of family relationships – in fact, several of the explanatory models for children's outcomes have to do with increased parental stress due to divorce and the subsequent negative effects of stress on parenting abilities (Ganong & Coleman, 2004; Simons, 1996). According to these models, poor parental adjustment, particularly for residential parents, results in parent–child relationships that are generally characterized by underinvolved parenting, parent–child conflicts, and inconsistent discipline (Amato, 1993; Hetherington, 1998). Single parents often face a great deal of stress and a lack of social support, both of which may diminish their parenting abilities. It has been suggested that newly remarried parents become depressed or preoccupied with the challenges of remarriage and stepfamily life, leading them to neglect their children or at least fail to maintain satisfying parent–child relationships (Hetherington, 1998). It should be noted that most research supporting these models is from secondary data sets, so knowledge of postdivorce parenting dynamics is incomplete.

Other reactions to divorce may serve to motivate an individual to work harder at remaining involved in their children's lives (if the person no longer resides with their children) or to focus their energies on maintaining a positive relationship with children and co-parents. There is some research on fathers that suggests that many fathers become more invested in their children after divorce, rather than less (Braver, 1998).

Adults' poor adjustment to divorce can also greatly reduce the chances of finding and developing new romantic relationships. In contrast, it could be argued that loneliness, stress and worry over finances, and other negative consequences of divorce can serve to motivate individuals to find new partners. Few scholars have examined the interconnections of adults' reactions to divorce and their subsequent dating behaviors.

Patterns of Adjustment

Despite the well-documented stress of divorce, researchers have found divorcing individuals to be resilient for the most part. Hetherington and Kelly (2002) identified six patterns of adjustment evident in the individuals in Hetherington's longitudinal studies. The *Enhanced* group, predominantly women, became more competent, well adjusted, and fulfilled over time. Working seemed to be related to resilience for the women, and 85% of them indicated they would work even if they did not have financial reasons for doing so. Work was a source of social support and romantic partners, and this group tended to remarry more successfully.

The *Goodenoughs* were the largest group in Hetherington's studies, and this group was composed fairly equally of men and women. Women in the Goodenough group dealt effectively for the most part with postdivorce stressors, but they were not as resilient as Enhancers, so tensions and challenges sometimes threw them off balance. Ten years after divorce, the Goodenough group's remarriages looked similar to their first marriages.

Men, in particular, appeared to cope with divorce and the accompanying stressors of caring for themselves by finding new partners. To avoid anxiety and depression, they tended to seek women who would look after them without being demanding or expecting much in return. Hetherington labeled those who were eager to find new partners *Seekers*. Perhaps not surprisingly, their second marriages were lower in satisfaction than their first marriages.

Hetherington labeled the often-stereotyped group of primarily men who engaged in behaviors such as buying convertibles, dressing youthfully, and having a lot of casual sex as *Swingers*. This style of coping was especially prominent the first year after divorce with nearly 25% of the men engaging in these behaviors. Many of them had been rather conventional before divorce, and they soon returned to more conventional behaviors. They became Goodenoughs over time, and they were no more likely to engage in extramarital affairs after remarrying than those in the other groups. Women, even if they had wanted to be Swingers, were unlikely to be able to sustain such a lifestyle. Women are far more likely to have physical custody of the children than are men, so they seldom have either the time or the money to live a swinging lifestyle.

The *Competent Loners* were a small group of mostly women (10% of Hetherington's sample at 1 year postdivorce and 15% at 10 years postdivorce) who were quite skilled and self-sufficient. These women were not seeking new partners although they were often involved in intimate relationships. Some remarried, but most were content to remain single.

The group that did not cope well, the Defeated, did especially poorly the first year after divorce. This group was large (about a third of the sample) and dominated by men. The gender difference diminished over time, and the size of the group became smaller, with 10% of the women and 12% of the men still in this category. The women who remained *Defeated* often did so because of poverty; they lacked education and job skills.

Postdivorce Relationships

Co-Parenting Relationships

One of the challenges of divorce for parents is to separate the marital and parental roles (Whiteside, 1998). The task is to maintain roles as co-parents while dissolving co-partner roles (Coleman & Ganong, 1995). Married parents typically merge these roles or blur the boundaries between them, and maintaining one without the other is difficult for some divorced people. Consequently, co-parenting is one of the most difficult aspects of postdivorce relating.

Ahrons (1983) coined the term *binuclear family* to describe postdivorce family structure – two households linked by the child. From her longitudinal data set, Ahrons identified five post-divorce co-parenting styles. In the case of *Dissolved Duos*, one parent, almost always a father, disappeared from the child's life. The co-parents no longer had any relationship at all, and one parent no longer had a relationship with the child. *Perfect Pals* continued to be best friends and to function as parents nearly identically to how they did prior to divorce. These parents attended school and other child-related events together and planned and talked about child-related issues regularly. Because the common expectation is that divorced couples will not get along, these couples puzzle others. Perfect Pals were unlikely to remarry, and it is surmised that many potential partners would be unable to handle the intimacy of a new partner who remained Perfect Pals with their ex-spouse. More study needs to be made of their postdivorce coping abilities. A less close but functional style was *Cooperative Colleagues*, a type of co-parenting typified by courtesy and respect for each other's parenting abilities and cooperation on issues related to the child. These couples would not refer to each other as best friends, but they managed to put aside their differences for the sake of the child. According to Ahrons, the keys to positive co-parenting are maintaining respect for the other parent, communicating constructively about the children as well as exchanging information and problem solving about them, and finding ways to share responsibility for child-rearing tasks. To successfully co-parent, couples have to believe it is important, that it is best for the children, and make it a priority (Whiteside, 1998). The majority of divorced couples are able to cooperate reasonably well as co-parents.

Less functional co-parenting styles included *Angry Associates* and *Fiery Foes*, two types that differed mainly in the intensity of their dysfunctional behaviors. These co-parents were unable to focus on the best interests of their children and spent their energies competing and fighting with each other. There was complete lack of respect for each other's parenting ability, and returning to court over custody and child support was common. Individuals in these co-parenting arrangements sometimes remarried to gain allies to help them fight the ex-spouse. These high-conflict parents may sabotage each other, withhold information, spend considerable time in court over custody issues, and even become neglectful and abusive (Whiteside, 1998).

CO-PARENTAL CONFLICT

Not surprisingly, high conflict between the ex-spouses often results in less contact between the noncustodial parent (typically the father) and the child. This usually means that relationships between the child and the noncustodial parent's extended family are cut off as well (Whiteside, 1998). Severing these ties can impoverish a child's life in terms of potential resources, knowledge of his or her heritage, and emotional support. In some instances, however, reduced contact may be a good thing. There is evidence that children who show the most problems are from families where the relationship between the ex-spouses is highly conflictual but they continue to maintain a great deal of contact (Amato & Booth, 1996).

As the divorce process continues, many of these warring couples resolve some of their conflicts and are able to establish clearer boundaries between parenting and their angry relationships with the ex-spouse. There is evidence that the longer and more conflictual the legal process, the worse the co-parental relationship. There is also evidence that fathers who initiate divorce proceedings and take more responsibility for the divorce are more likely to fulfill parental responsibilities (Baum, 2003). However, father's fulfillment of parental responsibilities is complicated. Child support policies have been predicated on the notion of fathers having only one set of children to support. In fact, increases in multiple marital and cohabiting relationships means that nearly 75% of remarried men have multiple sets of children to support (emotionally and financially) both inside and outside their current relationship. The more complex the father's parenting responsibilities, the less likely he is to meet them (Manning, Stewart, & Smock, 2003).

Attempts to educate divorcing parents through court-ordered programs seem to help parents focus more on their children's well-being and less on their anger at the other parent, although the research focus of these programs has primarily been on parents' perceived satisfaction with the program (Kelly, 2002). Utilizing mediation rather than the traditional legal system, which is adversarial, seems to be helpful as well (Hahn & Kleist, 2000; Kelly, 1996), although it is likely that couples who are already somewhat cooperative may be more likely to choose mediation than those who are highly conflicted. Parallel parenting, with parents doing the best they can when the child is with them but not sharing information or interacting with the other parent, seems to be a solution for some couples. However, when parents cannot communicate due to high levels of unresolved anger or distrust, a situation may develop in which the child has to pretend the other parent doesn't exist while spending time with one parent, which is stressful for children (Ricci, 1997). Johnston (1995) recommended that a co-parenting counselor or arbitrator may be necessary to help parents who are unable to relate in a reasonable way (e.g., without verbal abuse, physical threats, and sometimes violence). It is also important for parents engaging in parallel parenting to avoid relying on the child to carry messages back and forth.

Parent–Child Relationships

Much of the research on parent–child relationships has focused on how these relationships affect children's development after divorce (for reviews, see Amato, 2000 and Emery, 1999). However, researchers increasingly have turned attention to studying the dynamics of parent–child relationships after divorce. Most of these studies have been limited to the relationship between children and their nonresidential mother (Montgomery, Anderson, Hetherington, & Clingempeel, 1992). Studies of father–child relationships have primarily examined only the frequency of contact and not relationship quality. Considering that child outcome is negatively affected by parental conflict (Amato, Loomis, & Booth, 1995), it is likely that children who have high contact with their nonresidential fathers will do well if the parental relationship is low conflict.

Forming New Romantic Relationships After Divorce

Most divorced adults find another romantic partner. In the United States, the probability of cohabiting after the dissolution of first marriage is 70% after 10 years (Bramlett & Mosher, 2001); however, Black women are significantly less likely to cohabit after

first marriage than are Hispanic or White women. For many, cohabitation is a prelude to remarriage; for others, cohabitation is an alternative to legal unions (Booth & Crouter, 2002).

Census estimates project that in the United States nearly 85% of divorced people remarry (Kreider & Fields, 2002), although the likelihood of remarriage is much higher for White divorced women than for Black divorced women (Bramlett & Mosher, 2001). Although the remarriage rate is lower in other Western societies, most divorced people eventually cohabit or remarry (Allan et al., 2004; Wu & Penning, 1997).

REMARRIAGE

The United States has the highest remarriage rate in the world. About half of all U.S. marriages are remarriages for one or both partners (U.S. Census Bureau, 2000, Table 145), and more than 10% of U.S. remarriages are third- or higher order for one or both partners (National Center for Health Statistics, 1993). Remarriages are slightly more likely to end in dissolution than are first marriages (about 25% after 5 years; more probable for Black than White women and for women with children than for those without) (Bramlett & Mosher, 2001).

Divorced individuals in the United States tend to remarry quickly – on average, in less than 4 years (30% remarry within 1 year; Wilson & Clarke, 1992). Hetherington's data suggest that remarriage may be a path toward better adjustment for some divorced adults. For example, the Seekers in her study tried to find a new partner to alleviate anxiety and depression. Alternately, some argue that it is the other way around: Better adjusted adults are more likely to remarry. A causal link between psychological adjustment and remarriage has yet to be established, however. Amato (2000) posited that if the least fit were selected out of remarriage, the divorced population over time would be increasingly poorly adjusted. In support of Amato's argument, some researchers report that individual functioning improved over time only if they remarried (Ganong & Coleman, 2004).

For women, remarriage is often a way of improving economic circumstances. Although both men and women's living standards are reduced, "most women would have to make heroic leaps in the labor (or marriage) market to keep their losses as small as the losses experienced by the men from whom they separate" (McManus & Diprete, 2001, p. 266). It is unlikely that women often reveal to researchers that their purpose in remarrying was to establish financial security for their children, but it is obvious that this is often a factor (Weaver & Coleman, 2004). Additionally, the women who are least likely to remarry are those who are well educated, financially secure, and who do not have to depend on remarriage for financial security (Oh, 1986). The women most likely to remarry are those with fewer resources and greater economic demands (Schmiege, Richards, & Zvonkovic, 2001).

Regardless of their reasons, however, individuals in the United States are dedicated to the idea of partnerships, especially remarriage, after divorce. Remarriage nonetheless brings with it new challenges that many couples are not prepared to meet. Despite a rate of dissolution that is slightly higher than that for first marriages (Cherlin, 1992), there is little evidence that couples prepare for remarriage in any significant way other than cohabiting (Ganong & Coleman, 1989).

Dating after divorce can be awkward. Individuals who have not been in the "dating game" for a long period of time may not know what to do or how to act. Others may see dating as a chance to go wild and experience things they missed out on when they were dating before their first marriage (e.g., Hetherington's Swingers). Some may remarry quickly to avoid the awkwardness of dating, sometimes only to find themselves in another mediocre or bad marriage.

It is an almost universal finding that children have more difficulty adapting to parental remarriage than do the adults. Some adults may have been emotionally withdrawing from their spouse for years, so they were ready for new romantic relationships long before their marriages ended. The short courtships for remarriage would indicate that, indeed, many people first find a new partner and *then* get divorced. Children, however, are seldom as aware of the emotional divorce process as their parents, so surprise and a sense of loss are common among children. When they no longer share a household with both parents, their time with each parent is considerably less than it had been before divorce. If the nonresidential parent does not stay in close touch with the children (and as many as 50% of children lose contact with their fathers after divorce; Stephens, 1996), they may feel not just loss, but abandonment.

Relationships With Partners' Children

The development and maintenance of remarriages (or cohabiting partnerships) between divorced adults who have no children may not differ dramatically from relational dynamics in first marriages and cohabiting unions when adults do not have children. This is speculation because such relationships have not been studied. What is not speculative is the position that remarriages that create stepfamilies present challenges for adults and children (Ganong & Coleman, 2004). The process of developing a mutually satisfying stepparent–stepchild relationship is challenging because stepparents are trying to build these relationships within the context of ongoing parent–child relationships, ongoing co-parental ties between the stepchildren's parents, and multiple and possibly conflicting expectations of family members.

DEVELOPING STEPPARENT–STEPCHILD RELATIONSHIPS

Few researchers have examined the ways in which stepparents and stepchildren develop their relationships (for a review, see Ganong & Coleman, 2004). Hetherington and Clingempeel (1992) reported that stepfathers initially interacted like *polite strangers* with stepchildren, but over time they became less skilled at controlling and monitoring stepchildren. Bray and Kelly (1998) also found that stepfathers became less involved with stepchildren over the first 2 years, in part because children rebuffed their attempts to engage in "effective parenting skills" (p. 263). However, Bray found, as did Hetherington (1993; Hetherington, Cox, & Cox, 1982) in two earlier studies, that stepfathers who developed the closest relationships with stepchildren had focused on developing warm relationships that were characterized by a high degree of communication with them.

We studied the process of how stepparents, mostly stepfathers, attempted to elicit liking (affinity) from their stepchildren in a small sample (Ganong, Coleman, Fine, & Martin, 1999). We identified three patterns of stepparent affinity seeking. *Continuous affinity seekers* regularly tried to become friends and build affinity with stepchildren, both before and after the remarriage. The *early affinity seekers* initially tried to elicit liking from stepchildren but stopped doing so after remarriage. The early affinity seekers discontinued such efforts after they moved in with their stepchildren, assuming the role of parent, which they apparently saw as incompatible with getting their stepchildren to like them. Finally, one group of stepparents, the *nonseekers*, made few attempts to elicit affinity from their stepchildren. Continuous affinity seekers had the most cohesive relationships with stepchildren, according to both the stepparents and stepchildren. These stepparents engaged in dyadic interactions alone with the stepchildren that were chosen by the child, actions that allowed stepparents and stepchildren to get to know each other without being distracted by the presence and reactions of third persons. These stepparents were more likely to communicate warmth, empathy, and an understanding of children's needs and interests than were the other stepparents. These findings echoed those of earlier studies (Kelly, 1996) and shed light on why step relationships more often are characterized by liking and affection when stepparents focus on developing friendships with stepchildren before they attempt to discipline and set rules for them (Bray & Berger,

1993; Crosbie-Burnett & Giles-Sims, 1994; Hetherington & Clingempeel, 1992). The findings also suggest that affinity-seeking efforts need to be maintained for them to be effective. Disciplining appears to get in the way of affinity seeking, so it may be helpful for stepparents to focus on affinity developing and delay assuming a role as disciplinarian for as long as possible (Kelly, 1996).

What stepparents do to build good relationships with stepchildren is only part of the story. Relational development is a bi-directional process. Good step relationships are created when stepchildren respond to affinity-building efforts. A key to understanding how stepchildren affect relationship-building efforts by stepparents may be to know how they define their relationships with nonresidential parents and stepparents. For example, White and Gilbreth (2001) examined three perspectives on the importance of residential stepfathers and nonresidential fathers on stepchildren: an *accumulation model*, which implies that both men play important roles in children's lives; *a loss model*, which suggests that children only lose fathers, they don't gain stepfathers; and a *substitution model*, which proposes that stepfathers functionally replace nonresidential fathers. They found support for the accumulation model and recommended that researchers pay attention to how stepchildren feel about all of their parents, not just the ones in the household in which they live. Moreover, they argued from their findings that how children *feel about* their parents and stepparents predicts outcomes such as internalizing and externalizing behaviors better than contact or involvement with stepfathers and fathers do.

One fundamental question facing stepfamilies is: What kind of relationship is being developed? The type of residential step relationships appears to be the result of several processes. In the next section, we review stepfamily typologies that illustrate some processes. According to VanLear, Koerner, and Allen (this volume), "typologies act as tools for organizing our knowledge and understanding about human relationships . . . [and] provide parameters and limits for generalizations" (p. 106). We believe that typologies allow readers to look efficiently across studies and draw conclusions about commonalities and difference in stepfamilies. Of course, typologies are problematic if they restrict thinking about stepfamilies and if they do not adequately reflect the complexity of family patterns (VanLear et al., this volume).

Typologies of Stepfamily Functioning

Berger (1995) identified three types of stepfamilies (i.e., *Invented, Imported, and Integrated*). Invented stepfamilies ignored their past as though it did not exist. Stepfathers in Invented families had either not been previously married or had been briefly married but did not have children. These couples remarried when young and typically had at least one child in the new union. The stepfamily was considered the "real" family, everyone in the family used the same last name, children called the stepfather Dad, and family members seldom told others of their stepfamily status. Integrated families were those in which each spouse had been previously married and had children (usually adolescents or young adults) from that marriage. They seldom had children after remarrying; their focus was on the marital relationship. Integrated family members often used different last names, and they made no pretense at being anything other than a stepfamily. Children referred to the stepparents by their first names. Imported families functioned as a continuation of the previous family. The couple raised each other's children as though they were their own, and the stepfather adopted the role of the missing father. These families were less extreme forms of recreated nuclear families than were the Invented families. Berger did not find differences in family functioning or satisfaction between these stepfamilies.

Bray and Kelly (1998) identified three types of stepfamilies. *Neotraditional* families made up about 40% of the sample; these were stepfamilies that looked and acted as nuclear families. Neotraditionalists over time acquired characteristics of functional nuclear families – emotional closeness, close parent–child bond, satisfying marriages. Couples in these stepfamilies tended to nurture their relationships, shared a vision of marriage and family life, and agreed on parenting. The most important key to their success was agreeing on how to deal with their children.

Matriarchal stepfamilies (about 25%–30% of Bray's sample) had several defining characteristics. One key was that the parenting responsibilities belonged solely to the parent, typically the mother, and general decision-making power was in her hands as well. Stepfathers were interested in parenting but were willing to follow their wife's lead, which often meant helping the wife monitor the stepchild's activities. There was a fairly low level of cohesiveness in these stepfamilies, and they were vulnerable to change.

Romantic stepfamilies on the surface resembled Neotraditional families, and their goals were the same. However, the Romantics had difficult relations with stepchildren and former spouses, and they tended to fail to nurture the marital relationship. Their signature trait according to Bray was unrealistic expectations. They expected an instant transformation to a nuclear family. They seldom let go of unrealistic expectations despite many failures. These families were more likely than others to redivorce.

Burgoyne and Clark (1984) identified five stepfamily types. The *not really a stepfamily* group were basically reconstituted nuclear families. The couple remarried when the stepchild(ren) were quite young, and they reported that they did not consciously seek to recreate a nuclear family, things just fell into place that allowed them to live that way. The couple often had at least one mutual child, and they referred to themselves as *normal* families. The *looking forward to departure of children* families consisted of older remarrying couples with one or more sets of children who were already teenagers. They were too old to have mutual children in the new marriage, and they eagerly awaited the departure of the dependent children so that they could enjoy their new partnership more fully. *Progressive* stepfamilies did not try to imitate nuclear families or be conventional. Their conflicts with ex-spouses had been resolved, they had a pluralistic view of family life, and they depicted themselves as making choices with the goal of creating advantages for their children. They decided whether to have mutual children in light of this. They reported few sources of conflict, and they did not have financial worries. The *largely successful conscious pursuit of an ordinary family life together* stepfamilies, unlike the *not really a stepfamily* group, made serious efforts to be recreated nuclear families. They had mutual children to appear and feel more normal. Although they often initially struggled with this, the stepparents (usually stepfathers) transferred their affection and allegiance to their stepchildren. The last group, *conscious pursuit of an ordinary family life frustrated*, tried to become reconstituted nuclear families but were not successful in their attempts. This was often blamed on the noncustodial parent who was perceived as undermining the stepparents' efforts to replace them. Disputes over finances, custody, and property were common. Because of these continuing problems, these couples seldom had mutual children.

Stepfamily Trajectories

Braithwaite, Polson, Golish, Soukop, and Turman (2001) also identified five stepfamily types from interviews with one member of 51 stepfamilies who retrospectively recalled the first 4 years (or less if they had not been together that long) of their family life together. Thirty percent was in the *Accelerated* group, which was described as moving quickly toward "feeling like a family." These families basically recreated the nuclear family. *Prolonged* families were the next largest group; they did not compare themselves to the nuclear family but created their own definition of what it means to be a family. *Declining* stepfamilies were the smallest group. They quickly felt "like a family" and then regressed until

by the end of 4 years they felt a sense of impending doom and hopelessness about their families. They experienced loyalty conflicts, ambiguous and strained family roles, and boundary problems. *Stagnating* stepfamilies were also a small group, and they began with low feelings of family cohesiveness that continued over time. Although they sought to replicate the nuclear family, they were unable to do so, and the harder they tried the worse it got. *High-Amplitude Turbulent* families were diverse, unstable, and unpredictable. There was a lack of solidarity between the couple and expectations were unrealistic. Those who avoided conflict did more poorly than those who confronted the conflict.

Stepparent Typologies

Erera-Weatherly (1996) identified five stepparent styles from her in-depth study of 32 Israeli stepparents. Stepfathers only enacted the *biological parent style*. These stepfathers said that they felt and acted toward stepchildren identically to how they felt and acted toward their own children, which created conflict between stepparents and stepchildren and between the stepfathers and their wives. *Supergood stepmoms* consciously worked hard to be good parents to dispel the wicked stepmother stereotype. *Detached stepparents* had only minimal involvement with the stepchildren; they functioned this way after failing to succeed as more active stepparents. Stepmothers in this group were nonresidential, and detached stepfathers were residential. Wives of detached stepfathers often felt torn between the spouse and their children. *Uncertain stepparents*, usually stepfathers, often lacked parenting experience and were frustrated with how to interact with stepchildren. They experienced discipline problems and low levels of stepparent–stepchild intimacy. The *friendship style* appeared in stepfamilies that included an active nonresidential parent and was adopted by stepparents who cared for or at least accepted their stepchildren but did not try to take a parental role with their stepchildren.

How stepparents functioned in their roles depended on factors such as the stepparents' attitudes and personalities, their gender, the duration of the relationship, and the presence or absence of stresses and social supports. The stepchild's willingness to accept the stepparent was key, as was involvement of the nonresidential parent. When the nonresidential parent was actively involved, stepparents were relatively detached. A third factor was the tendency of some mothers to form alliances with their children that resulted in exclusion of the stepparent.

Typologies and Functioning

One thing that becomes clear from examining the various typologies of stepfamily functioning is that recreating the nuclear family is not only common, it is probably the leading way that stepfamilies try to live. Clinician/ and researcher James Bray shared,

> At first I thought the myth [of the nuclear family] was so popular because it expressed longing for a certain kind of family . . . but as the project progressed, I realized our participants clung to it because the nuclear-family myth speaks to certain fundamental human longings and desires. It is about the need to belong . . . to give and receive love, and the wish for a secure haven . . . to feel whole and authentic. (Bray & Kelly, 1998, p. 112)

It is perhaps what the Braithwaite et al. (2001) Accelerated group meant by "feeling like a family." Bray's Romantic group were the families in his study who had the least patience with recreating the nuclear family, and their rush to do so resulted in dysfunction and often divorce.

Although the nuclear family model was the most prevalent, there is evidence from multiple studies that there are other, less frequent approaches to creating a postdivorce stepfamily. One is the couple-oriented stepfamily, in which the adults focus their energies on each other. This style is often, but not always, accompanied by a pattern in which the stepparent, usually a stepfather, is emotionally detached from the stepchildren

and the mother is heavily invested in raising the children. Finally, there is the progressive stepfamily that works to develop into a unit whose relationships fit with their structure. These families are not limited generally by their structural configurations and may not appear to be similar – what they share is recognition that they are a postdivorce unit that extends beyond the household.

It is important to note, however, that in general marital and family satisfaction did not always differ in the way one might anticipate it would. Researchers have found little difference in marital or family satisfaction across typologies. This is true despite the fact that clinicians have argued for at least 2 decades against stepfamily members attempting to recreate the traditional nuclear family (see Ganong & Coleman, 2004). Perhaps more surprising is the fact that the recreated nuclear family is functional for many stepfamilies. At what cost to those no longer considered a part of the family we do not know, but considering the number of men who eventually lose contact with their children postdivorce, the costs may be minimal. Of course, we have little information regarding whether these men sever contacts with their children because they are not encouraged to participate in their lives (thus opening the door for the stepfamily to function as a nuclear family) or if they withdraw voluntarily from children's lives.

Conclusions

This review highlights the complexity of divorce and postdivorce relationships as well as the contrast between common perceptions of divorce and remarriage and the realities of these transitions. Divorce and remarriage are relationship processes that evolve over time but that are often expected to occur quickly. In addition, there are multiple ways in which these transitional processes unfold. Despite these diverse patterns, there is a tendency for adults to try to recreate nuclear family patterns. The complexity of family transitions, the contrast between myths and realities, and the tendency for individuals to try to recreate family patterns suggest the need for new ways of thinking about postdivorce relationships. Pinsof (2002) argued that the use of a dichotomous model (married vs. not married) to conceptualize intimate relationships leads to the view of marriage as good and divorce as bad. He proposes an alternate model of multiple pair-bonding arrangements (cohabitation with children, cohabitation without children, marriage, and elder cohabitation), which individuals move into and out of across the life span. This model views divorce and remarriage as normative transitions. Acceptance of the diversity of family structures and of family transitions as a normative part of the life course leads to the implication that all families need and deserve support to promote patterns of positive adaptation to life transitions.

References

Acock, A., & Demo, D. H. (1994). *Family diversity and well-being*. Thousand Oaks, CA: Sage.

Ahrons, C. R. (1983). Predictors of parental involvement postdivorce: Mothers' and fathers' perceptions. *Journal of Divorce, 6*, 55–69.

Ahrons, C. R. (1994). *The good divorce*. New York: HarperCollins.

Allan, G., Hawker, G., & Crow, S. (2004). Britain's changing families. In M. Coleman & L. Ganong (Eds.), *Handbook of contemporary families* (pp. 302–316). Thousand Oaks, CA: Sage.

Amato, P. (1993). Children's adjustment to divorce: Theories, hypotheses, and empirical support. *Journal of Marriage and the Family, 55*, 23–38.

Amato, P. (2000). The consequences of divorce for adults and children. *Journal of Marriage and the Family, 62*, 1269–1287.

Amato, P. (2004). Divorce in historical context: Changing scientific perspectives on children and marital dissolution. In M. Coleman & L. Ganong (Eds.), *Handbook of contemporary families* (pp. 265–281). Thousand Oaks, CA: Sage.

Amato, P., & Booth, A. (1996). A prospective study of parental divorce and parent–child relationships. *Journal of Marriage and the Family, 58*, 356–365.

Amato, P., Loomis, L., & Booth, A. (1995). Parental divorce, marital conflict, and offspring well-being during early adulthood. *Social Forces, 73*, 895–916.

Baum, N. (2003). Divorce process variables and the co-parental relationship and parental role fulfillment of divorced parents. *Family Process, 42*, 117–131.

Berger, R. (1995). Three types of stepfamilies. *Journal of Divorce and Remarriage, 35*–49.

Bohannan, P. (1970). Divorce chains, households of remarriage, and multiple divorces. In P. Bohannan (Ed.), *Divorce and after* (pp. 127–139). New York: Doubleday.

Booth, A., & Crouter, A. C. (2002). *Just living together: Implications of cohabitation on families, children, and social policy*. Mahwah, NJ: Erlbaum.

Braithwaite, D., Olson, L. N., Golish, T. D., Soukop, C., & Turman, P. (2001). "Becoming a family": Developmental processes represented in blended family discourse. *Journal of Applied Communication Research, 29*, 221–247.

Bramlett, M. D., & Mosher, W. D. (2001). *Cohabitation, marriage, divorce, and remarriage in the United States*. National Center for Health Statistics (Series 23, No. 22).

Braver, S. (1998). *Divorced dads: Shattering the myths*. New York: Jeremy Tarcher/Putnam.

Bray, J., & Berger, S. H. (1993). Developmental issues in stepfamilies research project: Family relationships and parent–child interactions. *Journal of Family Psychology, 7*, 76–90.

Bray, J., & Kelly, J. (1998). *Stepfamilies*. New York: Broadway Books.

Burgoyne, J., & Clark, D. (1984). *Making a go of it*. Boston: Routledge & Kegan.

Carriere, J. L. (1998). "Its déjà vu all over again": The Covenant Marriage Act in popular cultural perception and legal reality. *Tulane Law Review, 72*, 1701–1748.

Cherlin, A. (1992). *Marriage, divorce, remarriage*. Cambridge, MA: Harvard University Press.

Coleman, M., & Ganong, L. (1995). Family reconfiguring following divorce. In S. Duck & J. Wood (Eds.), *Confronting relationship challenges* (pp. 73–108). Thousand Oaks, CA: Sage.

Crosbie-Burnett, M., & Giles-Sims, J. (1994). Adolescent adjustment and stepparenting styles. *Family Relations, 43*, 394–399.

Cuber, J., & Harroff, P. (1965). *The significant Americans*. New York: Appleton-Century-Crofts.

Cummings, E. M., & Davies, P. (1994). *Children and marital conflict*. New York: Guilford Press.

DeGarmo, D. S., & Kitson, G. C. (1996). Identity relevance and disruption as predictors of psychological distress for widowed and divorced women. *Journal of Marriage and the Family, 58*, 983–997.

Emery, R. E. (1999). *Marriage, divorce, and children's adjustment* (2nd ed.). Beverly Hills, CA: Sage.

England, P. (2000). Marriage, the costs of children, and gender inequality. In L. Waite, C. Bachrach, M. Hindin, E. Thompson, & A. Thornton (Eds.), *The ties that bind* (pp. 320–342). New York: Aldine de Gruyter.

Erera-Weatherly, P. I. (1996). On becoming a stepparent: Factors associated with the adoption of alternative stepparenting styles. *Journal of Divorce and Remarriage, 25*, 155–174.

Ganong, L., & Coleman, M. (1989). Preparing for remarriage: Anticipating the issues, seeking solutions. *Family Relations, 38*, 28–33.

Ganong, L., & Coleman, M. (2004). *Stepfamily relationships*. New York: Kluwer Academic/Plenum.

Ganong, L., Coleman, M., Fine, M., & Martin, P. (1999). Stepparents' affinity-seeking and affinity-maintaining strategies with stepchildren. *Journal of Family Issues, 20*, 299–327.

Goode, W. J. (1993). *World changes in divorce patterns*. New Haven: Yale University Press.

Gottman, J. M. (1994). *What predicts divorce*. Hillsdale, NJ: Erlbaum.

Grall, T. (2000). *Child support for custodial mothers and fathers: 1997* (Current Population Reports, P60–212). Washington, DC: U.S. Government Printing Office.

Hagestad, G. O., & Smyer, M. A. (1982). Dissolving long-term relationships: Patterns of divorcing in middle age. In S. Duck (Ed.), *Personal relationships, Vol 4: Dissolving personal relationships* (pp. 155–188). New York: Academic Press.

Hahn, R., & Kleist, D. (2000). Divorce mediation: Research and implications for family and couples counseling. *The Family Journal, 8*, 165–171.

Hawkins, A. J., Nock, S. L., Wilson, J. C., Sanchez, L., & Wright, J. D. (2002). Attitudes about covenant marriage and divorce: Policy implications from a three-state comparison. *Family Relations, 51*, 166–175.

Hetherington, E. M. (1993). An overview of the Virginia Longitudinal Study of Divorce and Remarriage with a focus on the early adolescent. *Journal of Family Psychology, 7*, 39–56.

Hetherington, E. M. (Ed.). (1998). Applications of developmental science [Special issue]. *American Psychologist, 53*.

Hetherington, E. M., & Clingempeel, W. G. (1992). Coping with marital transitions: A family systems perspective. *Monographs of the Society for Research in Child Development, 57* (2–3, Serial No. 227).

Hetherington, E. M., Cox, M., & Cox, R. (1982). Effects of divorce on parents and children. In M. Lamb (Ed.), *Nontraditional families* (pp. 233–285). Hillsdale, NJ: Erlbaum.

Hetherington, E. M., & Kelly, J. (2002). *For better or for worse*. New York: Norton.

Hopper, J. (1993). The rhetoric of motives in divorce. *Journal of Marriage and the Family, 55*, 801–813.

Hopper, J. (2001). The symbolic origins of conflict in divorce. *Journal of Marriage and Family, 63*, 430–445.

Johnston, J. (1995). Children's adjustment in sole custody compared to joint custody families and principles for custody decision-making. *Family and Conciliation Courts Review, 33*, 415–425.

Kaslow, F. (2000). Families experiencing divorce. In W. Nichols, M. Pace-Nichols, D. Becvar, & A. Napier (Eds.), *Handbook of family development and intervention* (pp. 341–370). New York: Wiley.

Kayser, K. (1993). *When love dies: The process of marital disaffection*. New York: Guilford Press.

Kelly, J. (1996). A decade of divorce mediation research: Some answers and questions. *Family and Conciliation Courts Review, 34*, 373–386.

Kelly, J. (2002). Psychological and legal interventions for parents and children in custody and access disputes: Current research and practice. *Virginia Journal of Social Policy and Law, 10*, 129–163.

Kiecolt-Glaser, J. K., & Newton, T. L. (2001). Marriage and health: His and hers. *Psychological Bulletin, 127*, 472–503.

Kreider, R. M., & Fields, J. M. (2002). *Number, timing, and duration of marriage and divorce: 1996* (Current Population Reports, P70–80). Washington, DC: U.S. Government Printing Office.

Lorenz, F. O., Simons, R. L., Conger, R. D., Elder, G. H., Johnson, C., & Chao, W. (1997).

Married and recently divorced mothers' stressful events and distress: Tracing change across time. *Journal of Marriage and the Family*, 59, 219–232.

Mandell, D. (2002). *Deadbeat dads*. Toronto: University of Toronto Press.

Manning, W., Stewart, S., & Smock, P. (2003). The complexity of fathers' parenting responsibilities and involvement with nonresident children. *Journal of Family Issues*, 24, 645–667.

Marks, N. F. (1996). Flying solo at midlife: Gender, marital status, and psychological well-being. *Journal of Marriage and the Family*, 58, 917–932.

Mason, M. A., Fine, M., & Carnochan, S. (2004). Family law for changing families in the new millennium. In M. Coleman & L. Ganong (Eds.), *Handbook of contemporary families* (pp. 432–450). Thousand Oaks, CA: Sage.

McManus, P., & Diprete, T. (2001). Losers and winners: The financial consequences of separation and divorce for men. *American Sociological Review*, 55, 246–268.

Montgomery, M. J., Anderson, E. R., Hetherington, E. M., & Clingempeel, W. G. (1992). Patterns of courtship for remarriage: Implications for child adjustment and parent–child relationships. *Journal of Marriage and the Family*, 54, 686–698.

National Center for Health Statistics. (1993). *1988 marriages: Number of the marriage by bride and groom* [Computer program]. Washington, DC: NCHS Computer Center.

Nock, S. L., Wright, J. D., & Sanchez, L. (1999). America's divorce problem. *Society*, 36, 43–52.

Oh, S. (1986). Remarried men and remarried women: How are they different? *Journal of Divorce*, 9, 107–113.

Pinsof, W. M. (2002). The death of "till death us do part": The transformation of pair-bonding in the 20th century. *Family Process*, 41, 135–157.

Popenoe, D. (1996). *Life without father*. New York: Free Press.

Ricci, I. (1997). *Mom's house, Dad's house*. New York: Simon & Schuster.

Riessmann, C. K. (1990). *Divorce talk*. New Brunswick, NJ: Rutgers University Press.

Schmiege, C., Richards, L., & Zvonkovic, A. (2001). Remarriage: For love or money? *Journal of Divorce and Remarriage*, 36, 123–140.

Simons, R. (1996). *Understanding differences between divorced and intact families*. Thousand Oaks: Sage.

Smith, D. A., Vivian, D., & O'Leary, K. (1990). Longitudinal prediction of marital discord from premarital expression of affect. *Journal of Consulting and Clinical Psychology*, 58, 790–798.

Stephens, L. S. (1996). Will Johnny see Daddy this week? An empirical test of three theoretical perspectives of post divorce contact. *Journal of Family Issues*, 17, 466–494.

Sternberg, R. J. (1986). A triangular theory of love. *Psychological Review*, 93, 119–135.

Stewart, A. L. (1999). Covenant marriage: Legislating family values. *Indiana Law Review*, 32, 509–536.

Sweeney, M. (2002). Remarriage and the nature of divorce. *Journal of Family Issues*, 23, 410–440.

U.S. Bureau of the Census. (2000). *Statistical abstract of the United States: 2000*. Washington, DC: U.S. Government Printing Office.

U.S. Census Bureau (2003, December 2). *About half of custodial parents got full child support*. Retrieved May 2, 2004, from http://www.census.gov/Press-Release/www/releases/archives/ families_households/001575.html

Weaver, S. E., & Coleman, M. (2004). *Caught in the middle: Mothers in stepfamilies*. Manuscript submitted for publication.

White, L. K., & Gilbreth, J. G. (2001). When children have two fathers: Effects of relationships with stepfathers and noncustodial fathers on adolescent outcomes. *Journal of Marriage and Family*, 63, 155–167.

Whiteside, M. (1998). The parental alliance following divorce: An overview. *Journal of Marital and Family Therapy*, 24, 3–24.

Wilson, B. F., & Clarke, S. C. (1992). Remarriages: A demographic profile. *Journal of Family Issues*, 13, 123–141.

Wu, Z., & Hart, R. (2002). The effects of marital and nonmarital union transition on health. *Journal of Marriage and Family*, 64, 420–432.

Wu, Z., & Penning, M. J. (1997). Marital instability after midlife. *Journal of Family Issues*, 18, 459–478.

Part IV

RELATIONSHIPS ACROSS THE LIFE SPAN

CHAPTER 10

Relationships in Early and Middle Childhood

Willard W. Hartup

Close relationships outside the family begin to emerge in the second year of life. Toddlers exhibit preferences for certain children over others, and interactions between preferred partners are more reciprocal than interactions with other associates (Howes, 1983). Also, when preferred peers show distress, toddlers more often respond by offering comfort or alerting an adult than when nonpreferred peers are upset (Howes & Farver, 1987).

Close relationships among both younger and older children are usually described in terms of harmonious interaction, common interests, and social support. Qualities such as these are thought to be the basis of children's attraction to one another. Friends are believed to come together and maintain their relationships on the basis of common ground and expectations that cost–benefit ratios will be generally favorable in their interactions.

Friendships, however, frequently have a dark side, and even when attraction predominates, conflict and disharmony may be evident. Still other relationships are based almost entirely on mutual hatred, fear,

anxiety, and aversion. Peer relationships thus are diverse; enemies are salient in children's social networks as well as friends (Hartup & Abecassis, 2002).

Social scientists have had a long-standing interest in close relationships in early and middle childhood. Children's friendships began to be studied at about the same time that developmental psychology was emerging as a separate discipline: W. S. Monroe (1899), an American, published a seminal study of children's friendships at the close of the 19th century dealing with children's expectations about their friends, what is valued in these relationships, and the organization of clubs and gangs. European interest in children's relationships began with observational studies of social networks, especially as these differ from age to age (cf. K. Reininger, cited in Bühler, 1931).

Comparable studies dealing with enemies did not exist before the 1980s, although some small interest in these relationships among adults was expressed earlier (see Wiseman & Duck, 1995, for a review). On the other hand, certain "quasi-relationships," such as children's involvement with imaginary friends, have been long recognized as worth studying – especially in clinical and educational contexts (cf. Vostrovsky, 1895). Although the inclusion of imaginary companions in the relationships literature may require stretching one's conceptual categories, the documented functions of imaginary companions suggest that these phenomena have relationship-like features (Gleason, 2002).

Developmental scientists have thus been interested in children's relationships for a long time. Theoretical analysis and empirical studies of these relationships, however, were sporadic through the first two thirds of the 20th century. Certain early investigations are landmarks. Challman (1932), for example, published the first quantitative examination of friendship homophilies among preschool children in the 1930s, and at almost the same time, Green (1933) observed conflict behavior between preschool-age friends, as contrasted with the disagreements occurring between nonfriends. Mainly descriptive, these early studies were embedded in a larger effort made during this time to document the social competencies of children (Anderson & Anderson, 1946; Bühler, 1931). Sustained research on friendships in early and middle childhood did not begin until the 1970s and has expanded greatly in the decades since.

During this entire time, an integrated or unique set of theoretical principles designed to explain the formation and functioning of children's close relationships has not emerged. The major developmental theorists (e.g., Sigmund Freud, Jean Piaget, George Herbert Mead and the symbolic interactionists, and Albert Bandura and other social learning theorists) have all contributed ideas that have enriched research on children's relationships. For example, Piaget's notions about reciprocity and conflict among children (Piaget, 1932) formed the basis for James Youniss's (1980) analysis of reciprocity in the origins and functioning of childhood friendships. Piaget himself had little to say about these relationships, however, focusing instead on peer interaction more broadly as a force in cognitive development. Likewise, Freud had little to say about peer relationships, although Erikson (1950), in articulating his theory of psychosocial stages, recognized the intersection between childhood generativity and competence in peer relations. Finally, although the originators of contemporary social learning theory (Bandura, 1977) had little or nothing to say about the manner in which operant or observational learning works in the formation and functioning of friendships, efforts have been made through social exchange theory to apply these notions to children's relationships (Laursen, Hartup, & Koplas, 1996).

More explicit theoretical analyses of children's relationships have been formulated, but in only two cases: First, Harry Stack Sullivan (1953), who was a psychiatrist, acknowledged the importance of same-sex friendships in the juvenile and preadolescent "eras" to the individual's developing needs for companionship and intimacy and, more broadly, to the individual's sense of well-being. Robert Selman (1980), a psychologist, argued that developmental transformations in children's thinking about friendship relations appear in a more or less invariant order, an invariance that is closely linked to the development of perspective taking in early and middle childhood (discussed later). In each case, these theoretical formulations are relatively narrow; neither constitutes a comprehensive theory of friendship formation and functioning during childhood and adolescence. At the same time, each of these notions has served as a framework for important empirical work (cf. Buhrmester & Furman, 1986; Selman, 1980; Youniss, 1980).

The main goal of this chapter is to describe the current status of research dealing with children's relationships, including friendships, enemyships,[1] and other close relationships in which the child participates. First, I focus on friends, including what it means to children to have a friend as well as developmental implications. Second, mutual antipathies are discussed, including their incidence along with developmental implications. Third, bully–victim relationships are examined. Fourth, quasi-relationships (e.g., liking reciprocated by indifference; imaginary friends) are considered. Fifth, relationships among relationships (e.g., linkages between parent–child and peer relationships) are discussed. By bringing these diverse relationships into one essay, I show that within children's social networks, darker relationships coexist with brighter ones, and important developmental outcomes are associated with both (Hartup & Abecassis, 2002).

Friends

How Children Perceive Their Friends

Both continuity and discontinuity typify friendship expectations in early and middle childhood. Friends expect reciprocity (give and take) in their social exchanges at all ages, but children nevertheless describe their friendships differently as they grow older: Preschool-age children describe their friends concretely, referring to shared activities ("We play") whereas older children describe their friendship reciprocities in more nuanced terms such as loyalty and trustworthiness. Preadolescents emphasize sympathy and self-disclosure (Bigelow, 1977).

Selman (1980) has described this developmental progression as beginning with the child regarding friends as merely playmates (Stage 0), then as children who see one another as sources of gratification (Stage 1), then as children who see themselves as involved in two-way or reciprocal relationships (Stage 2), then as children who perceive these relationships as sources of intimacy and mutual support (Stage 3), and, finally, as individuals who regard their relationships as marked by both dependency on one another (e.g., each person relies on the other for psychological support) and independence (e.g., each person accepts the other's need to establish relationships with other persons and to grow through such experiences [Stage 4]).

So it is that reciprocity seems to be invariant in children's friendship expectations at all ages, thus constituting the "deep structure" of these relationships (Hartup, 1996; Youniss, 1980). At the same time, behavioral manifestations of friendship relations (i.e., their "surface structure") change with age. Some investigators (e.g., Bigelow, 1977; Selman, 1980) have argued that these changes occur in more or less discrete stages across childhood and adolescence that are closely linked to other changes in cognitive functioning. Most of the evidence, however, suggests that changes in friendship expectations occur gradually rather than abruptly (Berndt, 1981).

Whatever the case, these changes in friendship expectations are correlated with changes in cognition – in the number of constructs that children are able to apply to relationships and their increasing complexity (e.g., loyalty compared with play) as well as with better perspective taking. Friendships also become increasingly differentiated from other relationships (e.g., from parents and siblings) as children grow older. Friends, for example, are expected by older preschool-age children to provide one another with companionship and intimacy but not to supply compliance and control, which are more characteristic of parent–child relationships (Gleason, 2002). More fine-grained differentiations are made by school-age children and adolescents (Furman & Buhrmester, 1985).

Friendship Formation

Once two children meet, first encounters must produce some evidence of common ground for them to "hit it off." When this happens, a shift occurs in interpersonal attraction from "neutral" to "liking" and from an ego-centered orientation to a relationship-centered one (Gottman, 1983). Early manifestations of common ground, however, predict only small amounts of variance in relationship longevity. Over the long term, children must continually validate their common interests for these relationships to continue.

Friendships last somewhat longer among older children than younger ones (Epstein & Karweit, 1983) although terminations are frequent at all ages. Terminations occur for many reasons, although conflict and commitment violations are less likely to precipitate breakups than one might think. For example, friendships among first-grade children cease mainly because the children simply drift apart (Rizzo, 1989).

How Many Children Have Friends?

Although toddlers frequently display interpersonal preferences, these relationships are not as nuanced as friendships among older children and not every toddler has them. Among 4-year-olds, however, the word "friend" is frequently used, and about three quarters of children at this age are involved in friendships, as indicated by the amount of time they spend together as well as the reciprocal and affective nature of their interaction (Howes, 1983). These frequencies increase somewhat (to about 85%) in middle childhood. Friendship networks are also smaller among younger children than among older ones.

Children's friendships are gender concordant. Upward of 30% of preschool children's friendships are cross-sex (cf. Challman, 1932) but these percentages decline to about 5% during middle childhood, increasing once again as children approach adolescence (Sippola, Bukowski, & Noll, 1997). About the same percentage of boys and girls have friends, although friendship networks are somewhat smaller among girls than among boys.

How Children Interact with Their Friends

Children spend more time with their friends than with nonfriends, which partially accounts for the more frequent cooperation displayed by friends as well as their more frequent quarreling and fighting (Hartup, Laursen, Stewart, & Eastenson, 1988). These differences largely remain evident, however, when time spent together is controlled statistically.

In early childhood, behavioral differences between friends and nonfriends are most clear-cut in cooperation, behavioral reciprocities (Howes, 1983), and mutual pretend play (Howes & Unger, 1989). Also, during conflict resolution, friends use negotiation and disengagement more frequently than nonfriends but use resistance less often (Hartup et al., 1988).

Studies of school-age children, examined with meta-analysis (Newcomb & Bagwell, 1995), reveal differences between friends and nonfriends in four categories: *positive engagement* (friends talk, smile, and laugh more than nonfriends), *relationship mutuality* (friends are more supportive, more mutually oriented, and expect parity more frequently in their social exchanges than nonfriends), *task behavior* (friends spend more time discussing the task and more time on task than nonfriends), and *conflict management*. Once again, social support, emotional regulation, effective conflict management, and reciprocity turn out to be the behavioral hallmarks of children's friendships.

Are Friends More Similar to One Another Than Nonfriends?

The similarity–attraction hypothesis is affirmed in both early and middle childhood. The likelihood that two young children will be friends is a direct function of the number of behavioral attributes they share (Kupersmidt, DeRosier, & Patterson, 1995). Moreover, children who are strangers initially are more attracted to one another when cognitive and play styles are similar (Rubin, Lynch, Coplan, Rose-Krasnor, & Booth, 1994).

Greater similarity, indeed, is evident at all ages in gender, age, ethnicity, and sociometric status among friends than nonfriends. Behavioral concordances among young children and their friends are evident, too, although not as extensively as among older children. Greater similarity has been discovered among school-age children who are friends, compared with nonfriends, in prosocial behavior, antisocial behavior, shyness–dependency, depression, and achievement. These similarities extend to children's perceptions of both persons and relationships; that is, ratings of other children by friends are more concordant than ratings made by nonfriends (Haselager, Hartup, Van Lieshout, & Riksen-Walraven, 1998).

The homophilies existing in children's friendships derive from many sources. First, sociological forces bring similar children together in schools and other social institutions. Second, children are attracted to other children who are similar to themselves (Rubin et al., 1994). Third, social attraction may lead to the perception of similarities between oneself and one's partners as well as the reverse (Morry, 2003). Fourth, opposites do *not* attract in children's social relations; children actually dislike associates who are different from themselves (Rosenbaum, 1986). Fifth, once children become friends, mutual socialization increases their similarity to one another (Kandel, 1978). The relative importance of mutual selection and mutual socialization, however, depends on characteristics of the children themselves, the nature of their interaction, and the behavioral attributes being measured (Urberg, 1999).

At the moment, the manner in which these processes play out in the social development of individual children has not been documented. Although many more longitudinal studies are being conducted currently than in earlier times, friendship processes (including the interactions between children and their friends) have not been the major issues driving these investigations. Consequently, we know relatively little about the long-term history of friendships among individual children.

Developmental Implications

HAVING FRIENDS

Cross-sectional studies show that children who have friends, compared with those who do not, are more sociable, cooperative, altruistic, and self-confident and less lonely (Newcomb & Bagwell, 1995). Longitudinal studies are relatively rare but indicate that merely "having friends" in childhood may be most predictive of feelings of self-worth, family attitudes, and absence of depression in late adolescence. Indeed, some studies show that peer rejection is a better predictor of social competence in early adulthood (across domains ranging from aggressiveness

to social withdrawal) than friendship status (Bagwell, Newcomb, & Bukowski, 1998).

WHO ONE'S FRIENDS ARE

Friendships enhance social competence when a child's friends are socially competent, but not otherwise. For example, social adjustment improves across school transitions when friends are well adjusted, but otherwise not (Berndt, Hawkins, & Jiao, 1999). The child's resilience increases following marital transitions provided friends are well adjusted, but not otherwise (Hetherington, 1999). Finally, associating with antisocial friends increases a child's antisocial behavior more than contact with nonaggressive friends, especially among children who are themselves aggressive and rejected (Dishion, 1990).

Dyadic processes have been shown to depend on the characteristics of the children involved in the exchange. Aggressive boys and their friends, for example, provide more enticement for rule violations and engage in more rule-breaking behavior than nonaggressive boys and their friends as well as more intense conflicts. At the same time, nonaggressive friends show greater positive engagement, on-task behavior, and reciprocity in their interactions than aggressive boys and their friends (Bagwell & Coie, 2004). Friendships, therefore, provide different developmental contexts for children depending on who their partners are.

The mechanisms responsible for companion effects are not fully understood. Some of the differences in children's development that are traceable to characteristics of their partners may emanate from modeling or reinforcement of the normative behavior that the partners manifest. In other instances, conversations between friends may be pathways to behavior change, particularly conversations that are persuasive (Gottman & Parker, 1986). One must agree, though, that despite evidence supporting that friendship outcomes depend on who the child's friends are, the mechanisms responsible for these effects on socialization have been examined piecemeal rather than together. Once again, there is need for longitudinal study of friendship relations and their developmental outcomes.

FRIENDSHIP QUALITY (FEATURES)

Friendships vary in their social qualities, and these variations have adaptational implications. Social competence may not depend on merely having friends but on whether the child participates in a relationship in which partners support one another and refrain from contention and conflict. The cross-sectional evidence is relatively clear on this point: Supportiveness and harmony in friendship relations are linked to good social adaptation, whether measured in terms of sociability, social engagement, popularity, good social reputations, self-esteem, or avoidance of aggression (Hartup & Abecassis, 2002). Other more differentiated studies show that "prosocial friendships" are associated with school achievement and popularity, "antisocial friendships" with peer rejection and delinquency, and "socially withdrawn friendships" with anxiety, low self-confidence, depression, and peer rejection (Guroglu, Van Lieshout, & Haselager, 2004).

Other conditions sometimes moderate the effects of friendship quality: During school transitions, for example, supportiveness in a child's friendships predicts increasing sociability, positive attitudes about classmates, and popularity, but mainly when friendships are stable rather than unstable (Berndt et al., 1999). Another example: Antisocial behavior increases in preadolescence among aggressive but not nonaggressive children, but only among those who have "low-quality friendships" and not among children with "high-quality" ones (Poulin, Dishion, & Haas, 1999). Main effects thus do not give us more than an introduction to friendship quality and its developmental implications.

Enemies

Children's enemies have been studied much less extensively than their friendships. Often invisible owing to their avoidance of one another, enemies may nevertheless have considerable developmental significance. Evidence is examined in this section to determine whether it is better not to have enemies than to have them.

Who Is an Enemy?

Mutual antipathies are relatively easy to locate with sociometric interviews (two children say they don't like each other), but these relationships do not always involve the hostility and animosity that the word "enemies" suggests. Mutual antipathy is thus a better superordinate construct – one that encompasses "being enemies" as well as other relationships maintained on the basis of aversion.

Methodologies for identifying negative or aversive relationships are diverse. Mutual antipathies are sometimes identified by asking children to nominate classmates whom they "like least" and at other times by asking them to nominate classmates whom they "do not like" or "do not like at all." Still other investigators regard mutual antipathies as children who do not want to play with one another. Obviously, these variations constrain the identification of negative relationships: For example, two children who "least like" one another may simply not share interests. On the other hand, two children who "do not like one another at all" are almost certainly involved in a relationship that can be called antipathetic. To identify two children as enemies, though, requires questioning of the respondents beyond knowing whether they do not like one another; one needs also to know about the affective nature of their interactions (if they interact at all) and their feelings toward one another.

Why Do Children Dislike One Another?

Attribution studies demonstrate that enemies are believed to be more hostile than other children (Ray & Cohen, 1997), and persuasion studies suggest than enemies are seen as power-assertive, threatening, and uncooperative (Bernicot & Mahrokhian, 1989).

Little evidence suggests that children who dislike one another also fight a lot. In fact, preschool-age children do not often fight consistently with one particular opponent (Ross & Conant, 1992). On the other hand, casual observation suggests that avoidance is commonly used by children to "relate" to their enemies. Demonstrating avoidance with young children, however, is relatively difficult; observations can be misleading and self-reports unreliable.

Incidence

Little is known about the incidence of mutual antipathies among preschool-age children. Interviews were used in one instance (Hayes, Gershman & Bolin, 1980) and mutual dislike turned out to be extremely rare. Among school-age children, prevalence rates are not consistent across studies, most likely owing to methodological differences. Across six recent studies (see Hodges & Card, 2003), percentages ranged between 15% and 65% with a median of 30%.

Incidence depends on gender and age. One comprehensive study of fifth graders (Abecassis, Hartup, Scholte, Haselager, & Van Lieshout, 2002) revealed that 25% of fifth-grade boys were involved in same-sex antipathies but only 9% of girls, a difference that lessened with age; among adolescents, 19% of boys and 14% of girls had same-sex antipathies. No gender differences existed in involvement in mixed-sex (boy–girl) antipathies, which were approximately 16% for both sexes among both children and adolescents.

Taken together, the results of the six studies (see Hodges & Card, 2003) suggest that estimates of about 30% represent the proportion of children who have same-sex antipathies, mixed-sex antipathies, or both. These rates exceed the number of children who would mutually nominate one another by chance on a sociometric test (Abecassis et al., 2002) and also exceed the percentage of children ordinarily found to be socially rejected by their classmates. We do not know, however, whether the mutual antipathies identified in these studies by sociometric methods are recognized by the children as reciprocated rejection or whether they are regarded as relationships at all. Although we may possess a stable estimate of the incidence of mutual antipathies in middle childhood, we can say almost nothing about their salience to the children themselves.

Are Enemies Similar or Different from One Another?

Whether young children involved in mutual antipathies are similar or different from one another compared with "neutral" companions is not known. Card and Hodges (2003) reported, however, that the "relationship orientations" of school-age children with their respective parents are more different within mutual antipathies than within other dyads. Possibly, then, aversion ensues when children observe themselves to have different relationship expectations (especially with parents).

In another investigation, mutual antipathies among fifth graders were marked by greater differences between the individuals involved than between classmates who were neutral about each other – in antisocial behavior and social withdrawal as well as prosocial behavior and achievement (Hartup, Verhoeven, DeBoer, Scholte, & Van Lieshout, 2002). These results are consistent with evidence showing that children dislike others who are perceived as different from themselves (Rosenbaum, 1986).

Developmental Implications

Overrepresentation of children who are involved in mutual antipathies occurs among controversial and rejected children while underrepresentation occurs among popular, average, and neglected children (Abecassis et al., 2002; Hembree & Vandell, 2000). Results show further that although being disliked or unpopular is associated with involvement in mutual antipathies, substantial numbers of popular and average children also participate in these relationships. From 13% to 32% of popular and average children have mutual antipathies (see Hartup, 2003), demonstrating that having enemies is not limited to those children whose peer relations are troubled.

Comprehensive studies of 8- and 11-year-old children (Abecassis et al., 2002; Hembree & Vandell, 2000) show that with peer rejection factored out, involvement in mutual antipathies is significantly correlated with both antisocial behavior and social withdrawal in both sexes, whereas being negatively correlated with school achievement. In other instances, involvement in mutual antipathies and aggression were related but only under certain conditions: (a) when environments frequently expose children to aggression (Schwartz, Hopmeyer-Gorman, Toblin, & Abou-essedine, 2003) and (b) when antipathies involvement increases over time (Rodkin, Pearl, Farmer, & Van Acker, 2003). On balance, then, having enemies is a concomitant of risk in social development during childhood, but this concordance may be moderated by a variety of conditions.

Bully–Victim Relationships

Considerable information is available about bullying and victimization but dyads have not been studied in which one child bullies a specific victim over a substantial period. Bullying is generally defined as aggression occurring when there is an imbalance of power between the children (Olweus, 1993). We know that, somewhat surprisingly, bullying and victimization are correlated with one another, are relatively stable across time, and decline in frequency during middle childhood (Rigby, 2002). Although these results tell us something about bullying and about victimization separately, they do not reveal what bully–victim relationships are like, especially over time.

Both bullies and victims have more enemies than children who are nonbullies or nonvictims. Relationships with friends, however, moderate victimization (and, possibly, bullying). For example, among children who are at risk for victimization owing to both internalizing and externalizing dispositions, being bullied varies inversely with the number of friends the children have. Having numerous friends appears to provide protection, support, and advice to the potentially victimized child; friends are also feared by potential bullies (Hodges, Malone, & Perry, 1997). In addition, aggressive (externalizing) friends retaliate in defense of their friends, thereby protecting them from escalating victimization (Hodges & Perry, 1999).

Quasi-Relationships

Four types of quasi-relationships can be identified among children: (a) attraction reciprocated by indifference, (b) antipathy reciprocated by indifference, (c) attraction reciprocated by antipathy, and (d) imaginary friends. Among these quasi-relationships, unilateral friendships have been studied occasionally as well as imaginary ones; the other quasi-relationships have not.

Unilateral Friends

When one child is attracted to another and these feelings are not reciprocated, does their interaction represent a relationship? Although it is not difficult to argue that unilateral attraction constitutes something unique in social relations, these dyads function differently from mutual friends. Among young children, for example, common activities and positive evaluation occur less frequently in comments about associates when relationships are unilateral as opposed to mutual (Hayes et al., 1980). Among school-age children, unilateral friends know less about one another than mutual friends; they predict each other's characteristics less accurately and reciprocally. Unilateral friends are also less similar to one another in the total amount of knowledge they possess about their partners than mutual friends are (Ladd & Emerson, 1984).

Preschool-age children show both similarities and differences in the way these two kinds of friends resolve conflicts and behave afterward. First, conflicts among unilateral associates are more intense than among mutual friends, more likely to involve standing firm, and result in winners and losers. At the same time, unilateral friends are very similar to neutral dyads in these respects. Second, after the conflict, unilateral associates resemble mutual friends more than neutral associates do: They remain together and continue to interact whereas neutral associates do not (Hartup et al., 1988). Taken together, these results suggest that one-sided attractions are similar to neutral relationships during conflict resolution but to mutual attractions afterward.

Imaginary Friends

By the time children reach the preschool years, imaginary companions sometimes supplement other peer relationships. By age 4, some 20% of children have invisible friends and another 20% have personified objects (e.g., a bear that is treated as though it were human; Gleason, Sebanc, & Hartup, 2000). Early studies of these transitory phenomena were largely guided by psychoanalytic theory, especially the theoretical assumptions relating to the origins and meaning of children's fantasies. Results were inconsistent, although the findings clearly showed that imaginary companions are not more evident among troubled children than among better adjusted ones (Taylor, 1999).

More recent studies focus on the child's behavior with imaginary companions in relation to cognitive and social development (Gleason, 2002; Taylor, 1999). In general, children who have imaginary companions are more likely to be firstborn and only children than those without these companions, suggesting a "compensatory motivation" for their creation. Mothers believe that their children create these companions because

their children need a relationship, lack playmates, or experience a change in the family (e.g., birth of a sibling).

Children expect imaginary companions to provide them with the same social provisions as their "real" friends – provisions that differ from parent–child or sibling relationships. Parents provide instrumental help for the child; siblings provide conflict. Neither friends nor imaginary friends, however, are identified with either of these provisions. Real and imaginary friends, in contrast, are identified with social power. Imaginary friends are portrayed as objects of nurturance more frequently than real friends – the only major difference in the provisions children associate with these two types of partner (Gleason, 2002). More than exotic phenomena, then, imaginary companions seem to be linked to the young child's efforts to understand and differentiate the social world.

Relations Among Relationships

Most children have close relationships with a number of significant others. These relationships may be linked to one another in the sense that the quality of functioning in one may be associated with the quality of functioning in another. Attachment theory, for example, suggests the existence of continuities from one relationship to another (especially in their affective organization), both concurrently and across time (Bowlby, 1969). Other theories (e.g., social learning theory) lead to similar expectations, so that most psychologists view the child's social world as integrated. That is, the existence of interconnections among different relationships demonstrates that these same relationships are better regarded as constituent elements of "social networks" or "social systems" than as separate "social worlds."

Cross-time connections are also important because relationships are believed to combine with one another to determine developmental outcome. Two types of combinations can be identified that are significant in social development: (a) "moderator" effects, that is, when two relationships are associated with one another or with a later outcome under certain conditions but not others; and (b) "mediator" effects, that is, when the linkage between two relationships or between a relationship and some specific outcome are explained by some other condition (Collins & Roisman, 2003).

Parent–Child Relationships and Friendships

The quality of relationships between mothers and their offspring is associated with friendship quality among young children. Security in mother–infant relationships in both members of 4-year-old friendship pairs is associated with harmony and responsivity between the children (Park & Waters, 1989). Preschool children who have secure attachment histories are also not as likely to have negative and asymmetrical friendships as those who have insecure attachment histories (Youngblade & Belsky, 1992).

Longitudinal studies linking early and middle childhood show that the security of early attachment predicts friendship formation and functioning even when the effects of early peer competence are partialled out. Moreover, preschool peer competence (which is related to the earlier attachment history) continues to make a unique contribution to friendship functioning in middle childhood (Sroufe, Egeland, & Carlson, 1999).

The developmental effects of friendship quality are also known to depend on family conditions. For example, friendships that provide companionship, support, security, and closeness compensate for family vulnerabilities and stresses but, at the same time, provide few benefits when family environments are good (Gauze, Bukowski, Aquan-Assee, & Sippola, 1996).

Sibling Relationships and Friendships

Sibling relationships are sometimes regarded as "bridges" to peer relationships, but this is not the case. Overall, the evidence shows no consistent pattern in either the affective or social orientations of children with siblings compared with children who do not have them (Dunn, 2002; Kitzmann, Cohen, & Lockwood, 2002). Actually, sibling relationships and friendships constitute different social contexts. Conflicts between siblings are more intense than with friends, more likely to include aggression, and less likely to be resolved with negotiation and conciliation (DeHart, 1999). Children themselves recognize these differences in social context when they say that they expect conflict to be provided in their relationships with siblings more than with friends (Furman & Buhrmester, 1985). Something about general social understanding may be acquired in sibling relationships that transfers to friendships and other close relationships but demonstrating this notion has not been accomplished convincingly.

Friends and Enemies

Do friends who have enemies differ from friends who do not? Do enemies who have friends differ from enemies who do not? Contrasting friends, neither of whom has an enemy, with dyads who are neutral toward one another shows few differences. When one friend has an enemy and the other does not, dyads also do not differ extensively from neutral associates. When both friends have enemies, however, friendship dyads differ significantly from neutral ones in aggression and victimization, internalization, and antisocial behavior (Hartup et al., 2002). Clearly, involvement in mutual antipathies moderates children in friendship dyads in the direction of poorer adjustment.

Enemies who have mutual friends also differ from those who do not. Dyads comprising enemies who do not have friends, in contrast to neutral dyads, are more aggressive, antisocial, internalizing, and victimized. When only one child in a mutually antipathetic dyad has a friend, these deviations are attenuated: Enemy dyads differ from neutrals only in aggression and victimization. Even greater attenuation is evinced when both enemies have a friend. Moderating effects of having friends are thus noticeable among enemies, and similar effects of having enemies are noticeable among friends (Hartup et al., 2002).

Conclusion

The significance of peer relationships in early and middle childhood is tentatively established. Friendships, mutual antipathies, bully – victim relationships, and various quasi-relationships appear to be related to social adaptation both independently and in combination with one another. Friendship has received the lion's share of attention in the relationships literature, and other relationships need more attention than they have received thus far. To better specify the role that peer relationships play in child development, six factors need to be addressed (Hartup, 2003):

1. *Conceptualization and methodology*. Consensus does not exist on the best ways to identify close relationships in early and middle childhood. What, then, are the best ways to identify friendships, acquaintanceships, mutual antipathies, enemyships, bully–victim relationships, and relationships with imaginary friends?

2. *Salience*. The existence of close relationships in childhood is not questioned, but children's thinking about them has been explored superficially except in the case of friendships. What is the salience – both to the scientist and to children themselves – of animosities, bully–victim relationships, sibling bonds, and imaginary companions?

3. *Heterogeneity*. Research shows that children's friendships are not all alike. In what ways are mutual antipathies heterogeneous? Sibling relationships? Bully–victim relationships? Quasi-relationships such as those with imaginary companions?

4. *Dynamics*. What characterizes the social exchanges that exist between friends,

enemies, siblings, and bullies and their victims? In other words, what mechanisms of behavioral change are contained within these relationships?

5. *Antecedents*. What conditions in early development predict the formation and functioning of friendships, mutual antipathies, and bully–victim relationships among school-age children and adolescents? Child characteristics and the social context need to be explored as well as earlier experience in both parent–child and peer relationships.

6. *Developmental course*. When, in developmental terms, do specific relationships matter and why? Developmental models are needed to specify the manner in which childhood relationships change over time and combine with other experiences and conditions to affect the child's future development.

Answers to these questions require long-term effort. Both cross-sectional and longitudinal studies are needed. Beginnings have been made toward answering some of these questions: For example, evidence suggests that different relationships (e.g., friendships and mutual antipathies) make different contributions to the child's development. Relationships also seem to differ in the contributions they make to the lives of different children. These conclusions are tentative, however. So far, the evidence suggests that close relationships have considerable importance to the child's well-being. Beyond this, our knowledge about the importance of peer relationships in early and middle childhood is a long way from being complete.

Footnote

1. The word *enemyship* does not exist in English as an antonym for friendship, although equivalents exist in German, French, and other languages. This neologism is used sparingly in this chapter to refer to the relationship between enemies when other words or phrases are awkward or not precise.

References

Abecassis, M., Hartup, W. W., Haselager, G. J. T., Scholte, R., & Van Lieshout, C. F. M. (2002). Mutual antipathies and their significance in middle childhood and adolescence. *Child Development, 73*, 1543–1556.

Anderson, H. H., & Anderson, G. L. (1946). Social development. In L. Carmichael (Ed.), *Manual of child psychology* (pp. 1162–1215). New York: Wiley.

Bagwell, C., & Coie, J. D. (2004). The best friendships of aggressive boys: Relationship quality, conflict management, and rule-breaking behavior. *Journal of Experimental Child Psychology, 88*, 5–24.

Bagwell, C., Newcomb, A. F., & Bukowski, W. M. (1998). Preadolescent friendship and peer rejection as predictors of adult adjustment. *Child Development, 69*, 140–153.

Bandura, A. (1977). *Social learning theory*. Englewood Cliffs, NJ: Erlbaum.

Berndt, T. J. (1981). Relations between social cognition, nonsocial cognition, and social behavior: The case of friendship. In J. H. Flavell & L. Ross (Eds.), *Social cognitive development* (pp. 176–200). Cambridge, England: Cambridge University Press.

Berndt, T. J., Hawkins, J. A., & Jiao, Z. (1999). Influence of friends and friendships on adjustment to junior high school. *Merrill-Palmer Quarterly, 45*, 13–41.

Bernicot, J., & Mahrokhian, A. (1989). Asking and insisting after a refusal: How do 6- to 7-year olds proceed? *International Journal of Psychology, 24*, 409–428.

Bigelow, B. J. (1977). Children's friendship expectations: A cognitive developmental study. *Child Development, 48*, 246–253.

Bowlby, J. (1969). *Attachment and loss: Vol. 1. Attachment*. New York: Basic Books.

Bühler, C. (1931). The social behavior of the child. In C. Murchison (Ed.), *A handbook of child psychology* (pp. 393–431). New York: Russell & Russell.

Buhrmester, D., & Furman, W. (1986). The changing functions of friends in childhood: A neo-Sullivanian perspective. In V. J. Derlega & B. A. Winstead (Eds.), *Friendships and social interaction* (pp. 41–62). New York: Spinger-Verlag.

Card, N. A., & Hodges, E. V. E. (2003). Parent–child relationships and enmity with peers: The role of avoidant and preoccupied attachment. In E. V. E. Hodges & N. A. Card (Eds.), *Enemies and the darker side of peer relations* (pp. 5–22). San Francisco: Jossey-Bass.

Challman, R. C. (1932). Factors influencing friendships among preschool children. *Child Development, 3*, 146–158.

Collins, W. A., & Roisman, G. I. (2003, October). *Familial and peer influence in the development of competence during adolescence*. Paper presented at Marbach Conference, Zurich.

DeHart, G. B. (1999). Conflict and averted conflict in preschoolers' interactions with siblings and friends. In W. A. Collins & B. Laursen (Eds.), *Minnesota symposia on child psychology* (Vol. 30, pp. 281–303). Mahwah, NJ: Erlbaum.

Dishion, T. J. (1990). The peer context of troublesome child and adolescent behavior. In P. Leone (Ed.), *Understanding troubled and troublesome youth* (pp. 128–153). Newbury Park, CA: Sage.

Dunn, J. (2002). Sibling relationships. In P. K. Smith & C. H. Hart (Eds.), *Blackwell handbook of social development* (pp. 223–237). Oxford, England: Blackwell.

Epstein, J. L., & Karweit, N. (1983). *Friends in school*. New York: Academic Press.

Erikson, E. H. (1950). *Childhood and society*. New York: Norton.

Furman, W., & Buhrmester, D. (1985). Children's perceptions of the personal relationships in their social networks. *Developmental Psychology, 21*, 1016–1022.

Gauze, C., Bukowski, W. M., Aquan-Assee, J., & Sippola, L. (1996). Interactions between family environment and friendship and associations with self-perceived well-being during early adolescence. *Child Development, 67*, 2201–2216.

Gleason, T. R. (2002). Social provisions of real and imaginary relationships in early childhood. *Developmental Psychology, 38*, 979–992.

Gleason, T. R., Sebanc, A. M., & Hartup, W. W. (2000). Imaginary companions of preschool children. *Developmental Psychology, 36*, 419–428.

Gottman, J. M. (1983). How children become friends. *Monographs of the Society for Research in Child Development, 48* (3, Serial No. 201).

Gottman, J. M., & Parker, J. G. (Eds.). (1986). *Conversations of friends: Speculations on affective development*. New York: Cambridge University Press.

Green, E. H. (1933). Friendships and quarrels among preschool children. *Child Development*, 4, 237–252.

Güroğlu, B., Van Lieshout, C. F. M., & Haselager, G. J. T. (2004). *Heterogeneity of mutual friendship dyads in children and adolescents in school classes*. Unpublished manuscript, University of Nijmegen.

Hartup, W. W. (1996). The company they keep: Friendships and their developmental significance. *Child Development*, 67, 1–13.

Hartup, W. W. (2003). Toward understanding mutual antipathies in childhood and adolescence. In E. V. E. Hodges & N. A. Card (Eds.), *Enemies and the darker side of peer relations* (pp. 111–123). San Francisco: Jossey-Bass.

Hartup, W. W., & Abecassis, M. (2002). Friends and enemies. In P. K. Smith & C. H. Hart (Eds.), *Blackwell handbook of social development* (pp. 285–306). Oxford, England: Blackwell.

Hartup, W. W., Laursen, B., Stewart, M. A., & Eastenson, A. (1988). Conflict and the friendship relations of young children. *Child Development*, 59, 1590–1600.

Hartup, W. W., Verhoeven, M., De Boer, R., Scholte, R., & Van Lieshout, C. F. M. (2002, August). *Heterogeneity of mutual friendships and mutual antipathies: A cross-sectional study*. Paper presented at the biennial meetings of the International Society for the Study of Behavioural Development, Ottawa, Canada.

Haselager, G. J. T., Hartup, W. W., Van Lieshout, C. F. M., & Riksen-Walraven, M. (1998). Similarities between friends and nonfriends in middle childhood. *Child Development*, 69, 1198–1208.

Hayes, D., Gershman, E., & Bolin, L. (1980). Friends and enemies: Cognitive bases for preschool children's unilateral and reciprocal relationships. *Child Development*, 51, 1276–1279.

Hembree, S. E., & Vandell, D. L. (2000). *Reciprocity and rejection: The role of mutual antipathy and children's adjustment*. Unpublished manuscript, University of Wisconsin.

Hetherington, E. M. (1999). Social capital and the development of youth from nondivorced, divorced, and remarried families. In W. A. Collins & B. Laursen (Eds.), *Minnesota symposia on child psychology* (Vol. 30, pp. 177–209). Mahwah, NJ: Erlbaum.

Hodges, E. V. E., & Card, N. A. (Eds.). (2003). *Enemies and the darker side of peer relations*. San Francisco: Jossey-Bass.

Hodges, E. V. E., Malone, M. J., & Perry, D. G. (1997). Individual risk and social risk as interacting determinants of victimization in the peer group. *Developmental Psychology*, 33, 1032–1039.

Hodges, E. V. E., & Perry, D. G. (1999). Personal and interpersonal antecedents and consequences of victimization by peers. *Journal of Personality and Social Psychology*, 677–685.

Howes, C. (1983). Patterns of friendship. *Child Development*, 54, 1041–1053.

Howes, C., & Farver, J. (1987). Toddlers' responses to the distress of their peers. *Journal of Applied Developmental Psychology*, 8, 441–452.

Howes, C., & Unger, O. A. (1989). Play with peers in child care settings. In M. Bloch & A. Pellegrini (Eds.), *The ecological contexts of children's play* (pp. 104–119). Norwood, NJ: Ablex.

Kandel, D. B. (1978). Homophily, selection, and socialization in adolescent friendships. *American Journal of Sociology*, 84, 427–436.

Kitzmann, K. M., Cohen, R., & Lockwood, R. L. (2002). Are only children missing out? Comparison of the peer-related social competence of only children and siblings. *Journal of Social and Personal Relationships*, 19, 299–316.

Kupersmidt, J. B., DeRosier, M. E., & Patterson, C. P. (1995). Similarity as the basis for children's friendships: The roles of sociometric status, aggressive and withdrawn behavior, academic achievement, and demographic characteristics. *Journal of Social and Personal Relationships*, 12, 439–452.

Ladd, G. W., & Emerson, E. S. (1984). Shared knowledge in children's friendships. *Developmental Psychology*, 20, 932–940.

Laursen, B., Hartup, W. W., & Koplas, A. L. (1996). Toward understanding peer conflict. *Merrill-Palmer Quarterly*, 42, 76–102.

Monroe, W. S. (1899). Play interests of children. *American Educational Review*, 4, 358–365.

Morry, M. M. (2003). Perceived locus of control and satisfaction in same-sex friendships. *Journal of Personal Relationships*, 10, 495–509.

Newcomb, A. F., & Bagwell, C. (1995). Children's friendship relations: A meta-analytic review. *Psychological Bulletin*, 117, 306–347.

Olweus, D. (1993). *Bullying at school*. Oxford, England: Blackwell.

Park, K. A., & Waters, E. (1989). Security of attachment and preschool friendships. *Child Development*, 60, 1076–1081.

Piaget, J. (1932). *The moral judgment of the child*. Glencoe, IL: Free Press.

Poulin, F., Dishion, T. J., & Haas, E. (1999). The peer influence paradox: Friendship quality and deviancy training within male adolescent friendships. *Merrill-Palmer Quarterly*, 45, 42–61.

Ray, G., & Cohen, R. (1997). Children's evaluations of provocation between peers. *Aggressive Behavior*, 23, 417–431.

Rigby, K. (2002). Bullying in childhood. In P. K. Smith & C. H. Hart (Eds.), *Blackwell handbook of social development* (pp. 549–568). Oxford, England: Blackwell.

Rizzo, T. A. (1989). *Friendship development among children in school*. Norwood, NJ: Ablex.

Rodkin, P. C., Pearl, R., Farmer, T. W., & Van Acker, R. (2003). Enemies in the gendered societies of middle childhood: Prevalence, stability, associations with social status, and aggression. In E. V. E. Hodges & N. A. Card (Eds.), *Enemies and the darker side of peer relations* (pp. 73–88). San Francisco: Jossey-Bass.

Rosenbaum, M. E. (1986). The repulsion hypothesis: On the nondevelopment of relationships. *Journal of Personality and Social Psychology*, 51, 1156–1166.

Ross, H., & Conant, C. (1992). The social structure of early conflicts: Interaction, relationships, and alliances. In C. U. Shantz & W. W. Hartup (Eds.), *Conflict in child and adolescent development* (pp. 153–185). Cambridge, England: Cambridge University Press.

Rubin, K. H., Lynch, D. Coplan, R., Rose-Krasnor, L., & Booth, C. L. (1994). "Birds of a feather . . .": Behavioral concordances and preferential personal attraction in children. *Child Development*, 65, 1778–1785.

Schwartz, D., Hopmeyer-Gorman, A., Toblin, R. L., & Abou-ezzeddine, T. (2003). Mutual antipathies in the peer group as a moderating factor in the association between community violence exposure and psychosocial maladjustment. In E. V. E. Hodges & N. A. Card (Eds.), *Enemies and the darker side of peer relations* (pp. 39–54). San Francisco: Jossey-Bass.

Selman, R. L. (1980). *The growth of interpersonal understanding*. New York: Academic Press.

Sippola, L. K., Bukowski, W. M., & Noll, R. B. (1997). Dimensions of liking and disliking underlying the same-sex preference in childhood and early adolescence. *Merrill-Palmer Quarterly*, 43, 591–609.

Sroufe, L. A., Egeland, B., & Carlson, E. A. (1999). One social world: The integrated development of parent-child and peer relationships. In W. A. Collins & B. Laursen (Eds.), *Minnesota symposia on child psychology* (Vol. 30, pp. 241–261). Mahwah, NJ: Erlbaum.

Sullivan, H. S. (1953). *The interpersonal theory of psychiatry*. New York: Norton.

Taylor, M. (1999). *Imaginary companions and the children who create them*. New York: Oxford University Press.

Urberg, K. A. (1999). Introduction to invitational issue: Some thoughts about studying the influence of peers on children and adolescents. *Merrill-Palmer Quarterly*, 45, 1–12.

Vostrovsky, C. (1895). A study of imaginary companions. *Education*, 15, 393–398.

Wiseman, J., & Duck, S. (1995). Having enemies and managing enemies: A very challenging relationship. In S. Duck & J. Wood (Eds.), *Understanding relationship processes: Vol. 5. Confronting relationship challenges* (pp. 43–72). Thousand Oaks, CA: Sage.

Youngblade, L. M., & Belsky, J. (1992). Parent–child antecedents of five-year-olds' close friendships: A longitudinal analysis. *Developmental Psychology*, 28, 107–121.

Youniss, J. (1980). *Parents and peers in social development: A Sullivan–Piaget perspective*. Chicago: University of Chicago Press.

CHAPTER 11

Personal Relationships in Adolescence and Early Adulthood

W. Andrew Collins
Stephanie D. Madsen

Personal Relationships in Adolescence and Early Adulthood

Personal relationships loom large in both the popular lore and the research literature on adolescence and early adulthood. Explanations of the distinctive behaviors and attitudes of adolescents often point to the impact of the peer group and the young person's friends, and popular culture is suffused with images of "first love" and sexual awakening. Similarly, popular portrayals of early adulthood typically turn on events that occur in the context of friends and romantic partners; witness the popularity of long-running television hits such as *Friends*. Ironically, however, the behavioral and social science of these age periods commonly gives priority to individualistic accounts of behavior and development, neglecting their salient relational contexts. When relational contexts are considered, the individualistic bias favors constructs of distance (e.g., autonomy, identity) over notions of closeness (e.g., collaboration, mutuality). Only recently have calls for attention to relationships as key contexts for the development of individual competencies begun to redress the imbalance (e.g., Laursen & Bukowski, 1997; Reis, Collins, & Berscheid, 2000).

The focus of this chapter is the personal relationships of individuals during the years from age 12–18, the most commonly accepted age markers for adolescence, to ages 19–28, which has been suggested as the age range for early adulthood (Arnett, 2000; Collins & Van Dulmen, in press). The goals of the chapter are to distill from the literature evidence concerning how adolescents and early adults differ from older and younger age groups and to characterize differences between adolescents and early adults with regard to personal relationships.

As in other chapters in this volume, the term *relationship* refers to a pair of persons who are interdependent with each other, that is, each person affects and is affected by the behavior of the other person over time. Interdependence in relationships can vary in degree. Some pairs manifest a high degree of mutual impact over a period of years; the involvement and impact of other pairs may be more transitory. Longer term, more salient, and more mutually influential relationships correspond to the commonly used term *close* (Reis et al., 2000). For convenience, in this chapter the terms *close relationships* and *personal relationships* are used to refer explicitly to the two most salient types of interdependent relationships outside of the family, friendships and romantic relationships. Although familial relationships continue to be significant in the development of both adolescents and early adults (for a review, see Collins & Laursen, 2004), this chapter, like others in this volume, emphasizes close relationships beyond the family of origin.

The chapter is divided into four parts. The first part briefly characterizes the distinctive characteristics of adolescents and early adults as relationship partners and also outlines major conceptual approaches to the study of close relationships in these periods. The second part draws from research findings on friendships to identify distinctive features of these relationships in adolescence and in early adulthood. The third part turns to research findings to characterize romantic relationships in the two periods. Throughout these sections, themes that should be addressed in further research are noted.

Transitions in Relationships During Adolescence and Early Adulthood

The question of whether and in what ways the relationships of adolescents and early adults differ from those of other adults and children lurks, sometimes unrecognized, in current research on these age groups. Frequently, distinctiveness is simply assumed, often with the implication that the important differences are those that help to account for common problems associated with adolescents and youth (e.g., conformity to peers, social rejection, depression). Equally often, distinctiveness is ignored to use the relationships of youthful partners (e.g., college students) as exemplars of adult relationships generally. Consequently, the literature on college students sheds little light on the developmental questions that are the focus of this chapter (Brown,

Feiring, & Furman, 1999; Collins, 2003; Collins & Van Dulmen, in press).

Adolescents and Early Adults As Relationship Partners

Adolescence has been said to begin in biology and end in culture. This invocation of nature and nurture traditionally refers to the recognition that the normative psychological and behavioral markers of the period (e.g., intensified orientation to peers) reflect both biological maturation and social and cultural expectations. As relationship partners, adolescents experience extensive and rapid maturation and encounter equally dramatic changes in expectations for relating to others. By most of the usual criteria, 12 year olds, 15 year olds, and 18 year olds alike are categorized as adolescents, but members of these age groups also differ in physical and cognitive characteristics and elicit different expectations from others. For example, when adolescents experience conflicts with peers, negotiations take different forms from those in childhood because more advanced cognitive abilities permit more complex reasoning. At the same time, negotiations with friends and romantic partners are increasingly differentiated from negotiations with mere acquaintances. This pattern may reflect further maturation during adolescence that results in refined understanding of the requirements for maintaining and enhancing intimate friendships and romantic relationships versus more casual affiliations (Laursen & Collins, 1994).

By contrast, the markers of early adulthood are largely nonbiological. Arnett's (2000, in press) recent proposal that the years from the late teens to the late 20s constitute a distinctive period of experiences in social relationships stems partly from readily apparent social and demographic changes. Arnett argued that a prolonged period of uncertainty and temporizing has resulted from secular trends toward later marriage and childbearing, longer stints in education and other programs preparatory to career paths, and labor-market changes affecting the availability of long-term employment patterns. In this view, the early to middle 20s are a socially expected period of freedom and exploration before fully assuming adult roles and responsibilities. These presumed expectations support intense self-focus, experiencing a wide variety of relationships, and avoiding commitments to particular partners and lifestyle arrangements (Arnett, in press). Although research findings keyed to Arnett's predictions are sparse, his proposal raises provocative issues regarding whether close relationships in the teens and 20s are developmentally distinct or a combination of teenage patterns extended into the college and postcollege years (Collins & Van Dulmen, in press).

Conceptual Perspectives on Relationships During Adolescence

Formal theories of adolescent development provide contrasting accounts of differentiation and change in relationships. In this section, we briefly outline four general theoretical perspectives: (a) endogenous-change perspectives emphasize biological and motivational pressures toward alterations of relationships; (b) social–psychological perspectives focus on external pressures toward change and the interplay of external and internal factors; (c) attachment perspectives address the pressures toward continuity and coherence in primary aspects of dyadic relationships; and (d) interdependency perspectives emphasize the patterns of interaction and affect and the principles of exchange that characterize close relationships.

ENDOGENOUS-CHANGE PERSPECTIVES

Psychoanalytic and evolutionary views share two perspectives on relationships during adolescence. One is a focus on pubertal maturation in precipitating increased conflict and emotional distance in parent–child relationships and, correspondingly, an increased orientation to relationships beyond the family. The other is an emphasis on the functional significance of relationships and relationship changes.

Psychoanalytic and neo-analytic theorists (e.g., Blos, 1979; A. Freud, 1958) assumed that hormonal changes and the subsequent surge of sexual excitation at puberty generated increased pressures toward individuation from parents and greater involvement with age mates. Concomitant with these aspects of control and autonomy striving are the issues of personal integration and mastery encompassed by Erikson's (1968) concept of ego identity. Evolutionary views (Steinberg, 1988) also emphasize autonomy striving as a motivation for relationship changes. From this perspective, perturbations in parent–child relationships at puberty serve to facilitate formation of sexual relationships outside of the family group and, particularly for boys, to foster the socialization of autonomy. Corresponding increases in orientation to relationships with peers are viewed as a shift toward interpersonal objects appropriate to adult roles (Blos, 1979).

Endogenous-change perspectives have fewer direct implications for the transition to early adulthood, probably because biological change does not define this period. The emphasis on adaptation, however, does underscore the heretofore little considered possibility that the adaptive functions of close relationships in this later period may involve more subtle, complex processes than the adaptive functions of close relationships in adolescence.

SOCIAL–PSYCHOLOGICAL PERSPECTIVES

Social–psychological theories view relationship changes as a reflection of the stresses engendered by the multiple adaptations required during developmental transitions (Lewin, 1931; Reis et al., 2000). Life cycle changes in relationships in turn affect the individual development of both partners in the relationship (e.g., Hartup & Laursen, 1999).

Transitions to adolescence and then to early adulthood partly reflect maturational changes but appear to be affected even more extensively by age-graded expectations, tasks, and settings (Collins & Laursen,

2004). For adolescents, the confluence of maturational changes and age-graded social shifts can be seen in the comparatively greater decrements in seventh-grade girls' self-esteem if they are simultaneously experiencing pubertal maturation, beginning to date, and shifting from elementary to junior high school (Simmons & Blyth, 1987). In early adulthood, similar accumulations of stressors are apparent in less effective functioning if best friendships deteriorate during the transition to from high school to college (Oswald & Clark, 2003).

Although like other perspectives, the social–psychological viewpoint implies decreased stability followed by increasing stability between early and late adolescence, the course may be more episodic than other theories imply. From the perspective of social age grading, this episodic pattern reflects the periodic occurrence of age-graded transitions. An alternative, but conceptually consistent, prediction is that early adolescence might be a primary period of change, with gradual restabilization as appropriate accommodations are made to transitional status. Individuals may vary, moreover, as a function of timing of puberty (Collins & Laursen, 2004). Very early pubertal timing for girls may result in long-lasting perturbations in relationships (e.g., Caspi & Moffit, 1991; Magnusson, Stattin, & Allen, 1985).

ATTACHMENT PERSPECTIVES

The focus of attachment approaches is motivational tendencies toward functional similarities in relationships across time. Bowlby (1982) predicted that *internal working models* of relationships formed in early caregiver–child interactions would underlie stability across time in the *qualities* of relationships. These qualities are based in emotions associated with feelings of security and insecurity regarding one's close relationships.

Within this framework, specific interactions change as a function of developmental adaptations from one age period to the next. Despite these relatively superficial adaptations, however, the fundamental qualities of relationships are still rooted in internal working models that provide a functional similarity in relating from one developmental period to the next. These parallel patterns of behavior and affect across age periods have been attributed to stable *organizations* of behavior, mediated by internal working models formed in early caregiver–child relationships and repeatedly reconfirmed in subsequent interactions with others (Sroufe & Fleeson, 1988). Longitudinal findings show, for example, that interactions and the management of emotions with teachers and peers in early and middle childhood manifest similarities to assessments of caregiver–child attachment in infancy.

Differentiation among relationships results from certain cues or signals regarding what is expected from a particular other person. Although there is considerable coherence in adolescents' and early adults' reactions to certain types of actions by others, relationship partners nevertheless elicit different types of interactions. For example, aloof, ambivalent adolescents both elicit and actively respond to different types of overtures from peers than do more outgoing, relaxed, sociable children (Sroufe & Fleeson, 1988).

INTERDEPENDENCY PERSPECTIVES

Interdependency perspectives emphasize the joint patterns in which the actions, cognitions, and emotions of each member of the dyad are significant to the other's reactions (Hinde, 1997; Kelley et al., 1983). In contrast to attachment perspectives, close relationships are defined quantitatively, rather than qualitatively: A close relationship is one in which two persons interact with each other frequently, across a variety of settings and tasks, and exert considerable influence on each others' thoughts and actions. Typically, such relationships are not transitory, but exist for periods measured in months or years. It should be noted that closeness is independent of the emotional content of the relationship; interdependency may characterize relationships in which affective expression is largely negative, as well as those in which warm, positive emotions predominate.

In this perspective, adolescence can be characterized as a period during which interdependencies in familial relationships continue, although often in forms different from those in earlier life, whereas interdependencies with friends and romantic partners become more apparent. Some changes in individuals' competence for relating are required to create and maintain these interdependencies. In peer relationships, skills must be developed for maintaining interdependence on the basis of shared interests, commitments, and intimacy, even when contact is relatively infrequent (Parker & Gottman, 1989). Mismatches between expectancies about the relationship may precipitate conflicts, but these conflicts often stimulate adjustments of expectancies that gradually restore harmony (Collins, 1995). The process by which discrepant perceptions mediate changes in interactions is largely unstudied (see reviews by Collins, 1997; Laursen & Collins, 1994).

Differentiation among relationships is constrained partly by interrelations among the relationships in which most adolescents and early adults participate. For example, trust, communication, and conflict resolution within families have been found to be correlated with adolescents' intimacy and communication with peers (Youniss & Smollar, 1985), and the intimacy experienced in friendship may provide a model that enhances capacities for intimacy within families as adolescents mature (Youniss, 1980). Nevertheless, differences in the frequency, diversity, strength, and duration of relationships with parents or siblings and those with friends and acquaintances clearly produce contrasts among these relationship types. Characteristics of relationships with family members and friends are correlated with satisfaction with and longevity of romantic relationships in early adulthood (e.g., Parks & Eggert, 1991; Sprecher & Felmlee, 1992).

Close Relationships in Adolescence and Early Adulthood

Relationships with peers differ from those with family members in terms of the distri-

bution of power between participants and the permanence of the affiliation (Laursen & Bukowski, 1997). Peer relationships are voluntary and transient; participants freely initiate and dissolve interconnections. Neither party can impose the terms of social interaction on the other (Piaget, 1932/1965). Whether an affiliation persists hinges on mutually satisfactory terms and outcomes (Murstein, 1970). In this section we review research findings on the nature and significance of friendships and of romantic relationships during adolescence and early adulthood. We next consider the extent and implications of interrelations among personal relationships in these periods.

Friendships

Friendships are the most prominent feature of social relations in both adolescence and early adulthood. Adolescents commonly report that friends are their most important extrafamilial resources and influences, and relationships with friends consistently are implicated in variations in adolescent competence and well-being (Brown, 2004). Experiences with friends appear both to influence and moderate social adaptation and academic competence (Cairns & Cairns, 1994). In addition, as the first voluntary intimate relationships, adolescent friendships provide critical interpersonal experiences that establish a template for subsequent close relationships with peers, including romantic partners (Furman & Wehner, 1994; Sullivan, 1953).

Friends are frequent companions in early adulthood as well, getting together at least once a week for no specific purpose and somewhat less frequently for parties, movies, and concerts (Osgood & Lee, 1993). As in adolescence, close friends in early adulthood tend to be of the same sex, and women report more close friends than men (Jones, Bloys, & Wood, 1990).

CONCEPTS OF FRIENDSHIP

Adolescents typically experience considerable growth of conceptual and reasoning skills and as a consequence adopt more sophisticated views of close peer relationships than are typical of children (Selman, 1980). Adolescents increasingly regard companionship and sharing as necessary but no longer sufficient conditions for closeness in friendships; commitment and intimacy are expected as well, especially among girls and young women (Youniss & Smollar, 1985). This shift in friendship requirements from behavioral to emotional aspects may account partly for adolescents' perceptions that their friendship-making abilities are inferior to those they held in middle childhood (Barry & Wigfield, 2002).

Social–cognitive advances also underlie improved perspective taking abilities that can further bolster cognitive and affective ties between friends (Selman, 1980). For example, adolescents are better able to view friends' behaviors and emotions in terms of historical, biological, and social factors (Livesley & Bromley, 1973; Selman, 1980). Still, when the situation is ambiguous or multifaceted or when stereotypes can be easily applied, adolescents' reasoning skills may be overridden (Horn, 2003).

Developing cognitive abilities also are evident within friendships even in the early adult years. Conceptions of friendships remain malleable into the 20s, perhaps because the experiences of this age period require adjustments in previously held expectations of friends. Baxter, Dun, and Sahlstein (2001) studied early adults' implicit social rules regarding interactions with peers and found that rules concerning loyalty, honesty, and respect were especially salient. Social networks exerted their influence on the proper conduct of friendship primarily in an indirect manner by communicating general rules or beliefs about relationships, rather than providing instructions for specific relationships. Even more strongly than adolescents, early adults view interpersonal responsibilities in close relationships as obligatory. That is, once a relationship has begun, early adults do not consider it a matter of personal choice whether to meet a friend's needs, but rather a social obligation (Neff, Turiel, & Anshel, 2002). Such orientations may be helpful in sustaining friendships; relationships with a balance of functions fulfilled for each individual are more often marked by greater affection for the friend and greater satisfaction than relationships with an imbalance between partners (Mendelson & Kay, 2003).

Still-developing cognitive skills also play a role in interpersonal dynamics between friends. For example, individual differences in complexity of epistemological understanding have been linked to variations in approaches to conflict with friends. Women with more advanced ideas about knowledge are less likely to simply avoid conflict (or to agree to disagree) but instead productively engage in processing and exploring conflict (Weinstock & Bond, 2000). This finding suggests that early adults are still learning to approach conflicts in more constructive ways and that such advances may be tied to continuing cognitive development. Brain development that supports advances in executive regulatory functions may partly account for these effects (Siegel, 1999).

INTERACTIONS WITH FRIENDS

Relationships with friends change qualitatively during adolescence (Rubin, Bukowski, & Parker, 1998). Mutuality, self-disclosure, and intimacy with friends (defined as reciprocal feelings of self-disclosure and engagement in activities) increase markedly during adolescence (Furman & Buhrmester, 1992; Sharabany, Gershoni, & Hofmann, 1981). Intimacy in particular is closely related to satisfaction with friendships during early and middle adolescence (Hartup, 1996). Paradoxically, conflicts also are more likely between friends than between acquaintances in both childhood and adolescence. Within adolescence, topics of conflict reflect current concerns, with older adolescents reporting more conflicts regarding private disrespect and young adolescents voicing more concern about public disrespect and undependability (Shulman & Laursen, 2002). Still, compared with middle childhood, conflicts between friends increasingly are likely to be resolved effectively during adolescence and are less likely to disrupt friendships (Laursen & Collins, 1994).

Patterns of friendship qualities that are evident in adolescence continue in early adulthood. In particular, girls's and young women's friendships tend to emphasize emotional support and a communal or helping orientation, with women reporting that they receive greater emotional support and intimate disclosure than men report (Carbery & Buhrmester, 1998), whereas male friendships tend to center around shared activities (Sherman, DeVries, & Lansford, 2000). Despite these baseline differences, advances in friendship intimacy for both sexes continue across early adulthood (Reis, Lin, Bennett, & Nezlek, 1993).

Changes in interactions with friends also are evident, even across the relatively short span of early adulthood. As early adulthood progresses, everyday social interaction patterns change. Rochester Interaction Records from the same individuals at 18 and again at 26–31 (Reis et al., 1993) reveal more opposite-sex socializing and correspondingly less same-sex, mixed-sex, and group interaction. Further, more intimacy occurred in all types of interactions reported at the older age, compared with the younger. At roughly the same time, the overall frequency of leisure interactions with friends declines, a change that can be partially, but not completely, explained by the new family roles increasingly adopted in adulthood (Osgood & Lee, 1993). This instability in social interaction frequency is balanced by stability in social participation styles (Reis et al., 1993). That is, early adults who are highly social compared with their peers at the start of early adulthood tend to remain so later in early adulthood. Likewise, those who have relatively few social interactions with friends at the transition to early adulthood carry this pattern forward.

SELECTION OF FRIENDS

Adolescents choose friends who are similar to them on some dimensions and dissimilar on others. For example, European Americans and Asian Americans have friends who are similar in terms of substance use and academic orientation but dissimilar in

terms of ethnic identity, whereas African American adolescents show the reverse pattern (Hamm, 2000). It seems that rather than seeking friends who are identical to themselves, adolescents prefer to be around people whose similarity allows a comfort level for asserting and developing one's own identity.

Although less often studied than same-sex friendships, cross-sex friendships are a common experience in adolescence, with slightly fewer than half (47%) of adolescents reporting a cross-sex friendship (Kuttler, La Greca, & Prinstein, 1999). Such friendships are not associated inevitably with problematic social or behavioral functioning, although they are associated with perceptions of lower social acceptance. Indeed, cross-sex friendships may be considered a normative aspect of adolescent peer relations (for a review, see Hartup & Abecassis, 2002). Moreover, acknowledging friendships in mixed-gender groups is more normative in adolescence than in middle childhood, when gender segregation is the norm in mixed-gender groups (Maccoby, 1998).

FRIENDSHIP QUALITY AND INDIVIDUAL FUNCTIONING

Close relationships are primary settings for the acquisition of skills ranging from social competencies to motor performance (e.g., athletics, dancing) to cognitive abilities (Hartup, 1996). Poor-quality adolescent friendships (e.g., those low in supportiveness and intimacy) are associated with multiple outcomes, including incidence of loneliness, depression, and decreases in achievement in school and work settings (Hartup, 1996). Social development in and beyond adolescence thus requires continued experience in close relationships, but they and their relationship partners must adapt continually to the rapid changes of adolescence.

Girls report greater companionship, intimacy, prosocial support, and esteem support in their close friendships than boys do (Kuttler et al., 1999); however, this closeness may also create a vulnerability that could account for some negative features of girls' relationships. For example, girl's current friendships tend to be of shorter duration than boys' friendships, and more girls than boys report actions that have harmed existing friendships, as well as a history of dissolved friendships (Benenson & Christakos, 2003).

The impact of friendship quality on adjustment, however, may be stronger among male adolescents than it is among their female counterparts. For example, Hussong (2000) found that girls' adjustment (depression, substance use, positive affect) was affected most negatively by disengagement from friends, whereas boys showed the most deleterious impact of friends when the qualities of friendships were negative. Boys' vulnerability to negative friendship qualities may be exacerbated by greater conflict in male friendships, coupled with a tendency to avoid discussing these conflicts (Black, 2000).

FRIENDSHIPS IN SOCIAL NETWORKS.

Friends become increasingly salient as sources of support for emotional problems during adolescence. Adolescents' perceptions of parents as primary sources of support decline and perceived support from friends increases such that friendships are perceived as providing roughly the same (Helsen, Vollebergh, & Meeus, 2000; Scholte, van Lieshout, & van Aken, 2001) or greater (Furman & Buhrmester, 1992) support as parental relationships. Adolescents receiving little support from parents and greater support from friends report more emotional problems, however (Helsen et al., 2000).

As social roles change in early adulthood, the place of friends in social networks changes as well. Early adults who are similar in marital and parental status (i.e., who are either single, married without children, or married with children) have more similar friendship patterns than a randomly chosen group of early adults do (Carbery & Buhrmester, 1998; Fischer, Sollie, Sorrell, & Green, 1989; Reis et al., 1993). College entry, which often marks the transition from ado-

lescence to early adulthood, challenges early adults to distance themselves from friends from home to allow new supportive relationships to emerge in the college context. Research shows that social networks change gradually under these circumstances; at the end of the first 10 weeks in school, 40% of first-year college students listed no new friends in their social networks (and only 4% listed no friends from home). Best friendships from high school typically decline in satisfaction, commitment, rewards, and investments during the first year in college, although deterioration was less when friends maintained high levels of communication. When best friendships were maintained across this transition, the negative impact of loneliness was mitigated, relative to situations in which individuals did not retain their best friendships (Oswald & Clark, 2003). In the long term, however, failing to divest earlier friendships and affiliate with college friends is associated with loneliness and poor social acceptance and self-esteem in the college environment (Paul & Brier, 2001).

Romantic Relationships

Friendships and romantic relationships are tightly interwoven in adolescence and early adulthood. Unsupervised mixed-gender peer groups during adolescence provide opportunities and supportive environments for "pairing off" between group members. By midadolescence, most individuals have been involved in at least one romantic relationship; by the early years of early adulthood, most are currently participating in an ongoing romantic relationship (Collins, 2003). Middle and late adolescents (approximately ages 14–18) balance time spent with romantic partners with continued participation in same-sex cliques, gradually decreasing time in mixed-sex groups; by early adulthood, time with romantic partners increases further at the expense of involvement with friends and crowds (Reis et al., 1993). These and other findings are consistent with Dunphy's (1963) classic hypothesis regarding the emergence of romantic relationships (Connolly, Furman, & Konarski, 2000).

Most current findings imply that the growing nature and significance of romantic relationships during adolescence and early adulthood stem as much from a culture that emphasizes and hallows romance and sexuality as from physical maturation per se. Although individual differences in timing of romantic involvement sometimes have been attributed to the timing of puberty, studies have repeatedly demonstrated the independent contribution of social and cultural expectations, especially age-graded behavioral norms, to the initiation of dating (Feldman, Turner, & Araujo, 1999; Meschke & Silbereisen, 1997). Moreover, to the extent that physical maturation contributes to increased romantic interest and motivation, the relevant processes appear to occur earlier than the changes usually associated with puberty. The separate and joint effects of maturational and social and cultural factors are a primary focus of research today (Halpern, 2003).

Many, perhaps most, current findings portray the early adulthood years as part of a continuous progression toward the close relationships of adulthood (e.g., Hartup & Stevens, 1997). Existing findings point to a shift in the qualitative characteristics of dating relationships between the ages of 15 and 17 years, and dating among early adults seems similar in key ways to dating among late adolescents. After age 17, the likelihood of being involved in a romantic relationship changes little; partner selection tends to emphasize the personal compatibility, rather than solely on superficial features of appearance and social status, and couple interactions tend to be marked by greater interdependence and more communal orientations than was the case in early-adolescent relationships (Collins, 2003). Except for the larger proportions of married persons after age 28, however, there is currently little compelling evidence that either expectancies or behavior patterns differ between this older group and 18- to 28-year-olds. This section emphasizes these apparent continuities while noting some instances in which possible discontinuities have been reported.

CONCEPTS OF ROMANTIC RELATIONSHIPS

Representations of romantic relationships are linked to representations of other close relationships, especially relationships with friends, and these interrelated expectancies parallel interrelations in features such as support and control (Furman, Simon, Shaffer, & Bouchey, 2002; Furman & Wehner, 1994). Relationship representations, such as those associated with measures of attachment style, predict accommodation to potentially destructive behaviors by early adult romantic partners (e.g., Scharfe & Bartholomew, 1995) and also predict vulnerability to depression for individuals in romantic relationships (Davila, Steinberg, Kachadourian, Cobb, & Fincham, 2002).

In general, differences between midadolescents and 25-year-olds reflect increasing differentiation and complexity of *thoughts* about relationships, but continuity in *relationship motives, concerns, and expectations.* For example, in a longitudinal analysis of relationship narratives (Waldinger et al., 2002), the structure and complexity of narratives increased between midadolescence and age 25, whereas narrative themes were surprisingly similar across the 8- to 10-year gap between waves of the study. A desire for closeness was a dominant theme in the relationships of participants at both ages. Themes of distance also were present at both ages, although in adolescence, this theme was characterized by being on one's own, whereas at age 25 the emphasis was on independence (making autonomous decisions). Because U.S. respondents are highly likely to reflect the wish for independence throughout adulthood, these findings imply greater continuity than discontinuity between early adults and both foregoing and succeeding periods, although explicit comparisons have not yet been reported.

Emotions and cognitions are closely intertwined in romantic relationships and play a major role in determining their functional significance. For example, experiences that conform to idealized romantic scripts heighten positive emotions, and those that diverge from them are common sources for feelings of frustration, disappointment, and hurt. Moreover, tendencies to make attributions about the behavior of self and other are heightened in the early stages of romance, and because relevant cues are likely to be hidden, vague, or undifferentiated in this phase, misattributions are especially likely, often resulting in anxiety, anger, and distrust (for a review, see Larson, Clore, & Wood, 1999). Relationship cognitions and emotions, however, have been studied far more often in relationships *after* adolescence than in adolescent relationships (see Fletcher, Overall, & Friesen and Planalp, Fitness, & Fehr, both this volume). This is somewhat surprising given the common view of adolescence as a time of both intense and unpredictable emotionality and expanding, but still immature, cognitive abilities. Clues for further research on cognitive processes in adolescent romantic relationships come from findings that cognitive measures mediate relationship behavior and adjustment in samples of early adults. Among these are social goals (e.g., Sanderson & Cantor, 1995), attributions (e.g., Fletcher, Fincham, Cramer, & Herson, 1987), and relationship processes such as account making (Sorenson, Russell, Harkness, & Harvey, 1993). Fletcher, Overall, and Friesen (this volume) review relevant findings as well.

SELECTION OF PARTNERS

With whom adolescents and early adults have romantic experiences undoubtedly influences their developmental significance, just as the identity of friends helps to determine the impact of friendships (Hartup, 1996). Although social psychologists have accumulated a vast literature on processes of attraction and partner selection in adult relationships (Berscheid & Reis, 1998; also see Surra, Gray, Boettcher, Cottle, & Curran, this volume), little is known about either the nature of partner choices during adolescence or their significance. Findings from the National Longitudinal Study of Adolescent Health (commonly known as Add-Health) show that, like adults, male adolescents prefer same-age or younger prospective partners, whereas female adolescents prefer somewhat older partners (Carver, Joyner, & Udry, 2003).

Although developmental psychopathologists (e.g., Rutter, 1996) and life course researchers (e.g., Elder, 1998) have found that partner selection often constitutes a developmental turning point in adulthood, it is not known whether partner selection potentially plays an equally significant role during adolescence. This knowledge gap partly reflects two methodological realities (Reis et al., 2000). One is that studies of dating and other adolescent romantic relationships begin with existing couples who are long past the point of selection. The other is that the most common method, retrospective self-reports, is at least as limited in providing valid insights into selection as it is in providing insights into other aspects of behavior. Research that surmounts these problems may reveal that many of the correlations between involvement in romantic relationships and negative patterns of behavior and emotion are attributable to the characteristics of partners rather than to involvement in romantic relationships per se (Collins, 2003).

INTERACTIONS IN ROMANTIC RELATIONSHIPS

Content refers to the shared activities of relationship partners – what adolescent partners do together, how they spend their time, the diversity of their shared activities, and also activities and situations they avoid when together. By definition, more highly interdependent partners typically share a wider variety of activities than less close pairs, and many of those activities bear on the relationship itself (e.g., communicating, completing tasks together, enjoying common recreational activities, working toward common goals; Berscheid, Snyder, & Omoto, 1989; Hinde, 1997).

The few findings available imply that interactions with romantic partners are associated with distinctive patterns of experience for adolescents and early adults. Adolescents in romantic relationships, for example, report experiencing more conflict than other adolescents (Laursen, 1995). Moreover, conflict resolution between late-adolescent romantic partners more often involves compromise than conflict resolution in early-adolescent romantic pairs (Feldman & Gowen, 1998). Exchanges within the romantic relationships of older adolescents also are more likely to reflect greater interdependence and more communal orientations between the partners than is the case with early-adolescent romantic alliances (Laursen & Jensen-Campbell, 1999). Age-related patterns appear to have long-term implications. In longitudinal research in Germany (Seiffge-Krenke & Lang, 2002), quality of romantic relationships in middle adolescence was significantly and positively related to commitment in other relationships in early adulthood.

Unfortunately, little information is available on how time devoted to romantic relationships is spent or how teenage and early-adult romantic partners behave toward one another. Without such information, it is difficult to identify possible functions of the relationships, whether positive or negative, for long-term growth.

RELATIONSHIP QUALITY AND INDIVIDUAL
FUNCTIONING

Frequent conflicts mark romantic relationships, and mood swings, a stereotype of adolescent emotional life, are more extreme for those involved in romantic relationships (for a review, see Larson et al., 1999). In a finding that has become one of the most widely cited in the field, Joyner and Udry (2000) reported that participants in the Add-Health study who had begun romantic relationships in the past year manifested more symptoms of depression than adolescents not in romantic relationships. Recent findings have revealed important moderators of this global correlation (e.g., Ayduk, Downey, & Kim, 2001; Darling & Cohan, 2002; Davila

et al., 2002). For example, breakups, rather than involvement in a romantic relationship per se, may explain the elevated depressive symptoms reported by Joyner and Udry (2000); indeed, the most common trigger of the first episode of a major depressive disorder is a romantic breakup (Monroe, Rhode, Seeley, & Lewinsohn, 1999). Personality characteristics and the relationship history of one or both partners may exacerbate depressive reactions to relationship events as well (Ayduk et al., 2001).

Dating and romantic relationships also have an impact on psychosocial development during adolescence (Furman & Shaffer, 2003). Having a romantic relationship and the quality of that relationship are associated positively with romantic self-concept and, in turn, with feelings of self-worth (Connolly & Konarski, 1994; Kuttler et al., 1999), and longitudinal evidence indicates that by late adolescence, self-perceived competence in romantic relationships emerges as a reliable component of general competence (Masten et al., 1995). Whether adolescent romantic relationships play a distinctive role in identity formation during adolescence is not known, although considerable speculation and some theoretical contentions imply a link (e.g., Furman & Shaffer, 2003; Sullivan, 1953).

The most widely studied patterns have to do with variations in the *timing* of involvement in both romantic relationships and sexual activity, typically showing that early dating and sexual activity are risk factors for current and later problem behaviors and social and emotional difficulties (e.g., Davies & Windle, 2000; Zimmer-Gembeck, Siebenbruner, & Collins, 2001). A possibly complementary view is that timing of involvement is associated with familial and peer-group dysfunctions, which may be partly responsible for the risks attached to early romantic involvement (e.g., Collins, Hennighausen, Schmit, & Sroufe, 1997; Collins & Sroufe, 1999; Taradash, Connolly, Pepler, Craig, & Costa, 2001). Consistent with this pattern, poor relationships with parents and peers contribute to the incidence of both physical and relational aggression between romantic partners in late adolescence (Linder, Crick, & Collins, 2002).

Variations in relationship expectancies also reflect prior relationship experiences. The cognitive and behavioral syndrome known as rejection sensitivity arises from experiences of rejection in parent–child relationships and also in relations with peers and, possibly, romantic partners. Rejection sensitivity in turn predicts expectancies of rejection that correlate strongly with both actual rejection and lesser satisfaction in adolescent relationships (Downey, Bonica, & Rincon, 1999). Other individual differences play a role as well. In adult relationships, self-esteem, self-confidence, and physical attractiveness influence the timing, frequency, duration, and quality of relationships (Long, 1989; Mathes, Adams, & Davis, 1985; Samet & Kelly, 1987), and initial studies suggest a similar process in adolescent relationships (e.g., Connolly & Konarski, 1994).

Future Research on the Personal Relationships of Adolescents and Early Adults

Research comparing close relationships during childhood and adolescence has been far more extensive than comparisons of adolescent and early adult relationships. Consequently, transformations of relationship networks, changes in expectations of relationship partners, and relative likelihood of experiences of intimacy and social support in extrafamilial relationships during adolescence are well documented. Less is known about the distinctive qualities and functions of relationships after adolescence.

Consequently, the agenda for filling gaps in research on relationships during early adulthood is a lengthy one. Thus far, evidence based on data collected from early adults, although useful sources of descriptive information generally, cannot address the predictions of distinctiveness advanced by Arnett (2000, in press). Arnett's (in press) analyses of ethnographic reports of interviews with early adults provide information on the frequency and breadth of self-perceived distinctiveness of early adults but

neglect to assess similar themes in the discourse of middle and late adolescents on one hand, and those of "thirty somethings," on the other. The most compelling accounts would come from longitudinal data sets in which repeated accounts are sought from the same individuals across the three age periods, using standard reporting devices and standard metrics. Further research on the nature and significance of early adults' close relationships can be pursued most beneficially within the theoretical frameworks of the rapidly growing science of relationships (Reis et al., 2000).

Interrelations of Relationships

Research findings show that relationships become increasingly interrelated over time. Despite the stereotype of incompatible or contradictory influences of parents and friends, parent–child relationships set the stage for both the selection of friends and the management of these relationships (for a review, see Parke & Buriel, 1998). Links between qualities of friendships and romantic relationships, as well as between familial and romantic relationships, are equally impressive (Collins et al., 1997). At the same time, relationships with parents, friends, and romantic partners serve overlapping but distinctive functions. Typical exchanges within each of these types of dyads differ accordingly. In comparison to childhood relationships, the diminished distance and greater intimacy in adolescents' peer relationships may both satisfy affiliative needs and also contribute to socialization for relations among equals. Intimacy with parents may provide nurturance and support but may be less important than friendships for socialization to roles and expectations in late adolescence and early adulthood (Collins, 1997; Laursen & Bukowski, 1997).

Current research implies that relationships with parents, friends, and romantic partners increasingly overlap and complement each other as early adulthood approaches (Ainsworth, 1989; Collins & Laursen, 2000, 2004). Friends and romantic partners typically are the individuals with whom early adults most like to spend time (proximity seeking) and with whom they most want to be when feeling down (safe-haven function). Parents, however, are just as likely to be the primary source from which early adults seek advice and on whom they depend (Fraley & Davis, 1997). Hazan and Zeifman (1994) suggested that the apparent overlap among relationships reflects a change process in which components of attachment relationships (viz., maintaining proximity, using the other as a safe haven, and using the other as a secure base) are transferred sequentially from family members to extrafamilial partners. Family members' influence on adult friendship and romantic relationships should be better understood. These social spheres have typically and unfortunately been viewed as distinct systems, rather than mutually influential ones.

The social worlds of those involved in romantic relationships differ from those who are not because romantic partners quickly become dominant in the relationship hierarchy (Laursen & Williams, 1997). Although romantic interconnections initially are predicated on principles of social exchange, commitment drives participants to transform this voluntary relationship into one that is more obligatory and permanent (Laursen & Jensen-Campbell, 1999). Eventually, most early adults marry and reproduce, further transforming the relationship and marginalizing remaining friendships, thus effectively ending the peer group's dominance of relationship experiences (Collins & Laursen, 2000, 2004).

In general, qualities of friendships in middle and late adolescence are associated with concurrent qualities of romantic relationship (Collins, 2003; Furman et al., 2002). Representations of relationships show that working models of friendships and romantic relationships are interrelated as well (Treboux, Crowell, Owens, & Pan, 1994). Displaying safe-haven and secure-base behaviors with best friends is associated positively with displaying these behaviors with dating partners. Perhaps the growing importance of romantic relationships

makes the common relationship properties across types of relationships more apparent than before. It is equally likely, however, that the parallels between early adults' relationships reflect their common similarity to prior relationships with parents and peers (Owens, Crowell, Treboux, O'Connor, & Pan, 1995; Waters, Merrick, Treboux, Crowell, & Albersheim, 2000). It should be noted, however, that similarity is not the only criterion for interrelations among these relationships. For example, adolescents with insecure or otherwise unsatisfying relationships with parents initiate dating and sexual activity earlier than adolescents with more positive familial relationships. The quality of these apparently compensatory early involvements, however, is typically poorer than that of extrafamilial relationships for youth with more beneficent family histories (Collins, 2003). The nature and processes of these developmentally significant interrelations of relationships promise to become an increasingly prominent focus of future research.

Continuity in social networks from late adolescence also may set the stage for considerable influence from contexts of close dyadic relationships in the 18- to 28-year age period. Pertinent evidence comes from research in which the networks of parents and friends significantly influence continuation or dissolution of a romantic relationship. For example, Sprecher and Felmlee (1992) showed that network support for a relationship was associated positively with the quality of the relationship. Numerous other studies have shown that although couples vary in the degree to which they remain integrally involved with their former networks of kin and friends, those who do continue close involvements show effects of the support or interference they receive (e.g., Connolly & Goldberg, 1999; Parks & Eggert, 1991). Findings like these raise the possibility that involvement in and qualities of distinct dyads may moderate the effects of each other.

Early adults who are romantically uninvolved report greater reliance on friends than their romantically involved peers. Single adults name friends as their top companions and confidants and, along with mothers, the primary source for all facets of social support (Carbery & Buhrmester, 1998). Engagement and marriage are both linked to partial withdrawal from friends. Although total social network size remains the same after marriage, single adults have more friends than kin in their social network, whereas married adults report a balance of kin and friends (Fischer et al., 1989).

As the number of family roles increases, adults depend less on friends to satisfy their social needs. Although this change is most marked between the single and married phases of life, social networks are reorganized again across the transition to parenthood. Both mothers and fathers report a decline in the number of friends in their social networks after the birth of a child, but this decline is greater for fathers. Fathers also report less mutual support in friendship networks and less satisfaction with friendships over time compared with their wives (Bost, Cox, Burchinal, & Payne, 2002).

Conclusions

Research on relationships prior to adulthood seeks to describe and explain transformations in relationships under conditions of rapid and extensive changes in participants and in key contexts. Current findings on friendships and romantic relationships in the teens and 20s supplement and extend evidence from earlier periods that adaptations in relationships preserve their functional significance in the midst of change. Social networks expand during adolescence and early adulthood to include an increasing number and diversity of personal relationships, although these extrafamilial bonds also become increasingly interrelated with familial relationships by the late 20s. Although familial relationships often appear to decline in importance in this process, the decline is a relative rather than an absolute one. Individual adjustments and reactions by both parties are essential components in this developmental process.

These findings imply that broader perspectives are needed in research on development and change in relationships. Research largely has been directed toward interpersonal antecedents of deterioration and termination in voluntary adult relationships such as courtship and marriage. Integrating this tradition with perspectives on processes that link individual and relational changes is one possible step toward understanding how relationships are adapted to change in every period of life.

References

Ainsworth, M. D. S. (1989). Attachments beyond infancy. *American Psychologist, 44*, 709–716.

Arnett, J. J. (2000). Emerging adulthood: A theory of development from the late teens through the twenties. *American Psychologist, 54*, 317–326.

Arnett, J. J. (in press). *Emerging adulthood: The winding road from the late teens through the twenties.* New York: Oxford University Press.

Ayduk, O., Downey, G., & Kim, M. (2001). An expectancy-value model of personality diathesis for depression: Rejection sensitivity and depression in women. *Personality and Social Psychology Bulletin,* 868–877.

Barry, C. M., & Wigfield, A. (2002). Self-perceptions of friendship-making ability and perceptions of friends' deviant behavior: Childhood to adolescence. *Journal of Early Adolescence, 22*, 143–172.

Baxter, L. A., Dun, T., & Sahlstein, E. (2001). Rules for relating communicated among social network members. *Journal of Social and Personal Relationships, 18*, 173–199.

Benenson, J. F., & Christakos, A. (2003). The greater fragility of females' versus males' closest same-sex friendships. *Child Development, 74*, 1123–1129.

Berscheid, E., & Reis, H. T. (1998). Attraction and close relationships. In S. Fiske (Ed.), *Handbook of social psychology* (4th ed., pp. 193–281). New York: Addison-Wesley.

Berscheid, E., Snyder, M., & Omoto, A. (1989). The Relationship Closeness Inventory: Assessing the closeness of interpersonal relationships. *Journal of Personality and Social Psychology, 57*, 792–807.

Black, K. A. (2000). Gender differences in adolescents' behavior during conflict resolution tasks with best friends. *Adolescence, 35*, 499–512.

Blos, P. (1979). *The adolescent passage.* New York: International Universities Press.

Bost, K. K., Cox, M. J., Burchinal, M. R., & Payne, C. (2002). Structural and supportive changes in couples' family and friendship networks across the transition to parenthood. *Journal of Marriage and Family, 64*, 517–531.

Bowlby, J. (1982). *Attachment and loss: Vol. 1. Attachment.* New York: Basic Books. (Original work published 1969)

Brown, B. B. (2004). Adolescents' relationships with peers. In R. Lerner & L. Steinberg (Eds.), *Handbook of adolescent psychology* (pp. 363–394). New York: Wiley.

Brown, B. B., Feiring, C., & Furman, W. (1999). Missing the love boat: Why researchers have shied away from adolescent romance. In W. Furman, B. B. Brown, & C. Feiring (Eds.), *The development of romantic relationships in adolescence* (pp. 1–16). New York: Cambridge University Press.

Cairns, R. B., & Cairns, B. D. (1994). *Lifelines and risks: Pathways of youth in our time.* New York: Cambridge University Press.

Carbery, J., & Buhrmester, D. (1998). Friendship and need fulfillment during three phases of young adulthood. *Journal of Social and Personal Relationships, 15*, 393–409.

Carver, K., Joyner, K., & Udry, J. R. (2003). National estimates of adolescent romantic relationships. In P. Florsheim (Ed.), *Adolescent romantic relations and sexual behavior: Theory, research, and practical implications* (pp. 23–56). Mahwah, NJ: Erlbaum.

Caspi, A., & Moffitt, T. E. (1991). Individual differences are accentuated during periods of social change: The sample case of girls at puberty. *Journal of Personality and Social Psychology, 61*, 157–168.

Collins, W. A. (1995). Relationships and development: Family adaptation to individual change. In S. Shulman (Ed.), *Close relationships and socioemotional development* (pp. 128–154). New York: Ablex.

Collins, W. A. (1997). Relationships and development during adolescence: Interpersonal adaptation to individual change. *Personal Relationships, 4*, 1–14.

Collins, W. A. (2003). More than myth: The developmental significance of romantic relationships during adolescence. *Journal of Research on Adolescence, 13*, 1–24.

Collins, W. A., Hennighausen, K. H., Schmit, D. T., & Sroufe, L. A. (1997). Developmental precursors of romantic relationships: A longitudinal analysis. In S. Shulman & W. A. Collins (Eds.), *Romantic relationships in adolescence: Developmental perspectives* (pp. 69–84). San Francisco: Jossey-Bass.

Collins, W. A., & Laursen, B. (2000). Adolescent relationships: The art of fugue. In C. Hendrick & S. Hendrick (Eds.), *Close relationships: A sourcebook* (pp. 59–70). Thousand Oaks, CA: Sage.

Collins, W. A., & Laursen, B. (2004). Parent-adolescent relationships and influence. In R. Lerner & L. Steinberg (Eds.), *Handbook of adolescent psychology* (pp. 331–362). New York: Wiley.

Collins, W. A., & Sroufe, L. A. (1999). Capacity for intimate relationships: A developmental construction. In W. Furman, C. Feiring, & B. B. Brown (Eds.), *Contemporary perspectives on adolescent romantic relationships* (pp. 123–147). New York: Cambridge University Press.

Collins, W. A., & Van Dulmen, M. (in press). Friendships and romantic relationships in emerging adulthood: Continuities and discontinuities. In J. J. Arnett & J. Tanner (Eds.) (in press). *Coming of age in the 21st century: The lives and contexts of emerging adults.* Washington, DC: American Psychological Association.

Connolly, J. A., Furman, W., & Konarski, R. (2000). The role of peers in the emergence of heterosexual romantic relationships in adolescence. *Child Development, 71*, 1395–1408.

Connolly, J. A., & Goldberg, A. (1999). Romantic relationships in adolescence: The role of friends and peers in their emergence and development. In W. Furman, B. B. Brown, & C. Feiring (Eds.), *The development of romantic relationships in adolescence* (pp. 266–290). New York: Cambridge University Press.

Connolly, J. A., & Konarski, R. (1994). Peer self-concept in adolescence: Analysis of factor structure and of associations with peer experience. *Journal of Research on Adolescence, 4*, 385–403.

Darling, N., & Cohan, C. L. (2002, April). *Romantic anxiety, avoidance and middle adolescents' depressive symptoms.* In D. Welsh (Chair), When love hurts: Adolescent romantic relationships and depressive symptoms.

Symposium conducted at the meeting of the Society for Research in Adolescence, New Orleans, LA.

Davies, P. T., & Windle, M. (2000). Middle adolescents' dating pathways and psychosocial adjustment. *Merrill-Palmer Quarterly, 46,* 90–118.

Davila, J., Steinberg, S. J., Kachadourian, L., Cobb, R., & Fincham, F. (2002, April). *Early romantic experiences and depressive symptoms: Emerging depressogenic patterns.* In D. Welsh (Chair), When love hurts: Adolescent romantic relationships and depressive symptoms. Symposium at the conference of the Society for Research on Adolescence, New Orleans, LA.

Downey, G., Bonica, C., & Rincón, C. (1999). Rejection sensitivity and adolescent romantic relationships. In W. Furman, B. B. Brown, & C. Feiring (Eds.), *The development of romantic relationships in adolescence* (pp. 148–174). New York: Cambridge University Press.

Dunphy, D.C. (1963). The social structures of urban adolescent peer groups. *Sociometry, 26,* 230–246.

Elder, G. H., Jr. (1998). The life course and human development. In W. Damon (Gen. Ed.) & R. Lerner (Vol. Ed.), *Handbook of child psychology: Volume 1, Theoretical models of human development* (5th ed., pp. 939–991). New York: Wiley.

Erikson, E. H. (1968). *Identity: youth and crisis.* London: Faber & Faber.

Feldman, S. S., & Gowen, L. K. (1998). Conflict negotiations tactics in romantic relationships of high schoolers. *Journal of Youth and Adolescence, 27,* 691–717.

Feldman, S. S., Turner, R., & Araujo, K. (1999). The influence of the relationship context on normative and personal sexual timetables in youths. *Journal of Research on Adolescence, 9,* 25–52.

Fischer, J. L., Sollie, D. L., Sorrell, G. T., & Green, S. K. (1989). Marital status and career stage influences on social networks of young adults. *Journal of Marriage and Family, 51,* 521–534.

Fletcher, G. J. O., Fincham, F. D., Cramer, L., & Herson, N. (1987). The role of attributions in the development of dating relationships. *Journal of Personality and Social Psychology, 53,* 481–489.

Fraley, R. C., & Davis, K. E. (1997). Attachment formation and transfer in young adults' close friendships and romantic relationships. *Personal Relationships, 4,* 131–144.

Freud, A. (1958). Adolescence. In R. Eissler, A. Freud, H. Hartman, & M. Kris (Eds.), *Psychoanalytic study of the child* (Vol. 13, pp. 255–278). New York: International Universities Press.

Furman, W., & Buhrmester, D. (1992). Age and sex differences in perceptions of networks of personal relationships. *Child Development, 63,* 103–115.

Furman, W., & Shaffer, L. (2003). The role of romantic relationships in adolescent development. In P. Florsheim (Ed.), *Adolescent romantic relations and sexual behavior: Theory, research, and practical implications* (pp. 3–22). Mahwah, NJ: Erlbaum.

Furman, W., Simon, V. A., Shaffer, L., & Bouchey, H. A. (2002). Adolescents' working models and styles for relationships with parents, friends, and romantic partners. *Child Development, 73,* 241–255.

Furman, W., & Wehner, E. (1994). Romantic views: Toward a theory of adolescent romantic relationships. In R. Montemayor, G. R. Adams, & T. P. Gullotta (Eds.), *Advances in adolescent development: Volume 6, Personal relationships during adolescence* (pp. 168–195). Thousand Oaks, CA: Sage.

Halpern, C. T. (2003). Biological influences on adolescent romance and sexual behavior. In P. Florsheim (Ed.), *Adolescent romantic relations and sexual behavior: Theory, research, and practical implications* (pp. 57–84). Mahwah, NJ: Erlbaum.

Hamm, J. V. (2000). Do birds of a feather flock together? The variable bases for African American, Asian American, and European American adolescents' selection of similar friends. *Developmental Psychology, 36,* 209–219.

Hartup, W. W. (1996). The company they keep: Friendships and their developmental significance. *Child Development, 67,* 1–13.

Hartup, W. W., & Abecassis, M. (2002). Friends and enemies. In P. K. Smith & C. H. Hart (Eds.), *Blackwell handbook of childhood social development* (pp. 285–306). Oxford, England: Blackwell.

Hartup, W. W., & Laursen, B. (1999). Relationships as developmental contexts: Retrospective themes and contemporary issues. In W. A. Collins & B. Laursen (Eds.), *Relationships as developmental contexts: The Minnesota symposia on child psychology* (Vol. 30, pp. 13–35). Mahwah, NJ: Erlbaum.

Hartup, W. W., & Stevens, N. (1997). Friendship and adaptation in the life course. *Psychological Bulletin, 121*, 355–370.

Hazan, C., & Zeifman, D. (1994). Sex and the psychological tether. In K. Bartholomew & D. Perlman (Eds.), *Attachment processes in adulthood* (pp. 151–178). London: Kingsley.

Helsen, M., Vollebergh, W., & Meeus, W. (2000). Social support from parents and friends and emotional problems in adolescence. *Journal of Youth and Adolescence, 29*, 319–335.

Hinde, R. (1997). *Relationships: A dialectical perspective*. Hove, England: Psychology Press.

Horn, S. S. (2003). Adolescents' reasoning about exclusion from social groups. *Developmental Psychology, 39*, 71–84.

Hussong, A. M. (2000). Perceived peer context and adolescent adjustment. *Journal of Research on Adolescence, 10*, 391–415.

Jones, D. C., Bloys, N., & Wood, M. (1990). Sex roles and friendship patterns. *Sex Roles, 23*, 133–145.

Joyner, K., & Udry, J. R. (2000). You don't bring me anything but down: Adolescent romance and depression. *Journal of Health and Social Behavior, 41*, 369–391.

Kelley, H. H., Berscheid, E., Christensen, A., Harvey, J. H., Huston, T. L., Levinger, G., et al. (1983). *Close relationships*. New York: Freeman.

Kuttler, A. F., LaGreca, A. M., & Prinstein, M. J. (1999). Friendship qualities and social-emotional functioning of adolescents with close, cross-sex friendships. *Journal of Research on Adolescence, 9*, 339–366.

Larson, R. W., Clore, G. L., & Wood, G. A. (1999). The emotions of romantic relationships: Do they wreak havoc on adolescents? In W. Furman, B. B. Brown, & C. Feiring (Eds.), *The development of romantic relationships in adolescence* (pp. 19–49). New York: Cambridge University Press.

Laursen, B. (1995). Conflict and social interaction in adolescent relationships. *Journal of Research on Adolescence, 5*, 55–70.

Laursen, B., & Bukowski, W. M. (1997). A developmental guide to the organization of close relationships. *International Journal of Behavioral Development, 21*, 747–770.

Laursen, B., & Collins, W. A. (1994). Interpersonal conflict during adolescence. *Psychological Bulletin, 115*, 197–209.

Laursen, B., & Jensen-Campbell, L. A. (1999). The nature and functions of social exchange in adolescent romantic relationships. In W. Furman, B. B. Brown, & C. Feiring (Eds.), *The development of romantic relationships in adolescence* (pp. 50–74). New York: Cambridge University Press.

Laursen, B., & Williams, V. (1997). Perceptions of interdependence and closeness in family and peer relationships among adolescents with and without romantic partners. In S. Shulman & W. A. Collins (Eds.), *Romantic relationships in adolescence: Developmental perspectives. New directions for child development* (No. 78, pp. 3–20). San Francisco: Jossey-Bass.

Lewin, K. (1931). Experimental forces in child behavior and development. In C. Murchison (Ed.), *A handbook of child psychology* (2nd ed., pp. 590–625). Worcester, MA: Clark University Press.

Linder, J. R., Crick, N. R., & Collins, W. A. (2002). Relational aggression and victimization in young adults' romantic relationships: Associations with perceptions of parent, peer, and romantic relationship quality. *Social Development, 11*, 69–86.

Livesley, W. J., & Bromley, D. B. (1973). *Person perception in childhood and adolescence*. Oxford, England: Wiley.

Long, B. H. (1989). Heterosexual involvement of unmarried undergraduate females in relation to self-evaluations. *Journal of Youth and Adolescence, 18*, 489–500.

Maccoby, E. E. (1998). *The two sexes: Growing up apart, coming together*. Cambridge, MA: Harvard University Press.

Magnusson, D., Stattin, H., & Allen, V. L. (1985). Biological maturation and social development: A longitudinal study of some adjustment processes from mid-adolescence to adulthood. *Journal of Youth and Adolescence, 14*, 267–283.

Masten, A. S., Coatsworth, J. D., Neemann, J., Gest, S. D., Tellegen, A., & Garmezy, N. (1995). The structure and coherence of competence from childhood through adolescence. *Child Development, 66*, 1635–1659.

Mathes, E. W., Adams, H. E., & Davis, R. M. (1985). Jealousy: Loss of relationship rewards, loss of self-esteem, depression, anxiety and anger. *Journal of Personality and Social Psychology, 48*, 1552–1561.

Mendelson, M. J., & Kay, A. C. (2003). Positive feelings in friendship: Does imbalance in the relationship matter? *Journal of Social and Personal Relationships, 20*, 101–116.

Meschke, L. L., & Silbereisen, R. (1997). The influence of puberty, family processes, and leisure activities on the timing of first sexual experience. *Journal of Adolescence, 20*, 403–418.

Monroe, S. M., Rohde, P., Seeley, J. R., & Lewinsohn, P. M. (1999). Life events and depression in adolescence: Relationship loss as a prospective risk factor for first onset of major depressive disorder. *Journal of Abnormal Psychology, 108*, 606–614.

Murstein, B. I. (1970). Stimulus value role: A theory of marital choice. *Journal of Marriage and the Family, 32*, 465–481.

Neff, K. D., Turiel, E., & Anshel, D. (2002). Reasoning about interpersonal responsibility when making judgments about scenarios depicting close personal relationships. *Psychological Reports, 90*, 723–742.

Osgood, D. W., & Lee, H. (1993). Leisure activities, age, and adult roles across the life span. *Society and Leisure, 16*, 181–208.

Oswald, D. L., & Clark, E. M. (2003). Best friends forever?: High school best friendships and the transition to college. *Personal Relationships, 10*, 187–196.

Owens, G., Crowell, J., Pan, H., Treboux, D., O'Connor, E., & Waters, E. (1995). The prototype hypothesis and the origins of attachment working models: Adult relationships with parents and romantic partners. In E. Waters, B. Vaughn, G. Posada, & K. Kondo-Ikemura (Eds.), Caregiving, cultural, and cognitive perspectives on secure-base behavior and working models: New growing points of attachment theory and research. *Monographs of the Society for Research in Child Development, 60* (2–3, Serial No. 244), 216–233.

Parke, R. D., & Buriel, R. (1998). Socialization in the family: Ethnic and ecological perspectives. In W. Damon (Series Ed.) & N. Eisenberg (Vol. Ed.), *Handbook of child psychology: Volume 3. Social, emotional, and personality development* (5th ed., pp. 463–552). New York: Wiley.

Parker, J. G., & Gottman, J. M. (1989). Social and emotional development in a relational context: Friendship interaction from early childhood to adolescence. In T. J. Berndt & G. W. Ladd (Eds.), *Peer relationships in child development* (pp. 95–131). New York: Wiley.

Parks, M. R., & Eggert, L. L. (1991). The role of social context in the dynamics of personal relationships. In W. H. Jones & D. Perlman (Eds.),

Advances in personal relationships (Vol. 2, pp. 1–34). London: Kingsley.

Paul, E. L., & Brier, S. (2001). Friendsickness in the transition to college: Precollege predictors and college adjustment correlates. *Journal of Counseling and Development, 79*, 77–89.

Piaget, J. (1965). *The moral judgment of the child.* New York: Free Press. (Original work published 1932.)

Reis, H. T., Collins, W. A., & Berscheid, E. (2000). Relationships in human behavior and development. *Psychological Bulletin, 126*, 844–872.

Reis, H. T., Lin, Y., Bennett, M. E., & Nezlek, J. B. (1993). Change and consistency in social participation during early adulthood. *Developmental Psychology, 29*, 633–645.

Rubin, K. H., Bukowski, W. M., & Parker, J. G. (1998). Peer interactions, relationships, and groups. In W. Damon & N. Eisenberg (Eds.), *The handbook of child psychology: Volume 3. Social, emotional, and personality development* (pp. 619–700). New York: Wiley.

Rutter, M. (1996). Transitions and turning points in developmental psychopathology as applied to the age span between childhood and mid-adulthood. *International Journal of Behavioral Development, 19*, 603–626.

Samet, N., & Kelly, E. W. (1987). The relationship of steady dating to self-esteem and sex role identity among adolescents. *Adolescence, 22*, 231–245.

Sanderson, C. A., & Cantor, N. (1995). Social dating goals in late adolescence: Implications for safer sexual activity. *Journal of Personality and Social Psychology, 68*, 1121–1134.

Scharfe, E., & Bartholomew, K. (1995). Accommodation and attachment representations in young couples. *Journal of Social and Personal Relationships, 12*, 389–401.

Scholte, R. H. J., van Lieshout, C. F. M., & van Aken, M. A. G. (2001). Perceived relational support in adolescence: Dimensions, configurations, and adolescent adjustment. *Journal of Research on Adolescence, 11*, 71–94.

Seiffge-Krenke, I., & Lang, J. (2002, April). *Forming and maintaining romantic relations from early adolescence to young adulthood: Evidence of a developmental sequence.* In S. Shulman & I. Seiffge-Krenke (Cochairs), Antecedents of the Quality and Stability of Adolescent Romantic Relationships. Symposium at the conference of the Society for Research on Adolescence, New Orleans, LA.

Selman, R. (1980). *The growth of interpersonal understanding*. Orlando, FL: Academic.

Sharabany, R., Gershoni, R., & Hofmann, J. (1981). Girlfriend, boyfriend: Age and sex differences in intimate friendship. *Developmental Psychology, 17*, 800–808.

Sherman, A. M., DeVries, B., & Lansford, J. E. (2000). Friendship in childhood and adulthood: Lessons across the life span. *International Journal of Aging and Human Development, 51*, 31–51.

Shulman, S., & Laursen, B. (2002). Adolescents' perceptions of conflict in interdependent and disengaged friendships. *Journal of Research on Adolescence, 12*, 353–372.

Siegel, D. J. (1999). *The developing mind*. New York: Guilford Press.

Simmons, R. G., & Blyth, D. A. (1987). *Moving into adolescence*. Hawthorne, NY: Aldine.

Sorenson, K. A., Russell, S. M., Harkness, D. J., & Harvey, J. H. (1993). Account-making, confiding, and coping with the ending of a close relationship. *Journal of Social Behavior and Personality, 8*, 73–86.

Sprecher, S., & Felmlee, D. (1992). The influence of parents and friends on the quality and stability of romantic relationships: A three-wave longitudinal investigation. *Journal of Marriage and the Family, 54*, 888–900.

Sroufe, A., & Fleeson, J. (1988). Attachment and the construction of relationships. In R. Hinde & J. Stevenson-Hinde (Eds.), *Relations within families: Mutual influence* (pp. 26–47). Oxford, England: Oxford University Press.

Steinberg, L. (1988). Reciprocal relation between parent–child distance and pubertal maturation. *Developmental Psychology, 24*, 122–128.

Sullivan, H. S. (1953). *The interpersonal theory of psychiatry*. New York: Norton.

Taradash, A., Connolly, J. A., Pepler, D., Craig, W., & Costa, M. (2001). The interpersonal context of romantic autonomy in adolescence. *Journal of Adolescence, 24*, 365–377.

Treboux, D., Crowell, J. A., Owens, G., & Pan, H. S. (1994, February). *Attachment behaviors and working models: Relations to best friendship and romantic relationships*. Paper presented at the Society for Research on Adolescence, San Diego, California.

Waldinger, R. J., Diguer, L., Guastella, F., Lefebvre, R., Allen, J. P., Luborsky, L., & Hauser, S. T. (2002). The same old song? Stability and change in relationship schemas from adolescence to young adulthood. *Journal of Youth and Adolescence, 31*, 17–44.

Waters, E., Merrick, S., Albersheim, L., Treboux, D., & Crowell, J. (2000). Attachment from infancy to early adulthood: A 20-year longitudinal study of relations between infant Strange Situation classifications and attachment representations in adulthood. *Child Development, 71*, 684–689.

Weinstock, J. S., & Bond, L. A. (2000). Conceptions of conflict in close friendships and ways of knowing among young college women: A developmental framework. *Journal of Social and Personal Relationships, 17*, 687–696.

Youniss, J. (1980). *Parents and peers in social development*. Chicago: University of Chicago Press.

Youniss, J., & Smollar, J. (1985). *Adolescent relations with mothers, fathers, and friends*. Chicago: University of Chicago Press.

Zimmer-Gembeck, M., Siebenbruner, J., & Collins, W. A. (2001). The divergent influences of romantic involvement on individual and social functioning from early to middle adolescence *Journal of Adolescence, 24*, 313–336.

CHAPTER 12

Close Relationships in Middle and Late Adulthood

Rosemary Blieszner

Research on close relationships beyond the first half of life has burgeoned in the past few decades. Whereas earlier studies addressed a rather narrow range of variables and embodied a static conception of relationships, more recent investigations have given rise to very interesting relational issues, an array of emergent theoretical frameworks, and a dynamic perspective on changes in relational partners and their interaction patterns over the course of the adult years. The goal of this chapter is to highlight these new directions while providing a sense of the richness and diversity of relational experiences in middle and old age. Contrary to traditional stereotypes focusing on functional decline beyond youth, most adults in the second half of life experience vibrant and meaningful relationships with kin and friends.

The chapter begins with a brief history of research on adult close relationships and proceeds to a summary of key developmental milestones in middle and late adulthood that have implications for close relationships. Attention is given to structural features of relationship networks in the second half of life, as well as to dynamic inter-action processes. Influences on close relationships in adulthood and their effects on individuals are covered, then the last section provides a summary of recent theoretical and methodological advances in the study of close relationships during the second half of life. This tour of the literature is provided, of course, as a compendium of recent research for reference by those interested in adult development and aging. In addition, it serves as a cue for those studying earlier life relationships whose theories, methods, and results might be enhanced by taking a long-range perspective on social and personal interactions over the entire life course.

History of Research on Adult Close Relationships

Among the vast literatures on family and friend relationships in psychology, sociology, and communication studies, a sustained focus on close relationships in middle and old age is a relatively recent trend. About 35 years ago, the National Council on

Family Relationships established the tradition of publishing commissioned research reviews, including analyses of the literature on family relationships in the middle and later years (Allen, Blieszner, & Roberto, 2000; Brubaker, 1990; Mancini & Blieszner, 1989; Streib & Beck, 1980; Troll, 1971). By the mid-1990s, the field of family gerontology had sufficiently come of age to warrant compilation of its first handbook (Blieszner & Bedford, 1995). Relationship scholars also began to publish comprehensive works on adult friendships and social networks in recent decades (Adams & Blieszner, 1989; Blieszner & Adams, 1992; Fehr, 1996; Feld, 1997; Nardi, 1992; O'Connor, 1992; Rawlins, 1992; Wellman & Wortley, 1990). This focus on middle and later life relationships has occurred concurrently with both the emergence of the specialized field of personal relationships (Gilmour & Duck, 1986) and with conceptual and methodological advances in the life span developmental psychology and life course sociology perspectives that inform the field of social gerontology (Baltes, 1987, 1997; Elder, 1998). Thus, much of the recent work on close relationships in the second half of life is imbued with a developmental vantage point that investigates the occurrence of social interactions within the context of personal development, dyadic and network processes, and the larger social environment, all of which can influence close relationships.

At least four significant trends have occurred within this body of research. One is a shift from viewing elders as peripheral players to featuring them as central characters in families, as illustrated by the decade review articles. Concomitantly, attention has grown from focusing only on marital and parent–child relations to studies of siblings and even, in a few cases, of fictive kin in the lives of older adults. This work has been conducted by gerontologists, but as argued elsewhere, a full understanding of family life requires all researchers, not just gerontologists, to define family so as to include older members and study their contributions to family life (Bedford & Blieszner, 1997).

A second trend is movement from assessing very general variables and proxies of relational quality (e.g., equating frequency of contact with relationship harmony) to examining specific variables related to relationship structures, processes, and phases of development (Adams & Blieszner, 1998; Adams & Torr, 1998; Blieszner, 1995; Blieszner & Adams, 1992, 1998; de Jong Gierveld & Perlman, 2004; Lang & Fingerman, 2004). This work has resulted in broader and more nuanced knowledge about characteristics and dynamics of close relationships than was available before.

Advances in theory development and greater use of theory in studies of adult relationships have also occurred. Examples include family solidarity theory (Bengtson & Roberts, 1991) for explaining intergenerational patterns, the social convoy model (Kahn & Antonucci, 1980) for tracing changes in social networks over the life course, socioemotional selectivity theory (Carstensen, 1992) for understanding emotional regulation in late life, and a conceptual framework that integrates multiple sociological and psychological dimensions of friendship or other close relationships (Adams & Blieszner, 1994).

Finally, research methods and tools have improved over the years. Advances in statistical techniques such as development of multilevel modeling have permitted investigation of families as units of analysis and theory-based tests of causal relationships among variables (Teachman & Crowder, 2002; Townsend, Miller, & Guo, 2001; White, 2001). Greater use of longitudinal designs furthers understanding of the intersections between personal development and changes in family and friend relationships (e.g., Broese van Groenou & van Tilburg, 2003; Möller & Stattin, 2001; Reinhardt, Boerner, & Benn, 2003).

Taken together, these recent trends in family gerontology and close relationship scholarship not only have contributed new and more detailed knowledge about personal ties in middle and later life, they also suggest the exciting potential for stronger and more useful research results in the future.

This is important, because the aging of the baby boom cohort will yield unprecedented numbers of older adults who are likely to be pursuing increasingly diverse and complex varieties of family and social relationships.

Personal Development in Middle and Old Age

A useful framework for examining the maturational challenges and opportunities facing individuals in mid- and later life is Erikson's (1950) theory of psychosocial development. Erikson posited that individuals in middle age, being at the peak of their personality competence and having successfully resolved previous challenges related to establishing a personal identity and appropriate intimate relationships, would negotiate the middle years successfully by assuming responsibility for the well-being of future generations in the family and of the larger world in general. This characteristic, termed *generativity*, prompts guiding and mentoring behaviors within family, friend, work, and community relationships, as well as concerns about social causes and political issues. Those who are not successful in expressing generativity are characterized by excessive concern with their own needs and future, in a state labeled *ego stagnation*. Perceived nearness to death in old age prompts a life review process by which individuals assess their accomplishments and limitations. Those who attain basic satisfaction with and acceptance of the life they have lived, despite the problems and mistakes that might have occurred, proceed to a stage called *integrity* in which fear of death is minimized. In contrast, those who are dissatisfied with their life's activities and distressed at the probable lack of time left to overcome failures or accomplish significant goals, who thus may be fearful of death, are said to be suffering *despair*. Erikson acknowledged that most people would be located at a position between the two extremes of the generativity – stagnation and integrity – despair continua. Although research

on Erikson's hypotheses about generativity is in its infancy, McAdams (2001) provided a comprehensive overview of conceptual and empirical advances to date, which generally support the importance of generativity to midlife development. Likewise, studies of life review processes and the growing body of research on wisdom and spirituality in old age confirm the significance of attaining integrity for well-being at the end of life (McFadden, 1999; Sheldon & Kasser, 2001; Vaillant, 2003; Vaillant & Koury, 1993; Webster, 2003).

Understanding these personal developmental challenges in the second half of life provides background for comprehending and appreciating the motivations for and outcomes of enacting various family and friend relationships during that period. Close relationships provide myriad forms of instrumental and social support, emotional rewards, and foci for meaningful activities. Although these relationships occur at all stages of life and some ties (e.g., with siblings and friends) can endure through many decades, the intersections of personal and family developmental changes can lead to unique relational experiences associated with growing older. Some of these unique features are reflected in the structural form of the close relationships that exist.

Structural Features of Close Relationship Networks in Middle and Late Adulthood

Just as highlighting issues of personal development contributes to comprehending family interaction patterns in the second half of life, so does a summary of the structure of family and friend networks. The size and composition of networks provide the interpersonal context in which social interactions take place and have implications for the frequency and types of contacts that are made, the extent of support given and received, the self-disclosures exchanged, and many other dimensions of emotionally close connections.

Family Structures

The majority of adults in the United States are married, but the proportion is smaller in old age than earlier in adulthood (ages 35 to 54 years = 71.3%, 55 to 64 years = 74.2%, and 65 or older = 56.7%), and a notable sex difference in the proportion married exists between men and women aged 65 or older (75.7% versus 42.9%, respectively). The majority of households comprise family households (68%), usually of married couples (52%), but 32% of adults live in non-family households, including the 26% who live alone. Among persons aged 75 years or older, however, the proportion living alone is much higher (39.6%) because of the greater likelihood of being widowed (ages 35 to 54 years = 1.6%, 55 to 64 years = 6.7%, 65 to 74 = 19.6%, and 75 or older = 41%, U.S. Census Bureau, 2003).

Although few middle-aged adults have infants (2%) or preschool children (14%), the proportion of householders with children of any age at home remains above 50% even in the 45- to 54-year-old age group (Russell, 2001). Approximately 14% of men and 8% of women 18 to 34 years old are living with their parents (World Almanac and Book of Facts, 2003). Postponement of marriage, divorce, low wages, and unemployment contribute to young adults remaining in or returning to their family home. Among persons aged 65 years or older, 17.7% are grandparents living in households with one or more children, and 42% of them are responsible for rearing the grandchildren (U.S. Census Bureau, 2003). Given current rates of divorce and remarriage, stepfamilies are increasingly common, leading to new questions about the obligations of steprelatives to help one another across the generations (Ganong & Coleman, 1998a, 1998b).

Sibling ties in adulthood are a unique dimension of family structure because siblings share potentially the longest enduring close relationship of all. Studies using the National Survey of Families and Households show that adults tend to have at least monthly contact with their siblings for 60 or more years of adulthood and usually consider siblings as potential sources of support even if they do not actually help each other very often, particularly in advanced old age. Sister–sister relationships are strongest, and having living parents increases contact, affection, and exchanges of support among siblings (White, 2001; White & Reidmann, 1992).

Family structure has changed because of declining mortality and fertility. It is now increasingly common to have four or more generations alive, but successive generations typically include relatively fewer offspring than in the past (Bengtson, Rosenthal, & Burton, 1990; Lowenstein, 1999). This family pattern has implications that are potentially both positive (e.g., family members have opportunities to know relatives who are many decades older or younger than themselves, affection can deepen over many years of associating) and negative (e.g., younger persons may face responsibility for providing care to multiple generations of elderly relatives, conflicts can be quite long-standing). Because many families need assistance in providing care for aged members, home health care agencies have emerged to provide aides to old frail and homebound individuals. These aides, who often spend a lot of intimate time with their clients and develop close relationships with them, represent a new category of fictive kin for old people (Piercy, 2000), elevated to familylike status through a process of kin conversion (Allen et al., 2000). Similarly, relatives such as nieces who would not ordinarily be primary care providers for old people who have their own children, may indeed be tapped to fill such a role for childless elders through a process of kin upgrading (e.g., "My niece is like a daughter to me").

Family structure also changes for married middle-aged and old adults because of divorce and widowhood. Although adjustment to loss of a spouse through death has been widely investigated in the past (Lopata, 1996; Martin Matthews, 1991; Stroebe, Hansson, Stroebe, & Shut, 2001), little attention was paid to dating, remarriage, or other forms of repartnering in the second half of life. Recently, however, scholars have addressed not only remarriage, but also nonmarital cohabitation and, in northern and western Europe, couples in living apart together arrangements (LAT; sharing an intimate relationship while maintaining separate dwellings). According to the U.S. Census Bureau (2001), among all the unmarried partner households, 9.2% of the partners were men aged 55 and older and 5.5% were women in that age group. In Sweden, an estimated 4% of the adult population participates in LAT relationships, with the greatest proportion of them belonging to the young-old age category 65–74 years (Borell & Ghazanfareeon Karlsson, 2003); a representative sample of almost 4,500 older adults from the Netherlands revealed that among the 325 persons who had entered into a new partnership after divorce or widowhood, 21% were cohabiting and 24% were living in LAT partnerships (de Jong Gierveld, 2004). The chief reasons for pursuing LAT ties involve maintaining lifestyle autonomy and setting boundaries on traditional gender-based division of household labor (Borell & Ghazanfareeon Karlsson, 2003).

Friendship Structure

Estimates of the number of friends claimed by middle-aged and old adults range widely because of the varying definitions of *friend* and procedures used in research (e.g., focusing only on best friends versus eliciting names of friends from all contexts of life; Adams, 1989). In the Andrus Study of Older Adult Friendship Patterns that Rebecca Adams and I conducted using the latter method of identifying friend networks, the mean number of nonkin friends was 28.5 (range = 3–132), with an average of 10.8 of them deemed casual, 11.8 viewed as close, and 6.0 considered very close friends (Adams & Torr, 1998). It would be reasonable to expect that having a larger number of friends would afford more opportunities for receiving social support and other benefits of close relationships (Blieszner & Adams, 1992). But what might be the effects of friendship network size on problematic aspects of friendship?

A study of this question demonstrated that older adults with more friends were more likely to report having problematic friendships, but apparently they tolerated these relationships, because they rarely mentioned ending friendships on purpose, and they did not redefine problematic friendships as mere associations (Adams & Blieszner, 1998; Blieszner & Adams, 1998).

Findings across studies and age groups are consistent in showing that friendships tend to be homogeneous with respect to age, sex, race, class, power, and social status (Blieszner & Adams, 1992). In the Andrus Study, homogeneity of age within the close and very close friend portion of the networks was 33.5%, whereas sex homogeneity averaged 86.4%. An indicator of similarity in values and beliefs among friend network members is homogeneity of religious denomination, which averaged 40.6% in this research (Adams & Torr, 1998). Some people elect to make friends with persons who are somewhat or very different from themselves because they enjoy the stimulation of being introduced to new experiences and, in the case of old people, because they want to avoid having a network composed exclusively of age peers who are more likely to die than younger friends would be. Research on age segregation in the later years (Hagestad & Uhlenberg, 2005; Uhlenberg & de Jong Gierveld, 2004), however, shows that in both the United States and the Netherlands, only small proportions of old people have contact with nonkin children and young adults because of a range of social structural barriers (e.g., specialized schools, leisure settings, and physicians for children separate them from adults) and lifestyle options (e.g., not being employed or not engaging in volunteering in late adulthood limit opportunities to befriend younger persons).

A hallmark of friendship in middle and old age is that some of these relationships have endured for many decades and the partners have experienced numerous personal and family developmental transitions together. Long-term friends are thus important psychologically, even if actual contact is infrequent, because of the mutual perception that they embody deep understanding and commitment to providing support should any need arise (Shea, Thompson, & Blieszner, 1988). For example, in a study of recently formed versus long-standing friendships among residents of a newly constructed retirement community, old and new friends were liked about equally, but old friends were loved more dearly than new ones, even though interaction was much more frequent with new than with old friends (Shea et al., 1988). As this observation demonstrates, the structure of close relationships is directly associated with the interaction processes that take place within them. The next section, therefore, addresses key dynamic transactions that occur in families and friendships during the second half of life.

Interaction Processes in Middle and Late Adulthood Relationships

Close relationships encompass patterns of cognitive, affective, and behavioral activities occurring within and between the relational partners over time. These processes reflect the myriad ways both that relationships are enacted and sustained and that participants respond to them (Blieszner, 1995; Blieszner & Adams, 1992, 1998). Although it is common for relationship research in younger adulthood to focus on attraction, self-disclosure, and sexuality processes as described in other sections of this *Handbook*, studies of relationships in the second half of life have tended to address mainly social support, especially family caregiving. This focus is illustrated by the findings from a survey of all articles addressing midlife and later adulthood family relationships published in 13 journals during the 1990s (Allen et al., 2000). More than half of the publications concerned caregiving (32.6%), social support (13.7%), and intergenerational transactions (4.9%). When friendship in middle and late adulthood is the target of inquiry, a greater variety of relational processes has

been examined (Blieszner & Adams, 1992, 1998; Fehr, 1996; Rawlins, 1992).

Cognitive Processes

In keeping with the focus on caregiving in the family literature, one of the cognitive processes that has received much attention over the years is endorsement of filial responsibility norms and judgments of the extent to which filial responsibility is expected and displayed within parent–adult child dyads. Bromley and Blieszner (1997) investigated perceptions of parental expectations in a sample of adult children whose parents were healthy and not yet in need of assistance. These young adult and middle-aged offspring tended to believe that their parents would agree with a variety of filial expectations (e.g., "Adult children should give their parents financial help if they need it" and "Adult children should feel responsible for their parents"). These beliefs were not, however, associated with their being involved in helping their parents make plans for the future, which was rare in this sample. Most of the adult children had not gone beyond thinking about potential needs of their parents. Looking at reports of older parents themselves, Lee, Peek, and Coward (1998) found similar levels of endorsement of filial responsibility norms as Bromley and Blieszner did, with Blacks having significantly higher expectations than Whites. Hamon and Blieszner (1990) evaluated consensus on filial responsibility norms in parent–adult child dyads, finding strong endorsement among both the parents and their offspring that adult children should provide emotional support to parents and talk over important matters and available resources. The adult children, however, were much more inclined than their parents to consider it appropriate to make room in their homes for parents to move in during an emergency, provide care to sick parents, and sacrifice their personal freedom for the sake of helping their parents. Moving to dyads in which assistance was being provided, Walker, Pratt, Shin, and Jones (1990) assessed both mothers' and daughters' attributions about the daughters' motives for caring along a discretionary–obligatory continuum. The majority of women in both groups attributed helping to discretionary motives, and those who viewed helping as discretionary rated their relationships as more intimate than those who believed the assistance was based more on obligatory motives.

Another line of research on perceptions of family relationships concerns appraisals of troublesome relationships and the effects of such appraisals on psychological well-being. Using data from Swedish adults, Bedford (1992) found that viewing oneself as the least favored child in the family was associated with lower perceived relationship quality and more conflict with parents. However, in a study of U.S. adults and their problematic ties with siblings during childhood, Bedford (1998) found a significant association between positive reframing of negative experiences with siblings (i.e., perceived beneficial outcomes of competition and sibling rivalry) and positive affect, but no impact on negative affect. This implies that some adults can use effective strategies to cope with negative relational experiences from childhood.

Turning to cognitive aspects of nonkin close ties, adults engage in a multi-step decision-making process when forming friendships. First they eliminate people from the pool of potential friends who possess disliked characteristics or seem unsuitable as friends. Then they decide which of the remaining persons have desirable physical attributes, social skills, responsiveness, similarities, and other attractive characteristics (Fehr, 1996). Those are the people with whom they attempt to become friends. The limited research on appraisals of established friendships in middle and late adulthood shows that perceived similarity on values, interests, and background are key predictors of friendship, along with considering the person to be friendly, trustworthy, and easy to talk with (Blieszner, 1995; Johnson, 1989). In the Andrus Study, person perception was the most common of the 13 cognitive processes evident in participants' narratives

(91% of the sample mentioned friends' personal characteristics), followed by perceived similarities (83%), perceived understanding (42%), attributions (30%), relationship monitoring (30%), and perceived compatibility (25%; Blieszner, 1995).

Affective Processes

Evidence of emotional processes within family relationships in the second half of life comes mainly from studies of spouses and parents in which emotions are typically examined as outcomes of interaction but often not explicitly as interactive processes. Field, Minkler, Falk, and Leino (1993) studied the connection between stability or change in older adults' health over time, their contact with family members, and their feelings of satisfaction with various family relationships. As would be expected, those in better health had more contact with and felt closer to their relatives. Socioemotional selectivity theory (Carstensen, 1992) posits that emotional resources will be conserved for the most important relationships as older adults become increasingly frail, and more casual ties will be allowed to fade. Allen and Walker (1992) applied the concept of attentive love, originally formulated as a way of understanding mothers' caring for children, to the situation of daughters' caring for their mothers. In contrast to research focusing only on emotional stresses related to caregiving, Allen and Walker identified demonstrations of attentive love in the daughters' efforts to include their mothers in decisions about their own care, to preserve their mothers' dignity and autonomy, and to protect them from further health declines. Montgomery and Sorrell (1997) compared endorsement of different styles of love among 250 adults aged 17 to 70 who reported on romantic partners. The greatest differences occurred between young single persons and all married persons, with the young singles more likely to endorse types of love related to playing around (*ludus*) and fostering uncertainty (*mania*). The findings showed that romantic, passionate love (*eros*) and self-giving love (*agape*) occur within all stages of adulthood and are not just the province of the young.

For many people, emotional depth is one of the defining elements of friendship. Friendships provide opportunities for experiencing affection, happiness, excitement, and contentment as well as sadness, competitiveness, anger, and grief (de Vries, Blieszner, & Blando, 2002; Fehr, 1996; Nardi, 1992; O'Connor, 1992). Interactions with friends can alleviate feelings of loneliness, social isolation, and boredom (Larson, 1990). In the Andrus Study mentioned earlier, 19 affective processes were discerned in the participants' discussions of their friends, including feelings related to respect (mentioned by 49% of participants), liking (40%), feeling secure and that the friend is dependable (34%), enjoyment (25%), indifference (reflected in discussions of problematic friends, 25%), love (23%), and trust (23%). Note that the proportion of study participants referring to emotions was smaller than the proportions mentioning friend-related thoughts and actions. Often, they responded with statements about cognitive processes even when asked specifically how events and situations made them feel (Blieszner, 1995).

Interactions with relatives and friends do not always yield positive emotional reactions. Negative social exchanges such as offering intrusive or unsound advice, failing to be responsive in times of need, displaying insensitive or critical behavior, and conveying rejection or neglect of the person or relationship elicit distress, disappointment, frustration, anger, sorrow, and reservation about the partner or the relationship (Rook, Sorkin, & Zettel, 2004). These negative emotions detract from the health and well-being of the partners as well as from the quality of and satisfaction with the relationship.

Behavioral Processes

Although the number of behavioral processes that could be expressed in adult close relationships is vast, most of the family gerontology literature focuses on issues surrounding provision of assistance and caregiving (Allen et al., 2000). Family members supply instrumental, emotional, and social support to one another across the generations and throughout the life span. The nature of care and assistance, the types of support exchanged, and the extent of reciprocity change with shifts in developmental stages and normative roles of the individuals in the immediate and extended family. For example, in a follow-up study 12 years after the original data collection, Scott (1998) found that although old rural U.S. women had experienced family changes marked by death of their husbands, siblings, and adult children, they also experienced stability in that their remaining offspring continued to provide support and often helped more than they had in the past. Walter-Ginzburg, Blumstein, Chetrit, Gindin, and Modan (1999) found similar evidence of support stability in a longitudinal study of old Israelis that compared social networks and support received over 3.5 years. Probing into gender differences in family support to old relatives over a 2-year period, Gurung, Taylor, and Seeman (2003) demonstrated that the support men received increased for all types of support (more emotional, more instrumental, less negativity) from all sources, whereas the women received increased support in all three areas from their children, other relatives, and friends but not from their husbands. The fact that women reported fewer ties overall (an average of 9.53 compared with 10.77 for men) yet received more emotional support from a broader range of ties than the men suggests the advantages of maintaining a diverse social convoy, especially for women who are less apt to report receiving emotional support from their spouses. Nevertheless, even though the number of social ties tended to decline over time, the amount of support that the elders received did not, highlighting continuity of supportive exchanges across the adult years (Gurung et al., 2003). Data from Von Dras, Williams, Kaplan, and Siegler (1996) suggest that such gender differences are long-standing. Using a large representative sample of middle-aged Americans, they found that women reported both having greater availability of social support than men and also giving more support than they received. In contrast, Walter-Ginzburg and associates (1999) did not find gender differences in receipt of instrumental and emotional support among very old Israelis.

Some of the support that family members provide is direct care to frail or ill aged relatives. Caregiving ranges from occasional monitoring to providing daily assistance with all personal functions, household tasks, financial affairs, and arrangements with social and professional contacts. Much of this work is done by spouses (particularly wives) and adult children (usually daughters), although siblings, grandchildren, other relatives, friends, and neighbors also contribute various forms of aid (Lowenstein, 1999; Piercy, 1998; Stephens & Franks, 1999). Piercy (1998) pointed out that the complexities of helping dependent elders involve not only performing the various caregiving tasks, but also balancing the needs of other family members and the demands of the caregivers' personal responsibilities against the needs of the care recipients. Thus, although caring for family members can be satisfying and rewarding, it may simultaneously be stressful and demanding, especially when the care recipient is very frail or has dementia. Role and time conflicts, physical exhaustion, limitations on social activities, feelings of guilt or resentment, financial pressures, and worry about the future are some of the difficulties experienced by family caregivers (Stephens & Franks, 1999).

Friends provide extensive social and emotional support to one another, as well as occasional instrumental assistance. Friends display affection, bolster self-esteem, offer companionship, and impart advice and information (Blieszner & Adams, 1992; Dykstra, 1990). The effect of culture on norms for exchanges with friends is illustrated in research on confiding and self-disclosure in different countries. Whereas Parker and Parrott (1995) found that American elders were more likely to confide in family than friends for most functions of self-

disclosure, Siu and Phillips (2002) found that old women in Hong Kong were more likely to confide in and exchange intimate feelings and emotional support with friends as compared to relatives. In the Andrus Study, the participants identified at least 21 behavioral processes in the course of discussing their friendship interactions. The most frequently mentioned were related to contact (94% of the elders described what they did together), displays of support and caring (reported by 79% and 43% of participants, respectively), communication and self-disclosure (cited by 53% and 36%, respectively), and recommendations related to what one should avoid saying or doing when trying to form new friendships (stated by 66% and 47%, respectively; Blieszner, 1995).

The numerous interactive processes that form the substance and expression of close relationships in adulthood reflect the accumulation of ongoing development and experiences. In turn, the interactive processes and resulting relationships have many effects on the development and well-being of those who participate in them. The following section provides a summary of some exciting research that has extended static investigations of the effects of relationships to longitudinal analyses of these effects over both longer and shorter periods of the life span.

Influences on and Effects of Close Relationships in Middle and Late Adulthood

In keeping with the life span developmental perspective, scholars have recently begun to investigate the effects of early relational experiences on close relationships in the second half of life. Data from a prospective longitudinal study of Boston residents when they were 5 and 31 years old show that differences in adult value orientations could be traced back to treatment by parents in childhood (Kasser, Koestner, & Lekes, 2002). A Swedish prospective longitudinal study found that persons who had reported warm and trusting relationships with their parents during their adolescent years were likely to report satisfaction with their partner relationships in midlife, with ties between adolescent boys and their fathers being particularly influential in this regard (Möller & Stattin, 2001). A longitudinal follow-up investigation of middle-aged English women who had all experienced a poor relationship with one or more of their parents in childhood or adolescence likewise yielded evidence of the effects of earlier experiences on midlife relationships. On the one hand, women who displayed insecure (avoidant or ambivalent) attachment styles had significantly greater negative functioning in romantic relationships than those with a secure attachment style and were significantly more likely to have cohabited with a partner having a history of criminal offenses or substance abuse. On the other hand, women with secure attachment despite their childhood difficulties were more successful in their adult relationships (McCarthy, 1999). Based on an extensive review of 115 longitudinal studies about marriage in the United States, Karney and Bradbury (1995) developed a conceptual model of influences on marital stability and quality. They postulated that the capacity of couples to adapt to various stresses and sustain their marriages depends upon both the existing personal characteristics and vulnerabilities they bring into the marriage and the degree of stress they experience. Using a Dutch sample, Broese van Groenou and van Tilburg (2003) established a link between childhood and adult socioeconomic status and social network size in old age. Those with persistent low socioeconomic status tended to have smaller networks and to rely more on kin than nonkin for instrumental support compared with those whose socioeconomic circumstances improved over the course of life. That pattern potentially limits the sources of assistance and sustenance in late life for those with the fewest resources, who are already more vulnerable physically and socially than their more advantaged peers.

Relational events taking place within a narrower span of time also have effects on relationships and the persons involved in them. For example, when studying well-being in midlife, Vandewater, Ostrove, and Stewart (1997) examined personality and social role involvement in two longitudinal data sets from female college graduates. One group was assessed at ages 31, 43, and 48 and the other at ages 28 and 47. The researchers found evidence of the cumulative effects of experiences in social roles intersecting with personality development to influence well-being over time. Specifically, having multiple social roles in early adulthood predicted identity development, which in turn predicted midlife role variables that were related to midlife well-being. A second example comes from a 16-year, three-phase study of late-life friendship in Wales, in which Jerrome and Wenger (1999) found that many friendships faded away or were lost due to illness, relocation, or death. The effects of these relational changes varied, with some elders disengaging and finding contentment in a smaller network and others continuing to use social engagement skills to seek replacement friendships when needed. Coping strategies built up over a lifetime seemed to influence the relational strategies employed in old age. Also, friendship norms were more fluid than in earlier life; some elders made new friends with atypical partners, such as younger or opposite-sex persons.

Even short-term longitudinal studies are useful for documenting the effects of close relationships. Using daily diaries kept by old adults for 2 weeks, Nezlek, Richardson, Green, and Schatten-Jones (2002) identified connections between aspects of encounters with close others and psychological well-being. Particularly for spousal interactions, enjoyment, feeling in control, believing the partner to be responsive, and being socially active were positively related to measures of life satisfaction.

Close relationships can also be problematic, as when social network members are too demanding, are undependable, and get on one another's nerves (Antonucci, Akiyama, & Lansford, 1998). One of the key findings of research on the causes and consequences of relational difficulties in adulthood is that negative dimensions of interactions have stronger effects than positive ones on relationship quality and satisfaction. Rook (1990) identified potential explanations for this finding, including frequency and salience (rare unpleasant exchanges are more salient than frequent pleasant ones), attributions (the interpretation of negative behavior is less ambiguous than the interpretation of normative, positive behavior), and adaptive significance (people are more vigilant toward potential threats or risks than toward pleasures or benefits). Newsom, Nishishiba, Morgan, and Rook (2003) provided strong empirical confirmation of the greater salience of negative interactions in a short-term longitudinal study of exchanges in older adults' close relationships. A recent issue of the *Journal of Gerontology: Psychological Sciences* was devoted to negative interactions in close relationships (Lachman, 2003), providing insights into conflict and stress associated with particular relationships and situations.

Studies that link personal and relational characteristics and examine patterns of effects over time contribute greatly to extending knowledge and understanding about close relationships in the middle and later years. Findings such as those described in this section were not widely available previously, but the accumulation of longstanding data sets coupled with new statistical procedures contributes to building significant new research evidence. Another aid to the advancement of research on close relationships in middle age and the later years is the emergence of new theoretical perspectives. Some highlights are provided in the next section, along with additional examples of longitudinal studies and a summary of some interesting approaches to relationship interventions in the second half of life.

Advances in Research on Mid- and Late-Life Close Relationships

New Theoretical Perspectives

Several important theories for studying adult family and friend relationships were men-

tioned in the introduction. Besides those, new applications of existing theory and several new conceptualizations of relationships are discussed here. Attachment theory, long the province of research about children's ties with their mothers, has been extended into the adult years. The various attachment styles, whether secure, avoidant, or ambivalent, have differential implications for romantic relationships and approaches to parenting in adulthood, as well as for psychological well-being (Volling, Notaro, & Larson, 1998). McCarthy's (1999) study of relationship problems associated with poor attachment in middle-aged women was described previously.

Theories related to social and emotional regulation address other personal characteristics that affect relational dynamics. Carstensen's (1992) socioemotional selectivity theory, mentioned earlier, has given rise to studies of the motives and mechanisms for regulation of social relationships in late adulthood (Lang, 2001). Those who can proactively sustain or eliminate relationships according to their own goals fare better psychologically than those who are less successful at meeting their relational needs. Hansson's theory of relational competence (Hansson & Carpenter, 1994) provides a framework for examining the personal attributes and interpersonal skills of old adults that contribute to their success in initiating and enhancing relationships.

Several new frameworks are particularly appropriate for studying motives and dynamics in intergenerational relationships. Fingerman (1996) coined the term *developmental schism* to signify differences in developmental stage and socioemotional needs and goals of family members from different generations. When goals, expectations, and needs conflict, problems can arise in the relationship. Lüscher and Pillemer (1998) labeled contradictory attitudes or emotions toward the relational partner or the relationship itself as *intergenerational ambivalence*. In the case of aging mother–adult daughter relationships, an example of developmental schism would be the daughter's interest in offering suggestions related to the mother's health and safety conflicting with the mother's wish to retain her perceived right and responsibility to be the advice giver in the dyad. Intergenerational ambivalence would occur when the daughter both recognizes her duty to provide assistance to her frail mother and resents having to alter other plans to accommodate her mother's wishes. From the mother's point of view, intergenerational ambivalence would be reflected in ongoing love for her daughter coupled with disappointment in her daughter's lack of progress in achieving various adult statuses and roles.

Methodological Improvements

Throughout this chapter, I have referred to many short- and long-term longitudinal studies of close relationships in middle and old age. Grounded in assumptions that both relationships and relational partners change over time and searching for antecedents and consequences of interaction with significant others, these studies have contributed greatly to understanding relational dynamics. A special section of *Psychology and Aging* (Light & Hertzog, 2003) provides useful technical details on longitudinal methods. In addition, recent scholarship that places adult relationships in the context of development across the life span has employed a wider lens for examining close relationships than in the past, thus also expanding understanding of antecedents and consequences of dynamic interaction patterns. Lang and Fingerman's edited volume (2004) takes this approach from the perspective of different disciplines, examining structural features of relationships such as marriage, friendship, and parent–child associations along with processes such as emotion, stress, social support, and social cognition.

Another contribution to advancing research on relationships is use of relational dyads rather than collecting data only from individuals. For example, using a social context model, Townsend and associates (2001) probed depression as a relational rather than only an individual phenomenon. In a study of middle-aged and old married couples, they found that couple-related variables such as net worth were significant covariates of depression, along with individual-level variables such as sex, race, and health. Looking at a different topic, Lyons, Zarit, Sayer, and Whitlatch (2002) examined caregiving from the perspectives of caregivers and receivers. With this approach, the authors uncovered extensive discrepancies in appraisals of caregiving difficulties, even though both partners agreed on the care receivers' needs. This finding helps to explain the greater relationship strain reported by caregivers compared with care receivers. As these studies illustrate, dyadic data can yield insights into relational dynamics that are not apparent when only one partner is assessed.

Relationships Interventions

Another new focus in adult close relationship research is assessment of interventions aimed at improving relational functioning and reducing social isolation. Examples of the former are research-based recommendations for assisting with dilemmas experienced by adult children and their aging parents (Myers, 1988) and strategies aimed at helping grandparents who are rearing grandchildren (Roberto & Qualls, 2003). With regard to the latter, interventions designed to foster friendship formation and provide social support range from an educational program in the Netherlands that teaches appropriate expectations for friendship and skills for forming and maintaining friendships (Stevens, 2001), to a befriending program in the United Kingdom in which visitors are assigned to make short weekly visits to elderly clients (Andrews, Gavin, Begley, & Brodie, 2003), to an Internet training program for nursing home residents in the United States (White et al., 2002). Although these and other such interventions are usually deemed at least somewhat successful at reducing social isolation, Findlay (2003) reviewed evaluation results from 17 programs and found weak support for such claims, often because of methodological flaws. She pointed out that little is known about the long-term impact and cost-effectiveness of social intervention programs and called for evaluation research to be designed into future programs as they are implemented.

Conclusion

Since publication of the first decade review article on family gerontology (Troll, 1971) and the first compendium of research on late-life friendship (Adams & Blieszner, 1989), much progress has been made in the study of close relationships in the middle and later years. The quality of research has been bolstered by its grounding in life span development and life course perspectives and by incorporation of creative theoretical frameworks that permit not only solid description of relational phenomena but also explanation of findings. Research quality has also been enhanced by methods that support investigating the effects of earlier experiences on later development and of relationships as dynamic rather than merely static bonds. Attention has been given to the effects of relationship structures and interaction processes, and their implications for the formation and sustenance of relationships as well as changes in relationships and relational partners over time. The array of relationships investigated has broadened beyond a focus on marriage and parent–child ties to include a range of family and friend types. The field has matured enough to permit attempts at introducing intervention programs to strengthen relationships in the second half of life.

Still, research challenges remain for both gerontologists and scholars of other life stages. A fuller understanding of the role of old people in families and communities awaits more and detailed research with children and teenagers about their relationships with adult friends and relatives, not merely their perceptions of old people. When databases intended to provide the foundation for longitudinal analyses are created, they should include comprehensive rather than superficial relationship assessments to permit examination of the effects of relationship structures and interaction processes over the long term. All of the topics mentioned in this chapter warrant study in samples that reflect the diversity of the populations around the world, and more investigations are needed of new and varying types of family and friend experiences across social groups. Relationship structures and processes have been described, but further research is needed on their implications for personal and relational well-being. If rare forms of social support were tapped, such as studies of elderly brothers providing intensive caregiving or friends creating intentional living communities in retirement, new insights into personal and relational resiliency would emerge. In general, additional research on many topics related to close ties in the second half of life is needed, because the demographic transition that is taking place around the world (movement from high fertility and mortality to low fertility and mortality) means that the proportion of old people is increasing and more people are living to be very old (Kinsella, 1995). With that shift come numerous consequences for relationships among family members and friends of all ages.

References

Adams, R. G. (1989). Conceptual and methodological issues in studying friendships of older adults. In R. G. Adams & R. Blieszner (Eds.), *Older adult friendship: Structure and process* (pp. 17–41). Newbury Park, CA: Sage.

Adams, R. G., & Blieszner, R. (Eds.). (1989). *Older adult friendship: Structure and process*. Newbury Park, CA: Sage.

Adams, R. G., & Blieszner, R. (1994). An integrative conceptual framework for friendship research. *Journal of Social and Personal Relationships, 11*, 163–184.

Adams, R. G., & Blieszner, R. (1998). Structural predictors of problematic friendship in later life. *Personal Relationships, 5*, 439–447.

Adams, R. G., & Torr, R. (1998). Factors underlying the structure of older adult friendship networks. *Social Networks, 20*, 51–61.

Allen, K. R., Blieszner, R., & Roberto, K. A. (2000). Families in the middle and later years: A review and critique of research in the 1990s. *Journal of Marriage and the Family, 62*, 911–926.

Allen, K. R., & Walker, A. J. (1992). Attentive love: A feminist perspective on the caregiving of adult daughters. *Family Relations, 41*, 284–289.

Andrews, G. J., Gavin, N., Begley, S., & Brodie, D. (2003). Assisting friendships, combating loneliness: Users' views on a "befriending" scheme. *Ageing and Society, 23*, 349–362.

Antonucci, T. C., Akiyama, H., & Lansford, J. E. (1998). Negative effects of close social relations. *Family Relations, 47*, 379–384.

Baltes, P. B. (1987). Theoretical propositions of life-span developmental psychology: On the dynamics between growth and decline. *Developmental Psychology, 23*, 611–626.

Baltes, P. B. (1997). On the incomplete architecture of human ontogeny: Selection, optimization, and compensation as foundation of developmental theory. *American Psychologist, 52*, 336–380.

Bedford, V. H. (1992). Memories of parental favoritism and the quality of parent-child ties in adulthood. *Journal of Gerontology: Social Sciences, 47*, S149–S155.

Bedford, V. H. (1998). Sibling relationship troubles and well-being in middle and old age. *Family Relations, 47*, 369–376.

Bedford, V. H., & Blieszner, R. (1997). Personal relationships in later-life families. In S. Duck (Ed.), *Handbook of personal relationships* (2nd ed., pp. 523–539). New York: Wiley.

Bengtson, V. L., & Roberts, R. E. L. (1991). Intergenerational solidarity in aging families: An example of formal theory construction. *Journal of Marriage and the Family, 53*, 856–870.

Bengtson, V., Rosenthal, C., & Burton, L. (1990). Families and aging: Diversity and heterogeneity. In R. H. Binstock & L. K. George (Eds.), *Handbook of aging and the social sciences* (3rd ed., pp. 263–287). San Diego, CA: Academic.

Blieszner, R. (1995). Friendship processes and well-being in the later years of life: Implications for interventions. *Journal of Geriatric Psychiatry, 28*, 165–183.

Blieszner, R., & Adams, R. G. (1992). *Adult friendship*. Newbury Park, CA: Sage.

Blieszner, R., & Adams, R. G. (1998). Problems with friends in old age. *Journal of Aging Studies, 12*, 223–238.

Blieszner, R., & Bedford, V. H. (Eds.). (1995). *Handbook of aging and the family*. Westport, CT: Greenwood.

Borell, K., & Ghazanfareeon Karlsson, S. (2003). Reconceptualizing intimacy and ageing: Living apart together. In S. Arber, K. Davisons, & J. Ginn (Eds.), *Gender and ageing: Changing roles and relationships* (pp. 47–62). Maidenhead, England: Open University Press.

Broese van Groenou, M. I., & van Tilburg, T. (2003). Network size and support in old age: Differentials by socio-economic status in childhood and adulthood. *Ageing and Society, 23*, 625–645.

Bromley, M. C., & Blieszner, R. (1997). Planning for long-term care: Filial behavior and relationship quality of adult children with independent parents. *Family Relations, 46*, 155–162.

Brubaker, T. (1990). Families in later life: A burgeoning research area. *Journal of Marriage and the Family, 52*, 959–981.

Carstensen, L. L. (1992). Social and emotional patterns in adulthood: Support for socioemotional selectivity theory. *Psychology and Aging, 7*, 331–338.

de Jong Gierveld, J. (2004). Remarriage, unmarried cohabitation, living apart together: Partner relationships following bereavement or divorce. *Journal of Marriage and Family, 66*, 236–243.

de Jong Gierveld, J., & Perlman, D. (2004). *Longstanding non-kin relationships of (older) adults in the Netherlands and the U.S.A.* Manuscript submitted for publication.

de Vries, B., Blieszner, R., & Blando, J. A. (2002). The many forms of intimacy, the many faces of grief in later life. In K. J. Doka (Ed.), *Living with grief: Loss in later life* (pp. 225–241). Washington, DC: Hospice Foundation of America.

Dykstra, P. A. (1990). *Next of (non)kin*. Amsterdam: Swetz & Zeitlinger.

Elder, G. H., Jr. (1998). The life course and human development. In R. M. Lerner (Ed.), *Handbook of child psychology, Volume 1: Theoretical models of human development* (pp. 939–991). New York: Wiley.

Erikson, E. H. (1950). *Childhood and society* (2nd ed.). New York: Norton.

Findlay, R. A. (2003). Interventions to reduce social isolation amongst older people: Where is the evidence? *Ageing and Society, 23*, 647–658.

Fehr, B. (1996). *Friendship processes*. Thousand Oaks, CA: Sage.

Feld, S. L. (1997). Structural embeddedness and the stability of interpersonal relations. *Social Networks*, 19, 91–95.

Field, D., Minkler, M., Falk, R. F., & Leino, E. V. (1993). The influence of health on family contacts and family feelings in advanced old age: A longitudinal study. *Journal of Gerontology: Psychological Sciences*, 48, P18–P28.

Fingerman, K. L. (1996). Sources of tension in the aging mother and adult daughter relationship. *Psychology and Aging*, 11, 591–606.

Ganong, L. H., & Coleman, M. (1998a). An exploratory study of grandparents' and step-grandparents' financial obligations to grandchildren and stepchildren. *Journal of Social and Personal Relationships*, 15, 39–58.

Ganong, L. H., & Coleman, M. (1998b). Attitudes regarding filial responsibilities to help elderly divorced parents and stepparents. *Journal of Aging Studies*, 12, 271–290.

Gilmour, R., & Duck, S. (Eds.). (1986). *The emerging field of personal relationships*. Hillsdale, NJ: Erlbaum.

Gurung, R. A. R., Taylor, S. E., & Seeman, T. E. (2003). Accounting for changes in social support among married older adults: Insights from the MacArthur Studies of Successful Aging. *Psychology and Aging*, 18, 487–496.

Hagestad, G. O., & Uhlenberg, P. (2005). The social separation of old and young: A root of ageism. *Journal of Social Issues*, 61, 343–360.

Hamon, R. R., & Blieszner, R. (1990). Filial responsibility expectations among adult child–older parent pairs. *Journal of Gerontology: Psychological Sciences*, 45, P110–P112.

Hansson, R. O., & Carpenter, B. N. (1994). *Relationships in old age*. New York: Guilford Press.

Jerrome, D., & Wenger, G. C. (1999). Stability and change in late-life friendship. *Ageing and Society*, 19, 661–676.

Johnson, M. A. (1989). Variables associated with friendship in an adult population. *Journal of Social Psychology*, 129, 379–390.

Kahn, R. L., & Antonucci, T. C. (1980). Convoys over the life course: Attachment, roles, and social support. In P. B. Baltes & O. G. Brim, Jr. (Eds.), *Life-span development and behavior* (Vol. 3, pp. 253–286). New York: Academic Press.

Karney, B. R., & Bradbury, T. N. (1995). The longitudinal course of marital quality and stability: A review of theory, method, and research. *Psychological Bulletin*, 118, 3–34.

Kasser, T., Koestner, R., & Lekes, N. (2002). Early family experiences and adult values: A 26-year, prospective longitudinal study. *Personality and Social Psychology Bulletin*, 28, 826–835.

Kinsella, K. (1995). Aging and the family: Present and future demographic issues. In R. Blieszner & V. H. Bedford (Eds.), *Handbook of aging and the family* (pp. 32–56). Westport, CT: Greenwood.

Lachman, M. E. (Ed.). (2003). Negative interactions in close relationships. *Journal of Gerontology: Psychological Sciences*, 58B, P69–P137.

Lang, F. R. (2001). Regulation of social relationships in later adulthood. *Journal of Gerontology: Psychological Sciences*, 58B, P321–P326.

Lang, F. R., & Fingerman, K. L. (Eds.). (2004). *Growing together: Personal relationships across the life span*. Cambridge, England: Cambridge University Press.

Larson, R. (1990). The solitary side of life: An examination of the time people spend alone from childhood to old age. *Developmental Review*, 10, 155–183.

Lee, G. R., Peek, C. W., & Coward, R. T. (1998). Race differences in filial responsibility expectations among older parents. *Journal of Marriage and the Family*, 60, 404–412.

Light, L. L., & Hertzog, C. (Eds.). (2003). Special section: Applied longitudinal methods in aging research. *Psychology and Aging*, 18, 637–769.

Lopata, H. Z. (1996). *Current widowhood: Myths and realities*. Thousand Oaks, CA: Sage.

Lowenstein, A. (1999). Intergenerational family relations and social support. *Zeitschrift für Gerontologie und Geriatrie*, 32, 398–406.

Lüscher, K., & Pillemer, K. (1998). Intergenerational ambivalence: A new approach to the study of parent–child relations in later life. *Journal of Marriage and the Family*, 60, 413–425.

Lyons, K. S., Zarit, S. H., Sayer, A. G., & Whitlatch, C. J. (2002). Caregiving as a dyadic process: Perspectives from caregiver and receiver. *Journal of Gerontology: Psychological Sciences*, 57B, P195–P204.

Mancini, J. A., & Blieszner, R. (1989). Aging parents and adult children: Research themes in intergenerational relations. *Journal of Marriage and the Family*, 51, 275–290.

Martin Matthews, A. (1991). *Widowhood in later life*. Toronto: Butterworths/Harcourt.

McAdams, D. P. (2001). Generativity in midlife. In M. E. Lachman (Ed.), *Handbook of midlife development* (pp. 394–443). New York: Wiley.

McCarthy, G. (1999). Attachment style and adult love relationships and friendships: A study of a group of women at risk of experiencing relationship difficulties. *British Journal of Medical Psychology, 72*, 305–321.

McFadden, S. H. (1999). Religion, personality, and aging: A life span perspective. *Journal of Personality, 67*, 1081–1104.

Möller, K., & Stattin, H. (2001). Are close relationships in adolescence linked with partner relationships in midlife? A longitudinal, prospective study. *International Journal of Behavioral Development, 25*, 69–77.

Montgomery, M. J., & Sorell, G. T. (1997). Differences in love attitudes across family life stages. *Family Relations, 46*, 55–61.

Myers, J. E. (1988). The mid/late life generation gap: Adult children with aging parents. *Journal of Counseling and Development, 66*, 331–335.

Nardi, P. M. (Ed.). (1992). *Men's friendships.* Newbury Park, CA: Sage.

Newsom, J. T., Nishishiba, M., Morgan, D. L., & Rook, K. S. (2003). The relative importance of three domains of positive and negative social exchanges: A longitudinal model with comparable measures. *Psychology and Aging, 18*, 746–754.

Nezlek, J. B., Richardson, D. S., Green, L. R., & Schatten-Jones, E. C. (2002). Psychological well-being and day-to-day interaction among older adults. *Personal Relationships, 9*, 57–71.

O'Connor, P. (1992). *Friendships between women.* New York: Guilford Press.

Parker, R. G., & Parrott, R. (1995). Patterns of self-disclosure across social support networks: Elderly, middle-aged, and young adults. *International Journal of Aging and Human Development, 41*, 281–297.

Piercy, K. W. (1998). Theorizing about family caregiving: The role of responsibility. *Journal of Marriage and the Family, 60*, 109–118.

Piercy, K. W. (2000). When it is more than a job: Close relationships between home health aides and older clients. *Journal of Aging and Health, 12*, 362–387.

Rawlins, W. K. (1992). *Friendship matters.* New York: Aldine de Gruyter.

Reinhardt, J. P., Boerner, K., & Benn, D. (2003). Predicting individual change in support over time among chronically impaired older adults. *Psychology and Aging, 18*, 770–779.

Roberto, K. A., & Qualls, S. (2003). Intervention strategies for grandparents raising grandchildren: Lessons learned from the late caregiving literature. In B. Hayslip & J. Hicks Patrick (Eds.), *Working with custodial grandparents* (pp. 13–26). New York: Springer.

Rook, K. S. (1990). Stressful aspects of older adults' social relationships: Current theory and research. In M. A. P. Stephens, J. H. Crowther, S. E. Hobfoll, & D. L. Tennenbaum (Eds.), *Stress and coping in later-life families* (pp. 173–192). New York: Hemisphere.

Rook, K., Sorkin, D., & Zettel, L. (2004). Stress in social relationships: Coping and adaptation across the life span. In F. R. Lang & K. L. Fingerman (Eds.), *Growing together: Personal relationships across the lifespan* (pp. 210–239). Cambridge, England: Cambridge University Press.

Russell, C. (2001). *The baby boom: Americans aged 35 to 54* (3rd ed.). Ithaca, NY: New Strategist .

Scott, J. P. (1998). Family relationships of older, rural women: Stability and change. *Journal of Women and Aging, 10*, 67–80.

Shea, L., Thompson, L., & Blieszner, R. (1988). Resources in older adults' old and new friendships. *Journal of Social and Personal Relationships, 5*, 83–96.

Sheldon, K. M., & Kasser, T. (2001). Getting older, getting better? Personal strivings and psychological maturity across the life span. *Developmental Psychology, 37*, 491–501.

Siu, O-L., & Phillips, D. R. (2002). A study of family support, friendship, and psychological well-being among older women in Hong Kong. *International Journal of Aging and Human Development, 55*, 299–319.

Stephens, M. A. P., & Franks, M. M. (1999). Intergenerational relationships in later-life families: Adult daughters and sons as caregivers to aging parents. In J. C. Cavanaugh & S. K. Whitbourne (Eds.), *Gerontology: An interdisciplinary perspective* (pp. 329–354). New York: Oxford University Press.

Stevens, N. (2001). Combating loneliness: A friendship enrichment programme for older women. *Ageing and Society, 21*, 183–202.

Streib, G. F., & Beck, R. W. (1980). Older families: A decade review. *Journal of Marriage and the Family, 42*, 937–956.

Stroebe, M. S., Hansson, R. O., Stroebe, W., & Shut, H. (Eds.). (2001). *Handbook of bereavement research*. Washington, DC: American Psychological Association.

Teachman, J., & Crowder, K. (2002). Multilevel models in family research: Some conceptual and methodological issues. *Journal of Marriage and the Family, 64*, 280–294.

Townsend, A. L., Miller, B., & Guo, S. (2001). Depressive symptomatology in middle-aged and older married couples: A dyadic analysis. *Journal of Gerontology: Social Sciences, 56B*, S352–S364.

Troll, L. E. (1971). The family of later life: A decade review. *Journal of Marriage and the Family, 33*, 263–290.

Uhlenberg, P., & de Jong Gierveld, J. (2004). Age-segregation in later life: An examination of personal networks. *Ageing and Society, 24*, 5–28.

U.S. Census Bureau. (2001). *America's families and living arrangements: March 2000*. Table UC3. Opposite sex unmarried partner households by presence of own children under 18, and age, earnings, education, and race and Hispanic origin of both partners: March 2000. Retrieved May 17, 2004, from http://www.census.gov/population/socdemo/hh-fam/p20-537/2000/tabUC3.pdf

U.S. Census Bureau. (2003). *Statistical abstract of the United States: 2003* (Section 1. Population. No. 38, Persons 65 years old and over – grandparents, disability status, and language spoken at home: 2000; No. 63, Marital status of the population by sex and age: 2002; No. 65, Households and persons per household by type of household: 1990 to 2002). Retrieved March 20, 2004, from http://www.census.gov/prod/www/statistical-abstract-03.html

Vaillant, G. E. (2003). Mental health. *American Journal of Psychiatry, 160*, 1373–1384.

Vaillant, G. E., & Koury, S. H. (1993). Late midlife development. In S. I. Greenspan & G. H. Pollock (Eds.), *The course of life, Volume 6: Late adulthood* (rev. and exp. ed., pp. 1–22). Madison, CT: International University Press.

Vandewater, E. A., Ostrove, J. M., & Stewart, A. J. (1997). Predicting women's well-being in midlife: The importance of personality development and social role involvements. *Journal of Personality and Social Psychology, 72*, 1147–1160.

Volling, B. L., Notaro, P. C., & Larsen, J. J. (1998). Adult attachment styles: Relations with emotional well-being, marriage, and parenting. *Family Relations, 47*, 355–367.

Von Dras, D. D., Williams, R. B., Kaplan, B. H., & Siegler, I. C. (1996). Correlates of perceived social support and equality of interpersonal relationships at mid-life. *International Journal of Aging and Human Development, 43*, 199–217.

Walker, A. J., Pratt, C. C., Shin, H.-Y., & Jones, L. L. (1990). Motives for parental caregiving and relationship quality. *Family Relations, 39*, 51–56.

Walter-Ginzburg, A., Blumstein, T., Chetrit, A., Gindin, J., & Modan, B. (1999). A longitudinal study of characteristics and predictors of perceived instrumental and emotional support among the old-old in Israel. *International Journal of Aging and Human Development, 48*, 279–299.

Webster, J. D. (2003). An exploratory analysis of a self-assessed wisdom scale. *Journal of Adult Development, 10*, 13–22.

Wellman, B., & Wortley, S. (1990). Different strokes from different folks: Community ties and social support. *American Journal of Sociology, 96*, 558–588.

White, H., McConnell, E., Clipp, E., Branch, L. G., Sloane, R., Pieper, C., & Box, T. L. (2002). A randomized controlled trial of the psychosocial impact of providing Internet training and access to older adults. *Aging and Mental Health, 6*, 213–221.

White, L. (2001). Sibling relationships over the life course: A panel analysis. *Journal of Marriage and the Family, 63*, 555–568.

White, L. K., & Riedmann, A. (1992). Ties among adult siblings. *Social Forces, 71*, 85–102.

World Almanac and Book of Facts. (2003). *Young adults living at home in the U.S., 1960–2002*. Retrieved March 23, 2004, from http://www.infoplease.com/ipa/A0193723.html

Part V

INDIVIDUAL DIFFERENCES

CHAPTER 13

Personality and Relationships: A Temperament Perspective

Jeffry A. Simpson
Heike A. Winterheld
Jennie Y. Chen

Since the time of the ancient Greeks, people have assumed that personality traits affect what happens in close relationships. Indeed, many contemporary relationship models reserve a special place for how individual difference factors might affect both daily relationship function and long-term relationship quality (Karney & Bradbury, 1995). Throughout the 20th century, personality factors were examined in studies of romantic and other close relationships. As part of a special issue of the *Journal of Personality* (Cooper, 2002a) devoted to personality and relationships, Cooper and Sheldon (2002) traced 70 years of research. Table 13.1 shows the main foci of the work they surveyed, and their article provides more information on trends in the literature (e.g., the proportion of studies involving cross-sectional designs, self-report methods of data collection, and student samples increased from the 1950s until the 1990s).

Relatively meager progress, however, has been made toward understanding when, how, and why certain personality traits affect close relationships (Cooper, 2002b). This has led some scholars (e.g., Reis,

Capobianco, & Tsai, 2002) to question whether a focus on higher level personality traits is misplaced, and whether lower level measures that assess relationship-specific or partner-specific factors should be the principal focus of research. From the standpoint of personality psychology, however, neglecting the potential impact that higher level traits might have on relationships and interpersonal behavior is problematic. After all, one of the fundamental missions of personality psychology is to identify and understand how basic, cross-culturally robust personality dimensions influence individuals' thoughts, feelings, and behavior in important life contexts. Needless to say, few social contexts are more important than those that occur within close relationships.

Why has progress at the intersection of personality and relationships been so limited? To begin with, it is difficult to study the effects that individual differences have on ongoing dyadic relationships because individuals' reactions to events are colored not only by their own dispositions, motives, goals, and needs, but by their partners' as well. Complicating matters, personality and

Table 13.1. *Constructs and Measures Widely Used in 70 Years of Research on Personality and Close (Romantic) Relationships*

Construct	Percentage
Intraindividual and personality constructs[a]	
Broadband, multidimensional trait measures	37
Three/Five Factor Models	20
MMPI	7
Temperament	4
Other broadband	5
Personal adjustment/distress	27
Personality disorders	7
Midrange/narrow traits	63
Self-constructs	14
Interpersonal circumplex	14
Attachment styles	7
Aggressive traits	5
Gender-role attitudes	5
Social skills, competence	5
Socioemotional orientation	5
Impulsivity, sensation seeking	4
Relationship constructs[b]	
Global satisfaction/relationship adjustment	46
Relationship status/stability	26
Assortative mating/homogamy	24
Specific behaviors and dimensions	50
Intimacy, trust, caregiving	16
Sexual behavior	9
Communication, problem solving, decision making	8
Conflict	8
Violence, aggression, abuse	7
Power, dominance, equity	5
Role relationships/division of labor	4
Attraction	4
Other behaviors, dimensions	4

Note: Percentages sum to >100 because one study could examine multiple variables. Adapted from "Seventy years of research on personality and close relationships: Substantive and methodological trends over time," by M. L. Cooper and M. S. Sheldon, 2002, *Journal of Personality*, 70, pp. 800 and 803.
[a] Positive emotionality, negative emotionality, and constraint or extroversion, neuroticism, and psychoticism.
[b] Extroversion, neuroticism, conscientiousness, agreeableness, openness.

relationship researchers have not engaged in much cross-talk, a situation that has led each discipline to work with less-than-optimal knowledge of each other's cutting-edge the-

ories and ideas (Reis et al., 2002). Perhaps most important, however, investigators have not developed and tested models that specify when and how certain situations may interface with certain dispositions to activate specific relational schemas. Once activated, these schemas are likely to guide the way in which individuals feel, think, and behave during interactions with their partners, shunting relationships down different developmental pathways.

Our chapter is structured around the premise that certain personality traits may be markers of two biologically based systems that regulate perceptions and behavior in certain social contexts: (a) a behavioral activation or *approach system*, and (b) a behavioral inhibition or *avoidance system*. The approach system is believed to govern psychological tendencies to approach and acquire positive stimuli, outcomes, and goals, as reflected in appetitive (Gable & Reis, 2001) and promotion-focused (Higgins, 1998) orientations to relationships. The avoidance system, on the other hand, presumably regulates psychological tendencies to avert negative stimuli and outcomes, as evident in aversive or prevention-focused orientations.

The chapter contains three major sections. In the first section, we describe the two major dimensions of temperament and specify the major personality traits that map on to each one. We then discuss the theoretical and empirical ties that each dimension has with appetitive–promotion-focused tendencies and aversive–prevention-focused tendencies. In the second section, we provide a representative review of how traits believed to be markers of each dimension correlate with relationship outcomes, including relationship functioning, relationship quality, and relationship stability. In the final section, we introduce a process model that outlines the possible routes through which each temperament dimension might generate relationship outcomes, particularly perceptions of relationship quality. We suggest that certain situations may activate approach or avoidance motivations and their underlying relational schemas, especially in people who possess chronic approach or avoidance orientations. Once elicited, these schemas may influence patterns of interaction with and perceptions of relationship partners, which may then affect how individuals in approach or avoidance states view their relationships.

Major Personality Traits As Markers of Approach and Avoidance Temperaments

Personality psychology has three overarching goals: (a) to identify the basic dimensions (the "building blocks") of personality, (b) to understand their structure, and (c) to document the ways in which they systematically affect how individuals think, feel, and behave in important social contexts. Historically, these goals have been pursued using three distinct approaches to the study of personality (Clark & Watson, 1999): trait adjective approaches, affective disposition approaches, and motivational systems approaches.

Three Approaches to Personality

The *trait adjective approach* assesses traits by simply asking people (or their peers) to report what they are like on adjectives found in everyday language. This approach has produced two major models of personality: The Big Five traits (consisting of Openness to Experience, Conscientiousness, Extraversion, Agreeableness, and Neuroticism; Digman, 1990; John, 1990; McCrae & Costa, 1987), and the Big Three traits (consisting of Extraversion, Neuroticism, and Psychoticism; Eysenck & Eysenck, 1985). The neuroticism and extraversion measures identified in the Big Five model and in Eysenck's three-dimensional model are essentially identical (Costa & McCrae, 1992; Eysenck, 1992). A vast amount of research has revealed that highly neurotic people are more emotionally unstable, prone to anxiety and worries, and insecure about life. Highly extraverted people, by comparison, are more sociable, outgoing, impulsive, active, and optimistic.

A second tradition, the *affective disposition approach*, has identified two emotionality-based dimensions that are conceptually and empirically related to extraversion and neuroticism. Tellegen (1985) suggested that individual differences in affectivity (emotionality) form three basic dimensions, which he labeled positive emotionality, negative emotionality, and constraint. Watson and Clark (1993) referred to these same dimensions as positive temperament, negative temperament, and disinhibition. Considerable research has documented that people who score high in positive emotionality experience greater positive affect and approach life in a more positive, optimistic manner. Those who score high in negative emotionality experience more negative emotions and approach life in a more guarded, cautious manner.

A third tradition, the *motivational systems approach*, has attempted to identify major traits through the operation of motivational systems. This approach also has identified two conceptually similar dimensions – one that facilitates behavior and produces positive affect (approach motivation), and another that inhibits behavior and generates negative affect (Cacioppo & Berntson, 1994; Lang, 1995; Panksepp, 1998). Indeed, Gray (1970, 1990) claimed that basic individual differences exist within two separate biologically based systems, one that promotes behavior and positive affect (termed the behavior activation system or BAS) and one that inhibits behavior and generates negative affect (termed the behavioral inhibition system or BIS).[1]

There is growing consensus that each tradition has measured the same two fundamental dimensions (Elliot & Thrash, 2002; Watson, Wiese, Vaidya, & Tellegen, 1999). Adherents of each tradition assume that (a) both dimensions reflect distinct biologically based systems that may have evolved to serve unique functions, (b) each system operates within different neuroanatomical structures in the brain, and (c) individual differences on each dimension should be heritable, emerge early in development, and remain reasonably stable across the life span. Many scholars now believe that these dimensions are manifestations of adult *temperament* (Clark & Watson, 1999; Eysenck, 1970; McCrae et al., 2000; Zuckerman, 1991), which Allport (1937, pp. 54) defined as "the characteristic phenomena of an individual's emotional nature, including his [*sic*] susceptibility to emotional stimulation, his customary strength and speed of response, the quality of his prevailing mood, and all peculiarities of fluctuation and intensity of mood."[2]

Approach and Avoidance Temperament Dimensions

Certain individual difference measures anchor each temperament dimension. Elliot and Thrash (2002), for example, have shown that self-report measures of extraversion, positive emotionality, and the BAS all load highly on a single factor, which they labeled *approach temperament*. Measures of neuroticism, negative emotionality, and the BIS, in contrast, all load highly on an orthogonal factor termed *avoidance temperament* (see also Carver, Sutton, & Scheier, 2000; Gable, Reis, & Elliott, 2003). This research is consistent with earlier studies that have also found large bivariate correlations between the traits presumed to define each temperament dimension (see Elliot & Thrash, 2002).

Figure 13.1 depicts the approximate location of these trait measures within this two-dimensional space. According to Gray (1990), measures of the BAS and the BIS lie roughly 30 degrees counterclockwise from the extraversion and neuroticism axes, respectively. Within Eysenck and Eysenck's (1985) two-dimensional model of personality, therefore, the BAS primarily taps impulsivity (approaching possible rewards), whereas the BIS reflects general anxiety (avoiding possible punishments). Measures of emotional positivity are located slightly closer to the extraversion axis, whereas measures of emotional negativity fall nearer to the neuroticism axis (Watson et al., 1999).

In essence, the approach temperament dimension captures an individual's *general* sensitivity to potentially rewarding stimuli,

either actual or imagined. People who score high on this dimension are more cognitively aware of, emotionally responsive to, and behaviorally attracted to rewarding stimuli (Elliot & Thrash, 2002; Gray, 1990). As a result, they exhibit the sociable, outgoing, and optimistic features of extraverts, the elevated positive affect of persons who evince emotional positivity, and the impulsivity and behavioral facilitation characteristic of high BAS scorers.

The avoidance temperament dimension, on the other hand, reflects an individual's *general* sensitivity to actual or imagined negative or aversive stimuli. People who score high on avoidance are cognitively vigilant to, emotionally reactive to, and avoid or withdrawal from potentially punishing situations. Accordingly, they possess the anxiety-prone, emotionally unstable, and brooding characteristics of neurotics; the heightened negative affect of persons high in emotional negativity; and the restraint and behavioral inhibition of high BIS scorers.[3]

Multiple lines of research have identified the principal features of each orientation. Avoidance-oriented individuals (high BIS scorers), for example, report greater anxiety when they believe that unpleasant events will occur if they perform poorly on a task, whereas approach-oriented individuals (high BAS scorers) report greater happiness when they believe that rewards will follow good performances (Carver & White, 1994). In addition, avoidance-oriented people are biased to detect negative cues (especially those signaling potential loss), whereas approach-oriented people are biased to perceive positive cues, particularly those indicating potential gain (Derryberry & Reed, 1994). These differences may be partially rooted in brain functioning. Sutton and Davidson (1997) have confirmed that individuals who have different temperament orientations display different resting prefrontal brain asymmetries. Specifically, individuals who have an approach orientation (high BAS persons) have greater left prefrontal activation, whereas those with an avoidance orientation (high BIS persons) experience more right

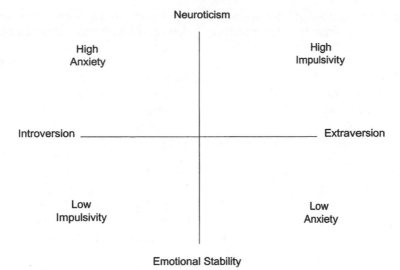

Figure 13.1. The approach and avoidance temperament dimensions within the extraversion–neuroticism circumplex model (Eysenck & Eysenck, 1985). High scores on the approach orientation lie between extraversion and high impulsivity. High scores on the avoidance orientation lie between neuroticism and high anxiety.

prefrontal activation. This research is illuminating because anticipating rewards is typically associated with greater left prefrontal activation, whereas fearing punishment corresponds to greater right prefrontal activation (Sobotka, Davidson, & Senulis, 1992). Most recently, Elliot and Thrash (2002) have shown that individuals who have approach tendencies (high BAS people) adopt mastery and performance-approach goals when engaging in tasks, but not performance-avoidance goals. Avoidance-oriented individuals (high BIS people), however, adopt performance-approach and performance-avoidance goals, but not mastery ones.

Appetitive–Promotion and Avoidance–Prevention Orientations in Relationships

Psychological processes that bear striking similarities to approach and avoidance tendencies may also govern how partners think, feel, and behave in close relationships. Gable and Reis (2001), for instance, proposed the existence of general two systems: an appetitive system (analogous to the approach system just discussed) and an aversive sys-

tem (analogous to the avoidance system). They claimed that the processes that regulate happy, fulfilling relationships (e.g., affiliation and intimacy) may be different from those that regulate reactions to negative relationship events (e.g., safety and security). As we shall see, various lines of evidence are consistent with this view.

Higgins (1998) has proposed a conceptually related two-dimensional model of self-regulatory systems that involve promotion and prevention foci. The promotion system facilitates the fulfillment of nurturance needs, hopes, and aspirations. The prevention system, in contrast, fosters the fulfillment of security needs, duties, and obligations. Similar to approach-oriented people, those who have a promotion-focus are sensitive to the presence and absence of positive outcomes (e.g., gains, rewards) and actively seek accomplishments. Analogous to avoidance-oriented people, those who have a prevention-focus are sensitive and reactive to the presence and absence of negative outcomes (e.g., losses, punishments), which they actively avoid to feel safe and secure. Unlike Gable and Reis's model, Higgins's model is structured around the specific self-regulation functions served by promotion and prevention tendencies.

A Representative Review of the Personality and Relationships Literature

Research investigating how approach and avoidance orientations might affect relationships is relatively new. Therefore, the personality traits that correspond with each orientation must be used to infer how each orientation is *likely* to be related to different relationship processes and outcomes. In this section, we present a selective yet representative review of what is currently known about how various trait markers of the approach and avoidance dimensions covary with measures of relationship functioning, quality, and stability in different contexts. Although the review covers multiple types of relationships (e.g., friendships, work relationships), most research has focused on the ways in which certain personality traits are differentially associated with outcomes in romantic relationships.

Markers of Approach and Relationship Outcomes

Several studies indicate that markers of the approach dimension – especially extraversion and positive affect – are associated with having more numerous and sometimes higher quality nonromantic relationships. In organizational settings, for instance, more extraverted people engage in more networking, socialize more, and become involved in more professional activities (Forret & Dougherty, 2001; Wanberg & Kammeyer-Mueller, 2000). In work settings, extraverts are more likely to use integrating and collaborating styles to manage conflicts and are less likely to use conflict avoidance tactics (Antonioni, 1998). During interactions with same-sex strangers, more extraverted people have higher quality interactions as rated by both themselves and observers (Berry & Hansen, 2000). When interacting with friends, they report feeling emotion-ally closer, which their friends corroborate (Berry, Willingham, & Thayer, 2000).

Similar effects have been found in other types of nonromantic relationships. Asendorpf and Wilpers (1998), for example, examined how personality is related to relationships with peers, mothers, fathers, and siblings across time. Extraversion and its subfactors (sociability and shyness) predicted various relationship outcomes, but not vice versa. After controlling for initial relationship quality, for instance, extraversion predicted higher rates of interaction in different types of relationships, forming more new relationships, and having better opposite-sex peer relationships (e.g., perceiving more support).[4] Over time, more extraverted people also report greater increases in the closeness and the importance of their relationships with friends and colleagues (Neyer & Asendorpf, 2001).

Parallel effects have been discovered for positive affectivity (PA). Individuals who report higher PA spend more time socializing with their friends (Watson, 1988; Watson, Clark, McIntyre, & Hamaker, 1992) and are involved in more different social interactions (Berry & Hansen, 1996). In terms of friendship quality, higher PA individuals also report feeling closer to their friends, find them less irritating, and have fewer conflicts (Berry et al., 2000). Connections between extraversion and PA and feelings of greater closeness appear to be mediated by how extraverts and high PA individuals handle interpersonal conflicts (Berry et al., 2000). For example, the relation between extraversion and feelings of greater closeness is mediated by the reluctance of extraverts to use exit tactics (active, destructive behaviors) during relationship conflicts. On the other hand, the relation between PA and feelings of greater closeness is mediated by the tendency of the friends of high PA individuals *not* to display neglect tactics (passive, destructive responses) during conflicts. Gable, Reis, and Elliott (2000) suggest that people who score higher in approach tendencies may experience greater positive affect because they are more often exposed to – or expose themselves to – positive daily events.

More research has investigated how markers of approach correlate with various outcomes in romantic relationships. With regard to relationship functioning, higher PA individuals are more likely to be involved in romantic relationships, report having higher quality relationships, and feel more committed to them (Berry & Willingham, 1997). When relationship conflicts arise, they display more active–constructive behaviors (voice tactics) and fewer passive–destructive (neglect tactics) and active–destructive (exit tactics) behaviors. In addition, the link between PA and heightened relationship quality appears to be mediated by high PA individuals' unwillingness to respond to relationship conflicts with exit tactics and by their tendency to use more voice tactics. PA often should be a good predictor of relationship quality during the early stages of relationship development when partners are polite, are learning much about one another, and are still displaying "good manners." However, NA should be – and usually is – a better predictor of relationship quality in more established relationships (Watson, Hubbard, & Wiese, 2000). Finally, Campbell, Simpson, Stewart, and Manning (2003) have found that more extraverted men display more leadership behaviors in small, all-male groups, but only when they are motivated to impress an attractive female evaluator.

A few studies indicate that markers of approach predict greater satisfaction in romantic relationships, but several do not. Watson et al. (2000) found that higher PA and extraversion both predicted greater marital satisfaction and that higher satisfaction was primarily a function of individuals' own traits rather than their partner's traits (see also Russell & Wells, 1994). Other studies, however, either have not found these effects (e.g., Botwin, Buss, & Shackelford, 1997; Kurdek, 1993) or have found extraversion to be negatively related to marital satisfaction (Lester, Haig, & Monello, 1989). In a comprehensive review of the literature, Karney and Bradbury (1995) concluded

that extraversion is associated with slightly greater marital satisfaction and marital instability, but these effects are small.

Having a chronic promotion-focus should be another good marker of an approach orientation. Studying friendship strategies used by chronically promotion-focused versus prevention-focused people, Higgins, Roney, Crowe, and Hymes (1994) documented that promotion-focused individuals typically select approach strategies when dealing with their friends (e.g., being generous and giving of oneself), whereas prevention-focused people habitually use avoidance strategies (e.g., trying not to neglect friends).

Most recently, Gable (2003) has shown that approached-based dispositional motives and current goals jointly predict less loneliness and more satisfaction in different types of close relationships over time. These effects are partially mediated by the greater exposure that approach-oriented people have to positive life events, which in turn facilitate their overarching goals of having happier, more satisfying relationships.

In sum, approach-oriented people become more actively involved in socially rewarding situations in different types of relationships. They may also play a direct role in creating and shaping positive relationship experiences, as indicated by the more constructive ways in which they manage conflict in their relationships. These propensities not only appear to affect the quality of their own experiences in social interactions (e.g., feeling closer to their relationship partners), they also seem to affect their partners' experiences. Nevertheless, the precise processes that generate these effects are not well understood.

Markers of Avoidance and Relationship Outcomes

Stronger and more consistent relationship effects have been documented for markers of avoidance. Using event-contingent sampling methods and examining mainly nonromantic interactions, Côté and Moskowitz (1998) found that highly neurotic people engage in fewer behaviors that typically generate positive affect (e.g., agreeable or slightly dominant acts) and experience less positive affect when they do. Conversely, such persons display more behaviors known to produce unpleasant affect (e.g., submissive and quarrelsome acts) and report greater negative affect when they do. Across time, more neurotic people are also more inclined to experience declines in security and closeness with friends and colleagues (Neyer & Asendorpf, 2001).

Furthermore, both higher NA persons and their friends report less emotional closeness and greater irritation (Berry et al., 2000). Higher NA individuals also report using more exit tactics during relationship conflicts, and they and their friends both report using more neglect tactics. Berry et al. (2000) also confirmed that more neurotic individuals have friends who, in a reciprocal manner, report feeling less close to them. This effect is mediated by highly neurotic individuals' greater use of exit tactics during relationship conflicts and by their *friends'* tendencies to display neglect tactics, perhaps to avoid aversive or relationship-damaging interactions. Gable et al. (2000) presented evidence that people who have avoidance tendencies may experience greater negative affect because of their stronger emotional reactions to negative daily events.

Studies of interactions between same-sex strangers, however, have not found that markers of avoidance predict less relationship quality (Berry & Hansen, 1996, 2000). Markers of avoidance, therefore, appear to have stronger and more pernicious effects on well-established nonromantic relationships than on newly developed ones. This suggests that the temperament dimensions might influence nonromantic relationships at different stages of relationship development, with approach orientations having stronger effects during relationship initiation and avoidance orientations having more powerful effects once relationships are established and require maintenance.

With regard to romantic relationships, robust effects have also been found for markers of avoidance. In terms of marital functioning, more neurotic individuals report poorer marital adjustment (Bouchard, Lussier, & Sabourn, 1999) and express or feel less positive affect and more negative affect when embroiled in marital conflicts (Geist & Gilbert, 1996). When addressing marital difficulties, highly neurotic spouses are also more likely to use distancing and avoiding tactics (Bolger & Zuckerman, 1995; Bouchard, 2003), which represent higher level emotion-focused coping strategies. Although such tactics can dissipate distress in the short term, they rarely yield good, permanent solutions to major marital problems.

Similar marital effects have been found for negative affectivity (NA), another marker of avoidance. In dating relationships, for instance, higher NA individuals report engaging in more active, destructive behaviors (exit tactics) combined with more passive, destructive behaviors (neglect tactics) when engaged in relationship conflicts (Berry & Willingham, 1997). In marriages, higher NA persons make more maladaptive attributions for their spouses' potentially negative actions (Karney, Bradbury, Fincham, & Sullivan, 1994). Not surprisingly, highly neurotic and high NA individuals both tend to have less satisfying marriages (Karney & Bradbury, 1995), not only concurrently (Karney & Bradbury, 1997; Thomsen & Gilbert, 1998) but also across large segments of time (Kelly & Conley, 1987). Furthermore, the spouses of highly neurotic people report greater marital dissatisfaction (Botwin et al., 1997), a pattern that also holds for the spouses of high NA individuals (Watson et al., 2000).

Russell and Wells (1994) have also documented that neuroticism predicts reduced personal happiness with marriage in both spouses. The relation between neuroticism and reduced happiness is mediated by each spouses' perceptions of lower marital quality. As a result, neuroticism also reliably forecasts greater marital instability and divorce (Kelly & Conley, 1987; Kurdek, 1993; Tucker, Kressin, Spiro, & Ruscio, 1998; for a review see Karney & Bradbury, 1995). Some of the strongest and most replicable associations between personality traits and relationship outcomes, in fact, have involved markers of avoidance, particularly neuroticism.

Possessing a chronic prevention focus should also be a prime marker of avoidance. Ayduk, May, Downey, and Higgins (2003) have investigated how being chronically prevention-oriented interacts with high rejection sensitivity (HRS) to predict coping when rejection seems imminent. HRS individuals who are also more prevention-focused use more covert and passive forms of negative coping (e.g., self-silencing) in these situations. Moreover, when they perceive rejection from a potential romantic partner or during real relationship conflicts, these individuals express greater passive hostility by being cold and distant, refrain from showing positive or accepting behaviors such as love or support, and suppress active hostility. These tactics reflect a heightened state of vigilance, which is a cardinal feature of the prevention system.

Gable (2003) has recently shown that people who possess avoidance-based motives and goals are lonelier, hold more negative social attitudes, and feel less secure about their relationships. These effects are partially mediated by the highly negative and reactive manner in which avoidance-oriented people respond to negative events that might destabilize the security of their relationship bonds.

To summarize, avoidance-oriented people react strongly and often negatively in different types of relationships, particularly when they encounter events that could destabilize their relationships. Indeed, they may aggravate negative relationship experiences through the corrosive and damaging ways in which they handle interpersonal conflicts. These tendencies may influence not only the quality of their own experiences (e.g., reduced satisfaction), but their partners' experiences as well. The processes responsible for these effects, however, remain poorly understood.

Linking Approach and Avoidance Orientations to Relationship Processes and Outcomes

To comprehend when, how, and why approach and avoidance orientations might affect relationships, one must first identify the major functions that each orientation serves. From an evolutionary perspective, the avoidance system might have evolved to help humans deal with immediate dangers in their environments rapidly and effectively. Although this system operates in all people, some individuals are more sensitive to negative events in their environments because of genetic differences that are likely to be reinforced by difficult or painful life experiences or by parents who were overprotective or overly punishing (Higgins & Silberman, 1998). Thus, when negative events are encountered, avoidance-oriented adults react more strongly to them, most likely because they have lower or more sensitive threat activation thresholds.

Approach tendencies may reflect an entirely separate evolved system, one that operates independently of the avoidance system. The approach system may motivate people to move toward potentially rewarding outcomes in their environments, which must often be actively sought or intentionally created. Because of genetic differences that may be amplified by a history of positive social experiences or by parents who encouraged accomplishment and risk taking (Higgins & Silberman, 1998), some individuals have lower approach activation thresholds, compelling them to pursue social rewards more frequently and more fervently.

Because the presence of rewards and costs may be uncorrelated in most situations, each evolved system should operate independently. Moreover, the two systems may be functionally and conceptually independent because they reflect the operation of two separate neurobiological systems in the brain, a proposition first introduced by Gray (1970) that has now received support from extensive neurophysiological research (e.g., Harmon-Jones & Allen, 1997; Sobotka, Davidson, & Senulis, 1992; Sutton & Davidson, 1997). Being managed by distinct neurobiological structures, the sensitivity levels of approach and avoidance systems can combine in various ways in different individuals (Carver & White, 1994). For example, some people should be low on both approach and avoidance tendencies (possibly resulting in indifference), whereas others should be high on both (perhaps generating ambivalence; see Gable et al., 2003). Still others should be low on approach and high on avoidance, or vice versa. Gable et al. (2003) suggested that under certain conditions, the behavioral manifestation of these two systems may be inversely related, occasionally concealing their functional independence. Cacioppo, Gardner, and Berntson (1997), in fact, found that people can either approach a stimulus or avoid it at any given moment, regardless of their attitude toward the stimulus. When extremely high levels of arousal are experienced, however, the two systems may functionally merge to minimize uncertainty, with high levels of one system effectively dampening the sensitivity of the other system. As a rule, however, approach and avoidance orientations ought to generate distinct patterns of relationship correlates similar to those discussed in the foregoing literature review.

Models of Personality and Relationships

Models explaining how personality traits could influence relationship processes and outcomes fall into two categories: general personality models, and models relevant to specific traits (e.g., approach and avoidance). A prime exemplar of a general personality model has been advanced by Reis et al. (2002). This model attempts to explain how personality traits generate different patterns of interaction in relationships (e.g., negative affect reciprocity, demand–withdrawal). According to this model, the situational context and personality traits of each partner should jointly affect routine interaction patterns in relationships. Traits may initially affect the types of situations that certain individuals choose to enter (transition into) or exit (transition out of), based on the perceived rewards versus costs of earlier interactions. Once in a situation, the situational context should govern whether a trait becomes activated and, if so, the degree to which it guides interpersonal expectations, information processing,

social behavior, and subjective emotional experiences.

Reis et al. (2002) also conjectured that traits should affect relationships most strongly in situations in which one partner feels vulnerable or both partners have competing motives or goals (i.e., "trust" situations; see Kelley et al., 2003). They surmised that partner and relationship-specific expectations should mediate connections between personality traits and interaction outcomes, with interpersonal expectations operating as interpretative filters or comparison standards. Thus, as relationships develop, general expectancies should give way to partner- and relationship-specific expectations, meaning that traits should exert weaker effects on relationships as they develop (see Zayas, Shoda, & Ayduk [2002] for a similar model).

Gable and Reis (2001) developed a more delimited model that explains how approach and avoidance orientations might influence relationships. Guided by evolutionary thinking, they proposed that the appetitive (approach) and aversive (avoidance) systems ought to affect different types of relationship outcomes and influence interpersonal behavior via distinct processes. In support of this, Gable et al. (2000) showed that individuals who score higher on avoidance measures experience more negative affect in their daily lives, most likely in response to their stronger emotional reactions to negative interpersonal events. Individuals scoring higher on approach measures, in contrast, experience more positive affect, ostensibly because they enter or create situations that facilitate positive moods. Accordingly, Gable and Reis (2001) proposed that the appetitive system fosters positive experiences in relationships (e.g., intimacy, feelings of emotional connection, enhanced personal growth) by motivating these people to select, create, or initiate positive interactions with relationship partners. The aversive system, on the other hand, regulates negative relationship experiences (e.g., feelings of uncertainty, jealousy, anger) by amplifying adverse emotional reactions in these people, especially

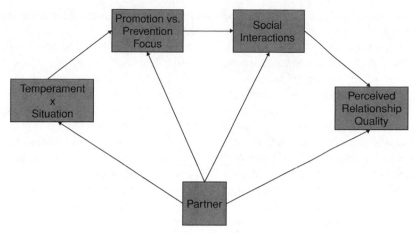

Figure 13.2. A model of how certain situations interact with the temperament dimensions en route to generating perceived relationship quality.

when negative social interactions are encountered.[5]

Extending this analysis, Gable (2003) proposed that approach and avoidance dispositional motivations may instigate more focused approach and avoidance goals in certain situations. She claimed that approach motivations and goals are likely to operate through differential exposure processes to achieve positive relationship outcomes (e.g., attaining satisfying intimate bonds), whereas avoidance motives and goals might operate via differential reactivity processes to avert negative relationship outcomes (e.g., losing secure bonds). If achieved, both outcomes should generate enhanced personal well-being, although approach-focused individuals should experience greater relationship quality. Gable also speculated that when relationship satisfaction is average or relationship prospects are unclear, dispositional motives should override situation-specific goals. However, when satisfaction is high or low, situational circumstances should have a stronger bearing on which specific goals individuals pursue.

A Process Model

Informed by previous findings and models, we have developed a process model that links approach and avoidance temperaments to relationship outcomes via partic-

ular modes of thinking, feeling, and interacting in romantic relationships. Our model attempts to explain how situational and individual difference factors might jointly influence perceived relationship quality and, for avoidance, perhaps even relationship stability. In essence, we propose that approach and avoidance temperaments should differentially affect perceptions of relationship quality through (a) the situations that approach- and avoidance-oriented individuals choose to enter, exit, or avoid with their relationship partners; (b) how they construe and frame situations once in them; (c) how they perceive their partners' behaviors, goals, intentions, and motives; and (d) how they then interact with their partners.

Figure 13.2 depicts the model once relationship partners have entered a specific situation. According to the model, certain situations ought to activate promotion or prevention foci in most people. Situations that are concordant with an individual's own chronic regulatory focus (i.e., prevention-activating situations for prevention-focused people and promotion-activating situations for promotion-focused people) should amplify the cognitive, emotional, and behavioral effects in these individuals. Once triggered, the activated focus should guide how individuals feel, think, and behave in interactions with their partners. Especially in situations that could be highly diagnostic of how partners really view one another and the relationship (e.g., in "trust" situations; Kelley et al., 2003), certain routine patterns of interaction might generate positive or negative short-term relationship outcomes, such as temporary shifts in perceptions of relationship quality, closeness, conflict, or support. If such patterns become stable "interaction signatures" that characterize a relationship, their repeated occurrence might eventually produce long-term changes in relationship perceptions and evaluations, fueling either relationship growth–enhancement or relationship damage–deterioration. We first discuss how approach-based motives and situations might impact relationships.

APPROACH MOTIVES AND SITUATIONS

As we have seen, traits that define an approach orientation tend to be associated with greater perceived relationship quality, especially when relationships are being formed. According to our model, these positive outcomes could be partly attributable to the situations that approach-oriented people selectively enter and, thus, to which they preferentially "expose" their developing relationships. When getting to know relationship partners, highly approach-oriented people may enter, create, or transform social interactions in ways that encourage greater openness, more rapid and intimate personal self-disclosure, and more mutual responsiveness. This, in turn, should foster greater intimacy at earlier points in relationship development (Reis & Shaver, 1988). Approach-oriented people might also enter or gravitate toward novel and challenging situations, which can accelerate self-expansion and promote feelings of greater closeness (Aron, Norman, Aron, & Lewandowski, 2002).

As shown in Figure 13.2, certain situations should activate the approach system in most people, particularly in those who possess a chronic (dispositional) approach orientation. For example, situations that are viewed as safe or benign (Friedman & Förster, 2001), those in which potential rewards far outstrip possible costs (Higgins, 1998), and those in which individuals believe they have greater power (Keltner, Gruenfeld, & Anderson, 2003) are all likely to launch the approach system, especially in highly approach-oriented people. Once this system is activated, individuals should enter a promotion-focused state.

Promotion-focused states have several cardinal features. In terms of emotional processes, promotion-focused people experience positive outcomes (e.g., gains, unexpected surprises by partners) more intensely than prevention-oriented people do, and therefore they report more cheerfulness-related emotions. Negative outcomes (e.g., losses, rejection by partners) are felt less intensely (Idson, Liberman, & Higgins, 2000). With regard to cognitive features, promotion-focused people exhibit more disjunctive thinking (believing that any successful route to achieving a promotion goal is a good one; Brockner, Paruchuri, Idson, & Higgins, 2002) and remain open to change in the hope of finding better ways to achieve their promotion goals (Liberman, Idson, Camacho, & Higgins, 1999). They also display riskier styles of cognitive processing and think more abstractly (Higgins, 1997), generate and endorse more hypotheses for interpersonal actions (Liberman, Molden, Idson, & Higgins, 2001), and take person and situation explanations into account when making inferences about others' behavior (Liberman et al., 2001). In terms of behavioral features, promotion-focused people eagerly approach matches to desired end states by pursuing multiple routes to attaining their goals (Higgins et al., 1994), use eagerness means (i.e., tactics that will advance goal attainment; Higgins et al., 2001), display more approach-related behaviors (Shah, Higgins, & Friedman, 1998), and feel greater motivation the closer they get to accomplishing their goals (Förster, Higgins, & Idson, 1998).

Collectively, these emotional, cognitive, and behavioral tendencies may lead people who are in promotion-focused states to enter, explore, and take fuller advantage of novel and challenging interactions with their partners. When doing so, they are likely to experience greater excitement, less boredom, more rapid self-expansion, and the type of pleasant interruptions believed to generate positive emotions (Berscheid, 1983). Novel or challenging activities may include attending cultural events together (e.g., concerts, plays), engaging in outdoor activities (e.g., skiing, hiking), or doing social activities (e.g., dancing). These tendencies might also help people in promotion-focused states to deal more effectively and constructively with interpersonal conflict because they experience negative emotions less intensely; because their more flexible, disjunctive styles of handling problems yields better resolutions; or because they find ways to promote closeness and intimacy, even during conflicts. Promotion-focused people may also display more pro-relationship behaviors and encourage their partners to do the same, which should enhance relationship quality (Kumashiro, Finkel, & Rusbult, 2002). They might also gravitate to "joint control" interactions in which both partners agree on what to do before a final decision is reached (Kelley et al., 2003). Couples who normally interact in joint control situations tend to be more happily married (Wagner, Kirchler, & Brandstatter, 1984).

Promotion-focused individuals might also perceive greater relationship quality due to their strong focus on achieving positive relationship outcomes. Because they are more sensitive to the presence and absence of positive outcomes, promotion-focused people might notice and give more "credit" when their partners display positive attributes or behaviors during interactions. To the extent that promotion-focused people define successful relationships as those that yield rewards and positive outcomes, their greater awareness and acknowledgment of positive partner behaviors should generate more intense positive emotions and, thus, heightened perceptions of relationship quality. When involved in relationships that provide fewer positive outcomes, promotion-focused people should experience relatively less intense negative emotions

and only moderately lower perceptions of relationship quality. According to our model, therefore, if individuals who are prone to experiencing promotion states (i.e., approach-oriented people) routinely engage in these positive types of interactions and have more positive perceptions of their partners' positive actions, this would explain why they perceive higher relationship quality, especially when initiating relationships.

Updegraff, Gable, and Taylor (2004) recently showed that highly approach-motivated people base their global judgments of satisfaction more on past positive emotional experiences and less on past negative experiences. They proposed that highly approach-motivated people not only experience more positive emotions across time, they also place greater weight on positive emotional experiences when judging their own well-being. Although this research was not conducted in a relationship context, it nevertheless supports the preceding propositions.

AVOIDANCE MOTIVES AND SITUATIONS

As reviewed earlier, traits that underlie the avoidance orientation are commonly associated with poorer relationship outcomes. These negative outcomes might, of course, be partly attributable to the situations that highly avoidance-oriented people either choose to enter (e.g., situations that typically provoke disagreements) or not to enter (e.g., situations that could be novel and exciting). The most deleterious effects of avoidance, however, are witnessed in well-established relationships that require maintenance.

Returning to Figure 13.2, a different set of situations should activate the avoidance system in most people, especially in those who have a chronic avoidance orientation. For example, situations perceived as threatening (Friedman & Förster, 2001), in which potential costs loom large relative to possible gains (Higgins, 1998), or in which individuals believe they have little power (Keltner et al., 2003) should elicit the avoidance system, particularly in highly avoidance-oriented people. Once activated, individuals should enter a prevention-focused state.

In terms of emotional processes, prevention-oriented people experience negative outcomes more intensely than promotion-oriented people do, and accordingly, they experience more agitation-related emotions. They also experience positive outcomes less intensely (Higgins, 1998; Idson et al., 2000). As for cognitive features, people in prevention-focused states engage in more conjunctive thinking (believing that multiple courses of action must all be successful to achieve their prevention goals; Brockner et al., 2002), and they prefer stability over change (e.g., staying with old, reliable solutions even when new ones might work better; Liberman et al., 1999). They also adopt more conservative cognitive processing styles and think more concretely (Higgins, 1997), generate and select fewer hypotheses for interpersonal actions (Liberman et al., 2001), and differentiate between person and situation explanations when making inferences about others' actions (Liberman et al., 2001). Elliot and Church (2003) proposed that prevention-focused states engender two self-protective cognitive strategies: defensive pessimism or self-handicapping (or both). With regard to behavioral characteristics, people in prevention-focused states avoid mismatches to desired end states (Higgins et al., 1994), focus on vigilance means (i.e., not using tactics that might impede goal attainment; Higgins et al., 2001), display more avoidance-related behaviors (Shah et al., 1998), and exhibit greater motivation the closer they are to the outcomes they want to avert (Förster et al., 1998).

Viewed together, these tendencies should lead prevention-focused people to manage relationship conflicts poorly, perhaps because they feel negative emotions more intensely, because their conservative, conjunctive styles of problem solving produce poorer resolutions, or because their strong security concerns overwhelm constructive behavioral responses. Prevention-focused people might also unwittingly create demand–withdrawal interaction patterns in their relationships, whereby the prevention-focused individual initially protests and issues demands, which then generates withdrawal on the part of the partner (Christensen & Heavey, 1990). Alternately, if individuals are involved with partners who confront relationship difficulties, people in prevention-focused states could become locked in escalating cycles in which negative affect is continually reciprocated. Couples who become entrenched in either of these negative interaction patterns tend to be less happy and are more likely to divorce (Gottman, 1994).

Prevention-focused individuals might also perceive lower relationship quality given their strong focus on avoiding negative relationship outcomes. Because of this focus, prevention-focused people may notice and place greater weight on their partners' negative attributes and behaviors during interactions. Given that prevention-focused people define successful relationships as those characterized by the absence of negative outcomes, their accentuated awareness and acknowledgment of negative partner actions might generate less intense positive emotions and, hence, more modest perceptions of relationship quality. When they find themselves in relationships that have negative outcomes, prevention-focused people should experience more intense negative emotions and very low perceptions of relationship quality. Thus, according to our model, if individuals who are vulnerable to experiencing prevention states (i.e., avoidance-oriented people) regularly have these damaging interaction patterns and harbor more negative perceptions of their partners' negative actions, this might explain why they report lower relationship quality.

THE ROLE OF THE PARTNER

Relationship partners assume a pivotal role in our model. As shown in Figure 13.2, partners influence not only the situational contexts in which many relationship interactions occur, they also act as one of the principle situational forces to which individuals are exposed each day. Over time, partners may affect an individual's chronic level of approach or avoidance as well as how often she or he enters promotion or prevention states. Shah (2003), in fact, confirmed that representations of significant others can implicitly affect an individual's own regulatory focus. Partners might also influence long-term relationship outcomes that are not mediated through the upstream variables in our model. Partners may, for example, leave relationships if new or better alternatives arise (Thibaut & Kelley, 1959), even if individuals are frequently in promotion states and the bulk of daily relationship interactions are positive and fulfilling. The fact that separate lines run from the "partner" to each of the other variables in Figure 13.2 signifies that partners are likely to have unique, independent effects on individuals at each juncture of our model.

QUALIFICATIONS

Several qualifications must be considered before applying this model. First, information must be gathered from both relationship partners. One reason for doing so is that certain dyad-level combinations of approach and avoidance orientations (such as two highly avoidant partners) or promotion and prevention states (such as two highly prevention-focused partners) may yield outcomes that are different from what might be expected based on each partner's individual-level scores. Second, several factors not represented in our model might also affect relationship quality. For instance, the quality or availability of alternative partners, assorted structural factors (e.g., religious beliefs, finances, children), or major life events (e.g., declining health, losing a job) should also affect relationship quality as it is perceived by one or both partners. Third, although the model is depicted as unidirectional, there are bound to be reciprocal feedback loops. Over time, for example, changes in perceived relationship quality might alter individuals' chronic approach or avoidance orientations; the situations they decide to enter, exit, or avoid with their partners; and their likelihood of entering promotion or prevention states. Fourth, our model may

account for variation in relationship quality better than variation in relationship stability (i.e., dissolution) because decisions to terminate a relationship are often made by only one partner. Finally, as partners gradually learn more about one another, partner- and relationship-specific beliefs and expectations should assume increasingly larger roles in shaping relationship outcomes.

Conclusion

One of the reasons little progress has been made toward understanding how personality traits affect relationship outcomes might be that sufficiently clear and precise models have not been proposed. Although tentative and most likely incomplete, our model suggests that certain trait-by-situation configurations should channel individuals into promotion- or prevention-focused states, which in turn should affect interaction patterns, perceptions, and judgments of relationship quality. If certain patterns become "interaction signatures" of relationships, their repeated occurrence could exert long-term effects on perceptions of relationship quality and, in the case of avoidance, perhaps relationship stability. What makes this model novel is its emphasis on how certain trait-by-situation configurations might activate more specific goal-oriented states that then promote recurrent interaction patterns and positive or negative perceptions of partners within close relationships.

Authors' Note

The writing of this chapter was partially support by the National Institutes of Health (grant MH49599-05).

Footnotes

1. There are, of course, more than three major approaches to the study of personality. Personality theorists have, for instance, used empirical keying techniques to identify major

dimensions of personality (see Burisch, 1984). They have also investigated how measures of Murray's (1938) primary needs organize and guide personality and social behavior, ranging from achievement (McClelland, Atkinson, Clark, & Lowell, 1953), to intimacy (McAdams, 1992), to power (Winter, 1973). However, neither empirical keying perspectives nor the fundamental needs perspective has identified higher order dimensions of personality similar to those discovered by the three major approaches discussed here.

2. Although correlated, the traits that measure each temperament dimension are conceptually distinct (Rusting & Larsen, 1997, 1999).

3. The approach and avoidance dimensions parallel Gray's (1990) behavioral activation system (BAS) and behavioral inhibition system (BIS) in several ways. Nevertheless, the two temperaments are believed to be associated with a larger network of semi-independent and interacting neuroanatomical structures and neurochemical/neuroendocrinological processes than is true of the BIS and the BAS (Cacioppo, Gardner, & Berntson, 1999; Panksepp, 1998). Thus, the temperament dimensions include, but are broader than, Gray's original conceptualization of the BIS and the BAS (Elliot & Thrash, 2002).

4. In this study, neuroticism did not interfere with the development of relationships, suggesting that neuroticism may be irrelevant when new relationships are being established.

5. This does not imply that the appetitive system is exclusively associated with "good" relationship outcomes and the aversive system is always associated with "bad" ones. Indeed, in some situations, a strong or highly activated appetitive system might lead to poor relationship outcomes, such as when an individual becomes obsessed with certain highly rewarding aspects of his or her relationship (e.g., good sex) and ignores other vital aspects (e.g., good communication). A strongly activated appetitive system might also lead individuals to become so focused on attaining rewarding relationship outcomes that they ignore or overlook negative information suggesting that their relationships are in jeopardy, such as not fully processing cues that their partners are unhappy about certain relationship matters. In other situations, a strong or highly activated aversive system might actually protect relationships from devastating consequences, such as when individuals exaggerate the poten-

tial costs of leaving a steady current partner for a highly provocative yet unstable or incompatible one. Given the heightened vigilance to negative outcomes that accompanies a highly activated aversive system, these individuals might also be more aware of potential threats to their relationships at an earlier stage, enabling them to address potential threats before they turn into severe problems. Neither system, therefore, is uniquely tied to the generation of "good" versus "bad" relationship outcomes.

References

Allport, G. W. (1937). *Personality: A psychological interpretation*. New York: Holt.

Antonioni, D. (1998). Relationship between the Big Five personality factors and conflict management styles. *International Journal of Conflict Management, 9*, 336–355.

Aron, A., Norman, C. C., Aron, E. N., & Lewandowski, G. (2002). Shared participation in self-expanding activities: Positive effects on experienced martial quality. In P. Noller & J. A. Feeney (Eds.), *Understanding marriage: Developments in the study of couple interaction. Advances in personal relationships* (pp. 177–194). New York: Cambridge University Press.

Asendorpf, J. B., & Wilpers, S. (1998). Personality effects on social relationships. *Journal of Personality and Social Psychology, 74*, 1531–1544.

Ayduk, O., May, D., Downey, G., & Higgins, E. T. (2003). Tactical differences in coping with rejection sensitivity: The role of prevention pride. *Personality and Social Psychology Bulletin, 29*, 435–448.

Berry, D. S., & Hansen, J. S. (1996). Positive affect, negative affect, and social interaction. *Journal of Personality and Social Psychology, 71*, 796–809.

Berry, D. S., & Hansen, J. S. (2000). Personality, nonverbal behavior, and interaction quality in female dyads. *Personality and Social Psychology Bulletin, 26*, 278–292.

Berry, D. S., & Willingham, J. K. (1997). Affective traits, responses to conflict, and satisfaction in romantic relationships. *Journal of Research in Personality, 31*, 564–576.

Berry, D. S., Willingham, J. K., & Thayer, C. A. (2000). Affect and personality as predictors of conflict and closeness in young adults' friendships. *Journal of Research in Personality, 34,* 84–107.

Berscheid, E. (1983). Emotion. In H. H. Kelley, E. Berscheid, A. Christensen, J. H. Harvey, T. L. Huston, G. Levinger, et al. (Eds.), *Close relationships* (pp. 110–168). New York: Freeman.

Bolger, N., & Zuckerman, A. (1995). A framework for studying personality in the stress process. *Journal of Personality and Social Psychology, 69,* 890–902.

Botwin, M. D., Buss, D. M., & Shackelford, T. K. (1997). Personality and mate preferences: Five factors in mate selection and marital satisfaction. *Journal of Personality, 65,* 107–136.

Bouchard, G. (2003). Cognitive appraisals, neuroticism, and openness as correlates of coping strategies: An integrative model of adaptation to marital difficulties. *Canadian Journal of Behavioural Science, 35,* 1–12.

Bouchard, G., Lussier, Y., & Sabourin, S. (1999). Personality and marital adjustment: Utility of the five-factor model of personality. *Journal of Marriage and the Family, 61,* 651–660.

Brockner, J., Paruchuri, S., Idson, L. C., & Higgins, E. T. (2002). Regulatory focus and the probability estimates of conjunctive and disjunctive events. *Organizational Behavior and Human Decision Processes, 87,* 5–24.

Burisch, M. (1984). Approaches to personality inventory construction: A comparison of merits. *American Psychologist, 39,* 214–227.

Cacioppo, J. T., & Berntson, G. G. (1994). Relationship between attitudes and evaluative space: A critical review, with emphasis on the separability of positive and negative substrates. *Psychological Bulletin, 115,* 401–423.

Cacioppo, J. T., Gardner, W. L., & Berntson, G. C. (1997). Beyond bipolar conceptualizations and measures: The case of attitudes and evaluative space. *Personality and Social Psychology Review, 1,* 3–25.

Cacioppo, J. T., Gardner, W. L., & Berntson, G. G. (1999). The affect system has parallel and integrative processing components: Form follows function. *Journal of Personality and Social Psychology, 76,* 839–855.

Campbell, L., Simpson, J. A., Stewart, M., & Manning, J. (2003). Putting personality in social context: Extraversion, emergent leadership, and the availability of rewards. *Personality and Social Psychology Bulletin, 29,* 1547–1559.

Carver, C. S., Sutton, S. K., & Scheier, M. F. (2000). Action, emotion, and personality:

Emerging conceptual integration. *Personality and Social Psychology Bulletin, 26,* 741–751.

Carver, C. S., & White, T. L. (1994). Behavioral inhibition, behavioral activation, and affective responses to impending reward and punishment: The BIS/BAS scales. *Journal of Personality and Social Psychology, 67,* 319–333.

Christensen, A., & Heavey, C. L. (1990). Gender and social structure in the demand/withdraw pattern of marital conflict. *Journal of Personality and Social Psychology, 59,* 73–81.

Clark, L. A., & Watson, D. (1999). Temperament: A new paradigm for trait psychology. In L. A. Pervin & O. P. John (Eds.), *Handbook of personality: Theory and research* (2nd ed., pp. 399–423). New York: Guilford Press.

Cooper, M. L. (Ed.). (2002a). Personality and close relationships [Special issue]. *Journal of Personality, 70*(6).

Cooper, M. L. (2002b). Personality and close relationships: Embedding people in important social contexts. *Journal of Personality, 70,* 757–782.

Cooper, M. L., & Sheldon, M. S. (2002). Seventy years of research on personality and close relationships: Substantive and methodological trends over time. *Journal of Personality, 70,* 783–812.

Costa, P. T., & McCrae, R. R. (1992). Revised NEO Personality Inventory (NEO-PI-R) and NEO Five-Factor Inventory (NEO-FFI) professional manual. Odessa, FL: Psychological Assessment Resources.

Côté, S., & Moskowitz, D. S. (1998). On the dynamic covariation between interpersonal behavior and affect: Prediction from Neuroticism, Extraversion, and Agreeableness. *Journal of Personality and Social Psychology, 75,* 1032–1046.

Derryberry, D., & Reed, M. A. (1994). Temperament and attention: Orienting toward and away from positive and negative signals. *Journal of Personality and Social Psychology, 66,* 1128–1139.

Digman, J. M. (1990). Personality structure: Emergence of the five-factor model. *Annual Review of Psychology, 41,* 417–440.

Elliot, A. J., & Church, M. A. (2003). A motivational analysis of defensive pessimism and self-handicapping. *Journal of Personality, 71,* 369–396.

Elliot, A. J., & Thrash, T. M. (2002). Approach-avoidance motivation in personality: Approach and avoidance temperaments and goals. *Journal of Personality and Social Psychology, 82*, 804–818.

Eysenck, H. J. (1970). *The structure of human personality* (3rd ed). London: Methuen.

Eysenck, H. J. (1992). Four ways five factors are not basic. *Personality and Individual Differences, 13*, 667–673.

Eysenck, H. J., & Eysenck, M. W. (1985). *Personality and individual differences: A natural science approach.* New York: Plenum Press.

Forret, M. L., & Dougherty, T. W. (2001). Correlates of networking behavior for managerial and professional employees. *Group and Organization Management, 26*, 283–311.

Förster, J., Higgins, E. T., & Idson, L. C. (1998). Approach and avoidance strength during goal attainment: Regulatory focus and the "goal looms larger" effect. *Journal of Personality and Social Psychology, 75*, 1115–1131.

Friedman, R. S., & Förster, J. (2001). The effects of promotion and prevention cues on creativity. *Journal of Personality and Social Psychology, 81*, 1001–1013.

Gable, S. L. (2003). *Approach and avoidance social motives and goals.* Unpublished manuscript, UCLA, Los Angeles, CA.

Gable, S. L., & Reis, H. T. (2001). Appetitive and aversive social interaction. In J. H. Harvey & A. E. Wenzel (Eds.), *Close romantic relationship maintenance and enhancement* (pp. 169–194). Mahwah, NJ: Erlbaum.

Gable, S. L., Reis, H. T., & Elliot, A. J. (2000). Behavioral activation and inhibition in everyday life. *Journal of Personality and Social Psychology, 78*, 1135–1149.

Gable, S. L., Reis, H. T., & Elliot, A. J. (2003). Evidence for bivariate systems: An empirical test of appetition and aversion across domains. *Journal of Research in Personality, 37*, 349–372.

Geist, R. L., & Gilbert, D. G. (1996). Correlates of expressed and felt emotion during marital conflict: Satisfaction, personality, process, and outcome. *Personality and Individual Differences, 21*, 49–60.

Gray, J. A. (1970). The psychophysiological basis of introversion–extroversion. *Behavior Research and Therapy, 8*, 249–266.

Gray, J. A. (1990). Brain systems that mediate both emotion and cognition. *Cognition and Emotion, 4*, 269–288.

Gottman, J. M. (1994). *Why marriages succeed or fail.* New York: Simon & Schuster.

Harmon-Jones, E., & Allen, J. J. B. (1997). Behavioral activation sensitivity and resting frontal EEG asymmetry: Covariation of putative indicators related to risk for mood disorders. *Journal of Abnormal Psychology, 106*, 159–163.

Higgins, E. T. (1997). Beyond pleasure and pain. *American Psychologist, 52*, 1280–1300.

Higgins, E. T. (1998). Promotion and prevention: Regulatory focus as a motivational principle. In M. P. Zanna (Ed.), *Advances in experimental social psychology* (Vol. 30, pp. 1–46). New York: Academic Press.

Higgins, E. T., Friedman, R. S., Harlow, R. E., Idson, L. C., Ayduk, O. N., & Taylor, A. (2001). Achievement orientations from subjective histories of success: Promotion pride versus prevention pride. *European Journal of Social Psychology, 31*, 3–23.

Higgins, E., Roney, C. J. R., Crowe, E., & Hymes, C. (1994). Ideal versus ought predilections for approach and avoidance distinct self-regulatory systems. *Journal of Personality and Social Psychology, 66*, 276–286.

Higgins, E. T., & Silberman, I. (1998). Development of regulatory focus: Promotion and prevention as ways of living. In J. Heckhausen & C. S. Dweck (Eds.), *Motivation and self-regulation across the life span* (pp. 78–113). New York: Cambridge University Press.

Idson, L. C., Liberman, N., & Higgins, T. E. (2000). Distinguishing gains from nonlosses and losses from nongains: A regulatory focus perspective on hedonic intensity. *Journal of Experimental Social Psychology, 36*, 252–274.

John, O. P. (1990). The "Big Five" factor taxonomy: Dimensions of personality in the natural language and in questionnaires. In L. A. Pervin (Ed.), *Handbook of personality: Theory and research* (pp. 66–100). New York: Guilford Press.

Karney, B. R., & Bradbury, T. N. (1995). The longitudinal course of marital quality and stability: A review of theory, method, and research. *Psychological Bulletin, 118*, 3–34.

Karney, B. R., & Bradbury, T. N. (1997). Neuroticism, marital interaction, and the trajectory of marital satisfaction. *Journal of Personality and Social Psychology, 72*, 1075–1092.

Karney, B. R., Bradbury, T. N., Fincham, F. D., & Sullivan, K. T. (1994). The role of negative affectivity in the association between attributions and marital satisfaction. *Journal of Personality and Social Psychology, 66*, 413–424.

Kelley, H. H., Holmes, J. G., Kerr, N. L., Reis, H. T., Rusbult, C. E., & Van Lange, P. A. M. (2003). *An atlas of interpersonal situations.* New York: Cambridge University Press.

Kelly, E. L., & Conley, J. J. (1987). Personality and compatibility: A prospective analysis of marital stability and marital satisfaction. *Journal of Personality and Social Psychology, 52,* 27–40

Keltner, D., Gruenfeld, D. H., & Anderson, C. (2003). Power, approach, and inhibition. *Psychological Review, 110,* 265–284.

Kumashiro, M., Finkel, E. J., & Rusbult, C. E. (2002). Self-respect and pro-relationship behavior in marital relationships. *Journal of Personality, 70,* 1009–1049.

Kurdek, L. A. (1993). Predicting marital dissolution: A 5-year prospective longitudinal study of newlywed couples. *Journal of Personality and Social Psychology, 64,* 221–242.

Lang, P. J. (1995). The emotion probe: Studies of motivation and attention. *American Psychologist, 50,* 372–385.

Lester, D., Haig, C., & Monello, R. (1989). Spouses' personality and marital satisfaction. *Personality and Individual Differences, 10,* 253–254.

Liberman, N., Idson, L. C., Camacho, C. J., & Higgins, E. T. (1999). Promotion and prevention choices between stability and change. *Journal of Personality and Social Psychology, 77,* 1135–1145.

Liberman, N., Molden, D. C., Idson, L. C., & Higgins, E. T. (2001). Promotion and prevention focus on alternative hypotheses: Implications for attributional functions. *Journal of Personality and Social Psychology, 80,* 5–18.

McAdams, D. P. (1992). The intimacy motive. In C. P. Smith, J. W. Atkinson et al. (Eds.), *Motivation and personality: Handbook of thematic content analysis* (pp. 224–228). New York: Cambridge University Press.

McClelland, D. C., Atkinson, J. W., Clark, R. A., & Lowell, E. I. (1953). *The achievement motive.* New York: Appleton-Century-Crofts.

McCrae, R. R., & Costa, P. T. (1987). Validation of a five-factor model of personality across instruments and observers. *Journal of Personality and Social Psychology, 52,* 81–90.

McCrae, R. R., Costa, P. T., Ostendorf, F., Angleitner, A., Hrebickova, M., Avia, M. D., et al. (2000). Nature over nurture: Temperament, personality, and lifespan development. *Journal of Personality and Social Psychology, 78,* 173–186.

Murray, H. A. (1938). *Explorations in personality.* New York: Oxford University Press.

Neyer, F. J., & Asendorpf, J. B. (2001). Personality-relationship transaction in young adulthood. *Journal of Personality and Social Psychology, 81,* 1190–1204.

Panksepp, J. (1998). *Affective neuroscience: The foundations of human and animal emotions.* New York: Oxford University Press.

Reis, H. T., Capobianco, A., & Tsai, F. F. (2002). Finding the person in personal relationships. *Journal of Personality, 70,* 813–850.

Reis, H. T., & Shaver, P. (1988). Intimacy as an interpersonal process. In S. Duck (Ed.), *Handbook of personal relationships: Theory, research, and interventions* (pp. 367–389). Oxford, England: Wiley.

Russell, R. J. H., & Wells, P. A. (1994). Predictors of happiness in married couples. *Personality and Individual Differences, 17,* 313–321.

Rusting, C. L., & Larsen, R. J. (1997). Extraversion, neuroticism, and susceptibility to positive and negative affect: A test of two theoretical models. *Personality and Individual Differences, 22,* 607–612.

Rusting, C. L., & Larsen, R. J. (1999). Clarifying Gray's theory of personality: A response to Pickering, Corr and Gray. *Personality and Individual Differences, 26,* 367–372.

Shah, J. (2003). The motivational looking glass: How significant others implicitly affect goal appraisals. *Journal of Personality and Social Psychology, 85,* 424–439.

Shah, J., Higgins, E. T., & Friedman, R. (1998). Performance incentives and means: How regulatory focus influences goal attainment. *Journal of Personality and Social Psychology, 73,* 447–458.

Sobotka, S. S., Davidson, R. J., & Senulis, J. A. (1992). Anterior brain electrical asymmetries in response to reward and punishment. *Electroencephalography and Clinical Neurophysiology, 83,* 236–247.

Sutton, S. K., & Davidson, R. J. (1997). Prefrontal brain asymmetry: A biological substrate of the behavioral approach and inhibition systems. *Psychological Science, 8,* 204–210.

Tellegen, A. (1985). Structures of mood and personality and their relevance to assessing anxiety, with an emphasis on self-report. In A. H. Tuma & J. D. Maser (Eds.), *Anxiety and the anxiety disorders* (pp. 681–706). Hillsdale, NJ: Erlbaum.

Thibaut, J. W., & Kelley, H. H. (1959). *The social psychology of groups*. New York: Wiley.

Thomsen, D. G., & Gilbert, D. G. (1998). Factors characterizing marital conflict states and traits: Physiological, affective, behavioral and neurotic variable contributions to marital conflict and satisfaction. *Personality and Individual Differences*, 25, 833–855.

Tucker, J. S., Kressin, N. R., Spiro, A., III, & Ruscio, J. (1998). Intrapersonal characteristics and the timing of divorce: A prospective investigation. *Journal of Social and Personal Relationships*, 15, 211–225.

Updegraff, J. A., Gable, S. L., & Taylor, S. E. (2004). What makes experiences satisfying? The interaction of approach–avoidance motivations and emotions in well-being. *Journal of Personality and Social Psychology*, 86, 496–504.

Wagner, W., Kirchler, E., & Brandstaetter, H. (1984). Marital relationships and purchasing decisions: To buy or not to buy, that is the question. *Journal of Economic Psychology*, 5, 139–157.

Wanberg, C. R., & Kammeyer-Mueller, J. D. (2000). Predictors and outcomes of proactivity in the socialization process. *Journal of Applied Psychology*, 85, 373–385.

Watson, D. (1988). Intraindividual and interindividual analyses of positive and negative affect: Their relations to health complaints, perceived stress, and daily activities. *Journal of Personality and Social Psychology*, 54, 1020–1030.

Watson, D., & Clark, L. A. (1993). Behavioral disinhibition versus constraint: A dispositional perspective. In D. M. Wegner & J. W. Pennebaker (Eds.), *Handbook of mental control* (pp. 506–527). Englewood Cliffs, NJ: Prentice Hall.

Watson, D., Clark L. A., McIntyre, C. W., & Hamaker, S. (1992). Affect, personality, and social activity. *Journal of Personality and Social Psychology*, 63, 1011–1025.

Watson, D., Hubbard, B., & Wiese D. (2000). General traits of personality and affectivity as predictors of satisfaction in intimate relationships: Evidence from self- and partner-ratings. *Journal of Personality*, 68, 413–449.

Watson, D., Wiese, D., Vaidya, J., & Tellegen, A. (1999). The two general activation systems of affect: Structural findings, evolutionary considerations, and psychobiological evidence. *Journal of Personality and Social Psychology*, 76, 820–838.

Winter, D. G. (1973). *The power motive*. New York: Free Press.

Zayas, V., Shoda, Y., & Ayduk, O. N. (2002). Personality in context: An interpersonal systems perspective. *Journal of Personality*, 70, 851–900.

Zuckerman, M. (1991). *Psychobiology of personality*. Cambridge, England: Cambridge University Press.

CHAPTER 14

Attachment Theory, Individual Psychodynamics, and Relationship Functioning

Phillip R. Shaver
Mario Mikulincer

Attachment theory (Bowlby, 1969/1982, 1973) has been extremely successful at stimulating research on the formation and quality of emotional bonds and the complex interplay between individual and relationship-level processes in all phases of the life span (Shaver & Hazan, 1993). In this chapter, we review and assess some of the empirical findings and propose integrative ideas concerning both normative and individual-difference aspects of personal relationships in adulthood. First, we present a theoretical model of the activation and psychodynamics of the attachment behavioral system in adulthood (Mikulincer & Shaver, 2003) and describe the intrapsychic and interpersonal manifestations of the sense of attachment security and the regulatory strategies of hyperactivation and deactivation. Next, we focus on romantic relationships, the site of some of the most important emotional bonds in adulthood, and explore implications of variations in attachment-system functioning for the formation and maintenance of these relationships. Specifically, we discuss (a) the contribution of these variations to relationship quality in differ-

ent stages of a romantic relationship (initiation, consolidation, and maintenance) and (b) the interpersonal processes that explain this contribution. Finally, we extend our theoretical analysis to other kinds of relationships, such as relationships within family systems, friendships, therapeutic relationships, and both intra- and inter-group relations.

Attachment Theory: Basic Concepts

In his classic trilogy, Bowlby (1969/1982, 1973, 1980) conceptualized the attachment behavioral system as an innate psychobiological system that motivates human beings of all ages (although most obviously so in infancy) to seek proximity to significant others (attachment figures) in times of need as a means of protecting oneself from threats and alleviating distress. Bowlby (1973) also described important individual differences in attachment-system functioning. Interactions with attachment figures who are available and responsive in times of need facilitate the optimal functioning of the attachment system, promote a sense of attachment security (a feeling or sense – "felt security" (Sroufe & Waters, 1977) – based on expectations that key people will be available and supportive in times of need), and lead to the formation of positive *working models* of relationships (mental representations of the self and others during attachment-related interactions). When attachment figures are not reliably available and supportive, however, a sense of security is not attained, negative working models of self and others are formed, and strategies of affect regulation other than appropriate proximity seeking are adopted.

In the late 1980s, Hazan and Shaver (1987; Shaver, Hazan, & Bradshaw, 1988) suggested extending Bowlby and Ainsworth's attachment theory (Ainsworth, Blehar, Waters, & Wall, 1978; Bowlby, 1969/1982), which was designed to characterize human infants' love for and emotional attachments to their caregivers, to create a framework for studying romantic love in adulthood. The core assumption was that romantic partners become most adults' primary attachment figures in adulthood, such that proximity maintenance to these partners in times of need becomes a crucial source of support, comfort, and reassurance (Zeifman & Hazan, 2000). The attachment behavioral system discussed by Bowlby (1969/1982) is often highly activated during couple interactions, separations, and losses; hence, individual differences in the functioning of that system are important for understanding variations in the quality of romantic relationships. It is important to remember that Hazan and Shaver (1987) did not equate romantic love with attachment, but argued that romantic relationships involve a combination of three innate behavioral systems: attachment, caregiving, and sex. The three systems often influence each other and work together to determine relationship characteristics and outcomes.

Attachment Styles

To study individual differences in attachment-system functioning within romantic relationships, Hazan and Shaver (1987) created a simple categorical measure of what has come to be called "attachment style." The three relational styles assessed by that measure – avoidant, anxious, and secure – were modeled after the three major patterns of infant–mother attachment described by Ainsworth et al. (1978). Infants and adults who have a secure attachment style find it relatively easy to trust others, open up emotionally, and feel confident about their partner's goodwill. Those with an anxious style are uncertain about being loved, worthy of love, or likely to be supported by a partner. This causes them to be unusually vigilant, dependent, intrusive, and excitable. Those with an avoidant style have learned to prefer to rely heavily on themselves and not openly seek support from a partner, even when (especially in the case of infants) such support is necessary for survival and optimal development. In adulthood, this "compulsively self-reliant" stance (Bowlby, 1969/1982) is often bolstered by self-glorification and disdain for others' neediness and weaknesses.

For a number of years, attachment researchers used the three-category measure of adult attachment style (see Shaver & Hazan, 1993, for a review). However, subsequent studies (e.g., Bartholomew & Horowitz, 1991; Brennan, Clark, & Shaver, 1998) indicated that attachment styles are more appropriately conceptualized as regions in a continuous two-dimensional space, an idea compatible with early dimensional analyses of infant attachment reported by Ainsworth and her colleagues (e.g., 1978, p. 102). The first dimension, attachment *avoidance*, reflects the extent to which a person distrusts relationship partners' goodwill and strives to maintain behavioral independence and emotional distance from partners. The second dimension, attachment *anxiety*, reflects the degree to which a person worries that a partner will not be available in times of need, partly because of doubts the person harbors about his or her own lovability and value. People who score low on both dimensions are said to be secure or to have a secure attachment style. Throughout this chapter, we refer to people with secure, anxious, and avoidant attachment styles, or people who are relatively anxious or avoidant. Although the categorical shorthand can mistakenly foster typological thinking, we are always referring to fuzzy regions in a two-dimensional space, a space in which people are continuously distributed.

Attachment styles are formed initially during early interactions with primary caregivers (as documented in an anthology edited by Cassidy and Shaver, 1999), but Bowlby (1973) contended that impactful interactions with others throughout life have the effect of updating a person's working models. Moreover, although attachment style is often conceptualized as a global orientation toward close relationships, there are theoretical and empirical reasons for believing that this style is part of a hierarchical cognitive network that includes a complex, heterogeneous array of episodic, relationship-specific, and generalized attachment representations (Mikulincer & Shaver, 2003; Overall, Fletcher, & Friesen, 2003). In fact, research indicates that (a) reports of attachment orientations can change, subtly or dramatically, depending on context and recent experiences (see Pietromonaco, Laurenceau, & Barrett, 2002, for a review), (b) people possess multiple attachment schemas (e.g., Baldwin, Keelan, Fehr, Enns, & Koh Rangarajoo, 1996), and (c) actual or imagined encounters with supportive or nonsupportive others can activate congruent attachment orientations (e.g., Mikulincer & Shaver, 2001), even if they are incongruent with a person's global attachment style.

Strategies of Responding to Activation of the Attachment System

Based on an extensive review of adult attachment studies, we (Mikulincer & Shaver, 2003; Shaver & Mikulincer, 2002) proposed a model of the dynamics of the attachment system in adulthood. Following Bowlby's (1969/1982) analysis, we assumed that the monitoring of unfolding events – both in the world and in a person's imagination – results in activation of the attachment system when a potential or actual threat is encountered. This activation is manifest in efforts to seek or maintain actual or symbolic proximity to external or internalized attachment figures. Once the attachment system is activated, a person, in effect, asks whether an attachment figure is sufficiently available and responsive. An affirmative answer results in the appropriate functioning of the attachment system, characterized by reinforced mental representations of attachment security and consolidation of security-based strategies of affect regulation (Shaver & Mikulincer, 2002). These strategies are aimed at alleviating distress, forming comfortable, supportive intimate relationships, and increasing personal adjustment. These strategies also set in motion a "broaden and build" cycle of attachment security (Shaver & Mikulincer, 2002), which facilitates other behavioral systems and broadens a person's perspectives and capacities.

Security-based strategies consist of declarative and procedural knowledge about the self, others, and affect regulation. The declarative knowledge consists of optimistic beliefs about distress management, optimistic and trusting beliefs about others' goodwill, and a sense of self-efficacy about dealing with threats. The procedural knowledge is organized around three main coping strategies: acknowledgment and display of distress, support seeking, and instrumental problem solving. Acknowledging and expressing feelings and seeking emotional support work in the service of downregulating distress so that problem-focused coping attempts can proceed effectively. These tendencies are the ones Epstein and Meier (1989) called constructive ways of coping – active attempts to remove the source of distress, manage the problematic situation, and restore emotional equanimity without generating negative side effects. Security-based strategies are characteristic of people who score relatively low on attachment anxiety and avoidance.

Perceived unavailability of an attachment figure results in attachment insecurity, which compounds the distress arising from an appraised threat. This state of insecurity forces a decision about the viability of proximity seeking as a protective strategy. The appraisal of proximity as viable or essential – because of attachment history, temperamental factors, or contextual cues – can result in energetic, insistent attempts to attain proximity, support, and love. These intense attempts are called *hyperactivating strategies* (Cassidy & Kobak, 1988), because they involve constant vigilance, intense concern, and prodigious effort until an attachment figure is perceived to be available and a sense of security is attained. Hyperactivating strategies, when used habitually, include overdependence on relationship partners as a source of protection; attempts to elicit a partner's involvement, care, and support through clinging and controlling responses; and cognitive and behavioral efforts aimed at minimizing distance from partners (Shaver & Hazan, 1993).

According to Shaver and Mikulincer (2002), hyperactivating strategies also involve increased vigilance to threat-related cues and a reduction in the threshold for detecting cues of attachment figures' unavailability – the two kinds of cues that activate the attachment system (Bowlby, 1973). They also intensify negative emotional responses to threatening events and heighten rumination on threat-related concerns, keeping these concerns salient in working memory. Because signs of attachment-figure unavailability and rejection are viewed as important threats, hyperactivating strategies foster anxious, hypervigilant attention to relationship partners and rapid detection of possible signs of disapproval, waning interest, or impending abandonment. As a result, minimal threat-related cues are easily detected, the attachment system is chronically activated, and psychological pain related to the unavailability of attachment figures is exacerbated. These concomitants of attachment-system hyperactivation account for many of the psychological correlates of attachment anxiety (see Mikulincer & Shaver, 2003, for a review).

Appraising proximity seeking as unlikely to alleviate distress results in the inhibition of the quest for support and active attempts to handle distress alone. These secondary approaches to affect regulation are called *deactivating strategies* (Cassidy & Kobak, 1988) because their primary goal is to keep the attachment system deactivated to avoid frustration and further distress caused by attachment-figure unavailability. These strategies involve denial of attachment needs; avoidance of closeness, intimacy, and dependence in close relationships; and maximization of cognitive, emotional, and physical distance from others. They also involve the dismissal of threat- and attachment-related cues, and suppression of threat- and attachment-related thoughts and emotions. These aspects of deactivation account for the psychological manifestations of avoidant attachment (again, see Mikulincer & Shaver, 2003, for a review).

In summary, each attachment-related strategy has a regulatory goal, which shapes cognitive and affective processes related to goal attainment. We believe these strategies are extremely relevant for understanding individual differences in the functioning and quality of romantic relationships in different stages of their development – initiation, consolidation, and maintenance. We also believe, and have preliminary evidence to show, that attachment-related strategies affect the quality of other kinds of relationships in adulthood, such as parent–child relationships, friendships, relationships with group members, and intergroup relations.

Attachment-Related Strategies and the Quality of Romantic Relationships

In this section, we present ideas and review research concerning the role played by attachment-related strategies in the formation and maintenance of long-lasting romantic relationships. Specifically, we focus on three stages of the development of romantic relationships (flirtation and dating, consolidation, and maintenance) and examine the contribution of attachment-related strategies (security based, hyperactivating, and deactivating strategies) to the interpersonal processes that determine relationship stability, quality, and satisfaction at each of these stages. In Table 14.1, we present a schematic

Table 14.1. *Attachment-Related Strategies and Interpersonal Processes in the Initiation, Consolidation, and Maintenance Stages of Romantic Relationships*

	Security-based strategies	Hyperactivating strategies	Deactivating strategies
Initiation Stage			
Interaction climate	Positive, warm emotional tone	Negative, anxious emotional tone	Emotional shallowness, detachment
Self-presentation	Balanced self-presentation	Self-defeating presentation	Self-inflating presentation
Self-disclosure	Responsive self-disclosure	Indiscriminate, effusive self-disclosure	Low levels of self-disclosure
Consolidation Stage			
Relational cognitions	Positive, optimistic beliefs	Dysfunctional, pessimistic beliefs	Dysfunctional, pessimistic beliefs
Perception of partner	Positive, constructive appraisals	Negative, destructive appraisals	Negative, destructive appraisals
Commitment	Strong commitment; positive appraisal of commitment	Weak commitment; doubts about partner's commitment	Weak commitment; negative attitude toward commitment
Support seeking	Seeking support in times of need	Reluctance to seek support or excessive reassurance seeking	Reluctance to seek support
Support provision	Sensitive, responsive caregiving	Compulsive, intrusive caregiving	Reluctance to provide support
Maintenance Stage			
Dyadic communication	Constructive, mutually sensitive, and positive	Demanding, anxious, and inaccurate	Withdrawn, cool, and hostile
Conflict-resolution strategies	Reliance on effective strategies, e.g., compromising, integrating	Reliance on strategies that lead to conflict escalation	Reliance on avoidant strategies that leave the conflict unresolved
Reactions to partner's negative behaviors	Constructive expressions of anger; relationship-repairing reactions; proneness to forgive	Intense, uncontrollable bouts of anger, hatred, and hostility; relationship-destructive reactions	Anger is suppressed, but expressed in nonspecific hostility, revenge seeking, and reluctance to forgive
Positive emotions toward partner	Admiration, respect, and gratitude	Ambivalent emotional reactions	Lack of admiration, respect, and gratitude
Expanding activities	Proneness to engage in novel, arousing activities	Reluctance to engage in novel, arousing activities	Reluctance to engage in novel, arousing activities
Quality of sexual activities	Sexual satisfaction and intimacy; sensitivity to partner's needs	Sex-related worries; engagement in sex to feel accepted and loved	Emotional detachment and lack of commitment during sexual activities
Attitudes toward fidelity	Investment in the relationship; no tendency to seek alternatives	Worries about losing partner; intense bouts of jealousy	Openness to relational alternatives; proneness to mate poaching

summary of the interpersonal processes that seem to be affected by attachment-related strategies during each of the three relationship stages.

Because the main focus of this section is to delineate the involvement of attachment-system functioning in the formation and maintenance of romantic relationships, we do not discuss the contribution of attachment-related strategies to the termination of these relationships. Nevertheless, it is important to mention that there is accumulating evidence regarding important attachment-style differences in the process of coping and adjustment with separation and loss. For example, whereas securely attached persons tend to cope constructively with the termination of a romantic relationship and maintain emotional equanimity during and after termination, less secure persons are more likely to rely on self-defeating strategies and become overwhelmed by distress and despair (e.g., Birnbaum, Orr, Mikulincer, & Florian, 1997; Simpson, 1990). Research also indicates that security-based strategies allow people to satisfy their attachment needs with alternative or new social ties without totally severing their previous emotional bonds. In contrast, hyperactivating strategies perpetuate emotional investment in ex-partners and distort, hasten, or impede the formation of new relationships, and deactivating strategies foster detachment from the former partner and denial of the importance of the lost relationship (Davis, Shaver, & Vernon, 2003; Fraley & Shaver, 1999; Mikulincer & Florian, 1996).

The Initial Stages: Flirting and Dating

Attachment-related strategies are active even at the very beginning of a romantic relationship, shaping the interpersonal processes that determine the quality of flirting and dating interactions and thereby affecting the chances of forming a more long-lasting emotional bond with a new romantic partner. Flirtatious interactions and first dates, mainly when their goal is more than sexual gratification, can activate the attachment system. These interactions are emotionally charged and can arouse fears of failure and rejection that can damage a person's sense of self-worth and activate habitual attachment-related strategies of affect regulation (Zeifman & Hazan, 2000). As a result, partners' cognitions, feelings, and behaviors during the initial stages of their relationship can be a direct reflection of their attachment working models and their methods of regulating the activation of their attachment systems. At this stage, one can observe the "purest" effects of chronic working models on relational behavior, because one has minimal information about a new partner's traits, and no unique pattern of relatedness has been formed between the partners.

Attachment-related strategies influence the emotional tone of flirtatious and dating interactions. Security-based strategies are constructive means of managing distress and transforming threats into challenges (Mikulincer & Shaver, 2003). As a result, secure individuals can effectively manage the threats involved in flirtatious and dating interactions, enjoy and savor the positive aspects of these interactions, and contribute to the creation and maintenance of a relaxed, positive emotional atmosphere. In contrast, the secondary attachment strategies, hyperactivation and deactivation, not only may fail to promote such an atmosphere, they may generate relational tension and distress that results in early breakups. During flirtation and dating, attachment anxiety can be directly manifested in needy, intrusive, "hungry" displays; exaggeration of the possibility of rejection; reactivation of memories of past rejections; and rumination on rejection-related thoughts, which in turn can intensify distress and lead to inappropriate and unsuccessful interactions. Attachment avoidance can be directly manifested in the adoption of an emotionally detached, purely sexual, or initially rejecting stance toward a potential partner, designed (perhaps unconsciously) to protect against potential threats to self-worth as well as engulfment in intimacy or threats to independence. As a result, these interactions may be emotionally shallow and lack the excitement and emotional involvement that otherwise characterize flirtatious and dating interactions.

EMOTIONAL TONE AND REACTIONS

Although adult attachment research has yet to provide a systematic examination of attachment-style differences in emotional reactions to flirting and dating, there are a few important pieces of evidence concerning associations between attachment orientations and the experience of positive emotions. For example, research has consistently shown that secure individuals score higher on self-report measures of joy, happiness, interest, love, and affection than do insecure individuals (see Mikulincer & Shaver, 2003, for a review). More important, in week-long diary studies in which participants completed the Rochester Interaction Record every time they engaged in a social interaction lasting 10 minutes or longer, anxious and avoidant participants experienced fewer positive emotions than secure participants (e.g., Tidwell, Reis, & Shaver, 1996; Pietromonaco & Feldman Barrett, 1997). Interestingly, the anxious participants were chronically worried about being disapproved of and rejected, whereas the avoidant participants felt bored and unengaged.

INTERPERSONAL PROCESSES: SELF-PRESENTATION AND SELF-DISCLOSURE

Attachment-related strategies are also involved in two important interpersonal processes that occur during the initial stages of a romantic relationship – self-presentation and self-disclosure. Self-presentation refers to the way people present themselves, which is likely to influence a potential partner's decision about whether to continue or end a budding relationship (Schlenker, 1980). Self-presentation involves a tactical choice concerning which aspects of the self to reveal to a partner, and it can be biased by secondary attachment strategies. On one hand, anxious people's urgent desire to achieve some sort of closeness, protection, support, or love can cause them to emphasize personal weaknesses and present themselves as helpless and needy in an effort to elicit a partner's compassion and sympathy. On the other hand, avoidant people's desire to keep their attachment system deactivated can cause them to communicate to a dating partner that they do not need anything and can handle life's threats and challenges alone, to present only personal strengths, and to inflate their self-image in the eyes of the partner even at the risk of diminishing the partner's own self-image.

There is empirical evidence concerning attachment-related biases in the process of self-presentation. In a series of four laboratory studies, Mikulincer (1998a) found that avoidant participants reacted to threats with more explicit and implicit positive self-presentation. However, this self-inflation tendency was inhibited by a message that broke the link between a positive self-view and self-reliance. Findings also revealed that persons scoring high on attachment anxiety reacted to threats with more explicit and implicit negative self-presentations, and this tendency was inhibited by a message that broke the link between self-devaluation and others' positive responses. These findings imply that (a) avoidant people tend to present themselves in a self-inflated manner to convince others of the avoidant person's strength and self-sufficiency, and (b) anxious people tend to present themselves in a self-devaluing manner in hopes of eliciting others' compassion and love. Interestingly, secure individuals in Mikulincer's (1998a) study evinced no notable bias of either kind in their self-presentations.

A second interpersonal process that facilitates the formation of intimate bonds is self-disclosure – the proneness to disclose and share personal information and feelings with a partner (Altman & Taylor, 1973; Greene, Derlega, & Mathews, this volume). Obviously, the inhibition of such a process during flirtation and dating can hinder the transition to a more committed and long-lasting relationship. However, premature and undifferentiated disclosure of highly personal information may also place a developing relationship in jeopardy. According to Altman and Taylor (1973), optimal self-disclosure should be regulated appropriately for each stage of a developing relationship. Very early in a new relationship, disclosure is typically limited to relatively superficial public information, and the rapid disclosure of very intimate concerns and feelings is perceived as a sign of maladjustment. As a relationship progresses, however, partners begin to exchange more personal information, including fears, secrets, and stories of painful experiences. At this stage, the inhibition of intimate disclosure is experienced as a sign of lack of trust or trustworthiness or as a lack of commitment to the relationship, which can obviously disrupt and endanger an emerging relationship.

Adult attachment research has consistently shown that attachment avoidance is associated with low levels of self-disclosure in dating relationships (e.g., Bradford, Feeney, & Campbell, 2002; Keelan, Dion, & Dion, 1998; Mikulincer & Nachshon, 1991) – a direct reflection of avoidant individuals' reluctance to engage in intimate interactions. Mikulincer and Nachshon (1991) also documented the ways in which attachment anxiety shapes self-disclosure. For anxiously attached individuals, self-disclosure can be a means of quickly merging with others, enlisting their help or support, and reducing their fear of rejection rather than enhancing reciprocal intimacy. As a result, although anxious people were found by Mikulincer and Nachshon (1991) to be highly disposed to self-disclose, they tended to disclose indiscriminately to people who were not yet prepared for intensely intimate interactions and tended to be unresponsive to their partner's disclosure. In fact, Mikulincer and Nachshon (1991) found that anxious people did not usually deal with a partner's disclosed information in their own disclosures, thereby endangering the formation of reciprocal intimacy.

Mikulincer and Nachshon (1991) also described the typical pattern of self-disclosure that characterizes securely attached persons – "responsive self-disclosure." Secure participants in their studies scored relatively high on measures of self-disclosure and responsiveness to a partner's disclosure. They disclosed more personal information to a high- than a low-disclosing partner; they were attentive to the issues raised in the partner's disclosure and expanded on them in their own discourse. This combination of self-disclosure and responsiveness to partner's disclosure is likely to be the best strategy for forming intimate, long-lasting relationships – those based on the kind of emotional bonds that secure individuals wish to create and maintain.

ATTACHMENT-STYLE DIFFERENCES AND DATING OUTCOMES

The attachment-style differences in the emotional tone of flirtatious and dating interactions, and in self-presentation and self-disclosure during these interactions, help to explain the recurrent finding that people, regardless of their own attachment style, report more positive emotions when imagining a relationship with a secure rather than an insecure partner (e.g., Chappell & Davis, 1998; Klohnen & Shanhong, 2003; Pietromonaco & Carnelley, 1994). In fact, several investigators who have constructed vignettes of potential partners differing in their attachment orientations have found that secure partners are preferred over insecure partners (e.g., Baldwin et al., 1996; Frazier, Byer, Fischer, Wright, & DeBord, 1996). This fits with our suspicion that the positive emotional tone and responsive self-disclosure of secure people make them generally the most attractive partners for people who are hoping to form intimate, emotional bonds.

The same interpersonal processes can explain the bulk of data documenting a positive association between attachment security and the perceived quality of dating relationships. More than 30 studies using different measures of attachment style and different scales measuring relationship satisfaction have found that secure individuals have higher levels of satisfaction with their dating relationships than their insecure counterparts (see Mikulincer, Florian, Cowan, & Cowan, 2002, for a detailed review of these studies). This finding has been replicated repeatedly using both cross-sectional and prospective research designs and cannot be explained by other personality factors, such as the "Big Five" personality traits, depression, self-esteem, or gender-role orientation (Mikulincer et al., 2002).

The Consolidation Stage in the Development of a Long-Lasting Romantic Relationship

In the course of a romantic relationship, couples usually make a transition from falling in love to loving each other. Flirtation and dating give way to longer, less arousing joint activities, and the sharing of intimate information and discussion of personal issues are supplemented or replaced by discussions of the prospect of implementing shared goals in a long-lasting relationship (e.g., Gagne & Lydon, 2001). Accordingly, the importance of emotional supportiveness, nurturance, and intimacy as determinants of relationship quality increases as initial attraction, passion, and sexual satisfaction recede in importance, and partners begin to make changes in their activities and living conditions that reflect their increasing commitment to a long-term relationship (e.g., Brehm, 1992; Huston & Burgess, 1979). As a result, the relationship partners gradually become primary attachment figures for each other – primary sources of support, reassurance, comfort, and relief in times of need (Zeifman & Hazan, 2000). All of these changes indicate that partners are consolidating their attachment bonds and setting the foundation for what they expect to be a long-lasting, highly committed, reciprocal relationship.

GOALS AND BELIEFS

During this transition stage, attachment-related strategies can facilitate or hinder the consolidation of a long-lasting relationship. Specifically, the interaction goals of relatively secure individuals (closeness, intimacy) and their positive working models of self and others favor the formation of optimistic expectations about the prospects of a long-lasting relationship and positive beliefs about the partner's trust-

worthiness, nurturance, supportiveness, and commitment. Moreover, these goals and beliefs encourage securely attached persons to commit to a long-lasting relationship (Morgan & Shaver, 1999), to treat their partner as a primary attachment figure (a target of support-seeking), and to become a primary attachment figure for their partner (a sensitive and responsive caregiver). In contrast, the interaction goals (self-focused search for security and support; deactivation of intimacy needs), regulatory strategies (rumination about relationship threats and worries; emotional distance, detachment, and self-reliance), and negative working models of insecurely attached (anxious and avoidant, respectively) individuals can negatively bias beliefs about the relationship and the partner, and thus inhibit support seeking, support provision, and commitment. As a result, securely attached partners have more chances of consolidating a long-lasting, reciprocal, and satisfactory relationship than do insecurely attached partners.

COGNITIONS AND PERCEPTIONS

Adult attachment studies have provided extensive information about the various interpersonal cognitions that can contribute to individual differences in the consolidation of a romantic relationship. Overall, insecure partners, compared with more secure partners, hold more negative interpersonal cognitions, such as pessimistic beliefs about romantic relationships (e.g., Carnelley & Janoff-Bulman, 1992; Pietromonaco & Carnelley, 1994), negative frames when thinking about these relationships (e.g., Boon & Griffin, 1996), and dysfunctional relational beliefs (e.g., Whisman & Allan, 1996).

There is also extensive evidence concerning the negative influence of insecure attachment strategies on perceptions of a romantic partner. Compared with secure individuals, insecurely attached people (a) hold more negative views of their romantic partner (e.g., Collins & Read, 1990; Feeney & Noller, 1991), (b) perceive their partner as less supportive (e.g., Collins & Read, 1990; Ognibene & Collins, 1998), and

(c) trust the partner less (e.g., Brennan & Shaver, 1995; Simpson, 1990). Both anxiety and avoidance are also associated with negative expectations concerning the partner's behavior (e.g., Baldwin, Fehr, Keedian, Seidel, & Thomson, 1993; Mikulincer & Arad, 1999) and with relationship-damaging explanations of the partner's negative behaviors (e.g., Collins, 1996; Mikulincer, 1998b). For example, Collins (1996) found that more anxious and avoidant people were more likely to attribute a partner's negative behavior to stable and global causes and to view these behaviors as negatively motivated.

TRUST

In a series of five studies, Mikulincer (1998b) systematically examined associations between attachment-related strategies and various aspects of trusting or distrusting one's romantic partner. The constructive nature of security-based strategies was evident in secure persons' tendency to have relatively fast access to memories of trust validation and to report more trust-validation episodes in their current relationship. Mikulincer (1998b) also found that secure people tend to attach relatively high importance to trust-validation episodes and to appraise them as reflecting their partner's beneficent disposition. The attachment strategies of insecure individuals were evident in their reactions to trust-violation episodes. Avoidant people increased their distance from their partner following a betrayal of trust and dismissed the importance of this threatening occurrence. Anxious people, in contrast, worried and ruminated during a trust-betrayal episode and reacted to it with strong negative emotion.

COMMITMENT

Attachment-related strategies also affect a person's commitment to a romantic relationship. Numerous studies have documented that secure individuals, compared with those who are insecure, report higher levels of commitment to their dating relationships (e.g., Shaver & Brennan, 1992; Simpson, 1990). In addition, Himovitch

(2003) recently found that secure people exhibited faster recall of episodes in which they or their partner strengthened their commitment to the relationship, and they appraised these episodes more positively. In contrast, insecure people emphasized the threats involved in relational commitment and displayed faster recall of episodes that led to a decrease in commitment. However, whereas avoidant individuals more rapidly accessed memories of episodes in which they decreased their commitment to the relationship, which we interpret as a clear sign of deactivating strategies, anxious individuals more rapidly accessed memories of episodes in which a partner decreased commitment to them, thereby manifesting their hypervigilance toward possible rejection.

SUPPORT SEEKING AND SUPPORT PROVISION

Adult attachment studies have also consistently documented insecure people's problems with support seeking and support provision. Several investigators have found that avoidant people are reluctant to appraise their romantic partner as a "safe haven" and seek support from the partner in times of need (e.g., Ognibene & Collins, 1998). The same phenomenon has been reported in studies examining actual support-seeking behavior in stressful laboratory situations (e.g., Collins & B. Feeney, 2000; Simpson, Rholes, & Nelligan, 1992; Simpson, Rholes, Orina, & Grich, 2002). For example, Simpson et al. (1992) told participants they would be exposed to a frightening, potentially painful laboratory procedure. The investigators then unobtrusively observed and coded participants' behavior while they were interacting with their romantic partner. It was found that avoidant participants, compared with secure ones, exhibited greater reluctance to seek proximity to and obtain comfort from their partners. With regard to anxiously attached individuals, findings reveal a more ambivalent reaction toward support seeking. Whereas anxious people are sometimes reticent about expressing their need for support, especially when they suspect that full revelation of their neediness will result in rejection (e.g., J. Feeney, 1999), they are also capable of excessive reassurance seeking from their romantic partner, which can be viewed by the partner as intrusive and demanding (Shaver, Schachner, & Mikulincer, 2005).

Insecure people's difficulties in providing support to a partner were first documented by Kunce and Shaver (1994), who constructed a self-report scale tapping caregiving behaviors in romantic relationships. They found that insecure individuals were less likely than their secure counterparts to say they provide emotional support. Moreover, whereas avoidant people's deactivating strategies led them to maintain distance from a needy partner, anxious people's hyperactivating strategies led them to report high levels of overinvolvement with partner's problems and a pattern of compulsive, intrusive caregiving. These findings have been replicated in subsequent, more behavioral studies (e.g., Carnelley, Pietromonaco, & Jaffe, 1996; J. Feeney, 1996; J. Feeney & Hohaus, 2001).

The link between attachment security and sensitive caregiving has been further documented in observational studies by B. Feeney and Collins (2001), Simpson et al. (1992), Rholes, Simpson, and Orina (1999), and Simpson et al. (2002), who videotaped heterosexual dating couples while one partner waited to endure a stressful task. Overall, compared with relatively secure participants, those who were less secure offered less comfort and reassurance to their distressed partner. Moreover, participants who were relatively secure and whose dating partners sought more support provided more support, whereas secure participants whose partners sought less support provided less. This finding indicates sensitive responsiveness: Secure participants recognized their partners' worries and tried to be especially warm and supportive, but they also recognized times when the partner was capable of proceeding autonomously, and they stood back and honored that autonomy. Compatible findings were obtained by Collins and B. Feeney (2000), who videotaped dating couples while one member of the couple disclosed a personal problem to the other. Insecure participants provided less instrumental support, were less responsive, and displayed more negative caregiving behaviors toward their distressed partner, compared with more secure participants.

A recent study conducted by Cobb, Davila, and Bradbury (2001) suggests that perceptions of a relationship partner's attachment style, not just a person's own attachment style, are important in determining the degree to which supportive caregiving will occur. The authors tested a mediation model in which positive perceptions of partner's security were associated with adaptive support behavior, which in turn predicted increases in relationship satisfaction. The findings supported the model and indicated that positive perceptions of a partner's security resulted in relationship enhancement partly by virtue of its influence on couple members' supportive interactions.

THE IMPORTANCE OF RELATIONSHIP-SPECIFIC ATTACHMENT

In this consolidation stage of a developing relationship, part of what partners are consolidating is a relationship-specific sense of attachment security (the extent to which each person feels that the partner will be available and supportive in times of need). This sense can be biased by a person's global working models of attachment relationships, but it can also be affected by a partner's actual supportive behaviors. In fact, the relationship-specific sense of security can become a potent regulator of attachment-system functioning as indicated by interpersonal cognitions and behaviors within the relationship, even if it does not fit a person's global working models. Indeed, Kobak and Hazan (1991) found that partners with a relatively strong relationship-specific sense of security were less rejecting and more supportive during problem-solving and confiding interactions (in the latter case, sharing a disappointment with one's partner). More important, Cozzarelli, Hoekstra, and Bylsma (2000) and Cowan and Cowan (2002) found that reports of secure attachment within a specific romantic relationship were more powerful predictors of satisfaction with that relationship than reports of global attachment security. This difference between global and relationship-specific levels of working models has recently been explored in detail by Overall et al. (2003).

Maintenance of a Long-Lasting Relationship

There is now good evidence that securely attached people maintain more stable romantic relationships than insecure people and report higher levels of marital satisfaction and adjustment (see Mikulincer et al., 2002, for a review). For example, Davila, Karney, and Bradbury (1999) collected data every 6 months for 3 years from newlywed couples and found that changes in husbands' and wives' reports of secure attachment predicted concurrent changes in both partners' reports of marital satisfaction. Studies of marriage have also linked attachment security with more marital intimacy (Mayseless, Sharabany, & Sagi, 1997), less marital ambivalence (Volling, Notaro, & Larsen, 1998), and stronger marital cohesion (Mikulincer & Florian, 1999). Not surprisingly, secure individuals are less likely to be divorced (e.g., Hazan & Shaver, 1987).

INTERPERSONAL PROCESSES INVOLVED
IN MAINTENANCE

Attachment-related strategies seem to be involved in several interpersonal processes that facilitate or hinder the maintenance of a satisfactory long-lasting relationship. One such process is marital communication. Several studies have found attachment security to be associated with more constructive, mutually sensitive patterns of dyadic communication and negatively associated with the demand–withdrawal pattern known to be destructive to relationship stability and satisfaction (e.g., J. Feeney, 1994; Fitzpatrick, Fey, Segrin, & Schiff, 1993). Moreover, secure partners have been found to maintain more positive patterns of nonverbal communication (expressiveness, pleasantness, attentiveness) than less secure partners (e.g., Guerrero, 1996; Tucker

& Anders, 1998) and to be more accurate in expressing their feelings and coding their partner's nonverbal messages (e.g., J. Feeney, 1994). Especially important is the fact that the association between attachment security and relationship satisfaction is mediated by a constructive, mutually sensitive pattern of communication (e.g., J. Feeney, 1994).

The way couples manage interpersonal conflicts is also an important link between attachment security and the maintenance of a satisfying and long-lasting relationship. Attachment-related strategies influence the methods couples adopt to manage inevitable interpersonal tensions (e.g., Gaines et al., 1997; Scharfe & Bartholomew, 1995). Specifically, secure people rely more heavily on effective conflict-resolution strategies – compromising and integrating their own and their partner's positions. They also display greater accommodation when responding to a partner's anger or criticism. In contrast, insecure people tend to rely on less effective conflict-resolution strategies, which leave conflicts unresolved and may even lead to conflict escalation. As usual, the different forms of insecurity encourage different ineffective means of dealing with distress: Whereas anxious people's hyperactivating strategies lead them to intensify conflict, avoidant people's deactivating strategies lead them to distance themselves from conflictual interactions and avoid engaging with their partner.

There are also attachment-related variations in people's reactions to a partner's negative behavior (e.g., Collins, 1996; Mikulincer, 1998c, Rholes et al., 1999). On one hand, secure individuals react to a partner's negative behavior with controlled expressions of anger, without extreme hatred or hostility, and this appears to have beneficial effects on their relationships. On the other hand, insecure people indulge themselves in uncontrolled bouts of anger, hatred, or feelings of resentment and hostility toward a partner. However, because deactivating strategies require the suppression of emotion, avoidant people's anger tends to be expressed only in unconscious or unintended ways and can take the form of nonspecific hostility. In contrast, anxiously attached individuals experience intense bouts of anger toward both the partner and the self, a manifestation of hyperactivating strategies (e.g., intense protest) and negative models of self.

Avoidant individuals' hostile attitudes toward relationship partners were also documented in Shaver and Mikulincer's (2003) recent study of forgiveness. Compared with less avoidant individuals, people who scored high on avoidance were less likely to forgive a partner who had hurt them. Moreover, when avoidant individuals were asked to recall an episode in which they forgave a relationship partner who had hurt them, they revealed a negative construal of these events. Their reactions were characterized by narcissistic wounds, thoughts about relationship deterioration, and lack of understanding of the partner's hurtful actions. Avoidant individuals' disinclination to forgive was also noted in a subsequent daily diary study in which participants reported their reactions to their partner's negative behaviors for a period of 21 days (Shaver & Mikulincer, 2003).

The maintenance of a long-lasting relationship also depends on the extent to which partners express affection, respect, admiration, and gratitude to each other and the extent to which they are able to create a climate of appreciation instead of criticism or contempt (Gottman, 1993). We have preliminary evidence that attachment security is related to the formation of such a climate and contributes to what Gottman (1993) called *marital friendship*. Specifically, secure people report more respect, admiration, and gratitude toward their romantic partner (Frei & Shaver, 2002; Shaver & Mikulincer, 2003) than insecure persons. In addition, we (Shaver & Mikulincer, 2003) found that when avoidant people were asked to recall an episode in which they felt grateful to a relationship partner, they tended to remember more negative experiences, involving more narcissistic threats and distrust and less happiness and love. People scoring high on attachment anxiety tended to remember more ambivalent experiences of gratitude-eliciting episodes: They recalled relatively high levels of security-related feelings, happiness, and love together with relatively high levels of narcissistic threats and inferiority feelings. Interestingly, data from a subsequent diary study (Shaver & Mikulincer, 2003) revealed that highly avoidant people experienced relatively low levels of gratitude even on days when they perceived a partner's behavior as positive. That is, a partner's positive behavior elicited gratitude mainly among participants who were not avoidant.

Another interpersonal process involved in the maintenance of a satisfying long-lasting relationship is the couple's engagement in novel, arousing activities that break their routines and "expand their selves" (to use the terminology favored by Aron, Norman, Aron, & Lewandowski, 2002). This engagement in shared expanding activities depends, however, on partners' openness to new experiences, their tolerance of novelty and ambiguity, and their inclination to explore. Adult attachment studies have consistently found that secure people are more likely than insecure ones to engage in exploration and exhibit higher levels of cognitive openness (e.g., Green-Hennessy & Reis, 1998; Mikulincer, 1997; Mikulincer & Arad, 1999). As a result, attachment security is likely to facilitate participation in shared self-expanding activities, which, in turn, will enhance relationship satisfaction.

Attachment security is also involved in the extent to which romantic partners satisfy their sexual needs (e.g., Brennan & Shaver, 1995; Tracy, Shaver, Albino, & Cooper, 2003). Attachment security is associated with sexual satisfaction and is conducive to genuine intimacy in sexual situations, including sensitivity and responsiveness to a partner's wishes and openness to mutual sexual exploration. In contrast, avoidant individuals tend to remain emotionally detached during sexual activities, another manifestation of their deactivating strategies, and anxiously attached individuals tend to hyperactivate sex-related worries and engage in sex primarily to placate a partner, feel accepted, and avoid abandonment (Davis, Shaver, & Vernon, 2004; Schachner & Shaver, 2004).

Insecure people's approach to sexual activities can also hinder marital satisfaction by fostering relational tensions related to fidelity, betrayal, and jealousy. For example, the reluctance of avoidant people to get emotionally involved with or committed to any particular sexual partner can foster positive attitudes toward extramarital affairs, which can place a marriage in jeopardy. Indeed, Schachner and Shaver (2002) recently found that attachment avoidance is associated with "mate poaching" – attempts to attract someone who is already in a relationship, and being open to being "poached" by others – and to low scores on a relationship exclusivity scale. In contrast, the tendency of anxious individuals to hyperactivate vigilance and concern regarding the possibility of losing their sexual partner can lead to intense bouts of jealousy, which in turn endanger relationship stability and quality. There is extensive evidence that anxiously attached individuals are prone to jealousy and tend to be overwhelmed by jealous feelings (e.g., Guerrero, 1998; Sharpsteen & Kirkpatrick, 1997). Furthermore, they tend to report high levels of suspicion and worry during jealousy-eliciting events and cope with them by engaging in intensive partner surveillance (Guerrero, 1998).

THE ROLE OF COPING AND THE OTHER PERSON
IN RELATIONSHIP MAINTENANCE

Beyond these important interpersonal processes, attachment security can contribute to maintenance of a long-lasting relationship by assisting partners in coping effectively with life difficulties, personal changes, and developmental transitions. The quality of a long-lasting relationship can be jeopardized by a broad array of extrarelational stressors (e.g., illness or injury, financial difficulties, problems at work); changes in a partner's identity, preferences, and values; and normative transitions that demand personal and dyadic readjustment (e.g., parenthood, aging). The optimistic and constructive regulatory strategies associated with attachment security, which facilitate coping with and adjusting to hardships, can facili-

tate rapid repair of individuals' feelings and relationship damage that may occur in conjunction with stress. In support of this idea, recent studies show that securely attached spouses deal more constructively with the transition to parenthood and are able to maintain high levels of marital satisfaction after becoming parents (e.g., Alexander, J. Feeney, Hohaus, & Noller, 2001; Simpson & Rholes, 2002). Moreover, Vasquez, Durik, and Hyde (2002) found that secure attachment facilitates coping with work-related stressors and inhibits the spread of work-related distress into the domain of marital satisfaction.

Before concluding this section, it is important to note that although our theoretical ideas and review of empirical studies are focused mainly on the contribution of a person's chronic attachment orientation to his or her relational cognitions and behaviors, the attachment system is affected by a relationship partner's behaviors, which are partly a function of the partner's attachment system. There is increasing evidence that one partner's attachment orientations add to the prediction of the other partner's relational cognitions and behaviors beyond the contribution made by the partner's own attachment orientation (e.g., Brennan & Shaver, 1995; Collins & Feeney, 2000; J. Feeney & Hohaus, 2001). Moreover, a person's scores on attachment anxiety and avoidance have differential effects on relational cognitions and behaviors depending on the partner's attachment orientation. These studies suggest a need for systemic models of attachment dynamics that characterize and explain the complex ways in which both partners' attachment systems shape the quality of their relationship.

Extending Adult Attachment Theory and Research to Other Kinds of Relationships

Although adult attachment research has focused mainly on dating and marital relationships, the interpersonal manifestations of attachment-related strategies are relevant to other kinds of relationships as well. Variations in attachment-system functioning bias access to specific mental representations of relationship partners and, with time, engender global attitudes toward closeness, support seeking, and support provision as well as recurrent problems in the interpersonal domain. These chronically accessible representations, global attitudes, and recurrent problems tend to crystallize in particular patterns of relatedness and profiles of relationship functioning, which become aspects of personality that can be manifested in different kinds of relationships. Research has shown, for example, that self-reports of attachment anxiety and avoidance are related to specific kinds of interpersonal problems, as measured by the Inventory of Interpersonal Problems (e.g., Bartholomew & Horowitz, 1991; Cyranowski et al., 2002).

Dyadic Relations

Following this line of reasoning, it has been proposed that attachment-related strategies are relevant to explaining the quality of best friendships that involve intimacy, support seeking, and support giving. Preliminary evidence suggests that the attachment-style differences observed in romantic relationships are replicated in the realm of close friendship. Specifically, secure, compared with insecure, individuals have more satisfying friendships (e.g., Bippus & Rollin, 2003; Markiewicz, Doyle, & Brendgen, 2001), display more intimate patterns of communication with their friends (e.g., Grabill & Kerns, 2000; Mayseless et al., 1997), and rely on more constructive strategies for resolving conflicts with friends (e.g., Bippus & Rollin, 2003; Creasey, Kershaw, & Boston, 1999). The interpersonal manifestations of attachment-related strategies were also observed in Mikulincer and Selinger's (2001) study of adolescents' same-sex friendships. Whereas secure adolescents flexibly engaged in a wide variety of activities (support seeking, creating opportunities to have fun) with their best friend, anxiously attached adolescents narrowed their interactions to the seeking of support

and reassurance, and avoidant adolescents tended to dismiss the importance of friendship and maintain emotional distance even from their best friend.

The interpersonal manifestations of attachment-related strategies should also be evident in every kind of relationship that involves support seeking and support giving, such as parent–child relationships and relationships between clients and therapists or counselors. With regard to parent–child relationships, Rholes, Simpson, Blakely, Lanigan, and Allen (1997), for example, reported that both avoidance and anxiety were associated with less (self-perceived) ability to relate to one's children and less expected warmth in child rearing among a sample of college students who were not yet parents. In observational studies of maternal behavior (e.g., Crowell & Feldman, 1988, 1991), secure mothers were warmer, more supportive, and more helpful toward their child and more attuned to their child's affect than insecure mothers. Similar associations between attachment style and caregiving have also been noted when observing fathers' interactions with their children (e.g., Cohn, Cowan, Cowan, & Pearson, 1992).

With regard to therapist–client relationships, more securely attached therapists tend to form stronger and more trusting therapeutic bonds with their patients – typically called a *working alliance* (e.g., Sauer, Lopez, & Gormley, 2003) and to respond more empathically to clients' narratives (Rubino, Barker, Roth, & Fearon, 2000). A client's attachment style also has important effects on the therapeutic relationship. Sauer et al. (2003) found that secure clients established better working alliances with their therapists, and Satterfield and Lyddon (1995) found that clients who felt they could depend on others to be available when needed were more likely to establish a secure personal bond with their therapist. Similar benefits of client security have been noted even in studies involving more severely troubled patients (Dozier, 1990). Greater patient attachment security was associated with better treatment compliance, whereas avoidant tendencies were associated with rejection of treatment providers, less self-disclosure, and poorer use of treatment.

Group Relations

Attachment theory is even useful for understanding intragroup relationships. People often feel attached to groups; they seek proximity with other group members in times of need; and the group as whole can be a source of support, comfort, and relief (e.g., Hogg, 1992). More specifically, Smith, Murphy, and Coats (1999) found that people can develop feelings of attachment anxiety and avoidance toward a group and that higher scores on group-specific attachment anxiety and avoidance are related to lower identification with social groups, stronger negative emotions toward groups, and lower perceived support from groups. Recently, Rom and Mikulincer (2003) found that people who are secure in their close relationships, compared with less secure people, have more positive memories of group interactions, appraise group interactions in more challenging and less threatening terms, react to these interactions with more positive affect, and function well, instrumentally and socioemotionally, during team work.

In a recent study, we (Mikulincer & Shaver, 2001) extended attachment theory to the realm of intergroup relationships, focusing on intergroup prejudice and hostility. We reasoned that if the sense of attachment security helps to regulate children's fear of strangers (which it does), it can also regulate adults' reactions to outgroup members, perhaps even members of groups that are in conflict with one's own. We hypothesized that the sense of attachment security would attenuate negative reactions to outgroups. In examining this hypothesis, we measured a person's chronic attachment style, contextually primed attachment security representations, and assessed evaluations and willingness to interact with a variety of outgroup members. We found that both the sense of chronic attachment security and the contextual priming of security representations were associated with more positive evaluations of outgroup members and heightened willingness to interact with them. These effects were mediated by threat appraisal and were found even when participants were led to believe they had failed on a cognitive task or their national group had been insulted by an outgroup member.

Conclusions

Attachment theory was originally created to explain the behavior of young children in relationships with their primary caregiver, usually mother, and the long-term personal and social outcomes of early secure or insecure relationships. The theory was broad from the start because Bowlby rooted it in psychoanalysis, primate ethology, control systems theory (an early form of cognitive psychology), and cognitive developmental psychology. He considered a vast amount of evidence related to emotions, attachments (which he conceptualized as emotional bonds), separation experiences, losses (especially through death), psychological defenses, and psychopathology. Amazingly, despite its original breadth, the theory and the evidence it encompasses and continues to generate is enormously greater now than when Bowlby was writing, thanks to the extension of the theory to adult romantic and marital relationships, close friendships, helping relationships, and intra- and inter-group processes. Underlying the continuously branching and expanding body of knowledge is a relatively simple model of the attachment behavioral system and the forms it takes in response to security-enhancing or security-denying relationships. The relational and affect-regulation strategies adopted by people with varying degrees of attachment security and types of insecurity play a huge role in interpersonal relations, are an important target for educational and clinical interventions, and are an endless source of fascination for researchers.

References

Ainsworth, M. D. S., Blehar, M. C., Waters, E., & Wall, S. (1978). *Patterns of attachment: Assessed in the strange situation and at home*. Hillsdale, NJ: Erlbaum.

Alexander, R., Feeney, J. A., Hohaus, L., & Noller, P. (2001). Attachment style and coping resources as predictors of coping strategies in the transition to parenthood. *Personal Relationships*, 8, 137–152.

Altman, I., & Taylor, D. (1973). *Social penetration: The development of interpersonal relationships*. New York: Holt, Rinehart, & Winston.

Aron, A., Norman, C. C., Aron, E. N., & Lewandowski, G. (2002). Shared participation in self-expanding activities: Positive effects on experienced marital quality. In P. Noller & J. A. Feeney (Eds.), *Understanding marriage: Developments in the study of couple relationships* (pp. 177–194). New York: Cambridge University Press.

Baldwin, M. W., Fehr, B., Keedian, E., Seidel, M., & Thomson, D. W. (1993). An exploration of the relational schemata underlying attachment styles: Self-report and lexical decision approaches. *Personality and Social Psychology Bulletin*, 19, 746–754.

Baldwin, M. W., Keelan, J. P. R., Fehr, B., Enns, V., & KohRangarajoo, E. (1996). Social–cognitive conceptualization of attachment working models: Availability and accessibility effects. *Journal of Personality and Social Psychology*, 71, 94–109.

Bartholomew, K., & Horowitz, L. M. (1991). Attachment styles among young adults: A test of a four-category model. *Journal of Personality and Social Psychology*, 61, 226–244.

Bippus, A. M., & Rollin, E. (2003). Attachment style differences in relational maintenance and conflict behaviors: Friends' perceptions. *Communication Reports*, 16, 113–123.

Birnbaum, G. E., Orr, I., Mikulincer, M., & Florian, V. (1997). When marriage breaks up: Does attachment style contribute to coping and mental health? *Journal of Social and Personal Relationships*, 14, 643–654.

Boon, S. D., & Griffin, D. W. (1996). The construction of risk in relationships: The role of framing in decisions about relationships. *Personal Relationships*, 3, 293–306.

Bowlby, J. (1969/1982). *Attachment and loss: Volume. 1. Attachment* (2nd ed.). New York: Basic Books. (Original work published 1969.)

Bowlby, J. (1973). *Attachment and loss: Volume. 2. Separation: Anxiety and anger*. New York: Basic Books.

Bowlby, J. (1980). *Attachment and loss: Volume. 3. Sadness and depression*. New York: Basic Books.

Bradford, S. A., Feeney, J. A., & Campbell, L. (2002). Links between attachment orientations and dispositional and diary-based measures of disclosure in dating couples: A study of actor and partner effects. *Personal Relationships*, 9, 491–506.

Brehm, S. S. (1992). *Intimate relationships*. New York: McGraw-Hill.

Brennan, K. A., Clark, C. L., & Shaver, P. R. (1998). Self-report measurement of adult attachment: An integrative overview. In J. A. Simpson & W. S. Rholes (Eds.), *Attachment theory and close relationships* (pp. 46–76). New York: Guilford Press.

Brennan, K. A., & Shaver, P. R. (1995). Dimensions of adult attachment, affect regulation, and romantic relationship functioning. *Personality and Social Psychology Bulletin*, 21, 267–283.

Carnelley, K. B., & Janoff-Bulman, R. (1992). Optimism about love relationships: General vs. specific lessons from one's personal experiences. *Journal of Social and Personal Relationships*, 9, 5–20.

Carnelley, K. B., Pietromonaco, P. R., & Jaffe, K. (1996). Attachment, caregiving, and relationship functioning in couples: Effects of self and partner. *Personal Relationships*, 3, 257–277.

Cassidy, J., & Kobak, R. R. (1988). Avoidance and its relationship with other defensive processes. In J. Belsky & T. Nezworski (Eds.), *Clinical implications of attachment* (pp. 300–323). Hillsdale, NJ: Erlbaum.

Cassidy, J., & Shaver, P. R. (Eds) (1999). *Handbook of attachment: Theory, research, and clinical applications*. New York: Guilford Press.

Chappell, K. D., & Davis, K. E. (1998). Attachment, partner choice, and perception of romantic partners: An experimental test of the attachment-security hypothesis. *Personal Relationships*, 5, 327–342.

Cobb, R. J., Davila, J., & Bradbury, T. N. (2001). Attachment security and marital satisfactions: The role of positive perceptions and social support. *Personality and Social Psychology Bulletin*, 27, 1131–1143.

Cohn, D. A., Cowan, P. A., Cowan, C. P., & Pearson, J. (1992). Mothers' and fathers' working models of childhood attachment relationships, parenting styles, and child behavior. *Development and Psychopathology*, 4, 417–431.

Collins, N. L. (1996). Working models of attachment: Implications for explanation, emotion, and behavior. *Journal of Personality and Social Psychology*, 71, 810–832.

Collins, N. L., & Feeney, B. C. (2000). A safe haven: An attachment theory perspective on support seeking and caregiving in intimate relationships. *Journal of Personality and Social Psychology*, 78, 1053–1073.

Collins, N. L., & Read, S. J. (1990). Adult attachment, working models, and relationship quality in dating couples. *Journal of Personality and Social Psychology*, 58, 644–663.

Cowan, P. A., & Cowan, C. P. (2002). What an intervention design reveals about how parents affect their children's academic achievement and behavior problems. In J. G. Borkowski, S. Ramey, & M. Bristol-Power (Eds.), *Parenting and the child's world: Influences on intellectual, academic, and social-emotional development* (pp. 75–98). Mahwah, NJ: Erlbaum.

Cozzarelli, C., Hoekstra, S. J., & Bylsma, W. H. (2000). General versus specific mental models of attachment: Are they associated with different outcomes? *Personality and Social Psychology Bulletin*, 26, 605–618.

Creasey, G., Kershaw, K., & Boston, A. (1999). Conflict management with friends and romantic partners: The role of attachment and negative mood regulation expectations. *Journal of Youth and Adolescence*, 28, 523–543.

Crowell, J. A., & Feldman, S. S. (1988). Mothers' internal models of relationships and children's behavioral and developmental status: A study of mother–child interaction. *Child Development*, 59, 1273–1285.

Crowell, J. A., & Feldman, S. S. (1991). Mothers' working models of attachment relationships and mother and child behavior during separation and reunion. *Developmental Psychology*, 27, 597–605.

Cyranowski, J. M., Bookwala, J., Feske, U., Houck, P., Pilkonis, P., Kostelnik, B., & Frank, E. (2002). Adult attachment profiles, interpersonal difficulties, and response to interpersonal psychotherapy in women with recurrent major depression. *Journal of Social and Clinical Psychology*, 21, 191–217.

Davila, J., Karney, B. R., & Bradbury, T. N. (1999). Attachment change processes in the early years of marriage. *Journal of Personality and Social Psychology*, 76, 783–802.

Davis, D., Shaver, P. R., & Vernon, M. L. (2003). Physical, emotional, and behavioral reactions to breaking up: The roles of gender, age, emotional involvement, and attachment style. *Personality and Social Psychology Bulletin*, 29, 871–884.

Davis, D., Shaver, P. R., & Vernon, M. L. (2004). Attachment style and subjective motivations for sex. *Personality and Social Psychology Bulletin*, 30, 1076–1090.

Dozier, M. (1990). Attachment organization and treatment use for adults with serious psychopathological disorders. *Development and Psychopathology*, 2, 47–60.

Epstein, S., & Meier, P. (1989). Constructive thinking: A broad coping variable with specific components. *Journal of Personality and Social Psychology*, 57, 332–350.

Feeney, B. C., & Collins, N. L. (2001). Predictors of caregiving in adult intimate relationships: An attachment theoretical perspective. *Journal of Personality and Social Psychology*, 80, 972–994.

Feeney, J. A. (1994). Attachment style, communication patterns, and satisfaction across the life cycle of marriage. *Personal Relationships*, 1, 333–348.

Feeney, J. A. (1996). Attachment, caregiving, and marital satisfaction. *Personal Relationships*, 3, 401–416.

Feeney, J. A. (1999). Adult romantic attachment and couple relationships. In J. Cassidy & P. R. Shaver (Eds.), *Handbook of attachment: Theory, research, and clinical applications* (pp. 355–377). New York: Guilford Press.

Feeney, J. A., & Hohaus, L. (2001). Attachment and spousal caregiving. *Personal Relationships*, 8, 21–39.

Feeney, J. A., & Noller, P. (1991). Attachment style and verbal descriptions of romantic partners. *Journal of Social and Personal Relationships*, 8, 187–215.

Fitzpatrick, M. A., Fey, J., Segrin, C., & Schiff, J. L. (1993). Internal working models of relationships and marital communication. *Journal of Language and Social Psychology*, 12, 103–131.

Fraley, R. C., & Shaver, P. R. (1999). Loss and bereavement: Attachment theory and recent controversies concerning grief work and the nature of detachment. In J. Cassidy & P. R. Shaver (Eds.), *Handbook of attachment: Theory, research, and clinical applications* (pp. 735–759). New York: Guilford Press.

Frazier, P. A., Byer, A. L., Fischer, A. R., Wright, D. M., & DeBord, K. A. (1996). Adult attachment style and partner choice: Correlational and experimental findings. *Personal Relationships*, 3, 117–136.

Frei, J. R., & Shaver, P. R. (2002). Respect in close relationships: Prototype definition, self-report assessment, and initial correlates. *Personal Relationships*, 9, 121–129.

Gagne, F. M., & Lydon, J. E. (2001). Mindset and close relationships: When bias leads to (in)accurate predictions. *Journal of Personality and Social Psychology*, 81, 85–96.

Gaines, S. O., Jr., Reis, H. T., Summers, S., Rusbult, C. E., Cox, C. L., Wexler, M. O., et al. (1997). Impact of attachment style on reactions to accommodative dilemmas in close relationships. *Personal Relationships*, 4, 93–113.

Gottman, J. M. (1993). *What predicts divorce? The relationship between marital processes and marital outcomes*. Hillsdale, NJ: Erlbaum.

Grabill, C. M., & Kerns, K. A. (2000). Attachment style and intimacy in friendship. *Personal Relationships*, 7, 363–378.

Green-Hennessy, S., & Reis, H. T. (1998). Openness in processing social information among attachment types. *Personal Relationships*, 5, 449–466.

Guerrero, L. K. (1996). Attachment-style differences in intimacy and involvement: A test of the four-category model. *Communication Monographs*, 63, 269–292.

Guerrero, L. K. (1998). Attachment-style differences in the experience and expression of romantic jealousy. *Personal Relationships*, 5, 273–291.

Hazan, C., & Shaver, P. R. (1987). Romantic love conceptualized as an attachment process. *Journal of Personality and Social Psychology*, 52, 511–524.

Himovitch, O. (2003). *The experience of commitment in couple relationships: An attachment theoretical perspective*. Unpublished doctoral dissertation, Bar-Ilan University.

Hogg, M. A. (1992). *The social psychology of group cohesiveness: From attraction to social identity*. New York: Harvester Wheatsheaf.

Huston, T. L., & Burgess, R. L. (1979). Social exchange in developing relationships: An overview. In R. L. Burgess & T. L. Huston (Eds.), *Social exchange in developing relationships* (pp. 3–28). New York: Academic Press.

Keelan, J. P. R., Dion, K. K., & Dion, K. L. (1998). Attachment style and relationship satisfaction: Test of a self-disclosure explanation. *Canadian Journal of Behavioural Science*, 30, 24–35.

Klohnen, E. C., & Shanhong, L. (2003). Interpersonal attraction and personality: What is attractive – self-similarity, ideal similarity, complementarity, or attachment security? *Journal of Personality and Social Psychology*, 85, 709–722.

Kobak, R. R., & Hazan, C. (1991). Attachment in marriage: Effects of security and accuracy of working models. *Journal of Personality and Social Psychology*, 60, 861–869.

Kunce, L. J., & Shaver, P. R. (1994). An attachment-theoretical approach to caregiving in romantic relationships. In K. Bartholomew & D. Perlman (Eds.), *Advances in personal relationships* (Vol. 5, pp. 205–237). London. Kingsley.

Markiewicz, D., Doyle, A., & Brendgen, M. (2001). The quality of adolescents' friendships: Associations with mothers' interpersonal relationships. *Journal of Adolescence*, 24, 429–445.

Mayseless, O., Sharabany, R., & Sagi, A. (1997). Attachment concerns of mothers as manifested in parental, spousal, and friendship relationships. *Personal Relationships*, 4, 255–269.

Mikulincer, M. (1997). Adult attachment style and information processing: Individual differences in curiosity and cognitive closure. *Journal of Personality and Social Psychology*, 72, 1217–1230.

Mikulincer, M. (1998a). Adult attachment style and affect regulation: Strategic variations in self-appraisals. *Journal of Personality and Social Psychology*, 75, 420–435.

Mikulincer, M. (1998b). Attachment working models and the sense of trust: An exploration of interaction goals and affect regulation. *Journal of Personality and Social Psychology*, 74, 1209–1224.

Mikulincer, M. (1998c). Adult attachment style and individual differences in functional versus dysfunctional experiences of anger. *Journal of Personality and Social Psychology*, 74, 513–524.

Mikulincer, M., & Arad, D. (1999). Attachment working models and cognitive openness in close relationships: A test of chronic and temporary accessibility effects. *Journal of Personality and Social Psychology, 77*, 710–725.

Mikulincer, M., & Florian, V. (1996). Emotional reactions to loss over the life span: An attachment perspective. In S. McFadden & C. Magai (Eds.), *Handbook of emotions, adult development, and aging* (pp. 269–285). New York: Academic Press.

Mikulincer, M., & Florian, V. (1999). The association between self-reports of attachment styles and representations of family dynamics. *Family Process, 38*, 69–83.

Mikulincer, M., Florian, V., Cowan, P. A., & Cowan, C. P. (2002). Attachment security in couple relationships: A systemic model and its implications for family dynamics. *Family Process, 41*, 405–434.

Mikulincer, M., & Nachshon, O. (1991). Attachment styles and patterns of self-disclosure. *Journal of Personality and Social Psychology, 61*, 321–331.

Mikulincer, M., & Selinger, M. (2001). The interplay between attachment and affiliation systems in adolescents' same-sex friendships: The role of attachment style. *Journal of Social and Personal Relationships, 18*, 81–106.

Mikulincer, M., & Shaver, P. R. (2001). Attachment theory and intergroup bias: Evidence that priming the secure base schema attenuates negative reactions to out-groups. *Journal of Personality and Social Psychology, 81*, 97–115.

Mikulincer, M., & Shaver, P. R. (2003). The attachment behavioral system in adulthood: Activation, psychodynamics, and interpersonal processes. In M. P. Zanna (Ed.), *Advances in experimental social psychology* (Vol. 35). San Diego, CA: Academic Press.

Morgan, H. J., & Shaver, P. R. (1999). Attachment processes and commitment to romantic relationships. In J. M. Adams & W. H. Jones (Eds.), *Handbook of interpersonal commitment and relationship stability* (pp. 109–124). New York: Plenum.

Ognibene, T. C., & Collins, N. L. (1998). Adult attachment styles, perceived social support, and coping strategies. *Journal of Social and Personal Relationships, 15*, 323–345.

Overall, N. C., Fletcher, G. J. O., & Friesen, M. D. (2003). Mapping the intimate relationship mind: Comparisons between three models of attachment representations. *Personality and Social Psychology Bulletin, 29*, 1479–1493.

Pietromonaco, P., & Carnelley, K. (1994). Gender and working models of attachment: Consequences for perceptions of self and romantic partners. *Personal Relationships, 1*, 63–82.

Pietromonaco, P. R., & Feldman Barrett, L. (1997). Working models of attachment and daily social interactions. *Journal of Personality and Social Psychology, 73*, 1409–1423.

Pietromonaco, P. R., Laurenceau, J., & Barrett, L. F. (2002). Change in relationship knowledge representations. In A. L. Vangelisti, H. T. Reis, & M. A. Fitzpatrick (Eds.), *Stability and change in relationships. Advances in personal relationships* (pp. 5–34). New York: Cambridge University Press.

Rholes, W. S., Simpson, J. A., Blakely, B. S., Lanigan, L., & Allen, E. A. (1997). Adult attachment styles, the desire to have children, and working models of parenthood. *Journal of Personality, 65*, 357–385.

Rholes, W. S., Simpson, J. A., & Orina, M. M. (1999). Attachment and anger in an anxiety-provoking situation. *Journal of Personality and Social Psychology, 76*, 940–957.

Rom, E., & Mikulincer, M. (2003). Attachment theory and group processes: The association between attachment style and group-related representations, goals, memory, and functioning. *Journal of Personality and Social Psychology, 84*, 1220–1235.

Rubino, G., Barker, C., Roth, T., & Fearon, P. (2000). Therapist empathy and depth of interpretation in response to potential alliance ruptures: The role of therapist and patient attachment styles. *Psychotherapy Research, 10*, 407–420.

Satterfield, W. A., & Lyddon, W. J. (1995). Client attachment and perceptions of the working alliance with counselor trainees. *Journal of Counseling Psychology, 42*, 187–189.

Sauer, E. M., Lopez, F. G., & Gormley, B. (2003). Respective contributions of therapist and client adult attachment orientations to the development of the early working alliance: A preliminary growth modeling study. *Psychotherapy Research, 13*, 371–382.

Schachner, D. A., & Shaver, P. R. (2002). Attachment style and human mate poaching. *New Review of Social Psychology, 1*, 122–129.

Schachner, D. A., & Shaver, P. R. (2004). Attachment dimensions and motives for sex. *Personal Relationships, 11*, 179–195.

Scharfe, E., & Bartholomew, K. (1995). Accommodation and attachment representations in couples. *Journal of Social and Personal Relationships, 12*, 389–401.

Schlenker, B. R. (1980). *Impression management: The self-concept, social identity, and interpersonal relations.* Monterey, CA: Brooks/Cole.

Sharpsteen, D. J., & Kirkpatrick, L. A. (1997). Romantic jealousy and adult romantic attachment. *Journal of Personality and Social Psychology, 72*, 627–640.

Shaver, P. R., & Brennan, K. A. (1992). Attachment styles and the "Big Five" personality traits: Their connections with each other and with romantic relationship outcomes. *Personality and Social Psychology Bulletin, 18*, 536–545.

Shaver, P. R., & Hazan, C. (1993). Adult romantic attachment: Theory and evidence. In D. Perlman & W. Jones (Eds.), *Advances in personal relationships* (Vol. 4, pp. 29–70). London: Jessica Kingsley.

Shaver, P. R., Hazan, C., & Bradshaw, D. (1988). Love as attachment: The integration of three behavioral systems. In R. J. Sternberg & M. Barnes (Eds.), *The psychology of love* (pp. 68–99). New Haven, CT: Yale University Press.

Shaver, P. R., & Mikulincer, M. (2005). Attachment-related psychodynamics. *Attachment and Human Development, 4*, 133–161.

Shaver, P. R., & Mikulincer, M. (2003, May). *Attachment, compassion, and altruism.* Paper presented at the Conference on Compassionate Love, Normal, IL.

Shaver, P. R., Schachner, D. E., & Mikulincer, M. (2005). Attachment style, excessive reassurance seeking, relationships processes, and depression. *Personality and Social Psychology Bulletin, 31*, 1–17.

Simpson, J. A. (1990). Influence of attachment styles on romantic relationships. *Journal of Personality and Social Psychology, 59*, 871–980.

Simpson, J. A., & Rholes, W. S. (2002). Attachment orientations, marriage, and the transition to parenthood. *Journal of Research in Personality, 36*, 622–628.

Simpson, J. A., Rholes, W. S., & Nelligan, J. S. (1992). Support seeking and support giving within couples in an anxiety-provoking situation: The role of attachment styles. *Journal of Personality and Social Psychology, 62*, 434–446.

Simpson, J. A., Rholes, W. S., Orina, M. M., & Grich, J. (2002). Working models of attachment, support giving, and support seeking in a stressful situation. *Personality and Social Psychology Bulletin, 28*, 598–608.

Smith, E. R., Murphy, J., & Coats, S. (1999). Attachment to groups: Theory and measurement. *Journal of Personality and Social Psychology, 77*, 94–110.

Sroufe, L. A., & Waters, E. (1977). Heart rate as a convergent measure in clinical and developmental research. *Merrill-Palmer Quarterly, 23*, 3–27.

Tidwell, M. C. O., Reis, H. T., & Shaver, P. R. (1996). Attachment, attractiveness, and social interaction: A diary study. *Journal of Personality and Social Psychology, 71*, 729–745.

Tracy, J. L., Shaver, P. R., Albino, A. W., & Cooper, M. L. (2003). Attachment styles and adolescent sexuality. In P. Florsheim (Ed.), *Adolescent romance and sexual behavior: Theory, research, and practical implications* (pp. 137–159). Mahwah, NJ: Erlbaum.

Tucker, J. S., & Anders, S. L. (1998). Adult attachment style and nonverbal closeness in dating couples. *Journal of Nonverbal Behavior, 22*, 124–109.

Vasquez, K., Durik, A. M., & Hyde, J. S. (2002). Family and work: Implications of adult attachment style. *Personality and Social Psychology Bulletin, 28*, 874–886.

Volling, B. L., Notaro, P. C., & Larsen, J. J. (1998). Adult attachment styles: Relations with emotional well-being, marriage, and parenting. *Family Relations, 47*, 355–367.

Whisman, M. A., & Allan, L. E. (1996). Attachment and social cognition theories of romantic relationships: Convergent or complementary perspectives? *Journal of Social and Personal Relationships, 13*, 263–278.

Zeifman, D., & Hazan, C. (2000). A process model of adult attachment formation. In W. Ickes & S. Duck (Eds.), *The social psychology of personal relationships* (pp. 37–54). New York: Wiley.

CHAPTER 15

"His" and "Her" Relationships? A Review of the Empirical Evidence

Emily A. Impett
Letitia Anne Peplau

Comparing the experiences of men and women in intimate relationships is a fascination – some might say an obsession – that has long intrigued laypeople and researchers alike. The public appears to crave information about how men and women differ in their approaches to love and relationships, a point reflected in the continuing popularity of John Gray's (1993) best-selling book, *Men are from Mars, Women are from Venus*. Social scientists, too, have tackled this topic. Thirty years ago, sociologist Jessie Bernard (1972) proposed that in every marriage there are actually two relationships – "his" and "hers." In the intervening years, relationship researchers have energetically investigated the possibility of important gender differences in close relationships, extending their analyses beyond marriage to include cohabiting partners, gay and lesbian couples (see Diamond, this volume), and other intimate relationships.

A comprehensive history of theory and research on gender in close relationships has yet to be written, but a few landmarks are illustrative. Early analyses, primarily by sociologists and anthropologists, focused on the family (see review by Glenn, 1987). Working from a functionalist perspective, theorists such as Parsons (1955) suggested that the existence of the traditional nuclear family provided evidence that differentiated male–female roles serve vital functions, including the socialization of children and the stabilization of adult personality. In the 1970s, emerging feminist perspectives criticized prevailing theories as justifying the status quo. Instead, feminist scholars urged analyses of male–female relationships that considered gender ideology, power inequalities, the division of labor, and the social context (e.g., Bernard, 1972). Although feminists often argued for the social origins of traditional gender patterns in relationships, the development of sociobiology provided an alternative perspective rooted in human evolution. Symons' (1979) influential book, *The Evolution of Human Sexuality*, laid the groundwork for evolutionary analyses of mate selection, parental investment, and other topics that continue to be studied today. In the 1970s, empirical projects such as the Boston Couples Study (e.g., Peplau, Hill, & Rubin, 1993) paid increasing attention to the impact of changing gender attitudes and roles on young couples. Early studies of gay and lesbian couples also began to appear (e.g., Peplau & Jones, 1982). The American Couples study (Blumstein & Schwartz, 1983) provided extensive survey data on thousands of couples, including not only married heterosexuals, but also cohabiting heterosexual, gay, and lesbian couples. Analytic reviews of research on women and men in personal relationships became more common (e.g., Glenn, 1987; Huston & Ashmore, 1986). Empirical research on gender in close relationships continued to grow in the 1980s and 1990s, and books devoted to this topic began to appear. These included *Gendered Relationships* (Wood, 1996), *Gender and Close Relationships* (Winstead, Derlega, & Rose, 1997), and *Gender and Families* (Coltrane, 2000a). A further indication of the wealth of research on gender and relationships comes from a search of the PsychINFO database, which, in February 2004, listed 1,042 articles, books, chapters, and dissertations published since 1960 that combined the thesaurus terms "human sex differences" and "couples."

A major critique of sex difference research is that many studies are purely descriptive (e.g., Yoder & Kahn, 2003). Those studies that are theory-based tend to focus on a limited set of experiences, with evolutionary theorists studying mate selection, social interdependence theorists studying commitment, social role theorists addressing the division of labor, and so on. This lack of theoretical grounding is problematic because gender itself does not provide an explanation for documented differences between the sexes. Demonstrating, for instance, that marriage is more beneficial for the health of husbands than of wives does not explain this gender effect. In other words, sex difference findings do not provide answers but rather lead to more questions. Observed male–female differences are likely to reflect a wide range of factors including an individual's biological makeup and personal dispositions, his or her loca-

tion in the social hierarchy of status and economic resources, attitudes about how men and women should behave in relationships, and the social opportunities available at a given historical moment (Winstead et al., 1997).

In this chapter, we take stock of the extensive empirical research comparing men's and women's experiences in intimate relationships. Of practical necessity, this review concentrates on six major domains: what men and women want in relationships, relationship orientation, sexuality, family work, power and influence, and health. We have selected areas in which there is sufficient empirical research to identify reliable patterns. In addition, this review is limited to adult romantic relationships and focuses on describing gendered patterns rather than tracing their origins. We hope that our review will spur relationship scholars to develop more integrative theoretical accounts of men's and women's experiences in close relationships.

What Men and Women Want in Relationships

We begin our review with research investigating whether women and men approach close relationships with different values and preferences in a mate.

Values about Relationships

Proponents of the position that women and men inhabit "different cultures" suggest that women and men hold distinctive standards for their intimate relationships and have different beliefs about effective communication (e.g., Wood, 1996). For example, whereas women may prefer emotion-focused messages that elaborate on a distressed person's feelings, men may prefer instrumentally oriented messages that focus on fixing a problem rather than expressing feelings. Empirical research provides little empirical support for this argument (see review by Burleson, 2003).

Instead, whereas women rate emotion-focused skills as more important than do men, and men rate instrumentally oriented skills as more important than do women, both sexes rate emotion-focused skills as considerably more important than instrumental skills. These results highlight the importance of examining both between-sex and within-sex effects. That is, although there are mean differences in the importance that men and women place on emotion-focused versus instrumental communication, both sexes value communication focused on emotions more highly.

Whereas the "different cultures" argument holds that women and men have different relational standards, the "different experiences" model holds that the sexes approach their relationships with the same values and goals, but that the behaviors typically displayed by women are more likely to fulfill men's relational standards. Available research supports the latter position. In an illustrative study, individuals in long-term relationships evaluated the importance of 30 relational standards (e.g., trust, affective accessibility, flexibility) as well as the degree to which their current relationship fulfilled each of these qualities (Vangelisti & Daly, 1997). Results showed that men and women attached equal importance to each of the relational standards, but men were more likely than women to report that their standards were fulfilled. Vangelisti and Daly suggested that women's caring and nurturing role, along with their more intimate style of interacting and communicating with a partner, create a context in which men's standards are more likely to be met than women's.

Another possibility is that men and women may have different standards for more specific things such as the preferred frequency of household work or sexual activity. For instance, men may have considerably lower standards than women for household work, and women may have lower standards than men for frequency of sexual activity. Differences in these more specific standards could set the stage for relationship conflict.

This would be a useful direction for future research.

Mate Preferences

What are men and women looking for in selecting a romantic partner? The extensive research on heterosexual mate selection documents two consistent sex differences. First, although both sexes appreciate good looks, men place greater value on the physical attributes of a partner than do women. For example, in a national survey of Americans, men were less willing than women to marry someone who was not "good looking" (Sprecher, Sullivan, & Hatfield, 1994). Second, women place greater emphasis on a partner's status and economic resources than do men. In a national survey, women indicated greater interest than men in marrying someone who had a steady job, earned more, and had more education (Sprecher et al., 1994). Men's greater interest in physical attractiveness and women's greater interest in status and resources have been found not only in the United States but in a wide range of other cultures as well (e.g., Buss & Schmitt, 1993).

However, digging deeper into findings about mate preference indicates that neither men nor women put good looks and economic resources at the top of their wish list. In a recent study that assessed 18 mate characteristics (Buss, Shackelford, Kirkpatrick, & Larsen, 2001), "good looks" ranked 8th on men's list (and 13th on women's list). "Good financial prospects" ranked 11th on women's list (and 13th on men's). At the top of both men's and women's lists were mutual attraction, dependability, emotional maturity, and a pleasing disposition. Taken together, these results find evidence of both gender similarities and gender differences. More broadly, they highlight the importance of taking a balanced view of gender comparisons, one that considers not only differences between the sexes but also individual differences among men and women, and features that are common to humans in general.

Relationship Orientation

Social theorists from diverse perspectives have proposed that women are more relationship-oriented than are men (e.g., Chodorow, 1978; Gilligan, 1982). Recent empirical studies provide converging support for this proposition (see Cross & Madson, 1997, for a review). Women's relatively greater relationship orientation is reflected in cognition (i.e., how individuals think about themselves in relation to others), motivation (i.e., the drive or desire to maintain relationships), and behavior (i.e., the activities that individuals engage in to maintain relationships).

Cognition

The ways people construe themselves in relation to important people in their lives indicate their relationship orientation. Research has identified two contrasting self concepts. For a person with an *independent self-construal*, self-definition is based to a large degree on his or her own unique attributes, and emphasis is placed on maintaining a sense of autonomy from others (Markus & Kitayama, 1994). In contrast, for a person with an *interdependent self-construal*, relationships are viewed as integral parts of his or her very being. Emphasis is placed on connection with others, so that the self is defined, at least in part, by important relationships with close others.

In U.S. society, women are more likely than men to construct an interdependent self-view, and men are more likely than women to construct an independent self-view. In a comprehensive review of research on gender and self-construal, Cross and Madson (1997) showed that women describe themselves in more relational terms, rank relationship-oriented aspects of their identity as more important, pay closer attention to others, talk more about their relationships, and have a better memory for close others and relationship events than do men. Across eight samples, women scored higher than men on a composite mea-

sure of the relational-interdependent self-construal (effect size of $d = -0.41$), more frequently endorsing such items as "My close relationships are an important reflection of who I am" (Cross, Bacon, & Morris, 2000). Some theorists have challenged this gender difference, asserting that whereas women's self-construal focuses on the self in intimate, dyadic relationships, men's focuses on the collective or group self (e.g., Baumeister & Sommer, 1997). Nonetheless, in the context of dyadic relationships (which is the focus of this review), women's and men's self-construals may differ in important ways.

Gender differences in self-construal can influence the characteristics that men and women value in an intimate relationship. Specifically, women may value closeness and intimate connections more than men, and men may value individuality and autonomy more than women. Indeed, a major source of conflict in marriage concerns the amount of closeness or intimacy that spouses desire in their relationships (see Eldridge & Christensen, 2002, for a review). In marriage, it is more often the wife who wants greater closeness and the husband who desires greater autonomy. Therapists report that the most common complaint of women in distressed marriages is that their husbands are too withdrawn, whereas men complain that their wives are overly expressive, emotional, and nagging (e.g., Markman & Kraft, 1989). These ideas are also consistent with research showing that women are most angry and upset when their partners behave in an inconsiderate, neglectful, emotionally restrictive, or condescending manner, whereas men are most angry and upset when their partners are possessive and dependent (Buss, 1991).

Consistent with what we might expect from research on self-construal, several studies have documented gender differences in adult attachment styles. Women are more likely than men to be "preoccupied" as measured by both self-reports and interviews (e.g., Scharfe & Bartholomew, 1994). That is, women place an extremely high value on feeling intimate with a romantic partner but are anxious about abandonment and fear that their partners will not want to get as close as they would like. In contrast, men in most cultures around the world are more likely than women to be "dismissing" (e.g., Schmitt, Alcalay, Allensworth, Allik, Ault, Austers, et al., 2003). Men are more likely to report that it is important to feel independent and self-sufficient, and they prefer not having to depend on others or have others depend on them.

Motivation

Evidence that women are more motivated than men to maintain their romantic relationships comes from research on commitment. Commitment has been defined as the degree to which an individual experiences long-term orientation toward a relationship, including the desire to maintain the relationship for better or worse (e.g., Rusbult, 1980). Although gender differences are not invariable, when they do arise, it is typically women who show greater relationship commitment. In a recent meta-analysis of 52 published and unpublished studies, Le and Agnew (2003) found a moderate effect size for gender ($d = -0.36$); women felt significantly more committed to their relationships than did men. Three important factors that influence commitment are relationship satisfaction, the quality of perceived alternatives to the current relationship, and the amount that a person has already invested in the relationship (see Rusbult & Van Lange, 1996, for a review). In the meta-analysis by Le and Agnew (2003), women were more satisfied ($d = -0.31$), felt that they had invested more into the relationship ($d = -0.13$), and perceived fewer alternatives to the current relationship ($d - 0.21$) than did men. In short, not only did women report "wanting" their relationships to continue – as indicated by their higher levels of satisfaction, they also reported "needing" their relationships to continue, reflected by their greater investments and fewer perceived alternatives.

This gender difference in commitment has also been documented in a gay and lesbian sample. Duffy and Rusbult (1985/1986) found that women, both heterosexual and lesbian, reported that they were more committed to maintaining their relationships and had invested more in their relationships than did men. In this sample, gay men reported the lowest levels of commitment and investment in their relationships. It will be valuable for future research to replicate the findings from this single study.

Behavior

For a relationship to persist over time, perhaps especially in societies where divorce is commonplace, partners need to engage in ongoing relationship "work" to maintain the relationship. In a typical study of relationship maintenance, dating or married participants indicate in an open-ended format the kinds of things they do to maintain their relationships (e.g., Stafford & Canary, 1991). Common strategies include acting cheerful around a partner, talking openly about the relationship, assuring a partner of one's love, surrounding the relationship with valued friends and family who support the relationship, and performing tasks. Although men and women do not differ in the types of behaviors they list as important, women report engaging in these behaviors more frequently than do men (e.g., Dindia & Baxter, 1987; Ragsdale, 1996).

Three maintenance strategies appear to be particularly gendered. First, women are more likely than men to express their love and affection for a partner (e.g., Ragsdale, 1996; Stafford, Dainton, & Haas, 2000). Second, women are more likely to engage in sexual activity that they do not desire in an effort to maintain a valued intimate relationship (see Impett & Peplau, 2003 for a review). Third, in communicating with their partner, women are more likely than men to report being cheerful and polite, and initiating open and direct discussions about the nature of their relationship (e.g., Dainton & Stafford, 1993).

Sexuality

In recent years, empirical research comparing men's and women's sexuality has flourished. A consensus appears to be emerging about several basic areas of difference (see reviews in Harvey, Wenzel, & Sprecher, 2004; Okami & Shackelford, 2001; Peplau, 2003). Our review focuses on five areas of difference.

Sexuality and Relationships

One consistent gender difference is women's greater tendency to emphasize relationships and commitment as a context for sexuality, and men's greater tendency to separate sexuality from love and commitment (see review by Peplau, 2003). For example, men and women differ in their definitions of "sexual desire." Women are more likely than men to "romanticize" the experience of sexual desire; men more often equate sexual desire with physical pleasure and sexual intercourse. In an illustrative study (Regan & Berscheid, 1996), more men (70%) than women (43%) believed that sexual desire was aimed at the physical act of sex. In contrast, more women (35%) than men (13%) cited love or emotional intimacy as the goal of sexual desire. Further, women's sex fantasies are more likely to include a familiar partner, to include affection and commitment, and to describe the setting for the sexual encounter. In contrast, men's fantasies are more likely to involve strangers, anonymous partners, or multiple partners and to focus on specific sex acts or body parts. Compared with women, men have more permissive attitudes toward casual premarital sex and toward extramarital sex. The size of these gender differences is relatively large, particularly for casual premarital sex ($d = 0.81$, Oliver & Hyde, 1993). The term *sociosexual orientation* has been used to capture this correlated set of sexual attitudes, preferences, and behaviors (see review by Simpson, Wilson & Winterheld, 2004). Significant gender differences are reliably found on measures of sociosexuality, both in the United States and in more than 50 other countries (Schmitt, Alcalay, Allik, Ault, Austers, Bennett, et al., 2003).

The gender difference in emphasizing the relational aspects of sexuality is also found among lesbians and gay men (see review by Peplau, Fingerhut, & Beals, 2004). Compared with gay men, lesbians have less permissive attitudes toward casual sex and are more likely to become sexually involved with partners who were first their friends. Lesbians' sex fantasies are more likely to be personal and romantic. Lesbians report having fewer lifetime sex partners than do gay men. Indeed, gay men report substantially more sex partners than either lesbians or heterosexuals and score significantly higher than other groups on a general measure of sociosexuality (Bailey, Gaulin, Agyei, & Gladue, 1994). Gay men in committed relationships are more likely than any group to report that they have sex with partners outside the relationship (Blumstein & Schwartz, 1983; Peplau, Fingerhut, & Beals, 2004).

Erotic Plasticity

Erotic plasticity is the extent to which an individual's sexual beliefs and behaviors can be shaped and altered by cultural, social, and situational factors. In a comprehensive review of empirical research, Baumeister (2000) showed that women's sexuality tends to be more malleable or "plastic" than men's. One sign of plasticity is that a person's sexual attitudes and behaviors are responsive to social and situational influences. Such factors as education, religion, and acculturation are more strongly linked to women's sexuality than to men's. For example, college education is associated with more permissive sexual attitudes and behavior, but this correlation is greater for women than for men. Another indicator of plasticity concerns changes in aspects of a person's sexuality over time. For example, the frequency of women's sexual activity is more variable than men's. If a woman is in an intimate relationship, she might have frequent sex with her partner. Following a breakup, however, she might have no sex at all, including masturbation, for several months. Men show less temporal variability: following a romantic breakup, men may substitute masturbation for interpersonal sex and so maintain a more constant frequency of sex. There is also growing evidence that women are more likely than men to change their sexual orientation over time (e.g., Diamond, 2003).

Sexual Desire

Many lines of research demonstrate that men show more interest in sex than do women (see review by Baumeister, Catanese, & Vohs, 2001). Compared with women, men think about sex more often. Men report more frequent sex fantasies and more frequent feelings of sexual desire. Across the life span, men rate the strength of their own sex drive higher than do their female agemates. Men are more interested in visual sexual stimuli and more likely to spend money on such explicitly sexual products and activities as x-rated videos and visits to prostitutes. Men and women also differ in their preferred frequency of sex. Masturbation provides a good index of sexual desire because it is not constrained by the availability of a partner. Men are more likely than women to masturbate, start masturbating at an earlier age, and do so more often. In a review of 177 studies, Oliver and Hyde (1993) found large male–female differences in the incidence of masturbation (effect size of $d = 0.96$). When dating and marriage partners disagree about sexual frequency, men usually want to have sex more often. In heterosexual couples, actual sexual frequency may reflect a compromise in the desires of the male and female partner. In gay and lesbian relationships, where sexual frequency is decided by partners of the same sex, lesbians report having sex less often than gay men or heterosexuals.

Caution is needed in interpreting evidence of men's greater sexual desire. First, it is important to avoid inadvertently using male standards such as penile penetration and orgasm as the basis for understanding women's sexuality. Some have suggested that other activities such as intimate kissing, cuddling, and touching may be uniquely important to women's erotic lives (e.g., Peplau & Garnets, 2000). This would be consistent with women's tendency to define sexual desire in romantic, relational terms. Second, because women's sexual desire may vary across the menstrual cycle, it may be more appropriate to describe women's desire as periodic rather than weak or limited (Gangestad & Cousins, 2001). Finally, as with all the male–female comparisons reviewed, there are many exceptions to this general pattern. Blumberg's (2003) recent study of "highly sexual" women is illustrative.

Sexual Aggression

A fourth gendered pattern concerns the association between sexuality and aggression. This link has been demonstrated in many domains. Andersen and her colleagues (1999) investigated the dimensions that individuals use to characterize their own sexuality. Both sexes described themselves along a dimension of being romantic, with some individuals seeing themselves as very passionate and loving, and others less so. Men's sexual self-concepts were also characterized by a dimension of aggression, reflected in men's self-ratings on such adjectives as aggressive, powerful, experienced, and domineering. There was no equivalent aggression dimension for women's sexual self-concepts. A second example concerns men's greater use of physical coercion to influence an intimate partner to have sex. It has been estimated that 62% of the sexual assaults committed against women are committed by relational partners (Christopher & Kisler, 2004). Many women who are battered by a boyfriend or husband also report sexual assaults as part of the abuse. Although men are sometimes victims of sexual aggression by women, this is relatively uncommon and less likely to involve sexual intercourse. Sexual aggression has been documented in both gay and lesbian relationships (Christopher & Kisler, 2004), although the use of convenience samples makes it difficult to ascertain typical rates of sexual aggression in this population. (For a review of violence in relationships, see Johnson, this volume.)

Gendered Patterns of Sexual Initiation and Response

Starting in the 1950s, U.S. researchers (e.g., Ehrmann, 1959) documented that in heterosexual couples men typically took the lead in initiating sexual intimacy and women served as gatekeepers, determining whether and when the couple engaged in sexual activities. This pattern was viewed as consistent with men's greater interest in sex and women's greater stake in preserving a good reputation and avoiding pregnancy. During the 1970s, when many young people were inspired by feminist ideas about sexual equality, researchers continued to find evidence that whether a dating couple had intercourse and how early in the relationship they did so were related to the woman's attitudes and prior experience more than to the man's (e.g., Peplau, Rubin, & Hill, 1977). There is considerable evidence for the persistence of this gendered pattern today. In heterosexual relationships, men are commonly more assertive and take the lead in sexual interactions (see Impett & Peplau, 2003, for a review). Early in a heterosexual relationship, men typically initiate touching and sexual intimacy. When college students describe a typical script for a first date, they consistently depict the man as the active partner who takes the lead in initiating sexual contact (Rose & Frieze, 1993). In ongoing relationships, men report initiating sex about twice as often as their female partners or age-mates (Impett & Peplau, 2003). To be sure, many women do initiate sex, but they do so less frequently than their male partners. As a result, women are more often in the position to respond. As in earlier eras, women sometimes act as gatekeepers, slowing the pace of sexual intimacy in a new relationship or determining whether a couple will have sex on a particular occasion.

One factor contributing to this gendered pattern is the persistence of a sexual double standard (see Crawford & Popp, 2003, for a review). Today, only a minority of religious and ethnic groups in the United States endorse an absolute double standard prohibiting sex outside marriage for women but not for men. Nonetheless, in many social settings, women are judged more harshly than men for initiating sexual activity, having casual sex, having sex at a young age, or having sex with many partners. Further, men may use more restrictive standards in evaluating a woman as a potential marriage partner versus a dating partner. Although the specifics of the sexual double standard differ across ethnic and social groups, the persistence of more permissive attitudes toward men's sexual activities continues.

Of course, women do not always strive to limit a couple's sexual activity but may instead welcome a male partner's sexual advances, either because of their own sexual desire or because of their concerns about the relationship. Recently, researchers have analyzed a gendered pattern of sexual initiation and response known as *sexual compliance* (see Impett & Peplau, 2003, for a review). This term refers to situations in which one partner consents to sexual activity that he or she does not personally desire. For example, despite personal misgivings, a teenage girl may agree to have sex with her older boyfriend to preserve their relationship. In ongoing male–female relationships, women are roughly twice as likely as men to report complying with a partner's request when they would personally prefer not to have sex. This pattern builds on many of the sex differences noted earlier including men's greater desire for sex, men's taking the lead to initiate sex, and women's more relational orientation to sex, which may encourage them to resolve a dilemma about unwanted sex by taking their partner's welfare into account.

Finally, although male–female differences in sexuality are larger than those found in areas of human cognition and social behavior such as math performance or interpersonal communication, they are not dichotomous. Researchers studying men's and women's sexuality have consistently emphasized the importance of within-sex variability (e.g., Simpson et al., 2004) and the impact of differences among social and ethnic groups (e.g., Crawford & Popp, 2003).

Family Work

A basic tenet of traditional marital roles has been a division of labor by sex, with men cast as economic providers and women as homemakers. During the past 50 years, women's participation in the paid labor force has increased dramatically, and attitudes about distinctive marital roles for men and women have decreased substantially (e.g., Twenge, 1997). Nonetheless, women continue to shoulder primary responsibility for homemaking and child care. Social scientists refer to the unpaid activities required to feed, clothe, shelter, and care for adults and children as *family work*.

Family Work Is Still Women's Work

The basic facts about family work are simple. Women who live with men typically do the majority of housework and, if they have children, the majority of child care. This is true whether the woman is a full-time homemaker, is employed part time, or has a full-time job (Shelton & John, 1996). Despite minor variations, the same pattern is found across U.S. ethnic groups (Coltrane, 2000b) and throughout the industrialized world (e.g., Batalova & Cohen, 2002). Consequently, marriage has opposite effects on the domestic labor performed by men and by women (Coltrane, 2000b). Single and cohabiting men do more housework than married men. Single and cohabiting women do less housework than married women.

In recent years, employed women in the United States have significantly decreased the amount of time they spend on housework: Those who can afford it often pay for domestic services, and Americans are eating fewer home-cooked meals. The amount of time that men devote to housework and child care has increased slightly over time. Together, these changes for women and men have decreased the gender gap in family work. Nonetheless, Coltrane's (2000b, p. 1212) recent review concluded that "the average woman still does about three times the amount of routine housework as the average man." Even when housework is shared or delegated to assistants, women typically act as household managers. Further, although it is not usually included in discussions of the division of family work, women are much more likely than men to provide care to family members, including aging parents and children who are ill or disabled (e.g., Cancian & Oliker, 2000). Not surprisingly, employed wives have less leisure time than their husbands.

Many factors affect the magnitude of sex differences in the division of labor (see reviews by Coltrane, 2000a, 2000b; Shelton & John, 1996). We highlight several consistent findings.

EMPLOYMENT AND INCOME

Not surprisingly, employed wives spend about a third less time on housework than do full-time homemakers. In general, the more hours a woman works outside the home and the more money she earns, the less work she does at home and the more balanced the division of labor. Although work hours and earnings can make a difference, most women nonetheless continue to do the majority of housework. Interesting exceptions to this pattern sometimes occur, for example, when work schedules constrain women's ability to perform domestic work. The impact of shift work is illustrative (e.g., Deutsch & Saxon, 1998). In some couples, particularly working-class couples with young children, husbands and wives work different shifts, perhaps with the husband working during the day and the wife leaving for a night shift just as her husband returns home. In such cases, it is more common for husbands to take charge of child care and housework in the wife's absence.

GENDER ATTITUDES

Individuals' attitudes about gender and marital roles are related to the amount of family work they perform, although the magnitude of this effect is often fairly small (e.g., Shelton & John, 1996). The match between partners' attitudes may be especially important. An analysis of data from the National Survey of Families and Households by

Greenstein (1996a) is illustrative. Men with nontraditional attitudes whose wives also had nontraditional attitudes did the most family work. Men with traditional attitudes did relatively little work regardless of their wives' attitudes. Other research has sought to understand how couples who have traditional gender attitudes interpret behaviors that are inconsistent with their ideology. Deutsch and Saxon (1998) studied traditional blue-collar married couples in which economic necessity led the wife to take a job and the husband to fill in as primary parent when his wife was at work. Despite their nontraditional behavior, these couples maintained the core belief that the husband was really the primary breadwinner and the wife was really the primary caregiver.

GAY AND LESBIAN COUPLES

Several studies have examined the division of labor in same-sex couples (see review by Peplau & Beals, 2004). Most lesbians and gay men are in dual-earner relationships, so that neither partner is the exclusive breadwinner and each partner has some degree of economic independence. The most common division of labor at home involves flexibility, with partners sharing domestic activities or dividing tasks according to personal preferences or time constraints. In an illustrative study, Kurdek (1993) compared the allocation of household labor in gay, lesbian, and heterosexual married couples, all of whom were cohabiting and childless. Among heterosexual couples, wives typically did most of the housework. In contrast, gay and lesbian couples were more equal in the division of labor. Gay male partners tended to arrive at equality by each partner specializing in certain tasks; lesbian partners were more likely to share tasks. A recent study comparing lesbian and gay couples who obtained civil unions in Vermont to heterosexual married couples also found much greater equality in housework among same-sex couples (Solomon, Rothblum, & Balsam, in press).

PARENTHOOD

Among heterosexual couples, the transition to parenthood typically increases the gen-der gap in family work, with many women adding primary responsibility for child care to their primary responsibility for housework and sometimes reducing their hours of paid work to compensate (Coltrane, 2000a). Fatherhood may also increase men's workload, but it appears that men are more likely to increase their family work by spending time with children rather than doing more housework. It has become more common on weekends to see fathers taking their children to the park or supermarket. A nationally representative study of families with at least one child under age 13 (Yeung, Sandberg, Davis-Kean, & Hofferth, 2001) documented this "weekend father" role among Anglo, Black, and Latino American families. During the week, these fathers spent much less time with their children than their wives did, but on weekends, fathers' time with children increased from 80% to 94% of mothers' time. For some activities, such as coaching or teaching a child sports, fathers spent considerably more time than mothers. On weekdays, dads who earned more money and had longer work hours spent less time with their children than dads with less demanding jobs. In contrast, fathers' work hours did not affect how much time they spent with children on the weekend.

Although research on parenthood among gay and lesbian couples is very limited, it suggests that same-sex partners continue to share major family responsibilities after the arrival of a baby. For example, Chan, Brooks, Raboy, and Patterson (1998) compared 30 lesbian couples and 16 heterosexual couples, all of whom became parents using anonymous donor insemination. In this highly educated sample, both lesbian and heterosexual couples reported a relatively equal division of paid employment, housework, and decision making. However, lesbian couples reported sharing child-care tasks more equally than did heterosexual parents.

Fairness and Marital Quality

In recent years, researchers have addressed a seeming paradox in male–female relationships: Although women perform the majority of family work, most partners view their division of labor as fair (Coltrane, 2000b; Shelton & John, 1996). If the observable "facts" of the matter do not fully determine assessments of fairness, what other factors make a difference? Individuals' gender attitudes appear to be important. Using the National Survey of Families and Households, Greenstein (1996b) found that wives are more likely to perceive the division of household labor as unfair if they have egalitarian rather than traditional gender attitudes. Based on models of justice (e.g., Major, 1993), it has been suggested that women will be most likely to perceive the division of labor as unfair when their relationship differs from their expectations, when they compare their own level of family work to that of their male partner (not to female peers), and when they perceive no legitimate justification for an unequal distribution of family work. Some support for these predictions has been found (Coltrane, 2000a, Kluwer, Heesink & van de Vliert, 2002). Finally, researchers are also investigating the symbolic meaning that partners attach to family work, for instance the extent to which women may view housework not merely as "work" but also as an important sign of love and caring for their family. Perceptions of fairness may have much to do with the broader meanings that individuals attach to housework and child care.

Marital quality is more closely linked to spouses' beliefs about their division of labor than to the actual amount of time each person contributes (see Shelton & John, 1996, for a review). Marital quality tends to be higher when spouses agree about the allocation of family work. Relationship satisfaction is also higher when partners perceived the distribution of family work to be fair, and this effect is stronger for wives with egalitarian rather than traditional attitudes (Greenstein, 1996b). In general, women are more likely than their husbands to have egalitarian attitudes about marital roles and to be dissatisfied with the balance of family work. If women voice concerns about fairness, relationship conflict may ensue. As Coltrane (2000b) noted, "Women are thus faced with a double bind: They can push for change, threatening the relationship, or they

can accept an unbalanced division of labor, labeling it 'fair' (p. 1225)."

Power and Influence

Traditional conceptions of marriage endorse the idea that the husband should be the head of the family, the patriarch with greater authority in leading the family and making important decisions. Newer conceptions of intimate relationships emphasize a more egalitarian model in which partners share in authority and influence (e.g., VanLear, Koerner, & Allen, this volume). Today, advocates for both positions can readily be found, with the traditional view most common among certain religious and ethnic communities and the egalitarian view gaining ground in the mainstream of life in the United States.

Power refers to one partner's ability to influence deliberately the behavior, thoughts, or feelings of the other. In some relationships, there is an imbalance of power, with one person making more decisions, controlling more of the joint activities and resources, winning more arguments and, in general, being in a position of dominance. In other couples, both partners are equally influential. Researchers often assess this balance of power by asking partners to give their personal evaluations of their relationship. Results of the American Couples Study (Blumstein & Schwartz, 1983) are typical. In this sample of more than 3,000 married couples, 64% reported that the balance of power in their marriage was equal. Most other couples said the husband was more powerful and less than 9% said the wife was dominant. Contrary to popular stereotypes, research on Mexican American and African American families has found similar patterns, with a majority of married couples reporting power equality (see Peplau & Campbell, 1989, for a review). Of course, relative equality of power can be achieved in a variety of ways, with some couples engaging in joint decision making and others dividing areas of responsibility based on gender roles or individual preferences.

Several factors can tip the balance of power in favor of one partner over the other, and these tend to favor the male partner in heterosexual couples (Peplau & Campbell, 1989). In heterosexual relationships, social norms traditionally cast the male partner as the initiator and leader. For example, the typical script for a first date depicts the man as taking the lead to ask the woman out, plan their activities, and pay their joint expenses (e.g., Rose & Frieze, 1993). The relative resources of the partners can also make a difference. The partner who earns more money, has more education, or has a more prestigious job tends to have a power advantage, especially if the partner with the greater resources is a man. In couples where the woman has a better job or earns more money, the result is more likely to be shared decision making (e.g., Tichenor, 1999). Research further suggests that the balance of power is affected by each partner's dependence on the relationship – that is, by their relative level of involvement or commitment. To the extent that one partner feels more committed to a relationship and less able to leave, he or she may be at a power disadvantage. This can affect both sexes, but may be somewhat more characteristic of women (e.g., Le & Agnew, 2003). In general relationship satisfaction is similar in egalitarian and male-dominant relationships but lower in female-dominant ones. As noted in a recent review, "Even today, female dominance in a heterosexual relationship is less acceptable to both parties than is male dominance" (Brehm, Miller, Perlman & Campbell, 2002, p. 323).

Lesbians and gay men tend to have egalitarian attitudes and norms about power that emphasize shared-decision making in intimate relationships (see review by Peplau & Spalding, 2000). In an early study, 92% of gay men and 97% of lesbians defined the ideal balance of power as one in which both partners were "exactly equal" (Peplau & Cochran, 1980). In a more recent study (Kurdek, 1995), partners in gay and lesbian couples responded to multiitem measures assessing various facets of equality in an ideal relationship. On average, both lesbians and gay men rated equality as quite important, with lesbians scoring significantly higher on the value of equality than did gay men. It has been estimated that about two thirds of lesbians and gay men describe their current relationship as equal in power, a figure comparable to that typically found for heterosexual couples. In same-sex couples, satisfaction is typically higher among those reporting equal rather than unequal power (Peplau & Spalding, 2000). Although research is limited, it seems likely that the same factors that affect the balance of power in heterosexual relationships – norms, resources, and relative involvement – also apply to lesbians and gay men.

Do men and women differ in the how they try to influence their romantic partners? This question has intrigued researchers for more than 2 decades, but as yet consistent answers have not emerged (e.g., Canary & Emmers-Sommer, 1997). Consider two examples. Some studies have found gender differences in the use of direct styles of influence among heterosexual couples, with men more likely to ask or bargain and women more likely to hint, pout, or withdraw (e.g., Falbo & Peplau, 1980). On closer examination, however, it was found that the tactics used by women were also the tactics used by partners who, regardless of gender, reported having less power in their relationship. This same link between power tactics and the perceived balance of power was also found among lesbians and gay men. In two laboratory experiments with mixed-sex and same-sex dyads, Sagrestano (1992) corroborated this finding, showing that when social power was manipulated such that one partner had greater expertise about the topic of conflict, the use of influence tactics was linked to expertise – not to gender. Men and women in similar power positions used the same strategies, with high-power individuals preferring persuasion, reasoning, and discussion.

In another line of work, Christensen and colleagues (see review by Eldridge & Christensen, 2002) investigated the demand–withdraw pattern of interaction during couple conflict. In this pattern, one partner seeks to discuss a relationship issue or problem and the other tries to avoid the topic. Overall, women are more likely to be the pursuer and men the distancing partner. Although gender socialization may contribute to this pattern by encouraging women to be expressive and relationship-oriented, it is only part of the story. Other factors also matter. In a study of gay, lesbian, and heterosexual couples, Walczynski (1997) found that the demand–withdraw pattern was linked to the partners' perception of power in the relationship. The partner who scored higher on power was more likely to be demanding in conflict discussions. The nature of the conflict itself is also important (Eldridge & Christensen, 2002). The wife–demand and husband–withdraw pattern is common when the wife wants a change in the relationship and the husband does not. In contrast, when the husband wants a change, both husband–demand and wife–demand are equally likely to occur. In short, there is no simple way to characterize "men's" and "women's" styles of influence. A range of factors including the goal of the influence attempt, the partners' relative power and expertise, and individual differences in personality can all make a difference.

Marriage and Health

Satisfying personal relationships enhance the mental and physical well-being of both women and men. Research demonstrating this point has focused on heterosexual marriage and includes studies with a diverse array of self-report and physiological measures (see reviews by Kiecolt-Glaser & Newton, 2001; Waite & Gallagher, 2000). Compared with their unmarried peers, married individuals are less likely to die from such leading causes of death as cancer, coronary heart disease, stroke, pneumonia, cirrhosis of the liver, automobile accidents, murder, and suicide. To some extent, this marriage benefit reflects selection effects: Healthy individuals are more likely to marry and stay married. However, there is growing evidence that marital relations can themselves enrich and prolong life. Gender also plays a role, and we will consider two sex

differences in detail. First, the health benefits of marriage are greater for men than for women, as are the detrimental effects of divorce and bereavement. Second, the health consequences of marriage are more closely linked to marital quality for women than for men.

Why Men Derive Greater Health Benefits From Marriage Do Women

Evidence from diverse sources documents that husbands tend to gain larger health benefits from marriage than do wives. For instance, unmarried women have a 50% greater mortality than married women, but unmarried men have a 250% greater mortality than married men (Ross, Mirowsky, & Goldsteen, 1990). Three explanations merit consideration.

THE SINGLE LIFE

Waite and Gallagher (2000) argued that "the reason that getting a wife boosts your health more than acquiring a husband is not that marriage warps women, but that single men lead such warped lives" (p. 164). Indeed, single men are much more likely than single women to drink to excess, drive too fast, get into fights, participate in dangerous sports, and engage in other unhealthy and risky behaviors (Umberson, 1987). Single women, in contrast, lead relatively settled, healthy lives, at least compared with single men. In short, men's health may improve dramatically through marriage because men often start off so poorly. A longitudinal study of 6,000 families is illustrative (Waite & Gallagher, 2000). Among singles, 8 out of every 10 women but only 6 out of 10 men who were alive at age 48 survived until at least age 65. In contrast, among the married, 9 of 10 men and women lived until retirement age.

HEALTH PROMOTION

Both husbands and wives benefit when a spouse attempts to protect their health (e.g., Umberson, 1992). However, women are more likely than men to engage in health-promoting activities by attempting to monitor and control their husband's health (Umberson, Chen, House, Hopkins,

& Slaten, 1996). Women generally possess greater knowledge than men about health-related issues and are more likely to monitor their own health status. Some married women extend these "social control" services to their husbands by discouraging drinking and smoking, cooking low-fat meals, scheduling medical appointments, and checking their husband's compliance with physicians' orders. In a study of married couples, 80% of men named their spouse as the primary person who tried to control their health, whereas only 59% of women listed their husband (Umberson, 1992). Women, in contrast, were more likely than men to report that their friends and female relatives attempt to influence their health behaviors.

EMOTIONAL SUPPORT

Emotional support, defined as "expressions of care, concern, love, and interest, especially during times or stress or upset" (Burleson, 2003, p. 2), has well-documented effects on physical and psychological health (Uchino, Cacioppo, & Kiecolt-Glaser, 1996). Men may benefit more from marriage than women because they rely on their wives as a primary source of emotional support and because women are good at giving the kinds of support that men want. Men typically name their wives as their sole or most important source of support and the one in whom they confide personal problems (e.g., Umberson et al., 1996). Women, in contrast, are more likely to turn to other female relatives and close friends for social support. Further, considerable evidence indicates that women are, on average, more skillful providers of emotional support than are men, providing messages that acknowledge, elaborate on, and legitimate their partner's concerns (e.g., MacGeorge, Clark, & Gillihan, 2002).

The Stronger Marital Quality–Health Link among Women Than Men

Women's health is more closely tied to the quality of their marriage than is true for men. In a comprehensive review, Kiecolt-Glaser and Newton (2001) presented evidence from dozens of studies showing that women's

physical health depends much more on the quality of the marriage than does men's. Across such diverse dependent measures as objective physiological responses, self-reported health, pain, and physiological assessments taken during marital interactions, marital quality was more strongly associated with health outcomes for women than for men. The gender differences in physiological reactions to marital conflict are particularly striking. For instance, even among a sample of relatively satisfied couples in stable and enduring marriages (lasting an average of 42 years), women's endocrine levels changed considerably more during conflicts than did men's (Kiecolt-Glaser et al., 1997). Most notably, these gender differences in response to marital conflict are at variance with broader physiological patterns of response to other types of acute stressors in which men show an elevated response.

In their review, Kiecolt-Glaser and Newton (2001) identified several gender-linked factors that may influence the greater association between marital quality and health outcomes for women than for men. First, women's interdependent traits and self-processes may make them more physiologically and psychologically responsive to the emotional quality of their marital interactions (Cross & Madson, 1997). Second, women's greater tendency to focus on others to the exclusion of themselves (referred to as "unmitigated communion") may increase their vulnerability to relationship stressors (see review in Helgeson, 1994). Third, the stress associated with wives' greater responsibility for household labor may contribute to pathways leading from marital functioning to health outcomes.

At present, systematic research on health among gay and lesbian couples is lacking. Given the current controversy about the merits of legalizing same-sex marriage, such research would be of great value.

Conclusion

In this review, we have identified six relatively well-documented differences between women and men in intimate relationships. Despite claims that men and women value widely different characteristics in their romantic partners, research shows that both sexes want partners who are honest, trustworthy, and responsive. Men's tendency to seek youth and beauty and women's tendency to seek social status and resources occur against this backdrop of commonality. Men and women in heterosexual relationships appear to have similar standards for the ingredients in a good relationship, but men may be more likely than women to have a partner who meets their expectations. There is evidence that relationships are more central to women's lives than to men's, as reflected in women's greater tendency to have an interdependent self-concept, to report greater commitment in relationships, and to engage in more relationship maintenance behaviors. Turning to sexuality, gender differences in sexual interest, erotic plasticity, sexual compliance, and sexual aggression are well documented, as is women's preference for close relationships as a context for sexuality. In heterosexual couples, women continue to perform the majority of housework and child care, even if they work full time for pay. Today, most couples, both heterosexual and same-sex, describe their relationships as relatively equal in power. When heterosexual relationships are unequal in power, however, it is more often the man who is dominant. A satisfying close relationship can promote both psychological and physical health, but these benefits appear to be greater for men than for women. Although research on lesbians and gay men is limited, gender seems to be a more important determinant of relationship experiences than sexual orientation. Many similarities exist between lesbian and heterosexual women and between gay and heterosexual men. The one major exception concerns the division of family work, where same-sex couples typically share housework and child care to a greater extent than heterosexuals.

Does Jessie Bernard's (1972) characterization of "his" and "her" marriages stand up to several decades of empirical research?

The answer depends on one's perspective. Some researchers and social commentators – the gender maximizers – view human experience through a lens of difference. Others – the gender minimizers – point to the basic humanity of both sexes and emphasize points of commonality. In some measure, the maximizer–minimizer controversy results from attending to different aspects of human behavior and experience. In everyday life, men and women often do engage in quite different activities. Women are more likely to cook for their family, change diapers, or remind a partner to refill a prescription. At a more basic level, however, men and women are remarkably similar – both fall in love, form enduring attachments, suffer the pain of loneliness, and benefit from social support. Differences between the sexes are never either–or dichotomies, but rather matters of degree. The variability within each sex is often profound. Some men take pride in sharing family work responsibilities. Some women are sexual enthusiasts who enjoy recreational sex with casual partners. "His" and "her" relationships are, depending on one's perspective, both similar and different.

Author's Note

The first author was supported by a Sexuality Research Fellowship from the Social Science Research Council. We are grateful to Cristina Nguyen for library assistance and to Adam Fingerhut, Steven Gordon, Martie Haselton, and Annette Stanton for valuable comments on an earlier draft of this paper.

References

Andersen, B. L., Cyranowski, J. M., & Espindle, D. (1999). Men's sexual self-schema. *Journal Personality and Social Psychology*, 76, 645–661.

Bailey, J. M., Gaulin, S., Agyei, Y., & Gladue, B. A. (1994). Effects of gender and sexual orientation on evolutionarily relevant aspects of human mating psychology. *Journal of Personality and Social Psychology*, 66, 1081–1093.

Batalova, J. A., & Cohen, P. N. (2002). Premarital cohabitation and housework: Couples in cross-national perspective. *Journal of Marriage and Family, 64*, 743–755.

Baumeister, R. F. (2000). Gender differences in erotic plasticity: The female sex drive as socially flexible and responsive. *Psychological Bulletin, 126*, 347–374.

Baumeister, R. F., Catanese, K. R., & Vohs, K. D. (2001). Is there a gender difference in strength of sex drive? *Personality and Social Psychology Review, 5*, 242–273.

Baumeister, R. F., & Sommer, K. L. (1997). What do men want?: Gender differences and two spheres of belongingness: Comment on Cross and Madson (1997). *Psychological Bulletin, 122*, 38–44.

Bernard, J. (1972). *The future of marriage*. New York: Bantam Books.

Blumberg, E. S. (2003). The lives and voices of highly sexual women. *Journal of Sex Research, 40*, 146–157.

Blumstein, P., & Schwartz, P. (1983). *American couples*. New York: Pocket Books.

Brehm, S. S., Miller, R. S., Perlman, D., & Campbell, S. M. (2002). *Intimate relationships* (3rd ed.). Boston: McGraw-Hill.

Burleson, B. R. (2003). The experience and effects of emotional support: What the study of cultural and gender differences can tell us about close relationships, emotion, and interpersonal communication. *Personal Relationships, 10*, 1–23.

Buss, D. M. (1991). Conflict in married couples: Personality predictors of anger and upset. *Journal of Personality, 59*, 663–688.

Buss, D. M., & Schmitt, D. P. (1993). Sexual strategies theory: An evolutionary perspective on human mating. *Psychological Review, 100*, 204–232.

Buss, D. M., Shackelford, T. K., Kirkpatrick, L. A., & Larsen, R. J. (2001). A half century of mate preferences: The cultural evolution of values. *Journal of Marriage and the Family, 63*, 491–503.

Canary, D. J., & Emmers-Sommer, T. M. (1997). *Sex and gender differences in personal relationships*. New York: Guilford Press.

Cancian, F. M., & Oliker, S. J. (2000). *Caring and gender*. New York: Altamira Press.

Chan, R. W., Brooks, R. C., Raboy, B., & Patterson, C. J. (1998). Division of labor among les-bian and heterosexual parents. *Journal of Family Psychology, 12*, 402–419.

Chodorow, N. (1978). *The reproduction of mothering*. Berkeley: University of California Press.

Christopher, F. S., & Kisler, T. S. (2004). Sexual aggression in romantic relationships. In J. Harvey, A. Wenzel, & S. Sprecher (Eds.), *The handbook of sexuality in close relationships* (pp. 287–309). Mahwah, NJ: Erlbaum.

Coltrane, S. (2000a). *Gender and families*. New York: Altamira Press

Coltrane, S. (2000b). Research on household labor. *Journal of Marriage and Family, 62*, 1208–1233.

Crawford, M., & Popp, D. (2003). Sexual double standards: A review and methodological critique of two decades of research. *Journal of Sex Research, 40*, 12–26.

Cross, S. E., Bacon, P. L., & Morris. M. L. (2000). The relational-interdependent self-construal and relationships. *Journal of Personality and Social Psychology, 78*, 791–808.

Cross, S. E., & Madson, L. (1997). Models of the self: Self-construals and gender. *Psychological Bulletin, 122*, 5–37.

Dainton, M., & Stafford, L. (1993). Routine maintenance behaviors: A comparison of relationship type, partner similarity and sex differences. *Journal of Social and Personal Relationships, 10*, 255–271.

Deutsch, F. M., & Saxon, S. E. (1998). Traditional ideologies, nontraditional lives. *Sex Roles, 38*, 331–362.

Diamond, L. M. (2003). Was it a phase? Young women's relinquishment of lesbian/bisexual identities over a 5-year period. *Journal of Personality and Social Psychology, 84*, 352–364.

Dindia, K., & Baxter, L. (1987). Strategies for maintaining and repairing marital relationships. *Journal of Social and Personal Relationships, 4*, 143–158.

Duffy, S. M., & Rusbult, C. E. (1985/1986). Satisfaction and commitment in homosexual and heterosexual relationships. *Journal of Homosexuality, 12*, 1–23.

Ehrmann, W. (1959). *Premarital dating behavior*. New York: Holt.

Eldridge, K. A. & Christensen, A. (2002). Demand–withdraw communication during couple conflict: A review and analysis. In P. Noller & J. A. Feeney (Eds.), *Understanding marriage: Developments in the study of couple interaction.* (pp. 289–322). New York: Cambridge University Press.

Falbo, T., & Peplau, L. A. (1980). Power strategies in intimate relationships. *Journal of Personality and Social Psychology, 38*, 618–628.

Gangestad, S. W., & Cousins, A. J. (2001). Adaptive design, female mate preferences, and shifts across the menstrual cycle. *Annual Review of Sex Research, 12*, 145–185.

Gilligan, C. (1982). *In a different voice: Psychological theory and women's development.* Cambridge, MA: Harvard University Press.

Glenn, E. N. (1987). Gender and the family. In B. B. Hess & M. M. Ferree (Eds.), *Analyzing gender: A handbook of social science research* (pp. 348–380). Newbury Park, CA: Sage.

Gray, J. (1993). *Men are from Mars, women are from Venus.* New York: HarperCollins.

Greenstein, T. N. (1996a). Husbands' participation in domestic labor: Interactive effects of wives' and husbands' gender ideologies. *Journal of Marriage and the Family, 58*, 585–595.

Greenstein, T. N. (1996b). Gender ideology and perceptions of the fairness of the division of household labor: Effects on marital quality. *Social Forces, 74*, 1029–1042.

Harvey, J., Wenzel, A., & Sprecher, S. (Eds.) (2004). *Handbook of sexuality in close relationships.* Mahwah, NJ: Erlbaum.

Helgeson, V. S. (1994). Relation of agency and communion to well-being: Evidence and potential explanations. *Psychological Bulletin, 116*, 412–428.

Huston, T. L., & Ashmore, R. D. (1986). Women and men in personal relationships. In R. D. Ashmore & F. K. Del Boca (Eds.), *The social psychology of female–male relations* (pp. 167–209). New York: Academic Press.

Impett, E., & Peplau, L. A. (2003). Sexual compliance: Gender, motivational, and relationship perspectives. *Journal of Sex Research, 40*, 87–100.

Kiecolt-Glaser, J. K., Glaser, R., Cacioppo, J. T., MacCallum, R. C., Snydersmith, M., et al. (1997). Marital conflict in older adults: Endocrinological and immunological correlates. *Psychosomatic Medicine, 59*, 339–349.

Kiecolt-Glaser, J. K., & Newton, T. L. (2001). Marriage and health: His and hers. *Psychological Bulletin, 127*, 472–503.

Kluwer, E. S., Heesink, J. A. M., & Van de Vliert, E. (2002). The division of labor across the transition to parenthood: A justice perspective. *Journal of Marriage and Family, 64*, 930–943.

Kurdek, L. A. (1993). The allocation of household labor in gay, lesbian, and heterosexual married couples. *Journal of Social Issues, 49*(3), 127–139.

Kurdek, L. A. (1995). Developmental changes in relationship quality in gay and lesbian cohabiting couples. *Developmental Psychology, 31*, 86–94.

Le, B., & Agnew, C. R. (2003). Commitment and its theorized determinants: A meta-analysis of the Investment Model. *Personal Relationships, 10*, 37–57.

MacGeorge, E. L., Clark, R. A., & Gillihan, S. J. (2002). Sex differences in the provision of skillful emotional support: The mediating role of self-efficacy. *Communication Reports, 15*, 17–28.

Major, B. (1993). Gender, entitlement, and the distribution of family labor. *Journal of Social Issues, 49*, 141–159.

Markman, H. J., & Kraft, S. A. (1989). Men and women in marriage: Dealing with gender differences in marital therapy. *Behavior Therapist, 12*, 51–56.

Markus, H. R., & Kitayama, S. (1994). A collective fear of the collective: Implications for selves and theories of selves. *Personality and Social Psychology Bulletin, 20*, 568–579.

Okami, P., & Shackelford, T. K. (2001). Human sex differences in sexual psychology and behavior. *Annual Review of Sex Research, 12*, 186–241.

Oliver, M. B., & Hyde, J. S. (1993). Gender differences in sexuality: A meta-analysis. *Psychological Bulletin, 114*, 29–51.

Parsons, T. (1955). The American family. In T. Parsons & R. F. Bales (Eds.), *Family, socialization, and interaction process* (pp. 3–33). New York: Free Press.

Peplau, L. A. (2003). Human sexuality: How do men and women differ? *Current Directions in Psychological Science, 12*(2), 37–40.

Peplau, L. A., & Beals, K. P. (2004). The family lives of lesbians and gay men. In A. L. Vangelisti (Ed.), *Handbook of family communication* (pp. 233–248). Mahwah, NJ: Erlbaum.

Peplau, L. A., & Campbell, S. M. (1989). The balance of power in dating and marriage. In J. Freeman (Ed.), *Women: A feminist perspective.* (4th ed.; pp. 121–137). Palo Alto, CA: Mayfield.

Peplau, L. A., & Cochran, S. D. (1980, September). *Sex differences in values concerning love relationships.* Paper presented at the annual meeting of the American Psychological Association, Montreal, Canada.

Peplau, L. A., Fingerhut, A., & Beals, K. (2004). Sexuality in the relationships of lesbians and gay men. In J. Harvey, A. Wenzel, & S. Sprecher (Eds.), *Handbook of sexuality in close relationships* (pp. 349–369). Mahwah, NJ: Erlbaum.

Peplau, L. A., & Garnets, L. D. (2000). A new paradigm for understanding women's sexuality and sexual orientation. *Journal of Social Issues*, 56, 329–350.

Peplau, L. A., Hill, C. T., & Rubin, Z. (1993). Sex-role attitudes in dating and marriage: A 15-year follow-up of the Boston Couples Study. *Journal of Social Issues*, 49(3), 31–52.

Peplau, L. A., & Jones, R. (Eds.) (1982). Homosexual couples [Special issue]. *Journal of Homosexuality*, 8(2).

Peplau, L. A., Rubin, Z., & Hill, C. T. (1977). Sexual intimacy in dating relationships. *Journal of Social Issues*, 33(2), 86–109.

Peplau, L. A., & Spalding, L. R. (2000). The close relationships of lesbians, gay men, and bisexuals. In C. Hendrick & S. S. Hendrick (Eds.), *Close relationships: A sourcebook* (pp. 111–123). Thousand Oaks, CA: Sage.

Ragsdale, J. D. (1996). Gender, satisfaction level, and the use of relational maintenance strategies in marriage. *Communication Monographs*, 63, 354–369.

Regan, P. C., & Berscheid, E. (1996). Beliefs about the state, goals, and objects of sexual desire. *Journal of Sex and Marital Therapy*, 22, 110–120.

Rose, S., & Frieze, I. H. (1993). Young singles' contemporary dating scripts. *Sex Roles*, 28, 499–509.

Ross, C. E., Mirowsky, J., & Goldsteen, K. (1990). The impact of the family on health: The decade in review. *Journal of Marriage and the Family*, 52, 1059–1078.

Rusbult, C. E. (1980). Commitment and satisfaction in romantic associations: A test of the investment model. *Journal of Experimental Social Psychology*, 16, 172–186.

Rusbult, C. E., & Van Lange, P. A. M. (1996). Interdependence processes. In E. T. Higgins & A. W. Kruglanski (Eds.), *Social psychology: Handbook of basic principles* (pp. 564–596). New York: Guilford Press.

Sagrestano, L. M. (1992). Power strategies in interpersonal relationships: The effects of expertise and gender. *Psychology of Women Quarterly*, 16, 481–495.

Scharfe, E., & Bartholomew, K. (1994). Reliability and stability of adult attachment patterns. *Personal Relationships*, 1, 23–42.

Schmitt, D. P., Alcalay, L., Allensworth, M., Allik, J., Ault, L., Austers, I., et al. (2003). Are men universally more dismissing than women? Gender differences in romantic attachment across 62 cultural regions. *Personal Relationships*, 10, 307–331.

Schmitt, D. P., Alcalay, L., Allik, J., Ault, L., Austers, I., Bennett, K. L., et al. (2003). Universal sex differences in the desire for sexual variety: Tests from 52 nations, 6 continents, and 13 islands. *Journal of Personality and Social Psychology*, 85, 85–104.

Shelton, B. A., & John, D. (1996). The division of household labor. *Annual Review of Sociology*, 22, 299–322.

Simpson, J. A., Wilson, C. L., & Winterheld, H. A. (2004). Sociosexuality and romantic relationships. In J. H. Harvey, A. Wenzel, & S. Sprecher (Eds.), *Handbook of sexuality in close relationships* (pp. 87–112). Mahwah, NJ: Erlbaum.

Solomon, S. E., Rothblum, E. D., & Balsam, K. F. (in press). Money, housework, sex, and conflict: Same-sex couples in civil unions, those not in civil unions, and heterosexual married siblings. *Sex Roles*.

Sprecher, S., Sullivan, Q., & Hatfield, E. (1994). Mate selection preferences: Gender differences examined in a national sample. *Journal of Personality and Social Psychology*, 66, 1074–1080.

Stafford, L., & Canary, D. J. (1991). Maintenance strategies and romantic relationship type, gender, and relational characteristics. *Journal of Social and Personal Relationships*, 8, 217–242.

Stafford, L., Dainton, M., & Haas, S. (2000). Measuring routine and strategic relational maintenance. *Communication Monographs*, 67, 306–323.

Symons, D. (1979). *The evolution of human sexuality*. New York: Oxford University Press.

Tichenor, V. J. (1999). Status and income as gendered resources: The case of marital power. *Journal of Marriage and the Family*, 61, 638–650.

Twenge, J. M. (1997). Attitudes toward women, 1970–1995. *Psychology of Women Quarterly*, 21, 35–51.

Uchino, B. N., Cacioppo, J. T., & Kiecolt-Glaser, J. K. (1996). The relationship between social support and physiological processes: A review with emphasis on underlying mechanisms and implications for health. *Psychological Bulletin, 119,* 488–531.

Umberson, D. (1987). Family status and health behaviors: Social control as a dimension of social integration. *Journal of Health and Social Behavior, 28,* 306–319.

Umberson, D. (1992). Gender, marital status and the social control of health behavior. *Social Science and Medicine, 34,* 907–917.

Umberson, D., Chen, M. D., House, J. S., Hopkins, K., & Slaten, E. (1996). The effect of social relationships on psychological well-being: Are men and women really so different? *American Sociological Review, 61,* 837–857.

Vangelisti, A. L., & Daly, J. A. (1997). Gender differences in standards for romantic relationships. *Personal Relationships, 4,* 203–219.

Waite, L. J., & Gallagher, M. (2000). *The case for marriage: Why married people are happier, healthier, and better off financially.* New York: Doubleday.

Walczynski, P. T. (1997). *Power, personality, and conflictual interaction.* Unpublished doctoral dissertation, University of California, Los Angeles.

Winstead, B. A., Derlega, V. J., & Rose, S. (1997). *Gender and close relationships.* Thousand Oaks, CA: Sage.

Wood, J. T. (Ed.). (1996). *Gendered relationships.* Mountain View, CA: Mayfield.

Yeung, W. J., Sandberg, J. F., Davis-Kean, P. E., & Hoferth, S. L. (2001). Children's time with fathers in intact families. *Journal of Marriage and Family, 63,* 136–154.

Yoder, J. D., & Kahn, A S. (2003). Making gender comparisons more meaningful. *Psychology of Women Quarterly, 27,* 281–290.

CHAPTER 16

The Intimate Same-Sex Relationships of Sexual Minorities

Lisa M. Diamond

The 1983 publication of Blumstein and Schwartz's *American Couples* marked a turning point in research on lesbian and gay relationships. During the 10 years before the publication of this volume, which reported the most detailed and thoroughgoing comparisons to date between heterosexual and same-sex couples, less than 50 books, chapters, or articles in the psychological literature had focused specifically on lesbian and gay couples. In the 10 years after the book's publication, the number of publications increased five-fold, and nearly doubled again during the next 10 years. The explosion of research on this topic reflects a growing awareness of the centrality of intimate relationships to the lives of lesbian, gay, and bisexual individuals – studies have found that between 40% and 60% of gay men and 50% and 80% of lesbians are partnered (reviewed in Peplau & Spalding, 2000), and the majority of lesbian, gay, and bisexual individuals would like the option of formalizing such relationships through same-sex marriage (Kaiser Foundation, 2001, November).

The sophistication of research on this topic has also increased over the past 20 years. Whereas early studies were characterized by small, homogeneous samples, collection of data from only one member of the couple, the use of measures with unknown psychometric properties, exclusive reliance on self-report data, and lack of long-term longitudinal assessment, all of these weaknesses have been remedied in more recent work. This has made it possible for researchers to move beyond the early focus on basic differences between same-sex and heterosexual couples to more complex investigations of why same-sex couples resemble and differ from heterosexual couples and from one another.

This chapter provides an overview of current research on same-sex intimate relationships, emphasizing the most central and well-researched domains: relationship initiation, maintenance, satisfaction, and dissolution, gender-related dynamics, sexuality and sexual exclusivity, and violence and abuse. The chapter begins with a discussion of the implicit theoretical frameworks that have guided research on this area and concludes by identifying some of the most interesting and complex questions that remain to be addressed by future research.

First, however, definitional issues require attention. Although the majority of research in this area addresses the *same-sex* intimate relationships of *openly identified* lesbians and gay men, this actually provides a somewhat restricted focus: not all lesbian- and gay-identified individuals participate in exclusively same-sex relationships, and not all individuals who participate in same-sex relationships identify as lesbian or gay. Such individuals (i.e., bisexual and "unlabeled" men and women) have been drastically understudied in relationship research, despite the fact that such individuals collectively outnumber openly identified lesbians and gay men (Laumann, Gagnon, Michael, & Michaels, 1994). In growing acknowledgment of this fact, researchers increasingly use the term *sexual minorities* to refer to all men and women whose same-sex attractions or behaviors place them outside conventional heterosexual norms. This chapter uses this terminology, but nonetheless retains the descriptors *lesbian, gay,* and *bisexual* when summarizing studies or research traditions that specifically recruited research participants on the basis of lesbian, gay and bisexual identification.

Theoretical Perspectives on Same-Sex Relationships

Although there is no unified body of psychological theory specifically purporting to explain how and why same-sex couples do and do not differ from heterosexual couples, much research is implicitly guided by two explanatory frameworks. The first emphasizes the impact of *social stigmatization and homophobia* on sexual-minority couples, and the second focuses on the influence of *gender-related dynamics* (i.e., combining two men or two women in the same relationships).

Stigmatization

Although tolerance and acceptance of same-sex sexuality have been gradually increasing (Loftus, 2001), considerable prejudice and sometimes outright condemnation continue to exist. A recent national survey by the Kaiser Foundation (2001) found that more than three fourths of lesbian, gay, and bisexual survey respondents reported experiencing some form of prejudice or discrimination. Social stigmatization creates a range of unique social and psychological challenges for same-sex couples, such as the threat of physical violence (i.e., Brenner, 1995), disapproval or denial of one's relationship from either partner's family of origin (Caron & Ulin, 1997; LaSala, 2000; Oswald, 2002; Patterson, 2000), and also low-level stressors such as difficulty making hotel room reservations (Jones, 1996), receiving poor service and rude treatment during routine shopping (Walters & Curran, 1996), or uncertainty about bringing one's partner to family functions (Caron & Ulin, 1997; Oswald, 2002).

Of course, such factors are likely to vary dramatically as a function of different cultures' attitudes toward same-sex sexuality. Given that the bulk of research on same-sex couples is conducted in the United States, it is important to keep in mind that Americans are particularly conservative in this regard. Widmer, Treas, and Newcomb's (1998) analysis of 24 industrialized countries participating in the International Social Survey Program found that 70% of Americans believe that homosexual sex is "always wrong," compared with 39% of Canadians, 58% of British, 45% of Spaniards, and 42% of West Germans. The most conservative attitudes were found in Northern Ireland (80% reporting "always wrong"), Hungary (83%), and the Philippines (84%), whereas the most accepting attitudes were found in the Netherlands (19%). Such variation must be taken into account when drawing inferences about the relevance of social stigma for same-sex couples across diverse cultural contexts. It also bears noting that no research has systematically tested whether same-sex couples living in more tolerant communities, cultures, or nations have substantially different relationship dynamics or outcomes than those living in more stigmatizing environments. Some research, however, has found that variation in gender- and sexuality-related childhood rejection relates to adult orientations toward interpersonal relationships (Allen & Land, 1999; Landolt, Bartholomew, Saffrey, Oram, & Perlman, 2004). Thus, links between social stigmatization of same-sex sexuality and couple functioning might be mediated by immediate, day-to-day stress *or* by cumulative influences on the development of interpersonal attitudes and orientations, both of which warrant substantive research attention.

Gender

Gender differences in interpersonal attitudes, cognitions, and behaviors, and their implications for couple functioning, have long been topics of vigorous research and debate, and studies of same-sex couples have provided unique opportunities to examine how broadly gender-related effects operate. One of the most common research questions is whether sexual-minority individuals arc "gender-inverted" in their interpersonal functioning, such that gay men resemble heterosexual women and lesbians resemble heterosexual men, or whether sexual minorities show the same gender differences in relationship behavior that have been long-observed among heterosexuals.

Research findings support the latter view. Although some sexual-minority men and women are, in fact, gender-*atypical* in appearance, behavior, or interests (reviewed in Bailey, 1996), this does not generally extend to relationship behavior. With respect to well-documented gender differences such as men's greater interest in casual sex, their greater emphasis on a partner's youth and physical attractiveness, and women's greater interest in emotionally invested relationships, gay men and lesbians show the same gender differences that

have been observed among heterosexuals (e.g., Bailey, Gaulin, Agyei, & Gladue, 1994; Hayes, 1995; Kenrick, Keefe, Bryan, & Barr, 1995). Some have interpreted these findings to indicate that men and women – regardless of sexual orientation – are endowed with fundamentally different mating "programs" that evolved to serve their distinct reproductive challenges (Bailey et al., 1994), whereas others have argued that sexual minorities simply undergo the same gender socialization as do heterosexuals (Ritter & Terndrup, 2002). Regardless of interpretation, such studies have proven valuable in prompting researchers to articulate and empirically test otherwise implicit assumptions about links between sexual orientation and gender-specific behavior. They have also prompted useful investigations of how *combining* two men or two women in a couple relationship tends to magnify gender-specific patterns. Results from such studies, some of which are reviewed subsequently, have helped to explain not only how same-sex relationships differ from those of heterosexuals, but how the relationships of sexual-minority *women* differ from those of sexual-minority *men*.

Keeping these implicit frameworks of gender and social stigma in mind helps to provide a context for interpreting the different ways in which research questions in this area have historically been formulated and answered. For example, studies that emphasize social stigmatization might presume that its effects are gender-neutral, and may therefore fail to compare female–female with male–male couples. In contrast, approaches that emphasize gender may fail to assess the specific sociocultural context in which different couples are embedded or to consider the possibility that "gender magnification" effects might vary as a function of local community attitudes toward homosexuality *and* toward gender conformity. Clearly, future research exploring the *intersections* of gender and social stigma will produce the most useful and informative results; for the time being, the extant findings reviewed here must be interpreted with an eye to what different studies do and do not assess and adjust for.

Relationship Initiation

Given the historical stigmatization and secrecy surrounding same-sex sexuality, much research on sexual minorities' relationships has focused on how they *find* eligible same-sex partners to begin with. Whereas older cohorts of sexual minorities did, in fact, rely on lesbian and gay bars and clubs to find potential partners (Berger, 1990), this is no longer necessarily the case. The progressively increasing societal openness regarding same-sex sexuality has allowed many sexual minorities to meet potential partners through a diverse range of channels, including work, school, friends, and recreational activities (Bryant & Demian, 1994; Elze, 2002). As for individuals living in more rural, isolated areas with smaller sexual-minority populations, the Internet has emerged into an important and highly utilized resource for finding and getting to know potential same-sex partners with minimal risk of exposure (Peplau & Beals, 2003).

Perhaps the most distinctive feature of sexual-minority relationship initiation is the tendency for sexual minorities to develop romantic relationships out of close same-sex friendships (Nardi, 1999; Rose & Zand, 2000). Lesbians, in particular, frequently follow a "friendship script" in developing new relationships, in which emotional compatibility and communication are as important – if not more important – than explicit sexual interest or interaction (Rose & Zand, 2000; Rose, Zand, & Cimi, 1993). Gay men also frequently become involved with same-sex friends, but these involvements sometimes remain exclusively sexual rather than developing into long-term partnerships (Nardi, 1999). Furthermore, in contrast to the "friendship script" of relationship development observed among lesbians, gay men's relationship scripts are more likely to involve the establishment of sexual intimacy prior to the development of emotional intimacy

(Rose et al., 1993). Lesbian couples have also been observed to follow a somewhat accelerated pathway to emotional exclusivity and commitment compared with heterosexuals and gay men. Cini and Malafi (1991) for example, found that lesbian couples often considered themselves an exclusive, emotionally involved couple by the fifth date. This emphasis on serious rather than casual involvement appears to become more pronounced at later stages of life. Rose and Zand (2000) found that among lesbians in middle and late adulthood, dating was so clearly oriented around the search for a potential long-term partner that women preferred to speak of themselves as "courting" than "dating." As noted earlier, these findings are consistent with gender differences that have been observed among heterosexuals, particularly regarding women's greater "relational" orientation in comparison to men (reviewed in Cross & Madson, 1997).

Relationship Maintenance and Satisfaction

Although same-sex relationships have been historically stereotyped as fleeting, unhealthy, and unhappy (Testa, Kinder, & Ironson, 1987), numerous studies over the past 20 years have confirmed that same-sex couples are generally as satisfied and dissatisfied as other-sex couples, for the same basic reasons: the balance of perceived rewards to perceived costs (Beals, Impett, & Peplau, 2002; Duffy & Rusbult, 1985). As with heterosexual couples, satisfaction in same-sex couples is positively associated with partners' similarity in attitudes and values (Kurdek & Schmitt, 1987; Kurdek & Schnopp-Wyatt, 1997) as well as demographic background (R. L. Hall & Greene, 2002), perceptions of fairness and equity (Eldridge & Gilbert, 1990; Kurdek, 1989, 1995, 1998b; Kurdek & Schmitt, 1986; Peplau, Padesky, & Hamilton, 1982; Schreurs & Buunk, 1996), and a mutual emphasis on dyadic attachment – that is, shared activities, togetherness, intimacy, commitment, and sexual exclusivity (Deenen, Gijs, & van

Naerssen, 1994; Eldridge & Gilbert, 1990; Peplau & Cochran, 1981).

Same-sex relationships also show similar levels of stability as heterosexual relationships. One survey found that 14% of lesbian couples and 25% of gay male couples had lived together for 10 or more years (Bryant & Demian, 1994). Blumstein and Schwartz's (1983) *American Couples* study found that over an 18-month period, 16% of the same-sex male and 22% of the same-sex female couples broke up, compared with 17% of the unmarried heterosexual couples and 4% of the married heterosexual couples. A more recent 5-year longitudinal study found breakup rates of 7% among married heterosexuals, 14% for cohabiting same-sex male couples and 16% for cohabiting same-sex female couples (Kurdek, 1998b).

Notably, several studies (Beals et al., 2002; Kurdek, 1992, 2000a) have found that the basic determinants of relationship stability are the same for same-sex couples as for heterosexual couples: specifically, the combination of *attractors* to the relationship, such as love and satisfaction, with psychological and structural *barriers to dissolution*, such as the lack of desirable alternatives, legal marriage, children, joint property, and so on, directly consistent with Rusbult's (1983) investment model. The lack of social–legal recognition for same-sex relationships means that same-sex couples automatically have fewer barriers to relationship dissolution than do married heterosexual couples, and this is directly consistent with the fact that their breakup rates are higher than those of married couples, but comparable to those of unmarried cohabiting heterosexuals (Kurdek, 1998b).

Determinants of relationship *satisfaction* are also similar across same-sex and heterosexual couples. Kurdek (1998b) found that relationship satisfaction in both types of couples was associated with appraisals of intimacy, autonomy, equality, and constructive problem solving. Additionally, trajectories of *change* in satisfaction over a 5-year period were the same across couple types. These findings are consistent with research indicating that same-sex couples use the same

basic strategies to maintain their relationships as do heterosexual couples. For example, Haas and Stafford (1998) found that the most common maintenance strategies reported by gay and lesbian individuals were sharing tasks, communicating about the relationship, and sharing time together, similar to the findings for heterosexual individuals (Dainton & Stafford, 1993).

Notably, Haas and Stafford (1998) also identified several maintenance strategies that are specific to sexual-minority couples, such as choosing to live, work, or socialize in environments accepting of lesbian, gay, and bisexual individuals, taking part in activities geared toward these populations, and being "out" as a couple. Yet the effects of such strategies may not be uniform across couples. Studies focusing on lesbians' openness versus secrecy about their relationships (Beals & Peplau, 2001; Caron & Ulin, 1997; Jordan & Deluty, 2000) have found that the impact of openness on relationship quality depends on whether it is met with acceptance versus rejection by family members, friends, and coworkers, as well as *correspondence* between partners' degrees of openness (Jordan & Deluty, 2000). Correspondence between partners has also been found to moderate the beneficial effects of lesbian, gay, and bisexual community involvement (Beals & Peplau, 2001).

Such findings raise important questions about the mechanisms through which gay-specific maintenance strategies operate. Some recent research suggests that these strategies might work both at the level of the dyad and at the level of the individual. Specifically, Elizur and Mintzer (2003) found that among gay men, having a positive gay identity and having strong social support from peers (both of which are likely fostered by living in gay-positive environments, participating in lesbian, gay, and bisexual activities, and "outness") were positively related to gay men's relationship durability and satisfaction. Furthermore, the effect of gay identification on these outcomes was found to be mediated by men's *self-acceptance*. This suggests, interestingly, that relationship maintenance strategies such as lesbian, gay, and bisexual community involvement might prove effective not only because they bolster social support for the dyad (which has been previously found to enhance sexual-minority relationship functioning, as reviewed by Green & Mitchell, 2002), but because they bolster each partner's positive self-concept as a gay individual. The notion that positive self-concepts can enhance relationship functioning is certainly not new to relationship research, but Elizur and Mintzer's work is one of the first to systematically examine how this dimension informs our understanding of the unique dynamics underlying sexual-minority relationships.

Another important moderator is obviously gender. Duffy and Rusbult (1985) found that in both same-sex and heterosexual relationships, women reported more commitment to maintaining their relationships than men. This, of course, is consistent with theory and research suggesting that women are socialized to define themselves and their self-worth in the context of their relationships (Cross & Madson, 1997), giving them a greater "stake" in relationship maintenance. Interestingly, Rusbult, Zembrodt, and Iwaniszek (1986) found that this phenomena is not simply linked with gender, but with adherence to traditional norms of femininity. They found that across both gender and sexual orientation, greater *psychological* femininity (as assessed through a personality inventory) was associated with tendencies to respond to relationship difficulties by attempting to improve them or to wait for them to improve, whereas psychological masculinity was associated with exiting problematic relationships or allowing them to deteriorate.

Altogether, this body of research suggests that although the determinants of relationship maintenance and satisfaction are largely similar across same-sex and heterosexual couples, same-sex couples are characterized by unique challenges and dynamics – partly as a function of partners' "matched" gender and partly as a function of social stigmatization – that remain important areas for future investigation.

Relationship Dissolution

The limited number of studies specifically comparing relationship dissolution across same-sex and heterosexual couples have generally found no significant differences in the reasons for and psychological effects of dissolution (Kurdek, 1997a). In both types of couples, dissolution can be longitudinally predicted from relationship qualities such as intimacy, equality, and problem solving (Kurdek, 1998b), as well as the experience and expectation of affectively positive partner interactions (Gottman et al., 2003), compared with equivalent analyses of heterosexual couples in Gottman & Levenson, 1992). Gottman and colleagues' series of studies (which, notably, followed same-sex couples over an unprecedented 12-year period) also found that among both same-sex and heterosexual couples, high physiological reactivity during couple interactions predicted later dissolution.

As just alluded to Kurdek (1998b) found that across same-sex and heterosexual couples, the strongest *unique* predictor of relationship dissolution over a 5-year period, adjusting for initial relationship quality, is the presence of barriers to leaving the relationship, consistent with the results of other research (Beals et al., 2002). In light of such findings, and in light of the steadily increasing efforts to secure formal recognition for same-sex relationships, one interesting question is whether couples who take legally binding steps to affirm their mutual commitment, such as registering for a civil union, will have lower breakup rates over time than couples that pursue public but nonlegal forms of recognition, such as commitment ceremonies, or couples who have not undergone a commitment ceremony but have established other legal ties to one another, such as taking the same last name (Suter & Oswald, 2003) or merging finances (Beals et al., 2002). Comparing breakup rates across such couples would provide a unique opportunity to compare directly the stabilizing effect of structural versus personal–moral dimensions of relationship commitment (Johnson, 1999). Additionally, given recent arguments over whether civil unions represent adequate substitutes for same-sex marriage, researchers might consider whether the specific degree, breadth, and perceived legitimacy of structural ties between same-sex partners is linearly related to their relationship stability.

Notably, some of these structural ties are more robust than couples may realize. Legal procedures for dissolving civil unions vary widely and are often poorly understood. For example, 85% of the same-sex couples who obtained official civil unions in Vermont by 2003 traveled there specifically for this purpose, and some have since discovered that they cannot formally dissolve such unions unless they are Vermont residents (Bernstein, 2003). Given such ambiguities, and sexual minorities' ambivalence about placing delicate matters of money and even child custody into the hands of potentially hostile court systems, some expect that same-sex couples might increasingly turn to professional mediators to assist with relationship dissolution (Walter, 2003), and the mediation field has shown increased awareness of – and calls for sensitivity to – their unique concerns (Felicio & Sutherland, 2001).

One issue that makes dissolution of same-sex relationships fairly unique is the tendency for sexual minorities to maintain close emotional ties – sometimes even best friendships – with their ex-partners after dissolution (Nardi, 1999; Shumsky, 2001), a phenomenon often attributed to the high value sexual minorities have been found to place on maintaining "chosen families" of supportive and accepting friends to compensate for troubled family ties (Nardi, 1992). The difficulties that long-standing "ex-lover" relationships introduce into individuals' new relationships has received some anecdotal and qualitative investigation (for examples, see Weinstock & Rothblum, 1996) but has not yet been the topic of systematic study across same-sex and heterosexual pairs. Given the contemporary prevalence of "blended" families, involving both stepparents and extended steprelatives, closer investigation of the strategies used by same-sex and heterosexual couples to balance ties to prior versus current partners is an important topic for future research.

Gender-Related Dynamics

As noted earlier, one of the most salient and unique dimensions of same-sex relationships is their potential to magnify gender-related dynamics. Numerous studies have investigated this phenomenon across a range of different relationship properties. With regard to individuals' perceptions of intimacy (typically of high value to women) versus autonomy (typically of high value to men) in their relationships, Kurdek (1998b) found mixed support for the notion that same-sex couples confer a "double-dose" of gender-linked relationship properties. Contrary to the notion that gay men should report uniquely high levels of autonomy, he found that both lesbian and gay male couples reported greater autonomy than did heterosexual couples.

As for intimacy, Kurdek detected a small but significant tendency for lesbian couples to report greater intimacy with their partners, assessed by self-reported factors such as shared time together and the degree to which partners maintained a "couple" identity. Similarly, Zacks, Green, and Marrow (1988) found that in comparison to heterosexual couples, lesbian couples reported higher levels of cohesion, adaptability, and satisfaction in their relationships, a result the authors attributed to women's gender role socialization. Recall, however, that lesbian couples have not been found to show greater relationship stability than either gay male or heterosexual couples. Rather, the results of Kurdek's (1998b) research suggest that having barriers to dissolving a relationship is more important for keeping it together than having a "double-dose" of female-typed relationship skills and maintenance strategies. In fact, some clinically oriented researchers have considered whether heightened levels of intimacy in female–female couples might actually prove *detrimental* by promoting excessive psychological "fusion" or "merger" between partners (Biaggio, Coan, & Adams, 2002; Nichols, 1987). Thus, this body of research has provided important correctives to many implicit assumptions about the role of "female-typed" intimacy skills in relationship maintenance and quality.

Another topic of interest with regard to gender magnification in same-sex couples concerns power and equality in domains ranging from decision making, influence strategies, household labor, and problem solving. Although stereotypes have historically presumed that same-sex couples implicitly designate one partner to take the classically "female" role and one partner to take the "male" role in these domains, research does not bear out this view. Rather, gay and lesbian couples place a high value on equity in their relationships, and lesbians in particular report particular success in achieving equitable arrangements (Peplau & Cochran, 1980). Strategies for achieving equity follow a number of different patterns. With respect to household responsibilities, research indicates that same-sex couples develop largely idiosyncratic arrangements, allowing their respective interests and desires to shape daily practice (Huston & Schwartz, 2002). Accordingly, it is not uncommon for same-sex partners to mix and match female-typed and male-typed tasks and roles (i.e., Amy handles auto maintenance and most of the cooking, and Deb takes care of social arrangements and financial planning). Overall, same-sex couples show more equitable distributions of household labor than do heterosexual couples (Kurdek, 1993; Patterson, 1995). However, male–male and female–female couples appear to operationalize equity in different ways, with male couples typically having each partner specialize in certain activities, whereas female couples tend to share task performance (Kurdek, 1993).

This is not to suggest, of course, that same-sex couples are uniformly successful in avoiding power differentials. For example, research has found that among both gay male and lesbian couples, income discrepancies tend to be associated with power differentials (Caldwell & Peplau, 1984; Harry, 1984; Harry & DeVall, 1978; Reilly & Lynch, 1990), more so for for gay men than for women (Blumstein & Schwartz, 1983). Research on influence strategies is also instructive. Historically, research in this area has differentiated between "weak," female-typed strategies (such as withdrawal or the expression of negative emotions) and "strong" male-typed strategies (such as bargaining, bullying, reasoning, or interrupting the other person). However, research comparing heterosexual couples to same-sex couples suggests that gender differences in the use of weak versus strong strategies have more to do with power than with gender (Falbo & Peplau, 1980; Howard, Blumstein, & Schwartz, 1986). Specifically, individuals who perceive themselves as more powerful tend to use stronger strategies, regardless of gender or sexual orientation, whereas individuals who perceive themselves as less powerful tend to use weaker strategies (Kollock, Blumstein, & Schwartz, 1986). Furthermore, Howard and colleagues (1986) found that for some influence strategies, the gender of one's *partner* proved more important than one's own gender: Specifically, manipulation and supplication were most common among individuals with male partners, regardless of the individual's gender.

Clearly, research on how each partner's gender – and gender socialization – shapes same-sex relationship dynamics has important implications for understanding such dynamics in *all* couples. Yet future investigations of such topics must be paired with more systematic assessments of individual differences *other than* gender to more clearly specify the mechanisms through which gender-related effects operate. For example, how might individual difference dimensions such as locus of control (Kurdek, 1997b, 2000b; Schmitt & Kurdek, 1987), attachment style (Gaines & Henderson, 2002; Kurdek, 2002), rejection sensitivity (Downey & Feldman, 1996), and affective states such as anxiety and depression

(Kurdek, 1997b, 1998a; Oetjen & Rothblum, 2000; Schmitt & Kurdek, 1987) mediate or moderate the effects of gender composition on couple functioning? Future research along these lines will enable researchers to explain not only differences between female–female, male–male, and male–female couples, but to identify and explain differences within each relationship type.

Sexual Behavior and Satisfaction

Sexuality obviously plays an important role in couple functioning, and it is particularly salient for same-sex couples given that society defines and categorizes lesbian, gay, and bisexual individuals on the basis of their sexuality. However, most research on sexuality among sexual minorities has focused on *individuals'* desires and behaviors rather than the *relationship* context of sexuality (reviewed in Peplau, Fingerhut, & Beals, 2004). The few data available suggest that, as with heterosexual couples (reviewed in Sprecher, Christopher, & Cate, this volume), same-sex couples' sexual satisfaction is strongly related to their global relationship satisfaction (Bryant & Demian, 1994; Deenen et al., 1994; Kurdek, 1991; Peplau & Cochran, 1981; Peplau, Cochran, & Mays, 1997). Interestingly, however, the type of sexual relationship that some same-sex couples consider satisfying differs from typical heterosexual norms. For example, as noted by Frye (1990), many lesbians endorse fairly broad conceptualizations of "sexual activity" that include behaviors such as hugging, cuddling, and fondling one another's bodies without necessarily attempting or achieving orgasm, whereas mainstream American adolescents and adults endorse more restrictive definitions of "sex" that focus on penetration and orgasm (Bogart, Cecil, Wagstaff, Pinkerton, & Abramson, 2000; Pitts & Rahman, 2001; Sanders & Reinisch, 1999). Yet notably, despite granting a less central role to orgasm in sexual activity, lesbian couples appear to have particularly high rates of orgasm (Jay & Young, 1979; Kinsey, Pomeroy, Martin, & Gebhard,

1953; Lever, 1994; Loulan, 1987; Peplau, Cochran, Rook, & Padesky, 1978). Also, lesbians appear to place a greater value than do heterosexual couples on equality in both initiating and refusing sexual activity, consistent with the fact that lesbian couples have been found to place a high emphasis on equality in their relationships in a variety of domains (Kurdek, 1995).

Considerable attention has been devoted to the phenomenon of sexual infrequency in long-term lesbian couples, sometimes called "lesbian bed death" (Iasenza, 2002). As reviewed by Peplau et al. (2004), the prevalence, causes, and relative "healthfulness" of diminished sexual frequency in lesbian couples have been hotly debated. Is it a dysfunctional consequence of excessive intimacy, a side effect of women's socialization toward sexual passivity and shame, or a methodological artifact of overly restrictive definitions of "sex" in conventional questionnaires? In wading through these debates, it becomes clear that research on the causes and consequences of this phenomenon would benefit greatly from more systematic integration with the research literature on heterosexual female sexuality, particularly female sexual dysfunction. A random, representative study of American adults found that more than 30% of women reported difficulties with sexual arousal and sexual desire (Laumann, Paik, & Rosen, 1999). Coupled with the tendency for women not to take the lead in initiating sexual activity as a result of conventional female socialization (Blumstein & Schwartz, 1983; Nichols, 1988, 1990), one might question whether most long-term heterosexual couples might also experience "bed death" if they did not have a reliably interested and initiatory male partner.

Some psychologists have argued that for some lesbian couples, low sexual frequency might be perfectly healthful to the extent that it meets both partners' needs (Fassinger & Morrow, 1995), whereas others may simply need to make specific efforts to respect and manage – rather than eradicate – differences between their sexual drives (M. Hall, 2001). Clearly, we need to maintain a critical perspective on contemporary definitions of – and proposed clinical treatments for – female sexual "problems" *in general* (Tiefer, 1999) to understand the causes and consequences of diminished sexual activity among lesbians. These topics will receive continuing research and debate in future years, particularly given the possibility that younger cohorts of sexual-minority women, who have grown up with more open and accepting environments regarding female sexuality, might show different patterns of sexuality in their long-term relationships.

Sexual Exclusivity

With respect to male couples, one factor that has received considerable attention concerns the degree of sexual exclusivity in the relationship. As documented by Blumstein and Schwartz (1983), male–male couples are more likely than either male–female or female–female couples to report engaging in extradyadic sexual activity, often with the explicit knowledge of their partner (see also Bryant & Demian, 1994; Harry, 1984; Harry & DeVall, 1978; McWhirter & Mattison, 1984; Peplau et al., 1997). Blumstein and Schwartz (1983) also found that gay male couples were less likely than lesbian or heterosexual couples to report that monogamy was important to them. However, such attitudes among gay men may be undergoing historical change. Contrary to what one might expect on the basis of findings published in the early 1980s, a 1994 survey ($N = 2,500$) conducted by *The Advocate* (Lever, 1994), a lesbian and gay magazine, found that although 48% of gay men reported having participated in extradyadic sexual activity in their relationships, more than 70% indicated that they preferred long-term monogamous relationships to other arrangements.

The degree to which extradyadic sexual activity and relationship satisfaction are associated with one another appears to depend on a number of factors, such as whether it is illicit versus part of a mutual relationship "contract" (Hickson et al.,

1992). Some couples, for example, view extradyadic sexual encounters as having positive effects on the primary relationship (Deenen et al., 1994). Yet even couples with positive attitudes toward – and explicit agreements permitting – extradyadic sex may find that they need to revise such agreements over time to account for unanticipated reactions and situations (LaSala, 2001). In making provisions for such opportunities within their relationships, some male couples define specific conditions under which extradyadic sex is and is not acceptable, often relating to safer sex practices, whether it occurs in the home, disclosure to or direct involvement of the other partner, and degree of emotional attachment to the other partner. Notably, gay men report feeling more threatened by a partner's emotional infidelity than sexual infidelity, exactly the reverse of heterosexual men (Dijkstra et al., 2001), perhaps reflecting gay men's expectation that men are generally more successful than women in separating love from sex, and hence in pursuing extradyadic sex that is, in fact, "just sex."

Given recent historical changes regarding attitudes toward, recognition of, and men's participation in committed same-sex partnerships, rates of – and rules about – extradyadic sexual activity may change, and deserve close attention. For example, one recent study of gay couples in Vermont that had obtained civil unions found that these couples reported lower rates of extradyadic sexual activity than have been found in prior research (Campbell, 2002). Longitudinal research is obviously necessary to determine whether such associations – if they are reliable – represent self-selection (i.e., the most exclusive couples are the ones most likely to seek legal recognition for their relationship) or whether the process of obtaining a civil union changes partners' attitudes toward – and behavior within – their relationships. Another topic for research is whether contemporary cohorts of young gay men, who are exposed to a far greater number of positive images of successful gay male couples than have been previous cohorts, might have significantly more optimistic expectations for forming stable and satisfying long-term relationships, and hence different attitudes about sexual exclusivity.

Violence and Abuse

Contrary to the notion that domestic violence is unique to the patriarchal dynamics of male–female pairings, recent years have seen increasing documentation of violence and abuse within same-sex relationships, ranging from physical behaviors such as hitting, slapping, scratching, and attacking with a weapon, to nonphysical behaviors such as threats, denigration, and sexual coercion (L. K. Burke & Follingstad, 1999; Regan, Bartholomew, Oram, & Landolt, 2002; Walder-Haugrud, 1999; C. M. West, 1998, 2002). Although accurate prevalence estimates are difficult to obtain, prior studies have found incidence rates ranging from 25% to 50% (Alexander, 2002; C. M. West, 2002). Notably, sexual-minority adolescents are not immune from these problems: Elze (2002) found that one third of female sexual-minority youths in northern England had experienced verbal or physical abuse in their dating relationships in the previous 12 months, including 28% of the girls who had only dated other girls.

Thus far, studies have found that the correlates of relationship violence in same-sex couples parallel those found in heterosexual couples, such as conflicts over dependency, jealousy, money, power, and substance abuse (McClennen, Summers, & Vaughan, 2002). Some unique patterns, however, have emerged. For example, a recent study of gay male couples (Regan et al., 2002) found that some forms of violence that typically occupy the upper end of the severity continuum for heterosexual couples, such as punching and hitting, tended to cluster with lower-severity violent behaviors among gay male couples. Alternatively, some behaviors that are lower in severity for heterosexual couples, such as twisting arms, pulling hair, and scratching, cluster with higher-severity violent behaviors among gay men. The authors suggested that men might resort to punching and hitting earlier in a male–male conflict than

in a male–female conflict, given that this behavior has more serious consequences when directed toward a weaker and smaller woman (and also potentially because some boys become accustomed to hitting and punching other boys in the context of childhood fights). With regard to hair pulling and scratching, they argued that these behaviors in gay male couples might index the escalation of a fight to a prolonged, close-proximity struggle. Unique dynamics have also been observed in lesbian couples. For example, one recent study (Miller, Greene, Causby, White, & Lockhart, 2001) found that physical *aggression* was more common than outright violence in lesbian relationships, and that it was best predicted by relationship fusion, whereas physical violence was best predicted by measures of control. Such findings raise important questions about how male and female socialization, as well as men's and women's different histories of physically aggressive conflicts in childhood, relates to the patterns of violence and abuse observed in male–female, male–male, and female–female couples.

Understanding such dynamics is critically important for the design and implementation of effective antiviolence interventions. For example, given that the overwhelming majority of domestic violence in heterosexual relationships is conducted by men, the training of clinicians and social workers may be inadequate to address the factors underlying female–female relationship violence. Additionally, it is important to consider whether sexual-minority relationships might be particularly vulnerable to relationship violence as a function of the stress and pressure of social stigmatization, or maladaptive patterns of social functioning derived from histories of parental or peer rejection or victimization. Such information might prove to be particularly important in preventing sexual-minority *youths* from developing stable, maladaptive patterns of dealing with social stigma *and* with relationship problems (see, for example, Lie, Schilit, Bush, Montagne, & Reyes, 1991).

Along the same lines, it is important to investigate larger social-structural responses to same-sex relationship violence (T. W.

Burke, Jordan, & Owen, 2002; Kuehnle & Sullivan, 2003; Potoczniak, Murot, Crosbie Burnett, & Potoczniak, 2003). Historically, much attention has been devoted to the ways in which institutionalized patriarchy and sexism contribute to male–female relationship violence by creating a climate of tolerance for male power over their female partners, both at the level of community norms and at the level of policing and legal responses to domestic violences. Among sexual-minority couples, the same question might be posed with respect to institutionalized and internalized homophobia (Tigert, 2001). Failures of local communities and policing-legal institutions to intervene actively in same-sex domestic violence might reflect and reinforce a sense that same-sex couples are less valuable individuals. Clearly, future research in this area is important for understanding the multiple ways in which the cultural stigmatization of same-sex sexuality influences sexual minorities' feelings and behaviors within their most intimate relationships.

Replacing Old Assumptions With New Questions: Cautions and Future Directions

In considering directions for future research on sexual-minority or same-sex relationships, it is important to remain mindful and critical of the cultural assumptions that typically underlie our research questions. For example, as noted earlier, the majority (specifically, 74%) of sexual minorities report wanting the option of legal same-sex marriage (Kaiser Foundation, 2001). Yet consider this finding more carefully: What do we know (or should we try and find out) about the one fourth of lesbian, gay, and bisexual individuals who don't want the option of legal marriage? Our historical emphasis on documenting that sexual minorities want and achieve the same types of long-term relationships as do heterosexuals can potentially blind us to important questions about alternative, unexpected relationship types and desires that might

challenge our own assumptions about the optimal form, duration, and developmental trajectories of same-sex and other-sex intimate relationships.

For example, many sexual-minority and heterosexual scholars and laypeople have responded to the historical exclusion of sexual-minority individuals from the institution of marriage with critical reflection about the political, social, legal, and personal meaning of marriage and "marriagelike" relationships. Some have come away from such reflections strongly critical of the patriarchal underpinnings of traditional marriage and the specter of religious or governmental regulation of personal relationships. Others, more provocatively, have argued that an even more dangerous problem is the hegemonic notion that exclusive, monogamous sexual and romantic partnerships are the most healthy, desirable, and worthy of legal recognition (for a range of views on these issues, see Butler, 2002; Ettelbrick, 1993, 2001; Kitzinger & Wilkinson, 2004; Sullivan & Landau, 1997; Warner, 1999). In light of these issues, some have argued that instead of advocating for same-sex marriage, activists should promote greater awareness and appreciation of alternative relationship practices among same-sex and other-sex couples, such as maintaining separate residences from a primary partner (Hess & Catell, 2001); pursuing multiple or nonmonogamous partnerships (Munson & Stelboum, 1999; Rust, 1996; C. West, 1996); developing romantic, emotionally primary, but nonsexual relationships (Rothblum & Brehony, 1993); or forgoing "primary" ties altogether in favor of "chosen families" of close friends (Nardi, 1999; Weinstock & Rothblum, 1996). Researchers should take our cue from these debates and devote increasing attention to the prevalence and long-term implications of such practices.

Another important area for future research concerns the relationship experiences of bisexual individuals, who have been historically underrepresented in research on sexual minorities. Despite recent increases in the cultural visibility and perceived legitimacy of "bisexual" as a stable sexual identity category (see Rust, 2000), it remains more highly stigmatized than exclusive homosexuality (Eliason, 1997; Eliason, 2001; Mulick & Wright, 2002; Paul, 1996) and is frequently misunderstood and denigrated even within lesbian and gay communities (Mohr & Rochlen, 1999; Mulick & Wright, 2002; Ochs, 1996; Rust, 1995). This can create particular problems for bisexual individuals whether they maintain long-term relationships with same-sex or other-sex partners. The social and psychological complexities involved in transitioning between successive same-sex and other-sex relationships also warrant close attention because these transitions often prompt feelings of having to "come out" – as lesbian or heterosexual – all over again (Diamond, 2000, 2003a).

Fluidity in sexual attractions and behavior, and the way in which it shapes and is shaped by relationship experiences, also warrants research attention, particularly among women. Researchers have long noted that some women appear to experience same-sex desires only in the context of a single, unexpectedly intense emotional bond (reviewed in Diamond, 2003b), and this phenomenon now appears to be related to the broader phenomenon of "situation-dependence" or "plasticity" in sexuality, which appears to be more common in women than in men and which cuts across sexual orientation (see Baumeister, 2000, for a comprehensive review). Given that intimate relationships appear to be among the most common triggers for sexual fluidity, future research should systematically investigate how common such experiences are among women and men, the mechanisms through which they operate, and their long-term implications for sexual experience and identity. Another fascinating topic with regard to fluidity concerns how same-sex and other-sex couples manage either partner's periodic experience – and potential expression – of desires that contradict his or her self-described sexual orientation. Some research in this vein has been conducted on bisexually attracted individuals in heterosexual relationships (Buxton, 2001; Edser & Shea,

2002; Reinhardt, 2002), but much more could be gained by a broader perspective that treats incongruencies among love, desire, and identity as its central focus, and this does not presume neat and impermeable boundaries between heterosexual and lesbian, gay, and bisexual individuals and life histories.

Finally, a fundamentally important priority for future research involves greater investigation of ethnic-minority same-sex relationships. Historically, the majority of research on same-sex couples has been conducted with White and middle-class samples; much greater research is needed dissecting the complex interacting influences of race, culture, and class on such relationships, particularly given that such factors often influence the degree to which one's family and local community tolerates or condemns same-sex sexuality (Chan, 1992; Collins, 1990; Hidalgo, 1984; Stokes, Miller, & Mundhenk, 1998). For example, some foreign languages have no positive or neutral terms for "lesbian," "gay," or "bisexual" (Espin, 1997), raising fascinating questions about how individuals with such backgrounds come to conceptualize same-sex relationships as they grow up and how they perceive and speak about such relationships in adulthood. Couples in which partners have different ethnic or socioeconomic backgrounds also pose particularly interesting and important questions: Research on a small group of African American lesbians, for example, has found that social class differences often posed salient and intractable problems for intimate relationships (R. L. Hall & Greene, 2002), often involving perceptions that a long-term involvement with a partner from a starkly different social class or ethnic background might further distance a sexual-minority from her family members and local community.

Conclusion

In sum, during the past 20 years, the volume and sophistication of research on same-sex intimate relationships has increased dramatically. In this chapter, I have focused on seven areas of research:

1. Relationship initiation, in which same-sex romantic relationships – particularly among women – are distinguished by the fact that they frequently emerge out of friendships;

2. Relationship maintenance and satisfaction, in which many of the same antecedent factors operate for same-sex as for other-sex relationships, although a number of maintenance strategies specific to same-sex couples have been documented;

3. Relationship dissolution, in which similar factors (e.g., the absence of barriers) operate in same-sex and other-sex couples, although sexual minorities are distinguished by a greater tendency to maintain close emotional ties to ex-partners after dissolution;

4. Gender dynamics, in which sexual minorities have been found to place a high value on equity in their relationships;

5. Sexual behavior, in which similar links between sexual satisfaction and global relationship quality have been detected in same-sex and other-sex couples, although studies of same-sex couples raise important definitional issues about the meaning of different sexual behaviors and experiences;

6. Sexual exclusivity, in which the historical finding of greater nonmonogamy among gay men appears to be shifting;

7. Violence and abuse, a relationship phenomenon that has received increasing attention and analysis in same-sex couples.

Overall, the research reviewed here demonstrates that the similarities between same-sex and other-sex couples outnumber the differences.

In considering the history and future of psychological research on sexual-minority relationships, the underlying cultural assumptions and unavoidable political dimensions that shape the asking and answering of questions about same-sex relationships warrant continual scrutiny. In an influential critique of early research on lesbian and gay individuals, Kitzinger (1987) pointed out that the long-standing emphasis on documenting the *lack* of significant mental health differences between gay and lesbian and heterosexual individuals might have appeared to represent the triumph of scientific objectivity over social prejudice, but in fact functioned to *reinforce* the social disenfranchisement of sexual-minority individuals by implicitly predicating their social acceptability on patterns of thought, feeling, and behavior that were judged "normal" and "healthy" by mainstream society. Her analysis demonstrates the importance of vigilantly monitoring the multiple sociocultural and political forces inescapably shaping the context in which research on sexual-minority relationships is conducted and interpreted. We must continually check and revisit our explicit and implicit theories of sexuality and relationships in order to appropriately represent how these phenomena develop, unfold, and interact within the life courses of diverse sexual-minority individuals. The end result of such efforts will be a deeper understanding of intimate relationships in the context of same-sex sexuality *and* a deeper understanding of same-sex sexuality in the context of intimate relationships.

References

Alexander, C. J. (2002). Violence in gay and lesbian relationships. *Journal of Gay and Lesbian Social Services: Issues in Practice, Policy, and Research, 14*, 95–98.

Allen, J. P., & Land, D. (1999). Attachment in adolescence. In J. Cassidy & P. R. Shaver (Eds.), *Handbook of attachment: Theory, research, and clinical applications* (pp. 319–335). New York: Guilford Press.

Bailey, J. M. (1996). Gender identity. In R. C. Savin-Williams & K. M. Cohen (Eds.), *The lives of lesbians, gays, and bisexuals: Children to adults* (pp. 71–93). Fort Worth, TX: Harcourt Brace.

Bailey, J. M., Gaulin, S., Agyei, Y., & Gladue, B. (1994). Effects of gender and sexual orientation on evolutionarily relevant aspects of human mating psychology. *Journal of Personality and Social Psychology, 66,* 1081–1093.

Baumeister, R. F. (2000). Gender differences in erotic plasticity: The female sex drive as socially flexible and responsive. *Psychological Bulletin, 126,* 347–374.

Beals, K. P., Impett, E. A., & Peplau, L. A. (2002). Lesbians in love: Why some relationships endure and others end. *Journal of Lesbian Studies, 6,* 53–63.

Beals, K. P., & Peplau, L. A. (2001). Social involvement, disclosure of sexual orientation, and the quality of lesbian relationships. *Psychology of Women Quarterly, 25,* 10–19.

Berger, R. M. (1990). Men together: Understanding the gay couple. *Journal of Homosexuality, 19,* 31–49.

Bernstein, F. A. (2003, April 6). Gay unions were only half the battle. *New York Times,* p. 2.

Biaggio, M., Coan, S., & Adams, W. (2002). Couples therapy for lesbians: Understanding merger and the impact of homophobia. *Journal of Lesbian Studies, 6,* 129–138.

Blumstein, P., & Schwartz, P. (1983). *American couples: Money, work, sex.* New York: Morrow.

Bogart, L. M., Cecil, H., Wagstaff, D. A., Pinkerton, S. D., & Abramson, P. R. (2000). Is it "sex"?: College students' interpretations of sexual behavior terminology. *Journal of Sex Research, 37,* 108–116.

Brenner, C. (1995). *Eight bullets: One woman's story of surviving anti-gay violence.* Ithaca, NY: Firebrand Books.

Bryant, A. S., & Demian. (1994). Relationship characteristics of American gay and lesbian couples: Findings from a national survey. *Journal of Gay and Lesbian Social Services, 1,* 101–117.

Burke, L. K., & Follingstad, D. R. (1999). Violence in lesbian and gay relationships: Theory, prevalence, and correlational factors. *Clinical Psychology Review, 19,* 487–512.

Burke, T. W., Jordan, M. L., & Owen, S. S. (2002). Cross-national comparison of gay and lesbian domestic violence. *Journal of Contemporary Criminal Justice, 18,* 231–257.

Butler, J. (2002). Is kinship always already heterosexual? *Differences: A Journal of Feminist Cultural Studies, 13,* 14–44.

Buxton, A. P. (2001). Writing our own script: How bisexual men and their heterosexual wives maintain their marriages after disclosure. *Journal of Bisexuality, 1,* 155–189.

Caldwell, M. A., & Peplau, L. A. (1984). The balance of power in lesbian relationships. *Sex Roles, 10,* 587–599.

Campbell, S. M. (2002, July). *Gay marriage: A descriptive study of civil unions in Vermont.* Paper presented at the International Conference on Personal Relationships, Halifax, Nova Scotia.

Caron, S. L., & Ulin, M. (1997). Closeting and the quality of lesbian relationships. *Families in Society, 78,* 413–419.

Chan, C. S. (1992). Cultural considerations in counseling Asian American lesbians and gay man. In S. H. Dworkin & F. J. Gutierrez (Eds.), *Counseling gay men and lesbians: Journey to the end of the rainbow* (pp. 115–124). Alexandria, VA: American Association for Counseling and Development.

Cini, M. A., & Malafi, T. N. (1991, March). *Paths to intimacy: Lesbian and heterosexual women's scripts of early relationship development.* Paper presented at the annual meeting of the Association for Women in Psychology, Hartford, CT.

Collins, P. H. (1990). Homophobia and Black lesbians. In P. H. Collins (Ed.), *Black feminist thought: Knowledge, consciousness, and the politics of empowerment* (pp. 192–196). New York: Routledge.

Cross, S. E., & Madson, L. (1997). Models of the self: Self-construals and gender. *Psychological Bulletin, 122,* 5–37.

Dainton, M., & Stafford, L. (1993). Routine maintenance behaviors: A comparison of relationship type, partner similarity, and sex differences. *Journal of Social and Personal Relationships, 10,* 255–272.

Deenen, A. A., Gijs, L., & van Naerssen, A. X. (1994). Intimacy and sexuality in gay male couples. *Archives of Sexual Behavior, 23,* 421–431.

Diamond, L. M. (2000). Sexual identity, attractions, and behavior among young sexual-minority women over a two-year period. *Developmental Psychology, 36,* 241–250.

Diamond, L. M. (2003a). Was it a phase? Young women's relinquishment of lesbian/bisexual identities over a 5-year period. *Journal of Personality and Social Psychology, 84,* 352–364.

Diamond, L. M. (2003b). What does sexual orientation orient? A biobehavioral model distinguishing romantic love and sexual desire. *Psychological Review, 110*, 173–192.

Dijkstra, P., Groothof, H. A. K., Poel, G. A., Laverman, T. T. G., Schrier, M., & Buunk, B. P. (2001). Sex differences in the events that elicit jealousy among homosexuals. *Personal Relationships, 8*, 41–54.

Downey, G., & Feldman, S. I. (1996). Implications of rejection sensitivity for intimate relationships. *Journal of Personality and Social Psychology, 70*, 1327–1343.

Duffy, S. M., & Rusbult, C. E. (1985). Satisfaction and commitment in homosexual and heterosexual relationships. *Journal of Homosexuality, 12*, 1–23.

Edser, S. J., & Shea, J. D. (2002). An exploratory investigation of bisexual men in monogamous, heterosexual marriages. *Journal of Bisexuality, 2*, 5–29.

Eldridge, N. S., & Gilbert, L. A. (1990). Correlates of relationship satisfaction in lesbian couples. *Psychology of Women Quarterly, 14*, 43–62.

Eliason, M. J. (1997). The prevalence and nature of biphobia in heterosexual undergraduate students. *Archives of Sexual Behavior, 26*, 317–326.

Eliason, M. J. (2001). Bi-negativity: The stigma facing bisexual men. *Journal of Bisexuality, 1*, 137–154.

Elizur, Y., & Mintzer, A. (2003). Gay males' intimate relationship quality: The roles of attachment security, gay identity, social support, and income. *Personal Relationships, 10*, 411–435.

Elze, D. E. (2002). Against all odds: The dating experiences of adolescent lesbian and bisexual women. *Journal of Lesbian Studies, 6*, 17–29.

Espin, O. M. (1997). Crossing borders and boundaries: The life narratives of immigrant lesbians. In B. Greene (Ed.), *Ethnic and cultural diversity among lesbians and gay men* (pp. 191–215). Thousand Oaks, CA: Sage.

Ettelbrick, P. (1993). Since when is marriage a path to liberation? In S. Sherman (Ed.), *Lesbian and gay marriage: Private commitments, public ceremonies* (pp. 20–26). Philadelphia: Temple University press.

Ettelbrick, P. (2001). Domestic partnership, civil unions, or marriage: One size does not fit all. *Albany Law Review, 64*, 905.

Falbo, T., & Peplau, L. A. (1980). Power strategies in intimate relationships. *Journal of Personality and Social Psychology, 38*, 618–628.

Fassinger, R. E., & Morrow, S. L. (1995). Overcome: Repositioning lesbian sexualities.

In L. Diamant & R. D. McAnulty (Eds.), *The psychology of sexual orientation, behavior, and identity: A handbook* (pp. 197–219). Westport, CT: Greenwood Press.

Felicio, D. M., & Sutherland, M. (2001). Beyond the dominant narrative: Intimacy and conflict in lesbian relationships. *Mediation Quarterly, 18*, 363–376.

Frye, M. (1990). Lesbian "sex." In J. Allen (Ed.), *Lesbian philosophies and cultures* (pp. 46–54). Albany: State University of New York Press.

Gaines, S. O., Jr., & Henderson, M. C. (2002). Impact of attachment style on responses to accommodative dilemmas among same-sex couples. *Personal Relationships, 9*, 89–93.

Gottman, J. M., & Levenson, R. W. (1992). Marital processes predictive of later dissolution: Behavior, physiology, and health. *Journal of Personality and Social Psychology, 63*, 221–233.

Gottman, J. M., Levenson, R. W., Gross, J., Frederickson, B. L., McCoy, K., Rosenthal, L., Ruef, A., & Yoshimoto, D. (2003). Correlates of gay and lesbian couples' relationship satisfaction and relationship dissolution. *Journal of Homosexuality, 45*, 23–43.

Green, R. J., & Mitchell, V. (2002). Gay and lesbian couples in therapy: Homophobia, relational ambiguity, and social support. In A. S. Gurman (Ed.), *Clinical handbook of couple therapy* (3rd ed., pp. 546–568). New York: Guilford Press.

Haas, S. M., & Stafford, L. (1998). An initial examination of maintenance behaviors in gay and lesbian relationships. *Journal of Social and Personal Relationships, 15*, 846–855.

Hall, M. (2001). Beyond forever after: Narrative therapy with lesbian couples. In P. J. Kleinplatz (Ed.), *New directions in sex therapy: Innovations and alternatives* (pp. 279–301). New York: Brunner-Routledge.

Hall, R. L., & Greene, B. (2002). Not any one thing: The complex legacy of social class on African American lesbian relationships. *Journal of Lesbian Studies, 6*, 65–74.

Harry, J. (1984). *Gay couples*. New York: Praeger.

Harry, J., & DeVall, W. B. (1978). *The social organization of gay males*. New York: Praeger.

Hayes, A. F. (1995). Age preferences for same- and opposite-sex partners. *Journal of Social Psychology, 135*, 125–133.

Hess, J., & Catell, P. (2001). Dual dwelling duos: An alternative for long-term relationships. In B. J. Brothers (Ed.), *Couples, intimacy issues, and addiction* (pp. 25–31). New York: Haworth Press.

Hickson, F. C. I., Davies, P. M., Hunt, A. J., Weatherburn, P., McManus, T. J., & Coxon, A. P. M. (1992). Maintenance of open gay relationships: Strategies for protection against HIV. *AIDS Care, 4,* 409–419.

Hidalgo, H. (1984). The Puerto Rican lesbian in the United States. In T. Darty & S. Potter (Eds.), *Women identified women* (pp. 105–150). Palo Alto, CA: Mayfield.

Howard, J. A., Blumstein, P., & Schwartz, P. (1986). Sex, power, and influence tactics in intimate relationships. *Journal of Personality and Social Psychology, 51,* 102–109.

Huston, M., & Schwartz, P. (2002). Gendered dynamics in the romantic relationships of lesbians and gay men. In A. E. Hunter (Ed.), *Readings in the psychology of gender: Exploring our differences and commonalities* (pp. 167–178). Needham Heights, MA: Allyn & Bacon.

Iasenza, S. (2002). Beyond "lesbian bed death": The passion and play in lesbian relationships. *Journal of Lesbian Studies, 6,* 111–120.

Jay, K., & Young, A. (1979). *The gay report: Lesbians and gay men speak out about sexual experiences and lifestyles.* New York: Summit Books.

Johnson, M. P. (1999). Personal, moral, and structural commitment to relationships: Experiences of choice and constraint. In J. M. Adams & W. H. Jones (Eds.), *Handbook of interpersonal commitment and relationship stability* (pp. 73–87). Dordrecht, The Netherlands: Kluwer Academic.

Jones, D. A. (1996). Discrimination against same-sex couples in hotel reservation policies. *Journal of Homosexuality, 31,* 153–159.

Jordan, K. M., & Deluty, R. H. (2000). Social support, coming out, and relationship satisfaction in lesbian couples. *Journal of Lesbian Studies, 4,* 145–164.

Kaiser Foundation. (2001, November). *Inside-out: Report on the experiences of lesbians, gays and bisexuals in America and the public's view on issues and policies related to sexual orientation.* Meno Park, CA.

Kenrick, D. T., Keefe, R. C., Bryan, A., & Barr, A. (1995). Age preferences and mate choice among homosexuals and heterosexuals: A case for modular psychological mechanisms. *Journal of Personality and Social Psychology, 69,* 1166–1172.

Kinsey, A. C., Pomeroy, W. B., Martin, C. E., & Gebhard, P. H. (1953). *Sexual behavior in the human female.* Philadelphia: Saunders.

Kitzinger, C. (1987). *The social construction of lesbianism.* London: Sage.

Kitzinger, C., & Wilkinson, S. (2004). Social advocacy for equal marriage: The politics of "rights" and the psychology of "mental health." *@SAP: Analyses of Social Issues and Public Policy, 4,* 173–194.

Kollock, P., Blumstein, P., & Schwartz, P. (1986). Sex and power in interaction: Conversational privileges and duties. *American Sociological Review, 50,* 34–46.

Kuehnle, K., & Sullivan, A. (2003). Gay and lesbian victimization: Reporting factors in domestic violence and bias incidents. *Criminal Justice and Behavior, 30,* 85–96.

Kurdek, L. A. (1989). Relationship quality for newly married husbands and wives: Marital history, stepchildren, and individual-difference predictors. *Journal of Marriage and the Family, 51,* 1053–1064.

Kurdek, L. A. (1991). Sexuality in homosexual and heterosexual couples. In K. McKinney & S. Sprecher (Eds.), *Sexuality in close relationships* (pp. 177–191). Hillsdale, NJ: Erlbaum.

Kurdek, L. A. (1992). Relationship stability and relationship satisfaction in cohabiting gay and lesbian couples: A prospective longitudinal test of the contextual and interdependence models. *Journal of Social and Personal Relationships, 9,* 125–142.

Kurdek, L. A. (1993). The allocation of household labor in gay, lesbian, and heterosexual married couples. *Journal of Social Issues, 49*(3), 127–139.

Kurdek, L. A. (1995). Developmental changes in relationship quality in gay and lesbian cohabiting couples. *Developmental Psychology, 31,* 86–94.

Kurdek, L. A. (1997a). Adjustment to relationship dissolution in gay, lesbian, and heterosexual partners. *Personal Relationships, 4,* 145–161.

Kurdek, L. A. (1997b). The link between facets of neuroticism and dimensions of relationship commitment: Evidence from gay, lesbian, and heterosexual couples. *Journal of Family Psychology, 11,* 503–514.

Kurdek, L. A. (1998a). The nature and predictors of the trajectory of change in marital quality over the first 4 years of marriage for first-married husbands and wives. *Journal of Family Psychology, 12,* 494–510.

Kurdek, L. A. (1998b). Relationship outcomes and their predictors: Longitudinal evidence from heterosexual married, gay cohabiting, and lesbian cohabiting couples. *Journal of Marriage and the Family, 60*, 553–568.

Kurdek, L. A. (2000a). Attractions and constraints as determinants of relationship commitment: Longitudinal evidence from gay, lesbian, and heterosexual couples. *Personal Relationships, 7*, 245–262.

Kurdek, L. A. (2000b). The link between sociotropy/autonomy and dimensions of relationship commitment: Evidence from gay and lesbian couples. *Personal Relationships, 7*, 153–164.

Kurdek, L. A. (2002). On being insecure about the assessment of attachment styles. *Journal of Social and Personal Relationships, 19*, 811–834.

Kurdek, L. A., & Schmitt, J. P. (1986). Relationship quality of partners in heterosexual married, heterosexual cohabiting, and gay and lesbian relationships. *Journal of Personality and Social Psychology, 51*, 711–720.

Kurdek, L. A., & Schmitt, J. P. (1987). Partner homogamy in married, heterosexual cohabiting, gay, and lesbian couples. *Journal of Sex Research, 23*, 212–232.

Kurdek, L. A., & Schnopp-Wyatt, D. (1997). Predicting relationship commitment and relationship stability from both partners' relationship values: Evidence from heterosexual dating couples. *Personality and Social Psychology Bulletin, 23*, 1111–1119.

Landolt, M. A., Bartholomew, K., Saffrey, C., Oram, D., & Perlman, D. (2004). Gender nonconformity, childhood rejection, and adult attachment: A study of gay men. *Archives of Sexual Behavior, 33*, 117–128.

LaSala, M. C. (2000). Gay male couples: The importance of coming out and being out to parents. *Journal of Homosexuality, 39*, 47–71.

LaSala, M. C. (2001). Monogamous or not: Understanding and counseling gay male couples. *Families in Society, 82*, 605–611.

Laumann, E. O., Gagnon, J. H., Michael, R. T., & Michaels, F. (1994). *The social organization of sexuality: Sexual practices in the United States.* Chicago: University of Chicago Press.

Laumann, E. O., Paik, A., & Rosen, R. C. (1999). Sexual dysfunction in the United States: Prevalence and predictors. *Journal of the American Medical Association, 281*, 537–544.

Lever, J. (1994, August 23). Sexual revelations. *The Advocate,* 17–24.

Lie, G. Y., Schilit, R., Bush, J., Montagne, M., & Reyes, L. (1991). Lesbians in currently aggressive relationships: How frequently do they report aggressive past relationships? *Violence and Victims, 6*, 121–135.

Loftus, J. (2001). America's liberalization in attitudes toward homosexuality. *American Sociological Review, 66*, 762–782.

Loulan, J. (1987). *Lesbian passion: Loving ourselves and each other.* San Francisco: Spinsters/Lute.

McClennen, J. C., Summers, A. B., & Vaughan, C. (2002). Gay men's domestic violence: Dynamics, help-seeking behaviors, and correlates. *Journal of Gay and Lesbian Social Services: Issues in Practice, Policy, and Research, 14*, 23–49.

McWhirter, D. S., & Mattison, A. M. (1984). *Male couple: How relationships develop.* Englewood Cliffs, NJ: Prentice Hall.

Miller, D. H., Greene, K., Causby, V., White, B. W., & Lockhart, L. L. (2001). Domestic violence in lesbian relationships. *Women and Therapy, 23*, 107–127.

Mohr, J. J., & Rochlen, A. B. (1999). Measuring attitudes regarding bisexuality in lesbian, gay male, and heterosexual populations. *Journal of Counseling Psychology, 46*, 353–369.

Mulick, P. S., & Wright, L. W., Jr. (2002). Examining the existence of biphobia in the heterosexual and homosexual populations. *Journal of Bisexuality, 2*, 45–64.

Munson, M., & Stelboum, J. P. (Eds.). (1999). *The lesbian polyamory reader: Open relationships, non-monogamy, and casual sex.* New York: Haworth Press.

Nardi, P. M. (1992). That's what friends are for: Friends as family in the gay and lesbian community. In K. Plummer (Ed.), *Modern homosexualities: Fragments of lesbian and gay experience* (pp. 108–120). London: Routledge.

Nardi, P. M. (1999). *Gay men's friendships.* Chicago: University of Chicago Press.

Nichols, M. (1987). Lesbian sexuality: Issues and developing theory. In Boston Lesbian Psychologies Collective (Ed.), *Lesbian psychologies* (pp. 97–125). Urbana: University of Illinois Press.

Nichols, M. (1988). Low sexual desire in lesbian couples. In S. R. Leiblum & R. C. Rosen (Eds.), *Sexual desire disorders* (pp. 387–412). New York: Guilford Press.

Nichols, M. (1990). Lesbian relationships: Implications for the study of sexuality and gender. In J. C. Gonsiorek & J. D. Weinrich (Eds.), *Homosexuality: Research implications for public policy* (pp. 350–364). Newbury Park, CA: Sage.

Ochs, R. (1996). Biphobia: It goes more than two ways. In B. A. Firestein (Ed.), *Bisexuality: The psychology and politics of an invisible minority* (pp. 217–239). Thousand Oaks, CA: Sage.

Oetjen, H., & Rothblum, E. D. (2000). When lesbians aren't gay: Factors affecting depression among lesbians. *Journal of Homosexuality, 39,* 49–73.

Oswald, R. F. (2002). Inclusion and belonging in the family rituals of gay and lesbian people. *Journal of Family Psychology, 16,* 428–436.

Patterson, C. J. (1995). Families of the baby boom: Parents' division of labor and children's adjustment. *Developmental Psychology, 31,* 115–123.

Patterson, C. J. (2000). Family relationships of lesbians and gay men. *Journal of Marriage and the Family, 62,* 1052–1069.

Paul, J. P. (1996). Bisexuality: Exploring/exploding the boundaries. In R. C. Savin-Williams & K. M. Cohen (Eds.), *The lives of lesbians, gays, and bisexuals: Children to adults* (pp. 436–461). Orlando, FL: Harcourt Brace College.

Peplau, L. A., & Beals, K. P. (2003). The family lives of lesbians and gay men. In A. L. Vangelisti (Ed.), *Handbook of family communication* (pp. 233–248). Mahwah, NJ: Erlbaum.

Peplau, L. A., & Cochran, S. D. (1980, September). *Sex differences in values concerning love relationships.* Paper presented at the American Psychological Association, Montreal, Canada.

Peplau, L. A., & Cochran, S. D. (1981). Value orientations in the intimate relationships of gay men. *Journal of Homosexuality, 6,* 1–19.

Peplau, L. A., Cochran, S. D., & Mays, V. M. (1997). A national survey of the intimate relationships of African American lesbians and gay men: A look at commitment, satisfaction, sexual behavior, and HIV disease. In B. Green (Ed.), *Ethnic and cultural diversity among lesbians and gay men: Psychological perspectives on lesbian and gay issues* (pp. 11–38). Thousand Oaks, CA: Sage.

Peplau, L. A., Cochran, S. D., Rook, K., & Padesky, C. (1978). Loving women: Attachment and autonomy in lesbian relationships. *Journal of Social Issues, 34*(3), 7–27.

Peplau, L. A., Fingerhut, A., & Beals, K. P. (2004). Sexuality in the relationships of lesbians and gay men. In J. H. Harvey, A. Wenzel, & S. Sprecher (Eds.), *Handbook of sexuality in close relationships* (pp. 349–369). Mahwah, NJ: Erlbaum.

Peplau, L. A., Padesky, C., & Hamilton, M. (1982). Satisfaction in lesbian relationships. *Journal of Homosexuality, 8,* 23–35.

Peplau, L. A., & Spalding, L. R. (2000). The close relationships of lesbians, gay man, and bisexuals. In C. Hendrick & S. S. Hendrick (Eds.), *Close relationships: A sourcebook* (pp. 111–123). Thousand Oaks, CA: Sage.

Pitts, M., & Rahman, Q. (2001). Which behaviors constitute "having sex" among university students in the UK? *Archives of Sexual Behavior, 30,* 169–176.

Potoczniak, M. J., Murot, J. E., Crosbie Burnett, M., & Potoczniak, D. J. (2003). Legal and psychological perspectives on same-sex domestic violence: A multisystemic approach. *Journal of Family Psychology, 17,* 252–259.

Regan, K. V., Bartholomew, K., Oram, D., & Landolt, M. A. (2002). Measuring physical violence in male same-sex relationships: An item response theory analysis of the conflict tactics scales. *Journal of Interpersonal Violence, 17,* 235–252.

Reilly, M. E., & Lynch, J. M. (1990). Power-sharing in lesbian partnerships. *Journal of Homosexuality, 19,* 1–30.

Reinhardt, R. U. (2002). Bisexual women in heterosexual relationship. *Journal of Bisexuality, 2,* 163–171.

Ritter, K. Y., & Terndrup, A. I. (2002). *Handbook of affirmative psychotherapy with lesbians and gay men.* New York: Guilford Press.

Rose, S., & Zand, D. (2000). Lesbian dating and courtship from young adulthood to midlife. *Journal of Lesbian Studies, 6,* 85–109.

Rose, S., Zand, D., & Cimi, M. A. (1993). Lesbian courtship scripts. In E. D. Rothblum & K. A. Brehony (Eds.), *Boston marriages* (pp. 70–85). Amherst: University of Massachusetts Press.

Rothblum, E. D., & Brehony, K. A. (Eds.). (1993). *Boston marriages.* Amherst: University of Massachusetts Press.

Rusbult, C. E. (1983). A longitudinal test of the investment model: The development (and deterioration) of satisfaction and commitment in heterosexual involvements. *Journal of Personality and Social Psychology, 45,* 101–117.

Rusbult, C. E., Zembrodt, I. M., & Iwaniszek, J. (1986). The impact of gender and sex-role orientation on responses to dissatisfaction in close relationships. *Sex Roles, 15,* 1–20.

Rust, P. R. (1995). *Bisexuality and the challenge to lesbian politics: Sex, loyalty, and revolution.* New York: New York University Press.

Rust, P. R. (1996). Monogamy and polyamory: Relationship issues for bisexuals. In B. A. Firestein (Ed.), *Bisexuality: The psychology and politics of an invisible minority* (pp. 127–148). Thousand Oaks, CA: Sage.

Rust, P. R. (Ed.). (2000). *Bisexuality in the United States: A reader and guide to the literature.* New York: Columbia University Press.

Sanders, S. A., & Reinisch, J. M. (1999). Would you say you "had sex" if . . . ? *Journal of the American Medical Association, 281,* 275–277.

Schmitt, J. P., & Kurdek, L. A. (1987). Personality correlates of positive identity and relationship involvement in gay men. *Journal of Homosexuality, 13,* 101–109.

Schreurs, K. M. G., & Buunk, B. P. (1996). Closeness, autonomy, equity, and relationship satisfaction in lesbian couples. *Psychology of Women Quarterly, 20,* 577–592.

Shumsky, E. (2001). Transforming the ties that bind: Lesbians, lovers, and chosen family. In E. Gould & S. Kiersky (Eds.), *Sexualities lost and found: Lesbians, psychoanalysis, and culture* (pp. 57–69). Madison, CT: International Universities Press.

Stokes, J. P., Miller, R. L., & Mundhenk, R. (1998). Toward an understanding of behaviourally bisexual men: The influence of context and culture. *Canadian Journal of Human Sexuality, 7,* 101–113.

Sullivan, A., & Landau, J. (Eds.). (1997). *Same-sex marriage: Pro and con.* New York: Vintage.

Suter, E. A., & Oswald, R. F. (2003). Do lesbians change their last names in the context of a committed relationship? *Journal of Lesbian Studies, 7,* 71–83.

Testa, R. J., Kinder, B. N., & Ironson, G. (1987). Heterosexual bias in the perception of loving relationships of gay males and lesbians. *Journal of Sex Research, 23,* 163–172.

Tiefer, L. (1999). "Female sexual dysfunction" alert: A new disorder invented for women. *Sojourner: The Women's Forum, 11.*

Tigert, L. M. (2001). The power of shame: Lesbian battering as a manifestation of homophobia. *Women and Therapy, 23,* 73–85.

Walder-Haugrud, L. K. (1999). Sexual coercion in lesbian and gay relationships: A review and critique. *Aggression and Violent Behavior, 6,* 139–149.

Walter, B. J. (2003). Lesbian mediation: Resolving custody and visitation disputes when couples end their relationships. *Family Court Review, 41,* 104–121.

Walters, A. S., & Curran, M. C. (1996). "Excuse me, sir? May I help you and your boyfriend?": Salespersons' differential treatment of homosexual and straight customers. *Journal of Homosexuality, 31,* 135–152.

Warner, M. (1999). *The trouble with normal: Sex, politics and the ethics of queer life.* New York: Free Press.

Weinstock, J. S., & Rothblum, E. D. (Eds.). (1996). *Lesbian friendships: For ourselves and for each other.* New York: New York University Press.

West, C. (1996). *Lesbian polyfidelity.* San Francisco: Bootlegger.

West, C. M. (1998). Leaving a second closet: Outing partner violence in same-sex couples. In J. L. Jasinski & L. M. Williams (Eds.), *Partner violence: A comprehensive review of 20 years of research* (pp. 163–183). Thousand Oaks, CA: Sage.

West, C. M. (2002). Lesbian intimate partner violence: Prevalence and dynamics. *Journal of Lesbian Studies, 6,* 121–127.

Widmer, E. D., Treas, J., & Newcomb, R. (1998). Attitudes toward nonmarital sex in 24 countries. *Journal of Sex Research, 35,* 349–358.

Zacks, E., Green, R.-J., & Marrow, J. (1988). Comparing lesbian and heterosexual couples on the circumplex model: An initial investigation. *Family Process, 27,* 471–484.

CHAPTER 17

Family Relationships and Depression

Deborah J. Jones
Steven R. H. Beach
Frank D. Fincham

Bronfenbrenner's (1986) ecological systems model emphasizes the importance of understanding individuals within the multiple contexts in which they live and interact. Consistent with this model, the role of the family context has received considerable attention in the research literature on mental health. The family context is generally characterized as dynamic, including the marital and parent–child, as well as sibling relationships, which are interrelated, each influencing and, in turn, being influenced by the other (see Erel & Burman, 1995, for a review). While healthy families, or families characterized by low levels of stress and conflict, have been linked to resilience and mental health and adjustment in both children and adults, unhealthy families, or families characterized by high levels of stress and conflict, have been linked to a wide range of adjustment difficulties, including mental illness (Cummings, Davies, & Campbell, 2000). Children who grow up in families characterized by high levels of conflict are more vulnerable to internalizing and externalizing problems and are more likely to engage in high-risk behaviors, including sub-stance use and sexual risk taking. Moreover, the consequences of family conflict may persist beyond childhood and adolescence into adulthood and affect not only individual adjustment (Jones, Forehand, & Beach, 2000) but also later adult romantic relationships (Delsing, Oud, DeBruyn, & van Aken, 2003; Sabatelli & Bartle-Haring, 2003).

Marital and parent–child relations also are associated with mental health and well-being in adulthood, prompting the development of marital- and family-based interventions to treat adult mental health problems, including mood disorders, anxiety disorders, and substance use disorders (see Baucom, Shoham, Mueser, Daiuto, & Stickle, 1998, for a review). One area in which the link between family relationships and mental health has been particularly well examined is depression.

Depression

It is not uncommon to hear someone say that they are feeling "depressed." Feeling sad is a virtually universal phenomenon and "sadness" and "depression" are often used interchangeably in the lay community. In the professional community, the definition of depression also varies. Some consider "clinical" depression, as diagnosed by the Diagnostic and Statistical Manual (4th ed., text revision); DSM-IV-TR; (American Psychiatric Association, 2000), the gold standard for clinical outcome research. A clinical diagnosis of depression, referred to as major depression in the DSM-IV-TR, requires an individual to have five symptoms for at least a 2-week period (e.g., depressed mood, anhedonia, loss of sleep, loss of appetite, suicidal ideation), with the symptoms representing a change in previous functioning. Additionally, one of the five symptoms has to be either depressed mood or anhedonia. Alternatively, others are more interested in subclinical depression, or any state in which depressive symptoms are present but in which they are not present in sufficient number or severity to quality for major depression, given that such milder forms of depression are far more common and also disruptive (Ingram & Siegle, 2002). Given the variability in the definition and use of the term, the term *depression* is used broadly throughout this chapter to refer to research examining both clinical depression and subclinical depressive symptoms.

Depression is the most common of all psychiatric disturbances, affecting nearly 20% of people in the United States at some point in their lives (Karno et al., 1987). Notably, the prevalence of depression prompted the World Health Organization to rank depression as the single most burdensome disease in the world (Murray & Lopez, 1996). Adding to the burden, depression is associated with poor physical health, with evidence mounting for an association between depression and cardiovascular disease in particular (e.g., Jones, Matthews, Bromberger, & Sutton-Tyrrell, 2003), as well as health-compromising behaviors (e.g., Roy, Mitchell, & Wilhelm, 2001). The economic costs of depression are also rising, with some estimates suggesting that lost work productivity associated with depression in the United States exceeds $33 billion

(Greenberg, Kessler, Nells, Finkelstein, & Berndt, 1996). For a significant portion of these individuals, depression will result in a suicide, with some estimates suggesting that 15% of depressed individuals will commit suicide (Hirschfeld & Goodwin, 1988).

In addition to health, workplace, and economic burdens associated with depression, there are also costs for family members. Depressed individuals are more likely to divorce (e.g., Wade & Cairney, 2000) and the children of depressed parents are more likely to experience depressive symptoms themselves (see Gotlib & Goodman, 1999, for a review). Thus, the family has become an important context within which to study and treat depressive symptoms in both children and adults. Surprisingly, however, reviews of the association between family distress and depression tend to focus either on adults or children, rather than on both as subsystems within a family context. Marital researchers tend to focus on the relation of marital distress and depression in adults, whereas child and family researchers tend to focus on the relation of family distress, including marital, parenting, and parent–child distress on child depression, with little communication between the two groups.

This chapter therefore integrates and summarizes the literature linking family relationship distress and depression, focusing on both children and adults within the family context. Understanding the association between family distress and depression, rather than studying children and adults separately, provides an opportunity to think within a developmental framework that has the potential to inform prevention and intervention efforts focusing on at-risk families, rather than targeting individuals. First, we review the literature linking family relationship distress in both adults and children. We then summarize the literature suggesting a bidirectional association between family relationship distress and depression. Finally, we discuss how our understanding of the interrelationship of family relationship distress and depression should guide our use of family-based prevention and intervention efforts. As such, this chapter is not meant as a review of the connections between the full spectrum of mental disorders and close relationships. The interested reader can find more general summaries regarding the role of close relationships in the development of mental disorders in Beach, Wamboldt, Kaslow, Heyman, and Reiss (in press) and Whisman and Bruce (1999). In addition, more information regarding the use of close relationships in the treatment of mental illness can be found in Baucom, Shoham, Mueser, Daiuto, and Stickle (1998), and a general theoretical formulation for the role of close relationships in mental health and well-being can be found in Baumeister and O'Leary (1995).

Family Relationship Distress and Depression in Adults

Recent estimates suggest that up to 20% of adults report significant depressive symptoms in the past 1 week to 6 months (Kessler, Avenevoli, & Merikangas, 2001). Rates of major depression are much lower, suggesting that more adults experience subclinical levels of depressive symptoms than depressive disorders. Whether focusing on major depression in particular, or depressive symptoms more generally, depressive symptomatology is associated with family relationship distress in adults.

Marital Distress and Depression in Adults

In a quantitative and exhaustive review of the marital literature, Whisman (2001) found that, across 26 cross-sectional studies, marital quality was negatively associated with depressive symptomatology for both women ($r = -0.42$) and men ($r = -0.37$), indicating a significant, albeit small, gender difference. Across 10 studies using diagnosed patient populations, Whisman (2001) found that the magnitude of the association was somewhat stronger for both women and men ($r = -0.66$). The average Dyadic Adjustment Scale (DAS) score for the diagnosed population was 93.7 (SD = 25.2), indicating that the average depressed individual is also maritally distressed (DAS cutoff = 97). Thus, marital relationships are often (but not always) distressed among depressed men and women. Serious marital dissatisfaction predicts increased risk for a major depressive episode in the year following initial assessment, even after controlling for history of depression (Whisman & Bruce, 1999), and marital conflict with physical abuse predicts increases in depressive symptoms over time controlling for earlier symptoms (Beach et al., 2004). In addition to the effect of the chronic stress of marital dissatisfaction, the effect of particular humiliating marital events is also substantial (Cano & O'Leary, 2000). Accordingly, the influence of marital context and marital events on depressive symptoms appears to be substantial. Interestingly, recent work suggests that the effect of marital satisfaction is a nonshared environmental effect and is not well modeled as resulting from the same genetic factors that produce vulnerability for depressive symptoms (Reiss et al., 2001). This means that it is not simply the case that the same genetic diathesis that produces depression also produces conflicted marital relationships. Accordingly, it appears that disturbance in intimate adult relationships is important in understanding the etiology of depressive symptoms for many individuals and will continue to be important as we develop a broad bio–psycho–social developmental model of depression.

Parent–Child Relationship Distress and Depression in Adults

It has long been noted clinically that depressed patients report considerable distress and difficulty in their parenting relationships (e.g., Weissman & Paykel, 1974), and some have attributed depressed mothers' level of dysphoria, at least in part, to her belief that she is an inadequate parent (Teti & Gelfand, 1991). Supplementing clinical observation and patient self-report is a large body of direct observation documenting problems in parenting behavior. In a review of 46 observational studies of the parenting behavior of depressed women, Lovejoy, Gracyk, O'Hare, and Neuman (2000) found evidence that depressed mothers displayed more withdrawn behavior with an overall average correlation between depression and withdrawn behavior of 0.14. They also found support for Forehand, Lautenschlager, Faust, and Graziano's (1986) hypothesis that depressed mothers display more negative parenting behavior, with an overall average correlation between depression and negative parenting behavior of 0.22, with a stronger effect for those in a current depressive episode than those with only a history of depression. As with marital relationships, there is reason to believe that many, but not all depressed persons, experience difficulty in the area of parenting.

Family Relationship Distress and Depression in Children and Adolescents

Up to 50% of children and adolescents report depressive symptoms in periods ranging from 1 week to 6 months, with less than 1% of children and 6% of adolescents meeting criteria for major depression (Kessler et al., 2001), again, suggesting that children and adolescents are more likely to experience depressive symptoms than disorders. Moreover, the prevalence of depression among young people has been rising, with higher rates of depression among adolescents in more recent than in earlier decades (Weissman, Bland, Joyce, & Newman, 1993). Accordingly, understanding correlates of child and adolescent depression, including the role of family relationship distress, is critical for prevention and intervention efforts (Kaslow, Deering, & Racusin, 1994).

Marital and Parent–Child Relationship Distress and Depression in Children

Bowlby's (1980) theory of attachment suggests that children with an insecure attachment style are predisposed to developing depression. In particular, children whose family environments lack security, comfort, and acceptance are less likely to view rela-

tionships positively and trustworthy and hence will be less satisfied and more wary of relationships in the future (Gotlib & Hammen, 1992).

Extreme family relationship distress is also associated with depressive symptoms in children. Infants exposed to serious abuse and neglect are more likely to evidence depressive symptoms (Trad, 1994). The infant's response to abuse, including failure to exhibit normal emotional expressions and heightened withdrawal, in turn, further interferes with the parent–child relationship, heightening the risk for low-self esteem, as well as further abuse in the future (Lamb, Gaensbauer, Malkin, & Schultz, 1985; Trad, 1987). Marital conflict between parents is also associated with other important family outcomes, including poorer parenting (see Erel & Burman, 1995), poorer child adjustment (see Grych & Fincham, 1990), problematic attachment to parents (e.g., Owen & Cox, 1997), increased likelihood of parent–child conflict (e.g., Margolin, Christensen, & John, 1996), and conflict between siblings (e.g., Brody, Stoneman, & McCoy, 1994). Indeed, when manipulated experimentally, marital conflict increased subsequent parent–son conflict (Jouriles & Farris, 1992), suggesting that marital conflict may lead to and cause disturbances in other family subsystems, which, in turn, may further increase a child's vulnerability for depression.

Aspects of marital conflict that have a particularly negative influence on children include more frequent, intense, physical, unresolved, child-related conflicts and conflicts attributed to the child's behavior (see Cummings & Davies, 1999; Fincham & Osborne, 1993). Accordingly, it may be that physical violence and physical altercations are particularly problematic with regard to child outcomes.

Moreover, the context of marital conflict in the home may be important for correctly specifying genetic effects. For example, women who were adopted soon after birth and who were at high genetic risk for depression showed no evidence of the disorder if they were reared in an adoptive family without marital difficulties or psychopathology in the rearing parents (Cadoret, Winokur, Langbehn, & Troughton, 1996). Accordingly, although individuals may be genetically vulnerable to depression, family relationships characterized by low levels of distress may offer some protection, whereas family relationships characterized by high levels of distress may exacerbate risk.

As children age, certain parenting styles are also associated with a vulnerability to depression. Children who perceive their parents as less warm and supportive and more controlling and intrusive are at greater risk for depression than their peers (e.g., Stein et al., 2000). The vulnerabilities associated with these parenting behaviors persist beyond childhood and adolescence and into young adulthood (Jones et al., 2000).

Families of depressed children are also higher in conflict than families of nondepressed children. Depressed children report higher levels of conflict in the parent–child, family, and marital relationships, including more verbal and physical aggression (see Kaslow et al., 1994, for a review). In particular, it is thought that marital conflict negatively affects the parent–child relationship and parenting behaviors which, in turn, increase children's vulnerability to depression. Importantly, the association between family relationship distress and child depression is not merely a function of depressed children perceiving their families more negatively. That is, both observations of family interactions and parent reports of their own parenting behavior confirms that families of depressed children have more negative interactions, are more hostile, and are more rejecting than families of nondepressed children (Lefkowitz & Tesiny, 1984).

Although the biological mechanisms by which family distress may affect depression is beyond the scope of this text, the animal literature offers an interesting possibility in terms of the link between family distress and child depression. For example, animal data suggest that poor maternal care (by rat dams of their pups) within the first 10 days of life can influence gene expression by leading to increased hippocampal glucocorticoid receptor messenger RNA expression and so to enhanced glucocorticoid feedback sensitivity. This appears to be the basis for lifetime sensitivity to stress of the maltreated pups (Liu et al., 1997). Extending this research, the family distress and depression literature suggests that family relationship characterized by high levels of distress may influence children's psychosocial adjustment directly, but also indirectly by modifying their physiological stress response systems and, in turn, emotional, cognitive, and behavioral functioning. Accordingly, some literature suggests that one's vulnerability to depression depends on early adverse family experiences.

Is Everyone at Equal Risk?

Are all persons equally reactive or vulnerable to negative interpersonal events? A large literature suggests that this is not the case. Personality variables (Davila, 2001), interpersonal sensitivities (Joiner, 2000), individual differences in biological vulnerability (Gold, Goodwin, & Chrousos, 1988), various negative childhood experiences (Hammen, Henry, & Daley, 2000; Kessler & Magee, 1993), and other individual difference variables have been linked to differential vulnerability to depression, differential vulnerability to stress, and differential vulnerability to recurrence. This literature suggests that everyone does not start with an equal chance of responding to negative interpersonal events with depression, but that early adverse experiences may exacerbate an individual's risk (see Goodman, 2002 for a review). Importantly, the adverse events examined to date have typically been associated with the family, with events ranging from maternal stress in utero and its effects on a fetus' physiological stress response system to infants' and children's exposure to maladaptive or inadequate parenting and its effect on children's emotional regulation and social interaction. Moreover, the impact of adverse experiences on predisposition for depression has to be considered within a developmental framework (see

Goodman, 2002, for a review). That is, depending on an individual's developmental accomplishments, adverse events may have more or less of an impact. At the earliest stages of development, maternal stress during pregnancy has been associated with emotional disturbances in children. Several theories attempt to account for this link, including that maternal stress leads to elevations in maternal cortisol (a primary stress response), which in turn crosses the placenta and may lead to irreversible elevations in infants' hypothalamic–pituitary–adrenal (HPA) activity (increased cortisol) and yield subsequent dysregulation of emotion and behavior (see Goodman, 2002, for a review). Experiences during infancy and early childhood may also shape an individual's vulnerability to depression. The primary focus of research in this area has been on maladaptive parenting, with findings suggesting that infants and children exposed to maladaptive parenting, including neglectful, harsh, and inconsistent parenting are more likely to experience difficulties with emotion regulation, social skills, and dysfunctional stress responses (see Goodman, 2002, for a review). Dysregulation in these physiological, emotional, and behavioral systems during early developmental periods may, in turn, increase an individual's predisposition to depression in response to stressors throughout the lifetime. In support of this hypothesis, Hammen and colleagues (2000) reported that young women with exposure to one or more childhood adversities, such as family violence or parental psychopathology, were more likely to become depressed following less overall stress than women without such adversity.

Of course, it is also the case that not all individuals who experience family distress experience depression. A thorough review of the full scope of the potential moderators of the link between early family distress and vulnerability for depression is beyond the scope of this chapter. Given the chapter's focus on the role of the family, however, one potential moderator merits mention: family support. The buffering role of social support against the development of depressive symptoms is well established (Cohen & Wills, 1985). Individuals who experience higher levels of social support generally experience lower levels of depressive symptoms. One mechanism by which social support may serve as a buffer against the development of depressive symptoms is by influencing the way individuals think about negative events (Cohen & Wills, 1985). That is, social support networks may encourage individuals to make more adaptive attributions about negative events, in turn, leading to lower levels of depressive symptoms. Consistent with this prediction, Joiner and colleagues (2001) demonstrated that higher levels of social support were associated with lower levels of depressive symptoms, and this association was partially mediated by individuals with higher levels of social support making more adaptive attributions about the causes of events. Importantly, family relations may serve as a significant source of support. Most notably, several theorists suggest that support from a marital partner may buffer the impact of family-of-origin distress on adult depression (see Coyne & Benazon, 2001, for a review). Evidence seems to suggest that a supportive spouse may prevent depression in response to stress in individuals who have a history of early family-of-origin distress, or at least delay the onset of the first episode. Accordingly, although the focus of this chapter is on the role of family distress and depression, it is important to note that families may also serve supportive roles.

What Comes First the Depression or the Family Distress?

As alluded to earlier, it is generally accepted that the association between family distress and depression is bidirectional. Specifically, possible causal relationships between family difficulties and depression include an effect of marital or family difficulties on depression, an effect of depression on marital or family difficulties, and a bidirectional pattern of causation. It is also possible that the nature of the relationship might change across different types of relationships, as a function of the number of episodes of depression experienced, as a function of age, or as a function of other personal or symptom characteristics. The potential complexity of the relationships is somewhat overwhelming relative to currently available analytic strategies (Beach, Davey, & Fincham, 1999), yet some generalizations can be made based on available evidence. In addition, a model is available to guide further investigation and to help draw implications for clinical intervention.

What generalizations can be drawn regarding the link between family relationships and depression? In the marital area, many theorists have adopted some variant of Hammen's (1991) stress generation theory to guide their theorizing about the link between marital discord and depression. Stress generation theory suggests a bidirectional pattern of causation between family relationships and depression. It is posited that depressed individuals can generate stress in their interpersonal environments in a variety of ways, but this interpersonal stress can also exacerbate depressive symptoms. Illustrating the vicious cycle between depressive symptoms and marital difficulties, Davila, Bradbury, Cohan, and Tochluk (1997) found that persons with more symptoms of depression were more negative in their supportive behavior toward the spouse and in their expectations regarding partner support. These negative behaviors and expectations, in turn, were related to greater marital stress. Finally, closing the loop, level of marital stress predicted subsequent depressive symptoms (controlling for earlier symptoms). Likewise, in his review of self-propagating processes in depression, Joiner (2000) highlighted the propensity for depressed persons to seek negative feedback, to engage in excessive reassurance seeking, to avoid conflict and so withdraw, and to elicit changes in the partner's view of them. In each case, the behavior resulting from the individual's depression carries the potential to generate increased interpersonal stress or to shift the response of others in a negative direction. Joiner suggested that increased

interpersonal negativity, in turn, helps maintain depressive symptoms.

Recent research also provides illustrations of the way in which stressful marital or family events can precipitate or exacerbate depressive symptoms among the vulnerable and so initiate the stress generation process. For example, Cano and O'Leary (2000) found that humiliating events such as partner infidelity and threats of marital dissolution resulted in a sixfold increase in diagnosis of depression and that this increased risk remained after controlling for family and personal history of depression. Further, Whisman and Bruce (1999) found that marital dissatisfaction increased risk of subsequent diagnosis of depression by 2.7-fold in a large, representative community sample, and again the increased risk remained significant after controlling for demographic variables and personal history of depression. As these studies suggest, marital distress and specific types of marital events may be sufficiently potent to precipitate a depressive episode. Thus, in the marital area, the broad outlines of the reciprocal relationship between depression and marital difficulties are already coming into focus.

In the area of parenting relationships, the reciprocal relationships between depression, parenting behavior, and parenting stress are also clear in broad brush. The data reviewed thus far, for example, suggest that parental depression is associated with a shift toward more lax, detached, inconsistent, and ineffective child management (see also Cummings & Davies, 1999, for a model and review), and problematic parenting practices in turn increase child deviance (e.g., Conger, Patterson, & Ge, 1995). As a consequence, depressed parents perceive their children as having more problems, their children do have more problems on average, and relationships between depressed parents and their children are more distressed. Recent research suggests that strained parent–child relationships may also predict maintenance of depressive symptoms (Jones, Beach, & Forehand, 2001). Jones et al. (2001) examined family stress generation among intact community families with adolescent children and found that mothers' depressive symptoms generated perceived stress in both marital and mother–adolescent relationships 1 year later. In turn, greater mother-reported family relationship stress was related to greater exacerbation of her depressive symptoms. It appears, therefore, that parenting behavior is another area in which stress-generation may connect depression and family relationships.

Role of Family-Based Treatments for Family Distress and Depression

What are the implications of stress generation theory for family interventions with depressed persons? If depressive symptoms are maintained by a vicious cycle in which symptoms lead to stress-generating processes which in turn help maintain symptoms, it should be useful to treat the stress-generating processes using efficacious interventions. Marital relationships and parenting relationships may provide excellent points of therapeutic intervention with depressed persons if (a) the stress-generating behaviors in each domain are amenable to change, (b) depressed persons can make the necessary changes in response to treatment, and (c) these changes can be maintained over time. Even if intervention in these domains did not produce rapid reduction in depressive symptoms, these are areas in need of attention by many depressed persons and appear to be implicated in the maintenance of depressive episodes via stress-generation processes. In fact, a growing body of literature suggests that failure to address marital and family issues in therapy for depression may interfere with the recovery process and increase the risk for relapse (cf. Hooley & Gotlib, 2000). Accordingly, the stress generation perspective suggests that the marital and parenting relationships may be particularly useful targets of intervention for depressed individuals. An intervention for a vicious cycle requires the application of some efficacious method for interrupting the cycle. Once the vicious cycle is interrupted, more beneficial feedback processes may be set in motion, perhaps without additional direct therapeutic intervention. Marital and parenting interventions therefore seem to be appropriate and promising starting points for family intervention with depressed adults.

Are There Effective Interventions for Both Depression and Family Distress?

We touch only briefly on the general efficacy of interventions here because this is the focus of another chapter in this volume (see Baucom et al., this volume), but family-based interventions have proven efficacious in the treatment of both family distress and depression.

With regard to marital distress, several approaches to marital therapy have been found to be efficacious, including behavioral marital therapy, cognitive–behavioral marital therapy, emotion-focused therapy, and insight-oriented marital therapy (see Baucom et al., 1998, for a comprehensive review). Behavioral marital therapy, in particular, is an efficacious and specific treatment for marital discord that has been successfully applied cross-culturally (Hahlweg & Markman, 1988), is well specified, and is widely available for clinical application on a broad scale (e.g., Markman, Stanley, & Blumberg, 1994). Likewise, parent management training (Patterson, 1982; Patterson, Reid, & Dishion, 1992) is an efficacious intervention for a range of child behavior problems including conduct disorder (Kazdin, 1998) and has been elaborated and applied to a range of child behavior problems (e.g., McMahon, Forehand, Griest, & Wells, 1981; Taylor & Biglan, 1998). Accordingly, there is substantial evidence to expect that depressed persons could be helped to enhance their functioning in these areas and so interrupt stress-generation processes triggered by an ongoing depressive episode. If so, one might expect benefit both with regard to greater relationship satisfaction and with regard to decreased symptoms over time.

Do these approaches work to alleviate not only family distress but also depression?

Given the reciprocal link between marital discord and depression, a number of clinicians and researchers have suggested that family-based interventions are indicated in treatment of depression. Several studies have examined well-specified approaches and have examined their efficacy in reducing symptoms of depression and in enhancing marital satisfaction. A recent review of this literature (Beach & Jones, 2002), suggests that efficacious forms for marital therapy can be safely and usefully applied to a depressed population. Furthermore, behavioral marital therapy (BMT) emerges as a specific and efficacious treatment for marital discord, even when the marital discord is occurring in the context of depression. That is, BMT has been shown in three independent studies to produce significant change in marital distress in a discordant and depressed population; in each case, it has outperformed a control group or an alternative intervention (or both; Beach & O'Leary, 1992; Emanuels-Zuurveen & Emmelkamp, 1996; Jacobson, Dobson, Fruzzetti, Schmaling, & Salusky, 1991). Because the marital relationship appears to be an important context for stress generation, successful intervention of this sort can be viewed as particularly promising and provides a strong rationale for recommending marital intervention, where appropriate, with depressed patients. Given the promising effects on reduction of depressive symptoms, it is important that work continues to establish as well that marital therapy may be an efficacious treatment for depression and to specify clearly the conditions under which it may serve as a treatment for depression in its own right.

Although the focus of relatively less research attention than marital therapy for depression, growing evidence suggests that parent training may also be an important intervention with depressed parents. Forehand, Wells, and Griest (1980) examined the effect of a parent training program, including teaching parents to use social reinforcement and time-out with their children, on both child and parent adjustment. Their findings revealed that mothers of clinic-referred, but not nonclinic-referred, children evidenced a significant reduction in depressive symptoms from pre- to post-treatment (for other demonstrations with depressive symptoms, see also Dadds & McHugh, 1992; and Webster-Stratton, 1994), suggesting that alleviation of parenting stress may also alleviate depressive symptoms.

In a direct test of the value of parent training for clinically depressed mothers, Sanders and McFarland (2000) compared two forms of behavioral family intervention to examine the effect of a parent training intervention (Behavioral Family Intervention; BFI) with that of a combination cognitive therapy-parent training intervention (Cognitive Behavioral Family Intervention; CBFI). Those assigned to the traditional Behavioral Family Intervention ($n = 24$, with 19 completing treatment) received instruction, role-playing, feedback, and coaching in the use of social learning principles. Those assigned to the cognitively enhanced BFI condition ($n = 23$, with 20 completing treatment) received cognitive interventions that were integrated into each treatment session and that were designed to increase personally reinforcing family activities, identify and interrupt dysfunctional child-related cognitions and automatic thoughts, and increase relaxation. In each case, therapy was provided individually once a week and was accompanied by two home visits each week. There were 12 sessions with either one or both parents present, with treatment completed over a 3 to 5 month time period.

Of importance for our review, both parenting interventions produced substantial reduction in depressive symptoms and negative cognitions, and there was no interaction of condition with time of assessment. There was also significant improvement in child behavior problems in both conditions. Significantly more mothers in the CBFI condition (72%) than in the BFI condition (35%) were nondepressed at follow-up, however, suggesting a superior effect for CBFI with regard to maternal depression at follow-up. Accordingly, it appears that a highly structured and comprehensive version of parent training can benefit parents who are depressed, but some direct attention to cognitive aspects of depression may enhance longer term effects on depression.

Another combination approach was attempted by Gelfand, Teti, Seiner, and Jameson (1996). They evaluated a multicomponent program in which registered nurses visited depressed mothers of infants at their homes to assess mothers' parenting skills, enhance mothers' self-confidence, and to reinforce mothers' existing parenting techniques. Depressed mothers were assigned either to the intervention group ($n = 37$) or the usual mental health care group (i.e., ongoing treatment with referral source). The intervention group involved assessment of mothers' needs and the development of individualized programs including modeling warm interactions with the infants, offering mild suggestions, and building self-confidence by appropriately reinforcing parenting skills. Nurses visited mothers and infants 25 times at 3-week intervals over a period of 6 to 12 months, then phased out home visits over four final visits. Although there were no differences on depression scores for mothers in the intervention and control group at study entry, mothers in the intervention group demonstrated significantly greater improvement in depressive symptoms posttherapy than those in usual care. Once again, this program suggests that parent training may be a useful point of intervention to break into a stress-generation process for some depressed individuals.

One reason that parent training might have been underinvestigated as an intervention for parents with a diagnosis of depression is that depressed parents seem to do somewhat less well in parent training than do other parents. For example, depressed mothers have greater difficulty learning parenting skills (e.g., Dumas, Gibson, & Albin, 1989) and are more prone to drop out of treatment prematurely (e.g., McMahon et al., 1981). Accordingly, one obstacle to the use of parent training may be providing it in a way that allows it to be successful with a depressed population. However, a similar objection might have been raised with regard to marital interventions for depression; there are also studies showing that depression predicts poorer response to treatment than in a general sample of couples seeking couples therapy (Sher, Baucom, & Larus, 1990; Snyder, Mangrum, & Wills, 1993) and that any serious individual problem predicts premature dropout from marital therapy (Allgood & Crane, 1991). In both cases, the data reviewed here suggest that appropriate delivery of the interventions in a manner targeted at depressed individuals can overcome whatever obstacles depressed persons may experience in untargeted marital and family interventions. Indeed, it is possible that the most important requirement for effective delivery of marital and family interventions for depression is recognition that one of the participants is depressed and so may require some special assistance.

In summary, sufficient evidence does not exist to demonstrate that parent training by itself is an efficacious intervention for major depression among parents dealing with problematic children. However, the research does suggest that parent training, itself an efficacious form of therapy for child-management problems, can be provided to depressed persons in a safe and efficacious manner and may have beneficial effects both with regard to child outcomes as well as with regard to parental depression. As the Sanders and McFarland (2000) study suggests, it will be useful to consider ways to enhance parent training to make it easier to consume for depressed parents and perhaps to enhance its long-term effects on depressive symptoms. Combinations with various elements of cognitive therapy may be useful in this regard.

Accordingly, there is substantial reason to expect that depressed persons could be helped to enhance their functioning in these areas and to interrupt stress-generation processes triggered by an ongoing depressive episode. If so, one might expect benefit both with regard to greater relationship satisfaction and with regard to decreased symptoms over time.

Summary and Conclusions

Depression is the most prevalent and burdensome of mental illnesses. It has long been known that there are strong links between family processes and depression. Increasingly it appears that depression can not be well understood from a developmental perspective or from a genetic perspective unless marital and family processes are included as contextual factors. Likewise, marital and parenting relationships appear to continue to exert important influence on depressive symptoms in adulthood. Accordingly, marital and family interventions are important in the treatment and management of depression as well as subclinical depressive symptoms. Although it might appear at first that family interventions would be more difficult to implement with depressed persons, and there is evidence that depression is associated with poorer outcomes for both marital therapy and parent training when clinicians are not prepared to work with depressed patients, in both cases it has been possible to overcome these difficulties by providing depressed persons with the additional help they may need for some aspects of the interventions. As a result, marital therapy has been established as an efficacious intervention for marital problems occurring in the context of depression, and parent training is well on its way to being established as an efficacious treatment for parenting problems in the context of depression. As a result, although there is considerable room for improvement, there is also reason for optimism that marital and parenting interventions will prove especially helpful in the treatment and, perhaps, the prevention of depressive episodes and elevated symptoms.

References

Allgood, S. M., & Crane, D. R. (1991). Predicting marital therapy dropouts. *Journal of Marital and Family Therapy, 17*, 73–79.

American Psychiatric Association. (2000). *Diagnostic and statistical manual of mental disorders* (4th ed., text rev.). Washington, DC: Author.

Baucom, D. H., Shoham, V., Mueser, K. T., Daiuto, A., & Stickle, T. R. (1998). Empirically supported couple and family interventions for marital distress and adult mental health problems. *Journal of Consulting and Clinical Psychology, 66*, 53–88.

Baumeister, R. F., & Leary, M. R. (1995). The need to belong: Desire for interpersonal attachments as a fundamental human motivation. *Psychological Bulletin, 117*, 497–529.

Beach, S. R. H., Davey, A., & Fincham, F. D. (1999). The time has come to talk of many things: A commentary on Kurdek (1998) and the emerging field of marital processes in depression. *Journal of Family Psychology, 13*, 663–668.

Beach, S. R. H., & Jones, D. J. (2002). Marital and family therapy for depression in adults. In I. H. Gotlib & C. L. Hammen (Eds.), *Handbook of depression* (pp. 422–440). New York: Guilford Press.

Beach, S. R. H., Kim, S., Cercone-Keeney, J. Gupta, M., Arias, I., & Brody, G. (2004). Physical aggression and depressive symptoms: Gender asymmetry in effects? *Journal of Social and Personal Relationships, 21*, 341–360.

Beach, S. R. H., & O'Leary, K. D. (1992). Treating depression in the context of marital discord: Outcome and predictors of response for marital therapy versus cognitive therapy. *Behavior Therapy, 23*, 507–258.

Beach, S. R. H., Wamboldt, M., Kaslow, N., Heyman, R., & Reiss, D. (in press). Describing Relationship Problems in DSM-V: Multiple routes to better inclusion. *Journal of Family Psychology*.

Bowlby, J. (1980). *Attachment and loss. Volume 3. Loss: Sadness and depression*. New York: Basic Books.

Brody, G. H., Stoneman, Z., & McCoy, J. K. (1994). Contributions of family relationships and child temperaments to longitudinal variations in sibling relationship quality and sibling relationship styles. *Journal of Family Psychology, 8*, 274–286.

Bronfenbrenner, U. (1986). Ecology of the family as a context for human development: Research perspectives. *Developmental Psychology, 22*, 723–742.

Cadoret, R. J., Winokur, G., Langbehn, D., & Troughton, E. (1996). Depression spectrum disease, I: The role of gene-environment interaction. *American Journal of Psychiatry*, 153, 892–899.

Cohen, S., & Wills, T. A. (1985). Stress, social support, and the buffering hypothesis. *Psychological Bulletin*, 98, 310–357.

Conger, R., Patterson, G., & Ge, X. (1995). It takes two to replicate: A mediational model of the impact of parents' stress on adolescent adjustment. *Child Development*, 66, 80–97.

Cano, A., & O'Leary, K. D. (2000). Infidelity and separations precipitate major depressive episodes and symptoms of non-specific depression and anxiety. *Journal of Consulting and Clinical Psychology*, 68, 774–781.

Coyne, J. C., & Benazon, N. R. (2001). Not agent blue: Effects of marital functioning on depression and implications for treatment. In S. R. H. Beach (Ed.), *Marital and family processes in depression: A scientific foundation for clinical practice* (pp. 25–43). Washington, DC: American Psychological Association.

Cummings, E. M., & Davies, P. T. (1999). Depressed parents and family functioning: Interpersonal effects and children's functioning and development. In T. Joiner & J. C. Coyne (Eds.), *Recent advances in interpersonal approaches to depression* (pp. 299–327). Washington, DC: American Psychological Association.

Cummings, E. M., Davies, P. T., & Campbell, S. B. (2000). *Developmental psychopathology and family process: Theory, research, and clinical implications*. New York: Guilford Press.

Dadds, M. R., & McHugh, T. A. (1992). Social support and treatment outcome in behavioral family therapy for child conduct problems. *Journal of Consulting and Clinical Psychology*, 60, 252–259.

Davila, J. (2001). Paths to unhappiness: The overlapping courses of depression and romantic dysfunction. In S. R. H. Beach (Ed.), *Marital and family processes in depression: A scientific foundation for clinical practice* (pp. 71–87). Washington, DC: American Psychological Association.

Davila, J., Bradbury, T. N., Cohan, C. L., & Tochluk, S. (1997). Marital functioning and depressive symptoms: Evidence for a stress generation model. *Journal of Personality and Social Psychology*, 73, 849–861.

Delsing, M. J. M. H., Oud, J. H. L., DeBruyn, E. E. J., & Aken, M. A. G. (2003). Current and recollected perceptions of family relationships: The social relations model approach to members of three generations. *Journal of Family Psychology*, 17, 445–459.

Dumas, J. E., Gibson, J. A., & Albin, J. B. (1989). Behavioral correlates of maternal depressive symptomatology in conduct-disorder children. *Journal of Consulting and Clinical Psychology*, 57, 516–521.

Emanuels-Zuurveen, L., & Emmelkamp, P. M. (1996). Individual behavioral-cognitive therapy vs. marital therapy for depression in maritally distressed couples. *British Journal of Psychiatry*, 169, 181–188.

Erel, O., & Burman, B. (1995). Interrelatedness of marital relations and parent–child relations: A meta-analytic review. *Psychological Bulletin*, 118, 108–132.

Fincham, F. D., & Osborne, L. (1993). Marital conflict and children: Retrospect and prospect. *Clinical Psychology Review*, 13, 75–88.

Forehand, R., Lautenschlager, G. J., Faust, J., & Graziano, W. G. (1986). Parent perceptions and parent–child interactions in clinic-referred children: A preliminary investigation of the effects of maternal depressive moods. *Behavior Research and Therapy*, 24, 73–75.

Forehand, R., Wells, K. C., & Griest, D. L. (1980). An examination of the social validity of a parent training program. *Behavior Therapy*, 11, 488–502.

Gelfand, D. M., Teti, D. M., Seiner, S. A., & Jameson, P. B. (1996). Helping mother fight depression: Evaluation of a home-based intervention for depressed mothers and their infants. *Journal of Clinical Child Psychology*, 24, 406–422.

Gold, P. W., Goodwin, F. K., & Chrousos, G. P. (1988). Clinical and biochemical manifestations of depression: Relation to the neurobiology of stress. *New England Journal of Medicine*, 319, 348–419.

Goodman, S. H. (2002). Depression and early adverse experiences. In I. H. Gotlib & C. L. Hammen (Eds.), *Handbook of depression* (pp. 245–267). New York: Guilford Press.

Goodman, S. H., & Gotlib, I. H. (1999). Risk for psychopathology in the children of depressed mothers: A developmental model for understanding mechanisms of transmission. *Psychological Review*, 106, 458–490.

Gotlib, I. H., & Hammen, C. L. (1992). *Psychological aspects of depression: Toward a cognitive-interpersonal integration.* Oxford: Wiley.

Greenberg, P., Kessler, R., Nells, T., Finkelstein, S., & Berndt, E. R. (1996). Depression in the workplace: An economic perspective. In J. P. Feighner & W. F. Boyer (Eds.), *Selective serotonin reuptake inhibitors: Advances in basic research and clinical practice* (pp. 327–363). New York: Wiley.

Grych, J. H., & Fincham, F. D. (1990). Marital conflict and children's adjustment: A cognitive-contextual framework. *Psychological Bulletin, 108,* 267–290.

Hahlweg, K., & Markman, H. J. (1988). Effectiveness of behavioral marital therapy: Empirical status of behavioral techniques in preventing and alleviating marital distress. *Journal of Consulting and Clinical Psychology, 56,* 440–447.

Hammen, C. (1991). *Depression runs in families: The social context of risk and resilience in children of depressed mothers.* New York: Springer-Verlag.

Hammen, C., Henry, R., & Daley, S. E. (2000). Depression and sensitization to stressors among young women as a function of childhood adversity. *Journal of Consulting and Clinical Psychology, 68,* 782–787.

Hirschfeld, R. M. A., & Goodwin, F. K. (1988). Mood disorders. In J. A. Talbott, R. E. Hales, & S. C. Yudofsky (Eds.), *Textbook of psychiatry* (pp. 403–441). Washington, DC: American Psychiatric Press.

Hooley, J. M., & Gotlib, I. H. (2000). A diathesis-stress conceptualization of expressed emotion and clinical outcome. *Applied and Preventive Psychology, 9,* 135–152.

Ingram, R. E., & Siegle, G. J. (2002). Contemporary methodological issues in the study of depression: Not your father's oldsmobile. In I. H. Gotlib & C. L. Hammen (Eds.), *Handbook of depression* (pp. 86–114). New York: Guilford Press.

Jacobson, N. S., Dobson, K., Fruzzetti, A. E., Schmaling, K. B., & Salusky, S. (1991). Marital therapy as a treatment for depression. *Journal of Consulting and Clinical Psychology, 59,* 547–557.

Joiner, T. E. (2000). Depression's vicious cycle: Self-propogating and erosive processes in depression chronicity. *Clinical Psychology: Science and Practice, 7,* 203–218.

Joiner, T. E. (2001). Nodes of consilience between interpersonal-psychological theories of depression. In S. R. H. Beach (Ed.), *Marital and family processes in depression: A scientific foundation for clinical practice* (pp. 129–138). Washington, DC: American Psychological Association.

Jones, D. J., Beach, S. R. H., & Forehand, R. (2001). Stress generation in intact community families: Depressive symptoms, perceived family relationship stress, and implications for adolescent adjustment. *Journal of Social and Personal Relationships, 18,* 443–462.

Jones, D. J., Forehand, R., & Beach, S. R. H. (2000). Maternal and paternal parenting during adolescence: Forecasting early adult psychosocial adjustment. *Adolescence, 35,* 513–530.

Jones, D. J., Matthews, K. A., Bromberger, J., & Sutton-Tyrell, K. (2003). Lifetime history of depression and carotid atherosclerosis in middle-aged women. *Archives-of-General-Psychiatry, 60,* 153–160.

Jouriles, E. N., & Farris, A. M. (1992). Effects of marital conflict on subsequent parent-son interactions. *Behavior Therapy, 23,* 355–374.

Karno, M., Hough, R. L., Burnam, A., Escobar, J., Timbers, D. M., Santana, F., & Boyd, J. H. (1987). Lifetime prevalence of specific psychiatric disorders among Mexican Americans in Los Angeles and non-Hispanic whites in Los Angeles. *Archives of General Psychiatry, 44,* 695–701.

Kaslow, N. J., Deering, C. G., & Racusin, G. R. (1994). Depressed children and their families. *Clinical Psychology Review, 14,* 39–59.

Kazdin, A. E. (1998). Psychosocial treatments for conduct disorder in children. In P. E. Nathan & J. M. Gorman (Eds.), *A guide to treatments that work* (pp. 65–89). London: Oxford University Press.

Kessler, R., Avenevoli, S., & Merikangas, K. R. (2001). Mood disorders in children and adolescents: An epidemiologic perspective. *Biological Psychiatry, 49,* 1002–1014.

Kessler, R. C., & Magee, W. J. (1993). Childhood adversities and adult depression: Basic patterns of association in a U.S. national survey. *Psychological Medicine, 23,* 679–690.

Lamb, M. E., Gaensbauer, T. J., Malkin, C. M., & Schultz, L. A. (1985). The effects of child maltreatment on security of infant–adult attachment. *Infant Behavior and Development, 8,* 35–45.

Lefkowitz, M. M., & Tesiny, E. P. (1984). Rejection and depression: Prospective and contemporaneous analyses. *Developmental Psychology*, 20, 776–785.

Liu, D., Diorio, J., Tannenbaum, B., Caldji, C., Francis, D., Freedman, A., et al. (1997). Maternal care, hippocampal glucocorticoid receptors, and hypothalamic-pituitary-adrenal responses to stress. *Science*, 277, 1659–1662.

Lovejoy, M. C., Gracyk, P. A., Hare, E., & Neuman, G. (2000). Maternal depression and parenting behavior: A meta-analytic review. *Clinical-Psychology-Review*, 20, 561–592.

Margolin, G., Christensen, A., & John, R. S. (1996). The continuance and spillover of everyday tensions in distressed and nondistressed families. *Journal of Family Psychology*, 10, 304–321.

Markman, H., Stanley, S., & Blumberg, S. I. (1994). *Fighting for your marriage*. San Francisco: Jossey-Bass.

McMahon, R. J., Forehand, R., Griest, D. L., & Wells, K. C. (1981). Who drops out of therapy during parent training? *Behavioral Counseling Quarterly*, 1, 79–85.

Murray, C. J. L., & Lopez, A. D. (Eds.). (1996). *The global burden of disease: A comprehensive assessment of mortality and disability from diseases, injuries, and risk factors in 1990 and projected to 2020*. Cambridge, MA: Harvard University Press.

Owen, M. T., & Cox, M. J. (1997). Marital conflict and the development of infant-parent attachment relationships. *Journal of Family Psychology*, 11, 152–164.

Patterson, G. R. (1982). *Coercive family processes*. Eugene, OR: Castilia.

Patterson, G. R., Reid, J. B., & Dishion, T. J. (1992). *Antisocial boys*. Eugene, OR: Castilia.

Reiss, D., Pedersen, N. L., Cederblad, M., Lichtenstein, P., Hansson, K., Neiderhiser, J. M., & Elthammar, O. (2001). Genetic probes of three theories of maternal adjustment: I. Recent evidence and a model. *Family Process*, 40, 247–259.

Roy, K., Mitchell, P., & Wilhelm, K. (2001). Depression and smoking: Examining correlates in a subset of depressed patients. *Australian and New Zealand Journal of Psychiatry*, 35, 329–335.

Sabatelli, R. M., & Bartle-Haring, S. (2003). Family-of-origin experiences and adjustment in married couples. *Journal of Marriage and Family*, 65, 159–169.

Sanders, M. R., & McFarland, M. (2000). Treatment of depressed mothers with disruptive children: A controlled evaluation of cognitive behavioral family intervention. *Behavior Therapy*, 31, 89–112.

Sher, T. G., Baucom, D. H., & Larus, J. M. (1990). Communication patterns and response to treatment among depressed and nondepressed maritally distressed couples. *Journal of Family Psychology*, 4, 63–79.

Snyder, D. K., Mangrum, L. F., & Wills, R. M. (1993). Predicting couples' response to marital therapy: A comparison of short- and long-term predictors. *Journal of Consulting and Clinical Psychology*, 61, 61–69.

Stein, D., Williamson, D. E., Birmaher, B., Brent, D. A., Kaufman, J., Dahl, R. E., et al. (2000). Parent–child bonding and family functioning in depressed children and children at high-risk for future depression. *Journal of the American Academy of Child and Adolescent Psychiatry*, 39, 1387–1395.

Taylor, T. K., & Biglan, A. (1998). Behavioral family interventions for improving child-rearing: A review of the literature for clinicians and policy makers. *Clinical Child and Family Psychology Review*, 1, 41–60.

Teti, D. M., & Gelfand, D. M. (1991). Behavioral competence among mothers of infants in the first year: The mediational role maternal self-efficacy. *Child Development*, 62, 918–929.

Trad, P. V. (1987). *Infant and childhood depression: Developmental factors*. New York: Wiley.

Trad, P. V. (1994). Depression in infants. In W. M. Reynolds & H. F. Johnston (Eds.), *Handbook of depression in children and adolescents* (pp. 401–426). New York: Plenum Press.

Wade, T. J., & Cairney, J. (2000). Major depressive disorder and marital transition among mothers: Results from a national panel study. *Journal of Nervous and Mental Disease*, 188, 741–750.

Webster-Stratton, C. (1994). Advancing video tape parenting training: A comparison study. *Journal of Consulting and Clinical Psychology*, 62, 583–593.

Weissman, M. M., Bland, R., Joyce, P. R., & Newman, S. (1993). Sex differences in rates of depression: Cross-national perspectives. *Journal of Affective Disorders Special Issue: Toward New Psychobiology of Depression in Women*, 29, 77–84.

Weissman, M. M., & Paykel, E. S. (1974). *The depressed woman: A study of social relationships*. Chicago: University of Chicago Press.

Whisman, M. A. (2001). The association between depression and marital dissatisfaction. In S. R. H. Beach (Ed.), *Marital and family processes in depression: A scientific foundation for clinical practice* (pp. 3–24). Washington, DC: American Psychological Association.

Whisman, M. A., & Bruce, M. L. (1999). Marital distress and incidence of major depressive episode in a community sample. *Journal of Abnormal Psychology, 108,* 674–678.

Part VI

BASIC PROCESSES

CHAPTER 18

Communication: Basic Properties and Their Relevance to Relationship Research

Alan L. Sillars
Anita L. Vangelisti

The terms *communication* and *relationship*, although not synonymous, are so entangled that it is difficult to talk about one concept without presuming the other. Within the academic study of communication, the term communication is invariably seen as a relational state, that is, as a "pattern of interconnections" (Rogers, 1998), whether between two people or between a source and audience at some broader level of analysis. Within the study of personal relationships, communication is seen as the means by which people construct and maintain relationships, along with a set of skills or skill deficits that contribute to relationship adjustment (Burleson, Metts, & Kirch, 2000). Thus, it is difficult to set clear boundaries on communication as a subtopic under personal relationships because relationships are entailed in all acts of communication and communication is the central process giving shape to relationships.

Given the difficulty of isolating, let alone reviewing, all of the literature on communication in personal relationships, we do not attempt such a review. Instead, we intend to talk about communication as a particular lens for analyzing personal relationships. Here again, there are a few alternative ways one could approach the task. Some reviews of equivalent scope compare and contrast perspectives on the study of communication (Baxter & Montgomery, 1996; Burleson et al., 2000; Roloff & Anastasiou, 2001). The perspectives examined in these reviews vary, ranging from strategic approaches (which emphasize the goals of communication) to functional approaches (which focus on the tasks or activities achieved through communication) to indexical approaches (which center on the outcomes associated with communication). Comparing and contrasting different perspectives can be a useful exercise for providing conceptual order and (if done evenhandedly) clarifying commonplace areas of argument between theoretical traditions (Craig, 1999). On the other hand, specific research programs are often hard to categorize under a few perspectives because their origins and purposes are quite diverse. Thus, we have yet to see much agreement on the criteria or vocabulary used to partition communication research according to broad perspectives. Further, by focusing on the distinguishing attributes of perspectives, we naturally foreground dissimilarities over similarities. This has the inadvertent consequence that central concepts and broadly shared assumptions receive less attention than concepts and assumptions that represent boundary issues.

In this chapter, we reverse the emphasis on competing perspectives, choosing instead to reflect on basic properties of communication that are often acknowledged across perspectives. We identify five such properties: *interdependence, reflexivity, complexity, ambiguity*, and *indeterminancy*. To be sure, there are specific debates related to each of these properties and the relevant ideas are not uniformly emphasized. Nonetheless, we maintain that there is wide agreement (or a least a lack of direct disagreement) about the basic properties themselves. Thus, these properties ground what we would characterize as a "communication perspective." In explicating and illustrating each of the five properties of communication, we further explore how the study of communication and the study of relationships intersect.

Interdependence

Interdependence refers to the idea, popularized by systems theorists, that messages simultaneously influence, and are influenced by, those messages that precede and follow. This mutual influence creates coherence between messages and across interactions and it accounts for the "relational" features of communication (i.e., pattern, process, and form), which exist in the connections between events or entities (Bateson, 1972; Rogers, 1998). Although similar to the conceptualization of interdependence put forth by Thibaut and Kelley (1959), this conceptualization is distinct in that it focuses on the mutual influence of messages rather than the ways that individuals affect each other's outcomes during interaction.

Interdependence is often seen as a defining feature of communication; in fact, some authors go so far as to define communication exclusively in terms of observed

(statistical) interdependence. That is, communication occurs when the probability of one person's behavior changes in response to another person's behavior and vice versa (see Cappella, 1988; Gottman, 1982). Definitions on this order, reflecting the influence of information theory and cybernetics, require no inferences about internal states and apply to a broad range of phenomena, potentially including machines, animals, and nonreflective human behavior. To be sure, other authors would see any definition of communication that makes no reference to intentions or symbols, for example, as incomplete and overly inclusive (e.g., Motley, 1990). Still, definitions of communication commonly include interdependence as at least a necessary, if insufficient, condition (e.g., Rogers, 1998).

Interdependence accounts for the central feature of living systems – *wholeness* (or *nonsummativity*). That is, the interdependent relationships between components, rather than the components themselves, account for the unique characteristics of the whole. The application of this principle to human communication suggests that the structure and complexity of a communication system is defined by interdependent patterns of interaction, rather than characteristics of people or messages per se. Thus, patterns are of primary interest, whereas objects (singular events or individual entities) are secondary (Rogers, 1998). Some past authors have argued on this basis that the primary focus of communication research should be the study of sequential interaction patterns (e.g., Fisher, 1975; Gottman, 1982). Although this argument did not fully carry the day, as witnessed by the eclectic nature of current communication research, several strong research traditions have emerged focused on mutual influence processes in interactions.

The theme of interdependence is quite pronounced, for example, in developmental studies of infant and child communication competencies. This research builds on the idea that, from birth, human beings are "primed for social interaction" (Barratt, 1995) and thus, infants and adults mutually regulate one another's behavior. For example, infants imitate adults' facial expressions and finger movements (Meltzoff & Moore, 1977), engage in coordinated vocal interactions with their primary caregiver in a way that approximates adult dialogue (Ginsburg & Kilbourne, 1988), adapt vocalizations and the latency of responses to those of their mother (Beebe, Jaffe, Feldstein, Mays, & Alson, 1985), and regulate activity levels in an effort to gain the attention of an unresponsive adult (Papousek, Papousek, & Haekel, 1987). Adult communication is similarly influenced by infants, in fact, a number of researchers suggest that infants exert more control over adult–infant interactions than do adults (e.g., Van Egeren, Barratt, & Roach, 2001). Van Egeren and Barratt (2004) explained that

> mothers tend to watch until the infant makes eye contact, which appears to activate the mother's vocalizing, smiling, and touching behaviors. . . . If the infant responds in some way, the chain of communication is continued and intensified until the infant breaks the cycle. (p. 298)

Interdependence in communication is most often conceptualized in terms of two opposite response tendencies – a tendency to reciprocate or match features of the other's communication versus a tendency to compensate (see Cappella, 1987). For example, studies of vocal behavior indicate that, under most conditions, conversational partners automatically adapt to each other to match behaviors such as speech rate and hesitation (Cappella & Planalp, 1981). In other circumstances, people may compensate for increases in physical proximity by decreasing eye gaze (Argyle & Dean, 1965) or the directness of body orientation (Pellegrini & Empey, 1970). Although the issue is beyond our scope here, the conditions under which individuals reciprocate versus compensate aspects of another's communication can be complex and have given rise to several alternative theories of interpersonal adaptation (see Burgoon, Stern, & Dillman, 1995).

Within the context of relationship research, the principle of interdependence is reflected in the study of dyadic interaction patterns. The concept of an *interaction pattern* presumes that there is a degree of redundancy – predictability as to the way events are ordered sequentially within interpersonal communication. Interaction patterns reveal a few basic things about communication in personal relationships. First, they demonstrate ways in which communication and relationships are coherent and structured. For example, people can carry on coherent conversations because they understand the (usually unspoken) rules associated with turn taking and topicality (e.g., Duncan & Fiske, 1977). They can gather information about others during initial interactions because they know that certain questions are appropriate and typically will obtain predictable responses (e.g., Berger, Gardner, Clatterbuck, & Schulman, 1976). This is not to say that such structures are necessarily highly predictable or static. Communication patterns fluctuate in response to day-to-day pressures such as economic stress (Conger, Ge, Elder, Lorenz, & Simmons, 1994). They change with relational events (Baxter & Bullis, 1986) and evolve with the passage of time (Dickson, Christian, & Remmo, 2004). Indeed one clear indication of mutual influence is the fact that communication rules may be augmented, suspended, or modified based on relationship history (e.g., Denzin, 1970). However, the changes are also, to some degree, patterned. It is this patterning that allows researchers to study developmental trends, to examine interactions that characterize different relational events, and to describe communicative responses to various social circumstances.

Second, interaction patterns reflect multiple systemic influences on communication, both of a proximal and distal nature. Every act of communication is enacted and interpreted within a particular "historical" context, including the time and place, relationship history, and history of the immediate encounter (Duck, 2002). Thus, a given communicative act is grounded in the overall context as well as the immediate actions that preceded it. For example, a considerable body of parent–child research is premised on a distinction between broad parenting styles (e.g., power-assertive versus inductive styles of parental discipline and persuasion). Yet these "styles" are, to some extent, an adaptation to specific contingencies within and across interactions, because parents typically mix elements of induction and power assertion, depending on how a child has misbehaved and whether children resist initial efforts to gain their compliance (Wilson, Whipple, & Grau, 1996). Similarly, a given infant-caregiver sequence may be influenced by factors that are external to the interaction itself, including socioecological sources of support and stress (Belsky, 1984). For example, if there has been a great deal of intense conflict in the relationship between the caregiver and his or her spouse, the caregiver's ability to attend to the infant's bids for attention may be diminished, thus disrupting reciprocity and affecting compatibility in this relationship (Belsky, 1984; Lamb & Gilbride, 1985).

Third, interaction patterns potentially reveal forms of relating that mediate relationship quality over time. This is suggested by the (presumably) bidirectional linkage between interaction patterns and relational outcomes (Cappella, 1987). That is, the mutual responsiveness (or reactivity) of individuals during communication predicts satisfaction, distress and so forth, over and above what one would assume based on overall communication base-rates. Indeed, much of the research on communication in marriage is concerned with identifying patterns of interaction that predict couple satisfaction versus distress. The most familiar connection of this sort is the especially high reciprocity of negative affect among dissatisfied married couples, over-and-above the amount of negativity shown by these couples generally (e.g., Gottman, 1994; Margolin & Wampold, 1981).

More recently, considerable attention has been given to a compensatory pattern that predicts marital dissatisfaction, referred to as the "demand–withdraw" pattern (i.e., one partner communicates in "demanding" ways, while the other tries to avoid the conversation). A number of studies have found

gender differences, such that wives engage in demanding behaviors more frequently than husbands, whereas husbands withdraw more often than wives (Baucom, Notarius, Burnett, & Haefner, 1990; Christensen & Shenk, 1991). However, there also is evidence that this pattern varies based on the topics discussed and the extent to which one person desires change on a particular issue more than the partner (Christensen & Heavey, 1990; Heavey, Layne, & Christensen, 1993). Some researchers have even found that husbands and wives sometimes reverse roles, with husbands engaging in demanding behavior and wives withdrawing, when husbands are the ones who desire change (Caughlin & Vangelisti, 1999; Klinetob & Smith, 1996). In either event, frequent use of the demand–withdraw pattern is symptomatic of marital dissatisfaction (e.g., Heavey et al., 1993), even after controlling for the effects of overall negativity in marriage (Caughlin & Huston, 2002).

Important questions remain about the causal impact of such interaction patterns on marital satisfaction and other relational outcomes (e.g., Bradbury, Rogge, & Lawrence, 2001; Erbert & Duck, 1997). As we note later in the section on indeterminancy, it can be misleading to regard messages (or interaction patterns) as having fixed effects on relational outcomes, without considering important contextualizing factors. Nonetheless, the research provides a convincing illustration that the (sequential) pattern of messages over multiple turns is itself, a key element of the context for a given act of communication.

Reflexivity

Reflexivity refers to the dual position of communication vis-à-vis relationship structure (i.e., rules, codes, situated identities, shared knowledge), in that communication both creates structure and is constrained by it. This idea reflects the classic sociological problem of agency versus structure (McPhee, 1998) but with a direct focus on dialogue as the generative mechanism for the cocreation and enactment of structure and with relationships as the level of analysis (Burleson et al., 2000). Fundamentally, the principle of reflexivity suggests that human relationships are constituted through communication. That is, communication is "essential" (Duck & Pond, 1988) and "strongly consequential" (Sanders, 1995). At the same time, "Emergent patterns of relational form are given life, rest on, and circle around the very processes from which they arise" (Rogers, 1998, p. 70). Thus, communication processes are both creative and reactive. People are "proactive actors who make communicative choices" but also "reactive objects, because their actions become reified in a variety of normative and institutionalized practices that establish the boundaries of subsequent communicative moves" (Baxter & Montgomery, 1996, p. 13).

Few authors dispute the idea that relationships are socially constructed through communication; however, certain research traditions focus on this theme, and others do not. Whereas some authors see relationship implications in all communication (e.g., Watzlawick, Beavin, & Jackson, 1967), discourse and conversation analytic scholars have been reluctant to study relationships because of the difficulty in documenting the "procedural relevance" of relationships to the way conversations are conducted (Mandelbaum, 2003). Mandelbaum offered a partial bridge, suggesting that the relationship implications of conversation are more apparent when the relative positioning of interactants is problematic. Speaking more broadly about relationship research, Burleson et al. (2000) distinguished between "consequential–cultural" approaches, which consider how communication fabricates, maintains, and modifies relational culture, versus "strategic–functional" approaches, which examine how people use communication in a more or less skillful manner to address relationship functions or goals. Close inspection of the researchers and authors identified with each approach suggests that there is a fuzzy boundary between the traditions, with at least occasional crossover. Nonetheless,

certain themes best exemplify investigation into the reflexive nature of communication and relationships (i.e., the consequential–cultural approach). A few such themes include the investigation of everyday discourse, relationship narratives or accounts, and relationship cultures.

Everyday Discourse

Duck (e.g., Duck, 1995; Duck & Pond, 1988) has built an extensive case for the symbolic force of everyday, routine conversations in creating, manifesting, and sustaining relationships. Essentially, Duck argued that relationships are ephemeral or transitory social objects, the "nature" of which depends on agreement within some community at a given rhetorical moment. By its very occurrence, talk serves to project an image of the relationship as real and enduring, thereby promoting its continuance. Talk also serves as a marker of the relationship. Once people agree that they are in a particular type of relationship and come to talk about it as such, their discourse changes in a number of ways. Thus, different topics are talked about, and these topics are understood in new light. Moreover, because partners (and others) inevitably have different perspectives on a relationship, talk in everyday life reflects an ongoing dialogue between alternative perspectives. Rather than reaching a final resolution at a given stage of relationship development, this dialogue is perpetually unfinished and largely manifested in ordinary, mundane communication.

Studies that explore the qualities of routine, everyday discourse have adopted diary methods to examine, for example, what people talk about, when, and with whom; how they identify and evaluate different forms of talk; how these features reflect different types of relationships; and so forth. For example, Duck, Rutt, Hoyhurst, and Strejc (1991) collected communication diaries from college students and found that most interactions were routine but satisfying, resulted in little change in the relationship, and differed according to gender, days of the week, and the type of relationship. In a study that combined diaries and other self-reports, Goldsmith and Baxter (1996) identified various types of speech events experienced by college students (e.g., gossip, joking around, serious relationship talk, making plans). Most of these were light, informal, and not explicitly goal directed. This lends some support to the idea that routine interactions are the basic fabric of relationships over more obviously strategic and instrumental forms of communication, at least when viewed in terms of the relative occurrence of speech events. The research also showed that different types of speech events predominate in different types of relationships (e.g., small talk among acquaintances, gossip among close friends), thus suggesting another way that relationships are constituted in talk.

Relationship Narratives and Accounts

The stories people tell about their relationships shape relationships by delineating and solidifying the rules and roles that define interactions (Jorgenson & Bochner, 2004). When people offer relational narratives or accounts to others, they position themselves and their partner with regard to each other and to a larger social world. They provide a particular portrayal of their relationship and, in the process, often show how, when, and why partners behave the way they do (Harvey, Weber, & Orbuch, 1990).

Some studies further suggest that the portrayals put forth in narratives are linked to relational quality. For instance, Buehlman, Gottman, and Katz (1992) found that married couples who described themselves as having overcome obstacles together had more stable, satisfying relationships than those who did not. The authors of this research suggested that couples who label themselves as resilient enter difficult situations with an optimistic attitude. Thus, these couples may be more ready and willing to encourage and comfort each other when adversity strikes.

Indeed, researchers and theorists who study narratives in close relationships underline the notion that people often behave in ways that confirm the perceptions they hold about their associations with others (e.g., Bruner, 1990; Byng-Hall, 1988). These scholars suggest that the stories individuals tell about their relationships affect the way they view their interpersonal associations and, as a consequence, shape the way they perceive and respond to partner behavior. Those who describe their relationships as optimistic and success-oriented thus will tend to view their partner's behavior through that orientation and will behave in ways that support their view.

Narratives also shape individuals' behavior when they are used to illustrate the rules and roles associated with relationships. For instance, families who consistently tell stories about a member being "strong," "mature," and "reliable" may create an environment in which it is difficult or uncomfortable for that person to express his or her insecurities. Because people are motivated to sustain their stories (Murray & Holmes, 1994), even in cases where the person is willing to discuss his or her fears, other family members may disregard them. In this way, stories embody prescriptions or standards that individuals use to evaluate themselves and their relational partners (Sternberg, 1996; Vangelisti, Crumley, & Baker, 1999). When narrators praise certain behaviors, note the usefulness of particular personality traits, or point out cases in which rules or roles are violated, they create and sustain prescriptions for enacting close relationships (Stone, 1988).

Relationship Cultures

The metaphor of "relationship culture," as it is generally used, also emphasizes the creative and emergent properties of communication, that is, relationships are conceived as establishing their own distinctive moral and social order, including private codes and unique interaction rules (Baxter, 1987; Denzin, 1970). Relationship cultures draw from conventions in the broader language community but are unique because of jointly constructed variations in routine and common conversational practices (Burleson et al., 2000). The joint construction of roles consistent with relational cultures is similar to processes that characterize the construction of social reality on a larger cultural scale (Berger & Luckmann, 1966) but with an additional dialectic involving the regulation of autonomy and privacy between the dyad (or family, etc.) and larger community (Montgomery, 1992).

There are quite a number of ways that relationship cultures manifest distinctive communicative practices. For example, over time, relational partners acquire private idioms (Hopper, Knapp, & Scott, 1981) and other special vocabulary, symbols of relationship identity (Baxter, 1987), routines and rituals (Bruess & Pearson, 1997), insider meaning (Hopper, 1981; Planalp & Garvin-Doxas, 1994), secrets (Vangelisti, 1994), and unique interaction rules (e.g., Planalp, 1993).

An issue that arises with respect to relational cultures specifically, and the property of reflexivity more generally, is how we should view the connection between relationships, communities, and societies (Montgomery, 1992). That is, to what extent are relationships a result of individualized, creative processes at the level of the dyad versus patterns, resources, and constraints that exist at a community or cultural level? There are broad differences in emphasis. At one end of the continuum are authors who emphasize the emergent, creative, and ephemeral nature of relationship patterns, picturing communication as a type of collaborative but improvisational art form, such as a dance or jazz ensemble (Baxter & Montgomery, 1996; Gottman, 1982; Rogers, 1998). At the other end, are authors who critique the tendency to regard interpersonal processes in isolation from broader social–cultural–historical forces (Lannamann, 1991; Sigman, 1998).

Montgomery (1992) offered a useful integrative statement about the interface of relational cultures and the larger society. She conceptualized this interface in terms of the negotiation of autonomy and connection between couples and society, suggesting that both act as communicative agencies. For example, couples may communicate to others how dependent or independent they are with regard to the rest of society by regulating their physical accessibility to others or using idiomatic speech in public. Simultaneously, social collectives, institutions, and networks act as communicative agencies through practices that carry implicit and explicit assertions about the autonomy of couples within society, such as those conveyed by the ceremonial options available for weddings or by the relationship advice that is received from members of social networks. The overall management of a couple's relation to the larger society also takes a variety of forms, such as oscillation between autonomy and connection, stressing autonomy and connection in different contexts, or consistently opting for one polarity over the other (Montgomery, 1992).

Complexity

A basic notion underlying much of the research on interpersonal communication is that communication conveys multiple messages simultaneously on different levels of analysis. In other words, "there is no such thing as a simple message" (Weakland, 1976, p. 117). The analytic separation of multiple meanings has roots in pragmatics (e.g., Austin, 1962) and interactional systems theory (Bateson, 1972; Watzlawick et al., 1967). However, analogous distinctions are commonplace throughout the literature on communication. Most basically, a number of authors distinguish between the literal or propositional content of a message and a second, pragmatic level of meaning. The second level of meaning, variously referred to as the "command" (Ruesch & Bateson, 1951), "relationship" (Watzlawick et al., 1967), "presentational" (Danziger, 1976), "illocutionary" (Searle, 1969), or "episodic" (Frentz & Farrell, 1976) aspect of meaning, includes the type of action and expected response conveyed (e.g., a request for information, a command), as well as the social or evaluative implications of the act (e.g., whether the act shows commitment, restraint, formality, independence, antagonism). The second level of meaning invokes a particular type of relationship and thus accounts for references to "relational communication." Whereas the first level of meaning is relatively explicit (that is, it is grounded in the formal coding rules of language or similar symbol systems), the second level of meaning is implicit in action. Thus, the "negotiation of relationships" is an implicit subtext to all communication, reflected in such things as the pragmatic form of utterances (and the responses they elicit), nonverbal signals, and various aspects of context (Watzlawick et al., 1967; Wilmot, 1980).

Authors connected with the *relational* perspective (e.g., Fisher & Drecksel, 1983; Rogers & Millar, 1988) have made the most direct attempt to operationalize relationship aspects of communication (hence, the name), particularly as these aspects were conceptualized within interactional systems theory. These authors have considered how the concepts of relationship *symmetry* and *complementarity* (i.e., relative dominance) might be manifested in terms of (a) the syntactic and pragmatic features of utterances (e.g., a question that extends the previous utterance versus a disconfirming statement) and (b) recurring message sequences. Although less obvious, a similar focus on implicit relationship negotiation is pervasive throughout much of the research on interpersonal communication. For example, research on communication in family conflicts is almost exclusively concerned with *how* families communicate about conflict and what this suggests about their relationships. Only rarely have researchers considered "content" features of conflict, for example, what families disagree about or what they decide to about it (see Sillars, Canary, & Tafoya, 2004). Similarly, the research on narratives, cited earlier, is not concerned with the stories per se but with how implicit features of stories and the process of storytelling connect with relationship roles and identities.

Along with the multiple levels of meaning that are associated with a given message, several other compelling features of interaction heighten the complexity of communication.

For one, messages are interpreted in terms of a surrounding matrix of messages, including extralinguistic and contextual cues that modify meaning (e.g., Duck, 2002; Wilmot, 1980). Participants to a conversation must integrate these multiple signals and then adapt and implement subsequent moves in a nearly instantaneous manner, to keep up with the normal pace of face-to-face communication (Bavelas & Coates, 1992; Kellerman, 1992). Further, extreme selectivity is required to discern the signals that are potentially meaningful because the stimuli generated during interaction are exceptionally rich and diverse. Street and Cappella (1985) noted the challenge this situation presents from the researcher's perspective:

> When one stops even for a moment to consider the diversity and kind of stimuli that are being generated during an interaction, a kind of despair creeps into the researcher's bones. How can anyone hope to study, let alone understand, the various verbal, vocal, and kinesic activities that people carry out while speaking and listening? What is worse, these auditory, visual, tactile and olfactory stimuli are information dense per unit of time. This means that they are changing a great deal over time. (p. 4)

Street and Cappella (1985) organized the many extralinguistic features of messages according to functional groupings, as a means of imposing order and showing relationships between diverse signals. These authors identify a tentative list of seven interaction functions: *coherence, intimacy, positive reinforcement, impression management, control, persuasion,* and *dominance–power.* Each function is associated with characteristic speech acts and nonverbal behaviors that are logically or empirically linked (or both) (e.g., intimacy reflects gaze, touch, and disclosure; impression management relates to verbal accounts, converging speech rates, smiling, and so on).

Although they do not focus on the issue directly, Street and Cappella (1985) appeared to regard the multiple functions of messages as overlapping systems that operate in tandem, rather than as competing explanatory frameworks. That is, messages presumably serve multiple (and perhaps several) functions simultaneously. Sigman (1998) reached a similar conclusion, although on quite different grounds (i.e., Sigman rejected the type of cognitive theorizing about communication that Street and Cappella embraced). According to Sigman, distinct rule sets govern the organization and coherence of face-to-face discourse versus the structure of relationships; however, these orders partly overlap in that the same unit of behavior (e.g., address terms) may serve multiple functions, and might be governed by more than one set of rules.

Jacobs (2002) also stressed the multifunctional nature of language; however, in his view it is important to recognize that multifunctionality might not be an additive process (one set of rules layered on top another) but rather an integrative one. That is, utterances reflect ways of responding in a unified manner to multiple demands and goals. Jacobs (2002) suggested, in concert with a number of others (see Tracy, 1989; Wilson & Sabee, 2003), that the ability to satisfy multiple demands and goals simultaneously is one of the central features of communication skill or competence.

An obvious question suggested by the complexity of face-to-face interaction is how people are able to pull it all off. That is, how do people manage to process diverse, rapidly changing stimuli, interpret these signals according to multilayered meanings and functions within a surrounding matrix of meanings, integrate this information with multiple and sometimes conflicting goals, and then reply appropriately in real time without disrupting the flow of natural conversation? This question is not easily answered. As Bavelas and Coates (1992) pointed out, the discrete operations and stages involved in cognitive models of speech comprehension and production are so complex, even when limited to isolated sentences rather than dialogue, that the models cannot possibly account for the rapidity with which individuals construct precisely fitted, improvised, and immediate responses during conversation. Bavelas (1990) observed that

"even the most banal conversation leaves current cognitive models in the dust" (p. 600).

Some authors, including many discourse and conversation analysts, deliberately avoid cognitive theorizing, at least in part, to avoid the untenable assumptions that can result from treating most discourse as a consciously strategic activity (see LeBaron & Koschmann, 2003; however, see Jacobs, 2002, regarding movement toward an inferential–strategic model of discourse). Other authors, who directly embrace cognitive concepts, provide several partial explanations concerning how participants are able to process and manage the complexity of communication. First, participants in communication are extremely selective about what signals they pay attention to. Further, they rely on conversational devices and interpretive principles to direct attention to the crux features of messages and contexts that reveal intended meaning (e.g., by sequencing information and marking topic shifts in ways that point to relevant background knowledge; see Tracy, 1985).

Second, people employ a number of mental shortcuts both when interpreting messages and when implementing or adapting communication strategies. Cognitive processing of communication is generally "geared to achieving the greatest possible cognitive effect for the smallest possible processing effort" (Sperber & Wilson, 1995, p.). This principle reflects the "cognitive miser" metaphor that is familiar within the social cognition literature (see Fletcher & Fincham, 1991), the metaphor being even more apropos of dialogue than "passive observer" contexts of social cognition, given the additional cognitive demands and constraints imposed by direct participation in communication (Waldron & Cegala, 1992).

One example of people acting to conserve cognitive resources during communication is Berger's (1998) demonstration that people alter lower order communicative plans (e.g., repeating oneself to be understood) before they alter higher order plans that are more effortful to implement and revise. In the realm of interpersonal and family conflict, Sillars and others (Sillars, 1998; Sillars, Roberts, Leonard, & Dun, 2000) have suggested that the cognitive demands of communication sharply constrain the complexity, flexibility, and objectivity of thought and talk during escalating arguments and marital quarrels. Although perspective-taking and cognitive complexity are often seen as important, if not essential, contributors to competence and adaptability in communication, Sillars et al. (2000) found few examples of conscious perspective-taking, an overriding tone of certainty, and limited consideration of alternative positions or interpretations in the thoughts that spouses reported during a marital conflict discussion, based on video-assisted recall methods.

A third consideration is that communicative functions may be served by behaviors that are both outside awareness and unintentional (Street & Cappella, 1985). When viewed in this manner, message "functions" refer to researcher-imposed analytic categories rather than levels of intended meaning. On the other hand, many communication processes that are intentional are nonetheless outside awareness (Hample, 1987).

In responding to the frequent confusion of intentionality and awareness, Kellermann (1992) argued that communication is both inherently strategic (intentional) and, at the same time, primarily automatic. Communication is inherently strategic in the sense that people communicate for a purpose (to fulfill needs) and that symbols are selected in a manner that is responsive to constraints (e.g., social appropriateness) and adjusted to purposes (e.g., giving comfort) on an ongoing, moment-to-moment basis. Further, much behavior that is goal-dependent, monitored, and adjusted on an ongoing basis occurs outside awareness. Such behavior is not limited to communication behaviors and routines that are initially mindful and then become automated through overlearning (as in the case of "mindless" behavior; Langer, 1989). Rather, most communication "strategies" are tacitly acquired and employed, in the same manner that individuals acquire and appropriately use language rules without ever being directly cognizant of them (Kellermann, 1992; see also Wilson & Sabee, 2003).

Hierarchical theories of message production (see Parks, 1994; Wilson & Sabee, 2003) help to explain how many aspects of communication can be simultaneously strategic and nonreflective. Generally speaking, these models assume that higher order knowledge structures (e.g., broad goals, plans, self-perceptions) exert control over the procedural operations involved in communication (e.g., organizing sensory input, synchronizing speech rhythms, selecting and integrating speech topics) without requiring direct attention to procedural operations, except where they become overtly problematic (e.g., one has difficulty pronouncing a name). The resulting process, as represented, for example, in Greene's (1997) revised action assembly theory, promotes extremely rapid processing of communication but in a manner that is also fallible, especially when there are competing goals (see Wilson & Sabee, 2003).

Ambiguity

A nearly universal assumption in the study of communication is that meanings are not "brute facts" but rather a product of negotiation (Montgomery, 1992; p. 484). This reflects the fact that the coding rules associated with language and other symbolic systems are incomplete. That is, the rules "underdetermine" the form and meaning of a message, always leaving it ambiguous to a degree (see Carston, 2002). Thus, mutual understanding is problematic and requires something beyond the application of a shared language (Sanders, Fitch, & Pomerantz, 2001). Even relatively simple and straightforward messages require considerable filling in of uncoded, taken-for-granted information (e.g., Hopper, 1981). In other cases, there may be no obvious correspondence between a string of signals and the meaning conveyed. Further, any particular message can mean multiple things depending on the context of occurrence (Jacobs, 2002).

These ideas contrast with a second view of communication, sometimes called the "conduit" metaphor (Reddy, 1979) or "transmission" model (Craig, 1999), which sees communication as a mechanical process of transferring information from the head of one person (source) to another (receiver) through reciprocal application of a shared code (i.e., "encoding" and "decoding"). This latter view is a frequent target of academic critiques, although, as Craig observed, the position critiqued tends to be a simplistic straw figure rather than a serious perspective with genuine adherents. On the other hand, the transmission model does seem to reflect popular and cultural assumptions about communication. For example, misunderstanding and a host of other interpersonal difficulties are most often attributed to a *lack* of communication – an emphasis that entirely neglects the more subtle aspects of communication (Sillars, 1998).

At the most basic level of analysis, ambiguity is reflected in linguistic underdeterminancy – the notion that no utterance fully encodes the thought or proposition it is used to express (Carston, 2002). Even the most explicit aspects of communication (i.e., literal meaning) rely on shared principles of inference that go beyond a surface reading of messages. Far greater potential ambiguity is associated with the sort of pragmatic meanings that are directly germane to the study of personal relationships, such as the speech acts reflected in various systems used to analyze marital and family interactions (e.g., "description," "agreement," "criticism," "validation"). The determination of a given speech act is ambiguous, because the same message can perform different actions (e.g., "How about telling him yourself?" can be a suggestion, challenge, criticism, rhetorical answer, or simple question depending on the context; Jacobs, 2002, p. 231). A single utterance can also serve as multiple acts simultaneously (e.g., "How much longer will you be?" can serve as an informational question, criticism, and indirect request [to hurry] all at the same time; Jacobs, 2002, p. 232).

Further, attempts to define the rules underlying the sequential use of speech acts (i.e., the "grammar of conversation") encounter the difficulty that many blatant rule violations are nonetheless coherent and meaningful (Jacobs, 2002).

Quite apart from the inherent ambiguities of language and other symbolic systems, there is also strategic ambiguity in communication, reflecting a speaker's effort at managing multiple and often conflicting goals. That is, through indirectness or obfuscation, a speaker might respond to the immediate pressure to say something coherent and appropriate, while at the same time trying to avoid saying anything too directly, in an effort to preserve good relations, show politeness, maintain personal boundaries, or avoid being pinned down (e.g., Bavelas, Black, Chovil, & Mullett, 1990; Craig, Tracy, & Spisak, 1986). The multifunctionality of such discourse both increases ambiguity (Craig et al., 1986) and invites selective responding because, with greater ambiguity, the listener is less constrained in furnishing an interpretation (Sanders, 1984).

Naturally, ambiguity in communication is affected by relationship history. In more intimate contexts, individuals may gain license to speak directly; moreover, they acquire shared knowledge and memories that facilitate understanding of complex and implicit aspects of intended meaning (Colvin, Vogt, & Ickes, 1997; Planalp & Garvin-Doxas, 1994). However, the ambiguity of communication is transformed rather than resolved by relational intimacy and shared history. Although intimacy may promote direct talk, it can also spark compensatory efforts to maintain autonomy and privacy in response to the potential transparency of close relationships. Strategic ambiguity is reflected, for example, in the case of an adolescent who reveals more to family outsiders than to insiders or the case of a spouse who speaks vaguely to avoid losing an argument. Further, there are distinctive biases associated with the way individuals interpret communication within close relationships, stemming from such things as the emotionality of close relationships and a tendency for long-established perceptions to become entrenched, thus promoting theory-driven processing of messages (Sillars, 1998).

Research confirms the intuitive point that pragmatic and relational meanings are often seen differently by relational "insiders" than "outsiders" (e.g., Surra & Ridley, 1991); however, insiders frequently diverge from one another as well. This is suggested, for example, by the generally low-to-moderate correspondence between parent and adolescent reports of family interaction (see Noller & Callan, 1988). Further, in dissatisfying relationships and conflictive encounters, spouses tend to "code" one another's communication in dissimilar terms, for example, by attributing negative intent to messages where none was reported by the sender (see Sillars et al., 2004 for a review) or by making self-serving attributions about who is disclosing, being attentive, and collaborating versus criticizing, distorting, and changing the topic (Sillars et al., 2000). Thus, participants will sometimes fashion different and incompatible views about the roles being played by each person within a communication sequence, as suggested by Watzlawick et al.'s (1967) notion of "punctuation" differences in interaction.

A further demonstration of the ambiguity of communication in personal relationships is the notably weak empirical connection between how directly people talk about their thoughts and feelings and the extent to which others show understanding of those same dispositions. Several studies of marital and dating partners have found weak or null associations between the amount of information directly disclosed during communication and mutual understanding (see Sillars, 1998; Thomas & Fletcher, 1997). Ickes (2003) explained this phenomena partly in terms of "motivated misunderstanding," the idea that people are sometimes motivated by desires and insecurities to maintain inaccurate conceptions about others, even in the face of explicit information that contradicts these conceptions. Further, people appear to lack accurate meta-knowledge about their degree of understanding or misunderstanding of others during communication, such

that confidence in one's inferences does not predict empathic accuracy (Ickes, 2003; Thomas & Fletcher, 1997).

Although relationship research often emphasizes idiosyncratic aspects of message interpretation, discourse and conversation scholars have quite rightly pointed out that despite the potential ambiguity of language and communication, people usually understand one another and demonstrate understanding at an extraordinary level of detail (Jacobs, 2002; Roberts & Bavelas, 1996). Understandings are established, confirmed, updated, and repaired publicly and interactively over the course of successive turns. For example, an answer confirms that the previous turn was a question (not an indirect request for action, etc.; Lawrence, 2003) and this understanding is apt to be further reinforced or repaired in subsequent turns. Similarly, the use of a gesture across multiple turns and participants can establish the meaning of the gesture (LeBaron & Koschmann, 2003). Lawrence (1999) was directly critical of what he saw as a preoccupation with problematic aspects of understanding in communication research, including much of the research on interpersonal relationships. According to Lawrence, the heavy emphasis on misunderstanding disregards evidence from conversational analytic and ethnomethodological sources that interactants routinely enact and preserve intersubjective understanding through a range of conversational structures and practices.

It is not clear that these two ways of thinking about understanding and misunderstanding are as directly opposed as Lawrence (1999) suggests, however because the different traditions emphasize different contexts of communication and levels of abstraction. Conversation analysts emphasize routine interactions, along with semantic and pragmatic meanings that have practical consequences for the composition and sequencing of turns (e.g., whether the turn was meant as a question or indirect request; whether "the doctor" refers to "our doctor" or another doctor; Lawrence, 1999, p. 271). Interpersonal communication researchers typically study more abstract inferences, often within the context of relationship conflict or other problematic interactions. A close analyses of routine interactions will certainly show that people are skilled at managing understanding, insofar as it has practical consequences for the coordinated construction of speaking turns. Nonetheless, there are clearly conversations, both disjointed and well coordinated, in which individuals derive entirely different impressions about what the interaction meant in terms of respect, commitment, concern, cooperativeness, or other abstract, relational dimensions of communicative intent. Such interactions occasionally have significant impacts on relationships, quite apart from the question of whether misunderstanding is the typical or exceptional state of affairs overall.

(Outcome) Indeterminancy

There are various respects in which one might say that communication is indeterminate, so we need to mark our use of the term in order to limit the argument. First, there is indeterminancy (or "underdeterminancy") of meaning that we have previously spoken about. Second, there is the argument, made by advocates of a "rules" perspective (e.g., Cushman & Whiting, 1972) that communication is indeterminate because acts are chosen, not compelled (i.e., a variant of the philosophical debate over "free will"). The implication for some is that communication is outside the appropriate realm of causal theories, because individuals retain ultimate control in deciding whether to follow or break communication rules (however, see Toulmin, 1970, on the compatibility of reasoned action and causal theories).

The third sense of indeterminancy, and the one we wish to focus on for the remainder of this section, is that there are few, if any, fixed effects of messages on people or relationships. Instead, the impacts of messages are contextual, historical, personal, and cultural. A primary objective of communication theory and research is to articulate the critical features of contextual, historical, personal, or cultural background

in a useful way. However, in many cases this proves to be exceedingly tricky, given the contradictory manner in which communication can operate. That is, communication is both transparent and opaque, unifying and divisive, and a source of satisfaction and despair.

To illustrate, consider two prominent metaphors that have anchored much of the research on communication in personal relationships. First, there is the metaphor of "relationship development" that evolved from research on self-disclosure and models of relationship change (e.g., Altman & Taylor, 1973; Berger et al., 1976; Knapp & Vangelisti, 2005, Miller & Steinberg, 1975). Roughly speaking, these models suggest that mutual disclosure and the accumulation of shared experience during relationship development leads toward intimate mutual knowledge, greater understanding, and more efficient and idiosyncratic ways of communicating. Second, there is the metaphor of "relational communication," referenced throughout this chapter. This metaphor suggests that relationships are continuously negotiated through the implicit subtext of communication. Further, the "relational communication" theme has emphasized aspects of communication that often lead people into trouble, including the confusing binds that result from paradoxical messages, the "imperviousness" of communicators, and other tendencies that Watzlawick and colleagues (1967) labeled "pathological communication."

These two traditions make an interesting contrast. On the one hand, you have people emphasizing how communication acts as a centrifugal force in drawing together the inferences and meanings of separate individuals. On the other hand, you have people speculating about how family members, who share the most intimate of connections, psychologically injure one another through obscure, contradictory, and otherwise misguided efforts at communication. Although these traditions highlight opposite impacts of intimate communication, both images have face validity. Indeed, many of the things we might observe about communication are contradicted when we shift the context, even slightly.

It is interesting to see how researchers have swung in the direction of one polarity or another, based on social trends and other influences. This is illustrated by literature on self-disclosure and related concepts. Following humanistic traditions in psychology, along with the idealistic mind-set of the late 1960s and early 1970s, writers originally emphasized the importance of self-disclosure to psychological and relational health. This was followed by critiques during the more pragmatic 1980s and early 1990s (e.g., Brown & Rogers, 1991; Parks, 1982), undressing the ideological treatment of openness and intimacy in writing about communication, and next by a wave of interest in privacy, secrecy, deception, and the "dark side of communication" (e.g., Cupach & Spitzberg, 1994). Recently, greater attention has been directed toward the balance between disclosure and privacy, as reflected, for example, in Petronio's (2002) "boundary management" perspective.

Inevitably, a certain distortion occurs any time that we talk about how communication works in "either–or" terms that are overly straightforward. Both general systems theory and dialectical theory make this point forcefully. General systems theory suggests that any final state or final condition can be achieved through different means and from different starting points (von Bertalanffy, 1968). This concept, labeled equifinality, defies the notion that, for example, communication goals only can be achieved using certain strategies; instead, multiple strategies may be employed to reach the same goal. Research supports this position, demonstrating that relational partners may use different techniques to persuade each other (Witteman & Fitzpatrick, 1986), express opposition (Sillars et al., 2004), and provide each other with support (Bolger, Zuckerman, & Kessler, 2000).

Although equifinality complicates the means by which relational partners reach particular outcomes, multifinality, a related component of general systems theory, suggests that the same starting point may result

in different outcomes. A communication strategy employed in one relationship may encourage satisfaction while, in another relationship, the same strategy may create distress. For instance, researchers have found that in some cases the expression of negative affect is harmful to relationships, whereas in others, it is positively associated with, or unrelated to, satisfaction (Fincham & Beach, 1999). It comes as no surprise that negative behavior is inversely associated with relational satisfaction overall (Gottman & Notarius, 2000; Noller & Fitzpatrick, 1990), yet it would be shortsighted to conclude that negative behavior is always "bad" for relationships.

Dialectical theory takes another approach to the problems associated with discussing communication in "either–or" terms. Rather than emphasize the various paths between starting points and outcomes, this theory suggests that the process of relating can be viewed as a dialogue about opposing or contradictory forces (Baxter & Montgomery, 1996). It "views communication in relationships as the dialectical tension of contradictory verbal-ideological forces, or discourses" (Baxter, 2004, p. 8). Dialectically minded scholars suggest, for example, that people desire both autonomy and connection in their personal relationships (Altman, Vinsel, & Brown, 1981). The way people negotiate these two opposing forces is part of what defines their relationship.

Although many, and probably most, communication researchers accept the basic arguments concerning dialectical contradictions and equifinality–multifinality, they may be less clear where to go with these arguments. For example, the most pervasive research strategy for assessing the impacts of communication on relationships is to evaluate the effects of communication strictly according to their observed association with relational satisfaction or distress. The persistent focus on relationship satisfaction and distress has certain unfortunate consequences (Sillars et al., 2004). For one, it encourages a tendency to see all communication in clinical terms, including normal variations in family interaction.

As we noted earlier, research examining the everyday or mundane aspects of social interaction can be as revealing as the study of problematic aspects of communication. Further, as Erbert and Duck (1997) observed, research dichotomizing adjusted–maladjusted groups often carries the implication that the interaction characteristics discriminating these groups can also be dichotomized as good–bad communication. However, studies suggest that "good," "sophisticated," or "skillful" communication does not necessarily distinguish satisfied from dissatisfied couples. Indeed, Burleson and Denton (1997) found no differences in the marital satisfaction of couples they defined as skilled and unskilled communicators. These researchers suggested that some couples who are unhappy may employ skillful, effective strategies to hurt each other. It also is possible that in unhappy or maladjusted relationships, "positive" communication behaviors serve negative functions and vice versa, as when positive behaviors reproduce unnecessary and damaging patterns of accommodation (Erbert & Duck, 1997).

Conclusion

The purpose of this chapter was to reflect on basic properties of communication that are acknowledged by scholars across different theoretical perspectives. At the outset, we argued that the terms *communication* and *relationship* are inextricably linked. Existing research and theory indicate that communication creates and sustains relationships and, as well, that relationships shape both the enactment and interpretation of communication. By articulating some of the basic properties of communication, we hoped not only to describe what it means to study relationships from a "communication perspective," but also to clarify some of the ways that communication and relationships intersect.

Although the properties we discuss – *interdependence, reflexivity, complexity, ambiguity,* and *indeterminacy* – are basic qualities of communication, they pose challenges to researchers and theorists that are notably complex. Perhaps the most obvious of these challenges is for researchers to continue to focus their attention on interactions and sequences of interactions, as opposed to individual strategies, turns, or utterances. Communication messages, like relationships, should not be treated as singular, isolated units. Instead, they should be studied in relation to one another. The literature suggests that patterns ranging from infants' bids for attention (Papousek, Papousek, & Haekel, 1987) to spouses' tendencies to approach or avoid conflict (Christensen & Heavey, 1990) are most clearly understood when examined together with the communication that precedes and follows them.

Another challenge that emerges from our discussion is for researchers to continue to address the multiple meanings, functions, and outcomes associated with communication behaviors. Communication, like relationships, is conceived, interpreted, and employed in different ways for different purposes. Because different meanings may be associated with a single message or set of messages, any given message may serve multiple functions and have multiple outcomes. Research on partners' tendency to avoid communication indicates that, indeed, avoidance is enacted in different ways and for different purposes (Caughlin & Afifi, 2004; Roberts, 2000). Such findings suggest that coding communication behaviors for singular, or even primary, meanings, functions, or outcomes must be done with care.

Yet another challenge for researchers involves the contextual nature of communication. Communication, like relationships, is situated; it only is fully understood when it is examined in context. Further, multiple contexts simultaneously affect and are affected by communication. Much of the literature on personal relationships examines communication in the context of satisfying or dissatisfying relationships, but satisfaction clearly is not the only variable that researchers might use to examine relational contexts, and relational contexts are not the only ones that influence communication.

Studies suggest that social, cultural, and historical environments also affect the ways people enact and interpret communication behaviors (e.g., Brown, Burton, & Sweeney, 1998; see Brown, Werner, & Altman, this volume for a review).

Clearly, addressing any one of these challenges – let alone all of them – is a big task. It is not a task that we anticipate researchers will be able to accomplish in a single study or even in a single program of research. Rather, like the development of relationships, we anticipate the development of research on communication in relationships to progress through the accidental and purposeful collaboration of multiple participants.

References

Altman, I., & Taylor, D. A. (1973). *Social penetration: The development of interpersonal relationships*. New York: Holt, Rinehart, & Winston.

Altman, I., Vinsel, A., & Brown, B. B. (1981). Dialectic conceptions in social psychology: An application to social penetration and privacy regulation. In L. Berkowitz (Ed.), *Advances in experimental social psychology* (Vol. 14, pp. 107–160). New York: Academic Press.

Argyle, M., & Dean, J. (1965). Eye contact, distance, and affiliation. *Sociometry, 28,* 289–304.

Austin, J. L. (1962). *How to do things with words.* Oxford: Clarendon.

Barratt, M. S. (1995). Communication in infancy. In M. A. Fitzpatrick & A. L. Vangelisti (Eds.), *Explaining family interactions* (pp. 5–33). Thousand Oaks, CA: Sage.

Bateson, G. (1972). *Steps to an ecology of mind.* New York: Ballantine.

Baucom, D. H., Notarius, C. I., Burnett, C. K., & Haefner, P. (1990). Gender differences and sex-role identity in marriage. In F. D. Fincham & T. N. Bradbury (Eds.), *The psychology of marriage* (pp. 150–171). New York: Guilford Press.

Bavelas, J. B. (1990). Nonverbal and social aspects of discourse in face-to-face interaction. *Text, 10,* 5–8.

Bavelas, J. B., Black, A., Chovill, N., & Mullett, J. (1990). *Equivocal communication.* Newbury Park, CA: Sage.

Bavelas, J. B., & Coates, L. (1992). How do we account for the mindfulness of face-to-face dialogue? *Communication Monographs, 59,* 301–305.

Baxter, L. A. (1987). Symbols of relationship identity in relationship cultures. *Journal of Social and Personal Relationships, 4,* 261–280.

Baxter, L. A. (2004). Relationships as dialogues. *Personal Relationships, 11,* 1–22.

Baxter, L. A., & Bullis, C. (1986). Turning points in developing romantic relationships. *Human Communication Research, 12,* 469–493.

Baxter, L. A., & Montgomery, B. M. (1996). *Relating: Dialogues and dialectics.* New York: Guilford Press.

Beebe, B., Jaffe, J. Feldstein, S., Mays K., & Alson, D. (1985). Interpersonal timing: The application of an adult dialogue model to mother–infant vocal and kinesic interactions. In T. M. Field & N. A. Fox (Eds.), *Social perception in infants* (pp. 217–248). Norwood, NJ: Ablex.

Belsky, J. (1984). The determinants of parenting: A process model. *Child Development, 55,* 83–96.

Berger, C. R. (1998). Message plans, communication failure, and mutual adaptation during social interaction (1998). In M. T. Palmer & G. A. Barnett (Eds.), *Progress in communication sciences, Volume XIV: Mutual influence in interpersonal communication: Theory and research in cognition, affect, and behavior.* Stamford, CT: Ablex.

Berger, C. R., Gardner, R. R., Clatterbuck, G. W., & Schulman, L. S. (1976). Perceptions of information sequencing in relationship development. *Human Communication Research, 3,* 34–39.

Berger, P., & Luckmann, T. (1966). *The social construction of reality.* New York: Doubleday.

Bolger, N., Zuckerman, A., & Kessler, R. C. (2000). Invisible support and adjustment to stress. *Journal of Personality and Social Psychology, 79,* 953–961.

Bradbury, T. N., Rogge, R. D., & Lawrence, E. (2001). Reconsidering the role of conflict in marriage. In A. Booth, N. Crouter, & M. Clements (Eds.), *Couples in conflict* (pp. 59–81). Hillsdale, NJ: Erlbaum.

Brown, B. B., Burton, J. R., & Sweeney, A. (1998). Neighbors, households, and front porches: New urbanist community tool or mere nostalgia? *Environment and Behavior, 30,* 579–600.

Brown, J., & Rogers, L. E. (1991). Openness, uncertainty, and intimacy: An epistemological reformulation. In N. Coupland, H. Giles, & J. M. Wiemann (Eds.), *"Miscommunication" and problematic talk* (pp. 146–165). Newbury Park, CA: Sage.

Bruess, C. J. S., & Pearson, J. C. (1997). Interpersonal rituals in marriage and adult friendship. *Communication Monographs, 64,* 25–46.

Bruner, J. (1990). *Acts of meaning.* Cambridge, MA: Harvard University Press.

Buehlman, K., Gottman, J. M., & Katz, L. (1992). How a couple views their past predicts their future: Predicting divorce from an oral interview. *Journal of Family Psychology, 5,* 295–318.

Burgoon, J. K., Stern, L. A., & Dillman, L. (1995). *Interpersonal adaptation: Dyadic interaction patterns.* Cambridge, England: Cambridge University Press.

Burleson, B. R., & Denton, W. H. (1997). The relationship between communication skill and marital satisfaction: Some moderating effects. *Journal of Marriage and the Family, 59,* 884–902.

Burleson, B. R., Metts, S., & Kirch M. W. (2000). Communication in close relationships. In C. Hendrick & S. S. Hendrick (Eds.), *Close relationships: A sourcebook* (pp. 245–258). Thousand Oaks, CA: Sage.

Byng-Hall, J. (1988). Scripts and legends in families and family therapy. *Family Process, 27,* 167–179.

Cappella, J. N. (1987). Interpersonal communication: Fundamental questions and issues. In C. R. Berger & S. H. Chaffee (Eds.), *Handbook of communication science* (pp. 184–238). Newbury Park, CA: Sage.

Cappella, J. N. (1988). Personal relationships, social relationships, and patterns of interaction. In S. W. Duck (Ed.), *Handbook of personal relationships* (pp. 325–342). Chichester, England: Wiley.

Cappella, J. N., & Planalp, S. (1981). Talk and silence sequences in informal conversations: Interspeaker influence. *Human Communication Research, 7,* 117–132.

Carston, R. (2002). *Thoughts and utterances: The pragmatics of explicit communication.* Cambridge, MA: Blackwell.

Caughlin, J. P., & Afifi, T. D. (2004). When is topic avoidance unsatisfying?: Examining moderators of the association between avoidance and dissatisfaction. *Human Communication Research, 30,* 479–513.

Caughlin, J. P., & Huston, T. L. (2002). A contextual analysis of the association between demand/withdraw and martial satisfaction. *Personal Relationships, 9,* 95–119.

Caughlin, J. P., & Vangelisti, A. L. (1999). Desire for change in one's partner as a predictor of the demand/withdraw pattern of marital communication. *Communication Monographs, 66,* 66–89.

Christensen, A., & Heavey, C. L. (1990). Gender and social structure in the demand/withdraw pattern of marital conflict. *Journal of Personality and Social Psychology, 59,* 73–81.

Christensen, A., & Shenk, J. L. (1991). Communication, conflict, and psychological distance in nondistressed, clinic, and divorcing couples. *Journal of Consulting and Clinical Psychology, 59,* 458–463.

Colvin, C. R., Vogt, D. S., & Ickes, W. (1997). Why do friends understand each other better than strangers do? In W. Ickes (Ed.), *Empathic accuracy* (pp. 169–193). New York: Guilford Press.

Conger, R., Ge, X., Elder, G., Lorenz, F., & Simmons, R. (1994). Economic stress, coercive family process, and developmental problems of adolescents. *Child Development, 65,* 541–561.

Craig, R. T. (1999). Communication theory as a field. *Communication Theory, 9,* 119–161.

Craig, R. T., Tracy, K., & Spisak, F. (1986). The discourse of requests: Assessment of a politeness approach. *Human Communication Research, 12,* 436–478.

Cupach, W. R., & Spitzberg, B. H. (Eds.). (1994). *The dark side of interpersonal communication.* Hillsdale, NJ: Erlbaum.

Cushman, D., & Whiting, G. C. (1972). An approach to communication theory: Toward consensus on rules. *Journal of Communication, 22,* 217–238.

Danziger, K. (1976). *Interpersonal communication.* New York: Pergamon.

Denzin, N. (1970). Rules of conduct and the study of deviant behavior: Some notes on the social relationship. In G. McCall, M. McCall, N. Denzin, G. Suttles, & S. Kurth (Eds.), *Social relationships* (pp. 62–94). Chicago: Aldine.

Dickson, F. C., Christian, A., & Remmo, C. J. (2004). An exploration of the marital and family issues of the later-life adult. In A. L. Vangelisti (Ed.), *Handbook of family communication* (pp. 153–174). Mahwah, NJ: Erlbaum.

Duck, S. (1995). Talking relationships into being. *Journal of Social and Personal Relationships, 12*, 535–540.

Duck, S. (2002). Hypertext in the key of G: Three types of "history" as influences on conversational structure and flow. *Communication Theory, 12*, 41–42.

Duncan, S., & Fiske, D. W. (1977). *Face-to-face interaction*. Hillsdale, NJ: Erlbaum.

Duck, S., Rutt, D. J., Hurst, M. H., & Strejc, H. (1991). Some evident truths about conversations in everyday relationships: All communications are not created equal. *Human Communication Research, 18*, 228–267.

Duck, S. W., & Pond, K. (1988). Friends, Romans, countrymen, lend me your retrospective data: Rhetoric and reality in personal relationships. In C. Hendrick (Ed.), *Review of social psychology and personality, Vol. 10: Close relationships* (pp. 3–27). Newbury Park, CA: Sage.

Erbert, L. A., & Duck, S. W. (1997). Rethinking satisfaction in personal relationships from a dialectical perspective. In R. J. Sternberg & M. Hojjat (Eds.) *Satisfaction in close relationships* (pp. 190–217). New York: Guilford Press.

Fincham, F. D., & Beach, S. R. H. (1999). Conflict in marriage: Implications of working with couples. *Annual Review of Psychology, 50*, 47–77.

Fisher, B. A. (1975). Communication study in system perspective. In B. D. Rubin & J. Y. Kim (Eds.), *General systems theory and human communication* (pp. 191–206). Rochelle Park, NJ: Hayden.

Fisher, B. A., & Drecksel, G. L. (1983). A cyclical model of developing relationships: A study of relational control interaction. *Communication Monographs, 1*, 66–78.

Fletcher, G. J. O., & Fincham, F. D. (1991). Attribution processes in close relationships. In G. J. O. Fletcher & F. D. Fincham (Eds.), *Cognition in close relationships* (pp. 7–36). Hillsdale, NJ: Erlbaum.

Frentz, T. S., & Farrell, T. B. (1976). Language-action: A paradigm for communication. *Quarterly Journal of Speech, 62*, 333–349.

Ginsburg, G. P., & Kilbourne, B. K. (1988). Emergence of vocal alternation in mother–infant interchanges. *Journal of Child Language, 15*, 221–235.

Goldsmith, D. J., & Baxter, L. A. (1996). Constituting relationships in talk: A taxonomy of speech events in social and personal relationships. *Human Communication Research, 23*, 87–114.

Gottman, J. M. (1982). Temporal form: Toward a new language for describing relationships. *Journal of Marriage and the Family, 44*, 943–962.

Gottman, J. M. (1994). *What predicts divorce: The relationship between martial processes and martial outcomes*. Hillsdale, NJ: Erlbaum.

Gottman, J. M., & Notarius, C. I. (2000). Decade review: Observing marital interaction. *Journal of Marriage and the Family, 62*, 927–947.

Greene, J. O. (1997). A second generation action assembly theory. In J. O. Greene (Ed.), *Message production: Advances in communication theory* (pp. 151–170). Mahwah, NJ: Erlbaum.

Hample, D. (1987). Communication and the unconscious. In B. Dervin & M. J. Voigt (Eds.), *Progress in communication sciences* (Vol. VIII, pp. 83–121). Norwood, NJ: Ablex.

Harvey, J. H., Weber, A. L., & Orbuch, T. L. (1990). *Interpersonal accounts: A social psychological perspective*. Oxford: Blackwell.

Heavey, C. L., Layne, C., & Christensen, A. (1993). Gender and conflict structure in marital interaction: A replication and extension. *Journal of Consulting and Clinical Psychology, 61*, 16–27.

Hopper, R. (1981). The taken-for-granted. *Human Communication Research, 7*, 195–211.

Hopper, R., Knapp, M. L., & Scott, L. (1981). Couples' personal idioms: Exploring intimate talk, *Journal of Communication, 31*, 23–33.

Ickes, W. (2003). *Everyday mind reading: Understanding what other people think and feel*. Amherst, NY: Prometheus Books.

Jacobs, S. (2002). Language and interpersonal communication. In M. L. Knapp & J. A. Daly (Eds.), *Handbook of interpersonal communication* (pp. 213–239). Thousand Oaks, CA: Sage.

Jorgenson, J., & Bochner, A. P. (2004). Imaging families through stories and rituals. In A. L. Vangelisti (Ed.), *Handbook of family communication* (pp. 513–538). Mahwah, NJ: Erlbaum.

Kellermann, K. (1992). Communication: Inherently strategic and primarily automatic. *Communication Monographs, 59*, 288–300.

Klinetob, N. A., & Smith, D. A. (1996). Demand–withdraw communication in marital interaction: Tests of interspousal contingency and gender role hypotheses. *Journal of Marriage and the Family, 58*, 945–958.

Knapp, M. L., & Vangelisti, A. L. (2005). *Interpersonal communication and human relationships* (5th ed.). Boston: Allyn & Bacon.

Lamb, M. E., & Gilbride, K. E. (1985). Compatibility in parent–infant relationships: Origins and processes. In W. Ickes (Ed.), *Compatible and incompatible relationships* (pp. 33–60). New York: Springer-Verlag.

Langer, E. (1989). *Mindfulness*. Reading, MA: Addison-Wesley.

Lannamann, J. (1991). Interpersonal research as ideological practice. *Communication Theory, 1*, 179–203.

Lawrence, S. G. (1999). The preoccupation with problems of understanding in communication research. *Communication Theory, 9*, 265–291.

Lawrence, S. G. (2003). Rejecting illegitimate understandings. In P. J. Glenn, C. D. LeBaron, & J. Mandelbaum (Eds.), *Studies in language and social interaction: In honor of Robert Hopper* (pp. 195–205). Mahwah, NJ: Erlbaum.

LeBaron, C. D., & Koschmann, T. (2003). Gesture and the transparency of understanding. In P. J. Glenn, C. D. LeBaron, & J. Mandelbaum (Eds.), *Studies in language and social interaction: In honor of Robert Hopper* (pp. 119–136). Mahwah, NJ: Erlbaum.

Mandelbaum, J. (2003). Interactive methods for constructing relationships. In P. J. Glenn, C. D. LeBaron, & J. Mandelbaum (Eds.), *Studies in language and social interaction: In honor of Robert Hopper* (pp. 207–219). Mahwah, NJ: Erlbaum.

Margolin, G., & Wampold, B. (1981). Sequential analysis of conflict and accord in distressed and nondistressed marital partners. *Journal of Consulting and Clinical Psychology, 49*, 554–567.

McPhee, R. D. (1998). Giddens' conception of personal relationships and its relevance to communication theory. In R. L. Conville & L. E. Rogers (Eds.), *Meaning of "relationship" in interpersonal communication* (pp. 83–106). Westport, CT: Praeger.

Meltzoff, A. N., & Moore, M. K. (1977). Imitation of facial and manual gestures by human neonates. *Science, 198*, 75–78.

Miller, G. R., & Steinberg, M. (1975). *Between people: A new analysis of interpersonal communication*. Chicago: Science Research Associates.

Montgomery, B. (1992). Communication as the interface between couples and culture. In S. Deetz (Ed.), *Communication Yearbook 15* (pp. 475–507). Newbury Park, CA: Sage.

Motley, M. T. (1990). On whether one can(not) not communicate: An examination via traditional communication postulates. *Western Journal of Speech Communication, 54*, 1–20.

Murray, S. L., & Holmes, J. G. (1994). Storytelling in close relationships: The construction of confidence. *Personality and Social Psychology Bulletin, 20*, 650–663.

Noller, P., & Callan, J. (1988). Understanding parent–adolescent interactions: Perceptions of family members and outsiders. *Developmental Psychology, 24*, 707–714.

Noller, P., & Fitzpatrick, M. A. (1990). Marital communication in the eighties. *Journal of Marriage and the Family, 52*, 832–843.

Papousek, M., Papousek, H., & Haekel, M. (1987). Didactic adjustments in fathers' and mothers' speech to their 3-month-old infants. *Journal of Psycholinguistic Research, 16*, 491–516.

Parks, M. R. (1982). Ideology in interpersonal communication: Off the couch and into the world. In M. Burgoon (Ed.), *Communication yearbook 6* (pp. 79–107). Beverly Hills, CA: Sage.

Parks, M. R. (1994). Communicative competence and interpersonal control. In M. L. Knapp & G. R. Miller (Eds.), *Handbook of interpersonal communication* (2nd ed., pp. 589–618). Thousand Oaks, CA: Sage.

Pellegrini, R. J., & Empey, J. (1970). Interpersonal spatial orientation in dyads. *Journal of Psychology, 76*, 67–70.

Petronio, S. (2002). *Boundaries of privacy: Dialectics of disclosure*. Albany: State University of New York Press.

Planalp, S. (1993). Friends' and acquaintances' conversations II: Coded differences. *Journal of Social and Personal Relationships, 10*, 339–354.

Planalp, S., & Garvin-Doxas, K. (1994). Using mutual knowledge in conversation: Friends as experts on each other. In S. Duck (Ed.), *Dynamics of relationships* (pp. 1–26). Thousand Oaks, CA: Sage.

Reddy, M. J. (1979). The conduit metaphor – A case of frame conflict in our language about language. In A. Ortony (Ed.), *Metaphor and thought* (pp. 284–324). Cambridge, England: Cambridge University Press.

Roberts, G. L., & Bavelas, J. B. (1996). The communicative dictionary: A collaborative theory of meaning. In J. Stewart (Ed.), *Reflections on the representational use of language* (pp. 135–160). Albany: State University of New York Press.

Roberts, L. J. (2000). Fire and ice in martial communication: Hostile and distancing behaviors as predictors of marital distress. *Journal of Marriage and the Family, 62*, 693–707.

Rogers, L. E. (1998) The meaning of relationship in relational communication. In R. L. Conville & L. E. Rogers (Eds.), *The meaning of "relationship" in interpersonal communication* (pp. 69–81). Westport, CT: Praeger.

Rogers, L. E., & Millar, F. E. (1988). Relational communication. In S. Duck (Ed.), *Handbook of personal relationships* (pp. 289–305). London: Wiley.

Roloff, M. E., & Anastoasiou, L. (2001). Interpersonal communication research: An overview. In W. B. Gudykunst (Ed.), *Communication yearbook 24* (pp. 51–70). Thousand Oaks, CA: Sage.

Ruesch, J., & Bateson, G. (1951). *The social matrix of psychiatry.* New York: Norton.

Sanders, R. E. (1984). Style, meaning, and message effects. *Communication Monographs, 51*, 154–167.

Sanders, R. E. (1995). A retrospective essay on the consequentiality of communication. In S. J. Sigman (Ed.), *Consequentiality of communication* (pp. 215–222). Hillsdale, NJ: Erlbaum.

Sanders, R. E., Fitch, K., & Pomerantz, A. (2001). Language and social interaction: Issues, theories, and prominent lines of research. In W. Gudykunst (Ed.), *Communication yearbook 24* (pp. 385–408). Thousand Oaks, CA: Sage.

Searle, J. R. (1969). *Speech acts.* London: Cambridge University Press.

Sigman, S. J. (1998). Relationships and communication: A social communication and strongly consequential view. In R. L. Conville & L. E. Rogers (Eds.), *The meaning of "relationship" in interpersonal communication* (pp. 47–67). Westport, CT: Praeger.

Sillars, A. L. (1998). (Mis)understanding. In B. H. Spitzberg & W. R. Cupach (Eds.), *The dark side of relationships* (pp. 73–102). Mahwah, NJ: Erlbaum.

Sillars, A., Canary, D. J., & Tafoya, M. (2004). In A. L. Vangelisti (Ed.), *Handbook of family communication* (pp. 413–446). Mahwah, NJ: Erlbaum.

Sillars, A., Roberts, L. J., Leonard, K. E., & Dun, T. (2000). Cognition during marital conflict: The relationships of thought and talk. *Journal of Social and Personal Relationships, 17*, 479–502.

Sperber, D., & Wilson, D. (1995). *Relevance: Communication and cognition* (2nd ed.). MA: Blackwell.

Sternberg, R. J. (1996). Love stories. *Personal Relationships, 3*, 59–79.

Stone, E. (1988). *Black sheep and kissing cousins: How our family stories shape us.* New York: Penguin Books.

Street, R. L., Jr., & Cappella, N. (1985). Sequence and pattern in communicative behavior: A model and commentary. In R. L. Street, Jr., & J. N. Cappella (Eds.), *Sequence and pattern in communicative behavior* (pp. 243–276). London: Edward Arnold.

Surra, C. A., & Ridley, C. (1991). Multiple perspectives on interaction: Participants, peers, and observers. In B. M. Montgomery & S. W. Duck (Eds.), *Studying interpersonal interaction* (pp. 35–55). New York: Guilford Press.

Thibaut, J. W., & Kelley, H. H. (1959). *The social psychology of groups.* New York: Wiley.

Thomas, G., & Fletcher, G. J. O. (1997). Empathic accuracy in close relationships. In W. Ickes (Ed.), *Empathic accuracy* (pp. 194–217). New York: Guilford Press.

Toulmin, S. (1970). Reasons and causes. In R. Borger & F. Cioffi (Eds.), *Explanation in the behavioural sciences* (pp. 1–26). Cambridge, England: Cambridge University Press.

Tracy, K. (1985). Conversational coherence: A cognitively-grounded rules approach. In R. Street & J. N. Cappella (Eds.), *Sequence and pattern in communicative behavior* (pp. 30–49). London: Edward Arnold.

Tracy, K. (1989). Conversational dilemmas and the naturalistic experiment. In B. Dervin, L. Grossberg, B. J. O'Keefe, & E. Wartella (Eds.), *Rethinking communication: Volume 2, Paradigm exemplars* (pp. 411–423). Newbury Park, CA: Sage.

Vangelisti, A. L. (1994). Family secrets: Forms, functions, and correlates. *Journal of Social and Personal Relationships, 11*, 113–135.

Vangelisti, A. L., Crumley, L., & Baker, J. (1999). Family portraits: Stories as standards for family relationships. *Journal of Social and Personal Relationships, 16*, 335–368.

Van Egeren, L. A., & Barratt, M. S. (2004). The development and origins of communication: Interactional systems in infancy. In A. L. Vangelisti (Ed.), *Handbook of family communication* (pp. 287–310). Mahwah, NJ: Erlbaum.

Van Egeren, L. A., Barratt, M. S., & Roach, M. A. (2001). Mother–infant responsiveness: Timing, mutual regulation, and interactional context. *Developmental Psychology, 37,* 684–697.

von Bertalanffy, L. (1968). *General system theory: Foundations, development, applications.* New York: Braziller.

Waldron, V. R., & Cegala, D. J. (1992). Assessing conversational cognition: Levels of cognitive theory and associated methodological requirements. *Human Communication Research, 18,* 599–622.

Watzlawick, P., Beavin, J., & Jackson, D. D. (1967). *Pragmatics of human communication: A study of interactional patterns, pathologies, and paradoxes.* New York: Norton.

Weakland, J. (1976). Communication theory and clinical change. In P. Guerin (Ed.), *Family therapy: Theory and practice* (pp. 111–128). New York: Gardner.

Wilmot, W. W. (1980). In D. Nimmo (Ed.), *Communication yearbook 4* (pp. 61–69). New Brunswick, NJ: Transaction Books.

Wilson, S. R., & Sabee, C. M. (2003). Explicating communicative competence as a theoretical term. In J. O. Greene & B. R. Burleson (Eds.), *Handbook of communication and social interaction skills* (pp. 3–50). Mahwah, NJ: Erlbaum.

Wilson, S. R., Whipple, E. E., & Grau, J. (1996). Reflection-enhancing regulative communication: How do parents vary across misbehavior types and child resistance? *Journal of Social and Personal Relationships, 13,* 553–569.

Witteman, H., & Fitzpatrick, M. A. (1986). Compliance-gaining in marital interaction: Power bases, processes, and outcomes. *Communication Monographs, 53,* 130–143.

CHAPTER 19

Social Cognition in Intimate Relationships

Garth J. O. Fletcher
Nickola C. Overall
Myron D. Friesen

Humans are the most cognitively complex animals on the planet. We spend inordinate amounts of time explaining, predicting, and attempting to control the world around us, and we are astonishingly successful at achieving such goals. Explaining the distant origins of such prodigious abilities is a question for evolutionary psychology. However, there is little doubt that the crucible within which humans learn to think consists of intimate relationships with parents and caretakers during childhood, and that both the nature and the functions of cognition in adulthood continue to be profoundly influenced by intimate relationships.

Thus, the study of cognition in intimate relationships holds out the promise of two fundamental payoffs. First, it contributes to our understanding of fundamental processes of cognition. Second, it helps us understand how intimate relationships work. Perhaps because of this double-barreled outcome, the study of social cognition within intimate relationship settings has become a massive area in social psychology (and related disciplines; see, for example, Fletcher & Clark, 2001). However, such research has not taken place in isolation. Three examples of the fruitful synergy that can exist across domains concern the application of social cognitive research and theorizing to the work on bias and accuracy, attachment theory, and evolutionary psychology.

In this chapter, we first provide a brief overview of the nature and functions of social cognition within intimate relationships, then apply this social cognitive perspective to three major topics within the relationship field, namely, bias and error, adult attachment, and mate selection (a major concern of evolutionary psychology). But first, a little history.

A Brief Historical Tour

The so-called cognitive revolution in psychology took place in the 1960s and 1970s, displacing behaviorism as the dominant paradigm. However, social psychology had already adopted a cognitive stance from the Second World War onward, and this approach also permeated the study of relationships and interpersonal attraction. Take, for example, Thibaut and Kelley's (1959) classic formulation of interdependence theory, which postulates that people assess their relationships by comparing what they have with both what they deserve and the available alternatives. At its core this model is a social cognitive theory.

Harold Kelley was also a key figure in the development of attribution theory (initially proposed by Fritz Heider in 1958). By the 1970s, attribution theory was one of the dominant paradigms in social psychology and was exported to many fields including the study of intimate relationships. Indeed, the study of cognition in intimate relationships was dominated in the 1970s and 1980s by the investigation of attributions (Fletcher & Fincham, 1991). However, attribution theory was developed prior to the emergence of social cognition in social psychology. The study of social cognition, in turn, largely borrowed its methodologies and concepts from cognitive psychology. Thus, the study of attributions in relationships faded in the 1990s and was gradually assimilated into more general social cognitive models (see Fletcher & Fitness, 1996).

The contemporary field concerned with cognition in close relationships uses both laboratory based methodologies (e.g., re-action-time studies) and concepts (e.g., automatic vs. controlled processing) borrowed from cognitive psychology. However, it also examines cognition amid the great complexity of intimate relationships as they are forged, maintained, and dissolved in real-world settings. Thus, researchers in this area happily swap from lab-based to survey research, from tightly controlled experimental studies with stripped-down stimuli to observational studies of behavioral interaction.

In the next section, we lay out a general social cognitive model. This model is partly our own invention, and thus the details may be arguable. However, the general outline would have considerable consensus in the field. Like all social cognitive models, this one splits the black box of cognition into two separate fields: stored knowledge structures (we call lay theories), and online process-

ing. In our discussion, we constantly juxtapose two separate but intertwined questions: what is the nature of such knowledge structures, and what is their function?

A Social Cognitive Approach

> ... there is nothing so practical as a good theory. –Lewin (1951)

Lay Relationship Theories

A plethora of terms have been coined to describe the elaborate knowledge structures that people develop concerning intimate relationships including *schemas, scripts, prototypes, working models, mental models,* and so forth. What are the functions of such knowledge structures? Exemplifying Lewin's quote, they seem to be associated with three basic lay aims: *explanation* (e.g., "I am nervous around Michael because he reminds me of my ex-boyfriend"), *prediction* (e.g., "If I tell Joan the truth, she will leave me"), and *control* or *influence* (e.g., trading in the sedan for a sports car to attract women). These are, of course, the familiar aims of scientific theories, which is one reason we like the term *lay relationship theories* to describe these knowledge structures.

Regardless of the way in which knowledge structures are conceptualized, everyone agrees that people do not store and retrieve exact replicas of every interpersonal experience. Instead, experiences are organized into generalized representations that summarize regularities encountered over time, including beliefs, expectations, interpersonal goals, and behavioral strategies. Whenever a relationship-relevant event occurs (from simply thinking of a close other to receiving a compliment from one's partner), such lay theories are activated automatically, guiding how the event is mentally processed and influencing both accompanying emotions and resultant behavior. Moreover, there is an emerging consensus that such theories are organized into a hierarchical network that ranges from general to specific forms.

We distinguish between three levels of lay intimate theories; *general social theories* that pertain generally to social interaction, *general relationship theories* that summarize knowledge specifically relevant to close relationships, and *local theories* that represent specific intimate relationships such as one's husband or ex-boyfriend. We describe each in turn, and analyze how their connections help drive the ABC (affect, behavior, and cognition) of human psychological phenomena in intimate relationships

General Social Theories

General social theories apply to all interpersonal relations, from a brief encounter with a stranger to daily interactions with one's spouse. People possess extensive knowledge about such interactions including a general folk theory (often termed theory of mind) that specifies when and how to produce mental attributions such as intentions, beliefs, attitudes, and personality traits. As previously noted, the most thoroughly researched model in relationship settings within this domain is attribution theory, which is concerned with how people explain their own and others' behavior.

People frequently and spontaneously talk about and explain intimate relationships, often with apparent enjoyment (Dunbar & Duncan, 1997; Fletcher & Fincham, 1991). Attribution theorists propose that what matters is not so much the content of the attributed cause, but where a particular causal explanation is located on a number of crucial dimensions, including locus (internal–external), stability, and specificity. Consider the following example:

> Imagine Susan and John on their first date. Throughout their conversation, John continually looks around the room and asks Susan to repeat herself. Susan initially explains his inattentiveness as self-absorption. However, John is attractive, and she warms to him. She then switches her explanation to account for his negative behavior as anxiety arising from being in an uncomfortable situation, the dreaded first date – maybe a second date is a good idea.

Note that in the first instance Susan attributes John's negative behavior to an internal, stable, and global characteristic (a relationship-negative pattern), whereas her latter attribution to the situation is external, unstable, and specific (a relationship-positive pattern). This example is not merely conjectural. There is a vast range of research that supports the hypothesis that these kinds of attributions have similar positive or negative effects in both dating and married relationships (see Fincham, 2001).

General Relationship Theories

General relationship theories are replete with beliefs, expectations, and concepts that are specifically concerned with close relationships of all kinds including intimate, sexual relationships. These theories can be idiosyncratic to some extent, depending on individual experiences. Nevertheless, relationship theories are derived from both culturally shared sources of information (e.g., media) and from hardwired evolutionary adaptations (more on this later). Thus, many core features of general relationship theories are similar across individuals. For example, people hold similar theories regarding the nature and roles of emotions in relationships, such as love, anger, and jealousy (Fitness, 1996), and have similar conceptualizations of concepts such as commitment (Fehr, 1999), respect (Frei & Shaver, 2002), the features of a "good" relationship (Hassebrauck, 1997), factors associated with relationship success and failure (Fletcher & Kininmonth, 1992), and mate selection criteria (Fletcher, Simpson, Thomas, & Giles, 1999).

Other types of general relationship theories have the same structure across individuals, although the actual content may differ. For example, there exist stable individual differences in attachment models, ideal standards, and what Knee and colleagues (2003) termed "growth and destiny beliefs." That is, individuals differ in the extent to which they believe and trust others will be available and responsive in times of need (see Shaver & Mikulincer, this volume), the importance they place on such standards as physical attractiveness in evaluating a potential or existent mate (Simpson, Fletcher, & Campbell, 2001), and the extent to which they believe relationship success is determined by destiny or through overcoming challenges (Knee et al., 2003). Individual differences in the content of these lay theories determine how the same relationship events are perceived and responded to. For example, individuals who ascribe to destiny beliefs are less satisfied with their relationships in the face of negative partner behavior or relationship experiences. In contrast, individuals who view relationship problems as challenges to be overcome remain satisfied and committed when their partners do not live up to their ideals or when they experience conflict within their relationships (Knee et al., 2003).

Regardless of the particular content, lay relationship theories pervasively influence affect, behavior, and cognition within relationships. Let us revisit our dating couple, Susan and John, in the course of their second date.

Susan notices that John dresses well and has a good job. This fits nicely with Susan's theory about the ideal man. However, caring and sensitivity are also critical for Susan; she seeks a long term relationship, and her last boyfriend was so concerned about his career, she felt he didn't have enough time for her. Similar feelings have plagued Susan's previous relationships, and deep down she fears that no one will ever really love her. As the discussion turns to their interests, Susan finds they have a lot of in common – "That's good," she thinks, "similarity is important in relationships." Maybe there is hope after all.

As this tale demonstrates, people enter social situations with preexistent mental dispositions (theories about relationships) that conspire to produce interpretations and explanations of behavior, evaluations of the partner and the relationship, and finally decisions about the course of the relationship.

Local Relationship Theories

If John and Susan's relationship continues, they will both develop elaborate local relationship theories of each other's personality, attributes and attitudes, and models of their relationship including how close and satisfied they are, how well they communicate, problems they currently have or may experience, and how their relationship is linked to friends and family. Such local theories become more complex and integrated over time, and steadily become entwined with representations and evaluations of the self (Aron, Aron, & Norman, 2001).

A critical point here is that local relationship theories are generated according to the way in which local theories overlap with preexistent general relationship theories. Thus, relationship evaluations are produced (in part) as a function of the extent to which perceptions and experiences match prior expectations and beliefs. For example, greater discrepancy between ideal standards concerning the degree of warmth and supportiveness and associated perceptions of partner behavior will be associated with more negative relationship evaluations and an increased probability of relationship dissolution (see Simpson et al., 2001).

Online Processing

Although the examples just used may leave the impression that people consciously draw on their theories, relationship theories are routinely accessed quite unconsciously (Fletcher, Rosanowski, & Fitness, 1994). In addition, the cognitive processing itself may be unconscious and automatic. This level of efficiency is necessary. A single interpersonal interaction requires many streams of cognitive processing to occur simultaneously. Partners must encode the verbal and nonverbal behavior (including facial expressions, eye contact, and gestures), while controlling their own behavior, making rapid judgments, and blending their thoughts, emotions, and behavior into a smoothly coordinated interaction. This is only achievable if such processing is conducted automatically and in parallel. There is considerable direct evidence for this thesis based on studies that use techniques that require individuals to carry out two tasks at the same time, thus loading their cognitive resources (e.g., Fletcher et al., 1994; Mikulincer, Gillath, & Shaver, 2002).

The extent to which relationship events are subject to in-depth conscious analysis will vary considerably depending on the stage of relationship, individual differences, and the situational context. In long-term stable relationships, a great deal of communication will become routine, resulting in overlearned and stereotypical sequences of behavior. Two kinds of events have been shown to snap people back into conscious, controlled cognition (often accompanied by emotion): negative events and unexpected events (Berscheid, 1983; Fletcher & Thomas, 1996).

Emotions

The study of social cognition in intimate contexts can ill afford to ignore the role of emotions, given that relationship cognition is so often "hot cognition," shot through with affect and evaluations. The functions of emotions in relationships are no different from their role generally (Fitness, Fletcher, & Overall, 2003). First, emotions (such as fear, anger, or love) both attract attention and provide the motivation to attain a goal. Second, they provide information that help people decide how to attain goals. Thus, in relationship settings there is evidence that feelings of love are associated with the desire to be physically close to the partner and to express such urges. Anger is associated with urges to confront the partner and seek redress, whereas hate is marked by the urge to avoid or escape from the partner (Fitness & Fletcher, 1993).

However, negative emotions provide a problem in relationships, given that their automatic full-blooded expression is likely to accelerate the demise of many relationships. Thus, individuals actively control and manage the expression of emotions like jealousy or anger (Fletcher, Thomas, &

Durrant, 1999). Indeed, the expression of emotions serves a range of communication goals that are important in intimate relationships. Drawing on Darwin's (1872) pioneering account, Clark and her colleagues have argued, for example, that the expression of emotions, such as anxiety and sadness, signals the need for comfort and support from the partner, whereas anger sets the scene for the partner to seek forgiveness (Clark, Fitness, & Brissette, 2001). Emotions are, thus, inextricably tied into both social cognition and the way that couples interact and negotiate issues within their relationships.

Fitness et al. (2003) argued that emotion lay theories can be categorized according to the same tripartite division that we previously laid out for cognitive lay theories. At the most general level individuals hold theories about the nature of emotions across domains, such as anger and love. These are often referred to as scripts, because they involve interactional sequences that unfold predictably over time (Fitness, 1996). At the next level down, people hold theories about emotions as they function in intimate sexual relationships. Finally, at the bedrock empirical level, people have theories about emotions as they function within specific relationships that take into account specific interactional patterns and the personalities of the individuals concerned.

We draw two main conclusions. First, emotions and cognitions are thoroughly intertwined and work together in normal social cognition. Thus, if John buys Susan a rose, she is likely to feel love or gratitude, but if Susan knows that John is aware she is allergic to roses, than she may feel contempt or anger. Second, studies of rare forms of brain damage that incapacitate emotions but leave other abilities and functions intact, have shown that people develop crippling deficits in social intelligence and managing interpersonal relationships (Damasio, 1994). Damasio's explanation is that without emotions, individuals are deprived of critical information. Thus, emotions are indispensable rather than inimical to rationality and good decision making.

This way of interpreting the role of emotions in relationships is not without controversy and appears at first blush to conflict with both conventional wisdom and a mass of scientific research showing that emotions like love can pitch people into rash decision making and motivate them to develop hopelessly biased and rose-tinted views of their partners and relationships. We deal with this argument in the next section.

With this brief sketch of a broad social cognitive account as background, we move into discussing the work concerning bias and error in relationship judgments followed by two popular areas that also embody the role of cognition in relationship settings: attachment theory and mate selection.

Bias and Accuracy in Relationship Judgments

> Love sees not with the eyes, but with the mind;
> And therefore is wing'd Cupid painted blind.
> William Shakespeare

The study of bias and accuracy in intimate relationship settings provides a particularly sharp test of two competing models that have been widely debated in the more general psychological literature. One general model (which we term the "love is blind" thesis) argues that normal, healthy, lay social cognition is typically positively biased, overoptimistic, and Pollyannaish. According to this approach, the motivation to retain a positive and healthy level of self-esteem, and by extension a positive level of relationship esteem, is assumed to be a pervasive motive. A second general model (which we call the "relationship reality" model) proposes that people are often motivated by the desire to be accurate in their relationship judgments, that such judgments are frequently accurate and that a firm grasp of relationship reality is necessary for healthy functioning relationships.

Both models appear plausible and are supported by impressive bodies of evidence (for recent reviews see Fletcher, 2002; Fletcher, Simpson, & Boyce, in press; Gagne & Lydon, 2004). In support of the "love is blind" model, for example, Murray and colleagues have produced an influential program of research (for a review, see Murray, 2001) that supports two major propositions. First, individuals routinely fight off doubts that corrode levels of commitment and trust by rewriting or restructuring local relationship theories. Second, as love's blinkers grow stronger and more opaque, individuals idealize their partners more, exaggerate the similarity between self and partner, and subsequently develop more stable and happier relationships (for both self and partner).

However, there is also considerable support for the relationship reality model. First, partners in romantic relationships tend to have similar relationship evaluations. Second, positive relationship evaluations are usually moderately correlated with the positivity of interactive behavior (as coded by external observers). Third, the evaluative valence of relationship judgments has been consistently shown to be one of the best predictors of relationship dissolution in both dating and married samples. Fourth, the mere fact that relationship dissolution is commonplace suggests that there are boundary conditions to the "love is blind" model. Fifth, an elaborate recent study by Thomas and Fletcher (2003) reported that, during problem-solving interactions, partners were superior in mind-reading each other's cognitions and emotions compared with either friends of the couples or strangers. Taken together, these five points convincingly suggest that the intimate relationship mind is locked onto the reality of relationships rather than to relationship illusions.

We suggest two ways to reconcile the competing claims advanced by the two accounts. First, contrary to common assumptions, bias and accuracy are relatively independent constructs. Thus, bias is not equivalent to inaccuracy or irrationality. Second, individuals' goals may sometimes be oriented toward relationship enhancement and esteem maintenance and sometimes toward truth and accuracy. We discuss each aspect in turn.

Consider the following example (adapted from Fletcher, 2002), picking up Susan and John's relationship again. Susan rates John (using 1–7 Likert scales, where 1 = *not like John at all* and 7 = *very much like John*) as being very honest (7), very sincere (6), sensitive (6), and moderately ambitious (5). Let us assume we have on hand benchmark ratings for John that are 100% accurate. These turn out to be honest (6), sincere (5), sensitive (5), and ambitious (4). Comparing the two sets of ratings, it is apparent that Susan is positively biased but accurate. That is, the mean level of Susan's judgments (6) is one unit higher than the benchmark ratings (5), but she is accurately tracking levels across personality traits ($r = 1.0$). However, if Susan produced ratings of 6, 7, 5, and 6 this would represent the same amount of positivity bias, but no accuracy. In this variation, the mean level of Susan's judgments is again one unit higher than the benchmark ratings, but she is not accurately tracking levels across traits ($r = 0.00$). Finally, Susan could be both unbiased and wildly inaccurate (with a pattern such as 3, 3, 7, and 7). That is, Susan's mean level of judgments is equivalent to the mean of the benchmark ratings (5), but she is tracking the traits inaccurately ($r = -0.71$).

In short, bias (assessed by comparing mean levels of positivity for the perceived judgments versus the reality benchmarks) and accuracy (assessed by using correlations between the perceived judgments and the reality benchmarks) can be relatively independent. Thus, the possibility is raised that individuals can have the best of both worlds and be both positively biased and accurate in judging their partner and relationship. For example, Murray, Holmes, Bellavia, Griffin, and Dolderman (2002) reported that women who were more egocentric (viewing their partners as more similar to self than was actually the case) also understood their partners more accurately.

An additional and quite different way in which bias has often been documented is in terms of the way in which preexis-

tent knowledge structures influence other judgments or memory processes. A massive list of such effects can be drawn up, including the way in which those in happier and more stable relationships exaggerate the extent to which they are similar to their partners (Murray et al., 2002), exaggerate the extent to which they were happy at prior times in their relationships (Karney & Frye, 2002), exaggerate the positive qualities of their partners (Murray, Holmes, & Griffin, 1996a), and exaggerate the extent to which their partners resemble their ideal partners (Murray, Holmes, & Griffin, 1996b), to name but a few.

However, demonstrations of such bias do not show that people are systematically irrational or that they are blind to the truth. Approaching data from the real world in a completely open-minded and atheoretical manner will reveal a blizzard of information, but little in the way of causal understanding. Thus, scientists of all stripes quite properly use their theories to explain or interpret data routinely and pervasively (Fletcher, 1996) and weight the import of the data accordingly (this is termed Bayes's theorem in probability circles). In the same fashion, laypeople will make judgments under conditions of uncertainty that reflect both the nature of the incoming data and their extant theories. For example, if Susan is asked to make judgments about how similar she is to John along some personality dimensions, she will do so (in part) by accessing both her general and her local partner and relationship theories. If Susan is in a very happy relationship and she believes that more similarity in relationships produces more successful relationships (a common belief), this will lead to biased judgments. In short, theory-guided judgments, either scientific or lay, are (by definition) biased judgments.

A second way of reconciling these two models is to admit that they are both true, but under different circumstances (on this view, Shakespeare's comment about Cupid being painted blind is half right). For example, the existence of extremely threatening events or relationship interactions may increase the accessibility and power of esteem-maintenance goals and subvert truth-seeking accuracy goals (see Ickes & Simpson, 2001). A compelling demonstration of this proposition was provided by Simpson, Ickes, and Blackstone (1995), who arranged for dating partners to rate photographs of attractive members of the opposite sex (with their own partners present). To juice up the threat, the photographs were of people supposedly on campus and available for dating. Individuals then both reported their own thoughts and feelings and attempted to mind-read their partners' thoughts and feelings while reviewing videotaped versions of the attractiveness rating session. The results showed that partners who were closer and more intimate produced more *inaccurate* mindreadings than those involved in less intimate relationships.

Conversely, when partners are involved in making decisions about relationship events that involve considerable escalations of commitment (e.g., getting married, having a baby), this may enhance the accessibility and power of relationship-reality goals that should counter the simple need to feel good about the relationship. The best evidence to date for this proposal has been provided by Gagne and her colleagues (see Gagne & Lydon, 2004, for a review), who have carried out a series of studies in which they have manipulated a deliberative (predecisional) versus an implemental (postdecisional) mind-set. For example, in one study (Gagne & Lydon, 2001, Study 3), individuals in dating relationships were required to either describe the pros and cons of an undecided relationship project (e.g., should they live together) or to describe how they planned to achieve a project to which they were already committed (e.g., finding a suitable apartment). Participants who were encouraged into a rational, evenhanded, deliberative frame of mind produced considerably more accurate predictions concerning how long their relationships would last, compared with those who were making the same prediction while in an esteem-maintenance, implemental mind-set.

Attachment Working Models

A child forsaken, waking suddenly,
Whose gaze afeard on all things round doth
* rove,*
And seeth only that it cannot see
The meeting eyes of love.
–George Eliot

The burgeoning study of adult attachment, based on Bowlby's developmental theory, was initiated by Hazan and Shaver's seminal study published in 1987. And, almost from the beginning, researchers have noted and exploited the links between social cognition and attachment theory. The reason for this natural alliance between the two domains lies in the nature of Bowlby's original theory, which posits that infants develop lay theories (termed working models) that organize and summarize their attachment interactions (see Shaver & Mikulincer, this volume) and provide expectations, emotional reactions, and attitudes regarding both the nature of self and others with respect to the likely provision of love and support. Thus, working models provide the mechanism and the link that explains how attachment experiences in infancy are carried into adulthood and why such working models are relatively stable in adulthood (see Fletcher, 2002).

Factor analytic studies have uniformly shown that adult working models are characterized by two relatively independent attachment dimensions: anxious attachment (anxiety over relationships and fear of being abandoned or unloved) and avoidant attachment (discomfort with and avoidance of closeness and intimacy; Brennan, Clark, & Shaver, 1998; Simpson, Rholes, & Phillip, 1996). Consistent with Bowlby's original formulation, working models were originally conceptualized as a species of general relationship theory (according to the tripartite taxonomy of relationship theories outlined previously). Moreover, again reflecting Bowlby's theory, they have often been defined as global and unitary theories that influence responses to any and all intimate relationships.

However, in a pioneering treatment of attachment theory from a social cognitive perspective, Collins and Read (1994) suggested that working models should be viewed in terms of a hierarchy with the top-most level occupied by the most general evaluative representation of self and others (based on a lifetime of attachment experiences). Further down are domain-specific models such as relationships with parents, friends, and romantic partners and, finally, at the bottom level reside models of specific local relationships. A considerable amount of research supports this kind of hierarchy (see Collins, Guichard, Ford, & Feeney, 2004). Perhaps the most direct evidence to date is provided by Overall, Fletcher, and Friesen (2003). In this study, participants completed standard attachment scales for the relationship domains of family, platonic friendships, and romantic partners, and also provided attachment ratings for three specific attachment relationships within each domain. Confirmatory factor analyses of various models showed that by far the best fit was provided by the Collins and Read hierarchical model, and this was true regardless of the measurement strategy, gender, and the relationship status of the participants.

Consistent with the cognitive approach previously specified, research evidence has steadily mounted showing that attachment working models direct and influence explanations, predictions, and behavioral regulation attempts. For example, Collins (1996) found that, consistent with their beliefs and expectations, highly anxious participants explained their partner's negative behavior with pessimistic causal attributions that were stable, global, and internal to the partner or relationship (e.g., insensitive). In contrast, secure individuals, low in attachment anxiety and avoidance, offered charitable explanations that were unstable, specific, and external (e.g., had a bad cold). Moreover, these effects held regardless of levels of relationship satisfaction. The same kind of attributional differences have been reported with studies that have assessed reactions to positive behaviors (Collins, Ford, Guichard,

& Allard, 2003, Study 2) and in the context of actual interactive behavior (Collins & Feeney, 2000).

Furthermore, there is increasing evidence that the influence of attachment working models occurs at both the controlled (conscious) and the automatic (unconscious) levels. For example, Baldwin, Fehr, Keedian, Seidel, and Thomson (1993) treated attachment-related expectations as if–then contingencies, in which particular contexts (e.g., closeness) are linked to particular outcomes (e.g., acceptance or rejection). To access if–then associations, Baldwin et al. employed a lexical decision task, which, after the presentation of a context string (e.g., interpersonal trust), required participants to identify whether a letter string is a word or a nonword (e.g., *hurt* or *care*). Reaction times in this task are indicative of how closely linked the context-target pair is in memory. When presented with the word string "If I trust my partner then my partner will…," avoidant participants responded faster to the word *hurt* and secure individuals to the word *care*, demonstrating the automatic activation of the outcome expectations associated with their working models (also see Baldwin & Meunier, 1999). Thus, expectations and predictions appear to come rapidly (and involuntarily) to the forefront of the relationship mind, shaping interpretations and guiding behavior.

This same methodology also allows access to the behavioral strategies that may be unconsciously initiated in response to a particular event. In examining trust-related coping strategies, Mikulincer (1998) found that after presentation of a context stem representing trust violation (e.g., "I trust my partner and he/she hurts me"), anxiously attached individuals identified the words *talk* and *worry* faster, and avoidantly attached individuals identified *escape* and *worry* faster. Consistent with their beliefs and expectations of others, avoidance is associated with withdrawal and anxiety over relationship stability and disclosure. Thus, individuals automatically react to a given event, particularly in times of stress (e.g., negative relationship event) when conscious effortful processing is limited and attachment representations are accessible and relevant.

Ready-made strategies may be employed automatically but are also likely to be guided by how an event is perceived and interpreted. For example, negative interpretations and attributions of relationship interactions (hypothetical or real life) arising from attachment anxiety or avoidance (or both), and the negative affect elicited, predict (and mediate) negative conflict behavior and relationship satisfaction (see Collins, 1996; Gallo & Smith, 2001). Regardless of whether behavior is influenced via cognitive and emotional reactions, or produced by the automatic activation of behavioral strategies, a large body of research has demonstrated that attachment working models predict behavior, such as communication, conflict-resolution style, and support seeking and giving, which, in turn, influence relationship quality and satisfaction (see Feeney, 1999; Simpson & Rholes, 1998).

The biased processing and behavioral outcomes associated with attachment suggest that working models, like other lay theories, should remain relatively stable. However, up to 30% of individuals demonstrate change in attachment classification when measured over periods of 1 week to 2 years (Baldwin & Fehr, 1995; Kirkpatrick & Hazan, 1994), suggesting that working models are open to revision. Importantly, change in attachment ratings over time is related to factors such as change in relationship status, satisfaction, and quality (e.g., Davila, Karney, & Bradbury, 1999; Hammond & Fletcher, 1991). These findings show that relatively permanent contextual changes can promote the modification of relationship representations. However, the ability to incorporate new or incongruent information into existing working models may also depend on the content of attachment working models. High attachment avoidance and anxiety is related to cognitive closure and rigidity and to a tendency to ignore or reject inconsistent information (e.g., Mikulincer, 1997; Mikulincer & Arad, 1999), making it especially hard to revise more negative representations.

Finally, harking back to our discussion of bias and accuracy, although attachment representations may systematically bias other judgments, this does not mean they inevitably lead to irrational or inaccurate judgments. Attachment working models, even avoidance, can be viewed as rational and optimal constructs designed to learn from the past and to protect and enhance the self (see Hinde, 1982). Moreover, bias and accuracy can happily coreside. For example, in Collins and Feeney's (2000) previously cited study, individuals' perceptions of their partners' level of support while discussing a stressful problem were biased by their attachment styles and their perceived satisfaction with the relationship. However, the same individuals simultaneously produced accurate judgments using observers' ratings of their partners' behavior as the reality benchmark.

Mate Selection (and Deselection)

Sometimes the most extreme passion is aroused – not by real-life love objects – but by partners who are barely known ... or who exist only in imagination. Berscheid and Walster (1978)

Once upon a time, in the 1960s and 1970s, the study of interpersonal attraction (at the psychological level) was dominated by social psychology, which focused on the whys and wherefores of attraction between strangers. This research was largely atheoretical, and the results read like a laundry list of factors that determined attraction including similarity, proximity, and physical attractiveness. In the 1980s and 1990s, the field moved toward the much greater complexity inherent in the development, maintenance, and dissolution phases of intimate relationships. However, the study of interpersonal attraction (now typically labeled *mate selection*) has once again become a hot topic, but under the new banner of evolutionary psychology.[1] Notably, this work is utterly different from the prior social psychological research. First, it has adopted a strong theoretical base, based on the evolutionary work of Darwin, and honed into modern psychological guise by figures such as Tooby, Cosmides, and Buss. Second, much of the work directly concerned with relationships has concentrated on sex differences, although attention has turned to within-sex differences more recently (Fletcher, 2002). Third, as will be seen, this work has important implications for a social cognitive approach.

There is no single evolutionary psychological theory. Nevertheless, there is widespread adherence to the aim of explaining the cognitive and emotional mechanisms of the contemporary human mind, through understanding how they evolved via natural and sexual selection in the ancestral environment. Just as with a social cognitive approach, it is posited that behavior at the proximal level is produced as a function of the interaction between such evolved dispositional states and the environment. Moreover, although controversial, even within evolutionary circles, it is commonly argued that the human mind contains many highly modular and specific adaptations, which were designed by evolution to solve particular problems in our ancestral environment.

Take the criteria that men and women use in selecting mates. From a social cognitive perspective, such criteria consist of cognitive–affective standards that are stored as components in the intimate relationship mind (as part of what we have termed general relationship theories). There is considerable evidence that men and women, across cultures, focus on the same features when looking for a mate in a long-term relationship (for reviews see Buss, 1999; Fletcher, 2002). The most valued factors are personality features such as intelligence, warmth, and trustworthiness. Physical attractiveness, good health, vitality, and either the actual possession of status and resources or the drive or potential to obtain them are also considered important but typically are rated somewhat less important than warmth and trustworthiness. Factor analytic studies of importance ratings of these kinds of individual items show that they neatly fall into

exactly these three categories (e.g., Fletcher et al., 1999; Fletcher, Tither, O'Loughlin, Friesen, & Overall, 2004).

Why are these three categories – warmth–trustworthiness, attractiveness–vitality, and status–resources – so important? A standard social cognitive approach is blithely indifferent to such a question, in stark contrast to evolutionary psychology. Gangestad and Simpson (2000) argued that these dimensions represent adaptations, designed to promote reproductive success via two distinct routes – either good investment or good genes. The possession of warmth and trustworthiness signals the capacity to be a good mate and parent (i.e., the motivation for good investment), whereas either the actual possession of status and resources, or the drive to obtain them, signal the ability to provide good investment for the family. The possession of attractiveness and vitality is the primary good genes factor, signalling high fertility and healthy genes.

The study of sex differences in mate selection has produced a particularly florid academic controversy along with considerable media attention, again with important implications for any social psychological or social cognitive account. The founding theory inevitably drafted into action by evolutionary psychology in this context is parental investment theory (Trivers, 1972). Parental investment theory explains what Darwin assiduously documented but failed to explain – that across species, males are promiscuous and females are choosy. Applied to humans, parental investment theory highlights the facts that women invest more in pregnancy and child rearing than do men, and women are capable of producing fewer children than are men. Thus, we should expect women to rate mate-selection criteria related to good investment as more important than criteria concerned with good genes (relative to men). Indeed, there is a wealth of evidence that women do rate status and resources as more important than men, whereas men cite physical attractiveness as more important than women and that men are more focused on short-term liaisons and sexual variety than women (see Buss, 1999; Fletcher et al., 2004).

However, Buss stressed the point that both long-term and short-term sexual relationships may have potential costs (as well as benefits), for both men and women, in terms of reproductive fitness (Buss & Schmitt, 1993). For example, women could benefit from short-term sexual liaisons by obtaining resources or picking up some superior genes. Indeed, there is accumulating evidence that both men and women rate physical attractiveness as more important in short-term flings than in long-term relationships but rate good investment criteria as less important in short-term flings (e.g., Fletcher et al., 2004).

Now, consider anew the findings mentioned previously that there exist strong within-sex individual differences in the importance attached to the three main categories of mate criteria (warmth–trustworthiness, attractiveness–vitality, and status–resources). From a social cognitive perspective, this finding suggests the existence of cognitive standards that vary in accessibility, that predate local relationships, and that can be used to accomplish some of the lay goals already described, such as evaluation, explanation, prediction, and regulation (see Simpson et al., 2001).

For example, to return to our fictional couple, if Susan places a high value on attractiveness and vitality, and her partner (John) has gained weight and turned into a couch potato, this will produce a large discrepancy between Susan's standard and her perception. This discrepancy should produce lower levels of relationship satisfaction, provide Susan with an explanation for her dissatisfaction, produce a gloomier prediction about the future of the relationship, and perhaps motivate Susan to attempt to change John's behavior (e.g., by dropping hints about joining a health club). There is accumulating evidence that supports this social cognitive account (Campbell, Simpson, Kashy, & Fletcher, 2001; Fletcher et al., 1999; Fletcher, Simpson, & Thomas, 2000).

Another important question concerns what causes individuals to set their mate selection standards at different levels. One answer, which has received considerable empirical support, is that people (quite rationally) calibrate their standards and expectations according to their own self-perceived mate value (see, for example, Campbell et al., 2001; Murray et al., 1996a). Moreover, the fact that people do not simply have one global self-perceived mate value means that they can afford to be picky on some domains but not others and that trade-offs across domains may be possible depending on the context. For example, Fletcher et al.'s (2004) findings suggest that women will select an attractive, cold man over a homely, warm man for a short-term fling, but will strongly prefer a homely, warm man to a cold, handsome man in a long-term relationship.

To conclude, a social psychological cum social cognitive approach suggests that essentially the same proximal-level processes operate throughout a relationship and do not cease after mate selection occurs. In addition, the picture emerging is one of massive flexibility, fluidity, and considerable control exerted by humans over all stages of relationship development. However, this does not gainsay the contribution of evolutionary psychology in this domain, which has helped establish the empirical claim that evolutionary processes have left indelible footprints on the intimate relationship mind.

Conclusion

The work summarized in this chapter supports the case that the study of social cognition in intimate contexts can make important and novel contributions to other scientific domains including those covered all too briefly in this chapter, namely, cognitive psychology, emotions, bias and accuracy, attachment theory, and, finally, evolutionary psychology. We have offered many examples of such contributions in this chapter. These include the structure and functions of relationship lay theories, the way in which emotion and cognitions are intertwined in relationship contexts, how social judgments in relationships can be both biased and accurate, the hierarchical nature of attachment working models, and the way in which we humans use mate selection processes in a flexible fashion to achieve multiple goals throughout relationships (and not just at the initial stages). Of course, as this chapter attests to, the process also works in reverse, with our understanding of social cognition in intimate contexts immeasurably enhanced by appropriating important elements, methods, and ideas from other domains (such as those just mentioned).

More generally, we believe work in this area supports two striking conclusions. First, a social cognitive approach can and does enrich our understanding of intimate relationships. Second, studying social cognition within the messy, complex, emotional, world of intimate relationships illuminates and expands our understanding of the most basic processes of cognition and emotion. And, this is simply because so much of the way that humans feel and think is rooted in close, interpersonal contexts.

Footnote

1. These points do not contradict the analysis by Surra, Gray, Boettcher, Cottle, and West (this volume) because they define the topic of mate selection far more broadly than we do here. We analyzed the number of journal articles that have the term mate selection in the abstract or title using the Web of Science search engine and excluding pure science journals to omit the work with animals other than humans. The figures were as follows: 1970–1979, 34 articles; 1980–1989, 62 articles; 1990–1999, 195 articles; 2000–2004, 106 articles. These figures are consistent with our impressions of the field.

References

Aron, A., Aron, E. N., & Norman, C. (2001). Self-expansion model of motivation and cognition in close relationships and beyond. In G. J. O. Fletcher & M. S. Clark (Eds.), *Blackwell hand-book of social psychology: Interpersonal processes* (pp. 478–501). Malden, MA: Blackwell.

Baldwin, M. W., & Fehr, B. (1995). On the instability of attachment style ratings. *Personal Relationships, 2*, 247–261.

Baldwin, M. W., Fehr, B., Keedian, E., Seidel, M., & Thomson, D. W. (1993). An exploration of the relational schemata underlying attachment styles: Self-report and lexical decision approaches. *Personality and Social Psychology Bulletin, 19*, 746–754.

Baldwin, M. W., & Meunier, J. (1999). The cued activation of attachment relational schemas. *Social Cognition, 17*, 209–227.

Berscheid, E. (1983). Emotion. In H. H. Kelley, E. Berscheid, A. Christensen, J., Harvey, T. Huston, G. Levinger, et al. (Eds.), *Close relationships* (pp. 110–68). San Francisco: Freeman.

Berscheid, E., & Walster, E. H. (1978). *Interpersonal attraction* (2nd ed.). Reading, MA: Addison-Wesley.

Brennan, K. A., Clark, C. L., & Shaver, P. R. (1998). Self-report measurement of adult attachment: An integrative overview. In J. A. Simpson & W. S. Rholes (Eds.), *Attachment theory and close relationships* (pp. 46–76). New York: Guilford Press.

Buss, D. M. (1999). *Evolutionary psychology: The new science of mind*. Boston: Allyn and Bacon.

Buss, D. M., & Schmitt, D. P. (1993). Sexual strategies theory: A contextual evolutionary analysis of human mating. *Psychological Review, 100*, 204–232.

Campbell, L., Simpson, J. A., Kashy, D. A., & Fletcher, G. J. O. (2001). Ideal standards, the self, and flexibility of ideals in close relationships. *Personality and Social Psychology Bulletin, 27*, 447–462.

Clark, M. S., Fitness, J., & Brissette, I. (2001). Understanding people's perceptions of relationships is crucial to understanding their emotional lives. In G. J. O. Fletcher & M. Clark (Eds.), *Blackwell handbook of social psychology: Interpersonal processes* (pp. 252–278). Malden, MA: Blackwell.

Collins, N. L. (1996). Working models of attachment: Implications for explanation, emotion and behavior. *Journal of Personality and Social Psychology, 71*, 810–832.

Collins, N. L., & Feeney, B. C. (2000). A safe haven: An attachment theory perspective on support seeking and caregiving in intimate relationships. *Journal of Personality and Social Psychology, 78*, 1053–1073.

Collins, N. L., Ford, M. B., Guichard, A., & Allard, L. M. (2003). *Working models of attachment and social construal processes in romantic relationships.* Unpublished manuscript, University of California at Santa Barbara.

Collins, N. L., Guichard, A., Ford, M. B., & Feeney, B. C. (2004). Working models of attachment: New developments and emerging themes. In W. S. Rholes & J. A. Simpson (Eds.), *Adult attachment: Theory, research, and clinical implications* (pp. 196–239). New York: Guilford Press.

Collins, N. L., & Read, S. J. (1994). Cognitive representations of attachment: The structure and function of working models. In K. Bartholomew & D. Perlman (Eds.), *Attachment processes in adulthood: Vol. 5. Advances in personal relationships* (pp. 53–90). London: Kingsley.

Damasio, A. R. (1994). *Descartes' error: Emotion, reason, and the human brain.* New York: Putnam.

Darwin, C. (1872). *The expression of the emotions in man and animals.* London: Murray.

Davila, J., Karney, B. R., & Bradbury, T. N. (1999). Attachment change processes in the early years of marriage. *Journal of Personality and Social Psychology, 76*, 783–802.

Dunbar, R. I. M., & Duncan, N. D.C. (1997). Human conversational behavior. *Human Nature, 8*, 231–246.

Feeney, J. A. (1999). Attachment romantic attachments and couple relationships. In J. Cassidy & P. R. Shaver (Eds.), *Handbook of attachment: Theory, research, and clinical applications* (pp. 355–377). New York: Guilford Press.

Fehr, B. (1999). Laypersons' perception of commitment. *Journal of Personality and Social Psychology, 76*, 90–103.

Fincham, F. D. (2001). Attributions in close relationships: From balkanisation to integration. In G. J. O. Fletcher & M. S. Clark (Eds.), *Blackwell handbook of social psychology: Interpersonal processes* (pp. 3–31). Malden, MA: Blackwell.

Fitness, J. (1996). Emotion knowledge structures in close relationships. In G. J. O. Fletcher & J. Fitness (Eds.), *Knowledge structures in close relationships* (pp. 195–217). Mahwah, NJ: Erlbaum.

Fitness, J., & Fletcher, G. J. O. (1993). Love, hate, anger and jealousy in close relationships: A cognitive appraisal and prototype analysis. *Journal of Personality and Social Psychology, 65*, 942–958.

Fitness, J., Fletcher, G. J. O., & Overall, N. C. (2003). Interpersonal attraction and intimate relationships. In M. A. Hogg & J. Cooper (Eds.), *The Sage handbook of social psychology* (pp. 258–278). Thousand Oaks, CA: Sage.

Fletcher, G. J. O. (1996). Realism versus relativism in psychology. *American Journal of Psychology, 109*, 409–429.

Fletcher, G. J. O. (2002). *The new science of intimate relationships.* London: Blackwell.

Fletcher, G. J. O., & Clark, M. S. (2001). *Blackwell handbook of social psychology: Interpersonal processes.* Malden, MA: Blackwell.

Fletcher, G. J. O., & Fincham, F. D. (1991). Attributional processes in close relationships. In G. J. O. Fletcher & F. D. Fincham (Eds.), *Cognition in close relationships* (pp. 6–34). Hillsdale, NJ: Erlbaum.

Fletcher, G. J. O., & Fitness, J. (Eds.). (1996). *Knowledge structures in close relationships.* Mahwah, NJ: Erlbaum.

Fletcher, G. J. O., & Kininmonth, L. (1992). Measuring relationship beliefs: An individual differences scale. *Journal of Research in Personality, 26*, 371–397.

Fletcher, G. J. O., Rosanowski, J., & Fitness J. (1994). Automatic processing in intimate contexts: The role of close-relationship beliefs. *Journal of Personality and Social Psychology, 67*, 888–897.

Fletcher G. J. O., Simpson, J. A. & Boyce, A, D. (in press). Accuracy and bias, in romantic relationships: An evolutionary and social psychological analysis. In M. Schaller J. A. Simpson, & D. Kenrick (Eds.), *Evolution and social psychology.* New York: Psychology Press.

Fletcher, G. J. O., Simpson, J. A., & Thomas, G. (2000). Ideals, perceptions, and evaluations in early relationship development. *Journal of Personality and Social Psychology, 79*, 933–940.

Fletcher, G. J. O., Simpson, J. A., Thomas, G., & Giles, L. (1999). Ideals in intimate relationships. *Journal of Personality and Social Psychology, 76*, 72–89.

Fletcher, G. J. O., & Thomas, G. (1996). Close relationship lay theories: Their structure and function. In G. J. O. Fletcher & J. Fitness (Eds.),

Knowledge structures in close relationships (pp. 3–24). Mahwah, NJ: Erlbaum.

Fletcher, G. J. O., Thomas, G., & Durrant, R. (1999). Cognitive and behavioral accommodation in relationship interaction. *Journal of Social and Personal Relationships, 16,* 705–730.

Fletcher, G. J. O., Tither, J. M., O'Loughlin, C. F., Friesen, M. D., & Overall, N. C. (2004). Warm and homely or cold and beautiful? Sex differences in trading off traits in mate selection. *Personality and Social Psychology Bulletin, 30,* 659–672.

Frei, J. R., & Shaver, P. R. (2002). Respect in close relationships: Prototype definition, self-report assessment, and initial correlates. *Personal Relationships, 9,* 121–139.

Gagné, F. M., & Lydon, J. E. (2001). Mindset and close relationship: When bias leads to (in)accurate predictions. *Journal of Personality and Social Psychology, 81,* 85–96.

Gagné, F. M., & Lydon, J. E. (2004). Bias and accuracy in close relationships: An integrative review. *Personality and Social Psychology Review, 8,* 322–338.

Gallo, L. C., & Smith, T. W. (2001). Attachment style in marriage: Adjustment and responses to interaction. *Journal of Social and Personal Relationships, 18,* 263–289.

Gangestad, S. W., & Simpson, J. A. (2000). The evolution of human mating: Trade-offs and strategic pluralism. *Behavioral and Brain Sciences, 23,* 573–644.

Hammond, J. R., & Fletcher, G. J. O. (1991). Attachment styles and relationship satisfaction in the development of close relationships. *New Zealand Journal of Psychology, 20,* 56–62.

Hassebrauck, M. (1997). Cognitions of relationship quality: A prototype analysis of their structure and consequences. *Personal Relationships, 4,* 163–185.

Hazan, C., & Shaver, P. R. (1987). Romantic love conceptualized as an attachment process. *Journal of Personality and Social Psychology, 52,* 511–524.

Heider, F. (1958). *The psychology of interpersonal relations.* New York: Wiley.

Hinde, R. A. (1982). Attachment: Some conceptual and biological issues. In C. M. Parkes & J. Stevenson-Hinde (Eds.), *The place of attachment in human behavior* (pp. 60–76). London: Tavistock.

Ickes, W., & Simpson, J. A. (2001). Motivational aspects of empathic accuracy. In G. J. O.

Fletcher & M. S. Clark (Eds.), *Blackwell handbook of social psychology: Interpersonal processes* (pp. 107–126). Malden, MA: Blackwell.

Karney, B. R., & Frye, N. E. (2002). "But we've been getting better lately": Comparing prospective and retrospective views of relationship development. *Journal of Personality and Social Psychology, 82,* 222–238.

Kirkpatrick, L. A., & Hazan, C. (1994). Attachment styles and close relationships: A four-year prospective study. *Personal Relationships, 1,* 123–142.

Knee, C. R., Patrick, H., & Lonsbary, C. (2003). Implicit theories of relationships: Orientations toward evaluation and cultivation. *Personality and Social Psychology Review, 7,* 41–55.

Lewin, K. (1951). *Field theory in social science.* New York: Harper & Row.

Mikulincer, M. (1997). Adult attachment style and information processing: Individual differences in curiosity and cognitive closure. *Journal of Personality and Social Psychology, 5,* 1217–1230.

Mikulincer, M. (1998). Attachment working models and the sense of trust: An exploration of interaction goals and affect regulation. *Journal of Personality and Social Psychology, 74,* 1209–1224.

Mikulincer, M., & Arad, D. (1999). Attachment working models and cognitive openness in close relationships: A test of chronic and temporary accessibility effects. *Journal of Personality and Social Psychology, 77,* 710–725.

Mikulincer, M., Gillath, O., & Shaver, P. R. (2002). Activation of the attachment system in adulthood: Threat-related primes increase the accessibility of mental representations of attachment figures. *Journal of Personality and Social Psychology, 83,* 881–895.

Murray, S. L. (2001). Seeking a sense of conviction: Motivated cognition in close relationships. In G. J. O. Fletcher & M. S. Clark (Eds.), *Blackwell handbook of social psychology: Interpersonal processes* (pp. 107–126). Malden, MA: Blackwell.

Murray, S. L., Holmes, J. G., Bellavia, G., Griffin, D. W., & Dolderman, D. (2002). Kindred spirits? The benefits of egocentrism in close relationships. *Journal of Personality and Social Psychology, 82,* 563–581.

Murray, S. L., Holmes, J. G., & Griffin, D. W. (1996a). The benefits of positive illusions: Idealization and the construction of satisfaction in close relationship. *Journal of Personality and Social Psychology, 70,* 79–98.

Murray, S. L., Holmes, J. G., & Griffin, D. W. (1996b). The self-fulfilling nature of positive illusions in romantic relationships: Love is not blind, but prescient. *Journal of Personality and Social Psychology, 71,* 1155–1180.

Overall, N. C., Fletcher, G. J. O., & Friesen, M. D. (2003). Mapping the intimate relationship mind: Comparisons between three models of attachment representations. *Personality and Social Psychology Bulletin, 29,* 1479–1493.

Simpson, J. A., Fletcher, G. J. O., & Campbell, L. (2001). The structure and function of ideal standards in close relationships. In G. J. O. Fletcher & M. S. Clark (Eds.), *Blackwell handbook of social psychology: Interpersonal processes* (pp. 86–106). Malden, MA: Blackwell.

Simpson, J. A., Ickes, W., & Blackstone, T. (1995). When the head protects the heart: Empathic accuracy in dating relationships. *Journal of Personality and Social Psychology, 69,* 629–641.

Simpson, J. A, & Rholes, W. S. (Eds.). (1998). *Attachment theory and close relationships.* New York: Guilford Press.

Simpson, J. A, Rholes, W. S., & Phillips, D. (1996). Conflict in close relationships: An attachment perspective. *Journal of Personality and Social Psychology, 71,* 899–914.

Thibaut, J. W., & Kelley, H. H. (1959). *The social psychology of groups.* Oxford, England: Wiley.

Thomas, G., & Fletcher, G. J. O. (2003). Mind-reading accuracy in intimate relationships: Assessing the roles of the relationship, the target, and the judge. *Journal of Personality and Social Psychology, 85,* 1079–1094.

Trivers, R. L. (1972). Parental investment and sexual selection. In B. Campbell (Ed.), *Sexual selection and the descent of man 1871–1971* (pp. 136–179). Chicago: Aldine.

CHAPTER 20

Emotion in Theories of Close Relationships

Sally Planalp
Julie Fitness
Beverley Fehr

Close relationships are so rich and multi-faceted that we can hope to explain them only by using several theories that range across levels of analysis, perspectives, and emphases. Yet despite the many differences among theories, they all have one element in common – emotion. Close relationships do not function well without emotion, and neither do the theories that have been developed to explain them.

As Berscheid noted 2 decades ago, to *be* close is at least in part to *feel* close, and social interaction, especially between intimates, is a crucible for emotion (Berscheid, 1983; Planalp, 1999). Feelings move infants and caregivers to form and protect bonds and to protest their loss. Inspired by emotion, acquaintances become friends, lovers, or life companions, but tortured by emotion, they may become distant or separate. Emotions are resources used to define and enact social norms and roles. In fact, it is hard to imagine a domain of close relationships that can do without emotion.

The primary aim of this chapter is to analyze the role of emotion in theories of close relationships and to consider how this role might be developed to enrich such theories. We have chosen seven theories of close relationship processes – or perhaps more accurately, families of theories – that incorporate emotion with varying degrees of depth and explicitness. Emotion can be seen as a prime mover in evolutionary and attachment theories, as a hidden dimension of social exchange theory, as kind of kinesthetic sense in dialectical theories, as a mysterious travel companion in stage theories, as a friendly collaborator in social cognitive theories, and as an instrument of negotiation in theories of social roles and power.

To illustrate the roles that the same emotions may play in each theoretical perspective, we put *love* and *anger*, in particular, under the spotlight. We chose love and anger because they are basic emotions that represent the fundamental dimension of valence that appears in most typologies of emotion terms (Shaver, Schwartz, Kirson, & O'Connor, 1987), and they play important roles in close relationships from a variety of perspectives. We begin by considering evolutionary approaches because evolution has made use of emotion to manage social bonds, especially among mammals.

Evolutionary Theory

Humans are profoundly social animals who depend on one another for their survival and well-being. But surviving and thriving in a complex social environment is not easy. Evolutionary theorists argue that the problems involved in successfully finding and retaining mates, parenting offspring, competing for resources, maintaining friendships for mutual support, managing conflicts, and negotiating shifting power and status dynamics have been challenging humans over many thousands of years of evolution. Today's humans manage these problems, at least in part, because they possess a variety of evolved, psychological mechanisms that enabled their *ancestors* to successfully manage them. We are the end products of a long line of successful reproducers (Buss & Kenrick, 1998).

Prime examples of such evolved psychological mechanisms are the emotions involved in the initiation, maintenance, breakdown, and repair of close relationships. Evolutionary theorists argue that emotions are hardwired "programs" that detect events that have recurred repeatedly over human evolution (e.g., the presence of a potential mate or rival; abandonment). Such events trigger discrete emotion programs and related perceptual, motivational, cognitive, and behavioral subprograms, selected over time as the most adaptive for dealing with such events (Cosmides & Tooby, 2000). Feeling anger toward a relationship partner, for example, signals that one's relational goals (such as monogamy) have been frustrated. What's more, anger motivates the kinds of coercive behaviors, including aggression, that may encourage the partner to meet one's goals (i.e., stop cheating). On the other hand, feeling love signals that one's relational goals have been facilitated by one's partner and motivates

adaptive responses such as increased commitment (Ellis & Malamuth, 2000).

If the evolutionary argument that anger and love are discrete emotion systems is true, then the activation of one system need not imply the deactivation of the other. In a study designed to test this proposition, Ellis and Malamuth (2000) found that individuals who felt more love for their partners were, indeed, more likely to demonstrate increased commitment behaviors (e.g., proposing marriage or maintaining dating exclusivity). However, they were *not* less likely to shout at their partners or throw things at them. Conversely, individuals who experienced more anger toward their partners were more likely to behave coercively (e.g., shout and throw things at them), but they were *not* less likely to demonstrate commitment behaviors such as proposing marriage or maintaining dating exclusivity. Clearly, then, anger and love coexist – sometimes uneasily – within close relationships, and both serve separate, but equally important goals.

To date, evolutionary theorists with an interest in close relationships have focused primarily on sexual attraction and mate selection strategies (Buss & Kenrick, 1998; Fitness, Fletcher, & Overall, 2003). Here, the emotions of romantic love and jealousy have assumed special significance as motivators of pair-bonding and mate-guarding behaviors (Planalp & Fitness, 1999). However, humans experience many more emotions than love, anger, and jealousy in close relationships, and according to the evolutionary perspective, each emotion has something to say about a relationship-relevant, adaptive problem. Grief, for example, is the price we pay for attachment – we are wired for pain because we need to love and be loved (see Archer, 1999). Similarly, emotions such as guilt, shame, fear, and loathing can be viewed as signals of how we're doing in the "survival stakes" – have I damaged an important relationship? Am I in danger of being abandoned? Is this person doing me harm?

Exploring the thoughts, feelings, and urges associated with these and other emotions sheds light on what Lazarus (1991) referred to as the "core relational themes" – adaptive problems – that have always confronted humans and enrich our understanding of an infinite variety of emotion-laden close relationship phenomena such as loneliness, rejection, attraction, repulsion, revenge, and forgiveness.

Emotions as Signals

Just as emotions let us know how we're doing and what's currently going right (or wrong) for us, so do emotional expressions communicate the same information to others. Thus, feelings of love inform us that our relationship goals are being met; however, the behaviors they motivate (e.g., buying an engagement ring) signal our commitment to a relationship partner who, in turn, may experience facilitation to his or her relationship goals and return our love. Similarly, expressing anger signals displeasure to a relationship partner; expressing sadness signals a need for comfort and care; expressing fear signals a need for protection; expressing guilt signals a desire to make up for a relationship transgression; and expressing joy signals that we are not currently needy, but rather have resources (including positive feelings) to share. In this sense, the expression of emotion is the currency of close relationships, and studies have confirmed that emotions are most likely to be expressed in so-called communal relationships in which people feel responsible for others' needs and believe others will be responsive to their needs (Clark, Fitness, & Brissette, 2001).

Marital interaction researchers have demonstrated the overall importance of emotional expressivity and empathic responding to spouses' relationship happiness (Gottman, 1994; Ickes, 1997; Noller & Ruzzene, 1991). However, not every expression of emotion sends a positive signal. An individual may be shamed by her partner's contempt, intimidated by her partner's anger, or frightened and frustrated by her partner's sadness and its message of neediness. An evolutionary approach enriches our understanding of the meaning of such emotional signals and their associated cognitions and motivations. It takes us beyond the proximal context (I'm expressing shame because you have criticized me) and adds another dimension to our understanding of the interaction: Personal devaluation is a survival threat; the feeling of shame alerts us to our lowered status and motivates behaviors such as defense or withdrawal, depending on the physical and psychological resources we bring to the interaction (Gilbert, 1998).

In summary, evolutionary approaches provide insights on the distal, as opposed to proximal, reasons for our emotions and motivations, and nowhere are these emotions and motivations so salient as within the context of our social and personal relationships (Fitness et al., 2003). We move now to consider a theory of relationship processes, originally formulated within an evolutionary framework that gives emotion a central role: attachment theory.

Attachment Theory

Every infant is born with a compelling need to establish an emotional bond with a primary caregiver (usually the mother) who provides security and a "safe haven" in a potentially dangerous world (Bowlby, 1969). Established bonds or secure attachments are the source of humans' first powerful experiences of love, trust, and joy. Disrupted or unpredictable bonds trigger intense negative emotions such as anxiety, anger, and sorrow (see Bowlby, 1973, 1980).

Hazan and Shaver (1987) applied Bowlby's theory to adult romantic relationships and inspired hundreds, if not thousands, of investigations into adult attachment. In this research, participants are typically asked to focus on a negative relationship event (e.g., conflict with their partner, being separated from their partner, a breakup experience) and report their emotional reaction to it (e.g., Feeney & Noller, 1992; Kobak & Hazan, 1991; Kobak & Sceery, 1988; Mikulincer & Florian, 1995; Mikulincer, Hirschberger, Nachmias, &

Gilliath, 2001; Mikulincer & Orbach, 1995; Simpson, 1990; Simpson, Rholes, & Nelligan, 1992). The typical finding is that people with secure attachment styles report less intense negative affect and regulate their emotions more effectively than those with insecure styles. Avoidant individuals tend to defensively minimize the experience of negative emotion, failing to acknowledge the distress that accompanies fractured attachment. Anxious–ambivalent individuals tend to experience especially high levels of negative affect, including anxiety and anger (Fraley & Shaver, 1997; Hazan & Shaver, 1987). Interestingly, Rowe and Carnelley (2003) recently demonstrated that participants primed with attachment security reported greater positive affect and less negaive affect than those primed with either an anxious or avoidant style. Thus, emotions such as love and anger may well serve as barometers of attachment security.

Failed Attachment and Negative Feelings

The emphasis in adult attachment work has been on emotions (typically the "negative" ones) as signals of distress and disrupted attachment. In line with the evolutionary perspective discussed earlier, anger is a crucially important emotion in this regard, and one that may actually go seriously awry in close relationships. Bowlby (1973), for example, described two types of anger that may arise in response to disrupted attachment: The anger of hope and the anger of despair. The anger of hope is aroused when the disrupted attachment is temporary. Similar to the coercive function of anger noted by Ellis and Malamuth (2000), the goal of "hopeful" anger is to overcome obstacles to reunion and discourage the attachment figure from leaving again. The response to repeated or permanent loss, however, is the anger of despair, an essentially dysfunctional cry of protest that cannot put a situation right. Importantly, Bowlby also noted that when partner-directed anger becomes so intense that aggressive or coercive behaviors are motivated more by revenge than

by deterrence, the feeling "ceases to be the 'hot displeasure' of anger and may become, instead, the 'malice' of hatred" (p. 288).

From an adult attachment perspective, then, anger may be simply regarded as a symptom or outcome of attachment disruption. However, a thoughtful consideration of anger, in all its rich varieties, invites many more questions than we currently have answers for. What kinds of attachment-related disruptions arouse the "anger of hope" in a close relationship, and what can shift such anger into a rage of despair? How do we move from there to anger's close cousins, hatred and contempt? Importantly, how do some relationship partners understand and manage their anger in a way that enables them to salvage and repair attachment bonds?

Successful Attachment and Positive Feelings

Although Bowlby noted the love and joy experienced when an attachment figure is "there for you," love per se is not often measured in attachment research. However, many studies have shown that people who report secure attachment to their romantic partner also report more frequent experiences of positive emotions such as happiness than those with an insecure style (e.g., Hazan & Shaver, 1987). Moreover, the same hormones (e.g., oxytocin) and feelings of warmth and tenderness are involved in both adult–infant attachment and adult–adult romantic love (see Fletcher, 2002, for a review). Love, then, is both a motivator of and reward for successful attachment, which in turn increases survival chances and reproductive opportunities. However, we still know little about the experience and expression of positive emotions in adult attachment relationships. For example, what kinds of feelings and emotions are associated with the experience of "being there" for a loved one, and how are such emotions expressed and received, depending on attachment styles? What is the role of positive emotions, such as joy, pride, and compassion, in strengthening attachment relationships?

Clearly, the emotions experienced and expressed by individuals with different kinds of attachment-related expectations are rich with meaning but as yet are poorly understood. For example, anxious–ambivalent individuals, who crave closeness but expect rejection, may engineer that outcome by way of their frequent displays of anger, anxiety, and jealousy. But what are their partners feeling in response to such emotion displays, and how do their emotional responses depend in turn on their attachment-related expectations?

Finally, it is assumed that attachment to a romantic partner mirrors (barring other major intervening events) attachment to one's primary caregiver in infancy. But why attach to an adult partner, and how is that process accomplished? Evolutionary theory may provide an answer to the former question. By establishing a strong bond with another person, we may be ensuring that there is at least one other person out there who will have a highly vested interest in ensuring our survival as well as that of our offspring. One must be careful, however, in choosing partners with whom to establish bonds. Some partners may not help at all, may not treat us fairly, or may not be dependable sources of resources needed to survive and thrive. Social exchange theory helps us address the issue of how people assess whether partners enhance or drain resources.

Social Exchange Theory

The language of social exchange theory draws on the terminology of cold financial calculation: rewards, costs, exchanges, comparison levels, short- and long-term profits, equity and inequity. The terms seem disconnected from and perhaps even antithetical to warm or even hot emotional processes, but are they? A closer look shows that the basic concepts and processes of social exchange theory can be viewed as deeply emotional (Planalp, 2003). Despite its cold exterior, social exchange theory may have a warm heart.

Basic Social Exchange Processes Have Emotional Parallels

The basic building blocks of social exchange theory are rewards and costs, which are experienced as positive and negative feelings. Perhaps either vocabulary will do, but what seem to register subjectively and in memory are affective associations with experiences rather than ledgers of profits or losses. Cosmides and Tooby (2000) argued from an evolutionary perspective that we must keep track of payoffs to make effective decisions about who to trust and how much to trust them. In survival terms, gullible or infinitely forgiving individuals are disadvantaged. Thus, our "stream of actions and daily experiences" is "affectively 'colored' by the assignment of these hedonic values" (p. 18). Evolution has, in effect, provided an affect-based accounting system that interfaces nicely with social exchange theory.

From this perspective, rather than computing profits and losses, people in close relationships may accumulate good and bad feelings toward others. Again, the emotions of love and anger play critical roles in signaling how we're doing, relative to our partners. Has my partner facilitated my goals as much as I have facilitated his (am I receiving as much love as I'm giving)? Has my partner frustrated my goals more than I have frustrated hers (am I feeling angrier and more resentful than she is)? Negative feelings can be ignored, of course, if one expects more positive feelings in the future, thus leading to the affective equivalent of absorbing short-term losses in the hopes of long-term gains. Still, anger may simmer, alerting us to the dangers of exploitation.

Comparison levels are also an integral part of emotion processes in that positive and negative emotions are triggered by deviations from expectations (Berscheid & Ammazzalorso, 2001). Organisms must save emotional energy for the unusual, but when the unusual becomes usual, they habituate. If expectations rise, it takes more to thrill us, and if they fall it takes less (Berscheid, 1983; Mandler, 1984). From an emotional point of view, comparison levels for alternatives are simply feelings toward A rather than B, which may, for example, be more positive than the current relationship (making the alternative tempting) but less positive than the comparison level (making it still not satisfying).

In social exchange theories, specifically equity theory, emotions play an explicit role as signals or outcomes of unfair exchanges. Underbenefited people feel angry, overbenefited people feel guilty, and both are motivated to set things right (although perhaps not so much the guilty as the angry). Emotion theorists have no quarrel with the basic conclusion, but they suggest complications because of the complex appraisal processes underlying emotional states (Scherer, Schorr, & Johnstone, 2001). For example, rather than feeling angry, underbenefited people may feel depressed if they believe they are helpless, hurt if they think the neglect is intentional, indifferent if they take it for granted, or guilty if they feel responsible for the inequity (Sprecher, 2001). Rather than guilt, overbenefited people may feel gratitude, hubris, contempt, happiness, or pride (Kuijer, Buunk, Ybema, & Wobbes, 2002). It depends on how they appraise the situation.

Feelings Are Shared, Not Exchanged

If one interprets social exchange theory literally, what is given is lost to the giver. It is important to get back because you could be left with nothing. Although that is certainly true of tangible commodities, just the opposite may be true for emotion. For love, it is certainly better to give *and* receive, but if love is unrequited, it may feel better to give without receiving than to receive without giving. In Baumeister and Wotman's words (1992):

> The would-be lover sees the situation as a high-stakes gamble, where there is a great deal to win or to lose – but the rejector sees it as a no-win proposition, where there is nothing to be gained and there is a real danger of unpleasantness. (p. 32)

Shared emotions seem to be more the rule than the exception, as described by Frijda (1988) in the law of comparative feeling. Shared feelings feel good; discrepancies feel bad. As the saying goes, "Home is where sorrow is divided and joy is multiplied." Witnessing good fortune or closeness that is not shared can produce envy, jealousy, or guilt. In fact, objective inequity such as unequal task sharing may be less of an issue than discrepancies between feelings. Knowing that your spouse is enjoying her friends when you are stuck doing dishes is not a problem if you enjoy doing dishes or if you hate the friends.

Sometimes, it seems, people do not exchange at all; they give without any expectation of getting. Selfless altruism seems to be common enough to beg for explanation, and it is a stretch for social exchange theory (Batson, 1998). Either helpers receive intangible benefits such as self-esteem, or their identities are fused with the persons being helped such that "I" becomes "We." What are the mechanisms for that fusion? People help to feel good about themselves, to escape bad feelings such as guilt, but most importantly because of feelings of compassion and genuine concern for others (Clary et al., 1998). Empathy and compassion seem much nobler than modified selfishness and just as basic to the human condition (Hoffman, 2001).

In conclusion, social exchange theories supplemented by concepts drawn from theories of emotion help to explain why people seek out one partner over another and how self-interest is amended or transformed by concerns for fairness and by compassion. What feels good or is rewarding for oneself and for others, however, is not fixed. Changing and sometimes seemingly contradictory needs can push and pull in different directions, leading theorists to turn to dialectical theory to understand them.

Dialectical Theory

Dialectical theory describes the processes of managing tensions between opposite ends of several continua that are basic to personal relationships: connectedness versus autonomy as the most central, but also predictability versus novelty, openness versus closedness, and others (Altman, Vinsel, & Brown, 1981; Baxter, 2004; Baxter & Montgomery, 1996; Rawlins, 1992). Given that relationships are constantly changing, how do people negotiate pushes and pulls in both directions? Just as an inherent kinesthetic sense enables tightrope walkers to adjust to changes in wind or rope, emotions are gauges that provide information about adjustments that may be needed to negotiate pushes and pulls from both ends of the dialectical continua.

Emotions as Dialectical Pushes and Pulls

According to dialectical theory, the tension between connectedness and autonomy is at the heart of all relationships. We know that human beings are not designed for isolation because it doesn't feel good (Baumeister & Leary, 1995). Solitary confinement is used as a form of torture, but less extreme isolation, whether physical or symbolic, can result in the more ordinary suffering labeled loneliness or rejection. Pulling in the same direction is love – that most desired of all emotions that propels physical and emotional closeness. Pulling in the opposite direction is our desire for autonomy and privacy that manifests in feeling smothered, socially overloaded (Petronio, 2000), or angry if you get in my way.

Similar tensions and emotional forces move people along other dialectical continua as well. Too much predictability makes for boredom that can be relieved by exciting activities that improve relationships or by love that expands the self (Aron & Aron, 1986; Aron, Norman, Aron, McKenna, & Heyman, 2000). On the other hand, too much excitement and uncertainty can be a drain, making familiar and routine activities feel reassuring (Berger & Bradac, 1982). Keeping feelings too closed off can perpetuate physiological arousal and unresolved issues to a degree that damages physical health (Pennebaker, 1997), but too much openness can leave people feeling vulnerable or ashamed (Kennedy-Moore & Watson, 1999).

Emotions as Signals of Dialectical Tensions

New adjustments and negotiations may be prompted by changes in life circumstances. Children leaving home can make parents crave connection or rejoice in their newfound autonomy. Relocating to a new place can make partners want to regain predictable daily routines or to escape to a novel vacation. Trauma can make people open up to others or close down by changing the subject. Feelings are what guide individuals and couples to action (or inaction) aimed at renegotiating the tensions between poles of the dialectical continua.

Even if people do nothing to change the objective situation, there seem to be emotional mechanisms that favor equilibrium over continuous change and adjustment. Emotions tend to be triggered by novelty (Mandler, 1984; Scherer, Schorr, & Johnstone, 2001) so that familiarity, no matter how nice or noxious, tends toward the emotionally bland. Long-distance couples get used to separation and new roommates adjust to forced togetherness. After a few years couples tune out the same old formerly-amusing, now-boring stories and think nothing of repeated quarrels (Berscheid, 1983). At some point, people no longer want to tell and even less to hear the earthquake story (Pennebaker, 1997), or they decide it's time to reveal the affair. In dialectical terms one would say that the dialectical tensions reach a temporary resolution, but in emotion terms one would say that people habituate to new circumstances (Frijda, 1988). The tightrope walker must constantly adjust to new gusts of wind, but if the wind comes constantly from the north, the adjustment becomes automatic, and it is as if there is no wind at all.

Despite differences in how individuals or pairs negotiate dialectical tensions, researchers have observed recurrent patterns in how people negotiate autonomy and connectedness. Interaction patterns change dramatically from the tentativeness of early acquaintanceship to the security of established relationships and for some also to the strain of dissolution, as described in stage theories.

Stage Theories

Stage theories of close relationships liken relationship development, continuation, and deterioration to climbing steps, walking around on a plateau, and sometimes descending back down. The number of steps or stages varies from theory to theory (e.g., 10 for Knapp, 1978; 5 for Levinger, 1983), but all stage theories assume that different relational patterns characterize each step. One of the most important tasks for stage theories is to explain what moves people up and down the staircase. Knapp outsourced the job to social exchange theory and dialectical theory (Knapp & Vangelisti, 2005), and Levinger offered a variety of explanations, but we argue that emotions are also at work in ways that are still a bit mysterious.

Emotions Change With Stages

Guerrero and Andersen (2000) reviewed literature on emotional dynamics across three general stages of relationships. They argued that initial encounters generate feelings of passion, infatuation, warmth, anticipation, and joy but also anxiety, uncertainty, fear, envy, and embarrassment. In long-term relationships partners maintain positive feelings through engaging in constructive actions, inhibiting negative behaviors, and maintaining equity. Relational endings sometimes bring relief, contentment, and even joy, but more likely anger, sadness, hurt, grief, loneliness, or guilt.

Do We Step Separately or Together?

The stair-step metaphor begs the question of whether relational partners are stepping up, down, or across together. If steps are defined by patterns of interaction, then both partners have to be on the same step because it takes two to interact, but if they are at least in part emotional, then it is a different story. Partners can be and often are out of step. Not only is love often unrequited, but so is anger, boredom, and hurt.

Perhaps we should ask why partners are ever on the same emotional step. Part of the answer seems to be that they work on it. They seek out shared experiences that are likely to be pleasant, saving the negative feelings and bad news for later (Aune, Buller, & Aune, 1996). Another part of the answer seems to be that it just works that way. Positive feelings tend to feed positive feelings, although not always. Saarni (1999) wrote of spirals of mutual liking, which probably occur without much effort. One person expresses liking, which feels good and is reassuring to the other, who reciprocates, leading to more and more liking. Discrepancies, however, feel bad (Frijda, 1988). When people anticipated experiencing emotionally evocative situations (such as winning a lottery) with friends, the emotions they expected to feel depended on how their friends felt. If their friends were disappointed in the winnings, they thought it would put a damper on their own enjoyment (Jakobs, Fisher, & Manstead, 1997).

How Do We Step Up or Down Together?

On intuitive and experiential levels, it seems obvious that emotions both produce and are produced by changes in relationships (Berscheid, 1983; Mandler, 1984). Curiosity or loneliness motivates you to strike up a conversation; you enjoy it, so you suggest an outing; your time together is boring, so you pursue it no further. That is the short and relatively pleasureless and painless version. Considering the variety of emotions that move people through and result from changes in stages of relationship, however, it is unlikely that emotions can explain development, continuation, and deterioration in any simple way.

Consider passionate love. It does not take a relational scholar to know that passion does not increase monotonically over the time course of a relationship, peaking after many years of marriage, and declining gradually if the marriage deteriorates. So does it have any correspondence with relational changes at all? Baumeister and Bratslavsky (1999) proposed that passion is a not function of intimacy per se, but of changes in intimacy. In short, when intimacy increases rapidly, as is common in the early stages of relationship development, passion is high. As intimacy becomes fully developed and can no longer increase as rapidly, passion declines. Abrupt decreases in intimacy also generate passion with negative valence, such as intense distress, whereas gradual declines may not produce such passionate negative feelings.

One emotional factor that may be directly associated with intimacy or stages of relational development is the degree to which each person feels that his or her emotional well-being depends on the relationship with the other (social exchange theorists would call it emotional investment). In the early stages of relationships, little is at stake beyond pleasant interactions, but pleasant interactions are addictive, and each partner may come to realize that they are happier together than apart. If they build a life together in advanced stages, their emotional well-being depends not just on shared interactions but on shared life experiences and goals. If the relationship declines, either those positive connections decline, negative connections increase, or both such that well-being depends on being away from one another rather than together.

Theorists have not addressed the question of why recurrent patterns are observed at different stages of relationship. It could because of biological drives for connection or because of logical imperatives such as partners' need to know about each other in order to coordinate. Or it could be that people have mental models of friendship or love that they enact in their own relationships as described by social cognitive theories.

Social Cognitive Theories

Social cognitive theorists also study emotion, particularly theorists with an interest in close relationships. Typically, however, social cognitive theorists are not so much con-

cerned with scientific accounts of the causes and functions of emotions as in so-called folk or lay accounts of such processes. This interest derives from the premise that people learn *about* emotions as they grow up, and it is their stored emotion knowledge structures, or scripts, that play a crucial role in their understanding, experience, and memory of emotion-related events in their close relationships.

The social cognitive theory that has been applied most explicitly to emotion is Rosch's (1973) prototype theory (see Mervis & Rosch, 1981, for a review). According to Rosch, many natural language concepts lack precise definitions. Instead, they are organized around their clearest cases or best examples, which are referred to as prototypes. Prototype theory originally was developed to account for the cognitive representation of object categories, such as furniture, fruit, and vehicles. Subsequently, Fehr and Russell (1984; see also Shaver, Schwartz, Kirson, & O'Connor, 1987) demonstrated that the concept of emotion was amenable to a prototype conceptualization; instances such as happiness, love, and sadness were considered by laypeople to be prototypical of the concept whereas awe, annoyance, and respect were considered nonprototypical.

The next development was to apply the theory to specific emotions, especially those that are relevant to close relationships. These included emotions such as love, hate, anger, joy, jealousy, and respect (e.g., Aron & Westbay, 1996; Fehr, 1988; Fehr & Russell, 1991; Fitness & Fletcher, 1993; Frei & Shaver, 2002; Lamm & Wiesmann, 1997; Regan, Kocan, & Whitlock, 1998; Russell & Fehr, 1994; Sharpsteen, 1993). This research has followed two major trajectories. One approach has been to specify the prototype structure of these concepts (i.e., identifying which types and features are considered central to a given emotion and which are considered peripheral). For example, it has been found that companionate-like features of love (e.g., trust, honesty, caring) are considered prototypical of the concept whereas passionate features (e.g., sexual attraction, increase in heart rate) are considered peripheral.

The other approach has been to ask laypeople to describe actual experiences of emotion (e.g., Fitness & Fletcher, 1993; Shaver et al., 1987). The assumption in these studies is that people will draw on their prototype of a particular emotion when reporting on an actual emotion experience. The intent is to map out laypeople's knowledge of prototypical emotion scripts, including antecedents, physiological components, behavioral tendencies, consequences, and so on. For example, Fitness and Fletcher (1993) found that laypeople conceptualize love in terms of positive thoughts – feeling warm and relaxed as caused by pleasant events and the like – whereas anger is conceptualized as involving negative thoughts and feelings, muscle tension, and as caused by the partner's negative behaviors. However, there were also similarities – both emotions were regarded as involving active engagement with the spouse, as being understandable, caused by the partner, and so on.

Both approaches have a common goal, namely, to uncover laypeople's cognitive representation of emotion. Although this goal has been successfully achieved, an unfortunate by-product is that prototype analyses of emotion have remained a largely "in the head" enterprise Yet, it would seem that this theory and the methodology based on it would be well suited to address important and interesting questions about emotion experience. As Fitness and Fletcher (1993) commented when describing cognitive theories of emotions such as prototype theory, "a cornerstone assumption of this work is that ... knowledge structures determine (or strongly influence) how different emotions are perceived, interpreted, labeled, and expressed" (p. 942). In other words, prototype researchers assume that people will draw on their prototype of a particular emotion when labeling or interpreting actual experiences of emotion and, importantly, when choosing a course of action. It is this issue that may well have the greatest relevance to close relationships. Framed in terms of love and anger, important questions are the following: How does

a person's cognitive representation of love or anger influence whether and how these emotions are expressed toward his or her partner? How does the partner's representation of love and anger influence his or her behavior? Importantly, how do matches and mismatches in partners' scripts for love and anger influence the course and outcome of emotion-laden interactions? These are the kinds of issues that will need to be explored in future research if we are to realize fully the value of prototype analyses of emotion concepts.

As anger bursts out of the individual and enters the social world through expression, it can sometimes seem to take on a life of its own. That is in part because messages of anger, shame, sympathy, and other emotions do not just express the internal states of individuals; they also negotiate social roles and power.

Theories of Social Roles and Power

Humans play a variety of relationship roles over the course of their lives, and every role comes with its own set of norms, rules, and expectations. Implicit within all such role identities are feelings and emotions. Thus, for example, it is acceptable for children, but not mothers, to have temper tantrums, and spouses should feel compassion, rather than contempt, for one another. There are also specific emotional role requirements for men and women. Brody (1999) documented the differences between men's and women's emotion roles in the family, with wives and mothers expected to carry the bulk of the so-called emotion work involved in nurturing and soothing others' feelings. Men's traditional role as family powerbrokers, on the other hand, involves more frequent (and acceptable) expressions of anger. Learning these kinds of gendered emotion rules is part and parcel of our emotion socialization as children (Fitness & Duffield, 2004).

So what happens when relationship partners break the rules and violate each others' expectations? Typically, emotion happens – indeed, perceived rule violation may generate the most dramatic and intense emotional responses, including abandonment, revenge, and murder. At a less drastic level, research on relational transgressions consistently shows that when one partner "breaks the rules," the other responds with hurt and anger. These emotional expressions, in turn, tend to generate anxiety, guilt, and even shame in the offender. Such emotional transactions play a crucial role in the negotiation of forgiveness, where the offender's guilt and remorse must be sufficient to "pay for" the victim's suffering (Fitness, 2001). Such emotional expressions also serve important functions in the proximal context, signaling a desire for continued attachment and emotional investment in the relationship.

Clearly, there are complex and subtle power plays at work here, with relationship partners' feelings and emotions signaling their positions (one-up, one-down) relative to each other and generating, in turn, the next moves in the drama. However, relatively little is known about emotion and power dynamics in close relationships – indeed, power is something of a dirty word in the close relationship context, with its connotations of coercion, manipulation, and exploitation. Yet power is an integral, inevitable, and inescapable feature of social relationships. We are all negotiating power with one another, all the time, via our feelings and emotions.

Emotions as Power and Status Signals

The basis of all power is dependency. To the extent that an individual relies on another for any valued resource (including love, or emotional investment in a relationship), then the holder of that resource has power over the individual who needs or wants it (Sprecher & Felmlee, 1997). Within every close relationship, then, there are both overt and covert power struggles involving issues of give and take, influence and resistance, control and subversion. For example, Retzinger (1991) described how spouses may jockey for position during marital quarrels by trading insults and put-downs. One partner's insult shames the other, who responds with defensive anger and a humiliating remark of his or her own, creating a relational interaction revolving around issues of power and subordination.

Perhaps one of the most insightful and potentially fruitful models of the relationship between power and emotion was proposed some years ago by Kemper (e.g., 1984, 1991). According to Kemper, two basic dimensions underlie every human interaction: power (feelings of control and dominance) and status (feelings of worthiness, esteem). Every relational exchange takes place along these two dimensions, with emotions signaling shifts in power–status dynamics. Thus, a perceived loss of power triggers anxiety; a perceived gain in power triggers pleasure. A perceived loss of status triggers hurt, depression, shame; a perceived gain in status, or esteem, elicits the happiness that comes from the feeling that one is a valued relationship partner.

There is considerable scope within this model to enrich our understanding of power and emotion dynamics within the close relationship context. As noted in previous sections of this chapter, relationship partners are constantly sending power and status signals to one another via their expressions of emotions like anger and love. The experience and expression of such emotions serve a vital informational function for humans who need to know how they are doing relative to others (i.e., how much power do they have, how much do others care about them; see Fitness & Duffield, 2004). Again, however, there is more to be learned about the varieties of anger and love that may be communicated within relationship contexts. Oatley and Jenkins (1996), for example, argued that contempt is "the emotion of complete rejection, of unmodulated power, treating the other as a nonperson" (p. 313). Similarly, Gottman (1994) argued that contempt is, in the long term, a corrosive marital emotion. However, we know little about its origins, associated motivations, and short- to medium-term relational consequences (shame, depression, or both?). Nor do we know about the emotions involved in people's strategies to gain and maintain power, or to regain lost status.

Power Shapes Emotions

According to a model recently proposed by Keltner, Gruenfeld, and Anderson (2003), having power is associated with holding resources, which generates positive emotions and "approach" tendencies – having power feels good. On the other hand, low power is associated with resource deficits and a felt incapacity to deal effectively with threat; this generates negative emotions (anxiety, depression) and "inhibition" tendencies. This implies that within the context of close relationships, having power may enable individuals to shape or control the emotions of their less powerful partners (see Gottman, Driver, Yashimoto, & Rushe, 2002). In a recent demonstration of such "emotional convergence," Anderson, Keltner, and John (2003) found that dating partners and roommates became more similar in their emotional responses over time, but that "the emotions of the relationship partner with lower power or status were better predicted by their partners' prior emotions than vice versa" (p. 1065). That is, high-power participants effectively shaped the emotions of low-power partners (and note that these findings did not relate to the gender of the participants).

Anderson et al. (2003) argued that although it may seem dysfunctional for low-power individuals to adapt emotionally to high-power individuals, the resulting emotional similarity may actually contribute to relationship cohesion and longevity. After all, low-power people have to put more effort generally into making relationships work because they depend on their partners more than their partners depend on them. It is also possible to make a sound evolutionary argument for why it is safer and more potentially adaptive for low-power individuals to keep high-power individuals happy. However, there is still much to be learned about the conditions under which partners may resist such emotional control and when emotional convergence may have dysfunctional outcomes (e.g., when a high-power partner's expressions of contempt are faithfully reproduced by the low-power partner as self-contempt and self-hatred).

Conclusions

What do various theories explain about close relationships and what role does emotion play? Evolutionary theory tells us that people need close relationships to survive and so emotions prompt efforts to establish, protect, and maintain strong bonds with parents, lovers, children, and other allies. Here, the emotions of love and anger play critical roles in partners' attempts to meet relationship goals and resolve relationship challenges.

Without strong social ties all human beings are vulnerable, but infants are almost completely helpless. Fortunately, they do have strong emotions (and lungs to match) that prompt them to maintain bonds or to protest their loss as described by attachment theory. Bonding patterns established in infancy may also carry over or become reestablished in adult relationships and emerge as emotional reactions to relationship challenges or loss.

Evolutionary and attachment theories have less to say about how to choose partners or allies. Infants should opt for dependable caregivers, but they seldom have a choice. Adults who want their genes to survive should choose fertile lovers, but what if he does not bring home the bison or she will not share? Social exchange theory provides a framework for understanding how relationships are negotiated so that both partners benefit. Emotions like love and anger are guides that lead toward rewarding partners and away from costly ones, toward fair exchanges and away from those where less is gained than given, and toward allies we can trust rather than those who are undependable.

Humans are deeply social beings, but unlike ants, we are also individuals who sometimes find sociality to be too much of a good thing. Dialectical theory addresses how people negotiate emotions that push and pull us between connectedness and autonomy, between novelty and predictability, between openness and protectiveness.

Individuals certainly figure out their own ways of negotiating dialectical tensions, but when many individuals establish the same patterns, those patterns serve as resources or expectations for others. Stage theories of relationship development describe typical patterns by which people move from being strangers with relative autonomy to close friends or spouses with greater connectedness, then perhaps back again to autonomy if the relationship declines or terminates. Somewhat different emotions characterize and move people through stages, from the excitement and anxiety of the early stages to the passion and compassion of developed relationships to the anger, hurt, and sadness of deterioration.

People also have mental models of socially developed guidelines for managing their feelings in interaction, as described by social cognitive theories. Prototypes or implicit theories of love, for example, show that trust, honesty, and caring are its central features whereas passion is more peripheral. Those looking for "true love," then, should seek trust, honesty, and caring, although it is not clear that they actually do in the throes of passion.

In addition to connection, social roles and power are negotiated through emotion and its expression. In marriages and families, power and status influence who is entitled to anger, love, and sympathy and who is responsible for providing comfort or inducing shame or guilt. Emotion also provides avenues not just for enacting established power relationships but also for negotiating power, such as when children throw temper tantrums, when couples try to outhumiliate one another in arguments, or when exchanges of mutual appreciation enhance the status of everyone.

Emotion is a common thread that runs through the theories of close relationships that we have analyzed. The thread is more or less visible, depending on the theory, but it is always there. Emotion may be indispensable to close relationships because it is arguably the most powerful mechanism that we have for monitoring the health and well-being of ourselves and of our relationships.

References

Altman, I., Vinsel, A., & Brown, B. B. (1981). Dialectic conceptions in social psychology: An application to social penetration and privacy regulation. In L. Berkowitz (Ed.), *Advances in experimental social psychology*, 14, 107–150.

Anderson, C., Keltner, D., & John, O. P. (2003). Emotional convergence between people over time. *Journal of Personality and Social Psychology*, 84, 1054–1068.

Archer, J. (1999). *The nature of grief: The evolution and psychology of reactions to loss.* New York: Routledge.

Aron, A., & Aron, E. N. (1986). *Love and the expansion of self.* Washington, DC: Hemisphere.

Aron, A., Norman, C. C., Aron, E. N., McKenna, C., & Heyman, R. E. (2000). Couples' shared participation in novel and arousing activities and experienced relationship quality. *Journal of Personality and Social Psychology*, 78, 273–284.

Aron, A., & Westbay, L. (1996). Dimensions of the prototype of love. *Journal of Personality and Social Psychology*, 70, 535–551.

Aune, K. S., Buller, D. B., & Aune, R. K. (1996). Display rule development in romantic relationships: Emotion management and perceived appropriateness of emotions across relationship stages. *Human Communication Research*, 23, 115–146.

Batson, C. D. (1998). Altruism and prosocial behavior. In D. Gilbert, S. Fiske, & G. Lindzey (Eds.), *The handbook of social psychology* (4th ed., pp. 282–316). New York: McGraw-Hill.

Baumeister, R. F., & Bratslavsky, E. (1999). Passion, intimacy, and time: Passionate love as a function of change in intimacy. *Personality and Social Psychology Review*, 3, 49–67.

Baumeister, R. F., & Leary, M. R. (1995). The need to belong: Desire for interpersonal attachments as a fundamental human motivation. *Psychological Bulletin, 117*, 497–529.

Baumeister, R. F., & Wotman, S. R. (1992). *Breaking hearts: The two sides of unrequited love*. New York: Guilford Press.

Baxter, L. A. (2004). Relationships as dialogues. *Personal Relationships, 11*, 1–22.

Baxter, L. A., & Montgomery, B. M. (1996). *Relating: Dialogues and dialectics*. New York: Guilford Press.

Berger, C. R., & Bradac, J. J. (1982). *Language and social knowledge*. London: Arnold.

Berscheid, E. (1983). Emotion. In H. H. Kelley, E. Berscheid, A. Christensen, J. H. Harvey, T. L. Huston, G. Levinger, et al. (Eds.), *Close relationships* (pp. 110–168). New York: Freeman.

Berscheid, E., & Ammazzalorso, H. (2001). Emotional experience in close relationships. In G. J. O. Fletcher & M. S. Clark (Eds.), *Blackwell handbook of social psychology. Volume 2: Interpersonal processes* (pp. 308–330). Oxford, England: Blackwell.

Bowlby, J. (1969). *Attachment and loss: Volume 1. Attachment*. New York: Basic Books.

Bowlby, J. (1973). *Attachment and loss: Volume 2. Separation, anxiety, and anger*. New York: Basic Books.

Bowlby, J. (1980). *Attachment and loss: Volume 3. Loss, sadness, and depression*. New York: Basic Books.

Brody, L. (1999). *Gender, emotion, and the family*. Cambridge, MA: Harvard University Press.

Buss, D., & Kenrick, D. (1998). Evolutionary social psychology. In D. Gilbert, S. Fiske, & G. Lindzey (Eds.), *The handbook of social psychology* (pp. 982–1026). New York: McGraw-Hill.

Clark, M., Fitness, J., & Brissette, I. (2001). Understanding people's perceptions of their relationships is crucial to understanding their emotional lives. In G. J. O. Fletcher & M. Clark (Eds.), *Blackwell handbook of social psychology. Volume 2: Interpersonal processes* (pp. 253–278). Oxford, England: Blackwell.

Clary, E. G., Snyder, M., Ridge, R. D., Copeland, J., Stukas, A. A., Haugen, J., & Miene, P. (1998). Understanding and assessing the motivations of volunteers: A functional approach. *Journal of Personality and Social Psychology, 74*, 1516–1530.

Cosmides, J., & Tooby, J. (2000). Evolutionary psychology and the emotions. In M. Lewis & J. Haviland-Jones (Eds.), *Handbook of emotions* (pp. 91–115). New York: Guilford Press.

Ellis, B., & Malamuth, N. (2000). Love and anger in romantic relationships: A discrete systems model. *Journal of Personality, 68*, 526–558.

Feeney, J. A., & Noller, P. (1992). Attachment style and romantic love: Relationship dissolution. *Australian Journal of Psychology, 44*, 69–74.

Fehr, B. (1988). Prototype analysis of the concepts of love and commitment. *Journal of Personality and Social Psychology, 55*, 557–579.

Fehr, B., & Russell, J. A. (1984). Concept of emotion viewed from a prototype perspective. *Journal of Experimental Psychology: General, 113*, 464–486.

Fehr, B., & Russell, J. A. (1991). The concept of love viewed from a prototype perspective. *Journal of Personality and Social Psychology, 60*, 425–438.

Fitness, J. (2001). Betrayal, rejection, revenge, and forgiveness. In M. Leary (Ed.), *Interpersonal rejection* (pp. 73–103). New York: Oxford University Press.

Fitness, J., & Duffield, J. (2004). Emotion and communication in families. In A. L. Vangelisti (Ed.), *Handbook of family communication* (pp. 473–494). Mahwah, NJ: Erlbaum.

Fitness, J., & Fletcher, G. J. O. (1993). Love, hate, anger, and jealousy in close relationships: A cognitive appraisal and prototype analysis. *Journal of Personality and Social Psychology, 65*, 942–958.

Fitness, J., Fletcher, G. J. O., & Overall, N. (2003). Attraction and intimate relationships. In M. Hogg & J. Cooper (Eds.), *The Sage handbook of social psychology* (pp. 258–278). Thousand Oaks, CA: Sage.

Fletcher, G. J. O. (2002). *The new science of intimate relationships*. Malden, MA: Blackwell.

Fraley, R. C., & Shaver, P. R. (1997). Adult attachment and the suppression of unwanted thoughts. *Journal of Personality and Social Psychology, 73*, 1080–1091.

Frei, J. R., & Shaver, P. R. (2002). Respect in close relationships: Prototype definition, self-report assessment, and initial correlations. *Personal Relationships, 9*, 121–139.

Frijda, N. H. (1988). The laws of emotion. *American Psychologist, 43*, 349–358.

Gilbert, P. (1998). What is shame? Some core issues and controversies. In P. Gilbert & B. Andrews (Eds.), *Shame: Interpersonal behavior, psychopathology, and culture* (pp. 3–38). New York: Oxford University Press.

Gottman, J. (1994). *What predicts divorce? The relationship between marital processes and marital outcomes*. Hillsdale, NJ: Erlbaum.

Gottman, J., Driver, J., Yoshimoto, D., & Rushe, R. (2002). Approaches to the study of power in violent and nonviolent marriages, and in gay male and lesbian cohabiting relationships. In P. Noller & J. Feeney (Eds.), *Understanding marriage* (pp. 323–347). New York: Cambridge University Press.

Guerrero, L. K., & Andersen, P. A. (2000). Emotion in close relationships. In C. Hendrick & S. S. Hendrick (Eds.), *Close relationships: A sourcebook* (pp. 171–183). Thousand Oaks, CA: Sage.

Hazan, C., & Shaver, P. (1987). Romantic love conceptualized as an attachment process. *Journal of Personality and Social Psychology, 52*, 511–524.

Hoffman, M. L. (2001). *Empathy and moral development*. New York: Cambridge University Press.

Ickes, W. (Ed.) (1997). *Empathic accuracy*. New York: Guilford Press.

Jakobs, E., Fischer, A. H., & Manstead, A. S. R. (1997). Emotional experience as a function of social context: The role of the other. *Journal of Nonverbal Behavior, 21*, 103–130.

Keltner, D., Gruenfeld, D. H., & Anderson, C. (2003). Power, approach, and inhibition. *Psychological Review, 110*, 265–284.

Kemper, T. D. (1984). Power, status, and emotions: A sociological contribution to a psychophysiological domain. In K. Scherer & P. Ekman (Eds.) *Approaches to emotion* (pp. 369–383). Hillsdale, NJ: Erlbaum.

Kemper, T. D. (1991). An introduction to the sociology of emotions. In K. T. Strongman (Ed.), *International review of studies on emotion* (pp. 301–349). Chichester, England: Wiley.

Kennedy-Moore, E., & Watson, J. C. (1999). *Expressing emotion: Myths, realities, and therapeutic strategies*. New York: Guilford Press.

Knapp, M. L. (1978). *Social intercourse: From greeting to goodbye*. Boston: Allyn & Bacon.

Knapp, M. L., & Vangelisti, A. L. (2005). *Interpersonal communication and human Relationships* (5th ed.). Needham Heights, MA: Allyn & Bacon.

Kobak, R. R., & Hazan, C. (1991). Attachment in marriage: Effects of security and accuracy of working models. *Journal of Personality and Social Psychology, 60*, 861–869.

Kobak, R. R., & Sceery, A. (1988). Attachment in late adolescence: Working models, affect regulation, and representations of self and others. *Child Development, 59*, 135–146.

Kuijer, R. G., Buunk, B. P., Ybema, J. F., & Wobbes, T. (2002). The relation between perceived inequity, marital satisfaction and emotions among couples facing cancer. *British Journal of Social Psychology, 41*, 39–57.

Lamm, H., & Wiesmann, U. (1997). Subjective attributes of attraction: How people characterize their liking, their love, and their being in love. *Personal Relationships, 4*, 271–284.

Lazarus, R. (1991). *Emotion and adaptation*. New York: Oxford University Press.

Levinger, G. (1983). Development and change. In. H. H. Kelley, E. Berscheid, A. Christensen, J. H. Harvey, T. L. Huston, G. Levinger, et al. (Eds.), *Close relationships* (pp. 315–359). New York: Freeman.

Mandler, G. (1984). *Mind and body*. New York: Norton.

Mervis, C. B., & Rosch, E. (1981). Categorization of natural objects. *Annual Review of Psychology, 32*, 89–115.

Mikulincer, M., & Florian, V. (1995). Appraisal of and coping with a real-life stressful situation: The contribution of attachment styles. *Personality and Social Psychology Bulletin, 21*, 406–414.

Mikulincer, M., Hirschberger, G., Nachmias, O., & Gilliath, O. (2001). The affective component of the secure base schema: Affective priming with representations of attachment security. *Journal of Personality and Social Psychology, 81*, 305–321.

Mikulincer, M., & Orbach, I. (1995). Attachment styles and repressive defensiveness: The accessibility and architecture of affective memories. *Journal of Personality and Social Psychology, 68*, 917–925.

Noller, P., & Ruzzene, M. (1991). Communication in marriage: The influence of affect and cognition. In G. J. O. Fletcher & F. Fincham (Eds.), *Cognition in close relationships* (pp. 203–233). Hillsdale, NJ: Erlbaum.

Oatley, K., & Jenkins, J. (1996). *Understanding emotions*. Cambridge, MA: Blackwell.

Pennebaker, J. W. (1997). *Opening up: The healing power of expressing emotions* (rev. ed.). New York: Guilford Press.

Petronio, S. (Ed.) (2000). *Balancing the secrets of private disclosures*. Mahwah, NJ: Erlbaum.

Planalp, S. (1999). *Communicating emotion: Social, moral, and cultural processes*. New York: Cambridge University Press.

Planalp, S. (2003). The unacknowledged role of emotion in theories of close relationships: How do theories feel? *Communication Theory, 13*, 78–99.

Planalp, S., & Fitness, J. (1999). Thinking/feeling about social and personal relationships. *Journal of Social and Personal Relationships, 16*, 731–751.

Rawlins, W. K. (1992). *Friendship matters: Communication, dialectics, and the life course*. New York: Aldine de Gruyter.

Regan, P. C., Kocan, E. R., & Whitlock, T. (1998). Ain't love grand! A prototype analysis of the concept of romantic love. *Journal of Social and Personal Relationships, 15*, 411–420.

Retzinger, S. M. (1991). *Violent emotions: Shame and rage in marital quarrels*. Newbury Park, CA: Sage.

Rosch, E. H. (1973). Natural categories. *Cognitive Psychology, 4*, 328–350.

Rowe, A., & Carnelley, K. B. (2003). Attachment style differences in the processing of attachment-relevant information: Primed-style effects on recall, interpersonal expectations, and affect. *Personal Relationships, 10*, 59–75.

Russell, J. A., & Fehr, B. (1994). The varieties of anger: Fuzzy concepts in a fuzzy hierarchy. *Journal of Personality and Social Psychology, 67*, 186–205.

Saarni, C. (1999). *The development of emotional competence*. New York: Guilford Press.

Scherer, K., Schorr, A., & Johnstone, T. (2001). *Appraisal processes in emotion*. New York: Oxford University Press.

Sharpsteen, D. J. (1993). Romantic jealousy as an emotion concept: A prototype analysis. *Journal of Social and Personal Relationships, 10*, 69–82.

Shaver, P., Schwartz, J., Kirson, D., & O'Connor, C. (1987). Emotion knowledge: Further explorations of a prototype approach. *Journal of Personality and Social Psychology, 52*, 1061–1086.

Simpson, J. A. (1990). Influence of attachment styles on romantic relationships. *Journal of Personality and Social Psychology, 59*, 971–980.

Simpson, J. A., Rholes, W. S., & Nelligan, J. S. (1992). Support seeking and support giving within couples in an anxiety-provoking situation: The role of attachment styles. *Journal of Personality and Social Psychology, 62*, 434–446.

Sprecher, S. (2001). A comparison of emotional consequences of and change in equity over time using global and domain-specific measures of equity. *Journal of Social and Personal Relationships, 18*, 477–501.

Sprecher, S., & Felmlee, D. (1997). The balance of power in romantic heterosexual couples over time from "his" and "her" perspectives. *Sex Roles, 37*, 361–380.

CHAPTER 21

Physiology and Interpersonal Relationships

Timothy J. Loving
Kathi L. Heffner
Janice K. Kiecolt-Glaser

During interpersonal interactions, a vast array of chemical, electrical, and mechanical activities are operating under each person's skin at any moment. Most concerted activities remain out of individuals' conscious awareness, but some "surface" and can be perceived by others. Psychophysiologists study these biological concomitants of social behaviors to better understand the social world; physiological indicators provide valuable information about cognitions, affect, and other internal states that individuals are either unwilling or unable to articulate in a self-report. Importantly, physiological responses also provide information about the stressful and emotional nature of social episodes or individuals circumstances. Not surprisingly, although personal relationships have the ability to enhance greatly one's quality of life, they can also cause serious harm. The quarrelsome couple, the husband who must cope daily with the strains of caregiving for his chronically ill wife, the woman who ruminates about the disagreement she had with her boyfriend the day before, and the lonely exemplify those vulnerable to health-compromising physiological wear and tear from ongoing or repeated engagement with stressful circumstances. Conversely, individuals embedded within positive social network structures, such as good marriages or supportive friendships, fare better with regard to morbidity and mortality and are less physiologically vulnerable when faced with stressful events.

Overview and Scope of the Chapter

Our focus in this chapter is how relationships affect the body's physiological systems (and vice versa). Although we do not focus on physical health outcomes per se (our attention is on how close relationships, including their characteristics, qualities, and dynamics, affect specific health-relevant physiological processes), we do note any links between physiological indicators and health outcomes when appropriate. We limit our review to adults and must neglect infant and child studies (Gunnar,

1992; Uvnaes-Moberg, Johansson, Lupoli, & Svennersten-Sjaunja, 2001).

We begin with a summary of the most commonly utilized physiological indicators, with the goal of providing a general knowledge base so that even the most novice readers have a frame of reference from which to evaluate the findings reported throughout the chapter. Consequently, our introduction is dense and initially focuses exclusively on physiology rather than relationships; it is our hope that by providing an in-depth discussion of physiological processes and systems, we allow for some illumination of the bigger picture that may serve as a resource in its own right. We then focus on the physiological consequences of social isolation (or the opposite, social embedment), including the physiological effects of social support and loneliness. We next devote attention to one area of inquiry that has received considerable empirical attention: the psychophysiology of marital interaction. By and large, our review focuses on the ways in which specific psychological and behavioral characteristics of relationships affect physiology; however, we also review existing literature on the reciprocal influence of physiology on relationship processes. Finally, we briefly address more recent advances in the field, closing with a few suggestions for future directions as well as a general assessment of the current state of the field.

Physiological Responses in the Study of Personal Relationship: Emphasis on Stress

Contemporary interpersonal psychophysiological research has typically emphasized the impact of relationship and affiliation-related processes on the body's responses to various intra- and extra-dyadic stressors. Understanding how the body's systems respond during stress provides a basis for evaluating and integrating research addressing physiological influences on relationship and physical health.

The Autonomic and Endocrine Systems: Pathways of Physiological Influence

The autonomic nervous system is a system of sensory and motor nerves that innervate the body's organ systems to regulate their activity. It is composed of the sympathetic nervous system, the parasympathetic nervous system, and the enteric nervous system. The enteric branch is responsible for regulation of the digestive tract, but digestion is also controlled by the sympathetic and parasympathetic branches. The sympathetic nervous system, essential for energy mobilization, and the parasympathetic nervous system, responsible for energy conservation, work together to maintain the body's normal functioning by continually making adjustments in response to normal metabolic demands, such as when we stand up. The sympathetic nervous system is largely responsible for the fight-or-flight response during threat or danger. Its activities promote the transfer of blood to the brain and the muscles, an increase in sugar levels in the blood, and heightened heart rate and other organ activity in preparation for physical exertion. Conversely, the parasympathetic nervous system plays essential roles in reproduction and energy storage. This system opposes activity of the sympathetic nervous system.

The endocrine system regulates functioning through the release of hormones that travel through the bloodstream to target organs. These hormones originate from endocrine glands whose activity is under the influence of the brain's pituitary gland as well as the autonomic nervous system. Two endocrine pathways are integral during the stress response: the *sympathetic adrenomedullary (SAM) pathway* and the *hypothalamic–pituitary–adrenocortical (HPA) pathway*. Both the SAM and HPA pathways begin at the hypothalamus, the key structure in the coordination of autonomic and endocrine function, and end at the adrenal glands, located above the kidneys.

Through direct sympathetic innervation from the hypothalamus that characterizes the SAM pathway, the adrenal medulla releases the catecholamines, epinephrine (adrenaline) and norepinephrine, into the bloodstream. Epinephrine acts on many tissues at one time and serves to coordinate many metabolic and behavioral responses during stress. Norepinephrine has minimal effects on the body when traveling though the bloodstream. However, when released via autonomic nerve pathways, norepinephrine increases general blood vessel constriction essential for blood pressure regulation. During activation of the SAM pathway, the HPA response also occurs, but effects are seen at a much slower rate. HPA release of adrenocorticotropin hormone (ACTH) into the bloodstream stimulates the adrenal cortex to secrete cortisol. Cortisol, a glucocorticoid hormone, is especially important for maintaining normal metabolic function but is also very important during the stress response; cortisol enhances the responses of the sympathetic nervous system and increases the release of glucose and stored fats for energy.

Physiological Indicators of Autonomic and Endocrine Activity

Numerous technologies are available to assess physiological function directly and indirectly, and our discussion provides information about some of the more common techniques currently in use. Those interested in pursuing additional measures and measurement techniques are encouraged to consult psychophysiological methods resources (e.g., Cacioppo, Tassinary, & Berntson, 2000; Stern, Ray, & Quigley, 2003).

GENERAL SYMPATHETIC ACTIVITY MEASUREMENT

Skin conductance or electrodermal response, one of the most widely measured physiological parameters (Stern, Ray, & Davis, 1980), is still commonly used today as an indicator of sympathetic nervous system activity (Dawson, Schell, & Filion, 2000). Electrodermal activity refers to the skin's varying ability to conduct electricity; changes result from increased or decreased perspiration

secretion by eccrine sweat glands. Although these glands cover most of the body, they are found in dense quantities on the palms and feet, and they are innervated by sympathetic nerve fibers. Sympathetic activation increases eccrine perspiration secretion, allowing an electrical signal to pass more readily between two electrodes placed on the eccrine glands.

CARDIOVASCULAR MEASURES

A large proportion of the psychophysiological research on personal relationships incorporates measurement of the cardiovascular system. Traditional cardiovascular parameters include heart rate and blood pressure, which are indirect indicators of autonomic activity (for example, blood pressure can rise because of norepinephrine activity at sympathetic nerve terminals), as well as sympathetically influenced endocrine activity (epinephrine released from the adrenal medulla can increase heart rate). Distinctions are often made between systolic (the maximum pressure in the arteries when the heart contracts) and diastolic blood pressure (pressure in the arteries when the heart is at rest). Heart rate can be assessed through measurement of the electrocardiogram (ECG) that reflects the natural electrical activity of the heart or more indirectly using methods that provide heart rate measures in addition to other parameters, such as automatic blood pressure assessment.

Cardiovascular indices not only provide inexpensive and reliable indicators of autonomic and endocrine system activity, but they characterize different motivational states (Tomaka, Blascovich, Kelsey & Leitten, 1993) and correlate with distinct coping opportunities (Hartley, Ginsburg, & Heffner, 1999). By assessing cardiac performance using impedance cardiography (a noninvasive technique to derive stroke volume and cardiac contractility measures) in conjunction with blood pressure measurement, more detailed information about substrates underlying cardiovascular changes is obtained. Measures of vascular resistance, such as total peripheral resistance (TPR) or finger pulse volume (FPV), provide information about the extent to which blood vessels are constricted or dilated.

ENDOCRINE MEASURES

Although cardiovascular measures can be used to infer relative activation of HPA or SAM pathways, hormones produced through these channels can be more directly assessed. Cortisol, the major HPA-derived hormone, has been the focus of considerable research in light of its significant effects on metabolic activity during stress, as well as its regulatory influence on other body systems, including the immune system. Rises in circulating cortisol are observed some time after the onset of acute physical or psychological stress (anywhere from 10 to 20 minutes), but cortisol also follows a diurnal pattern: levels are highest in the morning hours after waking and continue to fall throughout the day. Deviations from this pattern can be indicative of pathology, but are also tied to chronic stress (Spiegel & Giese-Davis, 2003) and even relationship functioning (Adam & Gunnar, 2001). Cortisol can be measured from blood and urine samples, but even more beneficial for social scientists is the ability to sample cortisol levels from saliva, an inexpensive and unobtrusive method. In conjunction with cortisol measures, ACTH provides further information about HPA activation because cortisol release is dependent on ACTH travel from the pituitary to the adrenals. Currently, ACTH must be attained through blood samples.

SAM-activated endocrine output of epinephrine and norepinephrine can also be assessed through blood or urine sampling, but the methods to assay these catecholamines are much more costly than those to assess cortisol. However, because SAM activity occurs much more quickly than HPA activity, researchers may be interested, for instance, in sampling circulating epinephrine to better understand temporal changes in sympathetic adrenal activation during acute stress.

Of particular relevance to close relationships researchers interested in pair bonding, oxytocin is an HPA-derived hormone released by the pituitary and is primarily responsible for milk release from the mammary glands and uterine contractions during labor. However, animal studies have demonstrated a role of oxytocin in mate pair bonding, suggesting it may have implications for social interactions (Taylor et al., 2000). Exciting ideas about oxytocin's possible role in relationships are briefly discussed at the chapter's end.

Potential Health Implications of Physiological Pathways

The physiological indicators of autonomic and endocrine activity can also provide a window into personal relationship processes that impact physical health. For instance, blood pressure reactivity to disagreements may indicate a heightened sensitivity to these conflicts, and exacerbated blood pressure responses and heightened vascular constriction may be tied to poor cardiovascular health outcomes (Saab & Schneiderman, 1993). Animal models and human studies alike provide compelling evidence for the cardiovascular reactivity–disease link (Blascovich & Katkin, 1993).

Psychoneuroimmunological studies of associations among stress, endocrine, and immune function also shed light on the ways close relationships may affect health processes. Interactions among SAM and HPA-activated endocrine responses and the immune system have been emphasized (Kiecolt-Glaser, McGuire, Robles, & Glaser, 2002), highlighting the role of stress reactivity in immune function. Epinephrine, in conjunction with cortisol, can dysregulate immune activity (Elenkov, Webster, Torpy, & Chrousos, 1999), and cortisol has multiple influences on immune function, including the trafficking of immune cells throughout the body and the ability of immune cells to kill antigen-infected cells (Miller, 1998), as well as the expression of latent viruses (Cacioppo, Kiecolt-Glaser et al., 2002) such as the Epstein–Barr virus, responsible for mononucleosis. Thus, endocrine concomitants of close relationship processes might indicate the situations and individual- or dyadic-level differences that potentially lead to immune-related health decrements.

Examining stress-associated immune modulation holds great promise for understanding the ways personal relationships impact health. The immune system is responsible for (a) distinguishing the "self," the body's normal cells, from the "nonself," foreign invaders or transformed cells, and (b) destroying the latter. These processes are performed through cellular and humoral immune responses operating across two categories of the immune system termed innate and acquired immunity. Measuring the performance and condition of the immune system typically takes two forms. Functional assays provide information on the ability of immune system cells to perform their job, and enumerative assays provide information regarding actual counts or percentages of specific immune cells (for a description of specific measures, see Kiecolt-Glaser & Glaser, 1995a).

As with other indices of physiological reactivity, however, assessing immune function alone cannot illuminate the links between interpersonal stressors and health outcomes. What is required is empirical attention to biological mechanisms mediating stress and health links. Maladaptive physiological responses to stress, such as repeated over- or underresponsiveness to stressors, lack of habituation to recurrent, similar stressors, or inadequate recovery from stress have been suggested as pathways through which stress can damage the body over time, leading to poor health outcomes and advanced aging (Cacioppo et al., 1998; McEwen, 2002). There are a growing number of studies of associations among stress, associated physiological responses, and health outcomes (for example, see Cohen, Doyle, Turner, Alper, & Skoner, 2003; Kiecolt-Glaser & Glaser, 1995b). Such studies, with the addition of interpersonal factors as moderators of these associations, are necessary to understand fully how social relations influence morbidity and mortality.

Not All Physiological Indicators Are Created Equal

The use of physiological indicators poses both methodological and interpretational challenges. For example, we noted earlier that catecholamines can only be assessed via blood or urine. This may prove difficult depending on the methodological design being employed (e.g., multiple assessments during a 30-minute conversation); however, utilization of a heparin well attached to a long polyethylene tube allows for repeated blood draws without frequent "sticks" (which also affect circulating hormone levels). In contrast, cortisol receives significant empirical attention both because of its function as a primary stress hormone, but also because it can be assessed relatively unobtrusively via saliva.

Consideration of the timing of biological samples and how they relate to the experimental procedure is also critical. Again, consider the catecholamines. Whereas cortisol and ACTH have a half life of 60–90 minutes and 10 minutes, respectively, the half-life for norepinephrine and epinephrine is significantly shorter – only 1 to 2 minutes (Baum & Grunberg, 1995; Rose, 1984). As a result, interpretation of change in physiological indicators that does not account for these differences in circulation life expectancy could be costly (e.g., inappropriately concluding that an intervention had no effect on norepinephrine because the blood or urine sample was collected too late to observe actual changes). Cardiovascular indices can also be difficult to interpret. For example, blood pressure can rise during stressful situations because of greater blood vessel constriction, a response that over time may have dire health consequences; however, blood pressure may also rise because the heart is pumping larger volumes of blood through the circulatory system, as is seen during healthful exercise. Impedance cardiography is useful for determining these sources of blood pressure changes, thus clarifying what implications such changes may have for individuals' health.

Ultimately, and a point we reiterate at the chapter's end, this type of work truly benefits from collaboration (see Kiecolt-Glaser & Glaser, 1995a, for a discussion of the various issues faced when assessing immunological outcomes). Deciding what physiological indicator to utilize as well as how and when to assess it is best done through consultation with those who are best equipped to answer these questions, including endocrinologists, immunologists, and psychophysiologists.

Summary

Psychophysiological researchers have contributed a wealth of knowledge regarding associations among social, psychological and physiological processes, but much remains to be done. Technological advances continue and will surely contribute to the study of biopsychosocial mechanisms. As discussed throughout this chapter, personal relationships play a central role in these mechanisms, contributing to our whole self, including our mental, emotional, and physical being. Examining autonomic, endocrine, and immune responses sheds light on the ways our close relationships produce or reduce stress in our lives and even set the stage for subsequent relationship functioning and health. Recent studies of physiological associations to disease and longevity suggest that cumulative biological mechanisms are important in predicting morbidity and mortality, and important for the study of personal relationships is early indication that positive cumulative relationships are tied to physiological function in the long term (Seeman, Singer, Ryff, Dienberg Love, & Levy-Storms, 2002), an issue we turn to next.

At the Heart of Relationships: A Fundamental Need for Affiliation

The need to belong "is a powerful, fundamental, and extremely pervasive motivation" (Baumeister & Leary, 1995). This proposition is impressively illustrated by longitudinal, prospective studies of various populations indicating increased mortality rates as a function of decreased social integration (Rutledge, Matthews, Lui, Stone, & Cauley, 2003), and myriad health and morbidity outcomes are associated with both the quality and quantity of an individual's social ties (Berkman, 1995). More recently, greater attention has been given to identifying potential mechanisms linking social relationships to health, with particular emphasis on social support. Whether in the context of marriage, family, or friendship, our affiliation with others (or a lack thereof) has powerful physiological consequences.

Being Socially Embedded: Physiological Correlates of Social Structures

Social integration is often operationalized based on various environmental characteristics proposed to reflect individuals' degree of social embedment, including their marital status, number of or degree of contact with relatives and friends, group affiliations, and the like (Berkman, Glass, Brissette, & Seeman, 2000). Importantly, recent research indicates an association between these structural indices of social network ties and physiological function and sheds light on mechanisms by which social integration may promote health. Seeman and her colleagues found decreases in urinary levels of epinephrine and norepinephrine for older men with greater social ties (Seeman, Berkman, Blazer, & Rowe, 1994), as well as reduced physiological activity across a range of indices in conjunction with increased social integration (Seeman et al., 2002). Older women evidenced weaker associations among social ties and physiological measures (Seeman et al., 1994), consistent with epidemiological reports of stronger relationships among social relationships and mortality for men (Kaplan et al., 1988). Given the prevalence of coronary-associated diseases and deaths and their suggested association with social integration (Krantz & McCeney, 2002; Smith & Ruiz, 2002), much of the psychophysiological research on social ties has emphasized cardiovascular function, with specific attention to blood pressure as a marker of disease risk. In general, greater numbers of social ties have been correlated with lower levels of resting blood pressure (Bland, Krogh, Winkelstein, & Trevisan, 1991), and, in contrast to the gender differences noted earlier with regard to endocrine and general measures of biological function, both men and women appear to experience the blood pressure benefits of social embedment (Uchino, Cacioppo, & Kiecolt-Glaser, 1996).

Being Socially Supported: Physiological Correlates of Social Relations

The *quality* of social relationships is also important, and perhaps most important, in predicting physiological function. Ryff and Singer (1998) suggest that having quality relations with others is indeed the most universally agreed upon component of well-being. Even marriage, which provides mental and physical health protection and promotion (Kiecolt-Glaser & Newton, 2001), can have fewer health benefits and may even be detrimental to physical well-being when troubled or dissatisfying (Gallo, Matthews, Troxel, & Kuller, 2003).

By far the most compelling evidence of social relationship quality and its effects on bodily functioning comes from research on social support. In a seminal review of the social support and physiology literature, Uchino and colleagues (1996) concluded that there are strong associations between social support and the cardiovascular, endocrine, and immune systems. Most social support studies emphasize functional support, such as instrumental or emotional support, and the quality of support received rather than structural characteristics such as network size. In general, higher levels of social support are related to numerous physiological markers of health, including fewer age-related decrements in cardiovascular function at rest (Uchino, Cacioppo, Malarkey, Glaser, & Kiecolt-Glaser, 1995), lower levels of catecholamines and cortisol (Seeman et al., 1994), lower levels of cortisol in women with metastatic breast cancer (Turner-Cobb, Sephton, Koopman, Blake-

Mortimer, & Spiegel, 2000), and better immune functioning, especially for individuals experiencing chronic stress (Esterling, Kiecolt-Glaser, Bodnar, & Glaser, 1994).

These correlational psychophysiological studies of integration and support represent an approach to the study of social relationships and health that emphasizes the broad, long-term impact personal relationships have on health-relevant biological mechanisms. The suggestion is that our relations with others can modify our regulatory bodily functions and set the stage for disease risk, for example, through bolstered immune function resulting from reduced anxiety and depression that good support affords during stress (Wills & Fegan, 2001). As such, an important contributor to our biological performance across time is our concurrent and recurring social emotional experience in key personal relationships (Ryff, Singer, Wing, & Love, 2001).

How might this long-term biological accumulation be borne out from our daily experience with relationships? One pathway by which health may be compromised is through the physiological wear and tear engendered by repeated physiological responses to stressors (McEwen, 1998). A psychophysiological account of the link between social support and health suggests attenuating effects of socially supportive others on acute physiological stress responses (DeVries, 2002). This buffering hypothesis has been investigated in laboratory studies by (a) relating measures of social support to stress reactivity and (b) manipulating the presence of others, as well as their specific supportive behaviors, during performance of stressful tasks. In light of the swift autonomic activation concurrent with acute stress, most of the research in this area has addressed cardiovascular reactivity. Recent advances in field methodologies, including ecological momentary assessment (Hufford, Shiffman, Paty, & Stone, 2001) and experience sampling (Csikszentmihalyi & Hunter, 2003) in conjunction with ambulatory physiological monitoring (Kamarck, Schwartz, Janicki, Shiffman, & Raynor, 2003), are fostering consideration of social support's buffering effects on everyday stress and concurrent physiological function (Holt-Lunstad, Uchino, Smith, Olson-Cerny, & Nealey-Moore, 2003).

Higher levels of self-reported naturalistic social support are associated with healthier physiological responses to stressors, including faster cardiovascular recovery from stress (Roy, Steptoe, & Kirschbaum, 1998) and less age-related increases in blood pressure in response to a stressor (Uchino, Kiecolt-Glaser, & Cacioppo, 1992). Broadwell and Light (1999) reported lower vascular resistance during rest, conversation about the day's events, and a marital conflict discussion for spouses high in family support. Heffner, Kiecolt-Glaser, Loving, Glaser, and Malarkey (2004) found higher cortisol responses to a marital conflict for younger, newlywed wives and older, long-married husbands who reported less satisfaction with the support they receive from their spouses. These data suggest that the pathways linking shorter term physiological processes to long-term health may well differ for wives and husbands across the life span. To address social support's buffering effects of stress on immune function, psychoneuroimmunology researchers have examined associations among social support self-reports and immune measures in the context of relatively longer term stressors, such as medical exams (Glaser et al., 1992), coping with disease (Dixon et al., 2001), caregiving (Kiecolt-Glaser, Dura, Speicher, Trask, & Glaser, 1991), and bereavement (Esterling, Kiecolt-Glaser, Bodnar, & Glaser, 1994). Overall, higher levels of social support when coping with moderate to severe stress can reduce the impact of these stressors on immune function.

Findings from laboratory studies manipulating support through a friend's or stranger's presence or absence during stressful tasks have been mixed (Uchino et al., 1996), likely due to the varying degree of perceived social evaluation while performing the traditional, stressful cognitive lab tasks (Stoney & Finney, 2000). Studies controlling for evaluation are more apt to produce results consistent with the buffering hypothesis (Fontana, Diegman, Villeneuve, & Lepore, 1999), and interestingly, nonevaluative support from a pet may provide the most benefit by buffering responses even in the presence of evaluative support, such as a human friend or spouse (Allen, Blascovich, & Mendes, 2002).

Modifying supportive behaviors and source of support explicitly have yielded stronger and more consistent results. In general, supportive behaviors before and during stressful tasks attenuate cardiovascular responses. This is especially true when supportive behaviors are performed by friends rather than strangers (Christenfeld et al., 1997), and when the quality of the friendship is purely positive, rather than perceived as ambivalent (Uno, Uchino, & Smith, 2002). However, support from female confederates reduced cardiovascular responses during an impromptu speech, whereas male confederate support did not (Glynn, Christenfeld, & Gerin, 1999), suggesting support from women strangers can be beneficial. Few studies have addressed acute support effects on cortisol reactivity to stress, but existing evidence warrants future attention to these associations. Men who received social support from their romantic partners had smaller anticipatory cortisol responses compared with men without support or who received support from a stranger prior to a public speaking task; in contrast, women had increased cortisol responses when receiving support from their partners (Kirschbaum, Klauer, Filipp, & Hellhammer, 1995). Both men and women receiving video-relayed support by a same-sex confederate evidenced attenuated cortisol reactivity to a demanding computer task compared with a no support group (Thorsteinsson, James, & Gregg, 1998).

Loneliness

As we note, the availability of support is an important component for maintaining positive physiological outcomes and simple structural measures of integration predict favorable outcomes. One mechanism for this latter relationship might be the consequential experience of loneliness for socially isolated persons. For example, coronary artery bypass surgery patients who endorsed the single item "I feel lonely" demonstrated significantly greater mortality rates 30 days and 5 years later relative to those who did not endorse the item (Herlitz et al., 1998).

Cacioppo and colleagues' studies of psychophysiological mechanisms associating loneliness to morbidity and mortality suggest a strong link between loneliness and autonomic activation (Cacioppo, Ernst, et al., 2000; Cacioppo, Hawkley, et al., 2002). Cacioppo, Hawkley, et al. (2002) had undergraduate participants complete four types of stress-inducing speeches as well as a mental arithmetic task. During all tasks, lonelier participants demonstrated lower heart rate levels and reactivity compared with nonlonely participants. Moreover, absolute blood pressure levels were similar across tasks for each group, although heart rate reactivity was lowest for lonely participants. This may seem counterintuitive; however, significant cardiovascular reactivity is *expected* in these types of situations, and an absence of such reactivity may be indicative of blunted or inadequate response by the system (McEwen, 1998). In an additional study, lonely individuals demonstrated higher total peripheral resistance and lower cardiac output than embedded (i.e., nonlonely) participants during a stressful task (Cacioppo, Hawkley, et al., 2002). Baseline systolic blood pressure and heart rate was also higher in older lonely participants versus younger lonely participants.

With regard to endocrine outcomes, much attention has been given to cortisol. Some work has reported increased cortisol levels in the lonely, but others have reported no differences (Cacioppo, Hawkley, et al., 2002; Kiecolt-Glaser, Ricker, et al., 1984). The type of loneliness assessed, as well as the timing of the cortisol measurement may warrant careful consideration. Trait loneliness was highly, positively correlated with undergraduates' salivary cortisol in the evenings, but not at any other time (Cacioppo, Ernst, et al., 2000). This might reflect the social context and timing of the sample; it is during the evenings that most social activity would occur for this undergraduate sample, a time when the discrepancy between desired and actual relationships would be most relevant and, thus, most likely to activate chronic loneliness (Cacioppo, Ernst, et al., 2000).

Feeling lonely also affects immune function. A series of studies on diverse samples have demonstrated immune system deficits in the lonely (Glaser, Kiecolt-Glaser, Speicher, & Holliday, 1985; Kiecolt-Glaser, Garner, et al., 1984; Kiecolt-Glaser, Speicher, Holliday, & Glaser, 1984), highlighting the health risks carried by this psychological state. Given the link between loneliness and depression (Russell, Peplau, & Cutrona, 1980), these results are not surprising (McGuire, Kiecolt-Glaser, & Glaser, 2002).

Summary

In sum, social integration is a key predictor of individuals' health outcomes, and the available evidence suggests a variety of physiological systems are involved. Both qualitative and quantitative indices of integration predict reduced cardiovascular arousal and more limited evidence suggests endocrine and immune benefits as well. Research into social support processes has offered the most explanations regarding a mechanism for these beneficial social integration effects, and work on loneliness suggests one mechanism whereby social isolation is detrimental (in addition to the lack of social support inherent in those circumstances). We now turn our attention to the physiological consequences produced by arguably our most important form of social integration: the romantic relationship.

From Pals to Pillow Talkers

In 1983, Levenson and Gottman (1983) reported an interesting result: In a sample of married couples, the more that one spouse's physiological arousal (e.g., heart rate, skin conductance, etc.) during a conflict discussion predicted the other spouse's physiological arousal, the lower the couples' overall marital satisfaction. The degree of prediction obtained with this measure of "physiological linkage" was substantial: It accounted for 60% of the variance in martial satisfaction (Levenson & Gottman, 1983). Subsequently, the impact of romantic relationships on physiological function (and vice versa) has received widespread empirical attention. Put simply, heterosexual marital relationships impact a host of spouses' physiological parameters. We know considerably less about nonmarital romantic relationships. Naturalistic as well as laboratory studies have illuminated a number of processes by which intimate relationships influence spouses' physiology.

Naturalistic Studies

Recently, studying couples in their natural settings has garnered increased interest. Carels and colleagues (Carels, Sherwood, Szczepanski, & Blumenthal, 2000) assessed associations among wives' marital quality and their ambulatory blood pressure at work and home. Wives reporting higher marital distress had higher blood pressure at home versus at work. Lower marital cohesion predicted elevated nighttime blood pressure and 24-hour diastolic blood pressure in mildly hyptertensive men and women (Baker et al., 1999). Gump, Polk, Kamarck, and Shiffman (2001) reported lower ambulatory blood pressure for individuals following social interaction with intimate partners relative to other persons or being alone. Interestingly, these effects were not moderated by relationship quality. Importantly, their sample consisted of married individuals as well as those living with a partner for more than three months. It is unclear whether relationship type might influence psychophysiological associations observed in naturalistic or even laboratory settings.

Clearly, investigating couples and couple members in their natural settings is ideal as it captures couples' ongoing, ordinary behavior without the constraints of experimenter observation, settings, and tasks. Technological advancements in ambulatory physiological monitoring, including the development of physiological equipment, and methods, such as salivary cortisol sampling, are contributing to the validity and reliability of naturalistic psychophysiological studies.

Laboratory Studies Utilizing the Problem-Solving Paradigm

Many laboratory marital interaction studies have followed similar experimental paradigms. Couples are asked to sit in silence, facing each other, for some period of time (e.g., 5 minutes). With a researcher, couples then identify two or more areas of marital disagreement based on partners' self-report ratings (Gottman, Markman, & Notarius, 1977); more recent work has taken care to identify and counterbalance "husband" and "wife" issues so that the topic initiator is taken into account (Caughlin & Vangelisti, 1999; Heavey, Layne, & Christensen, 1993). Couples are next instructed to work on resolving one or more identified issues as if they were at home. Interaction periods last from 10 to 30 minutes or more. From the beginning of the baseline session until, in many cases, a recovery period following the interaction, a range of physiological data are collected (e.g., cardiovascular measures, blood samples for purposes of endocrine and immune assays).

NOT BEING NASTY MATTERS MORE THAN BEING NICE

By and large, the physiological effects of these observed marital discussions are influenced by the presence or absence of negative behaviors (Ewart, 1993). This finding is best summarized by Ewart and colleagues 1991 article titled "High Blood Pressure and Marital Discord: Not Being Nasty Matters More Than Being Nice" (Ewart, Taylor, Kraemer, & Agras, 1991). In their sample of 43 hypertensive adults, hostile behaviors during a 10-minute discussion increased wives' blood pressure; positive and neutral behaviors had no impact. Husbands' blood pressure changes were only related to their speech rate.

This conclusion is not unique to cardiovascular reactivity. In a sample of 90 newlywed couples participating in an overnight study that included a 30-minute problem-solving discussion, Kiecolt-Glaser and colleagues demonstrated that (a) spouses' escalation of negative behaviors (e.g., criticizing, interrupting) accounted for large amounts of variance in change in wives', but not husbands', hormone levels (Kiecolt-Glaser et al., 1997); (b) spouses classified as low versus high immune responders were in marriages characterized by a greater frequency of negative behaviors (Kiecolt-Glaser et al., 1997); (c) spouses displaying more negative or hostile behaviors showed greater decrements on four functional immune measures and larger increases in blood pressure, with effects greater for wives than husbands and no effects for positive behaviors (Kiecolt-Glaser et al., 1993); and (d) wives' composite (average across the day) norepinephrine and cortisol levels were greater to the extent that their husbands' withdrew during the marital conflict following their negative behaviors, but no effects were found for husbands' endocrine responses (Kiecolt-Glaser et al., 1996).

Similar patterns are evidenced in other samples. In a sample of older adults, wives' (but not husbands') cortisol, ACTH, and norepinephrine increased when negative behaviors escalated, and spouses who displayed more negative conflict behaviors demonstrated weaker immune responses (Kiecolt-Glaser et al., 1997). In a sample of German couples, wives demonstrated greater cortisol responses to a conflict discussion than did husbands (Fehm-Wolfsdorf, Groth, Kaiser, & Hahlweg, 1999). Finally, in a study employing an extensive assortment of immune system indicators, two different measures of immune system function increased in spouses during a 15-minute conflict discussion (Dopp, Miller, Myers, & Fahey, 2000).

NOT BEING NASTY MATTERS MORE THAN BEING NICE... FOR WIVES?

A majority of the studies reviewed above as well as others have documented the differential impact of conflict discussions on wives relative to husbands (Dopp et al., 2000; Mayne, O'Leary, McCrady, Contrada,

& Labouvie, 1997). In their comprehensive review on the health impact of marriage, Kiecolt-Glaser and Newton (2001) concluded, "A... key theme among the interaction studies is the relatively greater physiological change shown in women; gender disparities were most obvious in relation to negative behavior" (p. 16). This summary is inconsistent with Gottman and Levenson's (1988) psychophysiological model of marital interaction, which suggests that men withdraw from conflict because of their greater conflict-associated physiological arousal relative to wives. The validity of Gottman and Levenson's model has been addressed elsewhere (Kiecolt-Glaser & Newton, 2001; Kiecolt-Glaser et al., 1996), and due to space limitations we do not revisit the issue here; however, a recent study (Denton, Burleson, Hobbs, Von Stein, & Rodriguez, 2001) testing the escape-avoidance model is worth mentioning in detail because it provides new insight into the demand–withdrawal communication pattern and highlights the importance of the interdependent dynamic between spouses rather than a focus on gender per se.

Denton et al. (2001) classified spouses as initiators (i.e., demand) or avoiders (i.e., withdraw) with respect to their general marital communication patterns. Consistent with past work (Heavey et al., 1993), husbands were more likely to be classified as avoiders and wives were more likely to be classified as initiators; however, during a structured interview, spouses classified as avoiders, *regardless of gender*, demonstrated greater increases in systolic blood pressure than did initiators. Furthermore, avoidant *wives* demonstrated greater systolic blood pressure reactivity than did initiator wives, and husbands demonstrated greater physiological arousal when they interacted with an avoidant wife (versus an initiator wife), especially when the husband was himself classified as an initiator. Denton et al. (2001) concluded that rather than a sole focus on gender, "our results suggest that physiological reactivity during confrontative interactions is a complex, joint function of one's own dispositions as well as the dispositions of one's spouse" (p. 416). These data highlight the need for further work exploring individual and couple-level predictors of the classic demand–withdrawal interaction sequence.

Moderators of Spouses' Physiological Reactivity During Discussions

The Denton et al. (2001) study highlights one moderator of discussion-induced physiological reactivity: the interdependent dynamic between spouses. Discussion-task characteristics as well as individuals' characteristics also influence physiological response patterns. Smith, Gallo, Goble, Ngu, and Stark (1998) asked spouses to discuss a number of topics (e.g., rent controls for campus-area housing) and randomly assigned them to same or opposing sides of the arguments. When forced to disagree during the discussions (labeled a communion stressor), wives, but not husbands, demonstrated elevated cardiovascular reactivity. When led to believe their part of the interaction would be critically evaluated (labeled an agency stressor), husbands, but not wives, displayed elevated reactivity.

In an additional study, husbands given an incentive to influence their wives during a nonmarital topic discussion demonstrated larger systolic blood pressure increases than did those not given an incentive. Wives' blood pressure did not increase (Brown & Smith, 1992). In further analyses, husbands' level of cynical hostility was associated with greater husbands' heart rate reactivity regardless of incentive, but only with increased systolic blood pressure when an incentive was present. Husbands' cynical hostility increased wives systolic blood pressure reactivity, but wives' cynical hostility had no effect on their own or husbands' cardiovascular reactivity (Smith & Brown, 1991). Less dominant spouses, based on spouses' ratings of dominance and submissiveness, displayed heightened blood pressure reactivity during discussion, except at very high levels of spouse dominance (Brown, Smith, & Benjamin, 1998). Interestingly the incentive condition tended to reduce the attenuation seen at high levels of spouse domination.

Similarly, Loving, Heffner, Kiecolt-Glaser, Glaser, and Malarkey (2004) demonstrated that relative levels of emotional involvement impacted spouses' ACTH and cortisol responses to marital conflict. Utilizing a principle of least interest approach (Waller & Hill, 1951) to delineating marital power, they compared spouses' reports of dependent love for one another. Less powerful spouses (i.e., spouses relatively more emotionally involved) displayed elevated ACTH responses to a conflict discussion, while shared power appeared to have a beneficial effect on wives' but not husbands' ACTH responses. Spouses' cortisol levels declined over time except for wives who were less powerful and for husbands who shared power with their wives. These data suggest that the particular dynamics couple members have already developed prior to their participation in marital interaction studies can significantly impact couple's physiological responses.

Recalling and Viewing Conflicts

Recalling or viewing marital conflict discussions can also have physiological consequences. For example, wives in distressed marriages demonstrate higher blood pressure than wives in nondistressed marriages when recalling a marital conflict (Carels, Szczepanski, Blumenthal, & Sherwood, 1998). Notably, it is not necessary to recall or view one's own problem discussion to invoke physiological responses. In a related vein, when individuals are asked to view the conflicts of other couples, married individuals best at rating the self-reported affect of other spouses who had engaged in the conflict discussion (i.e., other perception; Kenny, 1994) demonstrated patterns of physiological arousal while making the affect ratings that were similar to the physiological responses of the spouse who had actually engaged in the discussion (Levenson & Ruef, 1992).

Relationships in Context: Unique Psychophysiological Processes?

In this section, we have primarily focused on studies involving samples of married couples in light of the paucity of research with the nonmarried. We have mentioned two studies that utilized nonmarried samples (Gump et al., 2001; Kirschbaum et al., 1995). To our knowledge, with the exception of research on immune outcomes in HIV-Positive individuals following the loss of a partner (Kemeny et al., 1995; Leserman et al., 2000), no studies have investigated the psychophysiological processes involved in sexual-minority relationships. Thus, our understanding of these processes is really limited to the heterosexually married, with one exception: work on adult attachment utilizing heterosexual dating samples.

Adult attachment researchers have investigated how attachment processes might influence physiological responses to stressful situations within the context of dating relationships. These studies build on the social support literature reviewed earlier in which (typically) participants were asked to bring friends to serve as support provider (vs. a confederate). In a study of college women involved in a serious dating relationship, participants were led to believe that they would engage in an unspecified stressful task. Avoidant and anxious participants demonstrated greater anticipatory physiological arousal (heart rate and systolic blood pressure) when their partner was present versus when he was absent (Carpenter & Kirkpatrick, 1996). In another study (Feeney & Kirkpatrick, 1996), dating women performed a serial subtraction task, once in the presence of their male partner and once alone. Their partner was placed in sight, but prevented from being able to evaluate their partner during the task. Anxious and avoidant women displayed heightened physiological arousal in all conditions when they were first separated from their partner; the results were strongest for heart rate.

Few additional studies have investigated the physiology-attachment link in adults (or undergraduate samples; for an exception, see Scheidt et al., 2000). Given the hypothesized physiological underpinnings of attachment mechanisms (Diamond, 2001) as well as the significant role attachment plays in social support processes (Mikulincer & Florian, 1997), further empirical atten-

tion is certainly warranted. Diamond (2001) recently called for greater psychophysiological exploration of the attachment system, with a focus on the HPA and the parasympathetic branch of the autonomic nervous system. She also noted the important role that might be played by oxytocin (Diamond, 2001; Heinrichs, Baumgartner, Kirschbaum, & Ehlert, 2003).

Summary

Marital interaction research is particularly important for understanding the physiological consequences of relationship processes (e.g., behaviors, affect, marital dynamics, individual dispositions) and how such intimate affiliations may lead to morbid outcomes through their effects on the autonomic, endocrine, and immune systems. We now explore the reciprocal relationship: Can physiology affect the "health" of relationships?

Physiological Indicators As Predictors of Relationship Health

The notion that what happens *inside* couple members can affect couple functioning was first advanced by Levenson and Gottman (Gottman, 1993; Levenson & Gottman, 1983). The basic rationale behind their studies can be stated as follows: Individuals' physiological responses to interaction with, or the presence of, their partner might provide insights into some underlying currents within the relationship.

As noted at the outset of the section on marital interaction, Levenson and Gottman (1983) were able to explain 60% of the variance in spouses' average marital satisfaction scores from spouses' levels of physiological linkage during a conflict discussion. Subsequently, in 19 of the original 30 couples, greater overall arousal, but not physiological linkage, at Time 1 predicted declines in martial satisfaction over a 3-year period (Levenson & Gottman, 1985). What was most noteworthy about these latter findings is that their measure of physiological reactivity predicted changes in marital satisfaction much better than the use of observational data (accounting for over 80% of the variance in changes in marital satisfaction); however, the small sample size necessitates further replication of this result. More recently, husbands' physiological reactivity during an eyes-closed baseline preceding a discussion significantly predicted divorce (Gottman, 1993); on average, husbands who did divorce evidenced an 11-beat-per-minute greater heart rate than husbands who did not eventually divorce.

Hormone levels also relate to relationship outcomes (Kiecolt-Glaser, Bane, Glaser, & Malarkey, 2003). In a follow-up study of the newlywed couples mentioned earlier, stress hormones related to marital satisfaction and divorce 10 years after initial study participation. Spouses' epinephrine was 34% higher during the conflict discussion 10 years earlier for divorced versus intact couples, and divorced wives also had higher nighttime norepinephrine levels during the initial study. Among spouses not divorced, norepinephrine levels 10 years earlier distinguished satisfied from dissatisfied couples at the 10-year follow-up. In addition, wives' ACTH levels at the beginning of conflict were higher among those wives who were dissatisfied at follow-up. Furthermore, Cohan, Booth, and Granger (2003) demonstrated that concordance versus discordance of spouses' testosterone levels affects spouses' behaviors during conflict and social support discussions (Bradbury & Pasch, 1991). They argued that testosterone is a key variable in the marital behavior equation given its role in assertiveness and dominance. When husbands and wives were concordant for high testosterone levels, husbands were more positive and less negative during a conflict discussion. When wives were high and husbands were low on testosterone, husbands were more negative. During a social support interaction, husbands were more positive support providers when they and their wife had low levels of testosterone, but husbands were less positive when their testosterone levels were higher than their wives (Cohan et al., 2003).

Recent Developments

The field broadly construed as the psychophysiology of adult relationships extends beyond the primary physiological outcomes (and predictors) that we have focused on thus far. Oxytocin has been the subject of increasing interest in its role as a stress hormone and a promoter of bonding and attachment processes (Diamond, 2001; Taylor et al., 2000). What is particularly exciting about this work is that it incorporates aspects of mainstream relationships research (i.e., attachment theory) with psychophysiological mechanisms.

Research into the effects of steroidal chemosignals offers promise for increasing our understanding of, for example, attraction in relationships (Thornhill & Gangestad, 1999). McClintock and colleagues (Jacob, Kinnunen, Metz, Cooper, & McClintock, 2001; McClintock & Herdt, 1996), demonstrated that exposure to the chemosignal androstadienone affects a variety of brain areas, participant mood states, as well as other physiological indices (e.g., skin conductance and temperature). One unique study showed that positron emission tomography (PET) was able to identify brain areas activated by the hormone (Jacob et al., 2001). Magnetic resonance imaging is another methodology gaining favor with relationships researchers (Fisher, Aron, Mashek, Li, & Brown, 2002), and will likely become increasingly popular as researchers further explore the biology of close relationships.

Conclusion

Fifteen years ago, House, Landis, and Umberson (1988) commented: "The mechanisms through which social relationships affect health and the factors that promote or inhibit the development and maintenance of social relationships remain to be explored" (p. 540). Much has since been learned about the mechanisms responsible for the link between social relationships and health, and the underlying mechanisms (e.g., marital quality, dominance, behavior) are becoming clearer. However, in a recent editorial, House (2001) still noted similar inadequacies in the literature, particularly in our understanding of "the extent to which support or any other attribute or correlate of relationships can account for the robust and substantial impact of social relationships on health" (p. 273).

We encourage relationships researchers to take these comments to heart as they have the knowledge and tools about *close relationships* necessary to begin unraveling the processes and dynamics at play. Applications of attachment (Diamond, 2001), intimacy (Reis, 1990), and interdependence theory (Kelley & Thibaut, 1978), just to name a few, hold great promise for further understanding of why and how close relationships get under our skin. Advances in close-relationship methodologies may also be useful. For example, experimental social support studies rely heavily on trained confederates, and for good reason: "Natural" support providers (i.e., close friends or partners) bring a complex history with them to the laboratory making it difficult to control for extraneous effects; however, what if researchers wanted to investigate the effects of, for example, relationship closeness on social support provision and effects on physiological reactivity? The experimental induction of closeness paradigm seems perfectly suited for this inquiry (Aron et al., 1997). With this method, researchers can actually *manipulate* feelings of closeness between support recipient and provider and determine how this affects support seeking, provision, and physiological responses.

In sum, the complex set of dynamics that define close (and not so close) personal relationships hold profound implications for individuals' physiological functioning. With the advancement of new methods and technologies, and an intersection with psychophysiological and close relationships principles and theories, we can expect increasing resources devoted to a complete understanding of the role of close relationships in the mind–body equation.

Note

This research was supported in part by National Institutes of Health (NIH) grants P50 DE13749 and PO1 AG16321, by NIH General Clinical Research Center Grant MO1 RR0034, by Comprehensive Cancer Center Core Grant CA16058, and by NIH Training Grant T32 MH18831.

References

Adam, E. K., & Gunnar, M. R. (2001). Relationship functioning and home and work demands predict individual differences in diurnal cortisol patterns in women. *Psychoneuroendocrinology, 26,* 189–208.

Allen, K., Blascovich, J., & Mendes, W. B. (2002). Cardiovascular reactivity in the presence of pets, friends, and spouses: The truth about cats and dogs. *Psychosomatic Medicine, 64,* 727–739.

Aron, A., Melinat, E., Aron, E. N., Vallone, R. D., & Bator, R. J. (1997). The experimental generation of interpersonal closeness: A procedure and some preliminary findings. *Personality and Social Psychology Bulletin, 23,* 363–377.

Baker, B., Helmers, K., O'Kelly, B., Sakinofsky, I., Abelsohn, A., & Tobe, S. (1999). Marital cohesion and ambulatory blood pressure in early hypertension. *American Journal of Hypertension, 12,* 227–230.

Baum, A., & Grunberg, N. E. (1995). Measures of endocrine stress responses. In S. Cohen, R. C. Kessler, & L. G. Gordon (Eds.), *Measuring stress* (pp. 175–192). New York: Oxford Press.

Baumeister, R. F., & Leary, M. R. (1995). The need to belong: Desire for interpersonal attachments as a fundamental human motivation. *Psychological Bulletin, 117,* 497–529.

Berkman, L. F. (1995). The role of social relations in health promotion. *Psychosomatic Medicine, 57,* 245–254.

Berkman, L. F., Glass, T., Brissette, I., & Seeman, T. E. (2000). From social integration to health: Durkheim in the new millennium. *Social Science and Medicine, 51,* 843–857.

Bland, S. H., Krogh, V., Winkelstein, W., & Trevisan, M. (1991). Social network and blood pressure: A population study. *Psychosomatic Medicine, 53,* 598–607.

Blascovich, J., & Katkin, E. S. (1993). *Cardiovascular reactivity to psychological stress and disease*. Washington, DC: American Psychological Association.

Bradbury, T. N., & Pasch, L. A. (1991). Assessment of social support in marital interaction: The Social Support Interaction Coding System. *Archives of Psychiatric Diagnostics and Clinical Evaluation, 8*, 147–153.

Broadwell, S. D., & Light, K. C. (1999). Family support and cardiovascular responses in married couples during conflict and other interactions. *International Journal of Behavioral Medicine, 6*, 40–63.

Brown, P. C., & Smith, T. W. (1992). Social influence, marriage, and the heart: Cardiovascular consequences of interpersonal control in husbands and wives. *Health Psychology, 11*, 88–96.

Brown, P. C., Smith, T. W., & Benjamin, L. S. (1998). Perceptions of spouse dominance predict blood pressure reactivity during marital interactions. *Annals of Behavioral Medicine, 20*, 286–293.

Cacioppo, J. T., Berntson, G. G., Malarkey, W. B., Kiecolt-Glaser, J. K., Sheridan, J. F., Poehlmann, K. M., et al. (1998). Autonomic, neuroendocrine, and immune responses to psychological stress: The reactivity hypothesis. *Annals of the New York Academy of Sciences, 840*, 664–663.

Cacioppo, J. T., Ernst, J. M., Burleson, M. H., McClintock, M. K., Malarkey, W. B., Hawkley, L. C., et al. (2000). Lonely traits and concomitant physiological processes: The MacArthur social neuroscience studies. *International Journal of Psychophysiology, 35*, 143–154.

Cacioppo, J. T., Hawkley, L. C., Crawford, E., Ernst, J. M., Burleson, M. H., Kowalewski, R. B., et al. (2002). Loneliness and health: Potential mechanisms. *Psychosomatic Medicine, 64*, 407–417.

Cacioppo, J. T., Kiecolt-Glaser, J. K., Malarkey, W. B., Laskowski, B. F., Rozlog, L. A., Poehlmann, K. M., et al. (2002). Autonomic and glucocorticoid associations with the steady-state expression of latent Epstein–Barr virus. *Hormones and Behavior, 42*, 32–41.

Cacioppo, J. T., Tassinary, L. G., & Berntson, G. G. (Eds.) (2000). *Handbook of psychophysiology* (2nd ed.). New York: Cambridge University Press.

Carels, R. A., Sherwood, A., Szczepanski, R., & Blumenthal, J. A. (2000). Ambulatory blood pressure and marital distress in employed women. *Behavioral Medicine, 26*, 80–85.

Carels, R. A., Szczepanski, R., Blumenthal, J. A., & Sherwood, A. (1998). Blood pressure reactivity and marital distress in employed women. *Psychosomatic Medicine, 60*, 639–643.

Carpenter, E. M., & Kirkpatrick, L. A. (1996). Attachment style and presence of a romantic partner as moderators of psychophysiological responses to a stressful laboratory situation. *Personal Relationships, 3*, 351–367.

Caughlin, J. P., & Vangelisti, A. L. (1999). Desire for change in one's partner as a predictor of the demand/withdraw pattern of marital communication. *Communication Monographs, 66*, 65–89.

Christenfeld, N., Gerin, W., Linden, W., Sanders, M., Mathur, J., Deich, J. D., et al. (1997). Social support effects on cardiovascular reactivity: Is a stranger as effective as a friend? *Psychosomatic Medicine, 59*, 388–398.

Cohan, C. L., Booth, A., & Granger, D. A. (2003). Gender moderates the relationship between testosterone and marital interaction. *Journal of Family Psychology, 17*, 29–40.

Cohen, S., Doyle, W. J., Turner, R., Alper, C. M., & Skoner, D. P. (2003). Sociability and susceptibility to the common cold. *Psychological Science, 14*, 389–395.

Csikszentmihalyi, M., & Hunter, J. (2003). Happiness in everyday life: The uses of experience sampling. *Journal of Happiness Studies, 4*, 185–199.

Dawson, M. E., Schell, A. M., & Filion, D. L. (2000). The electrodermal system. In J. T. Cacioppo, L. G. Tassinary, & G. G. Berntson (Eds.), *Handbook of psychophysiology* (2nd ed., pp. 200–223). New York: Cambridge University Press.

Denton, W. H., Burleson, B. R., Hobbs, B. V., Von Stein, M., & Rodriguez, C. P. (2001). Cardiovascular reactivity and initiate/avoid patterns of marital communication: A test of Gottman's psychophysiologic model of marital interaction. *Journal of Behavioral Medicine, 24*, 401–421.

DeVries, A. C. (2002). Interaction among social environment, the hypothalamic–pituitary–adrenal axis, and behavior. *Hormones and Behavior, 41*, 405–413.

Diamond, L. M. (2001). Contributions of psychophysiology to research on adult attachment: Review and recommendations.

Personality and Social Psychology Review, 5, 276–295.

Dixon, D., Cruess, S., Kilbourn, K., Klimas, N., Fletcher, M. A., Ironson, G., et al. (2001). Social support mediates loneliness and human herpesvirus Type 6 (HHV-6) antibody titers. *Journal of Applied Social Psychology, 31,* 1111–1132.

Dopp, J. M., Miller, G. E., Myers, H. F., & Fahey, J. L. (2000). Increased natural killer-cell mobilization and cytotoxicity during marital conflict. *Brain, Behavior, and Immunity, 14,* 10–26.

Elenkov, I. J., Webster, E. L., Torpy, D. J., & Chrousos, G. P. (1999). Stress, corticotropin-releasing hormone, glucocorticoids, and the immune/inflammatory response: Acute and chronic effects. In M. Cutolo & A. T. Masi (Eds.), *Neuroendocrine immune basis of the rheumatic diseases* (Vol. 876, pp. 1–13). New York: New York Academy of Sciences.

Esterling, B. A., Kiecolt-Glaser, J. K., Bodnar, J., & Glaser, R. (1994). Chronic stress, social support, and persistent alterations in the natural killer cell response to cytokines in older adults. *Health Psychology, 13,* 291–299.

Ewart, C. K. (1993). Marital interaction – The context for psychosomatic research. *Psychosomatic Medicine, 55,* 410–412.

Ewart, C. K., Taylor, C. B., Kraemer, H. C., & Agras, W. S. (1991). High blood pressure and marital discord: Not being nasty matters more than being nice. *Health Psychology, 10,* 155–163.

Feeney, B. C., & Kirkpatrick, L. A. (1996). Effects of adult attachment and presence of romantic partners on physiological responses to stress. *Journal of Personality and Social Psychology, 70,* 255–270.

Fehm-Wolfsdorf, G., Groth, T., Kaiser, A., & Hahlweg, K. (1999). Cortisol responses to marital conflict depend on marital interaction quality. *International Journal of Behavioral Medicine, 6,* 207–227.

Fisher, H. E., Aron, A., Mashek, D., Li, H., & Brown, L. L. (2002). Defining the brain systems of lust, romantic attraction, and attachment. *Archives of Sexual Behavior, 31,* 413–419.

Fontana, A. M., Diegman, T., Villeneuve, A., & Lepore, S. J. (1999). Nonevaluative social support reduces cardiovascular reactivity in young women during acutely stressful performance situations. *Journal of Behavioral Medicine, 22,* 75–91.

Gallo, L. C., Matthews, K. A., Troxel, W. M., & Kuller, L. H. (2003). Marital status and quality in middle-aged women: Associations with levels and trajectories of cardiovascular risk factors. *Health Psychology, 22,* 453–463.

Glaser, R., Kiecolt-Glaser, J. K., Bonneau, R. H., Malarkey, W., Kennedy, S., & Hughes, J. (1992). Stress-induced modulation of the immune response to recombinant hepatitis B vaccine. *Psychosomatic Medicine, 54,* 22–29.

Glaser, R., Kiecolt-Glaser, J. K., Speicher, C. E., & Holliday, J. E. (1985). Stress, loneliness, and changes in herpes virus latency. *Journal of Behavioral Medicine, 8,* 249–260.

Glynn, L. M., Christenfeld, N., & Gerin, W. (1999). Gender, social support, and cardiovascular responses to stress. *Psychosomatic Medicine, 61,* 234–242.

Gottman, J. M. (1993). A theory of marital dissolution and stability. *Journal of Family Psychology, 7,* 57–75.

Gottman, J. M., & Levenson, R. W. (1988). The social psychophysiology of marriage. In P. Noller & M. A. Fitzpatrick (Eds.), *Perspectives on marital interaction* (pp. 182–199). Clevedon, England: Multilingual Matters.

Gottman, J., Markman, H., & Notarius, C. (1977). The topography of marital conflict: A sequential analysis of verbal and nonverbal behavior. *Journal of Marriage and the Family, 39,* 461–477.

Gump, B. B., Polk, D. E., Kamarck, T. W., & Shiffman, S. M. (2001). Partner interactions are associated with reduced blood pressure in the natural environment: Ambulatory monitoring evidence from a healthy, multiethnic adult sample. *Psychosomatic Medicine, 63,* 423–433.

Gunnar, M. R. (1992). Reactivity of the hypothalamic–pituitary–adrenocortical system to stressors in normal infants and children. *Pediatrics, 90,* 491–498.

Hartley, T. R., Ginsburg, G. P., & Heffner, K. (1999). Self presentation and cardiovascular reactivity. *International Journal of Psychophysiology, 32,* 75–88.

Heavey, C. L., Layne, C., & Christensen, A. A. (1993). Gender and conflict structure in marital interaction: A replication and extension. *Journal of Consulting and Clinical Psychology, 61,* 16–27.

Heffner, K. L., Kiecolt-Glaser, J. K., Loving, T. J., Glaser, R., & Malarkey, W. (2004). Spousal support satisfaction as a modifier of physiological responses to marital conflict in younger and older couples. *Journal of Behavioral Medicine*, 27, 233–254.

Heinrichs, M., Baumgartner, T., Kirschbaum, C., & Ehlert, U. (2003). Social support and oxytocin interact to suppress cortisol and subjective responses to psychosocial stress. *Biological Psychiatry*, 54, 1389–1398.

Herlitz, J., Wiklund, I., Caidahl, K., Hartford, M., Haglid, M., Karlsson, B. W., et al. (1998). The feeling of loneliness prior to coronary artery bypass grafting might be a predictor of short-and long-term postoperative mortality. *European Journal of Vascular and Endovascular Surgery*, 16, 120–125.

Holt-Lunstad, J., Uchino, B. N., Smith, T. W., Olson-Cerny, C., & Nealey-Moore, J. B. (2003). Social relationships and ambulatory blood pressure: Structural and qualitative predictors of cardiovascular function during everyday social interactions. *Health Psychology*, 22, 388–397.

House, J. S. (2001). Social isolation kills, but how and why? *Psychosomatic Medicine*, 63, 273–274.

House, J. S., Landis, K. R., & Umberson, D. (1988). Social relationships and health. *Science*, 241, 540–545.

Hufford, M. R., Shiffman, S., Paty, J., & Stone, A. A. (2001). Ecological Momentary Assessment: Real-world, real-time measurement of patient experience. In J. Fahrenberg (Ed.), *Progress in ambulatory assessment: Computer-assisted psychological and psychophysiological methods in monitoring and field studies* (pp. 69–92). Ashland, OH: Hogrefe & Huber.

Jacob, S., Kinnunen, L. H., Metz, J., Cooper, M., & McClintock, M. K. (2001). Sustained human chemosignal unconsciously alters brain function. *Neuroreport*, 12, 2391–2394.

Kamarck, T. W., Schwartz, J. E., Janicki, D. L., Shiffman, S., & Raynor, D. A. (2003). Correspondence between laboratory and ambulatory measures of cardiovascular reactivity: A multilevel modeling approach. *Psychophysiology*, 40, 675–683.

Kaplan, G. A., Salonen, J. T., Cohen, R. D., Brand, R. J., Syme, S. L., & Puska, P. (1988). Social connections and mortality from all causes and from cardiovascular disease: Prospective evidence from eastern Finland. *American Journal of Epidemiology*, 128, 370–380.

Kelley, H. H., & Thibaut, J. W. (1978). *Interpersonal relations: A theory of interdependence*. New York: Wiley.

Kemeny, M. E., Weiner, H., Duran, R., Taylor, S. E., Visscher, B., & Fahey, J. L. (1995). Immune system changes after the death of a partner in HIV-positive gay men. *Psychosomatic Medicine*, 57, 547–554.

Kenny, D. A. (1994). *Interpersonal perception: A social relations analysis*. New York: Guilford Press.

Kiecolt-Glaser, J. K., Bane, C., Glaser, R., & Malarkey, W. B. (2003). Love, marriage, and divorce: Newlyweds' stress hormones foreshadow relationship changes. *Journal of Consulting and Clinical Psychology*, 71, 176–188.

Kiecolt-Glaser, J. K., Dura, J. R., Speicher, C. E., Trask, O. J., & Glaser, R. (1991). Spousal caregivers of dementia victims: Longitudinal changes in immunity and health. *Psychosomatic Medicine*, 53, 345–362.

Kiecolt-Glaser, J. K., Garner, W., Speicher, C., Penn, G. M., Holliday, J., & Glaser, R. (1984). Psychosocial modifiers of immunocompetence in medical students. *Psychosomatic Medicine*, 46, 7–14.

Kiecolt-Glaser, J. K., & Glaser, R. (1995a). Measurement of immune response. In S. Cohen, R. Kessler, & L. G. Gordon (Eds.), *Measuring stress* (pp. 213–229). New York: Oxford Press.

Kiecolt-Glaser, J. K., & Glaser, R. (1995b). Psychoneuroimmunology and health consequences: Data and shared mechanisms. *Psychosomatic Medicine*, 57, 269–274.

Kiecolt-Glaser, J. K., Glaser, R., Cacioppo, J. T., MacCallum, R. C., Snydersmith, M., Kim, C., et al. (1997). Marital conflict in older adults: Endocrinological and immunological correlates. *Psychosomatic Medicine*, 59, 339–349.

Kiecolt-Glaser, J. K., Malarkey, W. B., Chee, M., Newton, T., Cacioppo, J. T., Mao, H., et al. (1993). Negative behavior during marital conflict is associated with immunological downregulation. *Psychosomatic Medicine*, 55, 395–409.

Kiecolt-Glaser, J. K., McGuire, L., Robles, T. F., & Glaser, R. (2002). Psychoneuroimmunology: Psychological influences on immune function and health. *Behavioral Medicine and Clinical Health Psychology*, 70, 537–547.

Kiecolt-Glaser, J. K., & Newton, T. (2001). Marriage and health: His and hers. *Psychological Bulletin, 127*, 472–503.

Kiecolt-Glaser, J. K., Newton, T., Cacioppo, J. T., MacCallum, R. C., Glaser, R., & Malarkey, W. B. (1996). Marital conflict and endocrine function: Are men really more physiologically affected than women? *Journal of Consulting and Clinical Psychology, 64*, 324–332.

Kiecolt-Glaser, J. K., Ricker, D., George, J., Messick, G., Speicher, C. E., Garner, W., et al. (1984). Urinary cortisol levels, cellular immunocompetency, and loneliness in psychiatric inpatients. *Psychosomatic Medicine, 46*, 15–24.

Kiecolt-Glaser, J. K., Speicher, C. E., Holliday, J. E., & Glaser, R. (1984). Stress and the transformation of lymphocytes by Epstein–Barr virus. *Journal of Behavioral Medicine, 7*, 1–12.

Kirschbaum, C., Klauer, T., Filipp, S. H., & Hellhammer, D. H. (1995). Sex-specific effects of social support on cortisol and subjective responses to acute psychological stress. *Psychosomatic Medicine, 57*, 23–31.

Krantz, D. S., & McCeney, M. K. (2002). Effects of psychological and social factors on organic disease: A critical assessment of research on coronary heart disease. *Annual Review of Psychology, 53*, 341–369.

Leserman, J., Petitto, J. M., Golden, R. N., Gaynes, B. N., Gu, H., Perkins, D. O., et al. (2000). Impact of stressful life events, depression, social support, coping, and cortisol on progression to AIDS. *American Journal of Psychiatry, 157*, 1221–1228.

Levenson, R. W., & Gottman, J. M. (1983). Marital interaction: Physiological linkage and affective exchange. *Journal of Personality and Social Psychology, 45*, 587–597.

Levenson, R. W., & Gottman, J. M. (1985). Physiological and affective predictors of change in relationship satisfaction. *Journal of Personality and Social Psychology, 49*, 85–94.

Levenson, R. W., & Ruef, A. M. (1992). Empathy: A physiological substrate. *Journal of Personality and Social Psychology, 63*, 234–246.

Loving, T. J., Heffner, K. L., Kiecolt-Glaser, J. K., Glaser, R., & Malarkey, W. (2004). Stress hormone changes and marital conflict: Spouses' relative power makes a difference. *Journal of Marriage and Family, 66*, 594–611.

Mayne, T. J., O'Leary, A., McCrady, B., Contrada, R., & Labouvie, E. (1997). The differential effects of acute marital distress on emotional, physiological and immune functions in maritally distressed men and women. *Psychology and Health, 12*, 277–288.

McClintock, M. K., & Herdt, G. (1996). Rethinking puberty: The development of sexual attraction. *Current Directions in Psychological Science, 5*, 178–183.

McEwen, B. S. (1998). Stress, adaptation, and disease. Allostasis and allostatic load. *Annals of the New York Academy of Sciences, 840*, 33–44.

McEwen, B. S. (2002). Sex, stress and the hippocampus: Allostasis, allostatic load and the aging process. *Neurobiology of Aging, 23*, 921–939.

McGuire, L., Kiecolt-Glaser, J. K., & Glaser, R. (2002). Depressive symptoms and lymphocyte proliferation in older adults. *Journal of Abnormal Psychology, 111*, 192–197.

Mikulincer, M., & Florian, V. (1997). Are emotional and instrumental supportive interactions beneficial in times of stress? The impact of attachment style. *Anxiety, Stress, and Coping, 10*, 109–127.

Miller, A. H. (1998). Neuroendocrine and immune system interactions in stress and depression. *Psychiatric Clinics of North America, 21*, 443–463.

Reis, H. T. (1990). The role of intimacy in interpersonal relations. *Journal of Social and Clinical Psychology, 9*, 15–30.

Rose, R. M. (1984). Overview of the endocrinology of stress. In G. M. Brown, S. H. Koslow, & S. Reichlin (Eds.), *Neuroendocrinology and psychiatric disorder* (pp. 95–122). New York: Raven Press.

Roy, M. P., Steptoe, A., & Kirschbaum, C. (1998). Life events and social support as moderators of individual differences in cardiovascular and cortisol reactivity. *Journal of Personality and Social Psychology, 75*, 1–9.

Russell, D., Peplau, L. A., & Cutrona, C. E. (1980). The revised UCLA Loneliness Scale: Concurrent and discriminant validity evidence. *Journal of Personality and Social Psychology, 39*, 472–480.

Rutledge, T., Matthews, K., Lui, L.-Y., Stone, K. L., & Cauley, J. A. (2003). Social networks and marital status predict mortality in older women: Prospective evidence from the

Study of Osteoporotic Fractures (SOF). *Psychosomatic Medicine, 65*, 688–694.

Ryff, C. D., & Singer, B. (1998). The contours of positive human health. *Psychological Inquiry, 9*, 1–28.

Ryff, C. D., Singer, B. H., Wing, E., & Love, G. D. (2001). Elective affinities and uninvited agonies: Mapping emotion with significant others onto health. In C. D. Ryff & B. H. Singer (Eds.), *Emotion, social relationships, and health* (pp. 133–175). London: Oxford University Press.

Saab, P. G., & Schneiderman, N. (1993). Biobehavioral stressors, laboratory investigation, and the risk of hypertension. In J. J. Blascovich & E. S. Kattkin (Eds.), *Cardiovascular reactivity to psychological stress and disease* (pp. 49–82). Washington, DC: American Psychological Association.

Scheidt, C. E., Waller, E., Malchow, H., Ehlert, U., Becker-Stoll, F., Schulte-Monting, J., et al. (2000). Attachment representation and cortisol response to the adult attachment interview in idiopathic spasmodic torticollis. *Psychotherapy and Psychosomatics, 69*, 155–162.

Seeman, T. E., Berkman, L. F., Blazer, D., & Rowe, J. W. (1994). Social ties and support and neuroendocrine function: The MacArthur studies of successful aging. *Annals of Behavioral Medicine, 16*, 95–106.

Seeman, T. E., Singer, B. H., Ryff, C. D., Dienberg Love, G., & Levy-Storms, L. (2002). Social relationships, gender, and allostatic load across two age cohorts. *Psychosomatic Medicine, 64*, 395–406.

Smith, T. W., & Brown, P. C. (1991). Cynical hostility, attempts to exert social control, and cardiovascular reactivity in married couples. *Journal of Behavioral Medicine, 14*, 581–592.

Smith, T. W., Gallo, L. C., Goble, L., Ngu, L. Q., & Stark, K. A. (1998). Agency, communion, and cardiovascular reactivity during marital interaction. *Health Psychology, 17*, 537–545.

Smith, T. W., & Ruiz, J. M. (2002). Psychosocial influences on the development and course of coronary heart disease: Current status and implications for research and practice. *Journal of Consulting and Clinical Psychology, 70*, 548–568.

Spiegel, D., & Giese-Davis, J. (2003). Depression and cancer: Mechanisms and disease progression. *Biological Psychiatry, 54*, 269–282.

Stern, R. M., Ray, W. J., & Davis, C. M. (1980). *Psychophysiological recording.* New York: Oxford University Press.

Stern, R. M., Ray, W. J., & Quigley, K. S. (2003). Psychophysiological recording. *Psychophysiology, 40*, 314–315.

Stoney, C., & Finney, M. L. (2000). Social support and stress: Influences on lipid reactivity. *International Journal of Behavioral Medicine, 7*, 111–126.

Taylor, S. E., Klein, L. C., Lewis, B. P., Gruenewald, T. L., Gurung, R. A. R., & Updegraff, J. A. (2000). Biobehavioral responses to stress in females: Tend-and-befriend, not fight-or-flight. *Psychological Review, 107*, 411–429.

Thornhill, R., & Gangestad, S. W. (1999). The scent of symmetry: A human sex pheromone that signals fitness? *Evolution and Human Behavior, 20*, 175–201.

Thorsteinsson, E. B., James, J. E., & Gregg, M. E. (1998). Effects of video-relayed social support on hemodynamic reactivity and salivary cortisol during laboratory-based behavioral challenge. *Health Psychology, 17*, 436–444.

Tomaka, J., Blascovich, J., Kelsey, R. M., & Leitten, C. L. (1993). Subjective, physiological, and behavioral effects of threat and challenge appraisal. *Journal of Personality and Social Psychology, 65*, 248–260.

Turner-Cobb, J. M., Sephton, S. E., Koopman, C., Blake-Mortimer, J., & Spiegel, D. (2000). Social support and salivary cortisol in women with metastatic breast cancer. *Psychosomatic Medicine, 62*, 337–345.

Uchino, B. N., Cacioppo, J. T., & Kiecolt-Glaser, J. K. (1996). The relationship between social support and physiological processes: A review with emphasis on underlying mechanisms and implications for health. *Psychological Bulletin, 119*, 488–531.

Uchino, B. N., Cacioppo, J. T., Malarkey, W., Glaser, R., & Kiecolt-Glaser, J. K. (1995). Appraisal support predicts age-related differences in cardiovascular function in women. *Health Psychology, 14*, 556–562.

Uchino, B. N., Kiecolt-Glaser, J. K., & Cacioppo, J. T. (1992). Age and social support: Effects on cardiovascular functioning in caregivers of relatives with Alzheimer's Disease. *Journal of Personality and Social Psychology, 63*, 839–846.

Uno, D., Uchino, B. N., & Smith, T. W. (2002). Relationship quality moderates the effect of social support given by close friends on cardiovascular reactivity in women. *International Journal of Behavioral Medicine, 9*, 243–262.

Uvnaes-Moberg, K., Johansson, B., Lupoli, B., & Svennersten-Sjaunja, K. (2001). Oxytocin facilitates behavioural, metabolic and physiological adaptations during lactation. *Applied Animal Behaviour Science, 72*, 225–234.

Waller, W., & Hill, R. (1951). *The family: A dynamic interpretation*. Ft. Worth, TX: Dryden Press.

Wills, T. A., & Fegan, M. F. (2001). Social networks and social support. In A. Baum, T. A. Revenson, & J. E. Singer (Eds.), *Handbook of health psychology* (pp. 209–234). Mahwah, NJ: Erlbaum.

Part VII

INTERACTIVE PROCESSES

CHAPTER 22

Self-Disclosure in Personal Relationships

Kathryn Greene
Valerian J. Derlega
Alicia Mathews

The following stories deal with thoughts and feelings about the self, and they illustrate dilemmas about whether to reveal highly personal information about oneself to significant others (a friend, a spouse or lover, and parents). If the following statements were true of you, would you share this material? If so, when, how, with whom, and in what detail?

I started dating a new guy from work, and it's still very exciting. We're taking it slow, so we haven't told many people. I wonder what will happen when they find out?

I am really unhappy and unmotivated most of the time. My friends see me as a happy person. They also see me as a goal-oriented person. The only person whom I can tell about how I really feel is my husband.

I got a great job offer in Atlanta last week. I want to talk to my girlfriend about it, but she wants to stay here, so I don't know what I'd say.

I am a gay man, but I have never talked to my parents about my sexual orientation.

In this chapter, we examine individuals' decision making about what, when, to whom, and how much to disclose personal feelings and thoughts. Although level of self-disclosure and personal relationships are not synonymous concepts, self-disclosure plays an important role in constructing what kind of relationships individuals have with each another (Harvey & Omarzu, 1997; Prager, 1995; Reis & Shaver, 1988). Self-disclosure, depending on reactions of relationship partners, also plays an important role in validating self-worth and personal identity (Beals, 2003; Greene, Derlega, Yep, & Petronio, 2003). This chapter reviews the historical background to self-disclosure research, definitions of self-disclosure, disclosure trajectories, reasons for and against disclosure, disclosure as a transactional process, disclosure message enactment, health consequences of disclosure, methodological trends in disclosure research, and opportunities for future research. To begin we put current work on self-disclosure and personal relationships into perspective by noting the contributions of pioneering researchers. Many of the testable hypotheses about self-disclosure were anticipated by the ideas and early research of these investigators.

Theoretical and Empirical Foundations: Contributions of Early Self-Disclosure Researchers

Sidney Jourard, a clinical psychologist, was an early proponent of self-disclosure research in his books and articles. See, for instance, *The Transparent Self* (1964, 1971a) and *Self-Disclosure: An Experimental Analysis of the Transparent Self* (1971b). Jourard was a visionary who argued that openness *in at least one significant relationship* was a prerequisite for a healthy personality. He published the first widely used scales measuring self-disclosure to friends, parents, and intimate partners (Jourard, 1964, 1971b).

Irwin Altman and Dalmas Taylor (1973) coauthored *Social Penetration: The Development of Interpersonal Relationships*. Altman and Taylor's book presents the first systematic theory and program of research – based on notions derived from social exchange and interdependence theories in social psychology – about the progression of close relationships (cognitively, emotionally, and behaviorally) as people move from being acquaintances to close relationship partners. Some of the most interesting research testing social penetration theory was based on studies of U.S. Navy volunteers who lived and worked together in small groups on simulated missions with no outside contact (Altman & Haythorn, 1965). Altman also introduced the notion of *dialectics* in the study of self-disclosure, whereby relationship partners struggle to balance oppositional needs such as "being both open and closed to contact" with one another in order to regulate privacy (Altman, Vinsel, & Brown, 1981, p. 127; also see Margulis, 2003,

for a recent review). Altman's ideas about dialectics are the foundation for an integrative theory of privacy recently constructed by Sandra Petronio (2002) in *Boundaries of Privacy*. Petronio extended Altman's dialectical conceptualization of privacy, showing how relationship partners rely on rules about control, ownership, and co-ownership of private information to open and close privacy boundaries (also see Derlega & Chaikin, 1977; Petronio, 1991).

Mirra Komarovsky, a sociologist, presented the first extensive study of self-disclosure in marital relationships in her book, *Blue-Collar Marriage* (1962). Based on an interview study of 58 married couples, she introduced many important lines of research in self-disclosure and close relationships, including the link between self-disclosure and marital satisfaction, mutuality of self-disclosure of couples, "taboo topics" in personal relationships (cf. Baxter & Wilmot, 1985; Roloff & Ifert, 2000), and how assumptions about a personal relationship (based on cultural background and gender) influence what couples disclose and avoid talking about in their marital communication.

Zick Rubin (1970) conducted influential early studies on disclosure reciprocity in naturalistic settings, such as in airport departure lounges and at bus stops. In the phenomenon of disclosure reciprocity (what Jourard, 1971a, 1971b, called the "dyadic effect"), one person's disclosure input encourages another's disclosure, which, in turn, may encourage the first person to disclose more, and so on. This reciprocal process of disclosure followed by disclosure contributes to people's knowledge about one another as well as to relationship development (see Dindia, 2000, 2002, for recent reviews of this literature). Rubin and his colleagues (see Rubin, Hill, Peplau, & Dunkel-Schetter, 1980) also popularized the notion that an "ethic of openness" underlies self-disclosure in intimate couples, especially for those who endorse equal roles for men and women in close relationships and at work. Rubin et al.'s (1980) research on the ethic of openness (part of the influential Boston Longitudinal

Dating Study; see Hill, Rubin, & Peplau, 1976) challenged preexisting views that men are inexpressive emotionally with their intimate partners.

Alan Chaikin and Valerian Derlega conducted many of the early studies on disclosure reciprocity and on social norms influencing the appropriateness of self-disclosure (e.g., Chaikin & Derlega, 1974a, 1974b; Derlega, Wilson, & Chaikin, 1976). They also integrated research via a functional model of self-disclosure focusing on the expressive value or instrumental effectiveness of self-disclosure (Derlega & Grzelak, 1979; also see Archer, 1987; Miller & Read, 1987), a privacy model emphasizing the role of self- and dyadic-boundaries regulating self-disclosure (Derlega & Chaikin, 1977), and reviews of the self-disclosure literature (e.g., Chaikin & Derlega, 1974c; Derlega & Chaikin, 1975; also see Cozby, 1973).

Richard Archer, John Berg, and Lynn Miller (in collaboration and separately) contributed important studies on the impact of self-disclosure for social attraction, interaction goals that motivate disclosure, and how to measure self-disclosure in close relationships. Archer documented how *personalistic* disclosures (where the disclosure input is uniquely intended for the disclosure recipient) may increase liking for the initial discloser (see Archer & Cook, 1986; Jones & Archer, 1976). Berg and his colleagues (e.g., Berg, 1986; Berg & Archer, 1980) demonstrated how conversational *responsiveness* ("the extent to which and the way in which one participant's actions address the previous actions, communications, needs, or wishes of another participant in that interaction;" Miller & Berg, 1984, p. 191) influences liking for a disclosure recipient. Miller pioneered a methodology (based on David Kenny's social relations model; see Kenny & La Voie, 1984) to partition how much of disclosure in a social interaction is due to what is unique to the partners in a close relationship as opposed to the personal characteristics of the disclosure or the disclosure recipient (see Miller & Kenny, 1986). Disclosure researchers are indebted to Miller, Berg, and Archer (1983) for constructing a psycho-metrically rigorous and easy-to-use index of self-disclosure as well as an individual differences measure of a listener's capacity to encourage self-disclosure from relationship partners (the "Opener scale").

Defining Self-Disclosure

Let us consider the question, "what is self-disclosure?" Researchers have not always agreed about how to define it. For instance, one could argue that all forms of verbal and nonverbal communication reveal something about the self, and, hence, any communicative act should be defined as self-disclosure. The jewelry or tattoos we have or *do not have* may reveal something unique about our personality, and they could be considered examples of self-disclosure. Or perhaps laughing or smiling might be considered examples of self-disclosure. However, these involuntary disclosures are different from what might be termed "willful disclosures" (Jourard, 1971a), where the "aim is to let another person know with no shadow of a doubt what you have done, what you feel, etc." (pp. 16–17). Consistent with the notion of willful disclosure, we define self-disclosure as an interaction between at least two individuals where one intends to deliberately divulge something personal to another (see Derlega, Metts, Petronio, & Margulis, 1993).

Self-disclosure is usually studied in terms of verbal messages that contain statements such as "I feel" and "I think," but nonverbal messages such as the clothes we wear as well as what we say may be examples of self-disclosure *if* the goal is to reveal something personal about ourselves that the other person did not know. As Rosenfeld (2000) aptly noted, "disclosure is the process that grants access to private things and to secrets" (p. 6).

Self-disclosure research often focuses on whether or not to reveal highly sensitive information (such as personal fears, deeply held religious convictions, potentially stigmatizing information), but self-disclosure also deals with less serious information (e.g., "I love home-made pizza"). Although

Table 22.1. *Dimensions of Disclosure Messages*

1. Transactional – self-disclosure is a complex process that may unfold over a number of occasions. For instance, it may be possible to identify a disclosure message (e.g., someone disclosing about their HIV positive status to a family member), but there is a "dynamic, continuous and circular process" (Dindia, 1998, p. 414) between relationship partners in "who" discloses and "what" is revealed or concealed. We use the terms "discloser" and the "disclosure target," but partners may take on (and switch) both roles in the disclosure process. A self-disclosure episode also involves multiple reactions (cognitive, emotional, and behavioral) by both the discloser and the disclosure target.
2. Reward value – there may be positive or negative outcomes from the disclosure for either (or both) the discloser or the disclosure target.
3. Informativeness – there are differences in how much information the disclosure message provides about the discloser. Does the disclosure provide information about the causes that underlie the discloser's behavior? This aspect of self-disclosure is traditionally defined in terms of topic breadth (the variety of topics disclosed) and depth (the level of intimacy of disclosure; see Altman & Taylor, 1973).
4. Accessibility – the ease or difficulty of divulging personal information in the interaction between the discloser and the target person.
5. Truthfulness – whether the disclosure taps information that is perceived to be about the "real" self or one's "true" thoughts and feelings.
6. Social norms – does the disclosure process support or deviate from existing sociocultural expectations about what, how, and when people should disclose or conceal information from one another?
7. Effectiveness – how much does the disclosure, as a communicative act, accomplish the discloser's as well as the listener's goals?

self-disclosure of everyday or even "superficial" information plays an important role in initiating as well as in maintaining a relationship, it is the disclosure of highly personal information that has many consequences for relationship development and maintenance. For instance, self-disclosure is an important ingredient in how researchers conceptualize romantic love (Rubin, 1970) and marital intimacy (Chelune, Waring, Vosk, Sultan, & Ogden, 1984).

Early research on self-disclosure focused on people revealing their "real self" or "essence" to at least one other person (Altman & Taylor, 1973; Fromm, 1956; Jourard, 1971a). It is worthwhile to distinguish, however, between *personal* self-disclosure (disclosure about oneself) and *relational* self-disclosure (disclosure that focuses on one's relationship with another person or interactions with others). Both forms of disclosure have consequences for the development and maintenance of close relationships (Derlega et al., 1993). Personal disclosures (e.g., "I had a terrific day at work") gives relationship partners "up-to-date" information about

what each person is thinking and feeling, but relational disclosures (e.g., "I can't imagine a better way to spend this holiday weekend than with you!") also informs partners about the state of their relationship and how they are getting along (cf. Waring, 1987).

Self-disclosure varies along a number of dimensions. Although not comprehensive, the list in Table 22.1 illustrates different features of self-disclosure messages. These dimensions of disclosure messages embody different lines of theory and research. A major portion of our own research on self-disclosure has focused on the subjective reasons for disclosure and nondisclosure in the pursuit of goals for oneself, the partner, and the relationship, what is referred to as *disclosure effectiveness* (Derlega & Grzelak, 1979; Greene et al., 2003).

Disclosure Trajectories

Important early theories of relationship development in the 1970s, such as social penetration (Altman & Taylor, 1973) and incremental exchange theory (Levinger & Snoek, 1972), emphasized how self-disclosure progresses in depth (sensitivity of material disclosed) and breadth (variety of topics disclosed) as relationships develop over time. According to this perspective, people would reveal more about their inner thoughts and feelings as their relationships and affection for one another developed over time. Disclosure gradually (or rapidly) accelerated with relationship development, in frequency, depth, and range of topics. Conversely, self-disclosure was assumed to decrease or decline in the same manner as a relationship deteriorated.[1] Consistent with these theories, Collins and Miller (1994) conducted a meta-analytic review documenting three distinct but overlapping mechanisms that account for the link between self-disclosure and relationship closeness: (a) people disclose more to someone whom they like, (b) people like someone more who discloses to them, and (c) people like someone more to whom they have disclosed personal information.

There is a generally linear association between self-disclosure and the development of a personal relationship, but relationship partners cycle between being open and closed about what they disclose to each other (Altman et al., 1981; Petronio, 2002). Relationships may also show alternate paths that defy the generally linear pattern. For example, couples who stay together may show a sharp decline in disclosure after an initial pattern of greater openness, or dating partners who "click" as a couple may display a high level of disclosure very quickly at the beginning of their relationship (e.g., Berg & Clark, 1986). On the other hand, "too much" self-disclosure early in a relationship may be associated with lower liking later on (Berg, 1984; also see Altman & Taylor, 1973).

Whatever the trajectory of disclosure over time in a relationship, early (e.g., Jourard, Altman & Taylor, Komarovsky) and contemporary researchers also report that all or most relationship partners will avoid talking about or conceal (or both) certain facts or feelings from significant others. This may happen because the material is considered a taboo topic (e.g., Baxter & Wilmot, 1985; Roloff & Ifert, 2000), too personal to divulge (Altman & Taylor, 1973), too undesirable for the partner to know (Afifi & Burgoon, 1998), too difficult to divulge (Derlega, Winstead, & Folk-Barron, 2000), too burdensome for the partner to worry about (Burke, Weir, & Harrison, 1976), or simply private information (Kelly, 2002; Petronio, 2002). Partners may even lie to each other to protect themselves from "unwanted access" (DePaulo, Wetzel, Weylin Sternglanz, & Walker Wilson, 2003, p. 293), and some individuals (termed "separates"; Fitzpatrick, 1987) may view self-disclosure and openness as incompatible with asserting autonomy in their personal relationships.

A comment on *mutuality* of disclosure between relationship partners: We have noted the generally linear progression of self-disclosure in developing personal relationships. However, as Komarovsky (1962) observed in her marital interviews, there is considerable mutuality in how much relationship partners disclose to one another. Relationship partners who disclose a lot also are likely to be the recipients of high levels of disclosure. Relationship partners who disclose little are also likely to be the recipients of low levels of disclosure. Partners in close relationships may or may not reciprocate self-disclosure in a single episode (e.g., I may want my intimate partner to simply listen as I seek her advice with a personal problem; see Berg & Archer, 1980). Many partners, however, are likely to approximate one another in their level of disclosure over time and in the course of their relationship (Dindia, 2002; Hendrick, 1981).

Disclosure Decision Making

Decisions about whether to disclose depend, in part, on an assessment of the relative benefits and costs to the discloser and the disclosure target (e.g., Kelly, 2002; Omarzu, 2000; Vangelisti & Caughlin, 1997). Disclosure decision making involves coping with "dialectical" dilemmas as relationship partners attempt to reconcile contradictory and incompatible personal needs – such

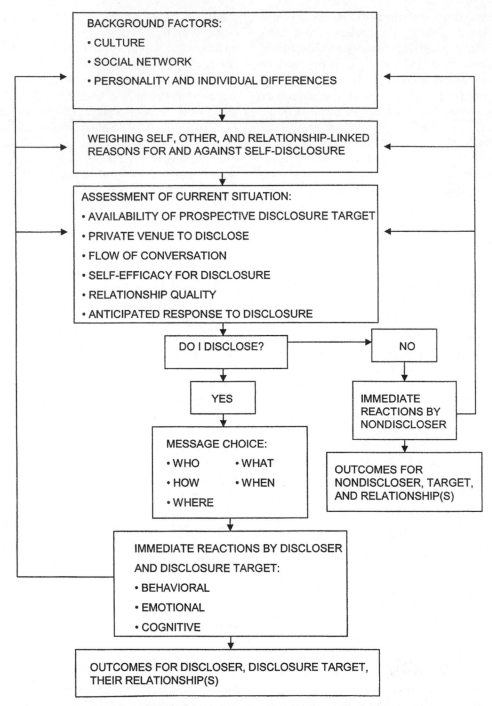

Figure 22.1. Model of disclosure decision making in a single episode.

as establishing connections with significant others (via openness) versus maintaining autonomy and independence (via concealment of private information from others;

e.g., Baxter & Montgomery, 1997; Dindia, 1998; Petronio, 2002).

Figure 22.1 presents a model of self-disclosure decision making, incorporating concepts from Derlega and Grzelak (1979), Greene et al. (2003), Omarzu (2000), and Petronio (2002). It includes both distal (cultural criteria, social network, and individual differences such as the personality and individual differences of the discloser and the disclosure target) and proximal factors (self, partner, and relationship-linked reasons for and against disclosing, and assessment of the current situation) that contribute to disclosure or nondisclosure. The prospective discloser weighs whether to disclose to significant others in the context of cultural attitudes about self-disclosure; access to a social network of family, friends, and coworkers; and individual difference variables such as gender, self-esteem, and attachment style. Then the prospective discloser, in coordination with the potential disclosure recipient, must assess the appropriateness of the situation (e.g., is there a private location to talk; does disclosure fit into the flow of the conversation; is there enough time available to talk; are the prospective discloser and disclosure recipient "getting along"; is the disclosure recipient being attentive and asking questions; is the response to the disclosure input likely to be positive or negative?). If a decision is made to disclose, then self-disclosure occurs (including to a particular target person, about specific content, at a particular level of disclosure intimacy, in a specific location, in person or by phone, e-mail, letter). The personal reactions of the discloser and the recipient (e.g., inferring mutual trust or mistrust, co-ownership of sensitive information) may, in turn, influence the outcomes experienced by both individuals (e.g., the partners in the relationship may click as friends; they may decide to meet at a future time to talk again; they may feel "intimate"). The model, as presented in Figure 22.1, also includes feedback loops. For instance, the immediate reactions of the discloser and the target (e.g., feeling emotionally close and labeling one another "close friends") may affect antecedent variables in the model (including perceptions about "who" in one's social network is a confidant, reweighing reasons for and against disclosure by the discloser as well as reassessing

the suitability of the situation for enacting disclosure) that predict subsequent disclosure or nondisclosure in the same and in future episodes.

The model in Figure 22.1 focuses on self-disclosure and nondisclosure in one episode, but self-disclosure (including "who" discloses, "what" is divulged, "how" the partners influence one another to disclose or not, and "when" and "where" disclosure occurs) is a *process* that unfolds over time – within a single conversation as well as across days, weeks, months, and even years of a personal relationship (e.g., Dindia, 1998, 2000; Greene et al., 2003). For instance, the disclosure recipient's responsiveness during a single episode (e.g., expressions of social support, asking questions, showing interest) as well as the potential discloser's own input (e.g., hinting about what one wants to say) may influence what is said at the time and influence disclosure decision making in future conversations. Also, despite the conceptual distinction between "discloser" and "disclosure recipient," partners in a relationship are likely to exchange roles of discloser and recipient within a conversation and across time as they coordinate their needs and expectations about disclosing or listening.

A key feature of disclosure decision making, according to the model in Figure 22.1, addresses people's self-reported reasons for *why* they disclose or do not disclose to a relationship partner. Consistent with attribution theories about communications and interactions in close relationships (see Manusov & Harvey, 2001), reasons for disclosure as well as nondisclosure reflect a self-focus, an other-focus, an interpersonal focus, and a situational–environmental focus (Burke et al., 1976; Derlega & Winstead, 2001; Derlega et al., 2000; for related research on reasons for keeping family secrets, see Vangelisti, 1994; Vangelisti & Caughlin, 1997; Vangelisti, Caughlin, & Timmerman, 2001).

The self-focused reasons for self-disclosure deal with the psychological and tangible benefits to the discloser and include catharsis, self-clarification, and seeking support. Other-focused reasons for self-disclosure include duty to inform and a desire to educate. Relationship-focused reasons include having a close and trusting relationship with one's partner, similarity or having something in common, and a desire to increase intimacy or closeness. Situational–environmental reasons include availability of the target person, the other person asked or "demanded" disclosure, and the other's involvement in the subject matter of the disclosure.

The self-focused reasons for nondisclosure deal with the psychological and physical costs based on divulging personal information and include fear of rejection and possible loss of privacy. Other-focused reasons for nondisclosure include the perception that the other person cannot or will not be helpful and protecting the relationship partner from being hurt or upset. Relationship-focused reasons include losing the relationship, dissimilarity, a superficial relationship, or the information is not significant or relevant for the relationship. Situational–environmental reasons include the possible disclosure target is unavailable or the person has prior knowledge already of the information.

The reasons for and against self-disclosure reflect the multiple goals that individuals have for what they divulge or do not divulge. People do not just reveal personal information to establish a closer relationship or conceal information to preclude a closer relationship (Burke et al., 1976; Derlega & Winstead, 2001; Omarzu, 2000). In close relationships, people pay attention to issues affecting their relationship partner (partner-focused) and the relationship itself (as well as self-focused and situation–environmental reasons) in deciding whether to disclose. It is also worthwhile noting that the reasons or explanations generated for self-disclosure (by the discloser as well as the disclosure target) may have consequences for relationship development – akin to a self-fulfilling prophecy. The discloser may feel closer to the target if the self-disclosure is attributed to liking for the partner. Also, the disclosure target may feel closer to the dis-

closer (and be more likely to disclose himself or herself) if it is inferred that liking or relationship closeness are the reasons for the discloser's behavior (Derlega, Winstead, Wong, & Greenspan, 1987; also see Harvey & Omarzu's 1997 theory on "minding the close relationship" for a detailed description of the role of attributions for self-disclosure in fostering relationship closeness).

Disclosure As a Transactional Process

Self-disclosure is important for achieving important goals (such as developing relationship closeness, gaining emotional support), but it is often just one component in a ongoing interaction involving disclosure input, reactions of the disclosure recipient, initial discloser's and recipient's perceptions of what happened, and so on. We illustrate how the "transactions" (Dindia, 1998) that occur between the discloser and the disclosure target (in particular, the immediate reactions of the disclosure recipient to the disclosure input; see Greene & Faulkner, 2002) contribute to the discloser's experience of intimacy and self-worth. We also describe how the particular cues and signals exchanged between the discloser and the prospective disclosure recipient during a social interaction influence disclosing behavior.

Development of Relationship Intimacy

Self-disclosure has an important role in the development of intimacy between romantic couples. For example, Rubin et al. (1980) examined the association between the level of self-disclosure to one's dating partner (the couples were "going together") and feelings of love and liking for the partner. Self-disclosure to one's dating partner was positively associated with self-reports of love (focusing on feelings of attachment, caring, and intimacy), but self-disclosure was only weakly associated with liking for one's partner. Nevertheless, sharing personal information per se between relationship partners may not by itself create intimacy. Consider, for instance, Reis and Shaver's (1988; also see Reis & Patrick, 1996) interpersonal process model of intimacy. According to this model, individuals disclose (or "self-express") personal thoughts and feelings; next there is an emotional or behavioral response by the disclosure recipient; then the initial discloser's reaction to the recipient's response is to feel understood. It is "feeling understood, validated, and cared for" that define an intimate interaction or intimate relationship in the Reis and Shaver model (Reis & Patrick, 1996, p. 536; also see Chelune, Robinson, & Kommor, 1984; Harvey & Omarzu, 1997; Prager, 1995).

A key feature in Reis and Shaver's intimacy process model is the disclosure recipient's conversational responsiveness (Miller & Berg, 1984), referring to "behaviors made by the recipient of another's communication through which the recipient indicates interest in and understanding of the communication" (Miller & Berg, 1984, p. 193). Responsiveness may be indicated by the content of the response (e.g., elaborating on what was said or making a matching disclosure), the style of the response (e.g., showing concern for what was said), and timing (e.g., whether there is an immediate response or a long delay before the recipient responds). Thus, the *response* is critical in understanding the disclosure process.

Laurenceau, Feldman Barrett, and Pietromonaco (1998) conducted two studies illustrating how recipient responsiveness to disclosure input contributes to the experience of intimacy in interactions. Research participants kept a daily diary record for 1 or 2 weeks (Studies 1 and 2, respectively) and recorded how much they (and the partner) disclosed. Self-disclosure and partner disclosure were both significant predictors of intimacy, but partner responsiveness also mediated the relationship between self-disclosure and intimacy. Greater disclosure by self and partner disclosure was associated with a perception of greater responsiveness by the partner that, in turn, was associated with a perception of higher intimacy of the interaction.[2]

Developing a Sense of Self-Worth

There is some question about the association between self-disclosure per se and mental health (e.g., Jourard, 1964; Kelly, 2002; Pennebaker, 1995), but there is no doubt that the mental health benefits of self-disclosure depend, in part, on the reactions of the disclosure recipient. Consider, for instance, a recent study on stigma management conducted by Beals (2003). Gay men and lesbians participated in a diary study and indicated whether they disclosed or concealed information about their sexual orientation when "disclosure opportunities" occurred during a 2-week time period. At the end of each day, participants completed measures of social support and psychological well-being, including positive affect, self-esteem, and satisfaction with life. Consistent with the notion that self-disclosure is a transactional process, Beals found that social support mediated the relationship between self-disclosure and well-being. That is, self-disclosure about sexual orientation was associated with greater social support and, in turn, greater social support was associated with greater psychological well-being.

Social Cues From the Prospective Disclosure Recipient Promoting Self-Disclosure

Someone may want to disclose personal information, but he or she may need to anticipate a positive (not a negative or neutral) response before being willing to make this decision (e.g., Altman & Taylor, 1973; Greene & Serovich, 1996). Signals or cues enacted by the prospective disclosure target during a disclosure episode (or in a relationship) may be crucial in deciding whether to disclose sensitive information. For instance, Petronio, Reeder, Hecht, and Mon't Ros-Mendoza (1996) found that prospective disclosers (who were victims of sexual abuse) looked for cues during a conversation signaling "tacit permission" (p. 187) to divulge potentially shameful and embarrassing information. Participants described two sorts of cues that signaled a "tacit permission" to self-disclose: inquiries suggesting concern and disclosure input by the other person.

Inquiries suggesting concern reflect an inference by the prospective discloser that the other person is attentive to the discloser's best interests and willing to listen. Petronio et al. (1996) gave the following example of the impact of the partner's expression of concern on self-disclosure about the sexual abuse:

> Participants in this study reported that when others asked questions such as, "Is everything all right? Are you O.K.?" followed by, "I am worried about you," they often interpreted these questions as indirect requests for information about the abuse, especially when they came from people they liked and trusted. The sympathetic nature of the inquiry was interpreted as communicating a willingness to receive disclosive information about sexual abuse. (p. 187)

Participants in Petronio et al. (1996) also disclosed in response to the other person's disclosure input, what we have referred to as disclosure reciprocity (also see Dindia, 2000). Reciprocity may occur because the other person's disclosure input was taken as a "request" or "consent" to talk oneself about a similar matter. Petronio et al. (1996) gave the following example of reciprocity:

> Jennifer stated that her sister revealed she had been abused by the stepfather and expected her to disclose in return. She said, "We were just talking about different little things. She was just basically telling me what she was doing. She wasn't living at home at the time. We were talking about her, the job she had, and stuff, and then she brought it up because she started talking about how it happened to her. Then she asked me. . . . I just said, well yes, it happened to me too." (pp. 188–189; italics in original)

This phenomenon of reciprocity may occur in the disclosure of other potentially stigmatizing information. For example, Greene et al. (2003, p. 105) found that people with HIV are more likely to disclose their HIV seropositive status to another person if the other first discloses about being HIV positive.

The examples of responding to general inquiries and the other's disclosure input illustrate how the disclosure process is a transaction between the "discloser" and the "disclosure recipient." In these illustrations, expressions of concern by the prospective disclosure target as well as the target's own self-disclosure affected participants' willingness to self-disclose.

Disclosure Message Enactment

How disclosure messages are enacted is an important feature of self-disclosure in personal relationships. When someone decides to disclose, he or she must choose what to say as well as how, when, where, and to whom. These message choices vary according to perceptions of the relationship. We describe various message features, including disclosure mode, context (including setting and timing), and content (directness, length, and associated information).

Disclosure Mode

The *mode* of disclosure (also termed *message channel*) can be face-to-face, non-face-to-face, or third-party (Greene et al., 2003). Face-to-face disclosure such as talking in person may be the most common, but the in-person interaction may be unpredictable and difficult to manage. For example, the discloser may be asked follow-up questions after the disclosure, perhaps ending up divulging much more information than was desired. Non-face-to-face disclosures (e.g., letter writing or an e-mail message) tend to be communicated in a manner that restricts how much the listener learns about the discloser. A benefit of non-face-to-face disclosure (e.g., an e-mail message) is that individuals may feel free to disclose openly in a manner that is not possible in face-to-face interactions (e.g., McKenna, Green, & Gleason, 2002), but fewer nonverbal cues are available to the interactants.

Yet not all disclosure is between just two people, and the third mode is having another person disclose one's personal information to others (either face-to-face or non-face-to-face). For example, someone with a serious illness may ask a sibling to tell the parents about the diagnosis. Although third-party disclosure may be intentional and deliberate, there is always the possibility that a disclosure recipient may violate the discloser's privacy either accidentally or deliberately by leaking confidential information to others. In research on HIV disclosure, individuals with HIV frequently report being upset by the loss of control of this information to a third party, especially in families (Greene & Faulkner, 2002).

Disclosure Setting

Along with the mode of disclosure, disclosure messages are set within contexts such as the place and time. The physical environment where people interact may influence how much and what people disclose (Werner, Altman, & Brown, 1992; also see Brown, Werner, & Altman, this volume). A person may choose to disclose at home to increase intimacy with the other person as well as to regulate privacy, yet another may choose to disclose in a public setting such as in a restaurant in hopes that the open setting may constrain the recipient's reaction. Also, what one person perceives as a private setting for disclosing personal information (e.g., talking on a cell phone while walking down a public street) may be perceived by another person as grossly inappropriate.

Disclosure Timing

Early studies of self-disclosure timing (in the 1970s and 1980s) often focused on disclosure between new acquaintances, finding that disclosure at the beginning of an interaction was often perceived as inappropriate and as violating social norms (e.g., Wortman, Adesman, Herman, & Greenberg, 1976). Less research is available on disclosure timing within close relationships, but Greene et al. (2003) provided a way to conceptualize timing on three levels: timing of

disclosure in a relationship, spontaneous versus preplanned disclosure, and timing of disclosure within a conversation.

Concerning timing of disclosure in a relationship, the prospective discloser may have to decide whether to disclose information immediately at the start of a relationship, after an important event has occurred, or wait until some future time. For example, if someone is diagnosed with a life-threatening disease, should that person tell friends (and family) immediately or wait (and how long)? Research indicates that people are likely to disclose to their loves ones (such as to a spouse or intimate partner) relatively soon after learning about a life-threatening illness, but decisions about when to disclose to children may be delayed because of age and maturity concerns (e.g., Greene et al., 2003; Schrimshaw & Siegel, 2002).

Disclosures may be either unplanned (spontaneous) or planned (occurring deliberately after a decision is made to disclose). People may prefer planned disclosure about potentially stigmatizing information because it maximizes privacy regulation (Petronio, 2002). When disclosure is unplanned, perhaps in response to a disclosure input or a direct question, someone may regret not having considered in detail the consequences of disclosing this information (e.g., gossip, being rejected).

Finally, the timing of disclosure in a conversation requires sequencing and a plan of action (see Derlega et al., 1993). If a person discloses *early* in a conversation, this may surprise the recipient but does ensure that the discloser does not "chicken out." For example, two people could sit down for lunch and one immediately blurts out, "I'm getting a divorce." If someone chooses to disclose in the *middle* of a conversation, prior time in the conversation can be used to assess the readiness of the prospective disclosure target to listen (e.g., whether the person is preoccupied by his or her own problems; see Petronio et al., 1996). With intermediate disclosure, it is also possible to foreshadow the disclosure, perhaps telling someone you "want to talk." For example, in the same lunch interaction the potential discloser asks how the disclosure target is doing, how work is going, how the family is, and if all is well then shares about the divorce (or chooses not to if the timing does not seem appropriate). For *late* disclosure, a person waits until the end of an interaction, for example, when the discloser target (or discloser) is leaving for the airport in 45 minutes and someone shares important information. The discloser may prefer late disclosure because it limits the interaction (and possible follow-up questions; see Greene et al., 2003), but the disclosure recipient may become upset or confused because there is no time to process the content of the disclosure or to be supportive.

Disclosure Message Features

Message features (directness, length, content) are another important aspect of self-disclosure in personal relationships. For instance, someone can discuss the same topic in a direct ("I just found out that I got a promotion") or in an indirect manner ("It's nice to finally have something good happen at work"; see Petronio, 1991). Direct, compared with indirect, disclosure messages may place more demands for a response from the disclosure recipient because the message is so clear. For instance, disclosing about the job promotion may require some sort of acknowledgment or an affirming statement, whereas a disclosure target may shrug off an equivocal comment about an unspecified event at work.

Disclosures may vary in length, but it is not always the case that greater length of disclosure is associated with greater depth of disclosure. For instance, a brief message (e.g., "I recently found out that I have breast cancer") may be more disclosing than, say, a convoluted description of a visit to a clinic for a mammogram or a vague general description of "I am not feeling very well these days." Sometimes people may give the appearance of disclosing intimately by increasing the amount of time spent talking about low-intimacy facts and feelings when they actually want to avoid divulging personal information (Derlega, Sherburne, & Lewis, 1998).

We should also note that the precise content of disclosure might differ, even when different persons are ostensibly revealing the same information. Someone who has missed work recently because of physical complications of HIV progression may reveal to a coworker, "I have HIV," whereas another person with the same diagnosis may simply say that "I have been sick." What the discloser said in these examples illustrates how someone can control the flow of information to a disclosure recipient and then influence the others' reactions (Petronio, 2002).

Alternative Disclosure Message Strategies

We have focused on verbal forms of disclosure, yet there are symbolic and non-verbal means of enacting self-disclosure in personal relationships. Particularly if verbal disclosure might be burdensome, symbolic disclosure may be an effective and efficient way of communicating information about the self to intimates. For instance, a person with HIV described how he had "HIV+" tattooed on his bicep to forewarn potential sexual partners:

> I was still going out, picking up guys, and I got tired of all the mess with talking about it, being safe.... [A] friend jokingly suggested I get this [points to tattoo] and I thought it would be the perfect solution. This way, there is no way he [a potential date] wouldn't know but we don't have to talk about it. (Greene et al., 2003, p. 117)

Sometimes these symbolic forms become almost habitual or automatic, but we focus on examples that are intentional in nature and thus qualify as disclosure. For example, wearing a special piece of jewelry, such as a pearl necklace given to a woman by her intimate partner as an anniversary gift. The woman assumes that her partner will recognize the significance of her gesture because it symbolizes their love. On the other hand, some alternative disclosure message strategies may be less clear, such as leaving a bank statement with a low balance in view in the hope that a relative will loan money!

Self-Disclosure, Relationships, and Health

In this section, we summarize research on the possible health ramifications of self-disclosure versus nondisclosure in personal relationships for coping with stressful and traumatic life events. Consider, for instance, the following study by Pennebaker and O'Heeron's (1984). Spouses of suicide and accidental-death victims completed a questionnaire about their coping strategies. The less the participants talked with friends, the greater the increase in health problems (e.g., weight change, headaches) from the year before the death of the spouse to the year after the death. Also, the more the participants talked with friends, the less they experienced intrusive thoughts (or ruminations) about the spouse's death. Pennebaker and O'Heeron suggested that the failure to talk with a confidant accounts for the unwanted thoughts about the spouse's death and contributes to health problems. Why might withholding information about stressful or traumatic events lead to psychological and physical problems, while disclosing may be healthy? We consider several possible mechanisms here.

Nondisclosure As Psychological Inhibition, Disclosure As Disinhibition

Concealing personal thoughts, feelings, and even actions could be a stressor on the body, ultimately increasing susceptibility to illness (e.g., Pennebaker, 1995). Disclosing, on the other hand, may reduce the negative effects of concealment, including improving health.

Research by Cole and colleagues (Cole, Kemeny, Taylor, Visscher, & Fahey, 1996) illustrates the notion that *psychological inhibition* (operationalized in Cole et al.'s study as concealing one's homosexual identity) may weaken immune function and influence disease progression. Participants were men with HIV who self-identified as either exclusively or predominantly homosexual. They were divided into an "open" versus a "closeted" group based on how much they reported disclosing or concealing their homosexual identity compared with other gay men. HIV progressed more rapidly

among the closeted compared with the open participants. Cole, Kemeny, Taylor, and Visscher (1996) conducted a related study on psychological inhibition among a group of gay men who were HIV seronegative. Participants who were closeted about their homosexual identity had a higher risk of cancer and infectious diseases (e.g., pneumonia, bronchitis). Given the results in Cole et al.'s studies, it is tempting to speculate that the link between psychological inhibition and health may occur across a variety of concealed psychological events (e.g., sexual orientation as well as other sensitive thoughts and feelings).

Nondisclosure As Suppression, Disclosure As Cognitive Processing

Suppressing thoughts and feelings via nondisclosure may have negative cognitive consequences. According to the preoccupation model of secrecy (Wegner & Lane, 1995), "secrecy sets into motion certain cognitive processes that create an obsessive preoccupation with the secret thought" (p. 31). Attempting not to think about a particular thought or feeling paradoxically increases intrusive thoughts about the information. The intrusive thoughts lead to further attempts at thought suppression, causing a "self-sustaining cycle of obsessive preoccupation with the secret" (Wegner & Lane, 1995, p. 33). For instance, Smart and Wegner (1999) found that concealing an eating disorder during a social interaction caused participants to become preoccupied with keeping the information a secret (e.g., increasing thought intrusions about the eating disorder).

From a cognitive processing perspective (Lepore, Ragan, & Jones, 2000), talking about stressful thoughts and feelings to a confidant enables someone to make sense of their experiences as well as desensitize them to upsetting or stress-related events. Someone who can put stressful thoughts and feelings into words (i.e., construct a narrative via talking or even writing about these events) may be better able to understand and find meaning in their experiences. Also, talking about stressful events may reduce their emotional impact. For instance, Lepore and Helgeson (1998) found that prostate cancer survivors who reported fewer constraints in talking about cancer with friends, relatives, and spouses were less distressed about intrusive thoughts associated with cancer.

DISCLOSURE IN THE CONTEXT OF "HELPFUL" VERSUS "UNHELPFUL" REACTIONS BY THE LISTENER

The possible benefits of self-disclosure in coping with stressful thoughts and feelings we have just described could be obtained from talking with a confidant or from writing or talking to oneself. In fact, most research on the physical and psychological health benefits of "self-disclosure" is based on expressive writing, that is, writing down personal thoughts and feelings on paper to oneself. One drawback, however, is that these conclusions based on writing are not always appropriate to generalize to disclosure that occurs between a discloser and disclosure recipient. The *social* benefits of self-disclosure depend, in part, on the reactions of the disclosure target and others (third parties) who find out about the private information (cf. Greene & Faulkner, 2002; Greene & Serovich, 1996). For instance, disclosure targets might be able to provide useful information or material assistance to the discloser to cope with health problems. The understanding and acceptance that others provide as listeners might also promote feelings of self-worth in the discloser (Beals, 2003) and decrease social isolation (Reis, Sheldon, Gable, Roscoe, & Ryan, 2000).

Nevertheless, there may be negative social consequences of self-disclosure for personal relationships. Talking about negative feelings in anticipation of an upsetting event may increase the discloser's stress (Costanza, Derlega, & Winstead, 1988), and the recipient (especially immediate family) may be "unhelpful" (Barbee, Derlega, Sherburne, & Grimshaw, 1998) and rejecting (Kelly, 2002). There may also be unreasonable physical and psychological burdens placed on the disclosure recipient who now "co-owns" the information (Petronio, 2002) and must manage it.

Given the risk of negative reactions by a disclosure recipient and concerns about regulating privacy, researchers recommend that prospective disclosers should exercise caution in deciding whether to disclose. For instance, Kelly (2002) suggested the following algorithm for deciding whether to reveal hidden information to a relationship partner. First, is the information private or secret ("private" refers to personal information which someone does not have a right to know, whereas "secret" refers to information that someone else may expect to have access)? If the information *is* secret, the next question would be, Is the other person an appropriate target for disclosure (someone "who will not tell others the secret, will not judge him negatively and will not reject him," Kelly, 2002, p. 199)? Next, is the secret likely to be found out by the other person anyway, and is keeping the secret troubling? If the other person is likely to find out about the secret and keeping the secret is emotionally upsetting, then a decision might be made to disclose the secret.

The research on the link between disclosure and health often focuses on the possible health benefits of self-disclosure in coping with negative life events and negative thoughts and feelings. But there may be psychological benefits from disclosing about pleasant events and positive emotions (e.g., getting a good grade, birth of a child, lower tuition rates). Gable, Reis, Impett, and Asher (2004) presented data on the phenomenon of *capitalization*, dealing with the benefits of sharing good things with significant others. Disclosing about positive personal events was associated with increases in daily positive affect as well higher relationship well-being (including intimacy and marital satisfaction) and was even more beneficial if the listener responded in an active and constructive manner to the information (e.g., "asks a lot of questions and shows genuine concern," p. 50). This research on capitalization illustrates a welcome trend in relationship research on how interactions about positive events between relationship partners promote personal health and relationship growth.

Methodological Trends and Future Research in Disclosure

Self-disclosure continues to be a significant area of relationship research, providing opportunities for both methodological and theoretical advancement. A recent methodological trend includes a greater reliance on diary studies (e.g., Lippert & Prager, 2001) that provide multiple observations from research participants on the predictors and consequences of self-disclosure. This kind of longitudinal data requires the use of statistical programs such as hierarchical linear modeling (HLM) that are appropriate for multilevel data. By asking participants to report their experiences on a daily basis (or more frequently) or after specific events have occurred, researchers can address questions such as the following: How much do individuals differ from one another over time in self-disclosure based on within-person (e.g., interactions in different types of relationships) and between-person (e.g., gender) variables? Are temporal changes in self-disclosure cyclical or linear in the development of different kinds of personal relationships?

Another important methodological development has been the extension of self-disclosure research to typically under-researched populations (e.g., stigmatized populations such as individuals with HIV, gay men and lesbians, or sexual abuse survivors). Studies with these populations test the strengths and weaknesses of theories and research about self-disclosure or personal relationships that have been developed primarily by studying undergraduate research participants.

Despite these important methodological advances, there is room for improvement in how research is conducted. There is a need for more research on the transactional nature of disclosure and the relational consequences of disclosure decisions. The focus of analysis in disclosure research has often been at the level of the individual (usually focusing on the discloser per se), but more attention can be focused on the dynamic interaction between the relationship partners (the "discloser" and the "disclosure recipient") as the process of self-disclosure unfolds within a single disclosure episode and over time. Videotapes of interaction episodes or diary records to be kept by relationship partners over time could be useful in documenting when and how self-disclosure occurs as well as its consequences.

Future research needs to disentangle the consequences for relationship functioning in cases when someone is told a particular piece of information by a discloser versus someone finding out about the information (see Greene & Faulkner, 2002). There are undoubtedly different ramifications for a personal relationship if someone acquires information (e.g., a diagnosis of a life-threatening illness) because they heard this information in a secondhand manner (e.g., via gossip) as opposed to hearing the information face-to-face during a self-disclosure episode.

People in self-disclosure studies often lament not knowing "what to say" or "how to say" something to their relationship partner. Burdening others with one's personal problems is another concern voiced by many (Burke et al., 1976; Derlega & Winstead, 2001). People also report that "some things are better left unsaid," even with relationship partners. Research should be conducted on disclosure skills, including knowing what to disclose, when to disclose, and how to disclose.

Finally, research is needed on the cultural criteria that influence self-disclosure. Although there is extensive research on, say, gender differences in self-disclosure (e.g., women in North America tend to disclose more than men, especially in same-sex interactions; cf. Dindia, 2002), more research is necessary on the psychological and social underpinnings of these effects. Also, there are cross-cultural differences in self-disclosure in different types of personal relationships (Yep, Reece, & Negrón,

2003). How different cultures conceptualize and express intimacy via self-disclosure and target responsiveness needs further examination.

Footnotes

1. There are relatively few studies examining disclosure in deteriorating relationships. In fact, there are many fewer studies of relationship breakups compared with relationship progression more generally. It is possible there is a sharp decline in disclosure with the breakup, yet there may also be a gradual lessening of disclosure with many peaks and valleys.

2. Lippert and Prager (2001) also conducted a related diary study focusing on predictors of daily experiences of intimacy between cohabiting couples. Consistent with Laurenceau et al. (1998), Lippert and Prager found that the perception of being understood by one's partner (together with interaction pleasantness, disclosure of private information, the expression of positive feelings, and the disclosure of emotions) predicted the perceived intimacy of daily interactions.

References

Afifi, W. A., & Burgoon, J. K. (1998). "We never talk about that": A comparison of cross-sex friendships and dating relationships on uncertainty and topic avoidance. *Personal Relationships, 5*, 255–272.

Altman, I., & Haythorn, W. W. (1965). Interpersonal exchange in isolation. *Sociometry, 23*, 411–426.

Altman, I., & Taylor, D. A. (1973). *Social penetration: The development of interpersonal relationships*. New York: Holt, Rinehart, & Winston.

Altman, I., Vinsel, A., & Brown, B. H. (1981). Dialectic conceptions in social psychology: An application to social penetration and privacy regulation. In L. Berkowitz (Ed.), *Advances in experimental social psychology* (Vol. 14, pp. 107–160). New York: Academic Press.

Archer, R. L. (1987). Commentary: Self-disclosure, a very useful behavior. In V. J. Derlega & J. H. Berg (Eds.), *Self-disclosure: Theory, research, and therapy* (pp. 329–342). New York: Plenum.

Archer, R. L., & Cook, C. E. (1986). Personalistic self-disclosure and attraction: Basis for relationship or scare resource. *Social Psychology Quarterly, 49*, 268–272.

Barbee, A. P., Derlega, V. J., Sherburne, S. P., & Grimshaw, A. (1998). Helpful and unhelpful forms of social support for HIV-positive individuals. In V. J. Derlega & A. P. Barbee (Eds.), *HIV and social interaction* (pp. 83–105). Thousand Oaks, CA: Sage.

Baxter, L. A., & Montgomery, B. M. (1997). *Dialectic approaches to studying personal relationships*. Mahwah, NJ: Erlbaum.

Baxter, L. A., & Wilmot, W. W. (1985). Taboo topics in close relationships. *Journal of Social and Personal Relationships, 2*, 253–269.

Beals, K. P. (2003). *Stigma management and well-being: The role of social support, cognitive processing, and suppression*. Unpublished doctoral dissertation, University of California, Los Angeles.

Berg, J. H. (1984). Development of friendship between roommates. *Journal of Personality and Social Psychology, 46*, 346–356.

Berg, J. H. (1986). Responsiveness and self-disclosure. In V. J. Derlega & J. H. Berg (Eds.), *Self-disclosure: Theory, research, and therapy* (pp. 101–130). New York: Plenum.

Berg, J. H., & Archer, R. L. (1980). Disclosure or concern: A second look at liking for the norm-breaker. *Journal of Personality, 48*, 245–257.

Berg, J. H., & Clark, M. S. (1986). Differences in social exchange between intimate and other relationships: Gradually evolving or quickly apparent. In V. J. Derlega & B. A. Winstead (Eds.), *Friendship and social interaction* (pp. 101–128). New York: Springer-Verlag.

Burke, R. J., Weir, T., & Harrison, D. (1976). Disclosure of problems and tensions experienced by marital partners. *Psychological Reports, 38*, 531–542.

Chaikin, A. L., & Derlega, V. J. (1974a). Liking for the norm-breaker in self-disclosure. *Journal of Personality, 42*, 117–129.

Chaikin, A. L., & Derlega, V. J. (1974b). Variables affecting the appropriateness of self-disclosure. *Journal of Consulting and Clinical Psychology, 42*, 588–593.

Chaikin, A. L., & Derlega, V. J. (1974c). *Self-disclosure*. Morristown, NJ: General Learning Press.

Chelune, G. J., Robinson, J. T., & Kommor, M. J. (1984). A cognitive interactional model of intimate relationships. In V. J. Derlega (Ed.), *Communication, intimacy, and close relationships* (pp. 11–40). Orlando, FL: Academic Press.

Chelune, G. J., Waring, E. M., Vosk, B. N., Sultan, F. E., & Ogden, J. K. (1984) Self-disclosure and its relationship to marital intimacy. *Journal of Clinical Psychology, 409*, 216–219.

Cole, S. W., Kemeny, M. E., Taylor, S. E., & Visscher, B. R. (1996). Elevated physical health risk among gay men who conceal their homosexual identity. *Health Psychology, 15*, 243–251.

Cole, S. W., Kemeny, M. E., Taylor, S. E., Visscher, B. R., & Fahey, J. L. (1996). Accelerated course of human immunodeficiency virus infection in gay men who conceal their homosexual identity. *Psychosomatic Medicine, 58*, 219–231.

Collins, N. L., & Miller, L. C. (1994). Self-disclosure and liking: A meta-analytic review. *Psychological Bulletin, 116*, 457–475.

Costanza, R. S., Derlega, V. J., & Winstead, B. A. (1988). Positive and negative forms of social support: Effects of conversational topics on coping with stress among same-sex friends. *Journal of Experimental Social Psychology, 24*, 182–193.

Cozby, P. C. (1973). Self-disclosure: A literature review. *Psychological Bulletin, 79*, 73–91.

DePaulo, B. M., Wetzel, C., Weylin Sternglanz, R., & Walker Wilson, M. J. (2003). Verbal and nonverbal dynamics of privacy, secrecy, and deceit. *Journal of Social Issues, 59*, 391–410.

Derlega, V. J., & Chaikin, A. L. (1975). *Sharing intimacy: What we reveal to others and why*. Englewood Cliffs, NJ: Prentice-Hall.

Derlega, V. J., & Chaikin, A. L. (1977). Privacy and self-disclosure in social relationships. *Journal of Social Issues, 33*(3), 102–115.

Derlega, V. J., & Grzelak, J. (1979). Appropriateness of self-disclosure. In G. J. Chelune (Ed.), *Self-disclosure: Origins, patterns, and implications of openness in interpersonal relationships* (pp. 151–176). San Francisco: Jossey-Bass.

Derlega, V. J., Wilson, J., & Chaikin, A. L. (1976). Friendship and disclosure reciprocity. *Journal of Personality and Social Psychology, 34*, 578–582.

Derlega, V. J., Metts, S., Petronio, S., & Margulis, S. T. (1993). *Self-disclosure*. Newbury Park, CA: Sage.

Derlega, V. J., Sherburne, S. P., & Lewis, R. J. (1998). Reactions to an HIV-positive man: Impact of his sexual orientation, cause of infection, and research participants' gender. *AIDS and Behavior, 2*, 239–248.

Derlega, V. J., & Winstead, B. A. (2001). HIV-infected person's attributions for the disclosure and nondisclosure of the seropositive diagnosis to significant others. In V. Manusov & J. H. Harvey (Eds.), *Attribution, communication behavior, and close relationships* (pp. 266–284). New York: Cambridge University Press.

Derlega, V. J., & Winstead, B. A., & Folk-Barron, L. (2000). Reasons for and against disclosing HIV-seropositive test results to an intimate partner: A functional perspective. In S. Petronio (Ed.), *Balancing the secrets of private disclosures* (pp. 53–69). Mahwah, NJ: Erlbaum.

Derlega, V. J., Winstead, B. A., Wong, P. T. P., & Greenspan, M. (1987). Self-disclosure and relationship development: An attributional analysis. In M. E. Roloff & G. R. Miller (Eds.), *Interpersonal processes: New directions in communication research* (pp. 172–187). Newbury Park, CA: Sage.

Dindia, K. (1998). "Going into and coming out of the closet": The dialectics of stigma disclosure. In B. M. Montgomery & L. A. Baxter (Eds.), *Dialectical approaches to studying personal relationships* (pp. 83–108). Mahwah, NJ: Erlbaum.

Dindia, K. (2000). Sex differences in self-disclosure, reciprocity of self-disclosure, and self-disclosure and liking: Three meta-analyses reviewed. In S. Petronio (Ed.), *Balancing the secrets of private disclosures* (pp. 21–35). Mahwah, NJ: Erlbaum.

Dindia, K. (2002). Self-disclosure research: Knowledge through meta-analysis. In M. Allen, R. W. Preiss, B. M. Gayle, & N. A. Burrell (Eds.), *Interpersonal communication research: Advances through meta-analysis* (pp. 169–185). Mahwah, NJ: Lawrence Erlbaum.

Fitzpatrick, M. A. (1987). Marriage and verbal intimacy. In V. J. Derlega & J. H. Berg (Eds.), *Self-disclosure: Theory, research, and therapy* (pp. 131–174). New York: Plenum.

Fromm, E. (1956). *The art of loving*. New York: Harper.

Gable, S. L., Reis, H. T., Impett, E. A., & Asher, E. R. (2004). What do you do when things go right? The intrapersonal and interpersonal benefits of sharing positive events. *Journal of Personality and Social Psychology, 87*, 228–245.

Greene, K., Derlega, V. J., Yep, G. A., & Petronio, S. (2003). *Privacy and disclosure of HIV in interpersonal relationships: A sourcebook for researchers and practitioners*. Mahwah, NJ: Erlbaum.

Greene, K., & Faulkner, S. L. (2002). Self-disclosure in relationships of HIV-positive African-American adolescent females. *Communication Studies, 53*, 297–313.

Greene, K., & Serovich, J. M. (1996). Appropriateness of disclosure of HIV testing information: The perspective of PLWAs. *Journal of Applied Communication Research, 24*, 50–65.

Harvey, J. H., & Omarzu, J. (1997). Minding the close relationship. *Personality and Social Psychology Review, 1*, 224–240.

Hendrick, S. S. (1981). Self-disclosure and marital satisfaction. *Journal of Personality and Social Psychology, 40*, 1150–1159.

Hill, C. T., Rubin, Z., & Peplau, L. A. (1976). Breakups before marriage: The end of 103 affairs. *Journal of Social Issues, 32*(1), 147–168.

Jones, E. E., & Archer, R. L. (1976). Are there special effects of personalistic self-disclosure? *Journal of Experimental Social Psychology, 12*, 180–183.

Jourard, J. M. (1964). *The transparent self*. New York: Van Nostrand.

Jourard, J. M. (1971a). *The transparent self* (2nd ed.) New York: Van Nostrand.

Jourard, J. M. (1971b). *Self-disclosure: An experimental analysis of the transparent self*. New York: Wiley-Interscience.

Kelly, A. E. (2000). Helping construct desirable identities: A self-presentational view of psychotherapy. *Psychological Bulletin, 126*, 475–494.

Kelly, A. E. (2002). *The psychology of secrets*. New York: Kluwer Academic/Plenum.

Kenny, D. A., & La Voie, L. (1984). The social relations model. In L. Berkowitz (Ed.), *Advances in experimental social psychology* (Vol. 18, pp. 139–180). New York: Academic Press.

Komarovsky, M. (1962). *Blue-collar marriage*. New York: Vintage.

Laurenceau, J. P., Feldman Barrett, L., & Pietromonaco, P. R. (1998). Intimacy as an interpersonal process: The importance of self-disclosure, partner disclosure, and perceived partner responsiveness in interpersonal exchanges. *Journal of Personality and Social Psychology, 74*, 1238–1251.

Lepore, S. J., & Helgeson, V. S. (1998). Social constraints, intrusive thoughts, and mental health after prostate cancer. *Journal of Social and Clinical Psychology, 17*, 89–106.

Lepore, S. J., Ragan, J. D., & Jones, S. (2000). Talking facilitates cognitive-emotional processes of adaptation to an acute stressor. *Journal of Personality and Social Psychology, 78*, 499–508.

Levinger, G., & Snoek, D. J. (1972). *Attraction in relationship: A new look at interpersonal attraction*. Morristown, NJ: General Learning Press.

Lippert, T., & Prager, K. J. (2001). Daily experiences of intimacy: A study of couples. *Personal Relationships, 8*, 283–298.

Manusov, V., & Harvey, J. H. (Eds.). (2001). *Attribution, communication behavior, and close relationships*. Cambridge, England: Cambridge University Press.

Margulis, S. T. (2003). On the status and contribution of Westin's and Altman's theories of privacy. *Journal of Social Issues, 59*, 411–429.

McKenna, K. Y. A., Green, A. S., & Gleason, M. E. J. (2002). Relationship formation on the Internet: What's the big attraction? *Journal of Social Issues, 58*, 9–31.

Miller, L. C., & Berg, J. H. (1984). Selectivity and urgency in interpersonal exchange. In V. J. Derlega (Ed.), *Communication, intimacy, and close relationships* (pp. 161–205). Orlando, FL: Academic Press.

Miller, L. C., Berg, J. H., & Archer, R. L. (1983). Openers: Individuals who elicit intimate self-disclosure. *Journal of Personality and Social Psychology, 44*, 1234–1244.

Miller, L. C., & Kenny, D. A. (1986). Reciprocity of self-disclosure at the individual and dyadic levels: A social relations analysis. *Journal of Personality and Social Psychology, 50*, 713–719.

Miller, L. C., & Read, S. J. (1987). Why am I telling you this? Self-disclosure in a goal-based model of personality. In V. J. Derlega (Eds.), *Self-disclosure: Theory, research, and therapy* (pp. 35–58). New York: Plenum.

Omarzu, J. (2000). A disclosure decision model: Determining how and when individuals will self-disclose. *Personality and Social Psychology Review, 4*, 174–185.

Pennebaker, J. W. (Ed.). (1995). *Emotion, disclosure, and health*. Washington, DC: American Psychological Association.

Pennebaker, J. W., & O'Heeron, R. C. (1984). Confiding in others and illness rate among spouses of suicide and accidental death victims. *Journal of Abnormal Psychology, 93*, 473–476.

Petronio, S. (1991). Communication boundary management: A theoretical model of managing disclosure of private information between marital couples. *Communication Theory, 1*, 311–355.

Petronio, S. (2002). *Boundaries of privacy: Dialectics of disclosure*. Albany: State University of New York Press.

Petronio, S., Reeder, H. M., Hecht, M. L., & Mon't Ros-Mendoza, T. M. (1996). Disclosure of sexual abuse by children and adolescents. *Journal of Applied Communication Research, 24*, 181–199.

Prager, K. J. (1995). *The psychology of intimacy*. New York: Guilford Press.

Reis, H. T., & Patrick, B. C. (1996). Attachment and intimacy: Component processes. In E. T. Higgins & A. W. Kruglanski (Eds.), *Social psychology: Handbook of basic principles* (pp. 523–563). New York: Guilford Press.

Reis, H. T., & Shaver, P. (1988). Intimacy as an interpersonal process. In S. W. Duck (Ed.), *Handbook of personal relationships: Theory, research and interventions* (pp. 376–389). Chichester, England: Wiley.

Reis, H. T., Sheldon, K. M., Gable, S. L., Roscoe, J., & Ryan, R. M. (2000). Daily well-being: The role of autonomy, competence, and relatedness. *Personality and Social Psychology Bulletin, 26*, 419–435.

Roloff, M. E., & Ifert, D. E. (2000). Conflict management through avoidance: Withholding complaints, suppressing arguments, and declaring topics taboo. In S. Petronio (Ed.), *Balancing the secrets of private disclosures* (pp. 151–163). Mahwah, NJ: Erlbaum.

Rosenfeld, L. B. (2000). Overview of the ways privacy, secrecy, and disclosure are balanced in today's society. In S. Petronio (Ed.), *Balancing the secrets of private disclosures* (pp. 3–17). Mahwah, NJ: Erlbaum.

Rubin, Z. (1970). Measurement of romantic love. *Journal of Personality and Social Psychology, 16*, 265–273.

Rubin, Z., Hill, C. T., Peplau, L. A., & Dunkel-Schetter, C. (1980). Self-disclosure in dating couples: Sex roles and the ethic of openness. *Journal of Marriage and the Family, 42*, 305–317.

Schrimshaw, E. W., & Siegel, K. (2002). HIV-infected mothers' disclosure to their uninfected children: Rates, reasons, and reactions. *Journal of Social and Personal Relationships, 19*, 19–43.

Smart, L., & Wegner, D. M. (1999). Covering up what can't be seen: Concealable stigma and mental control. *Journal of Personality and Social Psychology, 77*, 474–486.

Vangelisti, A. L. (1994). Family secrets: Forms, functions, and correlates. *Journal of Social and Personal Relationships, 11*, 113–135.

Vangelisti, A. L., & Caughlin, J. P. (1997). Revealing family secrets: The influence of topic, function, and relationships. *Journal of Social and Personal Relationships, 14*, 679–705.

Vangelisti, A. L., Caughlin, J. P., & Timmerman, L. (2001). Criteria for revealing family secrets. *Communication Monographs, 68*, 1–27.

Waring, E. M. (1987). Self-disclosure in cognitive marital therapy. In V. J. Derlega & J. H. Berg (Eds.), *Self-disclosure: Theory, research, and therapy* (pp. 283–301). New York: Plenum.

Wegner, D. M., & Lane, J. D. (1995). From secrecy to psychopathology. In J. W. Pennebaker (Ed.), *Emotion, disclosure, and health* (pp. 25–46). Washington, DC: American Psychological Association.

Werner, C. M., Altman, I., & Brown, B. B. (1992). A transactional approach to interpersonal relations: Physical environment, social context and temporal qualities. *Journal of Social and Personal Relationships, 9*, 297–323.

Wortman, C. B., Adesman, P., Herman, E., & Greenberg, R. (1976). Self-disclosure: An attributional perspective. *Journal of Personality and Social Psychology, 33*, 184–191.

Yep, G. A., Reece, S., & Negrón, E. L. (2003). Culture and stigma in a bona fide group: An analysis of boundaries and context in a closed support group for Asian Americans living with HIV infection. In L. R. Frey (Ed.), *Group communication in context: Studies of bona fide groups* (2nd ed., pp. 157–180). Mahwah, NJ: Erlbaum.

CHAPTER 23

Close Relationships and Social Support: Implications for the Measurement of Social Support

Barbara R. Sarason
Irwin G. Sarason

Scientific inquiry does not always proceed into a predictable pathway. The empirical investigation of the association between health outcomes and social relationships, from which the study of social support was born, began a little more than 30 years ago in 1976 with the publication of two papers, one by Cassel and one by Cobb, that stemmed from two very different scientific disciplines but which addressed the same general point that health, both physical and mental, was strongly affected by social aspects of the environment. Interest in the topic has grown so rapidly that a computer search of the psychological literature currently lists more than 21,000 publications dealing with social support.

Cassel (1976) in his paper, gave a wide-ranging review of epidemiological literature covering both animal and human health and well-being. The paper presented convincing evidence that the presence of others of the same species was linked to better health and to lower mortality rates for a wide variety of species. Cobb's paper (1976) had a different focus. He approached the association of health and presence of others from a clinical viewpoint and argued that, along with the support provided by others to a social support recipient, there was an additional and even more salutary communication. In Cobb's view the important aspect of supportive behavior of others was that it conveyed that an individual was valued and cared about and was part of a network of communication and mutual obligation.

Although Cobb's definition hinted at the importance of specific relationships in the effects produced by social support, most of those interested in social support assessment neglected this subtlety and instead emphasized the overall support available, regardless of its source. Many researchers focused on the presence of others in terms of the assistance they might provide, particularly in stressful situations. It had long been observed that some individuals handled stressful situations much better than others. What excited researchers was the possibility that help from others, whether it involved actual assistance or a virtual "pat on the back," might serve to moderate stress and ensure a more positive outcome. In studying what had now come to be called "social support" little attention was given to who did the supporting.

One partial exception to this rather cavalier attitude toward the source of the support was the work of Henderson (1977) who focused on two aspects of social support that he believed fulfilled very different roles in a person's life and health. He used a structured interview method to assess both the casual contacts with others that are part of a person's daily routine and also the role of the person with whom the support recipient felt most close. In the first case, he believed the casual contacts added to an individual's feelings of connection with others. Examples of this level of contact include casual greetings of neighbors and interactions at the bus stop with others who ride at the same time every day. In the second case, and for the present discussion the most relevant, the respondent was asked to select the individual with whom he or she had the most intimate or confiding relationship and then to respond to questions concerning the characteristics of that relationship. In his focus on this aspect of social support, Henderson was influenced by Bowlby's work on attachment (1969, 1977), discussed later in this chapter.

Despite Henderson's efforts, as the field of social support grew rapidly, the role of specific personal relationships was generally ignored. This was in part a function of the measuring instruments that began to be developed. Although a variety of questionnaires were created for research, most of them focused on asking the support recipient to report on the types and amount of support received and sometimes also the satisfaction with that support. One exception was the work of Procidano and Heller (1983), whose measure differentiated between support reported from family members and from friends. The second exception was the work of Sarason and his collaborators, who asked respondents to indicate by sets of initials specific individuals whom they considered to be available for support provision (I. G. Sarason, Levine, Basham, & Sarason, 1983). The rationale for this approach was that by focusing on actual relationships, the report of available support would be tied more closely to the individual's perceptions of each of these relationships and less to some general or global assessment that might be more affected by response bias. However, at this early stage neither Procidano and Heller nor Sarason et al. focused on specific relationships to the degree that now seems most productive.

Another way of assessing social relationships that included specific individuals but did not always focus on their supportive qualities was a network approach in which a schematic view of a person's relationships with others was developed. Using this method, some idea of the number of people considered part of the target person's network as well as the pattern of interrelationships among these individuals within the network could be constructed. However, within the field of psychology, the network methodology was not readily adapted to the statistical techniques available, so it was not often used as a research instrument. A somewhat simplified network approach was developed by Antonucci (1985), who used a diagram containing three concentric circles with the target person in the center to record not only the identity of specific people but also their perceived degree of closeness. This convoy model was especially useful in studying the changes in patterns as the target person grew older.

However, despite or in part because of the large number of measures that were, and are still being, developed and the various measurement approaches, the social support literature is replete with contradictions. Support was found to be at times a mediator and a times a moderator of stress (Cohen & Wills, 1985). In addition, support was sometimes found to be helpful and at other times either not effective or definitely negative in impact. Not only did these findings suggest that theory regarding social support needed to be refined, but they have also served as a major impediment to efficient and successful interventions. Relatively early in this flurry of test development, Heitzmann and Kaplan (1988) surveyed many of the available measures and the variables with which they correlated. They found that many, although not all, of the measures were sadly lacking in reliability and evidence of validity. They warned researchers that many of the results thus far available might be suspect as a result of the poor quality of many of the support measures used in the research. Later, B. R. Sarason, Shearin, Pierce, and Sarason (1987) compared several sets of measures by administering them to the same participants. Their work, as well as that of Barrera (1986), confirmed and strengthened the conclusion that results of using social support measures of different types were not at all comparable.

Most early questionnaire methods, and many still in use today, simply focus on whether people are available to provide support or companionship in each of a variety of situations. The support score consists of either the overall number of situations for which adequate support could be expected or divides these in some way, for instance, by the types of support, such as emotional support, information giving, and provision of concrete help, or the degree to which the support was satisfactory to the recipient or fit the situation. Alternately and less often, the number of people seen as support providers or the number of times help had been received over a specific period, for example, 6 months, is the focus of the measure. Although the various questionnaires assessing support availability show generally similar results, these reports of perceived available support do not correlate highly with reports of support that has been received (Barrera, 1986; B. R. Sarason et al., 1987). Further, only the measures that focus on available support are generally related to well-being and health outcomes. One reasonable explanation for this discrepancy is that people who receive a considerable amount of support are usually perceived by others to be in a very stressful situation, not to be coping well, or both (Dunkel-Schetter & Bennett, 1990).

Changing the Focus to Support in the Context of Relationships

Two conclusions have come from this work on social support. Both involve close personal relationships. The first relates to the importance of cognitive processes, influenced by earlier experience, in identifying the meaning of behaviors of others. The second suggests a focus on the dyadic aspects of social support. At least two individuals, the source of support and the intended recipient, are involved in every supportive transaction and in the majority of cases a close personal relationship exits between these two individuals. (The chapter on dyadic coping by Cutrona and Gardner in this volume reinforces the point that social support is an interactive process.)

Cognitive Processes and Social Support Perception

The importance of the cognitive aspects of social support or perceptions of availability as opposed to the behavioral aspects, such as receiving help, suggested that social support needs redefinition both to advance theory and to enhance prediction. A number of researchers had investigated perceptions of social support in the context of Bowlby's (1977) work on attachment (Henderson, 1977; B. R. Sarason et al., 1990). They suggested that early attachment experience might be an important determinant of support perceptions later in life, both on a cognitive level through expectations about relationship behavior and in the behavioral and emotional characteristics of the relationships formed in later life. The qualities of these past and present relationships could be expected to affect both current social support perception and provision. Recent work by Feeney and Cassidy (2003) demonstrated that despite how trained raters evaluated a taped laboratory-based conflict discussion between adolescents and their parents, when the adolescents rated the interaction immediately after it occurred, their ratings were generally congruent with their attachment status. Further, after 6 weeks had passed, the adolescents' perceptions of the interaction had shifted to bring them even more in line with their attachment-related representations of the parents. Thus, as time passed the attachment-related expectations were even more salient. These results are consistent with Bowlby's description of attachment schemata and the role they play in relationship expectations.

Bowlby and others also thought that these early relationship experiences might be important in later relationship choice. A number of researchers have supported this view by demonstrating that attachment status appears to be one determinant in later partner selection. Thus, partner choice may be determined in part by the apparent desire for predictable relationships. For example, those who are classified as securely attached are more likely than by chance to partner with someone of the same status (Collins & Read, 1990; J. Feeney, 1994). This argument has also been advanced as one explanation why some individuals consistently appear to make what might be considered "bad" relationship choices, for example, by perpetuating a childhood abusive relationship situation in the choice of an adult romantic partner (Sroufe & Fleeson, 1986). They suggested that this counterintuitive trend might be caused by the need for emotional regulation that was in part satisfied by the familiar type of relationship.

Specific Dyadic Relationships in Social Support Research

Relationship expectations also play a role in how supportive efforts are experienced. Several studies have shown that interpretation of the behaviors of one marital partner by the other can be predicted based on the couples' marital satisfaction. For example, in tension-provoking situations, individuals low in marital satisfaction tended to judge the intentions of their spouses more inaccurately than those high in marital satisfaction (Noller & Ruzzene, 1991). These researchers also found that husbands who were low in marital satisfaction tended to make more negative errors than those high in marital adjustment in interpreting their wives' behavior. Fincham and his colleagues have linked favorable causal attributions regarding spousal behavior to later marital satisfaction (Fincham & Bradbury, 1987, 1993). The meanings attached by recipients to efforts at support from others are also important

in assessing the impact of social support (Fisher, Nadler, & Whitcher-Alagna, 1982). For example, efforts to provide practical suggestions or even tangible assistance may carry with them negative appraisals in the eyes of the recipient, especially if the relationship is a generally conflictful one.

Often well-intentioned efforts to be supportive, either in a practical sense or through emotional support, can have a negative effect. Two general reasons have been suggested to explain why receipt of social support is not usually helpful in reducing distress in stressful situations. First, the support given may not be helpful or may even make things worse. Second, the receipt of support may have a negative effect on self esteem if the provider is not sensitive to the needs of the intended recipient. A study by Bolger and his associates (Bolger, Zuckerman, & Kessler, 2000) investigated support provision and receipt through a daily diary technique. The purpose of the study was to help clarify the general finding that in many cases actual support transactions do not aid adjustment to stressful life situations (Barrera, 1986; Dunkel-Schetter & Bennett, 1990; Wethington & Kessler, 1986), but perceptions of support availability are generally related to positive outcomes.

The participants in the Bolger et al. (2000) study were couples who lived together during the period when one of them, a law student, was preparing to take the bar exam. The use of the diary format and the participation of both members of the relationship dyad allowed the researchers to match reports of emotional support giving and emotional support receipt on a daily basis. The results indicated that support reported by the giver and acknowledged by the recipient was not helpful in allieviating stress and depressed mood. Instead, what the researchers called *silent support*, support reported to have been provided but not reported to have been received, was the effective factor in reducing depression level of the student preparing for the bar exam. The recipient apparently benefited from the support because it was not perceived as such, so there were no emotional costs from its receipt. Although some support may be carried out beyond the awareness of the recipient, such as dealing with problems before they come to the attention of the person under stress or what Coyne and Smith (1991) called protective buffering, Bolger et al. (2000) suggested that what was protective in this study was the skillful way the support was administered so that the recipient did not code the transaction as enacted support. This study illustrates how taking a dyadic view of social support in the context of close relationships can shed light on questions that have troubled researchers for a number of years.

Lehmann, Ellard, and Wortman (1986) also provided examples of attempts of emotional support offered in a stressful situation – in this case, to bereaved individuals. They suggested that the stressful nature of the bereavement situation made it more difficult for the would-be supporters to respond as sensitively as they might in more benign interactions. Some of the same reasoning was advanced by Coyne and Bandura and their colleagues (Coyne & Smith, 1991; Taylor, Bandura, Ewart, Miller, & DeBusk, 1985) in separate studies of spousal interactions in which one member had a serious medical condition. In both instances, provision of appropriate support, often encouragement following a medical regimen, was difficult for the well individual. It appeared that the potential loss of the spouse was so threatening that it interfered with support provision. Taylor et al. (1985) were able to demonstrate this by giving the patients' wives experience with the exercise regimen prescribed for their post–heart attack spouses. As a result the wives became more supportive of their husbands' participation because the exercise no longer appeared to them as too strenuous for someone who had experienced a heart attack.

These studies also illustrate that both relationship factors and the emotions engendered by stressful events involving a relationship partner affect the quality and appropriateness of support that might be given under other circumstances. Other examples of well-intentioned but misguided support efforts come from research on pain. Support by spouses and family members often serves as a deterrent for the person with the pain problems in resumption of normal levels of activity. This misguided support can either be in the form of offering concrete help that minimizes the patient's physical activity or emotional support that reduces patient motivation to become more active despite physicians' recommendations for resumption of more normal activity levels (Jamison & Virts, 1991; Turk, Kerns, & Rosenberg, 1992).

Social Support and the Negative Aspects of Relationships

Some of the earliest epidemiologically based work investigating the role of social support in future poor health or mortality used marital status as a measure of social support. Although this simple measure was somewhat useful in prediction when a very large sample was used, its predictive qualities for individuals were weakened because both positive and negative aspects of the relationship were ignored. Relatively early in the history of social support research Rook and Pietromonaco (1987) called attention to the *paradox of close relationships*, by which they meant that close relationships can be sources of conflict, strain, and disappointment, as well as of positive feelings and experiences. Coyne and DeLongis (1986), who were early in adopting the cognitive view of relationships discussed earlier, pointed out the importance of studying specific relationships not only in terms of the supportive behavior that occurred but how the behavior was interpreted. They noted that whether the behavior was interpreted by the recipient to be supportive was based not only on the behavior per se but also on other aspects of the relationship between the recipient and the supporter.

Yet despite this important insight, social support measures generally focused on positive aspects of general social interactions until the development of the Quality of Relationships Inventory (QRI) by Pierce and his associates (Pierce, Sarason, & Sarason, 1991). The QRI was designed to strengthen two of the weak points in social support assessment, its global nature and its removal from the context of other aspects of relationships. The QRI focused on aspects of an individual's relationship with a specific person, and it contained three separate scales by which to assess the relationship – support, depth or importance of the relationship in one's life, and conflict. Use of these scales made assessment of the cognitive aspects of social support more exact because the support could be seen in the context of these other aspects of the relationship between a particular pair of individuals. In both laboratory and in clinical settings, the QRI has been shown to enhance prediction of psychological health beyond that obtained from a general social support measure and demonstrated that social support perceptions are truly dyadic and specific to the individuals involved. For example, predictions based on a student's QRI about his or her mother predicted the student's appraisal of later behavior attributed to the mother, although the QRI data about his or her father did not (Pierce, Sarason, & Sarason, 1992). Even though the student's QRI ratings of the two parents were correlated, they were sensitive to differences in the two relationships.

Levels of Analysis in Social Support

Sarason and her colleagues (B. R. Sarason, Pierce, Bannerman, & Sarason, 1993) demonstrated that measures of perceived social support between family members were related but dyad specific. In a complex study, Branje and her colleagues (Branje, van Aken, & van Lieshout, 2002) expanded on this finding. In their study of dyadic support perceptions within families consisting of parents and two adolescent children, they found that four separate relationship-related support effects independently contributed to the prediction of the perceived relational support for each dyadic relationship. These effects included perceiver variance, that is,

the contribution of the recipient partner variance; the contribution of the support giver; relationship variance, that is, the role in the family (mother, father, older sibling, younger sibling); and family variance, that is, the general level of family support perceived by each participant. The percent of the variance contributed by each of these variables differed depending on the family relationship of the dyad members. For instance, the adolescents' support perceptions were mainly explained by either their own characteristics as perceivers or the general sense of support held by all family members. This finding buttresses the assertion by several authors that one aspect of social support is the general sense of support produced through early supportive interactions within the family as suggested by Bowlby's discussion of early attachment (Lakey & Dickinson, 1994; B. R. Sarason et al., 1993). In contrast, for the marital relationship, perceived support was predicted much more by the dyadic qualities of the relationship than any of the other variables. The results of the Branje et al. (2002) study suggest that relational factors are the primary predictors of perceived support within couple relationships and confirmed earlier findings by Lakey and his coworkers (Lakey, McCabe, Fisicaro, & Drew, 1996). The study illustrates the importance of several aspects of specific relationships in the provision of social support.

Other Relationship Functions to Consider

In considering what goes on in close relationships, it is obvious that they serve a number of different functions with respect to personal health and well-being. Social support is perhaps one of the most widely researched, but others – in particular, companionship and social control – also play important roles. One of the problems with many ways of assessing social support is that these aspects of interaction in close relationships are comingled so the definitions and conclusions continue to be fuzzy.

Companionship and Social Support Are Not the Same

Rook (1989) pointed out that many of the positive behaviors that occur in close relationships and contribute to positive outcomes should be classified as companionate, not as socially supportive. Unlike social support behaviors, which have an intended purpose, these companionship behaviors have no intrinsic function, yet they supply important pleasures that affect daily life. They provide satisfaction simply by participation. Companionate activities also have an important expressive function; they may have positive effects on mood and feelings of well-being. Rook (1989, 1990) found that companionship had a general effect on psychological well-being and served as a buffer against relatively minor life stresses. Social support, in contrast, often served to ameliorate major life stresses but had little or no effect on minor ones.

One way to help clarify this distinction between companionship and social support was advanced by Cutrona (1986) when she suggested that categorizing behavior in close relationships as socially supportive should be limited to those behaviors that occur when the recipient is perceived to be experiencing stress. Although this definition might be helpful, it is also problematic in its narrowness and also because most measures that assess social support include items that deal with companionship as well. An example of such an item might be, "When I want to go to the movies, there is someone I can ask to go with me."

Close Relationships and Social Control

Health psychologists use the term *social control* to draw attention to an important function of close relationships, such as marriage, in the regulation of healthful lifestyle and behavior. One effect of social control may be indirect. As a result of a sense of personal obligation to others, individuals involved in close personal relationships may refrain from risky activities such as scuba diving or rock climbing. Their concern for the consequences to others of their possible injury or death may serve as a deterrent for such activities and as a spur toward positive health behaviors. Large epidemiological surveys have shown that both marriage and parenthood often facilitate self-regulation by the choice of positive health behaviors and the reduction of negative ones (Umberson, 1987). However, these survey measures are not sensitive enough for prediction on an individual level.

Health psychologists have focused more attention on the second broad aspect of social control, the efforts of network members, especially those closest to an individual, to foster a change in his or her health-related behaviors. This may take the form of encouraging health promoting behaviors, monitoring health-related behaviors, or seeking to prohibit those that are potentially injurious to health. Marital partners who attempt to control the behaviors of their spouse are more likely to be women than men (Umberson, 1992). Perhaps for this reason, in terms of mortality, marriage has been found to be more beneficial for men than for women (Orth-Gomer, 1994). However, the degree of satisfaction in the marriage was found to be more important for health outcomes for women than for men. In a long-term study of marriages, women in marriages that the participants considered unsatisfactory in some way experienced more physical and mental health problems than did their husbands, whereas in marriages considered satisfactory to both husbands and wives, the health of both participants was equal (Levenson, Carstensen, & Gottman, 1993). Brown and Harris (1978) also found that women with unsatisfactory marital relationships were more protected from mental health problems if they had a close friend or confidant. In this case, the marital relationship served as a stressor rather than as a support.

It is likely that a spouse's attempts at social control may have negative effects on the marital relationship. One unanswered question is whether efforts to assert control, in themselves, provide the frustration or whether continued attempts to alter a partner's behavior tend to be accompanied by negative interactions within the couple. In either case, both participants may experience increased negative mood. Another question is whether the manner in which social control is attempted and whether the efforts are focused toward the elimination of negative health-related behaviors such as smoking or overuse of alcohol or toward the adoption of positive behaviors such as eating more fruits and vegetables or increasing exercise.

Little research has addressed these questions. An exception is a study that used a community-based sample rather than participants in a formal behavior change program to provide some insights into these issues. In this study, Lewis and Rook (1999) looked at the effects of efforts of encouragement both to stop behaviors that had a negative effect on health and to encourage those that might have a positive effect. They found that efforts at social control were quite commonly experienced among those they surveyed. Both married and unmarried people reported that they were the target of efforts at social control from people in their social network. This finding constitutes yet another argument as to the inadequacy of simply looking at whether a relationship exists rather than the qualities of a specific relationship. The reports of the participants indicated that among the most frequent efforts at social control they experienced were attempts to curb their smoking and drinking and efforts to encourage them to exercise. The more members of their network who participated in these social control efforts and the greater the frequency of their efforts, the less likely were the recipients to increase health enhancing behaviors and the more likely they were to increase their negative behaviors. Thus, the greater the pressure to change, the more reactance they experienced. In contrast, when only one particular person in the network was involved in the change efforts, the more likely the behaviors were to change in the desired direction. However, even in these instances, the size of the change was generally small and many of those reporting said they made no changes at all. Positive control strategies were more likely to produce change, but they also produced negative emotions in the change target, including guilt and feelings of sadness. Recipients of negative strategies such as nagging reported that not only did these not produce change, they also caused them to have feelings of irritation and hostility as well as sadness and guilt. The quality of the relationship between the person urging the change and the change target thus seemed to have suffered from the social control efforts.

A problem with applying the concept of social control to close relationships is that it is often difficult to define how the control is exerted. Is a wife's advising a husband to go to the doctor an example of social control? The answer probably depends on how the advice is given and the husband's readiness to take it. Given in a certain way, the advice might be received gratefully as an indication of caring, given in another, the advice might produce a negative reaction. Another study, focused on smoking cessation, indicated that the context of the relationship seems to mediate the impact of specific supportive or not supportive behaviors (Cohen & Lichtenstein, 1990). Social control in close relationships involves much more about the quality of the relationship than simply whether such a relationship exists.

The work on social control and health indicates that the quality of the relationship serves as a filter through which the behaviors of the partner or close network member are interpreted.

Attachment As an Interactive Process

The study of attachment has implications for a better understanding of both social support and dyadic relationships as well as the ability to form close, satisfying relationships that are the main sources of effective social support. For one thing, attachment style may influence perceptions of behavior in close relationships. Attachment security has been defined as an inner resource that helps to protect people in periods of stress (Mikulincer & Florian, 1998). In much research attachment style is conceived of as a traitlike characteristic developed as a function of early experience in a close relationship with a caregiver. In this view, neither the persons nor the situation are considered to be particularly important. This conception, although common and often unacknowledged, is related to an idea expressed by Bowlby (1988). He believed that attachment begins as an interactive process but that over time the patterns of attachment become increasingly the property of the child because they are internalized into what Bowlby called working models. However, as work on adult attachment has progressed, this view is clearly too simple. Hazan and Shaver (1987), whose work was primarily responsible for initiating interest in adult attachment, took a more complex view. They argued that the security in a particular relationship is likely to be a "joint function of attachment style and factors unique to *particular partners* and circumstances" (1987, p. 3) [emphasis added].

The picture may become even more complex if, as Kirkpatrick and Hazan (1994) viewed it, people seek out relationships and environments that are in accord with their existing views of the world. Not only does the attachment category of each partner seem to matter, but how they combine or interact is also important. In these studies of so-called couple types, only two attachment categories, secure and insecure, were ordinarily used, so that the participants fell into one of three categories, both secure, both insecure, or mixed (one secure, one insecure). To add to the complexity, the gender of the secure and insecure partners in mixed couples proved to be important (Sumer, 2000). Recent research has shown that interactional effects of the attachment dimensions of the two partners are quite common although the effects are more likely to be found for women than for men (Feeney, 2003). Feeney suggested that this may be a result of women's greater ability to buffer their partner's insecurity. There is some evidence that women may be more able to empathize with the emotional state of others and may be more likely to do so

(e.g., see Guerrero & Reiter, 1998). Thus, secure attachment status in women may more greatly facilitate partner interactions because women tend to be more active in offering support in close relationships than are men (Shumaker & Hill, 1991). Research also has revealed that women who are anxious about their relationship (insecurely attached) were particularly disadvantaged because their partners were less likely to offer support whether or not they were securely attached (Feeney, Noller, & Roberts, 2000).

Empathy, Close Relationships, and Social Support

As part of his theorizing on attachment, Bowlby (1977, 1988) emphasized the role of empathy and emotional sensitivity. He believed that secure attachment was brought about by what he called "sensitive parenting." By this he meant that the parent could understand and respond appropriately to the emotional needs of the child in a variety of situations. Bowlby suggested that a child's ability to respond sensitively to others arose in part from these early experiences and was a crucial feature in effective support provision and satisfaction in close relationships. Although this concept is appealing, research has been hampered by the difficulties of objectifying and measuring empathy and emotional sensitivity. More recently, research in the field of social psychology has explored empathic accuracy, a somewhat allied construct, although empathic accuracy is focused more on cognition and less on emotion and responding to others than attachment theory (Ickes, 1993, 1997).

Ickes developed a method for assessing empathetic accuracy in the interaction of strangers that was soon adapted to studies of couples in close relationships. The empathic accuracy studies led to some intriguing findings. In close relationship interactions, the participants did not seem to use behavioral information as a basis for empathetic judgments in any clear way (Thomas & Fletcher, 1997). Further, the longer the time in a well-functioning relationship, the less important empathic accuracy became. It was clearly important in the first 2 years of marriage, especially in dealing with relationship conflict, but then its strength began to weaken (Bissonnette, Rusbult, & Kilpatrick, 1997). In the early stages of marriage, accuracy inferring partner's thoughts and feelings enhances the relationship. As time goes on the relationship quality may be governed more by long-standing motives and habits rather than active efforts to understand what the partner is feeling and thinking. These findings have important implications for understanding social support perceptions in close relationships. Ickes's work may be interpreted as support for Bowlby's idea that satisfying relationships are built on the ability to perceive and respond to the thoughts and feelings of others. In Bowlby's view, this ability is fostered through early experiences with an empathetic and perceptive caretaker.

Bowlby also believed that early experience in relationships, if it is anxiety provoking, may result in the development of an anxious attachment style. Those who develop this type of relationship expectation may become skilled at scanning for clues as to what the other person is thinking or feeling because of a need to be on guard for possible threat. Work with empathic accuracy also shows this phenomenon. Simpson, Ickes, and Grich (1999) found that although highly anxious–ambivalent individuals were more empathically accurate in relationship-threatening situations, this resulted in greater distress and a feeling of decreased closeness. Thus, especially for certain types of individuals, enhanced understanding of what a partner is thinking or feeling may be detrimental to a relationship in circumstances in which partner's thoughts carry a negative message (Simpson, Orina, & Ickes, 2003).

Although the degree of overlap between Bowlby's and Ickes's approaches is not clear, both could be helpful in understanding more about how early attachment experiences affect both perceptions of availability of social support and the ability to provide appropriate support in close relationships. In addition to affecting the accurate perception of thoughts and feeling of others, working models derived from the initial attachment experience may affect how those thoughts and feelings are interpreted or the attributions made concerning them.

Attributions in Marital Relationships

The study of marital relationships is valuable because the marriage setting is a "laboratory" ideal for the study of social support and close relationships. The quality of their marital relationship is an important factor in how marital partners view each other and relationship-related negative events (Fincham & Bradbury, 1993). Spouses in positive relationships seem to make attributions that do not locate the cause of the problem in their partner but see it as a temporary thing unlikely to recur. In contrast, spouses in distressed relationships are likely to locate the cause of an untoward event in their partner and see it as stable or lasting and affecting many aspects of the relationship rather than a specific situation. However, both distressed and nondistressed couples showed a strong association between behavior and attributions (Johnson, Karney, Rogge, & Bradbury, 2001). Noller (1992) found that with respect to nonverbal behavior, spouses who were low in marital adjustment were not as accurate in their interpretations as spouses high in marital adjustment. In a study of married and unmarried couples involved in intimate romantic relationships, Manusov and her colleagues found that participants who had reported higher marital quality were more likely to note and to make attributions for positive behaviors than participants who had reported lower marital quality (Manusov, Floyd, & Kerssen-Griep, 1997).

Bringing Knowledge of Relationship Quality Into Social Support Research

We need to look beyond asking people about their overall or global level of social support.

Several recent developments can contribute to understanding the processes involved in social support and the consequences of social support. The study of close relationships and the support they provide seems promising. Work on attachment has shown that perceptions of the supportive aspects of relationships may be a function of the recipient's earlier relationship-related experiences.

It is also important to recognize that there are additional aspects of close relationships that may relate to the same types of outcomes that have been studied in the context of social support. To advance understanding of social support further, specific aspects of the relationship between the supporter and recipients, such as conflict should be considered. Also within a family setting, the individual dyadic relationships must be analyzed in addition to the overall gestalt of family integration and supportiveness. In stressful circumstances, where support most often seems appropriate, the effect of the stressor on the potential support giver as well as the intended recipient must also be taken into account. In some situations, a person attempting to give social support may be so distressed by the situation that support efforts can have a negative effect. For example, in recent years, the male partner of a woman giving birth is often encouraged to be present during labor and delivery to serve as a source of support. However, if he becomes upset in the situation, his efforts at support are likely to communicate his anxieties. In such cases, contrary to what might be expected, the presence of a supportive stranger, a trained paraprofessional who provides support may have a better outcome (Klaus & Kennell, 1997). The earlier examples of research on support efforts by wives of heart attack patients illustrate this same counterintuitive effect. In such situations, the needs of two people in a close relationship are in potential conflict in several ways. These include reconciling conflicting emotional needs, managing their distress as well as that of their partners, and providing appropriate practical support.

To understand how social support affects individuals, it is necessary to look at specific dyadic relationships and focus both on the interchanges within them and also consider other aspects of the quality of that relationship, such as the degree of conflict and the level of commitment it generally contains. This will enhance prediction by removing some of the "noise" in the association of the factors studied and should also provide clues as to the interpretation of behaviors of one individual by another. Looking at social support in the context of dyadic relationships is particularly essential. Not only are the perceptions of the recipient important, but those of the support giver are important as well. Just as the recipient may feel belittled or angry, rather than grateful, for the support, the giver may react with anger or may experience rejection by what he or she interprets a lack of appreciation of the supportive efforts.

Although the research examples given earlier in this chapter make clear the important insights by which the focus on dyadic relationships can enrich the support literature, efforts in this direction are relatively sparse. Yet lack of social support from partners has been identified by couples as one of the most important complaints leading to marital distress (Baxter, 1986). Marital satisfaction is associated in many studies with the provision of higher levels of social support to the partner (Acitelli & Antonucci, 1994; Cutrona, 1996). Further, social support within a marital couple has more than an effect on the immediate situation. It also makes a predictive contribution to marital satisfaction at least 2 years later and even when conflict behavior is considered, social support adds to the prediction of a positive outcome (Pasch & Bradbury, 1998).

Concluding Thoughts

The available evidence suggests the value of learning more about social support through the study of support efforts and expectations in the context of specific close relationships. This approach can profitably incorporate what research has shown about the importance of past relationship experience that affects the assessment of social support availability and how comfortable a person is with support receipt. In addition, focus on social support in a relationship context that takes account of the positive and negative aspects of the particular personal relationship involved is vital. Neglect of these variables not only may explain the many contradictions in the social support literature but also why so many supportive efforts fail.

References

Acitelli, L. K., & Antonucci, T. C. (1994). Gender differences in the link between marital support and satisfaction in older couples. *Journal of Personality and Social Psychology*, *76*, 688–698.

Antonucci, T. C. (1985). Social support: Theoretical advances, recent findings, and pressing issues. In I. G. Sarason & B. R. Sarason (Eds.), *Social support: Theory, research and applications* (pp. 21–38). Dordrecht, The Netherlands: Martinus Nijhoff.

Barrera, M., Jr. (1986). Distinction between social support concepts, measures, and models. *American Journal of Community Psychology*, *14*, 413–455.

Baxter, L. A. (1986). Gender differences in the heterosexual relationship rules embedded in breakup accounts. *Journal of Social and Personal Relationships*, *3*, 289–306.

Bissonnette, V. L., Rusbult, C. E., & Kilpatrick, S. D. (1997). Empathic accuracy and marital conflict resolution. In W. Ickes (Ed.), *Empathic accuracy* (pp. 251–281). New York: Guilford Press.

Bolger, N., Zuckerman, A., & Kessler, R. C. (2000). Invisible support and adjustment to stress. *Journal of Personality and Social Psychology*, *79*, 953–961.

Bowlby, J. (1969). *Attachment and loss: Vol. I. Attachment*. New York: Basic Books.

Bowlby, J. (1977). The making and breaking of affectional bonds: I. Aetiology and psychopathology in the light of attachment theory. *British Journal of Psychiatry*, *130*, 201–210.

Bowlby, J. (1988). Developmental psychiatry comes of age. *American Journal of Psychiatry*, *145*, 1–10.

Branje, S. J., van Aken, M. A., & van Lieshout, C. F. M. (2002). Relational support in families with adolescents. *Journal of Family Psychology*, *16*, 351–362.

Brown, G., & Harris, T. (1978). *Social origins of depression*. New York: Free Press.

Cassel, J. (1976). The contributions of the social environment to host resistance. *American Journal of Epidemiology*, *104*, 107–123.

Cobb, S. (1976). Social support as a moderator of life stress. *Psychosomatic Medicine*, *38*, 300–314.

Cohen, S., & Lichtenstein, E. (1990). Partner behaviors that support quitting smoking. *Journal of Consulting and Clinical Psychology*, *58*, 304–309.

Cohen, S., & Wills, T. A. (1985) Stress, social support, and the buffering hypothesis. *Psychological Bulletin*, *98*, 310–357.

Collins, N. L., & Read, S. J. (1990). Adult attachment: Working models, and relationship quality in dating couples. *Journal of Personality and Social Psychology*, *58*, 644–663.

Coyne, J. C., & DeLongis, A. M. (1986). Going beyond social support: The role of social relationships in adaptation. *Journal of Consulting and Clinical Psychology*, *54*, 454–460.

Coyne, J. C., & Smith, D. A. F. (1991). Couples coping with myocardial infarction: A contextual perspective on wives' distress. *Journal of Personality and Social Psychology*, *61*, 404–412.

Cutrona, C. E. (1986). Behavioral manifestations of social support: A microanalytic investigation. *Journal of Personality and Social Psychology*, *51*, 201–208.

Cutrona, C. E. (1996). Social support as a determinant of marital quality: The interplay of negative and supportive behaviors. In G. R. Pierce, B. R. Sarason, & I. G. Sarason (Eds.), *Handbook of social support and the family* (pp. 173–194). New York: Plenum.

Dunkel-Schetter, C., & Bennett, T. L. (1990). Differentiating the cognitive and behavioral aspects of social support. In B. R. Sarason, I. G. Sarason, & G. R. Pierce (Eds.), *Social support: An interactional view* (pp. 267–296). New York: Wiley.

Feeney, J. A. (1994). Attachment styles, communication patterns, and satisfaction across the life cycle of marriage. *Personal Relationships*, *1*, 333–348.

Feeney, J. A. (2003). The systemic nature of couple relationships: An attachment perspective.

In P. Erdman & T. Caffery (Eds.), *Attachment and family systems: Conceptual, empirical, and therapeutic relatedness* (pp. 139–163). New York: Brunner-Routledge.

Feeney, B. C., & Cassidy, J. (2003). Reconstructive memory related to adolescent-parent conflict interactions: The influence of attachment-related representations on immediate perceptions and changes in perceptions over time. *Journal of Personality and Social Psychology*, 85, 945–955.

Feeney, J. A., Noller, P., & Roberts, N. (2000). Attachment and close relationships (pp. 185–201). In C. Hendrick & S. S. Hendrick (Eds.), *Close relationships: A sourcebook*. Thousand Oaks, CA: Sage.

Fincham, F. D., & Bradbury, T. E. (1987). Marital satisfaction, depression, and attributions: A longitudinal analysis. *Journal of Personality and Social Psychology*, 53, 481–489.

Fincham, F. D., & Bradbury, T. E. (1993). The impact of attributions in marriage: A longitudinal analysis. *Journal of Personality and Social Psychology*, 64, 442–452.

Fisher, J. D., Nadler, A., & Whitcher-Algana, S. (1982). Recipient reactions to aid. *Psychological Bulletin*, 91, 27–54.

Guerrero, L. K., & Reiter, R. L. (1998). Expressing emotion: Sex differences in social skills and communicative responses to anger, sadness, and jealousy. In D. J. Canary & K. Dindia (Eds.), *Sex differences and similarities in communication* (pp. 321–350). Mahwah, NJ: Erlbaum.

Hazan, C., & Shaver, P. R. (1987). Romantic love conceptualized as an attachment process. *Journal of Personality and Social Psychology*, 52, 511–524.

Henderson, A. S. (1977). The social network, support, and neurosis: The function of attachment in adult life. *British Journal of Psychiatry*, 136, 574–583.

Heitzmann, C. A., & Kaplan, R. M. (1988). Assessment of methods for measuring social support. *Health Psychology*, 7, 75–109.

Ickes, W. (1993). Empathic accuracy. *Journal of Personality*, 61, 587–610.

Ickes, W. (Ed.). (1997). *Empathic accuracy*. New York: Guilford Press.

Jamison, R., & Virts, K. L. (1991). The influence of family support on chronic pain. *Behavior Research and Therapy*, 28, 283–287.

Johnson, M. D., Karney, B. R., Rogge, R., & Bradbury, T. N. (2001). The role of marital behavior in the longitudinal association between attributions and marital quality. In V. Manusov & J. H. Harvey (Eds.), *Attribution, communication, and close relationships* (pp. 173–192). Cambridge, England: Cambridge University Press.

Kirkpatrick, L. E., & Hazan, C. (1994). Attachment styles and close relationships: A four-year prospective study. *Personal Relationships*, 1, 123–142.

Klaus, M. H., & Kennell, J. H. (1997). The doula: An essential ingredient of childbirth rediscovered. *Acta Paediatrica*, 86, 1034–1036.

Lakey, B., & Dickinson, L. G. (1994). Antecedents of perceived support: Is perceived family environment generalized to new social relationships? *Cognitive Therapy and Research*, 18, 39–53.

Lakey, B., McCabe, K. M., Fisicaro, S. A., & Drew, J. B. (1996). Environmental and personal determinants of support perceptions: Three generalizability studies. *Journal of Personality and Social Psychology*, 70, 1270–1280.

Lehman, D. R., Ellard, J. H., & Wortman, C. B. (1986). Social support for the bereaved: Recipients' and providers' perspectives on what is helpful. *Journal of Consulting and Clinical Psychology*, 54, 438–446.

Levenson, R. W., Carstensen, L. L., & Gottman, J. M. (1993). Long-term marriage: Age, gender, and satisfaction. *Psychology and Aging*, 8, 301–313.

Lewis, M. A., & Rook, K. S. (1999). Social control in personal relationships: Impact on health behaviors and psychological distress. *Health Psychology*, 18, 63–71.

Manusov, V., Floyd, K., & Kerssen-Griep, J., (1997). Yours, mine, and ours: Mutual attributions for nonverbal behaviors in couples' interactions. *Communication Research*, 24, 234–260.

Mikulincer, M., & Florian, V. (1998). Attachment style and the mental representation of the self. *Journal of Personality and Social Psychology*, 69, 1203–1217.

Noller, P. (1992). Nonverbal communication in marriage. In R. S. Feldman (Ed.), *Applications of nonverbal behavioral theories and research* (pp. 31–59). Hillsdale, NJ: Erlbaum.

Noller, P., & Ruzzene, M. (1991). The effects of cognition and affect on marital communication. In G. J. O. Fletcher & F. D. Fincham (Eds.),

Affect and cognition in close relationships (pp. 203–233). Hillsdale, NJ: Erlbaum.

Orth-Gomer, K. (1994). International epidemiological evidence for a relationship between social support and cardiovascular disease. In S. A. Shumaker & S. M. Czaijkowski (Eds.), *Social support and cariovascular disease* (pp. 97–119). New York: Plenum.

Pasch, L. A., & Bradbury, T. N. (1998). Social support, conflict, and the development of marital dysfunction. *Journal of Consulting and Clinical Psychology, 66,* 219–230.

Pierce, G. R., Sarason, B. R., & Sarason, I. G. (1992). General and specific support expectations and stress as predictors of perceived supportiveness: An experimental study. *Journal of Personality and Social Psychology, 63,* 297–307.

Pierce, G. R., Sarason, I. G., & Sarason, B. R. (1991) General and relationship-based perceptions of social support: Are two constructs better than one? *Journal of Personality and Social Psychology, 61,* 1028–1039.

Procidano, M. E., & Heller, K. (1983). Measures of perceived social support from friends and from family: Three validation studies. *American Journal of Community Psychology, 11,* 1–24.

Rook, K. S. (1989). Strains in older adults' friendships. In R. G. Adams & R. Blieszner (Eds.), *Older adult friendships: Structure and processes* (pp. 164–194). Newbury Park, CA: Sage.

Rook, K. S. (1990). Social relationships as a source of companionship: Implications for older adults' psychological well-being. In B. R. Sarason, I. G. Sarason, & G. R. Pierce (Eds.), *Social support: An interactional view* (pp. 219–250). New York: Wiley.

Rook, K. S., & Pietromonaco, P. (1987). Close relationships: Ties that heal or ties that bind? In W. H. Jones & D. Perlman (Eds.), *Advances in personal relationships* (Vol. 1, pp. 1–35). Greenwich, CT: JAI Press.

Sarason, B. R., Pierce, G. R., Bannerman, A., & Sarason, I. G. (1993). Investigating the antecedents of perceived social support: Parents' view of and behavior toward their children. *Journal of Personality and Social Psychology, 65,* 1071–1085.

Sarason, B. R., Pierce, G. R., & Sarason, I. G. (1990). Social support: Sense of acceptance and the role of relationshhips. In B. R. Sarason, I. G., Sarason, & G. R. Pierce (Eds.), *Social support: An interactional view* (pp. 97–128). New York: Wiley.

Sarason, B. R., Shearin, E. N., Pierce, G. R., & Sarason, I. G. (1987). Interrelationships among social support measures: Theoretical and practical implications. *Journal of Personality and Social Psychology, 52,* 813–832.

Sarason, I. G., Levine, H. M., Basham, R. B., & Sarason, B. R. (1983). Assessing social support: The social support questionnaire. *Journal of Personality and Social Psychology, 49,* 469–480.

Shumaker, S. A., & Hill, D. R. (1991). Gender differences in social support and physical health. *Health Psychology, 10,* 102–111.

Simpson, J. A., Ickes, W., & Grich, J. (1999). When accuracy hurts: Reactions of anxious–ambivalent dating partners to a relationship-threatening situation. *Journal of Personality and Social Psychology, 76,* 754–769.

Simpson, J. A., Orina, M. M., & Ickes, W. (2003). When accuracy hurts and when it helps: A test of the empathic accuracy model in marital interactions. *Journal of Personality and Social Psychology, 85,* 881–893.

Sroufe, L. A., & Fleeson, J. (1986). Attachment and the construction of relationships. In W. W. Hartup & Z. Rubin (Eds.), *Relationships and development* (pp. 51–71). Hillsdale, NJ: Erlbaum.

Sumer, N. (2000, June). *The interplay between attachment models and interpersonal schemas among married couples.* Paper presented at the Second Joint conference of ISSPR and INPR, Brisbane, Australia.

Taylor, C. B., Bandura, A., Ewart, C. K., Miller, N. H., & DeBusk, R. F. (1985). Exercise testing to enhance wives' confidence in their husband's cardiac capability soon after clinically uncomplicated myocardial infarction. *American Journal of Cardiology, 55,* 635–638.

Thomas, G., & Fletcher, G. J. O. (1997). Empathetic accuracy in close relationships. In W. Ickes (Ed.). *Empathic accuracy* (pp. 194–217). New York: Guilford Press.

Turk, D.C., Kerns, R. D., & Rosenberg, R. (1992). Effects of marital interaction on chronic pain and disability: Examining the down side of social support. *Rehabilitation Psychology, 37,* 259–274.

Umberson, D. (1987). Family status and health behaviors: Social control as a dimension of social integration. *Journal of Health and Social Behavior, 28*, 306–319.

Umberson, D. (1992). Gender, marital status, and the social control of health behavior. *Social Science and Medicine, 34*, 907–917.

Wethington, E., & Kessler, R. C. (1986). Perceived support, received support, and adjustment to stressful life events. *Journal of Health and Social Behavior, 27*, 78–89.

CHAPTER 24

Understanding Couple Conflict

Galena H. Kline
Nicole D. Pleasant
Sarah W. Whitton
Howard J. Markman

Understanding Couple Conflict

Couple conflict is seen as a generic risk factor for a host of mental and physical health problems for adults and children (Coie et al., 1993). It has received widespread attention in the couple research field because of its links to relationship dissatisfaction, divorce, domestic violence, functioning at work, parenting, and child outcomes (for overviews, see Booth, Crouter, & Clements, 2001; Cox & Brooks-Gunn, 1999; for historical perspectives, see Raush, Barry, Hertel, & Swain, 1974; Gurman & Rice, 1975). Managing conflict is often a target, if not the main target, of couple interventions (Halford & Markman, 1997).

In this chapter, we first discuss what couple conflict is and provide examples of ways that researchers have measured conflict. Then, we provide a developmental context for couple conflict. We next examine the importance of understanding couple conflict because of its relation to relationship satisfaction and then discuss example risk factors for couple conflict. Lastly, we discuss specific, problematic patterns in how couples manage conflict and devote a significant amount of space to interventions for couple conflict.

Defining Conflict

Interpersonal conflict has been defined as an interaction between persons expressing opposing interests, views, or opinions (Bell & Blakeney, 1977) or, based on the work of Lewin (1948), as interactions in which partners "hold incompatible goals" (Bradbury, Rogge, & Lawrence, 2001). Some degree of conflict is typically considered a normative aspect of romantic relationships (Markman, Stanley, Blumberg, Jenkins, & Whiteley, 2004), and some have pointed out that it is not the amount of conflict that matters in relationships as much as the way conflict is handled (e.g., Markman, Renick, Floyd, Stanley, & Clements, 1993). Indeed, numerous studies have found associations between conflict management and relationship satisfaction (e.g., Gill, Christensen, & Fincham, 1999).

Aside from these definitions, there are many ways that researchers have conceptualized conflict. For example, some have made the distinction between overt and covert conflict (Beach, 2001; Whittaker & Bry, 1991), signifying that conflict is not always expressed *outwardly*. The majority of studies on couple conflict examine the more easily measured overt conflict, such as disagreements, arguments, verbal aggression, and, in some cases, physical violence, but it may also be important to examine conflict that may be expressed in other ways, such as avoidance of issues, negative body language, or spiteful behavior. While conflict can be considered on a continuum of severity, some have made the case that researchers should consider typologies of conflict (e.g., Gottman, 1993; Gottman, Markman, & Notarius, 1977; Ridley, Wilhelm, & Surra, 2001), especially violent conflict (Gelles, 1991; M. P. Johnson, 2001; Waltz, Babcock, Jacobson, & Gottman, 2000). While we include information on research that examines both violent and nonviolent conflict, the main focus of this chapter is on conflict without violence. The literatures on physical violence and conflictual interactions are somewhat distinct, and reviewing the violence literature is beyond the scope of this chapter. See Johnson's chapter in this volume for more information on couple violence.

Measuring Conflict

Measuring conflict accurately is important in research on couple relationships. Some scales are designed to measure the topics on which couples disagree. For example, the Marital Agendas Protocol (Notarius & Vanzetti, 1983; based on Knox, 1971) provides a list of possible topics of conflict, such as household tasks, money, children, jealousy, and in-laws and asks participants to rate the degree to which each area is a problem for the relationship.

A wide variety of scales is available for measuring how couples handle conflict. One of the most widely used instruments is the Conflict Tactics Scales (see Archer, 1999,

for a review). The measure asks individuals whether several behaviors have occurred and how frequently he or she and his or her partner have performed each one in the past year. The first version focused on couples' use of reasoning and on verbal and physical aggression in handling conflict (Straus, 1979). A 78-item revised version now includes subscales for minor and severe dimensions of negative conflict management, sexual coercion, physical injury, as well as distinctions between cognitive and emotional negotiation (positive forms of conflict management; Straus, Hamby, Boney-McCoy, & Sugarman, 1996). Other measures assess the broader construct of couple communication and many of these measures assess self-reported communication specifically about conflictual issues. For example, the Communication Patterns Questionnaire (Heavey, Larson, Zumtobel, & Christensen, 1996) measures several dimensions of communication about problems in relationships, including a measure of the demand–withdrawal pattern discussed later in this chapter. The Communication Skills Test, developed by Jenkins and Saiz (see Saiz, 2001; Stanley et al., 2001), is another example of a measure designed to assess several dimensions of communication about relationship problems (e.g., problem-solving skills, withdrawal, level of conflict, invalidation). A brief (eight-item) measure developed by Stanley and Markman (1997) is also available for assessing interaction characteristics predictive of relationship distress (e.g., negative escalation, invalidation, negative interpretations, withdrawal; see description in Kline, Stanley, et al., 2004).

Some measures are available to tap differential perspectives on conflict in the relationship. The Conflict Tactics Scale (described earlier) includes questions about one's partner's behavior and the Conflicts and Problem-Solving Scales asks participants to rate both themselves and their partners on dimensions of conflict, such as verbal aggression and collaboration (Kerig, 1996). These scales provide unique opportunities to examine both partners' views on conflict management.

Scales have also been designed specially to measure couple conflict in parental relationships. For example, the O'Leary–Porter Scale asks parents to rate items concerning how much interparental conflict their children witness (Porter & O'Leary, 1980). Additionally, the Children's Perceptions of Interparental Conflict Scale (Grych, Seid, & Fincham, 1992) and a briefer version of this measure developed for use with young adults (Kline, Wood, & Moore, 2003) address children's assessment of their parents' conflict.

Lastly, observational methods are often used to obtain independent ratings of couple communication and conflict. Although many observational coding systems examine broader issues in couple interactions, such as positive and negative dimensions of couple communication, many have subscales specifically examining couple conflict (Markman & Notarius, 1987). For example, the Interactional Dimensions Coding System has a conflict subscale that assesses the level of tension, hostility, disagreement, antagonism, and negative affect an individual displays during a videotaped interaction (Kline, Julien, et al., 2004). One benefit of using observational methods is that they contribute to a multimethod assessment of couple conflict when combined with self-report, making for a stronger, more well-rounded assessment of conflict. In addition, observational methods are designed to be objective. That is, raters do not rate partners' behavior based on what is socially desirable, nor are they influenced by outside factors that self-reporters might be influenced by (e.g., what happened between partners in the car just before completing the forms). While conflict during laboratory visits is likely prognostic of conflict at home, the conflict that couples display while being videotaped is likely less severe than at home (Fincham, 2003).

A Developmental Perspective

Stages of relationship development can be broadly characterized by dating, cohabitation, and marriage. Most adults will experience each of these stages at some point during their lives, and many couples move through them linearly, with around 65% of couples in the United States now living together before marriage (Bumpass & Lu, 2000). Each stage or type may be associated with different levels of conflict and different ways of managing conflict.

DATING

In most cases, dating relationships first occur in adolescence when individuals are beginning to form strong peer relationships and explore conflict-management styles within and outside the family (Hartup, 1992). Whereas conflict with romantic partners typically occurs less frequently than with family members during early and middle adolescence, conflict occurs as frequently with romantic partners as is it does with family members in late adolescence (Furman & Buhrmester, 1992). The way one handles conflict within family relationships are related to how one manages conflict in romantic relationships. As an example, Reese-Weber and Bartle-Haring (1998) found that negative conflict management styles in adolescent sibling relationships were related to styles in romantic relationships. In the same study, adolescents who used attacking, avoiding or compromising tactics with parents were likely to use these tactics with romantic partners. In a study of high schoolers, Feldman and Gowen (1998) examined several types of conflict management with romantic partners, including overt anger, violence, compromise, avoidance, distraction, and social support seeking. Compromise was reported most often, followed by distraction and avoidance; the use of compromise increased with age.

Adults, of course, also experience dating relationships. Much of the research on adult dating relationships, however, has focused on college students who may or may not adequately represent dating experiences of other adults (e.g., Larson, Peterson, Heath, & Birch, 2000; Levy, Wambolt, & Fiese, 1997; Reedy, 2002). One of the factors shown to affect conflict management within college student dating relationships is one's capacity for intimacy (i.e., self-disclosure, trust, and interdependence). Sanderson and Karetsky (2002) found that desiring intimacy in romantic relationships was associated with positive conflict management, such as the use of open discussion during conflict and showing concern for one's partner's feelings. The use of these conflict management strategies was also associated with increased relationship satisfaction (Sanderson & Karetsky, 2002).

COHABITATION

Research suggests that the conflict in cohabiting relationships versus dating and married relationships tends to be more violent. For example, cohabiters are nearly twice as likely as daters to be physically abusive toward their partners even when controlling for factors such as aggressiveness in adolescence, education level, stress, relationship duration, time spent together, relationship quality, balance of power, social ties, and religiosity (Kline, Stanley, et al., 2004; Magdol, Moffitt, & Caspi, 1998). Cohabitation appears to be a risk factor for violent conflict, particularly given that cohabiters have higher rates of partner violence than marrieds as well as daters (Stets, 1991).

MARRIAGE

The vast majority of research on conflict has been conducted with married couples. Indeed, nearly all of the research described in this chapter was conducted with married couples. Here, we highlight some basic findings about top issues and frequency of conflict in marriage.

What do couples experience conflict about most frequently? Longitudinal research suggests that before marriage, couples report money, jealousy, and relatives as top issues. Early in their marriages and just after the birth of a first child, the same couples reported money, sex, and communication as top issues, indicating that areas of conflict likely change with relationship development

(Storaasli & Markman, 1990). A national phone survey of married individuals asked in open-ended fashion about their top issues (Stanley, Markman, & Whitton, 2002). This research suggests that money is the top issue for first-time marriages, followed by children. However, for remarried couples, conflict over children was reported most often, followed by money (Stanley et al., 2002).

How often do couples experience conflict? According to some research, long-term married couples report only one or two disagreements per month (McGonagle, Kessler, & Schilling, 1992). Other research using observational coding of family dinners suggests one or two conflicts per *meal* (Vuchinich, 1987). It is important to note that individuals (both researchers and research participants) may have different ideas on what constitutes a disagreement, and in some cases, disagreements may not be associated with conflict per se. More research is needed to describe better the frequency of conflict in marriage, particularly research in which conflict is operationally defined clearly. Studies that employ daily diary methods (e.g., Almeida, McGonagle, Cate, Kessler, & Wethington, 2003) may be particularly useful in this area of research.

There may also be important changes in marital conflict (both in level and type) across the life span (see Zietlow & Sillars, 1988). For example, Jacobson and Christensen (1998), in their book on Integrative Couple Therapy, suggested that older couples are more difficult to treat with traditional behavioral techniques that teach conflict management skills. Further, they suggested that it may be that younger couples experience more overt conflict than older couples. For younger couples, conflict may be a key predictor of divorce. Older couples may be more likely to report a lack of positives aspects, such as intimacy and friendship, being the reason for desiring a divorce. These are empirical questions that future research could address.

Conflict, Relationship Satisfaction, and Divorce

It is generally recognized that destructive couple conflict (i.e., poorly managed conflict) is a risk for dissatisfaction and divorce (e.g., Clements, Stanley, & Markman, 2004) and 61% of divorced individuals cite "too much arguing" as a reason for divorce (C. A. Johnson et al., 2002). However, the connection between conflict and relationship outcomes is not exceedingly straightforward (for an overview, see Gill et al., 1999). Some suggest that low satisfaction leads to destructive conflict management (Marchand & Hock, 2000), whereas others have demonstrated that reductions in destructive conflict-management through preventive interventions are associated with higher satisfaction later on (Markman, Floyd, Stanley, & Storaasli, 1988).

Much longitudinal research has examined the effects of destructive conflict and marital outcomes (see Karney & Bradbury, 1995; Markman & Hahlweg, 1993). Markman and colleagues' early longitudinal research on whether couples' interactions predicted marital distress and divorce was the first to videotape couples discussing conflicts and have both the couples themselves as well as outside observers code the interactions (Markman, 1979; Markman, Duncan, Storaasli, & Howes, 1987; Markman & Hahlweg, 1993). This type of research identified several conflict-management characteristics that distinguished successful marriages from those that ended in divorce or distress (i.e., danger signs noted earlier such as invalidation, escalation, negative interpretations, and withdrawal). One of the most important findings from this early work was that these danger signs were apparent years before relationship dissatisfaction and distress developed. These findings led to a theory of marital dissolution that reflects a process of erosion (Markman, 1979; Stanley et al., 1999). According to this theory, deficits in conflict management exist in relationships from the start but become more important as couples try to negotiate expectations, problems, and stressors over time. Surprisingly (at the time), negative interaction was a stronger predictor of negative outcomes than positive interaction a predictor of positive outcomes. For example, couples headed for distress and divorce did not differ in amounts of validation during premarital conflict discussions but differed dramatically in terms of invalidation (e.g., put downs, criticism; Markman et al., 1987). Thus, couples destined to become distressed had more in common than couples destined to stay happy over time. The clinical implication of these findings was that interventions were developed to teach couples to avoid danger signs and manage conflict constructively, rather than teaching a formula for marital success (Notarius & Markman, 1993).

In more recent years, researchers have focused on ways to further examine the association between conflict and marital satisfaction. Gill et al. (1999) tested a social learning perspective (essentially suggesting that negativity leads to dissatisfaction) versus a negative confrontation model. The negative confrontation model was based on research suggesting that unpleasant interactions in which one partner (usually the female) confronts the other about marital problems are essential for resolving problems and achieving long-term marital satisfaction (Gottman & Krokoff, 1989; see Woody & Costanzo, 1990 for a critique of this study). Gill et al. (1999) found support for the social learning perspective, particularly for wives, in that aversive communication predicted declines in satisfaction, whereas positive communication predicted increases in satisfaction.

Other research on conflict and satisfaction has examined negative behavior in the context of the amount of positive behaviors in relationships. For example, based on their research, Notarius and Markman (1993) proposed a "relationship bank account" model. They coined the now well-know mathematical metaphor that one "zinger" can erase 5 or 10 positive acts of kindness. Stated another way, couples need to add deposits to the relationship bank account regularly to offset the inevitable negative interactions.

In a similar line of thinking, Gottman and colleagues (Gottman, 1993; Gottman & Levenson, 1992) divided married couples into two types based on the balance between negativity and positivity in their conflict interactions. In regulated (stable) couples, both partners show significantly more positive than negative speaker behavior during conflict discussions. In contrast, in nonregulated (unstable) couples, at least one partner showed more negative than positive conflict behaviors when speaking. There is evidence that these categories of conflict styles are predictive of couple outcomes. Nonregulated couples demonstrated significantly lower marital satisfaction and were more likely to consider ending their marriage, separate, and divorce during the following 4 years than regulated couples (Gottman, 1979; Gottman, 1993; Gottman & Levenson, 1992). Further, the ratio of negative to positive conflict behaviors best discriminated between regulated and nonregulated couples (i.e., the ratio did better at classifying couples than did the raw number of positive or negative behaviors or the difference between number of positive and negative codes; Gottman & Levenson, 1992). Based on these results, Gottman and colleagues proposed that marital stability may be based not in the ability to exclude all negative behaviors from conflicts, but in the ability to maintain a fairly high balance of positive to negative behaviors (positive to negative ratios of approximately five to one). Thus, multiple lines of research have suggested that it is important to consider positive and negative behavior in conflict management with regard to marital outcomes.

Another important distinction to make in regard to conflict and marital outcomes is dissatisfaction versus divorce. For example, in a longitudinal study, divorce was tied more closely to individual risk factors, whereas satisfaction was more related to observed conflict management (Rogge & Bradbury, 1999). Other longitudinal research corroborates the point that there may be differences in what predicts divorce versus dissatisfaction (Clements et al., 2004).

In conclusion, to attribute negative marital outcomes solely to a mismanagement of marital conflict would be too simplistic. Conflict is associated with satisfaction, but other factors, such as individual characteristics, life events, and the positive aspects of relationships, play important roles as well (Bradbury et al., 2001; Stanley, Blumberg, & Markman, 1999). Stanley et al. (1999) suggested that destructive conflict erodes the positive aspects in marriages, turning a loving relationship into one in which "the presence of the partner becomes increasingly associated with pain and frustration" (p. 282).

Correlates of and Risk Factors for Conflict

Another consideration in understanding couple conflict is the circumstances that may make some couples susceptible to conflict or may accompany conflict. Conflict has been associated with a host of risk factors, life changes, and consequences (see Almeida et al., 2003; Booth et al., 2001). In this section, we highlight a small sampling of factors associated with couple conflict; it is by no means an exhaustive list.

FAMILY BACKGROUND

There is a large body of research examining family background characteristics and child and adult outcomes. There are two important points to take from this literature that are relevant to this chapter. First, couple conflict can be detrimental to children in a variety of ways. A summary of the literature examining the negative effects of couple conflict for child outcomes is far beyond the scope of this chapter (for a review, see Grych & Fincham, 2001). Here, we highlight the second important point which is that some research indicates that parental conflict, particularly violence, may be a risk factor for marital conflict (Halford, Sanders, & Behrens, 2000). Thus, there may be an intergenerational transmission of conflict, although the mechanisms by which parental conflict and marital conflict are not exceedingly clear. In addition, research indicates that female parental divorce may be a risk factor for less effective and more negative conflict management (Sanders, Halford, & Behrens, 1999).

DEPRESSION

There is growing evidence that poor conflict-management increases spouses' risk for depression. An extended increase in marital arguments is the most frequent life event reported as preceding the onset of depression in married women (Paykel, 1969). Marital interactions of couples with one depressed member are characterized by negativity, decreased positivity and congeniality, asymmetry, and aggression (Hautzinger, Linden, & Hoffman, 1982; Hops, Biglan, Sherman, & Arthur, 1987; S. L. Johnson & Jacob, 1997; Whisman, Weinstock, & Uebelacker, 2002). Depressed spouses and their partners, in comparison with control couples, have been observed to have a more negative and impaired communication styles, including less constructive and more destructive problem solving, more negative feelings, and greater difficulty discussing problems (Coyne, Thompson, & Palmer, 2002). Low levels of self-disclosure (Brown & Harris, 1978) and diminished provision of emotional support (Daley & Hammen, 2002) between spouses are also associated with depression.

It is reasonable to presume that causality is bidirectional in such research. Just as conflict no doubt increases risk for depression, depression also affects the likelihood of conflict. In fact, observational data indicate that depressed individuals have a negative bias in the perceptions of their spouses' communications (Kowalik & Gotlib, 1987) and express lower rates of positive affect and higher rates of aggression toward their spouses (Biglan, 1985; Hops et al., 1987). Such findings support a view that patterns of poor conflict management are likely contributing to and being expressed from the presence of depression in marriage. It should also be noted that marital therapy has been shown to be effective treatment for depression (Beach, Fincham, & Katz, 1998).

PREMARITAL COHABITATION

Some research indicates premarital cohabitation may be associated with poorer conflict-management skills in marriage. Specifically, Cohan and Kleinbaum (2002) found that couples who lived together before marriage demonstrated more negative and less positive interaction skills during a videotaped conflict discussion. Similarly, Kline, Stanley et al. (2004) found that those who cohabited before engagement demonstrated poorer conflict-management skills during a conflict discussion and self-reported more verbal aggression than those who did not live together until after engagement or until marriage. Although it is difficult to discern why this cohabitation effect may occur, the results of both of these studies held up when controlling for length of cohabitation and sociodemographic factors such as religiosity, income, and age. Thus, it could be that there is something about the experience of cohabitation that is linked with poorer conflict management. Alternatively, it may be that couples who experience higher levels of conflict may decide to cohabit before deciding to marry because the conflict indicates to them a need to test their relationships before making a final decision. Some of these couples who are cohabiting as a test of the relationship may wind up marrying even though their conflict is not resolved (Kline, Stanley, et al., 2004).

PHYSIOLOGY

Researchers have begun examining what role physiology may play in couple conflict. For example, one study indicates that couples who demonstrate greater stress hormone reactivity during negative interactions during the first year of marriage may be more likely to experience divorce later (Kiecolt-Glaser, Bane, Glaser, & Malarkey, 2003). Thus, negative reactivity is an individual factor that appears to be associated with marital distress. Perhaps couples who had less hormone reactivity possess fewer "vulnerabilities" when dealing with the stress and conflict that all couples will face, allowing them a greater ability to adapt and experience better relationship outcomes overall (Karney & Bradbury, 1995). In addition, some have examined levels of testosterone during problem-solving tasks in a laboratory (Cohan, Booth, & Granger, 2003). In Cohan et al.'s study, there were important interactions between gender and levels of testosterone; low levels of testosterone in both partners seemed to be associated with more adaptive conflict management for husbands, whereas a high level of wife testosterone paired with a low level of husband testosterone was associated with more adaptive conflict management for wives. As the couple conflict field continues to expand, it is likely that more research will be conducted examining physiological risk factors and responses to conflict (see Loving, Heffner, & Kiecolt-Glaser's chapter in this volume for information on current directions in the study of physiology and interpersonal relationships). Ultimately, this line of research may lead to innovative new intervention strategies for couple conflict.

The Mechanics of Conflict Management

How do couples deal with conflict? In this section, we review some of the literature that describes the process of conflict management. It is important to note here that we typically use the term *conflict management* to describe how couples handle conflict in their relationships. Others use *conflict resolution* to describe this process. We chose conflict management because we believe that not all conflicts can be resolved. Not all conflict is destructive conflict, and what is most important is how couples manage conflict (Markman, Stanley, et al., 2004). Some conflicts will last throughout marriages, even happy marriages, but from our perspective, couples can learn better ways to understand areas of contention and manage them.

In terms of the mechanics of how couples deal with conflict, one early model for the process of conflict suggests that there are three distinct phases to couples' conflict discussions (Gottman et al., 1977). First, during the *agenda building* phase, both partners tend to present their perspectives

and feelings about the problem (at least in happy couples). Second, during the *arguing* phase, partners tend to attempt to persuade one another. Finally, during the *negotiation* phase, partners usually attempt to compromise and reach a resolution. The amount of time spent in each phase, as well as the behaviors observed in each phase, differs across couples.

Peterson (1983) also provided a comprehensive model for how conflict discussions begin and end. He suggested that predispositions for conflict around particular areas exist for most couples. Discussions about issues that partners feel strongly about and that have not been adequately resolved in the past may turn into destructive conflictual discussions with little provocation. Once a conflict discussion has started, it either moves toward direct negotiation or toward escalation and intensification of conflict. Peterson (1983) suggested that for conflict to end, the problem must be reframed to be less important than maintaining the relationship and the person making the first conciliatory move must acknowledge some personal responsibility for the conflict and an interest in negotiating a resolution.

More recent work examining the mechanisms of conflict has focused on partner's thoughts during conflict discussions. For example, Sillars, Roberts, Leonard, and Dun (2000) found that during conflict discussions, partners differed in their attention to issues, behaviors, and background knowledge surrounding the discussion. Many partners seemed to interpret the stream of communication in markedly different ways. Cognition during conflict discussions was also related to marital outcomes, in that angry, frustrated, and blaming thoughts were prevalent in severe conflicts and dissatisfied marriages. Satisfied couples expressed more optimism toward communication, reflected in a sense of impending resolution of conflict and faith that the partner is capable of understanding oneself.

The research detailed here suggests that both behavior and cognition must be examined to understand fully the mechanics of conflict management. With this background on the mechanics of conflict in mind, we next review specific patterns of conflict management. We focus on the demand–withdrawal pattern and Gottman's (1993) distinction between engagers and avoiders.

DEMAND–WITHDRAWAL PATTERN OF CONFLICT MANAGEMENT

Gender has been implicated in a destructive pattern that relationship researchers and therapists often cite: the demand–withdrawal pattern in which one partner typically retreats from conflict discussions and the other pursues (Caughlin & Huston, 2002; Christensen & Heavey, 1990; Markman, Silvern, Clements, & Kraft-Hanak, 1993). An example from a recent couples therapy session with the first author follows. Identifiable details have been modified to preserve confidentiality. The wife, Sally, a medical transcriptionist in her 40s, described to the therapist what happened over the weekend when she tried to talk to her husband, Scott, a police officer in his 40s, about landscaping their yard. She said that she asked Scott (while he was reading the newspaper) how much money he thought that they could spend and whether he was leaning toward rosebushes or rhododendrons in the front. He said that it was up to her. She apparently then answered in a somewhat agitated voice, "Well, I need your input because we have to talk about how much we can spend." Scott continued reading his newspaper. He reported during the session that he could tell his wife was becoming angry and that he did not want to "make things worse by talking." He reported that he felt like anything he said would have made her more mad, so he chose to be silent and "let her have time to calm herself down." What Sally did, though, was become even angrier, saying, "Why don't you ever listen to me?" Scott reported that he then told her he was going for a walk alone because their conversation was "going nowhere." Their issue then switched from being one about money and shrubbery to communication and caring. Sally was clearly pursuing Scott and demanding that they discuss an issue important to her and Scott was withdrawing, later

explaining in session that he did so because he did not know how to react to Sally in a way that would not make her angrier. Sally told the therapist that Scott's silence about things was exactly what made her most angry in their relationship.

Couples married less than 3 months have been shown to exhibit this pattern of demand and withdrawal, but with important qualifications (Vogel & Karney, 2002). Behavior during a marital interaction may be a function not of gender but of the investment of each spouse in the problem being discussed. When the husband viewed the topic as important, sex differences in withdrawal were greatly reduced. That is, when the husband selected the topic, there were no gender differences in terms of who played the demanding or withdrawing roles. However, in the same study, wives demanded more than husbands but without the corresponding greater withdrawal by husbands, which is different from what is observed in established relationships. Another interesting finding is that there was not a *pattern* of demand–withdrawal in this sample. Just because one partner demanded, it was not necessarily associated with corresponding withdrawal of the other partner. Instead, the withdrawal of one partner was associated with the withdrawal of the other. Similarly, demand by one partner was associated with demand by the other partner. This finding is not consistent with findings for established couples where there is a pattern of demand by the wife and withdrawal by the husband (e.g., Christensen & Heavey, 1990). The explanation the authors provide for this finding is that as the relationship deteriorates over time, the more typical demand–withdrawal pattern may emerge (Vogel & Karney, 2002).

In line with Vogel and Karney's (2002) findings, some researchers have found that who chooses the discussion topic moderates the demand–withdrawal pattern. That is, if the male chooses the discussion topic, he is less likely to withdrawal and more likely to be the pursuer, whereas if the female chooses the discussion topic, she is less likely to withdrawal and more likely to pursue (Christensen & Heavey, 1990). Other research suggests that the pattern may be linked to gender roles (i.e., femininity vs. masculinity) more than sex per se (Markman, Silvern, et al., 1993). Markman and colleagues found that men who rated themselves highly on indicators of femininity were less likely to withdrawal. In conclusion, the demand–withdrawal pattern is one that has received much attention in the couple conflict literature and is often recognized by couple therapists. For this reason, it is commonly targeted in prevention and therapy.

ENGAGERS VERSUS AVOIDERS

Gottman (1993) further divided the regulated–stable couples described earlier into conflict engagers versus avoiders, based on listener behavior during conflict interactions. Specifically, both partners in engager couples show more positive than negative listener behaviors, whereas avoiders demonstrated either more negative behaviors or equal numbers of positive and negative behaviors. Using clinical observations, Gottman described engagers as willingly and openly disagreeing and confronting conflict, in contrast to avoiders, who do not have specific strategies for resolving conflicts and tend to emphasize the acceptance and minimization of differences. To relate these types to the process of conflict discussion described earlier, avoiders tend to do little persuasion and often consider simply recognizing each person's perspective and the accepting the differences between perspectives as a complete discussion of the conflict. In contrast, conflict engagers demonstrate a great deal of persuasion throughout the conflict discussion, including during the agenda building phase, that for other couples is reserved for the expression of feelings.

In a parallel fashion, nonregulated couples were further classified as either hostile (more positive than negative listener behaviors) or hostile–detached (fewer or equal positive behaviors than negative behaviors). Anecdotally, hostile couples appeared directly engaged in the conflict and showed high levels of defensiveness, whereas hostile–detached couples were typically detached and emotionally uninvolved. This creates a descriptive typology of couples; however, Gottman (1993) did not demonstrate that these subgroups differed in terms of marital satisfaction or stability.

Other researchers have classified couples based on their conflict management styles. For example, Ridley and colleagues (2001) examined distancing versus engaging couples and couples in which partners were mismatched on these styles. The researchers report that these profiles were related to marital quality in that engaging couples reported the highest quality, distancing the lowest, and the mismatched couples were in the middle. It should be noted that much of the research on couple types grew out of the seminal work of Raush and colleagues (e.g., Raush et al., 1974).

Prevention and Intervention

A major theme in understanding the impact of conflict on romantic relationships is realizing that the amount of conflict may be less important than how that conflict is managed (Markman, Renick, et al., 1993). The finding mentioned earlier that seeds of future distress could be identified early in a relationship, while a couple was still happy and before children were born, gave way to divorce prevention and marriage education programs designed to teach couples skills to talk without fighting about the inevitable conflicts that most couples experience (e.g., Markman et al., 2004). Markman and colleagues noted that prevention programs need to teach couples how to handle conflict and regulate negative emotions, not because happy couples use these skills naturally, but because couples headed for distress naturally talk in destructive ways and need a safe way to talk about inevitable conflicts (and to handle negative emotions safely). In other words, couples need to learn safe ways to talk that counteract the dangerous communication patterns that predict negative outcomes (Markman, Stanley, et al., 2004).

Many intervention and prevention programs for couples include a component of teaching couples communication skills (e.g., Guerney, 1988; Jacobson & Christensen, 1998; Markman, Stanley, et al., 2004; Miller, Nunnally, & Wackman, 1975; also see Halford & Markman, 1997). Because the authors' expertise is with prevention programs, this section focuses on what prevention programs teach couples about conflict management.

A recent evaluation of the effectiveness of premarital prevention programs suggested that such programs are generally effective in producing immediate and short-term gains in conflict-management skills (Carroll & Doherty, 2003). Most programs employ a psychoeducational approach that includes lectures, discussions, and practice time for skills; such programs are often defined as "relationship education." The Premarital Relationship Enhancement Program (PREP; Markman, Stanley, et al., 2004) has the most empirical support for effectiveness (Halford, Markman, Kline, & Stanley, 2003). In a review of best practices in relationship education, four major components of such programs were identified: awareness, feedback, cognitive change, and skills training (Halford et al., 2003). Although all these components may have an impact on conflict management, it is the skills training portion of these programs that has the most significant implications for handling conflict. In PREP, for example, there is substantial emphasis early in the curriculum to prevent and remediate destructive conflict. Couples are taught to identify danger signs in conflict discussions (i.e., invalidation, negative escalation, withdrawal, and negative interpretations), and then they are taught the skills to reduce these danger signs (Markman, Stanley, et al., 2004). In an evaluation of PREP, couples rated the skills training in communication as the most helpful (Stanley et al., 2001).

SAFETY THEORY

Prevention programs are often based on theories or models of what makes a healthy relationship. Here, we describe the model on which PREP is based, highlighting how conflict fits into this theory called "safety theory" (Stanley et al., 2002) also referred to as the Baseball Model of Healthy Relationships (Markman, Stanley, et al., 2004).

Safety theory is based on Markman and Stanley's 25 years of research and intervention experience regarding how couples manage conflict and learn skills to better communicate. Safety theory is consistent with other theories of healthy family functioning, such as attachment theory (Furman & Flanagan, 1997), Jacobson and Christensen's (1998) work on acceptance, and emotional expression theory (S. M. Johnson, 1996). Safety theory suggests that there are two types of safety: safety in interaction (i.e., being able to talk openly and well (enough) about key issues) and safety in commitment (i.e., having the security of support and a sense of a clear future).

As described elsewhere (Markman, Kline, Rea, Piper Simms, & Stanley, 2005),

> Safety theory has guided our intervention work both in PREP and in our clinical practices. For example, if we had one session with a couple or one opportunity to educate a group of couples, based on research and clinical experience, we would help partners to take personal action to do two things: (a) help them stop (or avoid the tendency toward) fighting destructively and talk without fighting about important issues and (b) help them protect and preserve a lasting love though nurturing positive connections and being committed to one another. This will help couples be 'safe at home!'

From the description of safety theory, it is clear that healthy conflict management (part of safety in interaction) is a large component of what Markman and colleagues consider a healthy relationship. PREP focuses on helping couples better manage conflict by teaching them about danger signs in relationships (i.e., communication behaviors and patterns that are predictive of relationship erosion) and skills for structuring communication between partners that can help reduce destructive conflict patterns (i.e., the speaker–listener technique).

MODIFYING PROGRAMS TO ADDRESS SPECIFIC NEEDS OF COUPLES

Most intervention and prevention programs have been designed to be applicable to all couples. Although this was an important first step in the field, we believe it is important to begin to tailor programs to address differences that may exist between couples and cater more to the specific needs of couples. For example, the developers of PREP have begun to do this by supplying guidelines for working with different populations, such as low-income couples who may face unique problems (see http://www.PREPinc.com). In addition, when training leaders to deliver PREP, leaders are encouraged to modify the examples used and the language so that it fits best with the populations being served (Markman, Whitton, et al., 2004). As an illustration of ways in which interventions can be tailored to meet the particular needs of a specific group of people, we suggest ways in this chapter in which programs could be modified to better serve couples who are cohabiting or who cohabited before marriage. We chose cohabiting couples to use as an example because the United States is seeing such a dramatic shift in the number of couples that cohabit before or instead of marriage, and these issues are not typically addressed in prevention programs.

Cohabiting couples face special circumstances. As noted earlier, cohabiting couples show higher rates of conflict (Magdol et al., 1998) and research indicates that those who live together before to marriage and especially before engagement report more negative conflict than couples who do not live together before a commitment to marriage (Kline, Stanley, et al., 2004; Stanley, Whitton, & Markman, 2004). Because cohabiters appear to be at special risk for conflict, here we discuss specific intervention ideas for them.

It may be that cohabiting couples experience conflict around different issues than married couples or engaged couples who are not living together. For example, we outline

that, based on safety theory, feeling safe in the future of the relationship is a key component to a healthy relationship. Although little contemporary research has examined cohabiters' reasons for living together, many researchers speculate that some people who cohabit likely do so because they want to test the relationship before marriage (Popenoe & Whitehead, 2002). Conflict may be linked to this sense of wanting to test the relationship in several ways. First, couples with high levels of conflict during dating may sense a need to test the waters before making a commitment. That is, high levels of conflict may lead some couples to want to live together before marriage. Second, commitment levels and future plans may be a particular source of conflict for cohabiting couples, likely more so than married couples, who have received the most attention in the conflict intervention literature to date.

With these important considerations about cohabiting couples in mind, we suggest that intervention programs that focus on conflict management be modified to address the special circumstances surrounding cohabitation. Although many of the techniques, such as active listening and time-outs, will be useful with cohabiting couples, other issues need to be addressed. One such issue is how to deal with conflict surrounding commitment issues. Conflict around commitment may be especially tricky to handle because couples may not feel safe enough in the future of the relationship to manage conflict effectively. Thus, one tactic could be to help couples separate the conflict issue (e.g., housework, money, etc.) from the commitment issue. Cohabiting couples could be encouraged to hold discrete discussions (separated in time) for the conflict issues and commitment issues that may be underlying the conflict.

Future Directions

This chapter illuminates the need for much further research on conflict. Here we describe several areas where we see deficits and opportunities to further understand couple conflict.

One area that is particularly underresearched is the development of conflict-management skills. Little research has been conducted on adolescents' conflict-management skills in romantic relationships, and the potential links between conflict management in early romantic relationships and later relationships in young adulthood has, to our knowledge, not been examined. Similarly, to our knowledge, no research has examined the continuity of conflict-management skills from one adult romantic relationship to another. Doing so might help illuminate the individual contributions partners make to the quality of the couple's conflict management.

Related to issues surrounding the development of conflict management skills, is the issue of risk factors. Although many risk factors have been identified none of them are likely to be considered tried-and-true risk factors. Additionally, other important risk factors, such as mental health problems (other than depression), have not been well studied. Research on risk factors would aid in the development of prevention and intervention programs that could target high-risk individuals and couples.

In addition, conflict in populations other than heterosexual married couples needs to be studied. For example, some have begun studying conflict in gay and lesbian populations (e.g., Julien, Chartrand, Simard, Bouthillier, & Begin, 2003). Additionally, as we highlighted earlier, there is a lack of research on adult dating relationships that is not based on college students.

As other researchers have suggested (e.g., Fincham & Beach, 1999), it is important for research on conflict to continue to be theory driven. Much research on conflict has been based on theory; however, the couple conflict field lacks an integrative theory that combines the entirety of findings on conflict. Although developing such theory may seem a daunting task, it is important that we begin to consolidate findings, begin researching multiple risk factors at a time, and further examine the developmental tra-jectory of conflict over the span of relationships, beginning with adolescent dating and extending into late-life relationships. Having an integrative theory of conflict that combines risk factors, correlates, and a developmental perspective would push the couple conflict field much further along.

Acknowledgment

Support for this research and for preparation of this manuscript was provided in part by a grant from the National Institute of Mental Health: Division of Services and Intervention Research, Adult and Geriatric Treatment and Prevention Branch, grant 5-RO1-MH35525-12, "The Long-term Effects of Premarital Intervention" (awarded to Howard Markman, Scott Stanley, and Lydia Prado).

Suggested Further Reading

Booth, A., Crouter, A. C., & Clements, M. (Eds.). (2001). *Couples in conflict*. Mahwah, NJ: Erlbaum.

Cox, M. J., & Brooks-Gunn, J. (1999). *Conflict and cohesion in families: Causes and consequences*. Mahwah, NJ: Erlbaum.

Fincham, F. D., & Beach, S. R. H. (1999). Conflict in marriage: Implications for working with couples. *Annual Review of Psychology, 50*, 47–77.

Markman, H. J., Stanley, S. M., Blumberg, S. L., Jenkins, N., & Whiteley, C. (2004). *Twelve hours to a great marriage*. San Francisco: Jossey-Bass.

References

Almeida, D. M., McGonagle, K. A., Cate, R. C., Kessler, R. C., & Wethington, E. (2003). Psychosocial moderators of emotional reactivity to marital arguments: Results from a daily diary study. *Marriage and Family Review, 34*, 89–113.

Archer, J. (1999). Assessment of the reliability of the conflict tactics scales: A meta-analytic review. *Journal of Interpersonal Violence, 14*, 1263–1289.

Beach, S. R. H. (2001). Expanding the study of dyadic conflict: The potential role of self-evaluation maintenance processes. In A. Booth, A. C. Crouter, & M. Clements (Eds.), *Couples in conflict* (pp. 83–94). Mahwah, NJ: Erlbaum.

Beach, S. R. H., Fincham, F. D., & Katz, J. (1998). Marital therapy in the treatment of depression: Toward a third generation of therapy and research. *Clinical Psychology Review, 18*, 635–661.

Bell, E. C., & Blakeney, R. N. (1977). Personality correlates of conflict resolution modes. *Human Relations, 30*, 849–857.

Biglan, A. (1985). Problem-solving interactions of depressed women and their husbands. *Behavior Therapy, 16*, 431–451.

Booth, A., Crouter, A. C., & Clements, M. (Eds.). (2001). *Couples in conflict.* Mahwah, NJ: Erlbaum.

Bradbury, T., Rogge, R., & Lawrence, E. (2001). Reconsidering the role of conflict in marriage. In A. Booth, A. C. Crouter, & M. Clements (Eds.), *Couples in conflict* (pp. 59–81). Mahwah, NJ: Erlbaum.

Brown, G. W., & Harris, T. (1978). Social origins of depression: A reply. *Psychological Medicine, 8*, 577–588.

Bumpass, L. L., & Lu, H.-H. (2000). Trends in cohabitation and implications for children's family contexts in the United States. *Population Studies, 54*, 29–41.

Carroll, J. S., & Doherty, W. J. (2003). Evaluating the effectiveness of premarital prevention programs: A meta-analytic review of outcome research. *Family Relations, 52*, 105–118.

Caughlin, J. P., & Huston, T. L. (2002). A contextual analysis of the association between demand/withdraw and marital satisfaction. *Personal Relationships, 9*, 95–119.

Christensen, A., & Heavey, C. L. (1990). Gender and social structure in the demand/withdraw pattern of marital conflict. *Journal of Personality and Social Psychology, 59*, 73–81.

Clements, M. L., Stanley, S. M., & Markman, H. J. (2004). Before they said "I do": Discriminating among marital outcomes over 13 years based on premarital data. *Journal of Marriage and Family, 66*, 613–626.

Cohan, C., & Kleinbaum, S. (2002). Toward a greater understanding of the cohabitation effect: Premarital cohabitation and marital communication. *Journal of Marriage and Family, 64*, 180–192.

Cohan, C. L., Booth, A., & Granger, D. A. (2003). Gender moderates the relationship between testosterone and marital interaction. *Journal of Family Psychology, 17*, 29–40.

Coie, J. D., Watt, N. F., West, S. G., Hawkins, J. D., Asarnow, J. R., Markman, H. J., et al. (1993). The science of prevention: A conceptual framework and some directions for a national research program. *American Psychologist, 48*, 1013–1022.

Cox, M. J., & Brooks-Gunn, J. (1999). *Conflict and cohesion in families: Causes and consequences.* Mahwah, NJ: Erlbaum.

Coyne, J. C., Thompson, R., & Palmer, S. C. (2002). Marital quality, coping with conflict, marital complaints, and affection in couples with a depressed wife. *Journal of Family Psychology, 16*, 26–37.

Daley, S. E., & Hammen, C. (2002). Depressive symptoms and close relationships during the transition to adulthood: Perspectives from dysphoric women, their best friends, and their romantic partners. *Journal of Consulting and Clinical Psychology, 70*, 129–141.

Feldman, S. S., & Gowen, L. K. (1998). Conflict negotiation tactics in romantic relationships in high school students. *Journal of Youth and Adolescence, 27*, 691–717.

Fincham, F. D. (2003). Marital conflict: Correlates, structure, and context. *Current Directions in Psychological Science, 12*, 23–27.

Fincham, F. D., & Beach, S. R. H. (1999). Conflict in marriage: Implications for working with couples. *Annual Review of Psychology, 50*, 47–77.

Furman, W., & Buhrmester, D. (1992). Age and sex differences in perceptions of networks of personal relationships. *Child Development, 63*, 103–115.

Furman, W., & Flanagan, A. S. (1997). The influence of earlier relationships on marriage: An attachment perspective. In W. K. Halford & H. J. Markman (Eds.), *Clinical handbook of marriage and couples interventions* (pp. 179–202). New York: Wiley.

Gelles, R. J. (1991). Physical violence, child abuse, and child homicide: A continuum of violence, or distinct behaviors? *Human Nature, 2*, 59–72.

Gill, D. S., Christensen, A., & Fincham, F. D. (1999). Predicting marital satisfaction from behavior: Do all roads really lead to Rome? *Personal Relationships, 6*, 369–387.

Gottman, J. M. (1979). *Marital interaction: Experimental investigations*. San Diego: Academic Press.

Gottman, J. M. (1993). The roles of conflict engagement, escalation, and avoidance in marital interaction: A longitudinal view of five types of couples. *Journal of Consulting and Clinical Psychology, 61*, 6–15.

Gottman, J. M., & Krokoff, L. J. (1989). Marital interaction and satisfaction: A longitudinal view. *Journal of Consulting and Clinical Psychology, 57*, 47–52.

Gottman, J. M., & Levenson, R. W. (1992). Marital processes predictive of later dissolution: Behavior, physiology, and health. *Journal of Personality and Social Psychology, 63*, 221–233.

Gottman, J. M., Markman, H. J., & Notarius, C. I. (1977). The topography of marital conflict: A sequential analysis of verbal and nonverbal behavior. *Journal of Marriage and Family, 39*, 461–477.

Grych, J. H., & Fincham, F. D. (2001). *Interparental conflict and child development: Theory, research, and applications*. New York: Cambridge University Press.

Grych, J. H., Seid, M., & Fincham, F. D. (1992). Assessing marital conflict from the child's perspective: The Children's Perception of Interparental Conflict Scale. *Child Development, 63*, 558–571.

Guerney, B. G. (1988). Family relationship enhancement: A skill training approach. In L. A. Bond & B. M. Wagner (Eds.), *Families in transition: Primary prevention programs that work* (pp. 99–134). Thousand Oaks, CA: Sage.

Gurman, A. S., & Rice, D. G. (1975). *Couples in conflict*. New York: Aronson.

Halford, W. K., & Markman, H. J. (Eds.). (1997). *Clinical handbook of marriage and couples interventions*. Chichester, England: Wiley.

Halford, W. K., Markman, H. J., Kline, G. H., & Stanley, S. M. (2003). Best practice in couple relationship education. *Journal of Marital and Family Therapy, 29*, 385–406.

Halford, W. K., Sanders, M. R., & Behrens, B. C. (2000). Repeating the errors of out parents? Family-of-origin spouse violence and observed conflict management in engaged couples. *Family Process, 39*, 219–235.

Hartup, W. W. (1992). Conflict and friendship relations. In C. U. Shantz & W. W. Hartup (Eds.), *Conflict in child and adolescent development* (pp. 186–215). New York: Cambridge University Press.

Hautzinger, M., Linden, M., & Hoffman, N. (1982). Distressed couples with and without a depressed partner: An analysis of their verbal interaction. *Journal of Behavior Therapy and Experimental Psychiatry, 13*, 307–314.

Heavey, C. L., Larson, B. M., Zumtobel, D. C., & Christensen, A. (1996). The Communication Patterns Questionnaire: The reliability and validity of a constructive communication subscale. *Journal of Marriage and Family, 58*, 796–800.

Hops, H., Biglan, A., Sherman, L., & Arthur, J. (1987). Home observations of family interactions of depressed women. *Journal of Consulting and Clinical Psychology, 55*, 341–346.

Jacobson, N. S., & Christensen, A. (1998). *Acceptance and change in couple therapy: A therapist's guide to transforming relationships*. New York: Norton.

Johnson, C. A., Stanley, S. M., Glenn, N. D., Amato, P., Nock, S. L., Markman, H. J., et al. (2002). *Marriage in Oklahoma: 2001 baseline statewide survey on marriage and divorce (S02096 OKDHS)*. Oklahoma City: Oklahoma Department of Human Services.

Johnson, M. P. (2001). Conflict and control: Symmetry and asymmetry in domestic violence. In A. Booth, A. C. Crouter, & M. Clements (Eds.), *Couples in conflict* (pp. 95–104). Mahwah, NJ: Erlbaum.

Johnson, S. L., & Jacob, T. (1997). Marital interactions of depressed men and women. *Journal of Consulting and Clinical Psychology, 65*, 15–23.

Johnson, S. M. (1996). *The practice of emotionally focused marital therapy: Creating connection*. New York: Taylor and Francis.

Julien, D., Chartrand, E., Simard, M.-C., Bouthillier, D., & Begin, J. (2003). Conflict, social support and relationship quality: An observational study of heterosexual, gay male, and lesbian couples' communication. *Journal of Family Psychology, 17*, 419–428.

Karney, B. R., & Bradbury, T. N. (1995). The longitudinal course of marital quality and stability: A review of theory, method, and research. *Psychological Bulletin, 118*, 3–34.

Kerig, P. K. (1996). Assessing the links between interparental conflict and child adjustment: The Conflicts and Problem-Solving Scales. *Journal of Family Psychology, 10*, 454–473.

Kiecolt-Glaser, J. K., Bane, C., Glaser, R., & Malarkey, W. B. (2003). Love, marriage, and divorce: Newlyweds' stress hormones foreshadow relationship changes. *Journal of Consulting and Clinical Psychology*, 71, 176–188.

Kline, G. H., Julien, D., Baucom, B., Hartman, S. G., Gilbert, K., Gonzales, T., et al. (2004). The Interactional Dimensions Coding System: A global system for couple interactions. In P. Kerig & D. Baucom (Eds.), *Couple observational coding systems*. Mahwah, NJ: Erlbaum.

Kline, G. H., Stanley, S. M., Markman, H. J., Olmos-Gallo, P. A., St. Peters, M., Whitton, S. W., et al. (2004). Timing is everything: Pre-engagement cohabitation and increased risk for poor marital outcomes. *Journal of Family Psychology*, 18, 302–310.

Kline, G. H., Wood, L. F., & Moore, S. (2003). Validation of revised measures of family and interparental conflict for use with young adults. *Journal of Divorce and Remarriage*, 39, 125–142.

Kowalik, D. L., & Gotlib, I. H. (1987). Depression and marital interaction: Concordance between intent and perception of communication. *Journal of Abnormal Psychology*, 96, 127–134.

Knox, D. (1971). *Marriage happiness*. Champaign, IL: Research Press.

Larson, J. H., Peterson, D. J., Heath, V. A., & Birch, P. (2000). The relationship between perceived dysfunctional family-of-origin rules and intimacy in young adult dating relationships. *Journal of Sex and Marital Therapy*, 26, 161–175.

Levy, S. Y., Wambolt, F. S., & Fiese, B. H. (1997). Family-of-origin experiences and conflict resolution behaviors of young adult dating couples. *Family Process*, 36, 297–310.

Lewin, K. (1948). *Resolving social conflicts; selected papers on group dynamics*. Oxford, England: Harper.

Magdol, L., Moffitt, T. E., & Caspi, A. (1998). Hitting without a license: Testing explanations for differences in partner abuse between young adult daters and cohabitors. *Journal of Marriage and Family*, 60, 41–55.

Marchand, J. F., & Hock, E. (2000). Avoidance and attacking conflict-resolution strategies among married couples: Relations to depressive symptoms and marital satisfaction. *Family Relations*, 49, 201–206.

Markman, H. J. (1979). Application of a behavioral model of marriage in predicting relationship satisfaction of couples planning marriage. *Journal of Consulting and Clinical Psychology*, 47, 743–749.

Markman, H. J., Duncan, S. W., Storaasli, R., & Howes, P. (1987). The prediction and prevention of marital distress: A longitudinal investigation. In K. Hahlweg & M. Goldstein (Eds.), *Understanding major mental disorders: The contribution of family interaction research* (pp. 266–289). New York: Family Process Press.

Markman, H. J., Floyd, F. J., Stanley, S. M., & Storaasli, R. D. (1988). Prevention of marital distress: A longitudinal investigation. *Journal of Consulting and Clinical Psychology*, 56, 210–217.

Markman, H. J., & Hahlweg, K. (1993). The prediction and prevention of marital distress: An international perspective. *Clinical Psychology Review*, 13, 29–43.

Markman, H. J., Kline, G. H., Rea, J. G., Piper Simms, S., & Stanley, S. M. (2005). A sampling of theoretical, methodological, and policy issues in marriage education: Implications for family psychology. In W. M. Pinsof & J. Lebow (Eds.), *Family psychology: The art of the science*. Oxford/New York: Oxford University Press.

Markman, H. J., & Notarius, C. I. (1987). Coding and marital family interaction: Current status. In T. Jacob (Ed.), *Family Interaction and Psychology* (pp. 329–390). New York, NY: Plenum.

Markman, H. J., Renick, M. J., Floyd, F. J., Stanley, S. M., & Clements, M. (1993). Preventing marital distress through communication and conflict management training: A four and five year follow-up. *Journal of Consulting and Clinical Psychology*, 61, 70–77.

Markman, H. J., Silvern, L., Clements, M., & Kraft-Hanak, S. (1993). Men and women dealing with conflict in heterosexual relationships. *Journal of Social Issues*, 49(3), 107–125.

Markman, H. J., Stanley, S. M., Blumberg, S. L., Jenkins, N., & Whiteley, C. (2004). *Twelve hours to a great marriage*. San Francisco: Jossey-Bass.

Markman, H. J., Whitton, S. W., Kline, G. H., Thompson, H., St. Peters, M., Stanley, S. M., et al. (2004). Use of an empirically-based marriage education program by religious organizations: Results of a dissemination trial. *Family Relations*, 53, 504–512.

McGonagle, K. A., Kessler, R. C., & Schilling, E. A. (1992). The frequency and determinants of marital disagreements in a community sample. *Journal of Social and Personal Relationships*, 9, 507–524.

Miller, S., Nunnally, E., & Wackman, D. (1975). Minnesota Couples Communication Program (MCCP): Premarital and marital groups. In D. Olsen (Ed.), *Treating relationships* (pp. 21–40). Lake Mills, IA: Graphic.

Notarius, C. I., & Markman, H. J. (1993). *We can work it out: Making sense of marital conflict.* New York: Putnam.

Notarius, C., & Vanzetti, N. (1983). Marital Agendas Protocol. In E. Filsinger (Ed.), *Marriage and family assessment: A sourcebook for family therapy* (pp. 209–227). Beverly Hills, CA: Sage.

Paykel, E. S. (1969). Life events and depression: A controlled study. *Archives of General Psychiatry*, 21, 753–760.

Peterson, D. R. (1983). Conflict. In H. H. Kelley, E. Berscheid, A. Christensen, J. H. Harvey, T. L. Huston, G. Levinger, et al., *Close relationships* (pp. 360–396). New York: Freeman.

Popenoe, D., & Whitehead, B. (2002). *Should we live together? What young adults need to know about cohabitation before marriage.* Retrieved April 1, 2004, from http://www.smartmarriages.com/cohabit.html

Porter, B., & O'Leary, K. D. (1980). Marital discord and childhood behavior problems. *Journal of Abnormal Child Psychology*, 8, 287–295.

Raush, H. L., Barry, W. A., Hertel, R. K., & Swain, M. A. (1974). *Communication, conflict, and marriage.* San Francisco: Jossey-Bass.

Reedy, B. M. (2002). Family process as a mediator of the effects of parental divorce and alcoholism on young adult dating relationships. *Dissertation Abstracts International: Section B: The Sciences and Engineering*, 63 (1–B), 569.

Reese-Weber, M., & Bartle-Haring, S. (1998). Conflict resolution styles in family subsystems and adolescent romantic relationships. *Journal of Youth and Adolescence*, 27, 735–752.

Ridley, C. A., Wilhelm, M. S., & Surra, C. A. (2001). Married couples' conflict responses and marital quality. *Journal of Social and Personal Relationships*, 18, 517–534.

Rogge, R. M., & Bradbury, T. N. (1999). Recent advances in the prediction of marital outcomes. In R. Berger & M. T. Hannah (Eds.), *Preventive approaches in couples therapy* (pp. 331–360). Philadelphia: Brunner/Mazel.

Saiz, C. C. (2001). Teaching couples communication and problem-solving skills: A self-directed, videotape version of the prevention relationship enhancement program (PREP) (Doctoral dissertation, University of Denver, 2001). *Dissertation Abstracts International*, 62, 2076.

Sanders, M. R., Halford, W. K., & Behrens, B. C. (1999). Parental divorce and premarital couple communication. *Journal of Family Psychology*, 13, 60–74.

Sanderson, C. A., & Karetsky, K. H. (2002). Intimacy goals and strategies of conflict resolution in dating relationships: A mediational analysis. *Journal of Social and Personal Relationships*, 19, 317–337.

Sillars, A. L., Roberts, L., Leonard, K. E., & Dun, T. (2000). Cognition during marital conflict: The relationship of thought and talk. *Journal of Social and Personal Relationships*, 17, 479–502.

Stanley, S. M., Blumberg, S. L., & Markman, H. J. (1999). Helping couples fight for their marriages: The PREP approach. In R. Berger & M. T. Hannah (Eds.), *Preventive approaches in couples therapy* (pp. 279–303). Philadelphia: Brunner/Mazel.

Stanley, S. M., & Markman, H. J. (1997). *Marriage in the 90s: A nationwide random phone survey.* Denver, CO: PREP.

Stanley, S. M., Markman, H. J., Prado, L. M., Olmos-Gallo, P. A., Tonelli, L., St. Peters, M., et al. (2001). Community-based premarital prevention: Clergy and lay leaders on the front lines. *Family Relations*, 50, 67–76.

Stanley, S. M., Markman, H. J., & Whitton, S. W. (2002). Communication, conflict, and commitment: Insights on the foundations of relationship success from a national survey. *Family Process*, 41, 659–675.

Stanley, S. M., Whitton, S. W., & Markman, H. J. (2004). Maybe I do: Interpersonal commitment levels and premarital or nonmarital cohabitation. *Journal of Family Issues*, 5, 496–519.

Stets, J. E. (1991). Cohabiting and marital aggression: The role of social isolation. *Journal of Marriage and Family*, 53, 669–680.

Storaasli, R. D., & Markman, H. J. (1990). Relationship problems in the early stages of marriage: A longitudinal investigation. *Journal of Family Psychology*, 4, 80–98.

Straus, M. A. (1979). Measuring intrafamily conflict and violence: The Conflict Tactics (CT) Scales. *Journal of Marriage and Family, 41,* 75–88.

Straus, M. A., Hamby, S. L., Boney-McCoy, S., & Sugarman, D. B. (1996). The revised Conflict Tactics Scales (CTS2): Development and preliminary psychometric data. *Journal of Family Issues, 17,* 283–316.

Vogel, D. L., & Karney, B. R. (2002). Demands and withdrawal in newlyweds: Elaborating on the social structure hypothesis. *Journal of Social and Personal Relationships, 19,* 685–701.

Vuchinich, S. (1987). Starting and stopping spontaneous family conflicts. *Journal of Marriage and Family, 49,* 591–601.

Waltz, J., Babcock, J. C., Jacobson, N. S., & Gottman, J. M. (2000). Testing a typology of batterers. *Journal of Consulting and Clinical Psychology, 68,* 658–669.

Whisman, M. A., Weinstock, L. M., & Uebelacker, L. A. (2002). Mood reactivity to marital conflict: The influence of marital dissatisfaction and depression. *Behavior Therapy, 33,* 299–314.

Whittaker, S., & Bry, B. H. (1991). Overt and covert parental conflict and adolescent problems: Observed marital interaction in clinic and nonclinic families. *Adolescence, 26,* 865–876.

Woody, E. Z., & Costanzo, P. R. (1990). Does marital agony precede marital ecstasy? A comment on Gottman and Krokoff's "Marital interaction and satisfaction: A longitudinal view." *Journal of Consulting and Clinical Psychology, 58,* 499–501.

Zietlow, P. H., & Sillars, A. L. (1988). Life-stage differences in communication during marital conflicts. *Journal of Social and Personal Relationships, 5,* 223–245.

CHAPTER 25

Sexuality in Close Relationships

Susan Sprecher
F. Scott Christopher
Rodney Cate

Introduction

Relationships that include sexual desire and sexual expression are particularly salient in society and important to individuals. Moreover, our society emphasizes marriage as the premier dyadic relationship in which sex is expected to occur, although sex is also often viewed to be acceptable in close, dating relationships. Furthermore, many nonsexual close relationships, including parent–child relationships and friendships, provide socialization experiences related to sexuality. This chapter focuses on personal (close) relationships that are also sexual. Our chapter discusses how the sexual aspects of close relationships are intertwined with other aspects of the relationship, including satisfaction, affection, love, and conflict.

The research summarized in this chapter, although mostly conducted in the last 2 decades, was influenced by the pioneering work of such scholars as Ehrmann (1959), Kirkendall (1961), and Reiss (1960). These early scholars focused on how sexual standards and behaviors covary with relationship stages and experiences. Since 1990, an increasing number of scholars in various social science disciplines (psychology, sociology, family studies, communication) have integrated the study of sexuality with the study of close relationships. This interface was enhanced with the publication of two edited books that focused on sexuality in close relationships (McKinney & Sprecher, 1989, 1991) and a special issue of the journal *Personal Relationships* (Issue 4, 1995), coedited by two of the authors of this chapter, Christopher and Sprecher. In addition, Harvey, Wenzel, and Sprecher (2004) have recently edited the *Handbook on Sexuality in Close Relationships*. Some of the chapters of the Harvey et al. *Handbook* are referred to in this chapter, and we encourage readers who desire a more in-depth examination of these topics to see this *Handbook*.

We begin this chapter with a discussion of conceptual and methodological issues associated with the study of sexuality in close relationships and by presenting an overview of the patterns of sexual practices of adults (and adolescents).

Conceptual, Theoretical, and Methodological Issues

An important first step facing scholars who investigate sexuality in a relational context is to make decisions about how to conceptualize sexuality. Some have focused narrowly by positing that sex is a means to pass on one's genetic material (Buss, 1998)[1] or by querying solely on coital behavior (e.g., Maticka-Tyndale, Herold, & Oppermann, 2003). Others have incorporated a wider range of behaviors, including precoital interactions, oral–genital contact, and anal intercourse (e.g., Bogart, Cecil, Wagstaff, Pinkerton, & Abramson, 2000), and still others have taken a broader approach, conceptualizing sexuality as emerging from dyadic interaction (Christopher, 2001). From our perspective, conceptualizations of sexuality should recognize its multidimensional nature. They should include but not be limited to sexual behaviors that focus on caring, pleasure, or reproduction. Conceptualizing sexuality, however, must also take into account dynamic processes that provide a contextual meaning for such behaviors, including processes within the self (i.e., attitudes and self-definitions), dyadic interactions and relational conditions, and social forces that influence these behaviors (i.e., peers, parents, ethnicity, media).

Unfortunately, much of the past research in this area has been atheoretical and has not offered a specific conceptualization of sexuality. Scholars who have utilized theory have primarily relied on one of three frameworks: evolutionary theory, social exchange–based theories, or orientations that focus on the social construction of sexuality (for reviews of these theories, see DeLamater & Hyde, 2004; Weis, 1998). In addition, the relevance of attachment theory to the study of sexuality in close relationships has recently been highlighted. We briefly summarize these theories as they apply to the study of sexuality in close relationships.

Evolutionary theory (Buss, 1998) offers explanations specifically for gender differences in sexuality. It posits that differential reproductive strategies have evolved over time as a form of adaptation. This perspective begins by recognizing that men produce high numbers of sperm at a relatively constant rate. Men's successful reproduction is therefore most likely to occur by mating with as many women as possible thereby increasing the chances of multiple inseminations. Women, on the contrary, possess a limited number of eggs and have limited opportunities to conceive. Thus, women's best reproductive strategy is to procure mates with resources who will invest those resources in children. Men trade commitment for certainty of paternity from this perspective. This theory has been used to explain why men are more willing than women to seek short-term sexual partners and more variety in sex and are more likely to feel jealous about their partners' imagined or real extradyadic sexual encounters (see Buss, 1998, for a review).

Social exchange–based theories assume that sexual outcomes in relationships represent individuals' inherent wish to maximize rewards (i.e., love, services, sexual acts) and limit costs (i.e., punishments, pain, rewards foregone) and that relationships require investments if they are to last (e.g., Rusbult, 1983). Equity theory, an important theoretical offshoot of this framework (Sprecher, 1998), posits that satisfaction in a relationship is based on the judgments partners make about the proportion of rewards and costs each experiences relative to the other. Tests of social exchange models reveal that perceptions of inequality in rewards and costs are negatively related to sexual satisfaction and can contribute to the decision to engage in an extradyadic sexual liaison (see Byers & Wang, 2004, for a review). Other tests show that experiencing high sexual rewards and low sexual costs are positively related to coital frequency in long-term relationships (Lawrence & Byers, 1995).

Other theoretical models conceptualize sexuality as a social construction. One school of thought, as represented by script theory (Gagnon, 1990) and role theory (Stryker & Statham, 1985), views sexuality in terms of sexual roles and expectations. From this perspective, members of society construct these roles and then both positively and negatively sanction inappropriate sexual behavior. Symbolic interactionism, a related theory, posits that sexual roles and the meanings assigned to behaviors in the roles emerge from dyadic interaction (Longmore, 1998). Christopher's (2001) analysis of premarital sexuality represents one effort to integrate these two approaches. For example, he proposed that a couple's decision to engage in coitus is an outgrowth of each partner's sexual attitudes in conjunction with their relationship experiences. Moreover, he posited that the repertoire of possible sexual role choices is an outcome of the socialization efforts of peers, parents, and culture.

Finally, attachment theory is particularly relevant to the study of sexuality in close relationships. Shaver, Hazan, and Bradshaw (1988) proposed that adult romantic love is based on the integration of three behavioral systems: attachment, caregiving, and sexual mating. They argued that the primary dimension is attachment and that individual differences in attachment should be related to patterns of sexual mating (and caregiving). Feeney and Noller (2004) summarized their own research and that of others that show links between attachment styles or dimensions and sexuality. For example, they found that the avoidance attachment dimension is associated with more permissive attitudes about sex and that the secure attachment dimension is associated with mutually initiated sex and greater sexual enjoyment.

Methodological Issues

Sexuality research faces certain challenges because society deems most sexual interaction as private. For example, ethical constrictions limit the use of observation; studying couples engaging in in situ coitus is rare, although observation of flirting and related behaviors has been undertaken (i.e., Moore, 1985). Privacy considerations also mean that not everyone is willing to respond to sex-related questions in surveys or during interviews, the most common ways of collecting data in this field. Nonetheless, technolog-

ical advances in computer-assisted personal and telephone interviews have increased response rates to sensitive questions (Gribble, Miller, Rogers, & Turner, 1999).

Wiederman (2004) identified a number of additional methodological issues that can arise when investigating couples' sexuality. These include problems of nonrepresentative sampling, volunteer biases, a lack of convergence in partners' reports, and accuracy in individuals recalling relationship events. Analyzing couple data, with the lack of independence in partners' responses, poses additional challenges. Despite the conceptual and methodological challenges faced by sexuality researchers, considerable research has been done on sexuality in close relationships. Furthermore, methodological advances are being made to overcome these limitations, including event-sampling and diary studies, greater use of longitudinal research, development of valid and reliable multiple-item scales, and taking statistical dependence into account in statistical analyses (e.g., Wiederman, 2004).

Patterns of Sexual Behaviors in a Relational Context

In this section, we summarize the research that has focused on *patterns* of sexual behavior in society, based primarily on data collected in national samples and with an emphasis on the relational context of these sexual behaviors. Although most of the national data we summarize are from the U.S., we also highlight a few cross-cultural comparisons.

First Sexual Intercourse

National studies conducted with adolescents focus on the percentage of the participants who are sexually active by a particular age. Risman and Schwartz (2002) presented data from the Youth Risk Behavior Survey, which was conducted with national representative samples of high school students in the United States several times over the 1990s. They reported that in 1991, 54.1% of students aged 15 to 17 had engaged in sexual activity, but there was a decrease to 48.4% in the cohort surveyed in 1997. Further analyses conducted separately for male and female adolescents indicated that the decrease was greater for boys than girls. Risman and Schwartz concluded that today both boys and girls are likely to have their first sexual intercourse experience within a "relationship," in contrast to previous decades when many boys had first sex with a sexually experienced female outside of their social network.

Other national studies, such as the National Health and Social Life Survey (NHSLS; Laumann, Gagnon, Michael, & Michaels, 1994), have obtained retrospective data from adults on their premarital sexual activity. Such research indicates that by the age of 20, 80% to 90% of people have had sex and that the mean age of first sexual intercourse is around 16 to 17, although slightly higher for older generations and slightly lower for Blacks and Hispanics (e.g., Laumann et al., 1994). One of the most important predictors of early initiation to sex is being in a close, romantic relationship; hence, early initiation into dating is associated with early initiation into sex (e.g., Carver, Joyner, & Udry, 2003; Thornton, 1990).

Furthermore, research focused specifically on the experience of first sexual intercourse has found that most people report that it occurs in the context of a romantic relationship (Sprecher, Barbee, & Schwartz, 1995; Thornton, 1990). Even when first sex occurs in the context of romantic relationships, however, it can have different meanings for the partners depending on a number of factors, including whether they have expressed love to each other before having sex. Metts (2004), drawing from prior research on turning points in relationships (e.g., Baxter & Bullis, 1986), found that expressions of love and commitment before first sexual involvement in dating couples were associated with the greater likelihood that the sexual expression was perceived as a positive turning point and one that had positive outcomes for the relationship.

Number of Sexual Partners

For most people, sexual partners are typically also relational partners. That is, people usually feel affection, love, and commitment toward sexual partners and are involved with them in a relationship over time. Based on the General Social Survey (GSS) data, Smith (1998) reported that most sexual partners were described to be a married or cohabiting partner. Only 3% to 4% of sexual partners were prostitutes or one-night stands and another 4% to 5% were acquaintances (e.g., neighbors, coworkers) but not regular partners. In addition, national studies indicate that a majority of Americans have only one sexual–relational partner when asked about their sexual activity in a prior year. Only a small proportion of the participants report five or more sexual partners in the prior year, and they are primarily male, young, and not married or cohabiting (Laumann et al., 1994).

Over a lifetime, however, people accumulate sexual partners, and the number of partners may be increasing due to several social trends that have occurred over the past several decades. These trends include people entering marriage at a later age and the increased divorce rate, which allows for a period of postmarital sexual activity for many individuals (Smith, 1998).

For example, the respondents in the GSS reported an overall mean of seven partners during adulthood (Smith, 1998). For the NHSLS sample, Laumann et al. (1994) reported a median number of three partners for the entire sample. In almost all studies, including those conducted in countries other than North America, men report a greater number of sexual partners than do women (Wiederman, 1997). For example, Smith (1998) reported that the mean was 12.4 for men and 4.0 for women in the GSS. Several explanations have been offered for this gender difference, including that there is a small group of hypersexual women and prostitutes who have sex with many men. However, most experts argue that the gender differences can be best explained by the fact that men may exaggerate their reports of the number of sexual partners, whereas women may underreport (Laumann et al., 1994; Wiederman, 1997).

Men also both *desire* and *expect* to have more sexual partners in the future than do women (Schmitt, 2003; Simpson & Gangestad, 1991). This gender difference has been explained in various ways (e.g, Oliver & Hyde, 1993), including *differential socialization* (men may be socialized and rewarded for having more sexual partners) and *differential reproductive strategies based on evolutionary selection*.

Sexual Frequency

Large national data sets have also assessed how often people have sex. Although there is considerable variability in reports of sexual frequency, the overall average (mean or median) has been found to around 1 to 2 times a week. For example, with data from the National Survey of Family and Households (NSFH), Call, Sprecher, and Schwartz (1995) found that married respondents had an overall mean frequency of 6.3 times per month. In the NHSLS, the mean frequency of sexual activity was slightly more than 6.5 times per month (Laumann et al., 1994). Smith (1998) reported that married respondents in the GSS data reported engaging in sexual intercourse an average of 61 times per year, which is slightly more than once a week.

These national data sets and other large-scale studies (e.g., Blumstein & Schwartz, 1983; Edwards & Booth, 1976), as well as smaller geographically limited samples (Greenblat, 1983; James, 1983), also indicate that sex declines with age and number of years married. Thus, early in marriage, couples generally have sex frequently, but they do so less often over time. The decline appears to be due to psychological (attitudes about aging), social (children and busy jobs), and biological (illness) factors associated with the aging process (e.g., Call et al., 1995), as well as to a reduction in novelty associated with being with the same person for a long period of time. Relationship type also explains variance in sexual

frequency: Sex is more frequent in cohabiting relationships than in marital relationships even controlling for relationship length (e.g., Blumstein & Schwartz, 1983; Call et al., 1995; Laumann et al., 1994) and is also more frequent in gay relationships than in either lesbian relationships or heterosexual relationships (Blumstein & Schwartz, 1983). However, sexual frequency is generally not strongly associated with other social demographic characteristics, such as religion and socioeconomic status (e.g., Laumann et al., 1994). In a later section, we discuss the association between sexual frequency and sexual and relationship satisfaction.

Attitudes and Beliefs About Sexuality in a Relational Context

Sexual attitudes refer to what people think and feel about sexuality, for example, whether they approve of certain sexual behaviors (e.g., premarital sex) for themselves or others. In this section, we first discuss how people's attitudes about premarital sex depend on the relationship stage of the premarital relationships. Second, we describe research on other attitudes and beliefs people develop about sexuality in close relationships.

Premarital Sexual Standards and Relationship Stages

Sometimes only one question is included in a study to assess attitudes about premarital sexuality (e.g., "Do you approve of sexual intercourse before marriage?"), but most often multiple-item scales are used to assess the acceptance of sex for different relationship stages. The Reiss (1964) Premarital Sexual Permissiveness Scale was the first widely used sexual permissiveness scale. It asks respondents to indicate the acceptability of sexual behaviors for four levels of emotional involvement: no affection, strong affection, in love, and engaged. In a variation of Reiss's scale (Sprecher, McKinney, Walsh, & Anderson, 1988), respondents are asked about the acceptability of sex for five dating stages: first date, casually dating, seriously dating, preengagement (informal commitment to marry), and engagement.

When social scientists (e.g., Reiss, 1960, 1967) began studying college students' attitudes about premarital sexuality, the predominant sexual standards were the *abstinence standard* (the belief that sex is wrong for both men and women before marriage) and *the double standard* (greater sexual freedom for men than for women). More recently, however, young adults have been most likely to endorse a *permissiveness with affection standard* (sex is permissible in relationships with affection) and, to a lesser degree, a *permissiveness without affection standard* (sex is acceptable regardless of the emotional quality of the relationship; e.g., Sprecher & McKinney, 1993). These two standards (Reiss, 1967) have also been referred to as a *relational orientation* and a *recreational orientation*, respectively (e.g., DeLamater, 1989; Michael, Gagnon, Laumann, & Kolata, 1994).

For example, Sprecher (1989) and her colleagues (Sprecher & Hatfield, 1996; Sprecher et al., 1988) found that young adults (and especially women) expressed at least some disapproval of sexual intercourse on a first date and during casual dating, but generally approved of sexual intercourse for seriously dating and more committed stages (e.g., engagement). However, in their sample, 10% to 15% of young adults still endorsed an abstinence standard, that is, believed that sex should wait until marriage. Men were more accepting than were women of sexual behavior at early stages of the relationship (first date, casually dating), both for themselves and for others.

Other scales also measure attitudes about the appropriateness of sex in casual versus emotional contexts. For example, the Hendrick and Hendrick (1987) Sexual Attitudes Scale contains four subscales of sexual attitudes. The largest subscale, *Permissiveness*, measures acceptance of casual sex. Example items are, "I do not need to be committed to a person to have sex with him/her," and "The best sex is with no strings attached." In their research program, Hendrick and Hendrick (1987, 1995) have examined the links between sexual attitudes and love styles. Permissiveness has been found to be strongly associated with a *ludus* love style (a game-playing orientation), and also modestly *negatively* associated with *storge* (friendship love) and *agape* (selfless love). (We discuss the other subscales in the next section.)

Acceptance of sex for casual versus close relationship conditions is also assessed in Simpson and Gangestad's (1991) Sociosexuality Scale, which includes attitudinal and behavioral items that measure a *sociosexual orientation*. Two of the attitudinal items are, "Sex without love is OK," and "I would have to be closely attached to someone (both emotionally and psychologically) before I could feel comfortable and fully enjoy having sex with him or her." Those with a restricted sociosexual orientation need love, commitment, and emotional closeness before they would feel comfortable having sex. Unrestricted individuals, however, would feel comfortable having sex under more casual conditions. Simpson, Wilson, and Winterheld (2004) summarized research that has found that a more unrestricted sociosexual orientation is associated with being male, having dismissive–avoidant and fearful–avoidant attachment orientations, experiencing less commitment in relationships, and placing greater emphasis on selecting mates who are physically attractive and sexually experienced.

Beliefs About the Role of Sexuality in Relationships

People also form beliefs about the role of sexuality in established relationships. For example, some people believe that sex is essential to a good marriage, whereas others believe it is not that important (e.g., Fletcher & Kininmonth, 1992; Sprecher & Toro-Morn, 2002). In addition, people hold beliefs about specific aspects of sexuality, such as the sequence in which sexual behaviors should occur, whether one or both partners should initiate sex, and where and when sex should occur (e.g., Geer & Broussard, 1990).

We have already referred to the Hendrick and Hendrick (1987) Sexual Attitudes Scale.

The other subscales, in addition to permissiveness, refer to beliefs about specific practices or the role of sexuality in the relationship. The Sexual Practices subscale includes several items such as "Birth control is part of responsible sex" and "Using 'sex toys' during lovemaking is acceptable." The Communion subscale refers to the extent to which sexuality is viewed as a means for merging with the partner and includes such items as "A sexual encounter between two people deeply in love is the ultimate human interaction." The final subscale, Instrumentality, refers to the extent to which sex is seen as body focused versus person focused (e.g., "Sex is primarily a bodily function, like eating"). Hendrick and Hendrick (1987) found that men scored higher than women on permissiveness and instrumentality, but there were no gender differences on communion or sexual practices (similar results were found by Hendrick & Hendrick, 1995). Hendrick and Hendrick (1995) also reported that permissiveness and instrumentality are negatively associated with relationship satisfaction for both men and women. Beliefs about sexual practices were unrelated to satisfaction, and beliefs about sex as communion were positively associated with satisfaction.

Although Hendrick and Hendrick (1995) found associations between certain sexual beliefs (e.g., communion, instrumentality) and relationship satisfaction, Fletcher and Kininmonth (1992) found that the degree to which people believe that sex and passion are important for a successful and happy relationship is not associated with their relationship satisfaction. These beliefs were measured as a part of a larger Relationship Beliefs Scale (e.g., Fletcher & Kininmonth, 1992) and included such items as, "The best relationships are built on strong sexual attraction," "Without good sex relationships do not survive," and "Sexual compatibility is essential to good relationships." Fletcher and Kininmonth found that both student and nonstudent samples believe sex and passion are at least somewhat important to relationship success and that men rate passion as more important than do women.

In sum, people have diverse attitudes, standards, and beliefs about sexuality in close relationships. These attitudes and beliefs are likely to influence the meaning given to sexual acts in a current relationship. In addition, sexual attitudes and beliefs can influence initial attraction and relationship development, which we discuss in the next section.

Sexuality and Attraction and Relationship Development

People enter new relationships with a sexual history and a constellation of sexual beliefs and attitudes. These sexual standards and past sexual behaviors can influence their desirability as a dating or marriage partner to others. Two types of methods have been used to demonstrate the association between a person's sexuality and his or her mate desirability.

In one method, called mate selection studies (e.g., Buss, 1989a), people are presented with a list of traits or characteristics and are asked how much they would desire each trait in a partner. Included in this list are one or more traits associated with sexuality. The second method is experimental, in which participants are presented with information about a bogus stranger and asked how much they would be attracted to the person for a dating or marital relationship (e.g., Sprecher et al., 1991). The bogus stranger's degree of sexual experience is manipulated. Both methods generally demonstrate that low to moderate amounts of current or past sexual activities are desired more in a partner than is a history of many sexual partners or casual sexual activity (e.g., Bettor, Hendrick, & Hendrick, 1995; O'Sullivan, 1995; Sprecher, McKinney, & Orbuch, 1991; Sprecher, Regan, McKinney, Maxwell, & Wazienski, 1997).

There may be several explanations for why someone with less sexual experience is perceived to be more attractive than someone with more sexual experience, including (a) there is a greater risk of HIV and other STDs with a partner who has had many prior sexual partners or liberal sexual attitudes; (b) the implication may be that a person who has had multiple sexual partners may not remain faithful (research indicates that unfaithfulness is considered unattractive in a partner; e.g., Buss & Schmitt, 1993); and (c) the rewards associated with being someone's first or nearly first sexual partner. Although sexual experience does not generally contribute to attraction or desire, sexual passion and a high sex drive are valued traits in a partner (e.g., Buss & Schmitt, 1993; Regan, Levin, Sprecher, Christopher, & Cate, 2000; Sprecher & Regan, 2002). Furthermore, chastity or virginity, although valued more than sexual experience, is less important than other traits (e.g., kindness, physical attractiveness, social status) in the consideration of desirability of the partner (e.g., Sprecher et al., 1997).

The degree to which prior sexual experience is considered less desirable than lack of sexual experience, however, may depend on the relational context and the other person's sexual experience. Prior sexual experience can increase attraction or desirability when the target person is being considered for a short-term sexual relationship (e.g., Kenrick, Sundie, Nicastle, & Stone, 2001; Sprecher et al., 1991; Sprecher & Regan, 2002). In addition, people who themselves have extensive sexual experience are more attracted to someone with considerable sexual experience than are people with less or no sexual experience (e.g., Sprecher et al., 1997; Wiederman & Dubois, 1998).

The mate selection and experimental methods have also been used to examine whether the traits that attract people to someone as a sexual partner (i.e., sexual fling) are the same as those that attract them to someone for a long-term relationship. An attractive appearance has been found to be a more important determinant of desirability for a sexual relationship than for a long-term relationship (e.g., Regan, 1998; Regan & Berscheid, 1997; Sprecher & Regan, 2002). Furthermore, people are less demanding of a sexual partner than of a date or mate in regard to intrinsic personality characteristics (Sprecher & Regan, 2002).

Sexual attitudes and past sexual behavior affect not only initial attraction but also how soon the couple begins to have sex. If two partners enter the relationship with extensive prior sexual experience or liberal sexual attitudes, they are likely to have sex relatively early in their relationship, compared with their more sexually restrictive counterparts. Furthermore, the woman's previous sexual experiences have a greater impact than the man's in heterosexual relationships. For example, in the Boston Dating Couples Study, Peplau, Rubin, and Hill (1977) found that if the woman had previous sexual experience, the dating couple typically had sexual intercourse within 2 months, but if the woman was a virgin upon entering the dating relationship, the average time until sexual intercourse was more than 8 months. A man's prior sexual experience had much less influence on how soon the couple began having sex.

Sexual Expression, Sexual Satisfaction, and Relationship Quality

There is considerable empirical evidence supporting the interplay between the emotional and sexual aspects of close relationships. At the same time, it is not uncommon for people to experience emotional bonding in the absence of sexual desire for a specific person, or the reverse – sexual desire in the absence of emotional attachment (Diamond, 2003). However, it is safe to say that in romantically based relationships, the emotional–pair–bonding aspects are closely associated with the sexual aspects. In this section, we focus on this association of emotional and sexual aspects of romantic close relationships. We acknowledge that the link between emotional and sexual factors may be reciprocal and mediated by several sexual and nonsexual factors.

The Link between Sexual and Relationship Quality

The positive association between sexual satisfaction and relationship quality in close relationships has considerable empirical support. People who say they are sexually satisfied in their relationships are also likely to report higher levels of overall relationship satisfaction. This association has been found in marital (Blumstein & Schwartz, 1983; Cupach & Comstock, 1990; Edwards & Booth, 1994; Henderson-King & Veroff, 1994), dating–premarital (Byers, Demmons, & Lawrance, 1998; Davies, Katz, & Jackson, 1999; Sprecher, 2002), and homosexual couples (Kurdek, 1991). Sexual satisfaction is related not only to relationship satisfaction, it is also positively associated with other indicators of relationship quality, such as love (Aron & Henkemeyer, 1995; Grote & Frieze, 1998; Sprecher & Regan, 1998; Yela, 2000) and commitment or the likelihood that the relationship will last (Pinney, Gerrard, & Denney, 1987; Sprecher, 2002; Sprecher, Metts, Burleson, Hatfield, & Thompson, 1995; Waite & Joyner, 2001). The causal link between sexual and nonsexual aspects of relationships may be direct (e.g., when one increases, it causes increases in the other). On the other hand, it may be that sexual dimensions affect other relationship processes (e.g., sexual communication, conflict) that in turn lead to changes in general relationship dimensions. Conversely, changes in general relationship dimensions may affect relationship processes, which then induce changes in the sexual dimensions of a relationship. Unfortunately, there is surprisingly little work that directly investigates processes that might link the sexual and emotional–pair–bonding dimensions of relationships. Researchers have only indirectly studied such processes.

Processes That May Explain the Link between Sexual Satisfaction and Relationship Satisfaction

PHYSIOLOGICAL MECHANISMS

The link between sexual and global relationship satisfaction may be caused by physiological processes. There are no studies in humans that have explored this pathway. However, the existing animal research suggests that oxytocin, a neuropeptide hormone produced in the brain, may be responsible for the link between the sexual and nonsexual aspects of relationships. For exam-

ple, in nonhuman mammal experiments, the introduction of oxytocin into the brains of animals has been found to facilitate both interpersonal bonding and sexual interest and behavior (see Diamond, 2003, for a more complete discussion). In other words, it may be that when the sexual system is activated, oxytocin is released, which then activates the interpersonal bonding system; or the reverse may occur (e.g., activation of the bonding system leads to oxytocin release, which activates the sexual system). Physiological mediation of the association between the sexual and bonding systems is consistent with an evolutionary perspective. Ancestral individuals were likely to be reproductively successful when they could establish a strong interpersonal bond with a mate (Buss, 1994). For females, the strong bond reduced the likelihood that the male partner would allocate resources to other females. Furthermore, when a male established a close bond with a female, she would have been less likely to mate with someone else, thus increasing the likelihood of paternity for the male.

SEXUAL FREQUENCY

Sexual frequency is potentially one important mediator between sexual and nonsexual relationship satisfaction. Sexual frequency is related positively to sexual satisfaction (Blumstein & Schwartz, 1983) and general relationship satisfaction (Call et al., 1995), suggesting that it may account for the connection between sexual satisfaction and general relationship satisfaction. It is plausible that when people are generally satisfied with their partners, they may engage in more frequent intercourse, which may lead to greater sexual satisfaction. Increased sexual satisfaction may then lead to even more sexual intercourse, which could then promote greater overall global relationship satisfaction, thus establishing a cyclical process. Research has not addressed such cyclical–reciprocal processes, however.

In addition, we are not aware of any studies that have explored the processes that link sexual frequency with sexual and global relationship satisfaction. Exploring these processes could be facilitated by more theoretical work in the area. For example, why would increased sexual frequency lead to sexual satisfaction? From an exchange perspective, one might postulate that sexual frequency increases when partners perceive high rewards from both sexual and nonsexual aspects of the relationship. From a symbolic interaction perspective, increased sexual frequency might occur when people believe that they are competent in performing their role as wife, husband, or sex partner. Future research should address these issues.

SEXUAL COMMUNICATION

Sexual communication is related to both sexual (Byers & Demmons, 1999; Chesney, Blakeney, Cole, & Chan, 1981) and general relationship satisfaction (Byers & Demmons, 1999; Yelsma, 1986), suggesting that it might mediate between sexual and global relationship satisfaction. One important type of sexual communication, initiation or refusal of sexual interaction, is related to both sexual and global relationship satisfaction. Not surprisingly, increased refusals are related to lower sexual and relationship satisfaction, and increased levels of initiation are related positively to sexual and relationship satisfaction (Byers & Heinlein, 1989). Logically, when people are generally dissatisfied with a relationship, they may express their discontent through increased refusals to engage in sex, which then leads to increased sexual dissatisfaction. On the other hand, people who are dissatisfied with sex in the relationship may refuse initiations to avoid further aversive sexual interactions, which then can lead to lower general satisfaction.

A second possible communicative mediator of the link between sexual and relationship satisfaction is the expression of likes and dislikes for sexual behavior. Again, the disclosure of likes and dislikes to a partner is positively related to both sexual and global relationship satisfaction (Byers & Demmons, 1999; MacNeil & Byers, 1997; Purnine & Carey, 1997). These associations have been uncovered in both homosexual and heterosexual couples (Masters & Johnson, 1979).

Sexually satisfied people are likely to express their sexual likes and dislikes to each other. The resulting pleasure from engaging in preferred activities, or not engaging in disliked activities, may result in increased satisfaction in the relationship. However, an equally likely reverse path is that people who are satisfied with their relationships may feel comfortable disclosing their sexual likes and dislikes, thus leading to increased sexual satisfaction. Researchers have used exchange principles to explain the association of sexual communication with sexual and global relationship satisfaction (Byers & Demmons, 1999). However, symbolic interaction theory, which posits that relationships are negotiated and constructed through couples' communication, seems particularly applicable to research in this area.

When likes and dislikes differ between partners and partners refuse sexual initiations, conflict about sex can result. We turn to this topic next.

SEXUAL CONFLICT

Sexual conflict between partners may also link sexual and global relationship satisfaction in relationships. Relational conflict can arise when couples disagree about the frequency of sexual interaction, types of sexual activity, the inability to be sexually satisfied by the partner, and myriad other issues. However, the existing research on sexual conflict in ongoing romantic relationships is rather sparse.

Researchers have examined people's reports of conflict over sexual issues as it relates to sexual and nonsexual relationship quality. However, there are relatively few studies addressing these links. The existing studies have shown that sexual conflict is negatively associated with sexual and global relationship satisfaction in dating (Long, Cate, Fehsenfeld, & Williams, 1996) and married relationships (Buss, 1989b). In a dating study (Long et al., 1996), conflict over sexual issues (e.g., conflict over sexual frequency, amount of foreplay) was negatively related to both sexual and relationship satisfaction. Also, sexual conflict predicted general relationship satisfaction over and above the contribution of general conflict in the relationship in a 4-month follow-up of the respondents, suggesting a unique role for sexual conflict. A study with married individuals uncovered similar associations (Buss, 1989b). In this study, women experienced lower general satisfaction and sexual satisfaction the more their husbands were sexually aggressive. On the other hand, men were less generally satisfied and less sexually satisfied the more their wives were sexually withholding. In addition, Shackelford and Buss (1997) found that sexual conflict was negatively related to partners' esteem for their spouses. However, other research has failed to demonstrate that sexual conflict is related to general relationship satisfaction (Hurlbert, Apt, Hurlbert, & Pierce, 2000) but supported the link of sexual conflict with sexual satisfaction.

An evolutionary framework may be particularly useful in examining the role of sexual conflict in sexual and global relationship satisfaction. Evolutionary theory posits that sexual and other marital conflict lead to loss of esteem for the spouse (Shackelford & Buss, 1997). In early humans, such loss of spousal esteem would have motivated individuals to seek alternative partners with whom they would be more reproductively successful. Consequently, over historical time, present-day individuals retain the tendency for sexual conflict to be disruptive of committed relationships.

In summary, the association of sexual and global relationship satisfaction is well established. However, little is known about the mechanisms that link the two phenomena. Several mechanisms may link sexual and relationship satisfaction, such as physiological connections, coital frequency, sexual communication, and sexual conflict. In the next section, we discuss a more extreme type of sexual conflict, sexual aggression, as well as sexual jealousy.

The Dark Side of Sexuality

Although individuals are typically satisfied with their sexuality, sexuality can have a dark side. Individuals may suffer sexual dysfunction, partners can have extradyadic affairs, and couples may experience incompatibility. In this section, we focus on two common negative sides of sexuality: sexual aggression and sexual jealousy.

Sexual Aggression

Although most sexual interaction involves consensual acts between willing partners, this is not always the case. In fact, a recent national survey revealed that 17.6% of the females who participated were victims of rape or attempted rape (Tjaden & Thoennes, 2000). Intimate partners (current or former spouse, cohabitant, or a dating partner) accounted for 62% of the sexual assaults for women over age 18, and these individuals were more apt to injure their partner physically than were strangers or nonintimate acquaintances. Men who took part in the survey were not as likely to be victims; only 3% experienced rape or attempted rape. Their experiences were different from women's in other ways as well. Their assailants were more apt to be the same gender (male), their abuse typically occurred when they were under age 12, and intimate partners were much less likely to be perpetrators (only 18% of the cases).

RELATIONAL DYNAMICS OF SEXUAL AGGRESSION

A number of relational dimensions contribute to sexual aggression. Power is one dimension. Sexually aggressive single men and women, as well as sexually aggressive married men, exert control over their partners in areas of the relationship outside of the bedroom (Christopher & McQuaid, 1998; Finkelhor & Yllö, 1985). Commitment is another dimension. The chances of male sexual aggression increase with a commitment to monogamy among young single adults (Christopher, Owens, & Stecker, 1993) and adolescents (Small & Kerns, 1993). Moreover, some husbands see marriage as a license to victimize their wives sexually (Russell, 1990).

Two additional interrelated relational dimensions, consensual sexual behaviors and communication difficulties, play roles in sexual aggression in dating relationships. In some cases, consensual but noncoital behaviors preceded acts of single male sexual aggression (Kanin, 1970; Kanin & Parcell, 1977). At other times, couples have previously engaged in a given sexual act, but the woman is unwilling to do so at a particular time (Lloyd & Emery, 1991). Kanin (1970) speculated that women might not always understand that their dating partners become confused when they receive mixed signals of willingness. This may be especially true of men with a proclivity for using sexual aggression. It is not unusual for such single men to believe that their partners lead them on, even when this was not their partner's intention (Muehlenhard & Linton, 1987). Moreover, they may question the truthfulness of women's clear and direct messages of sexual refusal (Malamuth & Brown, 1994).

INDIVIDUAL TRAITS ASSOCIATED
WITH SEXUAL AGGRESSION

A number of traits characterize sexually aggressive men compared with their nonaggressive peers. Sex is often more central in lives of sexually aggressive men. Single sexually aggressive men report having more coital partners (Koss, Leonard, Beezley, & Oros, 1985) and are more likely to engage in coitus in uncommitted relationships (Lalumière & Quinsey, 1996). Sexually aggressive husbands may want sex up to 4 times a day and to engage in extreme sexual behaviors according to their wives (Finkelhor & Yllö, 1985). Not surprisingly, some sexually aggressive men, both single and married, find sex paired with violence arousing (Malamuth, 1986; Russell, 1990).

Other traits covary with the use of aggression. Single sexually aggressive men are more likely to accept rape myths and interpersonal violence (Byers & Eno, 1991) and feel hostile toward women (Malamuth, Lintz, Heavey, Barnes, & Acker, 1995). In addition, single sexually aggressive men, compared with nonaggressive peers, possess more traditional attitudes about women's place in society (Muehlenhard & Falcon, 1990) and more strongly endorse masculinity (Dean & Malamuth, 1997).

CONTEXTUAL INFLUENCES ASSOCIATED WITH
SEXUAL AGGRESSION

Single sexually aggressive men often join social groups with strong masculine orientations such as fraternities or sports teams (e.g., Frinter & Rubinson, 1993) and have friends who tend to be similarly aggressive toward their own dating partners (DeKeseredy & Kelly, 1995). These friends and social organizations likely support members' acts of sexual aggression by rewarding "sexual achievements" with increased social status (Koss & Dinero, 1988).

Another contextual influence on sexual aggression occurs on a cultural level. Legal support existed until recently in many states for husbands raping their wives (Russell, 1990). The lack of legal interdictions against husbands illustrates Burt's (1980) proposition that attitudinal support for men's sexual aggressiveness exists on a societal level. Investigations of this proposition generally confirm it but reveal that supportive attitudes are especially prevalent among single men who hold sex-role stereotyped beliefs (Lonsway & Fitzgerald, 1994). Even adolescents, particularly boys, often believe that it is permissible for a boy to force a girl to have sex under certain circumstances (Morrison, McLeod, Morrison, Anderson, & O'Connor, 1997).

Sexual Jealousy

Estimates of extradyadic affairs run as high as 30% in marriages (Laumann et al., 1994) and 40% in dating relationships (Wiederman & Hurd, 1999). Undoubtedly, these incidents or even the suspicion of these incidents likely trigger feelings of sexual jealousy (see Buunk & Dijkstra, this volume). Sexual jealousy occurs when partners suspect or know that their partner has had a sexual encounter with someone else (Guerrero, Spitzberg, & Yoshimura, 2004). Suspicions of an affair may be triggered by a partner's expression of relationship dissatisfaction, disengagement, unwillingness to spend time together, inconsiderateness, criticism, expressions of guilt, or reluctance to talk about a particular person (Shackelford

& Buss, 1997). These signs may also generate emotional jealousy or jealousy based on knowledge or suspicions that a partner is emotionally involved with another.

Explanations of jealousy have focused on its antecedents including evolution and biology, culture, personality, qualities of the relationship, situational factors, and intentionally induced jealousy (see Guerrero et al., 2004, for a review). Testing evolutionary-based hypotheses, however, has dominated this area of research. According to these hypotheses, extradyadic sexual involvement generates concerns about certainty of paternity for men. Men therefore would be more jealous than women when infidelity involves sexual acts. Women, on the other hand, can be certain of their maternal status but more concerned that their partner continue to provide resources; hence, women should be more jealous of acts of emotional infidelity (for reviews see Buss, 1998; Buunk & Dijkstra, 2000). Although findings from a number of studies support these hypotheses (Buss, 1998), some scholars challenge these results by citing a reliance on responses to hypothetical as opposed to actual experiences of infidelity and by reporting inconsistent findings when different response formats are used to examine the same manipulation (e.g., DeSteno & Salovey, 1996; Harris, 2002).

Thus far in this chapter, we have focused on sexuality in romantic and marital relationships. In this final section, we discuss parental and peer influence on sexuality, particularly among adolescents.

Sexuality As Affected by Parents and Peers

Scholars often depict sexual expression as a dyadic interaction that reflects individual choice. Research suggests, however, that social forces also influence sexuality. Much of this research has focused on sexual decision making in dating relationships. Parents and peers represent the most proximal of these forces and are discussed in this section. Religion and ethnicity are more distal influences on sexuality, and their discussion is beyond the scope of this chapter, but see Christopher (2001) for a discussion of the effects of these factors on adolescent and young adult sexuality.

Parents' sexual socialization of their children follows a developmental progression (see Christopher, 2001, for a discussion). During early childhood, *if* parents explain reproduction, they frequently leave out critical details even when their children are cognitively ready to understand them[2] (Goldman & Goldman, 1982; Raffaelli & Green, 2003). Many parents, in fact, delay talking to their children about sex and may unknowingly wait until their child is sexually active (K. S. Miller, Levin, Whitaker, & Xu, 1998). Even then, the likelihood of parents, usually mothers, conversing with their offspring about sex may be dependent on the comfort level of the parent (White, Wright, & Barnes, 1995).

Parents' effectiveness at socializing their adolescents in the area of sexuality is dependent on three central qualities of the parent–child relationship: closeness–support, control attempts, and monitoring (see B. C. Miller, 2002, for a review). Teens are more likely to adopt sexual attitudes that parallel their parents, and limit or delay their sexual involvement, if they feel close to their parents and believe their parents support them (Davis & Friel, 2001; Luster & Small, 1994). Teens are also more likely to delay sexual involvement if their parents exert moderate levels of control over their offspring's life rather than too little or too much (Hovell et al., 1994; B. C. Miller, McCoy, Olson, & Wallace, 1986) and if they monitor their teen's daily activities (Small & Luster, 1994).

Peers are an additional socialization influence on youth's sexuality (Gilmore et al., 2002). Early adolescents are often concerned with conformity to peer standards. Judgments about peer standards, however, are tied to teens' *perceptions* of their friends' sexual attitudes and behaviors. These perceptions are positively associated with early adolescents' own attitudes and behavior (Kinsman, Romer, Furstenberg, & Schwartz, 1998). Friends are also the most frequent source of teens' first romantic pairings, pairings which can include coital interaction (Carver et al., 2003).

The nature of peer influence changes as youth mature into single young adults. One of the developmental tasks these individuals face is to form an adult identity separate from one's family of origin. Not only do peers serve as models for sexual identities at this age (Laumann et al., 1994), but peers also support experimenting with adult roles (Berndt, 1996). It is not surprising then that young adults' perceptions of their friends' sexual behavior are positively related to their own sexual behavior (Cohen & Shotland, 1996; Maticka-Tyndale et al., 2003). It is important to note though that young adults' experimentation with sexual roles is additionally supported by societal attitudes that become increasingly permissive as youth age (Smith, 1994).

Conclusions and Future Research Directions

Several topics about sexuality in a relational context were discussed in this chapter including the role of sexuality in the attraction process, attitudes and beliefs about premarital sex and about the role of sex in relationships, as well as the complex associations between sexual satisfaction and relationship satisfaction. The phenomena of sexual aggression, sexual jealousy, and the role of parents and peers in influencing sexuality particularly among adolescents were explored. Finally, we summarized overall patterns of sexual behavior within a relational context and discussed methodological and theoretical issues in studying sexuality in a relational context. The research reviewed came from diverse sources and disciplines.

Our review of the literature concerning the link of sexuality with relationship dynamics showed that there is a great need for more research in this area. We believe that future research is needed in a number of specific areas. First, research should examine the mechanisms that link the sexual dimensions of relationships with general relationship dimensions; relational aspects such as sexual communication, sexual conflict, and other factors may be responsible for this association. The search for mediators might additionally include physiological mediators (see Diamond, 2003), motivated cognition, or positive illusion processes in relationships (Murray, 1999).

Second, examining the association of sexuality with close relationships could benefit from investigating more proximal relationship processes. This would require more attention to within-person or within-couple research designs compared with between-person designs that allow generalization of findings only to the group level. For example, daily diary designs and the use of multilevel modeling statistical methods (Bryk & Raudenbush, 1992) allow investigators to make conclusions at the daily level. A between-persons analysis of the link of sexual satisfaction with relationship satisfaction may allow one to conclude that on average (e.g., the group level), the two constructs are positively related. A within-person analysis of daily diary data might show that sexual and relationship satisfaction are positively related thereby allowing researchers to conclude that on *days* when sexual satisfaction is high, so is relationship satisfaction. Such data may prove useful for designing intervention programs addressing sexual issues in relationships.

Other researchers could help to illuminate the role of sexuality in marriage, a role that has been previously ignored. Christopher and Kisler (2004) speculated that marital partners have a number of sexual role expectations and seek therapy when expectations are violated; their assertion is worthy of empirical testing. Investigators of marital sexuality should additionally consider broadening the sexual variables they include beyond coital frequency. The saliency of sex, sexual variation, and sexual desire represent additional variables that could be explored.

We also encourage research on how changes in society, including in technology and the medicalization of sexuality, affect the sexual relationship of couples. For example, in the technology realm, the Internet provides ready access to sexual materials. Does such availability positively affect couples' sexuality? Couples can potentially use the Internet to increase sexual excitement, to learn about new techniques, or to obtain information for their sexual questions or problems. Contrarily, the ready availability of pornography or cybersexual relationships may promote secret liaisons, jealous reactions, or cause couples to redefine the boundaries of their relationship. These areas are worthy of investigation.

In the medical realm, we know little about how the availability of Viagra and other sex drugs has affected the sex lives of couples. Preliminary evidence (e.g., Pallas, Levine, Althof, & Risen, 2000) suggests that both men and their partners are satisfied with men's increased ability to maintain an erection. However, the long-term consequence for couples' relationships characterized by the use of these drugs has not been studied. Do they increase the desirability of the partners, the couple's intimacy, or their relationship satisfaction? How long do these effects last? These and many other issues could be examined in future research that focuses on sexuality in a relational context.

Footnotes

1. Sexuality should not be confused with sexual orientation, which focuses on the sex of one's partner.
2. This was not true of Scandinavian parents who typically provided detailed explanations of reproductions to their children (Goldman & Goldman, 1982).

References

Aron, A., & Henkemeyer, L. (1995). Marital satisfaction and passionate love. *Journal of Social and Personal Relationships*, 12, 139–146.

Baxter, L. A., & Bullis, C. (1986). Turning points in developing romantic relationship. *Human Communication Research*, 12, 469–493.

Berndt, T. J. (1996). Friendships in adolescence. In N. Vanzetti & S. Duck (Eds.), *A lifetime of relationships* (pp. 181–121). Pacific Grove, CA: Brooks/Cole.

Bettor, L., Hendrick, S. S., & Hendrick, C. (1995). Gender and sexual standards in dating relationships. *Personal Relationships*, 2, 359–369.

Blumstein, P., & Schwartz, P. (1983). *American couples: Money, work, sex*. New York: Morrow.

Bogart, L. M., Cecil, H., Wagstaff, D. A., Pinkerton, S. D., & Abramson, P. R. (2000). Is it "sex"?: College students' interpretations of sexual behavior terminology. *Journal of Sex Research*, 37, 108–116.

Bryk, A. S., & Raudenbush, S. W. (1992). *Hierarchical linear models: Applications and data analysis methods*. Newbury Park. CA: Sage.

Burt, M. R. (1980). Cultural myths and supports for rape. *Journal of Personality and Social Psychology*, 38, 217–230.

Buss, D. M. (1989a). Sex differences in human mate preferences: Evolutionary hypotheses tested in 37 cultures. *Behavioral and Brain Sciences*, 12, 1–49.

Buss, D. M. (1989b). Conflict between the sexes: Strategic interference and the evocation of anger and upset. *Journal of Personality and Social Psychology*, 56, 735–747.

Buss, D. M. (1994). *The evolution of desire: Strategies of human mating*. New York: Basic Books.

Buss, D. M. (1998). Sexual strategies theory: Historical origins and current status. *Journal of Sex Research*, 35, 19–31.

Buss, D. M., & Schmitt, D. P. (1993). Sexual strategies theory: An evolutionary perspective on human mating. *Psychological Review*, 100, 204–232.

Buunk, B. P., & Dijkstra, P. (2000). Extradyadic relationships and jealousy. In C. Hendrick & S. Hendrick (Eds.), *Close relationships: A sourcebook* (pp. 317–329). Thousand Oaks, CA: Sage.

Byers, E. S., & Demmons, S. (1999). Sexual satisfaction and sexual self-disclosure within dating relationships. *Journal of Sex Research*, 36, 180–189.

Byers, E. S., Demmons, S., & Lawrance, K. (1998). Sexual satisfaction within dating relationships: A test of the interpersonal exchange model of sexual satisfaction. *Journal of Social and Personal Relationships*, 15, 257–267.

Byers, E. S., & Eno, R. J. (1991). Predicting men's sexual coercion and aggression from attitudes, dating history, and sexual response. *Journal of Psychology and Human Sexuality, 4*, 55–70.

Byers, E. S., & Heinlein, L. (1989). Predicting initiations and refusals of sexual activities in married and cohabiting heterosexual couples. *Journal of Sex Research, 26*, 210–231.

Byers, E. S., & Wang. A. (2004). Understanding sexuality in close relationships from the social exchange perspective. In J. Harvey, A. Wenzel, & S. Sprecher (Eds.), *The handbook of sexuality in close relationships* (pp. 203–234). Mahwah, NJ: Erlbaum.

Call, V., Sprecher, S., & Schwartz, P. (1995). The incidence and frequency of marital sex in a national sample. *Journal of Marriage and the Family, 57*, 639–650.

Carver, K., Joyner, K., & Udry, J. R. (2003). National estimates of adolescent romantic relationships. In P. Florsheim (Ed.), *Adolescent romantic relationships and sexual behavior: Theory, research, and practical implications* (pp. 23–56). Mahwah, NJ: Erlbaum.

Chesney, A. P., Blakeney, P. E., Cole, C. M., & Chan, F. A. (1981). A comparison of couples who have sought sex therapy with couples who have not. *Journal of Sex and Marital Therapy, 7*, 131–140.

Christopher, F. S. (2001). *To dance the dance: A symbolic interactional exploration of premarital sexuality.* Mahwah, NJ: Erlbaum.

Christopher, F. S., & Kisler, T. S. (2004). Exploring marital sexuality: Peeking inside the bedroom and discovering what we don't know – but should! In J. Harvey, A. Wenzel, & S. Sprecher (Eds.), *The handbook of sexuality in close relationships* (pp. 371–384). Mahwah, NJ: Erlbaum.

Christopher, F. S., & McQuaid, S. (1998, June). *Dating relationships and men's sexual aggression: A test of a relationship-based model.* Biennial meeting of the International Society for the Study of Personal Relationships, Saratoga Springs, NY.

Christopher, F. S., Owens, L. A., & Stecker, H. L. (1993). An examination of single men and women's sexual aggressiveness in dating relationships. *Journal of Social and Personal Relationships, 10*, 511–527.

Cohen, L. L., & Shotland, R. L. (1996). Timing of first sexual intercourse in a relationship: Expectations, experiences, and perceptions of others. *Journal of Sex Research, 33*, 291–299.

Cupach, W. R., & Comstock, J. (1990). Satisfaction with sexual communication in marriage: Links to sexual satisfaction and dyadic adjustment. *Journal of Social and Personal Relationships, 7*, 179–186.

Davies, S., Katz, J., & Jackson, J. L. (1999). Sexual desire discrepancies: Effects on sexual and relationship satisfaction in heterosexual dating couples. *Archives of Sexual Behavior, 28*, 553–567.

Davis, E. C., & Friel, L. V. (2001). Adolescent sexuality: Disentagling the effects of family structure and family context. *Journal of Marriage and Family, 63*, 669–681.

Dean, K. E., & Malamuth, N. M. (1997). Characteristics of men who aggress sexually and of men who imagine aggressing: Risk and moderating variables. *Journal of Personality and Social Psychology, 72*, 449–455.

DeKeseredy, W. S., & Kelly, K. (1995). Sexual abuse in Canadian university and college dating relationships: The contribution of male peer support. *Journal of Family Violence, 10*, 41–53.

DeLamater, J. D. (1989). The social control of human sexuality. In K. McKinney & S. Sprecher (Eds.), *Human sexuality: The societal and interpersonal context* (pp. 30–62). Norwood, NJ: Ablex.

DeLamater, J., & Hyde, J. S. (2004). Conceptual and theoretical issues in studying sexuality in close relationships. In J. Harvey, A. Wenzel, & S. Sprecher (Eds.), *The handbook of sexuality in close relationships* (pp. 7–30). Mahwah, NJ: Erlbaum

DeSteno, D. A., & Salovey, P. (1996). Evolutionary origins of sex differences in jealousy: Questioning the fitness model. *Psychological Science, 7*, 367–372.

Diamond, L. (2003). What does sexual orientation orient? A biobehavioral model distinguishing romantic love and sexual desire. *Psychological Review, 110*, 173–192.

Edwards, J. N., & Booth, A. (1976). Sexual behavior in and out of marriage: An assessment of correlates. *Journal of Marriage and the Family, 38*, 73–81.

Edwards, J. N., & Booth, A. (1994). Sexuality, marriage, and well-being: The middle years. In A. S. Rossi (Ed.), *Sexuality across the life course* (pp. 233–259). Chicago: University of Chicago Press.

Ehrman, W. (1959). *Premarital dating behavior.* New York: Henry Holt.

Feeney, J. A., & Noller, P. (2004). Attachment and sexuality in close relationships. In J. Harvey, A. Wenzel, & S. Sprecher (Eds.), *The handbook* of sexuality in close relationships (pp. 183–201). Mahwah, NJ: Erlbaum.

Finkelhor, D., & Yllö, K. (1985). License to rape: Sexual abuse of wives. New York: Holt, Rinehart, and Winston.

Fletcher, G. J. O., & Kininmonth, L. A. (1992). Measuring relationship beliefs: An individual differences scale. Journal of Research in Personality, 26, 371–397.

Frinter, M. P., & Rubinson, L. (1993). Acquaintance rape: The influence of alcohol, fraternity membership, and sports team membership. Journal of Sex Education and Therapy, 19, 272–284.

Gagnon, J. H. (1990). The implicit and explicit use of the scripting perspective in sex research. Annual Review of Sex Research, 1, 1–43.

Geer, J. H., & Broussard, D. B. (1990). Scaling heterosexual behavior and arousal: Consistency and sex differences. Journal of Personality and Social Psychology, 58, 664–671.

Gilmore, M. R., Archibald, M. E., Morrison, D. M., Wilsdon, A., Wells, E. A., Hoppe, M. J., et al. (2002). Teen sexual behavior: Applicability of the theory of reasoned action. Journal of Marriage and Family, 64, 885–897.

Goldman, R., & Goldman, S. (1982). Children's sexual thinking. London: Routledge & Kegan Paul.

Greenblat, C. S. (1983). The salience of sexuality in the early years of marriage. Journal of Marriage and the Family, 45, 289–299.

Gribble, J. N., Miller, H. G., Rogers, S. M., & Turner, C. F. (1999). Interview mode and measurement of sexual behaviors: Methodological issues. Journal of Sex Research, 36, 16–24.

Grote, N. K., & Frieze, I. H. (1998). Remembrance of things past: Perceptions of marital love from its beginnings to the present. Journal of Social and Personal Relationships, 15, 91–109.

Guerrero, L., Spitzberg, B. H., & Yoshimura, S. M. (2004). Sexual and emotional jealousy. In J. Harvey, A. Wenzel, & S. Sprecher (Eds.), The handbook of sexuality in close relationships (pp. 311–345). Mahwah, NJ: Erlbaum.

Harris, C. R. (2002). Sexual and romantic jealousy in heterosexual and homosexual adults. Psychological Science, 13, 7–12.

Harvey, J., Wenzel, A., & Sprecher, S., Eds. (2004). Handbook of sexuality in close relationships. Mahwah, NJ: Erlbaum.

Henderson-King, D. H., & Veroff, J. (1994). Sexual satisfaction and marital well-being in the first years of marriages. Journal of Social and Personal Relationships, 11, 509–534.

Hendrick, S. S., & Hendrick, C. (1987). Multidimensionality of sexual attitudes. Journal of Sex Research, 23, 502–526.

Hendrick, S. S., & Hendrick, C. (1995). Gender differences and similarities in sex and love. Personal Relationships, 2, 55–65.

Hovell, M., Sipan, C., Blumberg, E., Atkins, C., Hofstetter, C. R., & Kreitner, S. (1994). Family influences on Latino and Anglo adolescents sexual behavior. Journal of Marriage and the Family, 56, 973–986.

Hurlbert, D. F., Apt, C., Hurlbert, M. K., & Pierce, A. P. (2000). Sexual compatibility and the sexual desire–motivation relation in females with hypoactive sexual desire disorder. Behavior Modification, 24, 325–347.

James, W. H. (1983). Decline in coital rates with spouses' ages and duration of marriage. Journal of Biosocial Science, 15, 83–87.

Kanin, E. J. (1970). Sex aggression by college men. Medical Aspects of Human Sexuality, 4, 28–40.

Kanin, E. J., & Parcell, S. R. (1977). Sexual aggression: A second look at the offended female. Archives of Sexual Behavior, 6, 67–76.

Kenrick, D. T., Sundie, J. M., Nicastle, L. D., & Stone, G. O. (2001). Can one ever be too wealthy or too chaste? Searching for nonlinearities in mate judgment. Journal of Personality and Social Psychology, 80, 462–471.

Kinsman, S. B., Romer, D., Furstenberg, F. F., & Schwartz, D. F. (1998). Early sexual initiation: The role of peer norms. Pediatrics, 102, 1185–1192.

Kirkendall, L. A. (1961). Premarital intercourse and interpersonal relationships. New York: Gramercy.

Koss, M. P., & Dinero, T. E. (1988). Predictors of sexual aggression among a national sample of male college students. In R. A. Prentky & V. L. Quinsey (Eds.), Human sexual aggression: Current perspectives. Annals of the New York Academy of Sciences, 528, 133–146.

Koss, M. P., Leonard, K. E., Beezley, D. A., & Oros, C. J. (1985). Nonstranger sexual aggression: A discriminant analysis of the psychological characteristics of undetected offenders. Sex Roles, 12, 981–992.

Kurdek, L. A. (1991). Sexuality in homosexual and heterosexual couples. In K. McKinney & S. Sprecher (Eds.), Sexuality in close relationships (pp. 177–191). Mahwah, NJ: Erlbaum.

Lalumière, M. L., & Quinsey, V. L. (1996). Sexual deviance, antisociality, mating effort, and the use of sexually coercive behaviors. *Personality and Individual Differences*, 21, 34–48.

Laumann, E. O., Gagnon, J. H., Michael, R. T., & Michaels, S. (1994). *The social organization of sexuality: Sexual practices in the United States*. Chicago: University of Chicago Press.

Lawrence, K., & Byers, E. S. (1995). Sexual satisfaction in long-term heterosexual relationships: The interpersonal exchange model of sexual satisfaction. *Personal Relationships*, 2, 267–285.

Lloyd, S. A. & Emery, B. (1991). The darkside of courtship: Violence and sexual exploitation. *Family Relations*, 40, 14–20.

Long, E. C. J., Cate, R. M. Fehsenfeld, D. A., & Williams, K. M. (1996). A longitudinal assessment of a measure of premarital sexual conflict. *Family Relations*, 45, 302–308.

Longmore, M. A. (1998). Symbolic interactionism and the study of sexuality. *Journal of Sex Research*, 35, 44–57.

Lonsway, K. A., & Fitzgerald, L. F. (1994). Rape myths: In review. *Psychology of Women Quarterly*, 18, 133–164.

Luster, T., & Small, S. A. (1994). Factors associated with sexual risk-taking behaviors among adolescents. *Journal of Marriage and the Family*, 56, 622–632.

MacNeil, S., & Byers, E. S. (1997). The relationships between sexual problems, sexual communication and sexual satisfaction. *Canadian Journal of Human Sexuality*, 6, 277–283.

Malamuth, N. M. (1986). Predictors of naturalistic sexual aggression. *Journal of Personality and Social Psychology*, 50, 953–962.

Malamuth, N. M., & Brown, L. M. (1994). Sexually aggressive men's perceptions of women's communications: Testing three explanations. *Journal of Personality and Social Psychology*, 67, 699–712.

Malamuth, N. M., Lintz, D., Heavey, C. L., Barnes, G., & Acker, M. (1995). Using the confluence model of sexual aggression to predict men's conflict with women: A 10-year follow-up study. *Journal of Personality and Social Psychology*, 69, 353–369.

Masters, W. H., & Johnson, V. (1979). *Homosexuality in perspective*. Boston: Little, Brown.

Maticka-Tyndale, E., Herold, E. S., & Oppermann, M. (2003). Casual sex among Australian schoolies. *Journal of Sex Research*, 40, 158–169.

McKinney, K., & Sprecher, S. (Eds.). (1989). *Human sexuality: The societal and interpersonal context*. Norwood, NJ: Ablex.

McKinney, K., & Sprecher, S. (Eds.). (1991). *Sexuality in close relationships*. Hillsdale, NJ: Erlbaum.

Metts, S. (2004). First sexual involvement in romantic relationships: An empirical investigation of communicative framing, romanticism, and attachment orientation in the passion turning point. In J. Harvey, A. Wenzel, & S. Sprecher (Eds.), *The handbook of sexuality in close relationships* (pp. 135–158). Mahwah, NJ: Erlbaum.

Michael, R. T., Gagnon, J. H., Laumann, E. O., & Kolata, G. (1994). *Sex in America: A definitive survey*. Boston: Little, Brown.

Miller, B. C. (2002). Family influences on adolescent sexual and contraceptive behavior. *Journal of Sex Research*, 39, 22–26.

Miller, B. C., McCoy, J. K., Olson, T., & Wallace, C. M. (1986). Parental discipline and control attempts in relation to adolescent sexual attitudes and behaviors. *Journal of Marriage and the Family*, 48, 503–512.

Miller, K. S., Levin, M. L., Whitaker, D. J., & Xu, X. (1998). Patterns of condom use among adolescents: The impact of mother–adolescent communication. *American Journal of Public Health*, 88, 1542–1544.

Moore, M. M. (1985). Nonverbal courtship patterns in women: Context and consequence. *Ethology and Sociobiology*, 6, 237–247.

Morrison, T. G., McLeod, L. D., Morrison, M. A., Anderson, D., & O'Connor, W. S. (1997). Gender stereotyping, homonegativity and misconceptions about sexually coercive behavior among adolescents. *Youth and Society*, 29, 134.

Muehlenhard, C. L., & Falcon, P. L. (1990). Men's heterosocial skill and attitudes toward women as predictors of verbal sexual coercion and forceful rape. *Sex Roles*, 23, 241–259.

Muehlenhard, C. L., & Linton, (1987). Date rape and sexual aggression in dating situations: Incidence and risk factors. *Journal of Counseling Psychology*, 34, 186–196.

Murray, S. L. (1999) The quest for conviction: Motivated cognition in romantic relationships. *Psychological Inquiry*, 10, 23–34.

Oliver, M. B., & Hyde, J. S. (1993). Gender differences in sexuality: A meta-analysis. *Psychological Bulletin*, 114, 29–51.

O'Sullivan, L. F. (1995). Less is more: The effects of sexual experience on judgments of men's and women's personality characteristics and relationship desirability. *Sex Roles, 33*, 159–181.

Pallas, J., Levine, S. B., Althof, S. E., & Risen, C. B. (2000). A study using Viagra in a mental health practice. *Journal of Sex and Marital Therapy, 26*, 41–50.

Peplau, L. A., Rubin, Z., & Hill, C. T. (1977). Sexual intimacy in dating relationships. *Journal of Social Issues, 33*, 86–109.

Pinney, E. M., Gerrard, M., & Denney, N. W. (1987). The Pinney Sexual Satisfaction Inventory. *Journal of Sex Research, 23*, 233–251.

Purnine, D. M., & Carey, M. P. (1997). Interpersonal communication and sexual adjustment: The roles of understanding and agreement. *Journal of Clinical and Consulting Psychology, 65*, 1017–1025.

Raffaelli, M., & Green, S. (2003). Parent–adolescent communication about sex: Retrospective reports by Latino college students. *Journal of Marriage and Family, 65*, 471–481.

Regan, P. C. (1998). Minimum mate selection standards as a function of perceived mate value, relationship context, and gender. *Journal of Psychology and Human Sexuality, 10*, 53–73.

Regan, P. C., & Berscheid, E. (1997). Gender differences in characteristics desired in a potential sexual and marriage partner. *Journal of Psychology and Human Sexuality, 9*, 25–37.

Regan, P. C., Levin, L., Sprecher, S., Christopher, F. S., & Cate, R. (2000). Partner preferences: What characteristics do men and women desire in their short-term sexual and long-term romantic partners? *Journal of Psychology and Human Sexuality, 12*, 1–21.

Reiss, I. L. (1960). *Premarital sexual standards in America.* New York: Free Press.

Reiss, I. L. (1964). The scaling of premarital sexual permissiveness. *Journal of Marriage and the Family, 26*, 188–198.

Reiss, I. L. (1967). *The social context of premarital sexual permissiveness.* New York: Holt, Reinhardt & Winston.

Risman, B., & Schwartz, P. (2002). After the sexual revolution: Gender politics in teen dating. *Contexts, 1*, 16–24.

Rusbult, C. E. (1983). A longitudinal test of the investment model: The development (and deterioration) of satisfaction and commitment in heterosexual involvements. *Journal of Personality and Social Psychology, 45*, 101–117.

Russell, D. E. H. (1990) *Rape in marriage: Expanded and rev. ed. with new introduction.* Bloomington: Indiana University Press.

Schmitt, D. P. (2003). Universal sex differences in the desire for sexual variety: Tests from 52 nations, 6 continents, and 13 islands. *Journal of Personality and Social Psychology, 85*, 85–104.

Shackelford, T. K., & Buss, D. M. (1997). Spousal esteem. *Journal of Family Psychology, 11*, 478–488.

Shaver, P. R., Hazan, C., & Bradshaw, D. (1988). Love as attachment: The integration of three behavioral systems. In R. J. Sternberg & M. Barnes (Eds.), *The psychology of love* (pp. 68–99). New Haven, CT: Yale University Press.

Simpson, J. A., & Gangestad, S. W. (1991). Individual differences in sociosexuality: Evidence for convergent and discriminant validity. *Journal of Personality and Social Psychology, 60*, 870–883.

Simpson, J. A., Wilson, C. L., & Winterheld, H. A. (2004). Sociosexuality and romantic relationships. In J. Harvey, A. Wenzel, & S. Sprecher (Eds.), *Handbook of sexuality in close relationships* (pp. 87–112). Mahwah, NJ: Erlbaum.

Small, S. A., & Kerns, D. (1993). Unwanted sexual activity among peers during early and middle adolescence: Incidence and risk factors. *Journal of Marriage and the Family, 55*, 941–952.

Small, S. A., & Luster, T. (1994). Adolescent sexual activity: An ecological, risk-factor approach. *Journal of Marriage and the Family, 56*, 181–192.

Smith, T. W. (1994). Attitudes toward sexual permissiveness: Trends, correlates, and behavioral connections. In A. S. Rossi (Ed.), *Sexuality across the life course* (pp. 63–97). Chicago: University of Chicago Press.

Smith, T. W. (1998). American sexual behavior: Trends, socio-demographic differences, and risk behavior. *GSS Topical Report No. 25.* Chicago: National Opinion Research Center, University of Chicago.

Sprecher, S. (1989). Premarital sexual standards for different categories of individuals. *Journal of Sex Research, 26*, 232–248.

Sprecher, S. (1998). Social exchange theories and sexuality. *Journal of Sex Research, 35*, 32–43.

Sprecher, S. (2002). Sexual satisfaction in premarital relationships: Associations with satisfaction, love, commitment, and stability. *Journal of Sex Research, 3*, 1–7.

Sprecher, S., Barbee, A., & Schwartz, P. (1995). Was it good for you, too?: Gender differences in first sexual intercourse experiences. *Journal of Sex Research, 32*, 3–15.

Sprecher, S., & Hatfield, E. (1996). Premarital sexual standards among U.S. college students: Comparison with Russian and Japanese students. *Archives of Sexual Behavior, 25*, 261–288.

Sprecher, S., & McKinney, K. (1993). *Sexuality*. Newbury Park, CA: Sage.

Sprecher, S., McKinney, K., & Orbuch, T. L. (1991). The effect of current sexual behavior on friendship, dating, and marriage desirability. *Journal of Sex Research, 28*, 387–408.

Sprecher, S., McKinney, K., Walsh, R., & Anderson, C. (1988). A revision of the Reiss Premarital Sexual Permissiveness Scale. *Journal of Marriage and the Family, 50*, 821–828.

Sprecher, S., Metts, S., Burleson, B., Hatfield, E., & Thompson, A. (1995). Domains of expression interaction in intimate relationships: Associations with satisfaction and commitment. *Family Relations, 44*, 203–210.

Sprecher, S., & Regan, P. C. (1998). Passionate and companionate love in courting and young married couples. *Sociological Inquiry, 68*, 163–185.

Sprecher, S., & Regan, P. C. (2002). Liking some things (in some people) more than others: Partner preferences in romantic relationships and friendships. *Journal of Social and Personal Relationships, 19*, 463–481.

Sprecher, S., Regan, P. C., McKinney, K., Maxwell, K., & Wazienski, R. (1997). Preferred level of sexual experience in a date or mate: The merger of two methodologies. *Journal of Sex Research, 34*, 327–337.

Sprecher, S., & Toro-Morn, M. (2002). A study of men and women from different sides of earth to determine if men are from Mars and women are from Venus in their beliefs about love and romantic relationships. *Sex Roles, 46*, 131–147.

Stryker, S., & Statham, A. (1985). Symbolic interaction and role theory. In G. Lindzey & E. Aronson (Eds.), *Handbook of social psychology* (pp. 311–377). New York: Random House.

Thornton, A. (1990). The courtship process and adolescent sexuality. *Journal of Family Issues, 11*, 239–273.

Tjaden, P., & Thoennes, N. (2000). *Full report of the prevalence, incidence, and consequences of violence against women: Findings from the national violence against women survey*. Washington, DC: National Institute of Justice and the Centers for Disease Control and Prevention (NCJ 183781).

Waite, L. J., & Joyner, K. (2001). Emotional satisfaction and physical pleasure in sexual unions: Time horizon, sexual behavior, and sexual exclusivity. *Journal of Marriage and Family, 63*, 247–264.

Weis, D. L. (1998). The use of theory in sexuality research. *Journal of Sex Research, 35*, 1–9.

White, C. P., Wright, D. W., & Barnes, H. L. (1995). Correlates of parent-child communication about specific sexual topics: A study of rural parents with school-aged children. *Personal Relationships, 2*, 327–344.

Wiederman, M. W. (2004). Methodological issues in studying sexuality in close relationships. In J. Harvey, A. Wenzel, & S. Sprecher (Eds.), *The handbook of sexuality in close relationships* (pp. 31–56). Mahwah, NJ: Erlbaum.

Wiederman, M. W. (1997). The truth must be in here somewhere: Examining the gender discrepancy in self-reported lifetime number of sex partners. *Journal of Sex Research, 34*, 375–386.

Wiederman, M. W., & Dubois, S. L. (1998). Evolution and sex differences in preferences for short-term mates: Results from a policy capturing study. *Evolution and Human Behavior, 19*, 153–170.

Wiederman, M. W., & Hurd, C. (1999). Extradyadic involvement during dating. *Journal of Social and Personal Relationships, 16*, 265–274.

Yela, C. (2000). Predictors of and factors related to loving and sexual satisfaction for men and women. *European Review of Applied Psychology, 50*, 235–243.

Yelsma, P. (1986). Marriage vs. cohabitation: Couples' communication practices and satisfaction. *Journal of Communication, 36*, 94–107.

Part VIII

THREATS TO RELATIONSHIPS

CHAPTER 26

Loneliness and Social Isolation

Jenny de Jong Gierveld
Theo van Tilburg
Pearl A. Dykstra

Given that all people seek happiness and all people desire to be happy, the feelings of loneliness as registered among adolescents, young adults (Marcoen, Goossens, & Caes, 1987; Sippola & Bukowski, 1999), midlife and older adults (see among many others, Lopata, 1996) reveal a major problem in society. Although there is a general core to loneliness – the evaluation of a discrepancy between the desired and the achieved network of relationships as a negative experience – the forms of loneliness and their antecedents vary enormously according to personal and contextual determinants. Despite the fact that loneliness is not treated as a specific clinical entity (Mijuskovic, 1996), Russell, Peplau, and Cutrona (1980) presented evidence on the uniqueness of loneliness as a phenomenon in its own right. After being largely ignored by social scientists until the mid-20th century, an ever-increasing flow of work since the 1970s amply testifies to the utility of loneliness as an important concept. This chapter addresses the concepts of loneliness and social isolation using theoretical ideas and empirical evidence from various sources and disciplines including psychology, sociology, and anthropology.

The Concepts of Loneliness and Social Isolation

Loneliness

The oldest publication about loneliness is *Über die Einsamkeit* (Zimmermann, 1785–1786). More recent efforts to conceptualize loneliness started in the 1950s with the publication "Loneliness" by Fromm Reichman (1959). Empirical research into loneliness was supported by the efforts of Perlman and Peplau (1981), who defined loneliness as "the unpleasant experience that occurs when a person's network of social relations is deficient in some important way, either quantitatively or qualitatively" (p. 31). A second definition of loneliness, frequently used in European countries, is formulated as follows:

Loneliness is a situation experienced by the individual as one where there is an unpleasant or inadmissible lack of (quality of) certain relationships. This includes situations, in which the number of existing relationships is smaller than is considered desirable or admissible, as well as situations where the intimacy one wishes for has not been realized. (De Jong Gierveld, 1987, p. 120)

Central to both definitions is that loneliness is a subjective and negative experience, and the outcome of a cognitive evaluation of the match between the quantity and quality of existing relationships and relationship standards. The opposite of loneliness is belongingness or embeddedness.

Social Isolation

Social isolation concerns the objective characteristics of a situation and refers to the absence of relationships with other people. The central question is this: To what extent is he or she alone? There is a continuum running from social isolation at the one end to social participation at the other. Persons with a very small number of meaningful ties are, by definition, socially isolated. Loneliness is not directly connected to objective social isolation; the association is of a more complex nature.

The Relationship Between Social Isolation and Loneliness

Loneliness is but one of the possible outcomes of the evaluation of a situation characterized by a small number of relationships. Socially isolated persons are not necessarily lonely, and lonely persons are not necessarily socially isolated in an objective sense. An individual who is well positioned in terms of objective social participation can occupy virtually any position on the subjective continuum. Where a person ends up on the subjective continuum depends on his or her relationship standards. Some people with a small number of social contacts might feel lonely; others might feel sufficiently embedded. An example of the latter situation is that of a person who prefers to be alone and opts for privacy as a means toward avoiding undesired social contacts and relationships. Acknowledging the importance of relationship standards, Perlman and Peplau

(1981) developed a cognitive or cognitive discrepancy theoretical approach to loneliness that focuses on the subjective evaluation of relationships in association with the personal standards for an optimal network of social relationships. The cognitive approach also considers the activities a person might undertake to restore the imbalance between the actual and the ideal situation. Thus, a person's position on the subjective continuum is affected not only by the type, nature and the saliency of the contacts missed, but also by the time perspective required to "solve" and upgrade problematic relationships, and the capacities to change the situation.

Types of Loneliness

Several components of loneliness can be distinguished. Zimmerman (1785/1786) differentiated between a positive and a negative type of loneliness. The positive type of loneliness is related to situations such as the voluntary withdrawal from the daily hassles of life and is oriented toward higher goals: reflection, meditation, and communication with God. Nowadays, the positive type of loneliness is more frequently referred to by a separate concept: privacy. Privacy is voluntary; it concerns a freely chosen situation of (temporary) absence of contacts with other people. The negative type of loneliness is related to an unpleasant or inadmissible lack of personal relationships and contacts with important others, as formulated in the definitions given in this chapter. This is the concept of loneliness that is nowadays used in theories and research. Moreover, it is the type of loneliness that best fits the everyday concept of loneliness.

Weiss (1973) differentiated between *emotional loneliness*, stemming from the absence of an intimate figure or a close emotional attachment (a partner, a best friend), and *social loneliness* stemming from the absence of a broader group of contacts, or an engaging social network (friends, colleagues, and people in the neighborhood). Emotional loneliness arises when a partner relationship dissolves through widowhood or divorce and is characterized by intense feelings of emptiness, abandonment, and forlornness. This type of loneliness is only solvable by starting a new intimate relationship. Social support from family and friends cannot compensate the loss of the attachment figure (Stroebe, Stroebe, Abakoumkin, & Schut, 1996). The social type of loneliness is related to the absence of a wider network of friends with common interests. According to Weiss (1973), social loneliness is frequently reported by young homemakers, who have moved to an area where they are newcomers. Their husbands, however supportive and intimate, cannot fill the gap that is caused by the absence of a group of friends and others with whom to socialize. The distinction between social and emotional loneliness has again been gaining attention. In recent years, researchers have used the two types to better understand the determinants and expressions of loneliness. Both the De Jong Gierveld loneliness scale (De Jong Gierveld & Van Tilburg, 1999a, 1999b; Dykstra & De Jong Gierveld, 2004; Van Baarsen, Snijders, Smit, & Van Duijn, 2001) and the Social and Emotional Loneliness Scale for Adults (SELSA); (DiTommaso & Spinner, 1993; Ernst & Cacioppo, 1999) have proved to be valid and reliable measuring instruments for emotional and social loneliness (see the next section for additional information).

Measuring Instruments

Loneliness has a negative connotation. Lonely people carry a social stigma. For those reasons it is embarrassing to talk about feelings of loneliness, in particular for men (Borys & Perlman, 1985), and people with deficiencies in their relationships do not always admit to being lonely. The use of direct questions including the words "lonely" or "loneliness" to investigate loneliness is likely to result in underreporting. Some loneliness scales consist of items excluding any reference to loneliness, whereas other scales include one or more such items. In discussing different measuring instruments, Shaver and Brennan (1991) argued that the exclusion of explicit references to loneliness gives rise to disagreements on

content validity. In their view, it is unclear whether one is measuring relationship satisfaction or loneliness. We disagree: Many instruments are validated by showing they correlate with self-reports of loneliness. We describe two loneliness scales that have no explicit references to loneliness and have been used in many research projects (Pinquart & Sörensen, 2001b).

The UCLA Loneliness Scale (Russell, Peplau, & Cutrona, 1980) has been translated into several languages. In the original version, all the items were worded in a negative or "lonely" direction. Because of concerns about how the negative wording of the items might affect scores (i.e., response sets), a revised version of the scale was developed that included items worded in a lonely and a nonlonely direction. The wording of the items and the response format have been simplified to facilitate administration of the measure to less educated populations (Russell, 1996).

De Jong Gierveld and colleagues conducted qualitative research as the first step in developing a loneliness scale. The 1985 version (De Jong Gierveld & Kamphuis, 1985; De Jong Gierveld & Van Tilburg, 1999a) consists of 11 items. Five items are positively phrased, and six are negatively phrased. The reliability and homogeneity of the scale have proven to be satisfactory in different Dutch samples adopting different modes of data collection (Van Tilburg & De Leeuw, 1991). Using the scale in self-administered questionnaires results in higher scale means than if the scale is used in face-to-face or telephone interviews (De Leeuw, 1992). This finding is in line with Sudman and Bradburn's (1974) observation that, compared with interviews, the more anonymous the setting in which self-administered surveys are completed, the more the results show self-disclosure and reduce the tendency of respondents to present themselves in a favorable light. The De Jong Gierveld scale was not developed to assess types of loneliness but rather to measure the severity of feelings of loneliness. Researchers can choose to use the scale as a one-dimensional measure. As a whole, the scale is moderately, yet sufficiently homogeneous. The items were, however, developed with Weiss's (1973) distinction between social and emotional loneliness in mind. For that reason, researchers can choose to use two subscales (one for emotional and one for social loneliness) that have moderate intercorrelations.

Conceptual Approaches to Understanding Loneliness

Several theoretical approaches have been used for analyzing loneliness (Derlega & Margulis, 1982; Perlman & Peplau, 1981). Weiss (1974), a leading proponent of the attachment perspective, suggested that there are different provisions of relationships (e.g., attachment, sense of worth, etc.), each associated with a specific type of relationships. He contended that as long as the provider is trustworthy, we can obtain guidance and assistance, often needed during stressful situations, and in alleviating loneliness. The main approaches to loneliness focus on individual-level characteristics that predispose people to become lonely or to persist in being lonely (Marangoni & Ickes, 1989; Rokach & Brock, 1996). In our view, greater insight into loneliness will be gained by bringing together individual level characteristics and contextual characteristics. Examples of the latter are sociocultural factors and sociostructural characteristics of the individual's environment. In this section, we start with a description of the individual level factors contributing to loneliness. We continue with the sociocultural factors that contribute to loneliness, more specifically, the social standards. Finally, the sociostructural factors modulating the risks of loneliness are addressed, particularly the socioeconomic characteristics of the contextual setting.

The Cognitive Approach to Loneliness (Individual Level)

Thanks to the efforts of Peplau and Perlman (1982) who, at the end of the 1970s, brought together loneliness researchers from the United States, Canada, and Europe, mea-

suring instruments and research into the determinants of loneliness became more or less "standardized." From that point in time, loneliness research in different regions of the world has been largely comparable in terms of design and theoretical modeling. Drawing on the *cognitive approach* to loneliness (Dykstra & De Jong Gierveld, 1994; Perlman & Peplau, 1981), analyses focus on subjective experiences and on cognitive processes that mediate the association between relationship characteristics and the experience of loneliness. A shortage of achieved as compared with desired relationships does not directly and inevitably lead to loneliness but is first perceived and evaluated. Social comparisons are key to this process. For example, social comparison may affect how large and important a social deficit is believed to be (Perlman & Peplau, 1981).

Researchers adopting the cognitive approach typically include the following characteristics in their models: (a) descriptive characteristics of the social network (intimate relationships as well as the broader group of acquaintances, colleagues, neighbors, and extended kin); (b) relationship standards, (c) personality characteristics (e.g., social skills, self-esteem, shyness, anxiety, introversion); and (d) background characteristics (e.g., gender and health). First, we address various components of the network of social relationships.

MARITAL AND PARTNER STATUS

From Durkheim onward, marriage has been seen as an avenue toward alleviating social isolation and loneliness. Research has repeatedly shown the protective effect of an intimate partner bond on the physical, financial and mental well-being of both men and women (Waite & Gallagher, 2000). Although, in Western and Northern Europe "new" partnerships such as consensual unions and "living apart and together" relationships are becoming increasingly popular, it is the content and not the form of the partner bond that matters (Coleman, Ganong, & Fine, 2000; De Jong Gierveld, 2004; Dykstra, 2004). A partner does not always provide protection against loneliness. Persons with a partner who is not their most supportive network member tend to be very lonely (Van Tilburg, 1988). Generally speaking, however, persons with a partner bond tend to be better protected from loneliness than persons without a partner bond (Dannenbeck, 1995; Wenger, Davies, Shahtahmasebi, & Scott, 1996).

Several mechanisms can explain why the absence of a partner in the household makes people more vulnerable to loneliness. First, a key structuring influence in the social network is missing: The size and broader composition of the network are strongly linked with the presence of a partner (Pinquart & Sörensen, 2001a). Persons living alone have smaller networks than those living with a partner. Second, when help is needed, the persons living alone lack in-house support and, by definition, have to orient themselves toward others outside the household. Third, living alone is, in many cases, the result of the dissolution of a partner relationship. Those who remain alone after the death of the partner are specifically at risk of loneliness, and the effects on the intensity of loneliness are recognizable over a long period of time (Lopata, 1996; Stevens, 1989). The effects of divorce on loneliness are also known to continue over long periods of time: Divorce in middle adulthood continues to affect feelings of loneliness even at older ages (Dykstra & De Jong Gierveld, 2004). Remarriage, unmarried cohabitation, and dating help to resolve loneliness to a certain extent. Findings reported by Peters and Liefbroer (1997) show that previous disruptions of partnerships have an effect on loneliness over and above current partner status.

KIN RELATIONSHIPS

Involvement in relationships other than a partner can also help to prevent or alleviate loneliness. Hagestad (1981, 1998) described the socially integrative role of the family, arguing that communication and historical conversations across generations help maintain continuity across life phases and strengthen a sense of belonging. The central-

ity of the parent–child bond in people's lives is undisputed (Rossi & Rossi, 1990). Adult children are an important source of companionship, closeness, and sharing, particularly for those who live alone. Dykstra (1993) and Pinquart (2003) have shown, for example, that contacts with children are more likely to reduce loneliness among formerly married than among married older adults. Divorce often impairs the relationship between parents and children, especially in the case of fathers (Kaufman & Uhlenberg, 1998; Kitson & Morgan, 1990). The low level of contact with adult children is the reason divorced fathers tend to be lonelier than divorced mothers (Pinquart, 2003). Siblings are special in many ways (Bedford, 1989; Cicirelli, 1995; Connidis, 1989; Gold, 1987): There is the common blood tie, the shared history of growing up together and of having the same background. The loss of a sibling has been found to contribute to loneliness among older persons (Gold, 1987). Siblings serve a particularly important function in alleviating the loneliness of those who lack the intimate attachment of a partner and have no children (Pinquart, 2003).

NONKIN RELATIONSHIPS

The importance of friends for psychological well-being is well documented (Blieszner & Adams, 1992; Rawlins, 1995): the joy of spending time together, the compassion evident in keeping up with personal ups and downs, and the exchange of ideas. Relationships with friends, colleagues, and other nonkin relationships serve to connect people to circles outside their immediate family. The benefits of belonging to a set of interlocking networks can lower the risks of social loneliness (Connidis & Davies, 1990; Wagner, Schütze, & Lang, 1999). Moreover, best friends can step in and function as confidants and in doing so help alleviate emotional loneliness, in particular, for never partnered or childless adults (Dykstra, 1993; Pinquart, 2003). Involvement in formal organizations is another source of sociability: Church attendance, activities in voluntary associations, and volunteer work bring people together and are a means of forming attachments (Pilusuk & Minkler, 1980) and in this way help to prevent or combat loneliness (Van Tilburg, De Jong Gierveld, Lecchini, & Marsiglia, 1998).

SIZE AND COMPOSITION OF THE NETWORK

Generally speaking, as the number of relationships in the social network increases and as the amount of emotional and social support exchanged increases, the intensity of loneliness decreases (Van Tilburg, 1988). The four closest ties in a person's network provide the greatest degree of protection against loneliness. The protection provided by additional relationships is marginal (Van Tilburg, 1990). Diversity across relationship types also serves to protect against loneliness. People with networks composed of both strong and weak ties are less prone to loneliness than people with strong ties only (Van Tilburg, 1990). Moreover, research (Dykstra, 1990; Silverstein & Chen, 1996) has shown that people with networks that consist primarily or entirely of kin ties are more vulnerable to loneliness than people with more heterogeneous networks. Those who are dependent on family members for social contacts because they lack alternatives tend to have the highest levels of loneliness.

RELATIONSHIPS STANDARDS

The cognitive approach to loneliness emphasizes that people evaluate whether their relationships measure up to their standards. Standards might be what a person aims for in relationships (e.g., a certain degree of intimacy, of frequency of contacts). Standards might also be desires to have specific types of relationships (e.g., an intimate partner, best friends, supportive colleagues). Standards develop over the course of life. Childhood experiences shape needs and desires for attachment (Bowlby, 1974), which are altered with new relationship experiences. Standards regarding partner relationships are a case in point. Research has shown that over the course of time, men and women who have lost their partner by death start downplaying the advantages of having a partner and start upgrading the advantages of being single (Dykstra & De Jong Gierveld, 1994; Stevens, 1989). In doing so, they free the way for other relationships. The less importance attached to having a partner, the less lonely the widowed were found to be.

PERSONALITY CHARACTERISTICS

People with poor social skills and psychological resources are likely to experience difficulty developing and maintaining relationships, and for that reason might feel lonely (Windle & Woods, 2004). Similarly, people with a neurotic or anxious personality might harbor unrealistic relationship standards, and their unmet social needs might give rise to feelings of loneliness (cf. Jones & Carver, 1991). Feeling socially uncomfortable, fear of intimacy, being easily intimidated by others, being unable to communicate adequately to others and developmental deficits such as childhood neglect and abandonment are reported by lonely people as the main causes of their feelings of loneliness (Rokach & Brock, 1996). Characteristics such as low self-esteem, shyness and low assertiveness can predispose people to loneliness and might also make it more difficult to recover from loneliness (Peplau & Perlman, 1982).

GENDER

Chodorow (1978) described the gender-specific socialization of men and women, arguing that men and women differ in the values they ascribe to different types of relationships. Men socialized to be emotionally independent prefer undemanding relationships and tend to rely on their wives and partners for social and emotional support. Women are socialized to have more complex affective needs in which an exclusive relationship to a man is not enough. Results from a meta-analysis (Pinquart & Sörensen, 2001a) of 102 studies that investigated gender differences in loneliness show that women report significantly higher levels of loneliness than men. This is more pronounced in studies in which loneliness is measured with single-item indicators than for studies using higher quality loneliness measuring instruments. This difference might be related to men's greater reluctance to report loneliness in response to direct questions (see the measurement section of this chapter; and Borys & Perlman, 1985). In multivariate analyses controlling for marital status, partner history, socioeconomic factors, and the functioning of the social network, the effect of gender on loneliness decreases (Baltes, Freund, & Horgas, 1999) and becomes insignificant for those in first marriages (Dykstra, 2004).

HEALTH

Loneliness is associated with a variety of measures of physical health. Those who are in poor health, whether this is measured objectively or subjectively, tend to report higher levels of loneliness (Havens, & Hall, 2001; Kramer, Kapteyn, Kuik, & Deeg, 2002; Mullins, Hall Elston, & Gutkowski, 1996; Penninx et al., 1999; Steverink, Westerhof, Bode, & Dittmann-Kohli, 2001). The causal mechanisms underlying the association between loneliness and health are not well understood, although new lines of research on the psychophysiology mechanisms and other pathways connecting loneliness and health outcomes (see Cacioppo et al., 2002; Hawkley & Cacioppo, 2003; Loving, Heffner, & Kiecolt-Glaser, this volume). Does Poor health lead to loneliness via difficulties in maintaining social relationships? Or does poor health lead to an increase in support and a decrease in loneliness? Penninx et al. (1999) and Van Tilburg and Broese van Groenou (2002) showed that investing in relationships by giving support might pay off in times of need: Poor health mobilizes network members and increases support giving. Does loneliness produce Poor health? Could they mutually influence each other? Perhaps there is no direct causation but rather an indirect relationship through a third factor. One possible reason for the loneliness–health association involves preventive health behaviors (see Cacioppo, Hawkley, & Bernston, 2003). Lonely individuals are less likely to engage in behaviors such as exercise, remember-ing to take medications or see their doctors, good nutrition, and relaxation (Aartsen, 2003; Mahon, Yarcheski, & Yarcheski, 2001; Pérodeau & du-Fort, 2000).

Loneliness in Context

Empirical studies have focused on individual-level determinants of loneliness. Much less attention has been paid to the ways in which social isolation and loneliness are patterned socially. A relatively new area of research concerns (a) the societal patterning of standards for evaluating one's social network of relationships and (b) the societal patterning of social and economic resources contributing to social integration. These contextual-level factors affect the intensity of loneliness either indirectly via the composition and size of the individual's network of relationships or directly via differences in the evaluation of a given context. Differences between neighborhoods in mutual concern for the other's well-being are an example of societal patterning of resources at the contextual level. As Thomése, Van Tilburg, and Knipscheer (2003) showed, as mutual concern for the other's well-being and the shared feeling of community embeddedness increase, the risk of loneliness at the individual level decreases.

In this section, we first address the outcomes of international comparative research into the relationship on socially differentiated standards and loneliness. Next we discuss theoretical ideas on contextual differences in social and economic resources and loneliness.

NORMATIVE CLIMATE

People's relationship standards are shaped by the normative climate in which they find themselves. The normative climate in and of itself can be conducive to loneliness. Norms and values affect people's ideas about the optimal size of the network, and the obligations and duties of family members.

Johnson and Mullins (1987) suggested that loneliness is high in collectivist-oriented communities where sensitivity to social exclusion is stronger than in individualistic communities. This hypothesis has been tested in a number of studies on differences between North America and Europe. Rokach, Orzeck, Cripps, Lackovic-Grgin, and Penezic (2001) compared Canadians and Croatians (from central-south Europe) assuming that North American culture poses a lower loneliness risk than European culture because of its emphasis on individual achievement and impersonal relationships. However, their findings revealed that Canadians experienced more loneliness than Croatians. Van Tilburg, Havens, and De Jong Gierveld (2004) observed, in line with Johnson and Mullins's hypothesis, that the likelihood of being emotionally lonely among older adults without a partner and of being socially lonely among all older adults in the study was highest in Tuscany, Italy, followed by the Netherlands and Manitoba, Canada. Swedish centenarians were more often lonely, in contrast to centenarians in Georgia, United States, who seldom reported being lonely (Martin, Hagberg, & Poon, 1997). Stack's (1998) analysis of World Values Surveys data showed that adults in Italy and Japan reported more loneliness than adults in the United States and Canada, whereas adults in a number of Western and Northern European countries as well as in Australia reported less loneliness than in the United States and Canada (after controlling for several individual characteristics such as marital and parental status, self-reported health, socioeconomic status, education, and gender). The assumed dichotomy of two types of cultures might be too simple. Differences within a cultural system are overlooked. Considerable variability exists *within* North America, for example, as illustrated by research among immigrants and people born and raised in North America where the experience of loneliness differed by country of origin and cultural background (Goodwin, Cook, & Yung, 2001; Rokach & Sharma, 1996). No one has yet offered a comprehensive explanation to account for the range of cultural differences that have been found.

A set of studies has examined differences in older adult loneliness across Europe (İmamoğlu, Küller, İmamoğlu, & Küller, 1993; Jylhä & Jokela, 1990). Findings showed that although living alone became progressively less common from Northern Europe to Southern Europe, experiences of loneliness progressively increased. According to the authors the crossnational differences are attributable to differences in normative climate. Living alone generally gives rise to loneliness, but this is the more so in countries where older adults without a partner are expected to live with their families (e.g., Greece, Italy) and the less so in countries where older adults without a partner prefer to live alone (e.g., Finland).

In general, the problems of lonely people cannot be regarded as individual failures only. Characteristics of the societal context, such as prevailing standards concerning matrimony and the nuclear family, the emphasis on individual fulfillment, and high expectations about romantic relationships might also be considered loneliness-provoking factors, especially so for those living on their own and parents without parents (Ernst & Cacioppo, 1999).

SOCIOECONOMIC CONTEXT

Perlman and Peplau (1981) argued that in any setting, factors that increase the frequency of interaction and foster group cohesiveness are likely to affect the incidence of loneliness. In our view, the dimension of socioeconomic equality versus inequality is among these factors. Unfortunately empirical research connecting socioeconomic inequality (a concept at the contextual level) to individual loneliness is virtually nonexistent. Phillipson (2004) has started a program of research in the United Kingdom that is oriented toward investigating the consequences of the deepening social and economic inequality and the socially deprived circumstances of groups of impoverished inhabitants of urban neighborhoods compared with the affluent subgroups, taking loneliness as the dependent variable (Phillipson, 2004). Research by Scharf, Phillipson, and Smith (2004) in some of the most deprived neighborhoods of the United Kingdom indicated significant numbers of people prone to social exclusion (e.g., from social relations, material resources, and basic services) and experiencing neighborhood exclusion. The risk of being affected by multiple forms of social exclusion and loneliness was greatest for those belonging to minority ethnic groups and the age group of 75 years and over.

In our view, the links between socioeconomic inequality and loneliness are a research area worth pursuing. In doing so, one can learn from research that investigates the relationship between socioeconomic inequalities and indicators of individuals' well-being, such as health, morbidity, and mortality.

O'Rand (2001) postulated that across industrialized countries, major structural and demographic changes have generated persistent social inequalities and shifts away from social welfare policies toward market-centered strategies for income and health maintenance. In her view, the growing economic and social inequalities within populations form the fundamental social condition that yields negative outcomes in health and well-being. O'Rand's concept of inequality consists of economic, social, and psychosocial components and operates multilevel: across societal planes, the state, and the neighborhood to the individual. The causal mechanism by which inequality affects well-being operates through people's perceptions of societal fairness more than directly on its own. O'Rand distinguished, on one hand, a direct pathway connecting inequality and persons' well-being via individuals' socioeconomic resources. On the other hand, there is an indirect pathway by which contextual level inequality and atomization at the community level reduce trust and increase persons' perceptions of relative deprivation, leading to negative outcomes.

Within the same paradigm, Wilkinson (1994) investigated the relationship between societal characteristics – gross national product per capita and differences in relative income – and life expectancy. He concluded that the Organization for Economic Co-operation and Development countries with the longest life expectancy are not the wealthiest but those with the smallest spread of incomes and the smallest proportion of the population in relative poverty. Wilkinson (1994) postulated that the link between socioeconomic inequalities and health or mortality is mediated by *cognitive processes* of social comparison, feelings of deprivation and disadvantage that can lead to depression. Kawachi, Kennedy, Lochner, and Prothow-Stith (1997) provided evidence for the link between social inequality at the macrolevel and perceived fairness and distrust at the microlevel. Using General Social Survey data from the United States, they found an inverse relationship between the degree of income inequality at the state level and the perceived lack of fairness and mistrust. The perceived lack of fairness was operationalized with the item, "Most people would try to take advantage of you if they got a chance," and social mistrust with the item, "Generally speaking, would you say that most people can be trusted or that you can't be too careful in dealing with people?" The concept of trust is also central in Ross, Mirowsky, and Pribesh's (2001) work on neighborhood disadvantage and powerlessness. Neighborhood disadvantage was measured as the sum of the percentage of households with incomes below the federal poverty line and the percentage of female-headed households with children. Results indicated that when controlled for individual disadvantage, residents of disadvantaged neighborhoods experienced lower levels of trust. Mistrust and absence of faith in other people promoted and reinforced a sense of powerlessness.

The promise of the previously described theoretical ideas for research into loneliness is that contextual and individual determinants might be integrated under an overarching cognitive theory, connecting social and economic inequality to the cognitive processes of persons' perceptions of societal fairness and trust, which in turn affect people's vulnerability to social isolation and loneliness. In the near future, the analyses and description of the core mechanisms of the overarching cognitive theory needs attention. Until now, this type of multilevel research is scarce. Moreover, some of the central theoretical concepts need better definitions and valid and reliable measuring instruments. We need to work toward a research and sample design that enables multilevel research into social isolation and loneliness.

Coping and Interventions

Some individuals recover from loneliness by using their own strategies, or by letting time do the healing. Others require outside professional help. The most obvious approach is to help people develop satisfying personal relationships (Rook, 1984). This can be done by improving how they interact with others through social skills training or forms of psychotherapy aimed at changing dysfunctional interpersonal dispositions (e.g., fear of rejection). It can also be done by improving opportunities for interactions through programs aimed at removing barriers for social interaction (e.g., providing transportation) or at bringing people together (e.g., discussion groups). Pilusuk and Minkler (1980) emphasized the importance of developing programs that have opportunities for so-called unintentional network building, that is, the development of friendships is a by-product of the shared activity, not the explicit purpose. Nevertheless, programs with an explicit focus on improving personal relationships have proven to be effective. In the Netherlands, the Friendship Enrichment Program (FEP) in which participants are taught how to nourish friendships and go about making friends has been successful in alleviating loneliness (Stevens, 2001; Stevens & Van Tilburg, 2000). The beneficial effects of the FEP might be limited to specific groups, however. The authors noted that the participants were self-selected and wanted to learn about friendship. The FEP might work best for individuals who actively want to become less lonely. Moreover, given that only women participated in the evaluation study, the question of whether men will also benefit from the FEP cannot be answered.

Interventions aimed at improving relationships might not always be feasible or appropriate, as in the case of people who have unrealistically demanding or excessive needs for support. Such people are more likely to benefit from cognitive interventions aimed at modifying relationship expectations. Individuals with severely limited physical mobility are likely to benefit from interventions aimed at increasing their repertoire of rewarding solitary activities. Rook (1984) pointed out that although encouraging lonely individuals to develop enjoyable solitary activities seems like a last resort, solitary activities relieve people from dependence on others and thus may increase their sense of personal control.

In a recent review of interventions targeting social isolation among the elderly, Findlay (2003) lamented the lack of evidence showing that they work. Few evaluative studies on the effectiveness of loneliness interventions have been carried out. The few studies that have been done are flawed by weak methodologies. Findlay concluded that future programs aimed at reducing social isolation should have evaluation built into them at inception. This advice is heeded in a program of research that is currently being carried out under the auspices of the Sluyterman van Loo Foundation in the Netherlands. This foundation commissioned 17 interventions aimed at reducing loneliness among the elderly under the condition that their effectiveness would be evaluated by the three authors of this chapter together with Tineke Fokkema of the Netherlands Interdisciplinary Demographic Institute. The interventions are diverse (e.g., home visits by volunteers, social program for nursing home residents, educational program for the hearing impaired, Internet usage). Under our supervision, the collection of data has been standardized as far as possible. Key variables such as loneliness, marital history, social network characteristics, relationship standards, and health and personality characteristics are measured the same way in each of the projects. All but two of the interventions are randomized control trials. A first report is scheduled for the end of 2005.

An Evaluative Conclusion

It is broadly agreed that loneliness is not directly connected to social isolation, that is, the absence of relationships with other people. Loneliness is defined as the negative outcome of a cognitive evaluation of a discrepancy between (the quality and quantity of) existing relationships and relationship standards. An increasing flow of work from disciplines such as psychology, sociology, and anthropology has broadened the understanding of the mechanisms behind the onset and continuation of loneliness. In doing so, next to background variables such as age, gender, and health, characteristics of the social network of relationships, personality characteristics, and relationship standards have been addressed. The socially isolating effects of deprivations brought by social and economic circumstances at the community or country level require further exploration. Future research should address the ways in which people's evaluations of their relationship networks are affected by the normative context in which they find themselves.

References

Aartsen, M. (2003). *On the interrelationships between cognitive and social functioning in older age*. Unpublished doctoral dissertation, Vrije Universiteit, Amsterdam.

Baltes, M. M., Freund, A. M., & Horgas, A. L. (1999). Men and women in the Berlin Aging Study. In P. B. Baltes & K. U. Mayer (Eds.), *The Berlin Aging Study; aging from 70 to 100* (pp. 259–281). Cambridge, England: Cambridge University Press.

Bedford, V. H. (1989). Understanding the value of siblings in old age: A proposed model. *American Behavioral Scientist, 33*, 33–44.

Blieszner, R., & Adams, R. (1992). *Adult friendship*. Newbury Park, CA: Sage.

Borys, S., & Perlman, D. (1985). Gender differences in loneliness. *Personality and Social Psychology Bulletin, 11*, 63–74.

Bowlby, J. (1974). *Attachment and loss Attachment:* Vol. 1. London: Hogart Press and the Institute of Psycho-Analysis.

Cacioppo, J. T., Hawkley, L. C., & Bernston, G. G. (2003). The anatomy of loneliness. *Current Directions in Psychological Science, 12*, 71–74.

Cacioppo, J. T., Hawkley, L. C., Crawford, E., Ernst, J. M., Burleson, M. H., Kowalewski, R. B., et al. (2002). Loneliness and health: Potential mechanisms. *Psychosomatic Medicine, 64*, 407–417.

Chodorow, N. (1978). *The reproduction of mothering: Psychoanalysis and the sociology of gender*. Berkeley: University of California Press.

Cicirelli, V. G. (1995). *Sibling relationships across the life span*. New York: Plenum Press.

Coleman, M., Ganong, L., & Fine, M. (2000). Reinvestigating remarriage: Another decade of progress. *Journal of Marriage and the Family, 62*, 1288–1307.

Connidis, I. A. (1989). Siblings as friends in later life. *American Behavioral Scientist, 33*, 81–93.

Connidis, I. A., & Davies, L. (1990). Confidants and companions in later life: The place of family and friends. *Journal of Gerontology: Social Science, 45*, 141–149.

Dannenbeck, C. (1995). Im alter einsam? Zur strukturveränderung sozialer beziehungen im alter [Lonely in later life? Changing social relationships in later life]. In H. Bertram (Ed.), *Das individuum und seine familie* (pp. 125–156). Opladen, Germany: Leske + Budrich.

De Jong Gierveld, J. (1987). Developing and testing a model of loneliness. *Journal of Personality and Social Psychology, 53*, 119–128.

De Jong Gierveld, J. (2004). Remarriage, unmarried cohabitation, living apart together: Partner relationships following bereavement or divorce. *Journal of Marriage and Family, 66*, 236–243.

De Jong Gierveld, J., & Kamphuis, F. H. (1985). The development of a Rasch-type loneliness-scale. *Applied Psychological Measurement, 9*, 289–299.

De Jong Gierveld, J., & Van Tilburg, T. G. (1999a). *Manual of the loneliness scale*. Vrije Universiteit Amsterdam, Department of Social Research Methodology.

De Jong Gierveld, J., & Van Tilburg, T. (1999b). Living arrangements of older adults in the Netherlands and Italy: Coresidence values and behavior and their consequences for loneliness. *Journal of Cross-Cultural Gerontology, 14*, 1–24.

De Leeuw, E. D. (1992). *Data quality in mail, telephone, and face-to-face surveys*. Unpublished doctoral dissertation, Vrije Universiteit Amsterdam.

Derlega, V. J., & Margulis, S. T. (1982). Why loneliness occurs: The interrelationship of social-psychological and privacy concepts. In L. A. Peplau & D. Perlman (Eds), *Loneliness. A sourcebook of current theory, research and therapy* (pp. 152–165). New York: Wiley.

DiTommaso, E., & Spinner, B. (1993). The development and initial validation of the social and emotional loneliness scale for adults (SELSA). *Personality and Individual Differences, 14,* 127–134.

Dykstra, P. A. (1990). *Next of non-kin. The importance of primary relationships for older adults' well-being.* Amsterdam/Lisse, the Netherlands: Swets & Zeitlinger.

Dykstra, P. A. (1993). The differential availability of relationships and the provision and effectiveness of support to older adults. *Journal of Social and Personal Relationships, 10,* 355–370.

Dykstra, P. A. (2004). Diversity in partnership histories: Implications for older adults' social integration. In C. Phillipson, G. Allan, & D. Morgan (Eds.), *Social networks and social exclusion: Sociological and policy issues* (pp. 117–141). London: Ashgate.

Dykstra, P. A., & De Jong Gierveld, J. (1994). The theory of mental incongruity, with a specific application to loneliness among widowed men and women. In R. Erber & R. Gilmour (Eds.), *Theoretical frameworks for personal relationships* (pp. 235–259). Hillsdale NJ: Erlbaum.

Dykstra, P. A., & De Jong Gierveld, J. (2004). Gender and marital-history differences in social and emotional loneliness among Dutch older adults. *Canadian Journal on Aging, 23,* 141–155.

Ernst, J., & Cacioppo, J. T. (1999). Lonely hearts: Psychological perspectives on loneliness. *Applied and Preventive Psychology, 8,* 1–22.

Findlay, R. A. (2003). Interventions to reduce social isolation amongst older people: Where is the evidence? *Ageing and Society, 23,* 647–658.

Fromm Reichmann, F. (1959). Loneliness. *Psychiatry, 22,* 1–15.

Gold, D. T. (1987). Siblings in old age: Something special. *Canadian Journal on Aging, 6,* 199–215.

Goodwin, R., Cook, O., & Yung, Y. (2001). Loneliness and life satisfaction among three cultural groups. *Personal Relationships, 8,* 225–230.

Hagestad, G. O. (1981). Problems and promises in the social psychology of intergenerational rela-

tions. In E. Shanas (Ed.), *Aging: Stability and change in the family* (pp. 11–46). New York: Academic Press.

Hagestad, G. (1998, October 1). *Towards a society for all ages: New thinking, new language, new conversations.* Keynote address at the Launch of the International Year of Older Persons 1999, United Nations, New York.

Havens, B., & Hall, M. (2001). Social isolation, loneliness, and the health of older adults. *Indian Journal of Gerontology, 14,* 144–153.

Hawkley, L. C., & Cacioppo, J. T. (2003). Loneliness and pathways to disease. *Brain, Behavior, and Immunity, 17,* S98–S105.

İmamoğlu, E. O., Küller, R., İmamoğlu, V., & Küller, M. (1993). The social psychological worlds of Swedes and Turks in and around retirement. *Journal of Cross-Cultural Psychology, 24,* 26–41.

Johnson, D. P., & Mullins, L. C. (1987). Growing old and lonely in different societies: Toward a comparative perspective. *Journal of Cross-Cultural Gerontology, 2,* 257–275.

Jones, W. H., & Carver, M. D. (1991). Adjustment and coping implications of loneliness. In C. R. Snyder & D. R. Forsych (Eds.), *Handbook of social and clinical psychology: The health perspective* (pp. 395–415). New York: Pergamon Press.

Jylhä, M., & Jokela, J. (1990). Individual experiences as cultural: A cross-cultural study on loneliness among the elderly. *Ageing and Society, 10,* 295–315.

Kaufman, G., & Uhlenberg, P. (1998). Effects of life course transitions on the quality of relationships between adult children and their parents. *Journal of Marriage and Family, 60,* 924–938.

Kawachi, I., Kennedy, B. P., Lochner, K., & Prothrow-Stith, D. (1997). Social capital, income inequality and mortality. *American Journal of Public Health, 87,* 1491–1498.

Kitson, G. C., & Morgan, L. A. (1990). The multiple consequences of divorce: A decade review. *Journal of Marriage and Family, 52,* 913–924.

Kramer, S. E., Kapteyn, T. S., Kuik, D. J., & Deeg, D. (2002). The association of hearing impairment and chronic diseases with psychosocial health status in older age. *Journal of Aging and Health, 14,* 122–137.

Lopata, H. Z. (1996). *Current widowhood: Myths and realities.* Thousand Oaks, CA: Sage.

Mahon, N., Yarcheski, A., & Yarcheski, T.-J. (2001). Mental health variables and positive health practices in early adolescents. *Psychological Reports*, 88, 1023–1030.

Marangoni, C., & Ickes, W. (1989). Loneliness: A theoretical review with implications for measurement. *Journal of Social and Personal Relationships*, 6, 93–128.

Marcoen, A., Goossens, L., & Caes, P. (1987). Loneliness in pre- through late adolescence: Exploring the contributions of a multidimensional approach. *Journal of Youth and Adolescence*, 16, 561–577.

Martin, P., Hagberg, B., & Poon, L. W. (1997). Predictors of loneliness in centenarians: A parallel study. *Journal of Cross-Cultural Gerontology*, 12, 203–224.

Mullins, L. C., Hall Elston, C., & Gutkowski, S. M. (1996). Social determinants of loneliness among older Americans. *Genetic, Social, and General Psychology Monographs*, 122, 453–473.

Mijuskovic, B. (1996). The phenomenology and dynamics of loneliness. *Psychology: A Journal of Human Behavior*, 33, 41–51.

O'Rand, A. M. (2001). Stratification and the life course; the forms of life-course capital and their interrelationships. In R. H. Binstock & L. K. George (Eds.), *Handbook of aging and the social sciences* (5th ed., pp. 197–213). New York: Academic Press.

Penninx, B. W. J. H., van Tilburg, T., Kriegsman, D. M. W., Boeke, A. J. P., Deeg, D. J. H., & van Eijk, J. T. M. (1999). Social network, social support, and loneliness in older persons with different chronic diseases. *Journal of Aging and Health*, 11, 151–168.

Peplau, L. A., & Perlman, D. (1982). Perspectives on loneliness. In L. A. Peplau & D. Perlman (Eds.), *Loneliness: A sourcebook of current theory, research and therapy* (pp. 1–18). New York: Wiley.

Perlman, D., & Peplau, L. A. (1981). Toward a social psychology of loneliness. In S. W. Duck & R. Gilmour (Eds.), *Personal Relationships. 3: Personal relationships in disorder* (pp. 31–56). London: Academic Press.

Pérodeau, G.-M., & du-Fort, G.-G. (2000). Psychotropic drug use and the relation between social support, life events, and mental health in the elderly. *Journal of Applied Gerontology*, 19, 23–41.

Peters, A., & Liefbroer, A. C. (1997). Beyond marital status: Partner history and well-being in old age. *Journal of Marriage and the Family*, 59, 687–699.

Phillipson, C. (2004). Review article: Urbanisation and ageing: Towards a new environmental gerontology. *Ageing and Society*, 25, 963–975.

Pilusuk, M., & Minkler, M. (1980). Supportive networks: Life ties for the elderly. *Journal of Social Issues*, 36(2), 95–116.

Pinquart, M. (2003). Loneliness in married, widowed, divorced, and never-married older adults. *Journal of Social and Personal Relationships*, 20, 31–53.

Pinquart, M., & Sörensen, S. (2001a). Gender differences in self-concept and psychological well-being in old age: A meta-analysis. *Journal of Gerontology: Psychological Sciences*, 56, 195–213.

Pinquart, M., & Sörensen, S. (2001b). Influences on loneliness in older adults: A meta-analysis. *Basic and Applied Social Psychology*, 23, 245–266.

Rawlins, W. K. (1995). Friendships in later life. In J. Coupland & J. F. Nussbaum (Eds.), *Handbook of communication and aging research* (pp. 227–257). Mahwah, NJ: Erlbaum.

Rokach, A., & Brock, H. (1996). The causes of loneliness. *Psychology, a Journal of Human Behavior*, 33, 1–11.

Rokach, A., Orzeck, T., Cripps, J., Lackovic-Grgin, K., & Penezic, Z. (2001). The effects of culture on the meaning of loneliness. *Social Indicators Research*, 53, 17–31.

Rokach, A., & Sharma, M. (1996). The loneliness experience in a cultural context. *Journal of Social Behavior and Personality*, 11, 827–839.

Rook, K. S. (1984). Promoting social bonding: Strategies for helping the lonely and socially isolated. *American Psychologist*, 39, 1389–1407.

Ross, C. E., Mirowsky, J., & Pribesh, S. (2001). Powerlessness and the amplification of threat: Neighborhood disadvantage, disorder, and mistrust. *American Sociological Review*, 66, 568–591.

Rossi, A. S., & Rossi, P. H. (1990). *Of human bonding: Parent-child relations across the life course*. New York: Aldine de Gruyter.

Russell, D., Peplau, L. A., & Cutrona, C. E. (1980). The revised UCLA Loneliness Scale: Concurrent and discriminant validity evidence. *Journal of Personality and Social Psychology*, 39, 472–480.

Russell, D. W. (1996). UCLA Loneliness Scale (Version 3): Reliability, validity, and factor structure. *Journal of Personality Assessment*, 66, 20–40.

Scharf, T., Phillipson, C., & Smith, A. E. (2004). Poverty and social exclusion: Growing older in deprived urban neighbourhoods. In A. Walker & C. Hagan Hennessy (Eds.), *Growing Older – Quality of Life in Old Age* (pp. 81–106). Maidenhead, England: Open University Press.

Shaver, P. R., & Brennan, K. A. (1991). Measures of depression and loneliness. In J. P. Robinson, P. R. Shaver, & L. S. Wrightsman (Eds.), *Measures of personality and social psychological attitudes* (pp. 197–289). San Diego, CA: Academic Press.

Silverstein, M., & Chen, X. (1996). Too much of a good thing? Intergenerational social support and the psychological well-being of older persons. *Journal of Marriage and Family, 58,* 970–982.

Sippola, L. K., & Bukowski, M. (1999). Self, other, and loneliness from a developmental perspective. In K. J. Rottenberg & S. Hymel (Eds.), *Loneliness in childhood and adolescence* (pp. 280–295). Cambridge, England: Cambridge University Press.

Stack, S. (1998). Marriage, family and loneliness: A cross-national study. *Sociological Perspectives, 41,* 415–432.

Stevens, N. (1989). *Well-being in widowhood: A question of balance.* Unpublished doctoral dissertation, Catholic University of Nijmegen, Nijmegen (the Netherlands).

Stevens, N. (2001). Combatting loneliness: A friendship enrichment programme for older women. *Ageing and Society, 21,* 183–202.

Stevens, N., & Van Tilburg, T. (2000). Stimulating friendship in later life: A strategy for reducing loneliness among older women. *Educational Gerontology, 26,* 15–35.

Steverink, N., Westerhof, G. J., Bode, C., & Dittmann-Kohli, F. (2001). The personal experience of aging, individual resources, and subjective well-being. *Journal of Gerontology: Psychological Sciences, 65B,* 364–373.

Stroebe, W., Stroebe, M., Abakoumkin, G., & Schut, H. (1996). The role of loneliness and social support in adjustment to loss: A test of attachment versus stress theory. *Journal of Personality and Social Psychology, 70,* 1241–1249.

Sudman, S., & Bradburn, N. M. (1974). *Response effects in surveys: A review and synthesis.* Chicago: Aldine.

Thomése, F., Van Tilburg, T., & Knipscheer, C. P. M. (2003). Continuation of exchange with neighbors in later life: The importance of the neighborhood context. *Personal Relationships, 10,* 535–550.

Van Baarsen, B., Snijders, T. A. B., Smit, J. H., & Van Duijn, M. A. J. (2001). Lonely but not alone: Emotional isolation and social isolation as two distinct dimensions of loneliness in older people. *Educational and Psychological Measurement, 61,* 119–135.

Van Tilburg, T. (1988). *Verkregen en gewenste ondersteuning in het licht van eenzaamheidservaringen* (Obtained and desired social support in association with loneliness). Unpublished doctoral dissertation, Vrije Universiteit, Amsterdam.

Van Tilburg, T. (1990). The size of the supportive network in association with the degree of loneliness. In C. P. M. Knipscheer & T. C. Antonucci (Eds.), *Social network research: Substantive issues and methodological questions* (pp. 137–150). Lisse, the Netherlands: Swets & Zeitlinger.

Van Tilburg, T., De Jong Gierveld, J., Lecchini, L., & Marsiglia, D. (1998). Social integration and loneliness: A comparative study among older adults in the Netherlands and Tuscany, Italy. *Journal of Social and Personal Relationships, 15,* 740–754.

Van Tilburg, T. G., & Broese van Groenou, M. I. (2002). Network and health changes among older Dutch adults. *Journal of Social Issues, 58,* 697–713.

Van Tilburg, T. G., & De Leeuw, E. D. (1991). Stability of scale quality under different data collection procedures: A mode comparison on the "De Jong Gierveld Loneliness Scale." *International Journal of Public Opinion Research, 3,* 69–85.

Van Tilburg, T. G., Havens, B., & De Jong Gierveld, J. (2004). Loneliness among older adults in the Netherlands, Italy, and Canada: A multifaceted comparison. *Canadian Journal on Aging, 23,* 169–180.

Wagner, M., Schütze, Y., & Lang, F. R. (1999). Social relationships in old age. In P. B. Baltes & K. U. Mayer (Eds.), *The Berlin Aging Study. Aging from 70 to 100* (pp. 282–301). Cambridge, England: Cambridge University Press.

Waite, L., & Gallagher, M. (2000). *The case for marriage: Why married people are happier, healthier and better off financially.* New York: Doubleday.

Weiss, R. S. (1973). *Loneliness: The experience of emotional and social isolation.* Cambridge, MA: MIT Press.

Weiss, R. S. (1974). The provisions of social relationships. In Z. Rubin (Ed.), *Doing unto others* (pp. 17–26). Englewood Cliffs, NJ: Prentice-Hall.

Wenger, C. G., Davies, R., Shahtahmasebi, S., & Scott, A. (1996). Social isolation and loneliness in old age: Review and model refinement. *Ageing and Society, 16,* 333–358.

Wilkinson, R. G. (1994). The epidemiological transition: From material scarcity to social disadvantage. *Daedalus, Journal of American Academy of Arts and Sciences,* 123(4), 61–77.

Windle, G., & Woods, R. T. (2004). Variations in subjective wellbeing: The mediating role of a psychological resource. *Ageing and Society, 24,* 583–602.

Zimmermann, J. G. (1785/6). *Über die einsamkeit* [About loneliness]. Frankfurt: Troppau.

CHAPTER 27

Stress in Couples: The Process of Dyadic Coping

Carolyn E. Cutrona
Kelli A. Gardner

One woman was propping her ill husband's pillow, serving him lunch, adjusting his oxygen, giving him his medication, reminding him of our appointment, and casually straightening the room with few wasted motions, while her husband boldly told the interviewer, "I don't receive help from others. I believe you should get things done on your own." (Hobfoll, 1998, p. 131)

Despite our ideals of individualism and independence, people rarely deal with stress in isolation. Although most of the research literature conceptualizes coping with stressful life events as a solitary activity, it is more accurate to view coping as a social phenomenon, an activity that is embedded in and has impact on the individual's social network (Lyons, Mickelson, Sullivan, & Coyne, 1998). As shown in the extract that opened this chapter, the contributions to successful coping made by network members are often integrated so flawlessly into daily routines, they are not noticed or properly appreciated. However, if the "unseen" helper is lost (i.e., dies or leaves), intense emotions of loss are experienced. In addition to per-

sonal grief, routines unravel and life becomes infinitely more difficult in the absence of the lost partner's previously unnoticed contributions (Berscheid, 1983). The illusion of independence is destroyed.

In this chapter, we discuss the processes that are set in motion when one or both members of a couple experience adversity. Because couples are highly interdependent, how they think about problems, how they try to solve problems, and the success of their problem-solving efforts are influenced by their partner. Coping is best construed as a combination of individual and joint efforts (Lyons et al., 1998). "Solo performances are rare and each event draws a cast of characters who confront the issue individually and together" (Lyons et al., 1998, p. 580). Furthermore, when people are embedded in an intimate relationship, solution of the immediate problem is not the only goal of coping. Protecting the relationship is as important as preventing harm to each individual. We describe current theories about how partners influence each other in each step of the coping process and summarize research on the consequences of good and poor dyadic coping. Interventions to promote positive dyadic coping in times of stress are briefly reviewed. Finally, directions for future research on dyadic stress and coping in the context of marriage will be suggested.

Dyadic Processes

Dyadic Stress

Most research on stressful life events has focused on the impact of negative events on individuals. However, events frequently affect multiple members of social groups. This chapter focuses on the marital dyad. Couples are clearly embedded in larger social contexts (e.g., nuclear and extended family, work and friendship networks, community organizations, neighborhoods, cultural groups). However, there is evidence that failures in coping at the dyadic level are particularly detrimental to well-being (Edwards, Nazroo, & Brown, 1988). We thus view our focus on dyadic stress and coping as an important first step in understanding the more complex phenomenon of social coping (cf. Hobfoll, 1998).

Dyadic stress is defined as an event or circumstance that affects both members of the couple and elicits joint appraisals, coping activities, and use of resources (Bodenmann, 1995; Lyons et al., 1998). Bodenmann (1995; 2005) distinguished between two types of dyadic stress: indirect and direct. In the case of indirect dyadic stress, the stressful event initially threatens the well-being of only one partner (e.g., a disappointing performance evaluation) but affects the other through its impact on the stress victim's behavior and emotional state (Conger et al., 1990), a process often referred to as "crossover" (Bolger, DeLongis, Kessler, & Wethington, 1989). For example, the stress that law and medical students experience during training has been shown to crossover and cause distress in their spouses (Katz, Monnier, Libet, Shaw, & Beach, 2000; Thompson & Bolger, 1999). If the stress victim is able to cope without emotional or behavioral spillover to the home environment, then the stress is individual

rather than dyadic. In the case of direct dyadic stress, both partners are affected at the same time and to a similar degree by the stressor (e.g., insufficient money to pay the rent).

Indirect dyadic stress poses multiple threats to each partner and to the relationship. The primary victim faces the direct consequences of the negative event (e.g., loss of status or assets, uncertainty regarding the future). He or she may be inattentive, irritable, and unsupportive in interactions with the spouse. In response, the unaffected partner may retaliate or withdraw. Research has shown, for example, that couples are more likely to have fights at home when the husband has had a difficult day at work (Bolger et al., 1989). Thus, both partners may lose the benefits of the other's companionship and support. In addition, the security of the relationship is threatened. Similar dynamics may unfold in the case of direct dyadic stress, but both partners face the direct consequences of the stressful event (e.g., serious illness in one of their offspring), depleting the psychological resources of both partners. At a time when they both need help in coping, they are both less likely to be able to help because of preoccupation with their own needs, as shown by Abbey and colleagues among couples coping with infertility (Abbey, Andrews, & Halman, 1995).

Dyadic Appraisals

In the classic model of stress proposed by Lazarus (Lazarus, 1966; Lazarus & Folkman, 1984), people's appraisals of the severity of the threat posed by an event (primary appraisal) and the adequacy of the resources available with which to confront the threat (secondary appraisal) determine the intensity of their emotional reactions to the event (e.g., anxiety, depression). Appraisals are not made in isolation (Bodenmann, 1995; Hobfoll, 1998; Hobfoll, Dunahoo, Ben-Porath, & Monnier, 1994; Lyons et al., 1998). Threat appraisals can spiral in intensity in a group setting, as evidenced by the "pressure cooker" effect found among Israeli women during the war between Israel and

Lebanon (Hobfoll & London, 1986). Women who sought each other for support experienced a higher level of distress than those who did not, the result of shared appraisals of threat and available defenses. Alternatively, threat appraisals may be lowered as a result of social interaction, when information is shared that eases unrealistic fears.

Bodenmann (1995) provided an analysis of the phases of individual and dyadic appraisals of stressful conditions. In his analysis, primary and secondary appraisals proceed in three phases. The three stages of primary appraisal are described first: (a) Each member of the couple evaluates the stressful event's threat to self, to the partner, and to the relationship; (b) each member of the couple tries to gauge the *partner's view* of the event's threat to self, to partner, and to the relationship; (c) finally, husband and wife compare each other's appraisals and try to reach a *consensus* view of the event's threat to each individual and to the relationship. In the secondary appraisal process, the resources available to deal with the stressful event are similarly appraised individually, from the partner's imagined perspective, and comparatively in an effort to reach a consensual view. An example illustrates these multiple stages of appraisal.

> *Mike and Pat have a 22-year-old daughter, Sonia, who came out to them as a lesbian several weeks after her graduation from college. It took Mike and Pat some time to adjust to this information, but they assured Sonia of their continuing love and agreed to meet Sonia's romantic partner, Eve. The first meeting with Eve was awkward, but as the evening went on, they found topics of joint interest and similar views on several issues, which gradually allowed them to relax. A month after they first met Eve, Sonia announced her intention to bring Eve to the family's Thanksgiving dinner, which would include grandparents, aunts and uncles, and cousins from Mike's side of the family, some of whom were quite traditional and conservative.*

In the primary appraisal process, Mike and Pat individually think through the possible consequences of their daughter's romantic partner's participation in Thanksgiving dinner for themselves, the other, and the relationship. For example, Pat might consider: "How will this affect my relationship with Mike's family? How will this affect Mike's relationship with his family? How will it affect our marriage?" Next, they each consider the other's probable appraisal in these areas. Pat's thoughts might include: "How does Mike think his mother will react? Will Mike think I am considering Sonia's feelings, but not his mother's? How will that affect his feelings toward me?" In the secondary appraisal process, in which coping resources are evaluated, Pat must consider her own level of self-control and ability to remain calm when responding to criticism from Mike's relatives, Mike's ability to support Pat through unpleasant family interactions, and the extent to which other sources of support (e.g., Pat's more liberal relatives, their minister, their friends) will affirm their decision to publicly accept their daughter's partner. She must also consider *Mike's views* of his ability to withstand family disapproval, her ability to support him, and the adequacy of outside sources of support. Of course, Mike goes through a similar set of primary and secondary appraisals.

Finally, if they are to work together to formulate an optimal way of handling the situation, it is advantageous for them to reach a consensus on their appraisals of both the threat and the resources they have available to deal with the threat. For example (in an ideal world), Mike and Pat might agree that their first priority is maintaining a good relationship with each other and with their daughter. If they agree that the threat to their primary family unit posed by disapproving relatives is manageable and that their resources as a couple and as a family are adequate to cope with disapproval by some of Mike's relatives, they can proceed in devising a strategy with their daughter and her partner for minimizing the potential unpleasantness of the holiday meal.

Although problem solving proceeds most smoothly when husband and wife reach consensus on both primary and secondary appraisals, Bodenmann (1995) argued that sometimes, different appraisals lead to more effective problem solution because each partner focuses on solving a different aspect of the situation. In our example, Pat might decide that the most severe threat is that their daughter may become clinically depressed if her father's relatives do not accept her partner. Thus, she may devote effort to reassuring Sonia that she and her father will stand with her no matter how the extended family reacts to her same-sex romantic partner. She may tell Sonia that the extended family's reaction is not important. Mike might decide that the most severe threat is that his mother's insensitive remarks may damage the relationship between his mother and his wife, a relationship that has already shown signs of strain. Thus, he may devote effort to preparing his mother, by revealing his daughter's homosexuality to her before the dinner, describing Eve in a positive manner, and making clear that his mother will be welcome at the dinner only if she can refrain from hurtful comments. He might ask Sonia to accompany him on one or more of these visits to his mother. In this latter scenario, Pat and Mike have selected different, but complementary strategies.

Sometimes, contrasting appraisals interfere with dyadic coping, as illustrated by the following scenario. Pat may conclude that the primary threat posed by the situation is to her daughter's mental health and Mike may conclude that the primary threat posed by the situation is to his family's image in the community. Pat will work to help her daughter retain her dignity and to care less about the family's opinion of her. Mike will try to convince Sonia to stay closeted and to lie about her relationship with Eve. He may ask her not to bring Eve to Thanksgiving dinner. In this case, Pat and Mike will be working at cross purposes. Their appraisals of the nature of the threat and the resources they have to deal with it have led them to behave in ways that will lead to conflict within their relationship and will probably prolong the discomfort experienced by all members of

the family. Their effectiveness as problem solvers will be low.

In sum, the appraisal process is complex, multifaceted, and firmly embedded in the relationship context of the marriage. When appraisals are consistent, joint problem solving proceeds most smoothly. Some discrepencies in appraisals may be adaptive if the result is that each partner "specializes" in solving a different component of the problematic situation. However, if appraisals suggest incompatible coping strategies, problem solving will be ineffective and the relationship may suffer.

Dyadic Coping

Dyadic coping is defined as the process of collaboration and sharing resources in response to a problem that affects both members of the couple, either directly or indirectly (Bodenmann, 1995, 2005; Lyons et al., 1998). Dyadic coping is distinguished from social support in that both individuals appraise the stressor as posing a threat to their well-being and both individuals take at least partial responsibility for dealing with it (Lyons et al., 1998). Although most instances of social support actually entail some degree of dyadic coping, most definitions of social support emphasize a one-way flow of resources to a single identified stress victim.

Bodenmann (2005) distinguishes between supportive dyadic coping and common dyadic coping. In supportive dyadic coping, one partner is primarily affected by the stressor, and the other partner is affected only indirectly. The spouse who is indirectly affected plays the role of "helper" to the spouse who is directly affected by the stressor. In common dyadic coping, both partners are directly affected by the stressor and they take on collaborative and relatively equal roles in efforts to solve the problem. In our example, Mike and Pat were both affected by their daughter's desire to introduce her same-sex partner to the family and engaged in common dyadic coping. However, if Mike and Pat had been newlyweds and Sonia were

Mike's daughter from a previous marriage, the problem of how to ease Sonia's partner into Mike's extended family might have been appraised as primarily Mike's problem, and Pat would have played a more secondary role, engaging in supportive dyadic coping.

As noted earlier, dyadic coping is directed toward multiple goals. These include dealing with one's own distress, taking instrumental steps to eliminate the problem, and dealing with the partner's distress and efforts to confront the problem (Coyne & Smith, 1991). In addition, protecting the long-term survival of the relationship from the effects of the stressor is a goal of dyadic coping. In the following section, empirical research on good and poor outcomes of dyadic coping is summarized. Research shows that sometimes the same dyadic coping behavior benefits one partner at the expense of another. The same dyadic coping behavior may also have different meaning and impact depending on the quality of the marital relationship within which it occurs. A variety of factors that can foster or prevent effective dyadic coping will be highlighted.

Empirical Research on Dyadic Coping

The Effects of Dyadic Coping

In this chapter, we focus on studies that explicitly tried to capture the dyadic nature of stressful life events or efforts to cope with these events. This dyadic perspective was reflected in the selection of study populations (i.e., couples facing a common stressor) or the use of measures that tapped coordinated coping activities or coping activities that were directed towards preserving the quality of the marital relationship.

Bodenmann (1995, 2005) conducted a series of studies to test the association between dyadic coping and marital outcomes. He created a measure of dyadic coping, the Dyadic Coping Scale (published in German as the FDCT-N; Bodenmann, 2000). The Dyadic Coping Scale assesses (a) supportive dyadic coping in which one

partner is the primary stress victim and the other assists in that person's coping efforts (e.g., "My partner gives me the feeling that he/she understands me"); (b) delegated coping in which one partner is the primary stress victim and the other takes over responsibilities for the stress victim to allow him or her to deal with the problem (e.g., "My partner takes on things that I normally do to help me out"); (c) common dyadic coping in which both partners are affected by the stressor and take relatively equal responsibility for dealing with the problem (e.g., "We help one another to put the problem in perspective and see it in a new light"); and (d) negative dyadic coping in which assistance is provided unwillingly, superficially, or in a hostile manner (e.g., "My partner provides support, but does so unwillingly"). Both emotion-focused (e.g., encouragement, understanding) and problem-focused coping assistance (e.g., advice, practical assistance) are assessed for supportive and common dyadic coping. Positive dyadic coping is the sum of scores on supportive dyadic coping, delegated coping, and common dyadic coping.

Among 1,200 married community-dwelling adults, Bodenmann (2005) found a highly significant correlation of 0.52 between positive dyadic coping and marital satisfaction. A meta-analysis of 13 studies that used the Dyadic Coping Scale (Bodenmann, 2005) found an average effect size for the relation between dyadic coping and marital satisfaction of 1.3, which would be classified as a "large" effect (Cohen, 1992). A 5-year longitudinal study examined the effects of dyadic stress and dyadic coping on relationship quality and stability (Bodenmann & Cina, 1999). Positive dyadic coping at the first assessment was a significant predictor of relationship quality 5 years later. Dyadic coping (positive and negative) and dyadic stress together predicted divorce with 73% accuracy. In an observational study that compared the behavior of couples who scored high versus low on marital satisfaction, positive dyadic coping was more frequent among satisfied couples, whereas negative dyadic coping (i.e., hostile, ambivalent, and superficial dyadic coping) was more frequent among dissatisfied couples (Bodenmann, 1990, 1995, 2000).

Unequal Benefits of Dyadic Coping

Dyadic coping sometimes benefits one partner more than the other, as illustrated in a study of couples in which the husband had suffered a myocardial infarction (Coyne, Ellard, & Smith, 1990; Coyne & Smith, 1991). The focus of the study was relationship-focused coping, that is, efforts to ease the partner's distress and preserve the relationship in the context of the husband's illness. Based on information gained from focus groups of patients and their wives, two primary types of relationship-focused coping emerged (Coyne et al., 1990). The first, active engagement, included constructive discussions with the partner, inquiring after the partner's well-being, and joint problem solving. The second, protective buffering, represented attempts to shield the partner from distress by hiding concerns, concealing worries, and giving in to avoid conflict. Surprisingly, active engagement showed little or no relation to outcomes when controlling for marital quality and medical variables. However, results showed that when wives engaged in protective buffering, their husbands' self-efficacy was increased. Wives paid a price for this strategy, in that it also predicted an increase in the wives' level of distress. Use of protective buffering by husbands increased husbands' distress in a separate study of couples in which the man had suffered a myocardial infraction (Suls, Green, Rose, Lounsbury, & Gordon, 1997). For both spouses and patients, concealing their own worries and dealing with problems alone was very stressful.

Moderation of Effects by Marital Quality

The impact of some dyadic coping behaviors differs as a function of the couple's level of marital satisfaction. In their study of heart attack patients, Coyne and Smith (1991) found that when husbands engaged in protective buffering, the effect on wives

was different among happy versus unhappy couples. Among unhappily married couples, husband protective buffering increased wives' distress. Among happily married couples, however, husband protective buffering had no adverse effect on wives' well-being. A similar pattern of results was found in a study of couples facing a range of shared negative life events (Edwards et al., 1988). Among happily married couples, failing to confide in the spouse about the event out of a desire to protect him or her did not increase rates of depression significantly over rates for those who did confide. Coyne and Smith (1991) speculated that in low-quality marriages, men engaged in "antagonistic cooperation" when they concealed their concerns and gave in during disagreements. Their attempts to protect their wives from stress were not effective because of the overall negative tone of their communication (e.g., "You don't need to know what I'm thinking! Just go about your business!"). Thus, it is important to evaluate the effects of dyadic coping in the context of the marital relationship in which it is embedded. The same behavior can have different meaning and impact when it is shown in happy versus unhappy marriages.

Barriers to Dyadic Coping

A range of factors can interfere with successful dyadic coping. These include the personality characteristics of the individuals, the severity of the stressor, the adequacy of available resources, differences in coping styles, different levels of optimism, fear of facing the problem directly, inability to relinquish or share control, resentment over perceived neglect of personal needs, depression, and anger over the injustice of the stressor. Each of these are considered briefly.

PERSONALITY

Personality characteristics can make dyadic coping more difficult. O'Brien and DeLongis (1996) examined the associations between personality characteristics and the use of relationship-focused coping. Relationship-focused coping was conceptualized as modes of coping aimed at "managing, regulating, or preserving relationships during stressful periods" (O'Brien & DeLongis, 1996, p. 782). In their view, an important component of relationship-focused coping is empathic responding to one's partner, including efforts to understand the other's point of view, vicariously experience the other's emotions, infer the other's emotional state from his or her behavior, and behave toward the other in a warm and accepting manner. O'Brien and DeLongis (1996) found that individuals high on neuroticism were less likely than other people to use empathic responding in stressors involving close relationships. With close others, high neurotics tended to use confrontation rather than empathy. The authors speculated that individuals high on neuroticism may find stressors that involve close others highly threatening, which may diminish their ability to use adaptive strategies. Neuroticism is a consistent predictor of poor marital outcomes (Karney & Bradbury, 1997), perhaps in part because people high on neuroticism use maladaptive approaches to stress-inducing situations, especially those that involve intimate relationships (O'Brien & DeLongis, 1996).

STRESS SEVERITY

Level of burden and available resources also may affect ability to use adaptive dyadic coping strategies. Kramer (1993) studied caregivers of Alzheimer's patients and examined both positive relationship-focused coping strategies (i.e., empathy, support provision, compromise) and negative relationship-focused coping strategies (i.e., confronting, ignoring, blaming, withdrawal). Kramer found that lower levels of stress, such as less severe patient impairment and higher levels of resources (e.g., income, support from network members) were associated with the use of positive relationship-focused strategies whereas high stress and low available resources were associated with negative relationship-focused coping. It is important to consider the context in which coping occurs. It is easier to cope constructively, in ways that foster a positive relationship climate, when the individual is not overwhelmed by situational demands and a lack of material and interpersonal resources.

DIFFERENCES IN COPING STYLES

Sometimes differences in the approaches that husbands and wives use to cope with dyadic stressors pose challenges to individual well-being and to the relationship. These differences can be especially problematic if individuals pressure each other to alter their coping behaviors. Among couples with a seriously ill child, Gottlieb and Wagner (1991) found that husbands coped by trying to avoid potentially overwhelming emotions and withdrawing into work and activities outside of the home. They pressured their wives to behave less emotionally and to concentrate on the daily requirements of caring for the ill child. By contrast, wives coped by venting about daily problems and airing their fears about the child's future. They pressured their husbands to become more involved emotionally and in the routines of daily care. Wives sought to comply with their husbands' wishes to be spared exposure to worrisome developments in the child's illness and to their own distress, although this frustrated their need to vent and their need for emotional connection. In sum, to win their husband's approval, wives adopted a "stoical" posture in husbands' presence. Although it eased immediate strains, it fostered considerable resentment and feelings of isolation among wives and, over an extended period of time, may have weakened the bonds of the relationship. Similar problems were found among couples facing a recent myocardial infarction when the husband was a "denier" (minimized the threat of the illness) and the wife was highly anxious (Stern & Pascale, 1979). Women were distressed by their spouse's inability to meet their needs for comfort and reassurance. Husbands could not tolerate discussions of the health problems they were trying to ignore.

Similarity of coping styles does not guarantee positive outcomes. Sometimes problems are created when both members of the couple cope in the same way. Among couples facing infertility, women who were low on emotional-approach coping (emotional processing and expression) were less depressed when their husband was high on this type of coping (Burghuis & Stanton, 2002). When women were high on emotional-approach coping, their husband's level on this strategy did not affect their well-being. Thus, it appeared that husbands could compensate for some coping activities that women found difficult. In a study of parents of children with cancer, symmetry in use of problem solving (both spouses high) was associated with lower marital satisfaction than complementary use (one high and one low; Barbarin, Hughes, & Chesler, 1985). Similar results were found among rheumatoid arthritis patients and their spouses (Revenson, 2003; Revenson & Cameron, 1992). Couples in which both partners used primarily problem-focused coping in response to the patient's illness showed the highest level of psychological distress, although their marital satisfaction did not seem to be negatively affected. Perhaps a primary focus on problem solving by both members of the couple leads to a sense of competition or vying for control. Perhaps when both partners focus on problem solving, neither partner takes responsibility for addressing the emotional burdens posed by family illness. Alternatively, perhaps both members of the couple find they must concentrate on problem-solving when the illness is particularly severe or when the patient's condition is deteriorating (Revenson, 2003; Revenson & Cameron, 1992). In the latter scenario, the severity of the patient's condition may drive both distress and concentration on problem solving.

EXPECTATIONS

Similarity in expectation level for positive outcomes appears to be important for good dyadic coping. In the same study of arthritis patients, complementary use of optimistic thinking (one spouse high, one spouse low) was associated with lower marital satisfaction than symmetry (both high or both low;

Revenson & Cameron, 1992). It may be devastating to one partner's sense of hope when the other partner cannot think optimistically. The partner who does not think optimistically may fear the let-down of letting one's hopes rise too high. Clearly, similarity in coping has different outcomes, depending on the specific type of coping under consideration.

EMOTIONS

Overwhelming fear may prevent effective dyadic coping. Among couples in which the wife had breast cancer, Wortman and Dunkel-Schetter (1979) found that spouses' fears led them to behave in ways that were distressing to the patient. The well spouse was frightened by his spouse's potentially fatal illness and either avoided discussing the illness or adopted a façade of cheery optimism. This cut off the patient from emotional intimacy and led her to feel that her own fears were not taken seriously. In a similar study of breast cancer patients and their spouses, patients were most satisfied in relationships where husbands expressed a high level of concern about recurrence or death (Lichtman, Taylor, & Wood, 1988). Patients were unhappy in their relationships when husbands downplayed women's fears of recurrence.

In other circumstances, fears of the well spouse may be manifested in intrusive and controlling behavior, especially when patient adherence to dietary and medical regimens is viewed as important to his or her survival (Coyne & Smith, 1991; Coyne, Wortman, & Lehman, 1988; Stern & Pascale, 1979). Spouses may become trapped in a battle over the patient's behavior in which the patient fights for autonomy, perhaps at the expense of behaviors that would benefit his or her recovery.

Depression often interferes with effective dyadic coping. There is some evidence that level of depression in the stress victim is a more powerful predictor of marital disruption than objective severity of the event, probably because of the disruptive effects of depression on marital interaction.

Observational studies provide convincing evidence that level of distress predicts a decline in warmth and an increase in hostility in marital interactions, which in turn, predicts erosion of marital quality (Cohan & Bradbury, 1997; Conger, Rueter, & Elder, 1999; Matthews, Conger, & Wickrama, 1996). The severity of the victim's distress predicted marital deterioration in the context of financial strain (Conger et al., 1999; Vinokur, Price, & Caplan, 1996), infertility (Abbey et al., 1995), breast cancer (Bolger, Foster, Vinokur, & Ng, 1996), and coronary bypass surgery (Kulik & Mahler, 1993). In a rare exception, a positive correlation was found among arthritis sufferers between patient level of depression and amount of social support received from the spouse (Revenson & Majerovitz, 1991).

Not only victim depression but also victim anger is associated with a decline in marital quality in the context of negative life events (Lane & Hobfoll, 1992). Among couples in which one member suffered from chronic obstructive pulmonary disease, patient anger and irritable behavior predicted spouse anger, both concurrently and over time. When both members of the couple are angry, it is difficult for them to provide comfort or support, and the bond between them may weaken significantly.

MARITAL STRAIN.

Dyadic coping suffers when the demands of the stressor reduce the amount of time and attention that spouses devote to one another. Perceived neglect may lead to resentment. Among couples in which one partner experienced the death of a parent, marital quality and perceived spousal support deteriorated (Umberson, 1995). The parent's final illness frequently took the bereaved partner from home for extended periods of time. After the parent died, the nonbereaved partner asserted his or her own needs and was often disappointed in the bereaved partner's inability to shift his or her attention back to the marital relationship. Among parents of children with cancer, husbands' marital satisfaction was tied to wives' availability at home, specifically the extent to which wives spent time at home versus at the hospital (Barbarin et al., 1985). Thus, disruptions in role performance and time spent together can have negative effects on couples' ability to retain a sense of closeness in times of stress (Bodenmann, 2005)

Interventions to Protect Marriages in the Context of Stressful Life Events

There are many interventions to help couples who are in the throes of a major life event cope more effectively. Interventions exist to aid new parents (Cowan & Cowan, 1997; Lichtenstein, 1993), parents of children entering kindergarten (Cowan & Cowan, 1997), parents of children with conduct problems (Eyberg & Robinson, 1982; Ireland, Sanders, & Markie-Dadds, 2003), parents of children with developmental disorders (Lichtenstein, 1993), and bereaved parents (Murray, Terry, Vance, Battistutta, & Connolly, 2000). Other interventions have been developed to help couples cope together with cancer (Blanchard, Toseland, & McCallion, 1996; Bultz, Speca, Brasher, Geggie, & Page, 2000; Christensen, 1983; Goldberg & Wool, 1985; Halford, Scott, & Smythe, 2000; Heinrich & Schag, 1985; Kayser, 2005; Sabo, Brown, & Smith, 1986; Samarel & Fawcett, 1992), dementia (Quayhagen et al., 2000), HIV/AIDS (Pakenham, Dadds, & Lennon, 2002; Pomeroy, Green, & Van Laningham, 2002), and the aftermath of military combat (Devilly, 2002).

Most interventions include education about the specific stressor (i.e., presentations by experts), tips on practical problem solving, and group discussion. Many of these intervention programs, however, fail to take into account that coping and stress are dyadic processes for individuals in ongoing relationships. We limit our focus to interventions that address the marital relationship as well as the specific stressor, with the objective not only to improve the quality of individual and dyadic coping but to maintain or improve the quality of the marital relationship.

In addition to psychoeducational and discussion components, these relationship-focused interventions typically address relationship skills of various types, most often problem-solving techniques and communication skills. Problem-solving assistance includes both methods for coping with the specific stressor (e.g., dealing effectively with the medical system in the context of breast cancer) and for dealing with stress-related problems in the relationship (e.g., what to do when one spouse wants to talk about the stressor and the other does not). A unique preventive intervention, Couples Coping Enhancement Training (CCET), was designed in Switzerland to prepare couples to deal with stressful events before they actually experience them (Widmer, Cina, Charvoz, Shantinath, & Bodenmann, 2005). The CCET integrates cognitive–behavioral approaches with concepts from theories of stress and coping. The CCET was designed to strengthen the individual and dyadic coping competencies of both partners, strengthen communication, and enhance problem-solving skills. Communication training includes both traditional components (e.g., clear communication, nondestructive conflict) and units on how to "protect" the quality of communication when it is challenged by stressful life events. Explicit coaching in effective individual and dyadic coping is included in the intervention. Couples are taught to discriminate among different kinds of stressful events (e.g., controllable vs. uncontrollable). They are shown techniques for effective planning and execution of coping strategies. They are taught about their own and their partner's preferred coping techniques and to recognize potential clashes that may result from differences in their coping styles. Couples are given opportunities to practice coordinated, cooperative coping skills. The dangers of overinvolvement or excessive dependency are discussed. The importance of continued communication is emphasized throughout all phases of the coping process.

CCET (Widmer et al., 2005) showed evidence of effectiveness when tested relative to comparison couples who were enrolled in a longitudinal study of marital functioning. Marital satisfaction increased significantly over a 1-year span in the intervention group, but no increase was seen in the comparison group. Women reported increased quality of marital communication, although men did not report any change. At the 1 year follow-up, observed increases in positive dyadic coping and decreases in negative dyadic coping were found in the intervention group relative to the comparison group.

A similar intervention, the Partners in Coping Program, was designed to enhance emotional support between partners and to facilitate dyadic coping among couples in which the wife had been diagnosed with breast cancer (Kayser, 2005). The program was individually administered to couples during the first year after diagnosis, while the woman was undergoing treatment, and consisted of nine 1-hour sessions. Fifty couples were randomly assigned to the Partners in Coping Program or to standard hospital services. Results showed that the intervention increased patient well-being, increased positive dyadic coping and communication about illness-related stressors, and decreased destructive coping. Unfortunately, some of the benefits of the treatment that were observed at the 6-month posttreatment follow-up had weakened considerably by the time of the 12-month follow-up.

Other interventions that include both marital and stressor-specific training have shown pre–post improvements in marital outcomes, such as Devilly's (2002) program for war veterans and their spouses, and Pomery and colleagues' (2002) program for couples in which one partner is HIV positive. Pakenham and colleagues' (2002) work with HIV-positive individuals and their spouses found that the marital outcomes of the intervention group remained stable, whereas marital satisfaction in control-group couples declined over the same period of time.

The evidence that relationship-focused interventions help couples cope with stress better than psychoeducational programs alone is somewhat mixed. Ireland, Sanders, and Markie-Dadds (2003) conducted two versions of the Positive Parenting Program (PPP) for parents of children with conduct disorders. The standard group offered only parenting skills training, whereas the extended group added marital-specific training, such as how to support partners' parenting and how to settle parenting-related disagreements. Marital satisfaction increased the same amount among couples in the maritally focused and standard groups; the maritally-focused group did not benefit more than the standard group. Quayhagen and colleagues (2002) studied the effectiveness of a problem-specific versus a maritally focused intervention for people with dementia and their caregiving spouses and found that marital satisfaction did not change significantly from pre- to post-intervention in either the intervention group or in the control group. Cowan and Cowan (1997) conducted an intervention for parents whose children were beginning kindergarten. Couples participated in groups that emphasized either parenting or marital concerns. Surprisingly, marital satisfaction increased for couples in the parenting-focused group but not for couples in the marital concerns group. Couples with a high level of conflict in their marriage who participated in the marital concerns group actually showed an increased level of conflict postintervention.

In sum, there appears to be evidence that couples benefit from interventions designed to help them cope with stressful life events, such as child health or behavior problems. It is less clear that the addition of an explicit marital component adds to the effectiveness of such interventions. However, few interventions have been rigorously tested in which a traditional psychoeducational intervention has been compared with a psychoeducational plus marital intervention. Several studies compared psychoeducational-only to marital-only interventions or reduced the amount of psychoeducational content in the combined programs. The psychoeducational component is important to give couples the knowledge they need to both make informed choices and feel a sense of control over the stressor. If this component is short-changed, couples may not have the tools they need to confront the practical aspects of the illness or problem. This may be one reason that maritally focused interventions have not shown clear superiority.

Alternatively, couples who participate in intervention programs may be higher functioning than those who do not participate. They may reach a ceiling in positive adjustment through participation in either kind of program. Thus, dramatic increases in marital adjustment may not be seen. Evidence that high-functioning couples are more likely than low-functioning couples to participate in preventive interventions was found in a study of premarital interventions (Sullivan & Bradbury, 1997). Similarly, Kayser (2005) found that couples who enrolled in her preventive intervention for breast cancer patients and their spouses began the program with high baseline levels of mutual emotional support.

Directions for Future Research

Research on dyadic stress and coping is in the early stages. Many important questions remain. Bodenmann's (1995, 2005) ideas about the stages of primary and secondary appraisal that occur within couples are largely untested. Thus, it would be useful to develop measures of personal appraisal, appraisal from the partner's perspective, and processes people go through in striving to achieve consistent appraisals of major threats. It would be useful to investigate consequences of consistent versus inconsistent appraisals within couples of both the major threat posed by events and the adequacy of resources to deal with them. It would be interesting to investigate the circumstances in which both members versus only one member of a couple define a given stressor as relevant to their well-being. There may be circumstances in which it is more adaptive to define a stressor as the province of one member only. In other words, there may be disadvantages to joint "ownership" of every problem.

It is not known whether certain components of dyadic coping are more beneficial than others. For example, the most important result of joint problem solving may be the cognition that one is not alone, that someone else knows and cares about the problems one is facing. It would be of interest to determine the extent to which defining a problem as dyadic rather than individual and attempting to work together actually results in superior problem solution.

Much of the experience of negative life events consists of waiting for events to unfold. For example, when a child is ill, recovery processes are slow and little can be done by parents to influence the outcome. One component of dyadic coping may be reassuring one another that they have done all that was possible (e.g., selected the most qualified physician or the best medical facility). Couples may reassure one another that they need not feel guilt for inactivity. Their most important function may be to help their partner survive lengthy waiting periods.

More research is needed on ways to handle apparent gender differences in coping styles. Are there benefits of making individuals aware of stylistic differences in coping styles? Can people be helped to make benign attributions (i.e., to gender-role socialization) rather than to engage in blame when differences arise in the need to vent emotions or avoid worrisome topics? Can compromises be devised in which individuals take turns accommodating to the coping needs of their partner and asking the partner to accommodate to their own needs? To what extent would such a strategy overwhelm the defenses of an individual whose primary weapon is denial?

Individuals often wish to shelter their spouse from distress. However, this technique can exact an emotional toll from the individual who seeks to protect and, in some circumstances, from the individual being protected. Overprotectiveness is a serious problem in some contexts, especially those involving a potentially life-threatening illness. Methods that enable people to work in teams of co-equals will be difficult to devise.

Patterns of overprotectiveness are built up over many years and rooted in fear of relinquishing control. Other ways of helping the overprotective spouse feel more secure are needed and probably must come from the patient whose survival is at issue.

Research suggests that when couples are able to face negative events as a unit, with a sense of "we-ness," events are less likely to damage the fabric of the relationship (Bodenmann, 2005; Cutrona, 1996). However, the research literature is replete with descriptions of problematic dyadic coping. This is not surprising, because when people are under stress, their energy and attention are deflected from their relationship to the demands of the taxing event or circumstances. Their emotions are intense and changeable, subject to variations in the stress-producing situation. Their worldview is in flux, as valued goals or love objects are threatened. In that context, people are not likely to be on their best "relationship behavior." Thus, there may be two critical components to relationship maintenance in the context of severe stress. The first is preventing hurtful or counterproductive interaction patterns, such as pressuring one's spouse to stop coping in a way that makes one uncomfortable (e.g., crying or expressing fear) or taking out one's frustrations on the spouse. Some negative coping is probably inevitable, given the context of high stress. Thus, the second critical component may be forgiveness. Individuals who are facing the potential loss of physical functions, valued achievements, or the presence of pain or suffering in a loved one cannot always be empathic or even reasonable. An intervention model that combines awareness of appraisal processes, the implications of conflicting primary and secondary appraisals, and instruction on how to cope together rather than at cross-purposes may work best if it is tempered with the expectation that people will fail. Such failures can be normalized, rather than construed as major betrayals ("How could he speak to me so sharply when our only child is undergoing major surgery tomorrow?"). Attributions to the situation rather than to flaws in the partner's character may be a critical component of the ability to forgive. ("He isn't angry with me, he is angry with the disease.") The most important contribution of interventions may be to educate people about the effects of stress on communication, the ability to express affection, and the capacity to process and react to information in a rational manner. It may be that our goal should not be "perfect dyadic coping" but multiple opportunities for redemption.

References

Abbey, A., Andrews, F. M., & Halman, L. J. (1995). Provision and receipt of social support and disregard: What is their impact on the marital life quality of infertile and fertile couples? *Journal of Personality and Social Psychology, 68,* 455–469.

Barbarin, O. A., Hughes, D., & Chesler, M. A. (1985). Stress, coping, and marital functioning among parents of children with cancer. *Journal of Marriage and the Family, 47,* 473–480.

Berscheid, E. (1983). Emotion. In H. H. Kelley, E. Berscheid, A. Christensen, J. H. Harvey, T. L. Huston, G. Levinger, et al. (Eds.), *Close relationships* (pp. 110–168). New York: Freeman.

Blanchard, C., Toseland, R., & McCallion, P. (1996). The effects of a problem-solving intervention with spouses of cancer patients. *Journal of Psychosocial Oncology, 14,* 1–21.

Bodenmann, G. (1990). *Ärgerregulation und deren Bedeutung für die Dyadische Interaktion.* [Anger regulation and its significance for dyadic interaction.] Unpublished master's thesis. Fribourg: University of Fribourg, Switzerland.

Bodenmann, G. (1995). A systemic-transactional conceptualization of stress and coping in couples. *Swiss Journal of Psychology, 54,* 34–49.

Bodenmann, G. (2000). *Stress und Coping bei Paaren* [Stress and coping in couples]. Gottingen, Germany: Hogrefe.

Bodenmann, G. (2005). Dyadic coping and its significance for marital functioning. In T. A. Revenson, K. Kayser, & G. Bodenmann (Eds.), *Couples coping with stress: Emerging perspectives on dyadic coping* (pp. 33–49). Washington, DC: American Psychological Association.

Bodenmann, G., & Cina, A. (1999). Der Einfluss von Stress, individueller Belastungsbewältigung und dyadischem Coping auf die Partnerschaftsstabilität: Eine 4-Jahres-Längsschnittstudie. *Zeitschrift für Klinische Psychologie, 28,* 130–139.

Bolger, N., DeLongis, A., Kessler, R. C., & Wethington, E. (1989). The contagion of stress across multiple roles. *Journal of Marriage and the Family, 51,* 175–183.

Bolger, N., Foster, M., Vinokur, A. D., & Ng, R. (1996). Close relationships and adjustment to a life crisis: The case of breast cancer. *Journal of Personality and Social Psychology, 70,* 283–294.

Bultz, B. D., Speca, M., Brasher, P. M., Geggie, P. H. S., & Page, S. A. (2000). A randomized controlled trial of a brief psychoeducational support group for partners of early stage breast cancer patients. *Psycho-Oncology, 9,* 303–313.

Berghuis, J. P., & Stanton, A. L. (2002). Adjustment to a dyadic stressor: A longitudinal study of coping and depressive symptoms in infertile couples over an insemination attempt. *Journal of Clinical and Consulting Psychology, 70,* 433–438.

Christensen, D. (1983). Postmastectomy couple counseling: An outcome study of a structured treatment protocol. *Journal of Sex and Marital Therapy, 9,* 266–275.

Cohan, C. L., & Bradbury, T. N. (1997). Negative life events, marital interaction, and the longitudinal course of newlywed marriage. *Journal of Personality and Social Psychology, 73,* 114–128.

Cohen, J. (1992). A power primer. *Psychological Bulletin, 112,* 155–159.

Conger, R. D., Elder, G. H., Jr., Lorenz, F. O., Conger, K. J., Simons, R. L., Whitbeck, L. B., et al. (1990). Linking economic hardship to marital quality and instability. *Journal of Marriage and the Family, 52,* 643–656.

Conger, R. D., Rueter, M. A., & Elder, G. H., Jr. (1999). Couple resilience to economic pressure. *Journal of Personality and Social Psychology, 76,* 54–71.

Cowan, C. P., & Cowan, P. A. (1997). Working with couples during stressful transitions. In S. Dreman (Ed.), *The family on the threshold of the 21st century: Trends and implications* (pp. 17–47). Mahwah, NJ: Erlbaum.

Coyne, J. C., Ellard, J. H., & Smith, D. A. (1990). Unsupportive relationships, interdependence, and unhelpful exchanges. In I. G. Sarason, B. R. Sarason, & G. Pierce (Eds.), *Social support: An interactional view* (pp. 129–149). New York: Wiley.

Coyne, J. C., & Smith, D. A. F. (1991). Couples coping with a myocardial infarction: A contextual perspective on wives' distress. *Journal of Personality and Social Psychology*, *61*, 404–412.

Coyne, J. C., Wortman, C. B., & Lehman, D. R. (1988). The other side of support: Emotional overinvolvement and miscarried helping. In B. H. Gottlieb (Ed.), *Marshalling social support* (pp. 305–330). Newbury Park, CA: Sage.

Cutrona, C. E. (1996). *Social support in couples*. Thousand Oaks, CA: Sage.

Devilly, G. J. (2002). The psychological effects of a lifestyle management course on war veterans and their spouses. *Journal of Clinical Psychology*, *58*, 1119–1134.

Edwards, A. C., Nazroo, J. Y., & Brown, G. W. (1988). Gender differences in marital support following a shared life event. *Social Science and Medicine*, *46*, 1077–1085.

Eyberg, S. M., & Robinson, E. A. (1982). Parent–child interaction training: Effects on family functioning. *Journal of Clinical Child Psychology*, *11*, 130–137.

Goldberg, R. J., & Wool, M. S. (1985). Psychotherapy for the spouses of lung cancer patients: Assessment of an intervention. *Psychotherapy Psychosomatics*, *43*, 141–150.

Gottlieb, B. H., & Wagner, F. (1991). Stress and support process in close relationships. In J. Eckenrode (Ed.), *The social context of coping* (pp. 165–188). New York: Plenum Press.

Halford, W. K., Scott, J. L., & Smythe, J. (2000). Couples and coping with cancer: Helping each other through the night. In K. B. Schmaling & T. G. Sher (Eds.), *The psychology of couples and illness: Theory, research, and practice* (pp. 135–170). Washington DC: American Psychological Association.

Heinrich, R. L., & Schag, C. C. (1985). Stress and activity management: Group treatment for cancer patients and spouses. *Journal of Consulting and Clinical Psychology*, *53*, 439–446.

Hobfoll, S. E. (1998). Our coping as individuals within families and tribes. In S. E. Hobfoll (Ed.), *Stress, culture, and community: The psychology and philosophy of stress* (pp. 119–140). New York: Plenum Press.

Hobfoll, S. E., Dunahoo, C. A., Ben-Porath, Y., & Monnier, J. (1994). Gender and coping: The dual axis model of coping. *American Journal of Community Psychology*, *22*, 49–82.

Hobfoll, S. E., & London, P. (1986). The relationship of self-concept and social support to emotional distress among women during war. *Journal of Social and Clinical Psychology*, *4*, 189–203.

Ireland, J. L., Sanders, M. R., & Markie-Dadds, C. (2003). The impact of parent training on marital functioning: A comparison of two group versions of the triple p-positive parenting program for parents of children with early-onset conduct problems. *Behavioural and Cognitive Psychotherapy*, *31*, 127–142.

Karney, B. R., & Bradbury, T. N. (1997). Neuroticism, marital interaction, and the trajectory of marital satisfaction. *Journal of Personality and Social Psychology*, *72*, 1075–1092.

Katz, J., Monnier, J., Libet, J., Shaw, D., & Beach, S. R. H. (2000). Individual and crossover effects of stress on adjustment in medical student marriages. *Journal of Marital and Family Therapy*, *26*, 341–351.

Kayser, K. (2005). Enhancing dyadic coping during a time of crisis: A theory-based intervention with breast cancer patients and their partners. In T. A. Revenson, K. Kayser, & G. Bodenmann (Eds.), Couples coping with stress: *Emerging perspectives on dyadic coping* (pp. 175–194). Washington, DC: American Psychological Association.

Kramer, B. J. (1993). Expanding the conceptualization of caregiver coping: The importance of relationship-focused coping strategies. *Family Relations*, *42*, 383–391.

Kulik, J. A., & Mahler, H. I. M. (1993). Emotional support as a moderator of adjustment and compliance after coronary artery bypass surgery: A longitudinal study. *Journal of Behavioral Medicine*, *16*, 45–63.

Lane, C., & Hobfoll, S. E. (1992). How loss affects anger and alienates potential supporters. *Journal of Consulting and Clinical Psychology*, *60*, 935–942.

Lazarus, R. S. (1966). *Psychological stress and the coping process*. New York: McGraw-Hill.

Lazarus, R. S., & Folkman, S. (1984). *Stress, appraisal, and coping*. New York: Springer.

Lichtenstein, J. (1993). Help for troubled marriages. In G. H. S. Singer & P. L. E. (Eds.), *Families, disability, and empowerment: Active coping skills and strategies for family interventions* (pp. 257 277). Baltimore, MD: Brookes.

Lichtman, R. R., Taylor, S. E., & Wood, J. V. (1988). Social support and marital adjustment after breast cancer. *Journal of Psychosocial Oncology*, *5*, 47–74.

Lyons, R. F., Mickelson, K. D., Sullivan, M. J. L., & Coyne, J. C. (1998). Coping as a communal process. *Journal of Social and Personal Relationships*, 15, 579–605.

Matthews, L. S., Conger, R. D., & Wickrama, K. A. S. (1996). Work-family conflict and marital quality: Mediating processes. *Social Psychology Quarterly*, 59, 62–79.

Murray, J. A., Terry, D. J., Vance, J. C., Battistutta, D., & Connolly, Y. (2000). Effects of a program of intervention on parental distress following infant death. *Death Studies*, 24, 275–305.

O'Brien, T. B., & DeLongis, A. (1996). The interaction context of problem-, emotion-, and relationship-focused coping: The role of the big five personality factors. *Journal of Personality*, 64, 775–813.

Pakenham, K. I., Dadds, M. R., & Lennon, H. V. (2002). The efficacy of a psychosocial intervention for HIV/AIDS caregiving dyads and individual caregivers: A controlled treatment outcome study. *AIDS Care*, 14, 731–750.

Pomeroy, E. C., Green, D. L., & Van Laningham, L. (2002). Couples who care: The effectiveness of a psychoeducational group intervention for HIV serodiscordant couples. *Research on Social Work Practice*, 12, 238–252.

Quayhagen, M. P., Quayhagen, M., Corbeil, R. R., Hendrix, R. C., Jackson, J. E., Snyder, L., et al. (2000). Coping with dementia: Evaluation of four nonpharmacologic interventions. *International Psychogeriatrics*, 12, 249–265.

Revenson, T. A. (2003). Scenes from a marriage: Examining support, coping, and gender within the context of chronic illness. In J. Suls & K. A. Wallston (Eds.), *Social psychological foundations of health and illness* (pp. 530–559). Malden, MA: Blackwell.

Revenson, T. A., & Cameron, A. E. (1992, August). *Coping processes among married couples with rheumatic disease*. Paper presented at the Annual meeting of the American Psychological Association, Washington, DC.

Revenson, T. A., & Majerovitz, D. M. (1991). The effects of chronic illness on the spouse: Social resources as stress buffers. *Arthritis Care and Research*, 4, 63–72.

Sabo, D., Brown, J., & Smith, C. (1986). The male role and mastectomy: Support groups and men's adjustment. *Journal of Psychosocial Oncology*, 4(1/2), 19–31.

Samarel, N., & Fawcett, J. (1992). Enhancing adaptation to breast cancer: The addition of coaching to support groups. *Oncology Nursing Forum*, 19, 591–596.

Stern, M. J., & Pascale, L. (1979). Psychosocial adaptation post-myocardial infarction: The spouse's dilemma. *Journal of Psychosomatic Research*, 23, 83–87.

Sullivan, K. T., & Bradbury, T. N. (1997). Are premarital prevention programs reaching couples at risk for marital dysfunction? *Journal of Consulting and Clinical Psychology*, 65, 24–30.

Suls, J., Green, P., Rose, G., Lounsbury, P., & Gordon, E. (1997). Hiding worries from one's spouse: Associations between coping via protective buffering and distress in male post-myocardial infarction patients and their wives. *Journal of Behavioral Medicine*, 20, 333–349.

Thompson, A., & Bolger, N. (1999). Emotional transmission in couples under stress. *Journal of Marriage and the Family*, 61, 38–48.

Umberson, D. (1995). Marriage as support or strain? Marital quality following the death of a parent. *Journal of Marriage and the Family*, 57, 709–723.

Vinokur, A. D., Price, R. H., & Caplan, R. D. (1996). Hard times and hurtful partners: How financial strain affects depression and relationship satisfaction of unemployed persons and their spouses. *Journal of Personality and Social Psychology*, 71, 166–179.

Widmer, K., Cina, A., Charvoz, L., Shantinath, S., & Bodenmann, G. (2005). Dyadic coping: Implications for prevention of marital distress. In T. A. Revenson, K. Kayser, & G. Bodenmann (Eds.), Couples coping with stress: *Emerging perspectives on dyadic coping*. (pp. 159–174). Washington, DC: American Psychological Association.

Wortman, C. B., & Dunkel-Schetter, C. (1979). Interpersonal relationships and cancer: A theoretical analysis. *Journal of Social Issues*, 35 (1), 120–155.

CHAPTER 28

Lying and Deception in Close Relationships

Mark L. Knapp

...it seems patently obvious that both the substance and the outcomes of deceptive transactions are markedly influenced by the nature of the communicators' relationship. (Miller, Mongeau, & Sleight, 1986)

Few would disagree with Miller, Mongeau, and Sleight's (1986) claim that the nature of one's relationship with another person will greatly influence the process of lying and deception. However, like other broad and unspecified conclusions about human behavior, it gets a bit gnarly when we start trying to specify precisely "the nature of the communicators' relationship," and "deceptive transactions." This chapter proceeds with the assumption that the closeness of a relationship will affect the frequency of lying, the motivation for lying, the things lied about, the interactive manifestations of the lying process, the awareness of and desire to detect deception, the accuracy of that detection, the methods used to detect deception, and the consequences of the deception. In order to understand lying and deception in close relationships, however, it is first necessary to establish what we mean by a close relationship because many of the features that make a relationship "close" are also the features that give shape to the manifestation and detection of duplicity in those relationships.

Close Relationships

Some researchers accept relationship labels like "friend" or "romantic partner" as sufficient indicators of closeness; others accept a response to a single, seven-point scale of relationship closeness as a satisfactory indicator of relationship closeness; still others equate measures of commitment with the degree of closeness in a relationship. However, as Parks and Floyd (1996) pointed out, these approaches don't tell us much about the meaning of closeness. It is possible that two people (or two couples) could use the same relationship label or the same response to the 7-point relationship scale and have very different views about what constitutes closeness or a close relationship.

In contrast, several scholars have identified specific characteristics people use as referents for relationships that they perceive as "close" (Aron, Aron, & Smollan, 1992; Berscheid et al., 1989; Davis & Todd, 1982; Fehr, 1993; Maxwell, 1985; Parks & Floyd, 1996). It is not always clear from these studies how these defining characteristics of close relationships are weighted or how the perceptions of these characteristics by each partner can be combined so that the relationship can be described as close. Nevertheless, the results of these studies do suggest four principles about close relationships that provide a useful context within which to better understand lying and deception in close relationships.

1. *People in close relationships are expected to recognize and respect the vulnerabilities that go with being in a close relationship.* As a consequence, *trust* (Davis & Todd, 1982; Fehr, 1993; Parks & Floyd, 1996), *honesty* (Fehr, 1993), *respect* (Davis & Todd, 1982; Fehr, 1993; Parks & Floyd, 1996), and *concern with relational outcomes* (Miller et al., 1986) coupled with the *giving and receiving of help* (Davis & Todd, 1982; Maxwell, 1985; Parks & Floyd, 1996) are recurring descriptors of close relationships. Lies or truths that are perceived as unfairly or harmfully taking advantage of a partner's vulnerabilities, then, are likely to be evaluated as negative; lies or truths that are perceived as serving to protect the vulnerabilities of one's partner or the relationship are likely to be evaluated less negatively or positively.

2. *People in close relationships feel sufficiently satisfied and emotionally invested in their relationship that they want it to continue.* Close relationships are described as feeling *natural, comfortable, and enjoyable* (Davis & Todd, 1982; Maxwell, 1985; Parks & Floyd, 1996); filled with *caring, warmth, acceptance, and the inclusion of oneself in the other* (Aron, Aron, & Smollan, 1992; Davis & Todd, 1982; Fehr, 1993; Parks & Floyd, 1996); and subject to *separation distress* (Maxwell, 1985). Both

lies and truths can make relationship life enjoyable and both lies and truths can be told in the pursuit of communicating caring, warmth, and acceptance. With an increasing sense of "we-ness" created by partners to a close relationship, the origins of, and complicity in, lies and truths is likely to be more ambiguous. In addition, the potential impact of lies and truths is also likely to increase as the desire to maintain a future for the relationship increases.

3. *People in close relationships have frequent opportunities to interact and mutually influence one another.* This principle is derived from studies of relationship closeness indicating that people in close relationships *seek out, spend time with, and frequently interact* with their partner (Berscheid & Peplau, 1983; Berscheid, Snyder, & Omoto, 1989; Maxwell, 1985; Miller et al., 1986; Parks & Floyd, 1996). During their time together, they seek advice, perspective, and exert influence on their partner's plans and activities (Berscheid & Peplau, 1983; Berscheid et al., 1989; Parks & Floyd, 1996). Thus, lies and truths are told and heard in a context in which recurring interactions are expected with each partner believing that their interaction can affect the behavior of their partner.

4. *People in close relationships believe they know and understand their partner well because they have acquired a great deal of general and personal information about him or her.* This principle is supported by descriptions of close relationships that involve *sharing attitudes, values, and interests* (Maxwell, 1985; Parks & Floyd, 1996); *disclosing to and confiding in one's partner* (Davis & Todd, 1982; Maxwell, 1985; Parks & Floyd, 1996); *communicating about issues that are important to the relationship* (Maxwell, 1985); *explicitly expressing the value of the relationship to one's partner* (Parks & Floyd, 1996); *believing the relationship is unique* (Davis & Todd, 1982); and *understanding one's partner* (Davis & Todd, 1982; Miller et al.,

1986; Parks & Floyd, 1996). The teller and the target of lies and truths, then, are both people who presume they have a reservoir of knowledge about the other. Sometimes people in close relationships reach a point where they are so confident (or so hopeful) about understanding their partner that they overlook or reinterpret behavior which contradicts what they think they know about their partner.

The preceding underscores some basic principles typically subscribed to by those who profess to have a close relationship. As such, they represent the basis for interpreting how and why duplicity manifests itself; how and why lie detection takes the form that it does; and how and why lies have the effects they do.

Doing Lying and Deception in Close Relationships

Attitudes Toward Honesty

Stewart, Stinnett, and Rosenfeld (2000) asked a hundred college men and women to rate the desirability of 19 characteristics that a dating partner might have. Each characteristic was rated twice, once for someone they would "date more than once" and once for someone with whom they could have a "long-term relationship, perhaps even marry." Some of the characteristics rated were an exciting personality, good health, adaptability, dependability, sense of humor, and kindness–understanding. It was trustworthy–honest, however, that received the highest rating (most desirable) for both short- and long-term relationships and for both men and women.

Boon and McLeod (2001) also found nearly a hundred college men and women endorsing the importance of honesty in close relationships, but only a third of these students sought the kind of complete and unrestrained honesty subscribed to by O'Neill and O'Neill (1972) and Blanton (1996). Endorsement of complete honesty in close relationships was more likely among those who also believed they had little chance of successfully lying to their partner. The other two thirds of these students acknowledged that even in close relationships there are conditions that demand one's partner be misled. This behavior was seen by some as not only appropriate but the right thing to do.

Thus, alone and outside of any particular context, people often believe honesty is an essential ingredient of close relationships and a goal each partner should strive to achieve (LaFollette & Graham, 1986). On the other hand, it is not uncommon for people to recognize that even in close relationships, there are likely to be situations in which honesty will not be practiced. Being honest, for example, may be deemed less important than some other important relationship goal such as building the self-esteem of one's partner, maintaining loyalty to another friend, or massaging truths that might hurt a loved one. In one study, couples who had been together an average of 27 months perceived that their partners were more honest than themselves (Cole, 2001).

Frequency of Lying

Rowatt, Cunningham, and Druen (1998) found both men and women saying they would be willing to lie about their intelligence, personal appearance, personality traits, income, past relationship outcomes, and career skills to a prospective date who was high in facial attractiveness. Even in get-acquainted conversations, participants are not averse to lying when they are asked to appear likable and/or competent (Feldman, Forrest, & Happ, 2002). So it seems that lies are common, even expected, in the interactions that serve as a launching pad for close relationships. Metts (1989) argued that the emphasis on finding out more and more about one's partner, so typical of dating relationships, is likely to foster more falsification than in established close relationships in which partners believe they already have a storehouse of information about their partner. In one survey of college students,

92% admitted to lying to a romantic partner about sexual issues (Knox, Schacht, Holt, & Turner, 1993). One book, written for men, even gives advice on "how to sound sincere," and "how to pretend sex is the furthest thing from your mind" (Casanova, 1999).

Lies don't cease when relationships are designated as "close," however; they just decrease in frequency. DePaulo and Kashy (1998) found both community leaders and students reporting that they told fewer lies (relative to the total number of interactions) to those with whom they had closer relationships. Lies occurred about once in every 10 interactions in a broad range of close relationships that included spouses, best friends, family, children, nonspouse romantic partners, and mothers. However, it is worth noting that lying in close relationships does not seem to be equally low for all types of relationships. The closeness of the relationship is only one factor governing the frequency of lying. More lies, for instance, were reportedly told to mothers and nonspouse romantic partners. One in every three transactions with nonspouse romantic partners were reported to involve lying.

Emotional closeness can be a powerful deterrent to lying in close relationships, and when lies do occur, they are often troubling for the liar. The processes that bring about closeness not only help to reduce the number of lies, they also provide the kind of bonding that serves as a safety net during times when the strength of that closeness is questioned. At the same time, however, close relationships create an environment in which any given lie can take a huge toll on the degree of closeness felt. It is not surprising that Cole (2001) found that increased perceptions of a partner's dishonesty were associated with lower levels of relationship satisfaction and commitment.

Types of Lies

Lies are often classified as a special form of the broader term, deception. DePaulo et al. (2003) defined *deception* as "a delib-

erate attempt to mislead others" (p. 74) and Knapp and Comadena (1979) defined *lying* as "the conscious alteration of information a person believes to be true in order to significantly change another's perceptions from what the deceiver thought they would be without the alteration" (p. 271). Definitions such as these are commonly used by social scientists who study the behavior of liars and the accuracy with which they can be detected. Conceptualizing lying and deception in this fashion can be useful, but it precludes self-deception, jointly constructed lies, and lies that are based on attributions rather than actual liar behavior – all of which are crucial for understanding lies in close relationships. The following illustrates some of the ways lies manifest themselves in close relationships.

LIES AND ATTRIBUTIONS OF LIES

Lies attributed to people in close relationships are not always lies. The dialogue associated with these attributions, however, may profoundly affect relationship closeness. This is a phenomenon research tells us little about (McCornack, Levine, Solowczuk, Torres, & Campbell, 1992). People in close relationships are familiar with their partner's communication style and do not expect their partner to lie to them. Nevertheless, one's motives for not saying something a partner thought should have been said, forgetting something a partner thought should have been reported, or misunderstanding something a partner thought should have been understood are all subject to attributions of deception. Accusing close relationship partners of lying when they don't believe they have can generate relationship-altering dialogue. Equivocal responses, which Bavelas, Black, Chovil, and Mullett (1990) say are used to avoid both lying and telling the truth, might well be labeled as a lie in daily interaction because of their evasive and ambiguous nature. Even changing one's self-presentation to fit a particular person or situation is subject to being perceived as "phony" or deceptive even though Bosson and Swann (2001) suggested that it may be quite genuine:

> *Like chameleons, people change the way they present themselves to different relationship partners; however, each self-presentation is a genuine reflection of the real self displayed in all sincerity. (p. 74)*

INDIVIDUAL LIES AND JOINTLY CONSTRUCTED LIES

We find it strangely amusing when Homer Simpson says, "It takes two people to lie, one to lie and one to listen," but academic researchers do tend to conceptualize and study lies as individual acts. Close relationships, however, are especially fertile ground for studying what Werth and Flaherty (1986) called collusion and Barnes (1994) called connivance. Connivance occurs when individuals in close relationships know they are being deceived by their partner, but deceptively act as if they didn't know. Other jointly managed lies occur when partners to a close relationship explicitly or implicitly agree to collaborate in a relationship lie. This happens when parties to an extramarital affair collaborate in deceiving others, when one partner authorizes a lie by telling his or her partner never to tell him or her if a particular thing happens, or when close friends testify to the strength of their bond by collaborating in a lie to another person. Jointly constructed lies may also be done interactively. A partner can make it clear that the punishment for telling the truth about an affair, for example, would be as severe as the punishment for lying about it – which, if lying occurs, means both partners played a role in constructing the lie.

LIES INVOLVING ACTIVE AND PASSIVE PARTICIPATION

Research typically focuses on lies of commission – false accounts, information, and stories that are invented by the liar. However, distinctions between lies of commission that invent a new reality for the target versus lies that involve secrets or simply allow the target to continue believing something false may be of special interest in close relationships in which partners believe they know so much about each other. Levenger and Senn (1967) found that concealing negative feelings, particularly about their mates, was far more characteristic of satisfied spouses than dissatisfied ones. Metts (1989) found spouses more likely to conceal information than to make deliberately false statements.

> *The pattern of deceptive communication reported here indicates that married respondents seem to take advantage of opportunities for concealment, opportunities frequently created by a lack of direct questioning from their partners. This raises the interesting possibility that once a relationship is institutionalized, partners are more likely to collude (consciously or unconsciously) in the accomplishment of deception, particularly when the information would drastically increase uncertainty or illuminate the state of the relationship. (p. 177)*

In addition to concealment, Nyberg (1993) pointed out a number of ways that partners to a close relationship can lie by "letting it happen" – that is, providing a wink or a short, ambiguous response that leads the target to a false belief or causes him or her to continue believing something false.

LIES TO SELF AND LIES TO OTHERS

Researchers typically study the process of lying to another person, but self-deception clearly plays an important role in close relationships (Baumeister, 1993; Baumeister & Wortman, 1992). Sometimes we don't want to see things as they are and convince ourselves through selective attention, biased reasoning, systematic ignoring, willful ignorance, or emotional detachment that certain things are not true. In a book about romantic relationships that focuses on the lies men sometimes tell women, Forward (1999) said the man's success in such situations is often contingent on lies women tell themselves – for example, "He would never lie to me," "Maybe he's lied to other women, but he won't lie to me," "Yes, he lies, but he loves me and that's all that matters," "He lies, but he's a victim of circumstances," "Yes, he lies, but

I can fix him," and "Yes, he lies, but it's my fault." An illustration of one woman's self-deception can be seen in this excerpt from an interview by Werth and Flaherty (1986):

> *Little by little things were happening that didn't make sense, but I can remember making excuses for them myself... I didn't want to believe there was anything to find out... so I was being deceived from two angles... I was deceiving myself... I didn't sit there when it was happening saying, "I am just fooling myself." You know, I, I, as I said, I made up a lot of excuses, and really believed them... I didn't confide in anyone, too, because I was afraid of what they would tell me. I wanted to believe everything was going to be fine and I wasn't being deceived. If I told someone else they might tell me I was being deceived and I didn't want to hear that... But as much as I wanted to be a detective and find him out, I didn't want to either. Because the truth – I was afraid more of the truth than living in the lie kind of. (p. 296)*

DePaulo and Bell (1996) found that people tended to be less honest when giving evaluative feedback to people they knew really cared about the subject of the evaluation. In the same way, there may be times when we are less honest with ourselves when we really care about and are heavily invested in the relationship that might be at risk. Dealing with the possibilities of rejection by one's partner and loss of the relationship may be a lot harder for some people than lying to themselves.

REPEATED AND ISOLATED LIES

Research typically focuses on a single interaction and a single lie. But partners to a close relationship interact with one another regularly and at least some lies will follow a developmental pattern. This may involve the necessity of repeating a lie or telling supplementary lies to lend support to the original lie. Topics of conversation and reports of events have a way of recycling in close relationships, so lies may have a long shelf life. Sometimes partners will even encourage the repeating of a lie to people outside the relationship – for example, "Bob was in Vietnam and saw some terrible things. Tell them, honey." Some things lied about are sufficiently complex, like an extramarital affair, that a variety of interconnected lies are needed to sustain both the activity and the lies associated with it.

SELF-SERVING AND OTHER-BENEFITING LIES

Lies are often classified according to the intended beneficiary, and this perception is, in turn, linked to the degree of disapproval. Lies told for the sole purpose of benefiting oneself are generally viewed more negatively than lies told with the goal of protecting another person from harm or trying to make him or her feel better. However, in close relationships, it is easy to see how one partner can serve him or herself by telling a lie that also benefits his or her partner. The demarcation between self and other in close relationships is, by definition, fuzzy at times – a condition that can make this method of distinguishing types of lies problematic.

HIGH-STAKES AND LOW-STAKES LIES

Lies can also be classified according to how much is gained or lost by their success or failure. Sometimes successful lies provide little gain for the liar and little punishment if they are uncovered. These are called low-stakes lies. With high-stakes lies, there is a nice reward when it goes undetected, but a severe punishment if it is discovered. Obviously, different combinations and strengths of rewards and punishments provide other types of lies – for example, significant rewards for a successful lie but not much punishment if it is unsuccessful. We would expect liars who perceive various degrees of perceived gain and punishment to manifest different behaviors. Even though partners to a close relationship may discuss the stakes involved in various types of lying as a part of general relationship talks, this method of classifying lies is based on liar perceptions at the time of the lie.

Motivation for Lying

People in close relationships lie for a variety of reasons, many of which are bound up with the nature of close relationships them-selves. One common reason for lying is to support and sustain our partners – to avoid hurting them, to tell them what they want to hear, to build and maintain their self-esteem, to help them accomplish their goals, and to show concern for their physical and mental states. Indeed, DePaulo and Kashy (1998) found what they called "altruistic" lies to be the most common type of lie told to friends and best friends. Lies told to close relationship partners are usually viewed by the lie teller as altruistically motivated, guilt inducing, spontaneous, justified by the situ-ation, and/or provoked by the lie receiver (Kaplan & Gordon, 2004). Metts (1989) also found people who reported the great-est degree of relationship commitment and closeness were also the people who reported more lies intended to support their partner. More satisfied couples may also tend to cre-ate a new partner reality through what Mur-ray and Holmes (1996) called "positive illu-sions" – seeing virtues in their partner that aren't there, turning faults into virtues, con-structing excuses for misdeeds, and so on. What may begin as lies of support or as positive illusions may later, with the effects of self-persuasion and/or the self-fulfilling prophecy, be viewed as fact. If there are permissible lies in close relationships, lying for the benefit of one's partner and lying to protect the relationship may be perceived as the most worthy intentions. Motives are not always mutually exclusive, however, so a lie that helps the target of the lie may also help the liar; a lie that hides a transgres-sion against the relationship may also pro-tect and sustain the relationship – until it is uncovered.

A number of characteristics of close rela-tionships may also provide an inviting basis for less altruistic lies – lies that primarily benefit the liar and may even harm the tar-get. For example, one might assume that the chance of being forgiven for any kind of lie is much higher in a close relationship, so why not lie and hope to be forgiven if found out? In addition, the punishment for lying about a particular issue in this rela-tionship may be perceived as about equal to the revelation of certain unwanted truths, so why not tell the lie (Ekman, 2001)? Part-ners to a close relationship may also provide an inviting climate for lies by making clear what they want and don't want to hear and by demonstrating the kind of unquestioned trust that says they can be easily duped. As a result, self-oriented lies used to accom-plish one partner's own goals, protect his or her own emotions, or retaliate against a partner suspected of lying (Cole, 2001) may not be common but may be present in close relationships. Cole also found that rela-tionship partners who had a higher fear of abandonment were also more likely to resort to deception.

Male and Female Lying

Lies in close relationships are told by both men and women. It isn't firmly established, but men may be particularly prone to lie about their past (Ross & Holmberg, 1990), and women may lie more in the pursuit of being supportive and positive (DePaulo & Bell, 1996). For better or worse, women may sacrifice some degree of honesty to com-municate the kind of support and protec-tion needed to sustain a close relationship. This doesn't mean men do not tell support-ive lies nor does it mean that women lie more often than men in close relationships, even though one therapist (Lerner, 1993) believes that American culture teaches women that pretending and "pleasing others" is an essen-tial part of their expected behavior in close relationships – so "imperceptibly woven into the fabric of daily life" that it sometimes "leads to the construction of a false self" (p. 122).

When it comes to assessing the "seri-ous" lies they've told in close relationships, women report being more upset than men. They also report more anxiety, fear, and remorse. In Kirkendol's study (1986) women said their serious lies to close friends were not undertaken without a lot of reflection, thought, and careful planning, but men often reported the need for greater planning with lies to casual friends.

Detection of Lies in Close Relationships

The interest in lie detection ability by those who form close relationships is not driven by the relatively few lies told in such relationships (DePaulo & Kashy, 1998) but by the fact that most of the "serious" lies people report telling are told to their partners in close relationships (Anderson, Ansfield, & DePaulo, 1999). Accurately detecting the lies of strangers on the basis of their verbal and nonverbal behavior is usually reported to be just above chance – a mean average across studies of about 54% (Malone & DePaulo, 2001). Levine, Park, and McCornack (1999) argued that even this rate of lie detection, which is the result of averaging across truthful and deceptive messages, is inflated by the fact that people are far more accurate in identifying truthful messages than lies, thereby making the accurate detection of *lies* significantly lower than chance. How does the closeness of one's relationship affect a person's ability to detect lies accurately on the basis of their partner's behavior? It depends.

Closeness May Effect Greater Accuracy *in Lie Detection*

People expect their lies to be detected more often by people who know them well (Burgoon, Buller, Dillman, & Walther, 1995), and they often are (DePaulo & Kashy, 1998). They expect it because they expect people in close relationships to be so familiar with their typical behavior that any deviations from that will be noticed. When people were repeatedly shown (up to four times) a video of a stranger's truthful communication behavior, this familiarity did serve to increase the viewer's accuracy in picking out the lies from subsequent video messages presented by the same stranger (Bauchner, Brandt, & Miller, 1977; Brandt, Miller, & Hocking, 1980; 1982; Feeley, deTurck & Young, 1995). Spouses in Comadena's (1982) study who had known each other an average of 46 months apparently relied on their familiarity to help them detect lies of their partner at a rate significantly higher than

their friends who had only known them an average of about 19 months. Anderson, DePaulo, and Ansfield (2002) found that the increasing familiarity of emotionally close friends made them report more accuracy in detecting each other's lies over a 6-month period of their friendship. These last two studies provide some data that show that familiarity with the behavior of a close relationship partner can provide a basis for greater accuracy in detecting his or her lies.

When suspicion of deceptive behavior is coupled with behavioral familiarity in close relationships, accuracy in detecting deception can increase (Stiff, Kim, & Ramesh, 1992). McCornack and Levine (1990b) studied couples who had been dating about a year. Some were dispositionally suspicious and some were not. Some were told their partner *may be* lying to them; some were told their partner *would be* lying to them; and some were not told anything. Without suspicion, people believed their partners were telling the truth, and detection accuracy was about where it would be with strangers – slightly above chance. People who were already dispositionally suspicious who were made moderately suspicious lowered their expectations for partner truth telling and increased their detection accuracy rate to 70%. Even though suspicion has the power to increase accuracy in lie detection, it may also be problematic if the suspected liar is not lying and resents the distrust that his or her partner's suspicion illustrates. Suspicion can also create more suspicion to the point where neither person trusts the other. Suspicious behavior also has a tendency to put the suspect on guard – possibly leading him or her to spend more time and energy covering up clues and creating new lies. DePaulo, Epstein, and Wyer (1993) say that women are more likely than men to be actively involved in seeking out the truth when suspicion is raised – talking to others, looking for behavioral and other evidence, and so on.

Closeness May Effect Greater Inaccuracy *in Lie Detection*

Familiarity in close relationships is a two-way street. As noted earlier, familiarity with one's partner can help a lie detector identify deviations from the liar's "normal" behavior, but the liar can also use familiarity to his or her advantage. High self-monitors who are lying in a close relationship are familiar with their own baseline behavior, which they will try to duplicate during periods of deception and prepare themselves with a ready explanations when they are unable to do so (Miller, deTurck, & Kalbfleisch, 1983). Effective liars in close relationships are also familiar with the routines and behavior of the lie detector and will use that knowledge to create maneuvers that will cover their own behavior. In short, liars know a lot of what the lie detectors know and will use that familiarity for their own ends during the lie–lie detection process.

Lie detection accuracy may also suffer in actual, ongoing close relationships because the detector is not a detached observer of the liar, but actively interacts with the liar while trying to assess his or her truthfulness. Research to date is largely based on detached observers judging monologues of others, but Burgoon, Buller, and Floyd (2001) indicated that accuracy is likely to decrease when the detector becomes an active participant. It is no doubt more difficult to make accurate attributions of deception when the person making the attribution is part of the very dialogue within which the lie takes shape.

Perhaps the single biggest contributor to decreased accuracy in lie detection in close relationships is when a detector puts a higher value on the closeness of the relationship than the need to uncover a lie that might decrease or eliminate that closeness. Anderson et al. (1999) put it this way:

> Therefore, the targets of self-serving lies may be motivated to let potential lies lie. This motivation may be especially great when the relationship is especially important. If, in fact, people in close relationships are particularly motivated to believe altruistic lies and to remain oblivious to self-centered ones, then their many experiences with each other's styles of communicating may come to naught. They could be equaled, or even outdone, by total strangers in the accuracy with which they detect their partner's lies. (p. 382)

People in close relationships are not averse to practicing "motivated inaccuracy" when perceiving their partner's behavior (Simpson, Ickes, & Blackstone, 1995; Sternglanz & DePaulo, 2004). Accurate perceptions in these studies were lowest when one partner expressed, but not too clearly, thoughts or feelings that might pose a threat to the relationship and the perceiver was highly committed to the relationship. In fact, relationship partners who tend to seek relationship-threatening information are also less trusting, more suspicious, and more likely to terminate their relationships (Ickes, Dugosh, Simpson, & Wilson, 2003). There is also a stronger "truth bias" among partners to close relationships. The presence of a strong truth bias (the extent to which they believe their partner is a truth teller) seems to be a standard feature of close relationships, which also contributes to inaccuracy in lie detection. Millar and Millar (1995) and Buller, Strzyzewski, and Comstock (1991) found more truth bias among friends than strangers. The process seems to work like this. Closeness gives people a greater amount of confidence that they know their partner's behavior which, in turn, leads to a bias toward believing their partner's behavior is truthful. This then leads to a lower rate of deception detection accuracy (Levine & McCornack, 1992; McCornack & Parks, 1986; Stiff et al., 1992).

Whether it is the truth bias or something else, there are times when people in close relationships sense deception and probably process certain related behaviors but have a hard time articulating what they are observing. This is illustrated in this interview by Werth and Flaherty (1986):

> It was like an atmosphere more than blatant evidence... It is so hard to grab on to something and say, "this is deceit" because it is just so much like a feeling you get when there is something amiss, something is wrong. It is in the atmosphere. It's just, and it might be... an uneasiness from the other person that you just, you know something is wrong, that it can't be the truth, and it might just be sort of a sensation

you get from nervousness or fidgetiness or uneasiness or..." (p. 297)

Other Ways Lies Are Detected

Detecting lies by observing the behavior of one's partner has been the predominant research paradigm to date (DePaulo et al., 2003), but Park, Levine, McCornack, Morrison, and Ferrara (2002) found several detection methods that were more common among undergraduate students, 33% of whom responded as a romantic partner, 40% as a friend, and 10% as a family member. So we can assume that experiences in close relationships were fairly well represented. By far, the two most common methods for uncovering lies among this sample were getting information from a third party and finding physical evidence that contradicted the liar's story. Sometimes lies in close relationships take a long time to discover, but sometimes the liar will confess as soon as the target shows any suspicion (Boon & McLeod, 2001), thus, obviating the need to look for any behavioral clues. Detection may also combine various methods of detection and generate new lies.

Consequences of Lies in Close Relationships

What one views as the consequences of lying and deception in close relationships depends on what type of lie (altruistic vs. self-interest) is in question; what is being lied about (an affair vs. saying you liked the outfit when you didn't); when the judgment is made (upon discovery vs. years later); and probably a number of other factors. The assessed consequences of close relationship lies will also vary depending on who is making the assessment. Liars often view their own behavior as far less harmful, offensive, and consequential than the target of the lie. Liars often describe extenuating circumstances that they view as justification for their lie(s), but targets often do not share those views (Gordon & Miller, 2000; McCornack & Levine, 1990a).

Consequences of Undiscovered Lies

Even though most of the consequences of deception in close relationships are examined in the context of discovered or revealed lies, there are, of course, lies that go undetected. What effect, if any, do these lies have on the relationship?

Metts (1989) asked people to describe a time when they didn't tell their relationship partner the whole truth. Over a third of them mentioned deceptions involving emotional information – for example, feelings of love and commitment. Thaler's (1991) account of his own relationship gives further insight into this process:

> *Amy has asked me on more than one occasion, "Do you love me?"... If I were always truthful, and sometimes I am not, I would confide to Amy the fluctuating tide of my emotions, a response that might stab into the heart of our relationship... So when Amy asks whether I love her, I always do, even if, at times, I don't. The lie is a support system that is part of the ritual of intimacy. It may not be truthful, but it is confirming. (pp. 16–17)*

By way of explanation, LaFollette and Graham (1986) pointed out that people's feelings about their partner are not always crystal clear and they worry about the communicative effects of trying to explain these complex and ambiguous states. They fear such a dialogue may cause more harm than good. So unambiguous declarations of love are proffered, the relationship is affirmed, and life is good. Liars feel especially good about lies that make their partner feel better, and these positive emotions permeate a variety of transactions in pleasant and constructive ways. As noted earlier, DePaulo and Kashy (1998) found these "other-oriented" or "altruistic" lies to be the norm in close relationships.

It is possible, however, for these seemingly insignificant deceptions designed to support the relationship to get out of hand. For example, suppose a woman lies to herself about her feelings for her husband – outwardly maintaining a love that isn't felt. At first it is merely done to cover up feelings that are confusing to her. She perceives nothing "wrong" or "bad" about her husband, so she is sure her feelings will eventually match her words. In time, however, she knows her declarations of love are a lie. Her husband does not question behavioral signs to the contrary because he wants (and needs) to believe she is lovingly devoted to him. Having perpetuated this lie for years, the wife suddenly decides to behave in line with her true feelings and tells her husband she is leaving him. The wife does not want to embarrass herself by admitting what she has done, and the husband is still unwilling to believe there were signs that showed a contrast to the feelings expressed by his wife. Thus, the infectious and coconstructed lies that led to the dissolution of this relationship remain in an undiscussed and undiscovered state.

Sometimes lies are not uncovered, but suspicion has been aroused to such an extent that trust in one's partner is negatively affected. To the extent that the lie or lies told have powerful effects on the liar (e.g., guilt, anger, fear, embarrassment), these effects may manifest themselves in almost any dialogue with the liar's partner. The target of the lie may wonder why, for no apparent reason, his or her partner seems so irritable over the slightest things. Sagarin, Rhoads, and Cialdini (1998) point out that liars will sometimes denigrate and distrust the target, trying to make themselves feel better by believing that their partner is just like they are – that they lie too, that they invited the lie by being such an easy dupe, that they created a situation where they were going to get just as much punishment for telling the truth as for lying, and so on.

Negative Consequences of Discovered Lies

"Serious" or "high-stakes" lies are not reported to be the most common type of lie in close relationships, but they are potentially the most damaging (Anderson et al., 1999; DePaulo & Kashy, 1998). Serious lies are often told to cover major transgressions of the relationship such as infidelity. In this case, then, both the lie and the thing lied about betray the bonds of closeness that form the heart of the relationship. Targets of these lies who have strong beliefs about the importance of honesty may have a strongly negative reaction to both the lie and the infidelity (Boon & McLeod, 2001), but the work of McCornack and Levine (1990a) indicates that it is the information covered by the lie that is the most decisive in whether the relationship is terminated or not.

Even though serious lies are not believed to be common in close relationships, it should be noted that it is not always easy to know what lies will emerge as serious and what lies will remain less serious. On the surface one would think that lies about one's feelings for one's partner would be in the serious category and occur infrequently. Yet when Metts (1989) asked people to describe a time when they didn't tell their relationship partner the whole truth, over a third of them mentioned deceptions involving emotional information – for example, feelings of love and commitment. LaFollette and Graham (1986) also say that there are times when one's feelings about one's partner are not always crystal clear and people worry that attempts to try to explain these complex and ambiguous states will cause more harm than good. Lies about relationship feelings are certainly capable of preserving closeness, but they are also especially well suited for dismantling the ties that bind.

Serious lies are capable of a wide variety of negative consequences for (a) the target of the lie (hurt feelings, lowered self-esteem, confusion, suspicion, desire for revenge [O'Hair & Cody, 1994], etc.); (b) the liar (loss of credibility, trust, respect); and (c) the relationship (lowered satisfaction or commitment [Cole, 2001], tension, etc.). Planalp and Honeycutt (1985) asked people to recall information that led them to question something basic to their relationship. Deception was one of the events recalled. Deception for these people in this context not only increased uncertainty about their relationship, it undermined their beliefs about all aspects of the relationship, including beliefs about themselves.

Adrienne Rich (1979) aptly captured the all-encompassing devastation some lies can have on close relationships.

> *Why do we feel slightly crazy when we realize we have been lied to in a relationship?*
>
> *We take so much of the universe on trust. You tell me: "In 1950 I lived on the north side of Beacon Street in Somerville." You tell me "She and I were lovers, but for months now we have only been good friends." You tell me: "It is seventy degrees outside and the sun is shining." Because I love you, because there is not even a question of lying between us, I take these accounts of the universe on trust: your address twenty-five years ago, your relationship with someone I know only by sight, this morning's weather. I fling unconscious tendrils of belief, like slender green threads, across statements such as these, statements made so unequivocally, which have no tone or shadow of tentativeness. I build them into the mosaic of my world. I allow my universe to change in minute, significant ways, on the basis of things you have said to me, of my trust in you.*
>
> *I also have faith that you are telling me things it is important I should know; that you do not conceal facts from me in an effort to spare me, or yourself, pain.*
>
> *Or, at the very least, that you will say, "There are things I am not telling you."*
>
> *When we discover that someone we trusted can be trusted no longer, it forces us to reexamine the universe, to question the whole instinct and concept of trust. For awhile, we are thrust back onto some bleak, jutting ledge, in a dark pierced by sheets of fire, swept by sheets of rain, in a world before kinship, or naming, or tenderness exist; we are brought close to formlessness.* (pp. 191–192)

Several studies portray the consequences of deception to be more substantial for women than men. Metts (1994) reported the women in her study were more sensitive than men to violations of the rules associated with close relationships. Women also seem to view deception as more unacceptable than men, see it as a more significant relational event, and react more strongly to its discovery. They report being more distressed and anxious than men on the discovery that their partner in a close relationship has lied to them (Levine, McCornack, & Avery, 1992) and more tearful and apologetic than men for the serious lies they tell. They may also maintain their bitterness about the transgression for a longer period of time than men (DePaulo et al., 1993).

Positive Consequences of Discovered Lies

Despite the emphasis on tragic consequences of serious lies in close relationships, some couples manage to make lemonade out of the life's lemons (Anderson et al., 1999). Surprisingly, research tells us little about how couples manage this feat. Data on relationship termination and other negative effects of serious lies and serious relationship transgressions are plentiful and tend to fit nicely within societal and perhaps even researchers' expectations. Data from couples who have worked through a serious lie about a serious violation of close relationship expectations are reported infrequently and may be far more difficult to obtain. This makes any conclusions about positive consequences of serious (or even less serious) lies in close relationships speculative at best.

Nevertheless, we know that some couples who have experienced serious lies that threaten their relationship manage to work effectively through their problems and regain a close relationship. Jang, Smith, and Levine (2002), in a study of attachment styles and deception in close relationships, found that both secure and anxious–ambivalent styles said they would continue a relationship even after finding out about a situation in which their partner deliberately misled them about "a matter of some consequence to the relationship." Termination of the relationship was the primary option for only the avoidant attachment style. Things that may work to the advantage of couples who cope effectively with a potentially harmful relationship lie (or lies) include: (a) a history of the liar doing many things with positive intentions and in the best interests of the relationship; (b) a plea from the liar for forgiveness and repeatedly demonstrating his or her commitment to rebuilding relational closeness; (c) a situation in which the discovery of the lie opened up issues for the couple that needed to be discussed for the survival and welfare of the relationship; (d) a situation in which the lie, by bringing the relationship to the edge of disaster, reminded both partners how much they wanted to save the relationship; and (e) a situation in which the process of mutually solving the problem or problems created by the lie serves to reestablish and strengthen relationship bonds.

Is Deception a "Dark Side" of Close Relationships?

In a word, no. Deception is a way of communicating and derives its goodness or badness from various contextual features – the intent behind it, the words and nonverbal behavior used in it's performance, the consequences that resulted, and so on. To say that deception is inherently evil or dark is as absurd as saying that disagreement is evil because it can lead to vicious fights, so we should try to eliminate any disagreements. There are good lies and bad lies; there are bad lies that can have good consequences; and there are bad truths. Should we call "truth" the dark side of relationships because someone tells the truth without regard for another person's feelings, tells the truth to mislead somebody, or tells the truth to someone who doesn't want to hear it?

Finkenauer and Hazam (2000) pointed out that the disclosure of truths and the keeping of secrets can contribute to marital satisfaction and closeness or detract from it. It all depends on how, why, when, and where it is done. Nyberg (1993) eloquently made the case when he said:

> Truth telling is a means for accomplishing purposes. So is deception. My approach to understanding of deception is not the usual one (top down) of focusing on the virtue of truth as a given, then finding ways to make benevolent compromises. It is rather to focus on human communication (bottom up), then to see what roles both play in

> furthering that process toward the achievement of worthwhile goals. (pp. 53–54)

Conclusion

Given the variety of ways "closeness" has been operationalized, coupled with the common reliance on self-reports to determine lying behavior, the findings presented in this chapter probably represent nothing more than a "good start" in trying to understand deception in close relationships. When experimental methods have been used, they usually involve single instances of serious or high-stakes lies viewed by a detached observer with the goal of identifying behavioral signs of deceit. This means we have a lot to learn about different types of jointly constructed lies, lies that are accomplished with more passive methods, how liars and lie detectors deal with the development of a series or "program" of lies, and the role of self-deception in both lying and lie detection.

A number of studies indicate conditions associated with relationship closeness that support both increased accuracy in lie detection and decreased accuracy. Features in close relationships such as frequency of interaction, proximity, and partner familiarity may help in detecting lies. Suspicion may also increase accuracy, but suspicious behavior can also decrease trust and closeness. A strong truth bias and the possibility that a partner who lies may not be considered as bad as the demise of the relationship with the liar will sometimes act against accurate lie detection. Exactly what conditions precipitate one approach or the other are not clear at this time, as are other questions about lie detection in close relationships. When there are false attributions about lies, how are they negotiated? How are observations of behavior combined with other methods to detect lies in close relationships? How do liars use their knowledge of the target's behavior and routines to fool them?

The potentially disastrous effects of serious lies on close relationships have received so much attention that we know relatively little about how couples achieve positive outcomes from lies that initially inflict relationship damage. In fact, we know relatively little about any kind of lie that has positive effects and any kind of truth that has negative effects in close relationships. Most surveys find that truth telling is considered a necessary feature in establishing and maintaining a close relationship, but most people in those same surveys are willing to admit that lying may play a worthwhile role in close relationships. It is possible, of course, that lies that provide the bonding elements for close relationships in everyday dialogue may not even be thought of as lies by the relationship partners.

References

Anderson, D. E., Ansfield, M. E., & DePaulo, B. M. (1999). Love's best habit: Deception in the context of relationships. In P. Philippot & R. S. Feldman (Eds.), *The social context of nonverbal behavior* (pp. 372–409). New York: Cambridge University Press.

Anderson, D. E., DePaulo, B. M., & Ansfield, M. E. (2002). The development of deception detection skill: A longitudinal study of same-sex friends. *Personality and Social Psychology Bulletin, 28,* 536–545.

Aron, A., Aron, E. A., & Smollan, D. (1992). Inclusion of the other in the self scale and the structure of interpersonal closeness. *Journal of Personality and Social Psychology, 63,* 596–612.

Barnes, J. A. (1994). *A pack of lies: Towards a sociology of lying.* New York: Cambridge University Press.

Bauchner, J. E., Brandt, D. R., & Miller, G. R. (1977). The truth/deception attribution: Effects of varying levels of information availability. In B. D. Ruben (Ed.), *Communication yearbook 1* (pp. 229–243). New Brunswick, NJ: Transaction Books.

Baumeister, R. F. (1993). Lying to yourself: The enigma of self-deception. In M. Lewis & C. Saarni (Eds.), *Lying and deception in everyday life* (pp. 166–183). New York: Guilford Press.

Baumeister, R. F., & Wortman, S. R. (1992). *Breaking hearts: The two sides of unrequited love.* New York: Guilford Press.

Bavelas, J. B., Black, A., Chovil, N., & Mullett, J. (1990). *Equivocal communication.* Newbury Park, CA: Sage.

Berscheid, E., & Peplau, L. A. (1983). The emerging science of relationships. In H. H. Kelley, E. Berscheid, A. Christensen, J. H. Harvey, T. L. Huston, G. Levinger, et al. (Eds.), *Close relationships* (pp. 1–19). New York: Freeman.

Berscheid, E., Snyder, M., & Omoto, A. M. (1989). The relationship closeness inventory: Assessing the closeness of interpersonal relationships. *Journal of Personality and Social Psychology, 57,* 792–807.

Blanton, B. (1996). *Radical honesty: How to transform your life by telling the truth.* New York: Delta.

Boon, S. D., & McLeod, B. A. (2001). Deception in romantic relationships: Subjective estimates of success at deceiving and attitudes toward deception. *Journal of Social and Personal Relationships, 18,* 463–476.

Bosson, J. K., & Swann, W. B., Jr. (2001). The paradox of the sincere chamelon: Strategic self-verification in close relationships. In J. H. Harvey & A. Wenzel (Eds.), *Close romantic relationships: Maintenance and enhancement* (pp. 67–86). Mahwah, NJ: Erlbaum.

Brandt, D. R., Miller, G. R., & Hocking, J. E. (1980). The truth/deception attribution: Effects of familiarity on the ability of observers to detect deception. *Human Communication Research, 6,* 99–110.

Brandt, D. R., Miller, G. R., & Hocking, J. E. (1982). Familiarity and lie detection: A replication and extension. *Western Journal of Speech Communication, 46,* 276–290.

Buller, D. B., Strzyzewski, K. D., & Comstock, J. (1991). Interpersonal deception: I. Deceivers' reactions to receivers' suspicions and probing. *Communication Monographs, 58,* 1–24.

Burgoon, J. K., Buller, D. B., Dillman, L., & Walther, J. B. (1995). Interpersonal deception: IV. Effects of suspicion on perceived communication and nonverbal behavior dynamics. *Human Communication Research, 22,* 163–196.

Burgoon, J. K., Buller, D. B., & Floyd, K. (2001). Does participation affect deception success? A test of the interactivity principle. *Human Communication Research, 28,* 503–534.

Casanova, N. (1999). *The Machiavellian's guide to womanizing.* Edison, NJ: Castle Books.

Comadena, M. E. (1982). Accuracy in detecting deception: Intimate and friendship relationships. In M. Burgoon (Ed.), *Communication yearbook 6* (pp. 446–472). Beverly Hills, CA: Sage.

Cole, T. (2001). Lying to the one you love: The use of deception in romantic relationships. *Journal of Social and Personal Relationships, 18*, 107–129.

Davis, K. E., & Todd, M. J. (1982). Friendship and love relationships. In K. E. Davis & T. O. Mitchell (Eds.), *Advances in descriptive psychology* (Vol. 2; pp. 79–122). Greenwich, CT: JAI Press, 1982.

DePaulo, B. M., & Bell, K. L. (1996). Truth and investment: Lies are told to those who care. *Journal of Personality and Social Psychology, 71*, 703–716.

DePaulo, B. M., Epstein, J., & Wyer, M. M. (1993). Sex differences in lying: How women and men deal with the dilemma of deceit. In M. Lewis & C. Saarni (Eds.), *Lying and deception in everyday life* (pp. 126–147). New York: Guilford Press.

DePaulo, B. M., & Kashy, D. A. (1998). Everyday lies in close and casual relationships. *Journal of Personality and Social Psychology, 74*, 63–79.

Depaulo, B. M., Lindsay, J. J., Malone, B. E., Muhlenbruck, L., Charlton, K., & Cooper, H. (2003). Cues to deception. *Journal of Personality and Social Psychology, 129*, 74–118.

Ekman, P. (2001). *Telling lies*. New York: Norton.

Feeley, T. H., deTurck, M. A., & Young, M. J. (1995). Baseline familiarity in lie detection. *Communication Research Reports, 12*, 160–169.

Fehr, B. (1993). How do I love thee? Let me consult my prototype. In S. Duck (Ed.), *Individuals in relationships* (pp. 87–120). Newbury Park, CA: Sage.

Feldman, R. S., Forrest, J. A., & Happ, B. R. (2002). Self-presentation and verbal deception: Do self-presenters lie more? *Basic and Applied Social Psychology, 24*, 163–170.

Finkenauer, C., & Hazam, H. (2000). Disclosure and secrecy in marriage: Do both contribute to marital satisfaction? *Journal of Social and Personal Relationships, 17*, 245–263.

Forward, S. (1999). *When your lover is a liar: Healing the wounds of deception and betrayal*. New York: HarperCollins.

Gordon, A. K., & Miller, A. G. (2000). Perspective differences in the construal of lies: Is deception in the eye of the beholder? *Personality and Social Psychology Bulletin, 26*, 46–55.

Ickes, W., Dugosh, J. W., Simpson, J. A., & Wilson, C. L. (2003). Suspicious minds: The motive to acquire relationship-threatening information. *Personal Relationships, 10*, 131–148.

Jang, S. A., Smith, S. W., & Levine, T. R. (2002). To stay or to leave? The role of attachment styles in communication patterns and potential termination of romantic relationships following discovery of deception. *Communication Monographs, 69*, 236–252.

Kaplan, M. E., & Gordon, A. K. (2004). The enigma of altruistic lying: Perspective differences in what motivates and justifies lie telling within romantic relationships. *Personal Relationships, 11*, 489–507.

Kirkendol, S. E. (1986). *Serious lies: First person accounts*. Unpublished master's thesis, University of Virginia.

Knapp, M. L., & Comadena, M. E. (1979). Telling it like it isn't: A review of theory and research on deceptive communications. *Human Communication Research, 5*, 270–285.

Knox, D., Schacht, C., Holt, J., & Turner, J. (1993). Sexual lies among university students. *College Student Journal, 27*, 269–272.

LaFollette, H., & Graham, G. (1986). Honesty and intimacy. *Journal of Social and Personal Relationships, 3*, 3–18.

Lerner, H. G. (1993). *The dance of deception: Pretending and truth-telling in women's lives*. New York: HarperCollins.

Levine, T. R., & McCornack, S. A. (1992). Linking love and lies: A formal test of the McCornack and Parks model of deception detection. *Journal of Social and Personal Relationships, 9*, 143–154.

Levine, T. R., McCornack, S. A., & Avery, P. B. (1992). Sex differences in emotional reactions to discovered deception. *Communication Quarterly, 40*, 289–296.

Levine, T. R., Park, H. S., & McCornack, S. A. (1999). Accuracy in detecting truths and lies: Documenting the "veracity effect." *Communication Monographs, 66*, 125–144.

Levinger, G., & Senn, D. J. (1967). Disclosure of feelings in marriage. *Merrill-Palmer Quarterly, 13*, 237–249.

Malone, B. E., & DePaulo, B. M. (2001). Measuring sensitivity to deception. In J. A. Hall & F. J. Bernieri (Eds.), *Interpersonal sensitivity: Theory and measurement* (pp. 103–124). Mahwah, NJ: Erlbaum.

Maxwell, G. M. (1985). Behavior of lovers: Measuring the closeness of relationships. *Journal of Social and Personal Relationships, 2*, 215–238.

McCornack, S. A., & Levine, T. R. (1990a). When lies are uncovered: Emotional and relational outcomes of discovered deception. *Communication Monographs, 57*, 119–138.

McCornack, S. A., & Levine, T. R. (1990b). When lovers become leery: The relationship between suspicion and accuracy in detecting deception. *Communication Monographs, 57*, 219–230.

McCornack, S. A., & Parks, M. R. (1986). Deception detection and relationship development: The other side of trust. In M. L. McLaughlin (Ed.), *Communication yearbook 9* (pp. 377–389). Beverly Hills, CA.: Sage.

McCornack, S. A., Levine, T. R., Solowczuk, K. A., Torres, H. I., & Campbell, D. M. (1992). When the alteration of information is viewed as deception: An empirical test of information manipulation theory. *Communication Monographs, 59*, 17–29.

Metts, S. (1989). An exploratory investigation of deception in close relationships. *Journal of Social and Personal Relationships, 6*, 159–179.

Metts, S. (1994). Relational transgressions. In W. R. Cupach & B. H. Spitzberg (Eds.), *The dark side of interpersonal communication* (pp. 217–239). Hillsdale, NJ: Erlbaum.

Millar, M., & Millar, K. (1995). Detection of deception in familiar and unfamiliar persons: The effects of information restriction. *Journal of Nonverbal Behavior, 19*, 69–84.

Miller, G. R., deTurck, M. A., & Kalbfleisch, P. J. (1983). Self-monitoring, rehearsal, and deceptive communication. *Human Communication Research, 10*, 97–117.

Miller, G. R., Mongeau, P. A., & Sleight, C. (1986). Fudging with friends and lying to lovers: Deceptive communication in personal relationships. *Journal of Social and Personal Relationships, 3*, 495–512.

Murray, S. L., & Holmes, J. G. (1996). The construction of relationship realities. In G. J. O. Fletcher & J. Fitness (Eds.), *Knowledge structures in close relationships* (pp. 91–120). Hillsdale, NJ: Erlbaum.

Nyberg, D. (1993). *The varnished truth: Truth telling and deceiving in ordinary life*. Chicago: University of Chicago Press.

O'Hair, H. D., & Cody, M. J. (1994). Deception. In W. R. Cupach & B. H. Spitzberg (Eds.), *The dark side of interpersonal communication* (pp. 181–213). Hillsdale, NJ: Erlbaum.

O'Neill, N., & O'Neill, G. (1972). *Open marriage*. New York: M. Evans.

Park, H. S., Levine, T. R., McCornack, S. A., Morrison, K., & Ferrara, M. (2002). How people really detect lies. *Communication Monographs, 69*, 144–157.

Parks, M. R., & Floyd, K. (1996). Meanings for closeness and intimacy in friendship. *Journal of Social and Personal Relationships, 13*, 85–107.

Planalp, S., & Honeycutt, J. M. (1985). Events that increase uncertainty in personal relationships. *Human Communication Research, 11*, 593–604.

Rich, A. (1979). *On lies, secrets, and silence: Selected prose*. New York: Norton.

Ross, M., & Holmberg, D. (1990). Recounting the past: Gender differences in the recall of events in the history of a close relationship. In J. M. Olson & M. P. Zanna (Eds.), *Self-inference processes: The Ontario Symposium* (Vol. 6, pp. 135–152). Hillsdale, NJ: Erlbaum.

Rowatt, W. C., Cunningham, M. R., & Druen, P. B. (1998). Deception to get a date. *Personality and Social Psychology Bulletin, 24*, 1228–1242.

Sagarin, B. J., Rhoads, K. V. L., & Cialdini, R. B. (1998). Deceiver's distrust: Denigration as a consequence of undiscovered deception. *Personality and Social Psychology Bulletin, 24*, 1167–1176.

Simpson, J. A., Ickes, W., & Blackstone, T. (1995). When the head protects the heart: Empathic accuracy in dating relationships. *Journal of Personality and Social Psychology, 69*, 629–641.

Sternglanz, R. W., & DePaulo, B. M. (2004). Reading nonverbal cues to emotions: The advantages and liabilities of relationship closeness. *Journal of Nonverbal Behavior, 28*, 245–266.

Stewart, S., Stinnett, H., & Rosenfeld, L. B. (2000). Sex differences in desired characteristics of short-term and long-term relationship partners. *Journal of Social and Personal Relationships, 17*, 843–853.

Stiff, J. B., Kim, H. J., & Ramesh, C. N. (1992). Truth biases and aroused suspicion in relational deception. *Communication Research, 19*, 326–345.

Thaler, P. (1991, June 9). The lies that bind. *New York Times Magazine*, pp. 15–18.

Werth, L. F., & Flaherty, J. (1986). A phenomenological approach to human deception. In R. W. Mitchell & N. S. Thompson (Eds.), *Deception: Perspectives on human and nonhuman deceit* (pp. 293–311). Albany: State University of New York Press.

CHAPTER 29

Temptation and Threat: Extradyadic Relations and Jealousy

Abraham P. Buunk
Pieternel Dijkstra

Infidelity has concerned our ancestors ever since the origin of the human species. Numerous historical, literary, anthropological, and other sources suggest that among humans the temptation to become involved in a sexual relationship outside one's marriage is, and always has been, a widespread phenomenon. Infidelity can take many forms, including one-night stands, passionate love affairs, sexual fantasies about someone else, mate exchange, extradyadic romantic attachments, flirting, and sex with prostitutes. In the recent literature on infidelity, two types – or aspects – of infidelity are often distinguished, *sexual* infidelity referring to extradyadic sexual relationships without emotional involvement and *emotional* infidelity referring to the development of extradyadic romantic feelings without becoming sexually involved with that other person (e.g., Buss, Larsen, Westen, & Semmelroth, 1992; Glass & Wright, 1992). Of course, in many cases of infidelity, both types of infidelity co-occur. In recent years, technological changes keep adding new dimensions to the dynamics of infidelity. Although since its beginning the telephone

has probably been used to keep in contact with extradyadic sexual partners, the rapid growth of cellular phones has made it easier to do so without the spouse noticing it. In addition, nowadays, infidelity may take the form of so-called virtual or cyberaffairs, in which individuals become romantically or sexually involved with someone else through the Internet or electronic communication.

What behaviors are exactly considered as unfaithful varies from individual to individual because of differences in relationship norms (cf. Drigotas, Safstrom, & Gentilia, 1999). When, for instance, someone feels that flirting with others does not contradict the norms that one has agreed to in the relationship, such behavior will not necessarily evoke jealousy. Nevertheless, in general, sexual relationships outside a committed relationship are considered a serious betrayal of one's partner, evoking – usually intense – feelings of jealousy. Despite the potentially disastrous consequences for committed relationships, many individuals still seek extradyadic sex. In this chapter, we discuss the incidence of infidelity, the societal context of extradyadic sexual relationships and jealousy, various theoretical perspectives on these phenomena, the factors associated with extradyadic sexual involvement, the effects of such involvement on the primary relationship, and the determinants of jealousy.

Infidelity

Incidence

Although extradyadic sex seems to occur regularly in contemporary Western society, there are few reliable data documenting the precise prevalence of such behavior. After reviewing 12 surveys of extramarital behavior, Thompson (1983) concluded that the probability that at least one partner in a marriage will have an extramarital relationship lies somewhere between 40% and 76%. Whereas 13% of the men and 21% of the women reported having been "purely" emotionally involved with someone else and 31% of the men and 16% of the women reported having had a "purely" sexual extradyadic affair, about 20% of both men and women reported having engaged in an extradyadic affair that included both sexual and emotional involvement. In many of these cases, an extramarital affair happens only once or twice in the lifetime of the individual involved, and at a given moment in time, most married people are not involved in extradyadic affairs. For instance, recently, Traeen and Stigum (1998) found, in a sample of 10,000 Norwegians, that, at the time of the study, 16% of the respondents reported having one or more parallel sexual relationships. However, "mild" forms of infidelity may occur much more often. Hicks and Leitenberg (2001), for instance, found that no less than 87% of their respondents (98% of men, 80% of women) reported having had extradyadic sexual fantasies in the past 2 months.

In general, extradyadic sex seems to occur more often in dating and cohabiting than in marital relationships (e.g., Buunk, 1980b; Treas & Giesen, 2000), whereas in gay relationships, extradyadic sex seems more

common, and in lesbian relationships less common than in heterosexual relationships (e.g., Blumstein & Schwartz, 1983). In addition, a higher lifetime incidence of extramarital sex is found among Blacks, remarried individuals, those in the highest and lowest education categories, those in urban areas and those low in religiosity (Atkins, Baucom, & Jacobson, 2001; Christopher & Sprecher, 2000; Weinberg & Williams, 1988). Although historically, men, more than women, engaged in extradyadic sexual behaviors (e.g., Thompson, 1983; Wiederman & Hurd, 1999), the difference between the sexes in rates of infidelity seems to be decreasing in younger individuals. The more similar rates of extramarital sex for men and women can at least partly be attributed to women's greater presence in the workforce and the financial independence and the opportunity for infidelity that come along with it (Atkins et al., 2001).

There is not only a considerable variety within Western society in the prevalence of extradyadic sex, but also a large cross-cultural variety in this respect. In general, extramarital sex is much more prevalent in African than in Asian countries (e.g., Caraël, Cleland, Deheneffe, Ferry, & Ingham, 1995). For example, in Guinea Bissau, 38% of the men and 19% of the women had had extradyadic sex in the past year, compared with only 8% of the men and 1% of the women in Hong Kong (e.g., Caraël et al., 1995), whereas in the Netherlands, 5% of all individuals with a steady relationship had in the previous year entered into casual extradyadic sex (Van Zessen & Sandfort, 1991). It must be emphasized that these figures concern the past year and that the lifelong incidence is likely to be considerably higher.

Norms with Respect to Extradyadic Sex

Even among those involved in extradyadic sex, such behavior is not necessarily approved of and perceived as morally right. Although during the "sexual revolution" of the 1970s, attitudes in some countries became somewhat more relaxed, in the past decades in Western society, attitudes have moved toward more disapproval of extramarital sex, especially among men (Thornton & Young-DeMarco, 2001). As a consequence, by the late 1990s, about 70% (Christopher & Sprecher, 2000) to 90% of U.S. men and women (Thornton & Young-DeMarco, 2001) said they believed that extramarital sex was always or almost always wrong. Although more so in the United States than in Western European countries such as Sweden and the Netherlands (Buunk & van Driel, 1989; Christensen, 1973), attitudes in these European countries have also become more restricted. For instance, in 1997 about 78% of Dutch respondents considered extradyadic sex wrong (Sociaal en Cultureel Rapport, 1998). Even extradyadic behaviors that do not have an explicit sexual content are often condemned, such as having dinner in a secluded place or dancing because they imply the risk of a developing sexual relationship (Weis & Felton, 1987). The disapproval of extradyadic sex also differs between ethnic groups. For instance, whereas about 30% of Asian Americans feel that violence is justified in case of a wife's sexual infidelity (Yoshioka, DiNoia, & Ullah, 2001), among Arab American immigrants 48% of the women and 23% of the men approve of a man slapping a sexually unfaithful wife, with 18% of the women even approving a man killing his wife if she were to have an affair (Kulwicki & Miller, 1999). In general, attitudes toward infidelity are more permissive among younger individuals, among the better educated and those from the upper middle class, among persons who are less religious, among those living in urban areas, and among those holding liberal political orientations (see Buunk & van Driel, 1989).

Despite the general disapproval of extradyadic sex all over the world, there is, and there has been in all periods of history, a double standard, that is, a stronger tendency to condemn extradyadic sex engaged in by women than extradyadic sex engaged in by men (e.g., McClosky & Brill, 1983). For instance, in many cultures, including ancient Mediterranean cultures such as Egyptians, Syrians, Hebrews, Romans, and Spartans, and Far Eastern cultures such as the Japanese and Chinese, only extramarital sex by women was legally defined as adultery and thus punishable by law. In the past, and still in many cultures, a wife's adultery has often been viewed as a provocation, allowing the cuckolded husband to exact revenge on the guilty parties (Daly, Wilson, & Weghorst, 1982). Also in contemporary North America, where a single standard of sexual behavior has officially become widely accepted, the double standard may still surface. For example, female adulterers are perceived as more responsible for their actions and as feeling more guilty following infidelity than male adulterers (Mongeau, Hale, & Alles, 1994). Moreover, whereas men who commit adultery tend to assume that this is something that most men do, women who commit adultery tend to view their behavior as rare and to feel unique in a negative sense (Van den Eijnden, Buunk, & Bosveld, 2000).

Theoretical Perspectives

There have been many theoretical perspectives from which jealousy and extradyadic sexual relationships have been analyzed. We confine ourselves here to three theories that have a firm basis in fundamental research, have an explanatory power for a wide range of phenomena, and in our view have become in recent years the most fruitful perspectives for studying close relationships (see also Buunk & Dijkstra, 2000). The three theories are social exchange theories, evolutionary psychology, and attachment theory.

SOCIAL EXCHANGE THEORIES

A social exchange framework, broadly, refers to any conceptual model that focuses on the exchange of resources between people or that refers to the major exchange concepts of rewards, costs, and reciprocity (Sprecher, 1998). In general, social exchange theories assume that individuals form and continue relationships on the basis of reciprocity in the exchange of costs and rewards in these relationships (Buunk & Schaufeli,

1999; Thibaut & Kelley, 1959). At least three specific social exchange models have been applied to extradyadic sex and jealousy: equity theory, interdependence theory, and the investment model (Sprecher, 1998).

First, according to equity theory, individuals who discover that they are in inequitable relationships will try to restore equity, with equity referring to the perceived balance in the relationship between partners' inputs and outcomes. Equity theory assumes that there are two types of inequity – feeling overbenefitted and feeling underbenefitted – that both lead to attempts to restore equity. Equity theory would therefore predict that inequity contributes to the likelihood of extradyadic involvement and may be a prominent reason for individuals to have extramarital affairs (e.g., Walster, & Walster, & Traupman, 1978). Extradyadic sex may then, unconsciously, be a way to restore inequity (Sprecher, 1998).

Second, whereas equity theory focuses on the principle of justice or fairness, interdependence theory focuses on the rewards and costs derived from the relationship for the individual. Key concepts in interdependence theory are the *comparison level* (CL), that is, the expectation of what someone thinks he or she deserves from such a relationship, and the *comparison level for alternatives* (CLalt), the lowest level of outcomes someone will accept in light of available alternative opportunities. In addition, as emphasized by Thibaut and Kelley (1959), partners become *dependent* on each other; that is, they develop the ability to control and influence each other's outcomes. As a consequence, in the course of the relationship, outcomes of both partners become intertwined, and positive experiences of the one may vicariously become rewards for the other ("I am happy because he or she is happy"). As a consequence, interdependence theory suggests that because someone who is more dependent has more to lose, among those highly dependent on the relationship the inclination to become involved in extradyadic sex will be lower whereas levels of jealousy will be higher. This will be particularly true for those with a high level of *relative dependency*, that is, those who feel more dependent on the relationship than does their partner (Buunk, 1991; Thibaut & Kelley, 1959).

Third, according to the investment model (Rusbult, 1983; see also Rusbult & Buunk, 1993), commitment is the primary force in relationships. Commitment is a psychological attachment to and a motivation to continue the relationship with the partner. It is supposedly based on a combination of high relationship satisfaction, low quality of alternatives, and a high level of investments in the relationship. According to the investment model, the likelihood of extradyadic sex increases as commitment erodes because of attractive alternatives, lowered satisfaction (outcome compared with CL), or low investments (Drigotas & Barta, 2001; Drigotas et al., 1999; Sprecher, 1998). The investment model may help explain why seemingly satisfied individuals still may be unfaithful because of low investments or attractive alternatives, and why an unsatisfied partner may remain faithful because of high investments in the relationship or the absence of alternatives. In addition, because they have more to lose when their relationship dissolves, committed individuals may experience more jealousy when confronted with a mate's infidelity than less committed individuals.

EVOLUTIONARY PSYCHOLOGY

This perspective is largely based on neo-Darwinistic theories in evolutionary biology and assumes that present-day humans are characterized by a complex set of mental mechanisms that have evolved because such mechanisms fostered reproductive success in ancestral times. Given the importance of the pair bond for reproductive success among humans, a universal concern with the potential threat of extradyadic sexual relationships to this bond is easy to explain. Nevertheless, according to evolutionary psychologists, in our ancestral past for females investing in a long-term relationship was virtually an absolute necessity to produce offspring who survive to reproduce.

In contrast, men had the potential to invest minimally – only one act of sexual intercourse at the theoretical low end – to reproduce. As a consequence, men would have evolved a stronger tendency than women to be open to casual extradyadic sex ("short-term mating"), more or less independent of the state of their marital relationship, and men could afford to be less selective in choosing partners for such casual encounters than women (Buss, 1994; Symons, 1979). However, although women may in general be somewhat more motivated to establish a committed long-term relationship than men ("long-term mating"; Buss, 1994), evolutionary psychologists have recently suggested that extradyadic sex may also have had considerable reproductive benefits for females. Women may, for instance, acquire better genes from higher value extrapair matings than from their regular mates or may use extradyadic sex as a means of replacing a primary partner (Buss, 2000).

Evolutionary psychologists have argued that because of men's and women's different reproductive biology, men and women will differ in several aspects of jealousy, such as the jealousy-evoking nature of rival characteristics and the type of infidelity they find most upsetting (Bjorklund & Shackelford, 1999; Buss et al., 1992, 1999; Daly et al., 1982; Okami, & Shackelford, 2001; Symons, 1979). Men have, in the course of evolution, confronted a problem not encountered by women, namely, that as a consequence of infidelity of their partner, men may unknowingly invest heavily in another man's offspring without passing on their own genes. Because investing in genetically unrelated offspring comes at substantial reproductive cost to the male, evolutionary psychologists have suggested that men's jealousy will be elicited primarily by signs of a mate's sexual infidelity. Although women do not suffer from uncertainty concerning the maternity of their offspring, they risk the loss of a man's resources if he directs his resources to alternative mates. Because men can copulate with women while minimizing their investments, cues to an emotional bond may be particularly reliable indicators to women

of the potential loss of their mate's investment. Jealousy in women would therefore be aroused primarily by signs to a mate's emotional unfaithfulness. With regard to rival characteristics, from an evolutionary-psychological perspective, one would expect men and women to feel the most jealousy in response to those rival characteristics that contribute most to the rival's value as a partner, and because different characteristics contribute to male and female value as partner, different rival characteristics should evoke jealousy in men and women.

ATTACHMENT THEORY

According to attachment theory, humans are born with a so-called attachment system that is activated in response to a potential separation from their caretaker, usually a parent. This attachment system then regulates emotions and behaviors aimed at reunion with the parent, such as anxiety and proximity seeking. Because of experiences with the way they are treated by their caregivers, children often develop a relatively consistent way of responding to separation from a parent, that is, a specific attachment style. For instance, if a caretaker is not very responsive to a child's distress, a child may unconsciously develop negative models of both the self ("I am not worthy of taking care of") and of others ("Others cannot be trusted"), which may cause the child to avoid contact with the caretaker. In addition to this fearful avoidant attachment style (guided by negative models of both self and others), Bartholomew (1990) also distinguished a dismissive avoidant attachment style (positive model of self, negative model of others), a preoccupied attachment style (negative model of self, positive model of others) and a secure attachment style (positive model of both self and others).

Although originally proposed to explain interactions between child and parents, attachment theory has been fruitfully applied to adult intimate relationships as well (e.g., Hazan & Shaver, 1987). In contrast to individuals with insecure attachment styles, individuals with a secure attachment style feel comfortable with intimacy and have long and stable relationships characterized by trust (Miller & Fishkin, 1997). Therefore, securely attached individuals, more than individuals with insecure attachment styles, seem in general to adopt a strategy of long-term mating and seem less likely to engage in extradyadic sex. Insecurely attached individuals may engage more often in extradyadic affairs because they experience more conflict in their relationships (Bogaert & Sadava, 2002). Because it is assumed that the attachment system regulates emotions and behaviors aimed at reunion with a partner, it can be hypothesized that the experience and expression of jealousy will also be partly a function of an individual's attachment style (Sharpsteen & Kirkpatrick, 1997). More specifically, attachment theory suggests that individuals with a disrupted attachment history are more likely to interpret the behavior of their spouse in terms of abandonment and therefore will have a lower threshold for adult jealousy.

More recently, several theorists have suggested or undertaken efforts to integrate the evolutionary psychological approach to understanding infidelity and jealousy with a social exchange framework (Buunk & Schaufeli, 1999; Drigotas & Barta, 2001; Shackelford & Buss, 2000), and respectively an attachment theoretical perspective (Bogaert & Sadava, 2002; Kirkpatrick, 1998). Indeed, these theories are largely compatible because of their different levels of explanation. Whereas evolutionary theory explains the *ultimate* motives for engaging in extradyadic sex and behaving jealously, that is, how such behaviors may have contributed to reproductive success in our evolutionary past, attachment theory and social exchange theories use more *proximate* levels of explanation. That is, attachment theory explains why some individuals, due to their childhood history, are more inclined to become jealous and have more problems building a committed, sexually exclusive relationship, whereas social exchange theories relate jealousy and extradyadic sex to processes of reciprocity and dependency in the relationship.

Correlates of Infidelity

Why do people engage in extradyadic sex? There are two major ways to examine the motives for extradyadic sex, and the first of these is asking people why they did so. The disadvantage of this method, of course, is that given the social undesirability of infidelity, individuals may feel they have to come up with "adequate" explanations for their behavior. As a consequence, the reasons given for extradyadic sex may not always reflect the true reasons behind this behavior. According to Atwater (1979), *justifications* (such as "I was deeply in love") are aimed at keeping one's self-image intact by accepting the responsibility for one's behavior, but denying that there is anything wrong with it. In contrast, with *excuses* (such as "it just happened") people deny responsibility for their actions but accept the negative value of their acts. A second way to learn more about the motives for extradyadic sex, is to examine the factors correlated with actual or intended involvement in extradyadic sex. For instance, when such involvement is associated with low marital satisfaction, one might conclude that infidelity often stems from marital problems. The limitation of this method is (to stay with this example) that such marital problems may be the consequence rather than the cause of extradyadic sex.

INDIVIDUAL CORRELATES

There is some evidence that individuals who engage in extradyadic sex are relatively often characterized by lower levels of well-being and mental health (e.g., Duckworth & Levitt, 1985; Sheppard, Nelson, & Andreoli-Mathie, 1995), and this seems to apply in particular to women. In a study among couples in their first year of marriage, Buss and Schackelford (1997) found that in general, the personality characteristics of wives were better predictors of her susceptibility to infidelity as perceived by herself and her husband. Especially wives low in conscientiousness, high in narcissism, and high in psychoticism (Buss & Schackelford, 1997) or suffering from a histrionic personality disorder (Apt & Hurlbert, 1994) seem to be inclined to be unfaithful. They may do so because, in part, these personality characteristics reflect insecure attachment styles (Buunk, 1997). Indeed, some studies have found that especially among women, an anxious–ambivalent attachment style is associated with a tendency to be unfaithful. Gangestad and Thornhill (1997) found that in women, anxious–ambivalence covaried positively and avoidance negatively with the number of extradyadic affairs, and Bogaert and Sadava (2002) found that women with anxious attachments had to deal with more infidelity (of themselves, their partners, or both) in their relationships (but see Miller & Fishkin, 1997, for evidence that insecurely attached men (but not women) seek more partners over a 30-year period than securely attached men).

In addition, extradyadic sex is more prevalent among individuals with a positive *attitude toward sexuality*. For example, individuals who have adopted an unrestricted sociosexual orientation – that is, who do not need a high degree of closeness or commitment before engaging in sex – are more likely to engage in extradyadic sex (e.g., Simpson & Gangestad, 1991; Treas & Giesen, 2000; Wiederman & Hurd, 1999). Seal, Agostinelli, and Hannet (1994) presented respondents with a script asking them to imagine a series of social interactions with an attractive opposite-sex stranger and found that those high in sociosexuality were more willing to pursue the relationship with the stranger in the scenario. In general, individuals may engage in extradyadic sex because it provides an opportunity for sexual variety and because it increases their self-esteem (Atwater, 1979; Buunk, 1980b; Sheppard et al., 1995; Treas & Giesen, 2000).

RELATIONSHIP CORRELATES

Several studies have found that, particularly among men, adultery often stems from feelings of sexual deprivation in the primary relationship. In contrast, among women emotional dissatisfaction with the relationship has been found to be related to adultery (e.g., Atkins et al., 2001; Buss & Shackelford, 1997; Buunk, 1980a; Edwards & Booth, 1976; Glass & Wright, 1985; 1992; Spanier & Margolis, 1983; Wiggins & Lederer, 1984). Furthermore, in line with equity theory, there is evidence that both individuals who feel underbenefited and those who feel overbenefited in their relationship report a greater number of extramarital affairs than individuals who experience equity (e.g., Walster, Walster, & Berscheid, 1978). Prins, Buunk, and VanYperen (1993) found that among women, but not men, the strength of extradyadic sexual desires and the frequency of affairs were related to the degree of reciprocity in the primary relationships, suggesting that among men the inclination to engage in extradyadic sex is a relatively autonomous motive that is to some extent independent of the state of the primary relationship (see also Buss & Shackelford, 1997).

In accordance with the investment model, lowered satisfaction, as well as lowered commitment have also been found to be important determinants of extradyadic sexual involvement or of the willingness to be involved in an extradyadic relationship (Buunk & Bakker, 1997a; Drigotas et al., 1999; Johnson & Rusbult, 1989; Treas & Griesen, 2000). In addition, there is evidence that, as interdependence theory would predict, extradyadic sex may be particularly likely to occur in relationships characterized by low dependency. Buunk (1980a), for instance, found that those who had been engaged in extradyadic sex, and were inclined to do so in the future, were lower in emotional dependency – a feeling of emotional attachment to the partner, accompanied by the perception that the relationship surpasses what one can expect in other relationships.

The personal and relational characteristics that we discussed thus far only *predispose* an individual to infidelity – that is, they may make individuals more open to temptation once the opportunity arises but do not necessarily always lead to infidelity. In fact, given factors such as the potential risk to their primary relationship, feelings of guilt and anxiety, and fears of pregnancy and venereal disease, becoming involved in extramarital relationships often implies a decision process in which the costs and benefits are identified and are compared with the expected values of alternative decisions. Meyering and Epling-McWerther (1986) found that in such a decision process, men were more affected by the perceived payoffs, including variation, and women more by the costs, including the probability of strong guilt feelings and the marriage being negatively affected.

Effects of Extradyadic Sex

Individuals involved in extramarital relationships often find themselves in a situation in which strong problems generated by their extramarital relationships conflict with the strong attraction to the extramarital partner. Indeed, such relationships often have a very high reward potential, including stimulating sex, personal growth, self-discovery, and the joys of courtship (Atwater, 1979; Buunk & Van Driel, 1989). For example, in a study conducted by Buunk (1980b), nearly all subjects emphasized the quality of the communication with the outside partner, and large majorities reported that new aspects of their personality emerged in this relationship and that the sexual aspect of their extramarital relationship was in several respects better than with their spouse. Such positive aspects are often overshadowed by the negative aspects of conducting an extradyadic sexual affair, such as strong anxiety and guilt feelings (Atwater, 1979), and by various practical problems, such as the necessity to have a private place to meet and the fact that one has to be careful in telephoning, writing, and seeing the extramarital partner. Moreover, because extradyadic sex often happens without protection of a condom, individuals engaging in extradyadic sex run the risk of getting infected with sexuality transmitted diseases (STDs) and of infecting their partners (e.g., Pulerwitz, Izazola-Licea, & Gortmaker, 2001). Indeed, the threat of AIDS has added a new dimension to the impact of extradyadic sexual relationships on the primary relationship. For instance, Buunk and

Bakker (1997a) found that as individuals felt less committed to their primary relationships, they were less inclined to protect their partner from becoming infected with STDs derived from their extrasexual relationships.

Extradyadic sexual relationships may have negative consequences not only for the individual, but may also constitute a serious threat to the quality and stability of the primary relationship. The adulterous individual may become attached to the extradyadic partner and begin to consider this partner as a serious alternative to the primary partner. Moreover, even when the individual has no intent to end the primary relationship, this relationship may in various ways look bleak compared with the romance and sexual excitement experienced in the extradyadic relationship. In an interesting approach, Charny and Parnass (1995) asked practicing therapists to describe in depth a specific extramarital affair with which they were familiar. According to these therapists, a one-time extramarital relationship had in more than half of the cases a negative impact on the marital relationship, including divorce and a high level of distress.

Most extradyadic relationships are kept secret from the primary partner, and even when this partner gets obvious clues that the other partner may be having an affair, such clues are often denied because the offended partners may not *want* to know they are being cheated on. According to Charny and Parnass (1995), nearly half of the cuckolded spouses did not consciously acknowledge the spouse's extramarital behavior, but there were indications that they knew about it. Remarkably, fully 58% of the betrayed spouses were seen as expressing explicit or tacit acceptance of their partner's affairs, whereas only 36% conveyed conscious active resistance to infidelity. On the other hand, some individuals are extremely jealous and are hypersensitive to every cue that their partner might be unfaithful. Shackelford and Buss (1997) identified a total of 14 types of cues that individuals assume may indicate emotional and sexual infidelity, including being angry and critical toward the partner, changes in normal routine and sexual behavior with the partner, increased sexual interest and exaggerated display of affection toward partner, physical signs of infidelity, sexual disinterest, passive rejection, and the reluctance to discuss a certain other person.

When extradyadic affairs come out in the open, they often have destructive results: Worldwide, adultery has been found to be a major cause of divorce (Betzig, 1989; Burns, 1984; Buss, 1994). Burns (1984), for instance, found that 31% of divorced people mentioned the husband's association with another woman as a cause of the breakdown of the marriage. It is difficult, however, if not impossible, to draw from this type of research firm conclusions about the consequences of extramarital relationships on the stability of marriages, especially because we do not know how many, and which couples, remain together despite an extramarital affair. In general, it seems that extradyadic sexual relationships will particularly likely lead to a divorce when they stem primarily from dissatisfaction with the primary relationship with the affair being a consequence rather than a cause of relational problems (Buunk, 1987a; Hunt, 1974; Spanier & Margolis, 1983). There is evidence that even when the spouse accepts the extradyadic sexual involvement such as in sexually open marriages, relational and sexual satisfaction decreases substantially over time (Buunk, 1987b).

Jealousy

Jealousy As a Response to a Partner's Actual or Imagined Infidelity

Although jealousy in close relationships may arise from many sources, including the partner's friends or the partner's work, extradyadic sex usually evokes the strongest jealousy – and vice versa, jealousy is the most common and universal response to the actual or suspected extradyadic sex of one's partner (Buss, 2000). Jealousy is aroused when a person is threatened with the loss of an important relationship to a rival and is strongly related to feelings such as

fear, suspicion, distrust, anxiety, and anger, betrayal, rejection, threat, and loneliness (e.g., Haslam & Bornstein, 1996; Knobloch, Solomon, & Cruz, 2001; Parrott, 2001). Jealousy may be aroused not only by a threat to the relationship, but also by a threat to one's self-esteem (e.g., Bringle & Buunk, 1985; Sharpsteen, 1995). According to the so-called sociometer hypothesis (Leary & Baumeister, 2000) self-esteem tracks social rejection, with infidelity being an important potential rejector (Shackelford, 2001). In case of actual or potential infidelity, and thus rejection, jealousy may help to restore self-esteem by maintaining a positive self-view (e.g., DeSteno & Salovey, 1996; Guerrero & Afifi, 1999).

Various typologies of jealousy have been proposed. Beginning with the work of Freud (1950), a distinction has been made in the clinical literature between normal or rational jealousy stemming from a realistic threat to the relationship and abnormal, pathological, or morbid jealousy that is aroused in the absence of such a threat. In a related vein, Parrott (1991, 2001) made a distinction between jealousy in response to a potential relationship threat ("suspicious" jealousy) and jealousy in response to a partner's extradyadic sex that has already occurred ("fait accompli" jealousy). Furthermore, various authors have distinguished state jealousy, that is, those feelings that are evoked by a jealousy event, from dispositional jealousy, that is, the individual propensity to respond in a jealous manner (e.g., Bringle & Evenbeck, 1979; Rich, 1991). More recently, scholars have emphasized the importance of communication between the jealous person and his or her partner, distinguishing between the experience and the expression of jealousy (e.g., Afifi & Reichert, 1996; Andersen, Eloy, Guerrero, & Spitzberg, 1995; Knobloch et al., 2001). According to these authors, the experience of jealousy comprises cognitions and emotions that in turn affect how people express their jealousy. In contrast, the expression of jealousy consists of behavioral and communicative reactions to jealousy.

Although all the typologies mentioned here are dichotomies, two comparable typologies have been proposed that distinguish between three types of jealousy. Pfeiffer and Wong (1989) made a distinction between three types: emotional, cognitive, and behavioral jealousy. Emotional jealousy entails feelings such as fear, anger, insecurity, and sadness; cognitive jealousy consists of paranoid thoughts and worries about the behavior of one's partner; and behavioral jealousy involves jealous actions such as spying on one's partner or rummaging through his or her belongings. In a related vein, Buunk (1991, 1997) made a distinction among reactive, anxious, and possessive jealousy. Reactive jealousy constitutes a direct response to an actual relationship threat, as is the case, for instance, when one's partner is flirting or having sex with someone else. Anxious jealousy refers to an active cognitive process in which the individual generates images of his or her partner becoming sexually or emotionally involved with someone else and experiences feelings of anxiety, suspicion, worry, distrust, and upset. Finally, possessive jealousy refers to the considerable effort jealous individuals can go to to prevent contact of their partner with a third person, such as opposing their partner's contact with opposite-sex individuals. In contrast to Pfeiffer and Wong's typology, Buunk's typology takes into account that jealousy may occur not only in response to an actual threat to the relationship, but also in the absence of such a threat. Whereas reactive jealousy constitutes a response to an actual relationship threat, both possessive and anxious jealousy may be evoked in response to a potential relationship threat or in the complete absence of such a threat.

Correlates of Jealousy

INDIVIDUAL CORRELATES OF JEALOUSY

Self-esteem is the most widely examined individual difference variable in jealousy research. Although several studies have found lowered self-esteem and increased jealousy to be related for both sexes (McIntosh, 1989; Mullen, 1994; Nadler & Dotan, 1992), a substantial number of studies found that, particularly among women, jealousy is related to low self-esteem (e.g., Buunk, 1997; Hansen, 1985; Mullen, 1994; Peretti & Pedowski, 1997). In addition, there is particularly consistent evidence for a positive association of jealousy with neuroticism. In general, neurotic individuals experience more jealousy than less neurotic individuals (e.g., Buunk, 1981, 1997; Melamed, 1991; Tarrier, Becket, Harwood, & Ahmed, 1989). An explanation for the findings that individuals with low self-esteem and neurotic individuals experience more jealousy is that they often feel more inadequate as a partner (Peretti & Pedowski, 1997). That is, they worry that they cannot measure up to their partner's expectations, are afraid that they are not what their partner is looking for, or perceive a negative discrepancy between their own desirability as a partner relative to their partner's (Buss, 2000). As a consequence, they feel more easily threatened by actual or potential rivals.

Although numerous other personality variables have been related to jealousy as well, most of these variables have been examined only in one or two isolated studies. For instance, jealous feelings, cognitions, or behaviors have been found to be negatively related to extraversion (e.g., Mathes, Roter, & Joerger, 1982; Tarrier et al., 1989) and positively to feelings of inadequacy (e.g., Buunk, 1997), gender-role traditionalism (Hansen, 1985), rigidity (e.g., Buunk, 1997), irrational thinking (e.g., Lester, Deluca, Hellinghausen, & Scribner, 1985), romanticism (e.g., Lester et al., 1985), trait anxiety (e.g., DeMoja, 1986; Jaremko & Lindsey, 1979), and need for control (e.g., Brainerd, Hunter, Moore, & Thompson, 1996).

Attachment theory suggests that individuals with a disrupted attachment history are more likely to interpret the behavior of their spouse in terms of abandonment and therefore will have a lower threshold for adult jealousy. When operationalized in terms of attachment history – that is, number of separations and losses during childhood, harshness of parental discipline, quality of parent–child relationships, and quality of child–peer relationships – no relation between attachment and jealousy emerges (Clanton & Kosins, 1991). In contrast, studies that have operationalized attachment in terms of individuals' attachment styles consistently found individuals with an insecure attachment style to be more jealous than individuals with a secure attachment style (e.g., Powers, 2000; Radecki-Bush, Farrell, & Bush, 1993), independent of the influence of personality characteristics such as self-esteem, neuroticism, and social anxiety on jealousy (Buunk, 1997). In particular, individuals with an anxious–ambivalent attachment style – the preoccupied attachment style in the conceptualization of Bartholomew (1990) – have been found to experience jealousy (e.g., Dobrenski, 2001). Findings on individuals with an avoidant attachment style – the dismissive attachment style in the conceptualization of Bartholomew (1990) – are somewhat contradictory. For example, Buunk (1997) found that avoidant-attached individuals reported more jealousy than securely attached individuals, whereas Guerrero (1998) found dismissing individuals to experience less fear when their relationship was threatened than securely attached individuals. With regard to specific types of jealousy, Knobloch et al. (2001) found that individuals high in anxiety over relationships, that is, individuals with negative self-models, were inclined to respond with more emotional jealousy, and, indirectly, also with more cognitive jealousy (see also Guerrero, 1998) whereas Buunk (1997) found that all three types of jealousy were experienced more intensely in anxious–ambivalent-attached individuals than in securely attached individuals. Because an anxious–ambivalent attachment style implies a "clinging" to the relationship out of fear of losing the partner, the link between this style and jealousy seems self-evident. A possible explanation for why an avoidant style may also be accompanied by jealousy is that avoidant individuals are actually quite dependent on their partner but feel that they are not meeting the needs of their partner by their distant attitude and are therefore concerned about losing their partner.

Attachment styles may also affect the behaviors individuals exhibit in response to suspected or actual infidelity. Securely attached persons tend to use more problem-focused coping, whereas individuals with insecure attachment styles use more emotion-focused coping strategies (Vocatura, 2000). More specifically, individuals with an avoidant attachment style, compared with individuals having other attachment styles, use less relationship-maintaining behaviors such as talking about the problem and coming to an understanding, are especially likely to direct their anger and blame against their rival, and are less likely to seek social support. Individuals with a preoccupied or anxious–ambivalent attachment style, on the other hand, are more likely to use surveillance behavior, such as looking through a partner's belongings, to blame themselves, and to resist expressing anger, presumably out of fear of rejection. In contrast, in response to a partner's infidelity, securely attached individuals express anger toward the partner and generally adopt more productive coping strategies aimed at maintaining their relationship (Guerrero, 1998; Leak, Gardner, & Parsons, 1998; Radecki-Bush et al., 1993; Sharpsteen & Kirkpatrick, 1997).

RELATIONSHIP CORRELATES

Most research examining the relationship characteristics associated with jealousy has focused in some way on the degree to which individuals feel dependent on their partner. As interdependence theory would predict, because someone who is more dependent has more to lose, jealousy will be more frequent and more intense among those highly dependent on the relationship. This issue has been examined mainly in the early jealousy literature, and studies in this area have generated mixed findings. In line with the theory's prediction, jealousy has been found to be more strongly related to loving than to liking (e.g., Pfeiffer & Wong, 1989; White, 1984), to be associated with emotional dependency (e.g., Buunk, 1995), to be negatively related to perceived alternatives to the present relationship (e.g., Hansen, 1985), and to be more prevalent in individuals who feel more involved in the relationship than their partner (e.g., White, 1981a). Other studies have, however, provided less unequivocal results. Buunk (1982a) found, for instance, that, although anticipated sexual jealousy correlated substantially with dependency in a student sample and in a general population sample, it did not in a sample of promiscuous individuals. Likewise, dependency has been found only to be moderately related to jealousy among women, not men (White, 1981b) and only in nonmarital relationships (Bringle, Renner, Terry, & Davis, 1983). In addition, although one might expect involvement to increase in the course of a relationship, relationship length has not been found to be consistently related to jealousy (Melamed, 1991; Pines & Aronson, 1983; Strzyzewski Aune, & Comstock 1997).

Another important relationship variable that has been studied in relation to jealousy is relationship satisfaction. In general the loss of a close relationship involves great costs, concerning not only the loss of important relationship rewards such as companionship, but also the loss of identity and self-esteem (Buss, 1994; Mathes, Adams, & Davies, 1985). On the basis of social exchange theory, it can therefore be expected that individuals who feel satisfied with their relationship will experience more intense jealousy because they fear losing a relatively high level of rewards. Support for this hypothesis has been found by Nadler and Dotan (1992) and Mathes et al. (1985). The latter found, for instance, that relatively jealous individuals had more stable and successful relationships than individuals who reported low jealousy. However, negative associations between jealousy and relational satisfaction also have been reported (e.g., Guerrero, Eloy, Jorgensen, & Andersen, 1993; Shackelford & Buss, 2000). These negative relations can be explained by the fact that jealousy may lead to negative relational outcomes, such as depression, divorce, and domestic violence (e.g., Barnett, Martinez, & Bluestein, 1995; Buss, 2000). As a consequence, jealousy may also lower relational outcomes and thus relational satisfaction. In addition, the association between jealousy and relationship satisfaction may depend on the type of jealousy. For example, cognitive jealousy has a stronger inverse relation with relational satisfaction than emotional jealousy (Andersen et al., 1995).

Various authors have argued that the level of outcomes provided by the partner is not as closely related to jealousy as is the degree of insecurity over these outcomes (Berscheid & Fei, 1977). Indeed, concerns about the viability of the relationship and relational uncertainty have been found to be tied inextricably to the manifestation of jealousy, especially cognitive jealousy (e.g., Afifi & Reichert, 1996; Knobloch et al., 2001). Insecurity over the relationship is assumed to be related to jealousy, because it can instill the fear that the partner may become attracted to someone else, risking the loss of important relationship rewards.

A partner's extradyadic sex may evoke particularly negative feelings for individuals when it has occurred unprotected because this may involve the risk of the transmission of sexually transmitted diseases. In a sample of adults, many of whom had been involved in extradyadic sex, Buunk and Bakker (1997b) examined three responses to unprotected extradyadic sex by one's partner: angry retreat (anger, upset, and inclination to leave the partner), accommodation (open communication aimed at preserving the relationship), and assertiveness (demanding precautionary measures from the partner). Women expressed more angry retreat and assertiveness but not more accommodation than men. Angry retreat was found particularly among individuals with a low intention to engage in extradyadic sex, accommodation was characteristic of those high in commitment, whereas assertiveness was especially common among those with a high intention to use condoms with new sexual partners.

Elicitors of Jealousy

The stimuli that elicit jealousy may vary considerably between individuals and between cultures. For example, in some cultures kissing is much more likely to evoke jealousy than in others, whereas in other cultures petting is a particularly salient jealousy-inducing event (Buunk & Hupka, 1987). In general, individuals do not become jealous when their partner ends the relationship for other reasons than attraction to a rival, such as when the partner is killed in an automobile accident (Mathes et al., 1985; Parrott, 1991). Therefore, for jealousy to occur, a rival is a necessary and defining condition. Overall, a rival who possesses qualities that are believed to be important to the opposite sex or to one's partner tends to evoke more feelings of jealousy than a rival who does not possess those qualities (e.g., DeSteno & Salovey, 1996; Dijkstra & Buunk, 1998; Mathes, 1991; White, 1981b). In addition, individuals tend to report more jealousy as their rivals possess more self-relevant attributes, such as intelligence, popularity, athleticism, and certain professional skills (e.g., DeSteno & Salovey, 1996; Rustemeyer & Wilbert, 2001).

Because jealousy is evoked by those characteristics that contribute most to the rival's value as a partner, one would, from an evolutionary–psychological perspective, expect women to feel more jealous than men when their rival is physically attractive and men to feel more jealous than women when their rival possesses status-related characteristics. Several studies have found support for this hypothesis (e.g., Buss et al., 1999; Dijkstra & Buunk, 1998, 2002; Yarab & Allgeier, 1999), even among homosexuals (Buunk & Dijkstra, 2001). The fact that homosexuals respond identically to heterosexuals to a rival's physical attractiveness and status-related characteristics, suggests that, independent of sexual orientation, sex or gender is in some way linked to a sensitivity to specific rival characteristics (or to a sensitivity to learn to respond to such characteristics).

Sexual VS. Emotional Infidelity

Until approximately a decade ago, jealousy research did not find consistent differences between men and women in the degree in which they experienced jealousy in response to infidelity: Most studies did not report a gender difference (for reviews, see Buunk, 1986; Buunk & Dijkstra, 2000). However, in the past decade, it has become clear that gender differences in jealousy may occur when the specific circumstances under which jealousy is aroused are taken into account. Because men have in the course of evolution faced the problem of paternity confidence, and women of securing the partner's investment of resources, from an evolutionary perspective, male jealousy would be specifically focused on the sexual aspects of the partner's extramarital activities and female jealousy on the emotional involvement of the partner with the rival (e.g., Buss, 2000; Buss et al., 1992; Bjorklund & Shackelford, 1999; Daly et al., 1982; Symons, 1979; Okami, & Shackelford, 2001). Until the 1990s, only indirect evidence was presented in support of this assumption. For example, men were found to experience their jealousy more in terms of sexual issues (Teismann & Mosher, 1978); across seven nations, men indicated significantly more so than women that they would become upset if their partner would have sexual fantasies about someone else (Buunk & Hupka, 1987); and among men, sexual aspects of extradyadic involvement evoked more jealousy, whereas in women jealousy was aroused more by the fact that the partner spent time with the rival (Francis, 1977; see also Buunk, 1984, 1986). Other indirect support for the stronger focus on sexual jealousy among men comes from a study by Buunk (1995), who found that women were less jealous the more extradyadic sexual affairs their husband had had, whereas jealousy stayed at the same level among men, no matter how many affairs the wife had previously. Indeed, from the perspective of paternity confidence, for men *any* act of intercourse with a third person is a potential threat. In contrast, for women an act of intercourse may only be a threat when the relationship is in jeopardy: when the partner has been unfaithful a number of times while maintaining his commitment, a woman may under some conditions adapt to her partner's infidelity.

In a more direct test of the gender difference predicted by evolutionary psychologists, Buss et al. (1992) developed a research paradigm in which they presented participants with dilemmas in which they had to chose between a partner's sexual unfaithfulness and a partner's emotional unfaithfulness as the most upsetting event. In support of the predicted gender difference, Buss et al. found that more men than women selected a partner's sexual infidelity as the most upsetting event, whereas more women than men reported a partner's emotional infidelity as the most upsetting event. In addition, these researchers found that participants were also more physiologically upset, as measured by heart rate, electrodermal response, corrugator supercilii contraction, in line with the predicted gender difference (see also Pietrzak, Laird, Stevens, & Thompson, 2002), although these physiological data could not be replicated by Grice and Seely (2000) nor by Harris (2000). Using the forced choice paradigm, however, this sex difference has since then been replicated several times, in, for instance, the United States, the Netherlands, China, Germany, Korea, Sweden, and Japan (e.g., Bailey, Gaulin, Agyei, & Gladue, 1994; Buss et al., 1999; Buunk, Angleitner, Oubaid, & Buss, 1996; Cann, Mangum, & Wells, 2001; Cramer, Abraham, Johnson, & Manning-Ryan, 2001; DeSteno & Salovey, 1996; Harris & Christenfeld, 1996; Wiederman & Kendall, 1999). Although some studies have not reported gender differences in the jealousy-evoking nature of sexual and emotional infidelity among homosexuals (e.g., Harris, 2002; Sheets & Wolfe, 2001), Dijkstra et al. (2001) found that the sex difference was reversed, with lesbian women showing more sexual jealousy than gay men and gay men showing more emotional jealousy than lesbian women. In line with the evolutionary perspective, this finding suggests that heterosexual as well as homosexual men and women find the same behavior of men (e.g., emotional infidelity) and of women (e.g., sexual infidelity) more threatening. In a similar vein, Fenigstein and Peltz (2002) found that mothers as well as fathers regard sexual infidelity as more distressing when committed by a daughter-in-law and emotional infidelity as more distressing when it involved a son-in-law. Furthermore, there is increasing

evidence that, rather than evoking merely upset, sexual and emotional jealousy evoke different emotional responses. In general, emotional infidelity is more likely to evoke feelings of insecurity and threat whereas sexual infidelity is more likely to evoke feelings of betrayal, anger, and repulsion (Buunk, 1995; Buunk & Dijkstra, 2004; Parrott, 1991; Shackelford, LeBlanc, & Drass, 2000).

It must be noted, however, that the evolutionary interpretation of the gender difference in emotional versus sexual jealousy has received serious criticism. First, it has been noted that although evolutionary psychologists have often framed men's and women's inclination to respond with jealousy to specific cues in absolute terms (e.g., "men primarily respond with jealousy to sexual cues of infidelity"), men are mostly equally split when it comes to choosing which type of infidelity they would find the most upsetting. Only in relative terms, that is, when the sexes are explicitly compared, do men seem to choose more often than women sexual infidelity as the most upsetting event (Buss et al., 1992, 1999; DeSteno & Salovey, 1996; Harris & Christenfeld, 1996; Hupka & Bank, 1996). In contrast, women choose emotional infidelity consistently as the more upsetting event. Second, there are indications that the gender difference depends on the use of the forced-choice paradigm. When using a different paradigm such as Likert scales to assess the upsetting nature of emotional and sexual infidelity, often no gender difference is found (e.g., DeSteno, Bartlett, Braverman, & Salovey, 2002; Wiederman & Allgeier, 1993). Therefore, some authors have claimed that the gender difference that supposedly supports the evolutionary view of jealousy is largely due to the experimental artifact of the choice format (DeSteno et al., 2002). Third, recent research has identified a variety of factors that may moderate the gender difference in emotional versus sexual jealousy. For example, the gender difference has been found to disappear when controlling for variables such as personal experiences with a partner's actual infidelity (Harris, 2002; Sagarin, Becker, Guadagno, Nicastle, & Millevoi, 2003), sexual orientation of the infidelity (Sagarin et al., 2003), cognitive constraint (DeSteno et al., 2002), and women's use of hormone-based birth control (Geary, DeSoto, Hoard, Sheldon, & Cooper, 2001).

In addition to the criticisms questioning the robustness of the gender difference in sexual versus emotional jealousy, a number of researchers have argued that the gender difference among heterosexuals generated by the Buss paradigm should not be attributed to innate differences, as Buss et al. (1992) did, but is more properly explained by how the sexes interpret evidence of infidelity of their partner (e.g., Harris, 2000; Harris & Christenfeld, 1996) or how the sexes view infidelity of members of the opposite sex in general. Adopting this last interpretation, DeSteno and Salovey (1996) postulated the so-called double-shot hypothesis, stating that emotional and sexual infidelity do not occur independently and that individuals will chose the type of infidelity as most upsetting that indicates most the occurrence of the other type of infidelity. Therefore, men will find a partner's sexual infidelity more distressing than her emotional infidelity because men believe that a woman's sexual unfaithfulness also indicates her emotional unfaithfulness, but not the opposite, whereas women will find a partner's emotional infidelity more upsetting than his sexual infidelity because women believe that a man's emotional unfaithfulness also implies his sexual unfaithfulness, but not the opposite. Although studies on this topic agree that men and women differ in their interpretation of evidence of infidelity in the hypothesized direction (Buss et al., 1999; DeSteno & Salovey, 1996; Wiederman & Allgeier, 1993; Wiederman & Kendall, 1999), some studies do indeed report relations between the gender difference in jealousy and the gender difference in beliefs about infidelity (e.g., DeSteno & Salovey, 1996; Harris & Christenfeld, 1996), whereas others do not (e.g., Cann et al., 2001; Cramer et al., 2001).

Coping With Jealousy

Coping with jealousy may not be limited to deliberate, conscious attempts to modify the threat but may also consist of unconscious instinctive reactions to a jealousy event (see also Bringle & Buunk, 1985). Therefore, coping strategies may include all those cognitive, emotional, or behavioral activities that result from a jealousy-evoking event and that are aimed at modifying the perception of the threat, or the actual threat, to one's relationship (see also Buunk & Dijkstra, 2000). Many ways of coping with jealousy have been identified, and several attempts have been made to summarize these into broader categories by the use of factorial analysis. Categories of coping strategies that are found recurrently are those referring to avoidance of the spouse, reappraisal of the situation, and communication with the partner, in particular, confronting the partner about the jealousy event (Buunk, 1982b; Hansen, 1991; McIntosh & Matthews, 1992). Although probably not very effective in dealing with jealousy, jealous individuals often feel depressed (e.g., Dobrenski, 2001; Jaremko & Lindsey, 1979; Radecki-Bush et al., 1993) and resort to violence (e.g., Daly et al., 1982; Follingstad, Bradley, Laughlin, & Burke, 1999). In the case of a relationship breakup due to a rival, jealous individuals may engage in stalking (Davis, Ace, & Andra, 2002). In general, individuals who stalk their ex-partners and individuals who use violence as a coping mechanism for jealousy share many of the same characteristics (Logan, Leukefeld, & Walker, 2000), such as emotional volatility, attachment dysfunction, and high rejection sensitivity (Douglas & Dutton, 2001).

Although there may be many coping strategies that individuals use when dealing with a jealousy-evoking event, we limit ourselves here to those coping strategies that have consistently been found to be often-used ways of coping with jealousy. A recurrent finding is that, in response to a jealousy-evoking event, women in particular have the tendency to think that they are "not good enough." For instance, they doubt themselves more than men do (Buunk, 1995), feel more insecure and undesirable (e.g., Shackelford et al., 2000), and try to make themselves look more attractive (e.g., Buss & Shackelford, 1997; Mullen

& Martin, 1994). In line with this, among women depression is a frequently reported consequence of their partner's infidelity (e.g., Cano & O'Leary, 2000). In contrast, men report more often that they would get drunk or high when confronted with a partner's infidelity (DeWeerth & Kalma, 1993; Shettel-Neuber et al., 1978) and use violence to prevent their partner from becoming unfaithful (Buss, 2000; Peters, Shackelford, & Buss, 2002). Actual homicide statistics, for instance, show that many more men than women commit homicides out of jealousy (Daly et al., 1982). However, studies that have asked participants what they *would* do if a jealousy-evoking event would occur consistently show that women in particular are inclined to endorse aggressive action against their rival (DeWeerth & Kalma, 1993; Paul, Foss, & Galloway, 1993). Possible explanations for this discrepancy are that women are more likely than men to admit intentions of violence toward their rival, women are less likely than men to convert their violent intentions into actual behavior, and, although women may physically injure their rivals, they do not kill them, whereas men do. Before acting aggressively in response to a partner's infidelity, however, to avoid infidelity, men are more inclined to act possessively toward their partners than are women (e.g., Paul et al., 1993), in particular, when their partner is young and attractive (Buss & Shackelford, 1997).

Conclusion

The temptation to engage in extradyadic sex and the tendency to respond with jealousy to such behavior by one's partner are interrelated and universal human phenomena that are both part of our human evolutionary heritage. Nevertheless, there is considerable variation across individuals, relationships, situations, and cultures in the likelihood that one will become involved in extradyadic sex and in the likelihood that one will exhibit various forms of jealousy. Although infidelity among women was historically subject to many more restrictions than it was for men,

in recent years, women seem to have caught up with men in terms of their involvement in extradyadic affairs. Jealousy seems more likely and extradyadic sex less likely the more a relationship is characterized by involvement, dependency, commitment, and secure attachment. The awareness of the potential negative effects that extradyadic relationships may have on primary relationships finds expression in a virtually universal normative disapproval of extradyadic sex. Ironically, the potential fury of jealousy also causes most affairs to be covert, which accentuates the aversive consequences following disclosure. Jealousy will, even among individuals who aim to have a sexually liberal lifestyle, reliably surface when an extradyadic sexual affair is disclosed or discovered. Although the robustness of this finding and its interpretation remain controversial, women seem to respond with more jealousy to an emotional attachment of their spouse to a third person, and men seem to respond with more jealousy to a sexual attachment of their spouse to a third person. Although having potentially destructive consequences, jealousy may basically be viewed as a response aimed at protecting the relationship, and, from an evolutionary perspective, one's reproductive opportunities. Technological changes such as cellular phones and the Internet may increase the options for engaging in various forms and degrees of extradyadic sexual and erotic involvement. Given the deeply rooted motivations that underlie jealous as well as adulterous tendencies, it would be unrealistic to expect that any interventions or cultural changes will ever eliminate the problems these tendencies may generate in intimate relationships.

References

Afifi, W. A., & Reichert, T. (1996). Understanding the role of uncertainty in jealousy experience and expression. *Communication Reports*, 9, 93–103.

Andersen, P. A., Eloy, S. V., Guerrero, L. K., & Spitzberg, B. H. (1995). Romantic jealousy and relational satisfaction: A look at the impact of jealousy experience and expression. *Communication Reports*, 8, 77–85.

Apt, C., & Hurlbert, D. F. (1994). The sexual attitudes, behavior, and relationships of women with histrionic personality disorder. *Journal of Sex and Marital Therapy*, 20, 125–133.

Atkins, D.C., Baucom, D. H., & Jacobson, N. S. (2001). Understanding infidelity: Correlates in a national random sample. *Journal of Family Psychology*, 15, 735–749.

Atwater, L. (1979). Getting involved: Women's transition to first extramarital sex. *Alternative Lifestyles*, 2, 33–68.

Bailey, J. M., Gaulin, S., Agyei, Y., & Gladue, B. A. (1994). Effects of gender and sexual orientation on evolutionary relevant aspects of human mating. *Journal of Personality and Social Psychology*, 66, 1081–1093.

Bartholomew, K. (1990). Avoidance of intimacy: An attachment perspective. *Journal of Social and Personal Relationships*, 7, 147–178.

Barnett, O. W., Martinez, T. E., & Bluestein, B. (1995). Jealousy and romantic attachment in maritally violent and nonviolent men. *Journal of Interpersonal Violence*, 10, 473–486.

Berscheid, E., & Fei, J. (1977). Romantic love and sexual jealousy. In G. Clanton & L. G. Smith (Eds.), *Jealousy* (pp. 101–110). Englewood Cliffs, NJ: Prentice Hall.

Betzig, L. (1989). Causes of conjugal dissolution: A cross-cultural study. *Current Anthropology*, 30, 676–694.

Bjorklund, D. F., & Shackelford, T. K. (1999). Differences in parental investment contribute to important differences between men and women. *Current Directions in Psychological Science*, 8, 86–89.

Blumstein, P., & Schwartz, P. (1983). *American couples*. New York: Morrow.

Bogaert, A. F., & Sadava, S. (2002). Adult attachment and sexual behavior. *Personal Relationships*, 9, 191–204.

Brainerd, E. G., Hunter, P. A., Moore, D., & Thompson, T. (1996). Jealousy induction as a predictor of power and other control methods in heterosexual relationships. *Psychological Reports*, 79, 1319–1325.

Bringle, R. G., & Buunk, B. P. (1985). Jealousy and social behavior: A review of person, relationship and situational determinants. In P. Shaver (Ed.), *Review of personality and social psychology* (Vol. 6, pp. 241–264). Thousand Oaks, CA: Sage.

Bringle, R. B., & Evenbeck, S. (1979). The study of jealousy as a dispositional characteristic. In M. Cook & G. Wilson (Eds.), *Love and attraction* (pp. 201–204). Oxford: Pergamon Press.

Bringle, R. G., Renner, P., Terry, R., & Davis, S. (1983). An analysis of situation and person components of jealousy. *Journal of Research in Personality*, 17, 354–368.

Burns, A. (1984). Perceived causes of marriage breakdown and conditions of life. *Journal of Marriage and the Family*, 46, 551–562.

Buss, D. M. (1994). *The evolution of desire: Strategies of human mating*. New York: Basic Books.

Buss, D. M. (2000). *The dangerous passion: Why jealousy is as necessary as love and sex*. New York: Free Press.

Buss, D. M., Larsen, R. J., Westen, D., & Semmelroth, J. (1992). Sex differences in jealousy: Evolution, physiology, and psychology. *Psychological Science*, 3, 251–255.

Buss, D. M., & Shackelford, T. K. (1997). Susceptibility to infidelity in the first year of marriage. *Journal of Research in Personality*, 31, 193–221.

Buss, D. M., Shackelford, T. K., Kirkpatrick, L. A., Choe, J., Lim, H. G., Hasegawa, M., et al. (1999). Jealousy and the nature of beliefs about infidelity: Tests of competing hypotheses about sex differences in the United States, Korea, and Japan. *Personal Relationships*, 6, 125–150.

Buunk, B. P. (1980a). Sexually open marriages: Ground rules for countering potential threats to marriage. *Alternative Lifestyles*, 3, 312–328.

Buunk, B. P. (1980b). Extramarital sex in the Netherlands: Motivations in social and marital context. *Alternative Lifestyles*, 3, 11–39.

Buunk, B. P. (1981). Jealousy in sexually open marriages. *Alternative Lifestyles*, 4, 357–372.

Buunk, B. P. (1982a). Anticipated sexual jealousy: Its relationship to self-esteem, dependency, and reciprocity. *Personality and Social Psychology Bulletin*, 8, 310–316.

Buunk, B. P. (1982b). Strategies of jealousy: Styles of coping with extramarital involvement of the spouse. *Family Relations*, 31, 13–18.

Buunk, B. P. (1984). Jealousy as related to attributions for the partner's behavior. *Social Psychology Quarterly*, 47, 107–112.

Buunk, B. P. (1986). Husband's jealousy. In R. A. Lewis & R. E. Salt (Eds.), *Men in families* (pp. 97–114). Beverly Hills, CA: Sage.

Buunk, B. P. (1987a). Conditions that promote breakups as a consequence of extradyadic involvements. *Journal of Social and Clinical Psychology, 5*, 271–284.

Buunk, B. P. (1987b). Long-term stability and change in sexually open marriages. In L. Shamgar-Handelman & R. Palomba (Eds.), *Alternative patterns of family life in modern societies* (pp. 61–72). Collana Monografie 1 Rome: Istituto di Ricerche sulla Popolazione.

Buunk, B. P. (1991). Jealousy in close relationships: An exchange-theoretical perspective. In P. Salovey (Ed.), *The psychology of jealousy and envy* (pp. 148–177). New York: Guilford Press.

Buunk, B. P. (1995). Sex, self-esteem, dependency and extradyadic sexual experiences as related to jealousy responses. *Journal of Social and Personal Relationships, 12*, 147–153.

Buunk, B. P. (1997). Personality, birth order and attachment styles as related to various types of jealousy. *Personality and Individual Differences, 23*, 997–1006.

Buunk, B. P., Angleitner, A., Oubaid, V., & Buss, D. M. (1996). Sex differences in jealousy in evolutionary and cultural perspective: Test from the Netherlands, Germany, and the United States. *Psychological Science, 7*, 359–363.

Buunk, B. P., & Bakker, A. B. (1997a). Commitment to the relationship, extradyadic sex, and AIDS-preventive behavior. *Journal of Applied Social Psychology, 27*, 1241–1257.

Buunk, B. P., & Bakker, A. B. (1997b). Responses to unprotected extradyadic sex by one's partner: Testing predictions from interdependence and equity theory. *Journal of Sex Research, 34*, 387–397.

Buunk, B. P., & Dijkstra, P. (2000). Extradyadic relationships and jealousy. In C. Hendrick & S. S. Hendrick (Eds.), *Close relationships: A sourcebook* (pp. 317–330). Thousand Oaks, CA: Sage.

Buunk, B. P., & Dijkstra, P. (2001). Evidence from a homosexual sample for a sex-specific rival-oriented mechanism: Jealousy as a function of a rival's physical attractiveness and dominance. *Personal Relationships, 8*, 391–406.

Buunk, B. P., & Dijkstra, P. (2004). Gender differences in rival characteristics that evoke jealousy in response to emotional versus sexual infidelity. *Personal Relationships, 11*, 395–418.

Buunk, B. P., & Hupka, R. B. (1987). Cross-cultural differences in the elicitation of sexual jealousy. *Journal of Sex Research, 23*, 12–22.

Buunk, B. P., & Schaufeli, W. B. (1999). Reciprocity in interpersonal relationships: An evolutionary perspective on its importance for health and well-being. In W. Stroebe & M. Hewstone (Eds.), *European Review of Social Psychology, 10*, 260–291.

Buunk, B. P., & Van Driel, B. (1989). *Variant lifestyles and relationships* Newbury Park, CA: Sage.

Cann, A., Mangum, J, & Wells, M. (2001). Distress in response to relationship infidelity: The roles of gender and attitudes about relationships. *Journal of Sex Research, 38*, 185–190.

Cano, A., & O'Leary, D. K. (2000). Infidelity and separations precipitate major depressive episodes and symptoms of nonspecific depression and anxiety. *Journal of Consulting and Clinical Psychology, 68*, 774–781.

Caraël, M., Cleland, J., Deheneffe, J. C., Ferry, B., & Ingham, R. (1995). Sexual behavior in developing counties: Implications for HIV control. *AIDS, 9*, 1171–1175.

Charny, I. W., & Parnass, S. (1995). The impact of extramarital relationships on the continuation of marriages. *Journal of Sex and Marital Therapy, 21*, 101–115.

Christensen, H. T. (1973). Attitudes toward marital infidelity: A nine-culture sampling of university student opinions. *Journal of Comparative Family Studies, 4*, 197–214.

Christopher, S. F., & Sprecher, S. (2000). Sexuality in marriage, dating, and other relationships: A decade review. *Journal of Marriage and the Family, 62*, 999–1017.

Clanton, G., & Kosins, D. J. (1991). Developmental correlates of jealousy. In P. Salovey (Ed.), *The psychology of jealousy and envy* (pp. 132–147). New York: Guilford Press.

Cramer, R. E., Abraham, W. T., Johnson, L. M., & Manning-Ryan, B. (2001). Gender differences in subjective distress to emotional and sexual infidelity: Evolutionary or logical inference explanation? *Current Psychology, 20*, 327–336.

Daly, M., Wilson, M., & Weghorst, S. J. (1982). Male sexual jealousy. *Ethology and Sociobiology, 3*, 11–27.

Davis, K. E., Ace, A., & Andra, M. (2002). Stalking perpetrators and psychological maltreatment of partners: Anger-jealousy, attachment insecurity, need for control, and break-up context. In K. E. Davis, I. H. Frieze, & R. D.

Maiuro (Eds.), *Stalking: Perspectives on victims and perpetrators* (pp. 237–264). New York: Springer.

DeMoja, C. A. (1986). Anxiety, self-confidence, jealousy, romantic attitudes toward love in Italian undergraduates. *Psychological Reports,* 58, 138.

DeSteno, D., Bartlett, M. Y., Braverman, J., & Salovey, P. (2002). Sex differences in jealousy: Evolutionary mechanism or artifact of measurement? *Journal of Personality and Social Psychology,* 83, 1103–1116.

DeSteno, D. A., & Salovey, P. (1996). Evolutionary origins of sex differences in jealousy? Questioning the fitness of the model. *Psychological Science,* 7, 367–372.

DeWeerth, C., & Kalma, A. P. (1993). Female aggression as a response to sexual jealousy: A sex role reversal? *Aggresive Behavior,* 19, 265–279.

Dijkstra, P., & Buunk, B. P. (1998). Jealousy as a function of rival characteristics: An evolutionary perspective. *Personality and Social Psychology Bulletin,* 24, 1158–1166.

Dijkstra, P., & Buunk, B. P. (2002). Sex differences in the jealousy-evoking effect of rival characteristics. *European Journal of Social Psychology,* 32, 829–852.

Dijkstra, P., Groothof, H. A. K., Poel, G. A., Laverman, T. G., Schrier, M., & Buunk, B. P. (2001). Sex differences in the events that elicit jealousy among homosexuals. *Personal Relationships,* 8, 41–54.

Dobrenski, R. A. (2001). Romantic jealousy: Symptoms, schemas, and attachment. *Dissertation Abstracts International,* 62 (6-B), 2954.

Douglas, K. S., & Dutton, D. G. (2001). Assessing the link between stalking and domestic violence. *Aggression and Violent Behavior,* 6, 519–546.

Drigotas, S. M., & Barta, W. (2001). The cheating heart: Scientific explorations of infidelity. *Current Directions in Psychological Science,* 10, 177–180.

Drigotas, S., Safstrom, C., & Gentilia, T. (1999). An investment model prediction of dating infidelity. *Journal of Personality and Social Psychology,* 77, 509–524.

Duckworth, J., & Levitt, E. I. (1985). Personality analysis of a swingers' club. *Lifestyles: A Journal of Changing Patterns,* 8, 35–45.

Edwards, J. N., & Booth, A. (1976). Sexual behavior in and out of marriage: An assessment of correlates. *Journal of Marriage and the Family,* 38, 73–81.

Fenigstein, A., & Peltz, R. (2002). Distress over the infidelity of a child's spouse: A crucial test of evolutionary and socialization hypotheses. *Personal Relationships,* 9, 301–312.

Follingstad, D. R., Bradley, R. G., Laughlin, J. E., & Burke, L. (1999). Risk factors and correlates of dating violence: The relevance of examining frequency and severity levels in a college sample. *Violence and Victims,* 14, 365–380.

Francis, J. L. (1977). Toward the management of heterosexual jealousy. *Journal of Marriage and Family Counseling,* 3, 61–69.

Freud, S. (1950). Certain neurotic mechanisms in jealousy, paranoia and homosexuality. *Complex,* 3–13.

Gangestad, S. W., & Thornhill, R. (1997). The evolutionary psychology of extrapair sex: The role of fluctuating asymmetry. *Evolution and Human Behavior,* 18, 69–88.

Geary, D. C, DeSoto, M. C., Hoard, M. K., Sheldon, M. S., & Cooper, L. M. (2001). Estrogens and relationship jealousy. *Human Nature,* 12, 299–320.

Glass, S. P., & Wright, T. L. (1985). Sex differences in type of extramarital involvement and marital dissatisfaction. *Sex Roles,* 12, 1101–1119.

Glass, S. P., & Wright, T. L. (1992). Justifications for extramarital relationships: The association between attitudes, behaviors, and gender. *Journal of Sex Research,* 29, 361–387.

Grice, J. W., & Seely, E. (2000). The evolution of sex differences in jealousy: Failure to replicate previous results. *Journal of Research in Personality,* 34, 348–356.

Guerrero, L. K. (1998). Attachment-style differences in the experience and expression of romantic jealousy. *Personal Relationships,* 5, 273–291.

Guerrero, L. K., & Afifi, W. A. (1999). Toward a goal-oriented approach for understanding communicative responses to jealousy. *Western Journal of Communication,* 63, 216–248.

Guerrero, L. K., Eloy, S. V., Jorgensen, P. F., & Andersen, P. (1993). Her or his? Sex differences in the experience and communication of jealousy in close relationships. In P. J. Kalbfleish (Eds.), *Interpersonal communication: Evolving interpersonal relationships* (pp. 109–132). Mahwah, NJ: Erlbaum.

Hansen, G. L. (1985). Perceived threats and marital jealousy. *Social Psychology Quarterly*, 48, 262–268.

Hansen, G. L. (1991). Jealousy: Its conceptualization, measurement and integration with family stress theory. In P. Salovey (Ed.), *The psychology of jealousy and envy* (pp. 211–230). New York: Guilford Press.

Harris, C. R. (2000). Psychophysiological responses to imagined infidelity: The specific innate modular view of jealousy reconsidered. *Journal of Personality and Social Psychology*, 78, 1082–1091.

Harris, C. R. (2002). Sexual and romantic jealousy in heterosexual and homosexual adults. *Psychological Science*, 13, 7–12.

Harris, C. R., & Christenfeld, N. (1996). Jealousy and rational responses to infidelity across gender and culture. *Psychological Science*, 7, 378–379.

Haslam, N., & Bornstein, B. H. (1996). Envy and jealousy as discrete emotions: A taxometric analysis. *Motivation and Emotion*, 20, 255–272.

Hazan, C., & Shaver, P. R. (1987). Romantic love conceptualized as an attachment process. *Journal of Personality and Social Psychology*, 52, 511–524.

Hicks, T. V., & Leitenberg, H. (2001). Sexual fantasies about one's partner versus someone else: Gender differences in incidence and frequency. *Journal of Sex Research*, 38, 43–50.

Hunt, M. (1974). *Sexual behavior in the 1970s.* Chicago: Dell.

Hupka, R. B., & Bank, A. L. (1996). Sex differences in jealousy: Evolution or social construction? *Cross Cultural Research: The Journal of Comparative Social Science*, 30, 24–59.

Jaremko, M. E., & Lindsey, R. (1979). Stress-coping abilities of individuals high and low in jealousy. *Psychological Reports*, 44, 547–553.

Johnson, D. J., & Rusbult, C. E. (1989). Resisting temptation: Devaluation of alternative partners as a means of maintaining commitment. *Journal of Personality and Social Psychology*, 57, 967–980.

Kirkpatrick, L. A. (1998). Evolution, pair-bonding, and reproductive strategies: A reconceptualization of adult attachment. In J. A. Simpson & W. S. Rholes (Eds.), *Attachment theory and close relationships* (353–393). New York: Guilford Press.

Knobloch, L. K., Solomon, D. H., & Cruz, M. G. (2001). The role of relationship development and attachment in the experience of romantic jealousy. *Personal Relationships*, 8, 205–224.

Kulwicki, A. D., & Miller, J. (1999). Domestic violence in the Arab American population: Transforming environmental conditions through community education. *Issues in Mental Health Nursing*, 20, 199–215.

Leak, G. K., Gardner, L. E., & Parsons, C. J. (1998). Jealousy and romantic attachment: A replication and extension. *Representative Research in Social Psychology*, 22, 21–27.

Leary, M. R., & Baumeister, R. F. (2000). The nature and function of self-esteem: Sociometer theory. In M. P. Zanna (Ed.), *Advances in experimental social psychology* (Vol. 32, pp. 1–62). San Diego, CA: Academic Press.

Lester, D., Deluca, G., Hellinghausen, W., & Scribner, D. (1985). Jealousy and irrationality in love. *Psychological Reports*, 56, 210.

Logan, T., Leukefeld, C., & Walker, R. (2000). Stalking as a variant of domestic violence: Implications from young adults. *Violence and Victims*, 15, 91–111.

Mathes, E. W. (1991). A cognitive theory of jealousy. In P. Salovey (Ed.), *The psychology of jealousy and envy* (pp. 52–79). New York: Guilford Press.

Mathes, E. W., Adams, H. E., & Davies, R. M. (1985). Jealousy: Loss of relationship rewards, loss of self-esteem, depression, anxiety, and anger. *Journal of Personality and Social Psychology*, 48, 1552–1561.

Mathes, E. W., Roter, P. M., & Joerger, S. M. (1982). A convergent validity study of 6 jealousy scales. *Psychological Reports*, 50, 1143–1147.

McClosky, H. B., & Brill, A. (1983). *Dimensions of tolerance: What Americans believe about civil liberties.* New York: Russell Sage.

McIntosh, E. G. (1989). An investigation of romantic jealousy among Black undergraduates. *Journal of Social Behavior and Personality*, 17, 135–141.

McIntosh, E. G., & Matthews, C. O. (1992). Use of direct coping resources in dealing with jealousy. *Psychological Reports*, 70, 1037–1038.

Melamed, T. (1991). Individual differences in romantic jealousy: The moderating effect of relationship characteristics. *European Journal of Social Psychology*, 21, 455–461.

Meyering, R. A., & Epling-McWerther, E. A. (1986). Decision-making in extramarital relationships. *Lifestyles: A Journal of Changing Patterns*, 8, 115–129.

Miller, L. C., & Fishkin, S. A. (1997). On the dynamics of human bonding and reproductive success: Seeking windows on the adapted-for human–environmental interface. In J. A. Simpson & D. T. Kenrick (Eds.), *Evolutionary social psychology* (pp. 197–235). Mahwah, NJ: Erlbaum.

Mongeau, P. A., Hale, J. L., & Alles, M. (1994). An experimental investigation of accounts and attributions following sexual infidelity. *Communication Monographs*, 61, 326–344.

Mullen, P. E. (1994). Jealousy: A community study. *British Journal of Psychiatry*, 164, 35–43.

Mullen, P. E., & Martin, J. L. (1994). Jealousy: A community study. *British Journal of Psychiatry*, 164, 35–43.

Nadler, A., & Dotan, I. (1992). Commitment and rival attractiveness: Their effects on male and female reactions to jealousy arousing situations. *Sex Roles*, 26, 293–310.

Okami, P., & Shackelford, T. K. (2001). Human sex differences in sexual psychology and behavior. *Annual Review of Sex Research*, 12, 186–241.

Parrott, W. G. (1991). The emotional experience of envy and jealousy. In P. Salovey (Ed.), *The psychology of jealousy and envy* (pp. 3–30). New York: Guilford Press.

Parrott, W. G. (2001). The emotional experiences of envy and jealousy. In W. G. Parrott (Ed.), *Emotions in social psychology: Essential readings* (pp. 306–320). Philadelphia: Psychology Press.

Paul, L., Foss, M. A., & Galloway, J. (1993). Sexual jealousy in young women and men: Aggressive responsiveness to partner and rival. *Aggressive Behavior*, 19, 401–420.

Peretti, P. O., & Pudowski, B. C. (1997). Influence of jealousy on male and female college daters. *Journal of Social Behavior and Personality*, 25, 155–160.

Peters, J., Shackelford, T. K., & Buss, D. M. (2002). Understanding domestic violence against women: Using evolutionary psychology to extend the feminist functional analysis. *Violence and Victims*, 17, 255–264.

Pfeiffer, S. M., & Wong, P. T. P. (1989). Multidimensional jealousy. *Journal of Social and Personal Relationships*, 6, 181–196.

Pietrzak, R. H., Laird, J. D., Stevens, D. A., & Thompson, N. S. (2002). Sex differences in human jealousy: A coordinated study of

forced-choice, continuous rating-scale, and physiological responses on the same subjects. *Evolution and Human-Behavior*, 23, 83–94.

Pines, A., & Aronson, E. (1983). Antecedents, correlates, and consequences of sexual jealousy. *Journal of Personality*, 51, 108–136.

Powers, A. M. (2000). The effects of attachment style and jealousy on aggressive behavior against a partner and a rival. *Dissertation Abstracts International*, 61 (6-B), 3325.

Prins, K. S., Buunk, B. P., & VanYperen, N. W. (1993). Equity, normative disapproval and extramarital relationships. *Journal of Social and Personal Relationships*, 10, 39–53.

Pulerwitz, J., Izazola-Licea, J. A., & Gortmaker, S. L. (2001). Extrarelational sex among Mexican men and their partners' risk of HIV and other sexually transmitted diseases. *American Journal of Public Health*, 91, 1650–1652.

Radecki-Bush, C., Farrell, A. D., & Bush, J. P. (1993). Predicting jealous responses: The influence of adult attachment and depression on threat appraisal. *Journal of Social and Personal Relationships*, 10, 569–588.

Rich, J. (1991). A two-factor model of jealous responses. *Psychological Reports*, 68, 999–1007.

Rusbult, C. E. (1983). A longitudinal test of the investment model: The development (and deterioration) of satisfaction and commitment in heterosexual involvements. *Journal of Personality and Social Psychology*, 45, 101–117.

Rusbult, C. E., & Buunk, B. P. (1993). Commitment processes in close relationships: An interdependence analysis. *Journal of Social and Personal Relationships*, 10, 175–204.

Rustemeyer, R., & Wilbert, C. (2001). Jealousy within the perspective of a self-evaluation maintenance theory. *Psychological Reports*, 88, 799–804.

Sagarin, B. J., Becker, V. D., Guadagno, R. E., Nicastle, L. D., & Millevoi, A. (2003). Sex differences (and similarities) in jealousy: The moderating influence of infidelity experience and sexual orientation of the infidelity. *Evolution and Human Behavior*, 24, 17–23.

Seal, D. W., Agostinelli, G., & Hannet, C. A. (1994). Extradyadic romantic involvement: Moderating effects of sociosexuality and gender. *Sex Roles*, 31, 1–22.

Shackelford, T. K. (2001). Self-esteem in marriage. *Personality and Individual Differences*, 30, 371–390.

Shackelford, T. K., & Buss, D. M. (1997). Cues to infidelity. *Personality and Social Psychology Bulletin, 23*, 1034–1045.

Shackelford, T. K., & Buss, D. M. (2000). Marital satisfaction and spousal cost-infliction. *Personality and Individual Differences, 28*, 917–928.

Shackelford, T. K., LeBlanc, G. J., & Drass, E. (2000). Emotional reactions to infidelity. *Cognition and Emotion, 14*, 643–659.

Sharpsteen, D. J. (1995). The effects of relationship and self-esteem threats on the likelihood of romantic jealousy. *Journal of Social and Personal Relationships, 12*, 89–101.

Sharpsteen, D. J., & Kirkpatrick, L. A. (1997). Romantic jealousy and adult romantic attachment. *Journal of Personality and Social Psychology, 72*, 627–640.

Sheets, V. L., & Wolfe, M. D. (2001). Sexual jealousy in heterosexuals, lesbians, and gays. *Sex Roles, 44*, 255–276.

Sheppard, V. J., Nelson, E. S., & Andreoli-Mathie, V. (1995). Dating relationships and infidelity: Attitudes and behaviors. *Journal of Sex and Marital Therapy, 21*, 202–212.

Shettel-Neuber, J., Bryson, J. B., & Young, L. E. (1978). Physical attractiveness of the "other person" and jealousy. *Personality and Social Psychology Bulletin, 4*, 612–615.

Simpson, J. A., & Gangestad, S. (1991). Individual differences in sociosexuality: Evidence for convergent and discriminant validity. *Journal of Personality and Social Psychology, 59*, 1192–1201.

Sociaal en Cultureel Rapport. (1998). Rijswijk, the Netherlands: Sociaal en Cultureel Planbureau.

Spanier, G. B., & Margolis, R. L. (1983). Marital separation and extramarital sexual behavior. *Journal of Sex Research, 19*, 23–48.

Sprecher, S. (1998). Social exchange theories and sexuality. *Journal of Sex Research, 35*, 32–43.

Strzyzewski Aune, K., & Comstock, J. (1997). Effect of relationship length on the experience, expression, and perceived appropriateness of jealousy. *Journal of Social Psychology, 137*, 23–31.

Symons, D. (1979). *The evolution of human sexuality.* Oxford, England: Oxford University Press.

Tarrier, N., Beckett, R., Harwood, S., & Ahmed, Y. (1989). Comparison of a morbidly jealous and a normal female population on the Eysenck Personality Questionnaire. *Personality and Individual Differences, 10*, 1327–1328.

Teismann, M. W., & Mosher, D. L. (1978). Jealous conflict in dating couples. *Psychological Reports, 42*, 1211–1216.

Thibaut, J. W., & Kelley, H. H. (1959). *The social psychology of groups.* New York: Wiley. (Reprinted by Transaction Books, New Brunswick, NJ, 1986.)

Thompson, A. P. (1983). Extramarital sex: A review of the research literature. *Journal of Sex Research, 19*, 1–22.

Thornton, A., & Young-DeMarco, L. (2001). Four decades of trends in attitudes toward family issues in the United States: The 1960s through the 1990s. *Journal of Marriage and the Family, 63*, 1009–1037.

Traeen, B., & Stigum, H. (1998). Parallel sexual relationships in the Norwegian context. *Journal of Community and Applied Social Psychology, 8*, 41–56.

Treas, J., & Giesen, D. (2000). Sexual infidelity among married and cohabitating Americans. *Journal of Marriage and the Family, 62*, 48–61.

Van den Eijnden, R. J. J. M., Buunk, B. P., & Bosveld, W. (2000). Feeling similar or feeling unique: How men and women perceive their own sexual behaviors. *Personality and Social Psychology Bulletin, 26*, 1540–1549.

Van Zessen, G. J., & Sandfort, T. M. (Eds.). (1991). *Seksualiteit in Nederland.* Amsterdam: Swets & Zeitlinger.

Vocatura, L. C. (2000). Predictors of coping styles in response to infidelity among college students. *Dissertation Abstracts International, 60* (11-B), 5796.

Walster, E., Walster, G. W., & Berscheid, E. (1978). *Equity: Theory and research.* Boston: Allyn and Bacon.

Walster, E., Walster, G. W., & Traupman, J. (1978). Equity and premarital sex. *Journal of Personality and Social Psychology, 36*, 82–92.

Weinberg, M. S., & Williams, C. J. (1988). Black sexuality: A test of two theories. *Journal of Sex Research, 25*, 197–218.

Weis, D. L., & Felton, J. R. (1987). Marital exclusivity and the potential for future marital conflict. *Social Work, 32*, 45–49.

White, G. L. (1981a). Relative involvement, inadequacy, and jealousy: A test of a causal model. *Alternative Lifestyles, 4*, 291–309.

White, G. L. (1981b). A model of romantic jealousy. *Motivation and Emotion, 5*, 295–310.

White, G. L. (1984). Comparison of four jealousy scales. *Journal of Research in Personality, 18*, 115–130.

Wiederman, M. W., & Algeier, E. R. (1993). Gender differences in sexual jealousy: Adaptionist or social learning explanation? *Ethology and Sociobiology, 14*, 115–140.

Wiederman, M. W., & Hurd, C. (1999). Extradyadic involvement during dating. *Journal of Social and Personal Relationships, 16*, 265–274.

Wiederman, M. W., & Kendall, E. (1999). Evolution, sex, and jealousy: Investigation with a sample from Sweden. *Evolution and Human Behavior, 20*, 121–128.

Wiggins, J. D., & Lerderer, D. A. (1984). Differential antecedents of infidelity in marriage. *American Mental Health Counselors Association Journal, 6*, 152–161.

Yarab, P. E., & Allgeier, E. R. (1999). Young adults' reactions of jealousy and perceived threat based on the characteristics of a hypothetical rival. *Journal of Sex Education and Therapy, 24*, 171–175.

Yoshioka, M. R., DiNoia, J., & Ullah, K. (2001). Attitudes toward marital violence. *Violence Against Women, 7*, 900–926.

CHAPTER 30

Violence and Abuse in Personal Relationships: Conflict, Terror, and Resistance in Intimate Partnerships

Michael P. Johnson

Violence occurs in all sorts of personal relationships. Parents hit their children, siblings have fights, girls slap their boyfriends, friends get into it, husbands terrorize their wives, and abused wives murder their husbands. Most of this violence receives little attention from scholars of personal relationships. For example, a 1997 handbook on personal relationships covers violence in only one section of one chapter (Klein & Johnson, 1997). However, in other disciplines such as family studies, social work, criminology, and sociology, there are research literatures (some small, some rather large) on most of these forms of violence. In the wake of the 20th century women's movement and the related cultural emphasis on gender equality, one of the largest of these literatures is focused on violence between intimate partners, including people who are dating, living together, married, or separated (Jasinski & Williams, 1998; Johnson & Ferraro, 2000). As a feminist sociologist, I work within and know best this literature, which is why this chapter focuses on intimate partner violence (IPV).

However, it may well be the case that the major lessons of the IPV literature are relevant for understanding violence in other kinds of personal relationships. I believe the two core lessons to be learned from work on IPV are simple, profound, and broadly applicable to violence in all types of personal relationships. First, one cannot understand violence in personal relationships without understanding its role in the relationship itself. Unlike most other kinds of violence (such as a mugging), which are essentially situational and do not involve a continuing relationship between the parties involved, personal relationship violence arises out of and shapes the dynamics of an ongoing relationship, the violence in some cases – but not always – being a central feature of the relationship.

Second, and more substantively, there are three quite different types of intimate partner violence, identified by their role in the control context of the relationship in which they are embedded. One type involves a violent attempt to take complete control or at least generally dominate the relationship (intimate terrorism), another involves violent resistance to such a control attempt (violent resistance), and the third is violence that is a product of particular conflicts or tensions within the relationship (situational couple violence). As this chapter shows, the nature of the control context is a major theme in the IPV literature, and although it has as yet received little attention in research on other types of personal relationships, there are hints of it in the parent–child literature.

Types of Intimate Partner Violence

These two core propositions are central to any theory of personal relationship violence. The three types of violence – intimate terrorism, violent resistance, and situational couple violence – have different origins, different dynamics, and different consequences. They therefore require different theoretical frameworks to explain them and different strategies for prevention and intervention. The failure to acknowledge these differences has led to major errors in the empirical literature on IPV, and perhaps in literatures on violence in other types of relationships. Unfortunately, until we carry out a broad program of research to investigate differences among the causes and consequences of the various types of IPV, we cannot know how widespread the errors are. Two examples, however, will illustrate the basic processes by which these errors are produced.

First, inadvertently aggregating different types of violence under one label produces data that are an "average" of the characteristics or correlates of the types that are aggregated. For example, a recent meta-analysis of the literature on the relationship between growing up in a violent home and subsequently becoming part of a violent marital relationship indicates quite small effects (Stith et al., 2000), calling into question what is often claimed to be one of the best established relationships in the IPV literature, the so-called intergenerational transmission of violence. The overall conclusion is that childhood experiences of family violence are *not* strongly related to adult IPV. However, that literature (and therefore the

meta-analysis) does not distinguish among types of violence, thus inadvertently aggregating whatever mix of types is found in the studies reviewed. Of course, this would not be a problem if the relationships of different types of violence to childhood experiences were the same. However, a recent study differentiating among the types finds that although situational couple violence is not strongly related to childhood experiences of violence, intimate terrorism is (Johnson & Cares, 2004). The "average" relationship thus does not represent the effect that is of most interest to most audiences: the effect on the likelihood of becoming an intimate terrorist – a wife beater.

The second type of error arises because different sampling strategies have different biases in terms of the types of violence they include. This is the error that produced the decades-long, and continuing, debate over the gender symmetry of domestic violence. Researchers using agency samples find domestic violence to be almost entirely male-perpetrated, whereas those using general survey samples find domestic violence to be gender-symmetric. As it turns out, general survey samples are dominated by situational couple violence, which is roughly gender-symmetric, and agency samples are dominated by intimate terrorism, which in heterosexual relationships is almost entirely male perpetrated (Johnson, 1995, 2001). It is important to remember that to most audiences, intimate terrorism is what the term *domestic violence* is all about. Thus, when we present conclusions about situational couple violence under the general rubric of domestic violence, we mislead the public in important ways, such as giving them the false impression that there are as many battered husbands as there are battered wives.

The typology of IPV presented here has its roots in this debate about gender symmetry. For decades, feminist theorists have argued that domestic violence is largely male perpetrated and rooted in the patriarchal traditions of the Western family (Dobash & Dobash, 1979). Family violence theorists, although acknowledging some role of gender in family violence, have argued that

Figure 30.1. Domestic violence–intimate terrorism.

domestic violence is rooted in the everyday tensions and conflicts of family life and that women are as violent as men in intimate relationships (Straus, 1999). We now know that they were both right but were not studying the same phenomenon. Two of the major types of IPV (intimate terrorism and violent resistance) are rooted in the dynamics of control and resistance that have been the focus of feminist theorists. Intimate terrorism and violent resistance comprise the bulk of the violence in the agency samples with which feminist theorists work. The third major type, situational couple violence, is rooted in the dynamics of family conflict that have been the focus of family violence theorists. Situational couple violence comprises the bulk of the violence in the general survey samples with which family violence theorists work. The three types constitute a typology of individual violence that is rooted in information about the couple and their relationship and defined by the control context within which the violence is embedded.

The Nature of Intimate Terrorism (IT)

In IT, the perpetrator uses violence in the service of general control over his or her part-

ner. The partner does not. The "control" that forms the basis of this typology of IPV and that is defining feature of IT is more than the specific, short-term control that is often the goal of violence in other contexts. The mugger wants to control you only briefly to take your valuables and move on, hopefully never to see you again. In contrast, the control sought in IT is general and long term. Although each particular act of intimate violence may appear to have any number of short term, specific goals, it is embedded in a larger pattern of power and control that permeates the relationship. This is the kind of violence that comes to mind when most people hear the term *domestic violence*. Figure 30.1 is a widely used graphical representation of partner violence deployed in the service of general control.

This diagram and the understanding of domestic violence that lies behind it were developed over a period of years from the testimony of battered women in the Duluth, Minnesota area, testimony that convinced the staff of the Duluth Domestic Abuse Intervention Project that the most important characteristic of the violence they encountered was that it was embedded in a general pattern of power and control (Pence

& Paymar, 1993). A pattern of power and control cannot, of course, be identified by looking at violence in isolation. It can only be recognized from information about multiple control tactics, allowing one to find out whether a perpetrator uses more than one of these tactics to control his or her partner, thus indicating an attempt to exercise general control.

A brief tour of the wheel, starting with economic abuse and moving through the other forms of control, might help to capture what Catherine Kirkwood calls a "web" of abuse (Kirkwood, 1993). It is not unusual for an intimate terrorist to deprive his[1] partner of control over economic resources. He controls all the money. She is allowed no bank account and no credit cards. If she works for wages, she has to turn over her paychecks to him. He keeps all the cash, and she has to ask him for money when she needs to buy groceries or clothes for herself or their children. He may require a precise accounting of every penny, demanding to see the grocery bill and making sure she returns every bit of the change.

This economic abuse may be justified through the next form of control, male privilege: "I am the man of the house, the head of the household, the king in my castle." Of course, this use of male privilege can cover everything. As the man of the house, his word is law. He doesn't have to explain. She doesn't disagree with him. She is to do his bidding without question. And don't talk back. All of this holds even more rigidly in public, where he is not to be humiliated by back talk from "his woman."

How does he use the children to support his control? First of all, they, too, know he is the boss. He makes it clear that he controls not only them, but their mother as well. He may use them to back him up, to make her humiliation more complete by forcing them into the room to assist him as he confronts her, asking them if he isn't right, and making them support his control of her. He may even have convinced them that he should be in charge, that he does know what is best (father knows best), and that she is incompetent or lazy

or immoral. In addition, he may use her attachment to the children as a means of control, by threatening to take them away from her or hurt them if she isn't a "good wife and mother." Of course, being a good wife and mother means doing as he says.

Then there's isolation. He keeps her away from everyone else. He makes himself her only source of information, of support, of money, of everything. In a rural setting, he might literally be able to isolate her, moving to a house trailer in the woods, with one car that he controls, no phone, keeping her there alone. In an urban setting, or if he needs her to go out to work, he can isolate her less literally, by driving away her friends and relatives and intimidating the people at work, so that she has no one to talk to about what's happening to her.

When she's completely isolated, and what he tells her about herself is all she ever hears about herself, he can tell her over and over again that she's worthless – humiliating her, demeaning her, emotionally abusing her. She's ugly, stupid, a slut, a lousy wife, an incompetent mother. She only manages to survive because he takes care of her. She'd be helpless without him. And who else is there to tell her otherwise? Maybe he can even convince her that she can't live without him.

If she resists, he can intimidate her. Show her what might happen if she doesn't behave. Scream at her. Swear at her. Let her see his rage. Smash things. Or maybe a little cold viciousness will make his point. Kick her cat. Hang her dog. That ought to make her think twice before she decides not to do as he says. Or threaten her. Threaten to hit her, or beat her, or pull her hair out, or burn her. Or tell her he'll kill her, and maybe the kids, too.

Pull all these means of control together, or even a few of them, and the abuser entraps and enslaves his partner in a web of control. If she manages to thwart one means of control, there are others at his disposal. Wherever she turns, there is another way he can control her. Sometimes she is ensnared by multiple strands. She can't seem to escape – she is trapped. But with the addition of violence, there is more to power and control than entrapment. There is terror.

For this reason, the diagram does not include the violence as just another means of control, another spoke in the wheel. The violence is depicted, rather, as the rim of the wheel, holding all the spokes together. When violence is added to such a pattern of power and control, the abuse becomes much more than the sum of its parts. The ostensibly nonviolent tactics that accompany that violence take on a new, powerful, and frightening meaning – controlling the victim not only through their own specific constraints but also through their association with the general knowledge that her partner will do anything to maintain control of the relationship, even attack her physically. Most obviously, the threats and intimidation are clearly more than idle threats if he has beaten her before. Even his "request" to see the grocery receipts, however, becomes a "warning" if he has put her into the hospital this year. His calling her a stupid slut may feel like the beginning of a vicious physical attack. As battered women often report, "All he had to do was look at me that way, and I'd jump." What is for most of us the safest place in our world – home – is for her a place of constant fear.

The Nature of Violent Resistance (VR)

What is a woman to do when she finds herself terrorized in her own home? At some point, most women in such relationships do fight back physically. For some, this is an instinctive reaction to being attacked, and it happens at the first blow – almost without thought. For others, it doesn't happen until it seems he is going to continue to assault her if she doesn't do something to stop him. For most women, the size difference between them and their male partner ensures that VR won't help, and may make things worse, so they turn to other means of coping. For a few, eventually it seems that the only way out is to kill their partner.

The critical defining pattern of violent resistance is that the resistor is violent but not controlling and is faced with a partner who is both violent and controlling, that is, he is an intimate terrorist. Violence in the face of IT may arise from any of a variety of motives. She may (at least at first) believe that she can defend herself, that her violent resistance will keep him from attacking her further. This may mean that she thinks she can stop him right now, in the midst of an attack, or it may mean that she thinks that if she fights back often enough, he will eventually decide to stop attacking her physically. Even if she doesn't think she can stop him, she may feel that he shouldn't be allowed to attack her without getting hurt himself. This desire to hurt him in return even if it won't stop him can be a form of communication ("What you're doing isn't right, and I'm going to fight back as hard as I can") or it may be a form of retaliation or payback, along the lines of "He's not going to do that without paying some price for it." In a few cases, she may be after serious retaliation, attacking him when he is least expecting it and doing her best to do serious damage, even killing him. There is another, more frequent motive for such premeditated attacks, however: escape. Sometimes, after years of abuse and entrapment, a victim of IT may feel that the only way she can escape from this horror is to kill her tormenter.

The Nature of Situational Couple Violence (SCV)

Probably the most common type of partner violence does not involve any attempt on the part of either partner to gain general control over the relationship. The violence is situationally provoked that is, the tensions or emotions of a particular encounter lead someone to react with violence. Intimate relationships, inevitably involve conflicts, and in some relationships, one or more of those conflicts may escalate to violence. The violence may be minor and singular, with one argument at some point in the relationship escalating to the level that someone pushes or slaps the other, is immediately remorseful, apologizes and never does it again. Or it could be a chronic problem, with one or both partners frequently resorting to violence, minor or severe.

The motives for such violence vary. A physical reaction might feel like the only way one's extreme anger or frustration can be expressed. It may well be intended to do serious injury as an expression of anger. It may primarily be an attempt to get the attention of a partner who doesn't seem to be listening. Or there could be a control motive involved, albeit not one that is part of a general pattern of coercive control. One partner may simply find that the argument is not going well for him or her and decide that one way to win this is to get physical.

The critical distinctions among types of violence have to do with general patterns of power and control, not with the ostensible motives for specific incidents of violence. Thus, many of the separate violent incidents of SCV may look exactly like those involved in IT or VR. The difference is in the general power and control dynamic of the relationship, not in the nature of any one assault. If it appears that neither partner is generally trying to control the other, that is, it is not the case that the relationship involves the use of a range of control tactics by one or both of the partners, then it is SCV. It is simply that one or more disagreements have resulted in violence. The violence may even be frequent, if the situation that provokes the violence is recurring, as when one partner frequently feels that the other is flirting, and the confrontations over that issue regularly lead one or the other of them to lash out. The violence may also be quite severe, including even homicide. What makes it SCV is that it is rooted in the events of a particular situation rather than in a relationship-wide attempt to control.

How Do We Know About These Types?

The descriptions of the three types of partner violence are derived from 30 years of social science research on violence between intimate partners, most of which did not make the distinctions that I describe. How, then, can we manage to come to conclusions about these different types of part-

ner violence from a research literature that doesn't distinguish among them? There are two answers to that question. First, some of the more recent research does operationalize the distinctions. Second, there are some "tricks" that can be used to tease information regarding the types out of the "old style" research that didn't make distinctions. One involves the sampling biases noted earlier. The violence in general survey research is almost entirely men's and women's SCV. Thus, any survey research that compares violent with nonviolent men or women – or victims with nonvictims – can be reliably assumed to tell us mostly about SCV. In contrast, the violence in agency samples is almost all men's IT and women's VR. Thus, agency-based studies can be used to inform us regarding those two types of violence. The second trick we can use with the old literature is to look for patterns that are associated with violence that shows the characteristics of each of the types. Here is an example. Violence that is frequent and severe is most likely to be IT. Violence that is infrequent and mild is more likely to be SCV. Thus, if studies show that anger-management therapy is only effective in the treatment of men whose violence is infrequent and mild, we have indirect support for the conclusion that it is effective for SCV but not effective for IT.

Correlates of the Types of Intimate Partner Violence

Here we face something of a dilemma. There is no shortage of comprehensive causal models, inventories, reviews, or meta-analyses of correlates of intimate partner violence (K. L. Anderson, 1997; Archer, 2000; Hotaling & Sugarman, 1986, 1990; Jasinski & Williams, 1998; O'Leary & Slep, 2003; Stith et al., 2000; Sugarman, Aldarondo, & Boney-McCoy, 1996; Sugarman & Frankel, 1996; Sugarman & Hotaling, 1989, 1997), but none of these papers or books makes the distinctions among types of intimate partner violence discussed earlier. Thus, we cannot be certain about which generalizations apply to which types of violence. For example, although there are perhaps hundreds of studies that purport to show that women are as violent as men in intimate relationships (Archer, 2000; Straus, 1999), a breakdown of IPV into types (Johnson, 2001) indicates that in heterosexual relationships, IT is almost entirely male perpetrated, violent resistors are almost all women, and SCV is not heavily gendered (at least not in terms of incidence, as discussed later).

Antecedents

GENDER

Let me begin with a reminder: The previous discussion indicates that perhaps the most important antecedent of IPV is gender, with IT being almost entirely male, VR female, and SCV more gender symmetric. Within each of these types, men's violence is more frequent and more severe than women's. It would not be wise, however, to think of gender only as a characteristic of perpetrators and victims of IPV. For over 2 decades now, feminist sociologists have admonished us to treat gender as an institution, not an individual characteristic. It has manifestations at all levels of social organization from the most macro of organizational contexts through the "meso" level of social interaction on down to the individual level of identities and attitudes (Ferree, Lorber, & Hess, 2000; Risman, 2004).

Thus, the role of gender in IPV is almost impossibly complex. First, sex–gender is important in heterosexual relationships simply because of average sex differences in size and strength. Second, the gendering of individual attitudes, values, knowledge, and skills affect partners' goals in their relationships and the means they use to attain them. Third, individual partners' attitudes regarding differences between men and women and the role of gender in relationships each play a part in the development of any particular relationship. Fourth, intimate partnership norms are heavily gendered, certainly in the midst of considerable historical change but rooted in a patriarchal heterosexual model that validates men's power (Dobash

& Dobash, 1979, 1992; Yllö & Bograd, 1988; Yllö & Straus, 1990). These norms affect the internal functioning of all relationships, regardless of the individual attitudes of the partners. For example, when a couple sets out to plan a wedding, they find their individual interests embedded in a larger social context that cannot be ignored. Finally, the gendering of the social context within which the relationship is embedded affects the resources the partners can draw on to shape the relationship and to cope with or escape from the violence. As an example, consider the major changes in the way the criminal justice system has reacted to domestic violence over the last 30 years (Dobash & Dobash, 1992).

There certainly is not enough space here to explicate the complex interaction of these gender-related factors in the shaping of different types of heterosexual IPV, but I would like to at least provide a few examples. First, in IT, the use of violence as one tactic in an attempt to exercise general control over one's partner requires more than violence. It requires a credible threat of a damaging violent response to noncompliance. Such a threat would be more credible coming from a man than a woman because of both the size difference and the cultures of masculinity and femininity. Second, with regard to SCV, the damage will be greater when perpetrated by a larger against a smaller partner (Felson, 1996), and the cultures of masculinity and femininity ensure that whatever the level of violence, its meaning will differ greatly depending on the gender of the perpetrator (Straus, 1999). Third, in cases of either IT or SCV, the reactions of criminal justice personnel are likely to differ as a function of the gender structure of the organization to which the officers belong, as well as the gender of the perpetrator (Buzawa & Buzawa, 1996).

Finally, much of this discussion of gender is relevant only to heterosexual relationships. In same-sex relationships, some aspects of gender will still be important (e.g., gender differences in individual attitudes and skills), others will be largely irrelevant (e.g., heterosexual relationship norms), and

THE CAMBRIDGE HANDBOOK OF PERSONAL RELATIONSHIPS

some will play themselves out in quite different ways (e.g., sex differences in size and strength will not be as likely to create differences within couples). Although we know considerably less about same-sex relationships than we do about heterosexual relationships, there is a growing literature that is important not only in its own right, but also because it sheds light on some of the inadequacies of theories rooted in research on heterosexual relationships (Renzetti, 1992, 2002; Renzetti & Miley, 1996).

PERSONALITY AND ATTITUDES

The work of Amy Holtzworth-Munroe and others on male perpetrators of IPV (Gondolf, 1988; Hamberger, Lohr, Bonge, & Tolin, 1996; Holtzworth-Munroe, 2002; Holtzworth-Munroe, Meehan, Herron, Rehman, & Stuart, 2000, 2003; Jacobson & Gottman, 1998; Ornduff, Kelsey, & O'Leary, 1995; Saunders, 1992, 1996; Waltz, Babcock, Jacobson, & Gottman, 2000) converges on the identification of two types of intimate terrorists. Holtzworth-Munroe referred to them as "borderline–dysphoric" and "generally violent–antisocial," whereas Jacobson and Gottman use the more colorful terms, "pit bulls" and "cobras." (I am going to call them "dependent intimate terrorists" and "antisocial intimate terrorists.") The dependent intimate terrorists score high on measures of borderline personality organization, dependency, and jealousy and seem to need general control to assuage their fear of losing their partner. The antisocial intimate terrorists are more generally violent and involved with delinquent peers, substance abuse, and criminal behavior; they are broadly willing to employ violence to have their way in many contexts. Both of these types score high on impulsivity, acceptance of violence, and hostile attitudes toward women and low on measures of social skills (Holtzworth-Munroe et al., 2000). The finding that intimate terrorists score high on hostility toward women is consistent with the meta-analysis of Sugarman and Frankel (1996) and of course harkens back to my discussion of gender as an institution. Sugarman and Frankel

found that intimate terrorists score higher on traditional gender attitudes than nonviolent men (effect size = 0.80 for studies that are probably dominated by IT, 0.54 when all studies are considered). Unfortunately, this important meta-analysis's support for feminist theory is often missed because Sugarman and Frankel's conclusions and abstract dismiss the finding.

SCV is included in Holtzworth-Munroe's work in what she calls the "family-only" cluster of perpetrators, a group of violent men whose violence is less severe than that of the intimate terrorists and who do not differ in personality or attitudes from nonviolent men. This pattern is supported by Sugarman and Frankel's finding that there are no differences in gender attitudes between violent and nonviolent men in studies that are probably dominated by SCV. Thus, it is clear that some elements of gender are *not* implicated in SCV.

As far as I know, there is no research on personality or attitudinal correlates of women's SCV, but Murray Straus has written a useful discussion of factors that might increase women's likelihood of being violent towards their partners. These factors include many features of gender as an institution, such as cultural norms regarding femininity, gender norms for conflict, sources of identity, and reactions of the criminal justice system (Straus, 1999, p. 31), some of which influence the personality and attitudes of women.

SO-CALLED INTERGENERATIONAL TRANSMISSION

Although childhood experiences of family violence are often touted as "the most widely accepted risk marker for the occurrence of partner violence" (Kantor & Jasinski, 1998, p. 16), in fact most studies find effect sizes on the order of 0.17 (Stith et al., 2000). It appears that "transmission" is hardly an appropriate metaphor (see also Johnson & Ferraro, 2000). However, a careful look at the Stith et al. meta-analysis and some recent research suggests that perhaps this is another case of misspecification through aggregation. A case *can* be made for a moderate effect of childhood experiences on IT and a minimal effect on SCV as follows. Because the literature is dominated by general surveys, the overall average effect size, which is quite small, reflects the impact of childhood experiences on SCV. However, Stith et al. find an interaction with sample type, in which the effect is much stronger (0.35) for agency samples, that is samples dominated by IT. More direct evidence comes from Johnson and Cares's (2004) finding of odds ratios of 2.40 (*ns*) and 7.51 ($p < 0.01$) for the effects of men's childhood experiences on SCV and IT, respectively.

SOCIAL CLASS AND OTHER ANTECEDENTS

Other widely accepted risk markers include occupation, education, race and ethnicity, marital status, age, and alcohol abuse, among others. However, the research that establishes these variables' relationships to IPV does not distinguish among IT, VR, and SCV. In some of my own unpublished analyses, I have found that once again, there are important differences among types of violence. For example, income is negatively related to SCV but not IT. Education is negatively related to both IT and SCV. Race is related to SCV (with African Americans at greater risk than Whites) but not IT. Age is negatively related to IT but not SCV. It is clear that we need research that differentiates among types of IPV before we can make useful statements about antecedents.

The Nature of the Relationship

CHARACTERISTICS OF THE VIOLENT ACTS

This is yet another area in which we clearly need further research. Johnson's (1995) review of the literature on men's violence indicated that IT (compared with SCV) involves a much higher average per-couple frequency of incidents, a much higher likelihood of escalation and therefore more severe violence, and a lower likelihood of mutual violence within an incident – all supported by data in Britain and the United States that operationalize the distinctions

(Graham-Kevan & Archer, 2003; Johnson, 2001).

What about women's violence? Women's violence in intimate relationships is almost entirely SCV. From reviews of the many studies done with general survey samples, which we can assume involve violence that is mostly SCV, a number of scholars have come to the oft-heard conclusion that women are as violent as men (Archer, 2000; Straus, 1999). This conclusion, however, is based on the virtually meaningless criterion of whether the respondent has been violent at least once within the time frame covered by the survey. These same scholars all agree that men's violence in these general survey samples (thus, SCV) involves more incidents, and produces more injuries and more fear than does women's violence. Thus, even with respect to SCV, men are, in fact, more violent than women.

Most of the remaining women's IPV is violent resistance, and what we know about that comes primarily from research using agency samples. That research indicates that, although many women dealing with an intimate terrorist partner do at some point respond with violence, most of them ultimately desist as they find that violence only puts them at further risk (Dasgupta, 2002; Gondolf & Fisher, 1988; Swan, 2000; Swan & Snow, 2002). However, there is a small but highly visible number of women entrapped in such relationships who finally resort to lethal violence to escape from their tormentor (Browne, 1987; O'Keefe, 1997; Roberts, 1996; Walker, 1989).[2]

OTHER CHARACTERISTICS OF THE RELATIONSHIP

The general dynamic of IT and violent resistance is captured in the many qualitative accounts of such relationships to be found in the literature, most of them involving interviews with either women contacted through agencies or volunteers who have left their abusive partners (Chang, 1996; Dobash & Dobash, 1979; Ferraro, 1996, 1997; Giles-Sims, 1983; Kirkwood, 1993; Pagelow, 1981; Pence & Paymar, 1993; Renzetti, 1992; Sev'er, 2002). Because of the broadly controlling behavior of intimate terrorists, the general characteristics of these relationships are shaped in large part by the intimate terrorist rather than the resistor. In the beginning, such relationships seem to follow a cycle identified early on by Lenore Walker (1979), a cycle in which the tension in the relationship builds until the terrorist erupts into violence, and the violence is followed by explanations, justifications, apologies, and romantic and attentive behavior (the so-called honeymoon stage). Eventually, the tension begins to build again, and the cycle repeats itself. More recent research suggests that in many cases the honeymoon stage becomes shorter and shorter over time, until there is no longer any honeymoon. The relationship becomes one of constant tension and attempts by the victim to attempt to figure out how to prevent or minimize the impending and inevitable violence.

Although this pattern gives the intimate terrorist considerable power in the relationship, it would be unwise to see him as entirely in control and his partner as merely a victim. Victims often do change their behavior in line with the intimate terrorists' interests in order to attempt to avoid or minimize violence, and sometimes they even seem to accept their partner's blaming of the violence on their own inadequacies as wives or mothers. However, over time the women involved in such relationships come to see the situation for what it is and turn to other means of coping with violence, including gathering the resources that will allow them to take themselves and their children out of the relationship safely (Campbell & Soeken, 1999; Campbell & Weber, 2000; Ferraro, 1997). These reactions of victims (some of whom become violent resistors) are discussed in the section on consequences of violence for the relationship.

Returning to our discussion of intimate terrorists, there is an important complication when it comes to the relationships in which they are involved. As noted earlier, the work of Holtzworth-Munroe and others indicates that there are two major types of intimate terrorists, and we actually know little about the differences between dependent intimate terrorists and antisocial intimate terrorists. It is likely that, beyond the general strategies of control that they share, their relationships with their partners are quite different. Dependent intimate terrorists are extremely emotionally dependent on the partners whom they abuse, become emotional basket cases during arguments, and are highly tenacious, willing to do anything to keep their partner (Jacobson & Gottman, 1998). Antisocial intimate terrorists are coldhearted men and not necessarily strongly emotionally tied to their partner. Although there is evidence that the dynamics and development of their relationships with their partners look quite different, we need considerably more research before we'll know exactly what the differences are.

The situation is even more unknown and probably more complicated with regard to SCV. The problem with this literature (as with many others) is that we have become so focused on averages and on "explaining" variance that we have paid no attention at all to the likely possibility that our general survey samples capture a number of types of SCV that involve quite different relationships. We will have to settle for a brief analysis of some of the major issues that need to be pursued. The major question is "What is the situational dynamic that produces the violence?"

My thoughts turn first to the large category of "violent relationships" in which there has been one and only one incident. Someone needs to ask those people what happened, and to look at characteristics of their relationships. I imagine that what we will find is that they range widely on any relationship variable we care to look at. There simply was one aberrant incident that could have happened in almost any relationship. That doesn't mean that there are no interesting questions to be pursued with regard to this group. We would like to know how they handled the incident, whether it had any short-term or long-term effects on their relationship, whether they took any steps to make sure it would never happen again, and so on.

Moving on to relationships in which there are multiple incidents of SCV, we might pursue what have been found to be some of the major correlates of IPV. A brief list would include alcohol and other substance abuse (Heyman, O'Leary, & Jouriles, 1995; Hutchison, 1999; Kantor, 1996; Moore, Greenfield, Wilson, & Kok, 1997; O'Leary & Schumacher, 2003; Stuart et al., 2002), jealousy and infidelity (Barnett, Martinez, & Bluestein, 1995; Dutton, Van Ginkel, & Landolt, 1996; Wilson & Daly, 1993), poverty (Benson, Fox, DeMaris, & Wyk, 2000; Gelles, 1993), and various communication patterns and skills (Cahn & Lloyd, 1996; Feldman & Ridley, 2000; Holtzworth-Munroe, Smutzler, & Stuart, 1998; Infante, 1989; Lloyd & Emery, 2000; Ridley & Feldman, 2003; Rogge & Bradbury, 1999). It is likely, however, that each of these, although a central factor in some relationships, plays no role at all in others. This is not a small matter, as success of various interventions would vary greatly depending on whether the chronic violence was a function of one partner's anger management problems, or the daily stresses of living in poverty, or the aggressiveness associated with alcohol abuse, and so on.

Consequences of the Violence

Most of the research on consequences is found in the feminist literature using agency samples, and therefore provides information regarding IT or VR. There are, however, some studies that might give us some insight into the impact of SCV, including a few that do make distinctions, and a number that use general survey data that are probably dominated by SCV.

HEALTH CONSEQUENCES

More than 1,000 women are killed by their male partners in the United States each year – mostly IT – and a little under 300 men are killed by their female partners – mostly VR (U.S. Federal Bureau of Investigation, 2003). These numbers are down considerably from the early 1990s, with the murders of husbands and boyfriends declining first and most steeply as the battered women's movement provided alternatives to women who had formerly been trapped in intimate terrorist relationships. More recently there have been somewhat smaller but consistent decreases for femicide, perhaps because preventive education is making a difference, but also because the movement is helping women to escape from intimate terrorists before they are murdered.

INJURIES

We have fairly good information regarding injuries incurred in IT and SCV. From agency studies, we know that the likelihood of serious injury is high for women experiencing IT (Campbell, 2002; Cantos, Neidig, & O'Leary, 1994). From the few studies operationalizing the types, we also know that average seriousness of injuries is clearly greater for IT than it is for SCV (Graham-Kevan & Archer, 2003; Johnson, 1999, 2000; Johnson, Conklin, & Menon, 2002; Johnson & Leone, in press; Leone, Johnson, Cohan, & Lloyd, 2004). Data from many general survey studies of IPV indicate that women sustain more severe injuries than do men in SCV (Archer, 2000; Straus, 1990). It is clear from qualitative agency data that violent resistance among women does sometimes inflict injury on their partners. However, if we can assume that couples in mandated domestic violence programs are mostly involved in male IT and female VR, then Cantos's (1994) data indicate that violent resistors are inflicting a much lower level of injury than are their intimate terrorist partners.

GENERAL HEALTH, INCLUDING
PSYCHOLOGICAL HEALTH

Campbell's general review (2002) concludes that "Increased health problems such as ... chronic pain, gastrointestinal, and gynecological signs including sexually-transmitted diseases, depression, and post-traumatic stress disorder are well documented by controlled research in abused women in various settings." Golding's (1999) meta-analysis is more specific: "The weighted mean prevalence of mental health problems among battered women was 47.6% in 18 studies of depression, 17.9% in 13 studies of suicidality, 63.8% in 11 studies of posttraumatic stress disorder (PTSD)." She also concluded, however, that these findings are variable across studies; I would suggest that this may be because they involve different mixes of SCV and IT. Two studies that do distinguish between IT and SCV indicate that effects on general health, depression, and posttraumatic stress disorder are minimal for SCV (Johnson & Leone, in press; Leone et al., 2004).

EFFECTS ON THE RELATIONSHIP

IPV of any sort is destructive to the relationship, as has been shown in a number of studies using general samples (for two longitudinal studies, see Rogge & Bradbury, 1999; Testa & Leonard, 2001). The effects of IT, however, are much more dramatic than those of SCV (Johnson et al., 2002). Although it is clear from decades of studies with agency samples that most women experiencing IT do eventually manage to escape (e.g., Campbell, Miller, Cardwell, & Belknap, 1994; Herbert, Silver, & Ellard, 1991), we continue to see articles with titles such as, "Why Do They Stay?" even in cases in which two thirds of the women had in fact already left their abusive partner (Herbert et al., 1991). Three explanations for this contradiction come to mind. First, I suppose that some writers simply feel that asking why they stay seems like a more interesting question than asking why or how they leave. Second, many of the samples studied include a large number of cases of SCV, few of which are serious enough to prompt anyone to consider ending the relationship. Third, and most important, IT almost always involves not only abuse, but entrapment (Johnson, 1998; Landenburger, 1989; Richie, 1996; Rosen & Stone, 1993). Leaving or threatening to leave one's abusive partner places women and their children at great risk of stalking, assault, and murder (Burgess, Harner, Baker, Hartman, & Lole, 2001; Hardesty, 2002; Morton, Runyan, Moracco, & Butts, 1998; Wilson, Daly, & Wright, 1993). As a result, leaving an IT relationship involves a complex process of gathering the information and resources required to allow a woman and her children to leave

the relationship *safely* (Campbell, Rose, Kub, & Nedd, 1998; Chang, 1996; Choice & Lamke, 1999; Kirkwood, 1993; Sev'er, 2002). Women experiencing IT go through a process of learning that the violence will be continuing, interpreting the causes of the violence, trying to cope with and stop the violence within the relationship, deciding it is necessary to leave, and gathering the necessary resources (M. A. Anderson et al., 2003; Arias & Pape, 1999; Barnett & LaViolette, 2000; Burke, Gielen, McDonnell, O'Campo, & Maman, 2001; Carlson, 1997; Choice & Lamke, 1997; Choice & Lamke, 1999; Merritt Gray & Wuest, 1995; Rose, Campbell, & Kub, 2000; Rosen & Stith, 1995; Sullivan & Davidson, 1991).

Lacunae

Much as I hate to end this section weakly, I have to say that we know almost nothing about the nature of or correlates of VR or SCV. Although there is some research regarding the impact of VR on the IT perpetrator's violence, addressing the question of whether violent resistance helps or makes things worse, there is very little on the conditions under which women do resist physically or on the impact of that resistance on the individuals involved or on their relationship. What little research there is focuses on the extreme cases in which women murder their abusive partners (Browne, 1987; O'Keefe, 1997; Roberts, 1996; Walker, 1989). As for SCV, what we think we know comes mostly from large-scale general surveys, which (a) involve an unknown mix of IT, VR, and SCV and (b) include none of the qualitative data that would provide real insight into the individual and relational dynamics of such relationships.

Violence Against Intimates Other Than One's Partner

Of course, there is violence against intimates other than one's partner. The 1985 National Family Violence Survey in the United States indicated, for example, that within a 1-year time frame, nearly 100% of U.S. parents had hit their children (aged 0–17) and 11% had used what the authors call "severe" violence (Straus & Gelles, 1990, p. 97). Furthermore, 80% of U.S. children had been violent toward their own brother or sister, 53% severely so, and 18% had been violent toward a parent. I am a bit surprised to find that there is essentially no recent literature on child violence toward parents and little on sibling violence (Duncan, 1999; Fair Brodeske, 2002; Wiehe, 1997), but reviews of the literature on parental violence toward children can be found under the rubrics of child abuse (Flett & Hewitt, 2002; Halperin, 1995; Hegar, Zuravin, & Orme, 1994; Larzelere & Johnson, 1999) and corporal punishment (Gershoff, 2002; Straus & Donnelly, 1994; Straus & Stewart, 1999).

The theoretical and empirical evidence for the importance of distinguishing among types of violence between partners on the basis of the control context of the violence is compelling. What about other types of personal relationships? In 2001, one of my students wrote an outstanding paper on violence in parent–child relationships, and I can do no better on this issue than to quote her:

> *The literature on this issue suggests that there are two types of parent-to-child abuse. The first is set in a context of general control, in which the parent seeks a wide scope of power over the child's life. This is comparable to Johnson's intimate terrorism. . . . The second type of child abuse is a result of a parent lashing out in anger or frustration, which is similar to Johnson's situational couple violence category. (Sobolewski, 2001, p. 27)*

Of course, the use of violence to control children is seen by many parents as a legitimate tool of socialization, to be used in the child's best interests. Sobolewski pointed out, however, that a number of theoretical statements and empirical pieces in the parenting literature identify *parent-centered* violence toward children in types that appear to correspond in many ways to IT and SCV. For example, Gough and Reavey (1997) identified three types of parental rationales

for violence,[3] two of which were parent-centered rationales, one which they call "individual (power assertive)," the other "cathartic (need relief)." The similarity to intimate terrorism and situational couple violence is striking (see also Dailey, 1979; Oldershaw, Walters, & Kordich, 1986). The third rationale is a "pedagogical" child-centered rationale that would hardly be considered appropriate for partner violence, although we might note that the traditional rationale for the "chastisement of wives" is rooted in the treatment of women as somewhat childlike and in need of direction from their husbands (Dobash & Dobash, 1979).

One other example of parallels in the parent–child literature will have to suffice to make my case here. Sobolewski (2001) pointed out that a number of studies seem to indicate that the type of sample can be important in terms of the type of parental violence that is detected, with general samples finding more cathartic violence (Bluestone & Tamis-LeMonda, 1999; Petersen, Ewigman, & Vandiver, 1994; Rodriguez & Green, 1997) and agency samples finding more power assertive violence (Oldershaw et al., 1986).

Conclusion

In thinking about directions for future research, I find myself drawn to a jigsaw puzzle metaphor. Many small pieces of the puzzle have yet to be filled in, pieces that will eventually fit together to give us the big picture. These small pieces involve all of the questions we have been asking for decades – questions now reframed in terms of different types of intimate partner violence. Is alcohol implicated in violent resistance in the same way it is implicated in intimate terrorism or situational couple violence? Is the impact of parental situational couple violence on children anything like the impact of parental intimate terrorism? Might couples counseling actually be a viable strategy for intervention in situational couple violence in ways that it is not for intimate terrorism? Is socioeconomic status an important factor in intimate terrorism, or only in situational couple violence?

Although we could go on and on listing the little questions, let me suggest that they can be effectively organized in terms of major areas of the big picture, that is, the major types of IPV. We do know a lot about intimate terrorism – from decades of quantitative and qualitative feminist research and activism. This section of the picture is held together by a dominant theme of gender – gender as an institution in the patriarchal norms of heterosexual relationships that have historically given men the right to control their wives (Dobash & Dobash, 1979; Wood, 2001); gender as it is embodied in individual differences such as male willingness to use violence to assert their masculinity (Wood, 2004), and in sex differences in size and strength that make male violence effective (Felson, 1996); and gender in organized societal reactions to intimate terrorism, reactions that have changed dramatically as a result of the second wave of the Western women's movement (Dobash & Dobash, 1992).

We know little, however, about violent resistance. Perhaps the silver lining in the gender symmetry fiasco is the renewed attention to the nature of women's intimate partner violence, including violent resistance (Renzetti, 2002; Straus, 1999; Swan, 2000; Swan & Snow, 2002). In general, however, feminist research has been focused so heavily on the behavior of male intimate terrorists that little attention has been paid to the dynamics of violent resistance. Although there is a small literature on women who kill their abusive partners, it is clear that there is a great need for research on the less dramatic violent resistance that characterizes most women's use of violence as a means of coping with an intimate terrorist.

With respect to situational couple violence, I would argue that despite 3 decades of research in the family violence tradition with large-scale survey samples that are probably dominated by SCV, we actually know much less about SCV than we do about IT. Perhaps we *can* simply take all of the family violence survey research, assume that

the results apply to SCV, and make our usual generalizations – but restricting them to situational couple violence. The example of intergenerational "transmission" (with the weak effects typically found in survey research appearing to be characteristic of SCV) suggests that such a strategy might work. I fear, however, that there may be a problem of types-within-types that will plague us with respect to SCV. We do not at this point have the body of qualitative research that we need to identify the interpersonal dynamics involved in types of SCV as different as (a) frequent, dangerous violence from one partner; (b) a single aberrant incident; and (c) a general pattern of mutual combat.

The big picture, therefore, is both disheartening and exciting. On one hand, the clear need to make major distinctions among types of IPV calls into question a massive literature that has produced glib overgeneralizations. There is no simple way to evaluate the distortions of decades of aggregating essentially different phenomena. On the other hand, we may be on the cusp of a slew of major breakthroughs such as the one in the gender symmetry debate. We are fortunate to be working at a time in which diligent attention to differences among the types of IPV is likely to produce major increases in the explanatory power of our theories and the effectiveness of our interventions.

Acknowledgment

Thank you to Maureen Mulderig for her thoughtful reactions to previous versions of this chapter.

Footnotes

1. I am going to use gendered pronouns here because the vast majority of intimate terrorists are men terrorizing female partners. That does not mean that women are *never* intimate terrorists. There are a small number of women who do terrorize their male partners (Steinmetz, 1977–1978), and there are also women in

same-sex relationships who terrorize their female partners (Renzetti & Miley, 1996).

2. There is so little IT among heterosexual women that we know very little about it, although I do have some unpublished data suggesting that the frequency and level of violence in women's IT is less than it is for men.

3. They actually identified four, but one of them is less a rationale than an explanation for violence – that the respondent learned to use corporal punishment from his or her parents.

References

Anderson, K. L. (1997). Gender, status, and domestic violence: An integration of feminist and family violence approaches. *Journal of Marriage and the Family, 59*, 655–669.

Anderson, M. A., Gillig, P. M., Sitaker, M., McCloskey, K., Malloy, K., & Grigsby, N. (2003). Why doesn't she just leave?: A descriptive study if victim reported impediments to her safety. *Journal of Family Violence, 18*, 151–155.

Archer, J. (2000). Sex differences in aggression between heterosexual partners: A meta-analytic review. *Psychological Bulletin, 126*, 651–680.

Arias, I., & Pape, K. T. (1999). Psychological abuse: Implications for adjustment and commitment to leave violent partners. *Violence and Victims, 14*, 55–67.

Barnett, O. W., & LaViolette, A. D. (2000). *It could happen to anyone: Why battered women stay* (2nd ed.). Thousand Oaks, CA: Sage.

Barnett, O. W., Martinez, T. E., & Bluestein, B. W. (1995). Jealousy and romantic attachment in maritally violent and nonviolent men. *Journal of Interpersonal Violence, 10*, 473–486.

Benson, M. L., Fox, G. L., DeMaris, A., & Wyk, J. V. (2000). Violence in families: The intersection of race, poverty, and community context. In G. L. Fox & M. L. Benson (Eds.), *Families, crime, and criminal justice* (pp. 91–109). New York: JAI.

Bluestone, C., & Tamis-LeMonda, C. S. (1999). Correlated of parenting styles in predominantly working and middle-class African American mothers. *Journal of Marriage and the Family, 61*, 881–893.

Browne, A. (1987). *When battered women kill.* New York: Free Press.

Burgess, A. W., Harner, H., Baker, T., Hartman, C. R., & Lole, C. (2001). Batterers' stalking patterns. *Journal of Family Violence, 16*, 309–321.

Burke, J. G., Gielen, A. C., McDonnell, K. A., O'Campo, P., & Maman, S. (2001). The process of ending abuse in intimate relationships: A qualitative exploration of the transtheoretical model. *Violence Against Women, 7*, 1144–1163.

Buzawa, E. S., & Buzawa, C. G. (1996). *Domestic violence: The criminal justice response.* Thousand Oaks, CA: Sage.

Cahn, D. D., & Lloyd, S. A. (Eds.). (1996). *Family violence from a communication perspective.* Thousand Oaks, CA: Sage.

Campbell, J. C. (2002). Health consequences of intimate partner violence. *Lancet, 359*, 1331–1336.

Campbell, J. C., Miller, P., Cardwell, M. M., & Belknap, R. A. (1994). Relationship status of battered women over time. *Journal of Family Violence, 9*, 99–111.

Campbell, J. C., Rose, L., Kub, J., & Nedd, D. (1998). Voices of strength and resistance: A contextual and longitudinal analysis of women's responses to battering. *Journal of Interpersonal Violence, 13*, 743–762.

Campbell, J. C., & Soeken, K. L. (1999). Women's responses to battering over time: An analysis of change. *Journal of Interpersonal Violence, 14*, 21–40.

Campbell, J. C., & Weber, N. (2000). An empirical test of a self-care model of women's responses to battering. *Nursing Science Quarterly, 13*, 45–53.

Cantos, A., Neidig, P. H., & O'Leary, K. D. (1994). Injuries of women and men in a treatment program for domestic violence. *Journal of Family Violence, 9*, 113–124.

Carlson, B. (1997). A stress and coping approach to intervention with abused women. *Family Relations, 46*, 291–298.

Chang, V. N. (1996). *I just lost myself: Psychological abuse of women in marriage.* Westport, CT: Praeger.

Choice, P., & Lamke, L. K. (1997). A conceptual approach to understanding abused women's stay/leave decisions. *Journal of Family Issues, 18*, 290–314.

Choice, P., & Lamke, L. K. (1999). Stay/leave decision-making processes in abusive dating relationships. *Personal Relationships, 6*, 351–367.

Dailey, T. B. (1979). Parental power breeds violence against children. *Sociological Focus, 12*, 311–322.

Dasgupta, S. D. (2002). A framework for understanding women's use of nonlethal violence in intimate heterosexual relationships. *Violence against Women, 8*, 1364–1389.

Dobash, R. E., & Dobash, R. P. (1979). *Violence against wives: A case against patriarchy.* New York: Free Press.

Dobash, R. E., & Dobash, R. P. (1992). *Women, violence, and social change.* New York: Routledge.

Duncan, R. D. (1999). Peer and sibling aggression: An investigation of intra- and extra-familial bullying. *Journal of Interpersonal Violence, 14*, 871–886.

Dutton, D. G., Van Ginkel, C., & Landolt, M. A. (1996). Jealousy, intimate abusiveness, and intrusiveness. *Journal of Family Violence, 11*, 411–423.

Fair Brodeske, L. J. (2002). *The comparison of mothers' perceptions of physically violent behavior between elementary school-age boys versus girls in sibling, friend, and acquaintance relationships.* Unpublished doctoral dissertation, Alliant International University, San Diego.

Feldman, C. M., & Ridley, C. A. (2000). The role of conflict-based communication responses and outcomes in male domestic violence toward female partners. *Journal of Social and Personal Relationships, 17*, 552–573.

Felson, R. B. (1996). Big people hit little people: Sex differences in physical power and interpersonal violence. *Criminology, 34*, 433–452.

Ferraro, K. J. (1996). The dance of dependency: A genealogy of domestic violence discourse. *Hypatia, 11*, 77–91.

Ferraro, K. J. (1997). Battered women: Strategies for survival. In A. Carderelli (Ed.), *Violence among intimate partners: Patterns, causes, and effects* (pp. 124–140). New York: Macmillan.

Ferree, M. M., Lorber, J., & Hess, B. B. (2000). Introduction. In M. M. Ferree, J. Lorber, & B. B. Hess (Eds.), *Revisioning gender* (pp. xv–xxxvi). Walnut Creek, CA: Alatamira.

Flett, G. L., & Hewitt, P. L. (2002). Personality factors and substance abuse in relationship violence and child abuse: A review and theoretical analysis. In C. Wekerle & A. M. Wall (Eds.), *The violence and addiction equation: Theoretical and clinical issues in substance abuse and relation-ship violence* (pp. 64–97). New York: Brunner Routledge.

Gelles, R. J. (1993). Through a sociological lens: Social structure and family violence. In R. J. Gelles & D. R. Loseke (Eds.), *Current controversies on family violence.* Thousand Oaks, CA: Sage.

Gershoff, E. T. (2002). Corporal punishment by parents and associated child behaviors and experiences: A meta-analytic and theoretical review. *Psychological Bulletin, 128*, 539–579.

Giles-Sims, J. (1983). *Wife battering: A systems theory approach.* New York: Guilford Press.

Golding, J. M. (1999). Intimate partner violence as a risk factor for mental disorders: A meta-analysis. *Journal of Family Violence, 14*, 99–132.

Gondolf, E. W. (1988). Who are those guys? Toward a behavioral typology of batterers. *Violence and Victims, 3*, 187–203.

Gondolf, E. W., & Fisher, E. R. (1988). *Battered women as survivors: An alternative to treating learned helplessness.* Lexington, MA: Heath.

Gough, B., & Reavey, P. (1997). Parental accounts regarding the physical punishment of children: Discourses of dis/empowerment. *Child Abuse and Neglect, 21*, 417–430.

Graham-Kevan, N., & Archer, J. (2003). Intimate terrorism and common couple violence: A test of Johnson's predictions in four British samples. *Journal of Interpersonal Violence, 18*, 1247–1270.

Halperin, D. S. (1995). Risk factors for child abuse and neglect in human parents: A review of the literature and a single institution experience. In C. R. Pryce & R. D. Martin (Eds.), *Motherhood in human and nonhuman primates: Biosocial determinants* (pp. 125–133). Basel, Switzerland: S. Karger.

Hamberger, L. K., Lohr, J. M., Bonge, D., & Tolin, D. F. (1996). A large sample empirical typology of male spouse abusers and its relationship to dimensions of abuse. *Violence and Victims, 11*, 277–292.

Hardesty, J. L. (2002). Separation assault in the context of postdivorce parenting: An integrative review of the literature. *Violence Against Women, 8*, 597–625.

Hegar, R. L., Zuravin, S. J., & Orme, J. G. (1994). Factors predicting severity of physical child abuse injury: A review of the literature. *Journal of Interpersonal Violence, 9*, 170–183.

Herbert, T. B., Silver, R. C., & Ellard, J. H. (1991). Coping with an abusive relationship: I. How and why do women stay? *Journal of Marriage and the Family, 53*, 311–325.

Heyman, R. E., O'Leary, K. D., & Jouriles, E. N. (1995). Alcohol and aggressive personality styles: Potentiators of serious physical aggression against wives? *Journal of Family Psychology, 9*, 44–57.

Holtzworth-Munroe, A. (2002). Standards for batterer treatment programs: How can research inform our decisions? *Journal of Aggression, Maltreatment and Trauma, 5*, 165–180.

Holtzworth-Munroe, A., Meehan, J. C., Herron, K., Rehman, U., & Stuart, G. L. (2000). Testing the Holtzworth-Munroe and Stuart (1994) batterer typology. *Journal of Consulting and Clinical Psychology, 68*, 1000–1019.

Holtzworth-Munroe, A., Meehan, J. C., Herron, K., Rehman, U., & Stuart, G. L. (2003). Do subtypes of maritally violent men continue to differ over time? *Journal of Consulting and Clinical Psychology, 71*, 728–740.

Holtzworth-Munroe, A., Smutzler, N., & Stuart, G. L. (1998). Demand and withdraw communication among couples experiencing husband violence. *Journal of Consulting and Clinical Psychology, 66*, 731–743.

Hotaling, G. T., & Sugarman, D. B. (1986). An analysis of risk markers in husband to wife violence: The current state of knowledge. *Violence and Victims, 1*, 101–124.

Hotaling, G. T., & Sugarman, D. B. (1990). A risk marker analysis of assaulted wives. *Journal of Family Violence, 5*, 1–13.

Hutchison, I. W. (1999). Alcohol, fear, and woman abuse. *Sex Roles, 40*, 893–920.

Infante, D. A. (1989). Test of an argumentative skill deficiency model of interspousal violence. *Communication Monographs, 56*, 163–177.

Jacobson, N., & Gottman, J. (1998). *When men batter women: New insights into ending abusive relationships*. New York: Simon & Schuster.

Jasinski, J. L., & Williams, L. M. (Eds.). (1998). *Partner violence: A comprehensive review of 20 years of research*. Thousand Oaks, CA: Sage.

Johnson, M. P. (1995). Patriarchal terrorism and common couple violence: Two forms of violence against women. *Journal of Marriage and the Family, 57*, 283–294.

Johnson, M. P. (1998, June). *Commitment and entrapment: Wife-beating in America*. Paper presented at the Ninth International Conference on Personal Relationships, Saratoga Springs, NY.

Johnson, M. P. (1999, November). *Two types of violence against women in the American family: Identifying patriarchal terrorism and common couple violence*. Paper presented at the National Council on Family Relations annual meetings, Irvine, CA.

Johnson, M. P. (2000, November). *Conflict and control: Symmetry and asymmetry in domestic violence*. Paper presented at the National Institute of Justice Gender Symmetry Workshop, Arlington, VA.

Johnson, M. P. (2001). Conflict and control: Symmetry and asymmetry in domestic violence. In A. Booth, A. C. Crouter, & M. Clements (Eds.), *Couples in conflict* (pp. 95–104). Mahwah, NJ: Erlbaum.

Johnson, M. P., & Cares, A. (2004, November). *Effects and noneffects of childhood experiences of family violence on adult partner violence*. Paper presented at the National Council on Family Relations annual meeting, Orlando, FL.

Johnson, M. P., Conklin, V., & Menon, N. (2002, November). *The effects of different types of domestic violence on women: Intimate terrorism vs. situational couple violence*. Paper presented at the National Council on Family Relations annual meetings, Houston, Texas.

Johnson, M. P., & Ferraro, K. J. (2000). Research on domestic violence in the 1990s: Making distinctions. *Journal of Marriage and the Family, 62*, 948–963.

Johnson, M. P., & Leone, J. M. (2005). The differential effects of intimate terrorism and situational couple violence: Findings from the National Violence Against Women Survey. *Journal of Family Issues, 26*, 322–349.

Kantor, G. K. (1996). Alcohol and spousal abuse: Ethnic differences. In M. Galanter (Ed.), *Recent developments in alcoholism*. New York: Plenum Press.

Kantor, G. K., & Jasinski, J. L. (1998). Dynamics and risk factors in partner violence. In J. L. Jasinksi & L. M. Williams (Eds.), *Partner violence: A comprehensive review of 20 years of research* (pp. 1–43). Thousand Oaks, CA: Sage.

Kirkwood, C. (1993). *Leaving abusive partners: From the scars of survival to the wisdom for change*. Newbury Park, CA: Sage.

Klein, R. C. A., & Johnson, M. P. (1997). Strategies of couple conflict. In S. Duck (Ed.), *Handbook of personal relationships: Theory, research, and interventions* (pp. 469–486). New York: Wiley.

Landenburger, K. (1989). A process of entrapment in and recovery from an abusive relationship. *Issues in Mental Health Nursing, 10*, 209–227.

Larzelere, R. E., & Johnson, B. (1999). Evaluations of the effects of Sweden's spanking ban on physical child abuse rates: A literature review. *Psychological Reports, 85*, 381–392.

Leone, J. M., Johnson, M. P., Cohan, C. M., & Lloyd, S. (2004). Consequences of male partner violence for low-income, ethnic women. *Journal of Marriage and Family, 66*, 471–489.

Lloyd, S. A., & Emery, B. C. (2000). The context and dynamics of intimate aggression against women. *Journal of Social and Personal Relationships, 17*, 503–521.

Merritt Gray, M., & Wuest, J. (1995). Counteracting abuse and breaking free: The process of leaving revealed through women's voices. *Health Care for Women International, 16*, 399–412.

Moore, K. J., Greenfield, W. L., Wilson, M., & Kok, A. C. (1997). Toward a taxonomy of batterers. *Families in Society: The Journal of Contemporary Human Services, 78*, 352–360.

Morton, E., Runyan, C. W., Moracco, K. E., & Butts, J. (1998). Partner homicide-suicide involving female homicide victims: A population based study in North Carolina. *Violence and Victims, 13*, 91–106.

O'Keefe, M. (1997). Incarcerated battered women: A comparison of battered women who killed their abusers and those incarcerated for other offenses. *Journal of Family Violence, 12*, 1–19.

Oldershaw, L., Walters, G. C., & Kordich, D. (1986). Control strategies and noncompliance in abusive mother–child dyads: An observational study. *Child Development, 57*, 722–732.

O'Leary, K. D., & Schumacher, J. A. (2003). The association between alcohol use and intimate partner violence: Linear effect, threshold effect, or both? *Addictive Behaviors, 28*, 1575–1585.

O'Leary, K. D., & Slep, A. M. S. (2003). A dyadic longitudinal model of adolescent dating aggression. *Journal of Clinical Child and Adolescent Psychology, 32*, 314–327.

Ornduff, S. R., Kelsey, R. M., & O'Leary, K. D. (1995). What do we know about typologies of batterers? Comment on Gottman et al. (1995). *Journal of Family Psychology, 9*, 249–252.

Pagelow, M. D. (1981). *Woman-battering: Victims and Their Experiences*. Newbury Park, CA: Sage.

Pence, E., & Paymar, M. (1993). *Education Groups for Men Who Batter: The Duluth Model*. New York: Springer.

Petersen, L., Ewigman, B., & Vandiver, T. (1994). Role of parental anger in low income women: Discipline strategy, perceptions of behavior problems, and the need for control. *Journal of Clinical Psychology, 23*, 435–443.

Renzetti, C. M. (1992). *Violent betrayal: Partner abuse in lesbian relationships*. Thousand Oaks, CA: Sage.

Renzetti, C. M. (2002). Special issue: Women's use of violence in intimate relationships, part 2 – Editor's note. *Violence Against Women, 8*, 1419–1419.

Renzetti, C. M., & Miley, C. H. (1996). *Violence in gay and lesbian domestic partnerships*. New York: Haworth Press.

Richie, B. (1996). *Compelled to crime: The gender entrapment of battered Black women*. New York: Routledge.

Ridley, C. A., & Feldman, C. M. (2003). Female domestic violence toward male partners: Exploring conflict responses and outcomes. *Journal of Family Violence, 18*, 157–170.

Risman, B. (2004). Gender as a social structure: Theory wrestling with activism. *Gender and Society, 18*, 429–450.

Roberts, A. R. (1996). Battered women who kill: A comparative study of incarcerated participants with a community sample of battered women. *Journal of Family Violence, 11*, 291–304.

Rodriguez, C. M., & Green, A. J. (1997). Parenting stress and anger expression as predictors of child abuse potential. *Child Abuse and Neglect, 21*, 367–377.

Rogge, R. D., & Bradbury, T. N. (1999). Till violence does us part: The differing roles of communication and aggression in predicting adverse marital outcomes. *Journal of Consulting and Clinical Psychology, 67*, 340–351.

Rose, L. E., Campbell, J., & Kub, J. (2000). The role of social support and family relationships in women's responses to battering. *Health Care for Women International, 21*, 27–39.

Rosen, K. H., & Stith, S. M. (1995). Women terminating abusive dating relationships: A qualitative study. *Journal of Social and Personal Relationships, 12*, 155–160.

Rosen, K. H., & Stone, J. C. (1993, November). *How women become entrapped in violent dating relationships*. Paper presented at the National Council on Family Relations annual meetings, Baltimore, MD.

Saunders, D. G. (1992). A typology of men who batter: Three types derived from cluster analysis. *American Orthopsychiatry, 62*, 264–275.

Saunders, D. G. (1996). Feminist-cognitive-behavioral and process-psychodynamic treatments for men who batter: Interactions of abuser traits and treatment model. *Violence and Victims, 4*, 393–414.

Sev'er, A. (2002). *Fleeing the house of horrors: Women who have left abusive partners*. Toronto: University of Toronto Press.

Sobolewski, J. (2001). *Parental control and children's social position as central features of physical violence against children: An extension of Johnson's typology of domestic violences*. Unpublished manuscript, Pennsylvania State University. University Park, PA.

Steinmetz, S. K. (1977–78). The battered husband syndrome. *Victimology, 2*, 499–509.

Stith, S. M., Rosen, K. H., Middleton, K. A., Busch, A. L., Lundeberg, K., & Carlton, R. P. (2000). The intergenerational transmission of spouse abuse: A meta-analysis. *Journal of Marriage and the Family, 62*, 640–654.

Straus, M. A. (1990). Injury and frequency of assault and the "representative sample fallacy" in measuring wife beating and child abuse. In M. A. Straus & R. J. Gelles (Eds.), *Physical violence in American families: Risk factors and adaptations to violence in 8,145 families* (pp. 75–91). New Brunswick, NJ: Transaction Press.

Straus, M. A. (1999). The controversy over domestic violence by women: A methodological, theoretical, and sociology of science analysis. In X. B. Arriaga & S. Oskamp (Eds.), *Violence in intimate relationships* (pp. 17–44). Thousand Oaks, CA: Sage.

Straus, M. A., & Donnelly, D. A. (1994). *Beating the devil out of them: Corporal punishment in American families*. New York: Lexington.

Straus, M. A., & Gelles, R. J. (1990). How violent are American families? Estimates from the National Family Violence resurvey and other studies. In M. A. Straus & R. J. Gelles (Eds.), *Physical violence in American families: Risk fac-tors and adaptations to violence in 8,145 families* (pp. 95–112). New Brunswick, NJ: Transaction Press.

Straus, M. A., & Stewart, J. H. (1999). Corporal punishment by American parents: National data on prevalence, chronicity, severity, and duration, in relation to child and family characteristics. *Clinical Child and Family Psychology Review, 2*, 55–70.

Stuart, G. L., Ramsey, S. E., Moore, T. M., Kahler, C. W., Farrell, L. E., Recupero, P. R., & Brown, R. A. (2002). Marital violence victimization and perpetration among women substance abusers: A descriptive study. *Violence Against Women, 8*, 934–952.

Sugarman, D. B., Aldarondo, E., & Boney-McCoy, S. (1996). Risk marker analysis of husband-to-wife violence: A continuum of aggression. *Journal of Applied Social Psychology, 26*, 313–337.

Sugarman, D. B., & Frankel, S. L. (1996). Patriarchal ideology and wife-assault: A meta-analytic review. *Journal of Family Violence, 11*, 13–40.

Sugarman, D. B., & Hotaling, G. T. (1989). Dating violence: Prevalence, context, and risk markers. In M. A. Pirog-Good & J. E. Stets (Eds.), *Violence in dating relationships: Emerging social issues* (pp. 3–32). New York: Praeger.

Sugarman, D. B., & Hotaling, G. T. (1997). Intimate violence and social desirability: A meta-analytic review. *Journal of Interpersonal Violence, 12*, 275–290.

Sullivan, C. M., & Davidson, W. S. (1991). The provision of advocacy services to women leaving abusive partners: An examination of short-term effects. *American Journal of Community Psychology, 19*, 953–960.

Swan, S. C. (2000). *Women who fight back: The development of a theory of women's use of violence in intimate relationships*. Paper presented at the National Institute of Justice Gender Symmetry Workshop, Arlington, VA.

Swan, S. C., & Snow, D. L. (2002). A typology of women's use of violence in intimate relationships. *Violence against Women, 8*, 286–319.

Testa, M., & Leonard, K. E. (2001). The impact of marital aggression on women's psychological and marital functioning in a newlywed sample. *Journal of Family Violence, 16*, 115–130.

U.S. Federal Bureau of Investigation. (2003). *Crime in the States 2002: Uniform Crime Reports*. Washington, DC: U.S. Government Printing Office.

Walker, L. E. (1979). *The battered woman*. New York: Harper & Row.

Walker, L. E. (1989). *Terrifying love: Why battered women kill and how society responds*. New York: Harper & Row.

Waltz, J., Babcock, J. C., Jacobson, N. S., & Gottman, J. M. (2000). Testing a typology of batterers. *Journal of Consulting and Clinical Psychology, 68*, 658–669.

Wiehe, V. R. (1997). *Sibling abuse: Hidden physical, emotional, and sexual trauma* (2nd ed.). Thousand Oaks, CA: Sage.

Wilson, M., & Daly, M. (1993). An evolutionary psychological perspective on male sexual proprietariness and violence against wives. *Violence and Victims, 8*, 271–294.

Wilson, M., Daly, M., & Wright, C. (1993). Uxoricide in Canada: Demographic risk patterns. *Canadian Journal of Criminology, 35*, 263–291.

Wood, J. T. (2001). The normalization of violence in heterosexual romantic relationships: Women's narratives of love and violence. *Journal of Social and Personal Relationships, 18*, 239–261.

Wood, J. T. (2004). Monsters and victims: Male felons' accounts of intimate partner violence. *Journal of Social and Personal Relationships, 21*, 555–576.

Yllö, K., & Bograd, M. (Eds.). (1988). *Feminist perspectives on wife abuse*. Newbury Park, CA: Sage.

Yllö, K., & Straus, M. A. (1990). Patriarchy and violence against wives: The impact of structural and normative factors. In M. A. Straus & R. J. Gelles (Eds.), *Physical violence in American families: Risk factors and adaptations to violence in 8,145 families* (pp. 383–399). Brunswick, NJ: Transaction Press.

Part IX
RELATIONAL QUALITIES

CHAPTER 31

Relationship Satisfaction

Frank D. Fincham
Steven R. H. Beach

In Western culture, the vast majority of people marry or cohabit, and expectations of couple relationships are high. Marriage is portrayed as providing lifelong companionship, romance, support, sexual fulfillment, and commitment. Yet a high proportion of couples experience an erosion of these positive qualities over time and, for some, relationship satisfaction erodes to the point where the relationship is terminated. For others, however, the barriers to separation, or the perceived absence of alternatives, may result in remaining married despite being unhappy with the relationship. It is not surprising, therefore, that some 40% of the problems for which people seek professional help in the United States concern their spouse or marriage, a proportion that is twice the size of any other problem area (Veroff, Kulka, & Douvan, 1981). When intimate relationships like marriage go wrong, the costs can be high; marital distress, separation, and divorce are associated with just about any physical or mental health problem one cares to name (see Fincham & Beach, 1999).

Emergence of Interest in Relationship Satisfaction

At the beginning of the 20th century, changing economic and social conditions called public attention to relationship problems in families and ushered in a period of emerging science. The desire to understand and remediate family problems led to direct study of family relationships using empirically based procedures. The two earliest studies in this domain were on sexual behavior (predating Kinsey by a decade) and both examined its role in relationship satisfaction or success (Davis, 1929; Hamilton, 1948).

The central status accorded relationship satisfaction in marital research became even more salient in two later projects that are often credited with establishing marital research as an area of empirical inquiry. Terman and colleagues' (1938) book, *Psychological Factors in Marital Happiness*, described a questionnaire study of 1,133 couples designed to identify the determinants of marital satisfaction. Burgess and Cottrell (1939) similarly reported a questionnaire study of 526 couples in *Predicting Success or Failure in Marriage*. Both books are classic texts and report studies that became the prototypes for later research in their attempt to identify correlates of marital satisfaction.

In short, satisfaction is viewed as the final common pathway that leads to relationship breakdown (Jacobson, 1985) and has been the dominant construct studied in the literature on relationships such as marriage. Not surprisingly, it has gained the attention of researchers from a variety of disciplines, including psychology, sociology, family studies, and communication. Initially researchers, mostly sociologists, paid greatest attention to identifying demographic correlates of marital satisfaction (the sociological tradition), a focus forgone in the late 1960s and 1970s when observation of couple behavior assumed center stage (the behavioral tradition). Beginning in the 1980s recognition of the limits of a purely behavioral account of marriage gave rise to study of variables such as cognition and affect that might mediate the relation between behavior and marital satisfaction (the mediational tradition). For a more complete historical account, see Fincham and Bradbury (1990).

Overview of Satisfaction in Close Relationships

Before providing a brief synopsis of major findings regarding relationship satisfaction, we briefly highlight salient features of scholarship on this topic.

The Nature of Relationship Satisfaction Research

A first important feature of writings on relationship satisfaction is that they focus almost exclusively on Western – and more particularly, North American – relationships. Moreover, with a few recent exceptions (e.g., Fletcher, Simpson, & Thomas, 2000; Hendrick, Dick, & Hendrick, 1998) most of the assessment devices used to study relationship satisfaction have focused on one particular relationship; marriage. This is both a strength and weakness. It is a strength in that there is a widespread agreement, although not consensus, in North American society that marriage is primarily for the benefit of the spouses rather than the extended family, society, the ancestors, deity or deities, and so on. Widespread agreement on the hedonic purpose of marriage has the potential to simplify the task of researchers engaged in assessing and understanding relationship satisfaction and thereby promote advances in understanding. On the other hand, there is the strong temptation to insert into our measures of satisfaction items that may not be applicable in other cultures. For example, an assessment of marital satisfaction that asks who the respondent would marry if she had her life to live over again (as in one of the most widely used measures of marital quality, the Marital Adjustment Test [MAT]; Locke & Wallace, 1959), is clearly not applicable in cultures in which arranged marriages are accepted practice. Likewise, questions assessing disagreements may be poor indicators of marital satisfaction in cultures in which disagreement with a spouse is discouraged.

Second, the literature on relationship satisfaction is characterized by a lack of adequate theory. As Glenn (1990) pointed out in regard to the study of marital satisfaction, most research is justified on practical grounds "with elements of theory being brought in on an incidental, ad hoc basis" (p. 818). Lack of attention to theory has had unfortunate consequences. For example, Spanier (1976) eliminated items from his influential measure (the Dyadic Adjustment Scale [DAS]) when they were positively skewed thereby assuming that items reflective of marital quality approximate a normal distribution. As Norton (1983) pointed out, however, such items may be less critical indicators or even irrelevant to marital quality if marital quality inherently involves skewed data because spouses tend to report "happy" marriages. Moreover, if the outcome predicted by marital quality is itself skewed (e.g., aggression), then a skewed predictor may be best (Heyman, Sayers, & Bellack, 1994). Conceptual confusion has resulted in a large number of terms, such as adjustment, success, happiness, companionship, or some synonym reflective of the quality of the relationship being used interchangeably to refer to satisfaction. As a result, some scholars have even called for elimination of such terms as *marital satisfaction* and *marital adjustment* from the literature (Trost, 1985).

Third, relationship satisfaction is almost exclusively assessed using self-report. However, self-reported satisfaction gives us little information on the processes involved in "the final common pathway" that results in relationship breakdown. Ironically, even behaviorally oriented psychologists who rejected the utility of self-report when they began to study marriage systematically in the 1970s used self-reported satisfaction as a criterion variable in their studies. Indeed, a primary goal was to account for variability in such reports of marital satisfaction. This feature of the literature is important when considering the two dominant approaches that have been used to study marital satisfaction. One approach has been to view marital quality as a characteristic of the relationship between spouses instead of, or in addition to, the spouses' feelings about the marriage. This approach has tended to favor use of such terms as adjustment. However, it is questionable whether spouses are the best, or even good, reporters of relationship properties. Self-report seems better suited to the second major approach to marital quality which focuses on how married persons feel about their marriage. This approach has tended to use such terms as marital satisfaction and marital happiness.

Fourth, it is not clear what most instruments of relationship satisfaction actually measure. Most frequently, measures comprise a polyglot of items, and responses to them are not conceptually equivalent. For example, on the MAT items include ratings of disagreement on eight issues (most, but not all, of which are scored from 0 to 5), and questions such as, "Do you ever wish you had not married?" (scored as 0, 1, 8, or 10 depending on responses). The inclusion of behavioral and subjective categories and the number and weighting of items used to assess each category varies across measures of marital satisfaction, making it unclear what these tools actually measure. The summation of various dimensions of marriage in omnibus measures of marital satisfaction (e.g., interaction, happiness) also precludes meaningful study of the interplay between such dimensions (e.g., interaction may influence satisfaction and vice versa).

Typically, an overall score is computed by summing over the items, but it is not clear how such a score should be interpreted. Although this problem was identified in the marital literature over 40 years ago (see Nye & MacDougall, 1959), it remains an issue. Dahlstrom (1969) described three levels at which responses to self-report inventories can be interpreted: they can be seen (a) as veridical descriptions of behavior (e.g., responses regarding frequency of disagreement reflect the actual rate of disagreement between spouses), (b) as potential reflections of attitudes (e.g., frequently reported disagreement may reflect high rates of disagreement but may also reflect the view that the partner is unreasonable, that the spouse feels undervalued, or some other attitude), and (c) as behavioral signs the meaning of which can only be determined by actuarial data (e.g., rated disagreement may reflect time spent together, respondents' self-esteem, frequency of intercourse, or a host of other variables). Few measures of relationship quality address the level at which responses are to be interpreted.

A fifth feature of relationship satisfaction research follows naturally from the last, namely, that our knowledge of the determinants and correlates of relationship satisfaction includes (an unknown number of) spurious findings. This is because of overlapping item content in measures of satisfaction and measures of constructs examined in relation to it. The often-documented association between self-reported communication (e.g., Marital Communication Inventory; "Do the two of you argue a lot over money?" "Do you and your and your spouse engage in outside activities together?") and marital satisfaction (DAS; "Indicate the extent of agreement or disagreement between you and your partner on: handling family finances," "Do you and your mate engage in outside interests together?") is a particularly egregious example of this problem. The resulting tautological association hinders theory construction and affects the credibility of research findings. Fincham and Bradbury (1987) discussed the dilemma caused by overlapping item content at some length showing that exclusion of the items common to both measures does not provide a satisfactory solution to this problem because they usually reflect overlap in the definition of the constructs.

Major Findings

Using quantitative measures of relationship satisfaction as criteria for group membership, a variety of studies have attempted to pinpoint what differentiates happy and unhappy relationships. However, the discovery of these correlates has been accompanied by "little or no explanation of why the correlations exist" (Raush, Barry, Hertel, & Swain, 1974, p. 4), and by the 1960s, there was considerable dissatisfaction with the research, particularly its reliance on self-report. In 1961, Raush et al. began to examine the overt behaviors of couples engaged in improvised marital conflicts in the laboratory.

Next, we briefly summarize what is has been learned about behavioral, cognitive, and emotive correlates of relationship satisfaction, recognizing that the distinctions among these three constructs are in many ways artificial.

BEHAVIOR

Attempts to identify the behavioral correlates of relationship satisfaction have taken two major forms. Using spouses as observers of their partners' behaviors, researchers have attempted to examine behaviors that covary with daily reports of marital satisfaction. A second strategy entailed laboratory observation of couples who reported high and low marital satisfaction.

The first point to note is that agreement between spouses in reports of daily marital behaviors is low (average 46%; Christensen

& Nies, 1980) and is not improved by training spouses as observers. Such findings raise questions about the epistemological status of spouse reports of partner behavior, suggesting that they may reflect more about the reporter's perceptions than the observed spouse's behavior. With this caveat in mind, it has been found that reported spouse behaviors covary only slightly with daily reports of satisfaction (the two variables share about 25% of their variance), the covariation remains slight even when lists of behaviors are customized for each couple, behaviors classed as affective are more highly related to satisfaction than other classes of behavior (e.g., instrumental), events experienced as displeasing (e.g., "spouse interrupted me") are more highly related to satisfaction ratings than events that are "pleasing," and the association between daily behaviors and satisfaction is higher in dissatisfied then satisfied spouses (see Weiss & Heyman, 1997, for a review).

Although questionable as veridical reports of partner behavior, some of the results obtained for spouse reports of behavior are remarkably consistent with the findings that emerge from observed couple interactions. For example, negative behaviors appear to distinguish more consistently satisfied from dissatisfied couples. Because several comprehensive reviews exist, we provide only a brief overview of findings (for reviews, see Gottman & Notarius, 2000; Kelly, Fincham, & Beach, 2003; Weiss & Heyman, 1997). Compared with satisfied couples, distressed couples show a range of dysfunctional communicative behaviors, including higher levels of specific negative behaviors such as criticisms and complaining, hostility, defensiveness, and disengagement, such as not responding or tracking the partner. Distressed couples also fail to listen actively to each other when interacting. We also know that these negative interactional behaviors are more likely to occur in some settings than others. Diary studies show that stressful marital interactions occur more frequently in couples' homes on days of high general life stress and at times and places associated with multiple competing demands and that topics of disagreements often coincide with the activities partners are engaged in at the time.

Recent research has shown that the giving and receipt of support behaviors are related to satisfaction and to important health outcomes. For example, wives' supportive behaviors predicted decreased satisfaction 24 months later independently of either partners' conflict behaviors and supportive behaviors moderated the association between conflict behavior and later marital deterioration with compromised conflict skills leading to greater risk of lower satisfaction in the context of poor support communication (Pasch & Bradbury, 1998; see also Bradbury, Fincham, & Beach, 2000).

With regard to sequences of behavior, the "signature" of dissatisfied couples is the existence of reciprocated negative behavior that tends to escalate in intensity. In fact, one of the greatest challenges for couples locked into negative exchanges is to find an adaptive way of exiting from such cycles (Gottman, 1998). This is usually attempted through responses designed to repair the interaction (e.g., metacommunication, "You're not listening to me") that are typically delivered with negative affect (e.g., irritation, sadness). Distressed couples tend to respond to the negative affect, thereby continuing the cycle. This makes their interactions more structured and predictable. In contrast, satisfied couples appear to be more responsive to the repair attempt and are thereby able to exit from negative exchanges early on. For example, a spouse may respond to "Please, you're not letting me finish" with "Sorry . . . please finish what you were saying." Their interaction therefore appears more random and less predictable.

A second interaction pattern commonly observed in dissatisfied couples is that one spouse pressures the other with demands, complaints, and criticisms, and the partner withdraws with defensiveness and passive inaction. This interaction pattern is commonly referred to as the demand–withdrawal pattern. Christensen and Heavey (1990) examined interactions of couples dis-

cussing a topic chosen by each spouse and found that frequency of demands by the female partner and withdrawal by the male partner were negatively related to marital satisfaction. That female-demand and male-withdrawal are associated with low relationship satisfaction is consistent with other gender differences in communication. In particular, women display more negative affect and behavior than do men, and male partners make more statements suggestive of withdrawal, such as not responding and making irrelevant comments (Weiss & Heyman, 1997).

However, inferring reliable gender differences in demand–withdrawal patterns would be premature. To clarify this issue, Heavey, Christensen, and Malamuth (1995) explored how demand–withdrawal patterns vary according to which partner's problem issue was discussed. When discussing the husband's issue, there were no systematic differences in the roles taken by each spouse. However, when discussing the wife's issue, women were much more likely to be demanding and men more likely to be withdrawing than the reverse. Similarly, Klinetob and Smith (1996) found that demand–withdrawal patterns switch polarity when the topics chosen for discussion clearly focus on an issue of change for each partner. These results provide good evidence that although men and women tend to play different roles in typical dysfunctional communications, these roles are sensitive to context and are particularly sensitive to whose issue is under discussion.

Finally, conflict interaction patterns seem to be relatively stable over time and to predict changes in marital satisfaction and marital stability (see Karney & Bradbury, 1995). For example, Gottman et al. (1998) found that active listening, anger, and negative affect reciprocity among newlyweds predicted marital satisfaction and stability 6 years later. However, the work on social support suggests it is important to consider such relations in a broader context (Pasch & Bradbury, 1998). In a similar vein, in the context of high levels of affectional expression between spouses, the inverse correlation between negative spouse behavior and marital satisfaction becomes significantly weaker (Huston & Chorost, 1994). Affectional expression is also important for understanding the association between the demand–withdrawal pattern and satisfaction; the demand–withdrawal pattern was unrelated to marital satisfaction in the context of high affectional expression but the two variables were inversely related in the context of average or low affectional expression (Caughlin & Huston, 2002).

COGNITION

The role of cognitive variables in understanding relationship satisfaction has received considerable attention (for reviews, see Fincham, 1994, 2001; Karney, McNulty, & Bradbury, 2001). Most research on cognition has studied the content of cognitions. For example, research examined unrealistic relationship beliefs early on (e.g., disagreement is destructive, partners cannot change, sexual perfectionism, mind reading is expected, and the sexes cannot change) showing that they are related to dissatisfaction, observed couple behavior, and couples therapy outcome.

In contrast, more recent studies have examined functional unrealistic beliefs. For example, Murray, Holmes, and Griffin (1996) investigated the extent to which idealized spousal qualities (e.g., kindness, affection, openness, patience, understanding, responsiveness, tolerance, and acceptance) were characteristic of happy dating and married couples. Happy couples were found to view their partners in a more positive light than their partners viewed themselves, and individuals were happier in their relationships when they idealized their partner and their partners idealized them. In a similar vein, Murray and her colleagues (2002) showed that egocentrically assuming similarities between partner and self that do not exist is characteristic of being in a satisfying relationship. This work showing that cognitive distortions are important in satisfied relationships is consistent with earlier work that shows happy spouses make

egocentric attributions for negative relationships events (e.g., arguments) but partner-centric attributions for positive relationships events (Fincham & Bradbury, 1989).

More work has been conducted on attributions in close relationships than on any other cognitive variable. Evidence for an association between attribution and relationship satisfaction is overwhelming, making it possibly the most robust, replicable phenomenon in the study of close relationships (Fincham, 2001). Specifically, certain attributions for relationship events (e.g., spouse arrives home late from work) can promote relationship satisfaction (e.g., she [he] was delayed by traffic," an attribution that locates cause outside of partner, is impermanent, does not influence other areas of the relationship, and absolves partner of blame) or dissatisfaction (e.g., she [he] is selfish and cares more about work than about me," which locates an unchanging cause – selfishness – with implications for many areas of the relationship and in the partner and makes the partner blameworthy). Alternative explanations for this attribution – satisfaction association that have been ruled out include anger and depression, general negative affectivity, measurement error, overlap between the assessment of attributions and satisfaction, and relationship violence (see Fincham, 2001).

The importance of attributions for relationship satisfaction is emphasized by longitudinal data showing that attributions may influence marital satisfaction. In each study, only the variance that attributions do not share with satisfaction is used to predict changes in satisfaction making it difficult to account for findings by arguing that attributions are a proxy index of relationship satisfaction. Four longitudinal studies show that attributions predict later satisfaction, a temporal relationship that is independent of partner depression. A fifth, more recent study spanning an 18-month period suggests that the association is mediated by the impact of attributions on efficacy expectations, which, in turn, influenced satisfaction (Fincham, Harold, & Gano-Phillips, 2000). Finally, Karney and Bradbury (2000) found that intraindividual changes in attribution and in marital satisfaction covaried. Moreover, controlling for within-subject covariation, initial attributions had greater effects on the trajectory of marital satisfaction than Time 1 satisfaction had on the trajectory of attributions. Specifically, more conflict-promoting attributions at Time 1 were associated with steeper declines in satisfaction and with satisfaction that covaried less with subsequent changes in attributions.

Relationship satisfaction is also related to a number of other cognitive variables. These include *working models of attachment*, with greater satisfaction being related to secure attachment (Meyers & Landsberger, 2002), and perception of the *partner and ideal standards discrepancies*, with smaller discrepancies being related to greater satisfaction (Campbell, Simpson, Kashy, & Fletcher, 2001). *Further, social comparison processes* affect relationship satisfaction as well, with greater downward comparison (and hence greater perceived superiority) being associated with greater satisfaction (Buunk & Ybema, 2003). *Memory is another cognitive factor* in that more satisfied partners believe their relationships have improved over the past by negatively biasing recall of the past (Karney & Coombs, 2000). Finally, *self-evaluation maintenance processes* influence satisfaction by changing the nature of couple communication, producing positive and negative emotional reactions to interactions involving the partner and moderating responses to differences in decision-making power in marital relationships (Beach et al., 1998; O'Mahen, Beach, & Tesser, 2000).

EMOTION

A variety of indices of emotion have been examined in marital research. An index of emotion which has long been utilized is nonverbal behavior. Although such assessment of affect is clearly simplistic, several fascinating findings support the centrality of affect in couple satisfaction. For example, affect codes are more powerful than verbal codes in discriminating satisfied from dissatisfied couples, with groups being distin-

guished by their use of neutral and negative, rather than positive, affect. Interestingly, although dissatisfied spouses are able to alter verbal behavior if instructed to pretend to be happily married, they are unable to change their nonverbal behavior (Vincent, Friedman, Nugent, & Messerly, 1979).

Other indices of emotion investigated include verbal report, "online" affect ratings, and physiological measures such as heart rate. As might be expected, satisfied partners score higher on self-report indices of emotion, suggesting that positive affect is an important component of marital satisfaction (although this finding is not surprising given that affect-related items appear in relationship satisfaction assessments). To investigate affective experience during interactions, partners have been asked to make continuous ratings of affect as they review a videotape of their interaction. Typically these consist of a rating dial with a semicircular arc, which is manipulated to represent how they felt (ranging from very negative to very positive). As might be expected, satisfied spouses experience problem-solving interactions with their partner as more positive than distressed couples.

Gottman and colleagues also took online measurements of automonic nervous system activity during the course of low- and high-conflict discussions. It was found that physiological interrelatedness (or "physiological linkage") between partners occurred at the times when negative affect was reported as occurring and being reciprocated, was higher in the high-conflict task compared with the low-conflict task, and was inversely related to marital satisfaction (see Gottman & Notarius, 2000). In contrast, Thomsen and Gilbert (1998) find greater synchrony or correspondence in physiological systems among satisfied than dissatisfied couples. Such discrepancies show that it can be difficult to obtain reliable physiological data during spontaneous social interaction (e.g., Sanders, Halford, & Behrens, 1999) and that, perhaps as a consequence, promising hypotheses involving physiological data (e.g., that arousal before and during marital interaction predicts later marital satisfaction) have not been supported on further analysis (Gottman & Levenson, 1992).

Notwithstanding these observations, there is strong evidence that emotion is an essential component of any complete understanding of relationship satisfaction and is integral to the experience of marital dissatisfaction. However, its exact role vis-à-vis change in satisfaction remains unclear because some studies show, for example, that negative affect is detrimental for marriage, and others show that negative affect promotes marital satisfaction or is unrelated to change in satisfaction (for discussions, see Fincham & Beach, 1999; Gottman & Notarius, 2000). Lack of replication across laboratories and even within laboratories is a problem, and it is unlikely that the role of affect in eroding or supporting relationship satisfaction will become clear without clarification of the conceptual underpinnings of affect-related constructs and refinement of the methods used to observe emotion and to document their impact on relationships over time.

CODA

The challenge for understanding relationship satisfaction given the overlap between it and other relevant constructs at both the conceptual level and the level of measurement operations, has already been noted. In a similar vein, the concept of sentiment override also poses a challenge to the validity of research findings on relationship satisfaction. Weiss (1980) coined the term sentiment override to describe the hypothesis that spouses respond noncontingently to partner behavior or questions about the marriage. In other words, partners simply respond to each other or research questions in terms of their dominant feeling or sentiment about the relationship, and this is reflected "in as many tests as one chooses to administer" (Weiss & Heyman, 1990, p. 92). Belief in this position is so strong that attempts to explain variance in relationship satisfaction using self-reports have been characterized as "invalid from a scientific standpoint" (Gottman, 1990, p. 79).

A fundamental task for the field is to show that any construct studied is not simply a proxy for relationship satisfaction. It is therefore useful to require that constructs studied do more than capture variance in commonly used measures of relationship satisfaction. A test of "surplus conceptual value" can be provided by controlling statistically the relationship satisfaction of both partners whenever two relationship variables are investigated lest any association between them simply reflect their status as proxies of relationship satisfaction.

Some Unresolved Issues: Toward a Resolution

One or Many?

One response to the issues just outlined has been the attempt to develop multidimensional measures of relationships satisfaction. Perhaps the most well developed of these is the Marital Satisfaction Inventory (MSI; Snyder, 1997). This measure includes a validity scale that attempts to provide a control for socially desirable responses, a global distress scale comprising items that tap the individual's overall dissatisfaction with the marriage, and nine scales assessing different dimensions of marital interaction (e.g., time together, disagreement about finances, sexual dissatisfaction). This psychometrically sophisticated instrument offers a profile of relationship satisfaction much like the Minnesota Multiphasic Personality Inventory (MMPI) offers a profile of individual functioning and, like the MMPI, offers actuarial data to assist in its interpretation. Unfortunately, the potential it offers for providing a more comprehensive picture of relationship satisfaction through profile analysis has not been realized, perhaps because of its length (150 items).

More important, the MSI accords one of its dimensions a special status in that the global distress scale is a criterion against which the remaining dimensions are validated. Hence, items that tap overall evaluations of the marriage are used to interpret the validity of items that assess various domains of the marriage. This is consistent with a pervasive tendency in the literature to favor global evaluations of the marriage, a preference that is not often explicitly discussed. Thus, for example, a single item in the MAT that assesses "marital happiness" is heavily weighted so that it accounts for 22% of the total possible test score. However, if all the items in the test were weighted equally, it would only account for 6.6% of the total possible score.

Not surprisingly, a second response to the circumstances described earlier has been to define relationship satisfaction as subjective, global evaluations of the relationship (e.g., Fincham & Bradbury, 1987; Norton, 1983). The strength of this approach is its conceptual simplicity; it avoids the problem of interpretation that arises in many omnibus measures of marital quality. Because it has a clear-cut interpretation, this approach allows the antecedents, correlates, and consequences of relationship satisfaction to be examined in a straightforward manner.

One criticism of this approach is the view that unidimensional, global scales "often do not provide much information beyond the fact that a couple is distressed" (Fowers, 1990, p. 370). However, the same is true of the most widely used scales of relationship satisfaction, the MAT and DAS. It therefore appears that any attempt to advance understanding of relationship satisfaction will have to offer a significant advantage over the MAT and DAS to overcome the familiarity bias that has developed concerning these two measures. The conceptual clarity and ease of measuring subjective, global evaluation of the relationship does so, suggesting that it replace the MAT and DAS in martial research. In the event that this standard is adopted, it will be important to reexamine accepted correlates of marital satisfaction to show that they do not represent spurious findings.

Variation on a Theme or Something New?

The attempt to conceptualize relationship satisfaction as a global evaluation of the relationship has focused on a bipolar conceptualization with dissatisfaction reflecting an evaluation of the relationship in which neg-

ative features are salient and positive features are relatively absent, and satisfaction reflecting an evaluation in which positive features are salient and negative features are relatively absent. This view has been challenged, however, on the basis that positive and negative evaluations in marriage can be conceptualized and measured as separate, but related, dimensions (Fincham, Beach, & Kemp-Fincham, 1997). Data obtained with a simple measure used to capture this two-dimensional conception of relationship satisfaction indicate that the dimensions have different correlates and account for unique variance in reported marital behaviors and attributions independently of individual affect. More important, the "surplus conceptual value" test was met as these findings held even when MAT scores were statistically controlled. Moreover, two groups of wives who were indistinguishable on MAT scores, those who were high in positivity and high in negativity (ambivalent wives) versus those who were low in positivity and low in negativity (indifferent wives), differed reliably in their behaviors and attributions (Fincham & Linfield, 1997).

This viewpoint may seem to be a variation on the previous theme of unidimensional versus multidimensional approaches to relationships satisfaction. On the other hand, it appears to be something new in that it alone in the field retains the advantage of the theoretical clarity found in the unidimensional, global evaluation perspective outlined in the last section while also capturing the advantages of a multidimensional approach. In addition, it has the clear advantage of allowing us to make distinctions that are not afforded by unidimensional measures and thereby open new areas of inquiry. For example, it allows study not only of happy (high in positivity and low in negativity), and unhappy spouses (high in positivity and high in negativity) but also ambivalent spouses (high in positivity and in negativity) and indifferent spouses (high in positivity and in negativity), two groups that have not received attention in prior research.

It also opens new avenues of inquiry in longitudinal research on marriage. For instance, it would be theoretically important if happily married spouses first increased negative evaluations only (became ambivalent) before then decreasing positive evaluations and becoming distressed, compared with a progression in which negative evaluations increased and positive evaluations decreased at the same time. Such progressions may, in turn, differ in important ways from one in which there is simply a decline in positive evaluations over time. Documenting the existence of different avenues of change in marital quality, examining their determinants, and exploring their consequences suggests a program of research that may do much to advance our understanding of how marriages succeed and fail.

Snapshot or Movie?

A recent important development is the notion that relationship satisfaction is appropriately conceptualized not as a judgment made at a single time point but as a trajectory that reflects fluctuations in satisfaction over time. Such a trajectory can be computed for individual partners and parameters of the trajectory, especially its slope, or rate of change, can be examined in relation to other variables of interest. From this perspective, relationship satisfaction at one point in time cannot be fully understood without reference to earlier or later data points. So, for example, a score of 105 on the MAT has a different meaning depending on whether the person scored 115 or 85 five months earlier. This approach has the advantage of fostering multiwave longitudinal research on relationships (two-wave longitudinal designs have dominated; see Karney & Bradbury, 1995) and encourages researchers to specify a model of marital change (two-wave longitudinal designs assume a simple linear model). Use of this approach to conceptualize and understand relationship satisfaction is increasing and has the potential to provide more a more refined picture of relationship satisfaction.

Enough: Will the Real Relationship Satisfaction Please Stand Up?

Confronted by various views of relationship satisfaction, it is tempting to want to iden-

tify the "real" relationship satisfaction. However, any attempt to identify the "real" meaning of relationship satisfaction is ultimately self-defeating. Instead, researchers are confronted by a situation analogous to that captured by the story of the blind men and the elephant. Each man describes what he can feel as an elephant and each is correct with the totality of the descriptions providing a more complete picture than any single description or any subset of descriptions. Similarly, there are several options available for understanding relationship satisfaction, and each, when precisely specified, has merit. For example, the rich, multidimensional picture provided by the MSI is clearly more valuable to the couple counselor than knowing the summary score on a unidimensional measure comprising global evaluations of the relationship.

In essence, unresolved issues as to the nature of relationship satisfaction can be resolved not by pitting different perspectives on relationship satisfaction against each other but by careful specification of their referents and the purposes for which they may be most suited. For instance, if one's purpose is to simply distinguish satisfied couples from couples who might need marital counseling, standard measures of couple satisfaction (e.g., MAT, DAS) are perfectly appropriate, and their inclusion of a heterogeneous set of items might even give them an edge *for this purpose* over measures that consist solely of global evaluation of the relationship. In contrast, more homogenous measures are clearly advantageous in theoretically driven research on the correlates of relationship satisfaction.

The New Frontier: Continuum or Category?

Research on relationship satisfaction has ignored a fundamental question that can be asked of many psychological constructs. For example, when we speak of depression, we commonly distinguish between symptoms of depression and the syndrome of depression. A basic issue in this field is whether there are cutting points between qualitatively distinct categories that reflect "upset/distress or life dissatisfaction" and "disorder/psychopathology." In an analogous manner, family psychologists are now beginning to ask whether we can show that the "manifestations of marital disorder tend to cluster or aggregate in recognizable patterns in the same way that the symptoms of individual psychiatric disorders cluster in identifiable syndromes" (First et al., 2002, p. 163). Simply stated, does relationship satisfaction reflect an underlying continuum or are there discontinuities in satisfaction?

Why is it important to understand the underlying structure of relationship satisfaction? First, the underlying structure has implications for the plausibility of linear versus nonlinear models in the study of relationships. Nonlinear models often imply discontinuities and if a continuous dimension underlies scores of relationship satisfaction, it might be taken as a strike against such theories. Second, dichotomizing a variable that could legitimately be treated as a continuous variable has the same effect on power as discarding more than a third of one's sample (Cohen, 1983). If there is no evidence of distinct categories of relationship satisfaction, dichotomizing data, as is often done in marital research, is wasteful and has the potential to lead to type two errors. Third, if there is no point of discontinuity in relationship satisfaction, one may question the validity of the distinction between therapy participants who have "recovered" and those who have not "recovered" following couple therapy. Accordingly, there are both theoretical and practical reasons to address the latent structure of relationship satisfaction.

Why Might One Expect Relationship Satisfaction to Be Well Represented as a Single, Continuous Dimension?

Reports of marital dissatisfaction appear to be linked to a dimension of individual negative affectivity (e.g., Karney & Bradbury, 1997). Likewise, the intraindividual changes produced by interaction patterns are well modeled as a linear effect over time (Karney & Bradbury, 1997). In addition, external life events influence level of satisfaction (Story & Bradbury, 2004). Accordingly, to the extent that variations in environmental events reflect a continuum of severity, they might be expected to stretch out the range of marital satisfaction scores in a relatively continuous manner. As a result of these influences, one might expect a fine gradation of different levels of satisfaction with no point of discontinuity or categorical differences.

Because traits such as neuroticism and negative affectivity represent subtle gradations of responsiveness to rewards or punishments, one might anticipate that the association between neuroticism and reported marital satisfaction would lead to a relatively continuous distribution of marital satisfaction scores in the general population. One might also expect marital satisfaction to reflect a continuum structure based on the broader literature regarding positive and negative affective reactions to events. If change in individual relationship satisfaction is related to perceptions of movement toward or away from important relationship or individual goals (e.g., Fincham & Beach, 1999), relationship distress could be viewed as feedback that goals are being met by the relationship or, conversely, that the relationship is blocking important individual goals. Because rate of progress toward important relationship goals may be variable and behavior in the service of goal attainment might be expected to require continuous adjustment, one might again expect a relatively continuous distribution of relationship satisfaction scores to result from such influences. Accordingly, there are a variety of empirical and theoretical considerations that would lead to the expectation that relationship satisfaction and distress is well represented as a continuum only.

Why Might One Expect Relationship Satisfaction to Be Categorical Rather Than a Single Continuous Dimension?

There are also, however, good reasons to expect discontinuity in relationship satisfaction. It has, for example, been known for some time that happy couples tend to overestimate positive qualities and underestimate negative qualities of partners, whereas unhappy couples tend to do the opposite (e.g., Murray, 1999). Indeed, attributional models of marital discord suggest that there are interpretive differences between couples that result in deterioration in marital satisfaction over time (see Fincham, 2001).

Biases in perception or interpretation, whether viewed as motivated or as merely a by-product of cognitive architecture, suggest the strong possibility that relatively subtle differences in initial biases could feed back on themselves, becoming exaggerated over time to create increasing divergence between happy and unhappy couples. In particular, one might anticipate that couples with negative biases could find themselves drawn inexorably into an increasingly negative view of the partner, whereas couples with more positive biases would find that they can readily explain away even those characteristics and behaviors that others might view as the "faults" of their partner (Murray, 1999). As a result, relatively minor initial differences in marital satisfaction could become exaggerated over time, leading to a bimodal distribution of outcomes.

As previously noted, marital interaction research also indicates that some couples are characterized by an increased likelihood of responding to a negative partner behavior with a negative behavior of their own (see Fincham & Beach, 1999; Gottman, 1998; Weiss & Heyman, 1997). This creates the potential for a behavioral feedback loop resulting in long chains of negative behavior. If these chains of negative behavior set the stage for further negative interaction in the future there is the potential for "causal loops" of the sort that are characteristic of close relationships (Kelley, Berscheid, Christensen, et al., 1983, pp. 58–62). Accordingly, some partners may become increasingly negative in their feelings toward each other as a function of their own internal couple dynamics without further influence from individual or external characteristics. At a minimum, these dynamics suggest the potential for some couples to "become stuck" in a negative pattern of interaction from which they find if very difficult to exit. This is a primary characteristic of

any proposed "marital disorder" (First et al., 2002). That is, there is the potential for well-documented interactional patterns to lead to a distinct "types" of marital satisfaction over time.

Consistent with the hypothesis of two distinct populations, Gottman (1994) discussed the possibility that rather continuous changes in the nature of a couple's interaction (p-space) could be related to an underlying discrete change in their perception of the partner (q-space). Such a discontinuity in perception of the partner and the associated felt well-being about the relationship would seem to require that categories underlie the distribution of marital satisfaction scores. This perspective is further elaborated in the nonlinear dynamical perspective espoused by Gottman et al. (2002) and leads to the expectation that there will be some evidence of categories in marital satisfaction scores among couples who have been married for several years.

How Can the Continuum–Category Issue Be Addressed?

Taxometric procedures (Waller & Meehl, 1998) have been developed to address the question of whether psychological constructs are best characterized as being dimensional only, or whether there is evidence of a latent categorical structure superimposed on the dimension of interest. If there is evidence of a latent categorical structure, the members of the group of interest are identified as members of the "taxon" and others are identified as members of the "complement." These procedures provide a set of tools to examine the underlying structure of relationship satisfaction.

Beach, Fincham, Amir, and Leonard (2005) used taxometric methods to analyze data from 447 couples in early marriage who had lived together for an average of 4.5 years. Using the MAT, they found evidence of a discontinuity in marital satisfaction scores such that approximately 20% of the sample experience marriage in a way that is qualitatively and not merely quantitatively different than their peers. They also showed that taxon and complement members differed on a number of relationship variables and that taxon membership moderated the contribution of leisure activities and negative partner behavior to satisfaction scores as measured by the Multidimensional Satisfaction Scale (MDS; Kearns & Leonard, 2004). The association for negative behavior was greater among the complement members than among members of the taxon (−0.547 vs. −0.445), conversely, the simple association for leisure activities was smaller for members of the complement than for members of the taxon (0.251 vs. 0.595). Thus, not only were the two groups different on a range of marital variables, they also appeared to show a different pattern of connections among marital variables.

To conclude, it is noteworthy that this attempt to study the underlying structure of relationship satisfaction differs dramatically from prior efforts that assumed an underlying continuum and have attempted to identify clusters of items that group together using such techniques as factor analysis. Early on, factor analytic approaches gave rise to the conclusion that "different operations designed to measure marital satisfaction converge and form one dimension" (Gottman, 1979, p. 5) a viewpoint supported by subsequent work that shows standard measures of relationship satisfaction intercorrelate highly (e.g., Heyman et al., 1994). With taxometric research on relationship satisfaction having only just begun, the jury is still out on whether relationship satisfaction is taxonic. We hope that it will not be too long before similarly strong conclusions to those just cited can be drawn about its taxonic, nature (or lack thereof). If relationship satisfaction proves to be taxonic, it will open up a new era of research in which it will be necessary to document correlates and consequences of taxon membership, the developmental trajectory of taxon members, and so on.

Conclusion

Romantic relationships do not invariably provide the benefits spouses hope and long for, and in Western societies the hedonic impact of this reality has been given a privileged position. As a result, a long and productive history of research has emerged on relationship satisfaction and its correlates. Primary among the findings in this research is clear evidence that relationship satisfaction is linked to problems in individual mental and physical health. It is also clear that a number of features characterize distressed couples, and research has moved on to address the more difficult problem of identifying reliable antecedents of marital dissatisfaction. Recent research and theory emphasize the utility of examining relationships in context and of studying both positive and negative aspects of the relationship. When this is done, it becomes clear that positive and negative aspects of relationships are not merely different ends of a bipolar dimension. Rather, they have the potential to interact in important ways to enrich our understanding of couple functioning. Finally, researchers have begun to take on the fundamental question of whether couples can be "categorized" as distressed or nondistressed.

References

Beach, S. R. H., Fincham, F. D., Amir, N., & Leonard, K. (2005). The taxometrics of marriage: Is marital discord categorical? *Journal of Family Psychology*, 19, 276–285.

Beach, S. R. H., Tesser, A., Fincham, F. D., Jones, D. J., Johnson, D., & Whitaker, D. J. (1998). Pleasure and pain in doing well together: An investigation of performance related affect in close relationships. *Journal of Personality and Social Psychology*, 74, 923–938.

Bradbury, T. N., Fincham, F. D., & Beach, S. R. H. (2000). Research on the nature and determinants of marital satisfaction: A decade in review. *Journal of Marriage and the Family*, 62, 964–980.

Burgess, E. W., & Cottrell, L. S. (1939). *Predicting success or failure in marriage*. New York: Prentice Hall.

Buunk, B. P., & Ybema, J. F. (2003). Feeling bad, but satisfied: The effects of upward and downward comparison upon mood and marital satisfaction. *British Journal of Social Psychology*, 42, 613–628.

Campbell, L., Simpson, J. A., Kashy, D. A., & Fletcher, G. J. O. (2001). Ideal standards, the self, and flexibility of ideals in close relationships. *Personality and Social Psychology Bulletin*, 27, 447–462.

Caughlin, J. P., & Huston, T. L. (2002). A contextual analysis of the association between demand/withdraw and marital satisfaction. *Personal Relationships*, 9, 95–119.

Christensen, A., & Heavey, C. L. (1990). Gender and social structure in the demand/withdraw pattern of marital conflict. *Journal of Personality and Social Psychology*, 59, 73–81.

Christensen, A., & Nies, D. C. (1980). The spouse observation checklist: Empirical analysis and critique. *American Journal of Family Therapy*, 8, 69–79.

Cohen, J. (1983). The cost of dichotomization. *Applied Psychological Measurement*, 7, 249–253.

Dahlstrom, W. G. (1969). Recurrent issues in the development of the MMPI. In J. M. Butcher (Ed.), *Research developments and clinical applications* (pp. 1–40). New York: McGraw-Hill.

Davis, K. B. (1929). *Factors in the sex life of twenty-two hundred women*. New York: Harpers.

Fincham, F. D. (1994). Cognition in marriage: Current status and future challenges. *Applied and Preventive Psychology: Current Scientific Perspectives*, 3, 185–198.

Fincham, F. D. (2001). Attributions and close relationships: From balkanization to integration. In G. J. Fletcher & M. Clark (Eds.), *Blackwell handbook of social psychology*. (pp. 3–31). Oxford, England: Blackwell.

Fincham, F. D., & Beach, S. R. H. (1999). Conflict in marriage: Implications for working with couples. *Annual Review of Psychology*, 50, 47–77.

Fincham, F. D., Beach, S. R., & Kemp-Fincham, S. I. (1997). Marital quality: A new theoretical perspective. In R. J. Sternberg & M. Hojjat (Eds.), *Satisfaction in close relationships* (pp. 275–304). New York: Guilford Press.

Fincham, F. D., & Bradbury, T. N. (1987). The assessment of marital quality: A reevaluation. *Journal of Marriage and the Family*, 49, 797–809.

Fincham, F. D., & Bradbury, T. N. (1989). Perceived responsibility for marital events: Egocentric bias or partner-centric bias? *Journal of Marriage and the Family*, 51, 27–35.

Fincham, F. D., & Bradbury, T. N., (Eds.). (1990). *The psychology of marriage: Basic issues and applications*. New York: Guilford Press.

Fincham, F. D., Harold, G., & Gano-Phillips, S. (2000). The longitudinal relation between attributions and marital satisfaction: Direction of effects and role of efficacy expectations. *Journal of Family Psychology*, 14, 267–285.

Fincham, F. D., & Linfield, K. J. (1997). A new look at marital quality: Can spouses feel positive and negative about their marriage? *Journal of Family Psychology*, 11, 489–502.

First, M. B., Bell, C. C., Cuthburt, B., Krystal, J. H., Malison, R., Offord, D. R., Reiss, D., Shea, T., Widdiger, T., Wisner, K. L. (2002). Personality disorders and relational disorders: A research agenda for addressing crucial gaps in DSM. In D. J. Kupfer, M. B. First, and D. A. Regier (Eds.), *A research agenda for DSM-V* (pp. 123–199). Washington, DC: American Psychiatric Association Press.

Fletcher, G. J. O., Simpson, J. A., & Thomas, G. (2000). The measurement of perceived relationship quality components: A confirmatory factor analytic approach. *Personality and Social Psychology Bulletin*, 26, 3, 340–354.

Fowers, B. J. (1990) An interactional approach to standardized marital assessment: A literature review. *Family Relations*, 39, 368–377.

Glenn, N. D. (1990). Quantitative research on marital quality in the 1980s: A critical review. *Journal of Marriage and the Family*, 52, 818–831.

Gottman, J. M. (1979) *Marital interaction: Experimental investigations*. New York: Academic Press.

Gottman, J. M. (1990). How marriages change. In G. R. Patterson (Ed.), *Depression and aggression in family interaction* (pp. 75–102). Hillsdale, NJ: Erlbaum.

Gottman, J. M. (1994). *What predicts divorce?* Hillsdale, NJ: Erlbaum.

Gottman, J. M. (1998). Psychology and the study of marital processes. *Annual Review of Psychology*, 49, 169–197.

Gottman, J. M., Coan, J., Carrere, S., & Swanson, C. (1998). Predicting marital happiness and stability from newlywed interactions. *Journal of Marriage and the Family*, 60, 5–22.

Gottman, J. M., & Levenson, R. W. (1992). Marital processes predictive of later dissolution: Behavior, physiology, and health. *Journal of Personality and Social Psychology*, 63, 221–233.

Gottman, J. M., & Notarius, C. I. (2000). Decade review: Observing marital interaction. *Journal of Marriage and the Family, 62*, 927–947.

Gottman, J. M., Murray, J. D., Swanson, C. C., Tyson, R., & Swanson, K. R. (2002). *The mathematics of marriage: Dynamic nonlinear models.* Cambridge, MA: MIT Press.

Hamilton, G. V. (1948). *A research on marriage.* New York: Lear.

Heavey, C. L., Christensen, A., & Malamuth, N. M. (1995). The longitudinal impact of demand and withdrawal during marital conflict. *Journal of Consulting and Clinical Psychology, 63*, 797–801.

Hendrick, S. S., Dicke, A., & Hendrick, C. (1998). The Relationship Assessment Scale. *Journal of Social and Personal Relationships, 15*, 137–142.

Heyman, R. E., Sayers, S. L., & Bellack, A. S. (1994). Global marital satisfaction versus marital adjustment: An empirical comparison of three measures. *Journal of Family Psychology, 8*, 432–446.

Huston, T. L., & Chorost, A. F. (1994). Behavioral buffers on the effect of negativity on marital satisfaction: A longitudinal study. *Personal Relationships, 1*, 223–239.

Jacobson, N. S. (1985). The role of observation measures in marital therapy outcome research. *Behavioral Assessment, 7*, 287–308.

Karney, B. R., & Bradbury, T. N. (1995). The longitudinal course of marital quality and stability: A review of theory, method, and research. *Psychological Bulletin, 118*, 3–34.

Karney, B. R., & Bradbury, T. N. (1997). Neuroticism, marital interaction, and the trajectory of marital satisfaction. *Journal of Personality and Social Psychology, 72*, 1075–1092.

Karney, B. R., & Bradbury, T. N. (2000). Attributions in marriage: State or trait? A growth curve analysis. *Journal of Personality and Social Psychology, 78*, 295–309.

Karney, B. R., & Coombs, R. H. (2000). Memory bias in long-term close relationships: Consistency or improvement? *Personality and Social Psychology Bulletin, 26*, 959–970.

Karney, B. R., Mc Nulty, J. K., & Bradbury, T. N. (2001). Cognition and the development of close relationships. In G. J. Fletcher & M. Clark (Eds.), *Blackwell handbook of social psychology* (pp. 32–59). Oxford, England: Blackwell.

Kearns J., & Leonard, K. (2004). Social networks, structural interdependence, and marital quality over the transition to marriage: A prospective analysis. *Journal of Family Psychology, 18*, 383–394.

Kelley, H. H., Berscheid, E., Christensen, A., Harvey, J. H., Huston, T. L., Levinger, G., McClintock, E., Peplau, L. A., & Peterson, D. R. (1983). Analyzing close relationships. In H. H. Kelley, E. Berscheid, A. Christensen, J. H. Harvey, T. L. Huston, G. Levinger, et al. (Eds.), *Close relationships* (pp. 20–67). New York: Freeman.

Kelly, A., Fincham, F. D., & Beach, S. R. H. (2003). Emerging perspectives on couple communication. In J. O. Greene & B. R. Burleson (Eds.), *Handbook of communication and social interaction skills* (pp. 723–752). Mahwah, NJ: Erlbaum.

Klinetob, N. A., & Smith, D. A. (1996). Demand–withdraw communication in marital interaction: Tests of interpersonal contingency and gender role hypotheses. *Journal of Marriage and the Family, 58*, 945–957.

Locke, H. J., & Wallace, K. M. (1959). Short marital adjustment prediction tests: Their reliability and validity. *Marriage and Family Living, 21*, 251–255.

Meyers, S. A., & Landsberger, S. A. (2002). Direct and indirect pathways between adult attachment style and marital satisfaction. *Personal Relationships, 9*, 159–172.

Murray, S. L. (1999). The quest for conviction: Motivated cognition in romantic relationships. *Psychological Inquiry, 10*, 23–34.

Murray, S. L., Holmes, J. G., & Griffin, D. W. (1996). The benefits of positive illusions: Idealization and the construction of satisfaction in close relationships. *Journal of Personality and Social Psychology, 70*, 79–98.

Murray, S. L., Holmes, J. G., Bellavia, G. Griffin, D. W., & Dolderman, D. (2002). Kindred spirits? The benefits of egocentrism in close relationships. *Journal of Personality and Social Psychology, 82*, 563–581.

Norton, R. (1983). Measuring marital quality: A critical look at the dependent variable. *Journal of Marriage and the Family, 45*, 141–151.

Nye, F. I., & MacDougall, E. (1959). The dependent variable in marital research. *Pacific Sociological Review, 12*, 67–70.

O'Mahen, H. A., Beach, S. R. H., & Tesser, A. (2000). Relationship ecology and negative communication in romantic relationships: A self-evaluation maintenance perspective. *Personality and Social Psychology Bulletin, 26*, 1343–1352.

Pasch, L. A., & Bradbury, T. N. (1998). Social support, conflict, and the development of marital dysfunction. *Journal of Consulting and Clinical Psychology, 66,* 219–230.

Raush, H. L., Barry, W. A., Hertel, R. K., & Swain, M. A. (1974). *Communication, conflict, and marriage.* San Francisco: Jossey-Bass.

Sanders, M. R., Halford, W. K., & Behrens, B. C. (1999). Parental divorce and premarital couple communication. *Journal of Family Psychology, 13,* 60–74.

Spanier, G. B. (1976). Measuring dyadic adjustment: New scales for assessing the quality of marriage and similar dyads. *Journal of Marriage and the Family, 38,* 15–28.

Snyder, D. K. (1997). *Manual for the Marital Satisfaction Inventory – Revised.* Los Angeles: Western Psychological Services.

Story, L. B., & Bradbury, T. N. (2004). Understanding marriage and stress: Essential questions and challenges. *Clinical Psychology Review, 23,* 1139–1162.

Terman, L. M., Buttenweiser, P., Ferguson, L. W., Johnson, W. B., & Wilson, D. P. (1938). *Psychological factors in marital happiness.* New York: McGraw-Hill.

Thomsen, D. G., & Gilbert, D. G. (1998). Factors characterizing marital conflict states and traits: Physiological, affective, behavioral, and neurotic variable contributions to marital conflict and satisfaction. *Personality and Individual Differences, 25,* 833–855.

Trost, J. E. (1985). Abandon adjustment! *Journal of Marriage and the Family, 47,* 1072–1073.

Veroff, J., Kulka, R. A., & Douvan, E. (1981). *Mental health in American: Patterns of help seeking from 1957–1976.* New York: Basic Books.

Vincent, J. P., Friedman, L. C., Nugent, J., & Messerly, L. (1979). Demand characteristics in observations of marital interaction. *Journal of Consulting and Clinical Psychology, 47,* 557–566.

Waller, N. G., & Meehl, P. E. (1998). *Multivariate taxometric procedures.* Thousand Oaks, CA: Sage.

Weiss, R. L. (1980). Strategic behavioral marital therapy: Toward a model for assessment and intervention. In J. P. Vincent (Ed.), *Advances in family intervention, assessment and theory* (Vol. 1, pp. 229–271). Greenwich, CT: JAI Press.

Weiss, R. L., & Heyman, R. E. (1990). Observation of marital interaction. In F. D. Fincham & T. N. Bradbury (Eds.), *The psychology of marriage* (pp. 87–117). New York: Guilford Press.

Weiss, R. L., & Heyman, R. E. (1997). A clinical-research overview of couple interactions. In W. K. Halford & H. J. Markman (Eds.), *The clinical handbook of marriage and couples interventions* (pp. 13–42). New York: Wiley.

CHAPTER 32

Romantic Love

Arthur Aron,
Helen E. Fisher,
Greg Strong

Romantic love appears to be a nearly universal phenomenon, appearing in every culture for which data are available (Janowiak & Fischer, 1992) and in every historical era (Hatfield & Rapson, 2002). Analogs to romantic love are found in a wide variety of higher animal species, and love may well have played a central role in shaping human evolution (Fisher, 1998, 2004). Romantic love seems to be a key factor in quality of life generally, being a source of both some of the greatest joys and some of the greatest problems, including depression, rage, stalking, suicide, and homicide (e.g., Ellis & Malamuth, 2000; for a review, see Meloy, 1998).

Given the prevalence and importance of romantic love, it is not surprising that it has been the subject of both artistic and scholarly attention from the earliest times. Among the most significant early scholarly treatments in Western culture is Plato's *Symposium*, a systematic analysis of the nature of love that continues to be influential today (e.g., Aron & Aron, 1991). There has been a continuous stream of interest in love since the classical Greeks, with landmarks that continue to be influential on contemporary thought, including Stendhal's (1822/1927) book-length essay *De l'amour* and the extensive discussions of the topic by Freud (e.g., 1927) and later writers emerging from that tradition, such as Theodore Reik (1944) and Carl Jung (e.g., 1959/1925). The 19th and early 20th century also saw interest in love, including sociologists studying the family (e.g., Westermarck, 1921), cultural anthropologists (e.g., Mead, 1928), and clinical writers outside of the Freudian tradition (e.g., Grant, 1957).

Scholarly work on romantic love in the last few decades has been primarily centered in social and personality psychology, largely starting with the groundbreaking work of Donn Byrne (1971) and other influential work on romantic attraction (e.g., Hatfield [Walster], Aronson, Abrahams, & Rottman, 1966) and Berscheid and Hatfield [Walster]'s (1969) significant distinction between companionate and passionate love. This work was quickly followed by important contributions of Rubin (1970, 1974) on loving and liking, Dutton and Aron (1974) on the arousal–attraction effect, and an influential book on attraction edited by Huston (1974). The 1980s set the stage for much of the current thinking on romantic love, including the development of lay understandings of love (Fehr, 1988), the influential extension of attachment theory to adult love (Hazan & Shaver, 1987; Shaver & Mikulincer, this volume), Sternberg's (1986) triangular theory of love, Tennov's (1979) descriptive work on intense passionate love, Aron and Aron's (1986) self-expansion model of love, evolutionary psychology approaches (e.g., Buss, 1989), and Hendrick and Hendrick's (1986) adaptation of Lee's (1977) model of types of love into a psychometrically solid and widely used multidimensional scale.

These trends from the 1960s through 1980s have all continued and expanded into the present, with the early 1990s bringing some new strands, such as a stronger interest in cultural differences (e.g., Hatfield & Rapson, 1996), work on unreciprocated love (Aron, Aron, & Allen, 1998; Baumeister, Wotman, & Stillwell, 1993), and love ideals (e.g., Fletcher, Simpson, Thomas, & Giles, 1999; Rusbult, Onizuka, & Lipkus, 1993). The major developments in the late 1990s and early 21st century have included a new exploration of love as an emotion (e.g., Gonzaga, Keltner, Londahl, & Smith, 2001) and the dramatic new developments in the biology of love (e.g., Fisher, 1998), notably including most recently the work on oxytocin and vasopressin in monogamous prairie voles (e.g., Carter et al., 1997; Lim, Murphy, & Young, 2004; Young, Wang, & Insel, 1998), the related work it has inspired in humans (e.g., Gonzaga, 2002), and the recent neuroimaging studies of romantic love (Aron, Fisher, Mashek, Strong, Li, & Brown, 2004; Bartels & Zeki, 2000).

This chapter is an overview of the current state of knowledge of romantic love, noting as appropriate both the sources of the ideas and the latest thinking and findings. We conclude with some comments on potential future directions.

What Is Romantic Love?

In this section, we first review research on how ordinary people construe love. Then we turn to how researchers have understood and measured love, organizing our discussion around the theme of types of love.

How Ordinary People Construe Love

Fehr (1988, 2001) suggested that the long-standing philosophical controversies over the meaning of love and the corresponding diversity of conceptual and operational definitions in the scientific literature are due to the possibility that ordinary people recognize instances of love not by their conforming to some formal definition but rather by their family resemblance to a prototypical exemplar (just as people seem to recognize something as a fruit by its similarity to an apple). Thus, Fehr (1988) adapted Mervis and Rosch's (1981) prototype approach to the topic of love. Specifically, she first had a group of participants simply list words that they considered the features of love. She then took the features listed by more than one individual and had another sample rate them for centrality to the concept. The result was striking agreement across persons in relative centrality of the different features, such that some features were central (e.g., caring, intimacy) and others, although clearly part of the concept, were more peripheral (e.g., butterflies in the stomach, euphoria). Additional studies demonstrated that the various prototypical features identified in this way, and particularly the most central features, were used by people to recognize instances of love and that these features structured processing and memory for love-related information.

One line of research emerging from Fehr's work has focused on generalizability. Fehr's studies were with North American students. However, replications with other age groups and in a number of other societies have produced sets of features of love with clear prototype structures, and in most cases even the actual content (the particular features and relative centrality of those features) have been found to be reasonably common across age groups and cultures (reviewed in Fehr, 2001). Another line of research emerging from Fehr's prototype work focuses on the latent structure of the prototypical love features. Across seven studies, Aron and Westbay (1996) identified and cross-validated three latent dimensions of these features, intimacy (which included mainly features with the highest centrality ratings), commitment (mainly the next most central items), and passion (mainly the least central items).

Other approaches to how ordinary people understand love have included Shaver, Schwartz, Kirson, and O'Connor's (1987) prototype work in which they found that love and joy are related or similar, but love is more personalized toward the object of affection, whereas joy is more general in nature. They also noted that people describe love as a form of social contact that is highly specific and focused on the love object, a desire to be near to, to touch, kiss (and so forth) the loved person. Yet another approach has been to focus not on prototypical features but on prototypical kinds of love. Thus Fehr and Russell (1991) found that maternal and friendship love were prototypical of love in general, but romantic and sexual love were not.

In sum, it appears that people have a common understanding of what love means in terms of its resemblance to a set of prototype features, that this kind of understanding is found almost everywhere, although there are some differences in its content across cultures; that in North American culture the central features tend to be related to intimacy, the next most central to commitment, and the more peripheral to passion; and that romantic love is not the most prototypical of love in general.

Scientific and Scholarly Delineations: Types of Love

Scientific and scholarly work on the nature of love has mainly emphasized identifying and differentiating subspecies or aspects of love. Most centrally is the distinction between romantic love (the focus of this chapter) and more general kinds of love, such as familial love, compassionate love for strangers, love of God, or love of country. As noted, the focus of this chapter is on romantic love, love in the context of romantic relationships – that is, relationships of the kind that typically have an explicit actual or potential sexual component, such as dating and marital relationships. Aron and Aron (1991) defined love as "the constellation of behaviors, cognitions, and emotions associated with a desire to enter or maintain a close relationship with a specific other person" (p. 26).

With regard to the relation of romantic love to other relationship constructs, Rubin (1970) explicitly distinguished loving from liking, and developed a measure that included separate scales for each. His 13-item love scale emphasizes dependence, caring, and exclusiveness and was validated in part by showing that college dating couples who scored higher on the scale gazed longer into their partner's eyes. His parallel liking scale, on the other hand, emphasizes similarity, respect, and positive evaluation. Importantly, the two scales were only moderately correlated. Indeed, in one study (Wong, 1989), intensity of unrequited love was positively correlated with the love scores and negatively correlated with liking scores. Rubin's scale has been widely used, and other researchers have found the conceptual distinction between liking and loving to be very useful (e.g., Davis & Todd, 1985; Sternberg, 1987).

Turning specifically to romantic love, a key distinction has been between passionate and companionate love. Berscheid and Hatfield [Walster] (1978) defined the first as "a state of intense longing for union with another" (p. 9). They defined companionate love as "the affection we feel for those with whom our lives are deeply entwined" (p. 9). Based on their definition of passionate love, Hatfield and Sprecher (1986) developed a Passionate Love Scale (PLS). Example items include "I would rather be with __ than with anyone else" and "I melt when looking deeply into __'s eyes." The PLS has been used successfully in a wide variety of studies, including studies that distinguish what it measures from companionate love (Sprecher & Regan, 1998); most recently, it was used in an functional magnetic resonance imaging (fMRI) study in which PLS scores correlated with activation in a region of the caudate associated with reward (Aron, Fisher, et al., 2004). The distinction between companionate and passionate love also maps on to a related distinction people have been shown to make between those whom they "love" and the subset of these with whom they are "in love," for whom they also typically report sexual desire (Myers & Berscheid, 1997).

There has been little explicit attention devoted to companionate love except as a conceptual counterpoint to passionate love. Thus, for example, Masuda (2003) conducted a meta-analysis comparing correlations of passionate and companionate love with satisfaction involving more than 33 studies by using a variety of measures to represent each construct (for passionate love measures, the mean disattenuated correlation with satisfaction was 0.64; for companionate love measures, the correlation was either 0.34 for studies using measures of "friendship love," or 0.72, for studies using other measures such as Rubin's liking or loving scales and measures of intimacy).

Another influential categorization focuses on "love styles." This was originally a circumplex model of three central and three secondary love types, based on a combination of historical conceptions and empirical analysis of interview reports (Lee, 1977). However, most research applications have employed the Hendrick and Hendrick (1986, 2003) measure, which treats Lee's styles as six relatively independent dimensions: eros (romantic, passionate love), ludus (game playing love), storge (friendship love), pragma (logical, "shopping-list" love), mania (possesive, dependent love), and agape (selfless love).

Yet another influential categorization of romantic love was developed by Sternberg (1986), based on his attempt to integrate the existing psychology and related literatures. Sternberg offers a triangular theory, which conceptualizes love in terms of intimacy, commitment–decision, and passion. Sternberg treated these three components as ingredients that in various combinations define types of love, such as "romantic love" (the combination of high intimacy, low commitment, and high passion) or "fatuous love" (high passion, low intimacy, and high commitment). Sternberg's three components correspond reasonably well with Aron and Westbay's (1996) later empirical identification of latent dimensions of lay conceptions of love and Sternberg's conceptualization has been independently influential (e.g., Acker & Davis, 1992). However, research using this conceptualization has been hampered by the lack of a strong measure. The questionnaire Sternberg (1997) developed has been difficult to use because of problems of discriminant validity among the scales assessing the three components (e.g., Whitley, 1993).

Hendrick and Hendrick (1989) factor analyzed many of the measures of love based on the typologies we have considered (as well as some others) and identified five latent dimensions. The first two factors, which accounted for most of the variance (34 and 14%), Fehr (2001) identified with passionate and companionate love, respectively. Hendrick and Hendrick commented that the last three factors are "less important but deserve mention" (p. 791). Factor 3 could be described as manic or ambivalent love, Factor 4 as security–closeness, and Factor 5 as a kind of solid, practical, nonerotic, friendship love.

Before concluding this section, we should also note that some of the relationship qualities identified as a part or type of love, also have often been distinguished from love. One such construct is commitment. Fehr (1988) demonstrated that lay conceptions of love and commitment are overlapping but not identical; Fehr's (2001) review of studies using measures of people's experience of the two constructs in actual relationships yielded a similar conclusion. Another such construct is closeness and intimacy (for a further distinction of closeness vs. intimacy, see Aron & Mashek, 2004). An interesting theoretical suggestion is that passionate love is a function of the rate of change in closeness (Aron & Aron, 1986) or rate of change in intimacy (Baumeister & Bratslavsky, 1999). However, there are no studies to date directly testing these predictions, and both closeness and intimacy seem tightly linked to love (e.g., Aron & Westbay [1996] found that the intimacy dimension was most central to the prototype of love, and Aron & Fraley [1999] found that closeness was highly correlated with measures of love).

One way to summarize much of this literature is in terms of passion, intimacy, and commitment. Passionate love has been distinguished from the outset from companionate love; it appears as a distinct factor in analyses of lay features of love; it is a strong factor when considering diverse measures of love; it is described as one of the three components in Sternberg's system; and it is described as eros or mania in Lee's and the Hendricks' system. Other types of romantic love are less clear-cut. Companionate love seems to comprise a combination of commitment and intimacy, is perhaps deeply linked with relationship satisfaction more generally, and seems strongly linked with types of love including friendship love, practical love, and all-giving (agape) love. Because most of these other topics have entire chapters devoted to them elsewhere in this volume (i.e., chapters on commitment and satisfaction), the main focus of this chapter is on romantic love (the passionate love aspect), although we continue to refer briefly to companionate love when there are unique relevant findings or thinking that may not be covered elsewhere in this volume.

The Biological Basis of Romantic Love

Based on a review of the relevant biological literature, Fisher (1998) hypothesized that avian and mammalian species have evolved three distinct brain systems for courtship, mating, reproduction, and parenting: (a) the sex drive, characterized by a craving for sexual gratification; (b) attraction ("favoritism," "sexual preference," or "mate choice"), characterized by focused attention on a preferred partner, heightened energy, motivation, and goal-oriented courtship behaviors; and (c) attachment, characterized by the maintenance of proximity, affiliative gestures, and expressions of calm when in social contact with a mating partner and separation anxiety when apart (as well as parental behaviors such as territory defense, nest building, mutual feeding, grooming, and other parental chores). Each emotion–motivation system is associated with a different constellation of brain circuits, different behavior patterns, and different affective states; each emotion–motivation system varies according to the reproductive strategy of each species; and each emotion–motivation system evolved to play a different role in courtship, mating, reproduction, and parenting. The sex drive evolved principally to motivate individuals to seek sexual union with a range of partners. Attraction evolved to motivate individuals to prefer particular mating partners and focus their courtship attention on these mates, thereby making a mate choice. The system for adult male–female attachment evolved primarily to motivate individuals to sustain affiliative connections long enough to complete species-specific parental duties.

From the perspective of the present chapter on human romantic love, we can equate Fisher's "attraction" with passionate love and Fisher's "attachment" with companionate love. (We return later to the issue of the distinction between the sex drive and romantic love.)

The Biology of Passionate Love

It is well established that many creatures have mate preferences and make mate choices. The phenomenon of mate choice is so common that the ethological literature regularly uses several terms to describe it, including "mate choice," "female choice," "mate preference," "individual preference," "favoritism," "sexual choice," and "selective perceptivity." Fisher (1998; Fisher et al.,

2002) argued that this brain system has a specific and distinct constellation of neural correlates; that this system operates in tandem with other neural systems, including the sex drive and specific sensory circuits for mate discrimination; that it is expressed at different times and to different degrees according to each species' specific reproductive strategy; and that this brain system evolved to enable the chooser to discriminate between courtship displays, prefer those that advertise superior genes, better resources, or more parental investment, and motivate the chooser to focus his or her courtship attention on and pursue specific mating partners.

In most species of mammals and birds, this excitatory state of attraction is brief. Feelings of attraction last only minutes, hours, days, or weeks. In humans, Fisher argued, the neural mechanism for attraction is more developed, forming the physiological basis of what is commonly known as passionate love, obsessive love, or romantic love.

Ethologists generally lump this system, attraction, with the sex drive and call this behavioral–physiological state "proceptivity." There are exceptions. Beach (1976) made a distinction between the sex drive and attraction, writing, "The occurrence or non-occurrence of copulation depends as much on individual affinities and aversions as upon the presence or absence of sex hormones in the female" (p. 131). Moreover, "proceptive and receptive behavior may depend upon different anatomical and neurochemical systems in the brain" (p. 131). Goodall (1986) wrote that "partner preferences, independent of hormonal influences, are clearly of major significance for chimpanzees" (p. 446).

Few scientists have considered the anatomic and neurochemical mechanisms that produce mate choice (see Fisher et al., 2002). However, Beach (1976) and Liebowitz (1983) proposed that the neurotransmitters associated with arousal, dopamine, or norepinephrine (or a combination of these) may be involved. Fisher (1998) hypothesized that attraction (romantic love) may be associated with *elevated*

activity of the brain's dopamine or norepinephrine and *decreased* activity of the brain's serotonin. These hypotheses are consistent with considerable correlational evidence. Characteristics of intense passionate love include focused attention, strong motivation, goal-oriented behaviors, heightened energy, sleeplessness, loss of appetite, feelings of euphoria, obsessive thinking about the beloved, and heightened attraction during adversity in the relationship (e.g., Tennov, 1979). Each of these characteristics are associated with elevated activities of central dopamine and norepinephrine or decreased activity of central serotonin in the corresponding brain regions (Flament, Rapoport, & Bert, 1985; Hollander et al., 1988; Schultz, 2000; Thoren, Asberg, & Bertilsson, 1980; Wise, 1989; see Fisher 1998). Passionate attraction takes a variety of graded forms, however, ranging from romantic love that is returned to unrequited love. So it is expected that these gradations of attraction are associated with different combinations of dopamine, norepinephrine, and serotonin, as well as with the activities of many other neural systems (Fisher, 1998).

Data from animal studies also support the hypothesis that elevated activities of central dopamine play a primary role in attraction in mammalian species. In rats, blocking the activities of dopamine diminishes specific proceptive behaviors, including hopping and darting (Herbert, 1996). Further, when a female lab-raised prairie vole is mated with a male, she forms a distinct preference for this partner. This preference is associated with a 50% increase of dopamine in the nucleus accumbens (Gingrich, Liu, Cascio, Wang, & Insel, 2000). In fact, when a dopamine antagonist is injected directly into the nucleus accumbens, females no longer prefer this partner and when a female is injected with a dopamine agonist, she begins to prefer a conspecific who is present at the time of infusion, even if the female has not mated with this male (Aragona, Yan, Curtis, Stephan, & Wang, 2003; Wang et al., 1999).

Two recent studies using fMRI lend relatively direct support to the dopamine hypothesis in humans. fMRI technology scans the brain to register blood flow changes in any or all brain regions that are either increasing or decreasing their metabolic activities. Bartels and Zeki (2000) scanned a group of participants who reported being "truly, deeply, and madly in love" (p. 3829), and compared brain activation when looking at the beloved partner versus when looking at familiar friends. They found a specific constellation of brain activity associated with looking at the beloved, including activity in the caudate nucleus. The caudate nucleus is largely associated with motivation and goal-oriented behaviors; 80% of receptor sites for dopamine reside here, and the caudate is a central part of the brain's "reward system," the system associated with the identification of, focus on, and motivation to win rewards. These data suggest that passionate romantic love is primarily a motivation system associated with dopamine pathways in the reward system of the brain.

Aron, Fisher, et al. (2004) conducted a similar study, but their participants were more recently and even more intensely in love than those in the Bartels and Zeki study. (In the Aron et al. sample, mean time in love was 7 months and mean PLS score was 8.54 on a 9-point scale; in the Bartels and Zeki sample, the corresponding means were 29 and 7.55 months). In the Aron et al. study, comparison of activations when looking at and thinking about a beloved (vs. looking at and thinking about familiar neutral individual) again yielded significant activation in the caudate. Indeed, in this study, the caudate activation was especially strong. Further, Aron et al. found that this caudate activation was significantly correlated (0.60) with scores on the PLS. (Bartels & Zeki did not test this correlation.) Most important, Aron et al. also found significant activity in the right ventral tegmental area, a region primarily associated with the production and distribution of dopamine to several other brain regions. These data further suggest that dopamine plays a central role in the focused attention, motivation, and goal-oriented behaviors associated with romantic love.

In sum, the considerable data on mate preference in mammalian (and avian) species, and the association of this mate preference with subcortical dopaminergic pathways in human and animal studies suggest that attraction in mammals (and its human counterpart, romantic love) is a specific biobehavioral brain system; that it is associated with at least one specific neurotransmitter, dopamine; and that this brain system evolved to facilitate a specific reproductive function: mate preference and pursuit of this preferred mating partner.

The Biology of Companionate Love

As noted earlier, companionate love overlaps with intimacy and commitment and general relationship satisfaction, topics treated elsewhere in this volume. Thus, the focus of this chapter is mainly on passionate love. Nevertheless, we should mention that there has been some important work on love more generally, specifically on adult male–female attachment behaviors in other mammalian species and fMRI data on maternal love in humans.

Several brain chemicals have been implicated in male–female bonding, group bonding, and mother–infant bonding in mammals (see Pedersen, Caldwell, Peterson, Walker, & Mason, 1992). Recent data indicate that oxytocin and vasopressin are the primary neurohormones associated with monogamous male–female attachment and monogamous parenting behaviors in mammals (Carter et al., 1997; Lim et al., 2004; Young et al., 1998;). Moreover, the distribution of receptor sites associated with these neurohormonal systems in the brain are directed by specific genes (Lim et al., 2004; Young, Nilsen, Waymire, MacGregor, & Insel, 1999) and these systems vary from one species to the next, contributing to species differences in male–female attachment (Lim et al., 2004).

Recent fMRI studies of humans have also begun to record the brain regions associated with maternal love (Bartels & Zeki, 2004; Swain et al., 2004), and some of these results suggest that central oxytocin and vasopressin systems also play a role in mother–infant attachment (Bartels & Zeki, 2004; Leckman et al., 2004). Researchers are beginning to pinpoint some of the neural mechanisms that most likely contribute to human attachment, specifically male–female companionate love and maternal love.

The Course of Love

Initial Attraction

Other chapters in this volume focus on attraction (see also Berschied & Reis, 1998) and courtship (see especially Surra, Gray, Boettcher, Cottle, & West). Thus, we review only briefly the extensive literature on romantic attraction, focusing specifically on the especially intense attractions commonly referred to as "falling in love."

Research over the years has identified several factors that lead to general liking, which also have been found to play a role in specifically romantic attraction. These include reciprocal liking (discovering that the other likes the self; e.g., Walster & Walster, 1963); desirability of the other (kindness, intelligence, humor, good looks, social status, etc.; e.g., Buss, 1989); similarity, especially of attitudes, personality, and demographic characteristics (e.g., Byrne, 1971; Laumann, Gagnon, Michael, & Michaels, 1994; Rushton, 1989); exposure (e.g., Zajonc, 1968); and social appropriateness, support, and encouragement from one's social network (e.g., Sprecher et al., 1994).

In the specific context of falling in love, reciprocal liking and desirability of the partner appear to be the most influential (Aron, Dutton, Aron, & Iverson, 1989), even across cultures (Buss, 1989; Sprecher et al., 1994). For example, Aron et al. (1989) reported that in their sample of Canadian college students who very recently fell in love, approximately 90% of accounts mentioned some indicator of perceiving the other was attracted to the self (with eye contact being a particularly common reported cue) and approximately 78% of accounts mentioned desirable characteristics. They commented that these data

suggest "people are just waiting for an attractive person to do something they can interpret as liking them" (p. 251).

Among desirable characteristics, across many cultures, kindness and intelligence (Buss, 1989) seem to be especially important for both women and men. Men and women do seem to vary in their mate preferences, however. Men are somewhat more likely to be attracted to women who show visual signs of youth, health, and beauty; women tend to be somewhat more attracted to men who exhibit signs of status and resources (e.g., Buss, 1989; Li, Bailey, & Kenrick, 2002).

Regarding similarity, perceived shared attitudes plays a highly consistent role across many experiments (Byrne, 1971), but when other variables are also free to vary, the effect sizes are often relatively small (e.g., Newcomb, 1956). Further, much of the effects may be due to reduced attraction to perceived dissimilars (Rosenbaum, 1986). It is also clear that perceived similarity is much more important than actual similarity (Berscheid & Reis, 1998). Personality similarity seems to play a much smaller role (Botwin, Buss, & Shackelford, 1997; Caspi & Herbener, 1993). In general dissimilarity ("opposites attract") seems to play little positive role in attraction, although there is some evidence that when one believes a relationship with an appropriate other is likely, one may prefer dissimilars over similars (Aron, Steele, & Kashdan, 2005).

Exposure or "propinquity" may function mainly as providing an opportunity. There is little direct evidence for it playing much of a direct role in falling in love (Aron et al., 1989; Sprecher et al., 1994), although the possibility that platonic friendships are a common beginning for romantic relationships given the romantic attractions they often include (Kaplan & Keys, 1997) may be due to such an effect.

Social appropriateness and the impact of social networks has been relatively unexplored. Sprecher et al. (1994) found that social networks play a more important role in Japanese than in American culture, perhaps consistent with the former being more collectivist. There is some evidence in

American culture for a "Romeo and Juliet Effect" in which romantic love is inversely correlated with parental approval (Driscoll, Davis, & Lipetz, 1972); however, most studies support the more universal pattern of parental approval being a positive factor (Sprecher, Felmlee, & Orbuch, 2002).

In addition to these general attraction variables, Aron et al. (1989) argued that there are at least three variables that appear to be specific to falling in love: arousal at time of meeting the partner (the "arousal–attraction effect"), readiness for falling in love, and "specific cues." The arousal–attraction effect has been demonstrated in a series of experiments including the Dutton and Aron (1974) "shaky bridge" study in which male participants were more attracted to a good-looking confederate when the participant met her on an anxiety-provoking suspension bridge than when they met her on a solid, low bridge. Subsequent studies (see Foster, Witcher, Campbell, & Green, 1998) have demonstrated the generalizability of the effect under a great variety of positive and negative sources of arousal, as well as supporting at least two mechanisms (reattribution of arousal and eliciting of a dominant response). One recent study (Lewandowski & Aron, 2004) showed the effect generalizes across women and men and holds even when the partner is not a confederate.

The main direct support for a readiness effect comes from the Aron et al. (1989) study in which it was mentioned with moderate frequency in accounts of falling in love and the Sprecher et al. (1994) cross-cultural study in which Russian, Japanese, and U.S. participants all rated it as being moderately important for falling in love. Indeed, it seems reasonable that people are less likely to fall in love with Person A when they have just fallen in love with Person B and may be more likely to fall in love when they have just broken up with someone.

The role of specific cues was first suggested by Binet (1887), the inventor of the intelligence test, who noted that individuals are often strongly attracted to others with some very specific characteristic (a color of hair, shape of face, way of walking, etc.), a theme extended by Grant (1957). Aron et al. (1989) found a number of accounts of falling in love that seemed especially well explained by such a phenomenon; perhaps consistent with studies showing that people often select romantic partners similar to their parents (e.g., Aron et al., 1974; Little, Penton-Voak, & Burt, 2003).

Effects of Falling in Love

Taking a largely qualitative approach, Tennov (1979) studied individuals who reported intense romantic love. As noted earlier, such individuals commonly report focused attention, strong motivation, goal-oriented behaviors, heightened energy, sleeplessness, loss of appetite, feelings of euphoria, obsessive thinking about the beloved, and heightened attraction during adversity in the relationship, characteristics that correspond well with those emphasized in Hatfield and Sprecher's (1986) PLS described earlier.

Is falling in love a good thing? Based on the self-expansion model (Aron, Aron, & Norman, 2001, reviewed below), Aron, Paris, and Aron (1995) predicted that falling in love, when reciprocated, would lead to an enhancement of the self-concept, including increased identity domain, greater sense of self-efficacy, and greater self-esteem. They studied two large samples of mainly first- and second-year U.S. college students, collecting data every 2 weeks over the first 10 weeks of the fall term. In both studies, at each testing participants completing a series of items about what had happened in the last 2 weeks, among which were items about whether they had fallen in love. In addition, in the first study, at each testing, they also answered an open-ended question "Who are you today?"; in the second study, they completed standard self-efficacy and self-esteem scales. About 25% of participants fell in love at some point over the 10 weeks. The key results were that participants who fell in love showed significant increases in diversity of the self-concept and increased self-efficacy and self-esteem from the testing session before to the testing session after they fell in love. These changes were significantly greater than the changes across other testing-to-testing periods for the participants who fell in love and also significantly greater than the average testing-to-testing changes for the participants who did not fall in love. Further, all of these results remained significant even after statistically controlling for mood changes associated with falling in love.

Unreciprocated Love

Of course, falling in love need not result in it being reciprocated. Baumeister et al. (1993) compared autobiographical accounts of being rejected and of being the object of someone's undesired attraction. They found that rejection can lead to strong organization as well as strong disorganization of thoughts, behaviors, and emotions; both the rejector's and rejectee's behaviors are mostly passive; and both wish (but don't necessarily act) for different behaviors and outcomes from the other and both usually end up disappointed.

Aron et al. (1998) found that intensity of unrequited love was predicted by three factors. The most important was perceived desirability of the partner and the relationship (e.g., high ratings for "How perfect is this person in your eyes?"); the second most important was perceived desirability of the state of being in love, whether reciprocated or not (e.g., "How fulfilling is it to love this person even though it is unrequited?"); and the least important (but still significant) was mistakenly believing at the outset that the other would reciprocate the love (e.g., "Even though you don't feel this person loves you as much as you would like, to what extent has this person done things that would make most people think he or she loves you?"). Aron et al. (1998) also found differences by self-reported attachment style. Secure individuals were least likely to experience unrequited love; when they did, they were the group with the strongest association with mistaken expectation of reciprocation. Avoidant individuals were the next most likely to experience unrequited love; when they did, they were the group with the strongest association with desirability of

the state of being in love. Finally, anxious–ambivalent individuals were the most likely to experience unrequited love and were the group with the strongest association with desirability of the partner (indeed, it was extremely strong for them, and intensity for them was negatively associated with desirability of the state of being in love).

Maintaining Love Over Time

Relationship satisfaction and measures of companionate love generally show declines over time after the initial relationship period (Karney & Bradbury, 1995; Tucker & Aron, 1993). Indeed, one 5-year longitudinal study of dating couples (Sprecher, 1999) found that although reports of love declined over each year, participants at the end of each year reported that they loved their partner more. Thus, it is possible that either people believe that love increases even when it does not (consistent with Karney & Frye's [2002] findings on recall of satisfaction), or perhaps the meaning of love changes so that what was considered love last year is now considered a shallow affection.

In any case, with regard to passionate love, the general view among love theorists has been that if a romantic relationship persists over time, passionate love declines over the first couple years (e.g., Huesman, 1980; Sternberg, 1986), and, if things are going well, companionate love correspondingly increases (e.g., Berscheid & Hatfield [Walster], 1969; Sternberg, 1986), creating perhaps a "warm afterglow" (Reik, 1944). Consistent with this view, cross-sectional data show that passionate love is higher at marriage than either just before the birth of a couple's first child or just before the last child leaves home, and longitudinal data show that it is higher before than after marriage (Tucker & Aron, 1993) and from the first to second year of marriage (Traupmann & Hatfield, 1981; Utne, 1977). Pineo (1961) found declines in self-report items of physical attraction and romantic feeling in 400 married couples from engagement to 20 years later.

Several theories have been offered to explain the general decline in passionate love over time. One approach emphasizes habituation (e.g., Aronson & Linder, 1965; Berger, 1988; Huesmann, 1980). Another view emphasizes the evolutionary value of passionate love for initiating and maintaining the relationship over the early stages, or long enough to conceive a child (e.g., Fisher, 1998, 2004). Yet another perspective emphasizes that passion arises from the rapid development of the relationship. Thus, Aron and Aron (1986) argued that passion arises from the intensity of the rapid self-expansion that occurs in the formation of a relationship as one comes to include the other in the self; after the other is largely included, the rate of expansion inevitably slows down. Baumeister and Bratslavsky (1999) offered a similar model, emphasizing that passion is a function of the rate of increase in intimacy and that as intimacy plateaus, passion decreases.

Nevertheless, while passionate love (and satisfaction and love of all kinds) generally declines over time, the view that passionate love *inevitably* declines has not been demonstrated. It is certainly clear that many long-term couples experience high levels of satisfaction (e.g., Cuber & Harroff, 1965). Indeed, in a 4-year longitudinal study of newlyweds, Karney and Bradbury (1997) found that about 10% maintained or increased their level of satisfaction. Perhaps more surprising, several cross-sectional studies have found a small percentage of individuals in long-term relationships of 20 years or more report very high levels of passionate love (reviewed in Tucker & Aron, 1993). Preliminary results of an interview study (Acevedo & Aron, 2005) suggest that at least some such reports may correspond to how the relationship is actually being experienced and not due merely to response bias or self-deception. Further, Aron, Norman, Aron, McKenna, and Heyman (2000) were able to increase reported passionate love (at least temporarily) in long-term relationship partners through an experimental task, suggesting there may be natural mechanisms that permit high levels of passionate love even in long-term relationships.

How Does Love Work? (Models of Love Processes)

In this section, we briefly review seven approaches that have been particularly influential in specifically focusing on understanding the dynamics of romantic love in general, and especially with regard to passionate love. Other important theoretical approaches in the relationship area, such as interdependence theory (Kelley & Thibaut, 1979), have only rarely been applied specifically to romantic love (e.g., Kelley, 1983; Rusbult et al., 1993)

Cultural Models

As noted at the outset, romantic love has been observed in every culture in which observers have reported on relevant topics and in every era of human history (Fisher, 2004; Hatfield & Rapson, 2002; Jankowiak & Fischer, 1992). However, the extent to which it is valued by a culture, the role it plays in marriage, and the traditional exemplars and narratives seem to differ greatly across cultures (e.g., Dion & Dion, 1988, 1996; Hatfield, Martel, & Rapson, in press; Hatfield & Rapson, 1996; Hendrick & Hendrick, 2003). For example, Dion and Dion focused on individualism and collectivistic views or attitudes. They argued that individualistic people may have a difficult time loving and becoming intimate with each other. The high divorce rate in the United States may be due to exaggerated feelings of individualism. As another example, Sprecher et al. (1994) compared love experiences of college students in the United States, Japan, and Russia. Across the three cultures, most participants had been in love at least once, erotic love was the most common style, most believed that love should be the basis of marriage, and desirable personality and physical appearance and reciprocal liking were most important for falling in love. There were also differences: Americans had more secure attachment, were higher on the eros and storge love styles and on passionate love, and considered physical appearance and similarity more important for falling in love.

Russians scored higher on avoidant attachment, ludus love style and agape style, and were most willing to marry someone they didn't love romantically (41% of Russian women and 30% of Russian men reported that); Russians rated familiarity high but personality and similarity low as reasons they had fallen in love. Japanese were least likely to be in love at the time and more likely to have never been in love; they had more avoidants, were less romantic, and considered social standing more important.

Overall, these examples and other studies of cultural (and subcultural) differences and similarities (e.g., Contreras, Hendrick, & Hendrick, 1996; Doherty, Hatfield, Thompson, & Choo, 1994; Kim, Hatfield, & Kim, 2004; Levine, Sato, Hashimoto, & Verma, 1995; Simmons, vom Kolke, & Shimizu, 1986) suggest that there is a core element of passionate love that arises in every culture and that may even have an evolutionary foundation, but how it is enacted may depend heavily on the cultural context.

Love As Emotion

Many emotion theorists have treated love as an emotion (e.g., Gonzaga et al., 2001) or even as a basic emotion (Shaver, Morgan, & Wu, 1996; Shaver et al., 1987), noting, for example, that it is typically the first response given when participants are asked for an example of an emotion and, particularly when one focuses on "moments of love," it shows many of the features of emotions. On the other hand, Aron and Aron (1991) argued that although love is highly emotional, it may be better characterized as a goal-oriented motivational state and not as a specific emotion in its own right, given that it tends to be hard to control, is not associated with any specific facial expression, and is focused on a specific reward. To date, this latter view is supported by two lines of research. First, in various studies (Acevedo & Aron, 2004a; Rousar, 1990) asking participants to check the emotions one feels or has felt when experiencing "love" (or "romantic love," "passionate love," or a "moment of passionate love"), many more emotions are checked than are checked for fear, anger,

sadness, or happiness; in each case, there were also more opposite valence emotions checked when rating experiences of love than experiences of fear and so forth. These results were predicted based on the idea that like other goal oriented states, love generates a variety of specific emotions according to the extent to which it is satisfied or frustrated. The second line of work is the recent fMRI studies of romantic love (Aron Fisher et al., 2005; Bartels & Zeki, 2000), which, as noted earlier, found activation across participants primarily in reward-related brain regions, with greater diversity of response in emotion-related regions.

At this point it seems clear that passionate love has a strong motivational component and functions much like a goal state. Nevertheless, it remains possible that love may also be a specific emotion or represent a specific motivational experience. Of course, both a constellation of emotions and several motivations are clearly involved, and definitions of what are called emotions versus motivations are somewhat overlapping.

Love As Sex

Ellen Berscheid (1988) made the influential comment that passionate love is "about 90% sexual desire unfulfilled." Clearly, sexual desire plays a significant role in passionate love. For example, in the lay prototype of love developed by Fehr (1988), many of the features identified by Aron and Westbay (1996) as part of the passion factor are sexual in nature, including sexual passion, sex appeal, and physical attraction. Similarly, the PLS Scale, the most widely used measure of passionate love, includes items that emphasize sexual desire, including "I sense my body responding when __ touches me," "In the presence of __, I yearn to touch, and be touched," and "Sometimes my body trembles with excitement at the sight of __" – all items that correlate highly with the other scale items.

Nevertheless, it does seem possible to distinguish passionate love from sexual desire. Conceptually, Aron and Aron (1991) argued that understandings of passionate love and sexuality fall on a continuum from love being the cause of sex to sex being the cause of love. In terms of evolutionary foundations, as noted earlier, Fisher (1998) argued that romantic attraction and the sex drive are associated with distinct brain systems and that each evolved to facilitate a different aspect of courtship, mating, and reproduction. Several studies also support their being such a distinction. Gonzaga et al. (2001) found positive correlations between love and sexual desire, but also that there are different cues and different behavioral responses. Another relevant line of thinking is Diamond's (2003) argument that sexual orientation does not completely predict the gender of objects of passionate love and that individuals sometimes appear to fall in love with partners of the "wrong" gender with whom they may have no initial desire to have sexual contact, even though they show all the other symptoms of passionate love. Finally, the two fMRI studies of romantic love (Aron Fisher et al., 2005; Bartels & Zeki, 2000) found activations that only minimally overlapped with activations that have been found in studies of sexual arousal (e.g., Arnow et al., 2002; Karama et al., 2002).

In sum, sexuality almost surely plays an important role in passionate love, but it is also conceptually and empirically distinguishable from it and cannot fully explain its functioning.

Love As Attachment

Attachment theory (Bowlby, 1969; Shaver & Mikulincer, this volume) has been among the most influential approaches to understanding romantic love and is the primary approach that emphasizes individual differences. The theory posits that love develops out of three behavioral systems that evolved to promote development and survival of infants in humans and perhaps other primates or even other species (Shaver, Hazan, & Bradshaw, 1988). These systems include attachment, caregiving, and sexuality. In human adults, according to this model, passionate love is a combination of the desire for attachment and sexuality. (Companionate love develops out of these systems plus the caregiving system.) Further, this model

emphasizes that early experience with caregivers (whether they serve as a reliable secure base for exploration and safe haven under threat) strongly shapes individual differences in adult love experiences. Thus, for example, those who have had inconsistent caregiving (those high on the anxious attachment or preoccupied dimension) are much more likely to experience intense passionate love and more likely to experience intense unrequited love, whereas those who experienced a consistent lack of security (those high on the avoidance dimension) are especially unlikely to experience passionate love in adulthood (Aron et al., 1998; Hendrick & Hendrick, 1989). Some preliminary evidence even suggests that the brain systems engaged by passionate love may be moderated by individual differences in attachment style (Aron, Fisher et al., 2004).

Love as a Story

Sternberg (1998) suggested that loving relationships can be described accurately by the people involved through narrative autobiographies, often suggesting culturally prototypical "stories." For example, the story of a couple locked in constant struggle is common, as is the story of couples growing to love each other over time. This approach seems promising given the general tendency for people to organize their world in narrative form and there has been some preliminary research support for the model (Sternberg, Hojjat, & Barnes, 2001).

Evolutionary Approaches

Because courtship and mate choice are central aspects of reproduction in higher animals, it seems plausible that the experiences, behaviors, and neural underpinnings of passionate love might be strongly shaped by evolution. Thus, as noted in the section on the biology of romantic love, Fisher (1998) proposed that the brain system for romantic attraction evolved to motivate individuals to select among potential mating partners, prefer particular conspecifics, and focus their courtship attention on these favored individuals, thereby conserving precious courtship and mating time and energy.

As also noted earlier, another important line of evolutionary thinking, largely based on parental investment theory (Trivers, 1972), has emphasized gender differences in what features are desirable in a mate and in the basis for jealousy (e.g., Buss & Schmitt, 1993). There have also been some approaches to the evolutionary basis of experience and behavior in romantic love arguing that the mating system exploits an evolved bonding module between infants and parent (Hazan & Diamond, 2000; Miller & Fishkin, 1997).

Self-Expansion Model

Aron and Aron's (1986) self-expansion model posits (a) a primary human motivation to expand one's self in terms of potential to attain desired goals and (b) that a main way that people seek to expand their self is in terms of "including others in the self" through close relationships so that the other's resources, perspectives, and identities are treated to some extent as one's own. Both principles have received considerable research support (for reviews, see Aron et al., 2001; Aron, Mashek, & Aron, 2004). In terms of romantic love, Aron et al. (2000) argued that the exhilaration and intense focused attention of passionate love arises from the rapid rate of including the other in the self often associated with forming a new romantic relationship. We have cited several relevant studies throughout this chapter. Companionate love, they argued, arises from the ongoing expansion offered by the partner and the potential for loss to the self of losing the partner. (For example, Lewandowski, Aron, Bassis, & Kunak, [2005] found that the degree of negative impact on the self-concept following relationship dissolution was predicted by degree of ongoing self-expansion that had been provided by the dissolved relationship.)

Summary and Conclusions

Romantic love is a nearly universal phenomenon that has been the subject of schol-

arly interest for centuries but has only in the last half century been a topic of systematic scientific study. What has been learned from this study is that romantic love is understood by ordinary people in terms of its resemblance to a standard prototype and is best understood by researchers for purposes of systematic analysis in terms of various types of love, most centrally in terms of a distinction between passionate and companionate love. There has been considerable recent progress in identifying the biological underpinnings of romantic love, including support from animal data and human neuroimaging studies for passionate love being linked with dopamine-based reward processes, whereas companionate love seems linked with bonding more generally and perhaps specifically with central oxytocin and vasopressin systems. The course of romantic love has been well delineated in terms of predictors of initial romantic attraction and diverse studies providing insights and suggested directions for future research regarding the effects of falling in love on the self, the processes and motivations associated with unrequited love, and the course of passionate love over time including potential moderators of that course. Finally, there are now at least seven major approaches to understanding romantic love that have served as the basis for much of the research on the topic. These approaches include cultural models, emotion models, attachment theory, love as sex, evolutionary theory, love as a story, and the self-expansion model.

We hope that this review has conveyed our view that the study of romantic love is both important and a thriving scientific endeavor, offering both a solid foundation and vast opportunities for significant future work.

References

Acevedo, B., & Aron, A. (2004a, July). *On the emotional categorization of love and beyond.* Paper presented at the International Association for Relationship Research Conference, Madison, WI.

Acevedo, B., & Aron, A. (2005, June). *Intense romantic love in longterm relationships*. Paper presented at the Positive Psychology Summer Institute, Philadelphia, PA.

Acker, M., & Davis, M. H. (1992). Intimacy, passion, and commitment in adult romantic relationships: A test of the triangular theory of love. *Journal of Social and Personal Relationships, 9,* 21–50.

Aragona, B. J., Yan, L., Curtis, J. T., Stephan, F. K., & Wang, Z. (2003). A critical role for nucleus accumbens dopamine in partner-preference formation in male prairie voles. *Journal of Neuroscience, 23,* 3483–3490.

Arnow, B. A., Desmond, J. E., Banner, L. L., Glover, G. H., Solomon, A., Polan, M. L., et al. (2002). Brain activation and sexual arousal in healthy, heterosexual males. *Brain, 125,* 1014–1023.

Aron, A., & Aron, E. N. (1986). *Love and the expansion of self: Understanding attraction and satisfaction.* New York: Hemisphere.

Aron, A., & Aron, E. N. (1991). Love and sexuality. In K. McKinney & S. Sprecher (Eds.), *Sexuality in close relationships* (pp. 25–48). Hillsdale, NJ: Erlbaum.

Aron, A., Aron, E. N., & Allen, J. (1998). Motivations for unreciprocated love. *Personality and Social Psychology Bulletin, 24,* 787–796.

Aron, A., Aron, E. N., & Norman, C. (2001). The self expansion model of motivation and cognition in close relationships and beyond. In G. Fletcher & M. Clark (Eds.), *Blackwell handbook in social psychology, Volume 2: Interpersonal processes* (pp. 478–501). Oxford: Blackwell.

Aron, A., Dutton, D. G., Aron, E. N., & Iverson, A. (1989). Experiences of falling in love. *Journal of Social and Personal Relationships, 6,* 243–257.

Aron, A., et al. (1974). Relationships with opposite-sexed parents and mate choice. *Human Relations, 27,* 17–24.

Aron, A., Fisher, H. E., Mashek, D., Strong, G., Shaver, P., Mikulincer, M., et al. (2004, August). *Individual differences in attachment anxiety and attachment avoidance: An fMRI study.* Paper presented at the Conference on Biological Basis of Personality and Individual Differences, Stony Brook, NY.

Aron, A., Fisher, H., Mashek, D., Strong, G., Li, H., & Brown, L. (2005). *Neural systems in intense romantic attraction: An fMRI study Journal of Neurophysiology, 94,* 327–337.

Aron, A., & Fraley, B. (1999). Relationship closeness as including other in the self: Cognitive underpinnings and measures. *Social Cognition, 17,* 140–160.

Aron, A., & Mashek, D. (2004). Conclusion. In D. Mashek & A. Aron (Eds.), *Handbook of closeness and intimacy* (pp. 415–428). Mahwah, NJ: Erlbaum.

Aron, A., Mashek, D., & Aron, E. N. (2004). Closeness, intimacy, and including other in the self. In D. Mashek & A. Aron (Eds.), *Handbook of closeness and intimacy* (pp. 27–41). Mahwah, NJ: Erlbaum.

Aron, A., Norman, C. C., Aron, E. N., McKenna, C., & Heyman, R. (2000). Couples' shared participation in novel and arousing activities and experienced relationship quality. *Journal of Personality and Social Psychology, 78,* 273–283.

Aron, A., Paris, M., & Aron, E. N. (1995). Falling in love: Prospective studies of self-concept change. *Journal of Personality and Social Psychology, 69,* 1102–1112.

Aron, A., Steele, J. L., & Kashdan, T. (2005). *When do opposites attract? Three studies from a self-expansion model perspective.* Manuscript under review.

Aron, A., & Westbay, L. (1996). Dimensions of the prototype of love. *Journal of Personality and Social Psychology, 70,* 535–551.

Aronson, E., & Linder, D. (1965). Gain and loss of esteem as determinants of interpersonal attraction. *Journal of Experimental Social Psychology, 1,* 156–171.

Bartels, A., & Zeki, S. (2000). The neural basis of romantic love. *NeuroReport, 11,* 1–6.

Bartels, A., & Zeki, S. (2004) The neural correlates of maternal and romantic love. *Neuroimage, 21,* 1155–1166.

Baumeister, R. F., & Bratslavsky, E. (1999). Passion, intimacy, and time: Passionate love as a function of change in intimacy. *Personality and Social Psychology Review, 3,* 49–67.

Baumeister, R. F., Wotman, S. R., & Stillwell, A. M. (1993). Unrequited love: On heartbreak, anger, guilt, scriptlessness, and humiliation. *Journal of Personality and Social Psychology, 64,* 377–394.

Beach, F. A. (1976). Sexual attractivity, proceptivity, and receptivity in female mammals. *Hormones and Behavior, 7,* 105–138.

Berger, C. R. (1988). Uncertainty and information exchange in developing relationships. In S. Duck (Ed.), *Handbook of personal relationships:*

Theory, research and interventions (pp. 367–389). Chichester, England: Wiley.

Berscheid, E. (1988). Some comments on love's anatomy: Or, whatever happened to old-fashioned lust? In R. J. Sternberg & M. L. Barnes (Eds.), *The psychology of love* (pp. 359–371). New Haven, CT: Yale University Press.

Berscheid, E., & Hatfield [Walster], E. H. (l969). *Interpersonal attraction.* New York: Addison-Wesley.

Berscheid, E., & Hatfield [Walster], E. H. (1978). *Interpersonal attraction* (2nd ed.). Reading, MA: Addison-Wesley.

Berscheid, E., & Reis, H. T. (1998). Attraction and close relationships. In S. Fiske, D. Gilbert, & G. Lindzey (Eds.), *Handbook of social psychology* (4th ed., pp. 193–281). Boston: McGraw-Hill.

Binet, A. (1887). Le fetishisme dans l'amour. *Revue philosophique, 24,* 260.

Botwin, M. D., Buss, D. M., & Shackelford, T. K. (1997). Personality and mate preferences: Five factors in mate selection and satisfaction. *Journal of Personality, 65,* 107–136.

Bowlby, J. (1969). *Attachment and loss, Volume 1: Attachment.* London: Hogarth Press and the Institute of Psycho-Analysis.

Buss D. M. (1989). Sex differences in human mate preferences: Evolutionary hypotheses tested in 37 cultures. *Behavioral and Brain Sciences, 12,* 1–49.

Buss, D. M., & Schmitt, D. P. (1993). Sexual strategies theory: An evolutionary perspective on human mating. *Psychological Review, 100,* 204–232.

Byrne, D. (1971). *The attraction paradigm.* New York: Academic Press.

Carter, C. S., DeVries, A. C., Taymans, S. E., Roberts, R. L., Williams, J. R., & Getz, L. L. (1997). Peptides, steroids, and pair bonding. In C. S. Carter, I. I. Lederhendler, & B. Kirkpatrick (Eds.), *The integrative neurobiology of affiliation* (Vol. 807, pp. 260–272). *Annals of the New York Academy of Sciences.*

Caspi, A., & Herbener, E. S. (1993). Phenotypic convergence and marital assortment: Longitudinal evidence. *Social Biology, 40,* 48–59.

Contreras, R., Hendrick, S. S., & Hendrick, C. (1996). Perspectives on marital love and satisfaction in Mexican American and Anglo couples. *Journal of Counseling and Development, 74,* 408–415.

Cuber, J. F., & Harroff, P. (1965). *The significant Americans: A study of sexual behavior among the affluent.* New York: Appleton-Century.

Curtis, J. T., & Wang, Z. (2003). Forebrain c-fos expression under conditions conducive to pair bonding in female prairie voles (*Microtus ochrogaster*). *Physiology and Behavior, 80,* 95–101.

Davis, K. E., & Todd, M. J. (1985). Assessing friendship: Prototypes, paradigm cases and relationship description. In S. Duck & D. Perlman (Eds.), *Understanding personal relationships: An interdisciplinary approach* (pp. 17–38). Thousand Oaks, CA: Sage.

Diamond, L. M. (2003). What does sexual orientation orient? A biobehavioral model distinguishing romantic love and sexual desire. *Psychological Review, 110,* 173–192.

Dion, K. L., & Dion, K. K. (1988). Romantic love: Individual and cultural perspectives. In R. J. Sternberg & M. L. Barnes (Eds.), *The psychology of love* (pp. 264–289). New Haven, CT: Yale University Press.

Dion, K. K., & Dion, K. L. (1996). Cultural perspectives on romantic love. *Personal Relationships, 3,* 5–18.

Doherty, R. W., Hatfield, E., Thompson, K., & Choo, P. (1994). Cultural and ethnic influences on love and attachment. *Personal Relationships, 1,* 391–398.

Driscoll, R., Davis, K. E., & Lipetz, M. E. (1972). Parental interference and romantic love: The Romeo and Juliet effect. *Journal of Personality and Social Psychology, 24,* 1–10.

Dutton, D. G., & Aron, A. (1974). Some evidence for heightened sexual attraction under conditions of high anxiety. *Journal of Personality and Social Psychology, 30,* 510–517.

Ellis, B., & Malamuth, N. M. (2000). Love and anger in romantic relationships: A discrete systems model. *Journal of Personality, 68,* 3525–556.

Fehr, B. (1988). Prototype analysis of the concepts of love and commitment. *Journal of Personality and Social Psychology, 55,* 557–579.

Fehr, B. (2001). The status of theory and research on love and commitment. In G. Fletcher & Clark (Eds.), *Blackwell handbook in social psychology, Volume 2: Interpersonal processes* (pp. 331–336). Oxford: Blackwell.

Fehr, B., & Russell, J. A. (1991). The concept of love viewed from a prototypical perspective. *Journal of Personality and Social Psychology, 60,* 425–438.

Fisher, H. E. (1998). Lust, attraction, and attachment in mammalian reproduction. *Human Nature, 9*, 23–52.

Fisher, H. E. (2004). *Why we love: The nature and chemistry of romantic love.* New York: Holt.

Fisher, H. E., Aron, A., Mashek, D., Li, H., Strong, G., & Brown, L. L. (2002). The neural mechanisms of mate choice. *Neuroendocrinology Letters* [Special Issue], 23 (Suppl. 4), 92–97.

Flament, M. F., Rapoport, J. L., & Bert, C. L. (1985). Clomipramine treatment of childhood obsessive-compulsive disorder: A double–blind controlled study. *Archives of General Psychiatry, 42*, 977–986.

Fletcher, G. J. O., Simpson, J. A., Thomas, G., & Giles, L. (1999). Ideals in intimate relationships. *Journal of Personality and Social Psychology, 76*, 72–89.

Foster, C. A., Witcher, B. S., Campbell, W. K., & Green, J. D. (1998). Arousal and attraction: Evidence for automatic and controlled processes. *Journal of Personality and Social Psychology, 74*, 86–101.

Freud, S. (1927). Some psychological consequences of anatomical distinction between the sexes. *International Journal of Psycho-Analysis, 8*, 133–142.

Gingrich, B., Liu, Y., Cascio, C., Wang, Z., & Insel, T. R. (2000). D2 receptors in the nucleus accumbens are important for social attachment in female prairie voles (*Microtus ochrogaster*). *Behavioral Neuroscience, 114*, 173–183.

Gonzaga, G. C. (2002). Distinctions between sexual desire and love in narrative report, nonverbal expression and physiology. *Dissertation Abstracts International: Section B: The Sciences & Engineering, 63* (2-B), 1087.

Gonzaga, G. C., Keltner, D., Londahl, E. A., & Smith, M. D. (2001). Love and the commitment problem in romantic relations and friendship. *Journal of Personality and Social Psychology, 81*, 247–262.

Goodall, J. (1986). *The chimpanzees of Gombe: Patterns of behavior.* Cambridge MA: The Belknap Press of Harvard University Press.

Grant, V. W. (1957). *The psychology of sexual emotions; The basis of selective attraction.* New York: Longmans, Green.

Hatfield, E., Martel, L. , & Rapson, R. L. (in press). Love and hate. In S. Kitayama & D. Cohen (Eds.), *Handbook of cultural psychology.* New York: Guilford Press.

Hatfield, E., & Rapson, R. L. (1996). *Love and sex: Cross-cultural perspectives.* Needham Heights, MA: Allyn and Bacon.

Hatfield, E., & Rapson, R. L. (2002). Passionate love and sexual desire. In H. T. Reis, M. A. Fitzpatrick, & A. L. Vangelisti (Eds.), *Stability and change in relationships* (pp. 306–324). New York: Cambridge University Press.

Hatfield, E., & Sprecher, S. (1986). Measuring passionate love in intimate relations. *Journal of Adolescelnce, 9*, 383–410.

Hazan, C., & Diamond, L. M. (2000). The place of attachment in human mating. *Review of General Psychology, 4*, 186–204.

Hazan, C., & Shaver, P. (1987). Romantic love conceptualized as an attachment process. *Journal of Personality and Social Psychology, 52*, 511–524.

Hendrick, C., & Hendrick, S. S. (1986). A theory and method of love. *Journal of Personality and Social Psychology, 50*, 392–402.

Hendrick, C., & Hendrick, S. S. (1989). Research on love: Does it measure up? *Journal of Personality and Social Psychology, 56*, 784–794.

Hendrick, C., & Hendrick, S. S. (2003). Romantic love: Measuring cupid's arrow. In S. J. Lopez & C. R. Snyder (Eds.), *Positive psychological assessment: A handbook of models and measures* (pp. 235–249). Washington, DC: American Psychological Association.

Herbert, J. (1996). Sexuality, stress and the chemical architecture of the brain. *Annual Review of Sex Research, 7*, 1–44.

Hollander, E., Fay, M., Cohen, B., Campeas, R., Gorman, J. M., & Liebowitz, M. R. (1988). Serotonergic and noradrenergic sensitivity in obsessive-compulsive disorder: Behavioral findings. *American Journal of Psychiatry, 145*, 1015–1017.

Huesmann, L. (1980). Toward a predictive model of romantic behavior. In K. Pope (Ed.), *On love and loving* (pp. 152–171). San Francisco: Jossey-Bass.

Huston, T. (Ed.). (1974). *Foundations of interpersonal attraction.* New York: Academic Press.

Jankowiak, W. R., & Fischer, E. F. (1992). A cross-cultural perspective on romantic love. *Ethnology, 31*, 149.

Jung, C. G. (1959). Marriage as a psychological relationship. In V. S. DeLaszlo (Ed.), *The basic writings of C. G. Jung* (R. F. C. Hull, Trans., pp. 531–544). New York: Modern Library. (Original work published 1925.)

Kaplan, D. L., & Keys, C. B. (1997). Sex and relationship variables as predictors of sexual attraction in cross-sex platonic friendships between young heterosexual adults. *Journal of Social and Personal Relationships, 14*, 191–206.

Karama, S., Lecours, A. R., Leroux, J. M., Bourgouin, P., Beaudoin, G., Joubert, S., & Beauregard, M. (2002). Areas of brain activation in males and females during viewing of erotic film excerpts. *Human Brain Mapping, 16*, 1–13.

Karney, B. R., & Bradbury, T. N. (1995). The longitudinal course of marital quality and stability: A review of theory, methods, and research. *Psychological Bulletin, 118*, 3–34.

Karney, B. R., & Bradbury, T. N. (1997). Neuroticism, marital interaction, and the trajectory of marital satisfaction. *Journal of Personality and Social Psychology, 72*, 1075–1092.

Karney, B. R., & Frye, N. E. (2002). "But we've been getting better lately": Comparing prospective and retrospective views of relationship development. *Journal of Personality and Social Psychology, 82*, 222–238.

Kelley, H. H. (1983). Love and commitment. In H. H. Kelley, E. Berscheid, A. Christensen, J. H. Harvey, T. L. Huston, G. Levinger, et al. (Eds.), *Close relationships* (pp. 265–314). New York: Freeman.

Kelley, H. H. & Thibaut, J. W. (1979). *Interpersonal relations: A theory of interdependence.* New York: Wiley-Interscience.

Kim, J., Hatfield, E., & Kim, J, (2004). Love types and subjective well-being: A cross cultural study. *Social Behavior and Personality, 32*, 173–182.

Laumann, E. O., Gagnon, J. H., Michael, R. T., & Michaels, S. (1994). *The social organization of sexuality: Sexual practices in the United States.* Chicago: University of Chicago Press.

Leckman, J. F., Feldman, R., Swain, J. E., Eicher, V., Thompson, N., & Mayes, L. C. (2004). Primary parental preoccupation: Circuits, genes and the crucial role of the environment. *Journal of Neural Transmission, 111*, 753–771.

Lee, J. A. (1977). A typology of styles of loving. *Personality and Social Psychology Bulletin, 3*, 173–182.

Levine, R., Sato, S., Hashimoto, T., & Verma, J. (1995). Love and marriage in eleven cultures. *Journal of Cross-Cultural Psychology, 26*, 554–571.

Lewandowski, G. W., & Aron, A. P. (2004). Distinguishing arousal from novelty and challenge in initial romantic attraction. *Social Behavior and Personality, 32*, 361–372.

Lewandowski, G. W., Aron, A. P., Bassis, S., & Kunak, J. (2005). *Losing a self-expanding relationship: Implications for the self-concept.* Manuscript under review.

Li, N. P., Bailey, J. M., & Kenrick, D. T. (2002). The necessities and luxuries of mate preferences: Testing the tradeoffs. *Journal of Personality and Social Psychology, 82*, 947–955.

Liebowitz, M. R. (1983). *The chemistry of love.* Boston: Little, Brown.

Lim, M. M., Murphy, A. Z., & Young, L. J. (2004). Ventral striatopallidal oxytocin and vasopressin V1a receptors in the monogamous prairie vole (*Microtus ochrogaster*). *Journal of Comparative Neurology, 468*, 555–570.

Little, A. C., Penton-Voak, I. S., & Burt, D. M. (2003). Investigating an imprinting-like phenomenon in humans: Partners and opposite-sex parents have similar hair and eye colour. *Evolution and Human Behavior, 24*, 43–51.

Masuda, M. (2003). Meta-analyses of love scales: Do various love scales measure the same psychological constructs? *Japanese Psychological Research, 45*, 25–37.

Mead, M. (1928). *Coming of age in Samoa: A psychological study of primitive youth for Western civilization.* New York: Morrow.

Meloy, J. R. (1998). *The psychology of stalking: Clinical and forensic perspectives.* New York: Academic Press.

Mervis, C. B., & Rosch, E. (1981). Categorization of natural objects. *Annual Review of Psychology, 32*, 89–115.

Meyers, S. A., & Berscheid, E. (1997). The language of love: The difference a preposition makes. *Personality and Social Psychology Bulletin, 23*, 347–362.

Miller, L. C., & Fishkin, S. A. (1997). On the dynamics of human bonding and reproductive success: Seeking windows on the adapted-for human environmental interface. In J. Simpson & D. T. Kenrick (Eds.), *Evolutionary social psychology* (pp. 197–235). Hillsdale, NJ: Erlbaum.

Newcomb, T. M. (1956). The prediction of interpersonal attraction. *American Psychologist, 11*, 575–586.

Pedersen, C. A., Caldwell, J. D., Peterson, G., Walker, C. H., & Mason, G. A. (1992) Oxytocin activation of maternal behavior in the rat. *Annals of the New York Academy Science, 652*, 58–69.

Pineo, P. C. (1961). Disenchantment in the later years of marriage. *Marriage and Family Living*, 23, 3–11.

Reik, T. (1944). *A psychologist looks at love*. New York: Farrar & Reinhart.

Rosenbaum, M. E. (1986). The repulsion hypothesis: On the nondevelopment of relationships. *Journal of Personality and Social Psychology*, 51, 1156–1166.

Rousar, E. E. (1990). *Valuing's role in romantic love*. Unpublished dissertation, California Graduate School of Family Psychology, San Rafel, CA.

Rubin, Z. (1970). Measurement of romantic love. *Journal of Personality and Social Psychology*, 16, 265–273.

Rubin, Z. (1974). From liking to loving: Patterns of attraction in dating relationships. In T. L. Huston (Ed.), *Foundations of interpersonal attraction* (pp. 383–402). New York: Academic Press.

Rusbult, C. E., Onizuka, R. K., & Lipkus, I. (1993). What do we really want? Mental models of ideal romantic involvement explored through multidimensional scaling. *Journal of Experimental Social Psychology*, 29, 493–527.

Rushton, J. P. (1989). Epigenesis and social preference. *Behavioral and Brain Sciences*, 12, 31–32.

Schultz, W. (2000). Multiple reward signals in the brain. *Nature Reviews. Neuroscience*, 1, 199–207.

Shaver, P. R., Hazan, C., & Bradshaw, D. (1988). Love as attachment: The integration of three behavioral systems. In R. J. Sternberg & M. L. Barnes (Eds.), *The psychology of love* (pp. 68–99). New Haven, CT: Yale University Press.

Shaver, P. R., Morgan, H. J., & Wu, S. (1996). Is love a "basic" emotion? *Personal Relationships*, 3, 81–96.

Shaver, P., Schwartz, J., Kirson, D., & O'Connor, C. (1987). Emotion knowledge: Further exploration of a prototype approach. *Journal of Personality and Social Psychology*, 52, 1061–1086.

Simmons, C. H., vom Kolke, A., & Shimizu, H. (1986). Attitudes toward romantic love among American, German, and Japanese students. *Journal of Social Psychology*, 126, 327–336.

Sprecher, S. (1999). "I love you more today than yesterday": Romantic partners' perceptions of changes in love and related affect over time. *Journal of Personality and Social Psychology*, 76, 46–53.

Sprecher, S., Aron, A., Hatfield, E., Cortese, A., Potapova, E., & Levitskaya, A. (1994). Love: American style, Russian style and Japanese style. *Personal Relationships*, 1, 349–369.

Sprecher, S., Felmlee, D., & Orbuch, T. L. (2002). Social networks and change in personal relationships. In A. L. Vangelisti, H. T. Reis, & M. A. Fitzpatrick (Eds.), *Stability and change in relationships* (pp. 257–284). New York: Cambridge University Press.

Sprecher, S., & Regan, P. C. (1998). Passionate and companionate love in courting and young married couples. *Sociological Inquiry*, 68, 163–185.

Stendhal (pseudonym for Beyle, M. H.) (1927). *On love* (V. B. Holland, Trans). New York: Boni & Liveright. (Original work published 1822.)

Sternberg, R. J. (1986). A triangular theory of love. *Psychological Review*, 93, 119–135.

Sternberg, R. J. (1987). Liking versus loving: A comparative evaluation of theories. *Psychological Bulletin*, 102, 331–345.

Sternberg, R. J. (1997). Construct validation of a triangular love scale. *European Journal of Social Psychology*, 27, 313–335.

Sternberg, R. J. (1998). *Love is a story: A new theory of relationships*. London: Oxford University Press.

Sternberg, R. J., Hojjat, M., & Barnes, M. L. (2001). Empirical tests of aspects of a theory of love as a story. *European Journal of Personality*, 15, 199–218.

Swain, J. E., Leckman, J. F., Mayes, L. C., Feldman, R., Constable, R. T., & Schultz, R. T. (2004). Neuural substrates and psychology of human parent-infant attachment in the early postpartum. *Biological Psychiatry*, 55, 1535.

Tennov, D. (1979). *Love and limerence: The experience of being in love*. New York: Stein & Day.

Thoren, P., Asberg, M., & Bertilsson, L. (1980). Clomipramine treatment of obsessive disorder: Biochemical and clinical aspects. *Archives of General Psychiatry*, 37, 1289–1294.

Traupmann, J., & Hatfield, E. (1981). Love and its effect on mental and physical health. In J. March, S. Kiesler, R. Fogel, E. Hatfield, & E. Shanas (Eds.), *Aging: Stability and change in the family* (pp. 253–274). New York: Academic Press.

Trivers, R. L. (1972). Parental investment and sexual selection. In B. Campbell (Ed.), *Sexual selection and the descent of man* (pp. 1871–1971). Chicago: Aldine.

Tucker, P., & Aron, A. (1993). Passionate love and marital satisfaction at key transition points in the family life cycle. *Journal of Social and Clinical Psychology*, 12, 135–147.

Utne, M. (1977). *Equity and intimate relations: A test of theory in marital interaction*. Unpublished doctoral dissertation, University of Wisconsin, Madison.

Walster, E., Aronson, V., Abrahams, D., & Rottman, L. (1966). The importance of physical attractiveness in dating behavior. *Journal of Personality and Social Psychology*, 4, 508–516.

Walster, E., & Walster, G. W. (1963). Effect of expecting to be liked on choice of associates. *Journal of Personality and Social Psychology*, 67, 402–404.

Wang, Z, Yu, G., Cascio, C., Liu, Y., Gingrich, B., & Insel, T. R. (1999). Dopamine D2 receptor-mediated regulation of partner preferences in female prairie voles (*Microtus ochrogaster*): A mechanism for pair bonding? *Behavioral Neuroscience*, 113, 602–611.

Westermarck, E. (1921). *The history of human marriage* (5th ed.). London: Macmillan.

Whitley, B. E. (1993). Reliability and aspects of the construct validity of Sternberg's Triangular Love Scale. *Journal of Social and Personal Relationships*, 10, 475–480.

Wise, R. A. (1989). Brain dopamine and reward. *Annual Review of Psychology*, 40, 191–225.

Wong, P. T. P. (1989, May). *Theory and measurement of unrequited love*. Paper presented at the Iowa Conference on Personal Relationships, Iowa City, IA.

Young, L. J., Nilsen, R., Waymire, K. G., MacGregor, G. R., & Insel, T. R. (1999). Increased affiliative response to vasopresin in mice expressing the V1a receptor from a monogamous vile. *Nature*, 400, 766–768.

Young L. J., Wang, Z., & Insel, T. R. (1998). Neuroendocrine bases of monogamy. *Trends in Neuroscience*, 21, 71–75.

Zajonc, R. B. (1968). Attitudinal effects of mere exposure. *Journal of Personality and Social Psychology Monograph Supplement*, 9, 1–27.

CHAPTER 33

Commitment

Caryl E. Rusbult
Michael K. Coolsen
Jeffrey L. Kirchner
Jennifer A. Clarke

The past 3 decades have witnessed dramatic growth in relationships science. Much of this work has sought to identify the determinants and consequences of positive affect – attraction, satisfaction, or love. For example, the goal of many studies is to explain the causes of attraction or love; measures of satisfaction frequently are employed as indices of couple well-being (for reviews, see Berscheid & Regan, 2005; Berscheid & Reis, 1998). The implicit or explicit assumption of this work is that if partners love each other and feel happy with their relationship, they should be more likely to remain involved with one another. In many respects, this point of view makes good sense: All things considered, it is easier to stick with a happy relationship than a miserable one.

Unfortunately, this conventional focus on the study of affective reactions fails to address three key questions: First, why do some relationships persist despite dissatisfaction – for example, why do unhappy partners sometimes remain together due to inertia or "for the sake of the children"? Second, why do some satisfying relationships end – why do people sometimes abandon rela-

tively happy relationships to pursue desirable alternative partners? Third, how can we account for persistence in the face of ordinary fluctuations in affect? Given that satisfaction ebbs and flows even in the most gratifying involvements, and given that tempting alternatives threaten even the most smitten partners, why do some relationships endure and thrive whereas others do not?

Over the course of the past 3 decades, questions such as these have inspired some social scientists to dedicate themselves to the study of commitment. Scientists working in this tradition believe that if we are to comprehend fully phenomena such as benevolent versus malevolent behavior, positive versus negative motivation, and tenacious persistence versus severance, understanding commitment may be as important as – perhaps more important than – understanding positive affect. The goal of this chapter is to review work in this tradition. We begin by describing several formal models of the causes of commitment. Next, we review empirical work that is relevant to assessing the validity of these models, discussing critical research findings and their implications for each model. Then we describe several important commitment processes, examining the generalizability of commitment phenomena, the role of commitment in inducing prosocial maintenance behaviors, the association of commitment with trust, and the phenomenon of deteriorating commitment. The chapter concludes with a review of contemporary trends in the commitment literature and suggestions for future research.

Formal Models of Commitment

In the following pages, we review the most prominent extant theories of commitment: Levinger's cohesiveness model, Rusbult's investment model, and Johnson's tripartite model. (We also briefly review Brickman's dialectical model.) Although these models differ in important ways, they share many common features, including the assertion that relationships may persist not only because of the positive qualities that draw partners to one another, but also because of the ties that bind partners to one another and the barriers that prevent them from dissolving their relationship. Indeed, the intriguing quality of these theories is the quality they share – their attempt to explain "unjustified persistence," or the tendency to remain involved in a relationship that is not particularly satisfying. The models were developed independently and emerged from differing theoretical traditions. This being the case, why do they share many common features?

We suggest that the models advanced by Levinger, Rusbult, and Johnson share many common features – particularly their emphasis on the constraints that may cause people to persist in unsatisfying relationships – because all three models were shaped by the scientific zeitgeist of the 1960s and 1970s. During these decades, the authors of these models were not alone in their attempt to explain unjustified persistence: During roughly the same period, social scientists from diverse fields simultaneously sought to understand unjustified persistence in nonromantic domains, studying commitment-relevant phenomena such as

dedicating unwarranted time or effort to an activity, increasing commitment to a losing enterprise, entrapment in escalating conflicts, and the manner in which investments, side bets, and sunk costs may induce perseverance at a line of action (e.g., Becker, 1960; Blau, 1967; Brockner, Shaw, & Rubin, 1979; Kiesler, 1971; Staw, 1976; Teger, 1980; Tropper, 1972). Thus, at the time during which Levinger, Rusbult, and Johnson advanced their theories of commitment processes, the theme of unjustified persistence was prominent throughout the social sciences.[1]

Cohesiveness Model – Levinger

The pioneering theory of relational commitment was advanced by George Levinger, who sought to identify abstract principles that would explain commonalities across diverse empirical findings regarding marital cohesiveness versus dissolution (Levinger, 1965, 1979). His model is based in part on the field theory concept of restraining forces (Lewin, 1951). Field theory describes two types of restraining force: the forces that exist between people and accordingly separate them from one another and the forces that surround people and accordingly bind them to one another. Levinger's model highlights three types of force: (a) *present attractions*, or the forces that draw individuals to their relationships; (b) *alternative attractions*, or the forces that pull individuals away from their relationships; and (c) *barriers*, or the forces that prevent individuals from leaving their relationships (see Table 33.1).

According to Levinger, attraction forces, including both present attractions and alternative attractions, rest on the positive outcomes derived from membership in a relationship, such as love, money, status, or other desirable resources. Levinger delineated three categories of attraction force: (a) material attractions, such as income and home ownership; (b) symbolic attractions, such as educational achievement or career status; and (c) affectional attractions, such as companionship and sexual fulfillment. Barrier forces influence the likelihood of remaining in a present relationship by

Table 33.1. *Similarities and Differences Among Commitment Models Advanced by Levinger, Johnson, and Rusbult*

	Levinger Cohesiveness Model	Rusbult Investment Model	Johnson Tripartite Model
Model Components			
Theoretical Construct			
Satisfaction Level	Present attractions	Satisfaction level	Personal commitment (also includes relational identity)
Alternative Quality	Alternative attractions	Quality of alternatives	Potential alternatives (part of structural commitment)
Investment Size	Barriers	Investment size	Irretrievable investments (part of structural commitment)
Moral Injunctions	Symbolic barriers (part of barriers)	Prescriptive support (part of investment size)	Moral commitment
Operational Definitions			
	No instrument developed to measure constructs	*Rusbult (1980a, 1983), Rusbult, Martz, & Agnew (1998) instruments*	*Adams & Jones (1997) and Stanley & Markman (1992) instruments approximate model*
Commitment Construct			
Theoretical Construct			
Commitment	Cohesiveness	Commitment level	Motivation to continue
Operational Definitions			
	No instrument developed to measure construct	*Rusbult (1980a, 1983), Rusbult, Martz, & Agnew (1998) instruments*	*No instrument developed to measure construct*

serving as deterrents to ending the relationship, even when attraction forces lessen or disappear. Paralleling the categories of attraction forces, Levinger delineated three categories of barriers: (a) material barriers, including the loss of income associated with separation and the expenses incurred in divorce; (b) symbolic barriers, such as concern about social disapproval or religious convictions regarding the indissolubility of marriage; and (c) affectional barriers, such as the presence of dependent children.

The three categories of force are assumed to exert independent effects on cohesiveness and probability of persisting in a relationship. If John perceives that the present attractions of his relationship with Mary are high, anticipates that the attractions of alternative relationships would be low, and there

are high barriers to terminating his relationship, he should be more likely to voluntarily persist. In contrast, to the extent that present attractions are low, alternative attractions are high, and barriers to termination are low, voluntary persistence should be less probable.

Investment Model – Rusbult

The investment model, a second formal model of commitment processes, was developed by Caryl Rusbult (1980a, 1983). Her model is based on the principles of interdependence theory, which argues that dependence is a central structural property of relationships, particularly insofar as we seek to understand persistence (Kelley & Thibaut, 1978; Thibaut & Kelley,

1959). According to interdependence theory, *dependence* describes the extent to which an individual "needs" a given relationship, or relies uniquely on the relationship for attaining desired outcomes.

Interdependence theory identifies two processes through which dependence grows. First, individuals become dependent to the extent that they enjoy high satisfaction. *Satisfaction level* describes the degree to which an individual experiences positive versus negative affect as a result of involvement (see Table 33.1). Satisfaction level increases to the extent that a relationship gratifies the individual's most important needs, including needs for companionship, security, intimacy, sexuality, and belongingness. Dependence is also influenced by the quality of available alternatives. *Quality of alternatives* describes the perceived desirability of the best available alternative to a relationship. Quality of alternatives increases to the extent that a person's most important needs could be fulfilled outside of the current relationship – in a specific alternative involvement, by the broader field of eligibles, by friends and family members, or on one's own.

Thus, interdependence theory suggests that dependence is greater when an individual wants to persist in a given relationship (i.e., satisfaction is high) and has no choice but to persist (i.e., alternatives are poor). Rusbult's model extends these claims in two respects. First, she has suggested that satisfaction and alternatives do not fully explain dependence. If dependence were based solely on the satisfactions derived from the current relationship in comparison to those anticipated elsewhere, few relationships would endure – a relationship would falter on the occasion of poor outcomes or the appearance of an attractive alternative. In point of fact, some relationships survive even though they are not very gratifying, even when attractive alternatives are available. How can we explain persistence in the face of tempting alternatives and fluctuating satisfaction?

The model asserts that dependence is also influenced by a third factor: *Investment size* describes the magnitude and importance of the resources that become attached to a relationship – resources that would decline in value or be lost if the relationship were to end. As a relationship develops, partners invest many resources directly into their relationship in the hope that doing so will improve it. For example, they may disclose their private thoughts to one another and may put considerable time and effort into their relationship. Moreover, indirect investments come about when originally extraneous resources become attached to a relationship, including mutual friends, personal identity, or children. Direct and indirect investments enhance dependence because the act of investment increases the costs of ending a relationship, serving as a powerful psychological inducement to persist.

The investment model further extends interdependence theory by suggesting that commitment emerges as a consequence of increasing dependence. *Commitment level* is defined as intent to persist in a relationship, including long-term orientation toward the involvement as well as feelings of psychological attachment to it (e.g., relational identity, or "we-ness"). How does commitment differ from dependence? Dependence is a structural property that describes the additive effects of wanting to persist (feeling satisfied), needing to persist (having high investments), and having no choice but to persist (possessing poor alternatives). As people become increasingly dependent they tend to develop strong commitment. Commitment is the sense of allegiance that is established to the source of one's dependence: Because John is dependent on Mary, he develops an inclination to persist with her, comes to think of himself as part of JohnandMary and tends to consider the broader implications of his actions – implications extending beyond his direct self-interest, including effects on the relationship next week and next month and next year. As such, the psychological experience of commitment reflects more than the bases of dependence out of which it arises. Commitment is the psychological state that directly influences everyday behavior in relationships, including decisions to persist – that is, commitment is argued to mediate the effects of the three bases of dependence.

Tripartite Model – Johnson

A third prominent model of commitment, the tripartite model, was developed by Michael Johnson (1973, 1991) and is based on the symbolic interactionist orientation (Alexander & Wiley, 1981; Mead, 1934). Importantly, Johnson's model departs from the previous two models in that rather than conceptualizing commitment as a unidimensional construct, he identified three distinct types of commitment: *personal commitment*, or wanting to remain in a relationship; *moral commitment*, or feeling morally obligated to remain in a relationship; and *structural commitment*, or feeling that one must remain in a relationship (i.e., experiencing constraints that prevent easy dissolution; see Table 33.1).

Personal commitment is said to comprise three components: attraction to one's partner; attraction to the relationship itself; and relational identity, or incorporating a relationship into one's self-concept. Moral commitment also comprises three components: the moral obligation not to divorce; the sense of personal obligation to one's partner; and the need to maintain consistency in one's beliefs and values. Structural commitment includes four components: potential alternatives to the present relationship; social pressure to remain involved in the relationship; termination procedures, defined in terms of the difficulties of ending a relationship (e.g., dividing possessions, legal divorce proceedings); and irretrievable investments, or desire to avoid feeling that time and resources were "wasted" on the relationship.

Importantly, Johnson proposed that the three types of commitment yield differential subjective experiences. The several types are experienced as either internal or external to the individual and are experienced in terms of either choice or constraint. Personal commitment – or wanting to continue – is based on the individual's internal desires, such that decisions based on personal commitment are

experienced as freely chosen rather than as constraining. Moral commitment – or feeling that one ought to continue – is also based on the individual's internal beliefs, but, at the same time, decisions based on moral commitment are experienced as constraining rather than as freely chosen. Structural commitment is based on factors that are external to the individual, such that decisions based on this type of commitment are experienced as constraining. Johnson also proposed that when Mary experiences strong personal and moral commitment, structural commitment does not come into play because it is unnecessary to sustain commitment. However, when Mary's personal commitment or moral commitment are depleted, structural considerations become important in shaping the decision to sustain versus terminate her relationship.

Dialectical Model – Brickman

There is also a fourth noteworthy commitment model – the dialectical model developed by Phillip Brickman (Brickman, Dunkel-Schetter, & Abbey, 1987). Brickman's model draws on the principles of opponent process theory, which posits that an initial affective experience is invariably followed by its opposite affective reaction (Solomon, 1980). For example, when Mary parachutes out of an airplane, she initially experiences terror; once she lands safely on the ground, this primary affective reaction is replaced by exhilaration, a secondary process that opposes and suppresses the primary experience of terror. As a result of repeated experience with a given event, the intensity of the initial affective reaction tends to weaken, and the opponent reaction becomes stronger and longer lasting. For example, a behavior performed by John initially may yield very gratifying outcomes for Mary. Yet over time and as a consequence of changes in expectations, the same behavior by John will inevitably be experienced as less and less satisfying, possibly even becoming tedious or unpleasant.[2]

Brickman's dialectical model applies the concept of opponent processes to understanding the development of commitment. To begin with, he noted that relationships are continually subject to challenges or stresses. For example, partners may experience doubts about their relationship, they may fight with one another, they may face situations in which their preferences are incompatible, or they may encounter tempting alternatives. When continuing at a line of behavior is opposed in some manner, the opposing factors must be reconciled – through a process of reinterpretation, or integration, they must be made compatible with the forces that attract one to a relationship. For example, when John becomes aware that Mary has an irritating habit, he may reinterpret it as an endearing quirk. When Mary finds that she is attracted to another man, she may mentally derogate the alternative and actively enumerate the many ways in which John is desirable. According to Brickman, such integration serves to strengthen commitment – that is, as a consequence of the integration process, commitment becomes stronger than it would have been in the absence of negative forces. (Quite literally, what doesn't kill a relationship will make it stronger.) As such, commitment is a dynamic phenomenon; the development of commitment rests on challenge and stress.

Empirical Tests of Commitment Models

As is evident based on the preceding review, Brickman's dialectical model differs qualitatively from the other three commitment models. Accordingly, in reviewing empirical findings relevant to the several models, we first address the models of Levinger, Rusbult, and Johnson. At the end of this section, we briefly review research relevant to Brickman's model.

Operational Definitions of Model Components

In reviewing empirical findings relevant to the models advanced by Levinger, Rusbult, and Johnson, it is important to note that the literatures relevant to these models vary in size. Far more studies have been designed as direct tests of Rusbult's investment model than have been designed as direct tests of the other two models. In large part, this discrepancy is attributable to the fact that the development of the investment model was immediately accompanied by the introduction of instruments to assess key model constructs, along with direct empirical tests of model predictions (e.g., Rusbult, 1980a, 1983; Rusbult, Martz, & Agnew, 1998; see Tables 33.1 and 33.2). Thus, clear operational definitions of investment model constructs have existed for some time. In contrast, operational definitions of key constructs from Johnson's tripartite model have only recently been developed (e.g., Adams & Jones, 1997; Stanley & Markman, 1992). And given that Levinger's cohesiveness model was developed mainly as an integrative tool – as a means of explaining commonalities across diverse findings – there is no instrument for assessing model constructs.

Moreover, given that commitment is a key variable in Rusbult's model, the instruments developed to measure investment model constructs also include a measure of commitment (see Tables 33.1 and 33.2). In contrast, given that Johnson's tripartite model identifies three distinct types of commitment (personal, moral, structural), no overall measure of commitment has been advanced; moreover, no instrument for tapping motivation to continue (Johnson's overarching construct) has yet been developed. In light of the differing availability of clear operational definitions for model constructs, it is easier to evaluate the validity of the investment model than it is to evaluate the validity of the cohesiveness and tripartite models.

Associations of Model Components with Commitment

The models of Levinger, Rusbult, and Johnson share many properties (see Table 33.1): First, all three models take account of satisfaction level, or the positive forces that draw one to a relationship – these forces

Table 33.2. *The Investment Model Scale*

Satisfaction Level

Facet Items

My partner fulfills my needs for intimacy (sharing personal thoughts, secrets, etc.).

My partner fulfills my needs for companionship (doing things together, enjoying each other's company, etc.).

My partner fulfills my sexual needs (holding hands, kissing, etc.).

My partner fulfills my needs for security (feeling trusting, comfortable in a stable relationship, etc.).

My partner fulfills my needs for emotional involvement (feeling emotionally attached, feeling good when another feels good, etc.).

Global Items

I feel satisfied with our relationship.

My relationship is much better than others' relationships.

My relationship is close to ideal.

Our relationship makes me very happy.

Our relationship does a good job of fulfilling my needs for intimacy, companionship, etc.

Quality of Alternatives

Facet Items

My needs for intimacy (sharing personal thoughts, secrets, etc.) could be fulfilled in alternative relationships.

My needs for companionship (doing things together, enjoying each other's company, etc.) could be fulfilled in alternative relationships.

My sexual needs (holding hands, kissing, etc.) could be fulfilled in alternative relationships.

My needs for security (feeling trusting, comfortable in a stable relationship, etc.) could be fulfilled in alternative relationships.

My needs for emotional involvement (feeling emotionally attached, feeling good when another feels good, etc.) could be fulfilled in alternative relationships.

Global Items

The people other than my partner with whom I might become involved are very appealing.

My alternatives to our relationship are close to ideal (dating another, spending time with friends or on my own, etc.).

If I weren't dating my partner, I would do fine; I would find another appealing person to date.

My alternatives are very attractive to me (dating another, spending time with friends or on my own, etc.).

My needs for intimacy, companionship, etc. could easily be fulfilled in an alternative relationship.

Investment Size

Facet Items

I have invested a great deal of time in our relationship.

I have told my partner many private things about myself (I disclose secrets to him/her).

My partner and I have an intellectual life together that would be difficult to replace.

My sense of personal identity (who I am) is linked to my partner and our relationship.

My partner and I share many memories.

Global Items

I have put a great deal into our relationship that I would lose if the relationship were to end.

Many aspects of my life have become linked to my partner (recreational activities, etc.), and I would lose all of this if we were to break up.

I feel very involved in our relationship, like I have put a great deal into it.

My relationships with friends and family members would be complicated if my partner and I were to break up (e.g., partner is friends with people I care about).

Compared with other people I know, I have invested a great deal in my relationship with my partner.

(continued)

Table 33.2. (*continued*)

Commitment Level

Global Items

I want our relationship to last for a very long time.

I am committed to maintaining my relationship with my partner.

I would not feel very upset if our relationship were to end in the near future.

It is likely that I will date someone other than my partner within the next year. (reverse-scored)

I feel very attached to our relationship – very strongly linked to my partner.

I want our relationship to last forever.

I am oriented toward the long-term future of my relationship (for example, I imagine being with my partner several years from now).

Note. Reliability and validity information is presented elsewhere (Rusbult, Martz, & Agnew, 1998). For facet items, 0 = *do not agree at all*, 3 = *agree completely*; for global items, 0 = *do not agree at all*, 8 = *agree completely*. Separately for each construct, scores for global items are averaged to form a single measure of each variable (facet items are not included in these calculations).

are termed *present attractions* (Levinger), *satisfaction level* (Rusbult), or *personal commitment* (Johnson). (However, Johnson's construct also includes some elements of what Rusbult would term *investment* – the involvement of one's identity in a relationship.) Second, all three models take account of the investments that tie one to a relationship – these forces are termed *barriers* (Levinger), *investment size* (Rusbult), or *irretrievable investments* (Johnson). (Johnson's structural commitment category also includes social pressure and termination procedures, as well as potential alternatives.) Third, all three models take account of alternative quality – these forces are termed *alternative attractions* (Levinger), *quality of alternatives* (Rusbult), or *potential alternatives* (Johnson). (Again, Johnson included potential alternatives in his structural commitment category.) Fourth, Johnson identified *moral commitment* as a separate category; Levinger included this variable in his barriers category, and Rusbult included it in her investments category.

How does the empirical literature square with these claims? Numerous studies have examined key predictions of the investment model (e.g., Bui, Peplau, & Hill, 1996; Cox, Wexler, Rusbult, & Gaines, 1997; Davis & Strube, 1993; Drigotas & Rusbult, 1992; Drigotas, Safstrom, & Gentilia, 1999; Duffy & Rusbult, 1986; Etcheverry & Agnew, 2004; Gaertner & Foshee, 1999; Kurdek, 1991, 1993; Lin & Rusbult, 1995; Morrow, Clark,

& Brock, 1995; Pistole, Clark, & Tubbs, 1995; Rusbult, 1980a, 1980b, 1983; Rusbult, Johnson, & Morrow, 1986; Rusbult & Martz, 1995; Rusbult et al., 1998; Rusbult, Verette, Whitney, Slovik, & Lipkus, 1991; Sanderson & Kurdek, 1993; Sprecher, 1988; Truman-Schram, Cann, Calhoun, & Van Wallendael, 2000; Van Lange, Agnew, Harinck, & Steemers, 1997; Van Lange, Rusbult et al., 1997). In a meta-analytic review of these and other empirical tests of the model, Le and Agnew (2003) concluded that "across 52 studies, including 60 independent samples and 11,582 participants, satisfaction with, alternatives to, and investments in a relationship each correlated significantly with commitment to that relationship" (p. 37; respective meta-analytic $rs = 0.68, -0.48,$ and 0.46).

Of course, in light of the parallels among models advanced by Levinger, Rusbult, and Johnson, many of these tests of the investment model could be construed as consistent with any one – or all – of the three models. In some respects, the models identify similar underlying constructs but with different names. Moreover, numerous extant studies were not designed as direct tests of any one of the models yet provide direct or indirect evidence of the impact on commitment of satisfaction, alternatives, investments, or moral injunctions or a combination of these (e.g., Attridge, Berscheid, & Simpson, 1995; Buunk, 1987; Felmlee, Sprecher, & Bassin, 1990; Gelles, 1980; Lund, 1985;

Lydon, Pierce, & O'Regan, 1997; Sabatelli & Cecil-Pigo, 1985; Secord, 1983; Simpson, 1987; South & Lloyd, 1995; Sprecher & Felmlee, 1992; Stanley & Markman, 1992; Straus & Gelles, 1986; Strube, 1988; Strube & Barbour, 1983; Thompson & Spanier, 1983; Udry, 1983; White, 1980). These studies, too, could be construed as consistent with any one – or all – of the models. Thus, there is abundant empirical evidence to support broad claims advanced in the models proposed by Levinger, Rusbult, and Johnson.

Associations of Model Components With Commitment and Persistence

All three models also propose that the net effect of factors promoting stability is to induce increased motivation to continue – this motivation is termed *cohesiveness* (Levinger), *commitment* (Rusbult), or *motivation* to continue (Johnson; see Table 33.1). In their meta-analytic review, Le and Agnew (2003) concluded that each of the three predictor variables in the investment model – satisfaction, alternatives, and investments – accounts for unique variance in commitment, and that these variables collectively explain nearly two thirds of the variance in commitment (61%). In turn, commitment reliably predicts persistence, accounting for 47% of the variance in stay–leave behavior. Of course, Rusbult's model alone represents commitment as an overarching construct that mediates the effects of other variables on persistence. At the same time, in light of broad commonalities among the models, this evidence can be construed as not only providing excellent support for the investment model, but also as providing some indirect support for the cohesiveness and tripartite models.

Factor Structure of Model Components

There are also noteworthy differences among the three models: First, they differ in how they categorize the variables that promote commitment. For example, Johnson's model suggests that social pressure, termination procedures, irretrievable investments, and potential alternatives "go together," in that all four are components of structural commitment; in contrast, Levinger and Rusbult would represent social pressure, termination procedures, and irretrievable investments as aspects of barriers (Levinger) or investments (Rusbult), and would represent potential alternatives as a separate force (see Table 33.1). Also, Johnson includes relational identity as a component of personal commitment, whereas Rusbult would include it as an aspect of investment size. Finally, Rusbult's model explicitly represents commitment as an independent construct (both theoretically and empirically), as an overarching subjective experience that exerts effects on behavior independent of its presumed causes (satisfaction, alternatives, investments).

How does the empirical literature square with these claims? Several authors have examined the factor structure of potential components of commitment, seeking to determine "what goes with what." Three studies by Rusbult et al. (1998) provide excellent support for the proposed factor structure of the investment model, revealing four distinct factors: satisfaction, alternatives, investments, and commitment (see Table 33.2). Each of the three presumed causes of commitment (satisfaction, alternatives, investments) account for unique variance in commitment level, and commitment significantly predicts later relationship status (persisted vs. ended). Two studies by Arriaga and Agnew (2001) were designed to examine a more finely articulated instrument for measuring the three hypothesized components of commitment – intent to persist (e.g., "I intend to stay in this relationship"), long-term orientation (e.g., "I imagine being with my partner several years from now"), and psychological attachment (e.g., "I feel very attached to our relationship – very strongly linked to my partner"). This work revealed that (a) each of the three components exhibits associations with dyadic adjustment (Spanier, 1976); (b) each of the three components exhibits associations with later relationship status (persisted vs. ended); (c) when pitted against one another as predictors of later relationship status, long-term orientation is the most powerful predictor; and (d) the three components fully mediate the associations of the three causes of commitment (satisfaction, alternatives, investments) with later relationship status. Thus, these studies provide good support for the investment model, demonstrating that (a) satisfaction, alternatives, and investments are distinguishable; and (b) as an overarching construct, commitment exerts effects that are independent of its presumed causes. Unfortunately, neither set of studies assessed the moral injunctions that may be relevant to understanding commitment; both sets of studies are therefore mute with respect to the distinctiveness of this factor.

Aspects of moral commitment *were* assessed in studies by Adams and Jones (1997), Johnson, Caughlin, and Huston (1999), and Stanley and Markman (1992). Moreover, each study revealed that moral commitment is distinct from other aspects of commitment: Stanley and Markman (1992) observed three factors – personal dedication (couple identity, primacy of relationship, alternative monitoring), constraint (termination procedures, alternatives, structural investments), and morality (morality of divorce). Adams and Jones (1997) also observed three factors – commitment to spouse (e.g., "I want to grow old with my spouse"), commitment to marriage (a morality factor; e.g., "I'm afraid that if I were to leave my spouse, God would punish me"), and feelings of entrapment (a constraints factor; e.g., "My family would strongly disapprove if I ended my marriage," "I've spent so much money on my relationship with my spouse that I could never divorce him or her") – and found that these factors exhibit the predicted associations with other established instruments for assessing commitment. Finally, Johnson et al. (1999) observed five factors – couple identity (e.g., "To what extent do you love [partner's name] at this stage?"), divorce attitudes (e.g., "Getting a divorce violates your religious belief"), consistency values (e.g., "It's important to stand by what you believe in"), partner contract (e.g., "You would feel bad about getting a divorce because you

promised..."), and marital satisfaction (traditional satisfaction items) – and found that measures of personal, moral, and structural commitment exhibit the predicted associations with each factor.[3] Thus, these studies support the claims that (a) moral commitment is a unique construct and (b) many aspects of structural commitment indeed "go together." Unfortunately, none of these studies examined whether the several subscales account for unique variance in relational criteria such as commitment, adjustment, or later status. In their defense, these studies did not examine such an overarching construct because (a) there is no extant instrument for tapping Johnson's overarching construct (motivation to continue) and (b) the goal of these studies was to advance and test a typology of commitment types, not to advance or test a predictive model of commitment and persistence.

Contribution of Moral Injunctions to Predicting Commitment

A second difference among the three models is that Johnson represents moral commitment as a component that should influence relationships in its own right, independent of personal and structural commitment (see Table 33.1). The models advanced by Levinger and Rusbult do not make such a claim. We are aware of only two studies that examined whether moral commitment accounts for unique variance in relational criteria beyond other components of commitment: In a study of marital relationships, Cox et al. (1997) examined satisfaction, alternatives, investments, personal prescriptive support (i.e., moral belief that one ought to persist in a relationship), and social prescriptive support (i.e., friends' and family members' support for persisting). These authors found that although all five measures were associated with commitment, personal prescriptive support (moral commitment) did not account for unique variance beyond satisfaction, alternatives, investments, and social prescriptive support.[4] In contrast, in a longitudinal study of persistence in long-distance dating relationships, Lydon et al. (1997) examined the power of enthusiastic commitment (enthusiasm, enjoyment) and moral commitment (obligation, duty) in predicting relational perseverance. These authors found that moral commitment, but not enthusiastic commitment, predicted the survival of relationships. Thus, there is mixed support for the claim that moral commitment accounts for unique variance in relational processes. Further time and effort should be dedicated to this issue.

Do Different Types of Commitment Yield Differential Experiences?

There is a third noteworthy difference among the models advanced by Levinger, Rusbult, and Johnson: Johnson's model proposes that the three components of commitment yield differential experiences (internal vs. external, choice vs. constraint), suggesting that the several types of commitment should exert differential effects on motivation. Whereas personal commitment may lead Mary to sacrifice cheerfully on John's behalf, structural commitment may cause her to feel trapped and resentful, thereby promoting neglectful or destructive behaviors. Interestingly, although Rusbult's investment model does not make direct claims regarding differences produced by varying combinations of satisfaction, alternatives, and investments, the theory on which the model is based *does* advance such claims. Specifically, interdependence theory distinguishes between voluntary dependence (based on high satisfaction) and nonvoluntary dependence (based on low satisfaction, poor alternatives), arguing that nonvoluntary dependence should yield entrapment and resentment (Thibaut & Kelley, 1959). These claims are compelling: Logically, it would seem that unhappy-but-committed people should differ meaningfully from happy-and-committed people. In our search for relevant empirical work, we located only two studies that revealed meaningful differences as a product of different types of commitment: Lydon et al. (1997) found that whereas

enthusiastic commitment was closely associated with satisfaction, moral commitment predicted increased investment and the probability that relationships persisted; in relationships that terminated, moral commitment predicted negative affect and symptoms of ill health. In addition, Frank and Brandstatter (2002) found that whereas approach commitment (attachment, identification with partner) was associated with promotion focus (universalism, humanism) and positive time spent with the partner, avoidance commitment (investment, moral obligation, prescriptive support) was associated with prevention focus (security, conformity, tradition) and less frequent positive affect. This issue, too, merits further empirical investigation.

Empirical Tests of Brickman's Dialectical Model

As noted earlier, Brickman's dialectical model advances claims that differ qualitatively from those advanced by Levinger, Rusbult, and Johnson. Few, if any, direct tests of Brickman's claims have been published. At the same time, it is noteworthy that dialectical phenomena are evident in much of the published work on maintenance mechanisms – work that is described briefly here and reviewed more extensively elsewhere (e.g., see Canary & Dainton, this volume). Paradoxically, the dialectical model suggests that challenge and stress can serve as a catalyst for strengthening commitment. For example, when John and Mary must choose between promoting their personal interests versus the interests of their relationship, John's decision to sacrifice his interests for the good of the relationship can serve as an investment, thereby strengthening his commitment. Further, for example, when Mary finds that she is attracted to a tempting alternative, she may cognitively derogate the alternative, thereby strengthening her commitment. As such, numerous studies of relationship maintenance processes provide indirect support for the *spirit* of Brickman's model: Uncertainty and doubt induce cognitive integration in the form of positive illusion, which in turn strengthens relationships; conflicting needs provide an occasion for partners to sacrifice on one another's behalf, which in turn strengthens relationships; attraction to tempting alternatives yields integration in the form of alternative derogation, which in turn strengthens relationships (e.g., Johnson & Rusbult, 1989; Murray & Holmes, 1999; Van Lange, Rusbult et al., 1997).

Commitment Processes

In the following pages, we review principles and findings regarding important commitment processes: Specifically, we examine work on the generalizability of commitment effects, the role of commitment in inducing prosocial maintenance behaviors, and the association of commitment with trust. We also describe the process by which commitment deteriorates and review some contemporary trends, including process-based models, work on the cognitive and affective properties of commitment, and findings regarding personal dispositions and commitment.

Generalizability of Commitment Phenomena

Earlier, we noted that relationships science has been characterized by an excessive focus on satisfaction level. The limitations of this orientation are clear in work regarding abusive relationships in that one of the more puzzling aspects of abuse concerns why people sometimes remain involved with violent partners. So long as researchers were blinded by the traditional satisfaction focus – by the assumption that partners persist because they love one another and feel happy with their relationship – this question was difficult to answer. Researchers tended to proffer answers emphasizing the weakness or irrationality of the abused individual. For example, abused women were assumed to remain in their relationships because they were masochistic, possessed low self-esteem, or suffered learned helplessness (e.g., Shainess, 1979; Walker, 1979).

Once researchers recognized the importance of commitment, it became evident that abuse victims may remain in their relationships because they are trapped – because they have poor alternatives (especially economic alternatives; e.g., limited financial resources, poor employment options) or because important investments bind them to their partners (e.g., young children, joint home ownership). Indeed, recent empirical work supports the claim that persistence in abusive relationships is at least partially attributable to poor alternatives and high investments (e.g., Rusbult & Martz, 1995; Straus & Gelles, 1990; Strube, 1988).

Other literatures, too, have been blinded by the traditional satisfaction focus. For example, until the early 1980s, organizational behavior researchers tended to assume that employees remained with their jobs largely due to job satisfaction. Here, too, recent work has revealed that people may remain with their jobs not only because they enjoy high job satisfaction, but also – or instead – because their employment alternatives are poor (e.g., few alternative jobs in the region) or because numerous important investments are linked to their jobs (e.g., nonvested retirement programs; e.g., Farrell & Rusbult, 1981; Koslowsky, Caspy, & Lazar, 1991; Meyer & Allen, 1997; Oliver, 1990; Rusbult & Farrell, 1983). The consumer behavior literature, too, has recently recognized that consumers may exhibit loyalty to a given brand not simply because they find use of the brand to be satisfying, but also because of poor alternatives or high investments (e.g., Beatty & Kahle, 1998; Coolsen, 2005; Fournier, 1998).

Commitment and Relationship Maintenance Phenomena

Of course, strong commitment does not magically cause relationships to persist. Rather, commitment promotes adaptive relationship-relevant acts, which in turn cause relationships to persist. Researchers frequently label these adaptive acts *relationship maintenance phenomena* (see Canary & Dainton, this volume). Some relationship maintenance phenomena are cognitive maneuvers that support the decision to persist. For example, people with strong commitment shield themselves from attractive alternative partners by cognitively derogating tempting alternatives ("he's gorgeous but dimwitted"; e.g., Johnson & Rusbult, 1989; Lydon, Meana, Sepinwall, Richards, & Mayman, 1999; Miller, 1997; Simpson, Gangestad, & Lerma, 1990). In a related vein, people with strong commitment react to periods of doubt or uncertainty by cognitively enhancing their partners and relationships: When Mary begins to worry about the declining quality of her sex life, she may react to such anxiety-generating thoughts by (a) developing unrealistically positive cognitions about John and their relationship (e.g., distorting the extent of John's intelligence and warmth) and (b) developing unrealistically negative cognitions regarding other people's relationships (e.g., bringing to mind vivid accounts of couple conflict or violence; e.g., Agnew, Loving, & Drigotas, 2001; Arriaga, 2002; Murray & Holmes, 1999; Murray, Holmes, & Griffin, 1996; Rusbult, Van Lange, Wildschut, Yovetich, & Verette, 2000).

Other relationship maintenance phenomena are behavioral. To begin with, people with strong commitment are inclined to accommodate rather than retaliate when their partners engage in potentially destructive behaviors; for example, when Mary says something rude to John, he may control his impulse to yell at her and instead simply ask her whether she had a bad day at work (e.g., Arriaga & Rusbult, 1998; Kilpatrick, Bissonnette, & Rusbult, 2002; Rusbult et al., 1991). In addition, committed people frequently sacrifice their personal interests to promote the interests of the partner and relationship; for example, when John and Mary are offered attractive jobs in distant cities, one or both may forgo their preferred job so the two of them can live in the same city (e.g., Powell & Van Vugt, 2003; Van Lange, Agnew et al., 1997; Van Lange, Rusbult et al., 1997). Further, when confronted with acts of betrayal, committed people exhibit greater tendencies to forgive; for example, when Mary discovers that John has lied to her about something impor-

tant, she may search for extenuating circumstances that help explain his behavior, acknowledge the role that she may have played in bringing about the lie, and find her way to forgive John for the incident (e.g., Cann & Baucom, 2004; Finkel, Rusbult, Kumashiro, & Hannon, 2002; McCullough et al., 1998).

Commitment and Trust: Mutual Cyclical Growth

Maintenance acts such as accommodation and sacrifice are beneficial not only because they prevent the escalation of conflict and yield better immediate outcomes, but also because they help each partner recognize the extent of the other's commitment. For this reason, the situations that call forth maintenance acts – for example, situations in which one person betrays the other or situations in which partners' preferences conflict – have been termed *diagnostic situations* (Holmes & Rempel, 1989; Kelley, 1983). Such situations are "diagnostic" in that it is possible to discern the strength of another's commitment *only* in situations wherein the behavior that benefits a relationship is at odds with the behavior that would benefit the individual: It is when John declines a job offer that he very much wants to accept that Mary can discern that he places the interests of their relationship above his personal interests. When John declines a job offer that does not interest him, Mary learns nothing about his commitment.

Why are diagnostic situations important? Confidence in a partner's commitment is reflected in *trust*, defined as the strength of one's conviction that the partner will be responsive to one's needs, now and in the future (Holmes, 1989; Holmes & Rempel, 1989). As such, one person's trust in the other is a rough gauge of the strength of the other's commitment; when John behaves well in a diagnostic situation (i.e., he accommodates, forgives, sacrifices), Mary develops increased trust in John (Wieselquist, Rusbult, Foster, & Agnew, 1999). As people become increasingly trusting, they become more willing to place themselves in vulnerable positions relative to the partner by becoming increasingly dependent – that is, they not only become more satisfied with the relationship, but are also more willing to drive away or derogate alternative partners (i.e., burn their bridges) and invest in the relationship in material and nonmaterial ways (i.e., throw in their lot with the partner).

Thus, John's increasing dependence yields strengthened commitment, which in turn causes him to exhibit a variety of prosocial maintenance acts. When Mary perceives such acts, she develops increased trust in John, which makes her more willing to become dependent on him, which promotes her own commitment and prosocial tendencies, which in turn strengthen John's own dependence and commitment... and so on, in a congenial pattern of mutual cyclical growth (or mutual cyclical deterioration, when circumstances go poorly). Which comes first, commitment or trust? In understanding real interaction in ongoing relationships, causes and effects are not so clearly distinguishable: In the context of temporally extended interactions with across-partner associations, John's prosocial motives and behaviors serve as the cause of Mary's enhanced trust; the products of her enhanced trust serve as the cause of her own strengthened commitment.

Deteriorating Commitment

Why does commitment decline? There are no extant typologies of the causes of deteriorating commitment. However, just as mutual cyclical growth describes a system in which commitment flourishes, such a model also provides insight into deteriorating commitment: To begin with, commitment may deteriorate because satisfaction level declines – John may no longer be capable of gratifying Mary's needs because he changes or because Mary and her needs change (e.g., she may become more concerned with her intellectual needs while John becomes a couch potato). Second, Mary may encounter an alternative partner who shows greater promise of fulfilling her needs (e.g., a new colleague may be exceptionally attractive). Third, it may become increasingly difficult to invest in the relationship, in that over time, necessary investments may become more effortful or costly (e.g., as the partners' interests evolve, it may become more difficult to engage in shared activities). Fourth, the partners may encounter diagnostic situations that extend beyond each person's relationship maintenance limits, in terms of motivation or ability; for example, they may confront conflicting interests requiring sacrifices that are of too great a magnitude (e.g., one wants to have children, the other does not). Fifth, partners may fail to perceive one another's maintenance acts; for example, Mary may be locked in her own perspective and fail to perceive John's generous, prosocial acts (e.g., she may be self-absorbed, insecure). Sixth, specific events in the relationship may rupture trust; for example, John may become involved in a "meaningless" extra-relationship involvement that Mary simply cannot forgive.

Interestingly, the very real deterioration of a relationship caused by one or more of these processes tends to be accompanied by cognitive maneuvers that support the decision to end a relationship (Rusbult et al., 2000). Specifically, the cognitive maintenance processes described earlier – tendencies to derogate alternatives and enhance the present relationship – "go into reverse," thereby justifying the decision to terminate a relationship. Mary may derogate John in relation to her available alternatives ("he's such a nebbish!"), she may exhibit excessively positive assessments of other people's relationships ("my girlfriends date men like Cary Grant!"), and she may develop unrealistically positive beliefs about her extra-relationship options ("I'd be much happier without him, even if I were on my own!"). Such cognitive maneuvers help individuals "talk themselves out of" their relationships, thereby rationalizing and defending the decision to break ties with a partner.

Other Commitment Processes

It is both a blessing and a curse that social scientists have increasingly dedicated themselves to the study of commitment. In light of the volume and vitality of the commitment literature – and in light of limits on what we can achieve in the space of a single chapter – it is not possible to comprehensively review the expanding literature regarding commitment processes. However, it is important to mention three contemporary themes, if only in a cursory manner. First, several models have been advanced to provide a more fine-grained analysis of the process by which commitment develops versus deteriorates. For example, above and beyond level of satisfaction and linear change in satisfaction, fluctuations in satisfaction appear to play a key role in predicting breakup (Arriaga, 2001). In addition, in predicting people's decisions to remain in versus terminate their relationships, it is important to understand the extent to which they depend on their partners – in relation to the broader social network – to gratify their most important needs (e.g., needs for companionship, security, identity; Drigotas & Rusbult, 1992). Moreover, and as noted earlier, research has recently begun to confirm the proposition that commitment is not a unidimensional construct; rather, different types of commitment (approach vs. avoidance, enthusiastic vs. moral) may exert differential effects on key relational criteria (both motivational and behavioral criteria; Frank & Brandstatter, 2002; Lydon et al., 1997).

Second, some contemporary work has examined important cognitive and affective properties of developing versus deteriorating commitment. For example, researchers have studied the perceptual, cognitive, and affective mental representation of commitment (e.g., among the committed, cognitive representations are characterized by greater plural pronoun use; Agnew, Van Lange, Rusbult, & Langston, 1998). In addition, the accessibility of commitment representations plays a role in promoting (vs. inhibiting) prosocial acts, in that accessibility moderates the association of commitment level with prosocial acts such as accommodation, sacrifice, and persistence (Etcheverry & Le, 2005). Researchers have also examined cognitive–affective phenomena such as the following: the relevance of implemental versus deliberative mind-set to predicting relationship survival (Gagne & Lydon, 2001); the role of love in motivating commitment-enhancing processes (Gonzaga, Keltner, Londahl, & Smith, 2001); the interaction of commitment with psychological threat in inducing jealousy (Rydell, McConnell, & Bringle, 2004); and the association of reasons for change in commitment (norms, network effects) with the speed and direction of change in relationships (Surra, Arizzi, & Asmussen, 1988). Importantly, romantic commitment serves a terror-management function, helping us cope with the anxiety and dread that otherwise accompanies thoughts about death (Florian, Mikulincer, & Hirschberger, 2002).

Third, some research has examined important dispositional influences on commitment. For example, narcissism appears to be problematic in ongoing relationships because narcissists more actively monitor alternative partners, perceive that their alternatives are superior, and accordingly experience weaker commitment to their partners (Campbell & Foster, 2002). Also, work regarding neuroticism demonstrates that the most problematic component of neuroticism is depression and that depression influences relationships primarily via its impact on attraction commitment (feeling less positive about one's relationship), not via its impact on constraint commitment (investing less, experiencing fewer barriers to termination; Kurdek, 1997).

Conclusions

Directions for Future Research

We propose that several types of research might enrich our understanding of important commitment processes. To begin with, and as noted earlier, it is important to continue studying the motivational and behavioral consequences of varying types of commitment – voluntary versus nonvoluntary commitment, choice versus constraint commitment, and moderation of component effects by satisfaction level (cf. Johnson, 1991; Thibaut & Kelley, 1959). In a related vein, a good deal remains to be learned about patterns of change in commitment; for example, we should attend more carefully to the consequences of linear versus nonlinear change in commitment as well as the impact of direction of change in combination with rate of change and fluctuations in level (cf. Kurdek, 2003). In addition, it is important to note that although we have learned a good deal about the cognitive concomitants of commitment, we know far less about its emotional or affective properties (cf. Frijda, 1988). And of course, it is important to recognize that humans are fundamentally social animals: We have always lived in groups; few phenomena are more "interpersonal" than human mating. Accordingly, it might be fruitful to examine predictions inspired by an evolutionary analysis (e.g., loyalty-relevant emotions, changing reproductive capacity, reactions to betrayal; cf. Kenrick & Trost, 2000; Ridley, 1996). In this regard, we believe that social neuroscience techniques might reveal theoretically meaningful physiological components of commitment phenomena (cf. Cacioppo, 2002).

Summary

The purpose of this chapter was to review the theoretical and empirical literature regarding commitment. Toward this goal, we introduced four prominent theories of commitment (those of Levinger, Rusbult, Johnson, and Brickman) and reviewed empirical work relevant to assessing the validity of these models. We also discussed the generalizability of commitment effects, outlined the role of commitment in promoting prosocial maintenance acts, described the interplay of one partner's commitment with the other's trust, and discussed the processes by which commitment deteriorates. Finally, we briefly reviewed important contemporary themes in the commitment literature, including novel process-based models, work on the cognitive and affective properties of commitment, and analyses of dispositional effects on commitment. It is our hope that this review may encourage other researchers to depart from the rather exclusive emphasis on positive affect that characterized early work in relationships science.

We also hope that this review may highlight the central role of commitment in promoting benevolent behavior, positive motivation, and tenacious persistence, thereby inviting further theoretical and empirical work regarding this critical property of ongoing relationships.

Footnotes

1. This body of work may well have been inspired by broader sociopolitical events, such as the Cold War arms race, or U.S. military involvement in Vietnam. Of course, we do not wish to suggest that the models of Levinger, Rusbult, and Johnson were directly inspired by events such as the Vietnam War. The point to be made is that during the 1960s and 1970s, a fascination with unjustified persistence was "in the air" from a scientific point of view.

2. The notion that the repeated experience of a given positive event will produce an increase in expectations – yielding reductions in the affective "power" of that event – is implicit in many psychological principles, including the concepts of satiation, declining marginal utility, and comparison level. Thus, the first bite of a chocolate bar is delicious, the second bite is tasty... and the sixth bite is merely good.

3. At the same time, these studies frequently assessed key variables using global attitudinal measures that were unrelated to the present relationship; for example, they assessed attitudes about the morality of divorce irrespective of the morality of divorce in the present relationship. It is perhaps not surprising that global attitudinal items such as these do not cluster with items that explicitly assess phenomena specific to the present relationship.

4. Of course, Johnson might argue that this study constitutes an invalid test of his claims, in that the criterion employed in this work was a variable that he would construe as a measure of personal commitment. (From the point of view of his model, there is no basis for predicting that moral commitment and personal commitment should be significantly associated.)

References

Adams, J. M., & Jones, W. H. (1997). The conceptualization of marital commitment: An integrative analysis. *Journal of Personality and Social Psychology, 72*, 1177–1196.

Agnew, C. R., Loving, T. J., & Drigotas, S. M. (2001). Substituting the forest for the trees: Social networks and the prediction of romantic relationship state and fate. *Journal of Personality and Social Psychology, 81*, 1042–1057.

Agnew, C. R., Van Lange, P. A. M., Rusbult, C. E., & Langston, C. A. (1998). Cognitive interdependence: Commitment and the mental representation of close relationships. *Journal of Personality and Social Psychology, 74*, 939–954.

Alexander, C. N., Jr., & Wiley, M. G. (1981). Situated activity and identity formation. In M. Rosenberg & R. H. Turner (Eds.), *Social psychology: Sociological perspectives* (pp. 269–289). New York: Basic Books.

Arriaga, X. B. (2001). The ups and downs of dating: Fluctuations in satisfaction in newly formed romantic relationships. *Journal of Personality and Social Psychology, 80*, 754–765.

Arriaga, X. B. (2002). Joking violence among highly committed individuals. *Journal of Interpersonal Violence, 17*, 591–610.

Arriaga, X. B., & Agnew, C. R. (2001). Being committed: Affective, cognitive, and conative components of relationship commitment. *Personality and Social Psychology Bulletin, 27*, 1190–1203.

Arriaga, X. B., & Rusbult, C. E. (1998). Standing in my partner's shoes: Partner perspective-taking and reactions to accommodative dilemmas. *Personality and Social Psychology Bulletin, 9*, 927–948.

Attridge, M., Berscheid, E., & Simpson, J. A. (1995). Predicting relationship stability from both partners versus one. *Journal of Personality and Social Psychology, 69*, 254–268.

Beatty, S., & Kahle, L. (1998). The involvement-commitment model: Theory and implications. *Journal of Business Research, 6*, 149–168.

Becker, H. S. (1960). Notes on the concept of commitment. *American Journal of Sociology, 66*, 32–40.

Berscheid, E., & Regan, P. (2005). *The psychology of interpersonal relationships*. Upper Saddle River, NJ: Pearson Education.

Berscheid, E., & Reis, H. T. (1998). Attraction and close relationships. In D. T. Gilbert, S. T. Fiske, & G. Lindzey (Eds.), *Handbook of social psychology* (4th ed., Vol. 2, pp. 193–281). New York: McGraw-Hill.

Blau, P. M. (1967). *Exchange and power in social life*. New York: Wiley.

Brickman, P., Dunkel-Schetter, C., & Abbey, A. (1987). The development of commitment. In P. Brickman (Ed.), *Commitment, conflict, and caring* (pp. 145–221). Englewood Cliffs, NJ: Prentice-Hall.

Brockner, J., Shaw, M. C., & Rubin, J. Z. (1979). Factors affecting withdrawal from an escalating conflict: Quitting before it's too late. *Journal of Experimental Social Psychology, 15*, 492–503.

Bui, K. T., Peplau, L. A., & Hill, C. T. (1996). Testing the Rusbult model of relationship commitment and stability in a 15-year study of heterosexual couples. *Personality and Social Psychology Bulletin, 22*, 1244–1257.

Buunk, B. (1987). Conditions that promote breakups as a consequence of extradyadic involvements. *Journal of Social and Clinical Psychology, 5*, 271–284.

Cacioppo, J. T. (2002). Social neuroscience in perspective: Understanding the pieces fosters understanding the whole, and vice versa. *American Psychologist, 57*, 819–831.

Campbell, W. K., & Foster, C. A. (2002). Narcissism and commitment in romantic relationships: An investment model analysis. *Personality and Social Psychology Bulletin, 28*, 484–495.

Cann, A., & Baucom, T. R. (2004). Former partners and new rivals as threats to a relationship: Infidelity type, gender, and commitment as factors related to distress and forgiveness. *Personal Relationships, 11*, 305–318.

Coolsen, M. K. (2005). Brand loyalty conceptualized as an interdependence process. *Business Research Yearbook, 12*, 611–614.

Cox, C. L., Wexler, M. O., Rusbult, C. E., & Gaines, S. O., Jr. (1997). Prescriptive support and commitment processes in close relationships. *Social Psychology Quarterly, 60*, 79–90.

Davis, L., & Strube, M. J. (1993). An assessment of romantic commitment among Black and White dating couples. *Journal of Applied Social Psychology, 23*, 212–225.

Drigotas, S. M., & Rusbult, C. E. (1992). Should I stay or should I go?: A dependence model of breakups. *Journal of Personality and Social Psychology, 62*, 62–87.

Drigotas, S. M., Safstrom, C. A., & Gentilia, T. (1999). An investment model prediction of dating infidelity. *Journal of Personality and Social Psychology, 77*, 509–524.

Duffy, S., & Rusbult, C. E. (1986). Satisfaction and commitment in homosexual and heterosexual relationships. *Journal of Homosexuality*, 12, 1–23.

Etcheverry, P. E., & Agnew, C. R. (2004). Subjective norms and the prediction of romantic relationship state and fate. *Personal Relationships*, 11, 409–428.

Etcheverry, P. E., & Le, B. (2005). Thinking about commitment: Accessibility of commitment and prediction of relationship persistence, accommodation, and willingness to sacrifice. *Personal Relationships*, 12, 103–123.

Farrell, D., & Rusbult, C. E. (1981). Exchange variables as predictors of job satisfaction, job commitment, and turnover: The impact of rewards, costs, alternatives, and investments. *Organizational Behavior and Human Performance*, 27, 78–95.

Felmlee, D., Sprecher, S., & Bassin, E. (1990). The dissolution of intimate relationships: A hazard model. *Social Psychology Quarterly*, 53, 13–30.

Finkel, E. J., Rusbult, C. E., Kumashiro, M., & Hannon, P. A. (2002). Dealing with betrayal in close relationships: Does commitment promote forgiveness? *Journal of Personality and Social Psychology*, 82, 956–974.

Florian, V., Mikulincer, M., & Hirschberger, G. (2002). The anxiety-buffering function of close relationships: Evidence that relationship commitment acts as a terror management mechanism. *Journal of Personality and Social Psychology*, 82, 527–542.

Fournier, S. (1998). Consumers and their brands: Developing relationship theory in consumer research. *Journal of Consumer Research*, 24, 343–373.

Frank, E., & Brandstatter, V. (2002). Approach versus avoidance: Different types of commitment in intimate relationships. *Journal of Personality and Social Psychology*, 82, 208–221.

Frijda, N. H. (1988). The laws of emotion. *American Psychologist*, 43, 349–358.

Gaertner, L., & Foshee, V. (1999). Commitment and the perpetration of relationship violence. *Personal Relationships*, 6, 227–239.

Gagne, F. M., & Lydon, J. E. (2001). Mind-set and close relationships: When bias leads to (in)accurate predictions. *Journal of Personality and Social Psychology*, 81, 85–96.

Gelles, R. J. (1980). Violence in the family: A review of research in the seventies. *Journal of Marriage and the Family*, 42, 873–885.

Gonzaga, G. C., Keltner, D., Londahl, E. A., & Smith, M. D. (2001). Love and the commitment problem in romantic relations and friendship. *Journal of Personality and Social Psychology*, 81, 247–262.

Holmes, J. G. (1989). Trust and the appraisal process in close relationships. In W. H. Jones & D. Perlman (Eds.), *Advances in personal relationships* (Vol. 2, pp. 57–104). London: Jessica Kingsley.

Holmes, J. G., & Rempel, J. K. (1989). Trust in close relationships. In C. Hendrick (Ed.), *Review of personality and social psychology* (Vol. 10, pp. 187–220). London: Sage.

Johnson, D. J., & Rusbult, C. E. (1989). Resisting temptation: Devaluation of alternative partners as a means of maintaining commitment in close relationships. *Journal of Personality and Social Psychology*, 57, 967–980.

Johnson, M. P. (1973). Commitment: A conceptual structure and empirical application. *Sociological Quarterly*, 14, 395–406.

Johnson, M. P. (1991). Commitment to personal relationships. In W. H. Jones & D. W. Perlman (Eds.), *Advances in personal relationships* (Vol. 3, pp. 117–143). London: Jessica Kingsley.

Johnson, M. P., Caughlin, J. P., & Huston, T. L. (1999). The tripartite nature of marital commitment: Personal, moral, and structural reasons to stay married. *Journal of Marriage and the Family*, 61, 160–177.

Kelley, H. H. (1983). Love and commitment. In H. H. Kelley, E. Berscheid, A. Christensen, J. H. Harvey, T. L. Huston, G. Levinger, et al., (Eds.), *Close relationships* (pp. 265–314). New York: Freeman.

Kelley, H. H., & Thibaut, J. W. (1978). *Interpersonal relations: A theory of interdependence.* New York: Wiley.

Kenrick, D. T., & Trost, M. R. (2000). An evolutionary perspective on human relationships. In W. Ickes & S. Duck (Eds.), *The social psychology of personal relationships* (pp. 9–35). New York: Wiley.

Kiesler, C. A. (1971). *The psychology of commitment: Experiments linking behavior to belief.* New York: Academic Press.

Kilpatrick, S. D., Bissonnette, V. L., & Rusbult, C. E. (2002). Empathic accuracy and accommodative behavior among newly married couples. *Personal Relationships*, 9, 369–393.

Koslowsky, M., Caspy, T., & Lazar, M. (1991). Cause and effect explanations of job satisfaction and commitment: The case of exchange commitment. *Journal of Psychology: Interdisciplinary and Applied*, 125, 153–162.

Kurdek, L. A. (1991). Correlates of relationship satisfaction in cohabiting gay and lesbian couples: Integration of contextual, investment, and problem-solving models. *Journal of Personality and Social Psychology*, 61, 910–922.

Kurdek, L. A. (1993). Predicting marital dissolution: A five year prospective longitudinal study of newlywed couples. *Journal of Personality and Social Psychology*, 64, 221–242.

Kurdek, L. A. (1997). The link between neuroticism and dimensions of relationship commitment: Evidence from gay, lesbian, and heterosexual couples. *Journal of Family Psychology*, 11, 503–514.

Kurdek, L. A. (2003). Methodological issues in growth-curve analyses with married couples. *Personal Relationships*, 10, 235–266.

Le, B., & Agnew, C. R. (2003). Commitment and its theorized determinants: A meta-analysis of the investment model. *Personal Relationships*, 10, 37–57.

Levinger, G. (1965). Marital cohesiveness and dissolution: An integrative review. *Journal of Marriage and the Family*, 27, 19–28.

Levinger, G. (1979). A social exchange view on the dissolution of pair relationships. In R. L. Burgess & T. L. Huston (Eds.), *Social exchange in developing relationships* (pp. 169–193). New York: Academic Press.

Lewin, K. (1951). *Field theory in social science*. New York: Harper & Row.

Lin, Y. H. W., & Rusbult, C. E. (1995). Commitment to dating relationships and cross-sex friendships in America and China: The impact of centrality of relationship, normative support, and investment model variables. *Journal of Social and Personal Relationships*, 12, 7–26.

Lund, M. (1985). The development of investment and commitment scales for predicting continuity of personal relationships. *Journal of Social and Personal Relationships*, 2, 3–23.

Lydon, J. E., Meana, M., Sepinwall, D., Richards, N., & Mayman, S. (1999). The commitment calibration hypothesis: When do people devalue attractive alternatives? *Personality and Social Psychology Bulletin*, 25, 152–161.

Lydon, J., Pierce, T., & O'Regan, S. (1997). Coping with moral commitment to long-distance dating relationships. *Journal of Personality and Social Psychology*, 73, 104–113.

McCullough, M. E., Rachal, K. C., Sandage, S. J., Worthington, E. L., Jr., Brown, S. W., & Hight, T. L. (1998). Interpersonal forgiving in close relationships II: Theoretical elaboration and measurement. *Journal of Personality and Social Psychology*, 75, 1586–1603.

Mead, G. H. (1934). *Mind, self, and society*. Chicago: University of Chicago Press.

Meyer, J. P., & Allen, N. J. (1997). *Commitment in the workplace: Theory, research, and application*. Thousand Oaks, CA: Sage.

Miller, R. S. (1997). Inattentive and contented: Relationship commitment and attention to alternatives. *Journal of Personality and Social Psychology*, 73, 758–766.

Morrow, G. C., Clark, E. M., & Brock, K. F. (1995). Individual and partner love styles: Implications for the quality of romantic involvements. *Journal of Social and Personal Relationships*, 12, 363–387.

Murray, S. L., & Holmes, J. G. (1999). The (mental) ties that bind: Cognitive structures that predict relationship resilience. *Journal of Personality and Social Psychology*, 77, 1228–1244.

Murray, S. L., Holmes, J. G., & Griffin, D. W. (1996). The self-fulfilling nature of positive illusions in romantic relationships: Love is not blind, but prescient. *Journal of Personality and Social Psychology*, 71, 1155–1180.

Oliver, N. (1990). Rewards, investments, alternatives, and organizational commitment: Empirical evidence and theoretical development. *Journal of Occupational Psychology*, 63, 19–31.

Pistole, M. C., Clark, E. M., & Tubbs, A. L., Jr. (1995). Love relationships: Attachment style and the investment model. *Journal of Mental Health Counseling*, 17, 199–209.

Powell, C., & Van Vugt, M. (2003). Genuine giving or selfish sacrifice?: The role of commitment and cost level upon willingness to sacrifice. *European Journal of Social Psychology*, 33, 403–412.

Ridley, M. (1996). *The origins of virtue: Human instincts and the evolution of cooperation*. New York: Penguin.

Rusbult, C. E. (1980a). Commitment and satisfaction in romantic associations: A test of the investment model. *Journal of Experimental Social Psychology*, 16, 172–186.

Rusbult, C. E. (1980b). Satisfaction and commitment in friendships. *Representative Research in Social Psychology*, 11, 96–105.

Rusbult, C. E. (1983). A longitudinal test of the investment model: The development (and deterioration) of satisfaction and commitment in heterosexual involvements. *Journal of Personality and Social Psychology, 45*, 101–117.

Rusbult, C. E., & Farrell, D. (1983). A longitudinal test of the investment model: The impact on job satisfaction, job commitment, and turnover of variations in rewards, costs, alternatives, and investments. *Journal of Applied Psychology, 68*, 429–438.

Rusbult, C. E., Johnson, D. J., & Morrow, G. D. (1986). Predicting satisfaction and commitment in adult romantic involvements: An assessment of the generalizability of the investment model. *Social Psychology Quarterly, 49*, 81–89.

Rusbult, C. E., & Martz, J. M. (1995). Remaining in an abusive relationship: An investment model analysis of nonvoluntary commitment. *Personality and Social Psychology Bulletin, 21*, 558–571.

Rusbult, C. E., Martz, J. M., & Agnew, C. R. (1998). The investment model scale: Measuring commitment level, satisfaction level, quality of alternatives, and investment size. *Personal Relationships, 5*, 357–391.

Rusbult, C. E., Van Lange, P. A. M., Wildschut, T., Yovetich, N. A., & Verette, J. (2000). Perceived superiority in close relationships: Why it exists and persists. *Journal of Personality and Social Psychology, 79*, 521–545.

Rusbult, C. E., Verette, J., Whitney, G. A., Slovik, L. F., & Lipkus, I. (1991). Accommodation processes in close relationships: Theory and preliminary empirical evidence. *Journal of Personality and Social Psychology, 60*, 53–78.

Rydell, R. J., McConnell, A. R., & Bringle, R. G. (2004). Jealousy and commitment: Perceived threat and the effect of relationship alternatives. *Personal Relationships, 11*, 451–468.

Sabatelli, R. M., & Cecil-Pigo, E. F. (1985). Relational interdependence and commitment in marriage. *Journal of Marriage and the Family, 47*, 931–937.

Sanderson, B., & Kurdek, L. A. (1993). Race and gender as moderator variables in predicting relationship satisfaction and relationship commitment in a sample of dating heterosexual couples. *Family Relations, 42*, 263–267.

Secord, P. F. (1983). Imbalanced sex ratios: The social consequences. *Personality and Social Psychology Bulletin, 9*, 525–543.

Shainess, N. (1979). Vulnerability to violence: Masochism as a process. *American Journal of Psychotherapy, 33*, 174–189.

Simpson, J. A. (1987). The dissolution of romantic relationships: Factors involved in relationship stability and emotional distress. *Journal of Personality and Social Psychology, 53*, 683–692.

Simpson, J. A., Gangestad, S. W., & Lerma, M. (1990). Perception of physical attractiveness: Mechanisms involved in the maintenance of romantic relationships. *Journal of Personality and Social Psychology, 59*, 1192–1201.

Solomon, R. L. (1980). The opponent-process theory of acquired motivation: The costs of pleasure and the benefits of pain. *American Psychologist, 35*, 691–712.

South, S. J., & Lloyd, K. M. (1995). Spousal alternatives and marital dissolution. *American Sociological Review, 60*, 21–35.

Spanier, G. B. (1976). Measuring dyadic adjustment: New scales for assessing the quality of marriage and similar dyads. *Journal of Marriage and the Family, 38*, 15–28.

Sprecher, S. (1988). Investment model, equity, and social support determinants of relationship commitment. *Social Psychology Quarterly, 51*, 318–328.

Sprecher, S., & Felmlee, D. (1992). The influence of parents and friends on the quality and stability of romantic relationships: A three-wave longitudinal investigation. *Journal of Marriage and the Family, 54*, 888–900.

Stanley, S. M., & Markman, H. J. (1992). Assessing commitment in personal relationships. *Journal of Marriage and the Family, 54*, 595–608.

Staw, B. M. (1976). Knee-deep in the big muddy: A study of escalating commitment to a chosen course of action. *Organizational Behavior and Human Performance, 16*, 27–44.

Straus, M. A., & Gelles, R. J. (1986). Societal change and change in family violence from 1975 to 1985 as revealed by two national surveys. *Journal of Marriage and the Family, 48*, 465–479.

Straus, M. A., & Gelles, R. J. (Eds.). (1990). *Physical violence in American families*. New Brunswick, NJ: Transaction.

Strube, M. J. (1988). The decision to leave an abusive relationship: Empirical evidence and theoretical issues. *Psychological Bulletin, 104*, 236–250.

Strube, M. J., & Barbour, L. S. (1983). The decision to leave an abusive relationship: Economic dependence and psychological commitment. *Journal of Marriage and the Family, 45*, 785–793.

Surra, C. A., Arizzi, P., & Asmussen, L. A. (1988). The association between reasons for commitment and the development and outcome of marital relationships. *Journal of Social and Personal Relationships, 5*, 47–63.

Teger, A. I. (1980). *Too much invested to quit.* New York: Pergamon.

Thibaut, J. W., & Kelley, H. H. (1959). *The social psychology of groups.* New York: Wiley.

Thompson, L., & Spanier, G. B. (1983). The end of marriage and acceptance of marital termination. *Journal of Marriage and the Family, 45*, 103–113.

Tropper, R. (1972). The consequences of investment in the process of conflict. *Journal of Conflict Resolution, 16*, 97–98.

Truman-Schram, D. M., Cann, A., Calhoun, L., & Van Wallendael, L. (2000). Leaving an abusive dating relationship: An investment model comparison of women who stay vs. women who leave. *Journal of Social and Clinical Psychology, 19*, 161–183.

Udry, J. R. (1983). The marital happiness/disruption relationship by level of marital alternatives. *Journal of Marriage and the Family, 45*, 221–222.

Walker, L. (1979). *The battered woman.* New York: Harper & Row.

Van Lange, P. A. M., Agnew, C. R., Harinck, F., & Steemers, G. E. M. (1997). From game theory to real life: How social value orientation affects willingness to sacrifice in ongoing close relationships. *Journal of Personality and Social Psychology, 73*, 1330–1344.

Van Lange, P. A. M., Rusbult, C. E., Drigotas, S. M., Arriaga, X. B., Witcher, B. S., & Cox, C. L. (1997). Willingness to sacrifice in close relationships. *Journal of Personality and Social Psychology, 72*, 1373–1395.

White, G. L. (1980). Physical attractiveness and courtship progress. *Journal of Personality and Social Psychology, 39*, 660–668.

Wieselquist, J., Rusbult, C. E., Foster, C. A., & Agnew, C. R. (1999). Commitment, prorelationship behavior, and trust in close relationships. *Journal of Personality and Social Psychology, 77*, 942–966.

CHAPTER 34

Intimacy in Personal Relationships

Jean-Philippe Laurenceau
Brighid M. Kleinman

Intimacy is a term that is inextricably tied to personal relationships and linked to the formation, maintenance, and dissolution of personal relationships. Our need as human beings to establish and maintain intimate attachments and connections with others has been identified as a fundamental human motivation (Baumeister & Leary, 1995; Ryan & Deci, 2000). Relationship researchers have investigated the role of intimacy in interpersonal relationships and several definitions and operationalizations of intimacy exist in the personal relationships literature (e.g., Argyle & Dean, 1965; Chelune, Robinson, & Kommor, 1984; Fisher & Stricker, 1982; Fruzzetti & Jacobson, 1990; Hatfield, 1984, 1988; McAdams, 1985, 1988; Patterson, 1976, 1982; Schaefer & Olson, 1981; Waring, 1984). These conceptualizations vary greatly and reflect the particular perspective on relationships taken by the particular researcher or theorist (Perlman & Fehr, 1987). Although each perspective has demonstrated explanatory power in its own right, theory and research on intimacy has lacked an overall conceptual model, leading some to refer to intimacy as the "proverbial

elephant" in the field of personal relationships, pieces of which relationship scientists in one way or another are all trying to grab (Acitelli & Duck, 1987).

Probably the first person to refer to the concept of intimacy as reflected within the current chapter is Harry Stack Sullivan (1953) who observed that "the developmental epoch of preadolescence is marked by . . . the manifestation of the need for interpersonal intimacy" (p. 246). Sullivan argued that beginning at about 9 or 10 years of age, children demonstrate a important interpersonal shift, from desiring the companionship and attention of others to desiring the companionship and attention of a *particular* other. Other early work by Erik Erikson (1963) points to the developmental "crisis" stage of intimacy versus isolation. Erikson argued that the capacity for true intimacy occurs in the mid-20s when the individual forms a stable identity and is able to disclose personally revealing information. Other early writing on intimacy also tended to focus on self-disclosure as the primary pathway to intimacy (Altman & Taylor, 1973). From this point in its history, the literature on intimacy has shown dramatic growth and has developed into an area of inquiry that moved from theoretical propositions to specific hypothesis testing using data collected from relationship partners.

The overarching purpose of this chapter is to provide a selective but comprehensive review of the theoretical and empirical literature on intimacy in personal relationships. With this in mind, our specific goals consist of reviewing existing conceptualizations of intimacy, noting some of the empirical work on intimacy and related processes, and identifying directions that warrant further theoretical and empirical attention. To accomplish this, we draw work from the many subdisciplines that make up relationship science (e.g., psychology, communication, sociology). A central assumption in our analysis is that intimacy is best conceptualized as a personal, subjective (and often momentary) sense of connectedness that is the outcome of an interpersonal, transactional process consisting of self-disclosure and partner responsiveness (Laurenceau, Rivera, Schaffer, & Pietromonaco, 2004; Prager, 1995).

Approaches Toward Conceptualizing Intimacy

A review of the literature suggests that existing theories, conceptualizations, and definitions of intimacy differ in their focus on locus of intimacy, determinants of intimacy, and the temporal nature of intimacy (Acitelli & Duck, 1987).

Locus of Intimacy

Locus refers to the level of analysis that is utilized when investigating intimacy. Definitions of intimacy tend to place the locus of intimacy on a continuum from a focus on individuals, to interactions that involve individuals, to relationships that emerge from interactions. Varying the focus of locus, intimacy has been conceptualized as either a quality of persons, a quality of interactions, or a quality of relationships. Although these three perspectives on intimacy may differ in the emphasis of locus, the conceptualizations in this section suggest that persons, interactions, and relationships are given varying degrees of attention.

INTIMACY AS A QUALITY OF PERSONS

As a quality of persons, intimacy has been described as a motivation, reflecting the needs of the individual. This perspective posits intimacy as a dispositional characteristic on which people demonstrate individual differences. Considering the distinction made between personality traits, schemas, and motives as dispositional characteristics (McAdams, 1984; McClelland, 1981), need for intimacy is best categorized as a motive.

Motives refer to the "why" that underlies an individual's behaviors and experiences and may be best understood as affective–experiential preferences that direct and guide behavior (McAdams, 1984). One of the primary human motives that consistently emerges in interpersonal relationships is that of communion, or intimacy (Bakan, 1966; Ryan & Deci, 2000). The identification of intimacy as a motivational force can be seen in the work of Harry Stack Sullivan (1953), where he ascribed tantamount importance to the need for intimacy in the development of the self-concept and self-esteem in children and adolescents. His discussion of intimacy best places it as a need to be met through a reciprocally validating, interpersonal relationship, although he described intimacy as "that type of situation involving two people which permits validation of all components of personal worth" (Sullivan, 1953, p. 246). When individuals are not able to satisfy their basic needs for intimacy in their interpersonal relationships, they experience anxiety, which may lead to the eventual development of psychopathology.

Intimacy motivation is more explicitly defined as the recurrent preference or drive for experiences of warm, close, and communicative interaction with others (McAdams, 1985). Thus, intimacy exists between people, whereas intimacy motivation exists within each person. This motivation is believed to represent a stable personality component on which individuals can differ. McAdams focused on the importance of individuals' intimacy motive to predicting "intimate" interactions and behaviors with others. Research has demonstrated that individual differences in motivations toward intimacy have resulted in predictions of intimate thoughts and behavior. In one longitudinal study, those high in intimacy motivation, relative to low scorers, reported greater marital enjoyment and personal adjustment (McAdams & Valliant, 1982). Moreover, individuals high in intimacy motivation spend more time during the day thinking about people and interpersonal relationships, talking with other people, and express more positive affect in interactions than individuals low in intimacy motivation (McAdams & Constantian, 1983).

INTIMACY AS A QUALITY OF INTERACTIONS

Intimacy can also be defined by what occurs in an interpersonal interaction. As a quality of interactions, intimacy has been conceptualized as an equilibrium level based on a process of behavioral exchanges. Argyle and Dean (1965) suggested that in any given interaction, there is a desired or comfortable level of intimacy that exists between individuals. Intimacy is reflected by behaviors such as increasing or decreasing interpersonal distance, making eye contact, or smiling. If one member of the couple were to engage in a behavior that would increase intimacy to a level beyond that which is desired or comfortable for the partner, a state of disequilibrium would occur. Interactants adjust their behaviors, usually through some form of approaching or distancing behavior, to maintain a comfortable level of closeness (Argyle & Dean, 1965). Some research has found, however, that increases in intimate behaviors were followed not by a decrease in these behaviors by the partner, but with a corresponding increase in intimate behavior by the partner (e.g., Chapman, 1975).

In an attempt to account for the possibility of either increasing or decreasing intimate behaviors in response to a change in the intimacy equilibrium, Patterson (1976) proposed the inclusion of a process in which individuals engage in cognitive labeling of a perceived change in arousal resulting from a perceived change in behavioral intimacy on the part of a partner. Consistent with the view of intimacy being a quality of interactions, this arousal model of interpersonal intimacy suggests that when an individual perceives a change in his or her partner's behavioral intimacy, the individual will perceive the change as either positively or negatively valenced. If the perceived change in arousal is positively valenced, the model would predict a reciprocation of the partner's behavior in the form of behaviors that increase closeness. If the perceived change in arousal is negatively valenced, the model would predict a distancing behavior that will compensate for the partner's change in behavioral intimacy. The arousal model of intimacy has received mixed empirical support, leading to a subsequent refinement of the model by including the functions of patterns of behavioral exchanges (Patterson, 1982, 1984).

From a more clinical perspective, some researchers have developed a conceptualization of intimacy based on the observations of behavior patterns in married couples. Fruzzetti and Jacobson (1990) indicated that although couples who seek marital therapy often describe their relationship problems as a loss of closeness or connection, an astute observer will note that indicators of these complaints lie in their pattern of behavioral exchanges. Intimacy may be understood as involving arousal–interaction feedback cycles that result in either conflict escalation–couple disengagement or conflict de-escalation–couple engagement (Fruzzetti & Jacobson, 1990). This behavioral conceptualization of intimacy posits the interaction of physiological arousal levels and behavioral interactions that lead to increased positive emotional experience, closeness, and understanding that may become reciprocally reinforcing. If spouses can learn that engaging in couple interactions often leads to the result of conflict resolution and closeness, they may begin to predict that future interactions will likely result in the same, encouraging trust and vulnerability. It should be noted that approaches to intimacy that focus on couple interaction also appear to include a person quality in that spouses may differ in their preferred or desired level of intimacy. Thus, each partner's desired level of intimacy will influence the exchange of behaviors in the direction that results in a range of comfort.

INTIMACY AS A QUALITY OF RELATIONSHIPS

Some theorists and researchers have discussed the use of intimacy as a description of the quality of a particular type or set of relationships. For example, Schaefer and Olson (1981) considered an intimate relationship as one in which individuals in a couple share experiences across a variety of areas and in which the experiences and relationship will continue over time. These shared areas of intimacy include social, emotional, intellectual, sexual, and recreational. Moreover, Waring and his colleagues (Waring, 1984; Waring & Reddon, 1983) defined an intimate relationship as consisting of eight facets: conflict resolution (the ability to resolve differences of opinion), affection (the expression of emotional closeness), cohesion (commitment to the relationship), sexuality (mutual fulfillment of sexual needs), identity (self-confidence and self-esteem), compatibility (ability to work and play together), expressiveness (self-disclosure of thoughts, beliefs, and attitudes), and autonomy (independence from family of origin). Another approach toward intimacy as a property of relationships comes from the application of equity theory to relationships (Walster, Walster, & Berscheid, 1978). Equity theory suggests that individuals attempt to maximize their outcomes in their relationships, in which outcomes are equal to rewards minus costs. Thus, the couple as a whole will attempt to maximize their collective rewards so long as the ratio between each member's costs and rewards is equal. Intimate relationships have been viewed as ones that are characterized by relationship equity (Hatfield, Traupmann, Sprecher, Utne, & Hay, 1985).

In general, intimate relationships are ones in which intimate interactions occur on a regular and consistent basis (Prager, 1995). An important distinction should be made between interactions and relationships when highlighting their link to intimacy. An interaction lasts as long as the behavior omitted by of each member of the dyad and can occur outside the context of a previously formed relationship. Specifically, intimate interactions are those that consist of both intimate behaviors and intimate experiences (Prager, 1995). Relationships, on the other hand, persist beyond specific interactions and the presence of any observable behaviors. Repeated intimate interactions produce "by-products" that become stable characteristics of intimate relationships and contribute to the judgment of a relationship as intimate or not (Duck & Sants, 1983; Prager, 1995). At least three relationship characteristics should be included in the definition of an intimate relationship: sustained affection, mutual trust, and partner cohesiveness (Prager, 1995). These three characteristics are not only a result of intimate interactions but also are needed to maintain and sustain interactions in a relationship. Somehow, these interactions over the history of the relationship contribute to the global judgment of the relationship as intimate or nonintimate. These observations point to the following conclusion: The degree of connectedness that may exist across interactions in an intimate relationship may wax and wane.

This disagreement over the locus of intimacy is reminiscent of the classic person–situation debate in personality and social psychology where the determinants of behavior were thought to reside either within the person or within the situation. It is now commonly accepted that behavior emerges from the interaction of both the person and the situation (Berscheid, 1999; Kenrick & Funder, 1988; Mischel & Shoda, 1998).

The Determinants of Intimacy

SELF-DISCLOSURE

Perlman and Fehr (1987) review several operationalizations and definitions of intimacy, all of which appear to have at least one aspect in common – a feeling of closeness developing from a communication process between partners. Therefore, it is not surprising that self-disclosure has traditionally been considered an important component and index of intimacy. Self-disclosure (see Greene, Derlega, & Mathews, this volume) refers to the verbal communication of personally relevant information, thoughts, and feelings to another and has been implicated as an important factor in the development of intimacy between individuals (Derlega, Metts, Petronio, & Margulis, 1993; Jourard, 1971). In Altman and Taylor's (1973) theory of social penetration, self-disclosure plays a central role in their proposed model of the development of intimacy in relationships. Individuals can influence the evolution of an emerging relationship by adjusting the breadth (the number of topics disclosed) and the depth of their self-disclosure (the degree of personal relevance). In addition, nonverbal behaviors (e.g., gaze, touch, body orientation) are expressions that can augment and interact with verbal self-disclosures to influence intimacy in a relationship (Patterson, 1984).

Intimacy and self-disclosure, however, are not synonymous constructs. Self-disclosure is an important part of the process of engaging in intimate interactions and developing intimate relationships but does not completely capture the phenomenon of intimacy (Reis & Patrick, 1996). Studies have suggested that self-disclosure is a related, but conceptually different, construct from intimacy (Laurenceau, Feldman Barrett, & Pietromonaco, 1998; Laurenceau, Feldman Barrett, & Rovine, 2005). Self-disclosure has been found to account for just below half of the variance in ratings of couples' level of intimacy (Waring & Chelune, 1983). Nevertheless, some investigations and definitions of self-disclosure treat them as largely equivalent constructs. For example,

Morton (1978) suggested a useful distinction between descriptive disclosures and evaluative disclosures in which descriptive referred to disclosure of private facts and information and evaluative refers to disclosure of feeling, opinion, and judgment. In discussing these dimensions, however, she referred to these types of expressions as both "disclosures" and "intimacy." Disclosure reciprocity plays an important role in the acquaintance process in which there is a strong demand for more immediate replies from a partner (Archer, 1979). Immediate reciprocity becomes less important as a relationship progresses, suggesting that other aspects of a partner's response may become more important as relationships grow.

RESPONSIVENESS

Although self-disclosure is central to the development of intimate relationships, some researchers have pointed to another variable, responsiveness, to help explain the development of intimacy in relationships. Miller and Berg (1984) stated that "responsiveness can be viewed as the extent to which and the way in which one participant's actions address the previous actions, communications, needs, or wishes of another participant in that interaction" (p. 191). To contribute to the development of intimacy in a relationship, an individual's responses have to demonstrate concern for the discloser. A response must be sincere and immediate, capture the content of the original communication, and meet the need of the discloser (Berg, 1987). Responsiveness has been found to play an important role in disclosure reciprocity, liking, and closeness in relationships (Berg & Archer, 1982). Recently, researchers have conceptualized responsiveness as a process whereby a person communicates understanding, validation, and caring in response to a partner's self-disclosure (Reis & Patrick, 1996; Reis & Shaver, 1988).

PERCEIVED PARTNER RESPONSIVENESS

As noted, partner responsiveness occurs when the listener's communication addresses the needs, wishes, or actions of the speaker (Berg, 1987; Davis, 1982; Miller & Berg, 1984). Some theorists, most notably Sullivan (1953), viewed perceptions of partner responsiveness as necessary in developing and sustaining intimate relationships, and ultimately mental health. In personal relationships, receiving validation and acceptance can often take on a self-esteem maintaining or protective function, in that individuals often seek to confirm their self-concept through the responses of others (Sullivan, 1953). Reis and Shaver (1988) argued that the speaker's perception and judgment of the listener's response as understanding, validating, and caring are important factors in the experience of intimacy, above and beyond the listener's actual responsiveness. Although a listener's response may be a genuine attempt to be understanding, validating, and caring, the speaker may not perceive the response as such. Ultimately, the extent to which a partner's responsiveness contributes to feelings of intimacy should be dependent on the speaker's perceptions of the quality of the partner's response (Laurenceau et al., 2004). Perceived partner responsiveness is posited to be a relationship construct that has been strongly implicated in several central relationship processes, including trust, comittment, and intimacy (Reis, Clark, & Holmes, 2004).

Temporal Aspects of Intimacy

Intimacy has been conceptualized as both a state and a process. Temporal stability is the important factor in this distinction, with a state being static and a process reflecting movement or fluctuation through time. Intimacy as a state can be viewed as a goal or product of a relationship (Duck & Sants, 1983). Once achieved, intimacy can be thought to remain relatively constant and always present in the relationship. For example, once a couple gets married, the relationship can be considered to reflect a higher level of intimacy compared with other types of relationships. Most likely, intimate relationships have some stable defining characteristics to be distinguished from noninti-

mate relationships. For example, an intimate relationship is one that is characterized by a high frequency of intimate behaviors and experiences (Prager, 1995). Models of intimacy as an equilibrium suggest that there is a state quality to intimacy that the couple as a whole is attempting to maintain through mutually influencing behaviors (Argyle & Dean, 1965; Patterson, 1982).

Nevertheless, most researchers who study intimacy suggest that it is best thought of as a process in constant development and variable over time (Duck & Sants, 1983; Laurenceau et al., 2004; Prager, 1995; Reis & Shaver, 1988). Thus, particular interactions over the course of the relationship can be experienced as either intimate or not. Models of intimacy must account for both its static and variable qualities. Although a particular interaction can be appraised as intimate, a relationship is made up of multiple interactions that are somehow "digested" and contribute to overall evaluations and judgments about the partner and the relationship itself (Chelune et al., 1984; Duck & Sants, 1983).

Decisions about the temporal nature of intimacy have definite implications for its measurement. Most, if not all, definitions of intimacy that have been reviewed in this chapter indicate that it is part of a process. However, several methods of measuring intimacy do not appear to capture this important temporal aspect. Cross-sectional self-report measures of intimacy can only reflect the more global view of the individual taken at one point in time. Nevertheless, authors of self-report measures have attempted to evaluate process aspects of intimacy using global scales (e.g., Schaefer & Olson, 1981; Waring, 1984). To tap into the variable nature of intimacy, we argue that measurements should ideally be taken at multiple points over time (Laurenceau & Bolger, in press).

Toward an Integrated Model of Intimacy

Some in the field of personal relationships have called for an integrated model of intimacy that captures and coalesces the multiple perspectives on this construct generated by previous theorists and researchers. To advance our understanding of intimacy, a theory must move toward integrating and developing a conceptualization that embraces all aspects of the phenomenon rather than fostering competition or exclusion. One model of intimacy, originally proposed by Reis and Shaver (1988), and later expanded (Reis & Patrick, 1996), provides a conceptualization of intimacy that encompasses its individual, interactional, and relationship qualities; incorporates its multiple components; addresses its temporal nature; and explicitly guides operationalization and measurement.

According to Reis and Shaver (1988), intimacy is an interpersonal, transactional process with two principal components: self-disclosure and partner responsiveness. Intimacy can be initiated when one person communicates personally relevant and revealing information to another person. Expressions may also be nonverbal in nature, standing as communications in their own right or amplifying verbal disclosures and behaviors (Keeley & Hart, 1994). For the intimacy process to continue, the listener must emit emotions, expressions, and behaviors that are both responsive to the specific content of the disclosure and convey acceptance, validation, and caring toward the individual disclosing. For the interaction to be experienced as intimate by the discloser, he or she must perceive both the descriptive qualities (understanding of content) and evaluative qualities (validation and caring) of the response.

In addition, the interpersonal process of intimacy, as a series of reciprocal disclosures occurring within the context of mutual partner responsiveness, can be influenced by individual differences such as personal needs, goals, and motives (Laurenceau et al., 2004; Reis & Patrick, 1996). For example, individuals high in intimacy motivation would be more likely to self-disclose and seek validation and acceptance from partners (McAdams, 1985). In an experience sampling study examining perceptions immediately following social interactions (Tidwell, Reis, & Shaver 1996), individu-

als with avoidant attachment styles reported less disclosure in their interactions with opposite-sex partners than those with secure and ambivalent attachment styles. Moreover, a consistent finding is that individuals with an insecure attachment style are less responsive than more securely attached individuals according to both objective third-party ratings and subjective reports (Collins & Feeney, 2004).

While the role of individual differences is acknowledged, the interpersonal process model of intimacy maintains a large focus on what specifically takes place in the interaction between partners (Acitelli & Duck, 1987; Berscheid, 1999). The model acknowledges that intimate relationships consist of repeated intimate interactions over time that contribute to more global evaluations of the quality of the relationship. For example, an individual's interpretation, assimilation, and expectations of repeated intimate interactions give rise to a general perception about relationships as satisfying, meaningful, and trustworthy (Prager, 1995; Reis, 1994). A methodological implication of a process model of intimacy is that it may be important to study the process by assessing self-disclosure and partner responsiveness repeatedly over time within a relationship.

A process view of intimacy also allows for a conceptual distinction between intimacy and other well-studied relationship constructs, such as relationship satisfaction, commitment, and trust. Although intimacy and satisfaction in personal relationships are linked, we argue they are not synonymous constructs when viewed over the course of time in a relationship. Intimacy is theorized to fluctuate from interaction to interaction based on the degree to which components of the intimacy process are present in the interaction. Satisfaction, on the other hand, should demonstrate greater stability from interaction to interaction. Intimacy and satisfaction may be difficult to separate when assessed cross-sectionally, underlying the importance of tapping the intimacy process over time within a relationship. We believe that these two constructs become separable when assessed over time where we would expect much greater moment-to-moment variability in intimacy than in satisfaction.

Some Critiques of Past Research and Future Directions

The existing work on intimacy that we have reviewed thus far is not without its limitations. In the remainder of this chapter, we discuss three issues that we believe have not been adequately addressed by existing research on intimacy in personal relationships. First, we discuss the individualistic view on intimacy in relationships that pervades many modern conceptions of intimacy. Second, we highlight the minor role that nonverbal (compared with verbal) communication has played in the literature on intimacy in personal relationships. Last, we explore the idea that individuals fluctuate between desiring more and less intimacy, leading us to propose a self-regulation framework for understanding variability in intimacy.

An Individualistic View of Intimacy

A notable tenet of existing models of intimacy (Reis & Shaver, 1988; Prager, 1995) is that intimacy is achieved when Partner A self-discloses and feels validated, cared for, and understood by Partner B's attempts at responsiveness. Although we agree that this model describes the intimacy process, we believe that in many ways it is decidedly one-sided. Is the experience of intimacy only achieved when one feels that a relationship partner is responding to one's needs? We argue that an individual may experience intimacy while *providing* understanding, care, and validation, as well as while receiving it. In other words, Partner B's feelings of intimacy may match Partner A's, even though A is the one being validated.

One type of important personal relationship that exemplifies this broader interpretation of intimacy is the parent–child relationship. Typically, responsiveness is provided by the parent to the child in response to expressed or latent needs. Young children are usually unable to provide the understanding, caring, and validation to a parent that might be the hallmark of adult intimate interactions as described in the earlier sections of this chapter. Yet despite the lack of caregiving from the child's side, parents still describe relationships with their children as intimate and report feelings of intimacy from interacting with them. Therefore, the act of caregiving itself can be a determinant of intimacy in addition to the receipt of caregiving. This form of responsive caregiving reflects the attachment and bonding that commonly occurs between parents and their children (Bowlby, 1982).

The therapist–client relationship may also be an example of a largely one-sided intimacy process. Although there are exceptions, many therapists do not engage in self-revealing disclosure with their clients, and clients do not attempt to validate their therapists. Yet often therapists report feelings of intimacy toward their clients (Fisher & Stricker, 1982). This likely occurs because effective therapists carefully track their clients' needs and use interventions that reflect responsiveness to clients' goals for behavior change (Bordin, 1979). If an exclusive focus on providing responsiveness produces intimacy in both the parent–child and the therapist–client relationship, then this aspect may generalize to other types of personal relationships. It is unclear to what degree the responder experiences intimacy following provision of responsiveness when compared to the recipient's experience of intimacy.

It is also important to note that the individualistic characterization of the intimacy process may only apply to Western cultures, in which individualism is pervasive in many aspects of life (Myers, 2000). In Eastern cultures, in which collectivism is the ubiquitous attitude, the act of providing responsiveness and caregiving may be more important to feelings of connectedness and intimacy than receiving care (Markus & Kitayama, 1991). Moreover, some two thirds of individuals in the world reside in collectivist countries where social norms revolve around meeting the other's needs and playing expected social roles (Triandis, 1995). Regarding intimacy processes, the central question in individualist cultures may be, "Do I feel understood, validated, and cared for by my partner in this interaction?", but perhaps the question in collectivist cultures is "Am I meeting my partner's needs in this interaction?" The specific determinants and processes reflective of intimacy in non-Western cultural contexts is an important direction for future research.

Nonverbal Communication in Intimacy

A common thread through most models of intimacy is the central role of communication between relationship partners. Close relationship researchers have had much to say on the topics of self-disclosure and partner responsiveness, believed to be central components of the intimacy process (e.g., Altman & Taylor, 1973; Laurenceau et al., 2004; Reis & Patrick, 1996; Reis & Shaver, 1988). The majority of this work has focused on verbal communication. The purpose of this section is to argue that nonverbal communication, although largely neglected, plays a crucial role in the intimacy process. First, nonverbal cues and behavior provide valuable clues about couples' interaction patterns and relationship outcomes. Second, nonverbal communication may actually be equally or more important in the self-disclosure process than verbal communication. Finally, the concept of nonverbal skill may be important in learning why couples may not understand each other or respond appropriately in intimate interactions.

NONVERBAL CUES IN INTIMATE RELATIONSHIPS

Nonverbal cues have been thought to contribute to intimacy in two ways. First, they communicate specific emotional messages, which may stand alone or be considered along with concurrent verbal messages. Second, nonverbal cues may intensify emotions that are experienced during intimate interactions (Argyle & Dean, 1965; Keeley & Hart, 1994; Patterson, 1982). There have

been many examples of both of these nonverbal processes in the literature. Reflecting the former, Patterson (1984) has shown that nonverbal behaviors such as gaze, touch, and posture interact with verbal expressions to affect the development of intimate interactions. Reflecting the latter, nonverbal cues can increase the likelihood of an intimate outcome, whereas others may decrease the possibility. Specifically, smiling, eye contact, and physical proximity tend to engross the listener, especially if the behaviors amplify the speaker's words (Argyle & Dean, 1965; Patterson, 1984).

Gender differences in nonverbal behaviors may also contribute important information to the intimacy process. Compared with men, women tend to smile more, use more eye contact, and generally communicate more emotion in their faces and postures (Hall, 1984). These findings suggest that women may be better at expressing their emotions and communicating their intended message. Observational studies have shown that husbands and wives use different nonverbal behaviors when delivering positive and negative messages (Noller, 1982; Noller & Gallois, 1986). In one study, across both genders, positive expressions tended to involve four behaviors: open smiles, closed smiles, eyebrow raises, and forward leans. Negative behaviors usually involved a frown and an eyebrow furrow (Noller & Gallois, 1986). Assessing behavior by gender, however, the authors discovered that women were much more likely to use the behaviors common to positive messages while delivering verbal communications, whereas men more often used ambiguous signals (e.g., eyebrow flash). For negative verbal messages, women tended to frown, whereas men were more likely to use an eyebrow raise – a signal that is more commonly used to accompany positive verbal messages. Thus, the authors concluded that wives' verbal and nonverbal messages were more congruent than those of their husbands. As Noller (1992) noted in a review of this and related work, "Is it any wonder, then, that husbands had difficulty getting across their positive messages...?" (p. 47).

NONVERBAL COMMUNICATION IN THE SELF-DISCLOSURE PROCESS

Self-disclosure is often described as solely a spoken process: the verbal communication of personal information, thoughts, and emotions (Laurenceau et al., 2004). In fact, Reis and Patrick (1996) explicitly broadened the self-disclosure component of the interpersonal process model to include "self-expression," reflecting both verbal and nonverbal revelation of self-relevant information and feelings. Other researchers also include nonverbal communication in the self-disclosure construct (Chelune et al., 1984). Although verbal messages are often the focus of disclosure research, nonverbal messages also play a crucial role.

Self-disclosures have been classified into two types: factual–descriptive (e.g., personal information, such as the number of one's siblings) versus emotional–evaluative (e.g., feelings about those siblings; Morton, 1978; Reis & Patrick, 1996). Emotional disclosures have been shown to be more important to intimate interactions because they encourage the knowledge, understanding, and validation of the inner aspects of the self (Laurenceau et al., 2004; Reis & Patrick, 1996). Because it has been established that the communication of emotional information is essential, we must therefore consider *how* it occurs. Although some part of that communication is verbal (Reis & Patrick, 1996), a much larger part of it is nonverbal. Research has shown that more emotional information is transmitted nonverbally than verbally (Mehrabian, 1968). For example, a frown or sad smile may be more poignant than a direct statement about one's sadness. Also, such statements carry more meaning if accompanied by the appropriate nonverbal signal of a frown rather than a smile. Nonverbal cues are often better indicators of feelings, emotions, and attitudes than are words (Feldman, Phillippot, & Custrini, 1991; Friedman, 1979a; Rosenthal, Hall, DiMatteo, Rogers, & Archer, 1979). In fact, when there is a discrepancy between verbal and nonverbal messages, people tend to believe the nonverbal ones (Bugental, Daswan, & Love, 1970).

Certain properties of nonverbal communication contribute to its subtle importance in self-disclosure and other relationship processes. For example, nonverbal communication is continuous. People may stop talking, but they cannot stop communicating nonverbal messages while in the company of others. As aptly put by Watzlawick, Beavin, and Jackson (1967, p. 49), "you cannot *not* communicate nonverbally!" (cf. Motley, 1990). Moreover, nonverbal communication takes place more outside of awareness than verbal communication (Ekman & Friesen, 1969; Friedman, 1979b). People are usually aware of the verbal content of their communication, but they are much less likely to be aware of the nonverbal signals they send or how those signals affect others. In addition, nonverbal errors are more likely to have a negative emotional impact than verbal mistakes (Nowicki & Duke, 2002). For example, standing too close may make an acquaintance uncomfortable, expressing angry facial cues while attempting to show compassion may dismay a relationship partner, but making a grammatical error in either of these situations will probably pass unnoticed. These properties of nonverbal behavior contribute to the concept of skill in nonverbal communication.

Rather than being simply a collection of automatic behaviors, the expression and processing of nonverbal behaviors are skills at which individuals can excel or fail, which has important implications for the intimacy process. For example, in one conceptualization, the decision to self-disclose in any given situation is based on goals, skills, and beliefs about how to accomplish these goals (Miller & Read, 1987). One skill involved may be expressive nonverbal skill, which is the ability to accurately display emotions to another. Because people vary in their ability levels of expressive behavior (e.g., women are more accurate nonverbal communicators than men; Hall, 1984), this skill probably influences the likelihood of the goal's achievement. A nonverbal error such as an angry facial expression in the presence of a subjective emotional experience of sadness, for example, may interfere with the intended goal. Consequently, self-disclosure in appropriate situations has been found to be associated with many traits, including social skills (Shaffer, Ruammake, & Pegalis, 1990).

NONVERBAL COMMUNICATION IN RESPONSIVENESS

Because of the importance of perceived partner responsiveness in the intimacy process, it appears essential that the listener be able to decode the speaker's nonverbal signals accurately to respond appropriately, in an understanding, caring, and validating manner. The concept of nonverbal receptiveness (also called nonverbal sensitivity or decoding) is important for partner responsiveness just as nonverbal expressiveness is important for self-disclosure. The discloser displays emotional nonverbal cues, and the listener decodes them. The listener then responds with nonverbal expressiveness, which the discloser perceives and uses to determine how to act next. One study that looked at this process found that when communicators attempted to increase intimacy through nonverbal cues (e.g., smiling, pleasant vocal expressions) partners responded by reciprocating those cues (Guerrero, Jones, & Burgoon, 2000). When communicators attempted to decrease intimacy (e.g., through hostile expressions), partners also responded reciprocally, indicating that partners monitor nonverbal indicators and use them as signals that drive their behaviors.

Because listeners depend on their partners' nonverbal cues to help them respond appropriately, it is essential that the listeners decode those cues accurately. However, a plethora of evidence suggests that people often misread nonverbal expressions in many adult friendships (Carton, Kessler, & Pape, 1999), child peer relationships (Nowicki & Carton, 1993), romantic relationships (Ickes, 1997), as well as teacher–student and other kinds of relationships (Rosenthal et al., 1979). These misreadings occur in several channels of nonverbal communication, such as facial expression (e.g., Ekman & Friesen, 1975), vocal expression (e.g., Scherer, Banse, & Wallbott, 2001), and postu-

ral expression (e.g., Patterson 1984). Perhaps these insights into nonverbal misinterpretations can help explain why there is often a discrepency between how partners are perceived to respond and how they actually respond (Reis et al., 2004).

FUTURE DIRECTIONS FOR NONVERBAL COMMUNICATION IN INTIMACY

There is evidence that nonverbal communication affects the outcomes of a wide variety of relationships. In married couples nonverbal behavior is more likely than verbal behavior to distinguish between distressed and undistressed pairs (Gottman, Markman, & Notarius, 1977). Poor nonverbal skills have been shown to be associated with less satisfying relationships for married couples (Kahn, 1970; Noller, 1980), romantic partners (Carton et al., 1999), roommates (Hodgins & Zuckerman, 1990), children's peer relationships (Nowicki & Carton, 1993), and adults in general (Rosenthal et al., 1979). A wealth of literature supports the conclusion that nonverbal skills are essential to relationship outcomes. Few studies, however, have focused on issues related to mechanism: *How* do nonverbal behaviors and skills affect relationship outcomes and processes? For example, studies have found that spouses low in marital adjustment were better at reading strangers' nonverbal skills than they were at reading their spouses' (Gottman & Porterfield, 1981; Noller, 1981). This finding suggests that nonverbal decoding ability may be specific to particular relationships. Noller (1980) also found that husbands are more likely to erroneously perceive responses as negative, whereas wives were more likely to erroneously perceive them as positive. More research of this nature is needed to determine how nonverbal behavior may play a role in maintaining or damaging an intimate interaction.

A recent unpublished study on the process of relationship formation in acquaintanceships suggests that the importance of nonverbal skill varies based on the current stage of the relationship and the gender of the participants (Kleinman & Nowicki, 2003). When men first met each other their nonverbal decoding skills were strongly related to their likeability; however, those skills became less important as they became closer friends. For women, on the other hand, general nonverbal skills were not significantly related to their likeability at first, but became important as the friendships grew. This study suggests that nonverbal communication skill may be extremely important to the understanding of relationship processes in addition to outcomes.

To create intimacy in an interaction, several nonverbal processes must occur. First, the discloser must display appropriate emotional nonverbal cues. Second, the listener must be able to decode them accurately. Third, the listener must then respond with appropriate nonverbal expressiveness. Finally, the original discloser must perceive these expressive cues accurately. In any interaction, this process is repeated continuously, and thus there is substantial room for error. This section has described research showing that nonverbal errors occur and that they are important in the intimacy process, but future research is needed to discover *where* in the process they occur, *why* they happen, and *how* to correct them.

An Emerging Self-Regulation View of Intimacy in Personal Relationships

Contrary to many depictions of intimacy in the popular press and media, ever-increasing levels of intimacy do not typically characterize personal relationships. Although most of us can imagine wanting more intimacy than we might currently be experiencing in a relationship, there is also the phenomenon of wanting less intimacy than is being currently experienced (Mashek & Sherman, 2004). For some, the prospect of increased levels of connectedness and closeness may trigger a fear of intimacy where individuals avoid intimate interactions. Fear in intimacy can come about because of the risk of rejection or discomfort with interpersonal closeness (Hatfield, 1984). There is likely an ongoing dialectic in our personal relationships between wanting more intimacy and wanting less intimacy, rather than steadily increasing levels

of intimacy (Prager & Roberts, 2004). Aptly put by Nowak and Vallacher (1998), "There is a limit to how close two people really want to be" (p. 203). As noted in an earlier section of this chapter, momentary intimacy fluctuates over time and interactions even in the most globally "intimate" and satisfied relationships.

A facet of the study of intimacy that has received relatively little attention are the putative regulatory process that may underlie the fluctuations in intimacy over time. In studies that have used intensive diary-based measurements of intimacy in personal relationships (e.g., Laurenceau et al., 1998; Laurenceau et al., in press) the behavior of intimacy and related variables demonstrate a great deal of variability over time. Consider the hypothetical case of Maria and Jose, a married couple who has allowed us to track their experience of intimacy on a daily basis. Figure 34.1 depicts the time series plot representing Maria and Jose's day-to-day ratings of intimacy.

From visual examination of the figure, several pieces of information can be gleaned. First, both Maria and Jose demonstrate a considerable degree of variability, suggesting that there are times when each wants more and wants less intimacy. Second, while both partners evidence daily fluctuations in intimacy, it can be seen that Maria's average level of intimacy is higher than that of Jose. Third, this average level may reflect some underlying equilibrium point around which daily intimacy ratings may vary. Moreover, Maria and Jose may each have their respective equilibria levels. Fourth, there seems to be synchrony between the partner's trajectories during certain portions over the 42-day diary period, suggesting some interdependence or coupling. How would we go about modeling these somewhat complex intimacy trajectories over time? Certainly, using linear, quadratic, or cubic time trends would do little to accurately describe this type of behavior. These seemingly chaotic day-to-day fluctuations may represent random noise, or rather, may represent something more meaningful and important that underlies variability in intimacy. One

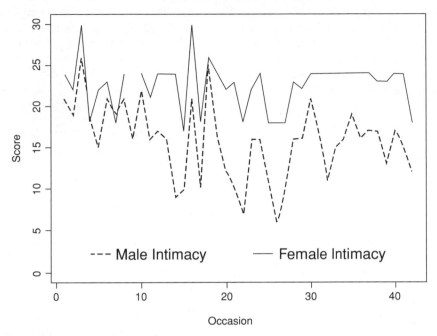

Figure 34.1. Time series of intimacy for hypothetical male and female partners in a married couple.

example of an approach intimacy regulation process is reflected in Maria wanting to experience more intimacy with Jose, and Jose behaving in ways that move him closer to her level. Jose, on the other hand, may not want to move closer to Maria's level of intimacy and engage instead in a solitary activity, an avoidance intimacy regulation process. Dynamical systems theory offers a potential way to examine these complex interpersonal processes.

In recent work (Boker & Laurenceau, in press), we have conceptualized intimacy from the framework of a self-regulating dynamical system that allows us (a) to integrate both the trait (i.e., equilibrium) and state (i.e., fluctuation) nature of intimacy and (b) to understand better how partners in personal relationships mutually influence each other's course of intimacy. Considering a dyad (e.g., marriage) as the system, we attempted to model a self-regulating intimacy process in each individual partner and a coupling between these dynamic processes. To empricially test these ideas,

we used second-order differential equations which enabled us to (a) formalize a test of self-regulation in partner variables measured over time and (b) examine how the regulating behavior of one partner may influence the other partner. Specifically, we found support for the hypothesis that in a well-adjusted marriage, the regulation of intimacy toward one's desired equilibrium level should be facilitated so as to prevent each partner from experiencing long-term extremes in levels of intimacy (i.e., too little intimacy or too much intimacy). We believe that this direction of work on examining the regulatory processes underlying intimacy has potential value for understanding better the ups and downs of intimacy in personal relationships.

Conclusion

Our aim in this chapter was to provide a selective but integrated review of both theoretical and empirical work on intmacy in personal relationships. We also sought to discuss potential issues and questions in the study of intimacy that are ripe for further theoretical development and investigation. There is no doubt that the ubiquitous experience of intimacy in personal relationships will continue to be considered and studied from a multidisciplinary approach in the field of relationship science.

References

Acitelli, L. K., & Duck, S. (1987). Intimacy as the proverbial elephant. In D. Perlman, & S. Duck (Eds.), *Intimate relationships* (pp. 297–308). Beverly Hills, CA: Sage.

Altman, I., & Taylor, D. A. (1973). *Social penetration: The development of interpersonal relationships*. New York: Holt, Rinehart & Winston.

Archer, R. L. (1979). Role of personality and the social situation. In V. J. Derlega (Ed.), *Self-disclosure* (pp. 28–58). San Francisco: Jossey-Bass.

Argyle, M., & Dean, J. (1965). Eye contact, distance, and affiliation. *Sociometry*, 28, 289–304.

Bakan, D. (1966). *The duality of human existence*. Chicago: Rand McNally.

Baumeister, R. F., & Leary, M. R. (1995). The need to belong: Desire for interpersonal attachments as a fundamental human motivation. *Psychological Bulletin*, 117, 497–529.

Berg, J. H. (1987). Responsiveness and self-disclosure. In V. J. Derlega & J. H. Berg (Eds.), *Self-disclosure: Theory, research, and therapy* (pp. 101–130). New York: Plenum Press.

Berg, J. H., & Archer, R. L. (1982). Responses to self-disclosure and interaction goals. *Journal of Experimental Social Psychology*, 18, 501–512.

Berscheid, E. (1999). The greening of relationship science. *American Psychologist*, 54, 260–266.

Boker, S. M., & Laurenceau, J-P. (in press). Dynamical systems modeling: An application to the regulation of the intimacy and disclosure in marriage. In T. A. Walls & J. L. Schafer (Eds.), *Models for intensive longitudinal data*. New York: Oxford University Press.

Bordin, E. S. (1979). The generalizability of the psychodynamic concept of the working alliance. *Psychotherapy: Theory, research, and practice*, 16, 252–260.

Bowlby, J. (1982). *Attachment and loss: Volume 1. Attachment* (2nd ed.). New York: Basic Books.

Bugental, D., Daswan, J., & Love, L. (1970). Perception of contradictory meanings conveyed by verbal and nonverbal channels. *Journal of Personality and Social Psychology*, 16, 647–655.

Carton, J., Kessler, E., & Pape, C. (1999). Nonverbal decoding skills and relationship well-being in adults. *Journal of Nonverbal Behavior*, 23, 91–101.

Chapman, A. J. (1975). Eye contact, physical proximity, and laughter: A reexamination of the equilibrium model of social intimacy. *Social Behavior and Personality*, 3, 143–155.

Chelune, G. J., Robinson, J. T., & Kommor, M. J. (1984). A cognitive interactional model of intimate relationships In V. J. Derlega (Ed.), *Communication, intimacy, and close relationships* (pp. 11–40). New York: Academic Press.

Collins, N. L., & Feeney B. C. (2004) An attachment theory perspective on closeness and intimacy. In D. J. Mashek & A. Aron (Eds.), *Handbook of closeness and intimacy* (pp. 163–187). Mahwah, NJ: Erlbaum.

Davis, D. (1982). Determinants of responsiveness in dyadic interaction. In W. Ickes, & E. S. Knowles (Eds.), *Personality, roles, and social behavior* (pp. 85–139). New York: Springer-Verlag.

Derlega, V. J., Metts, S., Petronio, S., & Margulis, S. T. (1993). *Self-disclosure*. Newbury Park, CA: Sage.

Duck, S. W., & Sants, H. K. A. (1983). On the origins of the specious: Are personal relationships really interpersonal states ? *Journal of Clinical and Social Psychology*, 1, 27–41.

Ekman, P., & Friesen, W. V. (1969). The repertoire of nonverbal behavior: Categories, origins, usage, and coding. *Semiotica*, 1, 49–98.

Ekman, P., & Friesen, W. V. (1975). *Unmasking the face*. Englewood Cliffs, NJ: Prentice Hall.

Erikson, E. H. (1963). *Childhood and society* (2nd ed. revised). New York: Norton.

Feldman, R. S., Philippot, P., & Custrini, R. J. (1991). Social competence and nonverbal behavior. In R. S. Feldman, & B. Rime (Eds.), *Fundamentals of nonverbal behavior* (pp. 329–350). New York: Cambridge University Press.

Fisher, M., & Stricker, G. (1982). *Intimacy*. New York: Plenum Press.

Friedman, H. (1979a). The concept of skill in nonverbal communication: Implications for understanding social interaction. In R. Rosenthal (Ed.), *Skill in nonverbal communication: Individual differences*. Cambridge, MA: Oelgeschalger, Gunn, & Hain.

Friedman, H. (1979b). The interactive effects of facial expressions of emotion and verbal messages on perceptions of affective meaning. *Journal of Experimental and Social Psychology, 15*, 453–469.

Fruzzetti, A. E., & Jacobson, N. S. (1990). Toward a behavioral conceptualization of adult intimacy: Implications for marital therapy. In E. A. Blechman (Ed.), *Emotions and the family: For better or for worse* (pp. 117–135). Hillsdale, NJ: Erlbaum.

Gottman, J. M., Markman, H., & Notarius, C. (1977). The topography of marital conflict: Sequential analysis of verbal and nonverbal behavior. *Journal of Marriage and the Family, 39*, 461–477.

Gottman, J. M., & Porterfield, A. L. (1981). Communicative competence in the nonverbal behavior of married couples. *Journal of Marriage and the Family, 43*, 817–824.

Guerrero, L. K., Jones, S. M., & Burgoon, J. K. (2000). Responses to nonverbal intimacy changes in romantic dyads: Effects of behavioral valence and degree of behavioral change on nonverbal and verbal reactions. *Communication Monographs, 67*, 325–346.

Hall, J. (1984). *Nonverbal sex differences: Communication accuracy and expressive style*. Baltimore: Johns Hopkins University Press.

Hatfield, E. (1984). The dangers of intimacy. In V. J. Derlega (Ed.), *Communication, intimacy, and close relationships* (pp. 207–220). New York: Academic Press.

Hatfield, E. (1988). Passionate and companionate love. In R. J. Sternberg, & M. L. Barnes (Eds.), *The psychology of love* (pp. 191–217). New Haven, CT: Yale University Press.

Hatfield, E., Traupmann, J., Sprecher, S., Utne, M., & Hay, J. (1985). Equity and intimate relationships: Recent research. In W. Ickes (Ed.), *Compatible and uncompatible relationships* (pp. 91–117). New York: Springer-Verlag.

Hodgins, H. S., & Zuckerman, M. (1990). The effect of nonverbal sensitivity on social interaction. *Journal of Nonverbal Behavior, 14*, 155–170.

Ickes, W. (Ed.). (1997). *Empathic accuracy*. New York: Guilford Press.

Jourard, S. M. (1971). *Self-disclosure: An experimental analysis of the transparent self*. New York: Wiley.

Kahn, M. (1970). Nonverbal communication and marital satisfaction. *Family Process, 9*, 449–456.

Keeley, M. P., & Hart, A. J. (1994). Nonverbal behavior in dyadic interaction. In S. W. Duck (Ed.), *Dynamics of relationships* (pp. 135–162). Thousand Oaks, CA: Sage.

Kenrick, D. T., & Funder, D.C. (1988). Profiting from controversy: Lessons form the person-situation debate. *American Psychologist, 43*, 23–34.

Kleinman, B. M., & Nowicki, S., Jr. (2003). The role of nonverbal communication skills in becoming sequainted. Unpublished honors thesis data. Emory University, Atlanta, GA.

Laurenceau, J-P., & Bolger, N. (in press). Using diary methods to study marital and family processes. *Journal of Family Psychology* [Special issue], *19*, 86–97.

Laurenceau, J-P., Feldman Barrett, L. A., & Pietromonaco, P. R. (1998). Intimacy as an interpersonal process: The importance of self-disclosure and perceived partner responsiveness in interpersonal exchanges. *Journal of Personality and Social Psychology, 74*, 1238–1251.

Laurenceau, J-P., Feldman Barrett, L., & Rovine, M. J. (2005). The interpersonal process model of intimacy in marriage: A daily-diary and multilevel modeling approach. *Journal of Family Psychology, 19*, 314–323.

Laurenceau, J-P., Rivera, L. M., Schaffer, A. R., & Pietromonaco, P. R. (2004). Intimacy as an interpersonal process: Current status and future directions. In D. J. Mashek & A. Aron (Eds.), *Handbook of closeness and intimacy* (pp. 61–78). Mahwah, NJ: Erlbaum.

Markus, H. R., & Kitayama, S. (1991). Culture and the self: Implications for cognition, emotion, and motivation. *Psychological Review, 98*, 224–253.

Mashek, D. J., & Sherman, M. D. (2004). Desiring less closeness with intimate others. In D. J. Mashek & A. Aron (Eds.), *Handbook of closeness and intimacy* (pp. 343–356). Mahwah, NJ: Erlbaum.

McAdams, D. P. (1984). Human motives and personal relationships. In V. J. Derlega (Ed.), *Communication, intimacy, and close relationships* (pp. 41–70). Orlando, FL: Academic Press.

McAdams, D. P. (1985). Motivation and friendship. In S. Duck & D. Perlman (Eds.), *Understanding personal relationships* (pp. 85–105). London: Sage.

McAdams, D. P. (1988). Personal needs and personal relationships. In S. W. Duck (Ed.), *Handbook of personal relationships* (pp. 7–22). Chichester, England: Wiley.

McAdams, D. P., & Constantian, C. A. (1983). Intimacy and affiliation motives in daily living: An experience sampling analysis. *Journal of Personality and Social Psychology, 45,* 851–861.

McAdams, D. P., & Valliant, G. E. (1982). Intimacy motivation and psychosocial adjustment: A longitudinal study. *Journal of Personality Assessment, 46,* 586–593.

McClelland, D. C. (1981). Is personality consistent? In A. I. Rabin, J. Aronoff, A. M. Barclay, & R. A. Zucker (Eds.), *Further explorations in personality* (pp. 87–113). New York: Wiley.

Mehrabian, A. (1968). Inference of attitudes from the posture, orientation, and distance of a communicator. *Journal of Consulting and Clinical Psychology, 32,* 296–308.

Miller, L. C., & Berg, J. H. (1984). Selectivity and urgency in interpersonal exchange. In V. J. Derlega (Ed.), *Communication, intimacy, and close relationships* (pp. 162–206). New York: Academic Press.

Miller, L. C., & Read, S. J. (1987). Why am I telling you this?: Self-disclosure in a goal-based model of personality. In V. J. Derlega, & J. H. Berg (Eds.), *Self-disclosure: Theory, research, and therapy* (pp. 35–58). New York: Plenum Press.

Mischel, W., & Shoda, Y. (1998). Reconciling processing dynamics and personality dispositions. *Annual Review of Psychology, 49,* 229–258.

Morton, T. L. (1978). Intimacy and reciprocity of exchange: A comparison of spouses and strangers. *Journal of Personality and Social Psychology, 38,* 72–81.

Motley, M. T. (1990). On whether one can(not) not communicate: An examination via traditional communication postulates. *Western Journal of Speech Communication, 54,* 1–20.

Myers, D. G. (2000). *The American paradox: Spiritual hunger in an age of plenty.* New Haven, CT: Yale University Press.

Noller, P. (1980). Misunderstandings in marital communication: A study of couples' nonverbal communication. *Journal of Personality and Social Psychology, 39,* 1135–1148.

Noller, P. (1981). Gender and marital adjustment level differences in decoding messages from spouses and strangers. *Journal of Personality and Social Psychology, 41,* 272–278.

Noller, P. (1982). Channel consistency and inconsistency in the communication of married couples. *Journal of Personality and Social Psychology, 43,* 732–741.

Noller, P. (1992). Nonverbal communication in marriage. In R. Feldman (Ed.), *Applications of nonverbal behavior: Theories and research* (pp. 31–59). Hillsdale, NJ: Erlbaum.

Noller, P., & Gallois, C. (1986). Sending emotional messages in marriage. *British Journal of Social Psychology, 25,* 287–297.

Nowak, A., & Vallacher, R. R. (1998). *Dynamical social psychology.* New York: Guilford Press.

Nowicki, S. J., & Carton, J. (1993). The measurement of emotional intensity from facial expressions. *Journal of Social Psychology, 133,* 749–755.

Nowicki, S. J., & Duke, M. P. (2002). *Will I ever fit in? The breakthrough program for conquering adult dyssemia.* New York: Free Press.

Patterson, M. L. (1976). An arousal model of interpersonal intimacy. *Psychological Review, 83,* 235–245.

Patterson, M. L. (1982). A sequential model of nonverbal exchange. *Psychological Review, 89,* 231–249.

Patterson, M. L. (1984). Intimacy, social control, and nonverbal involvement: A functional approach. In V. J. Derlega (Ed.), *Communication, intimacy, and close relationships* (pp. 105–132). New York: Academic Press.

Perlman, D., & Fehr, B. (1987). The development of intimate relationships. In D. Perlman & S. W. Duck (Eds.), *Intimate relationships: Development, dynamics and deterioration* (pp. 13–42). Beverly Hills, CA: Sage.

Prager, K. J. (1995). *The psychology of intimacy.* New York: Guilford Press.

Prager, K. J., & Roberts, L. J. (2004). Deep intimate connection: Self and intimacy in couple relationships. In D. Mashek & A. Aron (Eds.), *Handbook of closeness and intimacy* (pp. 43–60). Mahwah, NJ: Erlbaum.

Reis, H. T. (1994). Domains of experience: Investigating relationship processes from three perspectives. In R. Erber & R. Gilmore (Eds.),

Theoretical frameworks in personal relationships (pp. 87–110). Hillsdale, NJ: Erlbaum.

Reis, H. T., Clark, M. S., & Holmes, J. G. (2004). Perceived partner responsiveness as an organizing construct in the study of intimacy and closeness. In D. J. Mashek & A. Aron (Eds.), *Handbook of closeness and intimacy* (pp. 201–225). Mahwah, NJ: Erlbaum.

Reis, H. T., & Patrick, B. C. (1996). Attachment and intimacy: Component processes. In H. T. Higgins & A. W. Kruglanski (Eds.), *Social psychology: Handbook of basic principles* (pp. 523–563). New York: Guilford Press.

Reis, H. T., & Shaver, P. (1988). Intimacy as an interpersonal process. In S. W. Duck (Ed.), *Handbook of personal relationships* (pp. 367–389). Chichester, England: Wiley.

Rosenthal, R., Hall, J. A., DiMatteo, M. R., Rogers, P. L., & Archer, D. (1979). *Sensitivity to nonverbal communication: The PONS test*. Baltimore: Johns Hopkins University Press.

Ryan, R. M., & Deci, E. L. (2000). Self-determination theory and the facilitation of intrinsic motivation, social development, and well-being. *American Psychologist, 55*, 68–78.

Schaefer, M. T., & Olson, D. H. (1981). Assessing intimacy: The PAIR inventory. *Journal of Marital and Family Therapy, 7*, 47–60.

Scherer, K. R., Banse, R., & Wallbott, H. (2001). Emotion inferences from vocal expression correlate across language and culture. *Journal of Cross-Cultural Psychology, 32*, 76–92.

Shaffer, D. R., Ruammake, C., & Pegalis, L. J. (1990). The "opener": Highly skilled as interviewer or interviewee. *Personality and Social Psychology Bulletin, 16*, 511–520.

Sullivan, H. S. (1953). *The interpersonal theory of psychiatry*. New York: Norton.

Tidwell, M., Reis, H. T., & Shaver, P. R. (1996). Attachment, attractiveness, and daily social interactions: A diary study. *Journal of Personality and Social Psychology, 71*, 729–745.

Triandis, H. C. (1995). *Individualism and collectivism*. Boulder, CO: Westview Press.

Walster, E. H., Walster, G. W., & Berscheid, E. (1978). *Equity theory and research*. Boston: Allyn & Bacon.

Waring, E. M. (1984). The measurement of marital intimacy. *Journal of Marital and Family Therapy, 10*, 185–192.

Waring, E. M., & Chelune, G. J. (1983). Marital intimacy and self-disclosure. *Journal of Clinical Psychology, 39*, 183–190.

Waring, E. M., & Reddon, J. R. (1983). The measurement of intimacy in marriage: The waring intimacy questionnaire. *Journal of Clinical Psychology, 39*, 53–57.

Watzlawick, P., Beavin, J. H., & Jackson, D. D. (1967). *Human communication: Forms, disturbances, paradoxes*. Palo Alto, CA: Mental Research Institute.

Part X

CONTEXT

CHAPTER 35

Social Networks and Personal Communities

Graham Allan

Introduction

As others in this volume have indicated (see Perlman & Duck, this volume) after a somewhat uneven beginning, the study of personal relationships has moved on from a dominant focus on the traits and properties of individuals to a more broad-based concern with people's interactions and relationships. Moreover the field has embraced a degree of multidisciplinary tolerance that is relatively rare within the social science community. Nonetheless one can argue that the study of personal relationships remains rather "individualistic." Although personal relationships research is now less concerned with the individual as the prime focus of attention, it nonetheless tends to concentrate on individual relationships and see these as the key problematic. As Duck (1993) among others has been arguing for some time, understanding relationships also requires paying heed to the contexts in which they arise. Put simply, relationships do not occur in isolation, they are structured and framed at least in part by the broader contexts under which they develop, flourish, and eventually end.

By its nature, the notion of context is imprecise and broad. As Adams and Allan (1998) indicated in their discussion of friendship, there are different levels of context that personal relationships researchers need to consider. These include the personal environment level, the network level, the community level, and the societal level. It is the second of these, the network level, which is the main concern of this chapter. At the heart of this is the idea that individual relationships, be they relationships between family members, friends, sexual partners, colleagues, neighbors, or whatever, are elements within a broader constellation of relationships within which each individual is enmeshed. How this constellation of relationships is patterned, how the relationships within it are constructed, and what connections exist between relationships will be influenced by a wide range of factors – personal, social, and economic – and so inevitably vary between individuals. Nonetheless these relationships in which the individual is embedded are liable to cast a shadow over one another. Rather than being independent, different relationships are characterized as they are partly as a result of the influence of the other sets of relationships in which each of the individuals concerned is involved.

The aim of this chapter is to explore how researchers have attempted to incorporate this type of perspective into the study of personal relationships. Rather than focusing on specific relationships, whether defined by category or content, it reviews the ways scholars have examined the sets of personal ties which people generate, how these are shaped and patterned, and what overall impact they have. It starts by discussing the main traditions of social network analysis. It then reviews those ways which have been most influential in the field of personal relationships research, paying particular heed to research on relationship development and to researchers' efforts at collecting data on respondents' personal – or ego-centered – networks. Finally, it also focuses on the ways in which these sets of relationships change as the circumstances of people's lives alter and how social and economic transformations influence their configuration. In these ways, it seeks to illustrate how a social network perspective can contribute to the field of personal relationships research.

Conceptualizing Networks

The origins of social network research has been recounted on numerous occasions (e.g., Barnes, 1972; Scott, 2000; Wellman, 1988). In the United States, Moreno's (1934) work developing a sociometric approach was an early influence, although it was within British social anthropology that the concept of "social network" first came to prominence. Although Radcliffe-Brown (1940) had used the idea of network as a metaphor, John Barnes (1954) is generally credited with being the first to use the concept analytically to capture the structure of relationships in the Norwegian parish he was studying. Others including Bott (1957), Mitchell (1969), and Boissevain (1974) were influential in developing this tradition. Early network analysts in North America recognized

their debt to Barnes's (1954) and especially Bott's (1957) pioneering work, although their approach took a somewhat different path. There, network analysis was developed more by mathematically oriented sociologists than by social anthropologists. Drawing on graph and other mathematical theories, scholars such as White, Boorman, and Breiger (1976) and Burt (1980) explored the structural characteristics and properties of networks in an attempt to add greater precision to social network research (see Holland & Leinhardt, 1979; Scott, 2002). Indeed one of the attractions of the network approach was that it did appear to enable personal – and other types of – relationships to be mapped succinctly in ways that allowed precise structural comparisons to be made. This indeed was the fundamental promise of Bott's (1957) research which appeared to demonstrate that different network configurations led to different behavioural patterns (Milardo & Allan, 2000).

Arguably, since the 1970s the most influential network analyst from a personal relationships perspective has been Barry Wellman. In a series of reports based on data collected from East York, a suburb of Toronto, in the 1970s, Wellman consistently argued that a network approach is fundamental to understanding the character of contemporary society and the role that personal relationships play within this (Wellman, 1979, 1982, 1985; Wellman, Carrington, & Hall, 1988; Wellman & Wellman, 1992; Wellman & Wortley, 1990). He has been particularly concerned with the ways in which individuals are integrated into social life and how aspects of "community" are being transformed. His argument is that standard notions of community as used by political and social commentators, as well as some academics, are too all-embracing as well as too value-laden to be useful for analyzing the complexity of personal relationships that people sustain in industrial and other economically advanced societies. Instead, he and his colleagues have argued for the need to explore empirically the various relationships which individuals sustain, mapping these as networks that can then be analyzed with more sophistication than is ever possible with the use of constructs like community.

The focus of Wellman's approach is on what he termed "personal communities" – the relationships an individual sustains together with the relationships that exist between these others (Wellman, 1982; Wellman, Carrington, & Hall, 1988). In terms of network structure, different people have distinct configurations of relationships. Some, albeit a minority, are embedded in quite dense networks in which many of the others involved also sustain relationships with each other. Other people have networks which involve various subsets of relationships in which the others in each subset all know one another but with few relationships and little knowledge crossing between the subsets. In other cases, individual relationships may be more insulated, with those involved having relatively little to do with each other. Knowing about these different network constellations is clearly important if we are to understand the patterning of people's personal relationships and their consequent social integration.

In his concern for personal communities, Wellman's approach is rooted in the Bott tradition. Like Bott, he highlights the importance of interrogating the configuration of relationships comprising an individual's personal community. He wants to do this for two main reasons. First, such knowledge is valuable in its own right. In particular if comparisons of social integration are to be made between people, over time or across circumstance, then knowledge of the configuration of personal ties would appear to be a central element within this. Second, as Bott's work suggests, if there is any prospect of explaining behavior through personal network configuration, then evidently it is necessary to plot substantive differences in these networks accurately. There is a need to know not just the size and membership of the networks, but also such network configurational characteristics as their density (the number of relationships or "links" existing in a network as a proportion of the total number possible); the degree of clustering

(the extent to which there are certain sets – cliques – of individuals in the network who are highly connected to one another but less highly connected to other network members); and their centrality (the extent to which individuals have direct links with other individuals in the network). (For a full discussion of different measures of the configurational properties of networks, see Scott, 2000).

Although sophisticated measures of network patterns exist, the structure of a personal network remains highly dependent on what the analyst counts as warranting making a "link" between two individuals within the network. How are the relationships that count determined? What criteria does such a relationship need to meet to be included in the mapping? Whatever the answers given, these decisions govern the resultant constituted network. The issues involved here are more complex than they initially appear. In examining – or more accurately, constituting – networks, it is not solely a matter of whether a link exists, but what relevant properties that link has. Many relationships are multiplex, especially those that are of more consequence to individuals and their networks. Arguably, such complexity needs incorporating into the mapped network if the mapping is accurately to reflect the reality of people's personal communities (Milardo & Allan, 2000). This in turn makes analyzing and comparing network structures more complex. Although graph and other mathematical theories are capable of handling such complexity, a more interesting issue is whether social science research is capable of ascertaining the content of multiplex relationships sufficiently subtly and with sufficient accuracy.

Ego-Centered Networks

As can be recognized, the approach typified by the social network school of which Wellman is a proponent requires detailed information about the character of the range of ties in which an individual is involved and about the relationships which exist between those others who are party to this network. Such detailed information is rarely generated in what we can characterize as personal relationships research – in effect the type of research examined in this volume. Instead, where social networks are discussed, the term tends to be used simply as a proxy for the set of relationships an individual sustains. This is what Barnes (1972) referred to as an individual's "star," although this term is rarely used in the personal relationships literature. Within this literature the terms *personal network* or *ego-centered network* (or sometimes *ego-centric network*) are more common. In effect, these represent Wellman's personal community excluding whatever ties there are connecting the others in the network.

Even when the idea of network is used in this looser way, the criteria for including individuals in the constituted network are important. Milardo (1992) provided a useful summary of four major forms that have been drawn on by different researchers in constructing personal networks:

1. networks of significant others – those a respondent defines as important others in their lives, including family and friends;
2. exchange networks – those who provide support of different types or to whom support is given;
3. interactive networks – those with whom an individual interacts on a regular basis;
4. global networks – all those others personally known by the individual through whatever means.

As Milardo noted, there is generally a strong degree of overlap across these different networks. Nonetheless, they all are constructed differently, suggest different types of questions, and are designed to address different theoretical or substantive issues. As a consequence, the networks generated have different configurations and properties, notwithstanding any overlap there is between them.

These different approaches all have relevance for personal relationships researchers, although networks of significant others and exchange networks are the most pertinent and common within the personal relationships field. The whole topic of social support, however widely or narrowly this is defined, has received extensive attention from relationship researchers taking a network perspective. In particular, the part that different categories of others play in support provision – partners, children, friends, neighbors, and so on – has been researched widely, as has the overall composition of the network of others involved in giving assistance of different forms. Thus, some researchers have examined the patterns of support people in early phases of partnership–marriage or parenthood receive (Bost, Cox, & Payne, 2002; Felmlee, 2001; Kearns & Leonard, 2004). Others have been concerned with issues of support in later life (Aartsen, van Tilburg, Smits, & Knipscheer, 2004; Litwin, 2000; Wenger, 1995) or with particular transitions such as divorce or widowhood (Morgan, Carder, & Neal, 1997; Rands, 1988; Terhell, Broese van Groenou, & Tilburg, 2004). A principal concern with all these studies is with showing who it is that provides different forms of support in different circumstances and how that support is patterned within the context of the overall set of relationships in which the individual is involved.

A further topic that is core within the personal relationships field concerns the development, maintenance, and ending of relationships, especially intimate romantic–sexual relationships. Although these processes are generally examined within a dyadic framework, the part that other relationships play has also received attention. Sprecher, Felmlee, Orbuch, and Willetts (2002) provided a very good summary of recent work on the impact of networks on dating and marital relationships (see also Parks, 1997; Surra, 1988). They suggested that there are three major ways in which personal networks influence these relationships: opportunity; information; and support. Clearly the other relationships in which people are involved can act as a conduit for the development of romantic ties. Not only may friends, for example, exert direct and indirect influence over people's desire to engage in romantic relationships

(Simon, Eder, & Evans, 1992), but also, through network overlap, they can provide introductions and opportunities for potential partners to meet (Parks & Eggert, 1991). So, too, other members of the network may attempt to facilitate or discourage the continued development of the relationship. For example, research has shown that supportive networks tend to be associated with increased levels of attachment and commitment in the romantic dyad and reduced likelihood of breaking up (Parks, Stan, & Eggert, 1983; Sprecher & Felmlee, 2000).

Similarly, personal networks can have an impact on marital relationships. The most famous piece of research on this issue has already been referred to: Bott's (1957) much-debated analysis of conjugal relationships. Whether or not her arguments that dense networks helped generate segregated marital roles are accepted (Milardo & Allan, 2000), her work did establish the importance of viewing marital ties within the context of the networks those involved maintained. As with premarital couples, research has indicated that positive support from personal networks increases marital satisfaction and happiness, as does fuller integration of the couple in their shared network (Bryant & Conger, 1999; Orbuch, Veroff, & Hunter, 1999). Conversely, marriages can be affected negatively where one spouse, especially a wife, sustains high levels of interaction with dense networks of close friends (Burger & Milardo, 1995).

In important regards, these approaches are distinct from the social networks approach summarized earlier because the explanations they offer are not couched in configurational or even structural terms. Rather, somewhat more straightforwardly, they seek to recognize that dyadic relationships are not relationally isolated but are enacted within settings in which other relationships may be of consequence. Thus, the focus is predominantly on the different properties of both the individuals and the individual relationships which comprise the complex of relationships in which an individual is involved. In some regards, this type of approach does not seek to capitalize very

fully on the notion of network as structured configuration. Yet equally this comparatively loose usage of the term is common and conveys well the central notion that the sets of relationships in which people are embedded influence their behavior in significant ways.

The "Social Convoy" Approach

Whether researchers are concerned with ego-centered networks or fuller personal communities, they need to find ways of "capturing" and recording the relationships involved. Originally, as for example in Bott's research (1957), the questions posed were about who was known to the respondent, without much theorizing about what "known" meant. However, as discussed earlier, since then greater sophistication has been used in collecting data on personal networks, with the recognition that network structure is inevitably an artefact of the relational questions asked. The central issue though remains one of how to operationalize data collection in ways that allow for pertinent data on personal communities to be generated in forms which enable comparison between the properties of the component personal relationships and examination of the patterning of the personal communities. Moreover, other things being equal, it would seem sensible for the collection of information on who comprises an individual's personal community to be kept relatively straightforward so that it remains intuitively understandable to respondents. Once the names of network members are generated, then more complex questions, scales, and instruments can be administered as appropriate to the specifics of each project.

The approach used by Knipscheer, de Jong Gierveld, van Tilburg, and Dykstra (1995) has proved very successful. As part of the extensive "Living Arrangements and Social Networks of Older Adults" project in which a stratified sample of nearly 4,000 Dutch older adults were interviewed, information was collected on respondents' personal networks. The approach used was a structured one that involved asking a series of questions about different domains of social activity. These included the household, primary kin outside the household, colleagues and workmates, neighbors, and friends. For each domain, each respondent was asked about the relationships they sustained. They were then asked a wide range of questions about each of the specified relationships, including questions about patterns of interaction and services exchanged. This research has been very productive and resulted in a large number of articles, some based also on follow-up surveys of the same population. The sheer scale of the project means it has not been replicated elsewhere, although the approach to collecting respondents' personal networks is one that lends itself to replication. (See also Broese van Groenou & van Tilburg, 2003; Uhlenberg & de Jong Gierveld, 2004; van Tilburg & Broese van Groenou, 2002).

A quite different approach is the social convoy model, originally developed by Antonucci and her colleagues (Antonucci, 1986; Antonucci & Akiyama, 1987, 1995; Kahn & Antonucci, 1980). This has proved highly influential, especially in the field of social gerontology. The focus of this model is on the ways "individuals move through their lifetimes surrounded by people who are close and important to them and who have a critical influence on their life and well-being" (Antonucci & Akiyama, 1995, p. 356). As well as having a dynamic, life course element, it also offers a different notion of network structure to those in which configurational issues are dominant. Moreover, Antonucci and her colleagues have developed a simple, yet highly effective, means of researching social convoy membership.

The method involves providing respondents with a diagram of three concentric circles – somewhat like an archery board – with the word "you" in the center. The respondent is asked to place in the inner circle those people whom "you feel so close to that it's hard to imagine life without them" (Antonucci, Akiyama, & Lansford, 1998, p. 381). Those who were considered less close but still "very important" to the respondent are located in the middle circle. The outer circle contains those "people whom you haven't already mentioned who are close enough and important enough in your life that they should also be placed in your network" (Antonucci et al., 1998, p. 381). The result is a visual representation of those relationships that an individual considers most important in his or her life, together with a broad indication of their relative standing.

The benefits of Antonucci's approach have been demonstrated in a number of recent studies that have sought to capture the characteristics of people's personal communities (see, e.g., Morgan, Carder, et al., 1997; Pahl & Spencer, 2004; Phillipson, Bernard, Phillips, & Ogg, 2000; Wenger, 1995). Methodologically, a number of positive features of the approach can be identified. To begin with, it is one that intuitively makes sense to respondents. The idea of people being "closer" or "more important" to them is common in everyday discourse; moreover, representing this personal or social distance spatially in the concentric rings is readily understandable. Of course, this does not mean it is unproblematic. Respondents may struggle in some cases to locate people in a particular ring. Often they want to place one or more of their relationships on the lines of the rings rather than in the spaces between the lines. This, of course, is part of the benefit of the process. Wherever participants locate their different relationships within the concentric circles, they can be interrogated about how and why they reached the decisions they did. The criteria they are using and the contrasts they are making can be made explicit through discussion and comparison.

In addition of course, once the initial personal community has been mapped onto the concentric ring model, the researcher can ask other types of questions to extend the relational coverage. For example, they could ask the respondent about other kin or about colleagues or other friends. Alternatively, they may ask about different services and exchanges in which the individual is involved – from whom they give and receive different types of help or assistance. Or they may ask people about others on their phone or address lists. The point here is that Antonucci's method is extremely flexible. Methodologically its secret is that it allows a visual representation of relationships that requires respondents to make comparisons about the relative properties and qualities of the different relationships they include. Moreover, it is possible to add further rings to the diagram, although making the exercise too complex for respondents is likely to defeat the object. Much of the benefit of the method lies in its simplicity, which is compromised if the number of circles becomes too large.

Once researchers have established who is included in a respondent's social convoy, they are able to ask whatever questions in whatever format they want of the different people included in the diagram. These questions about individual relationships may be highly structured. For example, in theory there is no reason specific measurement scales and other such instruments could not be applied to each relationship in turn. Equally, though, this method of generating social convoys also allows for more qualitative approaches. In particular, as indicated earlier, the positioning of individual relationships within the concentric circles enables the researcher to ask a variety of questions about the rationale for this placement and to explore the histories and development of the different ties in a flexible fashion. It also allows for questioning about the linkages that exist between the relationships included (from ego's perspective) and consequently an examination of the configurational and density issues which have concerned social network analysts.

For researchers concerned with the patterning of personal relationships, Antonucci's social convoy approach combines intuitive simplicity with the capacity to ask detailed questions about the characteristics of different relationships. It also enables comparisons to be made across time. This may be done through respondents' retrospective accounts of changes in the character of their social convoys overall or through their recounting changes in the individual ties they include, although,

as with any retrospective reconstructions, there are inherent methodological difficulties with this. Equally, however, as Wenger's research (1995) has shown, the social convoy approach can be used effectively in longitudinal studies in which data are collected at different times. This allows a clear mapping of changes in the ways that people perceive their more significant relationships to have developed over time and how this has affected their overall social incorporation.

A social convoy approach does not entail using the analytical frameworks that have been developed for "standard" network studies. Some may see this as a significant disadvantage. There are certainly some empirical and theoretical concerns within the personal relationships field that do require the detailed mapping of ego-centered or more generalized networks, but there are many others that, although concerned with personal communities as sets of informal relationships, do not necessitate elaborate analysis of network configurational properties. Indeed, the social convoy approach is not particularly focused on issues of network configuration at all. Rather, those scholars who have drawn on it have more typically sought to describe personal communities in terms of the involvements people have with different categories of others and how this changes over time. As noted earlier, the approach itself allows all sorts of different questions to be asked of the relationships involved in the convoy (including configurational ones), but analysis is commonly built on categorizing the overall form of social participation and involvement of the individuals whose convoys are recorded. That is, researchers focus on the different memberships of the convoy, the role bases of those relationships (family, friends, colleagues, etc.), and the degree to which these are understood as important and central by the individual for their well-being. See, for example, the typologies created by Pahl and Spencer (2004) and Wenger (1995).

The details of these schemas are not important here. What is important is that they illustrate how a social convoy methodology can prove useful in personal relationships research. They show how this methodology allows aspects of personal community structure to be investigated as well as the "content" of individual relationships. Once the various patterns in people's social convoys are analyzed and typologies constructed, comparisons between various personal communities become possible. With knowledge of the different patterns occurring in people's personal communities, important comparative questions can also be addressed. In particular, it becomes possible to ask why different personal communities are structured as they are; what part different social and personal factors – age, gender, mobility histories, ethnicity, life course position, among others – play in this; what consequences various forms of personal community have for individuals; and how these patterns change over time, either gradually or as a result of some particular life event. Some of these sorts of questions have been posed successfully by social gerontologists using Antonucci's approach (Antonucci et al. 2001; Morgan, Carder, et al., 1997; Phillipson et al., 2000; Wenger, 1995; also see Blieszner, this volume), but there is evidently a need for better information than we have about the patterns found in the wider population. To be clear here, the suggestion is not that other network approaches are incapable of answering these sorts of questions. They are, provided that they collect data on the quality or content of the relationships involved in people's personal communities. The argument is, rather, that conventional network analysis can become overly concerned with structural or configurational issues and as a result be less successful in capturing other aspects of people's "micro-social worlds" (Pahl & Spencer, 2004) in ways that are important for understanding their lived experiences.

Changes in Personal Networks

The most common use of the social convoy idea has been in social gerontology and aging studies. Clearly, the analogy of peo-

ple's personal relationships being a social convoy with its implications of movement and change over time is readily compatible with a life course perspective. The convoy continues its passage with some of its members – relationships – being present more or less throughout, but others moving in or out of the convoy as the individual's life course develops. Whether or not a social convoy approach is adopted, the issue of change in people's personal communities is an important one for understanding the part played by different relationships in people's lives and the ways in which their personal worlds are constructed. Change is, of course, inevitable as people age, as they progress through the different phases of their life course, as contingencies of different orders strike, and as their needs for different types of support alter. Potentially, all such change can disrupt some existing relationships as well as providing opportunities for new ones to emerge and for others to be reframed.

Social scientific knowledge of the impact of different types of change on people's personal communities is, at best, limited. Some areas – in particular, how networks change in later life – have received some attention, (see, e.g., Broese van Groenou & van Tilburg 1997; van Tilburg & Broese van Groenou, 2002; Wenger & Jerrome, 1999). However, much of the research into networks in later life is concerned with the impact of infirmity and with examining who provides support as it is needed rather than with monitoring change in personal communities per se (see, e.g., Carpentier & Ducharme, 2003; Keating, Otfinowski, Wenger, Fast, & Derksen, 2003; Nocon & Pearson, 2000). Other areas of change in people's lives have received more limited attention, although there has been research on the impact of significant personal transitions, such as widowhood, divorce, job loss, and return to education (e.g., Larson, Wilson & Beley, 1994; Morgan & March, 1992; Morgan, Carder, et al., 1997; Morris & Irwin, 1992; Rands, 1988; Suitor, 1987; Suitor & Keeton, 1997; Terhell, Broese van Groenou & Tilburg, 2004.). However, perhaps not surprisingly, there has been little focus on more mundane changes in people's personal communities. Moving house, gaining promotion, or having another child, for example, may not have as dramatic an effect on our social routines as the ending of a marriage or long-term redundancy, but they are still likely to have some impact. They will influence whom we see, whom we have time for, and how we service different relationships. Similarly, other, even more routine changes in our lives – young children becoming more independent; adolescents leaving home; shifts in our work commitments or leisure pursuits – will also influence our participation in different social arenas. As this happens, so the relationships in our personal communities become modified and their content altered, in ways that are so unexceptional that we only rarely reflect on them.

Generally, there is a shortage of longitudinal material on what might be termed the routine *natural history* of personal communities – the ways in which different relationships unremarkably alter over time, some becoming more central in people's lives and others becoming of lesser consequence. Importantly, too, the studies there have been have tended to be short rather than long term. One exception here is Wellman's study of the networks of 33 respondents from his original Toronto sample of 845 whom he interviewed after a gap of 10 years (Wellman, Wong, Tindall, & Nazer, 1997). Another is Suitor and Keeton's (1997) restudy of Suitor's sample of school returners. What these studies indicate, not surprisingly, is that social change routinely occurs across the life course, affecting people's social location and in turn the sets of relationships they sustain. Although based on a shorter term study, Morgan and his colleagues (Morgan, Carder, et al., 1997; Morgan, Neal, & Carder, 1997) made the important point that although the personnel making up an individual's network may alter over time, the properties of the network itself can be more stable. In this study of widows, a core segment of key relationships remained relatively constant over the course of the research, whereas relationships that were more peripheral waxed and waned. Thus, as Morgan, Neal, et al. (1997) expressed it, "the stability of the aggregate properties in personal networks is much greater than the stability of the membership in these networks" (p. 22).

Late Modernity and Network Change

Clearly the different social and economic circumstances under which people live their lives will influence the ways in which their personal communities change. It is consequently unwise to attempt to generalize too much about any underlying patterns. However, personal relationships are rarely, if ever, static. The issues that concern personal relationships researchers are not just whether specific relationships continue over time, but also how and why their content alters. Of course, content can be understood in numerous ways, depending on the theoretical and substantive focus of the research. Indeed, what counts as change in a relationship is itself dependent on the criteria specified and how much change is needed for change to be recognized.

Thus, it can be argued that changes in personal communities are entirely normal, even if the more significant personnel in the middle of the social convoy tend to journey together longer. Moreover change in personal life is becoming more common under the social and economic transformations of "post" or "late" modernity. Potentially these changes are having an impact on all the relationships in an individual's social convoy and not just those at the periphery. There can be no doubting, for example, that traditional notions of family are currently being undermined by the changing demography of marriage and childbirth. Trends in divorce were the first indicator of this, but other changes are just as important. The growth of cohabitation as a normal form of partnership, increasing numbers of single-parent households, higher levels of births outside marriage, the preponderance of stepfamilies, and the numbers of people living alone are all indicative of changing patterns of family and household commitment (Coleman & Ganong, 2004; Duncan & Edwards, 1997; Lewis, 2001; Scott, Treas, & Richards, 2004). Such change has an impact not only on those most obviously involved but also on others in their family groupings.

These changes in family and household formation and dissolution can be understood as part of a broader set of changes that are affecting the social organization of people's personal relationships more generally. They reflect a growing individualization within contemporary society and a reduction in the traditional constraints exercised over personal and familial behavior. Writers like Giddens (1992) and Beck (1992; Beck & Beck-Gernsheim, 1995) have argued that contemporary material and social circumstances give people more choice over how they wish to live. Changes in women's social and economic location, linked to their readier control of fertility, have been particularly important in fostering greater freedom and diversity and in challenging the normality of "traditional" family and sexual templates. In this regard, lifestyle choices have become far more open than they were. This does not reflect a complete freedom; social and economic constraints still operate, albeit differentially depending on people's circumstances. What it does mean, though, is that in comparison to previous times, more people are more actively making decisions over how their lifestyles develop.

These changes in the freedoms there are to make lifestyle choices are structural, reflecting the changing social and economic order of the contemporary world. So, too, their consequences for the patterning of personal relationships and personal communities are structural. This is an issue that Pescosolido and Rubin (2000) developed in their important paper examining the character of affiliations in contemporary society. Taking Simmel (1955) as their starting point, their argument was that different forms of commitment and solidarity are generated under contemporary social conditions than was the case for most of the 20th century.

In particular, they suggested that individuals are no longer

> enmeshed within interconnected circles but rather stand outside of them, and their connections to institutions are multiple and often temporary, not single and life-long. Individuals, over time, have connections to many workplaces, to many families, perhaps even to more than one religion.(Pescosolido & Rubin, 2000, pp. 62–63)

In other words, whereas in the past there was an expectation of relative permanency in key areas of life, and consequently in personal communities, this expectation is now being undermined by the structural circumstances under which people currently forge their relationships. Like Giddens (1992), these authors are pointing to the increasing contingency, insecurity, and flexibility of contemporary relationships, be it within the spheres of employment, locality, or partnership ties.

Pescosolido and Rubin (2000) argued that a "spoke" model of social network formation is emerging as the dominant form in late modernity. In this, the individual is linked to a range of "connected but distinct social circles with some circles only loosely bound" (p. 62). This argument resonates well with Giddens's (1992) claims about the increasing flexibility in lifestyle construction. When, as in the past, social life is embedded in more closely overlapping circles premised on relatively long-lasting institutional relationships, the possibilities of diversity and choice in the constructions of self are limited. As involvement in personal relationships becomes more contingent and flexible, so the possibilities for individuals to highlight different elements of self-identity in different contexts and at different times increases, as does the control they can exercise over the character of their personal communities.

These processes clearly raise important issues for personal relationship research, three of which are highlighted here. First, while individuals may now have greater freedom over their lifestyle development, usually such decisions are not made in isolation. Rather they are informed by the sets of relationships in which the individual is involved. Some lifestyle changes may result from dissatisfaction with current relationships and routines, but more commonly individuals draw on (some of) their personal relationships to help them resolve the issues and dilemmas they are facing. Indeed, as in Jerrome's (1984) and Harrison's (1998) research, some of these relationships may be central in facilitating people's acceptance of dissatisfying elements in their structural location through providing alternative understandings of the self.

Second, and linked to this, personal relationships, and especially those which are seen as chosen rather than given, can play a significant part in helping individuals adapt their identities to changed circumstances. As discussed earlier, friendships, in particular, can be central to the ways in which individuals adapt to such changes as divorce, unemployment, or widowhood. In these circumstances, embracing a new identity may involve shedding some now less congruent relationships and developing new ones or, occasionally, rekindling older, neglected ties (Allan, 1989; Gerstel, 1988). These new ties provide greater congruence with the new status and through their associated relational activities and conversational topics facilitate and underpin the transition from past to present identity.

Third, if it is becoming more common for personal communities to contain discrete, nonoverlapping network segments, as Pescosolido and Rubin (2000) suggested, then not only is it easier for individuals to prioritize those others who share a similar identity to themselves, but equally individuals are able to emphasize different elements of the self in different contexts. The less network overlap there is, the more possibility there is of limiting the "spillover" from one setting to another. Thus, presenting somewhat different portrayals of the self in these different settings becomes more manageable. The classic example of this is found in studies of gay and lesbian lifestyles. Not

infrequently, some people in an individual's personal community will know about his or her gay or lesbian sexuality, but others will not. This is possible partly as a result of the discretion of those who do know but largely because the network is segmented in ways that result in those who do and do not know rarely having reason to meet (Weeks, Heaphy, & Donovan, 1999; Weston, 1991). Given contemporary trends in network formation, the differential presentation of aspects of the self is likely to become more common and contribute to the processes of identity construction that Giddens (1991, 1992) discusses. (For a fuller examination of some of these issues, see Allan, 2001.)

Conclusion

This chapter has been concerned with the wider relational context of personal relationships. It has focused on the ways in which different scholars have approached the study of social networks and personal communities, highlighting in particular the differential emphases that can be given to the configurational properties of networks. The premise of the chapter, as with all personal relationships research concerned with social networks, is that the individual relationships in which people are involved are patterned to some degree by the other relationships in which they are involved. Although this is not pertinent to all inquiry within the field of personal relationship, it is of relevance for many areas of research. Relationships do not exist independently of the contexts in which they are enacted, and generally other relationships form part of this context. It is important for many issues within personal relationships research that relationships are not overly individualized or treated inappropriately as though they stand alone.

What this means in practice obviously varies depending on the focus of the research. Detailed information about the content of other relationships or the configurational structure of personal communities is not always warranted. In this chapter, the potential value for personal relationships research of Antonucci's approach to collecting data on social convoys has been discussed. It is an approach that in some regards can be recognized as mediating between the "configurational" perspective characteristic of much social network analysis and the "personal star" perspective that is more commonly adopted by personal relationships researchers. It has the advantage of facilitating data collection through being visually intuitive for respondents while also enabling questions of different complexity to be asked about the constituent relationships. Moreover it permits, although does not require, wider network questions to be posed about the relationships that exist between the individuals the central ego includes.

Antonucci's social convoy approach is also well suited for considering changes in people's relationships. This can be done at an individual, life course level, with changes in relationships and networks being monitored as people age or experience lifestyle shifts. However, it also important to consider the impact of structural social changes on the patterning of people's relationships. As discussed toward the end of the chapter, social and economic transformations influence the construction and ordering of personal relationships. Although most apparent in contemporary demographic shifts affecting family life, the changes occurring with late modernity appear to be altering the constitution of personal communities in important ways. These changes are not experienced uniformly, but overall they foster a greater degree of contingency, flexibility and choice in the construction of micro-social worlds than was common in earlier periods.

This has two important consequences for people's personal communities. First, there is reduced expectation of permanency in their constituent relationships. In interactive fashion, increased contingency and flexibility in social life facilitates the exercise of greater choice and control over the form and continuation of relationships. As a result, assumptions of permanence in personal relationships are more questionable than they once were. Second, subsets of relationships within personal communities are more likely to be developed in relative isolation from one another, as outlined in Pescosolido and Rubin's spoke model of social life. This has major implications for self-identity and lifestyle choice, implications that are liable to affect how individuals construct and use their different personal relationships. It follows, of course, that these shifts in the patterning of personal communities also have significant implications for personal relationships researchers. These emergent changes represent new challenges for understandings of relational commitment, just as recent trends in family demography have generated new questions about the character of contemporary family solidarity.

References

Aartsen, M., van Tilburg, T., Smits, C., & Knipscheer, K. (2004). A longitudinal study of the impact of physical and cognitive decline on the personal network in old age. *Journal of Social and Personal Relationships*, 21, 249–266.

Adams, R., & Allan, G. (1998). Conceptualising friendship. In R. Adams & G. Allan (Eds.), *Placing friendship in context* (pp. 1–17). Cambridge, England: Cambridge University Press.

Allan, G. (1989). *Friendship: Developing a sociological perspective*. Hemel Hempstead, England: Harvester Wheatsheaf.

Allan, G. (2001). Personal relationships in late modernity. *Personal Relationships*, 8, 325–339.

Antonucci, T. C. (1986). Hierarchical mapping technique. *Generations*, 10, 10–12.

Antonucci, T. C., & Akiyama, H. (1987). Social networks in adult life: A preliminary examination of the convoy model. *Journal of Gerontology*, 4, 519–527.

Antonucci, T. C., & Akiyama, H. (1995). Convoys of social relations: Family and friendship within a life span context. In R. Blieszner & V. Hilkevitch Bedford (Eds.), *Handbook of aging and the family* (pp. 355–371). Westport, CT: Greenward Press.

Antonucci, T. C., Akiyama, H., & Lansford, J. E. (1998). Negative effects of close social relations. *Family Relations*, 47, 379–384.

Antonucci, T., Lansford, J., Schaburg, L., Baltes, M., Takahashi, K., Smith, J., et al. (2001). Widowhood and illness: A comparison of social network characteristics in France, Germany, Japan and the United States. *Psychology and Aging*, 16, 655–665.

Barnes, J. (1954). Class and committees in a Norwegian island parish. *Human Relations*, 7, 39–58.

Barnes, J. (1972). Social networks. *Module in anthropology* (No. 26). Reading, MA: Addison-Wesley.

Beck, U. (1992). *Risk society: Towards a new modernity*. London: Sage.

Beck, U., & Beck-Gernsteim, E. (1995). *The normal chaos of love*. London: Sage.

Boissevain, J. (1974). *Friends of friends*. Oxford: Blackwell.

Bost, K., Cox, M., & Payne, C. (2002). Structural and supportive changes in couples' family and friendship networks across the transition to parenthood. *Journal of Marriage and the Family*, 64, 517–531.

Bott, E. (1957). *Family and social network*. London: Tavistock.

Broese van Groenou, M., & van Tilburg, T. (2003). Network size and support in old age: Differentials by socio-economic status in childhood and adulthood. *Ageing and Society*, 23, 625–645.

Broese van Groenou, M., & van Tilburg, T. (1997). Changes in the support networks of older adults in the Netherlands. *Journal of Cross-Cultural Gerontology*, 12, 23–44.

Bryant, C., & Conger, R. (1999). Marital success and domains of social support in long-term relationships: Does the influence of network members ever end? *Journal of Marriage and the Family*, 46, 551–562.

Burger, E., & Milardo, R. (1995). Marital interdependence and social networks. *Journal of Social and Personal Relationships*, 12, 403–415.

Burt, R. (1980). Models of network structure. *Annual Review of Sociology*, 6, 79–141.

Carpentier, N., & Ducharme, F. (2003). Caregiver network transformations: The need for an integrated perspective. *Ageing and Society*, 23, 507–525.

Coleman, M., & Ganong, L. (2004). *Handbook of contemporary families*. Thousand Oaks, CA: Sage.

Duck, S. (Ed.). (1993). *Social contexts of relationships: Understanding relationship processes* (Vol. 3). Newbury Park, CA: Sage.

Duncan, S., & Edwards, R. (Eds.). (1997). *Single mothers in an international context*. London: UCL Press.

Felmlee, D. (2001). No couple is an island: A social network perspective on dyadic stability. *Social Forces*, 79, 1259–1287.

Gerstel, N. (1988). Divorce, gender and social integration. *Gender and Society*, 2, 343–367.

Giddens, A. (1991). *Modernity and self-identity*. Cambridge, England: Polity Press.

Giddens, A. (1992). *The transformation of intimacy*. Cambridge, England: Polity Press.

Harrison, K. (1998). Rich friendships, affluent friends: Middle-class practices of friendship. In R. G. Adams & G. Allan (Eds.), *Placing friendship in context* (pp. 92–116). Cambridge, England: Cambridge University Press.

Holland, P., & Leinhardt, S. (1979). *Perspectives on social network research*. New York: Academic Press.

Jerrome, D. (1984). Good company: The sociological implications of friendship. *Sociological Review*, 32, 696–718.

Kahn, R., & Antonucci, T. (1980). Convoys over the life course: Attachment, roles and social support. In P. Baltes & O. Brim (Eds.), *Life span development and behavior* (Vol. 3, pp. 253–286). New York: Academic Press.

Kearns, J., & Leonard, K. (2004). Social networks, structural interdependence, and marital quality over the transition to marriage: A prospective analysis. *Journal of Family Psychology*, 18, 383–395.

Keating, N., Otfinowski, P., Wenger, C., Fast, J., & Derksen, L. (2003). Understanding the caring capacity of informal networks of frail seniors. *Ageing and Society*, 23, 115–127.

Knipscheer, K., de Jong Gierveld, J., van Tilburg, T., & Dykstra, P. (Eds.). (1995). *Living arrangements and social networks of older adults*. Amsterdam: VU University Press.

Larson, J., Wilson, S., & Beley, R. (1994). The impact of job insecurity on marital and family relationships. *Family Relations*, 43, 138–143.

Lewis, J. (2001). *The end of marriage? Individualism and intimate relations*. Cheltenham, England: Edward Elgar.

Litwin, H. (2000). Activity, social network and well-being: An empirical examination. *Canadian Journal on Aging*, 19, 343–362.

Milardo, R. (1992). Comparative methods for delineating social networks. *Journal of Social and Personal Relationships*, 9, 447–461.

Milardo, R. M., & Allan, G. A. (2000). Social networks and marital relationships. In R. Milardo & S. Duck (Eds.), *Families as relationships* (pp. 117–33). Chichester, England: Wiley.

Mitchell, J. C. (Ed.). (1969). *Social networks in urban situations*. Manchester, England: Manchester University Press.

Moreno, J. (1934). *Who shall survive?* New York: Beacon Press.

Morgan, D., Carder, P., & Neal, M. (1997). Are some relationships more useful than others? *Journal of Social and Personal Relationships*, 14, 745–759.

Morgan, D., & March, S. (1992), The impact of life events on networks of personal relationships: A comparison of widowhood and caring for a spouse with Alzheimer's disease. *Journal of Social and Personal Relationships*, 9, 563–584.

Morgan, D., Neal, M., & Carder, P. (1997). The stability of core and peripheral networks over time. *Social Networks*, 19, 9–25.

Morris, L., & Irwin, S. (1992). Unemployment and informal support: Dependency, exclusion or participation? *Work, Employment and Society*, 6, 185–207.

Nocon, A., & Pearson, M. (2000). The roles of friends and neighbours in providing support for older people. *Ageing and Society*, 20, 341–367.

Orbuch, T., Veroff, J., & Hunter, A. (1999). Black couples, White couples: The early years of marriage. In M. Hetherington (Ed.), *Coping with divorce, single-parenting, and remarriage* (pp. 23–46), Hillsdale, NJ.: Erlbaum.

Pahl, R., & Spencer, L. (2004). Capturing personal communities. In C. Phillipson, G. Allan, & D. Morgan (Eds.), *Social networks and social exclusion* (pp. 72–96). Aldershot, England: Ashgate.

Parks, M. (1997). Communication networks and relationship life cycles. In S. Duck (Ed.), *Handbook of personal relationships* (pp. 351–72). New York: Wiley.

Parks, M., & Eggert, L. (1991). The role of social context in the dynamics of personal relationships. In W. Jones & D. Perlman (Eds.), *Advances in personal relationships* (Vol. 1, pp. 1–34). London: Jessica Kingsley.

Parks, M., Stan, C., & Eggert, L. (1983). Romantic involvement and social network involvement. *Social Psychology Quarterly*, 46, 116–131.

Pescosolido, B., & Rubin, B. (2000). The web of group affiliations revisited: Social life, postmodernism, and sociology. *American Sociological Review*, 65, 52–76.

Phillipson, C., Bernard, M., Phillips, J., & Ogg, J. (2000). *Family and community life of older people*. London: Routledge.

Radcliffe-Brown, A. R. (1940). On social structure. *Journal of the Royal Anthropological Institute*, 70, 1–12.

Rands, M. (1988). Changes in social networks following marital separation and divorce. In R. Milardo (Ed.), *Families and social networks* (pp. 127–146). Newbury Park, CA: Sage.

Scott, J. (2000). *Social network analysis: A handbook*. London: Sage.

Scott, J. (Ed.). (2002). *Social networks: Critical concepts in sociology* (Vol. 1). London: Routledge.

Scott, J., Treas, J., & Richards, M. (2004). *The Blackwell companion to the sociology of families*. Oxford: Blackwell.

Simmel, G. (1955). *Conflict and the web of group affiliations*. New York: Free Press.

Simon, R., Eder, D., & Evans, C. (1992). The development of feeling norms underlying romantic love among adolescent females. *Social Psychology Quarterly*, 55, 29–46.

Sprecher, S., & Felmlee, D. (2000). Romantic partners' perceptions of social network attributes with the passage of time and relationship transitions. *Personal Relationships*, 7, 325–340.

Sprecher, S., Felmlee, D., Orbuch, T., & Willetts, M. (2002). Social networks and change in personal relationships. In A. L. Vangelisti, H. T. Reis, & M. A. Fitzpatrick (Eds.), *Stability and change in relationships* (pp. 257–284). Cambridge, England: Cambridge University Press.

Suitor, J. (1987). Friendship networks in transition: Married mothers return to school. *Journal of Social and Personal Relationships*, 4, 445–461.

Suitor, J., & Keeton, S. (1997). Once a friend always a friend? Effects of homophily on women's support networks across a decade. *Social Networks*, 19, 51–62.

Surra, C. (1988). The influence of the interactive network on developing relationships. In R. Milardo (Ed.), *Families and social networks* (pp. 48–82). Newbury Park, CA: Sage.

Terhell, E., Broese van Groenou, M., & Tilburg, T. (2004). Network dynamics in the long-term period after divorce. *Journal of Social and Personal Relationships*, 21, 719–738.

Uhlenberg, P., & de Jong Gierveld, J. (2004). Age-segregation in later life: An examination of personal networks. *Ageing and Society*, 24, 5–28.

van Tilburg, T., & Broese van Groenou, M. (2002). Network and health changes among older Dutch Adults. *Journal of Social Issues*, 58, 697–713.

Weeks, J., Heaphy, B., & Donovan, C. (1999). Partnership rites: Commitment and ritual in non-heterosexual relationships. In J. Seymour & P. Bagguley (Eds.), *Relating intimacies* (pp. 43–63). Basingstoke, England: Macmillian.

Wellman, B. (1979). The community question: The intimate networks of East Yorkers. *American Journal of Sociology*, 84, 1201–1231.

Wellman, B. (1982). Studying personal communities. In P. Marsden & N. Lin (Eds.), *Social networks and social structure* (pp. 61–80). Beverly Hills, CA: Sage.

Wellman, B. (1985). Domestic work, paid work and net work. In S. Duck & D. Perlman (Eds.), *Understanding personal relationships* (pp. 159–191). London: Sage.

Wellman, B. (1988). Structural analysis: From method and metaphor to theory and substance. In B. Wellman & S. D. Berkowitz (Eds.), *Social structures: A network analysis* (pp. 19–61). Cambridge, England: Cambridge University Press.

Wellman, B., Carrington, P., & Hall, A. (1988). Networks as personal communities. In B. Wellman & S. D. Berkowitz (Eds.), *Social structures: A network analysis* (pp. 130–184). Cambridge, England: Cambridge University Press.

Wellman, B., & Wellman, B. (1992). Domestic affairs and network relations. *Journal of Social and Personal Relationships*, 9, 385–409.

Wellman, B., Wong, Y. R., Tindall, D., & Nazer, N. (1997). A decade of network change: Turnover, persistence and stability in personal communities. *Social Networks*, 19, 27–50.

Wellman, B., & Wortley, S. (1990). Different strokes for different folks: Community ties and social support. *American Journal of Sociology*, 96, 558–588.

Wenger, C. (1995). A comparison of urban with rural support networks: Liverpool and North Wales. *Ageing and Society*, 15, 59–81.

Wenger, C., & Jerrome, D. (1999). Change and stability in confidant relationships: Findings from the Bangor Longitudinal Study of Ageing. *Journal of Ageing Studies*, 13, 269–294.

Weston, K. (1991). *Families we choose*. New York: Columbia University Press.

White, H., Boorman, A., & Breiger, R. (1976). Social structure from multiple networks. *American Journal of Sociology*, 81, 730–780.

CHAPTER 36

Relationships in Home and Community Environments: A Transactional and Dialectic Analysis

Barbara B. Brown
Carol M. Werner
Irwin Altman

A Transactional and Dialectic Analysis

Our thesis is that relationships are inseparable from their settings; they do not simply take place against a backdrop of homes and communities. Although many researchers increasingly recognize the social, cultural, and historical aspects of relationships, they often ignore the physical environment, resulting in fragmented and incomplete descriptions of relationship processes. To be more holistic, we use transactional and dialectic perspectives and examine relationship openness and closedness among family members and between family and community in selected past and present times in the United States. We conclude by calling for transactional and dialectical research on new forms of homes and communities that allow different options for relationship openness and closedness in the future.

Transactional and Dialectic Concepts and Research

Transactional Worldview

The transactional world view promotes a distinctive holistic understanding of relationships as aspects of a multifaceted phenomenon, which always includes the physical environment (for details, see Altman, Brown, Staples, & Werner, 1992; Brown, Altman, & Werner, 1992, Brown, Werner, & Altman, 1998). Defined as "the study of the changing relationships among psychological and environmental aspects of holistic unities" (Altman & Rogoff, 1987, p. 21), our transactional approach was partially derived from philosophical analyses of Dewey and Bentley (1949) and Pepper (1942). Transactionalism treats relationships as unfolding in complex social, physical, historical, cultural settings that can be examined at multiple levels of scale and that exhibit both stability and change. A marriage, for example, defines and is defined by a holistic unity of stable and changing (a) physical environments of homes and communities; (b) relationships between spouses as well as with family, neighbors, and friends; and (c) cultural and historical forces. Separating the marital relationship from this rich contextual unity necessarily yields only a partial understanding of the relationship.

The transactional approach reflects a worldview that is distinctive from interactional and organismic worldviews more commonly used in science (Altman & Rogoff, 1987). Interactional approaches seek "the prediction and control of behavior and psychological processes" (Altman & Rogoff, 1987, p. 15), using models that involve independently defined elements. Like Newtonian billiard balls, elements involved in human relationships can be separately defined, manipulated, and studied. For example, early research manipulated perceived similarity to test its effect on subsequent liking, with similarity seen as causing greater liking, independent of other contextual considerations. A transactional approach, in contrast, eschews separating the world into independent elements and sees the meaning of any aspect of a setting as intrinsically linked to and defined by other aspects.

Organismic approaches involve "the study of dynamic and holistic psychological systems in which person and environment components exhibit complex, reciprocal relationships and influences" (Altman & Rogoff, 1987, p. 19). Just as the systematic relationships among neutrons, electrons, and protons define the atom, organized relationships among parts comprise human relationships. Organismic relationships are more than a simple sum of their parts. In addition, organismic relationships are presumed to strive for a teleological end state, such as homeostasis, or balance, or some "final" idealized goal. Instead of change being an intrinsic feature of relational processes, organismic change is typically in the service of achieving or maintaining the desired end

state (cf. Canary & Dainton, 2003), with complex and multidirectional causal pathways describing the dynamic system. A transactional approach, in contrast, does not presume a universal ideal end state but assumes that many states or directions of change are viable and ongoing throughout the relationship.

A distinctive feature of transactionalism is its emphasis on holism, with an underlying philosophy of science that highlights Aristotle's "formal cause" over the more traditional focus on "efficient cause" (i.e., cause–effect) relationships. That is, the goal of a transactional approach is to elucidate the patterned and changing nature of holistic events involving people, psychological and temporal processes, physical features, and cultural–historical forces. One could focus on a woman in a family, for example, but her behavior is made more intelligible by including her relationships with others and her home and community environments and cultural–historical context. Metaphors for a transactional approach include thinking of phenomena as historical events or ecological niches wherein the very meaning and actions of organisms are inseparable from, and mutually defined by, their contexts.

A focus on interdependence of people in contexts is common to many well-known approaches in psychology. For example, Altman and Rogoff (1987) described how Lewinian concepts of "life spaces" and psychological "fields" involve confluences of people and psychological environments; how ethogenic approaches of Harre and Secord emphasize how people and settings are connected by rules and roles; how Piagetian ideas of assimilation and accommodation describe how individuals change in ways inseparable from their contexts; and how Barker and Wicker's behavior streams and settings demonstrate the inseparability of people and context. Some of these approaches also have nontransactional aspects as well, such as homeostatic aspects of behavior settings or Piaget's stagelike progression, which point to particular ideal end states consistent with an organismic approach. Nevertheless, in the history of psychology, several approaches included the transactional goal of describing patterns of changing relations among humans and their settings.

Relationship Dialectics

The transactional worldview's emphasis on change fits well with dialectic analyses of relationships (Altman, Vinsel, & Brown, 1981). Indeed, we suggested that dialectic processes provide an essential "motor" to relationships (Werner, Altman, Brown, & Ginat, 1993). There are many views on dialectics. Our view emphasizes opposition, unity, and change, wherein opposing forces within each dialectic ebb and flow, exhibiting changing relative strengths over time. Yet the two sides form a unified whole, each giving meaning to the other, such as when we appreciate and understand positive affect better if we also experience negative affect. Flourishing scholarship since the early 1990s has resulted in many similar and overlapping definitions for opposing forces in dialectic processes (for reviews, see Montgomery & Baxter, 1998).

We identified three overarching dialectics that underlie much personal relationship research (Brown, Werner, & Altman, 1998). Thus, there are varying degrees of *engagement* in a relationship, varying feelings or *affect* about a relationship, and an array of ways to *regulate* an ongoing relationship. *Engagement* is "the degree and level of integration, involvement, connection, openness, interdependence, or association that relationship partners have with one another, in opposition to their degree and level of being individuated, uninvolved, disconnected, closed, independent, or separate from one another" (Brown et al., 1998, p. 142). Thus, forces toward involvement in a relationship are countered by demands and desires for solitude or for other activities. For example, spouses may enjoy their time with each other but also enjoy time apart for personal interests, other relationships, or for a certain amount of "breathing room." This blend of engagement, or openness and closedness, ebbs and flows both short

and long term. In the short term, one may be more open at certain times of the day, such as dinner, and more closed during rushed morning preparations for work. Over longer time periods, relationships may exhibit different blends of openness and closedness, such as yearly cycles involving holiday events or long-term patterns involving historical eras.

The *affect* dialectic involves positive and negative emotions and actions in a relationship. Positive affective qualities include love, liking, satisfaction, enjoyment, and friendliness; negative affective counterparts include hate, dislike, dissatisfaction, aversion, and unfriendliness. Tension between positive and negative affect is illustrated by spousal expressions of respect and love that are tempered by or alternated with exasperation and hostility, depending on the circumstances. Again positive and negative affect may vary in strength over short or long time periods.

Regulation involves oppositional processes of making decisions or creating rules and norms to guide the relationship. Decision making can involve "dominating, controlling, and offering direction versus submitting, resisting, and accepting direction" (Altman et al., 1992, p. 144). Or relationship guidance can come from rules, roles, and patterns of action that vary from highly structured to more ad hoc or spontaneous. For example, marital partners might divide labor predictably for certain tasks but negotiate or share other responsibilities on a case-by-case basis. Research suggests that relationship partners often negotiate both specific and general regulatory rules within relationships (Petronio, 2002).

Dialectics operate simultaneously and continuously, with engagement, affect, and regulation all defining the character of relationships. We presume there is no ideal or balanced blend of openness–closedness, positive–negative affect, or regulated–unregulated forces in relationships. Instead, viable relationships come in many forms and change in their relative strength of the dialectic oppositional forces. Similarly, physical environments embody the dialectics in various ways. Technological and architectural features often provide physical barriers or supports to relationship engagement opportunities. Gifts and environmental decorations often express and support affective features of relationships. Rules for claiming territories or using space often provide relationship regulation. Technological, social, and environmental aspects of relationships and ways of defining ideal relationships vary across cultures and historical eras. Sometimes the environmental aspects of relationships are changeable, such as a couple choosing to visit a certain restaurant to help achieve a certain mood, and sometimes they are quite stable, such as when a relationship is constrained by technological possibilities of the era, such as early Colonial families gathering in one area for warmth.

Status of Dialectic–Transactional Research

Dialectic and transactional approaches have been applied to several geographic and temporal scales. At microscales, research has demonstrated how students use the environment and activities to open themselves up and close themselves off from others throughout the course of a day, by opening and closing doors (Vinsel, Brown, Altman, & Foss, 1980) or adopting momentary variations in personal spacing (Altman, 1975). Over more macro temporal scales, such as the course of a relationship (Altman et al., 1981) or the temporal shifts and rhythms of a year (Werner, Haggard, Altman, & Oxley, 1988), people alter their relationships, with certain settings, times, and events fostering closer bonds and others fostering more closedness and uninvolvement. Even over broad historical eras, certain dialectic blends may characterize entire societies at certain points in time, such as when the relationship to kin is as strong as the marriage bond for certain Eastern cultures, such as the Taiwanese, but relationships to kin are less strong than the marriage bond for Western cultures, such as the Welsh (Altman et al., 1992).

We have applied transactional approaches to a variety of relationship issues. Historical work on Shaker communities reveals how community designs facilitated religious goals concerning engagement, affect, and regulation in heterosexual relationships (Isaac & Altman, 1998). Because pair bonds were considered a threat to the community, the design and use of the environment separated men and women in dining, work, and residential settings. Spontaneous affective expressions were allowed in religious but not interpersonal settings, and all heterosexual interactions occurred in regulated and supervised settings. Research on contemporary polygynous families in the United States also demonstrates how families use and manage the environment to support multiple husband–wife pair bonds (Altman & Ginat, 1996). Many aspects of the environment, from family positions within the wedding ceremony to the creation of distinct homes for new wives, help preserve the dyadic relationship in the context of the larger family. Finally, an ethnographic analysis demonstrated how courtships, weddings, and home place-making in many societies involve transactional unities of people, settings, and time (Altman et al., 1992). Where events occurred, what objects were used, who participated and the significance of their roles all reflected relationship processes. For example, in societies where marital bonds are relatively autonomous, newlyweds established their own independent homes after the ceremony. In contrast, in other societies, newlyweds move into a parental home and become subordinate to the parents. Different degrees of the dialectics of autonomy and connection allowed in these societies were manifested in housing, social practices, and rituals.

Several types of relationship research could be viewed as transactional with respect to selected aspects of the social environment or temporal aspects of relationships. Relationship researchers who focus on context often emphasize how the social context is important to dyadic relationships. For example, researchers have examined how friends and families may criticize or support the development of a relationship (e.g., Klein & Milardo, 2000) leading dyads to be especially careful about revealing or concealing their dyadic relationships (e.g., Baxter & Widenmann, 1993). Other research on important events or turning points in relationships illustrates how traditions, rituals, and activities together reinforce a certain definition of a relationship (Baxter & Erbert, 1999; Baxter, Braithwaite, & Nicholson, 1999; Braithwaite & Baxter, 1995). Physical environments of relationships are also sometimes acknowledged. For example, a retrospective study of a 50-year marriage indicated how a couple both selected and coped with housing and other physical settings in ways that revealed and changed their management of couple dynamics (Levinger & Levinger, 2003). Similarly, a study of couple place-making reveals how close, well-adjusted couples with long-term commitments are more likely to have dyadically meaningful objects, as opposed to individually meaningful objects, on display in rooms where they receive visitors, suggesting that positively valued symbols of couplehood may both reflect and prompt positive relationship features (Lohmann, Arriaga, & Goodfriend, 2003). In sum, some relationship research has emphasized the unity and inseparability of relationships with their social and temporal contexts, although much less attention has been given to physical aspects of relationships.

The limited use of a transactional framework may be due to a perception that the transactional approach is "difficult to be realized in the common research praxis" (Bonnes & Bonaiuto, 2002). Consequently, we have set forth guidelines for implementing a transactional worldview in a research program (Werner, Brown, & Altman, 2002). Transactional analyses proceed by exploring how people, psychological processes, settings, and time are inseparable aspects of a whole. Because it can be too complex to think about all aspects of a holistic unity at once, researchers are encouraged to think about them in subsets. For example, relationship processes can be examined with respect to physical environments and social settings,

or social and temporal processes, and a transactional whole can be gradually built across studies. In addition, researchers are urged to use multiple perspectives and sources of information about events and to be open to new insights that arise during the research process. The search for formal causes involves seeking the patterns of relationship among aspects of a phenomenon, with or without a search for efficient cause as well. The transactional approach defines these conceptual aspects of phenomena and the approach can be employed strategically to provide enhanced understanding of relationships in context.

Some researchers have adopted a dialectic approach, especially to social aspects of relationships (see Montgomery & Baxter, 1998, for a review). Dialectic approaches highlight oppositional qualities inherent in relationships. For example, research on privacy regulation, and the importance of keeping distance and reserve, served as an antidote to research that was focused exclusively on the benefits of openness and self-disclosure (Altman et al., 1981). Similarly, although relationship partners may strive for positive affect, negative affect is both inevitable and potentially useful in relationships (Baxter & West, 2003). In addition, dialectic approaches highlight how relationships are not static but change over time due to changing internal and external circumstances.

The following section applies the engagement dialectic to relationships in three U.S. historical eras. Although the analysis could examine all three dialectics – engagement, affect, and regulation – for brevity, we focus on the engagement dialectic, which is richly portrayed in the historical literature.

Physical Environments and Relationship Engagement across Historical Eras

Homes and communities are the principal places of relationships and offer rich insights into a host of societal and personal values and processes concerning relationships. These settings reflect technological, economic, and cultural forces in society. As insiders to our own relationships, it is sometimes difficult to recognize the daily operation of these forces. Yet transactional analyses of mainstream society in three very different eras in U.S. history demonstrate how dialectic processes, especially the engagement dialectic, are reflected in environmental opportunities and constraints.

Colonial Era (Mid-1600s)

ENGAGEMENT WITHIN THE HOME

Cultural, physical, technological, and religious forces helped define many early New England Puritan colonial families as highly engaged with each other inside the home and with the community. By today's standards, colonial housing involved large numbers of household and community members, sharing very little space as they performed many tasks. Inside the home, husbands, wives, children, neighbors, and apprentices interacted in close proximity to produce food, clothing, and other essentials as well as to experience births, weddings, deaths, and other key relationship events (Ierley, 1999). Middle-class houses might have only two lower rooms, and an upstairs sleeping loft, with many activities centrally located around one fireplace in winter or one open door in summer (Flaherty, 1972; Mintz & Kellogg, 1988). At night, children and apprentices shared sleeping mats, and parents and young children slept in the same room. During the day, all rooms were multifunctional, with even sleeping rooms used for work, social functions, and equipment. Householders were physically accessible to one another even when in different rooms, as evidenced by accounts of what was seen through knotholes or heard through poorly insulated floors (Flaherty, 1972). Thus the physical and technological environments, economic hardships, and cultural values created multifaceted household relationships. All support the claim that disengagement from others was less frequent in Colonial homes than in today's homes (Mintz, 2003).

At the same time, and consistent with our dialectic view, the colonial family achieved some separateness or disengagement. Few newly married couples lived with their parents (Hareven, 1991), providing some separation from parents in adulthood. Travel was slow, so out-of-town trips often separated family members for extended periods. Children were often sent away as teens to help other households, to be apprentices, and to learn independence. Rural places of retreat were available, and husbands worked outside more than wives (Mintz & Kellogg, 1988). Perhaps the most important way that family members distanced themselves from one another was through reserve in family interactions (Amato, 1986; Flaherty, 1972). Marriages were important economic and work relationships, not primarily affective love relationships. Thus historical accounts portray much openness in home relationships, tempered by closeness in the form of psychological reserve and times of separation.

ENGAGEMENT BETWEEN HOME AND COMMUNITY

Home–community relationships were also highly engaged in ways that would seem intrusive today. The colonial house offered an architecture of accessibility, with thin walls failing to disguise arguments and open doors inviting in neighbors. Childbirth, a family event in a birthing room today, was then "virtually a public event, almost a ritual, attended by many female friends and neighbors" (Wall, 1990, p. 95). The community, courts, and churches exercised much power over the constitution of the home, removing children who were considered unruly or inserting immigrants, prisoners, single men or women, or poor children into families who could provide needed order, discipline, and support (Mintz & Kellogg, 1988; Wall, 1990). Even spousal disagreements were subject to community intervention. Early courts pressured troubled couples to stay together, partly for community order but also because the labor of one adult was often insufficient for household economic survival, so divorce was often not a viable solution (Wall, 1990). The courts could mandate conditions for courtships, order home runaway spouses, bar relationships that might threaten marital stability, direct neighbors to monitor for marital disputes, and impose a variety of public humiliations. For example, one feuding couple had to sit in the public stocks; subsequently, the husband was admonished to "live peaceably with her" and she was told to "be orderly and not to gad abroad" with two men who threatened the marriage (Wall, 1990, p. 74). Consistent with a dialectic perspective, openness between homes and communities was combined with closedness. For example, men could own property and community authorities were expected to respect household boundaries of those who obeyed community laws.

In summary, dialectics of engagement in the early Colonial era reflected substantial openness within families and between families and community, and this ethos was reflected and supported by the physical environment. Although places affording separateness and isolation existed and were used, the daily routine and environment often put individuals in close contact with one another. Homes were small, simple, crowded, multipurpose spaces. From a transactional perspective, we believe it is critical to view Colonial family relationships as defining and defined by the contextual realities of the era's housing, technology, and cultural values. These conditions contrast considerably with conditions more than 200 years later, in the late Victorian era.

Late Victorian Era (Late 1800s)

ENGAGEMENT WITHIN THE HOME

The cultural, physical, and technological forces of the Victorian era supported more separation, individuality, and closedness between people within the home and between home and community. Social historians propose that resources such as wealth and leisure time are keys to supporting the more individualized relationships found in the Victorian era (Amato, 1986; Prost & Vincent, 1991; May, 1991). The industrial revolution of the 1800s allowed greater

wealth and required urbanization and a division of labor. Consequently, homes grew large but needed to be close to employment, so they were multistory and built close together. Separate and specialized roles for people and places were valued culturally (Klineberg, 1999) and enacted by those who could afford it (Spain, 1992). The design and technology of Victorian homes also supported separate places, activities, and roles for urban-employed husbands and domestically engaged wives, children, and servants. Heat was often available in many rooms so that people were no longer drawn by necessity to a common room fireplace. For wealthier Victorian families in the United States and Britain, servants had access to family members, although servants were expected to refrain from intimate interactions with employers and had separate living quarters, generally below stairs or in the attic. The editor of the *Saturday Review*, an important outlet for articulating values for Victorian households, claimed the ideal Victorian house was "where the family wished to live even when they disliked each other" (Hareven, 1991, p. 253). A house book author noted, "The chief object of the home is to give each individual a chance for unfettered development. Every soul is a genius at times and feels the necessity of isolation" (Cromley, 1991, p. 182).

When wealth allowed the largest possible housing, the theme of separation was carried to an extreme. A Victorian house manual recommended 27 separate rooms and a floorplan that emphasized the theme of separation, including separate stairwells for servant men, servant women, gentlemen, bachelors, and young ladies (Spain, 1992). As in the Colonial era, even furnishings were distinct, with larger chairs with armrests provided for men and smaller chairs without armrests for women (Green, 1983).

Separation was not complete, however, and the Victorian era also offered more opportunity for togetherness. Victorian families began to decorate Christmas trees, celebrate birthdays, and take family vacations, sometimes to second homes (Mintz, 2003). Those who could afford them built porches, comfortable venues for family and neighborhood leisure and interaction (Ierley, 1999). Thus some Victorians had the time and space to cultivate family engagements but also to achieve separation as desired.

ENGAGEMENT BETWEEN HOME AND COMMUNITY

Despite dense urban settlements, middle- to upper-class Victorians were fairly closed off from the community, especially from community visitors to the home – in contrast to Colonial times. Physically, Victorian homes were buffered externally with lawns, verandahs, and porches (McDannell, 1986) and internally with specialized parlors and hallways (Marsh, 1989). These buffers were consistent with cultural practices that favored regulated engagements with neighbors, such as the etiquette of formalized visiting patterns, whereby visitors presented their cards and householders decided whether to allow the visit. However, Victorian houses were not completely private havens, because a large service industry delivered meat, ice, messages, or coal and retrieved rags and refuse (Hareven, 1991). Although men had wide-ranging engagements around the town, cities were often unpleasant because of early industrial pollution, harsh working conditions, competition, and general danger. For women, cultural rules restricted their engagements outside the home. An exception involved downtown department stores, settings that connected women with their community. In addition to the sales floor, stores offered showers, letter writing rooms, and services that supported respectable community engagements (Bowlby, 2002). Consequently, Victorian men and women were engaged in their communities in ways that reflected the new separation of men from women, both spatially and by role.

In summary, the physical supports for the dialectic of openness and closedness shifted over the eras, from Colonial architecture favoring interpersonal accessibility to Victorian architecture enabling separation. Inside the Victorian home, divided spaces supported a cultural emphasis on separate roles and activities, although close affective ties were the norm more than previously. Victorian families were also fairly disengaged from intimate relations with communities, reflected in both physical buffers and psychological barriers of etiquette and reserve. Nevertheless, community engagements were available through home-based and downtown shopping encounters and through social engagements that followed the rules of etiquette for the era.

Early Suburban Era (Post-1900)

ENGAGEMENT WITHIN THE HOME

A backlash against Victorian separateness and formality paved the way for a suburban era of greater family togetherness and informality. The editor of the *Ladies Home Journal*, an influential magazine, refused to print home plans that contained a formal parlor instead of a more informal living room (Roth, 1991). Architect Frank Lloyd Wright criticized Victorian style as "boxes beside or inside other boxes, called rooms" (Marsh, 1989). Olmstead, the architect of Central Park, resented garden walls as "high dead walls ... as of a series of private madhouses" (Fishman, 1987, p. 130). These remarks reflect a changing society that perceived existing physical forms as barriers to new ideas favoring more open and informal family relationships. Thus, the dialectic of limited engagement in the Victorian era shifted to one emphasizing greater relative openness versus closedness in the post-1900 period.

New homes developed in the wake of these criticisms supported openness and informality. Homes were smaller, which also reflected the high costs of new construction technologies (e.g., indoor plumbing) and home amenities such as modern kitchen appliances (Spain, 1992). Floor plans of this time revealed less space devoted to individualistic pursuits and more space for common family activities (Marsh, 1989). Although bedrooms still provided enclaves for individual withdrawal (Cromley, 1991), opportunities for openness were provided by kitchen, dining, living, and backyard spaces that flowed together. Some Victorian-era separateness remained, notably the fact that fathers left the home to go to work and mothers were in charge of domestic life. Just as for Victorians, personal retreats were less available to women, who still spent more time than men in the company of others at home (Ahrentzen, Levine, & Michelson, 1989). However, children were no longer banished to spatially segregated quarters but were expected to share family time in common living spaces. Dinner times, for example, became nightly occasions for many families to interact and reinforce the separate roles of homemaker and breadwinner (Dreyer & Dreyer, 1973). In general, therefore, the engagement dialectic of the suburban era involved greater social contacts among family members, supported by home design and cultural values.

The 1950s ushered in the "golden age of domestic ideology" (May, 1991), with multiple supports for the ideal suburban family of a wage-earning father, a housewife, and children. These supports included the large number of World War II veterans seeking a peaceful life, a national economy reorienting from war to consumer goods, technologies for mass housing production, and policies that favored home purchases for white suburban men (Hayden, 1984). Suburban developments proliferated across the century so that, even now, many contemporary housing alternatives are measured against the suburban model.

ENGAGEMENT BETWEEN HOME AND COMMUNITY

Suburban communities were generally designed to be fairly separate from public places and downtown areas. Furthermore, community members, such as boarders and servants, rarely came to live with suburban families, furthering the separation between home and community. Suburban isolation was further supported by physical distance and transportation constraints, with early suburban women and children at home during the day when the husband had exclusive use of the family car. Modern technologies that encourage people to stay inside (e.g., heating and cooling systems, televisions,

telephones), large lot sizes, and economic independence from neighbors supported substantial disengagement between neighbors. The separation of the suburbs from the city often meant limited opportunities for community engagements. Women and children generally had only local community engagements to tie them to the community – typically church, school, and neighborhood associations (Hayden, 1984).

Problems With the Suburban Ideal

Even at the peak of popularity, there were signs that the suburbs were not ideal, especially for women. The original suburban home was designed for and encouraged development of a particular family type: one wage earner and one full-time homemaker with children. Since the 1960s, feminists in scholarly and popular sources portrayed the suburban ideal as especially isolating to women (May, 1991). Indeed, compared with societies in which women gather and socialize as they engage in household chores (Brolin, 1976), secluded suburban U.S. homes mean that housework is often done in isolation from other adults.

As U.S. women entered the paid labor force in the 1980s (Calthorpe, 1993), problems of physical isolation were lessened, albeit with new challenges of time constraints. Women left the home for workplaces, then returned home for their "second shift" of labor at home, leaving little time for family interaction. Some speculate that later suburban home designs and household equipment may have evolved to allow more time and opportunity for family engagements. Thus, the popularity of more open kitchen and family rooms (Hasell & Peatross, 1990) and labor-saving devices (Forty, 1986) may reflect the desire to provide more opportunity for family interaction. However, labor-saving technologies and designs often escalate standards for housekeeping, creating more opportunities for housework instead of freeing more time for family interaction (Forty, 1986), suggesting a continuing struggle to balance commitments to work and family life.

The suburban model remains popular, still bolstered by social desirability, personal preference, public policy, financing, zoning, and other legal supports. However, the suburban form is not suitable for everyone and may create problems of engagement inside the home as well as between homes and community. Thus, single-earner households often cannot afford suburban homes or may prefer an urban residence with closer shopping and transportation amenities. Even dual-earner suburban households may neglect relationship building and maintenance in the face of competing pressures to spend time maintaining the home and yard or commuting to jobs needed to finance the suburban lifestyle. Aging individuals may find themselves physically limited in their ability to maintain large suburban homes and landscaping, as well as being isolated from family and friends and lacking access to distant shopping and cultural opportunities.

These concerns have resonated with social philosophers interested in how physical environments have reduced residents' connections with community life (Calthorpe, 1993). In a wide-ranging review, Putnam (2000) traced the erosion of community ties to factors such as the technological advance of television, the economic demand to have two adults work full time to pay for expensive houses, and the advent of suburban sprawl. Suburban sprawl is implicated in multiple ways. People are discouraged from developing neighborhood ties by the loss of neighborhood interaction sites such as front porches, neighborhood schools and parks, and by the addition of wide streets and increasing traffic (Appleyard & Lintell, 1972; Brown, Burton, & Sweaney, 1998). People are drawn inside by home entertainment and thermal comfort; they are isolated from their neighborhoods by long hours devoted to commutes, work, shopping, and entertainment (Brown et al., 1998). Putnam (2000) even estimated that every additional 10 minutes commuting is linked to a 10% reduction in one's community ties. According to one analysis, today's homes emphasize "isolation and profit-making," not "ideals

such as neighbourliness and integration" (Friedman & Krawitz, 2002, p. 186). For significant numbers of people in modern U.S. society, physical environments of homes and communities do not mesh with the social relationships people have and desire. Mismatches between physical environments and relationship goals are fueling new proposals to reconnect homes to communities.

Currently, a variety of social movements encourage greater openness between home and community. Proponents of sustainable communities, new urbanism, smart growth, walkable communities, and healthy communities are proposing and building more pedestrian friendly neighborhoods meant to encourage community interaction and minimize isolating activities, such as long solo car commutes. By designing neighborhoods near needed services, such as schools and stores, and providing safe, tree-shaded walkways connecting homes and destinations, these new designs are intended to increase neighborhood use and relationships between home and community. Pedestrian-friendly places also reduce the dominance of the car by providing rear alley-fed garages, narrow streets, and reduced traffic speeds. Although streets used to be appropriated by children as play areas, fear of increased traffic levels in the West (O'Brien, 2003) and worldwide (Chawla & Malone, 2003) has restricted more children to home and away from community settings. In some countries neighborhoods have redesigned streets to ban or slow cars to restore children's play and adult friendships to the street (Skjaeveland & Garling, 2002).

Many other designs have been suggested to connect households to their communities (Calthorpe, 1993; Jacobs, 1961; Newman, 1972). Jacobs (1961) described intricate "ballets" on city streets in which residents' regular daily routines would intertwine and overlap to create a social setting. "The individual dancers and ensembles all have distinctive parts which miraculously reinforce each other and compose an orderly whole" (Jacobs, 1961, p. 50). Physical designs that support such interactions include small and narrow streets, short blocks that support easy pedestrian access to many destinations, pleasant plazas and parks, houses close to the street and windows for observing passersby, and shops and other activities to invite people to slow down, look, and acknowledge one another (Calthorpe, 1993; Jacobs, 1961).

Some of these changes include fairly radical alterations to the suburban model. Suburbs have traditionally been designed to separate households by income or family type and to buffer housing from work or other community necessities. In contrast, these new neighborhoods provide a range of housing sizes and costs to attract old and young, families and singles, poor and wealthy. Similarly, suburbs have traditionally been designed to separate land uses, so combining work, shopping, and home sites in close proximity is a substantial deviation from the suburban norm. Consequently, these communities are often controversial and research is needed to see how they might alter relationships. Some research shows that residents of such neighborhoods are indeed receiving the anticipated benefits. They walk more in the neighborhood, use neighborhood facilities more, endorse diverse housing forms, and know more neighbors (Brown & Cropper, 2001).

Summary

In sum, the configuration of openness and closedness of relationships within households and between households and communities has changed over long historical eras. The transactional perspective demonstrates how openness and closedness were manifested and supported, as well as discouraged, by the physical environment and cultural context. These three eras illustrate the value of a holistic analysis; only by examining how the environmental and cultural contexts are integral to the very definition and meaning of relationships are the historical shifts comprehensible. We now turn to our final issue: areas of needed research, especially given the many complex social, cultural, and physical environmental changes that are emerging worldwide.

Implications for Relationship Research in the 21st Century

What research is needed with respect to the dialectic processes of engagement as they are reflected in cultural and physical environmental changes? Indeed, we believe that the current era contains forces that will push U.S. society away from the heretofore idealized suburban model in favor of homes and communities that are better suited to current lifestyles, including emerging or previously neglected relationship forms. Furthermore, the changing ethnic, cultural, and national composition of American society is likely to involve pressures for new home and community designs that are more compatible with culturally distinct lifestyles, different from the idealized nuclear family of the suburban era.

In addition to changing social patterns, greater emphasis on sustainable human societies is suggesting changes in home and home–community relationships. Myriad factors including lifestyle preferences, the high costs of providing and maintaining infrastructure for large suburban developments, costs of commuting such as travel time and transportation, as well as concerns for environmental impacts are increasing interest in more compact, higher density city forms that allow people to walk, bike, or use transit for commuting and shopping, thereby reducing the need for roads and automobiles (see Brown, Werner, & Kim, 2003, for a review). Indeed, designers are experimenting with home and community designs that better support these myriad household forms, and research is needed to inform these immediate housing ideas as well as long-term community development plans. Under these complex changing circumstances, how can relationship researchers inform design decisions inside the home as well as between the home and community?

Changing Engagements

We center our analysis of future research needs around the engagement dialectic and suggest that research is needed on preferences for and satisfactions with different forms or amounts of openness and closedness. Our historical review showed that both openness and closedness are important and valued features of home and community relationships, but that historical eras offered distinct blends of openness and closedness that emphasized one or the other side of the dialectic. Trends for the future suggest a similar situation; both openness and closedness are important, but some households may want more openness or more closedness than current physical forms provide. Other households may prefer house forms that allow for greater variability in openness and closedness rather than a preference for one side relative to the other. We propose future research questions for relationships within the home and for relationships between residents and their immediate community.

ENGAGEMENT INSIDE THE HOME

People need home environments that allow them to regulate engagement (openness and closedness) with family members and with visitors. Changes in household composition and activities suggest that new layouts and configurations will be needed to support a variety of engagement goals. Single individuals, child-free couples, empty-nesters, home workers, and members of different ethnic groups may require different kinds of engagement and disengagement opportunities, and research is needed to identify those needs and evaluate various design innovations for their appropriateness and effectiveness.

One of environmental psychology's most well-researched areas is crowding and how people cope with greater openness than is desired, such as can occur in higher than desired densities. Crowding inside the home is related to more dysfunctional relationships. One reason for these poor relationships is that crowded individuals sometimes try to cope by withdrawing from family interaction. Although withdrawal as a coping mechanism might be acceptable and effective in alleviating the stress of crowding in public areas, the same techniques may

erode important family relationships (Evans, Rhee, Forbes, Allen, & Lepore, 2000). Negative crowding effects occur even in countries expected to have high tolerance for residential density, such as India (see Werner, Brown, & Altman, 1997, for a review), suggesting a limit to cultural adaptation to crowding. Research is needed on the use of physical environmental and interpersonal mechanisms for managing interactions under high density (Vinsel et al., 1980). For example, houses that provide layouts with more physical buffers, such as hallways or separate rooms, are associated with lower effects of crowding despite limited space (Evans, Lepore, & Schroeder, 1996). The key is to provide opportunities for people to get together as well as to stay apart when solitude is desired.

The recent popularity of working from home suggests another area where research is needed to understand how such work creates challenges for relationships. For the first time since the Colonial era, many people are trying to work from home. Modern home workers want to avoid commute time, achieve more family time, and prevent interruptions of traditional work environments. These desires, in conjunction with emerging technologies and supportive employer policies, make home-based work options possible for some. Although motivated to achieve a good blend of work and home life, many home-based workers actually spend longer hours at work because the work is so accessible. Furthermore, without the trappings of an off-site job, family, friends, and neighbors may impose on home workers, increasing the time needed to perform tasks (Gurstein, 2001; Johnson, 2003). In contrast, home workers sometimes feel too isolated from coworkers and find few stimulating relationships or places in the neighborhood. Instead of being an easy alternative to an office job, working from home requires that "separation, togetherness, and privacy all...be renegotiated" (Johnson, 2003, p. 31). Neighborhood work centers with fully equipped but temporary-use cubicles may provide physical supports for home–work separation, as well as workplace camaraderie and connection to the community, but without the time-consuming commute (Johnson, 2003).

A major recent societal shift involves more one- or two-person households of singles, empty-nesters, elders, or child-free couples. Because smaller households might prefer greater openness in their homes, some designers have created nontraditional designs for couples and singles. One design provides visual connections between the bedroom and more public areas of the house (Riley, 1999). As another example, bachelor housing has traditionally been spartan or makeshift, underscoring the idea that singlehood is a deviant identity that should only be temporary. In current designs for bachelors, the interior has sumptuous furnishings, serving as physical validation of the legitimacy of singlehood (Riley, 1999). Both cases suggest that child-free households adopt greater physical openness, but research is needed to evaluate how these designs serve relationships for single men, single women, and small households of various ages.

Research might also evaluate urban and suburban housing forms with respect to the openness and closedness goals of children and adolescents. Today's smaller family sizes mean fewer siblings with whom children can interact. In addition, children are often now provided their own bedrooms that support solitary uses (Sebba & Churchman, 1986), which may be desired sometimes but feel isolating at other times. On the other hand, children in many cultures have limited ability to regulate access to themselves, especially from parents, who may enter children's rooms without notice and to regulate their friendships and activities. This may be particularly contentious during the teen years, when children begin to assert their rights to keep others out of their rooms and to choose their own engagement times, locations, and partners (Altman & Chemers, 1980). As another example, some children complain of feeling too open and exposed in postdivorce homes, particularly when noncustodial parents live in housing without separate bedrooms for visiting children (Anthony, 1997). Either this creates

unresolvable tensions, or children seek out places to be on their own, alone or with friends, in homes, neighborhoods, and town centers (Clark & Uzzell, 2002). Adult sensitivity, professional interventions and skills training as well as appropriate environmental supports may all be needed to help families work through these changing situations.

Physical insulation of homes from their surroundings also creates engagement regulation dilemmas for those in abusive relationships. Although crime prevention programs emphasize using locks and bars to fortify the house against outside criminal intrusion, many individuals face their greatest risk of violence from household members (Goldsack, 1999). Abused women sometimes endure abuse at home rather than acknowledge the abuse publicly. One informant noted her dilemma: "I couldn't stay home even though I wanted to hide, and I couldn't leave the house . . . I look like shit. Everyone would know" (Dieckmann, 2000, p. 280). One environmentally oriented solution is a temporary restraining order, that strengthens the physical wall around the house with a legal one, thereby closing it off from an alleged abuser (Merry, 2001). Research is needed on how best to blend the safety of community oversight with desires for isolated living quarters.

Research also is needed to evaluate longstanding cultural assumptions about the proper degrees of openness inside one's home. When multiple families or generations share homes today, neighbors may complain because they fear that sharing will erode neighborhood property values and reputations and create traffic and population pressures. Yet some cultural groups prefer living in large, extended families. Pader (2002) recounted how two new college roommates found their sleeping arrangements to be uncomfortable and strange. The Latina roommate had never slept alone in a bed and her Caucasian roommate had never shared a bedroom. Pader traced restrictions on room sharing to late Victorian housing reformers who claimed that crowded tenements fostered sexual promiscuity and immorality. Pader countered that generations of Puritans – as well as many contemporary immigrant groups – managed shared living quarters without experiencing social collapse. Research is needed to examine processes by which different cultural groups manage interactions and how home layout supports or undermines desired access.

In summary, some households desire relatively more closedness, some desire relatively more openness, and some experience difficulties with the blend of openness and closedness in their present homes. These issues highlight the need to conduct research on how to provide environments and education to support a more flexible array of relationship needs.

ENGAGEMENT BETWEEN HOME AND COMMUNITY

Engagement patterns inside the home are paralleled by similar issues between the household and members of the community. Demographic shifts have meant that houses simply have fewer inhabitants or residents who spend less time at home. Smaller families, child-free couples, elderly people staying in their large homes, and women working longer hours outside the home all can involve fewer hours of togetherness at home. Research is needed on community forms that provide opportunities for both seclusion and interaction. For example, many people have limited mobility, which restricts their access to social contacts as well as limits their ability to shop, visit the doctor, and engage in other routine maintenance activities. Many elderly individuals live alone in suburban houses and may eventually face limitations on their abilities to drive (Burkhardt & McGavock, 1999). Research may examine relocation choices or a variety of mobility strategies as ways for addressing their unmet desires for social contacts.

Increasing recognition of the isolation of people with disabilities and elders has led to a growing movement to design what are called "visitable" houses, with a no-step entryway, and a ground-floor bathroom and bedroom so that when residents need a more supportive environment for themselves or visitors, they can have an environment that supports dignity, interaction, as well as seclusion (Urban Design Associates, 2000). Although most elderly and people with disabilities prefer to stay in their own homes, there are times when community helpers visit, which creates opportunities for social contact and support but also problems of physical vulnerability and psychological discomfort. Relationships with home health care workers can invade residents' typical expectations that they are in control of sociability and intimacy in the home (Ellefsen, 2002). Elderly residents dislike visiting caregivers' distancing strategies – looking at a watch, keeping a coat on, or referring to a time schedule. At the same time, elders feel overly exposed and humiliated when they need help with private bathroom functions, especially when high staff turnover brings a series of strangers into the home. Research is needed to see how residents cope with new patterns of time alone and new patterns of community visits by those who may provide both intimacy and intrusion.

Research is also needed on problems and solutions associated with greater proximity between households in denser community designs. "Proximity problems," such as barking dogs, noisy children, and contested parking spaces may erode the desired separation between homes and communities (Merry, 1987). Indeed, increases in car traffic and noise constitute a growing annoyance. In both the United States (Appleyard & Lintell, 1972) and other countries (Turgut & Cahantimur, 2003), residents simply stopped using the front yards or sidewalks in the face of increasing traffic volume and noise. Merry (1987) believed that diverse values among proximal residents facilitate intrusions. Whereas loud music might be acceptable in college dorms, it might be resented in more age-integrated communities. Research is needed on how to alleviate these problems, such as by strengthening physical sound barriers, providing age-segregated housing, enforcing good neighbor laws, or creating neighborhood mediators.

Low-income multifamily housing has often been designed in a way that discourages satisfying engagements among neighbors – engagements that can create neighborhood surveillance and safety. Residents of high-rise apartments suffer from crime and fear of crime when they cannot control who has access to the grounds and what the intruders do. When many neighbors share a common entryway, it is difficult to get to know one's neighbors and understand who might be engaging in criminal behavior (Newman, 1972). Furthermore, high-rise buildings make parental regulation of outdoor play difficult, requiring either long-distance surveillance from upper-floor windows or dedication of time to in-person oversight. In recent innovations in public housing, safe and user-friendly designs provide seating, attractive play areas, differentiation of the project from the public street, and window orientations that encourage both friendship formation and surveillance (Newman, 1972). More recent research shows that when public housing projects provide pleasant tree cover in outdoor play areas, children both play more and are more engaged with parental overseers (Taylor, Wiley, Kuo, Sullivan, 1998) and adults know more of their neighbors (Kuo, Sullivan, Coley, & Brunson, 1998). Research can suggest additional ways of increasing positive neighboring engagements with holistic interventions that address individual skills, economic opportunities, social relations, and defensible design.

We close our discussion of home–community engagements by describing two community forms designed to provide less and more engagement opportunities than traditional suburbs: gated communities and cohousing communities. Gated communities cater to a desire for physical separation from the larger community (McKenzie, 1994). Residents believe that such communities offer good financial investments, safety from crime and physical decay, good places for children, and protection from diverse people or housing forms (Low, 2001; Wilson-Doenges, 2000). Their private community associations assert a degree of control over

housing that has not been evident since the Colonial era in the United States. For example, residents have been cited for violations ranging from giving a goodnight kiss in a car in the community driveway, to flying the U.S. flag, to marrying a 45-year-old when the minimum resident age is 48, to walking out their back door too much and wearing a pathway in the grass, to owning a dog just over the 30-pound limit (McKenzie, 1994). These restrictions are accepted in the face of fears of kidnappers, burglars, and robbers that many residents said drove them from former ungated communities (Low, 2001). Low questioned whether gates can provide full security, given that residents talk about the need to improve gate security or build higher walls; yet other gated community residents report a stronger sense of safety and community despite crime rates comparable to nongated communities in some areas (Wilson-Doenges, 2000) but lower in others (Donnelly & Kimble, 1997).

A community form explicitly designed to encourage engagements among neighbors is cohousing. Typical cohousing developments include small neighborhood clusters of 10 or more residences, with fairly small individual dwellings grouped around a jointly owned common house. Cohousing residents are very engaged, making community decisions together and sharing cooking tasks for community dinners. The community building also brings residents together by providing common laundry facilities, amenities such as hobby rooms, or perhaps guest rooms or specialized workspaces. Cohousing communities typically limit parking to an edge or other restricted area to encourage pedestrian use. Residents are motivated to create cohousing to achieve closer neighborhood ties, good social opportunities for children, and more sustainable lifestyles (Fromm, 2000). Consistent with the dialectic view of relationships, cohousing groups also value some closedness and seclusion, with many groups explicitly acknowledging privacy as a community value. The community house provides a spacious place for social interaction, so that homes can be fairly secluded, if desired. Community members can also eat alone at home or skip meetings to achieve desired solitude. Thus, consistent with our dialectic perspective, even in the most open form of home–community relationships, residents can still achieve closedness and disengagement from the community.

Summary and Discussion

Research on past, present, and emerging home and community settings demonstrates how relationships are integral to their physical, cultural–historical, and social settings. A dialectical and transactional perspective gives us the tools to understand these issues with new insights. Examination of home and community relationships in Colonial, Victorian, and suburban eras showed that physical environments reflected and supported culturally prescribed blends of openness and closedness. Colonial homes were relatively open inside and also open to the community, although rural location and interpersonal reserve also provided separation. Victorian homes became fairly closed and individualistic, but times of family togetherness were also valued. Suburban homes emphasized openness within the home while maintaining relative closedness to the community. We reviewed research suggesting that this suburban ideal is not necessarily ideal for some demographic and cultural groups. We also suggested that increasing concerns about sustainability and providing accessible communities are leading to growing interest in higher density communities. Given changes in contemporary life, we suggested areas of research needed to understand how physical environments of homes and communities can enable people to have control over their openness–closedness with others.

Relationship members sometimes actively use the physical environment to achieve their desired relationships, such as moving to cohousing communities to achieve greater openness. At other times, people adapt to environmental circumstances without realizing potential consequences for relationships; for example, few suburbanites anticipated the impact of longer commutes on family time and community involvement. Perhaps because people tend to take the environment for granted, members of society may not realize how many competing visions exist for the best physical forms of relationships. For example, many people believed that the 1900s suburban model was ideal for children, despite research we reviewed that outlines worries about traffic dangers and isolation potentials within the suburban house. Research is needed to understand the advantages and disadvantages of different suburban forms for different kinds of users and with respect to multiple psychological processes and outcomes.

Just as the United States is debating alternatives to traditional suburban housing, many societies around the world are experiencing disruptions in their traditional housing, and struggling with the imposition of Western housing forms. Population, urbanization, and modernization pressures are disrupting many traditional communities. New dams, highways, and other projects have resulted in massive displacements of people. Often, these changes have unanticipated consequences for home and community relationships (Werner et al., 1997). For example, relocation of people from traditional homes and communities to government-provided housing can disrupt traditional extended family relationships both inside and outside of the home (Gauvain, Altman, & Fahim, 1983). Among Egyptian Nubians, traditional homes were clustered together so that family members could visit one another. When relocated for dam construction, families were not given adjacent homes, and women became isolated because they were afraid to travel to relatives' homes. Similarly, traditional homes in enclosed compounds had provided considerable buffering from visual intrusion, but the new-style homes were more open, creating discomfort inside the home. Many residents modified or redesigned their homes in attempts to restore their traditional cultural practices. Another example occurred in Damascus, Syria, where Western housing violated visual seclusion norms for women who were used to the spatial buffers of internal courtyards, screened doors, and louvered windows (Al-Kodmany, 2000). In this case, women simply avoided traditional outdoor activities and casual surveillance of the neighborhood to attain a proper separation from the community. Similar problems occurred in Accra, Ghana, where urbanization pressures and new Western housing forms without protected courtyard spaces left women without traditional secluded places for their ceremonies. Women adjusted by moving their ceremonies out to the street, and men cooperated by avoiding being in or watching the area, sustaining the rituals by providing "privacy in public" (Pellow, 2001). Among foreign-student families in the United States, achieving desired openness and closedness inside apartments was easier than achieving satisfactory engagements in the neighborhood, highlighting how cultural dissimilarities play out in neighborhood relationship difficulties (Harris, Werner, Brown, & Ingebritsen, 1995). Given rapid development and population pressures around the globe, we anticipate that many people will struggle to cope with housing environments that fail to support traditional needs for openness and closedness. The use of transactional and dialectical models will enable us to address important universal challenges in relationship engagement, affect, and regulation under conditions of societal change.

Our theme has been that interpersonal relationships are inseparable from their physical contexts. Given the emerging diversity of relationships and cultural backgrounds on the contemporary scene, we predict the development of an increasing variety of housing and community forms to meet peoples' needs for openness and closedness within the home and between homes and communities. Scholars can play a proactive role in meeting these needs. Instead of simply reacting to personal and societal upheavals, relationship researchers, design professionals, and urban planners should collaborate so that their collective and integrated expertise can identify holistic supports among people, relationships, and places. Healthy relationships require supportive physical settings. Effective environmental and architectural designs of buildings and cities require an understanding of the relationships they are intended to support. By acknowledging the interdependence and inseparability of relationships and settings, scholars can design, research, and envision new and appropriate ways to serve the diverse array of interpersonal relationships emerging in the 21st century.

References

Ahrentzen, S., Levine, D. W., & Michelson, W. (1989). Space, time, and activity in the home: A gender analysis. *Journal of Environmental Psychology, 4*, 123–131.

Al-Kodmany, K. (2000). Women's visual privacy in traditional and modern neighborhoods in Damascus. *Journal of Architectural and Planning Research, 17*, 283–303.

Altman, I. (1975). *The environment and social behavior.* Monterey, CA: Brooks/Cole.

Altman, I., Brown, B. B., Staples, B. A., & Werner, C. W. (1992). A transactional approach to close relationships: Courtship, weddings and place-making. In B. Walsh, K. Craik, & R. Rice (Eds.), *Person-environment psychology* (pp. 193–241). Hillsdale, NJ: Erlbaum.

Altman, I., & Chemers, M. M. (1980). *Culture and environment.* Belmont, CA: Wadsworth.

Altman, I., & Ginat, J. (1996). *Polygamous families in contemporary society.* New York: Cambridge University Press.

Altman, I., & Rogoff, B. (1987). World views in psychology: Trait, interactional, organismic and transactional perspectives. In D. Stokols & I. Altman (Eds.), *Handbook of environmental psychology, Volume 1* (pp. 1–40). New York: Wiley.

Altman, I., Vinsel, A., & Brown, B. B. (1981). Dialectic conceptions in social psychology: An application to social penetration and privacy regulation. In L. Berkowitz (Ed.), *Advances in experimental social psychology* (Vol. 14, pp. 107–160). New York: Academic Press.

Amato, J. (1986). A world without intimacy: A portrait of a time before we were intimate individuals and lovers. *International Social Science Review, 61*, 155–168.

Anthony, K. (1997). Bitter homes and gardens: The meanings of home to families of divorce. *Journal of Architectural and Planning Research, 14*, 1–19.

Appleyard, D., & Lintell, M. (1972). The environmental quality of city streets: The residents' viewpoint. *Journal of the American Institute of Planners, 38*, 84–101.

Baxter, L. A., Braithwaite, D. O., & Nicholson, J. H. (1999). Turning points in the development of blended families. *Journal of Social and Personal Relationships, 16*, 291–313.

Baxter, L. A., & Erbert, L. A. (1999). Perceptions of dialectical contradictions in turning points of development in heterosexual relationships. *Journal of Social and Personal Relationships, 16*, 547–569.

Baxter, L. A., & West, L. (2003). Couple perceptions of their similarities and differences: A dialectic perspective. *Journal of Social and Personal Relationships, 12*, 177–198.

Baxter, L. A., & Widenmann, S. (1993). Revealing and not revealing the status of romantic relationships to social networks. *Journal of Social and Personal Relationships, 10*, 321–337.

Bonnes, M., & Bonaiuto, M. (2002). Environmental psychology: From spatial–physical environment to sustainable development. In R. B. Bechtel & A. Churchman (Eds.), *Handbook of environmental psychology* (pp. 28–54). New York: Wiley.

Bowlby, R. (2002). *Carried away: The invention of modern shopping.* New York: Columbia University Press.

Braithwaite, D. O., & Baxter, L. A. (1995). "I do" again: The relational dialectics of renewing marriage vows. *Journal of Social and Personal Relationships, 12*, 177–198.

Brolin, B. (1976). Two case studies in the application of the modern ideology. *The failure of modern architecture.* New York: Van Nostrand Reinhold.

Brown, B. B., Altman, I., & Werner, C. M. (1992). Close relationships in the physical and social world: Dialectic and transactional analyses. In S. Deetz (Ed.), *Communication Yearbook 15* (pp. 509–522). Newbury Park, CA: Sage.

Brown, B. B., Burton, J. R., & Sweaney, A. (1998). Neighbors, households, and front porches: New Urbanist community tool or mere nostalgia? *Environment and Behavior, 30*, 579–600.

Brown, B. B., & Cropper, V. (2001). New Urban and standard suburban subdivisions: Evaluating psychological and social goals. *Journal of the American Planning Association, 67*, 402–419.

Brown, B. B., Werner, C. M., & Altman, I. (1998). Choicepoints for dialecticians: A dialectical/transactional perspective on close relationships. In B. Montgomery & L. Baxter (Eds.), *Dialectical approaches to studying personal relationships* (137–154). Mahwah, NJ: Erlbaum.

Brown, B., Werner, C. M., & Kim, N. (2003). Personal and contextual supports to change to transit use: Evaluating a natural transit intervention. *Analyses of Social Issues and Public Policy, 3*, 139–160.

Burkhardt, J. E., & McGavock, A. T. (1999). Tomorrow's older drivers: Who? How many? What impacts? *Transportation Research Record, 1693*, 62–70.

Calthorpe, P. (1993). *The next American metropolis: Ecology, community, and the American dream.* Princeton, NJ: Princeton Architectural Press.

Canary, D. J., & Dainton, M. (Eds.). (2003). *Maintaining relationships through communication: Relational, contextual, and cultural variations.* Mahwah, NJ: Erlbaum.

Chawla, L., & Malone, K. (2003). Neighborhood quality in children's eyes. In P. Christensen & M. O'Brien (Eds.), *Children in the city: Home, neighbourhood and community* (pp. 118–141). New York: Routledge Falmer.

Clark, C., & Uzzell, D. L. (2002). The affordances of the home, neighbourhood, school and town centre for adolescents. *Journal of Environmental Psychology, 22*, 95–108.

Cromley, E. C. (1991). A history of American beds and bedrooms. In T. Carter & B. L. Herman (Eds.), *Perspectives in vernacular architecture, IV* (pp. 177–186). Columbia: University of Missouri Press.

Dewey, J., & Bentley, A. F. (1949). *Knowing and the known.* Boston: Beacon Press.

Dieckmann, L. E. (2000). Private secrets and public disclosures: The case of battered women. In S. Petronio (Ed.), *Balancing the secrets of private disclosures* (pp. 275–286). Mahwah, NJ: Erlbaum.

Donnelly, P. G., & Kimble, C. E. (1997). Community organizing, environmental change, and neighborhood crime. *Crime and Delinquency, 43*, 493–511.

Dreyer, C. A., & Dreyer, A. S. (1973). Family dinner time as a unique behavioral habitat. *Family Process, 12*, 291–301.

Prost, A., & Vincent, G. (1991). *A history of private life: Volume 5, Riddles and identities in modern times*. Cambridge, MA: Harvard University Press.

Ellefsen, B. (2002). Dependency as disadvantage – patients' experiences. *Scandanavian Journal of Caring Sciences, 16*, 157–164.

Evans, G. W., Lepore, S. J., & Schroeder, A. (1996). The role of interior design elements in human responses to crowding. *Journal of Personality and Social Psychology, 70*, 41–46.

Evans, G., Rhee, E., Forbes, C., Allen, K. M., & Lepore, S. J. (2000). The meaning and efficacy of social withdrawal as a strategy for coping with chronic residential crowding. *Journal of Environmental Psychology, 20*, 335–342.

Fishman, R. (1987). *Bourgeois utopias: The rise and fall of suburbia*. New York: Basic Books.

Flaherty, D. H. (1972). *Privacy in Colonial New England*. Charlottesville: University of Virginia Press.

Forty, A. (1986). *Objects of desire*. New York: Pantheon.

Friedman, A., & Krawitz, D. (2002). *Peeking through the keyhole: The evolution of North American homes*. Montreal: McGill–Queens University Press.

Fromm, D. (2000). American cohousing: The first five years. *Journal of Architectural and Planning Research, 17*, 94–109.

Gauvain, M., Altman, I., & Fahim, H. (1983). Homes and social change: A cross cultural analysis. In N. R. Feimer & S. Geller (Eds.), *Environmental psychology: Directions and perspectives* (pp. 180–218). New York: Praeger.

Goldsack, L. (1999). A haven in a heartless world? Women and domestic violence. In T. Chapman & J. Hockey (Eds.), *Ideal homes? Social change and domestic life* (pp. 121–132). London: Routledge.

Green, H. (1983). *The light of the Victorian home: An intimate view of the lives of women in Victorian America*. New York: Pantheon.

Gurstein, P. (2001). *Wired to the world, chained to the home*. Vancouver: University of British Columbia Press.

Hareven, T. K. (1991). The home and the family in historical perspective. *Social Research, 58*, 253–285.

Harris, P. B., Werner, C. M., Brown, B. B., & Ingebritsen, D. (1995). Relocation and privacy regulation: A cross-cultural analysis. *Journal of Environmental Psychology, 15*, 311–320.

Hasell, M. J., & Peatross, F. D. (1990). Exploring connections between women's changing roles and house forms. *Environment and Behavior, 22*, 3–26.

Hayden, D. (1984). *Redesigning the American dream: The future of housing, work, and family life*. New York: Norton.

Isaac, J., & Altman, I. (1998). Interpersonal processes in nineteenth century utopian communities: Shakers and Oneida perfectionists. *Utopian Studies, 9*, 26–49.

Ierley, M. (1999). *Open house: A guided tour of the American home, 1637–present*. New York: Henry Holt.

Jacobs, J. (1961). *The death and life of great American cities*. New York: Vintage.

Johnson, L. C. (2003). *The co-workplace: Teleworking in the neighbourhood*. Vancouver: University of British Columbia Press.

Klein, R. C. A., & Milardo, R. M. (2000). The social context of couple conflict: Support and criticism from informal third parties. *Journal of Social and Personal Relationships, 17*, 618–637.

Klineberg, S. J. (1999). Gendered space: Housing, privacy and domesticity in the nineteenth-century United States. In I. Bryden & J. Floyd (Eds.), *Domesticating space: Reading the nineteenth-century interior* (142–161). Manchester, England: Manchester University Press.

Kuo, F. E., Sullivan, W. C., Coley, R. L., & Brunson, L. (1998). Fertile ground for community: Inner-city neighborhood common spaces. *American Journal of Community Psychology, 26*, 823–851.

Lohmann, A., Arriaga, X. B., & Goodfriend, W. (2003). Couple relationships and placemaking: Do objects in a couple's home reflect couplehood? *Personal Relationships, 10*, 437–449.

Levinger, G., & Levinger, A. C. (2003). Winds of time and place: How context has affected a 50-year marriage. *Personal Relationships, 10*, 285–306.

Low, S. (2001). The edge and the center: Gated communities and the discourse of fear. *American Anthropologist, 103*, 45–58.

Marsh, M. (1989). From separation to togetherness: The social construction of domestic space in American suburbs, 1840–1915. *Journal of American History, 76*, 506–527.

May, E. T. (1991). Myths and realities of the American family. In P. Aries & G. Duby (Eds.), *A history of private life: V: Riddles of identity in modern times* (pp. 539–592). Cambridge, MA: Harvard University Press.

McDannell, C. (1986). *The Christian home in Victorian America, 1840–1900.* Bloomington: Indiana University Press.

McKenzie, E. (1994). *Privatopia: Homeowner associations and the rise of residential private government.* New Haven, CT: Yale University Press.

Merry, S. E. (1987). Crowding, conflict, and neighborhood regulation. In I. Altman & A. Wandersman (Eds.), *Human behavior and environment, Vol. 9: Neighborhood and community environments* (pp. 35–68). New York: Plenum Press.

Merry, S. E. (2001). Spatial governmentality and the new urban order: Controlling gender violence through law. *American Anthropologist, 103*, 16–29.

Mintz, S. (2003). Digital history. Retrieved July 22, 2003, from http://www.digitalhistory.uh.edu

Mintz, S., & Kellogg, S. (1988). *Domestic revolutions: A social history of American family life.* New York: Free Press.

Montgomery, B. M., & Baxter, L. (Eds.). (1998). *Dialectical approaches to studying personal relationships.* Mahwah, NJ: Erlbaum.

Newman, O. (1972). *Defensible space: Crime prevention through urban design.* New York: Macmillan.

O'Brien, M. (2003). Regenerating children's neighborhoods: What do children want? In P. Christensen & M. O'Brien (Eds.), *Children in the city: Home, neighbourhood and community* (pp. 142–161). New York: Routledge Falmer.

Pader, E. (2002). Housing occupancy standards: Inscribing ethnicity and family relations on the land. *Journal of Architectural and Planning Research, 19*, 300–318.

Pellow, D. (2001). Cultural differences and urban spatial forms: Elements of boundedness in an Accra community. *American Anthropologist, 103*, 59–75.

Pepper, S. C. (1942). *World hypotheses: A study in evidence.* Berkeley: University of California Press.

Petronio, S. (2002). *Boundaries of privacy: Dialectics of disclosure.* Albany: State University of New York Press.

Putnam, R. D. (2000). *Bowling alone: The collapse and revival of American community.* New York: Simon & Schuster.

Riley, T. (1999). *The un-private house.* New York: Museum of Modern Art.

Roth, L. M. (1991). Getting the houses to the people: Edward Bok, the *Ladies' Home Journal*, and the ideal house. In T. Carter & B. L. Herman (Eds.), *Perspectives in vernacular architecture, IV* (pp. 187–196). Columbia: University of Missouri Press.

Sebba, R., & Churchman, A. (1986). The uniqueness of the home. *Architecture and Behavior, 3*, 7–24.

Skjaeveland, O., & Garling, T. (2002). Spatial-physical neighborhood attributes affecting social interactions among neighbors. In J. I. Aragones, G. Francescato, & T. Garling (Eds.), *Residential environments: Choice, satisfaction, and behavior* (183–203). Westport, CT: Bergin & Garvey.

Spain, D. (1992). *Gendered spaces.* Chapel Hill: University of North Carolina Press.

Taylor, A. F., Wiley, A., Kuo, F. E., & Sullivan, W. C. (1998). Growing up in the inner city: Green spaces as places to grow. *Environment and Behavior, 30*, 3–27.

Turgut, H., & Cahantimur, A. I. (2003). Tradition, change, and continuity: A dialectical analysis of social and spatial patterns in the home environment. In G. Moser, E. Pol, Y. Bernard, M. Bonnes, J. A. Corraliza, & M. V. Guiliani (Eds.), *People, places, and sustainability* (pp. 131–145). Seattle, WA: Hogrefe & Huber.

Urban Design Associates. (2000). *Strategies for providing accessibility and visitability for HOPE VI and mixed finance homeownership.* Washington, DC: U.S. Department of Housing and Urban Development.

Vinsel, A., Brown, B. B., Altman, I., & Foss, C. (1980). Privacy regulation, territorial displays, and effectiveness of individual functioning. *Journal of Personality and Social Psychology, 39*, 1104–1115.

Wall, H. M. (1990). *Fierce communion: Family and community in early America*. Cambridge, MA: Harvard University Press.

Werner, C. M., Altman, I., Brown, B. B., & Ginat, J. (1993). Celebrations in personal relationships: A transactional/dialectic perspective. In S. Duck (Ed.), *Social context and relationships, understanding relationship processes series* (Vol. 3, pp. 109–138). Newbury Park, CA: Sage.

Werner, C. M., Brown, B. B., & Altman, I. (1997). The physical environment and cross-cultural psychology. In J. W. Berry, M. H. Segall, & C. Kagitcibasi (Eds.), *Handbook of cross-cultural psychology* (2nd ed., Vol. 3, pp. 255–290). Boston: Allyn & Bacon.

Werner, C. M., Brown, B. B., & Altman, I. (2002). Transactionally oriented research: Examples and strategies. In R. B. Bechtel & A. Churchman (Eds.), *Handbook of environmental psychology* (pp. 203–221). New York: Wiley.

Werner, C. M., Haggard, L. M., Altman, I., & Oxley, D. (1988). Temporal qualities of rituals and celebrations: A comparison of Christmas Street and Zuni Shalako. In J. E. McGrath (Ed.), *The social psychology of time: New perspectives* (pp. 203–232). Beverly Hills, CA: Sage.

Wilson-Doenges, G. (2000). An exploration of sense of community and fear of crime in gated communities. *Environment and Behavior, 32*, 597–611.

CHAPTER 37

Relationships, Culture, and Social Change

Robin Goodwin
Urmila Pillay

The study of personal relationships (PRs) is an increasingly "mainstream" topic for social psychologists. Major international journals, such as the American Psychological Association's *Journal of Personality and Social Psychology*, regularly include papers on close relationships, and a growing number of texts and handbooks (such as the present volume) attest to the field's growing popularity among instructors, students, and researchers. Yet studies that consider relationships across culture are rare. In this chapter, we consider some key reasons why relationships should be considered in cross-cultural context and some of central issues around the definition of culture. We then go on to discuss cultural variations in the formation and maintenance of close relationships, family relations, and the broader social and supportive network (including that offered by friends and neighbors). We end with a consideration of the manner in which many long-assumed cultural differences in relationships are challenged by rapid social transitions in many parts of the world. Some dimensions of this change are then discussed in an attempt to

provide a more comprehensive understanding of relationships and culture.

Culture as the "Forgotten" Topic in Personal Relationships

A casual glance at the papers published in the two major specialist PR journals show a notable lack of cross-cultural research into personal relationships. For this chapter, we conducted a brief review of the 2001 and 2002 editions of the *Journal of Social and Personal Relationships* and *Personal Relationships*. Of a total of 135 articles published in these journals during these years, only two could be said to consider explicitly the role of culture in relationships and involved more than one cultural group (Goodwin, Cook, & Yung, 2002; Hetsroni, 2002), and a further two papers, both on attachment, compared relationship phenomena in one country with those found in other cultures (Onishi & Gjerde, 2002, in Japan; Alonso-Arbiol, Shaver, & Yárnoz, 2002, in the Basque country). Two further studies examined interethnic variations among different ethnic groups in the United States (Way, Cowal, Gingold, Pahl, & Bissessar, 2001) and Canada (Dayan, Doyle, & Markiewicz, 2001). Other studies that continued well-established North American research but were conducted outside of this continent commented little on the cultural setting of their studies. Instead, there was an assumption that any differences observed to previous findings were unrelated to the different cultural settings in which this work was conducted.

Why does this matter? Recently, several authors have outlined the advantages of taking a cross-cultural approach to the study of relationships (Goodwin, 1999; Hatfield & Rapson, 1996; Kagitcibasi, 1996). There are several theoretical reasons for studying relationships across cultures. First, there may be variation in the *relative magnitude* of different relationship phenomena. For example, in a cross-cultural comparison involving students from the United States, Turkey, and India, Medora, Larson, Hortacsu, and Dave (2002) found U.S. students to have the highest levels of romanticism. In an eight-country comparison, Neto et al. (2000) found Brazilians to be relatively high on pragmatic love styles, whereas the Angolans and Mozambicans were comparatively high on ludus (game-playing, noncommittal love). Second, culture can have a moderating impact on the association between individual-level factors (such as personality) and various relationship phenomena. Using data from the World Values Survey from 42 nations and almost 60,000 participants, Diener, Gohm, Suh, and Oishi (2000) found the relationship between marital status and subjective well-being to be moderated by culture, with being married having a stronger association with life satisfaction in collectively orientated as opposed to individually orientated cultures. The moderating influence of culture on psychological well-being may well be indicative of the differential role played by personality and other "internal" factors across cultures. As a result, loneliness might be a better predictor of life satisfaction in individualist

nations, where ecological factors and economic developments have freed up individuals to concentrate on the more emotional, less material, facets of their existence (Inglehart, 1997; see also de Jong Gierveld, van Tilburg, & Dykstra, this volume). Indeed, work in (relatively collectivist) Japan and the (more individualist) Australia demonstrates a stronger link between loneliness and life satisfaction in the latter nation (Schumaker, Shea, Monfries, & Groth, 1993). Finally, even when there are strong universal relational phenomena consistent across cultures, the ways in which these *influence actual behaviors* may differ. As we note later, individuals may feel passionately for each other in some cultures, but their passion may have relatively little impact on who they end up with as partners. Instead, pragmatic considerations (family pressures, but also basic economic realities) may have a far more significant role in partner choice.

Understanding the role of culture on personal relationship can also have important practical advantages. We can learn from cultures where they do it "better": for example, from those societies where relationship violence or child abuse are relatively unknown (Levinson, 1989). We can often disentangle the intertwined nature of variables in a cross-cultural context, unpacking, for example, how age and length of schooling separately influence human development in non-Western cultures where the two are not so related (Kagitcibasi, 1996). Increasing intercultural contact has a wide variety of impacts on interpersonal networks that could form several chapters in their own (see Berry, 1997, for an overview of the outcomes of acculturation strategies amongst migrant populations). An understanding of the dynamics of such contact means that we need not only to comprehend the niceties of intercultural contact (often described in rather stereotypical form in management training books) but must understand how such interactional expectations vary in accordance with the nature of the interactants (level of education, status, international experience, and expectations) and are themselves subject to regular change.

Finally, cross-cultural work also often draws our attention to the impact of sociohistorical forces on relationship behavior in a manner largely ignored by mainstream PR researchers, allowing us to understand relationships beyond the usual confines of the psychological laboratory. For example, in our own work in Eastern Europe (Goodwin, Nizharadze, Luu, Kosa, & Emelyanova, 2001), we found the association between stressful working conditions and social networks was complex in different cultures and that particular cultural traditions acted to ameliorate the effects of a stressful and busy lifestyle by allowing those working the longest hours to also be the most able to participate in important (and often expensive) exchanges of gifts and favors. Indeed, macro and ecological factors such as differences in financial resources and educational opportunities are likely to be important factors in support provision, with such factors influencing both the ability to provide support and the location, size, and homogeneity of the social network.

Defining and Distinguishing Cultures

Defining and categorizing culture is not a simple task. Culture is not something we can reach out and touch, but something that must inferred from the behavior of others (Rohner, 1984). As a result, most PR researchers – even those conducting explicitly cross-cultural investigations– have avoided the question of defining "culture," choosing instead to use country names as a proxy. Such a solution does, however, pose clear problems when there is considerable diversity within any one country (or indeed, sample).

Most formal definitions of culture suggest that shared and learned meanings are important when identifying a culture or cultural group (Rohner, 1984), although cultural products (such as buildings and other artifacts) may also be significant (Cole, 1990). Key from a PR perspective is the notion that culture is transmittable over time but modified from generation to generation (Rohner,

1984). Such transmission is most likely to occur within the framework of differing parenting and family patterns. In this chapter, we use the definition of culture provided by Fiske (2002, p. 85): culture is "a socially transmitted or socially constructed constellation consisting of such things as practices, competencies, ideas, schemas, symbols, values, norms, institution, goals, constitutive rules, artifacts and modification of the physical environment." Such a definition subsumes the values, norms and artifacts that influence an individual as well as his or her interaction pattern. This is particularly salient when one deals with personal relationships, as interaction with one another forms the basis of building any relationship, but these interactions take place within often highly significant physical settings (see Brown, Altman, & Werner, this volume).

Understanding the cultural makeup of any society also involves recognizing ethnic variations within that society and the possible importance of such diversity for relationship processes (Saroja, 1999). Most definitions of ethnicity recognize the close relationship between culture and ethnicity. For example, Wilkinson (1987) described an ethnic group as "a group of people who are of the same nationality or ancestry and who enact a shared culture and lifestyles" (p. 185). Although individuals may identify themselves to varying extents with their ethnic groups, others will often react to an individual in terms of his or her perceived group membership, even if that individual does not personally feel that they "belong" to a particular ethnic group (Berry, 1997).

In the last 2 decades a number of major international studies have sought to differentiate cultures empirically on the basis of their scores on key values. The most influential of these has been the dimensions that arose from Hofstede's (1980) seminal study of IBM employees of 50 nations and more than one hundred thousand respondents. In this study, Hofstede (1980) concluded that cultures vary along four dimensions: power distance (deference to authority), masculinity–femininity (relative emphasis on achievement or interpersonal harmony), uncertainty avoidance (stability and "planning ahead") and individualism–collectivism (which concerns the relationship between the individual and the group). Individualism–collectivism has been the most widely researched of these dimensions and is the focus of much of the review in the remainder of this chapter. Individualist cultures are those in which "individuals are loosely connected, and everyone looks after their own interests or those of their immediate family" (Hofstede, 1991, p. 2). Individualist cultures emphasize personal goals that might or might not overlap with those of their in-groups, but in which there is a conflict, they put their personal goals first (Singelis, Triandis, Bhawuk, & Gelfand, 1995). Collectivist cultures are ones in which "people from birth onwards are integrated into strong, cohesive in-groups, which throughout people's lifetime continue to protect them in exchange for unquestioning loyalty" (Hofstede, 1991, p. 2). In collectivist societies, the group is all important, and there is a need for group solidarity and shared activity. Western European nations, the United States, and Canada are high on individualism, whereas Asian, Latin American and African nations – and many U.S. minority groups from such regions – are more collectivist (Singelis et al., 1995). Although Hofstede (1980) provided dimension scores for each of these four dimensions, the dimensions are frequently (if controversially) treated as *categories* by cross-cultural researchers, who tend to classify culture "X" as an "individualist" or "collectivist" society.

Forming and Maintaining Close Relationships across Cultures

Most research into PR assumes that close relationships partners are chosen rather in the manner of an individual shopping in a supermarket, with individuals free to choose from a wide variety of products, in a multiplicity of shapes and sizes, from a range of different origins. Thus, although certain material constraints may operate to restrict the availability of those top-of-the-range partners (available only to the richest or most glamorous) and while other ecological restraints may serve to limit the availability of an ideal product (size of supermarket, range of goods, competition for particular items), the image is still of a large and free "open" field of partners from which a potential individual can choose.

In reality, this image is unlikely to be accurate even in the most individualistic of societies. Personal reputation, availability of social networks, and even opportunities to travel and shop around are basic limiters of choice in most cultures. However, in some cultures there is little opportunity to form any kind of romantic relationship outside of the most tightly restricted range. Indeed, we can plot a continuum ranging from those cultures in which partner choice is rarely restricted (usually those cultures where mate selection studies are conducted) to those cultures where partner choice might be prescribed as early as birth (Rosenblatt & Anderson, 1981).

Across the world, the majority of marriages are by arrangement, usually with the aid of matchmakers or relatives (Ingoldsby, 1995). Marriage in such cultures is not regarded as a union of two individuals but of two families, with the families likely to be similar in terms of values, customs, and norms. Saroja (1999), in her study on urban youth in India, showed arranged marriage to be preferred even in the most urbanized of areas, relieving young people from the personal responsibility of finding their own partner. Arranged relationships can be seen as invaluable in cementing family liaisons, helping build new economic ties, and maintaining the influence of the extended network on the new couple. Because such arrangements are of such significance to the wider family, opportunities for Western-style dating and partner choice outside of those approved as eligible is likely to be highly restricted (Hanassab & Tidwell, 1989). Different models of partner choice can be seen among different ethnic groups within one culture; in Britain, for example, partner choice among the White community is usually left to the individuals, although there may be some restrictions evident among those who belong to more religious communities. Among British Asians, however, marriages are frequently arranged by parents and go-betweens, with partner selection based primarily on caste, religious and social class lines. Arranged marriage is particularly prevalent among Britain's Muslim populations (primarily from Pakistan and Bangladesh; Beishon, Modood, & Virdee, 1998).

Where a relatively wide mate choice is available, preferences for a partner may follow broader cultural values. In more individualistic societies, for example, preference may be for partners possessing the more "individual" attributes such as kindness and understanding (Goodwin & Tang, 1991; Hatfield & Sprecher, 1995). In more sex-role orientated, "masculine" cultures such as Japan, health, wealth, and understanding are likely to be sought in husbands but less in boyfriends, whereas personality and affection are sought more in boyfriends than in husbands. In more "feminine" countries, these latter traits may be seen as equally desirable (Hofstede, 1996). It is, however, important not to overexaggerate such differences; as an individual ages in any culture the influence of pragmatic rather than hedonistic factors in partner choice is likely to increase, particularly if children are desired (or indeed are already present and a partner is required who is suitably caring and has appropriate resources). Similarly, personal ads in many cultures tend to include characteristics also present in a more traditional arranged marriage (such as social status, age, and the education of both the individual advertising and the partner sought).

In the last 2 decades, there has been something of a tension between the work of evolutionary psychologists (e.g., Buss, 1989), who have tended to stress universality in partner preferences, and social role theorists and cultural psychologists, who have emphasized the cultural variability in such preferences (e.g., Goodwin & Tang, 1991). Recent work on dynamical evolutionary psychology allows for some integration of these approaches by taking greater account of

mate proximity and sex ratios in the wider social environment (Kenrick, Li, & Butner, 2003). Key decisions about mating are then viewed in the context of the social networks that lead to short-term changes in behavior, with the theory allowing for fairly rapid updating of behaviors and a greater cultural flexibility in evolutionary models.

Because partner choice is restricted among some cultures and cultural groups, the role of love in the choice of marital partner is also likely to vary across the world. There is strong evidence that Western beliefs in the significance of love for marriage may not be universal (e.g., Levine, Sato, Hashimoto, & Verma, 1995). In cultures where marriages are arranged, love is often assumed to grow out of marriage, rather than to be a motivator for the formation of a particular relationship. In an oft-cited summary, Hsu (1981) observed: "An American asks. 'How does my heart feel?' A Chinese asks 'What will other people say?'" (p. 50). This does not mean that love does not exist in Chinese societies – in fact, anthropological studies have found love to exist in most societies, with most cultures possessing painful love songs and stories that illustrate the strong emotions love can evoke (Jankowiak & Fischer, 1992). However, because of the importance to family honor and economic success of an "appropriate" relationship match, in societies where marriage is arranged love is most likely to be sanctioned between only certain partners. For example, relationships in urban China are likely to be at least partly negotiated, with the choice of partner a joint effort between family and the individuals involved (Pimentel, 2000). Such sanctioned love can then act as important social glue, providing a strong binding force that brings (suitable) individuals and families together. As a consequence, idealistic views about spending time together as a couple outside the family, seen as central in many Western marriages, may have a far lesser role in predicting relationship quality in urban China (Pimentel, 2000).

Just as relationship formation may be at least partly dependent on the influence of significant external barriers so the pressures to maintain a relationship may be externally driven. In those societies in which arranged marriages dominate, divorce or even separation are often difficult or impossible (Hatfield & Rapson, 1996). Although marital dissatisfaction undoubtedly exists here as elsewhere, it is important not to exaggerate the unhappiness felt in many more traditional cultures. Instead, in such societies, different expectations about marriage may lead to different kinds of expectations as to what is – and is not – to be obtained from a marital relationship. For example, in our study of a large Hindu community in Britain, where marriages were mostly arranged by family members of community elders, the extended family provided considerable emotional and tangible support to the couple, significantly helping them in maintaining relationship harmony (Goodwin & Cramer, 2000).

One enduring debate has been the extent to which free-choice matches are happier than arranged marriages. This is difficult to assess because expectations for marriage differ, and in those societies in which arranged marriages predominate divorce is often difficult. To address this issue Xiaohe and Whyte (1990) tested a representative probability sample of 586 ever-married women in the Sichuan Province of mainland China. Their data suggested that women in arranged marriages were consistently less satisfied than those that had chosen their own partners. Controlling for a large number of measures (including age at marriage and family income), their study did suggest that freedom of mate choice was the strongest predictor of marital quality.

Work on social cognitions in close relationships has suggested that certain beliefs about relationships may be functional or dysfunctional (Epstein & Eidelson, 1981). "Functional" relationship beliefs – such as the belief that partners can change – may encourage relationship maintenance behaviors and help promote relationship quality (Karney, McNulty, & Bradbury, 2001). In contrast, "dysfunctional" relationship beliefs – such as disagreement is destructive – may restrict a partner's ability to deal with relational challenges (Karney & Bradbury, 1995). Dysfunctional beliefs are have been related to poor relationship quality and negative problem-solving behaviors (e.g., Emmelkamp, Krol, Sanderman, & Rüphan, 1987).

Goodwin and Gaines (2004) examined the association between relationship beliefs and marital quality among married participants from three former Communist nations: Hungary, Russia, and Georgia. As predicted, they found a significant overall correlation between dysfunctional beliefs and relationships quality. However, this association was moderated by country, with more than 4 times as much of the variance in relationship quality explained by relationship beliefs in Hungary than in the other two nations investigated. Hungary is the most individualistic country of these three nations, and one possibility is that individual cognitions play a greater role in relationship quality than other family and community factors in more individualistic societies. Indeed, Mastekaasa (1994) suggested that as environment becomes more rational and impersonal (characteristics often associated with individualism), the emotional intimacy of marriage becomes more important.

Family Relations and the Broader Social Network

Families are central in most societies but vary greatly in structure across cultures. As such, the family is often viewed as an ideal institution for cross-cultural study. Different living arrangements can also be found among different ethnic groups (Glick & Hook, 2002). Family structure can also be subject to relatively rapid social change, a change with potentially profound societal implications.

In some societies, family means the immediate family consisting of parents and children, whereas in other, largely collectivistic communities, it also includes other kin such as cousins, uncles, aunts, grandparents, and others (Ting & Chiu, 2002). In the traditional Chinese family, parents expect to live with their married sons, and taking care of elderly parents is an important family obligation (Ting & Chiu, 2002). In India, the family consists of a large, extended group of relatives (D'Souza, 2003). Assets are managed by the head of the family, usually the eldest male member. Sometimes, married sons choose to live separately, but rural sons are still likely to work on their share of the ancestral land. Daughters, once married, usually move to their husband's house to live. Such traditional families contrast markedly with the image of the conventional family often portrayed as prevalent in Britain and other industrialized nations. Such a family consists of a small nuclear unit of two parents, legally married with dependent children and residing in one distinct domestic unit. In reality, of course, it has long been recognized that family structure in most industrialized countries is diverse: As Oakley (1982) noted, the conventional family is just "one particular cultural interpretation of the 'facts' of sexuality and reproduction" (p. 123).

The role of culture is increasingly recognized by researchers in understanding parenting behaviour. Pinderhughes, Nix, Foster, and Jones (2001) suggested that there are two ways in which culture influences parenting, first by promoting unique, culture-specific styles of parenting and second by mediating the influence of parenting style on behavioral outcomes. Thus, for example, physical discipline has been associated with externalizing behavior among Whites, but not among Blacks (Deater-Deckard, Dodge, Bates, & Petti, 1996). Steinberg, Mounts, Lamborn, and Dornbush (1991) illustrated the differential impact that authoritative parenting can have on school performance of children belonging to different groups; authoritative parenting enhanced the performance of Whites and Latino adolescents but not that of Asians or African Americans. Differences also emerge when one considers the area of conflict that occurs between parents and adolescents. Compared with Hispanic and Black parents, White parents often disagree with their children over chores, and White families frequently report higher levels of conflict. This could be due

to the stress of independence and autonomy among White families, as well as their more authoritative parenting style (Barber, 1994).

Social Networks and Support

Social support is one of the most widely investigated areas of PR, and an increasing number of studies have considered the role of culture in defining different aspects of support. For the collectivist, the basic unit of survival is the group (Hui, 1988); hence, support from others is important in these societies and provides a strong buffer against life stresses (Triandis, Bontempo, Villareal, Asai, & Lucca, 1988). In contrast, individualists exhibit fewer skills for interacting intimately with others and are more emotionally detached from their in-groups (Triandis et al., 1988).

Social support is likely to emerge as a stronger predictor of well-being among collectivistic cultures than individualistic societies (Diener, Diener, & Diener, 1995). The source of support also plays an important role in influencing the well-being of the individual, although again cultural may moderate the appropriateness and impact of the support (Maton et al., 1996). In collectivists' cultures, families are more likely to be the prime providers of material and emotional support and informational guidance (Goodwin & Cramer, 2000). In a comparative study of the network systems of English-speaking and Spanish-speaking women, the more collectivist Spanish-speaking network was mainly composed of family members (Levitt, Weber, & Guacci, 1993). This may reflect the strong family obligations often observed in Spanish communities, which in turn limit contacts with individuals outside the home. However, Kagiticibasi (1996) argued that with an improvement in the economic situation in many collectivists' countries instrumental interdependence on families may weaken.

There are significant culture differences not only in network size and sources of support but also in network utilization. In the West, individuals are expected to solicit help from others actively (Kaniasty & Norris, 2000), whereas in Eastern cultures a greater sensitivity to others' needs and feelings may make help seeking less necessary (Pillay & Rao, 2002). In collectivists cultures where social connectedness is high, help is expected to be voluntarily provided, and asking for help may be regarded as socially demeaning (Pillay & Rao, 2002). In contrast, social support seeking is likely to be seen as self-threatening in individualist cultures, where even minimal dependence can have a damaging influence on the individual's self-esteem (Green & Rodgers, 2001). Nevertheless, this should not be taken to mean that some interdependence is not desired in individualist culture. Irrespective of culture, all individuals have a need to belong and to attach to others (Baumeister & Leary, 1995).

Apart from the family, friends and neighbors also form an important part of one's social support. Emphasizing the significance of friends and neighbors, Crow and Allan (1994) claimed that our "interlocking social network" consists of a combination of neighborhoods, kinship, and friendships. In individualists' cultures, friendship may be more plentiful and less enduring. Goodwin (1999) argued that Western friendship could be seen as "non-institutionalized institution" in which there are relatively few ritualistic ties and relationships are built on "voluntary interdependence." Among Korean and Caucasian students, You and Malley-Morrison (2000), found that Korean students reported less intimate relationships with, and less positive expectations of, close friends than Caucasian American college students. In their study of friendship in North America and West Africa, Adams and Plaut (2003) found that Ghanaians had a more cautious approach to friendship and did not regard companionship or emotional support as the core feature of friendship. Goodwin (1999) maintained that many of the most obvious differences between friendships across cultures can be traced to the significance of hierarchy within a society. In Chinese society, friendship is the only equal relationship within the Confucian system and as a result is highly valued.

Although few studies have focused on comparison of neighbor relations across cultures, there are some data on neighbor relations in ethnically diverse neighborhood. Homogeneity of neighborhood is an important factor determining attachment to one's area. This homogeneity facilitates both greater interaction and more involvement with the organization of neighborhood. Persistent stereotypes also, of course, influence the nature of interethnic relations within neighborhoods. Emerson, Chai, and Yancey (2001) showed that Whites preferred the presence of Asians and Hispanics neighbors to those of Blacks due to negative stereotypic associations linking Blacks with crime and low educational achievement.

Relationships, Culture, and Social Change

Just as PR researchers have largely ignored culture as an independent or moderating variable in their research, they have also largely neglected the role of social change and its implications for the way in which people interrelate with others. Yet even a cursory glance at the world news demonstrates clear ways in which we might expect significant economic and political transitions to influence our personal relationships. What, for example, happens to people's support networks when individuals feel they can no longer trust their friends or even family members, such as during a period of oppressive dictatorship? What happens when long-established rules about generational respect are reversed, such as during the Cultural Revolution in China? Who decides who can date whom when a society becomes more religious, as happened after the fall of the shah in Iran? Such societal changes can seriously challenge the established "cross-cultural differences" observed by those who study personal relationships, making many such prior observations redundant.

Just as we can study the influence of culture on relationships on several dimensions, we can also identify different ways in which cultural change might influence personal relationships. First, we might differentiate between those aspects of relationships that are most likely to vary following social changes and those likely to remain stable (Goodwin & Neto, 2003). Stable aspects of relationships are likely to include ones based on universally expressed emotions or relationship ideals, such as erotic and manic love styles, and *ideal* preferences for a partner. Less stable aspects include the more environmentally determined *actual* love choices and "realistic" or pragmatic partner preferences. Buss, Shackleford, Kirkpatrick, and Larsen (2001) reviewed partner preferences over a more than 50-year period using the same instrument (1939, 1956, 1967, 1977, 1984, and 1996). Over this time period, they found important generational shifts in mate preferences. Both men and women increasingly valued mutual attraction and love, education and intelligence, sociability and good looks, and decreased their stress on refinement, neatness, and chastity. Men increasingly valued similar educational background and good financial prospects and decreasingly valued a woman being a good cook and housekeeper, whereas women placed less value on ambition and industriousness. Partner preferences across genders became generally similar over this time period, with men's preferences moving toward those of women.

Second, we can differentiate between relative *surface changes* in relationships activities (peripheral, largely behavioral changes that may have little impact on more deeply held values or norms) and *deeper relationship changes* (more substantial changes that may influence both the values of the individual and his or her relationships with their extended community). For example, the introduction of new technology is often seen as revolutionary in the way we interrelate with others and may certainly offer new ways of communicating with others. However, such communication changes may remain relatively superficial, not greatly influencing the content of the communication. We can contrast this with deeper changes in relationship longevity and com-

mitment. Here, often one major transforming influence is changes in the economic situation. In India, there has been an increase in family breakdown over the past decade at both the familial level, where the joint family system is moving toward nuclearization, and at the marital level, where there is increased rate of divorce. The Indian agrarian economy is dominated by the joint family system but with urbanization and industrialization, the family has ceased to be the unit of production (D'Souza, 2003). In contrast, more and more young people have left traditional jobs and moved to the cities in search of a job as well as better living conditions. This has laid the foundation for the break up of the joint family system, and has also contributed to the growth of supplemented and other varieties of nuclear families (Singh, 2001). Such changes have resulted in changes in relationships among the members of the family, particularly with respect to family obligations and childrearing (Singh, 2001). As a result modern Indian families are small and nuclear, with parents working outside the home. Economic pressures can also have direct effect on relations within the marriage: In a longitudinal study of family stress during the Czech transformation from Communism, economic pressures were shown to make both husbands and wives irritable, undermining marital stability (Hraba, Lorenz, & Pechacova, 2000).

Although such changes are undoubtedly significant, they are best viewed in terms of adjustments to environmental conditions. Indeed, many of the warnings of the "end of intimacy," which imply that modern, "rational" societies undermine relationships (e.g., Putnam, 2000; Ritzer, 2002), are likely to be exaggerated. For example, there has been a steady decline in the number of marriages per 1,000 persons in Britain (Goodwin, Christakopoulou, & Panagiotidou, in press). Fewer couples now marry in church, and the number of marriages where both partners were marrying for the first time in 2000 accounted for just 58% of marriages. There is also a tendency for people to marry for the first time somewhat later in life in recent years. The average family size is decreasing and is projected to fall below two children per woman for women born around 1960 (Office of National Statistics, 2002). At the same time, the majority of the adult population can be classified as being very "family-centered" and a "belief" in conventional marriage remains strong (Lewis, 2000). Family members are still connected by a network of mutual aid that takes many different forms, ranging from child care and caring for the elderly to the provision of substantial intergenerational financial and moral support. Kagitcibasi (1996) described three forms of family pattern: the interdependent, collectivist family; the independent, individualist family; and a new synthetic family form she termed *emotional dependency*. This final type combines social structural and economic change alongside cultural continuity, with the resulting synthesis providing a new adjustment to environmental demands. In this family type material dependencies may decrease with socioeconomic development, but emotional dependencies may even increase, with individuals adjusting their communications to meet the opportunities and realities of their new living arrangements (Kagitcibasi, 1996). Similarly, Goodwin et al. (2002), in a cross-cultural study of loneliness among Italian, Anglo-Canadian, and Chinese Canadian, provided data that challenges the postmodern hypothesis that young people today are more lonely because their self-centered, individualistic nature. Instead, such individuals have formed a range of alternative emotional relationships, often outside the family, which serve to maintain emotional connectedness and psychological well-being.

One, largely neglected aspect of personal relationships and social change has been the impact of large-scale political change and conflict. Cha (1994) provided an historical interpretation of the changes in family alliances in South Korea. In the 1950s, the hardships of the Korean War led to a great emphasis on materialistic values, such as money, power, and social status. The industrialization of the 1960s promoted values of self-reliance, with diligence as a value actively promoted by the military government. In the 1970s, the traditional values of loyalty and filial piety declined. Instead, the influence of the extended family and clan was replaced by the school as a focus for collective identity.

Changes in divorce laws can have a significant impact on relationship stability and the way in which individuals decide to dissolve a particular relationship (Fine & Fine, 1994). Fine and Fine argued that these changes have been bidirectional in influence: Although they have followed existing cultural values, they have at the same time been important in helping change societal perspectives on marriage and divorce. It is important here to remember that there can be considerable diversity in divorce rates even within a single religious or cultural group. Divorce, for example, is relatively rare among many Muslims populations across the world (e.g., Goodwin et al., in press), but divorce rates are relatively high among Muslims in Southeast Asia. This is indicative of the limited restrictions imposed on Muslim men who want to divorce in this region (Heaton, Cammack, & Young, 2001). In general, in societies where women are less economically dependent on men and where fewer stigmas are attached to divorce, there has been a recent increase in the divorce rate (Heaton et al., 2001).

Conclusion

This review provides only a small flavor of some of the complexities of cultural variation in personal relationships and the complex ways in which cultural and social changes may influence such relationships. At present, large questions remain about why cultural differences exist, and the role of the ecological setting in helping frame different kinds of relationships in different cultures. Such work needs to be conducted with a sensitivity to the pitfalls of measuring responses across cultures (such as acquiescence biases and response sets; see Van de Vijver & Leung, 1997). In addition, it is clear that simple classifications of relationship differences between cultures need to consider a whole range of other factors, and should strive to combine analysis of the *macrocontext* (the dominant cultural norms and resources) along with *mesocontextual factors* and *microcontextual factors* and the individual personalities and values of the couple concerned. The challenge now is for relationship researchers to develop explicitly more complete and embracing analyses of relationships that include these additional levels of analysis, to help us better understand relationships across cultures.

References

Adams, G., & Pault, V. C. (2003). The cultural grounding of personal relationship: Friendship in North American and West African worlds. *Personal Relationships, 10*, 333–347.

Alonso-Arbiol, I., Shaver, P. R., & Yárnoz, S. (2002). Insecure attachment, gender roles, and interpersonal dependency in the Basque Country. *Personal Relationships, 9*, 479–490.

Barber, B. K. (1994). Cultural, family and personal contexts of parent–adolescent conflict. *Journal of Marriage and the Family, 56*, 375–386.

Baumeister, R. F., & Leary, M. R. (1995). The need to belong: Desire for interpersonal attachments as a fundamental human emotion. *Psychological Bulletin, 112*, 461–484.

Beishon, S., Modood, T., & Virdee, S. (1998). *Ethnic minority families*. London: Policy Studies Institute.

Berry, J. W. (1997). Immigration, acculturation, and adaptation. *Applied Psychology: An International Review, 56*, 5–68.

Buss, D. M. (1989). Sex differences in human mate preferences: Evolutionary hypotheses tested in 37 cultures. *Behavioral and Brain Sciences, 12*, 1–14.

Buss, D. M., Shackleford, T. K., Kirkpatrick, L. E., & Larsen, R. J. (2001). A half century of mate preferences: The cultural evolution of values. *Journal of Marriage and Family, 63*, 491–503.

Cha, J.-H. (1994). Aspects of individualism and collectivism in Korea. In U. Kim, H. C. Triandis, C. Kagitcibasi, S-C. Choi, & G. Yoon (Eds.), *Individualism and collectivism: Theory, method, and applications* (pp. 157–174). Thousand Oaks, CA: Sage.

Cole, M. (1990). Cultural psychology: A once and future discipline? In J. Berman (Ed.), *Nebraska Symposium on Motivation: Vol. 37. Cross-cultural perspectives: Current theory and research in motivation* (pp. 279–335). Lincoln: University of Nebraska Press.

Crow, G., & Allan, G. (1994). *Community Life: An introduction to local social relations*. Hemel Hempstead, England: Harvester Wheatsheaf.

Dayan, J., Doyle, A., & Markiewicz, D. (2001). Social support networks and self-esteem of idiocentric and allocentric children and adolescents. *Journal of Social and Personal Relationships, 18*, 767–784.

Deater-Deckard, K., Dodge, K. A., & Bates, J. E., & Petti, G. S. (1996). Physical discipline among African American and European American mothers: Links to children's externalizing behaviors. *Developmental Psychology, 32*, 1065–1072.

Diener, E., Diener, M., & Diener, C. (1995). Factors predicting subjective well-being of nations. *Journal of Personality and Social Psychology, 69*, 851–864.

Diener, E., Gohm, C. L., Suh, E., & Oishi, S. (2000). Similarity of the relations between marital status and subjective well-being across cultures. *Journal of Cross-Cultural Psychology, 31*, 419–436.

D'Souza, V. S. (2003). Societal development and the changing Indian family In R. S. Bhatti, M. Varghese, & A. Raghuram (Eds.), *Changing marital and family systems challenges to conventional models in mental health* (pp. 46–57). Bangalore, India: National Institute of Mental Health and Neuro Sciences.

Emerson, M. O., Chai, K. J., & Yancey, G. (2001). Does race matter in residential segregation? Exploring the preferences of White Americans. *American Sociological Review, 66*, 922–935.

Emmelkamp, P. M., Krol, B., Sanderman, R., & Rüphan, M. (1987). The assessment of relationship beliefs in a marital context. *Personality and Individual Differences, 8*, 775–780.

Epstein, N., & Eidelson, R. J. (1981). Unrealistic beliefs of clinical couples: Their relationship to expectations, goals, and satisfaction. *American Journal of Family Therapy, 9*, 13–22.

Fine, M. A., & Fine, D. R. (1994). An examination and evaluation of recent changes in divorce laws in five Western countries: The critical role of values. *Journal of Marriage and the Family, 56*, 249–263.

Fiske, A. P. (2002). Using individualism and collectivism to compare cultures – A critique of the validity and measurement of the constructs: Comment on Oyserman et al. (2002). *Psychological Bulletin, 128*, 78–88.

Glick, J. E., & Hook, J. V. (2002). Parents' coresidence with adult children: Can immigration explain racial and ethnic variation? *Journal of Marriage and the Family, 64*, 240–253.

Goodwin, R. (1999). *Personal relationships across cultures*. London: Routledge.

Goodwin, R., Christakopoulou, S., & Panagiotidou, V. (in press). Family structure in Britain. In J. Georgas, J. W. Berry., F. van de Vijver., C. Kagitcibasi & Y. H. Poortinga (Eds.), *Family structure and function across cultures: Psychological variations*. Cambridge, England: Cambridge University Press.

Goodwin, R., Cook, O., & Yung, Y. (2002). Cultural predictors of life satisfaction in the UK and Italy. *Personal Relationships, 8*, 225–230.

Goodwin, R., & Cramer, D. (2000). Marriage and social support in a British Asian community. *Journal of Community and Applied Social Psychology, 10*, 49–62.

Goodwin, R., & Gaines, S. O. (2004). Relationships beliefs and relationship quality across cultures: Country as a moderator of dysfunctional beliefs and relationship quality in three former Communist societies. *Personal Relationships, 11*, 267–279.

Goodwin, R., & Neto, F. (2003, July). *Universal and relative relationship phenomena: A new theoretical framework for research across cultures*. Paper presented at the International Association for Cross-Cultural Psychology Conference, Budapest.

Goodwin, R., Nizharadze, G., Luu, L. A. N., Kosa, E., & Emelyanova, T. (2001). Social support in changing Europe: An analysis of three post-communist nations. *European Journal of Social Psychology, 31*, 379–393.

Goodwin, R., & Tang, D. (1991). Preferences for friends and close relationship partners: Cross-cultural comparison. *Journal of Social Psychology, 131*, 579–581.

Green, B. L., & Rodgers, A. (2001). Determinants of social support among low-income mothers: A longitudinal analysis. *American Journal of Community Psychology, 29*, 419–441.

Hanassab, S., & Tidwell, R. (1989). Cross-cultural perspective on dating relationships of young Iranian women: A pilot study. *Counselling Psychology Quarterly, 2*, 113–121.

Hatfield, E., & Rapson, R. L. (1996). *Love and sex: Cross-cultural perspectives*. Boston: Allyn and Bacon.

Hatfield, E., & Sprecher, S. (1995). Men's and women's mate preferences in the United States, Russia, and Japan. *Journal of Cross-Cultural Psychology, 26*, 728–750.

Heaton, T. B., Cammack, M., & Young, L. (2001). Why is the divorce rate declining in Indonesia? *Journal of Marriage and the Family, 63*, 480–490.

Hetsroni, A. (2002). Differences between Jewish–Israeli and Arab–Israeli college students in attitudes toward date selection and sex relations: A research note. *Personal Relationships, 9*, 507–517.

Hofstede, G. (1980). *Culture's consequences: International differences in work-related values*. Beverly Hills, CA: Sage.

Hofstede, G. (1991). *Cultures and organizations: Software of the mind*. London: McGraw-Hill.

Hofstede, G. (1996). Gender stereotypes and partner preferences of Asian women in masculine and feminine cultures. *Journal of Cross-Cultural Psychology, 27*, 533–46.

Hraba, J., Lorenz, F. O., & Pechacova, Z. (2000). Family stress during the Czech transformation. *Journal of Marriage and the Family, 62*, 520–553.

Hsu, F. L. (1981). *Americans and Chinese: Passage to differences* (3rd ed.). Honolulu: University Press of Hawaii.

Hui, C. H. (1988). Measurement of individualism–collectivism. *Journal of Research in Personality, 22*, 17–36.

Inglehart, R. (1997). *Modernization and postmodernization: Cultural, economic, and political change in 43 societies*. Princeton, NJ: Princeton University Press.

Ingoldsby, B. B. (1995). Mate selection and marriage. In B. B. Ingoldsby & S. Smith (Eds.), *Families in multicultural perspective* (pp. 143–160). New York: Guilford Press.

Jankowiak, W. R., & Fischer, E. F. (1992). A cross-cultural perspective on romantic love. *Ethology, 31*, 149–155.

Kagitcibasi, C. (1996). *Family and human development across cultures*. Mahwah, NJ: Erlbaum.

Kaniasty, K., & Norris, F. H. (2000). Help-seeking comfort and receiving social support: The role of ethnicity and context of need.

American Journal of Community Psychology, 28, 545–581.

Karney, B. R., & Bradbury, T. N. (1995). The longitudinal course of marital quality and stability: A review of theory, method, and research. *Psychological Bulletin, 118,* 3–34.

Karney, B. R., McNulty, J. K., & Bradbury, T. N. (2001). Cognition and the development of close relationships. In G. J. O. Fletcher & M. S. Clark (Eds.), *Interpersonal processes* (pp. 32–59). Oxford: Blackwell.

Kenrick, D. T., Li, N. P., & Butner, J. (2003). Dynamical evolutionary psychology: Individual decision rules and emergent social norms. *Psychological Review, 110,* 3–28.

Lewis, C. (2000). *A man's place in the home: Fathers and families in the UK.* York, England: Joseph Rowntree Foundation.

Levine, R., Sato, S., Hashimoto, T., & Verma, I. (1995). Love and marriage in eleven cultures. *Journal of Cross-Cultural Psychology, 26,* 554–571.

Levinson, D. (1989). *Family values in cross-cultural perspective.* Newbury Park, CA: Sage.

Levitt, M. J., Weber, R. A., & Guacci, N. (1993). Convoys of social support: An intergenerational analysis. *Psychological Aging, 8,* 323, 326.

Mastekaasa, A. (1994). Marital status, distress, and well-being: An international comparison. *Journal of Comparative Family Studies, 25,* 183–206.

Maton, K. L., Teti, D. M., Corns, K. M., Viera-Baker, C. C., Lavine, J. R., Gouze, K. R., & Keating, D. P. (1996). Cultural specificity of support sources, correlates and contexts: Three studies of African–American and Caucasian youth. *American Journal of Community Psychology, 24,* 551–587.

Medora, N. P., Larson, J. H., Hortaçsu, N., & Dave, P. (2002). Perceived attitudes towards romanticism: A cross-cultural study of American, Asian-Indian, and Turkish young adults. *Journal of Comparative Family Studies, 33,* 155–171.

Neto, F., Mullet, E., Deschamps, J-C., Barros, J., Benvindo, R., Camino, L., et al. (2000). Cross-cultural variations in attitudes toward love. *Journal of Cross-Cultural Psychology, 31,* 626–635.

Oakley, A. (1982). Conventional families. In N. Rapaport, M. P. Fogarty, & R. Rapaport (Eds), *Families in Britain* (pp. 123–137). London: Routledge & Kegan Paul.

Office of National Statistics. (2002). *UK 2002, Official Yearbook of the UK.* London: The Stationery Office.

Onishi, M., & Gjerde, P. F. (2002). Attachment strategies in Japanese urban middle–class couples: A cultural theme analysis of asymmetry in marital relationships. *Personal Relationships, 10,* 435–455.

Pillay, U., & Rao, K. (2002). The structure and function of social support in relation to help-seeking behavior. *Family Therapy, 29,* 153–167.

Pimentel, E. E. (2000). Just how do I love thee? Marital relations in urban China. *Journal of Marriage and the Family, 62,* 32–47.

Pinderhughes, E. E., Nix, R., Foster, E. M., Jones, D., & The conduct problem prevention research group. (2001). Parenting in context: Impact of neighborhood poverty, residential stability, public services, social networks, and danger on parental behaviors. *Journal of Marriage and Family, 63,* 941–953.

Putnam, R. D. (2000). *Bowling alone: The collapse and revival of American community.* New York: Simon & Schuster.

Ritzer, G. (2002). *McDonaldization: A reader.* Thousand Oaks, CA: Pine Forge Press.

Rohner, R. (1984). Toward a conception of culture for cross-cultural psychology. *Journal of Cross-Cultural Psychology, 15,* 111–138.

Rosenblatt, P. C., & Anderson, R. M. (1981). Human sexuality in cross-cultural perspective. In M. Cook (Ed.), *The bases of human sexual attraction* (pp. 215–250). London: Academic Press.

Saroja, K. (1999). Intercaste marriage and social dynamics in India: A critique. *Indian Journal of Social Work, 60,* 183–192.

Schumaker, J. F., Shea, J. D., Monfries, M. M., & Groth, M. G. (1993). Loneliness and life satisfaction in Japan and Australia. *Journal of Psychology, 127,* 65–71.

Singelis, T. M., Triandis, H. C., Bhawuk, D. S., & Gelfand, M. (1995). Horizontal and vertical dimensions of individualism and collectivism: A theoretical and measurement refinement. *Cross Cultural Research, 29,* 240–275.

Singh, Y. (2001). *Social change in India: Crisis and resilience.* New Delhi: Har-Anand.

Steinberg, L., Mounts, N. S., Lamborn, S. D., & Dornbush, S. M. (1991). Authoritative parenting and adolescent adjustment across varied ecological niches. *Journal of Research on Adolescence, 1,* 19–36.

Ting, K., & Chiu, S. W. K. (2002). Leaving the parental home: Chinese culture in an urban context. *Journal of Marriage and the Family, 64*, 614–626.

Triandis, H. C., Bontempo, R., & Villareal, M. J., Asai, M., & Lucca, M. (1988). Individualism and collectivism: Cross-cultural perspectives on self-ingroup relationships. *Journal of Personality and Social Psychology, 54*, 323–338.

Van de Vijver, F., & Leung, K. (1997). *Methods and data analysis for cross-cultural research.* Thousand Oaks, CA: Sage.

Way, N., Cowal, K. Gingold, R., Pahl, K., & Bissessar, N. (2001). Friendship patterns among African American, Asian American, and Latino adolescents from low-income families. *Journal of Social and Personal Relationships, 18*, 29–53.

Wilkinson, D. (1987). Ethnicity. In M. B. Sussman & S. K. Steinmetz (Eds.), *Handbook of marriage and the family* (pp. 183–210). New York: Plenum Press.

Xiaohe, X., & Whyte, M. (1990). Love matches and arranged marriages: A Chinese replication. *Journal of Marriage and the Family, 52*, 709–722.

You, H. S., & Malley-Morrison, K. (2000). Young adult attachment styles and intimate relationships with close friends: A cross-cultural study of Koreans and Caucasian Americans. *Journal of Cross-Cultural Psychology, 31*, 528–534.

CHAPTER 38

Personal Relationships: On and Off the Internet

Jeffrey Boase
Barry Wellman

From Computer-Mediated Small Groups to the Internet

That the internet is a communication medium for personal relationships is obvious. That the nature of the internet affects the nature of personal relationships has often been proclaimed – recall Marshall McLuhan's "the medium is the message" but less often proven – especially in field studies. How might the internet have an impact?

Early debates about computer-mediated relationships began before the Internet. Research was dominated by social psychologistic lab experiments focusing on (a) how different types of computer-mediated communication among dyads fit specific *tasks* and (b) how *group norms* determine the appropriateness of using different media in particular situations (see the review in Haythornthwaite & Wellman, 1998). Researchers examined whether the limited "social presence" of computer media (compared with face-to-face contact) affected

the media people choose to use, their perception of the messages they received, and their perception of the people who sent messages to them (see Kling, 1996; Sproull & Kiesler, 1991). For example, Daft and Lengel (1986) argued that people should choose rich media (e.g., face-to-face contact) over less rich media (e.g., impersonal written documents) when communicating equivocal or difficult messages. Researchers also found that users considered the lower social presence of email to be less appropriate for intellectually difficult or socially sensitive communications (Fish, Kraut, Root, & Rice, 1993), and that the type of information exchanged affected the types of media used (Markus, Bikson, El-Shinnawy, & Soe, 1992). This laboratory-based research often treated people as if they did not have positions in social systems and often assumed that they had free choice about which media to use. Reading this literature is to enter a world that pays scant attention to matters such as power, gender, socioeconomic status, norms, differential resources, or complex bundles of interactions and alliances (see also the critique in Walther, 1997)

Although the internet has captured popular attention as a communication and information medium, a substantial body of research has developed only recently that places understanding of computer-mediated communication in broader social contexts. Unlike the earlier lab experiments on dyads and small groups, internet research of personal relations has been principally based on surveys, interviews, and observations of how people use computer-mediated communication in the context of their everyday lives. In the past decade, research has moved from social accounting – asking how many people use the internet to communicate – to delving more into how the internet intersects with their social practices.

This chapter discusses the role of the internet in personal relationships. It starts with a brief description of the socially relevant characteristics of internet technology and a summary of the debate between utopian and dystopian accounts of internet use on personal relationships. Both of these accounts are inadequate because they take a technologically deterministic approach that ignores the causal role of the individual's need to maintain offline social relationships. Research that examines the internet's role in facilitating communication between family and friends, and in forming new social ties and neighboring relations shows that the internet is neither destroying nor radically altering society for the better. Rather, research results point to the need for a more holistic account of internet use that places internet use in the broader context of all personal relationships. They suggest that the interpersonal patterns associated with internet use are the continuation of a shift in the nature of personal networks that began well before the advent of the internet. This shift toward "networked individualism" involves the transition from spatially proximate and densely knit communities to which people belong to more spatially dispersed and sparsely knit personal networks in which people maneuver.

The Social Affordances of the Internet

What are the social affordances of the internet, to use Bradner, Kellogg, and Erickson's (1999) term for how its technical characteristics affect possibilities, opportunities, and constraints for personal relationships?

1. Because internet communication is largely distance-independent in use and cost, it may support more interactions with a greater number of spatially dispersed network members.

2. The asynchronous nature of the internet, in which senders and receivers of messages do not have to be online simultaneously, also supports interactions at great distances and among people with different temporal rhythms.

3. The rapidity of internet interactions compared with intermittent face-to-face meetings and phone calls may foster a high velocity of interpersonal exchange, sometimes ill considered.

4. The reduced social presence of the internet may limit its ability to support emotional, nuanced, and complex interactions.

5. The text-only nature of almost all internet messages can reduce perceived hierarchies as gender, social class, ethnicity, age, lifestyle, and so on are less visible.

6. The absence of direct visual or audio feedback in internet exchanges may encourage more extreme forms of communication, sometimes called flaming. People may input messages to screen that they would never say to another person palpably present in person or on the telephone.

7. The ability of email to be forwarded to others supports transitive, indirect contact, as when messages get sent to friends of friends. This aids the exchange of information that cuts across group boundaries. Such crosscutting ties link and integrate social groups, increasing societal connectivity.

8. The ability of internet messages to be sent to many people simultaneously allows

people to remain in contact with multiple social circles.

9. The internet's velocity, transitivity, and multiple message characteristics indirectly connect the wired world in six steps or less. Yet there is significant decoupling in social networks. Hence, information diffuses rapidly through computer-supported social networks, but neither universally nor uniformly.

Utopianism and Dystopianism

Early accounts of the internet's role in personal relationships tended to be assertions and anecdotes. Utopian writers argued that the internet contained an enormous potential that would revolutionize society for the better. They praised the internet's ability to bring together disparate people from around the world into what Marshall McLuhan called the "global village": The internet would allow relationships to flourish in an environment of equality and respect. This world would be so immersive that people would be able to escape the mundane routine of everyday life, becoming at one with collective intelligence (i.e., de Kerckhove, 1997). As John Perry Barlow, a leader of the Electric Frontier Foundation (and songwriter for the Grateful Dead), wrote in 1995:

> With the development of the Internet, and with the increasing pervasiveness of communication between networked computers, we are in the middle of the most transforming technological event since the capture of fire. I used to think that it was just the biggest thing since Gutenberg, but now I think you have to go back farther (p. 36).... In order to feel the greatest sense of communication, to realize the most experience,... I want to be able to completely interact with the consciousness that's trying to communicate with mine. Rapidly... We are now creating a space in which the people of the planet can have that kind of communication relationship. (Barlow, Birkets, Kelly, & Slouka, 1995, p. 40)

At the same time as these utopian writers were praising the internet, another group of dystopian writers were taking the opposite position. Dystopian writers found life online to be problematic, arguing that online relationships would never measure up to face-to-face relationships of real life. Online life would only take time away from the more emotionally satisfying relationships that could be found offline. In doing so, it would erode the fabric of community life, leaving individuals isolated and alienated (i.e., Kroker & Weinstein, 1994; Stoll, 1995). They worried that ephemeral online identities would trump their offline counterparts. Along these same lines of reasoning, Sherry Turkle (1995) argued that the ability to create multiple personalities in this online world would be so emotionally engaging that it would fracture identity, leading to multiple personality disorders. Anecdotes of gender deception were told and retold (Dery, 1997; Van Gelder, 1985; selections from Bell & Kennedy, 2000).

Many of these utopian and dystopian accounts were written by a small number of academics and hi-tech corporate folks who were early users when the pre-'90s internet was only open to them. By focusing only on internet use common to their lifestyles and personal interests, they failed to consider how most of the population actually *does* use the internet. In doing so, they lost perspective of the internet's true potential for society at large, relying on hyped conjecture rather than informed theorizing. This failure to place internet use into a broader pattern of common social tendencies means that utopian and dystopian writers share an overly simplistic view of internet use. Both assume that the internet actually *does* have the power to pull people away from their everyday lives and immerse them in a world that is radically different from the one in which they previously lived. This assumption – often referred to as technological determinism – attributes a large amount of causal power to the technology itself, ignoring the complex array of social factors that determine how the internet is actually used by the general population. Although the internet does have social affordances – technologically produced social opportunities and constraints – we show that its technology does not determine its interpersonal use.

This lack of context is most evident in arguments made by utopian writers. By arguing that the internet has caused the breakdown of physical constraints, allowing people to connect all over the world, utopian writers fail to acknowledge that this has already been happening for decades. By way of mass transportation and the telephone, people have been maintaining a significant number of their relationships with people who are not located within the neighborhood locale (Wellman, 1979; Wellman & Gulia, 1999). While it is true that the internet enables people to communicate around the world at a relatively low cost, the point being made here is that these geographic networks already existed before the internet was invented. For this reason, it was not internet technology that caused the breakdown of physical barriers, but rather the widespread desire for long-distance communication that helped lead to widespread adoption of the internet. Contrary to technologically deterministic assumptions, internet use has been the effect and not the cause of distant communication with spatially dispersed relations.

Both utopian and dystopian writers also fail to consider social context when they assume that the internet offers an experience that is so immersive, it is divorced from the kinds of interactions that routinely occur in everyday life. They rarely acknowledged that many relationships did not rely exclusively on "real," in-person contact before the advent of the internet. Instead, a large portion of people's personal relationships were geographically dispersed, relying on a mixture of telephone and only intermittent face-to-face contact (Fischer, 1992; Wellman & Tindall, 1993). Moreover, there is evidence that a large majority of the social interactions that occur online are between people who also know each other offline (Quan-Haase & Wellman, 2002). By ignoring the

reality of present-day relationships, they falsely assume that the internet is actually responsible for this shift and that it would continue to amplify these social tendencies to the point where individuals no longer socialized in person at all. Although it may be true that some of these writers were never intending to give an account of how the internet is really used, much of the hype they created has spilled over into the media stories and common perceptions about the internet's impact on society.

Fortunately, a body of research about internet use has been accumulating. Although these studies do much to shed light on the ways that the internet is actually being used by the general population, they share common assumptions with both utopian and dystopian thinkers. Many of these studies frame their research questions as addressing the *effects* of internet use. By way of example, one of the most comprehensive and informative summaries of this kind of research is titled *Social Consequences of Internet Use* (Katz & Rice, 2002). These "consequences" are often conceptualized in terms of interaction with friends and family, or formation of new online friendships and neighboring relations. By making internet use appear causally prior to these outcomes, this research often does not include social factors that play a fundamental role in shaping internet use.

Although the theoretical justification for these studies may attribute more causal power to the internet than necessary, these empirical studies do much to enrich our understanding of internet use. These projects often drew on large samples of people, asking questions about internet habits, mental health, and social interaction with friends and family. Findings from these studies will be used to examine the following issues:

1. Does internet use detract from time spent with friends and family?
2. To what extent are people engaged in online relationships?
3. Does the internet affect neighborhood community?

These three issues will help address utopian and dystopian arguments, by providing some evidence about the extent to which people engage in online relationships and if this new connectivity is associated with a change in their lives offline.

After using the current body of research to address these three questions, we then interpret these empirical observations in a way that contextualizes their existence in the somewhat new and emerging theoretical position of networked individualism.

Contact With Friends and Family – Online and Off

In 1998, the dystopian perspective gained some empirical support when a group of researchers at Carnegie Mellon University published a paper, "Internet Paradox: A Social Technology That Reduces Social Involvement and Psychological Well-Being?" (Kraut et al., 1998). Using systematic evidence, Kraut and colleagues argued that despite the internet's function as a social tool, new internet users experienced lower levels of face-to-face communication with close friends and family. They also found that their internet newbies displayed symptoms of depression, stress, and loneliness after going online. The results of this study captured widespread media coverage, confirming in the minds of many that the internet is detrimental to social relationships and mental well-being.

These same respondents were asked a similar set of questions on three follow-ups after the initial observation, results of which were reported in the paper, "Internet Paradox Revisited" (Kraut et al., 2002). These results showed that the negative effects of internet use had dissipated three years later. There were generally positive effects of internet use on social relationships and psychological well-being, especially among people who were highly extroverted. Earlier findings of negative social and psychological outcomes were explained as an effect of inexperience when people first go online. These findings also suggest that internet use

itself does not necessarily cause strictly positive or negative outcomes, but rather that internet use is very much tied to preexisting dispositions, such as extroversion.

Research that records daily activities by use of time diaries finds little evidence of the internet harming social relationships or detracting from time spent socializing in person. Robinson, Kestnbaum, Neustadtl, and Alvarez (2002) used time diary results drawn from a sample of 948 Americans, finding few differences in offline communication patterns (in person and by telephone) between internet and non-internet users. Anderson and Tracey (2001) also used longitudinal time-use diary data drawn from 2,600 individuals living in 1,000 U.K. households, along with qualitative interviews, to examine internet use in daily life. They found little change in time use once respondents gained internet connections. However, they did find that major lifestyle changes, such as changing jobs, very often triggered both the adoption of the internet and changes in daily activities. This implies that relationships between internet adoption and changes in lifestyle are caused by more fundamental events over the life course. Contrary to the musings of both utopian and dystopian pundits, the internet does not have the power to alter people's daily activities significantly.

One exception to these findings is a study by Nie and Hillygus (2002) that used time diaries to track everyday activities at regular 6 hour intervals. The sample used 6,000 American respondents, who were representative of the American population, except that they surfed the Web using the Microsoft Web-TV set-top box. Although the demographic composition of Nie's sample is similar to the demographic composition of the general U.S. population, his respondents were atypical because they were early adopters of a new technology and were using a device that was more media oriented than a typical internet terminal. Nie argued that time spent online is largely asocial because it detracts from time spent with others in person. Nevertheless, Nie's findings fly in the face of other time diary studies that also draw on large representative samples. Moreover, the shift in leisure use from TV watching to internet communication is undoubtedly a shift toward more social behavior.

With the exception of Nie, these time diary results are generally consistent with other large-scale surveys that measure social activity that occurs both online and offline. These surveys also find little connection between internet activity and regular social engagements. Findings from a representative sample of 1,800 Americans in 2000 found no difference in levels of telephone use between users and nonusers of the internet (Katz & Rice, 2002). Another survey by the same researchers compared the levels of involvement in religious organizations, leisure organizations, and community organizations, of internet and non-internet users. They found no association between levels of involvement in these activities and internet use (Katz & Aspden, 1997). Another large-scale sample of 3,533 Americans collected by the Pew Internet and American Life Project indicated that internet users were significantly more likely to visit with friends and family, even when controlling for demographic factors (Katz & Rice, 2002). Quan-Haase and Wellman (2002) also examined this issue using the results of a survey that was posted on the National Geographic Web site during the fall of 1998. Their analysis showed that the amount of reported contact through email was not related to decreased amounts of in-person contact or telephone contact. Findings from these studies all indicated that internet use does not detract from amounts of contact with people offline. Given the consistency of these findings, we conclude that people have not radically altered their lives because of the internet.

Because time spent online does not detract from time spent with friends and family, presumably the time spent online is taking away from time that could be spent on other activities. A number of studies have examined this issue, often comparing measures of time spent online with measures of time spent using tradition media, for example, TV watching. A special issue of the journal *IT and Society* includes arti-

cles on 11 such studies (see the introduction by Robinson, 2002, for a summary of the results). As with many studies in social science, differing sources of data, methodology, and measurements often lead to discrepancies in results. In general, these articles showed moderate evidence that internet use was associated with a decrease in the amount of time spent watching TV (Nie & Hillygus, 2002; Pronovost, 2002; Robinson et al., 2002) and sleeping (Fu, Wang, & Qiu, 2002; Nie & Hillygus, 2002; Robinson et al., 2002).

A few longitudinal studies have examined which activities are displaced once people go online. Longitudinal studies are especially apt to answer this question, because they allow researchers to see how fluctuations in internet use are associated with changes in time spent on other daily activities. Findings from a large Swedish study of approximately 1,000 respondents between 1997 and 2001 found that going online leads to a decrease in hours spent watching TV (Franzen, 2000, 2003). Similar but qualified results were found in a random-sample U.S. panel survey of 1,222 persons in 2001 and 963 of those same people in 2002 (Kraut, Kiesler, Boneva, & Shklovski, in press). Rather than lumping all kinds of internet activity into a single measure of internet use, this survey distinguished among a number of kinds of online activities, such as "communicating with friends," "getting news online," or "playing games." Using the internet to meet new people was associated with lower levels of watching TV, whereas using the internet for entertainment or commerce was not. This more refined measure shows that particular kinds of online activities are associated with particular kinds of offline activities. Those who use the internet for social purposes will be less likely to watch TV, and those using the internet for entertainment purposes will continue to seek entertainment through TV watching. This indicates that the needs of people must be understood to make sense of how the internet is used in everyday life. Again, this is in contrast to utopian or dystopian perspectives that assume the internet itself has the power to alter lifestyles.

Although the evidence has generally shown that internet use is not associated with less time spent on social activities, knowing that internet use does not detract from time spent offline with close friends and family says little about the effects of internet use on time spent with these social ties. A recent report by the Pew Internet and American Life Project reports that 93% of those with internet access send email (Fallows, 2004). As much of this email could be sent to close friends and family, it is quite possible that this added contact may strengthen relationships and lead to more contact offline. Then again, this contact may simply add on to offline contact but not increase the frequency or amount of time spent with close friends and family offline.

Longitudinal studies show a positive association between internet use and offline interaction with close friends, but not with family. This finding comes from a recent meta-analysis of 16 data sets that contain measures of internet use and offline social interaction with friends and family (Shklovski, Kiesler, & Kraut, in press). These studies were all conducted between 1995 and 2003, some of them using cross-sectional sampling design and others using longitudinal design. Although measures differed somewhat between studies, they all shared common conceptions of internet use and offline interaction, making comparisons possible. Rather than comparing each measure directly, the total effects of associations between internet use and offline interaction with friends and family for each study were standardized by using a Fisher's Z transformation. Results varied significantly, depending on the survey design. Cross-sectional surveys generally showed a negative association between internet use and interaction with friends. In contrast, longitudinal surveys found a positive association between internet use and interaction with friends. Longitudinal studies found little association between internet use and interaction with family.

To explain these findings, Shklovski et al. (in press) theorized that email is used both to strengthen friendships and schedule more in-person meetings. It strengthens friendships because email may act as an extra source of stimulus, serving as a reminder of the sender and thereby reaffirming the existence of the relationship. Email may also be used more instrumentally as a way of scheduling meetings. Its nonintrusive and asynchronous nature affords the possibility of communicating in a way that is sensitive to the schedules of both parties. The sender can send an email at any time, and the receiver can read and respond to the email at a time that is convenient. This is in contrast to meetings that are arranged by telephone, when the caller very often interrupts the activity of the person on the other end of the line.

Although friendships are more fluid and often require active tie maintenance, family relationships more often involve routine interactions. This would be especially true for household members by virtue of their shared living space. These relationships would tend to benefit less from email exchange, because much interaction could occur during everyday routine. Family relationships are often more stable, requiring less active maintenance. Because email may be suited for affirming the existence of a relationship, increasing its strength, and arranging offline events, it would be less useful in family relationships, which are mostly involuntary and reliant on routine interaction.

Forming Relationships Online

Although research shows that the internet is often used to contact existing relationships, there has been interest in the potential of the internet to create new relationships. Much of the hype surrounding the internet has been about the possibility of people becoming immersed in relationships with people who they have never seen or touched in "real" life. Some scholars writing about the internet portray users so taken with online relationships that their ties with offline friends and family recede into the background (e.g., Chayko, 2002; Kendall, 2002; Rheingold, 2000; Turkle, 1995). Although the evidence suggests that internet use is not associated with declines in contact with friends or family, scholars have yet to explore systematically the issue of the internet's role in the formation of new relationships.

The current body of internet research indicates that the internet has not caused a widespread flourishing of new relationships that are disembodied, existing only in the realm of an immersive online world. In reality, only a relatively small proportion of internet users have ever met someone new online. Two large-scale national surveys done in 1995 and 2000 indicate that only about 10% of internet users have ever met someone new online (Katz & Aspden, 1997; Katz & Rice, 2002). It is probably safe to assume that at least some of these relationships were short lived, fizzling over time. Many of the relationships that do continue to exist for a longer duration tend to migrate offline. Evidence for this has been found in two studies of relationships formed through online newsgroups showing that the desire to meet internet friends in person is common among those who make new friends online (Parks & Floyd, 1996; McKenna, Green, & Gleason, 2002). This is not to deny that an online forum might be important to making new friends, especially when physical or psychological barriers make in-person meetings difficult (McKenna et al., 2002). For example, this research indicated that people who felt physically isolated or dissatisfied with their own self-image were more prone to use an online forum for making friends. Nevertheless, once the friendship was established, there was a common desire to meet in person, implying that people wanted a broader range of interactions than online communication can easily supply.

These findings can be summarized as follows. First, a relatively small minority of internet users actually use the internet to communicate with people that they do not already know from their everyday lives. Second, of the small minority who do form relationships online, those relationships often become incorporated into offline life. In other words, it is not the case that the internet has immersed people into a new world of social relationships with others who they

never see in the flesh. Although the internet does create a new venue through which people may form new relationships, at present, this venue represents only one small aspect of the internet's role in personal relationships for a majority of its users.

Neighboring and the Internet

Typically, neighboring relationships tend to comprise only a small proportion of personal relationships. Early studies in the Toronto area of East York show that most social interaction occurs with people who live outside of their neighborhoods but within their metropolitan area (Wellman, 1979; Wellman, Carrington, & Hall, 1988). However, a recent study in a Toronto suburb has shown that internet use can be associated with an increase in contact between neighbors. This suburb was dubbed "Netville" by Hampton and Wellman (2002, 2003) because of its high-speed internet service. However, 35% of the 109 homes did not receive the service, creating a convenient comparison group. This internet service differed from dial-up internet connections because it could be on 24/7, without tying up the household telephone line and at no additional cost. It was also 10 times faster than most of the present-day broadband connections.

Of all the internet-based services offered to those living in Netville, the neighborhood discussion list was used most heavily. On this discussion list, neighborhood members could broadcast email messages to their neighbors, about a variety of topics, often soliciting services such as child care or lawn maintenance. These email messages increased overall levels of neighborhood contact, increasing the number of neighborhood ties, the amount of regular contact between neighbors, and the number of household visits to neighboring homes. "Wired" residents knew the names of 25 neighbors, whereas the "nonwired" residents only knew the names of 8. This increase in online contact resulted in more informal offline, in-person contact, where wired residences talked to an average of 6 neighbors on a regular basis, while the nonwired residents talked to an average of only three. Moreover, the wired residents made 50% more visits to their neighbors' homes, in comparison with the nonwired residents (for more detail, see Hampton & Wellman, 2003).

Although the high-speed internet connection and community-oriented message board helped residents increase their contact with local neighborhoods, it also helped them maintain relationships with friends and family who were more geographically distant. By virtue of being in a new neighborhood, Netville residents had left friends and family behind when they moved. Only the wired residents used the internet to maintain levels of contact with these friends and family that were similar to levels of contact before the move. Maintaining personal relationships that are both local and nonlocal is a social phenomenon that Hampton and Wellman (2002) referred to as "glocalization."

A study of two Israeli suburbs by found similar results, although not to the same extent. Although membership in neighbor-based mailing lists did not increase the total amount of neighborhood interaction, it did increase the number of people known in the community. As with the studies of online relationship formation, many people who first met on these mailing lists were likely to move their relationships offline and meet in person (Mesch & Levanon, 2003).

These findings indicate that internet-based email systems do have the potential to enhance neighborhood relationships. There may be two reasons why this is the case. First, of all the internet software offered to those in Netville, it was the email-based system that was used most often. Similarly, it was use of an email-based system in the Israeli study that led to an increased awareness of other neighbors. It is likely the familiarity of email software that helped lead to its widespread adoption in these communities. Second, these emailing lists were used because they offered the potential to fulfill instrumental purposes that would exist in any neighborhood. It was not the intrinsic appeal of an online world that lured these people to talk to their neighbors. It was the fact that these email lists supplement needs that were lacking in offline life. Again it is

apparent that online activity is best understood when considering needs that exist offline in the realm of everyday life.

Up to this point, we have drawn on a number of empirical studies to argue that the internet is not detracting from social relationships or radically altering the way people live their lives. The findings from these studies can be summarized as follows:

1. Internet use is not associated with decreases in time spent on social activities. Internet use is associated with relatively high levels of offline contact with friends, but not family.

2. Only a small percentage of internet users meet new people online. Relationships formed online rarely stay there.

3. Internet use has the potential to enhance neighborhood relationships.

The remainder of this chapter will use a theoretical position that explains these empirical findings by pointing to changes in the patterns of social relationships that have been occurring since the industrial revolution. This discussion uses Barry Wellman's theory of networked individualism, or what might also be named "individualized networking," in conjunction with the writings of Robert K. Merton (1957) and Rose Laub Coser (1975). Although more research is needed to verify the connection between networked individualism and the current body of empirical findings, the following discussion serves two purposes. First, it shows how accounting for social tendencies within modern life can help make sense of the current body of empirical findings. Second, it gives a theoretical direction to future projects that seek to explain how internet use fits within broader patterns of everyday life.

Toward a Theory of Networked Individualism

Wellman argues that since the industrial revolution, the rise of mass transit and telecommunication systems have allowed a shift in the nature of social relationships, especially in metropolitan centers where these kinds of systems tend to be more readily accessible. He argues that this shift, which he calls "networked individualism," has at least three important characteristics:

1. Relationships are both local and long distance.
2. Personal networks are sparsely knit but include densely knit groups.
3. Relationships are more easily formed and abandoned.

These three attributes are discussed in turn.

First, unlike the geographically limited small-town communities of preindustrial society, relationships in modern societies can be maintained over greater distance. Wellman first argued this point in his 1979 article "The Community Question," where he found evidence that a majority of the relationships maintained in an urban area of Toronto were with people who lived just outside of the neighborhood boundary. Contrary to common notions of community as being fixed to a particular locale, these urbanites maintained their own personal communities by traveling to make in-person visits and phoning to maintain contact between these visits. While it is true that neighborhood contact still exists, it only comprises a relatively small portion of a person's total social network.

Second, this and other studies indicated that relationships in contemporary societies are not with one particular group of densely knit individuals. Instead, many relationships are with multiple small groups or individuals. Many of these people will not know each other, or will only know of each other to a small extent. In this sense, every individual has her own personal community, because it is rare for two people to have exactly the same set of relationships. Even among married couples, husbands and wives will tend to know different sets of people at their workplaces and elsewhere.

Third, many relationships are transitory. The high divorce rate in industrialized countries indicates that even relationships people have vowed to maintain over the course of their lives often fall by the wayside. The transitory nature of relationships is even more evident among relationships that are not so strong. People will often form many sets of relationships throughout their lives, especially with career changes that have become common place in the current service-based economic system of First World countries. This issue is elaborated in greater detail later, when discussing Georg Simmel's (1903) theory of modern life.

We would like to further develop this theory of networked individualism by adding two more attributes:

4. Although homophily still exists, many relationships are with people from different social backgrounds.
5. Some social ties are strong, but many more are weak.

Georg Simmel (1903), Rose Laub Coser (1975), and Mark Granovetter (1973) all discussed these two important attributes of modern life. Simmel and Coser argued that interacting with people from different social backgrounds has become fundamental to life in contemporary societies. This is especially true for those who live in urban areas and those of high socioeconomic status. Having smooth interactions with people from these different backgrounds has become so important that people have developed an elaborate set of roles. Networked individuals use this knowledge when interacting with people from different social backgrounds. Because many of their contacts do not know each other, they are in fact switching between different social networks, accessing new ideas or information that are common to those groups. Second, many of these relationships tend to be weak, in the sense that they tend to lack high amounts of emotional intimacy and tend to be more temporary in nature. This has the advantage of allowing networked individuals to maintain relatively large social networks that allow them access to new ideas and information (Granovetter, 1973).

Having discussed the nature of networked individualism and developed it further, we revisit each of its five attributes and connect them to a general discussion about internet use. In doing so, we use this theory to interpret the empirical research that was summarized earlier and use theoretical conjecture when the research fails to address particular points of interest. Throughout this discussion, we focus on email use, because it is the most common of internet activities among American users (Pew, 2004) and the focus of many of the studies discussed in this chapter.

MAINTAINING LOCAL AND LONG DISTANCE RELATIONSHIPS

The connection between the widespread adoption of the internet and the rise of geographically dispersed relationships is fairly straightforward. As many scholars made clear, internet communication need not be limited by physical constraint. It is possible to communicate to anyone who has access to a computer and internet connection, anywhere in the world. Yet people do not always use the internet to communicate with others on the other side of the world. As the empirical research we have reviewed indicates, much of the communication that takes place on the internet is with people who are known offline. This is not surprising when considering that a majority of social relationships are with people who are close enough to have in-person contact, but just distant enough that they are not seen unless special trips are made. The ability to send messages quickly to people who are at least somewhat distant is likely why people use CMC (computer mediated communication) with their friends and family. This supports Shklovski et al.'s (in press) argument that internet users may experience increased amounts of offline contact because they are using email to arrange in-person meetings and strengthen relationships with people known offline. Moreover, the importance of the internet in maintaining relationships that are physically distant was also found in the Netville project described earlier. In this project it was found that the internet was used to maintain both local and nonlocal relationships.

SPARSELY AND DENSELY KNIT NETWORKS

The sorts of communication afforded by CMC can be useful in maintaining a network that is sparsely knit. As CMC is often carried out as one-on-one exchange, it is particularly conducive to maintaining relationships with people who do not know each other. Unlike in-person communication that sometimes leads to contact between different network members by virtue of inhabiting a common space, the direct and autonomous nature of CMC allows for the maintenance of multiple relationships with people who need not even be aware of each other's existence. At the same time, email affords the ability to broadcast single messages to large groups of people. This often makes the coordination of group events and interactions much easier.

Although many relationships are often formed with people who have mutual friends, the internet also affords the formation of relationships between those who do not share common social relationships. Although people in societies that are traditionally composed of tightly bounded groups might disapprove of forming relationships with others who share no common social connection, this behavior might be more acceptable in societies composed of loosely knit networks. Even if people do disapprove of forming relationships online, it is more difficult for them to enforce these sanctions because it is in tightly bounded groups where social disapproval often leads to complete withdrawal of all social relationships. Not surprisingly, the formation of online relationships and the ability to communicate individually makes internet use particularly conducive to the loosely bounded networks of networked individuals.

MAKING AND BREAKING RELATIONSHIPS

The transitory nature of many relationships implies that social relationships are not only being lost, they are also being formed. High turnover creates a demand for the internet as a means both to form new relationships and to build on existing relationships. For example, Hampton and Wellman (2002) found that people moving to a suburb used the internet to maintain ties with former neighbors. As the research discussed earlier indicates, the internet is being used for both purposes, although more often for the latter. Although online forums are not particularly common ways to meet new people, they nevertheless aid those who might have trouble forming relationships by typical means offline. For the rest of the population, internet use provides a way to maintain new relationships by "keeping in touch" and arranging times to meet in person. The Netville project also indicates that the internet can be used to form new relationships among neighbors. Moreover, we theorize that CMC might also be particularly useful in ending relationships because it may be emotionally easier to ignore email messages than to ignore people in face-to-face situations.

SWITCHING BETWEEN RELATIONSHIPS

Email is a "lean" medium in that it does not allow for visual or auditory cues that convey emotion. For example, unlike in-person conversations, email does not allow for the communication of emotion through facial expression or tone of voice. This is not to say that email does not allow for the exchange of any emotion, but rather that there are few cues available for self-expression. Because email is a lean medium, it provides an easy avenue for communication with people from diverse social backgrounds. As argued earlier, communicating with people from different backgrounds often requires the ability to orient one's behavior toward an appropriate role. Although email may require orientation, such as appropriate language use, it does not include the many social cues that are communicated through body language and appearance. This is not to say that people who are heavy internet communicators do not have the ability to take on appropriate roles, but rather that communication by email minimizes the effort required to take on such roles. This makes it less time-consuming and cognitively less draining to maintain social ties by way of short text-based online interactions. Of course, as the research herein suggests, networked individuals also would like to see their network members in person from time to time, but email helps minimize the effort needed to maintain these diverse social ties.

STRONG AND WEAK TIES

There are at least two ways that CMC affords the maintenance of strong and weak tie relationships. First, CMC allows people to arrange in-person meetings, sometimes more conveniently than by telephone. The most prevalent form of CMC, email, is asynchronous, meaning that both parties do not need to be engaged in the communication process at the same time. An email can be sent off at a time that is convenient and without fear of disrupting the activity of the receiver. This is useful in strong tie relationships because it allows for asynchronous coordination of everyday activities, such as shopping. For example, instead of interrupting a spouse at work, a short email can be sent asking him or her to pick up some milk on the way home from work. The asynchronous nature of email also affords the opportunity to contact weak ties in a way that is not intrusive or disruptive. Moreover, it allows them to send detailed messages asynchronously in a way that could not be done simply by leaving telephone messages.

CMC's second advantage to maintaining weak tie relationships is the way that it allows people to keep in touch. Both email and instant messaging allow individuals the opportunity to send short messages quickly to those whom they do not see on a regular basis. This makes CMC especially useful, because weak ties are not often seen frequently in person. These messages may not contain immediately useful information, but they do serve to promote the feeling that the relationship still exists. This increases the likelihood that people will meet with each other in person at future dates. The very act of sending a short message is a reminder that they are still part of someone's social world.

Conclusions

Early writings about the internet's role in society often made assertions that were either extremely optimistic or extremely pessimistic. Both these groups of utopian and dystopian writers share a common assumption that the internet has the power to consume people, totally leading them to form completely new kinds of relationships. In doing so, these writers took a technologically deterministic approach that failed to consider the importance of relationships as they already existed. A growing body of scholarly research has begun to address this issue by providing evidence about the relationship between internet use and contact with friends and family, the extent to which the internet is used to form new relationships, and the internet's role in neighboring relations. Findings from these studies indicate that internet use is not associated with low levels of time spent with friends and family. Instead, internet use is associated with high levels of contact with friends. These studies also indicate that only a small minority of internet users actually meet new people online. When this does happen, these online relationships tend to migrate offline. Finally, the internet may be used to increase contact among neighbors, although this will often happen when there is a specific need to connect. All in all, these studies indicate that the internet is neither destroying nor radically enhancing society. Rather, the internet is adding to the overall volume of communication, helping to maintain the kinds of relationships that have existed for decades.

To help explain the workings of "everyday life," we have discussed and developed Wellman's theory of networked individualism. This theoretical position takes into consideration broad changes in social relationships that have occurred since the widespread adoption of mass transit and communication. It accounts for some of these empirical findings by making explicit five attributes of modern relationships, arguing that they tend to be physically distant, sparsely knit, transitory, socially diverse, and weak in strength. The internet use allows people to maintain networks that are physically distant, because it allows quick and cheap distant communication. The ability to communicate one-on-one makes it particularly useful for those who wish to maintain relationships in sparsely knit networks. The high turnover of transitory networks makes email particularly

convenient when maintaining new relationships and for dropping relationships when they go sour. Email's lack of social cues minimizes the effort required to adopt suitable roles, which is important to maintaining socially diverse relationships. Finally, email affords the ability to maintain larger networks of weak-tie relations, acting as a means to arrange in-person meetings and renew the existence of these relationships.

Although the existing body of scholarly research fits with the ideal type of the networked individual, much research is needed to verify this connection and address some outstanding issues. Similarly, although the findings of Kraut et al. (2002) indicate that internet use is not associated with depression among experienced users, more research is needed to address the psychological effects of networked individualism. Does the constant access to new and diverse people that the internet helps to facilitate really lead to overstimulation and disaffection, as suggested by Simmel (1903)? Or, is this internetaided lifestyle associated with cognitive flexibility, openness to new cultures, and perhaps social tolerance? Does the maintenance of weak ties through the use of email networks allow people to maintain larger networks, which in turn grant them access to new ideas, information, and other resources? Research questions come as abundantly to us as spam on email.

Acknowledgments

We have benefited from the advice of Shyon Baumann, Wenhong Chen, Bernie Hogan, Tracy Kennedy, and Janet Salaff. Our research has been supported by the Social Science Research Council of Canada (grant and fellowship) and Microsoft Research.

References

Anderson, B., & Tracey, K. (2001). Digital living: The impact (or otherwise) of the internet on everyday life. *American Behavioral Scientist, 45*, 456–475.

Barlow, J. P., Birkets, S., Kelly, K. & Slouka, M. (1995, August). What are we doing on-line? *Harper's*, pp. 35–46.

Bell, D., & Kennedy, B. M. (2000). *The cybercultures reader*. London: Routledge.

Bradner, E., Kellogg, W., & Erickson, T. (1999, April). Social affordances of BABBLE. Presented at the *CHI Conference*. Pittsburgh, PA.

Chayko, M. (2002). *Connecting: How we form social bonds and communities in the internet age*. Albany: State University of New York Press.

Coser, R. L. (1975). The complexity of roles as a seedbed of individual autonomy. In L. A. Coser (Ed.), *The idea of social structure: Papers in honor of Robert K. Merton* (pp. 237–263). New York: Harcourt Brace Jovanovich.

Daft, R. L., & Lengel, R. H. (1986). Organizational information requirements, media richness and structural design. *Management Science*, 32, 554–571.

Dery, M. (1997). *Escape velocity: Cyberculture at the end of the century*. New York: Grove Press.

de Kerckhove, D. (1997). *Connected intelligence: The arrival of the Web society*. Toronto: Somerville House.

Fallows, D. (2004). Spam is beginning to undermine the integrity of email and degrade life online. Pew Internet & American Life Project. Retrieved May 30, 2004, from http://www.pewinternet.org/pdfs/PIP_Spam_Report.pdf.

Fischer, C. (1992). *America calling: A social history of the telephone to 1940*. Berkeley: University of California Press.

Fish, R. S., Kraut, R. E., Root, R. W., & Rice, R. (1993). Video as a technology for informal communication. *Communications of the ACM*, 36, 48–61.

Franzen, A. (2000). Does the internet make us lonely? *European Sociological Review*, 16, 427–438.

Franzen, A. (2003). Social capital and the internet: Evidence from Swiss panel data. *Kyklos*, 53, 341–360.

Fu, S. J., Wang, R., & Qiu, Y. (2002). Daily activity and internet use in dual-earner families: A weekly time-diary approach. *IT and Society*, 1, 37–43.

Granovetter, M. (1973). The strength of weak ties. *American Journal of Sociology*, 78, 1360–1380.

Hampton, K., & Wellman, B. (2002). The not so global village of Netville. In B. Wellman & C. Haythornthwaite (Eds.), *The internet in everyday life* (pp. 345–371). Oxford, England: Blackwell.

Hampton, K., & Wellman, B. (2003). Neighboring in Netville: How the internet supports community and social capital in a wired suburb. *City and Community*, 2, 277–311.

Haythornthwaite, C., & Wellman, B. (1998). Work, friendship and media use for information exchange in a networked organization. *Journal of the American Society for Information Science*, 49, 1101–1114.

Katz, J., & Aspden, P. (1997). A nation of strangers? *Communications of the ACM*, 40, 81–86.

Katz, J. E., & Rice, R. E. (2002). *Social consequences of internet use: Access, involvement, and interaction*. Cambridge, MA: MIT Press.

Kendall, L. (2002). *Hanging out in the virtual pub: Masculinities and relationships online*. Berkeley: University of California Press.

Kling, R. (Ed.). (1996). *Computerization and controversy: Value conflicts and social choices* (2nd ed.). San Diego, CA: Academic Press.

Kraut, R., Kiesler, S., Boneva, B., Cummings, J., Helgeson, V., & Crawford, A. (2002). Internet paradox revisited. *Journal of Social Issues*, 58, 49–74.

Kraut, R., Patterson, M., Lundmark, V., Kiesler, S., Mukhopadhyay, T., & Scherlis, W. (1998). Internet paradox: A social technology that reduces social involvement and psychological well-being? *American Psychologist*, 53, 1017–1031.

Kraut, R. E., Kiesler, S., Boneva, B. & Shklovski, I. (in press). Examining the impact of Internet use on TV viewing: Details make a difference. In R. Kraut, M. Brynin, & S. Kiesler (Eds), *Domesticating Information Technology*. Oxford, England: Oxford University Press.

Kroker, A., & Weinstein, M. A. (1994). *Data trash: The theory of the virtual class*. New York: St. Martin's Press.

Markus, M. L., Bikson, T., El-Shinnawy, M., & Soe, L. (1992). Fragments of your communication: E-mail, v-mail, and fax. *The Information Society*, 8, 207–226.

McKenna, K. Y. A., Green, A. S., & Gleason, M. E. J. (2002). Relationship formation on the internet: What's the big attraction? *Journal of Social Issues*, 58, 9–31.

Merton, R. K. (1957). *Social theory and social structure*. New York: Free Press.

Mesch, G. S., & Levanon, Y. (2003). Community networking and locally-based social ties in two suburban localities. *City and Community*, 2, 335–351.

Nie, N. H., & Hillygus, D. S. (2002). Where does internet time come from?: A reconnaissance. *IT and Society*, 1, 1–20.

Parks, M. R., & Floyd, K. (1996). Making friends in cyberspace. *Journal of Communication*, 46, 80–97.

Pew. (2004). *Internet activities*. Retrieved July 17, 2004, from http://www.pewinternet.org/trends/Internet_Activities_4.23.04.htm.

Pronovost, G. (2002). The internet and time displacement: A Canadian perspective. *IT and Society*, 1, 44–52.

Quan-Haase, A., & Wellman, B. (2002). Capitalizing on the net: social contact, civic engagement, and sense of community. In B. Wellman & C. Haythornthwaite (Eds.), *The internet in everyday life* (pp. 291–324). Oxford, England: Blackwell.

Rheingold, H. (2000). *The virtual community* (rev. ed.). Cambridge, MA: MIT Press.

Robinson, J. P. (2002). Introduction to issue 2: IT, mass media and other Activity. *IT and Society*, 1, i–viii.

Robinson, J. P., Kestnbaum, M., Neustadtl, A., & Alvarez, A. (2002). Information technology and functional time displacement. *IT and Society*, 1, 21–36.

Shklovski, I., Kiesler, S., & Kraut, R. (in press). *The Internet and social interaction: A meta-analysis and critique of studies, 1995–2003*. In R. Kraut, M. Brynin, & S. Kiesler (Eds.), *Domesticating information technology*. Oxford, England: Oxford University Press.

Simmel, G. (1903). The metropolis and mental life. In K. Wolff (Ed.), *The sociology of Georg Simmel* (pp. 409–424). Glencoe, IL: Free Press.

Sproull, L., & Kiesler, S. (1991). *Connections*. Cambridge, MA: MIT Press.

Stoll, C. (1995). *Silicon snake oil: Second thoughts on the information highway*. New York: Doubleday.

Turkle, S. (1995). *Life on the screen: Identity in the age of the internet*. New York: Simon & Schuster.

Van Gelder, L. (1985, October). The strange case of the electronic lover. *Ms*, 94–104, 117–123.

Walther, J. (1997). Group and interpersonal effects in international computer-mediated collaboration. *Human Communication Research*, 23, 342–369.

Wellman, B. (1979). The community question: The intimate networks of East Yorkers. *American Journal of Sociology*, 84, 1201–1231.

Wellman, B., Carrington, P., & Hall, A. (1988). Networks as personal communities. In B. Wellman & S. D. Berkowitz (Eds.), *Social structures: A network approach* (pp. 130–184). Cambridge, England: Cambridge University Press.

Wellman, B., & Gulia, M. (1999). Net surfers don't ride alone: Virtual communities as communities. In B. Wellman (Ed.), *Networks in the global village* (pp. 331–366). Boulder, CO: Westview Press.

Wellman, B., & Tindall, D. (1993). Reach out and touch some bodies: How telephone networks connect social networks. *Progress in Communication Science*, 12, 63–94.

Part XI

MAINTENANCE AND REPAIR OF RELATIONSHIPS

CHAPTER 39

Maintaining Relationships

Daniel J. Canary
Marianne Dainton

Simple Question, Complex Answer

The question is simple: Why do some relationships succeed and others do not? However, the question defies a simple answer. One reason for this defiance concerns how *relational maintenance* as a rallying point for relationship scholars represents a relatively new enterprise; according to Perlman (2001), a focus on relationship maintenance did not emerge until the late 1980s. Although previous researchers included variables that referenced *maintenance*, the construct as a major domain of inquiry was not systematically examined until recently (Perlman, 2001). Since the 1980s, researchers who directly examined maintenance processes have discussed fundamental issues with regard to defining maintenance, explaining maintenance processes, and testing maintenance behaviors as both independent and dependent factors (see Dindia, 2000, for a review). In brief, the first generation of research on maintenance has established the nature, function, and scope of maintenance activities.

In this chapter, we describe the first generation of research that focuses on various processes directly related to the question of why some relationships succeed and others do not with an eye toward what should be done now as we embark on the second generation. Of course, many of the other chapters in this volume provide evidence, however implicitly, about relational maintenance. The chapters on satisfaction (Fincham & Beach, this volume) and commitment (Rusbult, Coolsen, Kirchner, & Clarke, this volume), for example, directly implicate maintenance processes. Other chapters, such as the chapters on social support (Sarason & Sarason, this volume) and temptation and jealousy (Buunk & Dijkstra, this volume), also suggest why some relationships might succeed and others fail.

Our chapter, however, focuses on the means by which people maintain their close, personal relationships. Specifically, in this chapter we address variations in the meaning of the term *maintenance*, as well as variations in the techniques used to maintain relationships (e.g., cognitively, systemically, through a larger social network, and through cultural prescription). We introduce two overarching perspectives associated with maintenance, the centrifugal perspective and the centripetal perspective, along with research and theory that illustrate these approaches. We then summarize what we know about factors that moderate relational maintenance, including factors internal and external to the relationship. Finally, we address implications of this first generation of research.

Defining Maintenance

Our first order of business is to identify what we mean by *maintenance*. Duck (1988) offered the first dedicated treatment of the various forms of maintenance. He argued that maintenance involves efforts to sustain the existence of a relationship, to keep a relationship from becoming more intimate, and to stabilize a relationship that has gone through tough times. Later, Dindia and Canary (1993) presented four definitions of relational maintenance. First, these authors suggested that maintenance can be conceived as the *process of keeping a relationship in existence*. This definition is most consistent with the notion of stability in the family sciences (e.g., Lewis & Spanier, 1979).

Second, Dindia and Canary argued that maintenance refers to the *process of keeping a relationship in a specified state or condition*. Accordingly, such a definition suggests that maintenance functions to sustain desired relational characteristics, such as intimacy, commitment, love, and so on. According to this definition, a relationship that is stable but lacks such important features represents a hollow shell.

Third, Dindia and Canary (1993) proposed that maintenance can be defined as the *process of keeping a relationship in satisfactory condition*. The usefulness of this definition is in its ability to differentiate between stability and quality. This sort of distinction is helpful when seeking to explain seeming anomalies such as stable, unhappy marriages (Heaton & Albrecht, 1991). The emphasis

of this definition is on global experience of satisfaction rather than with any specific qualitative characteristics.

Finally, Dindia and Canary (1993) proposed that maintenance references a *process of keeping a relationship in repair*. This definition includes two elements: preventative maintenance and fixing a relationship in disrepair. At first glance, these two efforts appear conceptually distinct, although Dindia and Baxter (1987) and later Dindia (1994) found that the strategies for maintenance and repair largely overlap.

A fifth definition of maintenance has emerged, and this concerns keeping a relationship *sustained*. Montgomery (1993) initially offered this term to reflect how couples manage dialectical tensions, for example, how partners respond to simultaneous needs for autonomy and connection. Her rationale was that the term maintenance implies an emphasis on the status quo as a fixed entity, a rationale that Rawlins (1994) shared.

Most authors appear to latch on to one of these definitions, suggesting a lack of consensus on the term. As Perlman (2001) observed, "There is disagreement over whether relational maintenance is designed to maintain the current level of intimacy or to either maintain or enhance that level" (p. 360). Still other scholars consider maintenance as a temporal stage – the period between relational development and dissolution (Stafford, 1994).

We do not view the term *maintenance* as reflecting stasis without change. Rather, we view maintenance as actions and activities in which partners engage to sustain desired relational properties, for example, how commitment or love might be promoted (e.g., Weigel & Ballard-Reisch, 1999). In our view, a focus on the means whereby partners maintain a relationship provides sufficient breadth because it allows scholars using different theoretical perspectives to focus on the same phenomenon. Moreover, the definition implies a focus on the interplay between people's goals for their close relationships and how they attempt to achieve those goals. For example, maintaining liking might be primary for some people, whereas maintaining commitment might be primary for other individuals. Given this definitional background, we turn our attention to the varying ways that scholars have examined maintenance processes in various contexts.

Maintenance in Context

Much of the research into relational maintenance has focused on specific techniques that relational partners can use to maintain their relationship. These techniques occur across various levels of hierarchy. Dainton (2003) argued that maintenance activity occurs in four contexts: the self (which references psychological or individual influences on the process), the system (which refers to behaviors enacted within the relational system), the network (which involves the influences of the larger community in which the system is embedded), and the culture (which references the historical patterns of ideas, beliefs, rules, and roles for that relational type). Because the terms *self* might imply the self concept literature for some readers, the *self context* has been relabeled here as the *cognitive context*. We briefly review each of these contexts.

The Cognitive Context

As indicated earlier, the cognitive context refers to the noninteractive processes that individuals enact for relational purposes. These processes most often take the form of cognitions. Acitelli (2001) argued that relationships can be maintained simply by thinking about them, or *attending* to them. For example, Rusbult, Drigotas, and Verette (1994) proposed that relationships can be maintained by partners engaging in various mental activities that accrue from being committed to one's partner (e.g., derogation of alternatives). We review these cognitions later. In a related vein, Murray, Holmes, and Griffin (1996) argued that idealizing one's partner works in a self-fulfilling way. Murray et al. found that highly idealized people remained in their relationships through times of trouble more than did people who were less idealized, and idealized

partners reported more increased satisfaction and decreased ambivalence with regard to their partner over a year's time.

Other scholars talk about the importance of particular cognitions during critical periods. Wilmot (1994), for example, argued that two ways to rejuvenate relationships are to *accept and forgive* and to *reassess the importance of the relationship*. Similarly, Roloff and Cloven (1994) suggested that cognitions can play a vital role when individuals are faced with a partner's relational transgression. They posited that individuals might use *reformulation*, wherein the individual changes the nature of his or her understanding of the relationship so that the act is no longer viewed as a transgression, *minimization*, which recasts the transgression so that it is no longer perceived as a threat, or *justification*, which involves a focus on the reasons for staying in the relationship. Using an empathic accuracy model, Simpson, Ickes, and Orina (2001) suggested that when the relationship is threatened, partners can use tactics to increase ambiguity and thereby minimize the perceived threat. Specifically, Simpson et al. suggested that partners can *not attend to, selectively attend to,* or *distort their interpretation* of what their partner is saying or doing. They also suggest that partners can *shift their attention* to irrelevant issues or *refuse to think* at all about the threat.

In sum, several scholars have identified specific thoughts that function to sustain a relationship. We turn our attention next to the behavioral level of maintenance.

The Relational System Context

The most frequent focus of maintenance research has been the identification of behaviors or interactions that relational partners can enact to sustain their relationship (Dindia, 2003). Numerous typologies of such behaviors exist (for a review, see Dindia, 1994). For instance, Stafford and Canary's (1991) initial research on the topic generated five positive and proactive maintenance strategies, which have become widely used (Dindia, 2000). *Positivity* refers to attempts to make interactions pleasant. These include acting nice and cheerful when one does not feel that way, performing favors for the partner, and withholding complaints. *Openness* involves direct discussion about the relationship, including talk about the history of the involvement, rules made, and personal disclosure. *Assurances* involve support of the partner, comforting the partner, and making one's commitment clear. *Social networks* refers to relying on friends and family to support the relationship (e.g., having dinner every Sunday at the in-laws). Finally, *sharing tasks* refers to doing one's fair share of household chores. Based on an inductive analysis, Canary, Stafford, Hause, and Wallace (1993) added five other strategies: *joint activities* (e.g., spend time together), *cards, letters, calls* (e.g., write emails, notes), *avoidance* (e.g., plan separate activities), *antisocial acts* (e.g., act moody), and *humor* (e.g., teasing each other).

An alternative typology is provided by Baxter and colleagues, who have used a dialectical approach to understand relational maintenance. To manage contradictory tensions, a dialectical approach suggests that relational partners might invoke one or more of eight strategies (Sahlstein & Baxter, 2001). These include *denial* (reject the existence of a tension), *disorientation* (partners ignore their abilities to manage tensions actively), *spiraling inversion* (partners respond to first one, then the other pole), *segmentation* (partitioning the relationship by topic or activity), *balance* (compromise is achieved by partially fulfilling the demands of each pole), *integration* (both poles are responded to simultaneously, as through rituals), *recalibration* (a temporary synthesis of the contradiction such that opposing forces are no longer viewed as opposite), and *reaffirmation* (a celebration of the stimulation that contradictory tensions provide).

Early on, Duck (1988) questioned the extent to which maintenance behaviors are intentionally enacted. This issue is central because it addresses whether maintenance as a process requires effort and planning or occurs as a by-product of relating. Dindia (2000) argued that three possible relationships link strategic and routine maintenance. First, some behaviors might start as strategies but over time become routine. Second, some behaviors might be performed primarily strategically by some people and primarily routinely by others. Finally, the same behavior might on some occasions be used strategically and on other occasions be used routinely by the same relational partner. Early evidence supports all three of the proposed links.

Moreover, Dainton and Aylor (2002) found that the same behaviors are used intentionally and unintentionally, with those routine behaviors (i.e., unintentionally) predicting slightly more of the variation in relational satisfaction and commitment than do the strategic enactment of maintenance. Dainton and Aylor (2002) speculated that maintenance might be performed routinely until something happens to disrupt the routine. At that point, relational partners might turn to strategic maintenance enactment. As such, routine maintenance might be used during times when preferred levels of satisfaction and commitment are experienced, and strategic maintenance might be enacted during times of perceived uncertainty.[1]

The research described thus far adopts an individualistic bent, focused on the cognitions of individuals and on how individuals might manage their relationships by enacting particular behaviors. The last two contexts, the network context and the cultural context, broaden our scope considerably. However, relatively little maintenance research has focused on these two contexts.

The Network Context

The network context recognizes that relationships are always embedded in larger networks of social relationships. Few studies have directly assessed how social networks inhibit or facilitate relational maintenance (but see Allan, this volume).

Scholars have recognized that social networks play an important role in the *stability* of romantic relationships (Attridge, 1994). Klein and Milardo (2000), for example, studied how third parties influence couple conflict. Among other findings, Klein and Milardo found that women's contentiousness and men's lack of accommodation were positively linked to whether the women and men had support from their different social networks. Also, Felmlee, Sprecher, and Bassin (1990) found that a lack of support from social networks accelerates the time taken to separate from one's partner.

Felmlee (2001) noted that social networks can facilitate *or* inhibit the stability of dating relationships. She found that the perceptions of the partner's parental support and friendship support promoted relational stability but that one's own parental support did not add to relational stability. Rather, a combination of friendship support and disapproval from one's own parents facilitated relational stability. Felmlee offered two alternative explanations for the Romeo and Juliet effect that she found (as have others): (a) individuals engage in psychological reactance when a parent disapproves of the relationship (i.e., Brehm, 1966), and (b) parental disapproval "encourages couples to confront and resolve potential relationship problems raised by family members, and that this interactive process strengthens the relationship" (Felmlee, 2001, p. 1280). In addition, the *perception* of support from friends appears to be more critical than is the friends' actual support (Felmlee, 2001).

A handful of studies have examined how people *use* their social networks as resources to sustain their close relationships. This issue is different from noting how social networks affect the stability of relationships. For instance, Stafford and Canary (1991) found that purposefully relying on one's friends and family for relational support is positively associated with liking the partner, with commitment, and with satisfaction. This finding has been replicated (e.g., Canary & Stafford, 1992, 2001). Their measure of support is rather global and includes items such as "[My partner] showed s/he was willing to do things with my friends or family" and "[My partner] included our friends or family in our activities." More research is needed to specify the range of behaviors in which people engage to enlist their friends and families to support their romantic relationships.

In addition, relationships vary in their need for network support. For example, Haas (2003) and Gaines and Agnew (2003) argued that a lack of societal support for gay and lesbian relationships and for intercultural relationships makes network support even more important for people in these relationships. Likewise, Felmlee et al. (1990) found that ethnic differences accelerate the rate of dissolution for romantic partners. One question that arises from this research concerns the strategies that people in nonnormative relationships can use to secure support from their social network.

The Cultural Context

Cultures include values and beliefs about relationships, as well as rules for enacting them (Smith, 1966). Accordingly, cultures have a profound impact on how and why relationships might be maintained (Goodwin & Pillay, this volume). Despite the importance of culture in understanding relationships, few scholars have studied the impact of culture on relational maintenance behaviors. Indeed, much of the research has focused on White, middle-class romantic relationships in the United States, so much so that Stafford (2003) questioned whether what we have learned thus far about maintenance might in fact be merely uncovering a cultural ideology about relationship enactment.

There are exceptions. As indicated above, Yum and Canary (2003) studied relational maintenance in Korea compared with that in the United States. They found that for Korean participants, cultural rules for maintenance were more important than maintenance behaviors. For example, one cultural rule is *eui-ri*, which refers to the extent one is expected to be attached and loyal to one's husband and wife. For instance, practicing *eui-ri* requires one not to have sexual intercourse before marriage. Consistent with these observations, Yum (2003; Yum & Canary, 1997) found that U.S. participants engaged in a higher frequency of maintenance behaviors and that maintenance behaviors were stronger predictors of important relational characteristics for the U.S. versus Korean samples. Also, Ballard-Reisch, Weigel, and Zaguidoulline (2003) found that beliefs about marriage in Russia influence maintenance efforts because these cultural beliefs imply that systemic relationship maintenance is not necessary. Again, these findings are understood within the culture's own historical development with regard to marriage.

Using an understanding of culture that is based in ethnicity, Gaines and colleagues studied relationships in which the partners represent different ethnic cultures (Gaines & Agnew, 2003). Using Rusbult's investment model as a theoretic frame (discussed later), these authors suggested that the lower relational stability among intercultural couples can be traced to a larger number of perceived alternatives than those in intracultural relationships, and a decreased amount of social support.

Perspectives on Maintenance

One of the more compelling questions regarding maintenance concerns whether relationships remain stable unless some event disrupts them or whether relationships are inherently unstable and people must expend energies to keep them intact. The view that relationships are inherently stable reflects a *centripetal* analogue, whereas the view that people must work to stay together represents a *centrifugal* analogue (Duck, 1988). Of course, the answer to the question regarding which approach appears more accurate defies an absolute answer. Indeed, the universe of relationships are composed of many forces, some of which are centripetal and some of which are centrifugal.

Centripetal Analogues

One popular axiom is that relationships are easy to get into and hard to get out of, and evidence exists to support this axiom.

Attridge (1994) reviewed various "barriers" to dissolving romantic relationships, including reviews of the following: Levinger's (1965) use of the term; Michael Johnson's model of personal, structural, and moral commitment; Rusbult's investment model; and Lund's barrier model. Attridge noted that both internal and external barriers prevent people from treating marriages like blind dates and that smart relational partners would make use of barriers to keep their relationships intact (e.g., remind the partner of religious premises of marriage).

In terms of internal barriers that Attridge (1994) reviewed, the first is commitment. His sense of commitment reflects a moral obligation to keeping one's vows. Next, one's religious beliefs regarding the sanctity of marriage compel people to remain. Also, one's self-identity – that is, viewing oneself in terms of the relationship – acts as a barrier to dissolution. Next, irretrievable personal investments (such as spending time with the partner) work against dissolution. Finally, Attridge argued that the presence of children acted as an internal barrier, especially for women; women who have children are more likely to remain in a marriage than are women without children.

In terms of external barriers, Attridge (1994) cited several. Not surprisingly, these include legal barriers, financial obligations, and social networks that promote the bond. In addition to these, we would add a perception of a lack of alternatives. Both Rusbult and Johnson's models indicate that having no perceived alternatives increases one's commitment to the partner. Both Johnson (2001) and Rusbult and Martz (1995) have shown that abused women remain in these marriages because they perceive that they have no alternative associations or resources that they can leverage to leave their unhappy state. Conversely, Heaton and Albrecht (1991) found that "social contact – whether having potential sources of help, receiving help, or spending social and recreational time away from home – is positively associated with instability" (p. 755; that is, the likelihood that an unsatisfying relationship will terminate).

Referring to more garden-variety experiences, Duck (1994) argued that partners remain together because they establish a rhetorical vision of their relationship that carries them into the future. This vision is created and re-created through mundane interaction. Duck (1994) summarized his view accordingly:

> Thus, in the seemingly trivial talk that bombards us daily, people are signifying the essence of their relationships with each other and doing so because they share enough understanding of one another to make this mutual interpretation possible. Everyday talk continues relationships because it continues to embody partners' understanding or shared meaning, and it continues to represent their relationship to one another in ways that each accepts and is comfortable with, or which "ratify" the relationship. (p. 54)[2]

In Duck's view, then, people do not calculate the rewards and costs in the creation of their interdependence. Relationships are built through and by interaction. In this manner, they obtain momentum for continuing, and some event must occur to tear them apart.

Centrifugal Analogues

Clearly, we have adopted the position that people must expend efforts in order to maintain their relationships. For example, Canary and Stafford (1993) stated, "It is naïve to assume that people continue in their relationships until they happen to fall apart; it appears that something more than momentum keeps dyads bonded" (p. 240). As indicated, we emphasize the sustenance of fundamental relational qualities, such as commitment, liking, love, and control mutuality (i.e., the extent to which the partners agree on who has rightful influence power). Relationships that lack these and similar features are nominal relationships.

Consistent with research that examines marital stability more generally, we view communication behaviors as initial forces that affect relationships, and marriage in particular (e.g., Gottman & Levenson, 2000; Huston, Caughlin, Houts, Smith, & George,

2001). In this vein, relational characteristics represent *outcomes* of maintenance activities. The effect sizes of the five maintenance strategies initially reported by Stafford and Canary (1991) on fundamental characteristics have been rather large, ranging from 10% to 80% (e.g., Canary & Stafford, 1992; Weigel & Ballard-Reisch, 1999). Also, research shows that maintenance strategies provide the bases for increases in intimacy (Guerrero, Eloy, & Wabnik, 1993). That is, the use of maintenance behaviors helps dating partners develop their involvements. Moreover, people who do not engage in maintenance behaviors are more likely to de-escalate or terminate their relationships (Guerrero et al., 1993). Furthermore, the research shows that these maintenance strategies have different functional utility. For example, commitment to one's partner is most strongly predicted by use of assurances, whereas liking the partner is most strongly predicted by positivity (Canary & Stafford, 1994).

Yet the functional utility of maintenance behaviors does not endure for long. In other words, the half-life of maintenance behaviors is brief. Canary, Stafford, and Semic (2002) conducted a panel study examining married partners' maintenance activity and relational characteristics (liking, commitment, and control mutuality) at three points in time, each a month apart. They found that maintenance behaviors are strongly associated with relational characteristics concurrently, but that the effects completely fade within a month's time (when controlling for the previous months' reports). Thus, it appears that maintenance strategies must be used continuously if they are to sustain desired relational characteristics. Being positive, assuring the partner of one's love and commitment, sharing tasks, and so forth represent proactive relational behaviors to be sure, but they must be enacted on a regular basis to matter.

Theoretic Examples

To illustrate how theories might reflect the centripetal and centrifugal views, we highlight two theoretical approaches to maintenance. Both fall within the social exchange camp: Rusbult's investment model and our own application of equity theory. In our view, Rusbult's model elaborates on processes that represent centripetal forces because it highlights features of the relationship that promote continued commitment and maintenance activities are seen as products of that commitment.[3]

This model begins with interdependence theory (Kelley, 1979; Kelley & Thibaut, 1978). More specifically, Rusbult adopted Kelley and Thibaut's ideas that stable and satisfying relationships occur when the partner compares favorably to one's ideal and to alternatives. Rusbult adds a third component that represents the *investments* one has in the relationship (e.g., time, effort expended). These three factors predict commitment, which reflects a personal desire to remain in the relationship indefinitely. Rusbult et al. (1994) argued that commitment is *macromotive*. That is, commitment filters the link between the three initial factors and maintenance activities, and the extent of commitment dictates whether someone engages in relational maintenance.

Rusbult et al. (1994) described several kinds of cognitions that serve to maintain a relationship. The first is *deciding to remain* in the relationship, which obviously reflects the extent to which a person is committed. Next, *perceived relational superiority* refers to the idealistic belief that one's relationship is better than other relationships. Next, Rusbult et al. (1994) noted that *derogation of alternatives* serves maintenance functions by devaluating potential alternatives. Rusbult et al. also noted that committed individuals would have a *willingness to sacrifice* self-interests for the good of the relationship (see Rusbult et al., this volume). Similarly, Rusbult and Buunk (1993) suggested that *managing jealousy and extrarelational involvements* serve maintenance functions (see also Buunk & Dijkstra, this volume).

Finally, Rusbult (1987) identified variations in the way that people respond to their partners during troubled times. These *tendencies to accommodate* reflect two dimensions: passive versus active and constructive versus destructive. *Exit* is an active and destructive behavior that includes threats to leave the partner; *voice* is an active and constructive strategy that involves discussing the problem without hostility; *Loyalty* is a passive and constructive approach that involves giving in to the partner; and *Neglect* is a passive and destructive approach that includes passive–aggressive reactions. Several studies have shown that committed individuals are more likely to engage in the more civil forms of accommodation – *voice* and *loyalty* – and that these behaviors have a more positive associations than do *neglect* or *exit* with relational quality.

Moreover, tendencies to accommodate the partner are affected by features that constitute commitment (Rusbult, 1987). For instance, the use of voice most likely occurs when satisfaction, investment, and alternatives are high, whereas loyalty is the preferred response in relationships marked by high satisfaction and investment but low alternatives. Moreover, individual differences are theoretically mediated by the relational factors of satisfaction, investment, and availability of alternatives (Rusbult, Verette, Whitney, Slovik, & Lipkus, 1991, p. 57). For instance, perspective-taking (i.e., understanding one's partner from his or her perspective) is said to increase positive accommodation behaviors to the extent that it also links positively to satisfaction and investments (or negatively associates with viable alternatives; Rusbult et al., 1991). Tests of Rusbult's model have largely endorsed its basic tenets, as reported elsewhere (Canary & Zelley, 2000). Whereas Rusbult's investment model indicates that maintenance activities are the products of commitment, the following model holds that commitment and other relational features are the products of maintenance activities.

EQUITY THEORY

We have been part of a program of research that has applied equity theory propositions to understand why people use maintenance behaviors. In brief, equitable treatment leads to the use of maintenance strategies, and maintenance behaviors then bring about relational characteristics. In this sense, we have adopted a centrifugal perspective.

Equity is based on the *principle of distributive justice*, which holds that rewards should be distributed according to who provides the most inputs into the dyadic or group system (Deutsch, 1985). Equitable relationships exist when the ratios of outcomes to inputs are the same for both partners. However, when one person has a greater outcome–input ratio than his or her partner, that person is *overbenefited*; when one experiences a lower outcome–input ratio when compared with the partner, then one is *underbenefited*.

Consistent with other social exchange approaches, equity theory holds that people attempt to maximize their rewards and reduce their costs. Equity theory holds that people seek rewards in a fair manner and they attempt to restore equity when the balance of rewards and costs has become inequitable (for reviews, see Hatfield, Traupmann, Sprecher, Utne, & Hay, 1985; Van Yperen & Buunk, 1990). For example, a person can withhold inputs (e.g., not do household chores, not be positive or assuring) or they can persuade their partner to do more (e.g., cook more, be more positive). Or the partner can engage in more radical forms of equity restoration (e.g., punish the partner, leave the field).

Equity theory suggests that people who feel equitably treated engage in and perceive their partner's maintenance strategies more than do people who perceive that they are overbenefited or underbenefited. Research applying equity theory to the realm of maintenance has largely supported these predictions (Canary & Stafford 1992, 1993, 2001; Messman, Canary, & Hause, 2000; Vogl-Bauer, Kalbfleisch, & Beatty, 1999). For example, in Canary and Stafford (1992), wife assessments of equity predicted both wife and husband reports of partners' *positivity, openness, assurances*, and *social networks*; husband asssessments of equity affected perceptions of the partner *sharing tasks,*

positivity, and *assurances*.[4] In a word, people decide to engage in maintenance behaviors because of their levels of satisfaction and equity. In turn, maintenance behaviors act as forces to sustain desired relational characteristics, such as commitment.

Moderating Factors

More than a decade ago, Duck (1994) used the analogy of car ownership for understanding the process of relational maintenance. To keep an automobile running, he said, one has to service the vehicle appropriately, doing both preventative maintenance as well as prompt repairs. The point was to differentiate between the everyday, routine activities that can sustain a relationship and the conscious and strategic efforts that are less frequent yet more memorable to the relational partners.

To build on Duck's analogy a bit further, if we really want to use the metaphor of relational maintenance as car ownership, we also have to consider a number of other factors. For example, one should consider *differences in maintaining various types* of vehicles (maintaining a classic '57 Chevy is different from maintaining a 2004 BMW), *how personal preferences influence maintenance* (are you the type of person who thinks about oil changes before or after the warning light comes on?), *what happens when you are dealing with other people on the road* (you stopped for the light but the person behind you didn't – crunch!), *what happens over time* (will you still love your car after it loses the "new car smell?"), and finally, *how culture affects maintenance* (a taxi ride in London is quite different from a taxi ride in St. Martin, thanks in part to variations in vehicle maintenance). The next section discusses each of the aforementioned issues: maintenance in different relational types, individual factors that moderate maintenance processes, and external factors that influence maintenance.

Relational Type

Fitzpatrick identified three pure relational types (where both husband and wife agree on their relational schemata): *traditional*, which involves conventional beliefs about relationships, high interdependence of relational partners, and moderate amounts of conflict over important issues; *independent*, which involves nonconventional beliefs about relationships, moderate interdependence, and much conflict; and *separate*, which involves conventional beliefs but little interdependence and conflict (Fitzpatrick, 1988a; see also VanLear, Koerner, and Allen, this volume).

Gottman (1994) reported similar couple types based on observational analyses (pp. 158–211). Gottman discovered two types of conflict engagers. The first includes the *validating* couple, which tends initially to minimize conflict through validating each other, increase disagreement, but then appear to resolve differences. He equated validating couples to Fitzpatrick's traditional type. The second is the *volatile* couple, which maintains a high level of disagreement and criticism throughout the conversation. Gottman equated volatile couples to Fitpatrick's independent type. One type of nonengaged couple was found – the *avoiders*. As implied in the term, the avoiders do not want to discuss conflict directly and they minimize disagreement. Avoiders were seen as similar to Fitzpatrick's separate type. Other research generally supports these equations; that is, couple types vary in their conflict tactics in ways that are consistent with Gottman's speculation (e.g., Burggraf & Sillars, 1987; Fitzpatrick, 1988b).

Some evidence shows that when the husband and the wife do not agree on their relational schemata (i.e., the couple is classified as "mixed"), relational disruption ensues. For example, the most common mixed type involves a separate male and a traditional female. Research has shown that men and women in this relationship respond to each other stereotypically (e.g., men do not disclose and women seek disclosure), and they disagree on how interdependent they should be (Fitzpatrick & Best, 1979; Fitzpatrick, Vance, & Witteman, 1984). The implication is that regardless of their reported satisfaction, neither person will enact the behaviors that maintain the relationship as the partner wants it to be, because both people adopt different schemata for what the relationship should entail. Gottman (1994) speculated that one reason people adopt a particular type is to match their own preferred modes of emotional expression. An important relational maintenance strategy, then, would occur at the beginning of any involvement – assess the other person's view of what a long-term relationship should entail.

In a study that directly examined maintenance behaviors across relational types, Weigel and Ballard-Reisch (1999) found that four maintenance activities were differentially enacted based on couple type: Traditional and Independent couples reported greater use of openness and assurances than did separate couples; traditional couples reported greater use of sharing tasks than did either independent or separate couples; and traditional couples also reported greater use of shared network than did separate couples. Dainton and Stafford (2000) also found that couple type contributed to the prediction of maintenance enactment, although in this study, couple type did not account for as much variability in maintenance enactment as did reciprocity.

Besides different types of marriages, people maintain other kinds of relationships – parent, friend, lover, colleague, and so on. (for a review of maintenance in various kinds of relationships, see Canary & Dainton, 2003). It makes sense that the processes associated with the maintenance of these different relational forms would vary because each of these relational types serve different functions (Burleson & Samter, 1994). However, few studies have compared directly how maintenance is achieved in different types of relationships. One exception is Canary et al. (1993), who compared the frequency of maintenance behaviors identified for the romantic, friendship, family, and coworker contexts. They found that several behaviors (positivity, openness, and assurances) were nominated more frequently in romantic relationships than in friendships, and that others (assurances, sharing tasks, and cards, letters, calls) were described more frequently in family relationships than in friendships.

The study of the maintenance of close relationships other than romantic involvements remains in its infancy. A focus on the maintenance of friendship is relatively new, for example, with focus being placed on the identification of friendship maintenance behaviors (e.g., Dainton, Zelley, & Langan, 2003), motives associated with maintaining cross-sex relationships as platonic (e.g., Messman et al., 2000), and dialectical tensions associated with managing friendships (e.g., Rawlins, 1994). Current interest has also focused on the maintenance of family relationships (e.g., Vogl-Bauer et al., 1999) and, intriguingly, on the maintenance of undesired relationships (e.g., Hess, 2003).

Individual Factors: Attachment and Sex

Not only does the type of relationship affect relational maintenance, but the type of people involved in the relationship also affects maintenance. This section focuses on three individual factors that have garnered attention in the maintenance field. Note that the treatment of these topics is intentionally brief; additional information about attachment and sex is available in other chapters in this volume. Other factors, such as personality (the Big Five; locus of control, etc.), are probably linked to maintenance activities as well.

Turning to attachment, and despite the boom of research using attachment theory explanations, little published research has clearly connected attachment to maintenance (Shaver & Mikulincer, this volume). To our knowledge, only two studies have empirically made this link. Simon and Baxter (1993) found that securely attached individuals (vs. people in other attachment groups) in romantic relationships used more prosocial maintenance behaviors but no difference occurred among attachment groups in the use of antisocial behaviors. Bippus and Rollin (2003) replicated their findings using a sample of people reporting on friendships. Despite the dearth of empirical investigation, we believe that attachment theory provides a powerful theoretical lens for the study of maintenance processes.

Finally, sex (as well as gender) has been studied by scholars interested in relational maintenance (see also Impett & Peplau, this volume). Most of the research has reported that women (vs. men) use more relational maintenance behavior, specifically openness and sharing tasks (e.g., Canary & Stafford, 1992, 1994; Dainton & Stafford, 1993; Ragsdale, 1996). However, other research shows that men use more maintenance behaviors (Stafford & Canary, 1991), and one study found a disordinal interaction between sex and strategy type (i.e., although women rely more on openness and sharing tasks, men rely somewhat more on positivity and assurances, Canary et al., 2002). Also, the effect sizes of such research are typically small (Dindia, 1998).

To determine whether differences are really due to biological sex, or whether gender might play an important role, Stafford, Dainton, and Haas (2000) ran a series of regressions using sex and gender (femininity and masculinity) as the predictor variables, and the use of maintenance behaviors as the independent variables. They found that gender was a superior predictor than sex. Specifically, femininity was the primary predictor of every maintenance behavior, with sex appearing in only two of the seven equations. Similar results for sex versus gender were reported by Rusbult et al. (1991).

External Factors: Networks, Culture, and Time

Earlier in this chapter, we discussed how social networks and the larger culture might influence relational maintenance. We do not repeat that information here, other than to acknowledge again the importance of recognizing that relationships are embedded within a network of relationships and are influenced by larger cultural prescriptions for relationships.

We look at the impact of time developmentally. For example, a longstanding assumption is that in established relationships much communication involves taken-for-granted presumptions and expec-tations, and "habits of adjustment to the other person become perfected and require less participation of the consciousness" (Waller, 1951, p. 311). This would imply that over time maintenance would be achieved routinely rather than strategically. Indeed, Sillars and Wilmot (1989) discussed the like-lihood that the longer a couple is together their interactions become more routine and their communication becomes less explicit. Research supports these presuppositions. For example, Dindia and Baxter (1987) found that the longer a couple was mar-ried the fewer strategies they used iden-tified as part of their maintenance reper-toire. Using different methods, Dainton and Aylor (2002) found that the use of strate-gic maintenance was negatively associated with relational length and that the use of routine maintenance was positively associ-ated with relational length. However, other research reports more subtle differences. In a cross-sectional study, Stafford and Canary (1991) found that married, engaged, and seri-ously dating partners more likely engaged in assurances and sharing tasks than did people who were casually dating. Also, engaged cou-ples and seriously dating couples reported more openness and positivity than did mar-ried people. Clearly, the image presented by these findings requires clarification in future studies.

Conclusions

Although the systematic study of relational maintenance constitutes a relatively new area of inquiry for personal relationship scholars, the amount of energy expended on the topic over the past 15 years has yielded important insights into the question regard-ing why some couples succeed and oth-ers fail. Debate over definitional issues and whether momentum works for or against relational health has prompted scholars to clarify their assumptions regarding mainte-nance processes. In addition, researchers are now turning their attention to maintenance processes in contexts other than U.S. het-erosexual romantic involvements (Canary &

Dainton, 2003). In these senses, the first gen-eration of *maintenance* research is giving way to the second generation, and some conclu-sions might be drawn regarding our under-standing of maintenance processes.

First, *maintenance as an activity probably involves all four uses of the term* that Dindia and Canary (1993) reviewed. In the world of real people, to maintain a relationship surely involves keeping it stable, achieving partic-ular characteristics (e.g., liking and commit-ment), achieving satisfaction, and repairing it when problems occur (and they certainly will). Naturally, scholarly definitions have relevance-determining aspects that help to guide research. Yet we need to realize that over the course of a long-term relation-ship, different forms of maintenance must be used. Such adaptation likely helps cou-ple success. In addition, these definitions are *not* mutually exclusive.

For instance, and in the face of our own defi-nition, we assume that stability constitutes a necessary feature of relational maintenance (Dindia, 2001). The idea of maintaining a relationship that no longer exists might be defensible and the notion that terminating a relationship to salvage it might be thinkable, but in our view such concepts stretch the boundaries of the maintenance construct. That is, one might engage in individual main-tenance activities (e.g., derogation of alter-natives), but if one's partner is not there then the exercise reflects an unreal world.

Our observation that different forms of maintenance are required in the same rela-tionship is not new (Duck, 1988). It is pos-sible that a developmental purpose under-lies the use of various forms of maintenance. That is, once a sense of stability (in terms of interdependence) is established, then part-ners hone their relational definitions (to make their relationships as they want them) and become sensitive to how satisfied they are. When problems arise, they repair their close relationships. If no repair occurs, then satisfaction diminishes, and partners assess what must be done to define their rela-tionships again. Failing that, stability might be in jeopardy. This general developmental pattern of maintenance is highly specula-tive and monolithic. Of course, we believe that variations on the general theme exists (e.g., maintenance forms and related behaviors overlap) and that more critical thinking on the topic is needed.

Second, *the examination of various contexts shows that maintenance occurs at multiple levels – the self, the dyadic system, the network, and the culture.* Researchers have presented fascinating material regarding how people change their thinking to maintain their personal relationships (e.g., idealizing their partner) and how people use various maintenance behaviors to sustain desired relational characteristics. We know much less about how people *use* social networks and how cultures function to promote or demote maintenance of relationships. In particular, theoretical models that show why social networks are critically important to relational stability would help researchers target specific relationally promoting and demoting behaviors.

Unearthing the assumptions that cultures contain about relationships is a more difficult enterprise. The existing research suggests that some norms are quite powerful, whereas other cultural norms are less so (Yum, 2003; Yum & Canary, 2003). Not only do cultural norms differ in their normative force, they also vary qualitatively in reflecting various historical, political, and religious bases. More effort is needed to unearth the manner in which cultures act as a canvas for people's relational constructions.

Third, it appears clear that *relationships are maintained through both types of forces – centripetal and centrifugal.* Adopting one approach over the other appears to us as both necessary and naïve. Again, one must adopt a perspective to do good research. At the same time, in the world of real people, both types of forces function to maintain relationships. We proffer an initial attempt to synthesize these approaches.

The centripetal factors and behaviors appear to work more directly on relational stability, whereas the centrifugal forces and behaviors appear to work more directly on defining and sustaining the feature characteristics of the relationship (e.g., commitment, liking, control mutuality). Another way of saying this is that some products of

relating include the creation of a rhetorical vision for the future, economic dependence and interdependence, one's personal identity, and other important elements (e.g., children). These products also act as constraints or barriers to dissolution (Attridge, 1994), and they require little strategic effort to make them salient.

Relationships with barriers are probably stable, but they do not necessarily contain characteristics that demarcate a high-quality relationship. To ensure the continuation of such qualities, one needs to engage in individual and relational strategies that help create and sustain liking, love, commitment, and so forth. That is, one must engage in proactive and positive behaviors to countermand centrifugal forces pulling down perceptions of one's likeability, lovingness, commitment, and so forth. Telling your partner that you love him or her once a month does little to assure your partner of your commitment. Likewise, acting positive only on the weekends probably does little to sustain impressions that one is likeable.

As the reader can ascertain, the answer to the question posed at the beginning of this chapter requires scholars to look within and between definitions, contexts, and approaches. The answer to what makes some relationships successful and others not resides in the ability to understand that the differences among approaches do not disqualify what each brings to the discussion. Indeed, it appears that the first generation of maintenance research has provided various answers to the question. We hope that the issues discussed here will provide some incentive to the next generation of researchers interested in relational maintenance processes.

Footnotes

1. We also recognize research suggests people learn language pragmatically; that is, people learn and use messages because they function to help achieve goals. Because they are implicitly learned, messages are inherently strategic (Kellermann, 1992). Future research is warranted to parse when the same maintenance behaviors might be used as effortful attempts

to sustain desired relational characteristics versus routinized patterns that fly beneath the radar of intentional action.

2. In his chapter, Duck (1994) provided several memorable quotes, several more pithy than this one. However, this one appears to summarize his views. We do want to share one other: "Relationships, like conferences, keep going because they are filled with juicy meaning for the partners. *Period*" (p. 51).

3. We have no idea whether Caryl Rusbult would agree with our placement of her theory in this general camp.

4. Ragsdale (1996) argued that Canary and Stafford's (1992) findings were ambiguous because a few of the univariate tests did not reveal significant findings that supported the multivariate tests, apparently under the false assumption that each univariate test must reflect the multivariate test. Ragsdale held that interdependence theory, versus equity theory, could predict the five maintenance strategies of positivity, openness, assurances, tasks, and networks. Ragsdale (1996) found no mutivariate or univariate support for his argument, nor did he test for the curvilinear effects that equity theory would call for.

References

Acitelli, L. K. (2001). Maintaining and enhancing a relationship by attending to it. In J. H. Harvey & A. Wenzel (Eds.), *Close romantic relationships: Maintenance and enhancement* (pp. 153–167). Mahwah, NJ: Erlbaum.

Attridge, M. (1994). Barriers to dissolution of romantic relationships. In D. J. Canary & L. Stafford (Eds.), *Communication and relational maintenance* (pp. 141–164). San Diego, CA: Academic Press.

Ballard-Reisch, D., Weigel, D., & Zaguidoulline, M. (2003). Maintaining marriages in Russia: Managing social influences and communication dynamics. In D. J. Canary & M. Dainton (Eds.), *Maintaining relationships through communication: Relational, contextual, and cultural variations* (pp. 255–276). Hillsdale, NJ: Erlbaum.

Bippus, A. M., & Rollin, E. (2003). Attachment style differences in relational maintenance and conflict behaviors: Friends' perceptions. *Communication Reports, 16,* 113–124.

Brehm, J. W. (1966). *A theory of psychological reactance*. New York: Academic Press.

Burggraf, C. S., & Sillars, A. L. (1987). A critical examination of sex differences in marital communication. *Communication Monographs, 54,* 276–294.

Burleson, B. R., & Samter, W. (1994). A social skills approach to relationship maintenance: How individual differences in communication skills affect the achievement of relationship functions. In D. J. Canary & L. Stafford (Eds.), *Communication and relational maintenance* (pp. 61–90). New York: Academic Press.

Canary, D. J., & Dainton, M. (Eds.). (2003). *Maintaining relationships through communication: Relational, contextual, and cultural variations*. Hillsdale, NJ: Erlbaum.

Canary, D. J., & Stafford, L. (1992). Relational maintenance strategies and equity in marriage. *Communication Monographs, 59,* 243–267.

Canary, D. J., & Stafford, L. (1993). Preservation of relational characteristics: Maintenance strategies, equity, and locus of control. In P. J. Kalbfleisch (Ed.), *Interpersonal communication: Evolving interpersonal relationships* (pp. 237–259). Hillsdale, NJ: Erlbaum.

Canary, D. J., & Stafford, L. (1994). Maintaining relationships through strategic and routine interaction. In D. J. Canary & L. Stafford (Eds.), *Communication and relational maintenance* (pp. 3–22). San Diego, CA: Academic Press.

Canary, D. J., & Stafford, L. (2001). Equity in maintaining personal relationships. In J. H. Harvey & A. E. Wenzel (Eds.), *Close romantic relationships: Maintenance and enhancement* (133–150). Mahwah, NJ: Erlbaum.

Canary, D. J., Stafford, L., Hause, K. S., & Wallace, L. A. (1993). An inductive analysis of relational maintenance strategies: Comparisons among lovers, relatives, friends, and others. *Communication Research Reports, 10,* 5–14.

Canary, D. J., & Stafford, L., & Semic, B. A. (2002). A panel study of the associations between maintenance strategies and relational characteristics. *Journal of Marriage and the Family, 64,* 395–406.

Canary, D. J., & Zelley, E. D. (2000). Current research programs in relational maintenance behaviors. In M. E. Roloff (Ed.), *Communication yearbook 23* (pp. 305–339). Thousand Oaks, CA: Sage.

Dainton, M. (2003). Erecting a framework for understanding relational maintenance: An epilogue. In D. J. Canary & M. Dainton (Eds.), *Maintaining relationships through communication: Relational, contextual, and cultural variations* (pp. 299–321). Hillsdale, NJ: Erlbaum.

Dainton, M., & Aylor, B. A. (2002). Routine and strategic maintenance efforts: Behavioral patterns, variations associated with relational length, and the prediction of relational characteristics. *Communication Monographs, 69,* 52–66.

Dainton, M., & Stafford, L. (1993). Routine maintenance behaviors: A comparison of relationship type, partner similarity and sex differences. *Journal of Social and Personal Relationships, 10,* 255–271.

Dainton, M., & Stafford, L. (2000). Predicting maintenance enactment from relational schemata, spousal behavior, and relational characteristics. *Communication Research Reports, 17,* 171–180.

Dainton, M., Zelley, E., & Langan, E. (2003). Maintaining friendships throughout the lifespan. In D. J. Canary & M. Dainton (Eds.), *Maintaining relationships through communication: Relational, contextual, and cultural variations* (pp. 79–102). Hillsdale, NJ: Erlbaum.

Deutsch, M. (1985). *Distributive justice: A social-psychological perspective.* New Haven, CT: Yale University Press.

Dindia, K. (1994). A multiphasic view of relationship maintenance strategies. In D. J. Canary & L. Stafford (Eds.), *Communication and relational maintenance* (pp. 91–114). New York: Academic Press.

Dindia, K. (1998, May). *Men are from North Dakota, women are from South Dakota: Sex similarities and differences.* Keynote address given at the meeting of the International Network for the Study of Personal Relationships, Norman, OK.

Dindia, K. (2000). Relational maintenance. In C. Hendrick & S. S. Hendrick (Eds.), *Close relationships: A sourcebook* (pp. 287–300). Thousand Oaks, CA: Sage.

Dindia, K. (2003). Definitions and perspectives on relational maintenance communication. In D. J. Canary & M. Dainton (Eds.), *Maintaining relationships through communication: Relational, contextual, and cultural variations* (pp. 1–30). Hillsdale, NJ: Erlbaum.

Dindia, K., & Baxter, L. A. (1987). Strategies for maintaining and repairing marital relationships. *Journal of Social and Personal Relationships, 4,* 143–158.

Dindia, K., & Canary, D. J. (1993). Definitions and theoretical perspectives on maintaining relationships. *Journal of Social and Personal Relationships, 10,* 163–173.

Duck, S. W. (1988). *Relating to others.* Chicago: Dorsey.

Duck, S. W. (1994). Steady (s)he goes: Relational maintenance as a shared meaning system. In D. J. Canary & L. Stafford (Eds.), *Communication and relational maintenance* (pp. 45–60). New York: Academic Press.

Felmlee, D. H. (2001). No couple is an island: A social network perspective on dyadic stability. *Social Forces, 79,* 1259–1287.

Felmlee, D. H., Sprecher, S., & Bassin, E. (1990). The dissolution of romantic relationships: A hazard model. *Social Psychology Quarterly, 53,* 13–30.

Fitzpatrick, M. A. (1988a). *Between husbands and wives: Communication in marriage.* Newbury Park, CA: Sage.

Fitzpatrick, M. A. (1988b). Negotiation, problem solving and conflict in various types of marriages. In P. Noller & M. A. Fitzpatrick (Eds.), *Perspectives on marital interaction* (pp. 245–270). Philadelphia: Multilingual Matters.

Fitzpatrick, M. A., & Best, P. (1979). Dyadic adjustment in relational types: Consensus, cohesion, affectional expression, and satisfaction in enduring relationships. *Communication Monographs, 46,* 167–178.

Fitzpatrick, M. A., Vance, L., & Witteman, H. (1984). Interpersonal communication in the causal interaction of marital partners. *Journal of Language and Social Psychology, 3,* 81–95.

Gaines, S. O., Jr., & Agnew, C. R. (2003). Relationship maintenance in intercultural couples: An interdependence analysis. In D. J. Canary & M. Dainton (Eds.), *Maintaining relationships through communication: Relational, contextual, and cultural variations* (pp. 231–254). Hillsdale, NJ: Erlbaum.

Gottman, J. M. (1994). *What predicts divorce? The relationship between marital processes and marital outcomes.* Hillsdale, NJ: Erlbaum.

Gottman, J. M., & Levenson, R. W. (2000). The timing of divorce: Predicting when a couple will divorce over a 14-year period. *Journal of Marriage and the Family, 62,* 737–745.

742 THE CAMBRIDGE HANDBOOK OF PERSONAL RELATIONSHIPS

Guerrero, L. K., Eloy, S. V., & Wabnik, A. I. (1993). Linking maintenance strategies to relationship development and disengagement: A reconceptualization. *Journal of Social and Personal Relationships, 10,* 273–283.

Haas, S. (2003). Relationship maintenance in same-sex couples. In D. J. Canary & M. Dainton (Eds.), *Maintaining relationships through communication: Relational, contextual, and cultural variations* (pp. 209–230). Hillsdale, NJ: Erlbaum.

Hatfield, E., Traupmann, J., Sprecher, S., Utne, M., & Hay, M. (1985). Equity in close relationships. In W. Ickes (Ed.), *Compatible and incompatible relationships* (pp. 91–117). New York: Springer-Verlag.

Heaton, T. B., & Albrecht, S. L. (1991). Stable unhappy marriages. *Journal of Marriage and the Family, 53,* 747–758.

Hess, J. A. (2003). Maintaining undesired relationships. In D. J. Canary & M. Dainton (Eds.), *Maintaining relationships through communication: Relational, contextual, and cultural variations* (pp. 103–126). Hillsdale, NJ: Erlbaum.

Huston, T. L., Caughlin, J. P., Houts, R. M., Smith, S. E., & George, L. J. (2001). The connubial crucible: Newlywed years as predictors of marital delight, distress, and divorce. *Journal of Personality and Social Psychology, 80,* 237–252.

Johnson, M. P. (2001). Conflict and control: Symmetry and asymmetry in domestic violence. In A. Booth, A. C. Crouter, & M. Clements (Eds.), *Couples in conflict* (pp. 95–104). Mahwah, NJ: Erlbaum.

Kellermann, K. (1992). Communication: Inherently strategic and primarily automatic. *Communication Monographs, 59,* 288–300.

Kelley, H. H. (1979). *Personal relationships: Their structures and processes.* Hillsdale, NJ: Erlbaum.

Kelley, H. H., & Thibaut, J. W. (1978). *Interpersonal relations: A theory of interdependence.* New York: Wiley.

Klein, R. C. A., & Milardo, R. M. (2000). The social context of couple conflict: Support and criticism from informal third parties. *Journal of Social and Personal Relationships, 17,* 618–637.

Levinger, G. (1965). Marital cohesiveness and dissolution: An integrative review. *Journal of Marriage and the Family, 27,* 19–28.

Lewis, R. A., & Spanier, G. B. (1979). Theorizing about the quality and stability of marriage. In W. R. Burr, R. Hill, F. I. Nye, & I. L. Reiss (Eds.), *Contemporary theories about the family* (Vol. 2, pp. 268–294). New York: Free Press.

Messman, S. J., Canary, D. J., & Hause, K. S. (2000). Motives to remain platonic, equity, and the use of maintenance strategies in opposite-sex friendships. *Journal of Social and Personal Relationships, 17,* 67–94.

Montgomery, B. M. (1993). Relationship maintenance versus relationship change: A dialectical dilemma. *Journal of Social and Personal Relationships, 10,* 205–233.

Murray, S. L., Holmes, J. O., & Griffin, D. W. (1996). The self-fulfilling nature of positive illusions in romantic relationships: Love is not blind, but presient. *Journal of Personality and Social Psychology, 71,* 1155–1180.

Perlman, D. (2001). Maintaining and enhancing personal relationships: Concluding commentary. In J. H. Harvey & A. Wenzel (Eds.), *Close romantic relationships: Maintenance and enhancement* (pp. 357–377). Mahwah, NJ: Erlbaum.

Ragsdale, J. D. (1996). Gender, satisfaction level, and the use of relational maintenance strategies in marriage. *Communication Monographs, 63,* 354–369.

Rawlins, W. K. (1994). Being there and growing apart: Sustaining friendships during adulthood. In D. J. Canary & L. Stafford (Eds.), *Communication and relational maintenance* (pp. 275–294). New York: Academic Press.

Roloff, M. E., & Cloven, D. H. (1994). When partners transgress: Maintaining violated relationships. In D. J. Canary & L. Stafford (Eds.), *Communication and relational maintenance* (pp. 23–43). New York: Academic Press.

Rusbult, C. E. (1987). Responses to dissatisfaction in close relationships: The exit-voice-loyalty-neglect model. In D. Perlman & S. Duck (Eds.), *Intimate relationships: Development, dynamics, and deterioration* (pp. 209–237). Newbury Park, CA: Sage.

Rusbult, C. E., & Buunk, B. P. (1993). Commitment processes in close relationships: An interdependence analysis. *Journal of Social and Personal Relationships, 10,* 175–204.

Rusbult, C. E., Drigotas, S. M., & Verette, J. (1994). The investment model: An interdependence analysis of commitment processes and relationship maintenance phenomena. In D. J. Canary & L. Stafford (Eds.), *Communication and relational maintenance* (pp. 115–140). New York: Academic Press.

Rusbult, C. E., & Martz, J. M. (1995). Remaining in an abusive relationship: An investment model analysis of nonvoluntary dependence. *Personality and Social Psychology Bulletin*, 21, 558–571.

Rusbult, C. E., Verette, J., Whitney, G. A., Slovik, L. F., & Lipkus, I. (1991). Accommodation processes in close relationships: Theory and preliminary evidence. *Journal of Personality and Social Psychology*, 60, 53–78.

Sahlstein, E. M., & Baxter, L. A. (2001). Improvising commitment in close relationships: A relational dialectics perspective. In J. H. Harvey & A. Wenzel (Eds.), *Close romantic relationships: Maintenance and enhancement* (pp. 115–132). Mahwah, NJ: Erlbaum.

Sillars, A. L., & Wilmot, W. W. (1989). Marital communication across the lifespan. In J. F. Nussbaum (Ed.), *Lifespan communication: Normative processes* (pp. 225–253). Hillsdale, NJ: Erlbaum.

Simon, E. P., & Baxter, L. A. (1993). Attachment-style differences in relationship maintenance strategies. *Western Journal of Communication*, 57, 416–430.

Simpson, J. A., Ickes, W., & Orina, M. (2001). Empathic accuracy and preemptive relationship maintenance. In J. H. Harvey & A. Wenzel (Eds.), *Close romantic relationships: Maintenance and enhancement* (pp. 27–46). Mahwah, NJ: Erlbaum.

Smith, A. G. (1966). *Communication and culture*. New York: Holt, Rinehart & Winston.

Stafford, L. (1994). Tracing the threads of spider webs. In D. J. Canary & L. Stafford (Eds.), *Communication and relational maintenance* (pp. 297–306). New York: Academic Press.

Stafford, L. (2003). Maintaining romantic relationships: Summary and analysis of one research program. In D. J. Canary & M. Dainton (Eds.), *Maintaining relationships through communication: Relational, contextual, and cultural variations* (pp. 51–78). Hillsdale, NJ: Erlbaum.

Stafford L., & Canary, D. J. (1991). Maintenance strategies and romantic relationship type, gender, and relational characteristics.

Journal of Social and Personal Relationships, 8, 217–242.

Stafford, L., Dainton, M., & Haas, S. (2000). Measuring routine and strategic relational maintenance: Scale development, sex versus gender roles, and the prediction of relational characteristics. *Communication Monographs*, 67, 306–323.

Van Yperen, N. W., & Buunk, B. (1990). A longitudinal study of equity and satisfaction in intimate relationships. *European Journal of Social Psychology*, 20, 287–309.

Vogl-Bauer, S., Kalbfleisch, P. J., & Beatty, M. J. (1999). Perceived equity, satisfaction, and relational maintenance strategies in parent–adolescent dyads. *Journal of Youth and Adolescence*, 28, 27–49.

Waller, W. (1951). *The family: A dynamic interpretation*. New York: Cordon.

Weigel, D. J., & Ballard-Reisch, D. D. (1999). All marriages are not maintained equally: Marital type, marital quality, and the use of maintenance behaviors. *Personal Relationships*, 6, 291–303.

Wilmot, W. W. (1994). Relationship rejuvenation. In D. J. Canary & L. Stafford (Eds.), *Communication and relational maintenance* (pp. 253–271). New York: Academic Press.

Yum, Y. O. (2003). The relationships among loneliness, self/partner constructive maintenance behavior, and relational satisfaction in two cultures. *Communication Studies*, 54, 451–467.

Yum, Y. O., & Canary, D. J. (2003). Maintaining relationships in Korea and the United States: Features of Korean culture that affect relational maintenance beliefs and behaviors. In D. J. Canary & M. Dainton (Eds.), *Maintaining relationships through communication: Relational, contextual, and cultural variations* (pp. 277–298). Hillsdale, NJ: Erlbaum.

Yum, Y. O., & Canary, D. J. (1997, June). *The role of culture in the perception of maintenance behaviors and relational characteristics: A comparison between the U.S. and Korea.* Paper presented at the meeting of the International Network for the Study of Personal Relationships, Miami University, Oxford, OH.

CHAPTER 40

The Treatment of Relationship Distress: Theoretical Perspectives and Empirical Findings

Donald H. Baucom
Norman B. Epstein
Susan Stanton

For most individuals in Western countries, adulthood is associated with a married lifestyle, with more than 90% of the population becoming married by age 50 (McDonald, 1995). Unfortunately, the benefits that individuals expect to derive from marriage often do not translate into gratifying relationships, or satisfaction erodes over time. As a result, divorce rates are high in Western countries. The divorce rate for first marriages is approximately 40% to 45% in the United States, Australia, and the United Kingdom, and approximately 35% in Germany (Australian Bureau of Statistics, 2001; United States Bureau of Census, 2002).

Given the alarming rate of both marital distress and dissolution, it is fortunate that clinicians and researchers have devoted considerable effort to developing and evaluating interventions for treating marital problems. In the current chapter, we provide an overview of the major models of couple therapy[1] that have empirical support for their efficacy. This decision to include only approaches with current empirical support is not intended to imply that other approaches are not useful for couples; we

hope that investigators interested in other couple therapy approaches such as Bowen's family systems therapy (Kerr & Bowen, 1988), structural family therapy (Minuchin & Nichols, 1998), narrative therapy (Freedman & Combs, 2002), solution-focused therapy (Hoyt, 2001), and brief strategic therapy (Shoham & Rohrbaugh, 2001) will conduct well-controlled treatment outcome investigations to evaluate their efficacies. In addition, the field awaits evaluation of the efficacy of interventions for individuals in committed relationships who are not married.

The field of marital and couple therapy has existed for many decades, with its roots in the 1930s practice of marriage counseling and the establishment of centers such as Emily Mudd's pioneering Marriage Council of Philadelphia (Bischof & Helmeke, 2003). The American Association of Marriage Counselors (AAMC), established in 1945, included practitioners from a variety of fields, such as social workers, physicians, clergy, and family guidance specialists, who used a variety of interventions in the absence of any theoretical base. As the field of family therapy developed around systems theory concepts, the name of AAMC was changed in 1970 to the American Association of Marriage and Family Counselors, and its current name of the American Association for Marriage and Family Therapy (AAMFT) was adopted in 1978. Given the overarching systems theory view that dominated AAMFT, couple therapy tended to be viewed as a subtype of family therapy rather than a specialty in its own right, and charismatic leaders who developed a variety of theoretical approaches to family and couple therapy dominated the field. Overall, schools of family therapy gained many adherents despite little empirical research on their efficacy.

Only in the 1970s did well-controlled investigations evaluating the efficacy of specific approaches begin to appear, particularly as research-oriented psychologists increasingly became involved in the field (Jacobson, 1978). In the 1990s, a major emphasis on empirically supported interventions or evidence-based practice emerged more broadly within clinical psychology. Given that couple researchers had been evaluating their treatments for 2 decades when this emphasis within clinical psychology gained momentum, a large number of investigations had already been completed. In discussing the efficacy of various approaches to couple therapy, we have adopted the criteria set forth by Chambless and Hollon (1998) for empirically supported interventions. Briefly, for a treatment to be evaluated as efficacious, these authors propose that it be superior to a wait-list condition or equivalent to another efficacious treatment; moreover, there must be sufficient statistical power to detect treatment effects. Successful implementation of treatments by therapists other than the originators of the treatment is another prerequisite for defining an intervention as efficacious. Thus, Chambless and Hollon require that the efficacy of a treatment must be corroborated by at least two independent teams of investigators and that the preponderance of the evidence must support its efficacy. If the intervention has been successful in only one study or in multiple studies by the same investigator, then the intervention is described as "possibly efficacious" (see Chambless & Hollon, 1998), and the special issue of the *Journal of Consulting and Clinical Psychology* [Kendall & Chambless, 1998] for an in-depth discussion of the strengths and weaknesses of this approach to evaluating psychotherapy research). Based on these criteria, we discuss three broad approaches to couple therapy with empirical support: (a) behavioral couple therapy and its variants, including cognitive–behavioral and integrative behavioral couple therapy; (b) emotionally focused couple therapy; and (c) insight-oriented couple therapy.

The different approaches to couple therapy vary greatly with regard to their positions on three dimensions. First, theoretical approaches vary in the degree to which they focus on overt behavioral patterns versus on internal experiences such as cognitions and emotions. Second, approaches vary in whether they focus on the roles that the individual members play in the development and functioning of the marriage or on the couple's dyadic interaction patterns and other relationship characteristics. Third, approaches differ in the extent to which they focus on the present or more proximal factors versus more historical or distal factors in addressing relationship distress. Therefore, we describe how each approach addresses each of these three dimensions. No approach focuses exclusively on one pole of these dimensions, but there are notable differences in their relative emphases.

Models Based on Behavioral Perspectives

Behavioral Couple Therapy

As suggested by the title of the model, behavioral couple therapy (BCT) takes a systematic approach to the assessment and modification of couples' behaviors (e.g., Jacobson & Margolin, 1979; Stuart, 1980). Behavioral couple therapy was developed in the 1960s and 1970s from the theoretical models of social exchange theory (Thibaut

& Kelley, 1959) and social learning theory (Bandura, 1977). Social exchange theory proposes that a person's level of relationship satisfaction depends on his or her ratio of positive to negative experiences in that relationship. Social learning theory suggests that members of a couple shape each other's behavior by providing positive or negative consequences for each other's actions.

BASIC CONCEPTS

Behavior. Empirical investigations have supported the social exchange conceptualization of intimate relationships, such that self-reported relationship satisfaction is correlated (a) positively with the frequencies of partners' positive actions and (b) negatively, to an even stronger degree, with the frequencies of the partners' negative actions (Weiss & Heyman, 1990). Thus, distressed couples are more likely to demonstrate a high rate of negative behaviors and a low rate of positive behaviors; conversely, nondistressed spouses are more likely to engage in more positive behaviors toward their partners than negative ones (Gottman, 1994). In accordance with social learning theory, other findings indicate that distressed married couples are more prone than nondistressed couples to aversive, destructive patterns of communication, such as a demand–withdrawal pattern in which one partner pursues an issue while the other withdraws (Christensen & Heavey, 1990; Christensen & Shenk, 1991). Furthermore, distressed couples are more likely to engage in exchanges in which one person's hurtful comment is reciprocated with greater intensity by the receiving partner.

Cognition. As discussed subsequently, behavioral couple therapy has evolved into cognitive–behavioral couple therapy, a therapeutic modality that places significant emphasis on partners' cognitions about each other and their relationship. Even from a more behavioral perspective, however, cognitions are important because of their relationship to behavior. First, the impact of a partner's behaviors as positive or negative

depends, in part, on the recipient's subjective experience and evaluation of these behaviors (Baucom & Epstein, 1990). For example, a wife may buy her husband a trendy outfit as a gift for no particular occasion. The husband may either interpret this behavior as a loving and thoughtful act, based on his inference that she was thinking of him and thought the outfit would look good on him, or he may interpret her gesture as an indication of her dissatisfaction with his wardrobe and an attempt to improve his appearance. These different interpretations of the same behavior likely would have differing impacts on the husband's feelings and subsequent behavior toward his wife. Behavioral couple therapists also assume that people choose to engage in a particular behavior because of their expectancies about the consequences, or rewards and punishments, they will receive from their partners.

Affect. In addition to cognition, behavioral couple therapists have noted that affect has a great influence on couples' behaviors and relationship satisfaction. Studies of couples' conversations have shown that distressed partners are more likely to respond negatively to each other's expressions of negative affect than are members of nondistressed couples (negative reciprocity); furthermore, these expressions of negative affect are not as likely to be offset by high levels of positive affect as they are in nondistressed relationships (Gottman, 1994).

CONTRIBUTION OF THE COUPLE VERSUS THE INDIVIDUAL IN COUPLE DISTRESS

With a major focus on interactive processes as a primary source of couple distress, behavioral couple therapists place a strong emphasis on the contribution of the couple as a dyad rather than the individual's unique characteristics. Although partners bring learned behaviors from the past into their current relationships, social learning theory emphasizes that a spouse's behavior is both learned and influenced by the other partner's behavior. Over time, spouses' influence on each other becomes a stronger predictor of current behavior than the influences of previous close relationships. The behavioral approach also is based on social exchange theory principles that link the couple's satisfaction to higher ratios of pleasing versus displeasing behaviors that are exchanged. Thus, the behavioral model suggests that a couple's ability to maintain a satisfying relationship is based on the partners' skills for providing each other with reinforcing and effective behavioral exchanges. As a result, the therapeutic interventions are focused primarily on altering behavioral exchanges between the partners and developing more effective communication skills. In early behavioral models, little attention was given to understanding the unique characteristics of each partner, and how individual factors, including both strengths and vulnerabilities, contribute to marital adjustment.

Proximal Versus Distal Factors in Understanding Relationship Discord

Behavioral couple therapy has a strong emphasis on the present, exploring how couples interact with each other and communicate with each other. Historical perspectives are addressed primarily in terms of understanding how well entrenched a behavioral interaction pattern might be and the various contexts in which it has occurred over time.

APPROACHES TO TREATMENT

Behavior. Because a central tenet of the behavioral model is that distress is caused by a low ratio of positive to negative exchanges, behavioral couple therapists have used behavior-exchange procedures such as "love days" (Weiss, Hops, & Patterson, 1973) or "caring days" (Stuart, 1980). These procedures involve each partner agreeing to enact certain positive behaviors requested by his or her partner to increase the percentage of positive exchanges. Similarly, couples have been taught to develop behavioral contracts in which each person agrees to behave in specific ways desired by the partner and then receives reinforcement for these actions. Although behavioral contracting appears to be less emphasized in current

behavioral approaches to assisting distressed couples, it served as a major intervention strategy in many of the treatment outcome investigations that have been conducted. In addition, to increase the likelihood that couples will experience more reinforcing interactions, behavior therapists teach couples specific communication skills and guidelines for (a) expressing thoughts and feelings, (b) engaging in empathic listening, and (c) problem solving. It is assumed that by developing these skills, couples will enhance their abilities to negotiate more satisfying solutions to conflicts, as well as their abilities to experience more intimacy through skillful expression of feelings. As a result, couples will decrease negative reciprocity and increase positive reciprocity in their communication and overall relationship.

Cognition. In the early texts on behavioral couple therapy, Jacobson and Margolin (1979) recommended that therapists instruct couples to monitor and record their cognitions at home, and Stuart (1980) promoted the concept of relabeling, which involves challenging the partners to alter their negative interpretations of ambiguous actions on each other's part. Unfortunately, descriptions of cognitive restructuring in early behavioral texts are brief, and they typically do not give therapists a great deal of guidance in how to accomplish this goal. It also should be noted that cognitive interventions were not systematically employed in the treatment outcome studies that were conducted, which we discuss subsequently. Thus, despite the theoretical recognition of the role of cognitions in influencing the behaviors of spouses, the original BCT interventions did not address cognitions directly.

Affect. Behavioral approaches to couple relationships have viewed emotions (e.g., joy, anger, sadness) as reactions to specific behavioral interactions. Distress is viewed as resulting from particular behavioral patterns that are repetitive, ingrained, and reciprocal. Consequently, behaviorists' approaches to modifying affect typically have depended on the behavioral interventions described previously. However, this approach of altering affect through changing behavior may be problematic for some distressed couples (Epstein & Baucom, 2002). Specific behavior changes may not be powerful enough to overcome existing negative feelings toward the partner due to "sentiment override," with research findings indicating limited associations between partner behaviors and overall relationship satisfaction (e.g., Halford, Sanders, & Behrens, 1993; Iverson & Baucom, 1990).

Theoretical models of relationship distress and related interventions continue to evolve over time, and this has been the case with behavioral perspectives on relationship functioning. As a result, two noteworthy behaviorally oriented approaches have evolved in the past 15 years: cognitive–behavioral couple therapy and integrative behavioral couple therapy.

Cognitive–Behavioral Couple Therapy

Cognitive–behavioral couple therapy (CBCT) evolved from behavioral couple therapy and is consistent with trends during the 1980s and 1990s in the overall field of behavior therapy to incorporate cognitive factors into behavioral conceptualizations of maladaptive responses. Consequently, most of the BCT theoretical perspectives and interventions described previously have been incorporated into CBCT. The much greater emphasis on cognition in the original formulation of cognitive–behavioral couple therapy is its primary difference from BCT. Whereas BCT practitioners noted the importance of cognitions to behavior change without explicitly targeting cognitions in treatment, the CBCT model also proposes that cognitive change is important in its own right. That is, in many instances, the members of a couple might *not* need to change their behavior to increase their relationship satisfaction; instead, if they come to interpret or understand each other's behavior differently, then positive relationship adjustment might occur. For example, a husband with an extreme standard

for his wife's behavior (e.g., that if she is committed to the family, she should stay home with the children and give up her career) might be dissatisfied if she does not meet this standard, perhaps interpreting her pursuit of a career as indicating a lack of family commitment. Helping him to reevaluate and reduce the stringency of his standard might be the intervention of choice, rather than a behavior change on either person's part. Thus, CBCT builds on the behavioral model by suggesting that increasing relationship satisfaction involves a balance of behavioral and cognitive changes, both of which hold the potential for important emotional change.

BASIC CONCEPTS

Overall, CBCT incorporates basic behavioral perspectives on the role of behavior and affect in relationship functioning. Its major contribution involves the development and elaboration of the role of cognitions in relationship distress. Thus, a brief description of the cognitive perspective is provided.

Cognition. CBCT researchers have identified five major types of cognitions involved in couple relationship functioning (Baucom, Epstein, Sayers, & Sher, 1989). Empirical studies suggest that these cognitions are associated with, or even lead to, partners' negative affective and behavioral responses to each other (Epstein & Baucom, 1993, 2002; Fincham, Bradbury, & Scott, 1990; Noller, Beach, & Osgarby, 1997). The first three cognitions involve evaluations of specific events. *Selective attention* involves how each member of a couple idiosyncratically notices, or fails to notice, particular aspects of relationship events. Selective attention contributes to distressed couples' low rates of agreement about the occurrence and quality of specific events, as well as negative biases in perceptions of each other's messages (Noller et al., 1997). *Attributions* are inferences made about the determinants of partners' positive and negative behaviors. The tendency of distressed partners to attribute each other's negative actions to global, stable traits has been referred to as "distress-maintaining attributions" because they leave little room for future optimism that one's partner will behave in a more pleasing manner in other situations (Holtzworth-Munroe & Jacobson, 1985). Bradbury and Fincham (1990) have thoroughly reviewed and noted the empirical support for the importance of partners' attributions in relationship functioning. *Expectancies*, or predictions that each member of the couple makes about particular relationship events in the immediate or more distant future, are the last type of cognitions involving specific events. Negative relationship expectancies have been associated with lower satisfaction, stemming from pessimism about improving the relationship (Fincham & Bradbury, 1989; Pretzer, Epstein, & Fleming, 1991).

The fourth and fifth categories of cognition are forms of what cognitive therapists have referred to as basic or core beliefs shaping one's experience of the world. These include (a) *assumptions*, or beliefs that each individual holds about the characteristics of individuals and intimate relationships, and (b) *standards*, or each individual's personal beliefs about the characteristics that an intimate relationship and its members "should" have (Baucom & Epstein, 1990; Baucom et al., 1989). Couples' assumptions and standards are associated with current relationship distress, either when these beliefs are unrealistic or when the partners are not satisfied with how their personal standards are being met in their relationship (Baucom, Epstein, Rankin, & Burnett, 1996; Halford, Kelly, & Markman, 1997).

CONTRIBUTIONS OF THE COUPLE VERSUS THE INDIVIDUAL IN COUPLE DISTRESS

Cognitive–behavioral couple therapists see relationship problems as developing not only from behavioral excesses and deficits within the couple, but also from each individual's cognitions that either elicit distress or impede the resolution of conflicts (Epstein, Baucom, & Rankin, 1993). Thus, some of the problematic cognitions that the therapist identifies may have developed from each individual's history, including previous romantic relationships, a person's family of origin, and society at large, as well as from their current relationship. For example, depending on how a husband experienced his mother's domination and control over his father's daily activities, he might overgeneralize and predict that his wife will eventually try to control his every move, even if she presently exhibits no overt signs of making such attempts. Thus, many of the problematic behavioral interactions between spouses may evolve from the partners' relatively stable cognitions about the relationship. Unless these cognitions are taken into account, successful intervention is likely to be compromised. Therefore, cognitive–behavioral couple therapists attend to how each person thinks about and experiences the relationship. In this way, the unique characteristics, learning histories, and current thoughts and cognitions of each partner are integrated into the couple's ongoing interactions.

PROXIMAL VERSUS DISTAL FACTORS IN UNDERSTANDING RELATIONSHIP DISCORD

Given that CBCT derived from BCT, it also emphasizes the present relative to the past. However, to the degree that an individual's distorted cognitions are rooted in the past, such historical precedents are noted so that an individual can learn to differentiate between what he or she learned in the past versus what is occurring in the present.

APPROACHES TO TREATMENT

The various interventions described in BCT apply to CBCT as well, again with the major contribution of CBCT being an increased focus on interventions to directly alter cognitions.

Cognition. The cognitive–behavioral approach (Baucom & Epstein, 1990; Epstein & Baucom, 2002) has integrated assessment and intervention procedures from cognitive therapies (Beck, Rush, Shaw, & Emery, 1979; Meichenbaum, 1985) with traditional skills-oriented behavioral strategies. CBCT teaches partners to monitor and test the appropriateness of their cognitions. It incorporates some standard cognitive restructuring strategies, such as (a) considering alternative attributions for a partner's negative behavior; (b) asking for behavioral data to test a negative perception concerning a partner (e.g., that the partner never complies with requests); and (c) evaluating extreme standards by generating lists of the advantages and disadvantages of expectations to live up to this standard.

Integrative Behavioral Couple Therapy

Christensen and Jacobson developed integrative behavioral couple therapy (IBCT; Christensen, Jacobson, & Babcock, 1995; Jacobson & Christensen, 1996) to build on behavioral couple therapy by emphasizing emotional acceptance. IBCT includes a core assumption that there are genuine incompatibilities in all couples that are not amenable to change and that partners' emotional reactions to each other's behavior are as problematic, or more so, than the behavior itself. Attempting to cajole or force one's partner to change often can lead to a resistance to change. Therefore, interventions focus on a balance between active change in partners' behavior and the achievement of acceptance between partners regarding behavior that is unlikely to change.

BASIC CONCEPTS

IBCT incorporates many of the concepts from BCT and CBCT but places an increasing focus on emotional reactions that partners have in response to the difficulties they encounter in their relationships. The importance of constructive–behavioral interactions and cognitively viewing each other's behaviors in realistic ways remain central to IBCT. The major differentiation of IBCT from BCT is IBCT's emphasis on acceptance between partners for incompatibilities that are unlikely to be responsive to behavioral change. Although Christensen and Jacobson described acceptance as a largely emotional process, it is difficult to differentiate between the cognitive and affective changes that are necessary in the acceptance

process. Unless such differentiations can be demonstrated empirically, it might be best to refer to an emphasis on an internal, subjective affective–cognitive shift that is critical for accepting one's partner.

CONTRIBUTIONS OF THE COUPLE VERSUS THE INDIVIDUAL IN COUPLE DISTRESS

IBCT continues to incorporate the BCT emphasis on couples' maladaptive interaction patterns and thus places a significant focus on the couple as a unit. Although these couple-level interaction patterns are the major grist for the acceptance mill, acceptance itself is an internal, subjective experience that exists on an individual level. Thus, IBCT attempts to promote acceptance in each partner and the couple as a unit and regards the partners' individual differences as a means for reducing maladaptive interaction patterns that have been due to a lack of acceptance.

PROXIMAL VERSUS DISTAL FACTORS IN UNDERSTANDING RELATIONSHIP DISCORD

Given its derivation from CBT, IBCT also emphasizes the present. However, acceptance can involve being aware of the vulnerabilities that an individual has developed in the past, perhaps before the current relationship.

APPROACHES TO TREATMENT

Affect. In addition to the use of typical behavioral interventions just described to promote behavior change, IBCT employs three major strategies to promote acceptance: empathic joining around the problem, unified detachment from the problem, and tolerance building (Christensen et al., 1995; Jacobson & Christensen, 1996). During empathic joining, the IBCT therapist elicits vulnerable feelings (such as sadness) that may underlie partners' observed negative emotional reactions (such as anger) about an area of concern, encourages expression and elaboration of these vulnerable feelings, and communicates empathy for these understandable reactions. As a result, the therapist attempts to build empathy between the partners for each other. During unified detachment from the problem, the therapist helps the couple step back from the problem and assume a more descriptive and less evaluative stance toward the problem. The therapist may engage the couple in an effort to describe (without evaluating) the common sequence that they go through, to specify the triggers that activate each other and escalate negative emotions, to create a name for their problematic pattern, and to consider variations in their interaction pattern and factors that might account for these variations. The therapist then might encourage both members of the couple to engage deliberately in the problematic sequence in the session or at home so that they can become more aware of their pattern and take it less personally. In tolerance building, the therapist helps the couple remember the positive aspects and benefits of their individual differences, as well as the negative implications of their differences.

EMPIRICAL SUPPORT FOR BEHAVIORALLY ORIENTED INTERVENTIONS

BCT. Behavioral couple therapy is the most widely evaluated couple treatment, having been a focus of approximately two dozen well-controlled treatment outcome studies, suggesting adequate power for meta-analyses to detect effects. Behavioral couple therapy has been reviewed in detail in several previous publications, including findings from specific investigations (e.g., Alexander, Holtzworth-Munroe, & Jameson, 1994; Baucom & Epstein, 1990; Baucom, Shoham, Mueser, Daiuto, & Stickle, 1998; Bray & Jouriles, 1995) as well as meta-analyses (Baucom, Hahlweg, & Kuschel, 2003; Dunn & Schwebel, 1995; Hahlweg & Markman, 1988; Shadish & Baldwin, 1993; Shadish et al., 2002). All of these reviews reach the same conclusion: Behavioral couple therapy is an efficacious intervention for maritally distressed couples.

A large number of investigations have satisfied efficacy criteria by comparing behavioral couple therapy with wait-list control conditions, consistently finding that behavioral couple therapy is more effica-

cious than the absence of systematic treatment. Several early investigations of behavioral couple therapy also have compared it with nonspecific or placebo treatment conditions, with behavioral couple therapy generally being more efficacious than nonspecific treatment conditions (Azrin et al., 1980; Crowe, 1978; Jacobson, 1978). Also, meta-analyses have confirmed these findings (Dunn & Schwebel, 1995; Hahlweg & Markman, 1988; Shadish & Baldwin 1993; Shadish et al., 2002). Baucom et al. (2003) concluded that compared with waiting list control groups, BCT has an average effect size[2] of 0.72, which is consistent among studies conducted in several countries.

Regarding clinically significant change (Jacobson, Follette, & Revenstorf, 1984), between one third and two thirds of couples will be in the nondistressed range of marital satisfaction after receiving behavioral couple therapy. Most couples appear to maintain these gains for short time periods (6 to 12 months); however, long-range follow-up results are not as encouraging. In a 2-year follow-up of BCT, for example, Jacobson, Schmaling, and Holtzworth-Munroe (1987) found that approximately 30% of couples who had recovered during therapy had relapsed subsequently. In addition, Snyder, Wills, and Grady-Fletcher (1991) reported that 38% of couples receiving BCT had divorced during a 4-year follow-up period. Thus, brief behavioral couple therapy improvements are not maintained for many couples over a number of years, although some couples maintain and even improve on their gains.

CBCT. The efficacy of cognitive interventions has been explored in two ways – as the sole intervention or as part of a broader set of therapeutic strategies to assist distressed couples. Huber and Milstein (1985) compared cognitive couple therapy with a waiting-list control condition. Their cognitive couple therapy focused primarily on irrational relationship standards and assumptions that were highlighted by Epstein and Eidelson (1981), along with specific irrational marital beliefs noted by

Ellis (1978). Six weeks of cognitive couple therapy was more effective than the waiting-list condition. Applying the Chambless and Hollon criteria (1998), conjoint cognitive therapy would be classified as a possibly efficacious treatment for marital distress.

In current practice, cognitive interventions are typically used with a variety of behavioral interventions, as well as interventions focusing on couples' emotions. Based on the description of cognitive–behavioral couple therapy provided earlier, Baucom and colleagues (Baucom & Lester, 1986; Baucom, Sayers, & Sher, 1990) supplemented traditional behavioral couple therapy with cognitive restructuring interventions targeted at couples' marital attributions and their marital standards. In these two studies, both traditional behavioral couple therapy and cognitive–behavioral couple therapy were more effective than a waiting-list condition in improving the couples' marital adjustment and communication. However, there were no significant differences between the two treatment conditions. These results were replicated in a similar investigation by Halford et al. (1993). Furthermore, the magnitude of change produced for various dependent measures appears to be consistent with what has been found in a number of behavioral couple therapy investigations. Compared with a waiting-list control group, Baucom et al. (1990) found in their larger study that CBCT has an effect size of 0.52. They also found that approximately 43% of the couples had moved into the nondistressed range following treatment. Thus, the findings to date suggest that CBCT is as efficacious as BCT alone and shows more improvement than wait-list conditions, but it does not produce enhanced treatment outcomes. In interpreting these findings, it is important to note that couples were randomly assigned to treatment conditions. Some couples might benefit more from a central focus on cognitive change, whereas others may need extensive alterations in how they behave toward each other. At present, no reported investigations have addressed this matching issue.

IBCT. Christensen et al. (2004) recently completed the first large-scale randomized, controlled trial of IBCT, comparing it with BCT as described by Jacobson and Margolin (1979). This study, including 134 couples, is the largest trial of therapy to date for distressed couples and has adequate power to detect treatment differences, compared with the small sample sizes included in most other treatment studies. The findings indicated that in terms of improving marital adjustment, both treatments resulted in gains from pretest to posttest, and there were no overall differences between the two conditions at posttest. However, couples in the two treatments demonstrated different *patterns* of change over the course of treatment. Couples in BCT improved more quickly than couples in IBCT, but their level of improvement flattened out near the end of treatment. Meanwhile, IBCT couples showed slow but steady improvement during treatment, with no flattening out over time. The proportion of couples showing clinically significant improvement into the nondistressed range was not different for the two treatments (52% and 44% for IBCT and BCT, respectively) and was similar to what has been demonstrated for BCT in other investigations. Likewise, the within group effect size of IBCT was $d = 0.86$, almost identical to the average within group effect size of BCT ($d = 0.82$), seen across 17 investigations of BCT (Baucom et al., 2003). Thus, similar to CBCT, IBCT appears to be of benefit to couples, and the magnitude of its effects is similar to those of BCT (the follow-up results have not yet been published, and thus, differential long-term effects are yet to be known).

Emotionally Focused Couples Therapy

Emotionally focused couple therapy (EFCT), developed by Johnson and Greenberg (1985; Greenberg & Johnson, 1988), has its roots in experiential therapies and emphasizes understanding individuals' subjective experiences, in particular their emotional responses, in their intimate relationships. Johnson and Denton (2002) noted that EFCT represented an important shift away from the prevailing emphasis on behavior and cognition in the marital field. EFCT draws substantially from attachment theory (Bowlby, 1989), which describes how humans have an innate need for emotional attachment to nurturant others, beginning in infancy and continuing throughout life. Based on the degree to which an individual's early caretakers are physically and psychologically available, a child develops either a secure or an insecure attachment style. Empirical evidence has lent support to the concept that the attachment style or pattern that an individual develops during childhood tends to be stable into adulthood, although significant experiences in adult relationships are capable of altering an individual's attachment pattern (Berman, Marcus, & Berman, 1994; Davila, Burge, & Hammen, 1997; Rothbard & Shaver, 1994; Waters, Hamilton, & Weinfield, 2000). Theory and research have identified up to three types of insecure adult attachment: dismissing–avoidant, preoccupied (anxious–ambivalent), and fearful–avoidant (Ainsworth, Blehar, Waters, & Wall, 1978; Bartholomew & Horowitz, 1991; Hazan & Shaver, 1987), but all of them involve a cognitive component or "working model" in which the individual is sensitive to the likelihood that significant others will not meet his or her needs for emotional attachment. According to attachment theory, when an individual perceives that a significant other such as a spouse is not available, this elicits vulnerable "primary" emotions such as anxiety internally but also may elicit "secondary" emotions such as anger expressed toward the spouse. Johnson and Greenberg (1985) developed EFCT as a means of helping partners understand their own and each other's emotional responses due to attachment concerns and to find more constructive forms of behavior to increase intimacy and fulfill attachment needs.

BASIC CONCEPTS

Behavior. The EFCT model draws on family systems theory in positing that a cou-

ple's dysfunctional responses to the partners' attachment needs typically form a negative interaction pattern (Johnson, 1996; Johnson & Denton, 2002). On one hand, each person attempts to elicit caring responses from the other in ways that backfire (e.g., nagging, clinging, criticism) or withdraws from the other in a self-protective manner. On the other hand, the recipient of these negative actions responds negatively (counterattacking, withdrawing) rather than providing nurturance. EFCT focuses on negative interaction cycles between partners as well as the two individuals' emotional experiences associated with attachment needs.

Cognition. Attachment theory that forms a key part of the foundation of EFCT describes "working models" or cognitive schemas that individuals hold about themselves (as lovable or not) and about significant others (as available for nurturance or not). However, the proponents of EFCT (Johnson, 1996; Johnson & Denton, 2002; Johnson & Greenberg, 1985) emphasize that emotions organize partners' perceptions and attachment behaviors toward each other. Johnson and Denton (2002) state that change does not occur through insight but rather through new emotional experiences involving attachment interactions between partners. Thus, an individual comes to view a partner more as a secure source of nurturance based on interactions with the partner that elicit more positive emotions.

Affect. In couples' relationships, insecure partners use a variety of strategies to cope with their primary emotions such as fear or sadness concerning being neglected or abandoned. Some coping strategies involve expression of anger or other secondary emotions and attempts to coerce the partner to provide intimacy, whereas others involve emotional states such as apathy or contempt and behavior such as distancing. It also is assumed that as long as individuals are experiencing strong attachment fear, they will be unable to communicate constructively with each other. However, EFCT proposes that when partners have opportunities to feel emotionally soothed in interactions with each other, they will be less likely to respond with negative emotions and behavior toward each other. When an individual expresses primary attachment emotions such as sadness and anxiety, this communicates the individual's needs to the partner who is the potential caregiver, which in turn should elicit comforting responses from the caregiver.

CONTRIBUTIONS OF THE COUPLE VERSUS THE INDIVIDUAL IN COUPLE DISTRESS

The central role of attachment needs in the theoretical base of EFCT clearly identifies characteristics of the individual partners that contribute to marital distress. Kobak, Ruckdeschel, and Hazan (1994) noted that when individuals' working models are secure, they expect that caregivers will attend to their attachment needs. Consequently, secure individuals are more likely to express their emotions so as to facilitate attachment (e.g., expressing anger as a reflection of concern about distance in the relationship rather than as a personal attack on the caregiver). In contrast, individuals with insecure attachment working models commonly expect that direct expressions of attachment needs and emotions will lead to negative responses from a significant other, which results in a high level of anxiety about their ability to maintain the attachment. As described earlier, strategies for coping with attachment fears, such as detachment or hypervigilance and exaggerated expressions of emotion, are unlikely to elicit the desired nurturing responses, and the partner is unlikely to decipher the vulnerable attachment needs underlying such behavior. The individual's insecure working model is reconfirmed when the caregiver does not respond in a comforting, nurturing manner.

Thus, the characteristics of the two individuals shape the couple's interactions, but the dyadic pattern that arises between partners also plays a crucial role in maintaining marital distress. Research studies have found that adults with insecure attachment patterns tend to use less constructive conflict-resolution tactics in intimate relationships, as well as more negative conflict-management behavior, including psychological and physical abuse (Bookwala, 2002; Bookwala & Zdaniuk, 1998; Creasey, 2002; Dutton, Saunders, Starzomski, & Bartholomew, 1994; Roberts & Noller, 1998). Furthermore, the EFCT focus on dyadic couple interaction patterns is supported by studies indicating the combinations of two partners' attachment styles that are associated with levels of marital distress. For example, Fisher and Crandell (2000) found that clinical couples in which one partner had a preoccupied attachment style (anxious about losing the other's nurturance) and the other had a dismissing–avoidant style (more comfortable when autonomous) were characterized by conflict and a demand–withdrawal interaction pattern.

PROXIMAL VERSUS DISTAL FACTORS IN UNDERSTANDING RELATIONSHIP DISCORD

EFCT acknowledges that attachment concerns in the current relationship might be greatly influenced by historical factors and experiences that an individual had in earlier relationships, including family of origin and earlier romantic relationships. However, the focus within treatment is on the current relationship and attachment issues that are operating in the present.

APPROACHES TO TREATMENT

Behavior. EFCT proponents suggest that adults' perception of threats to their attachment relationships elicits natural negative behavioral responses. To change such problematic responses, the therapist creates a safe setting in sessions for each person to explore, understand, and reveal his or her primary (insecure) emotions and gain empathy for the partner's attachment needs. The therapist assists individuals in developing more constructive interactions with their partners, such as direct, nonhostile communication, that increase the probability of receiving reassuring responses and greater intimacy (Johnson & Denton, 2002; Johnson & Greenberg, 1995). Although the therapist and couple may set general goals of improving communication and relationship functioning, they typically do not identify and focus on specific behavioral targets or skills training. The therapist "reframes" negative behavior in terms of vulnerabilities and attachment needs and encourages further expressions of vulnerability. Presumably, understanding oneself and one's partner more clearly provides the context for adaptive behavior change.

Cognition. Emotionally focused therapists believe that relationship distress is caused by insecure attachment styles that include cognitive schemas in the form of "working models" of self in relation to a significant other and that these schemas typically are formed in the individuals' earlier attachment relationships. However, in EFCT, little attention is paid to fostering insight about earlier origins of attachment responses; rather, the focus is on the partners understanding each other's adaptive needs for closeness and nurturance within the current relationship, so that they can seek and provide for these needs in more positive ways. Each person's expressions of vulnerability should foster empathy from the other partner. The empathic shift toward viewing the partner's negative behavior as arising from attempts to cope with vulnerable feelings rather than from malicious motives results in a significant cognitive change in the individual's attributions about the partner.

Affect. A central goal of EFCT is to access the partners' insecure attachment styles through identifying the secondary emotions typically expressed to each other and the underlying vulnerable primary emotions associated with attachment insecurity. The therapist not only reflects back an individual's expressions of emotion regarding the partner and relationship, but also probes for vulnerable feelings (Johnson & Denton, 2002). By increasing partners' mutual empathy for each other's attachment fears and understanding of the more benign reasons for each other's misguided negative behavioral security-seeking strategies, therapists help

sooth the individuals and create opportunities for them to meet each other's attachment needs better (Johnson, 1996; Johnson & Denton, 2002; Kobak et al., 1994). Thus, affect is the therapist's window into the partners' attachment styles and the means for increasing more mutually satisfying interactions between partners.

EMPIRICAL SUPPORT FOR EMOTIONALLY FOCUSED COUPLE THERAPY

Several investigations of EFCT have addressed its efficacy, and the findings to date indicate that it is of significant benefit to distressed couples (Baucom et al., 1998; Johnson, Hunsley, Greenberg, & Schindler, 1999). Approximately a half dozen controlled studies have found EFCT to be superior to a wait-list control group (e.g., Denton, Burleson, Clark, Rodriguez, & Hobbs, 2000), with one study finding greater marital satisfaction for EFCT couples than BCT couples at posttreatment and at 8-week follow-up (Johnson & Greenberg, 1985). Johnson (2002) described a meta-analysis of the four most methodologically rigorous outcome studies on EFCT and reports that EFCT produced recovery rates from relationship distress (into the nondistressed range) of 70% to 73%, as well as an effect size of 1.3, all higher than has been found for BCT, CBCT, and ICBT. However, most studies on EFCT have treated couples who range from nondistressed to moderately distressed, so further studies are needed to test the efficacy of EFCT with more highly distressed couples. In the one study with more distressed couples, Goldman and Greenberg (1992) found that the 14 couples in EFCT and 14 couples in systemic couple therapy were not different from each other at posttest, but at a 4-month follow-up, the systemic therapy was superior to EFCT because the EFCT couples experienced significant relapse during the follow-up period. Goldman and Greenberg (1992) caution that with severely distressed couples, a time-limited course of EFCT might not be sufficient to create a level of intimacy between partners necessary to maintain posttreatment gains. Considering the overall results from these empirical investigations, Baucom et al. (1998) classified EFCT as an efficacious treatment in assisting moderately distressed couples.

Similar to Baucom et al.'s (1990) study adding cognitive restructuring to BCT, James (1991) compared 12 sessions of traditional EFCT with an enhanced version of EFCT that included 8 sessions of EFCT and 4 sessions of communication training (similar to communication training seen in BCT). Both treatments, with 14 couples in each condition, were superior to the wait-list condition that also included 14 couples in terms of marital functioning but the two treatment groups did not differ significantly. James (1991) reported that approximately 90% of couples receiving the two versions of EFCT improved with treatment, and 75% were no longer distressed at the end of treatment. These high rates of improvement must be considered in light of James's finding that even 50% of his waiting-list couples improved without treatment, perhaps because of the moderate marital distress level of the study's sample. The small sample size and lack of statistical power in the study make it difficult to interpret the lack of a difference between the traditional and enhanced EFCT conditions. At posttherapy, the effect size for the difference between the traditional EFCT and waiting-list conditions was 0.85, and the effect size for the difference between the EFCT plus communication training versus the waiting list condition was 1.07.

Insight-Oriented Couple Therapy

Just as there is no singular behavioral approach to marital distress and couple therapy, there is no one approach to understanding and treating marital distress that focuses on the role of insight in fostering change. In general, these approaches are labeled psychodynamic and have in common an emphasis on early relationship experiences in understanding current adult intimate relationships such as marriage (in contrast to EFCT, which emphasizes the couple's cur-

rent relationship). Although psychodynamic approaches continue to be popular among couple therapists, little empirical research has been conducted on their efficacy, with one notable exception – Snyder's insight-oriented couple therapy (IOCT; Snyder & Wills, 1989). IOCT is based on a premise that relationship problems are derived from emotional injuries that partners experienced in prior relationships and that left the individuals with vulnerabilities and defensive strategies designed to protect them from further hurt. Individuals are helped to see how their negative emotional and behavioral responses within their current relationship are influenced by distressing experiences that they had in prior relationships and that the coping strategies that were adaptive in those relationships are inappropriate for achieving emotional intimacy and other personal needs in their marriage. These interventions contribute to "affective reconstruction," or insight into one's interpersonal conflicts and coping patterns that identifies distortions and inappropriate solutions for achieving intimacy in one's relationship that are rooted in the past.

BASIC CONCEPTS

Behavior. IOCT is based on a premise that adults' negative behavioral responses in their relationships are influenced by previous relationship experiences that compromise an individual's ability to respond adaptively to the present relationship. As in other insight-oriented approaches, the individual's internalized "introjects," or schemas concerning intimate relationships, create a tendency to behave in particular ways to cope with perceived relationship dynamics. Marital distress is increased by the partners' previously developed behavioral strategies for protecting themselves from relationship injuries.

Cognition. IOCT views individuals' cognitions regarding intimate relationships as a system of internalized representations that function as models of how relationships should and do work. These internalized representations comprise characteristics that the client either observed or experienced in early relationships with parents or similar significant caregiving figures. These representations may be beyond awareness but are influential in how the person interacts with his or her partner and how the individual interprets current situations in the relationship. For example, a woman whose parent(s) devalued her abilities on the basis of her gender while she was growing up may have developed limited self-esteem and a schema that significant others do not value her. Subsequently, she may perceive any disagreement from her husband as a devaluation of her and respond with hurt feelings and behavioral withdrawal.

Affect. IOCT therapists propose that emotions experienced within the context of interacting with a partner have a major impact on the overall relationship. The individual's developmental history presumably influences many of these emotional responses to one's mate. Although a couple's distress also may be due to current stressors in the partners' life together and inadequate skills for coping with them, negative emotions tied to past relationship injuries tend to color present interactions. In "affective reconstruction," these emotions and their origins must be identified so that the partners can differentiate between past and present relationship experiences and develop more constructive strategies for emotional gratification and reduction of negative affect such as anxiety.

CONTRIBUTIONS OF THE COUPLE AND THE
INDIVIDUAL IN COUPLE DISTRESS

Of all the models presented in this chapter, the IOCT model tends to place the most emphasis on the individual's contribution to the relationship. Although IOCT therapists pay considerable attention to the couple's interaction patterns, they largely focus on the personal histories that the individual partners bring to the relationship. A major goal of therapy is to make each partner's affectively charged relationship schemas and associated strategies for coping with significant others clearer to both members of the couple and to develop the individuals' empathy with each other as each struggles to correct distorted schemas. Affective reconstruction capitalizes on the likelihood that each person's dysfunctional patterns of relating to significant others will be elicited in conjoint couple sessions more than in individual therapy, making them more apparent to the therapist and couple and accessible for therapeutic intervention.

PROXIMAL VERSUS DISTAL FACTORS IN
UNDERSTANDING RELATIONSHIP DISCORD

As noted earlier, IOCT assumes that current relationship difficulties often derive from earlier relationship traumas or difficulties. Thus, a major emphasis is placed on exploring and attempting to understand these earlier difficulties, consistent with the psychodynamic priority placed on insight into the role of the past on current functioning.

APPROACHES TO TREATMENT

Behavior. In IOCT, the therapist identifies for the couple how their current negative affect and interaction patterns are emotional responses and coping strategies developed in response to emotional injuries in past relationships. The therapist reframes these negative responses as normal and encourages the partners to view them in a more benign manner and to self-disclose their more vulnerable feelings within their relationship. A primary emphasis is placed on gaining insight into how previous relationship injuries contribute to current interaction patterns.

Cognition. IOCT and other relatively psychodynamically oriented therapists believe that much of a couple's distress results from underlying processes and schemas that are generally accessible but often beyond awareness. Therefore, the therapy focuses on identifying the content of these internalized representations derived from distressing experiences in past relationships and then interpreting them to clients to create insight into the effects of their relationship histories on their current maladaptive reactions to their partners. It is assumed that this insight then helps the individuals to modify their schemas and their continuing problematic relationship patterns in light of current awareness. The focus is on producing more realistic views of each other in the present relationship rather than focusing on resolving old issues with significant others from past relationships, such as parents (Snyder & Schneider, 2002).

Affect. IOCT therapists consider clients' emotional responses to be a key source of information about partners' internal dynamics. Moments in which an individual experiences emotion toward the partner during therapy sessions are viewed as potential windows into unconscious material from earlier developmental stages. These earlier experiences are presumed to have contributed to the current distressing emotions and associated dysfunctional behavior toward a partner. When appropriate, the therapist attempts to identify and interpret the intrapsychic, developmental meaning of these emotional responses and encourages the individual to self-disclose about vulnerable feelings. Each person is encouraged to identify relationship themes involving past disappointments and injuries. By helping the couple understand the significance of their negative emotions and their developmental origins, the therapist helps the partners tolerate anxiety. Furthermore, each partner becomes better able to provide for the other's personal needs because of their increased understanding of, and empathy for, each other.

EMPIRICAL SUPPORT FOR INSIGHT-ORIENTED
COUPLE THERAPY

Snyder and Wills (1989) compared the relative efficacy of IOCT and traditional behavioral couple therapy (BCT), both delivered for a mean of 19 sessions, and found both treatments to be efficacious relative to a waiting list condition. On the Global Distress Scale of the Marital Satisfaction Inventory, the IOCT versus waiting-list control comparison effect size was 1.15, and the BCT versus control group effect size was 0.85. There were no differences between

IOCT and BCT, however, in altering marital adjustment. Furthermore, at posttest, the two therapies had similar percentages of couples who moved from the distressed range of relationship functioning to the nondistressed range (40% of IOCT couples and 55% of BCT couples, compared with only 5% of waiting-list couples). Whereas IOCT and BCT were comparable on marital adjustment at a 6-month follow-up, Snyder et al. (1991) recontacted 96% of the treated couples 4 years after the completion of therapy and found that significantly more of the BCT couples (38%) had experienced divorce relative to the IOCT couples (3%). In the longest follow-up period of any couple interventions to date, IOCT couples also reported significantly higher levels of marital adjustment than BCT at the 4-year follow-up. Because finding meaningful differences between active treatment conditions is rare in the field of couple therapy, Snyder et al.'s findings call for replication to determine whether the long-term impact of IOCT is consistently superior to skills-based behavioral interventions. Based on the results from this one investigation, IOCT can be classified as possibly efficacious.

Integration and Conclusions

Considering the centrality that marriage holds in the lives of most adults and the high divorce rate, it is striking that controlled outcome studies have been conducted with only a few of the major theoretical approaches to treating relationship distress, as described in this chapter. The outcome evidence for behavioral (and its derivatives), emotionally focused, and insight-oriented approaches tends to be encouraging. The positive impacts demonstrated in investigations of behavioral, cognitive, and affective interventions of BCT, CBCT, IBCT, EFCT, and IOCT need not be the basis for competition among approaches but rather the grounds for seeking integration of models and procedures to maximize our ability to be of help to couples who are struggling with the most significant relationships in their lives. At times the concepts and terms used by different approaches seem to be incompatible, but our review suggests that the areas of overlap are substantial. The functioning of an intimate relationship includes behavioral interactions between the two individuals (including ingrained patterns), the often idiosyncratic cognitions that each person holds regarding the other, and a range of positive and negative emotional responses that influence cognitive appraisal as well as types of behavior toward the partner. Consequently, all of the approaches reviewed here have much to offer the researcher who is attempting to understand couple functioning and the clinician whose goal is to alleviate conflict and distress, because they all address behavior, cognition, and emotion. Furthermore, they vary in their focus on the two individuals' characteristics versus influences of the couple as a dyad, but they all attend to both realms.

Some significant steps toward theoretical and procedural integration in couple therapy have been developed in recent years. Epstein and Baucom (2002) described an enhanced cognitive–behavioral couple therapy that incorporates a greater focus on containing or eliciting emotions and broadens the focus of assessment and intervention to include relatively equal attention to characteristics of the two individuals, their dyadic interaction patterns, and the interpersonal and physical environments that comprise the context within which the couple functions. The individual level includes each person's developmental history, personality characteristics, needs and motives, and any psychopathology that he or she brings to the relationship. At the dyadic level, the couple's communication and problem-solving skills that have long been foci of BCT practitioners still are staples of enhanced cognitive–behavioral therapy. Environmental factors, such as extended family members, jobs, and social institutions (e.g., schools), commonly present in close relationships have not previously been incorporated into the empirically supported couple interventions discussed here and require attention in future treatment research. Although environmental demands may challenge a couple's ability to adapt, they also may be vital sources of resources to help the couple cope with life stressors.

Similarly, Snyder and Schneider's (2002) recent pluralistic approach to affective reconstruction broadens Snyder's earlier IOCT and assumes that relationship problems are influenced by multiple factors and require a multidimensional conceptual model and varied interventions. This pluralistic approach combines insight into developmental processes with behavioral, cognitive, and structural interventions intended to improve couples' relationship skills, enhance intimacy, reduce stressors in the partners' lives, and eliminate negative defensive coping strategies. Snyder and Schneider described a hierarchical model of intervention that includes the components of (a) developing a collaborative alliance with the couple; (b) containing disabling relationship crises; (c) strengthening the marital dyad through positive interactions and increased goodwill; (d) promoting relationship skills for expressiveness, empathic listening, conflict resolution, parenting, financial management; and time management; (e) challenging partners' cognitive distortions contributing to relationship distress; and (f) exploring the individuals' psychological injuries in past relationships that affect their current negative emotional and behavioral responses to each other. In-depth exploration of negative impacts that psychological injuries from earlier relationships have on current emotional and behavioral responses to a partner are combined with practical training in behavioral skills to reduce stress on the couple and enhance intimacy (which can reduce the effects of old emotional wounds). Emotionally focused therapy proponents have not pursued integration with other approaches to a significant extent, but there seems to be great potential for using concepts and methods from other theoretical approaches in the service of modifying problematic responses to insecure attachments.

Overall, we propose that some of the common elements in the effective approaches that we have reviewed include (a) broadening partners' perspectives on sources of their difficulties as a couple, as well as on their strengths as a couple; (b) increasing the partners' abilities to differentiate between the strengths and problems within their current relationship, versus characteristics that occurred in prior relationships; (c) motivating and directing the couple to reduce behavioral patterns that maintain or worsen relationship distress; and (d) increasing the range of constructive strategies that partners have available for influencing each other. We propose that efficacious interventions from all of the approaches that we reviewed have aspects of these features in common, as well as an overarching ability to increase partners' hope or positive expectancies that efforts that they make in therapy and in their daily life as a couple can increase mutual goodwill, intimacy, and relationship satisfaction. Future intervention research can benefit by including specific interventions that address these factors and multiple assessment measures that can measure changes in those areas.

Whereas this discussion of common elements of efficacious treatment highlights the issues that should be emphasized in couple-therapy, this might not be all that is essential for efficacious treatment. In addition, the overall quality of the couple-therapist relationship (i.e., therapeutic alliance) might be an important factor in efficacious treatment. Although the quality of the therapeutic alliance in explaining treatment effects has not been investigated empirically in couple therapy, the therapeutic alliance has received considerable attention in psychotherapy research more generally. A recent meta-analysis of psychotherapy concluded that the therapeutic alliance explains between 38% and 77% of the variance in treatment outcome, whereas specific techniques account for only 0% to 8% of the variance (Wampold, 2001). Furthermore, Fitzpatrick, Stalikas, and Iwakabe (2001) demonstrated that the impact of specific techniques was dependent on the quality of the therapeutic alliance. Thus, focusing on certain issues within the couple's relationship within the context of a positive, safe therapeutic relationship might provide an optimal context for couples to relate to each other in a more constructive manner.

Footnotes

1. The term "couple therapy" will be employed in this chapter because it is the term commonly used in the field at present. However, the reader should be aware that in almost of the empirical investigations to date, couples receiving intervention have been married; thus, the applicability of the findings to unmarried, committed couples is unclear.

2. A between-group effect size is merely the difference in means between two treatment conditions expressed in standard score form; that is, it can be calculated by calculating the difference between the means of the two interventions, divided by the standard deviation of the control group. Glass, McGraw, and Smith (1981) proposed the following guidelines for different sizes of effect sizes: $0.2 = $ small; $0.5 = $ medium; $0.8 = $ large.

References

Ainsworth, M. S., Blehar, M. C., Waters, E., & Wall, S. (1978). *Patterns of attachment: A psychological study of the strange situation*. Hillsdale, NJ: Erlbaum.

Alexander, J. F., Holtzworth-Munroe, A., & Jameson, P. B. (1994). The process and outcome of marital and family therapy: Research review and evaluation. In A. E. Bergin & S. L. Garfield (Eds.), *Handbook of psychotherapy and behavior change* (4th ed., pp. 595–630). New York: Wiley.

Australian Bureau of Statistics. (2001). *Marriage and divorces, Australia*. Canberra: Australian Bureau of Statistics.

Azrin, N. H., Besalel, V. A., Betchel, R., Michalicek, A., Mancera, M., Carroll, D., et al. (1980). Comparison of reciprocity and discussion-type counseling for marital problems. *American Journal of Family Therapy, 8*, 21–28.

Bandura, A. (1977). *Social learning theory*. Englewood Cliffs, NJ: Prentice-Hall.

Bartholomew, K., & Horowitz, L. M. (1991). Attachment styles among young adults: A test of a four-category model. *Journal of Personality and Social Psychology, 61*, 224–226.

Baucom, D. H., & Epstein, N. (1990). *Cognitive–behavioral marital therapy*. New York: Brunner/Mazel.

Baucom, D. H., Epstein, N., Rankin, L., & Burnett, C. K. (1996). Understanding and treating marital distress from a cognitive–behavioral orientation. In K. S. Dobson & K. D. Craig (Eds.), *Advances in cognitive–behavioral therapy* (pp. 210–236). Thousand Oaks, CA: Sage.

Baucom, D. H., Epstein, N., Sayers, S. L., & Sher, T. G. (1989). The role of cognitions in marital relationships: Definitional, methodological, and conceptual issues. *Journal of Consulting and Clinical Psychology, 57*, 31–38.

Baucom, D. H., Hahlweg, K., & Kuschel, A. (2003). Are waiting list control groups needed in future marital therapy outcome research? *Behavior Therapy, 34*, 179–188.

Baucom, D. H., & Lester, G. W. (1986). The usefulness of cognitive restructuring as an adjunct to behavioral marital therapy. *Behavior Therapy, 17*, 385–403.

Baucom, D. H., Sayers, S. L., & Sher, T. G. (1990). Supplementing behavioral marital therapy with cognitive restructuring and emotional expressiveness training: An outcome investigation. *Journal of Consulting and Clinical Psychology, 58*, 636–645.

Baucom, D. H., Shoham, V., Mueser, K. T., Daiuto, A. D., & Stickle, T. R. (1998). Empirically supported couples and family therapies for adult problems. *Journal of Consulting and Clinical Psychology, 66*, 53–88.

Beck, A. T., Rush, A. J., Shaw, B. F., & Emery, G. (1979). *Cognitive therapy of depression*. New York: Guilford Press.

Berman, W. H., Marcus, L., & Berman, E. R. (1994). Attachment in marital relations. In M. B. Sperling & W. H. Berman (Eds.), *Attachment in adults: Clinical and developmental perspectives* (pp. 204–231). New York: Guilford Press.

Bischof, G. H., & Helmeke, K. B. (2003). Couple therapy. In L. L. Hecker & J. L. Wetchler (Eds.), *An introduction to marriage and family therapy* (pp. 297–336). New York: Haworth Press.

Bookwala, J. (2002). The role of own and perceived partner attachment in relationship aggression. *Journal of Interpersonal Violence, 17*, 84–100.

Bookwala, J., & Zdaniuk, B. (1998). Adult attachment styles and aggressive behavior within dating relationships. *Journal of Social and Personal Relationships, 15*, 175–190.

Bowlby, J. (1989). The role of attachment in personality development and psychopathology. In S. Greenspan & G. Pollock (Eds.), *The course of life: Volume 1. Infancy* (pp. 229–270). Madison, CT: International Universities Press.

Bradbury, T. N., & Fincham, F. D. (1990). Attributions in marriage: Review and critique. *Psychological Bulletin, 107*, 3–33.

Bray, J. H., & Jouriles, E. N. (1995). Treatment of marital conflict and prevention of divorce. *Journal of Marital and Family Therapy, 21*, 461–473.

Chambless, D. L., & Hollon, S. (1998). Defining empirically supported therapies. *Journal of Consulting and Clinical Psychology, 66*, 7–18.

Christensen, A., Atkins, D., Berns, S., Wheeler, J., Baucom, D. H., & Simpson, L. (2004). Traditional versus integrative behavioral couple therapy for significantly and chronically distressed married couples. *Journal of Consulting and Clinical Psychology, 72*, 176–191.

Christensen, A., & Heavey, C. L. (1990). Gender and social structure in the demand/withdraw pattern of marital conflict. *Journal of Personality and Social Psychology, 59*, 73–81.

Christensen, A., Jacobson, N. S., & Babcock, J. C. (1995). Integrative behavioral couple therapy. In N. S. Jacobson & A. S. Gurman (Eds.), *Clinical handbook of couple therapy* (pp. 31–64). New York: Guilford Press.

Christensen, A., & Shenk, J. L. (1991). Communication, conflict, and psychological distance in nondistressed, clinic, and divorcing couples. *Journal of Consulting and Clinical Psychology, 59*, 458–463.

Creasey, G. (2002). Associations between working models of attachment and conflict management behavior in romantic couples. *Journal of Counseling Psychology, 49*, 365–375.

Crowe, M. J. (1978). Conjoint marital therapy: A controlled outcome study. *Psychological Medicine, 8*, 623–636.

Davila, J., Burge, D., & Hammen, C. (1997). Why does attachment style change? *Journal of Personality and Social Psychology, 73*, 826–838.

Denton, W. H., Burleson, B. R., Clark, T. E., Rodriguez, C. R., & Hobbs, B. V. (2000). A randomized trial of emotionally focused therapy for couples in a training clinic. *Journal of Marital and Family Therapy, 26,* 65–78.

Dunn, R. L., & Schwebel, A. I. (1995). Meta-analytic review of marital therapy outcome research. *Journal of Family Psychology, 9,* 58–68.

Dutton, D. G., Saunders, K., Starzomski, A., & Bartholomew, K. (1994). Intimacy–anger and insecure attachment as precursors of abuse in intimate relationships. *Journal of Applied Social Psychology, 24,* 1367–1386.

Ellis, A. (1978). Family therapy: A phenomenological and active directive approach. *Journal of Marital and Family Therapy, 4,* 43–50.

Epstein, N., & Baucom, D. H. (1993). Cognitive factors in marital disturbance. In K. S. Dobson & P. C. Kendall (Eds.), *Psychopathology and cognition* (pp. 351–385). San Diego, CA: Academic Press.

Epstein, N., & Baucom, D. H. (2002). *Enhanced cognitive–behavioral therapy for couples: A contextual approach.* Washington, DC: American Psychological Association.

Epstein, N., Baucom, D. H., & Rankin, L. A. (1993). Treatment of marital conflict: A cognitive-behavioral approach. *Clinical Psychology Review, 13,* 45–57.

Epstein, N., & Eidelson, R. J. (1981). Unrealistic beliefs of clinical couples: Their relationship to expectations, goals and satisfaction. *American Journal of Family Therapy, 9*(4), 13–22.

Fincham, F. D., & Bradbury, T. N. (1989). The impact of attributions in marriage: An individual difference analysis. *Journal of Social and Personal Relationships, 6,* 69–85.

Fincham, F. D., Bradbury, T. N., & Scott, C. K. (1990). Cognition in marriage. In F. D. Fincham & T. N. Bradbury (Eds.), *The psychology of marriage: Basic issues and applications* (pp. 118–149). New York: Guilford Press.

Fisher, J., & Crandell, L. (2000). Patterns of relating in the couple. In C. Clulow (Ed.), *Adult attachment and couple psychotherapy: The "secure base" in practice and research* (pp. 15–27). London: Brunner-Routledge.

Fitzpatrick, M. R., Stalikas, A., & Iwakabe, S. (2002). Examining counselor interventions and patient progress in the context of the therapeutic alliance. *Psychotherapy, 38,* 160–170.

Freedman, J. H., & Combs, G. (2002). Narrative couple therapy. In A. S. Gurman & N. S. Jacobson (Eds.), *Clinical handbook of couple therapy*

(3rd ed., pp. 308–334). New York: Guilford Press.

Glass, G. V., McGraw, B., & Smith, M. L. (1981). *Meta-analysis in social research.* Beverly Hills, CA: Sage.

Goldman, A., & Greenberg, L. (1992). Comparison of integrated systemic and emotionally focused approaches to couples therapy. *Journal of Consulting and Clinical Psychology, 60,* 962–969.

Gottman, J. M. (1994). *Why marriages succeed or fail.* New York: Simon & Schuster.

Greenberg, L. S., & Johnson, S. M. (1988). *Emotionally focused therapy for couples.* New York: Guilford Press.

Hahlweg, K., & Markman, H. J. (1988). Effectiveness of behavioral marital therapy: Empirical status of behavioral techniques in preventing and alleviating marital distress. *Journal of Consulting and Clinical Psychology, 56,* 440–447.

Halford, W. K., Kelly, A., & Markman, H. J. (1997). The concept of a healthy marriage. In W. K. Halford & H. J. Markman (Eds.), *Clinical handbook of marriage and couples interventions* (pp. 3–12). Chichester, England: Wiley.

Halford, W. K., Sanders, M. R., & Behrens, B. C. (1993). A comparison of the generalization of behavioral martial therapy and enhanced behavioral martial therapy. *Journal of Consulting and Clinical Psychology, 61,* 51–60.

Hazan, C., & Shaver, P. (1987). Romantic love conceptualized as an attachment process. *Journal of Personality and Social Psychology, 52,* 511–524.

Holtzworth-Munroe, A., & Jacobson, N. S. (1985). Causal attributions of married couples: When do they search for causes? What do they conclude when they do? *Journal of Personality and Social Psychology, 48,* 1398–1412.

Hoyt, M. F. (2002). Solution-focused couple therapy. In A. S. Gurman & N. S. Jacobson (Eds.), *Clinical handbook of couple therapy* (3rd ed., pp. 335–369). New York: Guilford Press.

Huber, C. H., & Milstein, B. (1985). Cognitive restructuring and a collaborative set in couples' work. *American Journal of Family Therapy, 13*(2), 17–27.

Iverson, A., & Baucom, D. H. (1990). Behavioral marital therapy outcomes: Alternative interpretations of the data. *Behavior Therapy, 21,* 129–138.

Jacobson, N. S. (1978). Specific and nonspecific factors in the effectiveness of a behavioral approach to the treatment of marital discord. *Journal of Consulting and Clinical Psychology*, 46, 442–452.

Jacobson, N. S., & Christensen, A. (1996). *Integrative couple therapy: Promoting acceptance and change*. New York: Norton.

Jacobson, N. S., Follette, W. C., & Revenstorf, D. (1984). Psychotherapy outcome research: Methods for reporting variability and evaluating clinical significance. *Behavior Therapy*, 15, 336–352.

Jacobson, N. S., & Margolin, G. (1979). *Marital therapy: Strategies based on social learning and behavior exchange principles*. New York: Brunner/Mazel.

Jacobson, N. S., Schmaling, K. B., & Holtzworth-Munroe, A. (1987). Component analysis of behavioral marital therapy: 2-year follow-up and prediction of relapse. *Journal of Marital and Family Therapy*, 13, 187–195.

James, P. S. (1991). Effects of a communication training component added to an emotionally focused couples therapy. *Journal of Marital and Family Therapy*, 17, 263–275.

Johnson, S. M. (1996). *The practice of emotionally focused marital therapy: Creating connection*. New York: Brunner/Mazel.

Johnson, S. M. (2002). Marital problems. In D. H. Sprenkle (Ed.), *Effectiveness research in marriage and family therapy* (pp. 163–190). Alexandria, VA: American Association for Marriage and Family Therapy.

Johnson, S. M., & Denton, W. (2002). Emotionally focused couple therapy: Creating secure connections. In A. S. Gurman & N. S. Jacobson (Eds.), *Clinical handbook of couple therapy* (3rd ed., pp. 221–250). New York: Guilford Press.

Johnson, S. M., & Greenberg, L. S. (1985). Differential effects of experiential and problem-solving interventions in resolving marital conflict. *Journal of Consulting and Clinical Psychology*, 53, 175–184.

Johnson, S. M., & Greenberg, L. S. (1995). The emotionally focused approach to problems in adult attachment. In N. S. Jacobson & A. S. Gurman (Eds.), *Clinical handbook of couple therapy* (pp. 121–141). New York: Guilford Press.

Johnson, S. M., Hunsley, J., Greenberg, L., & Schindler, D. (1999). Emotionally focused couples therapy: Status and challenges. *Clinical Psychology: Science and Practice*, 6, 67–79.

Kendall, P. C., & Chambless, D. L. (Eds.). (1998). Empirically supported psychological therapies [Special issue]. *Journal of Consulting and Clinical Psychology*, 66, 3–167.

Kerr, M., & Bowen, M. (1988). *Family evaluation*. New York: Norton.

Kobak, R., Ruckdeschel, K., & Hazan, C. (1994). From symptom to signal: An attachment view of emotion in marital therapy. In S. M. Johnson & L. S. Greenberg (Eds.), *The heart of the matter: Perspectives on emotion in marital therapy* (pp. 46–71). New York: Brunner/Mazel.

McDonald, P. (1995). *Families in Australia: A socio-demographic perspective*. Melbourne: Australian Institute of Family Studies.

Meichenbaum, D. (1985). *Stress inoculation training*. New York: Pergamon Press.

Minuchin, S., & Nichols, M. P. (1998). Structural family therapy. In F. M. Dattilio (Ed.), *Case studies in couple and family therapy: Systemic and cognitive perspectives* (pp. 108–131). New York: Guilford Press.

Noller, P., Beach, S. R. H., & Osgarby, S. (1997). Cognitive and affective processes in marriage. In W. K. Halford & H. J. Markman (Eds.), *Clinical handbook of marriage and couples interventions* (pp. 43–71). Chichester, England: Wiley.

Pretzer, J., Epstein, N., & Fleming, B. (1991). Marital Attitude Survey: A measure of dysfunctional attributions and expectancies. *Journal of Cognitive Psychotherapy: An International Quarterly*, 5, 131–148.

Roberts, N., & Noller, P. (1998). The association between adult attachment and couple violence. In J. A. Simpson & W. S. Rholes (Eds.), *Attachment theory and close relationships* (pp. 317–350). New York: Guilford Press.

Rothbard, J. E., & Shaver, P. (1994). Continuity of attachment across the lifecourse: An attachment-theoretical perspective on personality. In M. B. Sperling & W. H. Berman (Eds.), *Attachment in adults: Theory, assessment, and treatment* (pp. 31–71). New York: Guilford Press.

Shadish, W. R., & Baldwin, S. A. (2002). Meta-analysis of MFT interventions. In D. H. Sprenkle (Ed.), *Effectiveness research in marriage and family therapy* (pp. 339–370). Alexandria, VA: American Association for Marriage and Family Therapy.

Shadish, W. R., Montgomery, L. M., Wilson, P., Wilson, M. R., Bright, I., & Okwumabua, T. (1993). Effects of family and marital psychotherapies: A meta-analysis. *Journal of Consulting and Clinical Psychology, 61,* 992–1002.

Shoham, V., & Rohrbaugh, M. J. (2002). Brief strategic couple therapy. In A. S. Gurman & N. S. Jacobson (Eds.), *Clinical handbook of couple therapy* (3rd ed., pp. 5–25). New York: Guilford Press.

Snyder, D. K., & Schneider, W. J. (2002). Affective reconstruction: A pluralistic, developmental approach. In A. S. Gurman & N. S. Jacobson (Eds.), *Clinical handbook of couple therapy* (3rd ed., pp. 151–179). New York: Guilford Press.

Snyder, D. K., & Wills, R. M. (1989). Behavioral versus insight-oriented marital therapy: Effects on individual and interspousal functioning. *Journal of Consulting and Clinical Psychology, 57,* 39–46.

Snyder, D. K., Wills, R. M., & Grady-Fletcher, A. (1991). Long-term effectiveness of behavioral versus insight-oriented marital therapy: A 4-year follow-up study. *Journal of Consulting and Clinical Psychology, 59,* 138–141.

Stuart, R. B. (1980). *Helping couples change: A social learning approach to marital therapy.* New York: Guilford Press.

Thibaut, J. W., & Kelley, H. H. (1959). *The social psychology of groups.* New York: Wiley.

United States Census Bureau. (2002). *Number, timing and duration of marriages and divorces: 1996.* Washington, DC.

Wampold, B. E. (2001). *The great psychotherapy debate: Models, methods, and findings.* Mahwah, NJ: Erlbaum.

Waters, E., Hamilton, C. E., & Weinfield, N. S. (2000). The stability of attachment security from infancy to adolescence and early adulthood: General information. *Child Development, 71,* 678–683.

Weiss, R. L., & Heyman, R. E. (1990). Observation of marital interaction. In F. D. Fincham & T. N. Bradbury (Eds.), *The psychology of marriage: Basic issues and applications* (pp. 87–117). New York: Guilford Press.

Weiss, R. L., Hops, H., & Patterson, G. R. (1973). A framework for conceptualizing marital conflict, a technology for altering it, some data for evaluating it. In M. Hersen & A. S. Bellack (Eds.), *Behavior change: Methodology, concepts and practice* (pp. 309–342). Champaign, IL: Research Press.

Part XII

CONCLUSION

CHAPTER 41
Bringing It All Together: A Theoretical Approach

Patricia Noller

The task of writing a concluding chapter to a handbook with the scope of this one is obviously difficult. It was a challenge to find a way to draw together the themes that emerge from all these chapters. I finally decided, with inspiration from Planalp, Fitness, and Fehr, to organize my comments around the various theoretical perspectives that tend to be most prominent in research on personal relationships. I have not been as ambitious as Planalp and her colleagues, however, and have limited my comments to five theoretical perspectives: social exchange perspectives, sociocognitive theories, attachment theory, evolutionary theories, and social roles and power.

Given that these various perspectives have not been given equal treatment by the chapter authors, I have not given them equal treatment either. In addition, taking a theoretical perspective has meant that some chapters in this volume have received little or no mention, whereas others tend to be mentioned more frequently. I find it necessary to quote Harvey and Wenzel and note that, despite my best efforts, I almost certainly "will not do justice to the nuances of these approaches," nor will I do justice to the large amount of research that has gone into writing the various chapters.

As will be obvious to readers, most of the theoretical perspectives that I have included involve not a single theory but a number of theories that tend to come under the same "umbrella" perspective. The social exchange perspective is an obvious example, with interdependence theory (Kelley & Thibaut, 1978), equity theory (Hatfield, Utne, & Traupmann, 1979), and the investment model (Rusbult, 1980) all coming under the umbrella of the social exchange perspective. The sociocognitive perspective and the evolutionary perspective also include a number of related theoretical perspectives clustered under the one umbrella.

My goal in discussing each theoretical perspective is to draw together the comments of the various authors about the ways that the various theoretical perspectives relate to the particular content areas being discussed and then to discuss the usefulness of that perspective to research on personal relationships. I finally comment on possible directions for future research.

Social Exchange Theories

Social exchange processes are mentioned in at least 13 of the chapters in this volume. As noted already, the social exchange perspective has spawned a number of more specific theories, in particular, interdependence theory, equity theory, and the investment model. In their discussion of mate selection and dating relationships, Surra, Gray, Boettcher, Cottle, and West (this volume) note that social exchange processes have been consistently studied in this type of research and that issues about justice, equity, and fairness in dating and romantic relationships have been a focus from the earliest reviews to the most recent ones.

Perlman and Duck, in their introductory chapter to this volume, comment on the fact that scholars associated with interdependence theory (e.g., Kelley and Rusbult) are among the most frequently cited in the 1990s. They note that interdependence theory "clearly has become an important perspective for understanding close relationships." Proponents of equity theory, such as Hatfield and Sprecher, are also listed among the top 20 most frequently cited scholars in the area of personal relationships.

There are arguments about the extent to which social exchange processes are relevant to close relationships such as marriage, and more recently there has been a shift from an emphasis on "tit-for-tat" exchanges to more cooperative approaches such as seeking to meet one another's needs (e.g., see Clark and Mills's [1979] discussion of exchange versus communal relationships). I believe that Harvey and Wenzel are correct in claiming that exchange processes may become more salient when a relationship is in trouble: "Indeed, when a relationship becomes distressed, it is quite possible that each individual focuses his or her attention on the quid pro quo of social exchange and is quick to identify instances of relationship inequity."

Thus social exchange processes may be more relevant to relationships that are struggling, with the members of the couple becoming more concerned about what they are getting out of the relationship and less concerned with meeting the needs of the partner. Unfortunately, tracking rewards and costs at this stage is unlikely to help the partners rediscover their love for one another or their commitment to the relationship.

Surra et al. maintain that, as for the study of committed relationships, in the study of dating and mate selection, the emphasis has shifted from a focus on tit-for-tat exchanges to a focus on norms that encourage cooperation in close relationships. They do acknowledge, however, that the rewards partners receive from the interactions in their relationships are powerful predictors of satisfaction with that relationship. In addition, they note that the perceived quality of investments in and available alternatives to the relationship predict both satisfaction and commitment. In other words, a relationship is likely to be maintained when there are few desirable alternatives and there has been a sizeable investment of time, energy, and resources in the current relationship.

As Canary and Dainton note in their chapter on maintenance processes, interdependence theory promotes the view that romantic relationships (including marriage) are stable and satisfying when the partner can be compared favorably with an individual's ideal and with perceived alternatives. In developing her investment model, Rusbult (1980) adds a third factor focusing on the investments an individual has in the relationship (such as energy, time, shared history, and children), with the three factors (ideal, alternatives, and investment) predicting that person's level of commitment to the relationship. Canary and Dainton see the willingness to be involved in maintenance processes as a function of the level of commitment to the relationship.

Proponents of equity theory take the view that individuals tend to be happier in relationships that are fair and equitable, that is, where partners perceive that the ratios of rewards to inputs experienced by each partner are equal. When they are in relationships that they perceive as unfair, they attempt to restore equity by either reducing their own inputs or by trying to increase the rewards from the partner. According to Canary and Dainton, partners' willingness to engage in maintenance behaviors depends on their satisfaction and perceived level of equity, and engaging in maintenance behaviors tends to keep commitment high.

Cutrona and Gardner in their chapter relate exchange processes to the problem of work–family spillover and show that an initial negative event (for example, for the husband at work) may lead to the affected person being unsupportive in his or her interactions with the partner, followed by the unaffected partner withdrawing. The consequences for the relationship are that neither partner will experience any real sense of support and companionship from the other, and the relationship itself may be threatened if such occurrences are frequent.

The association between social exchange processes and self-disclosure is the focus of the chapter by Greene, Derlega, and Mathews. They note that decisions about whether to disclose something personal about oneself to a partner depend on their assessment of the relative costs and benefits of disclosing such material in that relationship. This assessment would include their expectation of how the partner is likely to respond to such a disclosure. Greene et al., in line with Reis and Shaver (1988), underline the importance of the partner's response to the impact of that disclosure on the relationship and to future decisions about disclosure in that relationship.

The ratio of positive and negative behaviors during conflict interactions is also critical to relationships as viewed from a social exchange perspective, as Kline, Pleasant, Whitton and Markman point out in their chapter. The study of conflict communication in married couples, however, has shown that negative behavior tends to have a stronger impact on relationship satisfaction than positive behavior. Notarius and Markman (1993), for example, have proposed a bank account model where positive behaviors are seen as deposits and negative behaviors are seen as withdrawals. They note, however, that one very negative behavior can wipe out a number of positive ones.

This problem of the stronger effects of negative behaviors than positive behaviors on satisfaction in adult relationships is discussed by Blieszner. She reports work by Rook (1990), who identified possible explanations for the potential of relatively rare negative behaviors to wipe out the impact of positive ones. Rook suggested that the salience of negative behavior (perhaps just because it is less common), the less ambiguous interpretation of negative behavior, and the vigilance that individuals tend to exercise toward behavior that is potentially threatening all contribute to this effect. Another factor relevant to this issue of the power of negative behavior is what Sillars and colleagues (Sillars, Leonard, Roberts, & Dun, 2002) called the high reciprocity of negative affect, particularly among distressed couples. Thus negative behavior tends to beget negative behavior with ever-increasing intensity.

In their chapter on the sexual relationship, Sprecher, Christopher, and Cate focus on social exchange processes and suggest that frequency of sexual intercourse is likely to increase when the sexual relationship and the nonsexual aspects of the relationship are both highly rewarding. In discussing the sexual relationships of homosexual couples, Diamond notes that exchange theory principles are relevant, with the balance of perceived rewards and costs being just as important in assessing sexual satisfaction for same-sex couples as for heterosexual couples.

In discussing social exchange processes and emotion, Planalp, Fitness, and Fehr debunk the idea that social exchange processes are cold and calculating and argue that "the basic concepts and processes of social exchange theory can be viewed as deeply emotional." For example, they note that rewards and costs are often experienced as positive and negative feelings. In addition, our reactions to inequity and inequality in our relationships are likely to be highly emotional, and indeed such social exchange concepts as comparison levels and comparison levels for alternatives are basically about positive and negative feelings toward the partner and toward potential alternatives. Overall, adding the emotional component to social exchange theories helps to increase our understanding of partner selection and the development of relationships.

Extradyadic sexual involvement and jealousy can also be related to interdependence theory according to Buunk and Dijkstra. They note that interdependence theory would seem to predict that individuals who are highly dependent on their partners are less likely than more independent individuals to become involved in affairs; in addition, the probability of an extradyadic affair increases as investment in the current relationship decreases. On the other hand, highly dependent partners are more likely to be jealous, especially if they are satisfied with their current relationship and are afraid of losing the rewards that relationship provides. Being more dependent on the relationship than their partner is also likely to increase the probability of jealousy. Buunk and Dijkstra see having an extramarital affair as involving a social-exchange-type decision process involving the assessment of costs and benefits, and they note that men tend to focus more on the possible benefits, whereas women tend to focus more on the possible costs. Perhaps that is why some men at least seem to "rush headlong" into affairs without considering the consequences for themselves or their families.

As part of our discussion of the social exchange perspective, it is important to note that much couple therapy is based on a social exchange perspective. As Baucom, Epstein, and Stanton point out, behavioral marital therapy (BMT) is based on social exchange principles. Therapists working from this perspective aim to increase the ratio of positive to negative exchanges between the couple and to increase the skills of the partners in providing one another with positive rewards and reinforcing exchanges. To increase the couple's potential for rewarding exchanges and to increase the likelihood that they will reinforce appropriate behavior, therapists tend to teach specific communication skills such as nonblaming ways of expressing thoughts and feelings, empathic listening, and problem solving.

Although there is some controversy about the extent to which social exchange processes are relevant to committed relationships that are going well, it is clear that people want their relationships to be fair and equitable, and exchange processes tend to become the focus when relationships are not going well. Perhaps the reason that BMT tends to be successful in promoting increased marital happiness is because of its focus on just those exchange processes that have become so salient for those struggling in their relationships. In addition, exchange processes are relevant to so many aspects of our close personal relationships, including mate-selection, commitment, self-disclosure, dealing with conflict, the sexual relationship, extradyadic sexual involvement, and jealousy.

Harvey and Wenzel see the social exchange perspective as less influential now than it has been in the past, with approaches such as communal love providing some balance. They go on to argue, however, that "even communal relationships involve implicit considerations of equity or reciprocity." In addition, they see the interdependence model as providing a sophisticated explanation for the ways individuals seek to address both their own needs and expectations, and those of their relationship.

Sociocognitive Theories

With the emphasis on observational methodologies and the importance of obtaining an "objective" view of relationship behavior so prevalent in the '70s and '80s, I believe that we lost a necessary emphasis on understanding the meaning of partner behavior for individuals. There seemed to be an assumption that a behavior always has the same meaning. Yet as Harvey and Wenzel note, "Because of the extensive history that couples develop, seemingly minute relationship events often hold a great deal of meaning to one or both partners, which can prompt behavior that is much more extreme than would seem warranted to an outside observer."

The point is that it is not enough to observe a couple's behavior, we need also to understand the meaning of that behavior for the partners engaging in the interaction. The sociocognitive perspective has brought some balance and put the emphasis back on understanding the cognitive processes that can be powerful drivers of partner behavior.

It is important to point out that there is no single sociocognitive perspective, but a group of theories that focus on the role of cognition in individual behavior and functioning. These theories are important to relationship researchers because individuals' cognitions about themselves, about their partners, and about their relationships can affect the quality of those relationships. As Fletcher, Overall, and Friesen note,

> More generally, we believe work in this area supports two striking conclusions. First, a social cognitive approach can, and does, enrich our understanding of intimate relationships. Second, studying cognition within the messy, complex emotional world of intimate relationships illuminates and expands our understanding of the most basic processes of cognition and emotion. This is simply because so much of the way that humans feel and think is rooted in close interpersonal contexts.

Theories that belong in this group include attribution theory and cognitive–behavioral theory. Other major theories of relationships that include a sociocognitive component are discussed in greater detail in other sections. For example, attachment theory focuses on working models but also involves a more comprehensive focus on relational processes, The investment model includes the cognitive variable of commitment, but because of its relation to interdependence theory, has also been considered in the section on social exchange processes.

Fincham and Beach suggest that the evidence for an association between attributions and relationship satisfaction is one of the most robust findings in the area of close relationships. These authors also note that many cognitive variables, apart from attributions, are associated with relationship satisfaction. Their list includes discrepancies between the partner's behavior and one's ideal standards, social comparison processes such as seeing one's relationships as superior to the norm, memory processes that lead to the recall of positive versus negative memories, and self-evaluation maintenance processes that serve to maintain self-esteem even when one compares poorly with the partner.

It is also important to note that cognitions can operate at several levels of analysis. For example, Goodwin and Pillay focus on culture, which is likely to have an impact on individuals' beliefs, schemas, values, and goals. Within any culture, however, individuals may have different types of experiences in the family that will have an impact on their values, beliefs, standards, schemas, and working models, and these cognitions will affect the quality and stability of their relationships. For example, Goodwin and Pillay make the point that in many cultures, marriage is seen as between two families rather than as between two individuals, as it is generally seen in the west. In addition, because those in "traditional" cultures have different expectations about marriage, they are also likely to expect different benefits than those in more individualistic cultures who focus on love and intimacy. For example, Greene et al. discuss cultural impacts on attitudes about self-disclosure. Noting that family and individual variables such as gender, self-esteem, and attachment style also have an influence, they also comment on the finding of cross-cultural differences in disclosure in different types of relationships.

Goodwin and Pillay acknowledge the tension between evolutionary psychologists who tend to stress what they consider universal aspects of partner choice and cultural psychologists who tend to emphasize the ways in which cultures vary in how these choices are made, depending at least in part on whether those cultures are individualistic or collectivist, "masculine" or "feminine." (I discuss evolutionary theories in a later section.) These authors also focus on the relationship between the cultural environment and expectations about marriage and suggest that as the environment becomes more rational and impersonal, couples put more emphasis on intimacy in their marriages.

In their discussion of passionate love, Aron, Fisher, and Strong emphasize the work of Dion and Dion (1988) on the effects of individualistic and collectivistic attitudes on love and on the potentially negative effects of excessive individualism on a person's ability to be involved in a committed relationship and to be intimate with a partner. Aron et al. argue that although passionate love exists in every culture, how it is enacted is likely to depend on cultural beliefs about what is appropriate. They suggest that the high levels of divorce in the United States (and other Western cultures) may be related to the strong emphasis on individualism in that culture.

Harvey and Wenzel raise the issue of the lack of direct empirical support for the proposition that cognition actually causes changes in behavior. At the same time, they note that the way that individuals interpret events in their relationship is likely to affect their emotional reaction and their subsequent behavior. Indeed, a prominent program for teaching couples to communicate more effectively (Miller, Nunnally, & Wackman, 1975) makes just that assumption. It is also important to emphasize here that understanding a person's interpretation of partner behavior may be as important as observing that behavior. Research methods aimed at seeking to understand partners' thoughts and feelings have been developed for just this purpose (Manusov, 2002; Schweinle & Ickes, 2002; Sillars et al., 2002).

From a sociocognitive perspective, as Planalp et al. note, individuals tend to store emotional knowledge as scripts or prototypes as they grow and develop, and these scripts and prototypes can play a crucial role in their understanding of how emotions function in close relationships. These authors are, however, critical of the prototype approach because it has remained a cognitive approach to emotion rather than taking the further step of applying the theory and methodology to increasing our understanding of how people experience emotion in their relationships and how their prototypes influence the manner in which they express emotions in their relationships.

Jones, Beach, and Fincham explore the associations between negative cognitions and depression in families. They note the role of positive attributions about the causes of negative events in buffering individuals against becoming depressed following such events. An interesting finding was that those with high levels of social support were more likely to make these adaptive attributions. Although the role of attributions in the etiology and maintenance of depression has been well established, the association is likely to be mediated by other variables such as social support as just noted, and the process is likely to be somewhat circular, with negative attributions increasing depressive feelings, and depressive feelings increasing negative attributions in an escalating pattern.

Jones et al. also explored the effectiveness of what they called a cognitively enhanced behavioral family intervention (BFI) in treating depressed mothers by providing them with a classic behavioral family intervention as well as cognitive interventions that were designed to increase the extent to which the family involved itself in personally reinforcing family activities. They found that those mothers involved in the cognitively enhanced intervention were more likely to be nondepressed at the follow-up session than were those who were involved in the standard BFI. This effect was not because the children's behavior improved, because their behavior improved in the classic BFI as well, but because the mothers had been helped to change their negative patterns of thinking.

Although BMT began with a strong focus on the actual interactional behavior of the partners, it has now developed into cognitive – behavioral couple therapy (CBCT) and places a similar emphasis on the attitudes of the partners to each other and to the relationship. Problematic cognitions in this model include selective attention, attributions, expectancies, assumptions, and standards. As noted by Baucom et al., CBCT also focuses on the partners' subjective evaluations of partner behavior. They point out that if partners change their cognitions about a particular spouse behavior, relationship satisfaction may increase without any need for the actual behavior to change (Markman, Stanley, & Blumberg, 1994). For example, changing attributions about the intention or causality of a partner's behavior may reduce the perceived negativity of that behavior and make it more acceptable and less threatening to the spouse. CBCT helps couples to pay attention to their cognitive processes and to use specific cognitive restructuring techniques such as considering alternative attributions for their partner's behavior.

Jones et al. discuss a range of cognitive variables related to why people stay in relationships. Commitment seems to be the strongest predictor of relational stability, and other factors include religious beliefs about the sanctity of marriage, viewing one's identity in terms of the relationship, personal investments in the relationship, and children. Le and Agnew (2003) conducted a meta-analysis to test Rusbult's (1980) investment model of commitment. They found that Rusbult's three variables of satisfaction with, alternatives to, and investment in the relationship were significantly related to commitment to that relationship and together accounted for two-thirds of the variance in commitment. Gender attitudes involve another set of cognitive variables that can have an impact on behavior. For example, Impett and Peplau show how gender attitudes and the consequent attitudes to family roles affect the amount of family work in which people engage. As would be expected, where both members of a couple are nontraditional in their gender attitudes, the husband is likely to be more involved in family work than other husbands. These researchers also show how core beliefs can be maintained, even when circumstances require changes in behavior, such as when the wife in a working-class couple is employed outside the home because of her greater ability to get a job and the husband cares for the children.

In their chapter on conflict, Kline et al. comment on work by Sillars (e.g., Sillars, Roberts, Leonard, & Dun, 2000) focusing on partners' thoughts during conflict discussions. They found that partners would often interpret the same communication in totally different ways. When dissatisfied couples engaged in severe conflicts, the thoughts they reported tended to be angry and blaming, whereas the thoughts of satisfied couples tended to be more optimistic about achieving understanding from the partner and a resolution to the conflict.

In discussing lying and deception in close relationships, Knapp notes that individuals in close relationships are likely to endorse the importance of honesty in close relationships, although most may also see a place for "not telling the partner everything," and for even misleading the partner at times. Some respondents even saw telling lies to the partner as being the right thing to do in some situations. Presumably such "lies" may be told to avoid hurting the partner, to deal with a partner's anxieties, or to curb a partner's attempts at control.

Knapp raises the issue of whether there are times in close relationships when partners are accused of being deceptive when that is not their intention. One example he provides is Bavelas's notion of equivocal communication, which can be used to avoid either telling a lie or telling the truth (Bavelas, Black, Chovil, & Mullett, 1990). Other examples include forgetting to tell the partner something that he or she thought should have been told (e.g., about a short business trip coming up) and not saying something that the partner thinks should have been said (e.g., expressing true feelings about a particular situation). It is clear that attributions for these behaviors are likely to be critical to the relationship, and attributing them to deceptive motives could lead to suspicion and mistrust, and even the destruction of the relationship.

A similar problem can arise with regard to interpretations of a partner's attempts at offering social support, as Sarason and Sarason point out. They also note that expectations about the relationship are likely to have an impact on how support behaviors are interpreted and experienced. Relationship satisfaction, a higher level cognitive variable, also affects the ways that such behaviors are understood. Weiss (1984) introduced the concept of *sentiment override* as a type of halo effect whereby the global level of satisfaction affects interpretations and attributions for partner behavior, as well as expectations about future behavior, making it difficult for couples low in relationship satisfaction to change their behavior and improve their relationships, without the help of a therapist who can challenge those cognitions. Fincham and Beach also see sentiment override as challenging the validity of measures of relationship satisfaction. Nevertheless, it is important to assess partners' attitudes to their relationships and how those attitudes, even if they can be described as biased, relate to behavior in that relationship.

Sillars and Vangelisti, in their discussion of communication in relationships, focus on the finding, from narrative research, that people in relationships often behave in ways that confirm their perceptions of that relationship. For example, they suggest that those who are optimistic about their relationships are likely to view their partner's behavior through an optimistic lens and expect (and probably encourage) positive behavior from the partner. Perceptions of the relationship may also be manifest in interaction rules, private idioms, symbols of relationship identity, and routines and rituals that may also suggest an optimistic or pessimistic perception of the relationship. Reflecting on the complexity of face-to-face interaction and the extent to which relational communication can be seen as a consciously staged activity, Sillars and Vangelisti ask,

> How do people manage to process diverse, rapidly changing stimuli; interpret these signals according to multilayered meanings and functions within a surrounding matrix of meanings; integrate this information with multiple and sometimes conflicting goals; and then reply appropriately in real time, without disrupting the flow of natural conversation?

As Fincham and Beach note in their discussion of recent studies about idealization in couples, cognitive distortions in a positive direction tend to be characteristic of happy couples. Those who idealize their partners and who tend to see their partners in a more positive light than their partners view themselves are likely to be happier than other couples. The attributions of these couples are likely to be affected, and they are likely to blame themselves for negative events and give their partners the credit for positive events (Murray, Holmes, Bellavia, Griffin, & Dolderman, 2002).

To the extent that traits are associated with cognitive processes such as motives, goals, expectations, and attributions, so they are likely to have an impact on close personal relationships. For example, Simpson, Winterheld, and Chen suggest (following Reis, Capobianco, & Tsai, 2002) that the relation between personality traits and relationship outcomes should be mediated by expectations related to the partner and the relationship that have presumably developed over the course of that relationship. They further suggest that as the relationship develops, general expectations (such as those driven by attachment insecurity) should give way to these specific types of expectations that are based on actual experiences in the relationship. It is important to remember, however, earlier cautions about the difficulty of changing destructive cognitions.

Sexuality is an area where cognitions are likely to have important effects, as Sprecher et al. note. For example, whether individuals approve of certain sexual behaviors (e.g., sex before marriage, petting, oral sex) is likely to have an impact on their approach to sex in relationships and to the meaning that sex has for them. There has been a lot of change in sexual standards over the last 40 years, at least in the dominant culture, with young adults less likely in the current climate than in the past, to endorse an abstinence standard and more likely to endorse a permissiveness standard (with or without the requirement of affection). These authors also note that individuals (and even partners) can have different beliefs about the role of sexuality in relationships, with some partners placing less emphasis on the importance of sex than others. Other areas where beliefs may differ include the timing, location, and initiation of sexual activity.

In developing their sexual standards and attitudes, adolescents may be torn between the standards of the youth culture in which they are involved and standards presented by parents and religious leaders. Because adolescents tend to be so concerned about conforming to the standards of their peers and being accepted by them, they are likely to become more involved sexually than they actually are comfortable being, particularly if they are insecure in attachment or low in self-esteem (or both).

Hartup discusses the changes that occur for children and adolescents in their cognitions about relationships, cognitions that are closely linked to other developments in cognitive functioning. These changes include changes in expectations of friendship and changes in the level of complexity they can apply to their relationships. Children also increase their ability to take the perspective of another as they mature.

Appraisals of relationships and attitudes about filial responsibility are the cognitive variables most likely to be related to the close relationships of adults in middle and late adulthood, according to Blieszner. There is evidence (e.g., Bedford, 1998) that those who can reframe their negative relationship experiences from childhood to focus on the positive aspects of those relationships are more likely to be happy at this later stage. Norms about filial responsibility are also important for the young adult and middle-aged offspring of elderly parents, particularly understanding the level of agreement between themselves and their parents about the extent to which help should be offered and accepted when necessary.

Surra et al. cite the work of Casper and Sayer (2000) in showing that beliefs about cohabitation affect whether couples are likely to remain in a cohabiting relationship or move on to marriage. Casper and Sayers showed that those who see cohabitation as an alternative to marriage are likely to stay in a cohabiting relationship longer than

those who believe that cohabitation is a stage on the way to marriage.

Thus, there is a lot of evidence in this volume supporting the powerful role that cognitions can play in personal relationships. Whether our focus is on cognitions at the cultural level or at the interpersonal level, they seem to have powerful effects on relationship behavior and satisfaction. Also, the effects are likely to be reciprocal, with cognitions affecting relationship satisfaction and satisfaction affecting cognitions. The effectiveness of therapies that involve a focus on changing cognitions about partners and relationships in improving relationship satisfaction and vulnerability to such problems as depression further supports the importance of cognition to our individual mental health and to our relationships. Rather than (or perhaps as well as) being what we eat, we are also how we think.

Attachment Theory

Since the publication of Hazan and Shaver's (1987) seminal paper on adult attachment, a huge literature has been produced relating attachment theory to a range of interpersonal situations and behaviors. In addition, several scholars who work from an attachment perspective (Shaver, Simpson, Noller) are included among the 20 most cited scholars who study personal relationships. In this volume, attachment theory is mentioned in at least 18 chapters and has been shown to be relevant to a number of relationship variables. Canary and Dainton, for example, have described attachment theory as providing "a powerful theoretical lens for the study of maintenance processes."

In their chapter on dating and mate selection, Surra et al. comment about the focus on attachment security as a causal condition for partner choice. They present three hypotheses that involve using attachment theory to predict mate selection. The attachment-security hypothesis proposes that individuals will choose partners who offer the possibility of forming a secure attachment bond; the similarity hypothesis proposes that individuals will choose partners with similar attachment styles (that is, who endorse similar working models of self and others as they do) and the complementary hypothesis proposes that individuals will choose partners who endorse models that complement their own. Surra et al. note that these hypotheses have received mixed support. Clearly more research is needed to test these possibilities.

Recent data showing that early relationships with parents, as reflected in attachment style, have an impact on adults' experiences of love are discussed by Aron et al. in their chapter on romantic love. Preoccupieds, who are more likely to have experienced inconsistent caregiving, are more likely than the other styles to experience intense passionate love, and avoidants who have generally been subject to a consistent lack of security are the least likely to experience passionate love as adults. Aron et al. also comment on some recent preliminary evidence suggesting a link between attachment style and brain activity related to passionate love. Using Shaver, Hazan, and Bradshaw's (1988) model involving the three behavioral systems of attachment, sexuality, and caregiving, Aron et al. argue that passionate love involves a combination of desire for attachment and sexuality, and that companionate love develops out of these systems and the parenting system. It is important to keep in mind, however, that couple relationships also involve caregiving, and this caregiving is likely to be dysfunctional when the carer is insecure in attachment.

Planalp et al. describe attachment theory as a theory about relationships that gives emotional processes a central role. Overall, those who are secure in attachment generally react with less intense affect to negative events in their relationships and are better able to regulate their emotions than those who are insecure. However, as these researchers point out, there is much about the association between attachment and emotion that we do not understand, particularly with regard to the management of negative emotions such as anger. One fascinating finding to which they refer involves the way that anxious individuals, who fear being rejected and abandoned, and whose greatest need is for closeness, tend to bring about what they fear most by their negative behavior.

De Jong Gierveld, van Tilburg, and Dykstra have shown the relevance of insecure attachment to the problems of lonely people whose difficulties are often created by developmental deficits such as childhood neglect and abandonment and driven by fear of rejection (Rokach & Brock, 1996). They suggest that lonely people can be helped by therapy that aims to change such dysfunctional interpersonal dispositions as fear of rejection, which seems to have a powerful effect on interpersonal behavior. For example, Greene et al. show that this fear of rejection is also associated with problems in self-disclosure, a behavior central to the maintenance of healthy and satisfying relationships. There is also evidence that a capacity for intimacy, or self-disclosure, so difficult for insecurely attached individuals, especially avoidant individuals, is also important for conflict management (Kline et al.).

On the other hand, as Shaver and Mikulincer show, those who are secure in attachment see self-disclosure as the best strategy for forming and maintaining intimate relationships. These individuals are able to engage in genuine intimacy through their "responsive self-disclosure," which involves disclosing personal information about oneself, but also being attentive to a partner's disclosures and responding with sensitivity to them. This sensitivity and responsiveness are seen as carrying over into the sexual relationship, with attachment security being related to sexual satisfaction. Avoidants, however, are more likely to respond with emotional detachment rather than sexual intimacy, and the sexual experiences of anxiously attached individuals are likely to be affected by their concerns about abandonment and their overwhelming desire to please their partners and to feel accepted.

Buunk and Dijkstra, in their chapter on jealousy and extradyadic relationships, also discuss the link between attachment insecurity and sexual relationships and note that women who are anxiously attached are more likely to be unfaithful as well as to have to deal with infidelity in their relationships. In addition, levels of anxiety and number of affairs are correlated, whereas avoidance is negatively correlated with number of affairs. They also report evidence that insecurely attached men report seeking more partners over a 30-year period.

The possibility that those who have had a disrupted attachment history are likely to be more prone to jealousy because of their tendency to interpret spouse behavior in terms of their fear of abandonment, is also raised by Buunk and Dijkstra. Although this hypothesis was not supported in a study focusing on attachment history, it is important to keep in mind that only those who are high on the anxiety dimension (that is, preoccupieds and fearfuls) are likely to interpret spouse behavior in terms of abandonment and react with jealousy. Those high on avoidance are more likely to react with increased detachment.

It is clear that attachment theory, as Hartup notes, implies continuities from one relationship to another and over time, although the extent to which attachment styles differ from one relationship to another and in the same relationship over time is still a controversial issue. As Fletcher et al. point out, however, the evidence is accumulating in support of a hierarchical model as proposed by Collins and Read (1994). In their discussion of the implications of individuals' cognitive processes for the quality of their relationships, Fletcher et al. argue that these working models of attachment provide the mechanism for this consistency and help to explain how experiences in infancy carry over into adult relationships.

Insecure attachment can lead to a range of negative behaviors and emotions. For example, Knapp shows that partners who are high in fear of abandonment are more likely than those in the other attachment groups to resort to deception as a relational strategy. In addition, according to Fletcher et al., insecurely attached individuals are more likely than secure individuals to be rigid in their thinking and to have a tendency to ignore or reject information that does not fit with

their framework. Such a strategy makes it difficult for individuals to revise their views or to change their negative perceptions that may hinder their attempts at problem solving. Jones et al. also comment on the negative effects of insecure attachment, in terms of children whose early experiences in the family may increase their risks of becoming depressed. These children are likely to have negative views of close relationships, to be low in trust, and to be wary of becoming involved too deeply. As these authors point out, a supportive partner can help such individuals cope with stress without succumbing to bouts of depression, but their insecurity may inhibit their attempts at finding such supportive relationships.

Sarason and Sarason speak to this issue of attachment and social support when they note that one aspect of social support is a general sense of support that comes with secure attachment and is produced through those early supportive interactions in the family. For those who do not develop that general sense of support, that is, those who are insecure, their sense of social support is likely to be affected both by their difficulty in developing the kinds of relationships that will provide high levels of support, but also their difficulty in perceiving or accepting support even when it is provided. If, as these authors note, social support is an inner resource that helps to protect people in times of stress, those who are insecure in attachment are also likely to have problems coping effectively with the inevitable times of stress that we all have to face.

In her chapter on relationships in middle and late adulthood, Blieszner notes the association between childhood relationships with parents, and relationships and well-being later in life. She reports a study of middle-aged women who had experienced negative relationships with at least one of their parents during childhood. Those who were secure in attachment despite their negative experiences as children had more satisfying relationships as adults, whereas those who were insecure in attachment tended to be involved in less satisfying relationships that were often quite dysfunctional.

Emotion focused couple therapy (EFCT), based on humans' innate need for emotional attachment, seeks to help couples change their negative interaction cycles that tend to arise because one partner's attempts to elicit caring responses provoke a negative response by the other. According to Baucom et al., EFCT helps couples deal with their attachment issues, because the therapist focuses on creating a safe environment in which partners can gain a greater understanding and empathy with regard to each other's attachment needs. Partners can also learn to respond more positively to one another's expression of those needs and to provide understanding and comfort when necessary. Baucom et al. point out, however, that EFCT does not focus on trying to understand the origins of attachment insecurity but rather on helping couples to deal with one another's current needs for nurturance and closeness.

During the almost 20 years of work on adult attachment theory, provoked by the seminal paper of Hazan and Shaver (1987), the theory has been applied to a range of interpersonal variables in close relationships. Originally proposed as a theory of romantic love, it has developed into an important and powerful theory about the antecedents of individual and partner functioning in personal relationships. Although much of the early research was rather simplistic, focusing primarily on differences between the three attachment groups proposed by Hazan and Shaver, the development of multidimensional measures and the focus on partner as well as individual functioning and on different relationship contexts has increased the sophistication of the research being published. In fact, Rholes and Simpson (2004) claimed that "Attachment theory is among the most sweeping, comprehensive theories in psychology today." They see attachment theory as offering "a biosocial, lifespan account of how close relationships form, are maintained, and dissolve" as well as an account of "how relationships influence, sometimes permanently, the persons involved in them" (p. 3).

More work is still needed to deal with a number of ongoing controversies in the literature. The first concerns the measurement of attachment style and whether self-report measures can tap into the unconscious as well as the conscious aspects of attachment (Shaver & Mikulincer, 2004). This issue is primarily provoked by the claims of Mary Main and her colleagues, although my own view is that Main's Adult Attachment Interview is measuring coherence of attachment, rather than attachment style. A second issue is that of the stability of attachment and the factors that predict change versus stability. A third important issue is understanding the processes by which attachment affects relationships, as well as individual health and well-being.

Evolutionary Theory

As Fletcher et al. note, there is no single evolutionary psychological theory. In fact, evolutionary approaches are about trying to explain particular human behaviors by increasing our understanding of the processes of natural and sexual selection through which they are assumed to have evolved. Evolutionary approaches have been applied to such aspects of close relationships as attraction and mate selection, gender differences, emotion including jealousy, sexual behavior, couple conflict, and temperament. Perlman and Duck note that an evolutionary perspective is currently growing in significance and that scholars working from an evolutionary perspective, such as Buss and Simpson, are listed among the top 20 eminent scholars in personal relationships.

Impett and Peplau point out that there has been extensive research on heterosexual mate selection, with two consistent sex differences being documented. The first finding is that men put more emphasis on the physical appearance of a potential partner than women do. This difference is generally explained from an evolutionary perspective in terms of men looking for female partners likely to bear healthy children who will carry on their genes into the future. As Aron, et al. note, visual signs of youth, health, and beauty seem to be the critical indicators of fertility. The second consistent finding concerns the greater focus of women on the status and economic resources of potential partners. This finding is generally explained in terms of a woman's need to find a mate who will be able to support her and her children. There is also evidence, as Aron and associates note, that characteristics such as kindness and intelligence are considered desirable across many cultures.

Sprecher et al. report that another common finding in studies of sexual behavior conducted from an evolutionary perspective is that men report both desiring and expecting to have more sexual partners throughout their lives than do women. According to an evolutionary perspective, it is to men's advantage to have as many partners as possible because they can then spread their seed widely (and take little responsibility for the progeny?), whereas it is to women's advantage to have a single committed mate who will provide for her and their offspring (Buss, 1988). Aron and colleagues suggest that passionate love could be seen as having evolutionary value in terms of maintaining the relationship, at least over the early stages.

If we consider the health of the family system, however, the family is best supported in the context of a committed couple (preferably expressing that commitment through marriage) who are not only committed to each other, but also to their children (see Noller, 1996). In this context, children have a better chance of being brought up in an environment that offers security and stability. It is interesting to note that Buss (1988) took the view that the most prototypical acts of love from an evolutionary perspective were agreeing to marry and remaining faithful when separated.

Buunk and Dijkstra make the point that from an evolutionary perspective, females of earlier times had to invest in a long-term relationship to produce healthy offspring that would then survive to reproduce themselves. Sprecher et al. reinforce this perspective when they claim that a strong bond with a male was important to ensure that the male allocated all his resources to her and did not share them with other females. A committed pair bond also enabled the male to be more confident that the children produced by the female were actually his own. In similar vein, Aron and colleagues claim that "The neural circuitry for adult male–female attachment evolved primarily to motivate individuals to sustain affiliative connections long enough to complete species-specific parental duties."

In considering the importance of the pair bond, Sprecher et al. discuss the possibility of an association among sexual activity, interpersonal bonding, and the release of oxytocin. They suggest two possibilities: first that activation of the sexual system releases oxytocin, which activates the interpersonal bonding system, or second, that activation of the bonding system leads to the release of oxytocin, which then activates the sexual system. Either way, the interpersonal bond is important in ensuring the stability of family life. Aron et al. also claim that scientists are beginning to increase our understanding of the neural mechanisms most likely to play a role in the development of human attachments including maternal and romantic love. Oxytocin and vasopressin seem to be the main neuropeptides involved in pair bonding in humans, as well as in the development of romantic love.

In their discussion of evolutionary approaches to emotion, Planalp et al. see the approach as increasing our understanding of what emotional signals mean, and also to a greater understanding of the associated cognitions and motivations, at a more distal level than we usually think about these issues. They note that from an evolutionary perspective, "Personal devaluation is a survival threat; the feeling of shame alerts us to our lowered status and motivates behaviors such as defense or withdrawal, depending on the physical and psychological resources we bring to the interaction."

Buunk and Dijkstra present an evolutionary perspective on the particular emotion of jealousy in close relationships. They argue that because of men's greater concern with partner attractiveness and women's greater concern about partner resources, women are more likely to experience jealousy when their potential rival is attractive, whereas men are more likely to experience jealousy if their potential rival is higher in status and resources. Buunk and Dijkstra also argue that because of men's and women's different attitudes to reproduction (men are concerned about paternity confidence and women about securing the partner's investment in them and their offspring), men's and women's jealousy is going to be differentially focused.

According to this perspective, men will be more concerned about their female partner's sexual involvement with another man, whereas women will be more concerned about their male partner's emotional investment in another woman and taking resources from her and her offspring. This possibility has been supported in a study by Buss, Larsen, Westen, and Semmelroth (1992), who found that men tended to report that a partner's sexual infidelity would be more upsetting than her emotional infidelity. Women, on the other hand, tended to report that they would be more upset by emotional infidelity than sexual infidelity. This finding is reminiscent of the double standard, with men seen from an evolutionary perspective as having more to gain than women by infidelity and promiscuity and yet being more upset by the infidelity of a partner (see Buunk & Dijkstra for alternative explanations for the finding).

Simpson et al. focus on approach and avoidance tendencies, which they see as central to temperament. They see these dimensions as reflecting distinct biologically based systems that have evolved to serve particular functions. The approach system tends to motivate people toward rewarding outcomes, whereas the avoidance system tends to involve stronger emotional reactions to negative events, with highly avoidant individuals tending to experience more negative

affect in their daily lives (Gable & Reis, 2001) than those who are predominantly affected by approach motives.

Thus the contribution of evolutionary psychology to our understanding of personal relationships is primarily in terms of attraction and mate-selection. The two primary findings concerning mate preferences can also be applied to jealousy in relationships, with males being more jealous when their rival is rich in resources and women being more jealous when their rival is physically attractive. Passionate love can be seen as both a motivator of a couple getting together in the first place and a maintainer of the relationship so that children can be supported. Sex is also seen as helping to maintain relationships, with links among sexual activity, interpersonal bonding, and the release of oxytocin that aids bonding and increases the possibility of a stable environment in which children can be supported.

Harvey and Wenzel provide a critique of the evolutionary perspective, noting that the data collected about dating and mating preferences are often "far removed from any type of investigation of the slow unfolding of biologically driven evolutionary processes." They report a study (Shackelford & Buss, 1997) in which participants were asked to rate the likelihood that they would engage in a range of extramarital behaviors, including having an affair. As Harvey and Wenzel note, "Not only are such measures indirect tests of evolution, they also are hypothetical in nature, with an unclear link to the frequency of actual affairs in this case." These authors also describe the theory as gross and simplistic and as unable to explain the variations in dating and mating behavior that occur at an interpersonal level as individuals of the opposite sex initiate and develop relationships with one another.

Harvey and Wenzel view more positively the more recent evolutionary thinking that has included the possibility that dating and mating selections are also affected by individuals' thoughts and feelings (Buss, Haselton, Shackelford, Bleske, & Wakefield, 1999). They see this perspective as "striking a more reasoned chord about dating and mating activities" and as likely to find more acceptance among relationship researchers than the more extreme versions of the theory that have been criticized as making excuses for male philandering as well as encouraging gender stereotyping.

Social Roles and Power

Personal relationships involve a number of different roles that are discussed in this book, including romantic partner, husband, wife, parent, child, sibling, and friend. As Planalp et al. note, each role involves its own set of norms, rules, and expectations about how a person in that role is expected to behave. Roles are a central concept of symbolic interactionism (Stryker, 1972) and are expectations about behavior that are based on positions in the family.

Roles also involve various levels of social power, and how much power is involved in a role will vary from culture to culture. For example in very traditional cultures, husbands are likely to have considerably more power than wives, although in Western cultures we have seen more emphasis on equity and equality over recent years. Of course, as Johnson notes, in some couple relationships power is exerted through the use of violence.

Individuals generally occupy multiple roles at the same time. A woman may be a wife, mother, daughter, sister, and occupy a particular work role all at the same time. In addition, a woman may occupy all these roles and also be a carer for an ageing parent. A man may be a husband, father, son, brother, and also occupy a particular work role. Blieszner reports that those who occupy multiple social roles in early adulthood are likely to have well-developed identities, and there is evidence that identity development is associated with well-being at midlife.

Parents always have power over children, although exerting power can become more difficult as children get older. Some researchers argue for a gradual change in the parent–child relationship in adolescence, with a more equal relationship being negotiated between parents and adolescents. In this way, adolescents gradually attain more autonomy and more control over their own lives (Noller, 1994). In fact, one of the notable absences from this volume is any focus on parent–child relationships. Parent–child relationships are implicit in discussions of attachment theory, but there is little discussion of the processes involved in these relationships. The editors decided to minimize the emphasis on parent–child relationships in this volume because the primary focus of the book is on voluntary relations. Nonetheless, no treatment of close relationships is complete without consideration of parent–child and other kin relations.

Hartup focuses on issues of power and control in children's peer relationships. He argues that sibling relationships and friendships are very different because of the different social contexts in which they operate and argues against the notion that sibling relationships can be regarded as "bridges" to peer relationships. Although he agrees that a general social understanding may be transferred from sibling relationships to friendships, he sees the association as not sufficiently proven. Hartup also focuses on the problems of bullying and victimization in children's peer relationships, and the role of an imbalance of power between children in encouraging bullying. In a more positive vein, he also notes that having a lot of friends can help alter the balance of power and provide protection and support that may act as a deterrent to would-be bullies.

In couple relationships, it is important, as Harvey and Wenzel point out, to reach agreement about who can rightfully exercise power and in what areas. They also note that even in communal relationships, where partners are seen as responding to need rather than operating on exchange principles, it is difficult for partners to avoid, at least implicitly, issues of equity and reciprocity. Of course, in communal relationships, reciprocity and equity should be considered over a longer time span, rather than partners expecting, for example, immediate reciprocation.

Use of power can be a difficult issue in modern relationships where at least a semblance of equality is required and where even discussing the issue of power and control may be problematic. In this situation, arguments about relatively trivial issues such as what to watch on television, what movie to see, and where to eat can really be about who has power. As Greene et al. suggest, intimacy may also be affected, if partners view the expectation of self-disclosure and openness as infringing their need for autonomy or control over their own lives.

Cutrona and Gardner note that the sense of independence of individuals in couple relationships can often be an illusion that is not fully faced until the partner is no longer available. They argue that daily routines are often carried out so smoothly that the various roles that partners play can be virtually invisible and may only be acknowledged when the realization comes that life is more difficult without the partner.

When relationship partners do not meet each other's expectations or break rules, Planalp et al. argue, emotion is the most likely response. Partners are likely to respond with hurt and anger when the other breaks relationships rules and does not live up to the agreements that have been made. Transgressions that produce these emotional reactions may be as minor as failing to call when they were going to be late to as serious as having an affair. Of course, the ultimate emotional reaction would be to engage in violence to exert one's power over the transgressor. Planalp et al. argue that partners send each other messages of power and status through their expressions of emotions such as anger and love, but that we know little about how individuals use emotions to maintain power or to regain status that has been lost.

Issues about autonomy and power are most clearly seen in violent relationships. As Johnson explains, power is central to the issue of what he calls intimate terrorism, which he sees as "embedded in a larger pattern of power and control that permeates the relationship." His position is supported by the research of Pence and Paymar (1993) and the Duluth Domestic Abuse Intervention Project. As Johnson points out, multiple control tactics are often used, mostly by men, with the perpetrator exercising control by demanding complete obedience from his partner, denying her economic resources, keeping her isolated from sources of support, and threatening her access to the children if she does not do his bidding. In this situation, the female partner has virtually no autonomy. This type of violence is to be distinguished from common or situational couple violence, which tends to be mutual, less severe, less likely to escalate, and not part of a general pattern of control. By making such clear distinctions between different types of violence, Johnson has shed light on the controversy in the literature between those who use primarily "shelter" samples in their research and see violence as perpetrated only by men and those who use community samples and see violence as frequently mutual.

Thus, issues of power and control can be present in a range of personal relationships, from the peer relationships of children through parent–child relationships and couple relationships. Sometimes the degree of power to be exerted is legitimized in the role that is occupied. For example, we expect parents to exercise power, although there are rightly concerns in our modern Western society when this power is abused. At least in Western society, we expect equity and equality in our couple relationships, although for many, these qualities represent the ideal rather than the reality. Of course, power can be exercised subtly, or blatantly. The ultimate abuse of power occurs in couples in whom husbands exercise power through the use of force and in the service of male privilege batter their wives into submission. As Johnson notes, "the abuser entraps and enslaves his partner in a web of control." This blatant abuse of power cannot be condoned by any civilized society, and many societies, including my own, are finally conducting educational campaigns focusing on the criminal nature of such behavior.

An Integrative Theory?

Harvey and Wenzel discuss the different contributions made by each of the major theories to our understanding of close personal relationships and the ways each is limited in terms of its contribution and application. They do, however, make an interesting attempt to provide a unifying model by highlighting the need for relationship variables stemming from more than one approach to be included in studies. For example, as noted earlier, although evolutionary theory may be able to explain general behavioral tendencies with regard to mating and dating, it cannot explain individual differences in the ways individuals interact in their relationships. Attachment theory, on the other hand, is able to explain how individual differences in early experiences with parents can make individuals more prone to negative interactions, because of their basic beliefs about their own unworthiness and the lack of dependability of others. In addition, attachment theory is a sociocognitive theory and, as Harvey and Wenzel point out, could form the basis for a "taxonomy of relational schemas" that actually drive behavior. Further, from an attachment theory perspective, there are likely to be individual differences in individuals' propensity to be successfully involved in a communal relationship, because insecure people may be more prone to focus on a perceived lack of equity and equality in their relationships. As Harvey and Wenzel explain: "It is not difficult to imagine the manner in which an avoidant or anxious–ambivalent attachment style would interfere with giving or receiving selfless benefits from one's partner."

Suggestions for Future Research

Although an enormous amount of research on close personal relationships has been reviewed in this volume, there is undoubtedly still much more to be done. As always, new findings tend to raise new questions. A number of authors have raised issues that should be tackled in future research, and I try to summarize some of these here.

Fincham and Beach are concerned, as some of us have been for a long time, about the ways that relationship satisfaction is measured in our studies. They recognize that evaluative measures are more valid for assessing satisfaction than are descriptive measures, which assume that the same behaviors are problematic for all couples and which often (e.g., Dyadic Adjustment Scale; Spanier, 1976) confound the independent variable of relationship satisfaction with dependent variables such as affection and communication. These researchers are, however, also concerned about the relationship between positivity and negativity. If positivity and negativity are independent dimensions as some researchers suggest, should we be using measures that assess both of these dimensions of satisfaction rather than relying on only one of them?

Surra and her colleagues emphasize the need for researchers to pay careful attention to relationship status in studies of the effects of romantic attachment on relationships. They make this argument because of studies that show that marital status is associated with more positive perceptions of a partner for insecure individuals than for secure individuals. I am inclined to agree that we need to pay attention to relationship status, because there are many areas where this variable is related to important differences. For example, there is evidence that couples who cohabit after they have committed to each other through engagement are less likely to be subject to the increased rate of divorce once married that applies to couples who cohabit without commitment.

Collins and Madsen argue that we need to know more about the role that partner selection plays during adolescence. Suggested research questions include the association between negative patterns of partner behavior and emotion and involvement in romantic relationships. In other words, do adolescents just want to be in relationships for the sake of being in relationships, and how important are characteristics of partners to the relationship choices they make?

Kashy, Campbell, and Harris make a plea for a greater use of dyadic data, noting that in their limited survey of articles published in the relationship journals, 70% involved individual-level data. They argue that given what we know about the causal connections in close relationships between one partner's thoughts, feelings, and behaviors and those of the other partner, much more emphasis needs to be placed on the collection and analysis of dyadic level data. They also argue for greater use of the more sophisticated methods of analyzing dyadic level data such as the social relations model (SRM), structural equation modeling (SEM), and hierarchical linear modeling (HLM). Of course, it is important to keep in mind that for at least some of these techniques, large samples and more elaborate data collection methods are required. For example, in using SRM, data must be collected on the same person interacting with a number of interaction partners, and in using SEM, large samples are needed. The advantages of HLM, as noted by Kashy et al., are that

> It is a technique that allows researchers to examine simultaneously the effects of individual-, dyad-, and even group-level variables, and it can also be used to examine longitudinal data both for individuals and for dyads. . . . (It) is a very flexible data analytic strategy that can handle a variety of nested data structures relevant to relationship researchers.

Coleman, Ganong, and Leon call for more work on a range of issues related to postdivorce families. One interesting area involves studying those postdivorce parents who have been labeled "perfect pals" in Ahrons' (1994) typology. It may be important for us to understand how these couples are able to stay good friends and parent their children effectively without the conflict that can be so ubiquitous in these relationships. A second area of further study suggested by these researchers is related to remarriage. They raise the question of whether those who remarry become better adjusted, or whether the better adjusted are more likely to remarry? Although this issue is still controversial, there is evidence that individual functioning is more likely to improve over time for individuals who remarry. A further question raised by Coleman et al. concerns the quality of relationships between nonresident fathers and children, an area where there is little research. Although a sample of nonresident fathers may be difficult to access, it should be possible to obtain at least the children's perspectives on such relationships.

Brown, Werner, and Altman also raise the issue of potential problems for children of divorce who may move between homes and not really have any space to call their own. This issue is likely to be especially problematic in the homes of noncustodial parents where they may spend every second weekend but never feel as though they really belong.

In focusing on issues of openness and closedness in family relationships, Brown et al. argue that more research is needed on preferences for and satisfaction with different forms or amounts of openness and closedness. They also suggest that we need a better understanding of the effects of the physical environment on family relationships, particularly with regard to large families that often have to cope with crowded conditions. How do family members regulate opportunities for getting together as well as for staying apart under these conditions? A further important question, particularly applicable in our modern age, relates to the effects on children and other family members of children being supported in solitary activities in their own rooms where they are likely to have televisions, computers, videos, and game machines and spend a lot of time – not only in sedentary activities but also in solitary activities.

Brown et al. also raise the difficulty of maintaining privacy and dignity for elderly people who need help with bathroom functions. At this stage, the elderly will probably have to move out of their own homes and may even need to go into a nursing home if they need high levels of care. In this situation, it may be difficult for them to feel comfortable when their once private bodily functions are being regularly exposed to multiple individuals. We need research to understand how elderly people cope with this situation and the extent to which nursing-home staff are trained to understand the difficulties and maintain as much privacy and dignity for the elderly person as possible. For example, I know that although there is an increase in the number of male nurses working in institutions, many elderly women are very uncomfortable with the possibility of being showered by a male.

Allan complains that so much of the research into social networks in later life focuses on the impact of various types of infirmity, whereas there is little research that involves monitoring change in social networks per se. We need to understand how people cope as members leave their networks, through divorce, relocation, or death, and the extent to which other network members change their roles, or new network members come in to replace those who have left. As people become more infirm, of course, the potential for meeting new network members probably decreases.

In their discussion of relational maintenance, Canary and Dainton emphasize that maintenance can occur at multiple levels, including at the network and cultural levels. They argue that we know little about how people use social networks in helping them to maintain their relationships, although we do know that women tend to discuss their relationships with friends more than men do. We also need to understand how cultures (and perhaps subcultures) function to promote or to play down the importance of maintenance activities. The marriage enrichment movement, for example, puts a lot of emphasis on maintenance activities and working on relationships and aims to provide couples with skills for dealing constructively with the issues in their relationships.

Although the research of the last 2 or more decades has increased our understanding of a range of relationships and relationship processes, there is still much to learn. I would join with Charania and Ickes in emphasizing the "benefit of obtaining multiple perspectives, through multiple methods." As I have emphasized elsewhere (e.g., Noller & Feeney, 2004), we need data about behavior, about cognition, and about emotional reactions. We need to choose methods that will answer the research questions we are raising and to remember with Charania and Ickes that "every research method has at least some limitations," even observation. We also need to use more representative samples and stop assuming that 19- and 20-year-olds are the experts on love and relationships. They are not. As Charania and Ickes note, citing Sears (1986):

> Social psychologists have saturated the research enterprise with unrepresentative findings having only limited generality through their many studies of college students who are tested in laboratory situations.

We must resolve to do better by using more representative samples and multiple methods so that we really can increase our understanding of close personal relationships and the important ways they function in our lives.

References

Ahrons, C. R. (1994). *The good divorce*. New York: Harper & Collins.

Bavelas, J. B., Black, A., Chovil, N., & Mullett, J. (1990). *Equivocal communication*. Newbury Park, CA: Sage.

Bedford, V. H. (1998). Sibling relationship troubles and well-being in middle and old age. *Family Relations, 47*, 369–376.

Buss, D. M. (1988). Love acts: The evolutionary biology of love. In R. J. Sternberg & M. L. Barnes (Eds.), *The psychology of love* (pp. 100–118). New Haven, CT: Yale University Press.

Buss, D. M., Haselton, M. G., Shackleford, T. K., Bleske, A., & Wakefield, J. C. (1999). Interactionism, flexibility and inferences about the past. *American Psychologist, 54*, 443–445.

Buss, D. M., Larsen, R. J., Westen, D., & Semmelroth, J. (1992). Sex differences in jealousy: Evolution, physiology, and psychology. *Psychological Science, 3*, 251–255.

Casper, L. M., & Sayer, C. (2000). *Cohabitation transitions: Different attitudes and purposes, different paths.* Paper presented at the Annual Meeting of the Population Association of America, Los Angeles, CA.

Clark, M. S., & Mills, J. (1979). Interpersonal attraction in exchange and communal relationships. *Journal of Personality and Social Psychology, 37,* 12–24.

Collins, N. L., & Read, S. J. (1994). Cognitive representations of attachment. The structure and function of working models. In K. Bartholomew & D. Perlman (Eds.), *Attachment processes in adulthood: Volume 5 Advances in personal relationships* (pp. 53–90). London: Kingsley.

Dion, K. L., & K. K. (1988). Romantic love: Individual and cultural perspectives. In R. J. Sternberg & M. L. Barnes (Eds.), *The psychology of love* (pp. 100–118). New Haven, CT: Yale University Press.

Gable, S. L., & Reis, H. T. (2001). Appetitive and aversive social interaction. In J. H. Harvey & A. E. Wenzel (Eds.), *Close relationship maintenance and enhancement* (pp. 169–194). Mahwah, NJ: Erlbaum.

Hatfield, E., Utne, M. K., & Traupmann, J. (1979). Equity theory and intimate relationships. In R. L. Burgess & T. L. Huston (Eds.), *Social exchange in developing relationships.* New York: Academic Press.

Hazan, C., & Shaver, P. R. (1987). Romantic love conceptualized as an attachment process. *Journal of Personality and Social Psychology, 52,* 511–524.

Kelley, H. H., & Thibaut, J. W. (1978). *Interpersonal relations; A theory of interdependence.* New York: Wiley-Interscience.

Le, B., & Agnew, C. R. (2003). Commitment and its theorized determinants: A meta-analysis of the investment model. *Personal Relationships, 10,* 37–57.

Manusov, V. (2002). Thought and action: Connecting attributions to behaviors in married couples' interactions. In P. Noller & J. A. Feeney (Eds.), *Understanding marriage: Developments in the study of couple interaction* (pp. 14–31). New York: Cambridge University Press.

Markman, H. J., Stanley, S., & Blumberg, S. L. (1994). *Fighting for your marriage: Positive steps for preventing divorce and preserving a lasting love.* San Francisco: Jossey-Bass.

Miller, S., Nunnally, E. W., & Wackman, D. B. (1975). *Alive and aware.* Minneapolis, MN: Interpersonal Communications Program.

Murray, S. L., Holmes, J. G., Bellavia, G., Griffin, D. W., & Dolderman, D. (2002). Kindred spirits? The benefits of egocentrism in close relationships. *Journal of Personality and Social Psychology, 82,* 563–581.

Noller, P. (1994). Relationships with parents in adolescence: Process and outcome. In R. Montemayor, G. R. Adams, & T. P. Gullotta (Eds.), *Personal relationships during adolescence.* Thousand Oaks, CA: Sage.

Noller, P. (1996). What is this thing called love? Defining the love that supports marriage and family. *Personal Relationships, 3,* 97–115.

Noller, P., & Feeney, J. A. (2004). Studying family communication: Multiple methods and multiple sources. In A. L. Vangelisti (Ed.), *Handbook of family communication.* Mahwah, NJ: Erlbaum.

Notarius, C. I., & Markman, H. (1993). *We can work it out: Making sense of marital conflict.* New York: Putnam.

Pence, E., & Paymar, M. (1993). *Education groups for men who batter: The Duluth model.* New York: Springer.

Reis, H., Capobianco, A., & Tsai, F. F. (2002). Finding the person in personal relationships. *Journal of Personality, 70,* 813–850.

Reis, H., & Shaver, P. R. (1988). Intimacy as an interpersonal process. In S. W. Duck (Ed.), *Handbook of personal relationships* (pp. 367–389). Chichester, England: Wiley.

Rholes W. S., & Simpson, J. A. (2004). Attachment theory; basic concepts and conemporary questions. In W. S. Rholes & J. A. Simpson (Eds.), *Adult attachment: Theory, research, and clinical implications* (pp. 3–14). New York: Guilford Press.

Rokach, A., & Brock, H. (1996). The causes of loneliness. *Psychology: A Journal of Human Behavior, 33,* 1–11.

Rook, K. S. (1990). Stressful aspects of older adults' social relationships: Current theory and research. In M. A. P. Stephens, J. H. Crowther, S. E. Hobfoll, & D. L. Tennenbaum (Eds.), *Stress and coping in later-life families* (pp. 173–192). New York: Hemisphere.

Rusbult, C. E. (1980). Commitment and satisfaction in romantic associations: A test of the investment model. *Journal of Experimental Social Psychology, 16,* 172–186.

Schweinle, W. E., & Ickes, W. (2002). On empathic accuracy and husbands' abusiveness: The "overattribution bias." In P. Noller & J. A. Feeney (Eds.), *Understanding marriage: Developments in the study of couple interaction* (pp. 228–250). New York: Cambridge University Press.

Sears, D. O. (1986). College sophomores in the laboratory: Influences of a narrow data base on social psychology's view of human nature. *Journal of Personality and Social Psychology, 51,* 515–530.

Shackelford, T. K., & Buss, D. M. (1997). Cues to infidelity. *Personality and Social Psychology Bulletin, 23,* 1034–1045.

Shaver, P. R., Hazan, C., & Bradshaw, D. (1988). Love as attachment: The integration of three behavioral systems. In R. J. Sternberg & M. L. Barnes (Eds.), *The psychology of love* (pp. 68–99). New Haven, CT: Yale University Press.

Shaver, P. R., & Mikulincer, M. (2004). What do self-report attachment measures assess? In W. S. Rholes & J. A. Simpson (Eds.) *Adult attachment: Theory, research, and clinical implications* (pp. 17–54). New York: Guilford Press.

Sillars, A. L., Leonard, K. E., Roberts, L. J., & Dun, T. (2002). Cognition and communication during marital conflict: How alcohol affects subjective coding of interaction in aggressive and nonaggressive couples. In P. Noller & J. A. Feeney (Eds.), *Understanding marriage: Developments in the study of couple interaction* (pp. 85–112). New York: Cambridge University Press.

Sillars, A. L., Roberts, L. J., Leonard, K. E., & Dun, T. (2000). Cognition during marital conflict: The relationship of thought and talk. *Journal of Social and Personal Relationships, 17,* 479–502.

Spanier, G. B. (1976). Measuring dyadic adjustment: New scales for assessing the quality of marriage and similar dyads. *Journal of Marriage and the Family, 38,* 15–28.

Stryker, S. (1972). Symbolic interaction theory: A review and some suggestions for comparative family research. *Journal of Comparative Family Studies, 3,* 17–32.

Weiss, R. L. (1984). Cognitive and behavioral measure of marital interaction. In K. Hahlweg & N. S. Jacobson (Eds.), *Marital interaction: Analysis and modification* (pp. 232–252). New York: Guilford Press.

Author Index

Subject Index

marriage(s) (*cont.*)
    effects on domestic labor, 281
    egalitarian model, 283
    emotional climate of, 132–133
    emotional intimacy in individualistic cultures, 700
    facilitating self-regulation, 435
    fewer health benefits when troubled or dissatisfying,
       391
    for the first time later in life, 703
    focusing on change in, 131
    forecasts of eventual, 121
    frequency of conflict in, 448
    health and, 285–287
    heightened focus on positive elements of, 147–149
    husband as the head of the family, 283
    increase in the age at, 121
    majority by arrangement across the world, 698
    majority of research assessing marital satisfaction, 132
    median age of first, 121
    movement from a vital to a devitalized, 159
    not all beginning with high levels of positive affect,
       138
    observable behaviors and subjective factors in, 131
    overall emotional tenor of, 132
    patriarchal underpinnings of traditional, 304
    positive and negative aspects of, 133
    predicting changes in the emotional climate of,
       144–146
    primarily for the benefit of the spouses, 580
    proportion dissolving, 157
    regarded as a union of two families, 698
    relationship progressing toward, 114
    role of sexuality in, 476
    supportive behaviors in, 147
Marriage and Family Living, 14. See also *Journal of*
    Marriage and the Family
marriage behavior, demographic changes in, 121
Marriage Council of Philadelphia, 745
marriage counseling, practice of, 745
marriage enrichment movement, 787
marriage literature, notions of accommodation in, 141
marriage markets, 120–122
marriage rates, positive effects of economic
    opportunities, 122
marriage squeeze
    effects of, 121
    producing, 121
marriage stage of relationship development, 448
marriage typologies, 93
married couples
    behavior patterns in, 639
    SRM used to study communication within, 77
    types based conflict interactions, 450
married individuals as healthier, 285
married life style, adulthood associated with, 745
married student housing at Massachusetts Institute of
    Technology, 15
Married-Happy couples, 134
Married-Not Happy couples, 134
Masculinity-Femininity dimension, 697
mastery goals, adoption of, 235
masturbation as a good index of sexual desire, 279
MAT (Marital Adjustment Test)
    comprising a polyglot of items and responses to
      them, 581
    not a cross cultural measure, 580
    replacing in marital research, 587

simple item assessing marital happiness heavily
    weighted, 587
mate availability, marriage markets operating on the
    principle of, 121
mate characteristics, recent study assessing, 275
mate choice, 362–364. *See also* mate preferences
    anatomical and neurochemical mechanisms
      producing, 600
    contemporary patterns much broader than just
      marriage, 122
    criteria men and women use in, 363
    defining the study of, 116
    directed by innate mechanisms, 123
    phenomenon of, 599
    sex differences in, 363
    standards, 364
    steadily decreasing emphasis on, 119
    as a strong predictor of marital quality, 700
    studies, 469
    as a theme of articles on dating and mate selection,
      119
    using attachment theory to predict, 777
mate criteria, strong within-sex individual differences,
    364
mate poaching, 264
mate preferences. *See also* mate choice
    among women and men, 275
    generational shifts in, 703
mate selection. *See* mate choice
material attractions, 616
material barriers, 617
material constraints, restricting the availability of
    partners, 698
maternal behavior, observational studies of, 265
maternal cortisol, stress leading to elevations in, 318
maternal love, 597
maternal stress during pregnancy, 318
mating in the context of social networks, 699
mating "programs", different for men and women, 295
mating system, exploiting an evolved bonding module,
    608
Matriarchal stepfamilies, 168
maximizer-minimizer controversy on gender
    differences, 287
McLuhan, Marshall, 711
meanings
    attached by recipients to efforts at support from
      others, 432
    as a product of negotiation in communication, 340
measure of commitment in Rusbult's model, 620
measures of effect size in meta-analysis, 63
media, collecting self-report data through, 55
mediating model, 41
mediation
    of same-sex couples assisting with relationship
      dissolution, 299
    utilizing, 164
mediational tradition in the study of marital
    satisfaction, 580
"mediator" effects, 186
medical records for sampling elderly populations, 64
meetings, arranging in-person through CMC, 720
memory, negatively biasing recall of the past, 585
men. *See also* males
    attracted to women showing visual signs of youth,
      health, and beauty, 602
    citing physical attractiveness as more important, 363

concerned about ability to reproduce, 123
coping with divorce by finding new partners, 163
deriving greater health benefits from marriage, 285–286
emotion roles in the family, 378
emphasis on the physical appearance of a potential partner, 780
engaging more in extradyadic sexual behaviors, 534
exhibiting more jealousy, 123
feelings of sexual deprivation, 539
focused on short-term liaisons and sexual variety, 363
genetically wired differently from women, 36
getting drunk or high when confronted with a partner's infidelity, 548
greater reluctance to report loneliness, 491
inclination to engage in extradyadic sex as a relatively autonomous motive, 539
inclined to act possessively toward their partners, 548
increasing family work by spending time with children, 282
jealous over status-related characteristics, 545
jealousy focused upon the sexual aspects of the partner's extramarital activities, 545
killed by female partners, 567
lifestyle of single, 285
likely to construct an independent self-view, 276
likely to report their relational standards fulfilled, 275
most upsetting spousal behavior, 276
permissive in sexual behavior, 123
placing greater value on physical attributes of a partner, 275
with potential to invest minimally, 537
preferring relationships with youthful and reproductively vital women, 36
producing high numbers of sperm at a relatively constant rate, 464
prone to lie about their past, 523
receiving social support from romantic partners, 392
reporting a greater number of sexual partners, 466
reporting a partner's sexual infidelity more upsetting, 546, 782
separation from women in Victorian communities, 680
showing more interest in sex than do women, 279
socializing to be emotionally independent, 490
stronger relationships among social relationships and mortality for, 390
taking the lead in sexual activities, 280
trading commitment for certainty of paternity, 464
using ambiguous signals delivering verbal communications, 645
using more maintenance behaviors, 737
using violence to in response to infidelity, 548
violence more frequent and more severe than women's, 563
wide-ranging engagements around the town, 680
mental disorders, development of, 315
mental dispositions, pre-existent, 356
mental health
association with self-disclosure, 417
linked to healthy families, 313

mental health problems
among battered women, 567
development of marital- and family-based interventions to treat, 313
mental illness, linked to unhealthy families, 313
mental shortcuts, interpreting messages and implementing communication strategies, 339
Merton, Robert K., 717
mesocontextual factors, 705
message channel. See mode of disclosure
message features in self-disclosure, 420
message sequences, recurring, 338
messages
ambiguity of, 340
extra-linguistic features of, 338
fixed effects of, 343
interpreted in terms of a surrounding matrix, 338
multiple functions of as overlapping systems, 338
simultaneously influencing and influenced by, 332
theory-driven processing of, 342
meta-analysis, 20, 63–64
metaphors for a transactional approach, 674
methodological improvements in studying adult family and friend relationships, 222
methodological innovations since 1978, 20
methodology effect on the quality and interpretation of data, 51
methods
general types of, 92
for typing relationships, 92–93
microcontextual factors, 705
microscales, dialectic and transactional approaches applied to, 676
microsocial worlds, 664
Microsoft Web-TV set-top box, 713
middle and late adulthood relationships, 216–219
middle and old age, personal development in, 213
middle circle in the social convoy model, 662
midlife development, 213
Milardo, 25
Miller, Lynn, 411
minding the close relationship theory, 416
mindless behavior, 340
minimization, 729
misattributions in the early stages of romance, 200
misreadings of nonverbal expressions, 647
misunderstanding
attributing to a lack of communication, 341
heavy emphasis on, 342
mixed couples, families headed by, 100
mixed model analysis of variance, 77
Mixed Model of SPSS, 81
Mixed relational type, 736
mixed-mode surveys, 66
mixed-sex (boy/girl) antipathies, 183
MMPI, compared to the MSI, 586
mode of disclosure, 418
models, 96, 240–241
moderating model, 41
"moderator" effects, 186
moderator variables, 106
money as the top issue for first-time marriages, 448
monogamous relationships, preference for among gay men, 302
Monroe, Will S., 14
Montgomery, 23